CLYMER®

MERCURY/MARINER

TWO-STROKE OUTBOARD SHOP MANUAL

75-250 HP • 1998-2002 (Includes Jet Drive Models)

The World's Finest Publisher of Mechanical How-to Manuals

PRIMEDIA
Business Magazines & Media

P.O. Box 12901, Overland Park, KS 66282-2901

Copyright ©2002 PRIMEDIA Business Magazines & Media Inc.

FIRST EDITION
First Printing September, 2002

Printed in U.S.A.

CLYMER and colophon are registered trademarks of PRIMEDIA Business Magazines & Media Inc.

This book was printed at Von Hoffmann an ISO certified company.

ISBN: 0-89287-796-0

Library of Congress: 2002111258

AUTHOR: Mark Rolling.

TECHNICAL PHOTOGRAPY: Mark Rolling.

TECHNICAL ILLUSTRATIONS: Mike Rose.

WIRING DIAGRAMS: Bob Caldwell.

EDITORS: Jason Beaver and James Grooms.

PRODUCTION: Shara Pierceall.

COVER:Photo courtesy of Godfrey Marine, Elkhart, Indiana.

Contents

Quick Reference Data

VEHICLE HISTORY DATA

MODEL:_____ YEAR:_____

VIN NUMBER:_____

ENGINE SERIAL NUMBER:_____

CARBURETOR SERIAL NUMBER OR I.D. MARK:_____

Record the numbers here for your reference.

MAINTENANCE SCHEDULE

Maintenance interval	Maintenance required
Before each use	Check the lanyard switch operation* Inspect the propeller for damage Check the propeller nut tightness Inspect the fuel system for leakage Check the outboard mounting bolt tighteness Check the steering for binding or looseness Check the shift and throttle control
After each use	Flush the cooling system Wash debris from the gearcase
After the first 10 days of operation	Check the gearcase lubricant level
Every 30 day or 50 hours of usage	Check the gearcase lubricant level (continued)

MAINTENANCE SCHEDULE (continued)

Maintenance interval	Maintenance required
Once a season or 100 hours of usage	Lubricate the steering system
	Lubricate tiller control pivots*
	Lubricate the tilt and swivel shaft
	Lubricate the shift and throttle linkages/cables
	Check the tightness of all accessible fasteners
	Clean and inspect the spark plugs
	Remove carbon from the combustion chambers
	Inspect fuel filters for contamination
	Check control cable adjustments
	Adjust the carburetors*
	Test and inspect the battery
	Check ignition timing
	Check trim/tilt fluid level (Chapter Eleven)
	Clean and inspect sacrificial anodes
	Lubricate the drive shaft splines
	Lubricate the propeller shaft splines
	Change the gearcase lubricant
	Lubricate the starter motor pinion
	Clean remote fuel tank filter*
	Change the water separating filter (EFI)*
	Inspect or replace the water pump impeller
	Replace the compressor air filter (Optimax)*
	Clean the compressor cooling water strainer*
Before long term storage	Drain and refill the gearcase lubricant

*This maintenance item does not apply to all models.

LUBRICANT CAPACITIES

Model	Oil capacity	Gearcase capacity
65 jet, 75 hp and 90 hp	1 gal. (3.8 liter)*	22.5 oz. (665 ml)*
80 jet and 100-125 hp (except 115 Optimax)	1.4 gal (5.3 liter)*	22.5 oz. (665 ml)*
105 jet and 140 jet	12.9 qt. (12.2 liter)	–
135-200 hp (except Optimax)	12.9 qt. (12.2 liter)*	22.5 oz. (665 ml)*
115-175 hp Optimax models	13.5 qt. (12.8 liter)*	22.5 oz. (665 ml)*
200/225 hp Optimax, 225 hp and 250 hp	13.5 qt. (12.8 liter)	28.0 oz. (828 ml)*

*Approximate capacity. Always add lubricant until it reaches the full level.

SPARK PLUG RECOMMENDATIONS

Model	Recommended plug	Spark plug gap
65 jet, 75 hp and 90 hp	NGK BUHW-2	Surface gap plug
Alternate plug (resistor type)	NGK BUZHW-2	Surface gap plug
80 jet, 100 hp, 115 hp and 125 hp	NGK BP8H-N-10	0.040 in. (1.0 mm)
Alternate plug (resistor type)	NGK-BPZ8H-N-10	0.040 in. (1.0 mm)
105 jet and 140 jet		
1998 and 1999	NGK BU8H	Surface gap plug
2000-on	NGK BPZ8HS-10	0.040 in. (1.0 mm)
135-200 hp (except Optimax)		
1998 and 1999	NGK BU8H	surface gap plug
2000-on	NGK BPZ8HS-10	0.040 in. (1.0 mm)

(continued)

SPARK PLUG RECOMMENDATIONS (continued)

Model	Recommended plug	Spark plug gap
115-150 hp (Optimax models)	NGK PZFR5F-11	0.040 in. (1.0 mm)
Alternate plug	NGK ZFR5F-11	0.040 in. (1.0 mm)
Alternate plug	Champion RC12MC4	0.040 in. (1.0 mm)
200 and 225 hp (Optimax models)		
1998 and 1999	NGK PZFR5F-11	0.040 in. (1.0 mm)
Alternate plug	NGK ZFR5F-11	0.040 in. (1.0 mm)
2000	Champion QC12GMC	0.040 in. (1.0 mm)
2001-on	NGK PZFR5F-11	0.040 in. (1.0 mm)
225 and 250 hp (except Optimax)	Champion QL77CC	0.035 in. (0.9 mm)

BATTERY CAPACITY

Accessory draw	Provides continuous power for:	Approximate recharge time
80 amp-hour battery		
5 amps	13.5 hours	16 hours
15 amps	3.5 hours	13 hours
25 amps	1.6 hours	12 hours
105 amp-hour battery		
5 amps	15.8 hours	16 hours
15 amps	4.2 hours	13 hours
25 amps	2.4 hours	12 hours

STANDARD TORQUE SPECIFICATIONS

Screw or nut size	in.-lb.	ft.-lb.	N•m
U.S. Standard			
6-32	9	–	1.0
8-32	20	–	2.3
10-24	30	–	3.4
10-32	35	–	4.0
12-24	45	–	5.1
1/4-20	70	–	7.9
1/4-28	84	–	9.5
5/16-18	160	13	18.1
5/16-24	168	14	19.0
3/8-16	–	23	31.1
3/8-24	–	25	33.8
7/16-14	–	36	48.8
7/16-20	–	40	54.2
1/2-13	–	50	67.8
1/2-20	–	60	81.3
Metric			
M5	36	–	4.1
M6	70	–	8.1
M8	156	13	17.6
M10	–	26	35.3
M12	–	35	47.5
M14	–	60	81.3

Chapter One

General Information

This detailed, comprehensive manual contains complete information on maintenance and overhaul. Hundreds of photos and drawings guide the reader through every step-by-step procedure.

Troubleshooting, tune-up, maintenance and repair procedures are not difficult with the necessary tools and equipment, and the ability to use them. Anyone with some mechanical ability can perform most of the procedures in this manual. See Chapter Two for more information on tools and techniques.

A shop manual is a reference. Clymer books are designed for finding information quickly. All chapters are thumb tabbed and important topics are indexed at the end of the manual. All procedures, tables, photos and instructions in this manual assume the reader may be working on the machine or using the manual for the first time.

Store the manual with other tools in the workshop or boat. It will help in gaining a better understanding of how the boat runs, and help to lower repair and maintenance costs.

MANUAL ORGANIZATION

Chapter One provides general information useful to boat owners and mechanics.

Chapter Two discusses the tools and techniques for preventative maintenance, troubleshooting and repair.

Chapter Three provides troubleshooting procedures for all engine systems and individual components.

Chapter Four provides maintenance, lubrication and tune-up instructions.

Additional chapters cover storage, adjustment and specific repair instructions. All disassembly, inspection and assembly instructions are in step-by-step form. Specifications are included at the end of the appropriate chapters.

WARNINGS, CAUTIONS AND NOTES

The terms, WARNING, CAUTION and NOTE have specific meanings in this manual.

A WARNING emphasizes areas where injury or even death could result from negligence. Mechanical damage may also occur. WARNINGS *are to be taken seriously.*

A CAUTION emphasizes areas where equipment damage could occur. Disregarding a CAUTION could cause permanent mechanical damage, though injury is unlikely.

A NOTE provides additional information to make a step or procedure easier or clearer. Disregarding a NOTE could cause inconvenience, but would not cause equipment damage or personal injury.

TORQUE SPECIFICATIONS

Torque specifications throughout this manual are given in foot-pounds (ft.-lb.), inch-pounds (in.-lb.) and newton meters (N•m). Torque wrenches calibrated in meter-kilograms can be used by performing a simple conversion: move the decimal point one place to the right. For example, 4.7 mkg = 47 N•m. This conversion is accurate enough for mechanical repairs even though the exact mathematical conversion is 3.5 mkg = 34.3 N•m.

ENGINE OPERATION

All marine engines, whether two- or four-stroke, gasoline or diesel, operate on the Otto cycle of intake, compression, power and exhaust phases. A two-stroke engine requires one crankshaft revolution (two strokes of the piston) to complete the Otto cycle. All Mercury and Mariner engines covered in this manual are of the two-stroke design. **Figure 1** shows typical gasoline two-stroke engine operation.

Optimax models use a direct fuel injection system. On these models, fuel is injected directly into the combustion chamber after the exhaust port is covered; preventing unburned fuel from exiting along with the exhaust gases. Compared to typical two-stroke engines, direct fuel injected engines run smoother, emit far less unburned fuel, use less oil and provide improved fuel economy. **Figure 2** shows direct injection two-stroke engine operation.

FASTENERS

The material and design of the various fasteners used on marine equipment are specifically chosen for performance and safety. Fastener design determines the type of tool required to work with the fastener. Fastener material is carefully selected to decrease the possibility of physical failure or corrosion. See *Galvanic Corrosion* in this chapter for information on marine materials.

Threaded Fasteners

Nuts, bolts and screws are manufactured in a wide range of thread patterns. To join a nut and bolt, the diameter of the bolt and the diameter of the hole in the nut must be the same. The threads must also be compatible.

Determine if the threads on the fasteners are compatible by turning the nut on the bolt (or bolt into its respective opening) with fingers only. Make sure both pieces are clean. If much force is required, check the thread condition on each fastener. If the thread condition is good but the fasteners jam, the threads are not compatible.

Four important specifications describe the thread:
1. Diameter.
2. Threads per inch.
3. Thread pattern.
4. Thread direction.

Figure 3 shows the first two specifications. Thread pattern is more subtle. Italian and British standards exist, but the most commonly used by marine equipment manufacturers are American and metric. The root and top of the thread are cut differently as shown in **Figure 4**.

Most threads are cut so the fastener must be turned clockwise to tighten it. These are called right-hand threads. Some fasteners have left-hand threads; they must be turned counterclockwise for tightening. Left-hand threads are used in locations where normal rotation of the equipment would loosen a right-hand threaded fastener. Fasteners with left-hand threads are identified in the instructions.

Machine Screws

There are many different types of machine screws (**Figure 5**). Most are designed to protrude above the secured surface (rounded head) or be slightly recessed below the surface (flat head). In some applications, the screw head is recessed well below the fastened surface. **Figure 6** shows a number of screw heads requiring different types of turning tools. See Chapter Two for detailed information.

Bolts

Commonly called bolts, the technical name for these fasteners is cap screw. They are normally described by diameter, threads per inch and length. For example, 1/4-20 × 1 indicates a bolt that is 1/4 in. in diameter with 20 threads per inch, and is 1 in. long. The measurement across two flats on the head of the bolt indicates the proper wrench size to use.

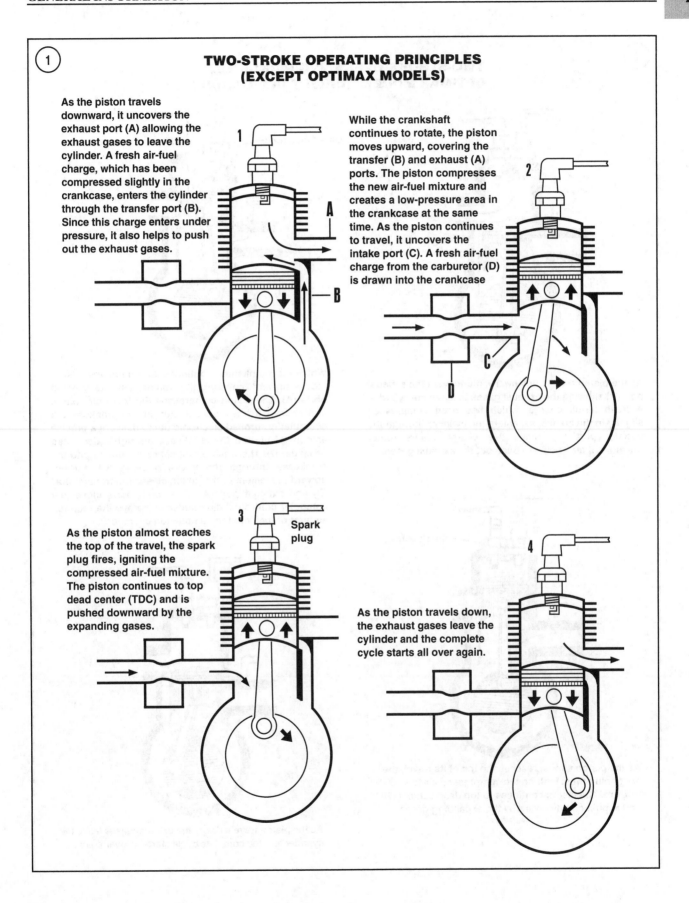

① TWO-STROKE OPERATING PRINCIPLES (EXCEPT OPTIMAX MODELS)

As the piston travels downward, it uncovers the exhaust port (A) allowing the exhaust gases to leave the cylinder. A fresh air-fuel charge, which has been compressed slightly in the crankcase, enters the cylinder through the transfer port (B). Since this charge enters under pressure, it also helps to push out the exhaust gases.

While the crankshaft continues to rotate, the piston moves upward, covering the transfer (B) and exhaust (A) ports. The piston compresses the new air-fuel mixture and creates a low-pressure area in the crankcase at the same time. As the piston continues to travel, it uncovers the intake port (C). A fresh air-fuel charge from the carburetor (D) is drawn into the crankcase

As the piston almost reaches the top of the travel, the spark plug fires, igniting the compressed air-fuel mixture. The piston continues to top dead center (TDC) and is pushed downward by the expanding gases.

As the piston travels down, the exhaust gases leave the cylinder and the complete cycle starts all over again.

②

TWO-STROKE OPERATING PRINCIPLES
OPTIMAX MODELS (DIRECT INJECTION)

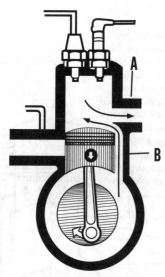

1

As the piston travels downward, it uncovers the exhaust port (A) allowing the exhaust gases to leave the cylinder. A fresh air-oil charge, which has been compressed slightly in the crankcase, enters the cylinder through the transfer port (B). Since this charge enters under pressure, it also helps to push out the exhaust gases.

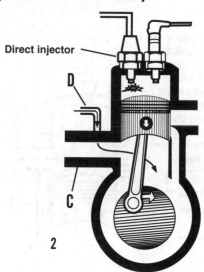

2

While the crankshaft continues to rotate, the piston moves upward, covering the transfer (B) and exhaust ports (A). The piston compresses the fresh air charge and creates a low-pressure area in the crankcase. A computer controlled electronic pump delivers a precise amount of oil into the crankcase through a dedicated passage (D). The fresh air-oil charge is drawn into the crankcase through the intake opening (C). Further upward movement of the piston closes the transfer port (B) and exhaust port (A). After both ports close, the computer controlled direct injector sprays the required amount of fuel into the combustion chamber.

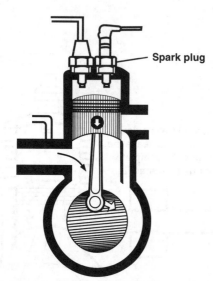

3

As the piston almost reaches the top of its travel, the spark plug fires, igniting the compressed air-fuel mixture. The piston continues to top dead center (TDC) and is pushed downward by the expanding gases.

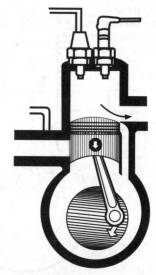

4

As the piston travels down, the exhaust gases leave the cylinder and the complete cycle starts all over again.

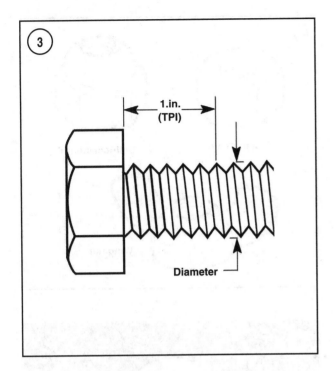

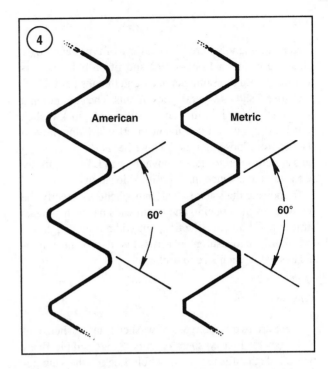

③

④

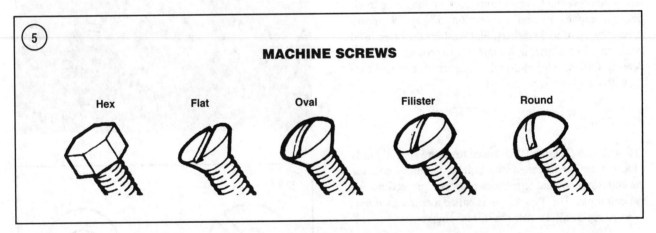

⑤ **MACHINE SCREWS**

Hex   Flat   Oval   Filister   Round

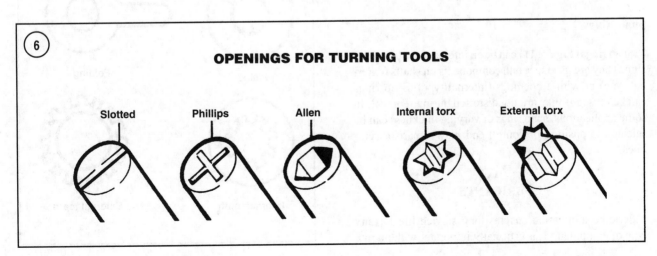

⑥ **OPENINGS FOR TURNING TOOLS**

Slotted   Phillips   Allen   Internal torx   External torx

Nuts

Nuts are manufactured in a variety of types and sizes. Most are hexagonal (six-sided) and fit on bolts, screws and studs with the same diameter and threads per inch.

Figure 7 shows several types of nuts. The common nut is usually used with some type of lockwasher. Self-locking nuts have a nylon insert that helps prevent the nut from loosening; no lockwasher is required. Wing nuts are designed for fast removal by hand. Wing nuts are used for convenience in non-critical locations.

To indicate the size of a nut, manufacturers specify the diameter of the opening and the threads per inch. This is similar to a bolt specification, but without the length dimension. The measurement across two flats on the nut indicates the wrench size to use.

Washers

There are two basic types of washers: flat washers and lockwashers. Flat washers (**Figure 8**) are simple discs with a hole that fits the screw or bolt. Lockwashers are designed to prevent a fastener from working loose due to vibration, expansion and contraction. **Figure 9** shows several types of lockwashers. Flat washers are often used between a lockwasher and a fastener to provide a smooth bearing surface. This allows the fastener to be turned easily with a tool.

Cotter Pins

Cotter pins (**Figure 10**) are used to secure special kinds of fasteners. The threaded stud, bolt or shaft has a hole for the cotter pin; the nut or nut lock piece has projections for the cotter pin. This type of nut is called a *castellated nut*. Always replace the cotter pin if it is removed.

Snap Rings

Snap rings (**Figure 11**) can be an internal or external design. They are used to retain components on shafts (external type) or within openings (internal type). Snap rings can be reused if they are not distorted during removal. In some applications, snap rings of varying thickness can be selected to position or control end play of parts assemblies.

LUBRICANTS

Periodic lubrication ensures long service life for any type of equipment. It is especially important with marine

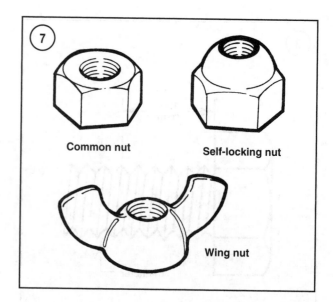

Common nut   Self-locking nut

Wing nut

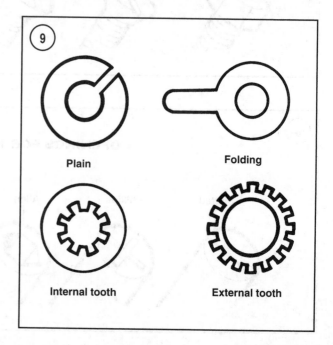

Plain   Folding

Internal tooth   External tooth

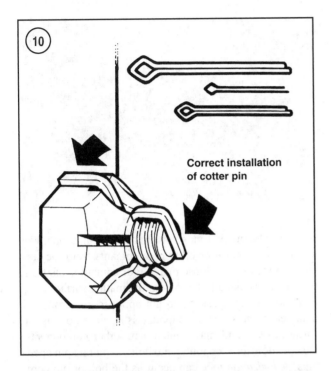

Correct installation
of cotter pin

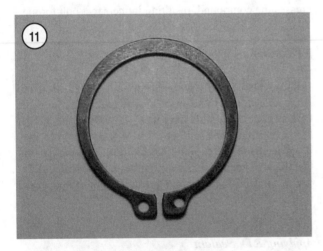

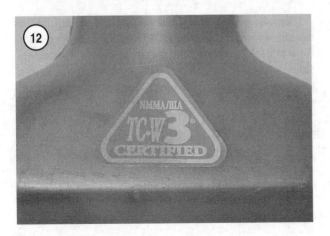

equipment because of exposure to salt, brackish or polluted water and other harsh environments. The *type* of lubricant used is just as important as the lubrication service itself; although, in an emergency, the wrong type of lubricant is better than none at all. The following sections describe the types of lubricants most often used on marine equipment. Follow the equipment manufacturer's recommendations for the lubricant types.

Generally, all liquid lubricants are called *oil*. They may be mineral-based (including petroleum bases), natural-based (vegetable and animal bases), synthetic-based or emulsions (mixtures). *Grease* is an oil thickened with additives, and maybe enhanced with anticorrosion, antioxidant and extreme pressure (EP) additives. Grease is often classified by the type of thickener added; lithium and calcium soap are the most commonly used.

Two-stroke Engine Oil

Lubrication for a two-stroke engine is provided by oil mixed into the incoming air or air-fuel mixture. Some of the oil mist settles in the crankcase, lubricating the crankshaft, bearings and lower end of the connecting rod. The rest of the oil enters the combustion chamber to lubricate the piston, rings and the cylinder wall. This oil is then burned with the air-fuel mixture during the combustion process.

Engine oil must have several special qualities to work well in a two-stroke engine. It must mix easily and stay in suspension with gasoline. When burned, it cannot leave behind excessive deposits. It must also withstand the high operating temperatures associated with two-stroke engines.

The National Marine Manufacturer's Association (NMMA) has set standards for oil used in two-stroke, water-cooled engines (TC-W). This is the NMMA TC-W grade (**Figure 12**). It indicates the oil's performance in the following areas:

1. Lubrication (prevention of wear and scuffing).
2. Spark plug fouling.
3. Piston ring sticking.
4. Preignition.
5. Piston varnish.
6. General engine condition (including deposits).
7. Exhaust port blockage.
8. Rust prevention.
9. Mixing ability with gasoline.

In addition to oil grade, manufacturers specify the ratio of gasoline to oil required during break-in and normal engine operation.

Gearcase Oil

Gearcase lubricants are assigned SAE viscosity numbers under the same system as four-stroke engine oil. Gearcase lubricant falls into the SAE 72-250 range. Some gearcase lubricants, such as SAE 85-90, are multi-grade.

Three types of marine gearcase lubricant are generally available: SAE 90 hypoid gearcase lubricant is designed for older manual-shift engines; Type C gearcase lubricant contains additives designed for the electric shift mechanisms; High viscosity gearcase lubricant is a heavier oil designed to withstand the shock loading of high-performance engines or engines subjected to severe duty use. Always use a gearcase lubricant of the type specified by the gearcase manufacturer.

Grease

Greases are graded by the National Lubricating Grease Institute (NLGI). Greases are graded by number according to the consistency of the grease. These ratings range from No. 000 to No. 6, with No. 6 being the most solid. A typical multipurpose grease is NLGI No. 2. For specific applications, equipment manufacturers may require grease with an additive such as molybdenum disulfide (MOS_2).

GASKET SEALANT

Gasket sealant is used instead of pre-formed gaskets on some applications, or as a gasket dressing on others. Three types of gasket sealant are commonly used: gasket sealing compound, room temperature vulcanizing (RTV) and anaerobic. Because these materials have different sealing properties, they cannot be used interchangeably.

Gasket Sealing Compound

Gasket sealing compound is a non-hardening liquid is used primarily as a gasket dressing. Gasket sealing compound is available in tubes or brush top containers. When exposed to air or heat it forms a rubber-like coating. The coating fills in small imperfections in gasket and sealing surfaces. Do not use gasket sealing compound that is old, has began to solidify or has darkened in color.

Applying Gasket Sealing Compound

Carefully scrape residual gasket material, corrosion deposits or paint from the mating surfaces. Use a blunt tip scraper and work carefully to avoid damaging the mating

surfaces. Use quick drying solvent and a clean shop towel to wipe residual oil or other contaminants from the surfaces. Wipe or blow loose material or contaminants from the gasket. Brush a light coat on the mating surfaces and both sides of the gasket. Do not apply more compound than necessary. Excess compound is squeezed out as the surfaces mate and may contaminate other components. Do not allow the compound into bolt or aligning pin openings. A *hydraulic lock* can occur as the bolt or pin compresses the compound, resulting in incorrect bolt torque.

RTV Sealant

RTV sealant is a silicone gel supplied in tubes. Moisture in the air causes RTV to cure. Always place the cap on the tube as soon as possible after using RTV. RTV has a shelf life of approximately one year and will not cure properly if the shelf life has expired. Check the expiration date on the tube and keep partially used tubes tightly sealed. RTV can generally fill gaps up to 1/4 in. (6.3 mm) and works well on slightly flexible surfaces.

Applying RTV Sealant

Carefully scrape all residual sealant and paint from the mating surfaces. Use a blunt tip scraper and work carefully to avoid damaging the mating surfaces. Remove residual sealant from bolt or aligning pin openings. Use a quick drying solvent and a clean shop towel to wipe all oil residue or other contaminants from the surfaces.

Apply RTV sealant in a continuous bead 0.08-0.12 in. (2-3 mm) thick. Circle all mounting bolt or aligning pin holes unless otherwise specified. Do not allow RTV sealant into bolt or aligning pin openings. A *hydraulic lock* can occur as the bolt or pin compresses the sealant, resulting in incorrect bolt torque. Tighten the mounting fasteners within ten minutes after application.

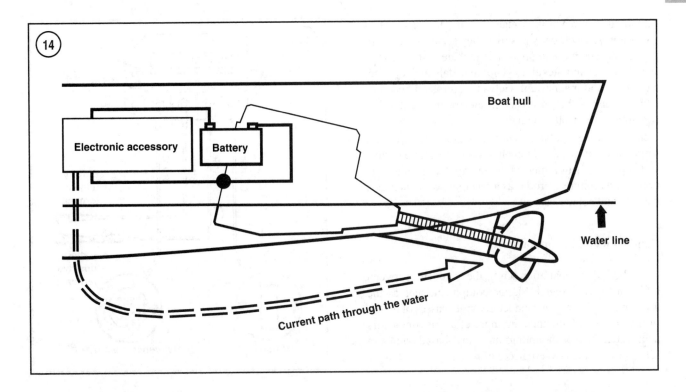

(14)

Electronic accessory

Battery

Boat hull

Water line

Current path through the water

Anaerobic Sealant

Anaerobic sealant is a gel supplied in tubes (**Figure 13**). It only cures in the absence of air, as when squeezed tightly between two machined mating surfaces. For this reason, it will not spoil if the cap is left off the tube. Do not use anaerobic sealant if one of the surfaces is flexible. Anaerobic sealant can fill gaps up to 0.030 in. (0.8 mm) and generally works best on rigid, machined flanges or surfaces.

Applying Anaerobic Sealant

Carefully scrape all residual sealant from the mating surfaces. Use a blunt tip scraper and work carefully to avoid damaging the mating surfaces. Clean sealant from bolt or aligning pin openings. Use a quick drying solvent and shop towel to wipe oil residue or other contaminants from the surfaces. Apply anaerobic sealant in a 0.04 in. (1 mm) thick continuous bead onto one of the surfaces. Circle bolt and aligning pin openings. Do not get sealant into bolt or aligning pin openings. A *hydraulic lock* can occur as the bolt or pin compresses the sealant, resulting in incorrect bolt torque. Tighten the mounting fasteners within ten minutes after application.

GALVANIC CORROSION

A chemical reaction occurs whenever two different types of metal are joined by an electrical conductor and immersed in electrolyte. Electrons transfer from one metal to the other through the electrolyte and return through the conductor.

The hardware on a boat is made of many different types of metal. The boat hull acts as a conductor between the metals. Even if the hull is wooden or fiberglass, the slightest film of water (electrolyte) within the hull provides conductivity. This combination creates a good environment for electron flow (**Figure 14**). Unfortunately, this electron flow results in galvanic corrosion, causing one of the metals to be corroded or eaten away. The amount of electron flow and, therefore, the amount of corrosion depends on the following factors:

1. The types of metal involved.
2. The efficiency of the conductor.
3. The strength of the electrolyte.

Metals

The chemical composition of the metals used in marine equipment has a significant effect on the amount and speed of galvanic corrosion. Certain metals are more resistant to corrosion than others. These electrically negative metals are commonly called *noble*; they act as the cathode in any reaction. Metals that are more subject to corrosion are electrically positive; they act as the anode in a reaction. The more *noble* metals include titanium, 18-8 stainless steel and nickel. Less *noble* metals include zinc, aluminum and magnesium. Galvanic corrosion becomes more severe as the difference in electrical potential between the two metals increases.

In some cases, galvanic corrosion can occur within a single piece of metal. Common brass is a mixture of zinc and copper. When immersed in electrolyte, the zinc portion of the mixture corrodes as a reaction occurs between the zinc and copper particles.

Conductors and Insulators

The hull of the boat often acts as the conductor between different types of metal. Marine equipment, such as the drive unit can act as the conductor. Large masses of metal, firmly connected together, are more efficient conductors than water. Rubber mountings and vinyl-based paint can act as insulators between pieces of metal.

Electrolyte

The water in which a boat operates acts as the electrolyte for the corrosion process.

Cold, clean freshwater is the poorest electrolyte. Pollutants increase conductivity; brackish or saltwater is an efficient electrolyte. The better the conductor, the more severe and rapid the corrosion. This is one of the reasons that most manufacturers recommend a freshwater flush after operating in polluted, brackish or saltwater.

Slowing Corrosion

Because of the environment in which marine equipment operates, preventing galvanic corrosion is practically impossible. There are several ways to slow the process. These are *not* substitutes for the corrosion protection methods discussed under *Sacrificial Anodes* and *Impressed Current Systems* in this chapter, but they can help these methods reduce corrosion.

Use fasteners of a metal more noble than the parts they secure. If corrosion occurs, the parts they secure may suffer but the fasteners will be protected. The larger secured parts are more able to withstand the loss of material. Major problems could arise if the fasteners corrode to the point of failure.

Keep all painted surfaces in good condition. If paint is scraped off and bare metal is exposed, corrosion rapidly

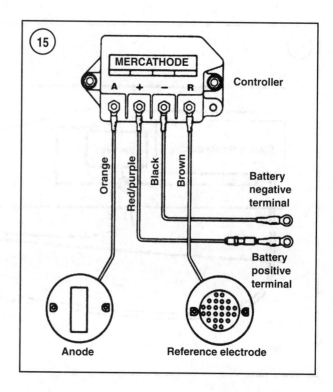

increases. Use a vinyl- or plastic-based paint, which acts as an electrical insulator.

Do not apply metal-based antifouling paint to metal parts of the boat or the drive unit. When applied to metal surfaces, it will react with the metal, and corrosion between the metal and the layer of paint occurs. Maintain a minimum 1 in. (25 mm) border between the painted surface and metal parts. Organic-based paints are available for use on metal surfaces.

Corrosion protection devices must be immersed in the electrolyte with the boat to provide protection. If the gearcase is raised out of the water when the boat is docked, anodes on the gearcase may be removed from the corrosion process rendering them ineffective. Never paint anodes or other protection devices. Paint or other coatings insulate them from the corrosion process.

Changes in the boat's equipment, such as the installation of a new stainless steel propeller, changes the electrical potential and may cause increased corrosion. Keep this in mind when adding equipment or changing exposed materials. Add additional anodes or other protection as required. Repairing corrosion damage usually costs more than additional corrosion protection.

Sacrificial Anodes

Sacrificial anodes are designed to corrode. They act as the anode in *any* galvanic reaction that occurs; any other

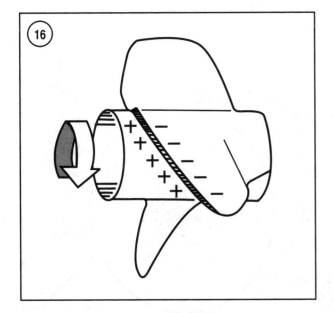

metal in the reaction acts as the cathode and is not damaged.

Anodes are usually made of zinc, which is far from resistant to oxidation and corrosion. Later model Quicksilver anodes are an aluminum and indium alloy. This alloy is less noble than the aluminum alloy in drive system components, providing the desired sacrificial properties. The aluminum and indium alloy is more resistant to oxide coating than zinc anodes. Oxide coating occurs as the anode material reacts with oxygen in the water. An oxide coating acts as an insulator, dramatically reducing corrosion protection.

Anodes must be used properly to be effective. Simply fastening anodes onto the boat in random locations will not properly reduce corrosion.

First determine how much anode surface is required to adequately protect the equipment's surface area. The Military Specification MIL-A-818001 states that one square inch of new anode protects either:

1. 800 square inches or freshly painted steel.
2. 250 square inches of bare steel or bare aluminum alloy.
3. 100 square inches of copper or copper alloy.

This rule applies for a boat at rest. When operating, additional anode area is required to protect the same surface area.

The anode must have a good electrical connection with the metal that it protects. If possible, attach an anode to all metal surfaces requiring protection.

Good quality anodes have inserts made of a more noble material around the anode fastener holes. Otherwise, the anode could erode away around the fastener hole, allowing the anode to loosen and possibly fall off, loosing needed protection.

Impressed Current System

An impressed current system can be added to any boat. The components of the commonly used Quicksilver Mercathode System (**Figure 15**) include the anode, controller and reference electrode. The anode in this system is coated with a very noble metal, such as platinum. It is almost corrosion-free and can last indefinitely. The reference electrode, under the boat's waterline, allows the control module to monitor the potential for corrosion. If electrical current flow reaches the point indicating galvanic corrosion, the control module applies positive battery voltage to the anode. The current flows from the anode to all other metal components, regardless of how noble or non-noble. The electrical current from the battery counteracts the galvanic reaction and dramatically reduces corrosion.

Only a small amount of current is needed to counteract corrosion. The control module uses input from the sensor to provide only the amount of current needed to suppress galvanic corrosion. Most systems consume a maximum of 0.2 Ah at full demand. Under normal conditions, these systems can provide protection for 8-12 weeks without recharging the battery. This system must have constant connection to the battery. Often the supply to the system is connected to a battery switching device and is inadvertently shut off by the operator when the boat docked.

An impressed current system is more expensive to install than sacrificial anodes, but the long-term cost may be lower due to low maintenance requirements and superior protection.

PROPELLERS

The propeller is the final link between the boat's drive system and the water. A perfectly maintained engine and hull are useless if the propeller is the wrong type or has deteriorated. Although propeller selection for a specific application is beyond the scope of this manual, the following sections provide the basic information needed to make an informed decision. A marine dealership is the best source for a propeller recommendation.

Propeller Operation

As the curved blades of a propeller rotate through the water, a high-pressure area forms on one side of the blade and a low-pressure area forms on the other side of the blade (**Figure 16**). The propeller moves toward the low-pressure area, carrying the boat with it.

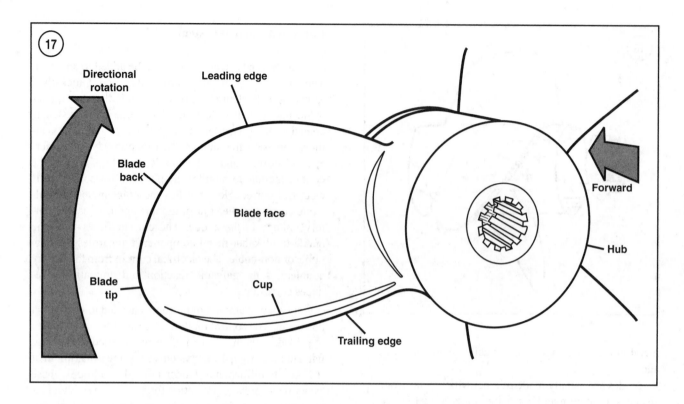

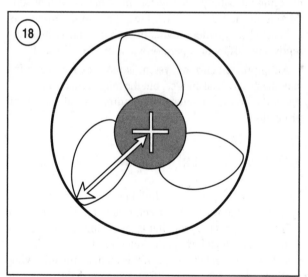

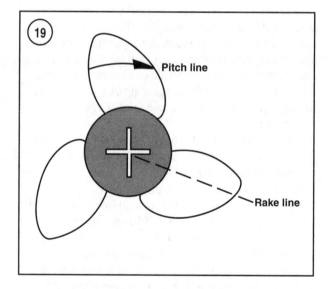

Propeller Parts

Although a propeller is usually a one-piece unit, it is made of several different parts (**Figure 17**). Variations in the design of these parts make different propellers suitable for different applications.

The blade tip is the point on the blade furthest from the center of the propeller hub or propeller shaft bore. The blade tip separates the leading edge from the trailing edge.

The leading edge is the edge of the blade nearest the boat. During forward gear operation, this is the area of the blade that first cuts through the water.

The trailing edge is the surface of the blade furthest from the boat. During reverse gear operation, this is the area of the blade that first cuts through the water.

The blade face is the surface of the blade that faces away from the boat. During forward gear operation, high-pressure forms on this side of the blade.

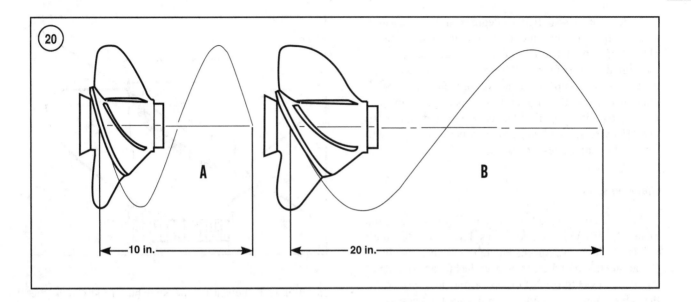

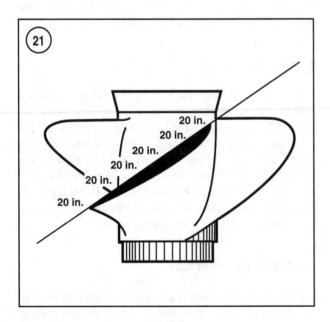

The blade back is the surface of the blade that faces toward the boat. During forward gear operation, low-pressure forms on this side of the blade.

The cup is a small curve or lip on the trailing edge of the blade. Cupped propeller blades generally perform better than noncupped propeller blades.

The hub is the central portion of the propeller. It connects the blades to the propeller shaft. On most drive systems, engine exhaust is routed through the hub; in this case, the hub is made up of an outer and inner portion, connected by ribs.

The diffuser ring is used on through hub exhaust models to prevent exhaust gasses from entering the blade area.

Propeller Design

Changes in length, angle, thickness and material of propeller parts make different propellers suitable for different applications.

Diameter

Propeller diameter is the distance from the center of the hub to the blade tip, multiplied by two. It is the diameter of the circle formed by the blade tips during propeller rotation (**Figure 18**).

Pitch and rake

Propeller pitch and rake describe the placement of the blades in relation to the hub (**Figure 19**).

Pitch describes the theoretical distance the propeller would travel in one revolution. In A, **Figure 20**, the propeller would travel 10 inches in one revolution. In B, **Figure 20**, the propeller would travel 20 inches in one revolution. This distance is only theoretical; during operation, the propeller achieves only 75-85% of its pitch. Slip rate is the difference in actual travel relative to the pitch. Lighter, faster boats typically achieve a lower slip rate than heavier, slower boats.

Propeller blades can be constructed with constant pitch (**Figure 21**) or progressive pitch (**Figure 22**). Progressive pitch starts low at the leading edge and increases toward the trailing edge. The propeller pitch specification is the average of the pitch across the entire blade. Propellers with progressive pitch usually perform better than constant pitch propellers.

Blade rake is specified in degrees and is measured along a line from the center of the hub to the blade tip. A blade perpendicular to the hub (**Figure 23**) has 0° rake. An angled blade (**Figure 23**) has a rake determined by its difference from perpendicular. Most propellers have rakes ranging from 0-20°. Lighter, faster boats generally perform better with propellers that have a greater amount of rake. Heavier, slower boats generally perform better with a propeller that has less rake.

Blade thickness

Blade thickness is not uniform at all points along the blade. For efficiency, blades are as thin as possible at all points while being strong enough to move the boat. Blades are thicker where they meet the hub and thinner at the blade tips (**Figure 24**) to support the heavier loads at the hub section of the blade. Overall blade thickness is dependent on the strength of the material used.

When cut from the leading edge to the trailing edge in the central portion of the blade (**Figure 25**), the propeller blade resembles an airplane wing. The blade face, where high-pressure exists during forward gear rotation, is almost flat. The blade back, where low-pressure exists during forward gear rotation, is curved with the thinnest portions at the edges and the thickest portion at the center.

Propellers that run only partially submerged, as in racing applications, may have a wedge shaped cross-section (**Figure 26**). The leading edge is very thin. The blade thickness increases toward the trailing edge, where it is thickest. This propeller is very inefficient when completely submerged.

Number of blades

The number of blades used on a propeller is a compromise between efficiency and vibration. A one-bladed propeller would be the most efficient, but it would create an unacceptable amount of vibration. As blades are added, efficiency decreases, but so does vibration. Most propellers have three or four blades, representing the most practical trade-off between efficiency and vibration.

Material

Propeller materials are chosen for strength, corrosion resistance and economy. Stainless steel, aluminum, plastic and bronze are the most commonly used materials. Bronze is quite strong but rather expensive. Stainless steel is more common than bronze because of its combination of strength and lower cost. Aluminum alloy and plastic

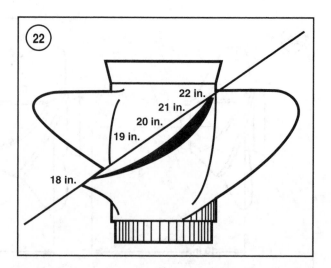

materials are the least expensive but usually lack the strength of stainless steel. Plastic propellers are more suited for low horsepower applications.

Direction of rotation

Propellers are made for both right-hand and left-hand rotation. Right-hand is the most commonly used. As viewed from the rear of the boat while in forward gear, a right-hand propeller turns clockwise and a left-hand propeller turns counterclockwise. When detached from the boat, the propeller's direction of rotation is determined by the angle of the blades (**Figure 27**). A right-hand propeller's blade slants from the upper left to the lower right; a left-hand propeller's blades are the opposite.

Cavitation and Ventilation

Cavitation and ventilation are *not* interchangeable terms. They refer to two distinct problems encountered during propeller operation.

To understand cavitation, consider the relationship between pressure and the boiling point of water. At sea level, water boils at 212° F (100° C). As pressure increases, such as within an engine cooling system, the boiling point of the water increases. The opposite is also true. As pressure decreases, water boils at a temperature lower than 212° F (100° C). If the pressure drops low enough, water boils at normal room temperature.

During normal propeller operation, low pressure forms on the blade back. Normally the pressure does not drop low enough for boiling to occur. However, poor propeller design, damaged blades or the wrong propeller can cause unusually low pressure on the blade surface (**Figure 28**).

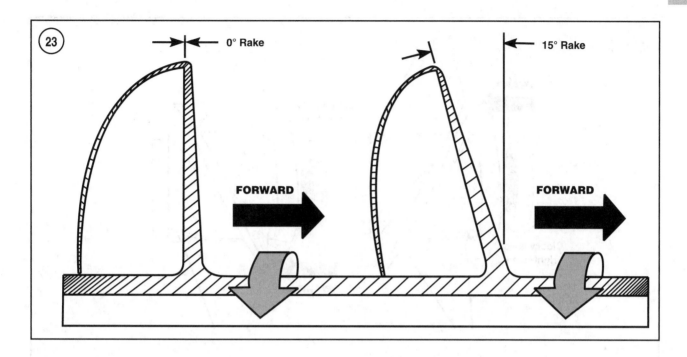

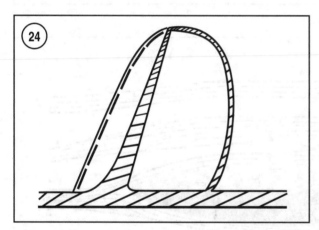

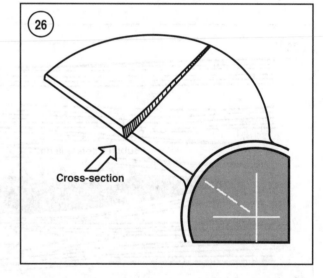

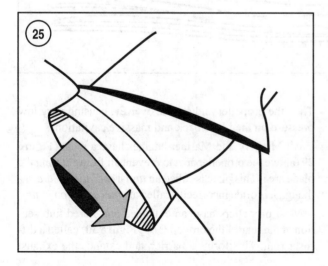

If the pressure drops low enough, boiling occurs and bubbles form on the blade surfaces. As the boiling water moves to a higher pressure area on the blade, the boiling ceases and bubbles collapse. The collapsing bubbles release energy that erodes the surface of the propeller blade.

Corroded surfaces, physical damage or even marine growth combined with high speed operation can cause low pressure and cavitation on gearcase surfaces. In such cases, low pressure forms as water flows over a protrusion or rough surface. Boiling water causes bubbles to form and collapse as they move to a higher pressure area toward the rear of the surface imperfection.

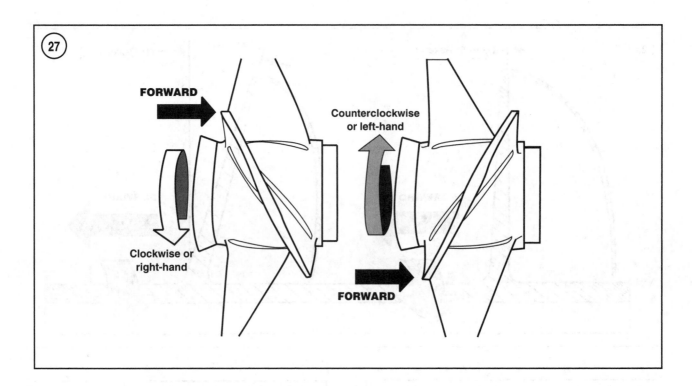

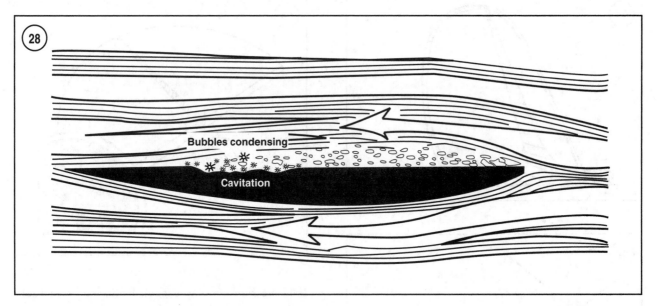

This entire process of pressure drop, boiling and bubble collapse is called *cavitation*. The ensuing damage is called *cavitation burn*. Cavitation is caused by a decrease in pressure, *not* an increase in temperature.

Ventilation is not as complex as cavitation. Ventilation refers to air entering the blade area, either from above the surface of the water or from a though-hub exhaust system. As the blades meet the air, the propeller momentarily looses it contact to the water, losing most of its thrust.

Then the propeller and engine overrev, causing very low pressure on the blade back and massive cavitation.

All Mercury and Mariner engines have a plate (**Figure 29**) above the propeller area to prevent air from entering the blade area. This plate is called an *anti-ventilation plate*, although it is often incorrectly called an *anticavitation plate*.

Most propellers have an extended and flared hub section at the rear of the propeller (A, **Figure 30**) called a diffuser ring. This forms a barrier, and extends the exhaust

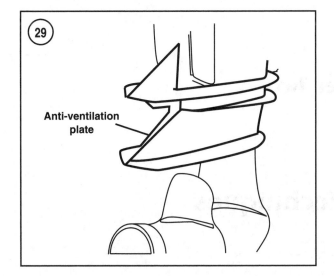

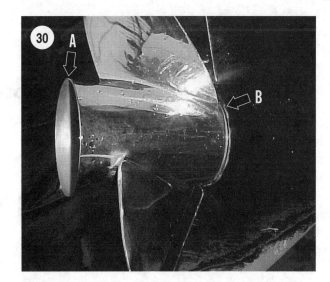

passage far enough aft to prevent the exhaust gases from ventilating the propeller.

A close fit of the propeller to the gearcase (B, **Figure 30**) keeps exhaust gasses from exiting and ventilating the propeller. Using the wrong propeller attaching hardware can position the propeller too far aft, preventing a close fit. The wrong hardware can also allow the propeller to rub heavily against the gearcase, causing rapid and permanent wear to both components. Wear or damage to these surfaces allows the propeller to ventilate.

Chapter Two

Tools and Techniques

This chapter describes the common tools required for engine repairs and troubleshooting, and techniques that make the work easier and more effective. Some procedures in this book require special skills or expertise; in some cases, it is better to entrust the job to a dealership or qualified specialist.

SAFETY FIRST

Professional mechanics can work for years and never suffer a serious injury. Follow a few simple rules and using common sense to avoid injury. Ignoring the rules can lead to physical injury and/or damaged equipment.

1. Never use gasoline as a cleaning solvent.

2. Never smoke or use a torch near flammable liquids, such as cleaning solvent. Dirty or solvent soaked shop towels are extremely flammable. When working in a garage, remember that most home gas appliances have pilot lights.

3. Never smoke or use a torch in an area where batteries are being charged. Highly explosive hydrogen gas is formed during the charging process.

4. Use the proper size wrench to avoid damaged fasteners and bodily injury.

5. When loosening a tight or stuck fastener, consider what could happen if the wrench should slip. Take the necessary precautions.

6. Keep the work area clean, uncluttered and well lit.

7. Wear safety goggles while using any type of tool, especially when drilling, grinding or using a cold chisel.

8. Never use worn or damaged tools.

9. Keep a Coast Guard approved fire extinguisher handy. Make sure it is rated for gasoline (Class B) and electrical (Class C) fires.

BASIC HAND TOOLS

A number of tools are required for maintenance and repair. Most of these tools are also used for home and automobile repairs. Some tools are made especially for working on marine engines; these tools can be purchased from a dealership. Using the required tools always makes the job easier and more effective.

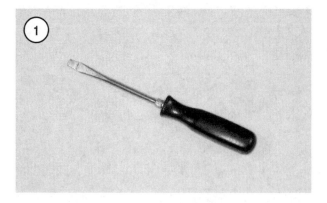

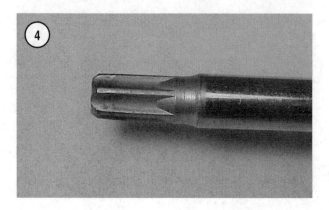

2

Keep the tools clean and in a suitable box. Keep them organized and stored with related tools. After using a tool, wipe off dirt and grease with a shop towel.

The following tools are required to perform virtually any repair job. Each tool is described and the recommended size is given for starting a tool collection. Additional tools and some duplication may be added with increased familiarity with the equipment. You may need all standard U.S. size tools, all metric size tools or a mixture of both.

Screwdrivers

A screwdriver (**Figure 1**) is a very basic tool, but if used improperly, it can do more damage than good. The slot on a screw has a definite dimension and shape. Always use a screwdriver that comforts to the shape of the screw. Use a small screwdriver for small screws and a large one for large screws, or the screw head will be damaged.

Three types of screwdrivers are commonly required: a slotted (flat-blade) screwdriver (**Figure 2**), Phillips screwdriver (**Figure 3**) and Torx screwdriver (**Figure 4**).

Screwdrivers are available in sets, which often include an assortment of slotted, Phillips and Torx blades. If purchasing them individually, buy at least the following:

1. Common screwdriver—5/16 × 6 in. blade.
2. Common screwdriver—3/8 × 12 in. blade.
3. Phillips screwdriver—No. 2 tip, 6 in. blade.
4. Phillips screwdriver—No. 3 tip, 6 in. blade.
5. Torx screwdriver—T15 tip, 6 in. blade.
6. Torx screwdriver—T20 tip, 6 in. blade.
7. Torx screwdriver—T25 tip, 6 in. blade.

Use screwdrivers only for driving screws. Never use a screwdriver for prying or chiseling. Do not attempt to remove a Phillips, Torx or Allen head screw with a slotted screwdriver; the screw head can be damaged to the point that the proper tool is unable to remove it.

Keep screwdrivers in the proper condition so they will last longer and perform better. Always keep the tip of a common screwdriver in good condition. Carefully re-grind the tip to the proper size and taper if it becomes worn or damaged. The sides of the blade must be parallel and the blade tip must be flat. Replace a Phillips or Torx screwdriver if its tip is worn or damaged.

Pliers

Pliers come in a wide range of types and sizes. Pliers are useful for cutting, gripping, bending and crimping. Never

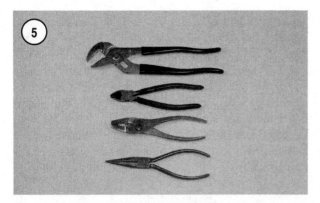

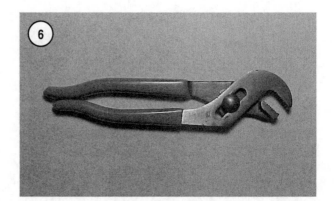

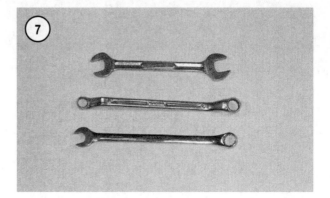

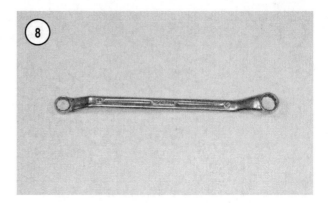

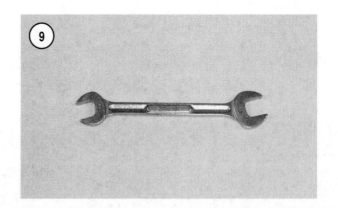

use pliers to cut hardened objects, or to turn bolts or nuts. **Figure 5** shows several types of pliers.

Each type of pliers has a specialized function. General purpose pliers are mainly used for gripping and bending. Locking pliers are used for gripping objects very tightly, like a vise. Needlenose pliers are used to grip or bend small objects. Adjustable or slip-joint pliers (**Figure 6**) can be adjusted to grip various sized objects; the jaws remain parallel for gripping objects such as pipe or tubing. There are many more types of pliers. The ones described here are the most common.

Box- and Open-end Wrenches

Box- and open-end wrenches (**Figure 7**) are available in sets in a variety of sizes. The number stamped near the end of the wrench refers to the distance between two parallel flats on the hex head bolt or nut.

Box-end wrenches (**Figure 8**) provide a better grip to the nut and are stronger than open end wrenches. An open-end wrench (**Figure 9**) grips the nut on only two flats. Unless it fits well, it may slip and round off the points on the nut. A box-end wrench grips all six flats. Box-end wrenches are available with 6-point or 12-point opening. The 6-point opening provides superior holding power; the 12-point allows a shorter swing for working in tight quarters.

Use an open-end wrench if a box-end wrench cannot be positioned over the nut or bolt. To prevent damage to the fastener, avoid using an open-end wrench if a large amount of tightening or loosening torque is required.

A combination wrench (**Figure 10**) has both a box-end and open-end. Both ends are the same size.

Adjustable Wrenches

An adjustable wrench (**Figure 11**) can be adjusted to fit virtually any nut or bolt head. However, it can loosen and

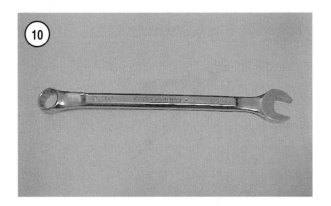

slip from the nut or bolt, causing damage to the nut and possible physical injury. Use an adjustable wrench only if a proper size open or box-end wrench is not available. Avoid using an adjustable wrench if a large amount of tightening or loosening torque is required.

Adjustable wrenches come in sizes ranging from 4 to 18 in. overall length. A 6 or 8 in. size is recommended as an all-purpose wrench.

Socket Wrenches

A socket wrench (**Figure 12**) is generally faster, safer and more convenient to use than a common wrench. Sockets, which attach to a suitable handle, are available with 6-point or 12-point openings, and 1/4, 3/8, and 1/2 in. drive sizes. The drive size corresponds with the square hole that mates with the ratchet or flex handle.

Torque Wrenches

A torque wrench (**Figure 13**) is used with a socket to measure how tight a nut or bolt is installed. They come in 1/4, 3/8, and 1/2 in. drive sizes. The drive size corresponds with the square hole that mates with the socket.

A typical 1/4 in. drive torque wrench measures torque in in.-lb. increments, and has a range of 20-150 in.-lb. (2.2-17 N•m). A typical 3/8 or 1/2 in. torque wrench measures torque in ft.-lb. increments, and has a range of 10-150 ft.-lb. (14-203 N•m).

Impact Driver

An impact driver (**Figure 14**) makes removal of tight fasteners easy, and reduces damage to bolts and screws. Interchangeable bits allow use on a variety of fasteners.

Snap Ring Pliers

Snap ring pliers, also called circlip pliers, are necessary to remove snap rings. Snap ring pliers (**Figure 15**) usually come with different size tips; many designs can be switched to handle internal or external type snap rings.

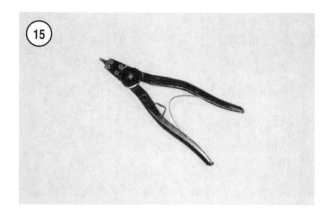

Hammers

Use the correct hammer (**Figure 16**) for the necessary repairs to prevent damage to other components. Use a plastic or rubber tip hammer for most repairs. Soft-faced hammers filled with buckshot (**Figure 17**) produce more force than a rubber or plastic tip hammer, and are sometimes necessary to remove stubborn components.

Never use a metal-faced hammer as severe damage to engine components or tools will occur. The same amount of force can be produced with a soft-faced hammer.

Feeler Gauges

A feeler gauge has either a flat or wire measuring gauge (**Figure 18**). Wire gauges are used to measure spark plug gap; flat gauges are used for other measurements. A non-magnet (brass) gauge may be specified when working around magnetized components.

Other Special Tools

Many of the maintenance and repair procedures require special tools (**Figure 19**). Most of the tools are available from marine dealerships. The remainder are available from tool suppliers. Instruction on their use and the manufacture's part numbers are included in the appropriate chapter.

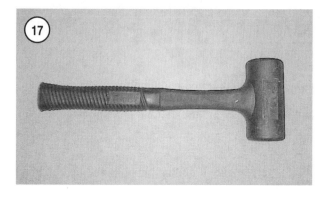

Some special tools can be made locally by a qualified machinist, often at a lower price. Many marine dealerships and rental outlets will rent some of the required tools. Using makeshift tools may result in damaged parts that cost far more than the recommended tool.

TEST EQUIPMENT

This section describes equipment for testing, adjustments and measurements on marine engines. Most of these tools are available from a local marine dealership or automotive parts store.

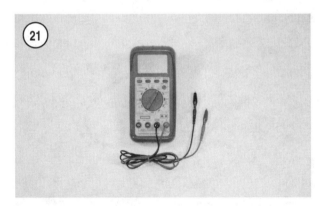

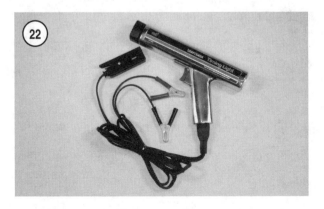

Multimeter

A multimeter is invaluable for electrical troubleshooting and service. It combines a voltmeter, ohmmeter and an ammeter in one unit. It is often called a VOM.

Two types of mutimeter are available: analog and digital. On analog meters (**Figure 20**), a moving needle and marked bands on the meter face indicate the volt, ohm and amperage scales. An analog meter must be calibrated each time the battery or scale is changed.

A digital meter (**Figure 21**) is ideal for electrical troubleshooting because it is easy to read and more accurate than an analog meter. Most models are auto-ranging, have automatic polarity compensation and have internal overload protection circuits.

Either type of meter is suitable for most electrical testing described in this manual. An analog meter is better suited for testing pulsing voltage signals such as those produced by the ignition system. A digital meter is better suited for tests involving very low resistance or voltage reading (less than 1 volt or 1 ohm). The test instructions indicate if a specific type of meter is required.

The ignition system produces electrical pulses that are too short in duration for accurate measurement with a common multimeter. Use a meter with peak volt reading capability for ignition system testing. This type of meter utilizes special circuits that capture and display the peak voltage reached during the pulse. Unless specified, use the appropriate scale in the DVA function when testing the ignition system.

Scale selection, meter specifications and test lead connection points vary by the manufacturer and model of the meter. Read the instructions supplied with the meter before performing any test. The meter and certain electrical components on the engine can be damaged if tested incorrectly. Have the test performed by a qualified professional if you are unfamiliar with the testing or general meter usage. The expense to replace damaged equipment can far exceed the cost of having the test performed by a professional.

Strobe Timing Light

A timing light is necessary to set the ignition timing while the engine is running. By flashing a light at the precise instant the spark plug fires, the position of the timing mark can be seen. The flashing light makes a moving mark appear to stand still next to a stationary timing mark.

Suitable timing lights (**Figure 22**) range from inexpensive models to expensive models with a built-in tachometer and timing advance compensator. A built-in tachometer is very useful as most ignition timing specifications refer to a specific engine speed.

A timing advance compensator can delay the strobe enough to bring the timing mark to a certain place on the scale. Although useful for troubleshooting, this feature should not be used to check or adjust the base ignition timing.

Tachometer/Dwell Meter

A portable tachometer (**Figure 23**) is needed for tuning and testing engines. Ignition timing and carburetor adjustments must be performed at a specified engine speed. Tachometers are available with either an analog or digital display.

Carburetor adjustments are performed at idle speed. If using an analog tachometer, choose one with a low range of 0-1000 rpm or 0-2000 rpm and a high range of 0-6000 rpm. The high range setting is necessary for testing, but lacks the accuracy needed at lower speeds. At lower speeds, the meter must be capable of detecting changes of 25 rpm or less.

Digital tachometers (**Figure 24**) are generally easier to use than most analog tachometers. Their measurements are accurate at all speeds without the need to change the range or scale. Many of these use an inductive pickup to receive the signal from the ignition system.

A dwell meter is often incorporated into the tachometer to allow testing and/or adjustments to engines with a breaker point ignition system. The engines covered in this manual are all equipped with a transistorized ignition system and a dwell meter is not required.

Compression Gauge

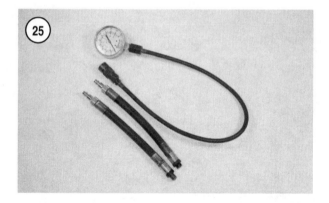

A compression gauge (**Figure 25**) measures the amount of pressure created in the combustion chamber during the compression stroke. Compression indicates the general engine condition making it one of the most useful troubleshooting tools.

The easiest gauge to use has screw-in adapters that fit the spark plug holes. Press-in, rubber tipped gauges are also available. This gauge must be held firmly into the spark plug opening to prevent air leakage and inaccurate compression measurements. Only use a good quality gauge and check its accuracy by measuring the compression on a well performing engine. False measurement can lead to needless and expensive power head repair.

Hydrometer

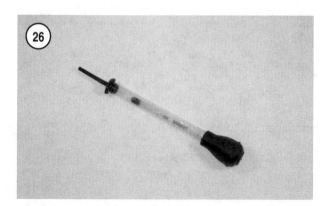

A hydrometer measures the specific gravity of the electrolyte in the battery. The specific gravity indicates the

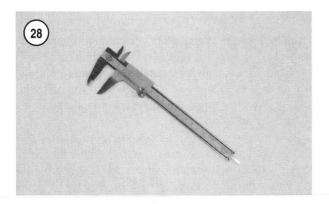

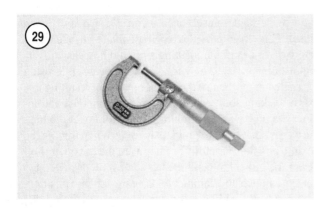

of parts assemblies. It also measures free movement between the gear teeth (backlash) in the drive unit.

Vernier calipers (**Figure 28**), micrometers (**Figure 29**) and other precision tools are used to measure the size of parts, such as the piston.

Precision measuring equipment must be stored, handled and used carefully or it will not remain accurate.

BASIC SERVICE METHODS

Most of the service procedures are straightforward and can be performed by anyone handy with tools. Consider the necessary skill, tools and equipment before attempting repairs involving major disassembly of the engine or drive unit.

Marine engines are subjected to conditions very different from most engines. They are repeatedly subjected to a corrosive environment followed by long periods of non-use. This increases corrosion damage to fasteners, causing difficulty or breakage during removal.

Some operations, for example, require the use of a press. Other operations require precision measurement. Have the procedure(s) or measurement(s) performed by a professional if the correct equipment or experience is lacking.

Working With Electrical Components

All models covered in this manual use a transistorized ignition system. The components of the system are able to withstand a rigorous marine environment. However, they can be damaged under certain circumstances, such as operating the engine with the spark plug lead(s) disconnected. Always ground disconnected spark plug leads before operating the starter.

Battery Precautions

Disconnecting or connecting the battery can create a surge of current throughout the electrical system. This surge can damage certain components of the charging system. Always make sure the ignition switch is in the *off* position before connecting or disconnecting the battery or changing the selection on a battery switch (**Figure 30**).

Always disconnect both battery cables and remove the battery from the boat for charging. If the battery cables are connected, the charger may induce a damaging surge of current into the electrical system. During charging, batteries produce explosive and corrosive gasses. These gasses can cause corrosion within the battery compartment and create an extremely hazardous condition.

battery's state of charge by measuring the density of the electrolyte as compared to pure water. Choose a hydrometer (**Figure 26**) with automatic temperature compensation; otherwise, the electrolyte temperature must be measured to determine the actual specific gravity.

Precision Measuring Tools

Various tools are required to make precision measurements. A dial indicator (**Figure 27**), for example, determines piston position in the cylinder, runout and end-play

The cables must be disconnected from the battery prior to testing, adjusting or repairing many of the systems or components on the engine. This prevents damage to test equipment, ensures accurate testing or adjustment and ensures safety. Always disconnect or connect the battery cables in the appropriate order.

1. To disconnect the battery cables, disconnect the negative then the positive cable.

2. To connect the battery cables, connect the positive then negative cable.

Preparation for Disassembly

Repairs go much faster if the equipment is clean. There are special cleaners, such as Gunk or Bel-Ray Degreaser, for washing engine related and non-electrical components. Spray or brush on the cleaning solution, let it stand, then rinse it off with a garden hose. Clean oily or greasy parts with a cleaning solvent after removal.

Use pressurized water to remove marine growth, corrosion or mineral deposits from external components, such as the gearcase, drive shaft housing and clamp brackets. Avoid directing pressurized water directly at seals or gaskets. Pressurized water can flow past seal and gasket surfaces and contaminate lubricating fluids.

WARNING
Never use gasoline as a cleaning agent. It presents an extreme fire hazard. Always work in a well-ventilated area if using cleaning solvent. Keep a Coast Guard approved fire extinguisher, rated for gasoline fires in the work area.

Removal and disassembly to access defective parts is much of the cost of taking the vessel to a dealership. Frequently, most of the disassembly can be performed and the defective part or assembly can be taken to the dealership for repair.

Before beginning repair work, read the appropriate procedure in this manual. Study the illustrations and text to fully understand what is involved to complete the repair. Make arrangements to purchase or rent all required special tools and equipment before starting the repair.

Because of the extreme demands placed on marine equipment, keep several points in mind when performing service and repairs. Following these general suggestions can improve the overall life of the machine and help avoid costly problems.

1. Unless otherwise specified, apply a locking compound to all bolts and nuts even if they are secured with a lockwasher. If a locking compound is called for, use only the specified grade of threadlocking compound. A screw

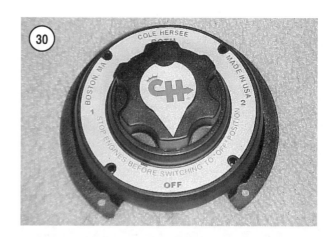

or bolt lost from an engine cover or bearing retainer could easily cause serious and expensive damage before the loss is noticed. When applying threadlocking compound, use only enough to lightly coat the threads. If too much is used, it can work down the threads and bind parts not meant to be stuck together.

2. Be careful when using air tools to remove stainless steel nuts or bolts. The threads of stainless steel fasteners are easily damaged by the heat generated if spun rapidly. To prevent thread damage, apply a penetrating oil as a cooling agent and loosen or tighten them slowly.

3. When straightening the tab of a fold-over lockwasher, use a wide-blade chisel, such as an old and dull wood chisel. This chisel provides a better contact surface than a screwdriver or pry bar, making straightening easier. During installation, use a new fold-over lockwasher. Reusing the same tab may cause the washer to break, resulting in a loss of locking ability and a loose piece of metal in the engine. If a new washer is not available, fold over a tab on the washer that was not previously used. When folding the tab into position, carefully pry it toward the flat on the bolt or nut. Use pliers to bend the tab against the fastener. Do not use a punch and hammer to drive the tab into position. The resulting fold may be too sharp, weakening the washer and increasing its chance of failure.

4. Use only authorized replacement parts when replacing missing or damaged bolts, screws or nuts. Many fasteners are specially hardened for the application. The wrong bolt can easily cause serious and expensive damage.

5. Install only authorized gaskets. Unless specified otherwise, install them without sealant. Many gaskets are made with a material that swells when it contacts oil. Gasket sealer prevents them from swelling as intended and can result in oil leaks. Authorized gaskets are cut from material of a precise thickness. Installation of a too thick or too thin gasket in a critical area could cause expensive damage.

Disassembly Precautions

During disassembly, keep a few general precautions in mind. Force is rarely needed to separate parts. If parts fit tightly, such as a bearing on a shaft, there is usually a tool designed to separate them. Never use a screwdriver to separate parts with a machined mating surface, such as cylinder heads and manifolds. The surfaces will be damaged and could cause a leak.

Make diagrams or take photographs wherever similar-appearing parts are found. For example, cylinder head bolts are often different lengths. Disassembled parts can be left for several days or longer before work is resumed. Carefully arranged parts can get disturbed.

Cover all openings after removing parts to keep dirt, insects or other parts from entering.

Tag all similar internal parts for location and mounting direction. Reinstall all internal components in the same locations and mounting directions as removed. Record the thickness and locations of shims as removed. Place small bolts and parts in plastic sandwich bags. Seal and label the bags with masking tape.

Tag all wires, hoses and connection points, and make a sketch of the routing. Never rely on memory alone; it may be several days or longer before work is resumed.

Protect all painted surfaces from physical damage. Never allow gasoline or cleaning solvent on these surfaces.

Assembly Precautions

No parts, except those assembled with a press fit, require unusual force during assembly. If a part is hard to remove or install, find out why before proceeding.

When assembling parts, start all fasteners, then tighten them evenly in an alternating or crossing pattern unless a specific tightening sequence or procedure is given.

When assembling parts, install all shims, spacers and washers in the same position and location as removed.

Whenever a rotating part butts against a stationary part, look for a shim spacer or washer. Use new gaskets, seals and O-rings if there is any doubt about the conditions of the used ones. Unless otherwise specified, a thin coat of oil on gaskets may help them seal more effectively. Use heavy grease to hold small parts in place if they tend to fall out during assembly.

Use emery cloth and oil to remove high spots from piston surfaces. Use a dull scraper to remove carbon deposits from the cylinder head, ports and piston crown. *Do not* scratch or gouge these surfaces. Wipe the surfaces clean with a *clean* shop towel when finished.

If the carburetor must be repaired, completely disassemble it and soak all metal parts in a commercial carburetor cleaner. Never soak gaskets and rubber or plastic parts in these cleaners. Clean rubber or plastic parts in warm soapy water. Never use a wire to clean out jets and small passages; they are easily damaged. Use compressed air to blow debris from all passages within the carburetor body.

The break-in procedure for a newly rebuilt engine or drive is the same as a new engine. Use the recommended break-in oil and follow the instructions provided in the appropriate chapter. Take the time to do the job right.

Removing Frozen Fasteners

When a nut or bolt corrodes and cannot be removed, several methods may be used to loosen it. First, apply penetrating oil, such as Liquid Wrench or WD-40 available at hardware or automotive supply stores. Apply it liberally to the threads and allow it to penetrate for 10-15 minutes. Tap the fastener several times with a small hammer; do not hit it hard enough to cause damage. Reapply the penetrating oil if necessary.

For stuck screws, apply penetrating oil as described, then insert a screwdriver in the slot. Tap the top of the screwdriver with a hammer. This loosens the corrosion in the threads. If the screw head is too damaged to use a screwdriver, grip the head with locking pliers to loosen it.

A Phillips, Allen or Torx screwdriver may start to slip in the screw during removal. If this occurs, stop immediately and apply a dab of valve lapping compound to the tip of the screwdriver. Valve lapping compound or a special screw removal compound (**Figure 31**) is available from most hardware and automotive parts stores. Insert the driver into the screw and apply downward pressure while

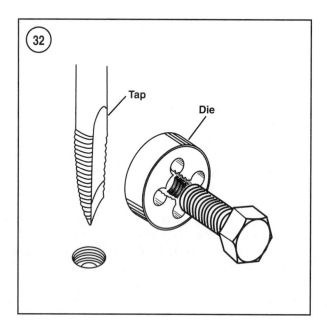

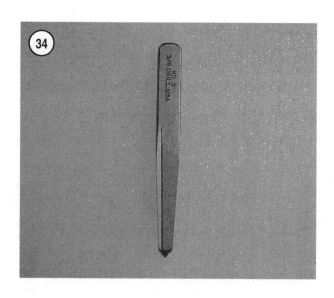

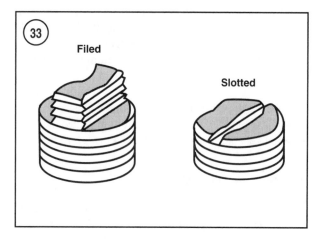

turning. The gritty material in the compound improves the grip to the driver, allowing more force to be applied before it will slip. Keep the compound away from other engine components. It is very abrasive and can cause rapid wear if applied to moving or sliding surfaces.

Avoid applying heat unless specifically instructed. Heat can warp or remove the temper from parts.

Damaged Thread Repair

Occasionally, threads are stripped through carelessness or impact damage. Often the threads can be repaired by using a tap (for internal threads) or die (for external threads) (**Figure 32**).

Damaged threads in a housing or component can often be repaired by installing a threaded insert.

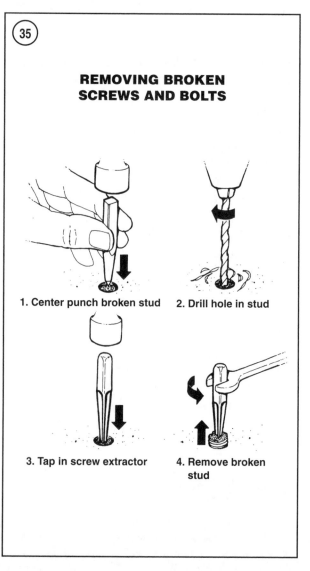

REMOVING BROKEN SCREWS AND BOLTS

1. Center punch broken stud

2. Drill hole in stud

3. Tap in screw extractor

4. Remove broken stud

2

Removing Broken Bolts or Screws

The head of a bolt or screw may unexpectedly twist off during removal. Several methods are available for removing the remaining portion of the bolt or screw.

If a large portion of the bolt or screw projects out, try gripping it with locking pliers. If the projecting portion is too small, file it to fit a wrench or cut a slot in it to fit a screwdriver (**Figure 33**). If the head breaks off flush or cannot be turned with a screwdriver or wrench, use a screw extractor (**Figure 34**). To do this, center punch the remaining portion of the screw or bolt (**Figure 35**). Select the proper size extractor for the fastener. Using the drill bit size specified on the extractor, drill a hole into the fastener. Do not drill deeper than the remaining fastener. Carefully tap the extractor into the hole (**Figure 35**). Back the remnant out with a wrench on the extractor.

Chapter Three

Troubleshooting

Troubleshooting is the process of testing individual systems to quickly isolate good systems from defective or inoperative system(s). When a system is identified as defective, troubleshooting continues with testing of the individual components of the suspect system. Perform one test procedure at a time to determine the condition of each component. Occasionally a component in a system cannot be isolated for testing. In this case, other components are tested and eliminated until the suspect component is identified as defective by the process of elimination. When troubleshooting, always test systems before components and be methodical. Haphazardly jumping from one system or component to another may eventually solve the problem, but will waste time and effort. Use the various system diagrams provided in this manual to identify all components in a system. Test each component in a rational order to determine which component has caused the system to fail.

After noticing a symptom, such as a noticeable decrease in performance or unsatisfactory operating characteristic, consider the following questions:

1. Did the problem occur all at once (suddenly) or was its onset gradual?
2. Is there a specific rpm or load at which the problem occurs?
3. Does the weather (extreme cold or heat) affect the symptom?
4. Has any recent service work been performed?
5. Has the engine recently come out of storage?
6. Have the fuel suppliers or fuel grades been changed recently?
7. Is the manufacturer's recommended oil being used?
8. Have any accessories been added to the boat or motor recently?

Simple things like failing to prime the fuel system, attach the safety lanyard and incorrect starting procedures have caused many problems for boat operators.

Before beginning troubleshooting procedures, perform a thorough visual inspection of the unit. Check the condition of the battery cable connections at both ends, all electrical harness connectors and terminals, fuel quantity, quality and supply, indications of engine overheating, evi-

dence of fuel, oil and water leaks, and mechanical integrity (loose fasteners, cracked or broken castings). Take your time and examine components closely. Use your hands to touch, feel and wiggle components.

Be realistic about the level of skill required to complete a procedure. Avoid major disassembly which will make you feel compelled to continue work well beyond your qualifications. Service departments tend to charge heavily to reassemble an engine and some will refuse to take on such a job.

Performing lubrication, maintenance and engine tune-up procedures as described in Chapter Four reduce the need for troubleshooting. However, because of the harsh and demanding environment in which the outboard motor operates, troubleshooting at some point in the motors serviceable life is inevitable.

This chapter contains troubleshooting procedures. Once the defective component is identified, refer to appropriate chapter for removal and installation procedures. **Tables 1-3** list starting, fuel and ignition system troubleshooting. **Tables 4-15** list test specifications.

SAFETY PRECAUTIONS

Wear approved eye protection (**Figure 1**) at all times, especially when machinery is in operation and hammers are being used. Wear approved ear protection during all running tests and in the presence of noisy machinery. Keep loose clothing tucked in and long hair tied back. Refer to *Safety* in Chapter Two for additional safety guidelines.

Always disconnect the negative battery cable before making or breaking an electrical connection. When performing tests that require cranking the engine without starting, disconnect and ground the spark plug leads to prevent accidental starts and sparks.

Securely cap or plug all disconnected fuel lines to prevent fuel discharge when the motor is cranked or the primer bulb is squeezed.

Read all manufacturer's instructions and safety sheets for test equipment and special tools being used.

Do not substitute parts unless they meet or exceed the original manufacturer's specifications.

Never run an outboard motor without an adequate water supply. Never run an outboard motor at wide-open throttle without an adequate load. Never exceed 3000 rpm in neutral (no load).

Safely performing on-water tests requires two people. One person to operate the boat, the other to monitor the gauges or test instruments. All personnel must remain seated inside the boat at all times. Do not lean over the transom while the boat is under way. Use extensions to allow all gauges and meters to be located in the normal seating area.

A test propeller is an economical alternative to the dynometer. A test propeller is also a convenient alternative to on-water testing. Test propellers are made by turning down the diameter of a standard low pitch aluminum propeller until the recommended wide-open throttle engine speed can be obtained with the motor in a test tank or backed into the water on the trailer. Be careful when the boat is tied to a dock as considerable thrust is developed by the test propeller. Some docks may not be able to withstand the load.

Propeller repair stations can provide the modification service. Normally, approximately 1/3 to 1/2 of the blades are removed. However, it is better to remove too little than too much. It may take several tries to achieve the correct full throttle speed, but once it is achieved, no further modifications will be required. Many propeller repair stations have experience with this type of modification and may be able to recommend a starting point.

Test propellers also allow simple tracking of engine performance. The full throttle test speed of an engine fitted with a correctly modified test propeller can be recorded and tracked from season to season. It is not unusual for a new or rebuilt engine to show a slight increase in test propeller engine speed as complete break-in is achieved. The engine generally holds this speed over the normal service life of the engine. As the engine begins to wear out, the test propeller engine speed will show a gradual decrease that deteriorates to a marked or drastic decrease as the engine nears the point of failure.

OPERATING REQUIREMENTS

All two-stroke engines require three basic conditions to run properly: correct air and fuel mixture from the carburetor, crankcase and combustion chamber compression and adequate spark delivered to the spark plug at the correct time. Remember fuel, compression and spark

(**Figure 2**) when troubleshooting. If any of these are lacking, the motor will not run. First, verify the mechanical integrity of the engine by performing a compression test (Chapter Four). Once compression has been verified, test the ignition system with an air gap spark tester. Finally, check on the fuel system. Troubleshooting in this order provides the quickest results.

If the engine has been sitting for any length of time and refuses to start, check the battery to make sure it is adequately charged, then inspect the battery cable connections at the battery and the engine. Examine the fuel delivery system. This includes the fuel tank, fuel pump, fuel lines, fuel filters and carburetor(s). Rust or corrosion may have formed in the tank, restricting fuel flow. Gasoline deposits may have gummed up carburetor jets and air passages. Gasoline may have lost its potency after standing for long periods. Condensation may have contaminated the fuel with water. Connect a portable tank containing fresh fuel mix to help isolate the problem. Do not drain the old gasoline unless it is at fault. Always dispose of old gasoline in accordance with EPA regulations.

Two-Stroke Crankcase Pressure

The following troubleshooting procedure requires a multimeter and adapter cables. However, the system is designed for easy troubleshooting diagnosis by using the Merc/Mariner Quicksilver Digital Diagnostic Terminal (DDT). This system displays sensor inputs and actuator outputs at the ECM.

A two-stroke engine cannot function unless the crankcase is adequately sealed. If fuel and ignition systems test satisfactorily and a compression test indicates that the combustion chamber (piston, rings, cylinder walls and head gasket) is in acceptable condition, test the crankcase sealing. As the piston travels downward, the crankcase must pressurize and push the air/fuel mixture into the combustion chamber as the intake ports are uncovered. As the piston travels upward, the crankcase must create a vacuum to pull the air/fuel mixture into the crankcase from the carburetor in preparation for the next cycle. Refer to Chapter Two for operational diagrams of a typical two-stroke engine.

Leaks in the crankcase cause the air/fuel charge to leak into the atmosphere under crankcase compression. During the intake stroke, crankcase leaks cause air from the atmosphere to be drawn into the crankcase, diluting the air/fuel charge. The result is inadequate fuel in the combustion chamber. On multiple cylinder engines, each crankcase must be sealed from all other crankcases. Internal leaks allow the air/fuel charge to leak to another cylinder's crankcase, rather than travel to the correct combustion chamber.

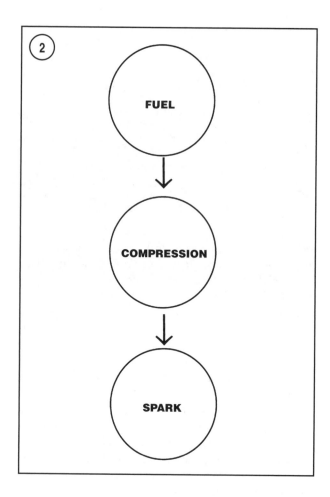

The function of the lower piston ring on most two-stroke engines is crankcase compression. It is difficult to test this ring. A standard compression test tests the upper compression ring, not the lower ring. A symptom of lower ring failure is the inability to idle at the recommended idle speed. The engine runs fine at higher speeds, but slowly dies at idle speed.

External crankcase leaks can be identified with a visual inspection for fuel residue leaking from crankcase parting lines, upper and lower crankshaft seals, reed valves, and intake manifolds. Pressure leaking out of the crankcase can be identified with a soap and water solution. Air leaking into the crankcase can be found by applying oil to the suspect sealing area. The oil will be drawn into the crankcase at the point of the leak.

Internal leaks are difficult to identify. If there are fittings on each crankcase for fuel pumps, primers or recirculation systems, a fuel pressure/vacuum gauge can be attached. As the engine is cranked over, a repeating pressure/vacuum cycle should be observed on the gauge. The pressure reading should be substantially higher than the vacuum reading. All cylinders should read basically

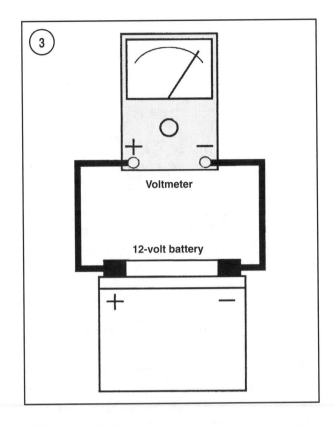

Voltmeter

12-volt battery

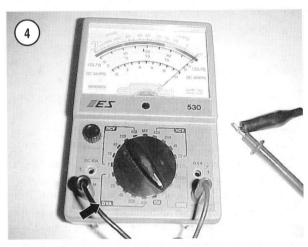

the same. If this test is not possible, test the fuel and ignition systems. As a final resort, disassemble and internally inspect the engine.

TERMINOLOGY AND TEST EQUIPMENT

Voltage

Voltage is the pressure in an electrical circuit. The more pressure, the more work that can be done. Voltage can be

visualized as water pressure in a garden hose. The more pressure, the further the water can be sprayed. You can have water present in the hose, but without pressure, you cannot accomplish anything. If the water pressure is too high, the hose will burst. When voltage is excessive, it will leak past insulation and arc to ground. Voltage is always measured with a voltmeter in a simple parallel connection. The connection of a voltmeter directly to the negative and positive terminals of a battery is an example of a parallel connection (**Figure 3**). Nothing has to be disconnected to make a parallel connection.

DC Voltage

DC voltage is direct current. The electricity always flows in one direction. All circuits associated with the battery are DC circuits.

AC Voltage

AC voltage is alternating current. The current flows in one direction momentarily, then switches to the opposite direction. The frequency at which AC voltage changes direction is hertz. In typical outboard motors, the charging system's stator output is AC voltage. In larger, inboard motors, AC voltage is typically created by a dedicated AC generator (genset) that powers high load devices such as air-conditioning and appliances. Shore power is also AC voltage. Standard AC voltmeters take an average reading of the fluctuating voltage signal. RMS (root mean square) AC voltmeters use a different mathematical formula to determine the value of the voltage signal. RMS meters should only be used where specified, since the difference in readings between a standard AC meter and a RMS AC meter is significant.

DVA Voltage

DVA stands for direct voltage adapter. This measures AC voltage at the absolute peak or highest value of the fluctuating AC voltage signal. Peak readings are substantially higher than standard or RMS AC values and are typically used when testing marine CD (capacitor discharge) ignition systems. Failure to use a meter with a DVA scale can lead to a misdiagnosis and the replacement of good components. See **Figure 4** for a typical multimeter with a DVA scale.

Amperes

Current is the actual flow of electricity in a circuit and is measured in Amperes (amps). Current can be visualized as water flowing from a garden hose. There can be pressure in the hose, but if it is not allowed to flow, no work can be done. The higher the flow of current, the more work that can be done. However, when too much current flows through a wire, the wire will overheat and melt. Melted wires are caused by excessive current, not excessive volts. Amps are measured with an ammeter in a simple series connection. A circuit must be disconnected and the ammeter spliced into the circuit. An ammeter must have all of the current flow through it. Always use an ammeter that can read higher than the anticipated current flow. Always connect the positive (red) lead of the ammeter to where the electricity is coming from (electrical source) and the negative (black) lead of the ammeter to where the electricity is going (electrical load) (**Figure 5**).

Many digital multimeters use an inductive or clamp-on ammeter test lead (**Figure 6**). These leads read the magnetic field strength created by current flowing through a wire. No direct electrical connection is required.

A simple form of ammeter is the direct reading ammeter (**Figure 7**). These meters also use the inductive principle for readings.

Watts

Watts (W) is the measurement unit for power in an electrical circuit. Watts rate the ability to do electrical work. The easiest formula for calculating watts is to take the system voltage times the amps flowing. 12-volt system times 10 amp alternator equals 120 watt maximum load. Amp load can be calculated by dividing watts by voltage. 12-watt radio divided by 12-volt system uses 1 amp of current. When calculating load on a charging system, remember the system cannot carry more load than it is rated for or the battery discharges during engine operation.

Ohms

Ohms is the measurement unit for resistance in an electrical circuit. Resistance causes a reduction in current flow and a reduction in voltage. Visualized as a kink in a garden hose, which would cause less water (current) to flow and cause less pressure (volts) to be available downstream from the kink. Ohms are measured with self-powered ohmmeters. Ohmmeters send a small amount of electricity into a circuit and measure how hard

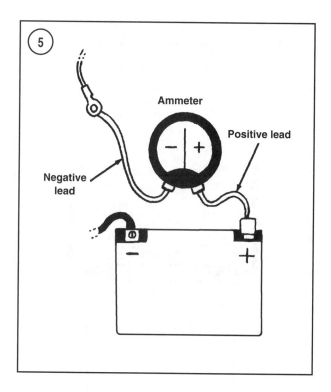

they have to push to return the electricity to the meter. An ohmmeter must only be used on a circuit or component that is disconnected from any other circuit or component and has no voltage present.

Voltage Drop Test

Since resistance causes voltage to drop, resistance can be measured on an active circuit with a voltmeter. A voltage drop test measures the difference in voltage from the beginning of the tested circuit to the end of the tested circuit while the circuit is being operated. If the circuit has no resistance, there will be no voltage drop and the meter will read zero volts. The more resistance the circuit has, the higher the voltmeter reading. Generally, voltage drop readings of one or more volts are considered unsatisfactory. The chief advantage to the voltage drop test over an ohmmeter resistance test is that the circuit is tested while under operation. A zero reading on a voltage drop test is good, while a battery voltage reading would signify an open circuit.

The voltage drop test provides an excellent means of testing solenoid relays, battery cables and other high current positive and negative electrical leads. As with the ammeter, always connect the positive (red) lead of the voltmeter to where the electricity is coming from (electrical source) and the negative (black) lead of the voltmeter to where the electricity is going (electrical load).

Multipliers

When using an analog multimeter to measure ohms, the scale choices will typically be labeled R × 1, R × 10, R × 100 and so on. These are resistance scale multipliers. R × 100 means to multiply the meter reading by 100. If the needle indicates a reading of 75 ohms while set to the R × 100 scale, the actual resistance reading is 75 × 100 or 7500 ohms. Note the scale multiplier when using an analog ohmmeter.

Diodes

Diodes are one-way electrical check valves. A series of diodes used to change AC current to DC current is a rectifier. Single diodes prevent reverse flow of electricity and are typically called blocking diodes. Diodes can be tested with an analog meter set to any ohmmeter scale other than *low* or with a digital multimeter set to the diode test scale. A good diode tested with an analog ohmmeter indicates a relatively low reading in one polarity and a relatively high reading in the opposite polarity. A good diode tested with a digital multimeter reads a voltage drop of approximately

0.4-0.9 volts in one polarity and an open circuit (OL or OUCH) in the opposite polarity.

Analog Multimeter

When using an analog meter to read ohms, recalibrate (zero) the meter each time the scale or range is changed. Normally the ohmmeter leads are connected for calibration; however, some meters require the leads to be separated for calibration when using the low ohms scale. Always follow the manufacturer's instructions for calibration. When checking for shorts to ground, calibrate on the highest scale available. When checking diodes, calibrate on the R × 10 scale or higher. Never use the *low* scale, if so equipped, to test a diode or short to ground. When checking for a specific ohm value, set the ohmmeter on a scale that allows reading the specification as near the middle of the meter movement as possible. Analog meters allow easy visual identification of erratic or fluctuating readings.

Digital Multimeter

Digital multimeter displays are easy to read. Most digital meters are autoranging. They automatically shift to the scale most appropriate for displaying the value being read. Be careful to read the scale correctly. Fluctuating readings can be frustrating to read as the display will change several times a second. Quality digital multimeters typically have a bar graph located below the digital number display. The bar graph allows easy interpretation of fluctuating readings. The scale range and multiplier (if applicable) are displayed alongside the actual reading. Most quality digital meters have a special diode test scale that measures the voltage drop of the diode, instead of the resistance. Do not attempt to use the digital multimeter's ohms scale to test diodes, as the readings are inconsistent. The digital multimeter is protected by internal fuses. Buy several spare fuses at the time of purchase.

Adapters are available for temperature readings, inductive ammeter readings and many other functions. **Figure 8** shows a typical digital multimeter.

Test Light

The test light (**Figure 9**) is a useful tool for simple troubleshooting, such as starter circuits. A test light must not be used on electronic circuits, such as modern ignition and fuel injection circuits. The current draw of the test lamp can damage delicate electronic circuits. Never use a test light to measure specific voltage. Before beginning troubleshooting with a test lamp, connect the test lamp directly to the battery and note the bulb brightness. Reference other readings against this test. If the bulb is not as bright as when attached to the battery, there is a problem.

Connect the test lamp lead directly to the positive battery terminal to check ground circuits. When the test lamp probe is connected to any ground circuit, the light should glow brightly.

Electrical Repairs

Check all electrical connections for corrosion, mechanical damage, heat damage and loose connections. Clean and repair all connections as necessary. All wire splices or connector repairs must be made with waterproof marine grade connectors and heat shrink tubing. A Quicksilver electrical hardware repair kit and crimping pliers are available to repair the serviceable connectors and make wire splices on the engine. Heat shrink connectors and heat shrink tubing for making other waterproof connections and repairs are also available from Quicksilver. Marine and industrial suppliers are also good sources for electrical repair equipment.

NOTE
On engines equipped with an ECM (electronic control module), any electrical connection or repair that does not have perfect continuity will affect the signal being sent to or from the ECM, effectively throwing the system out of calibration. This will always have a detrimental effect on engine operating quality, performance and reliability.

STARTING SYSTEM

All models covered in this manual are equipped with electric start systems. The starter motor mounts vertically on the engine. When battery current is supplied to the starter motor, the pinion gear engages the teeth on the engine flywheel (**Figure 10**, typical). Once the engine starts, the pinion gear disengages from the flywheel.

The starting system requires a fully charged battery to provide the large amount of electrical current necessary to operate the starter motor. Electric start models are equipped with an alternator to charge the battery during operation.

The typical electric starting system consists of the battery, starter switch, neutral safety switch, starter solenoid, starter motor, starter drive and related wiring (**Figure 11**). The neutral safety switch allows starter engagement only

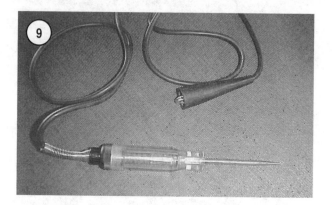

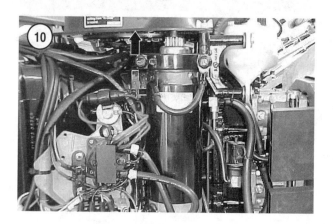

when the gear shift is in NEUTRAL. Tiller handle models have the neutral safety switch mounted on the engine. Remote control models have the neutral safety switch mounted in the remote control box. Remote control models incorporate a 20 amp fuse to protect the remote control key switch circuits. The fuse is located on the engine, between the starter solenoid and the boat main harness connector.

The neutral safety switch is on the positive side of the solenoid. Engaging the starter switch allows current to flow to the starter solenoid coil windings. When the cur-

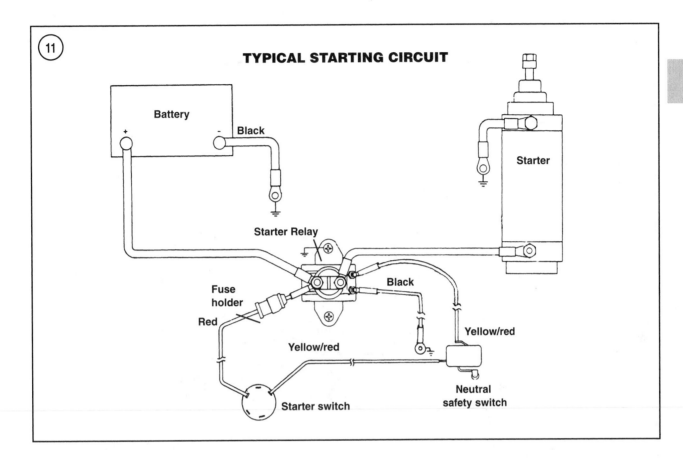

TYPICAL STARTING CIRCUIT

3

rent path is complete, the solenoid contacts close, allowing current to flow from the battery through the solenoid to the starter motor.

Solenoid design varies, but all solenoids use two large terminal studs (battery positive and starter cables) and two small terminal studs (black and yellow/red primary wires). The cable connecting the battery to the starter solenoid is red or black with red sleeved ends. The cable connecting the starter solenoid to the starter motor is yellow/black with yellow sleeved ends or black with red sleeved ends.

CAUTION
To prevent starter damage, do not operate the starter motor continuously for more than 30 seconds. Allow the motor to cool for at least two minutes between attempts to start the engine.

Troubleshooting Preparation

If the following procedures do not locate the problem, refer to **Table 1** for additional information. Before troubleshooting the starting circuit, check for the following:

1. The battery is fully charged.
2. The shift control lever is in NEUTRAL.
3. All electrical connections are clean and tight.
4. The wiring harness is in good condition with no worn or frayed insulation.
5. The fuse protecting the starter switch is not blown.
6. The power head and gearcase are not faulty.

NOTE
Unless otherwise noted, perform all tests with the terminals connected.

Starter Motor Turns Slowly

1. Make sure the battery is in acceptable condition and fully charged. See Chapter Seven.
2. Inspect all electrical connections for looseness or corrosion. Clean and tighten them as necessary.
3. Check for the proper size and length of battery cables. Refer to Chapter Seven for recommended minimum cable gauge sizes and lengths. Replace cables that are too short or move the battery to shorten the distance between the battery and starter solenoid.

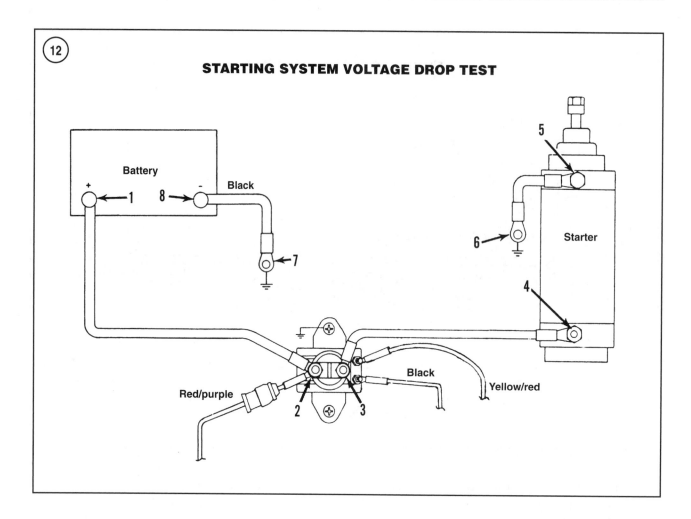

STARTING SYSTEM VOLTAGE DROP TEST

4. Disconnect and ground the spark plug leads to the engine to prevent accidental starting. Turn the flywheel clockwise by hand and check for mechanical binding. If mechanical binding is evident, remove the lower gearcase to determine if the binding is in the power head or the lower gearcase. If no binding is evident, other than normal crankcase compression and water pump impeller drag, continue to Step 5.

5. Perform the starting system voltage drop test as described in the next section.

6. Check the starter motor current draw as described in this chapter.

Starting system voltage drop test

As described in this chapter, resistance causes a reduction in current flow and voltage drop. Excessive resistance in the battery cables, starter solenoid and starter cable restricts the current flow to the starter, causing the starter to turn the motor slowly. Slow cranking speeds cause low ignition system output and hard starting.

Use the following procedure to determine if any of the cables or the starter solenoid is the source of a voltage drop causing slow cranking speeds. If the problem is intermittent, try gently pulling, bending and flexing the cables and connections during the test. Sudden voltmeter fluctuations indicate a poor connection has been located.

A voltage drop test measures the difference in voltage from the beginning of a circuit or component to the end of the circuit or component. If there is resistance in the circuit, the voltage at the end of the circuit is less than the voltage at the beginning. The starter must be engaged to take a voltage drop reading. A voltmeter reading of 0 (zero) means that there is no resistance in the test circuit. A reading of battery voltage means that the circuit is completely open (battery voltage going in and nothing coming out).

Refer to **Figure 12** for this procedure. Clean, tighten, repair or replace cables or solenoids with excessive voltage drop.

1. Disconnect and ground the spark plug leads to the engine to prevent accidental starting.

2. Connect the positive voltmeter lead to the positive battery terminal (1, **Figure 12**). Connect the negative voltmeter lead to the positive solenoid terminal (2, **Figure 12**).

3. Engage the electric starter and observe the meter. A meter reading of more than 0.3 volts indicates excessive resistance in the positive battery cable. Clean the connections, repair the terminal ends or replace the positive battery cable.

CAUTION
Do not connect the positive voltmeter lead in Step 4 until after the engine begins cranking. The open solenoid will read battery voltage and could damage a voltmeter set to a very low volts scale. Also, disconnect the voltmeter before stopping cranking.

4. Connect the negative voltmeter lead to the starter side of the solenoid (3, **Figure 12**). Engage the electric starter. While the engine is cranking, touch the positive voltmeter lead to the battery cable positive solenoid terminal (2, **Figure 12**). Note the meter reading, remove the positive voltmeter lead and stop cranking. A meter reading of more than 0.2 volts indicates the starter solenoid has excessive internal resistance and must be replaced.

5. Connect the positive voltmeter lead to the starter side of the solenoid (3, **Figure 12**) and the negative voltmeter lead to the starter motor terminal (4, **Figure 12**). Engage the electric starter and observe the meter. A meter reading of more than 0.2 volts indicates excessive resistance in the starter motor cable. Clean the connections, repair the terminal ends or replace the starter motor cable. If the starter motor has a ground cable, repeat this test with the positive voltmeter lead connected to the starter end of the starter ground cable (5, **Figure 12**) and the negative voltmeter lead connected to the engine end of the ground cable (6, **Figure 12**).

6. Connect the positive voltmeter lead to the engine end of the negative battery cable (7, **Figure 12**) and the negative voltmeter lead to the negative battery terminal (8, **Figure 12**). Engage the electric starter and observe the meter. A meter reading of more than 0.3 volts indicates excessive resistance in the battery negative cable. Clean the connections, repair the terminal ends or replace the negative battery cable.

Starter Motor Does Not Turn

A test light or voltmeter are both acceptable tools for troubleshooting the starter circuit. When using a voltmeter, all test readings should be within 1 volt of battery voltage. Readings of 1 volt or more below battery voltage

indicates problems (excessive resistance) with the circuit being tested. If using a test light, first connect the test light directly to the battery and note the bulb brightness. Reference other readings against this test. If the bulb is not as bright as when attached to the battery, the resistance is excessive.

CAUTION
Disconnect and ground the spark plug leads to the engine to prevent accidental starting during all test procedures.

Refer to **Figure 13** for this procedure. Refer to the individual model wiring diagrams at the end of the book.

1. Connect the test lamp lead to the positive terminal of the battery and touch the test lamp probe to metal anywhere on the engine block. If the test lamp does not light or is dim, the battery ground cable connections are loose or corroded, or there is an open circuit in the battery ground cable. Check connections on both ends of the ground cable.

2. Place the shift lever into NEUTRAL and connect the test lamp lead to a good engine ground.

3. Connect the test lamp probe to the starter solenoid input terminal (1, **Figure 13**). If the test lamp does not light or is very dim, the positive battery cable connections are loose or corroded, or there is an open in the cable between the battery and the solenoid. Clean and tighten connections or replace the battery cable as required.

4. Remove the 20 amp fuse and connect the test lamp probe to the input side of the fuse holder (2, **Figure 13**). If the lamp does not light, repair or replace the wire between the starter solenoid and the fuse holder.

5. Inspect the 20 amp fuse. Install a known good fuse into the fuse holder. Unplug the main eight-pin connector and connect the test light probe to pin No. 8 of the main engine harness connector. If the test lamp does not light, repair or replace the wire between the fuse holder and the main engine harness connector.

6. Reconnect the main harness connector and access the key switch on the dash or in the remote control box. Connect the test lamp probe to terminal B on the key switch (3, **Figure 13**). If the lamp does not light, repair or replace the wire between pin No. 8 of the main boat harness connector and the key switch terminal B.

7. Connect the test lamp probe to the key switch terminal S (4, **Figure 13**). Turn the key switch to the start position. If the test lamp does not light, replace the key switch.

8A. *Remote control models*—Remove the cover from the remote control box and connect the test lamp probe to the key switch side of the neutral safety switch (5, **Figure 13**). Turn the key switch to the start position. If the test lamp

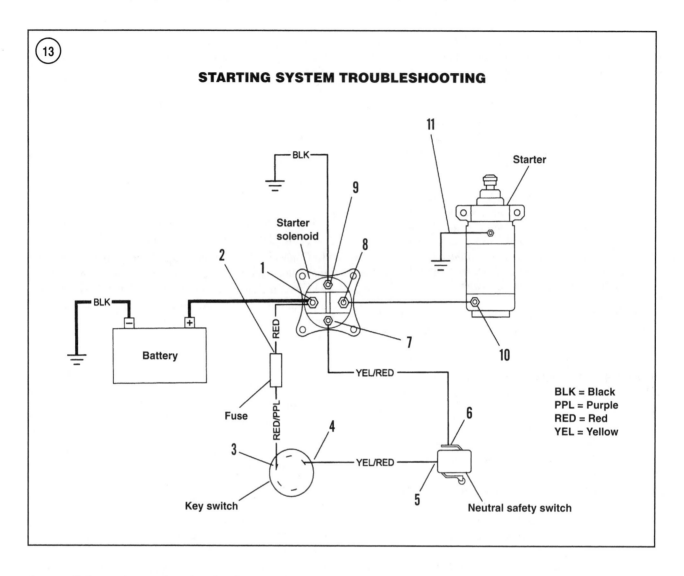

STARTING SYSTEM TROUBLESHOOTING

BLK = Black
PPL = Purple
RED = Red
YEL = Yellow

does not light, repair or replace the wires between the neutral safety switch and the key switch.

8B. *Tiller control models*—The switch is in the tiller control housing. Connect the test lamp probe to the key switch side of the neutral safety switch (5, **Figure 13**). Turn the key switch to the start position. If the test lamp does not light, repair or replace the wire between the neutral safety switch and the starter switch.

9. Move the test lamp probe to the solenoid side of the neutral safety switch (6, **Figure 13**). Turn the key switch to the start position. If the test lamp does not light, make sure the shift control is still in neutral and retest. Replace the neutral safety switch if the lamp does not light.

10. Connect the test lamp probe to the yellow/red terminal on the starter solenoid (7, **Figure 13**). Turn the key switch to the start position. If the test lamp does not light, repair or replace the wire between the neutral start switch

and the starter solenoid. This includes the main harness connector pin No. 7.

11. Connect the test lamp probe to the starter solenoid terminal leading to the starter motor (8, **Figure 13**). Turn the key switch to the start position. If the test lamp does not light, connect the test lamp lead to the positive battery terminal and connect the test lamp probe to the small black (ground) terminal of the starter solenoid (9, **Figure 13**). If the test lamp does not light, repair or replace the ground wire between the starter solenoid and the engine block. If the test lamp only lights during the ground wire test, replace the starter solenoid.

12. Connect the test lamp lead to a good engine ground. Connect the test lamp probe to the starter motor terminal (10, **Figure 13**). Turn the key switch to the start position. If the test lamp does not light, repair or replace the cable between the starter solenoid and the starter motor. If the test lamp lights, proceed to Step 13.

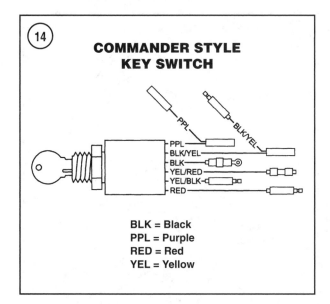

**COMMANDER STYLE
KEY SWITCH**

PPL
BLK/YEL
PPL
BLK/YEL
BLK
YEL/RED
YEL/BLK
RED

BLK = Black
PPL = Purple
RED = Red
YEL = Yellow

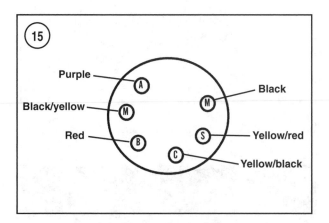

Purple — A
Black — M
Black/yellow — M
Red — B — S — Yellow/red
C — Yellow/black

13. *Starter equipped with a ground cable*—Inspect the ground cable for loose connections, corrosion and damage. Clean, tighten or repair it as necessary. If the starter still will not engage, remove the starter for replacement or repair.

14. *Starter not equipped with a ground cable*—Remove the starter and inspect it for paint or corrosion on the mounting bolts and bosses. If paint or corrosion is found, clean the mounting bolts and bosses. Reinstall the starter and test the starter engagement. If the starter still will not engage, remove the starter for replacement or repair.

Ignition Switch Test

The following procedure tests the ignition switch on models equipped with Quicksilver Commander remote control assemblies and standard aftermarket remote controls or dash-mounted key switches. This test may not be valid on *all* models equipped with aftermarket controls and electrical harnesses.

The ignition switch and main wiring harness can be tested at the main engine wiring harness connector, eliminating the need to disassemble the control box or remove the key switch from the dash panel. Refer to the wiring diagrams at the end of the manual for the main engine wiring harness connector pin locations and wire color code identification. When testing at the main engine harness connector, connect the ohmmeter to the appropriate pins based on the wire color codes called out in the following text. Testing at the main engine harness connector will not isolate a bad wiring harness from the key switch. If the switch and harness fails the test procedure at the main harness connector, disconnect and retest the key switch to make sure the main harness is not faulty. Test the key switch by itself as follows:

Use an ohmmeter set on the R × 1 scale to test the key switch circuits. Refer to **Figure 14** for Mercury/Mariner switches or **Figure 15** for typical aftermarket switches.

NOTE
Mercury/Mariner switches typically use short color-coded wires with bullet connectors. Aftermarket switches typically use screw terminals that are labeled with abbreviations. When testing at the main harness connector, consult the wiring diagrams at the end of the manual for pin locations.

1. Disconnect the negative battery cable from the battery.
2. Access the key switch and disconnect the wires from the bullet connectors or key switch terminals. If the key switch is located in the remote control, refer to Chapter Fourteen and disassemble the control to the point necessary to access the terminals. Note the color code and terminal markings of aftermarket switches.
3. Connect one ohmmeter lead to the switch red/purple wire (BAT, B or B+ terminal) and the other ohmmeter lead to the purple wire (A, ACC or IGN terminal). When the switch is in the *off* position, the meter should indicate no continuity.
4. Turn the switch to the on or run position. The ohmmeter should indicate continuity.
5. Turn the switch to the start or crank position. The ohmmeter should indicate continuity.
6. Turn the switch to the off or stop position. Connect one ohmmeter lead to the black/yellow wire (first M terminal) and the other ohmmeter lead to the black wire (second M terminal). The ohmmeter should indicate continuity.
7. While observing the meter, turn the switch to the on, run and start positions. The ohmmeter should indicate no continuity in both positions.

8. Turn the switch to the off or stop position. Connect one ohmmeter lead to the red/purple wire (BAT, B or B+ terminal) and the other ohmmeter lead to the yellow/black wire (C terminal). The ohmmeter should indicate no continuity.

9. Turn the switch to the on or run position. The ohmmeter should indicate no continuity. Press in on the key to engage choke or prime. The ohmmeter should indicate continuity in choke or prime.

10. Turn the switch to the start or crank position. The ohmmeter should indicate no continuity. Press in on the key to engage the choke or prime. The ohmmeter should indicate continuity in choke or prime.

11. Replace the key switch if it is faulty.

Starter Solenoid Bench Test

NOTE
All engine wiring harness wires must be disconnected from the solenoid for this test.

Solenoids vary from engine to engine, but all solenoids have two large terminal studs and two small terminal studs. Refer to **Figure 16** for this procedure.

1. Disconnect the negative battery cable from the battery.

2. Disconnect all wires from the solenoid terminal studs. If necessary, remove the solenoid from the engine.

3. Connect an ohmmeter set to the R × 1 scale to the two large terminal studs (1 and 2, **Figure 16**). If the ohmmeter indicates continuity, replace the solenoid.

4. Attach a 12-volt battery with suitable jumper leads to the two small terminal studs (3 and 4, **Figure 16**). Polarity is not important for this test. An audible click should be heard as wires connect and the solenoid engages. If the ohmmeter does not indicate continuity, replace the solenoid.

5. Reconnect all wires. Connect the negative battery cable last.

Starter Motor Current Draw Tests

Load test

Make sure the ammeter can read higher than the anticipated highest amp reading (**Table 4**). The spark plugs must be installed for the load test.

1. Disconnect the negative battery cable from the battery.

2A. *On 2001-on Optimax models*—Disconnect the starter motor wire (**Figure 17**) from the inner large terminal on the starter mounted solenoid. The inner terminal does not use an insulator over the terminal.

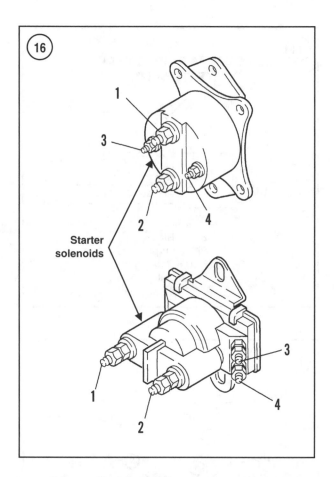

2B. *All other models*—Disconnect the starter motor wire from the starter motor (**Figure 18**, typical).

3. Securely connect the ammeter positive lead to the starter motor wire. Insulate the connection with electrical tape to prevent accidental arcing.

4. Securely connect the ammeter negative lead to the starter motor or starter mounted solenoid terminal. Disconnect and ground the spark plug leads to the engine to prevent accidental starting.

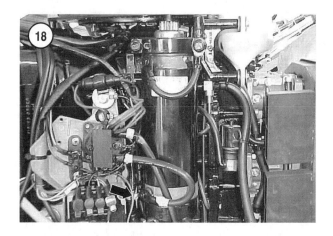

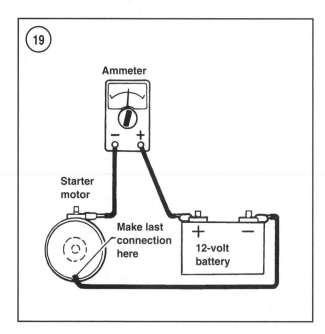

5. Reconnect the negative battery cable.

6. Crank the engine to check the current draw. If the current draw exceeded the specification in **Table 4**, repair or replace the starter motor.

No-load test

If starter system troubleshooting indicates that additional starter motor tests are necessary, use the starter no-load current draw test as an indication of internal starter condition. Make sure the ammeter can read higher than the anticipated highest amp reading (**Table 4**).

1. Remove the starter motor assembly as described in Chapter Seven. Place the starter motor in a vise or another holding fixture. Do not damage the starter motor by overtightening the vise.

2. Obtain a fully charged battery that meets the requirements for the engine being tested. See Chapter Seven.

3A. 2001-on Optimax models use heavy gauge jumper cables and connect the ammeter in series with the positive battery cable and the starter motor terminal. Connect another heavy gauge jumper cable to the negative battery terminal and the starter ground.

3B. *All other models*—Using heavy gauge jumper cables, connect the ammeter in series with the positive battery cable and the starter motor terminal. Connect another heavy gauge jumper cable to the negative battery terminal. See **Figure 19**.

> *WARNING*
> *Make the last battery connection to the starter frame in Step 4. **Do not** create any sparks near the battery or a serious explosion could occur.*

4A. On 2001-on Optimax models, connect a jumper wire to the positive battery cable. When ready to perform the test, touch the other end of the jumper wire to the small terminal on the starter mounted solenoid.

4B. When ready to perform the no-load test, quickly and firmly connect the remaining connection to the starter motor frame (**Figure 19**).

5. Observe the amperage reading, then disconnect the jumper cables and wires from the starter and battery.

6. If the amperage reading is not within the specification in **Table 4**, repair or replace the starter motor. See Chapter Seven. Refer to **Table 1** for additional starter motor symptoms and remedies.

BATTERY CHARGING SYSTEM

An alternator charging system is used on all electric start models. The charging system keeps the battery fully charged and supplies current to run accessories. Charging systems can be divided into two basic designs: integral regulated (**Figure 20**, typical) and external (belt driven) regulated (**Figure 21**, typical). All Optimax, 225 hp and 250 hp models use an external (belt driven) regulated charging system. All other models use the integral regulated system.

Integral systems use permanent magnets mounted in the flywheel and a stator coil winding mounted to the power head. As the flywheel rotates, the magnetic fields in the flywheel pass through the stator coil windings, inducing AC (alternating current).

The rectifier portion of the rectifier/regulator changes the AC to DC, while the regulator portion monitors system voltage and controls the charging system output ac-

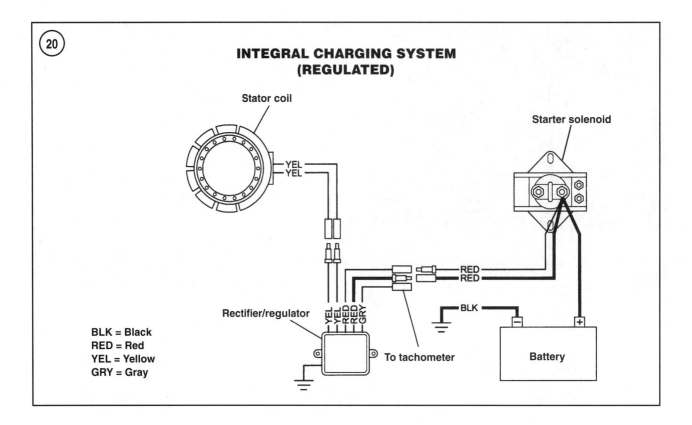

INTEGRAL CHARGING SYSTEM (REGULATED)

Stator coil

Starter solenoid

YEL
YEL

RED
RED

BLK

Rectifier/regulator

To tachometer

Battery

BLK = Black
RED = Red
YEL = Yellow
GRY = Gray

cordingly. The regulator controls the output of the charging system to keep system voltage at approximately 14.5 volts. The large red wire of the rectifier/regulator is DC output. The small red wire is the sense terminal which allows the regulator portion to monitor system voltage (**Figure 20**).

The integral charging system also provides the signal for the tachometer. The tachometer counts AC voltage pulses coming out of the stator before the AC voltage is rectified to DC. Tachometer failure on models with integral charging systems is related to the charging system, not the ignition system. The tachometer connects to the rectifier/regulator gray wire (**Figure 20**).

Refer to **Table 5** for typical charging system problems and solutions. Refer to the wiring diagrams at the end of the manual.

External regulated systems use a belt-driven, excited rotor and internally regulated 60 amp alternator similar to many automotive designs (**Figure 21**). The alternator has no permanent magnets. The voltage regulator sends current through the rotor windings to create an electromagnetic field. The output of the alternator can be controlled by changing the strength of the rotor magnetic field. The alternator is not serviceable and is available only as an assembly. This system is used on all Optimax, 225 and 250

hp models. The tachometer signal on these models is produced by the electronic control module (ECM).

Malfunctions in the charging system generally cause the battery to be undercharged and on integral systems, the tachometer to read erratically or fail. The following conditions will cause rectifier/regulator or alternator failure.

1. Reversing the battery cables.
2. Disconnecting the battery cables while the engine is running.
3. Loose connections in the charging system circuits, including battery connections and ground circuits.

NOTE
The 40 amp integral charging system is two separate 20 amp charging systems. Half of the stator windings are connected to the upper regulator/rectifier assembly and the remaining stator windings are connected to the lower regulator/rectifier. If one regulator/rectifier fails, the charging system will still function, but at half of its rated output. Test each regulator/rectifier assembly separately.

CAUTION
If an integral regulated charging system must be operated with the battery removed or disconnected, disconnect and insulate

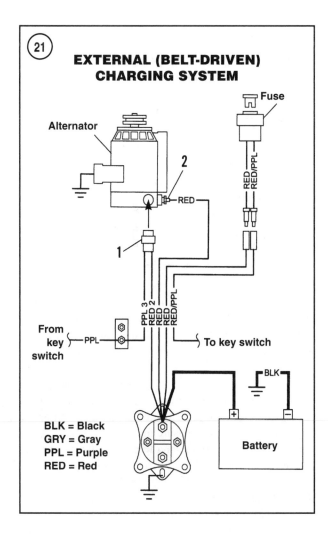

EXTERNAL (BELT-DRIVEN) CHARGING SYSTEM

BLK = Black
GRY = Gray
PPL = Purple
RED = Red

4. Check the wiring harness between the stator and battery for damaged insulation, and corroded, loose or disconnected connections. Repair or replace the wiring harness as necessary.

   a. On integral systems, visually inspect the stator windings for discoloration and burned windings. Replace any stator that shows evidence of overheating.

   b. On external systems, check belt tension and adjust as necessary. See Chapter Four.

CAUTION
Unless otherwise noted, perform all voltage tests with the wires connected, but with the terminals exposed to accommodate the test lead connection. All electrical components must be securely grounded to the power head any time the engine is cranked or started, or the components will be damaged.

Current Draw Test

Use this test to determine if the total load of the engine electrical system and boat accessories exceeds the capacity of the charging system.

NOTE
If a clamp-on or inductive ammeter is used, install the probe on the positive battery cable near the battery and go to Step 3. If a conventional ammeter is used, make sure the ammeter is rated for at least 50 amps.

1. Disconnect the negative battery cable from the battery.
2. Disconnect the positive battery cable from the battery. Securely connect the ammeter between the positive battery post and the positive battery cable. Reconnect the negative battery cable.
3. Turn the ignition switch to the ON or RUN position and turn on all accessories. Note the ammeter reading. Turn the ignition switch to the OFF or STOP position and turn off all accessories.
4. Refer to **Table 6** for charging system maximum output. If the ammeter reading exceeds the rated capacity of the charging system, the battery will discharge. If necessary, reduce the accessory load connected to the charging system.

Troubleshooting Integral Regulated Models (Except 40 Amp)

NOTE
A regulated charging system only puts out the current necessary to maintain 14.5 volts

(tape or sleeve) both stator yellow (or one yellow and one gray) wires on both ends of the connection. Never attempt to operate external regulated charging systems without a battery connected. ECM equipped engines, 225 and 250 hp models (carbureted and EFI) and all Optimax models will not start without battery voltage.

Inspection (All Models)

Before performing the troubleshooting procedure, check the following:

1. Make sure the battery is properly connected. If the battery polarity is reversed, the rectifier or voltage regulator will be damaged.
2. Check for loose or corroded connections. Clean and tighten them as necessary.
3. Check the battery condition. Recharge or replace the battery as necessary.

at the battery. If the battery is fully charged, the alternator will not produce its rated output unless enough accessory demand is present. If a clamp-on or inductive ammeter is used, install the probe on the rectifier/regulator large red wire and go to Step 4.

1. Disconnect the negative battery cable from the battery.

2. Connect an ammeter of sufficient size to measure the maximum rated output of the charging system in *series* between the large red positive output wire of the rectifier/regulator and the red positive output terminal of the rectifier/regulator (**Figure 22**). Connect the positive lead of the ammeter to the rectifier/regulator wire (male bullet connector) and the negative lead of the ammeter to the rectifier/regulator engine harness wire (female bullet connector). Make sure the connections are secure and insulated from other wires or grounds.

3. Reconnect the negative battery cable.

4. Install a shop tachometer according to its manufacturer's instructions.

5. Connect a voltmeter to the battery terminals.

CAUTION
*Do not run the engine without an adequate water supply and do not exceed 3000 rpm without an adequate load. Refer to **Safety Precautions** at the beginning of this chapter.*

6. Start and operate the engine at the rpm in **Table 6** while noting the ammeter and voltmeter readings. If the voltage exceeds 12.5 volts, turn on accessories or attach accessories to the battery to maintain battery voltage at 12.5 volts or less. If the amperage output is less than specified, continue to Step 7. If the amperage output is within the specification, turn off or disconnect the accessories and run the engine at approximately 3000 rpm while observing the voltmeter. As the battery approaches full charge, the voltage should rise to approximately 14.5 volts and stabilize. If the voltage stabilizes at approximately 14.5 volts, the voltage regulator is functioning correctly. If the voltage exceeds 15 volts, go to Step 7 and check the rectifier/regulator sense circuit voltage.

7. To test the rectifier/regulator sense circuit, disconnect the rectifier/regulator small red wire from the engine harness. Connect the positive lead of a voltmeter to the engine harness side of the small red wire (male bullet connector) and the negative lead of the voltmeter to the negative battery terminal. The voltmeter should read battery voltage. If the voltage is more than 0.5 volt below battery voltage, clean and tighten the connections, or repair

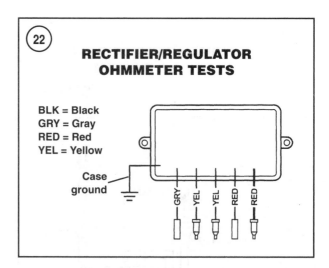

RECTIFIER/REGULATOR OHMMETER TESTS

BLK = Black
GRY = Gray
RED = Red
YEL = Yellow

Case ground

GRY YEL YEL RED RED

or replace the wire between the regulator small red wire and the battery. If the voltage is within 0.5 volt of battery voltage, go to Step 9 and check the stator for shorts to ground. If the stator tests good, replace the rectifier/regulator.

8. To check the resistance of the stator, disconnect the negative battery cable. Disconnect the two yellow stator wires from the rectifier/regulator. Set an ohmmeter on the appropriate scale and measure the stator resistance. Connect one lead of the ohmmeter to each of the stator wires and note the readings. Replace the stator if the resistance is not within the specification in **Table 7**.

9. To check the stator for shorts to ground, set the ohmmeter on its highest scale. Connect one lead of the ohmmeter to a clean engine ground. Connect the other lead alternately to each of the two yellow stator wires. If the ohmmeter reads *continuity*, the stator is shorted to ground and must be replaced.

10. To check the diodes in the rectifier/regulator, disconnect the negative battery cable. Disconnect the two red, two yellow and one gray rectifier/regulator wires (**Figure 22**). Connect the ohmmeter positive lead, calibrated on the appropriate scale to read 100-400 ohms, to the rectifier/regulator large red wire. Connect the ohmmeter negative lead to one of the rectifier/regulator yellow AC wires. Replace the rectifier/regulator if the reading is not 100-400 ohms. Repeat the test for the other yellow AC wire.

11. Connect the ohmmeter negative lead, set on the appropriate scale to read 40,000 ohms or greater, to the rectifier/regulator large red wire. Connect the ohmmeter positive lead to one of the rectifier/regulator yellow AC wires (**Figure 22**). Note the meter reading. Repeat the test for the other yellow AC lead. One yellow wire should read no continuity. The other lead should read 40,000 ohms or

more. Replace the rectifier/regulator if the readings are not as specified.

12. To check the rectifier/regulator silicon controlled rectifier (SCR) in each yellow wire, set an ohmmeter to the highest ohms scale. Connect the ohmmeter negative lead to one of the rectifier/regulator yellow AC wires. Connect the ohmmeter positive lead to the rectifier/regulator metal case ground (**Figure 22**). Replace the rectifier/regulator if a the reading is lower than 10,000 ohms. Repeat the test for the other yellow AC wire.

13. To check the rectifier/regulator tachometer circuit, set an ohmmeter on the high-ohms scale. Connect the ohmmeter negative lead to the rectifier/regulator metal case ground (**Figure 22**). Connect the ohmmeter positive lead to the rectifier/regulator tachometer (gray) lead. Replace the rectifier/regulator if the reading is not 10,000-50,000.

14. To check the continuity of the rectifier/regulator positive wire to the battery, make sure the negative lead of the battery is disconnected. Make sure the rectifier/regulator large red wire is disconnected from the rectifier/regulator. Calibrate an ohmmeter to a high-ohms scale. Connect one lead of the ohmmeter to the battery positive terminal. Connect the other lead of the ohmmeter to the rectifier/regulator end of the wire that connects to the rectifier/regulator large red wire. If the circuit does not have a zero or very low resistance reading, repair or replace the wire, connections and fuse between the rectifier/regulator and the battery.

15. Reconnect all wires.

Troubleshooting Integral Regulated 40 Amp Models

The 40 amp system is two separate 20 amp systems in parallel. Test each system individually. The two short yellow stator wires and the upper regulator make up one 20 amp system. The two long yellow stator wires and the lower regulator make up the second 20 amp system. Refer to **Table 6** and **Table 7** for specifications and to the wiring diagrams at the end of the manual.

NOTE
A regulated charging system only puts out the current necessary to maintain 14.5 volts at the battery. If the battery is fully charged, the alternator will not produce its rated output unless enough accessory demand is present. If a clamp-on or inductive ammeter is being used, install the probe on the top rectifier/regulator large red wire and go to Step 4.

1. Disconnect the negative battery cable from the battery.

2. Connect an ammeter, of sufficient size to measure the maximum rated output of the charging system, in *series* between the large red output wire of the top rectifier/regulator and the wire that was connected to it (**Figure 23**). Connect the positive lead of the ammeter to the rectifier/regulator wire and the negative lead of the ammeter to the rectifier/regulator engine harness wire. Make sure the connections are secure and insulated from other wires or grounds.

3. Disconnect the two long yellow stator wires from the lower voltage regulator. Insulate (tape or sleeve) both ends of the wires from each other and from ground.

4. Reconnect the negative battery cable.

5. Install a shop tachometer according to the manufacturer's instructions.

6. Connect a voltmeter to the battery terminals.

CAUTION
*Do not run the engine without an adequate water supply and do not exceed 3000 rpm without an adequate load. Refer to **Safety Precautions** at the beginning of this chapter.*

7. Start and operate the engine at the rpm specified in **Table 6** while observing the ammeter and voltmeter readings. If the voltage exceeds 12.5 volts, turn on accessories or attach accessories to the battery to maintain battery voltage at 12.5 volts or less. If amperage output is less than specified in **Table 6**, continue to Step 9. If amperage output is within specification, turn off or disconnect the accessories and run the engine at approximately 3000 rpm while observing the voltmeter. As the battery approaches full charge, the voltage should rise to approximately 14.5 volts and stabilize. If the voltage stabilizes at approximately 14.5 volts, the voltage regulator is functioning correctly. If the voltage exceeds 15 volts, go to Step 8 and test the top rectifier/regulator sense circuit.

8. To test the rectifier/regulator sense circuit, disconnect the top rectifier/regulator small red wire from the engine harness. Connect the positive lead of a voltmeter to the engine harness side of the small red wire and the black lead of the voltmeter to the negative battery terminal. If the voltmeter reads more than 0.5 volts below battery voltage, clean and tighten the connections, or repair or replace the wire between the regulator small red wire and the battery. If the voltage is within 0.5 volts of battery voltage, go to Step 10 and check the stator for shorts to ground. If the stator tests good, replace the rectifier/regulator.

9. To check the resistance of the stator, proceed as follows:

   a. Disconnect the negative battery cable.

3

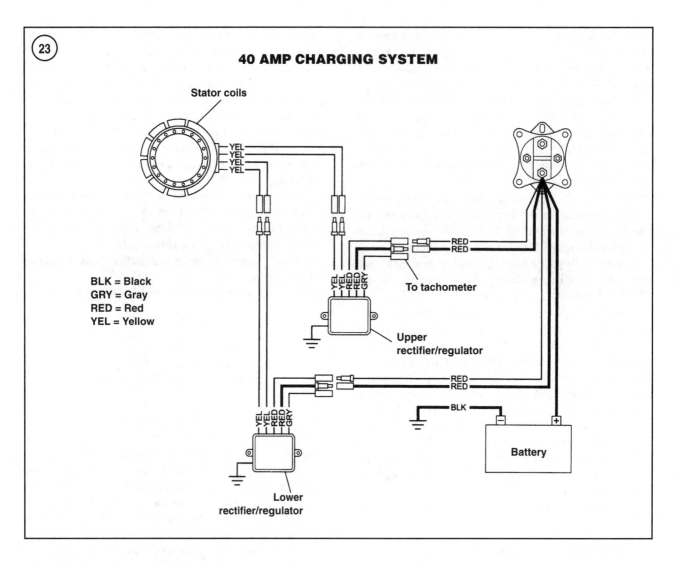

40 AMP CHARGING SYSTEM

Stator coils

YEL
YEL
YEL
YEL

BLK = Black
GRY = Gray
RED = Red
YEL = Yellow

RED
RED

To tachometer

YEL
YEL
RED
RED
GRY

Upper
rectifier/regulator

RED
RED

BLK

Battery

YEL
YEL
RED
RED
GRY

Lower
rectifier/regulator

b. On 1998 and 1999 models, disconnect the two short yellow stator wires from the top rectifier/regulator. Connect one lead of the ohmmeter to each of the stator wires.

c. On 2000-on models, disconnect the connector with two yellow wires from the top rectifier/regulator. Touch one lead of the ohmmeter to each of the terminals within the connector (stator side).

d. Replace the stator if its resistance is not within the specification **Table 7**.

e. Repeat this step using the longer yellow stator wires (1998 and 1999 models) or connector (2000-on) to the lower rectifier/regulator.

10. To check the stator for shorts to ground, calibrate the ohmmeter on the highest ohms scale. Connect one lead of the ohmmeter to a clean engine ground. Connect the other lead alternately to each of the two yellow stator wires or terminal in the yellow wire connectors (2000-on). If the

ohmmeter reads *continuity*, the stator is shorted to ground and must be replaced.

NOTE
On all 2000-on models, the rectifier/regulator has a red and red/blue wire in place of the two red wires used on 1998 and 1999 models.

11. To check the diodes in the top rectifier/regulator, disconnect the negative battery cable. Disconnect the two red (or red and red/blue), two yellow and one gray top rectifier/regulator wires (**Figure 22**). Connect the ohmmeter positive lead, calibrated on the appropriate scale to read 100-400 ohms, to the rectifier/regulator large red or red/blue wire. Connect the ohmmeter negative lead to one of the rectifier/regulator yellow AC wires. Replace the rectifier/regulator if the reading is not 100-400 ohms. Repeat the test for the other yellow AC wire.

12. Connect the ohmmeter negative lead, calibrated on the appropriate scale to read 40,000 ohms or greater, to the top rectifier/regulator large red or red/blue wire. Connect the ohmmeter positive lead to one of the two rectifier/regulator yellow AC wires (**Figure 22**). Note the meter reading. Repeat the test for the other yellow AC wire. One yellow wire should read no continuity. The other lead should read 40,000 ohms or greater. Replace the rectifier/regulator if the readings are not as specified.

13. To check the top rectifier/regulator silicon controlled rectifier (SCR) in each yellow wire, calibrate an ohmmeter on the highest ohms scale. Connect the ohmmeter negative lead to one of the rectifier/regulator yellow AC wires. Connect the ohmmeter positive lead to the rectifier/regulator metal case (**Figure 22**). Replace the rectifier/regulator if the reading is lower than 10,000 ohms. Repeat the test for the other yellow AC wire.

14. To check the top rectifier/regulator tachometer circuit, calibrate an ohmmeter on the high-ohms scale. Connect the ohmmeter negative lead to the rectifier/regulator metal case. Connect the ohmmeter positive lead to the rectifier/regulator tachometer (gray) wire (**Figure 22**). Replace the rectifier/regulator if the reading is not 10,000-50,000 ohms.

15. To check the continuity of the top rectifier/regulator positive wire to the battery, make sure the negative cable of the battery is disconnected. Make sure the rectifier/regulator large red or red/blue wire is disconnected from the rectifier/regulator. Calibrate an ohmmeter to a high-ohms scale. Connect one lead of the ohmmeter to the battery positive terminal. Connect the other lead of the ohmmeter to the rectifier/regulator end of the wire that connects to the rectifier/regulator large red or red/blue wire. If the circuit does not have a zero or very low resistance reading, repair or replace the wire, connections and fuse between the top rectifier/regulator and the battery.

16. Repeat this procedure for the two longer yellow stator leads and the lower voltage regulator. Disconnect and insulate (tape or sleeve) both ends of the two short yellow stator wires from the upper voltage regulator before beginning. If both upper and lower regulators output 19-21 amps at 5000 rpm and voltage is regulated to approximately 14.5 volts, the system is functioning correctly.

17. Reconnect all wires.

Troubleshooting External 60 Amp Models

Refer to **Table 6** for specifications and to the wiring diagrams at the end of the manual.

1. Check and adjust belt tension as specified in Chapter Four.

2. Install a shop tachometer according to the manufacturer's instructions.

3. Connect a voltmeter to the battery terminals.

CAUTION
Do not run the engine without an adequate water supply and do not exceed 3000 rpm without an adequate load. Refer to Safety Precautions at the beginning of this chapter.

4. Start and operate the engine at the rpm specified in **Table 6** while noting both the ammeter and voltmeter readings. If the voltage stabilizes at approximately 14.5 volts as the battery approaches full charge, the voltage regulator is functioning correctly. If the voltage is below 13.5 volts or exceeds 15.1 volts, go to Step 5.

5. To test the alternator sense circuit, disconnect the alternator two-wire (red and purple) plug from the alternator. Connect the positive lead of a voltmeter to the red wire (1, **Figure 21**) (pin No. 2). Connect the negative lead of the voltmeter to the negative battery terminal. If the voltage is more than 0.5 volts below battery voltage, clean and tighten the connections, or repair or replace the red wire between the alternator two-wire plug and the battery. If the voltage is within 0.5 volts of battery voltage, go to Step 6.

6. To test the alternator excite circuit, disconnect the alternator two-wire (red and purple) plug from the alternator. Connect the positive lead of a voltmeter to the purple wire (1, **Figure 21**) (pin No. 3). Connect the negative lead of the voltmeter to the negative battery terminal. Turn the ignition switch to the ON or RUN position. The voltmeter should read battery voltage. Turn the ignition switch to the OFF or STOP position. If the voltage is more than 1 volt below battery voltage, clean and tighten the connections, or repair or replace the circuit (including the key switch and 20 amp fuse) between the alternator two-wire plug and the battery. If the voltage is within 1 volt of battery voltage, go to Step 7.

7. To test the alternator output circuit, connect the positive lead of a voltmeter to the alternator output terminal B (2, **Figure 21**). Connect the negative lead of the voltmeter to the negative battery terminal. If the voltage is more than 0.5 volts below battery voltage, clean and tighten the connections, or repair or replace the wire between the alternator output terminal B and the battery. If the voltage is within 0.5 volts of battery voltage, go to Step 8 and test the amperage output.

NOTE
If a clamp-on or inductive ammeter is used, install the probe on the alternator output large red wire (terminal B) and go to Step 9.

8. Disconnect the negative battery cable from the battery.

9. Connect an ammeter of sufficient size to measure the maximum rated output of the charging system (60 amps) in *series* between the alternator output terminal and the large red wire (2, **Figure 21**). Connect the positive lead of the ammeter to the alternator output terminal and the negative lead to the large red wire. Make sure the connections are secure and insulated from other wires or grounds.

10. Reconnect the negative battery cable.

> *CAUTION*
> *Due to the high output of this alternator, the regulator must be bypassed to check the rated output of the alternator. Bypass the regulator by grounding terminal F (field) on the lower end frame of the alternator. Do not keep terminal F grounded longer than necessary or the battery will be overcharged and damaged.*

11. Fabricate a tool (**Figure 24**) from a stiff piece of wire. Insert the tool through the access hole (**Figure 25**) in the lower end cover of the alternator and ground the terminal F. A jumper wire may be used to ensure that the tool is securely grounded to the power head.

12. Start and operate the engine at the rpm in **Table 6** while observing the ammeter. If the alternator output is as specified, the charging system is working correctly. If the output is less than specified, remove the alternator, and check for paint and corrosion on the mounting brackets. Reinstall the alternator and retest the output. If the output is still unsatisfactory, replace the alternator.

ELECTRICAL ACCESSORIES

The wiring harness used between the ignition switch and outboard motor is adequate to handle the electrical requirements of the outboard motor and the dash mounted gauges. It cannot handle the electrical requirements of accessories. Whenever an accessory is added, run new wiring between the battery and the accessory. Install a separate fuse panel on the instrument panel.

If the ignition switch requires replacement, *never* install an automotive switch. Only use a switch approved for marine use.

IGNITION SYSTEM

This section describes troubleshooting the ignition system. If a defective component has been identified, refer to Chapter Seven for component removal and replacement procedures.

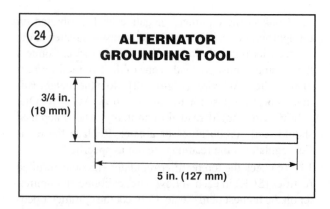

Troubleshooting Notes and Precautions (All Models)

Observe the following troubleshooting precautions to avoid injury and/or damage to the ignition system.

1. Do not reverse the battery connections. Reverse battery polarity will damage electronic components.

2. Do not spark the battery terminals with the battery cable connections to determine polarity.

3. Do not disconnect the battery cables while the engine is running.

4. Do not crank or run the engine if any electrical components are not grounded to the power head.

5. Do not touch or disconnect ignition components while the outboard is running, while the ignition switch is ON or while the battery cables are connected.

6. Do not rotate the flywheel when performing ohmmeter tests. The meter will be damaged.

7. If a sudden unexplained timing change is noted:
   a. Check the trigger magnets in the hub of the flywheel, if so equipped, for damage or a possible shift in magnet position. If the magnets are cracked, damaged or have shifted position, replace the flywheel. See Chapter Seven.
   b. Check the flywheel key for wear or damage. See Chapter Seven.

8. The ignition system on electric start models requires the electric starter to crank the engine at normal speed in order for the ignition system to produce adequate spark. If the starter motor cranks the engine slowly or not at all, refer to *Starting System* in this chapter before continuing.

9. The spark plugs must be installed during troubleshooting. The ignition system must produce adequate spark at normal cranking speed. Removing the spark plug(s) raises the cranking speed and may mask a problem in the ignition system at lower cranking speeds.

10. Check the battery cable connections, on models so equipped, for secure attachment to both battery terminals and the engine. Clean corrosion from all connections. Dis-

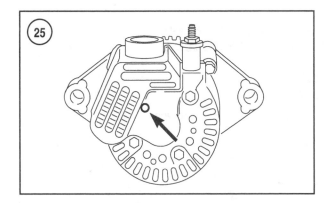

card wing nuts and install corrosion resistant hex nuts at all battery cable connections. Place a corrosion-resistant locking washer between the battery terminal stud and battery cable terminal end to ensure a positive connection. Loose battery connections can cause many different symptoms.

11. Check all ignition component ground wires for secure attachments to the power head. Clean and tighten all ground wires, connections and fasteners as necessary. Loose ground connections and loose component mounting hardware can cause many different symptoms.

Resistance (Ohmmeter) Tests

The resistance specifications in the following procedures are based on tests performed at room temperature. Actual resistance readings obtained during testing are generally slightly higher for hot components. In addition, resistance readings may vary depending on the manufacturer of the ohmmeter. Many ohmmeters have difficulty reading less than 1 ohm accurately. If this is the case, specifications of less than 1 ohm generally appear as a very low continuity reading. Due to these variables, use caution when considering the replacement of an electrical component that tests only slightly out of specification.

NOTE
Terminal stud style switch boxes have the color code abbreviations embossed into the switch box at each wire terminal stud. To remove the switch box wires, unsnap the rubber cap and remove the nut holding the wire to be removed. Reinstall the nut on the terminal to prevent its loss.

Direct Voltage Tests

Direct voltage tests are designed to check the voltage output of the ignition stator and the switch box (CDM).

The test procedures check voltage output at normal cranking speed. If an ignition misfire or failure occurs only when the engine is running and cranking speed tests do not show any defects, perform the output tests at the engine speed which the ignition symptom or failure occurs.

Table 8 lists the cranking and high-speed running voltages for all applicable tests. When checking the DVA voltage output of a component, observe the meter needle for fluctuations, which indicate erratic voltage output. The voltage output of the ignition stator and switch box (CDM) change with engine speed, but they should not be erratic.

The term *peak volts* is used interchangeably with *DVA (direct volts adapter)*. The Mercury Marine 91-99750 multimeter has a DVA scale that should be used whenever the specification is in peak volts or DVA. A DVA adapter (part No. 91-98045) is available to adapt any analog voltmeter capable of reading at least 400 DC volts. If the DVA or peak volts specification is listed as polarity sensitive, reverse the meter test leads and retest if the initial reading is unsatisfactory.

WARNING
High voltage is present during ignition system operation. Do not touch ignition components, wires or test leads while cranking or running the engine.

CAUTION
*Do not run the engine without an adequate water supply and do not exceed 3000 rpm without an adequate load. Refer to **Safety Precautions** at the beginning of this chapter.*

CAUTION
Unless otherwise noted, perform all direct voltage tests with the wires connected, but with the terminals exposed to accommodate test lead connections. Ground all electrical components to the power head before cranking or starting the engine, or the components will be damaged.

CAPACITOR DISCHARGE MODULE (CDM) IGNITION (65 JET AND 75-125 HP, EXCEPT 105 JET AND 115 OPTIMAX)

This CDM ignition is an alternator driven, capacitor discharge module system with mechanical spark advance. It is used on all 1998-on three and four cylinder two-stroke models. Ignition test harness part No.

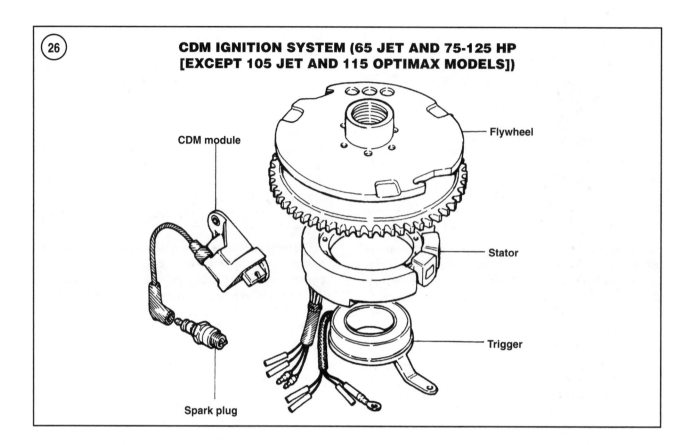

(26) CDM IGNITION SYSTEM (65 JET AND 75-125 HP [EXCEPT 105 JET AND 115 OPTIMAX MODELS])

CDM module

Flywheel

Stator

Trigger

Spark plug

84-825207A2 is required to test the CDM system without damaging the wiring harness and connectors.

The major components (**Figure 26**) include:

1. *Flywheel*—The flywheel inner magnet is for the trigger coil and provides timing information. The outer magnets are for the ignition stator and battery charging stator.

2. *Ignition stator coils*—The stator consists of one winding around three bobbins. The ignition stator is not grounded to the power head. The ignition stator provides power to the CDMs. Stator output is always AC (alternating current) voltage.

> *NOTE*
> *The ignition stator circuit must be complete from the stator to a CDM and back to the stator through a different CDM in order for the system to function.*

a. *Three-cylinder models (**Figure 27**)*—The voltage return path for cylinder No. 1 CDM is *either* cylinder No. 2 or No. 3 CDM. The voltage return path for cylinder No. 2 and No. 3 CDMs is through cylinder No. 1 CDM.

b. *Four-cylinder models (**Figure 28**)*—The voltage return path for cylinder No. 1 and No. 2 CDMs is through *either* cylinder No. 3 or No. 4 CDM. The

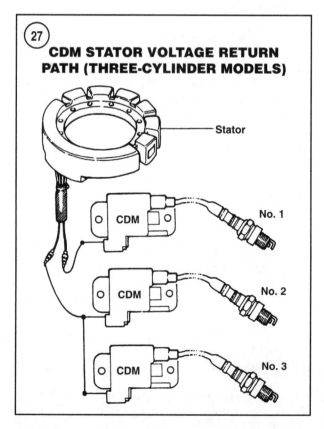

(27) CDM STATOR VOLTAGE RETURN PATH (THREE-CYLINDER MODELS)

Stator

CDM — No. 1

CDM — No. 2

CDM — No. 3

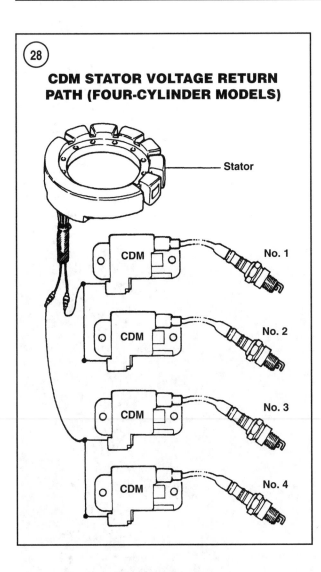

(28)

CDM STATOR VOLTAGE RETURN PATH (FOUR-CYLINDER MODELS)

Stator

CDM — No. 1

CDM — No. 2

CDM — No. 3

CDM — No. 4

voltage return path for cylinder No. 3 and No. 4 CDMs is through *either* cylinder No. 1 or No. 2 CDM.

3. *Trigger coil*—The trigger coil is rotated by a mechanical linkage to change the trigger's position relative to the flywheel. This movement advances or retards the ignition spark timing.

a. *Three-cylinder models*—The trigger coil has three windings grounded by a common black wires. The three individual trigger wires are brown, white and purple. Failure of the common black wire can cause an erratic or no spark condition on all cylinders. Failure of a single trigger wire will cause the loss of spark on one cylinder.

b. *Four-cylinder models*—The trigger coil has four windings grounded by a common black wire. The four individual trigger wires are brown, white, purple and blue. Failure of the common black wire can

cause an erratic or no spark condition on all cylinders. Failure of a single trigger wire will cause the loss of spark on one cylinder.

4. *CDMs*—There is one CDM for each cylinder. The CDM integrates the CD module (switch box) and ignition coil into one unit. The rectifier in each CDM transforms the ignition stator AC voltage into DC voltage so it can be stored in the CDM capacitor. The capacitor holds the voltage until the silicon controlled rectifier (SCR), an electronic switch, releases the voltage to the integral ignition coil primary windings. The SCR is triggered by the trigger coil signal. The ignition coil transforms the relatively low voltage from the capacitor into voltage high enough (45,000 volts) to jump the spark plug gap and ignite the air/fuel mixture.

5. *Spark plugs*—There is one spark plug for each cylinder. Use only the recommended spark plugs or power head damage may occur. Resistor or suppressor plugs are designed to reduce radio frequency interference (RFI) that can cause interference with electrical accessories. Use the recommended RFI spark plug if RFI is suspected of causing interference or malfunction of electrical accessories.

6. *Stop circuit*—The stop circuit is connected to one end of the capacitor in each CDM. Whenever the stop circuit is connected to ground the capacitor is shorted out and cannot store electricity. Therefore no voltage is available to send to the ignition coil windings and the ignition system ceases producing spark.

NOTE
The 65 jet, 80 jet, 100 hp, 115 hp and 125 hp models are equipped with a rpm limit module. The rpm limit module is connected to the CDM's stop circuit (black/yellow). When engine speed exceeds the preprogrammed limit, the rpm limit module momentarily shorts the black/yellow lead to ground, limiting engine speed.

Troubleshooting

Refer to **Tables 8-10** at the end of the chapter for specifications refer to the wiring diagrams at the end of the manual. Read *Troubleshooting Notes and Precautions (All Models)* at the beginning of the ignition section before continuing.

The recommended troubleshooting procedure is listed below.

1. Preliminary checks.
2. Ground circuit verification test.
3. Stop circuit isolation test.
4. Ignition stator output test.
5. Ignition stator resistance test.

6. Trigger output test.
7. Stop circuit output test.
8. CDM resistance test (optional).

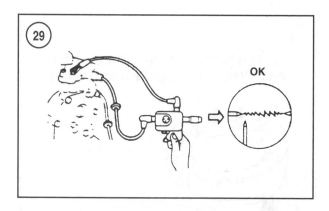

> *WARNING*
> *High voltage is present in the ignition system. **Never** touch or disconnect ignition components while the engine is running.*

> *CAUTION*
> *Do not run the engine without an adequate water supply and do not exceed 3000 rpm without an adequate load. Refer to **Safety Precautions** at the beginning of this chapter.*

> *NOTE*
> *All CDMs must be connected when troubleshooting the system. On three-cylinder models, disconnecting cylinder No. 1 CDM will cause a loss of spark on all cylinders. On four-cylinder models, disconnecting any CDM will cause a loss of spark on two of the remaining cylinders. On all models, disconnecting either stator will cause a loss of spark on all cylinders.*

Preliminary checks

1. Disconnect the spark plug wires from the spark plugs and install an air gap spark tester (part No. FT-11295 or equivalent) to the spark plug wires. Connect the alligator clip of the spark tester to a clean engine ground. Set the spark tester air gap to 7/16 in. (11.1 mm). See **Figure 29**.

2. Make sure the safety lanyard is installed on the safety lanyard switch and the ignition switch is in the RUN position.

3. Crank the engine while observing the tester. If there is a crisp, blue spark at each air gap, the ignition system is functioning correctly. If the engine will not start or does not run correctly, check the spark plugs and ignition timing. If the engine backfires or pops when attempting to start, remove the flywheel and check for a sheared flywheel key. If there is no spark, weak spark or erratic spark, continue to the *Ground circuit verification* test.

Ground circuit verification test

> *NOTE*
> *To prevent damage to the connector pins, use test harness adapter (part No. 84-825207A2) for all tests involving connection to the CDMs and engine harness connectors (**Figure 30**, typical).*

1. Disconnect all of the CDM plugs and connect the test harness adapter (part No. 84-825207A2) to the ignition wiring harness connector of the cylinder No. 1 CDM. Do not connect the test harness to the CDM. Calibrate an ohmmeter to the highest scale available. Connect one lead of the ohmmeter to a clean engine ground and connect the other ohmmeter lead to the black wire of the test harness. If the ohmmeter reads high resistance or no continuity, repair or replace the engine harness black wire or CDM connector as necessary.

2. Repeat Step 1 for each of the CDM harness connectors.

3. To verify the grounding of the ignition component mounting plate, connect one lead of an ohmmeter calibrated to the highest scale to a clean engine ground and the other lead to the ground lead terminal(s) (A, **Figure 31**, typical) on the ignition component mounting plate. If the ohmmeter reads high resistance or no continuity, tighten, repair or replace the ground path(s) (wires and ground stud) as required.

Stop circuit isolation test

> **WARNING**
> *To prevent accidental starting, remove the spark plug leads from the spark plugs and install the spark gap tester (part No. FT-11295 or equivalent) to the spark plug leads. Connect the alligator clip of the spark tester to a clean engine ground. See **Figure 29**.*

1. Isolate the stop circuit from the CDM ignition system by disconnecting the black/yellow bullet connector. This connector is in the tie-strapped bundle of leads near the voltage regulator (B, **Figure 31**, typical). Make sure the black/yellow lead is not touching other leads or ground.

2. Crank the motor and observe the spark tester. If there is now a good spark, the key switch, safety lanyard switch, rpm limit module (if equipped) or main engine harness black/yellow lead has shorted to ground. Test, repair or replace the circuit or component as necessary.

Ignition stator output test

> **WARNING**
> *To prevent accidental starting, remove the spark plug leads from the spark plugs and*

*install the spark gap tester, part No. FT-11295 or equivalent, to the spark plug leads. Connect the alligator clip of the spark tester to a clean engine ground. See **Figure 29**.*

1. Install the test harness (part No. 84-825207A2) between the cylinder No. 1 CDM and the ignition harness. Set the multimeter to the 400 DVA scale. Connect the meter positive lead to the test harness green wire and the meter negative lead to the test harness black lead.

2. Crank the engine while observing the meter reading. Refer to **Table 8** for specifications. The meter should indicate at least the minimum specification in **Table 8**. Repeat the test for each remaining CDM. If only one CDM is below specification, replace that CDM and retest. If all stator voltage readings are below the specification, go to *Ignition stator resistance test*.

3. If all CDM ignition stator voltages are below specification and stator resistance tests are within specification, perform the stop circuit output test in this section or replace each CDM one at a time with a known good CDM until the defective CDM is located.

Ignition stator resistance test

1. To check the resistance of the stator windings, disconnect the green/white and white/green stator wire bullet connectors from the engine wire harness. Calibrate an ohmmeter to the appropriate scale to read 600-750 ohms. Connect the positive ohmmeter lead to the stator assembly white/green wire and the negative ohmmeter lead to the stator assembly green/white wire. Note the meter reading. If the resistance is not within the specification in **Table 9**, the stator is defective and must be replaced. If the resistance is within specification, continue to Step 2.

2. To check the ignition stator windings for shorts to ground, calibrate an ohmmeter to the highest scale available. Connect one ohmmeter lead to a good engine ground and the other ohmmeter lead alternately to the ignition stator green/white and white/green wires while observing the meter. If the meter indicates continuity, the stator or stator wires are shorted to ground. Replace the stator if no faults are found with the wires.

Trigger output test

> **NOTE**
> *Pin C of the CDM connector is the trigger wire. The trigger wires on the ignition harness are color coded for each cylinder. Cylinder No. 1 uses a purple trigger wire,*

cylinder No. 2 uses a white trigger wire, cylinder No. 3 uses a brown trigger wire and cylinder No. 4 uses a dark blue trigger wire. Connecting the wrong trigger wire to the wrong CDM will cause the engine to fire out of time.

WARNING
*To prevent accidental starting, remove the spark plug leads from the spark plugs and install the spark gap tester (part No. FT-11295 or equivalent) to the spark plug leads. Connect the alligator clip of the spark tester to a clean engine ground. See **Figure 29**.*

1. Install the test harness part No. 84-825207A2 between the cylinder No. 1 CDM and the ignition harness.
2. Set the multimeter to the lowest DVA scale. Connect the meter positive lead to the test harness white wire and the meter negative lead to the test harness black wire. Crank the engine while observing the meter reading. If trigger voltage is below the specification in **Table 8**, replace the trigger and retest. If trigger voltage is above specification, replace the cylinder No. 1 CDM. Repeat the test for each remaining CDM.

NOTE
If trigger voltage remains low after a new trigger is installed, replace the CDM to which the low reading trigger wire is connected.

Stop circuit output test

The stop circuit output test checks the internal stop circuit of each CDM. Perform this test only after all of the preceding tests have been completed.

WARNING
*To prevent accidental starting, remove the spark plug leads from the spark plugs and install the spark gap tester (part No. FT-11295 or an equivalent) to the spark plug leads. Connect the alligator clip of the spark tester to a clean engine ground. See **Figure 29**.*

1. Install the test harness (part No. 84-825207A2) between the cylinder No. 1 CDM and the ignition harness. Set the multimeter to the 400 DVA scale. Connect the meter positive lead to the test harness black/yellow wire and the meter negative lead to the test harness black.
2. Crank the engine while observing the meter reading. Each CDM should show at least the minimum specifica-

tion in **Table 8**. Repeat the test for each remaining CDM. Replace any CDM that has a stop circuit output below the minimum specification.

CDM resistance test

Refer to **Table 10** for specifications. Test harness part No. 84-825207A2 is required for this test.
1. Connect the test harness part No. 84-825207A2 to the CDM. Do not connect the test harness to the ignition harness. This test is for the CDM only.
2. Calibrate the ohmmeter on an appropriate scale to read the specifications in **Table 10**.

NOTE
The following test includes a diode test. The ohmmeter readings may be reversed depending on the polarity of the ohmmeter being used. If test results are incorrect, reverse the test lead connection points. If the test is correct with the leads reversed, the diode is probably functioning correctly.

3. Connect the meter test leads to the pins and terminals specified in **Table 10**. Record the resistance readings.
4. If the resistance is not within the specification in **Table 10** for each test, replace the CDM.

RPM Limit Module

The 65 jet, 85 jet and 100-125 hp models (except 105 jet and 115 Optimax) are equipped with a rpm limit module. The rpm limit module is connected to the CDM's stop circuits (black/yellow wire). If engine speed exceeds the pre-programmed limit, the rpm limit module momentarily shorts the black/yellow wire to ground, limiting engine speed. There are four wires on the rpm limit module. The purple lead is power for the module from the key switch. The brown lead is connected to the brown trigger coil wire and is an rpm signal for the module. The black/yellow wire is connected to the CDM's stop circuit and is shorted to ground by the module to control engine speed by switching the ignition system on and off. The black wire is the ground path for the module.

Troubleshooting the rpm limit module

Refer to the wiring diagrams at the end of the manual.

CAUTION
*Do not run the engine without an adequate water supply and do not exceed 3000 rpm without an adequate load. Refer to **Safety***

Precautions at the beginning of this chapter.

NOTE
If the rpm limit module is suspected of causing a high speed misfire, verify the operating speed of the engine using a shop tachometer. Also, make sure the boat's tachometer, if equipped, is set correctly. The high speed misfire may be caused by the engine over-speeding without the operators knowledge.

1. If the rpm limit module is suspected of causing a no-spark, weak spark, erratic spark or misfire while running, disconnect the black/yellow and brown engine harness bullet connectors at the rpm limit module.

2. Retest spark output or run the engine to the speed at which the misfire occurs. If the spark output is now satisfactory or the misfire is no longer present, the rpm limit module is defective and must be replaced.

3. If the rpm limit module is suspected of not functioning when necessary, check the ground wire for secure attachment to the power head. Clean and tighten the connection as necessary to ensure a good ground path.

4. Disconnect the purple wire bullet connector from the rpm limit module. Connect the positive lead of a voltmeter, set to read 20 volts DC, to the engine harness purple wire bullet connector. Connect the negative lead of the voltmeter to a good engine ground. When the ignition key is ON, the voltmeter should read within 1 volt of battery voltage. When the key is OFF, the voltmeter should read zero volts. If the meter reading is below specification with the key on, repair or replace the purple wire circuit from the key switch to the engine harness rpm limit module bullet connector.

5. Check the brown rpm limit module engine harness wire for continuity to the brown trigger coil wire by disconnecting the engine harness brown wire from the trigger coil bullet connector and the rpm limit module bullet connector. Calibrate an ohmmeter to the R × 1 scale. Connect one ohmmeter lead to the trigger coil end of the engine harness brown wire. Connect the other ohmmeter lead to the rpm limit module end of the engine harness brown wire. If the ohmmeter does not read continuity, repair or replace the engine harness brown lead.

6. Check the black/yellow rpm limit module engine harness wire for continuity to each CDM. Disconnect the engine harness black/yellow wire from the rpm limit module bullet connector. Disconnect the engine harness four-pin connector at each CDM. Connect the CDM test harness (part No. 84-825207A-2) to the cylinder No. 1 CDM engine harness connector. Calibrate an ohmmeter to the R ×

1 scale. Connect one ohmmeter lead to the rpm limit module end of the engine harness black/yellow wire. Connect the other end to the CDM test harness black/yellow bullet connector. If the ohmmeter does not read continuity, repair or replace the engine harness black/yellow wire between the rpm limit module and the cylinder No. 1 CDM engine harness connector.

7. Repeat Step 6 for each CDM engine harness connector.

8. Reconnect all leads when finished.

ALTERNATOR DRIVEN IGNITION (1998 AND 1999 105 JET AND 135-200 HP MODELS [EXCEPT OPTIMAX MODELS])

The AD-CDI ignition is an alternator driven, capacitor discharge ignition system with mechanical spark advance. It is used on 1998 and 1999 135-200 hp, except Optimax, models. Capacitor discharge module (CDM) ignition is used on 2000-on models.

On EFI models, the ignition system operates independently of the fuel injection system. However, the fuel injection ECM requires input from the inner switch box primary ignition coil wires for cylinders No. 1, No. 3 and No. 5. An ignition failure on one of these cylinders will cause two cylinders not to receive fuel, since the ECM will not receive a fuel injector trigger signal from the ignition system.

Refer to **Figure 32** for an operational diagram of the AD-CDI six-cylinder ignition system. The major components include:

1. *Flywheel*—The flywheel inner magnets are for the trigger coil and provide timing information. The outer magnets are for the ignition stator and battery charging stator.

2. *Ignition stator (charge) coils*—The stator is equipped with two low- and two high-speed windings and a ground wire. The ignition stator provides the power the two switch boxes need to operate the ignition system. Low-speed windings provide most of the electricity for cranking and idle. High-speed windings provide most of the electricity for cruising and wide open throttle. Stator output is always AC (alternating current) voltage. The ignition stator has one set of wires banded with a yellow sleeve for identification. The yellow banded ignition stator wires must be connected to the same switch box as the yellow banded trigger coil wires. The non-yellow banded ignition stator wires must be connected to the same switch box as the non-yellow banded trigger coil wires. Normally the yellow banded wires go to the outer switch box.

3. *Trigger coil*—The trigger coil tells the switch box when to fire the ignition coils. A mechanical linkage ro-

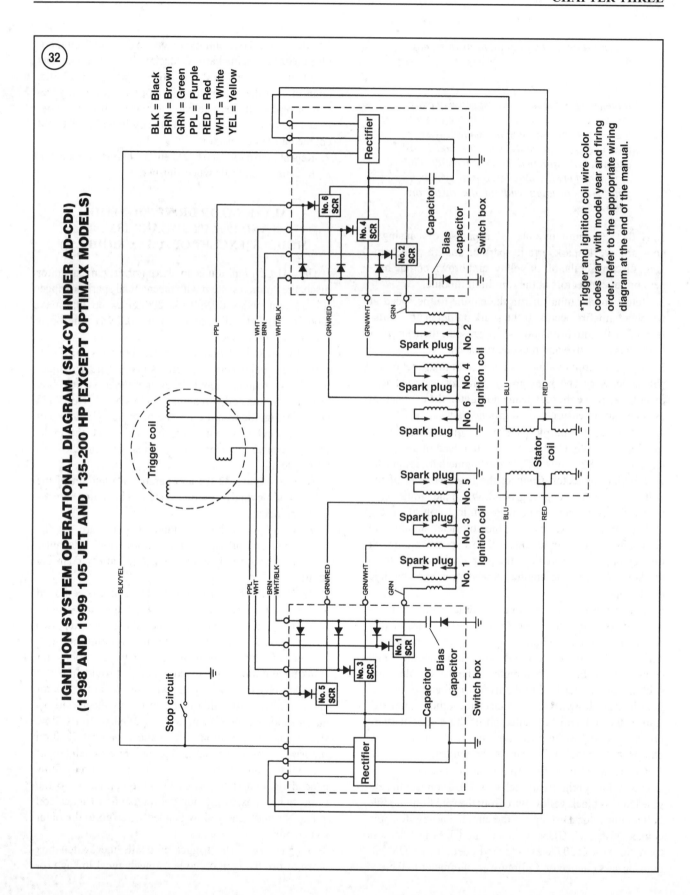

IGNITION SYSTEM OPERATIONAL DIAGRAM (SIX-CYLINDER AD-CDI) (1998 AND 1999 105 JET AND 135-200 HP [EXCEPT OPTIMAX MODELS)

BLK = Black
BRN = Brown
GRN = Green
PPL = Purple
RED = Red
WHT = White
YEL = Yellow

*Trigger and ignition coil wire color codes vary with model year and firing order. Refer to the appropriate wiring diagram at the end of the manual.

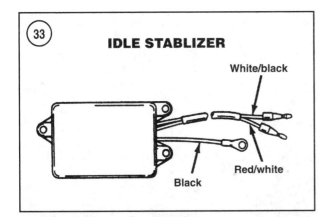

IDLE STABLIZER

White/black

Red/white

Black

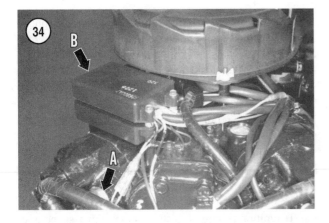

tates the trigger coil to change the trigger's position relative to the flywheel. This advances or retards the ignition spark timing. The trigger coil has three windings. Each winding has two wires. One wire from each winding goes to each switch box. The trigger coil has three wires banded with a yellow sleeve for identification. The yellow banded trigger coil wires must connect to the same switch box as the yellow banded ignition stator wires. The non-yellow banded trigger coil wires must connect to the same switch box as the non-yellow banded stator wires. Normally the yellow banded leads go to the outer switch box. The three individual trigger wires on each switch box are brown, white and purple. Failure of a single trigger winding or wire will cause the loss of spark on two cylinders on opposing cylinder banks.

4. *Switch boxes*—These models use two switch boxes with terminal stud connectors. All 2000-on models use a CDM ignition system that does not require switch boxes. The switch boxes store the electricity from the ignition stator windings until the trigger coils tell them to send the electricity to the ignition coils. The switch box uses an internal rectifier to change the ignition stator AC voltage to DC (direct current) voltage. The DC voltage is stored in a

capacitor, an electrical storage tank, until it is released by a SCR (silicon controlled rectifier), which is an electronic switch. There is one SCR for each cylinder. The SCR is controlled by the trigger coil. The switch boxes incorporate a bias circuit primarily used to stabilize ignition spark advance and to keep the two switch boxes from interfering with each other. A separate test is necessary to make sure the bias circuit is functioning correctly on each switch box. Switch boxes must be grounded to each other and the engine block anytime the engine is cranked or run.

5A. *Idle stabilizer module*—An idle stabilizer (**Figure 33**) module is connected to the switch box bias circuit. When idle speed drops below a preprogrammed value, additional spark advance is added through the bias circuit to stabilize engine speed.

5B. *Detonation sensor and module*—The 200 hp EFI models are also equipped with a detonation sensor (A, **Figure 34**) and module (B, **Figure 34**) which detects potentially damaging spark knock (abnormal combustion) and retards ignition spark advance up to 8°. The detonation module also signals the fuel system ECM (electronic control module) to enrich fuel flow up to 15 percent. Reducing spark advance and enriching fuel prevents spark knock under normal operating conditions.

6. *Ignition coils*—There is one ignition coil for each cylinder. The ignition coil transforms the relatively low voltage from the switch box into voltage high enough (35,000 volts) to jump the spark plug gap and ignite the air/fuel mixture.

7. *Spark plugs*—There is one spark plug for each cylinder. Only use the recommended spark plugs or engine damage could occur. Resistor or suppressor plugs are designed to reduce RFI (radio frequency interference) emissions that can cause interference with electrical accessories. Use the recommended RFI spark plug if RFI is suspected of causing interference or malfunction of electrical accessories.

8. *Stop circuit*—The stop circuit is connected to one end of the capacitor in each switch box. Whenever the stop circuit is connected to ground, the capacitors are shorted to ground and cannot store electricity. Therefore, no voltage is available to send to the ignition coils and the ignition system ceases producing spark.

NOTE
The 105 and 140 jet models are equipped with an rpm limit module. The rpm limit module is connected to the switch box stop circuit (black/yellow wire). When engine speed exceeds the preprogrammed limit, the rpm limit module momentarily shorts the black/yellow wire to ground, limiting engine speed.

Troubleshooting

Refer to **Table 8** and **Table 9** for specifications and the wiring diagrams at the end of the manual. Read *Troubleshooting Notes and Precautions (All Models)* at the beginning of the ignition section before continuing. Test harness part No. 91-1443A1 has a six position rotary switch and six long test leads that allow connection to as many as six different test points. The harness allows testing on a running motor from the passenger compartment. A typical use of the harness is to check all six switch box outputs at the engine speed that the ignition symptom is occurring.

The recommended troubleshooting procedure is listed below.

1. Preliminary checks.
   a. Spark test.
   b. Stop circuit isolation.
   c. Idle stabilizer module isolation test.
   d. Detonation sensor module isolation test (200 EFI models).
2. Switch box stop circuit test.
3. Ignition stator output test.
4. Ignition stator resistance test.
5. Switch box bias test.
6. Trigger resistance test.
7. Switch box output test.
8. Ignition coil ohmmeter test.

WARNING
*High voltage is present in the ignition system. **Never** touch or disconnect ignition components while the engine is running.*

CAUTION
*Do not run the engine without an adequate water supply and do not exceed 3000 rpm without an adequate load. Refer to **Safety Precautions** at the beginning of this chapter.*

Preliminary checks

NOTE
Weak, intermittent or no spark at two cylinders (one cylinder on each bank) usually indicates a defective trigger coil. Weak, intermittent or no spark at three cylinders (one complete bank) usually indicates a defective stator assembly or switch box. Weak, intermittent or no spark at one cylinder usually indicates a defective spark plug, ignition coil or switch box.

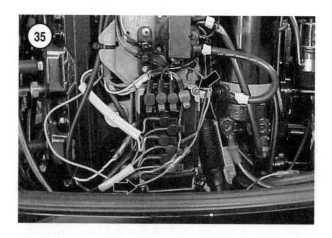

1. Disconnect the spark plug leads from the spark plugs and install an air gap spark tester (part No. 91-850439 or an equivalent) to the spark plug leads. Connect the alligator clip of the spark tester to a clean engine ground. Set the spark tester air gap to 7/16 in. (11.1 mm). See **Figure 29**.

2. Make sure the safety lanyard is installed on the safety lanyard switch and the ignition switch is in the run position.

3. Crank the engine while observing the tester. If there is a crisp, blue spark at each air gap, the ignition system is functioning correctly. If the engine will not start or does not run correctly, check the spark plugs and ignition timing. If ignition timing is unstable at cranking speed and idle speed, go to *Switch box bias test* in this section. If there is no spark, weak spark or erratic spark, continue to Step 4.

CAUTION
*Remove the switch boxes from the power head to access the inner switch box wire terminals. Ground the switch boxes to the power head before cranking or starting the engine, or the switch boxes may be damaged. Connect a suitable jumper wire securely between **both** switch boxes and a good engine ground before cranking the engine in the following tests.*

4. Remove the screws (**Figure 35**) securing the switch boxes to the power head. Without disconnecting any switch box wires, separate the inner and outer switch boxes. Do not lose the spacers between switch boxes at each mounting screw.

5. Disconnect the stop circuit black/yellow wires from *both* switch box terminal studs. Crank the engine while observing the spark tester. If there is now a good spark, a short to ground is present in the key switch, safety lanyard switch, rpm limit module (if equipped) or the main engine

harness black/yellow wire. Test, repair or replace the circuit or component as necessary.

6. To isolate the idle stabilizer module from the ignition system, disconnect the white/black and red/white wires from the idle stabilizer module bullet connectors (**Figure 33**). Crank the engine while observing the spark tester. If there is now a good spark, replace the idle stabilizer and retest the spark output.

7. On 200 hp EFI models, isolate the detonation sensor module from the ignition system by removing the screws (**Figure 35**) securing the switch boxes to the power head. Without disconnecting any switch box wires, separate the inner and outer switch boxes. Do not lose the spacers between switch boxes at each mounting screw. Disconnect the detonation module white/black wires from each switch box. Crank the engine while observing the spark tester. If there is now a good spark, replace the detonation sensor module and retest spark output.

Switch box stop circuit tests

WARNING
*To prevent accidental starting, remove the spark plug leads from the spark plugs and install the spark gap tester (91-850439) to the spark plug leads. Connect the alligator clip of the spark tester to a clean engine ground. See **Figure 29**.*

CAUTION
*Remove the switch boxes from the power head to access the inner switch box wire terminals. Ground the switch boxes to the power head before cranking or starting the engine, or the switch boxes may be damaged. Connect a suitable jumper wire securely between **both** switch boxes and a good engine ground before cranking the engine in the following tests.*

1. Remove the screws (**Figure 35**) securing the switch boxes to the power head. Without disconnecting any switch box wires, separate the inner and outer switch boxes. Do not lose the spacers between switch boxes at each mounting screw.

2. Connect the meter negative lead to a good engine ground and the meter positive lead to the black/yellow terminal stud on the outer switch box.

3. Set the meter selector switch to 400 DVA.

4. Crank the engine while noting the test meter.

5. Move the meter positive lead to the black/yellow terminal stud on the inner switch box.

6. Crank the engine while noting the test meter.

7. If the stop circuit voltage is not within the specification in **Table 8** at both switch boxes, go to *Ignition stator output test* in this section.

8. If the stop circuit voltage is above the specification at one or both switch boxes, either the switch box(es) or the trigger coil assembly is defective. Test the trigger coils as described under *Trigger coil ohmmeter tests* in this section. If the trigger coils are within specification, replace the switch box(es) that exhibits high stop circuit voltage and retest.

9. If the stop circuit voltage is below specification at one or both switch boxes, disconnect the black/yellow stop circuit wire from both switch box terminal studs.

10. Recheck the stop circuit voltage at both switch boxes (Steps 2-6). If the stop circuit voltages are now within the specified range, the stop circuit is partially shorted to ground and must be repaired. If the stop switch voltage is still below specification, go to *Ignition stator output tests* in this section.

Ignition stator output tests

WARNING
*To prevent accidental starting, remove the spark plug leads from the spark plugs and install the spark gap tester (part No. 91-850439) to the spark plug leads. Connect the alligator clip of the spark tester to a clean engine ground. See **Figure 29**.*

CAUTION
*Remove the switch boxes from the power head to access the inner switch box wire terminals. Ground the switch boxes to the power head before cranking or starting the engine, or the switch boxes may be damaged. Connect a suitable jumper lead securely between **both** switch boxes and a good engine ground before cranking the engine in the following tests.*

NOTE
*A malfunctioning idle speed stabilizer module may cause the test results to be inaccurate. Disconnect the red/white bullet connector from the idle speed stabilizer module (**Figure 33**) before performing the ignition stator output test.*

1. To test the ignition stator low-speed winding output, connect the meter negative lead to a good engine ground and the meter positive lead to the inner switch box blue ignition stator wire terminal stud.

2. Set the meter selector switch to 400 DVA.

3. Crank the engine and note the meter.

4. If the low speed stator output voltage is not within the cranking speed specification in **Table 8**, test the resistance of the ignition stator low-speed windings as described in the next section.

5. Repeat the low-speed output test for the outer switch box blue/white ignition stator wire.

6. To test the stator high-speed winding output, connect the meter negative lead to a good engine ground and the meter positive lead to the inner red ignition stator wire terminal stud on the switch box.

7. Verify the meter is still set to the 400 DVA scale.

8. Crank the engine and note the meter.

9. If the high speed stator output voltage is not within the cranking speed specification in **Table 8**, test the resistance of the ignition stator high-speed windings as described in the next section.

10. Repeat the high-speed output test for the outer switch box red/white ignition stator wire.

Ignition stator resistance tests

1. Disconnect the ignition stator blue and red wires from the inner switch box, and disconnect the blue/white and red/white wires from the outer switch box terminal studs. Disconnect the blue and red wires from the inner switch box terminal studs.

2. To check the resistance of the ignition stator low-speed windings, calibrate an ohmmeter on the appropriate scale to read the low winding specifications in **Table 9**.

3. Connect the ohmmeter negative lead to the ignition stator blue wire and the ohmmeter positive lead to the ignition stator red wire.

4. If the resistance reading is not within the low speed winding specification in **Table 9**, replace the stator coil assembly and retest spark output.

5. Repeat Steps 2-4 using the ignition stator blue/white and red/white wires.

6. To check the resistance of the ignition stator high-speed windings, calibrate an ohmmeter on the appropriate scale to read the high-speed winding specifications in **Table 9**.

7. Connect the ohmmeter negative lead to a good engine ground and the ohmmeter positive lead to the red ignition stator lead.

8. If the resistance reading is not within the high speed winding specification in **Table 9**, replace the stator coil assembly and retest spark output.

9. Repeat Steps 6-8 using the ignition stator red/white lead.

Switch box bias test

> *WARNING*
> *To prevent accidental starting, remove the spark plug leads from the spark plugs and install the spark gap tester (part No. 91-850439) to the spark plug leads. Connect the alligator clip of the spark tester to a clean engine ground. See **Figure 29**.*

> *CAUTION*
> *The switch box bias circuit voltage output is DC (direct current). Do not use the DVA scale or adapter for this test.*

> *NOTE*
> *A malfunctioning idle speed stabilizer or detonation sensor module may cause the following test results to be inaccurate. Disconnect the white/black wire from the idle stabilizer bullet connector (**Figure 33**). On 200 hp EFI models, also disconnect the white/black detonation sensor module wires from both switch boxes before proceeding.*

1. To check the switch box bias circuit output, connect the positive lead of a DC voltmeter set to the 20 VDC scale to a clean engine ground. Connect the negative lead of the DC voltmeter to the outer switch box white/black wire terminal stud.

2. Crank the engine while observing the meter. The meter should indicate 2-10 volts DC.

> *NOTE*
> *The detonation sensor module on 200 hp EFI models completes the bias circuit between the two switch boxes. Check the bias circuit voltage on both switch boxes.*

3. On 200 hp EFI models, repeat Steps 1-2 for the inner switch box white/black terminal stud.

4. If switch box bias is above the specified voltage, one or both switch boxes are defective. Disconnect all leads from both switch box white/black terminal studs. Set an ohmmeter on the appropriate scale to read 1300-1500 ohms.

5. Connect one ohmmeter lead to the inner switch box white/black wire terminal stud. Connect the other ohmmeter lead to the inner switch box case ground.

6. If the ohmmeter does not read 1300-1500 ohms, replace the switch box and retest the switch box bias circuit voltage.

7. Repeat Steps 4-6 for the outer switch box.

8A. On 200 hp EFI models, if the ohmmeter tests are within specification, but the bias circuit voltage is still below specification for both switch boxes, replace both

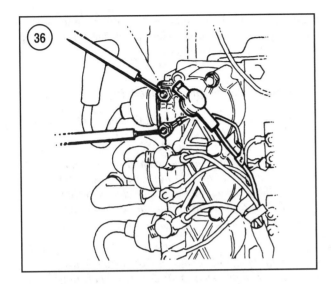

3. Connect one ohmmeter lead to the trigger coil brown wire without the yellow sleeve and the other ohmmeter lead to the trigger coil white wire with the yellow sleeve.

4. If the resistance reading is not 1100-1400 ohms, replace the trigger coil and retest the spark output.

5. Repeat the test for the second trigger coil winding. Connect one ohmmeter lead to the white trigger coil wire without the yellow sleeve and the other ohmmeter lead to the purple trigger coil wire with the yellow sleeve.

6. If the resistance reading is not 1100-1400 ohms, replace the trigger coil and retest the spark output.

7. Repeat the test for the third trigger coil winding. Connect one ohmmeter lead to the trigger coil purple wire without the yellow sleeve and the other ohmmeter lead to the trigger coil brown wire with the yellow sleeve.

8. If the resistance reading is not 1100-1400 ohms, replace the trigger coil and retest the spark output.

switch boxes and retest the switch box bias circuit voltage. If the bias circuit voltage is below specification on one switch box, replace the suspect switch box and retest the switch box bias circuit voltage.

8B. On carbureted models, if the ohmmeter tests are within specification, but the bias circuit voltage is below specification, one or both switch boxes are defective. Replace the outer switch box and retest the switch box bias circuit voltage. If the reading is still below specification, replace the inner switch box and retest switch box bias circuit voltage.

NOTE
*A frequent cause of switch box bias failure is a poor ground to the adjacent switch box. If repeated bias failure occurs in the same switch box, inspect the other switch box ground. If the ground is clean, tight and appears to be in acceptable condition, the manufacturer recommends replacing **both** switch boxes.*

Trigger coil resistance test

NOTE
Ohmmeter tests require connection to one wire from the yellow banded trigger harness and one wire from the non-yellow banded trigger coil harness.

1. Disconnect the brown, white and purple trigger coil wires from the terminal studs of both switch boxes.

2. Set an ohmmeter on the appropriate scale to read 1100-1400 ohms.

Switch box output test

WARNING
*To prevent accidental starting, remove the spark plug leads from the spark plugs and install the spark gap tester (part No. 91-850439) to the spark plug leads. Connect the alligator clip of the spark tester to a clean engine ground. See **Figure 29**.*

NOTE
The inner switch box controls the ignition coils for cylinders No. 1, No. 3 and No. 5. The outer switch box controls the ignition coils for cylinders No. 2, No. 4 and No. 6.

1. To check the switch box voltage output to the ignition coils, connect the meter positive lead to the cylinder No. 1 ignition coil positive primary terminal. Connect the meter negative lead to the cylinder No. 1 ignition coil negative primary terminal (black wire). See **Figure 36**.

2. Set the meter selector switch to 400 DVA.

3. Crank the engine while noting the meter reading.

4. If the meter reading is below the specification in **Table 8**, continue to the ignition coil ohmmeter test. If the ignition coil ohmmeter tests are within specification, replace the switch box and retest the spark output. If the ignition coil tests are not within the specification, replace the ignition coil(s) and retest the spark output. If the meter reading is within the specification, but there is no spark, weak spark or erratic spark, continue to the ignition coil ohmmeter test.

5. Repeat the test procedure for the remaining ignition coil(s).

Ignition coil resistance test

1. To check the ignition coil primary resistance, calibrate an ohmmeter to the appropriate scale to read the primary resistance specification in **Table 11**.

2. Disconnect the spark plug leads. Carefully remove the spark plug leads from the ignition coils. Disconnect the switch box primary wire from each ignition coil positive primary terminal stud.

3. Connect the ohmmeter negative lead to the cylinder No. 1 ignition coil negative terminal. Connect the ohmmeter positive lead to the cylinder No.1 ignition coil positive terminal stud.

4. If the meter reading is not within the primary resistance specification in **Table 11**, replace the ignition coil and retest the spark output. If the meter reading is within specification, go to Step 5. Repeat the test for the remaining ignition coils.

5. To check the ignition coil secondary resistance, calibrate the ohmmeter on the appropriate scale to read the secondary resistance specification in **Table 11**.

6. Connect the ohmmeter positive lead to the cylinder No. 1 ignition coil spark plug tower. Connect the ohmmeter negative lead to the cylinder No. 1 ignition coil primary positive terminal stud.

7. If the meter reading is not within the specification in **Table 11**, replace the ignition coil and retest the spark output. If the meter reading is within specification and all other ignition components are within specification, but there is still no spark, weak spark or erratic spark, replace the ignition coil(s) and retest the spark output. Repeat the test for the remaining ignition coils.

8. To check the ignition coil spark plug wires for continuity, calibrate an ohmmeter to the R × 1 scale. Connect one ohmmeter lead to each end of the spark plug wire. Gently twist and flex the spark plug lead while observing the meter. If the meter indicates a high reading or fluctuates when the wire is flexed, replace the spark plug wire. Repeat the test for the remaining spark plug wires.

RPM Limit Module

The 105-140 jet models are equipped with a rpm limit module. The rpm limit module is connected to the switch box stop circuits (black/yellow wire). If engine speed exceeds the preprogrammed limit, the rpm limit module momentarily shorts the black/yellow wire to ground, limiting engine speed. There are four wires on the rpm limit module. The purple wire is power for the module from the key switch. The brown wire connects to the brown trigger coil wire and is an rpm signal for the module. The black/yellow wire is connected to the switch box stop circuits and is

shorted to ground by the module to control engine rpm by switching the ignition system on and off. The black wire is the ground path for the module.

Troubleshooting the rpm limit module

Refer to the wiring diagrams at the end of the manual.

> *CAUTION*
> *Do not run the engine without an adequate water supply and do not exceed 3000 rpm without an adequate load. Refer to **Safety Precautions** at the beginning of this chapter.*

> *NOTE*
> *If the rpm limit module is suspected of causing a high-speed misfire, verify operating speed of the engine using a shop tachometer. Also make sure the boat's tachometer, if equipped, is set correctly. The high-speed misfire may be caused by the engine over-speeding without the operator's knowledge.*

1. If the rpm limit module is suspected of causing no spark, weak spark, erratic spark or misfire while running, disconnect the rpm limit module black/yellow wires from the engine harness or outer switch box.

2. Disconnect the brown rpm limit module wire from the outer switch box.

3. Retest spark output or run the engine to the speed at which the misfire occurs. If the spark output is now satisfactory or the misfire is no longer present, the rpm limit module is defective and must be replaced.

4. If the rpm limit module is suspected of not functioning when necessary, check the ground wire for secure attachment to the power head. Clean and tighten the connection as necessary to ensure a good ground path.

5. Disconnect the purple wire bullet connector at the rpm limit module. Connect the positive lead of a voltmeter, set to read 20 VDC, to the engine harness purple wire bullet connector. Connect the negative lead of the voltmeter to a good engine ground. When the ignition key is *on*, the voltmeter should read within 1 volt of battery voltage. When the key is *off*, the voltmeter should read zero volts. If the meter reading is below specification, repair or replace the purple wire circuit from the key switch to the engine harness rpm limit module bullet connector.

6. Check the brown rpm limit module engine harness wire for continuity to the brown trigger coil wire. Disconnect the engine harness brown wire from the switch box terminal stud and the rpm limit module bullet connector. Calibrate an ohmmeter to the R × 1 scale. Connect one

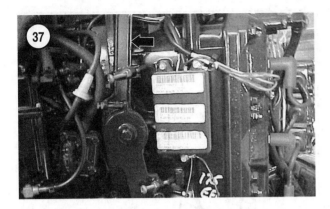

ohmmeter lead to the switch box end of the engine harness brown wire. Connect the other ohmmeter lead to the rpm limit module end of the engine harness brown wire. If the ohmmeter does not read continuity, repair or replace the engine harness brown wire.

7. Check the black/yellow rpm limit module engine harness wire for continuity to the switch box. Disconnect the engine harness black/yellow wire at the rpm limit module bullet connector and at the switch box terminal stud. Calibrate an ohmmeter to the R × 1 scale. Connect one ohmmeter lead to the switch box end of the engine harness black/yellow wire and the other ohmmeter lead to the rpm limit module end. If the ohmmeter does not read continuity, repair or replace the engine harness black/yellow wire.

8. Reconnect all wires when finished.

Idle Stabilizer Module Troubleshooting

All 1998 and 1999 models are equipped with an idle stabilizer module. The module is a solid-state, non-serviceable device and must be replaced if not functioning correctly. Whenever engine speed drops below approximately 550 rpm, the idle stabilizer electronically advances ignition timing through the switch box bias circuit. The idle stabilizer can advance ignition timing a maximum of 9° above normal base timing. The additional timing advance raises the engine speed to 550 rpm and the module returns ignition timing to normal operation. The idle stabilizer module has three wires. The red/white wire provides power to the module from the ignition stator high-speed winding, the white/black wire is connected to the switch box bias circuit to allow the idle stabilizer module to control ignition timing and the black wire is ground. See **Figure 33**. Test the idle stabilizer as follows:

CAUTION
*Do not run the engine without an adequate water supply and do not exceed 3000 rpm without an adequate load. Refer to **Safety***

***Precautions** at the beginning of this chapter.*

Refer to the wiring diagrams at the end of the manual.

1. Connect a timing light to the No. 1 top starboard spark plug wire. Connect an accurate tachometer to the engine following its manufacturer's instructions.

2. Start the engine and allow it to warm to operating temperature. Reduce the engine speed to approximately 600-650 rpm.

3. Slowly pull forward on the spark advance lever (**Figure 37**) to retard the timing and reduce the engine speed. Use the timing light to observe the timing as the spark advance lever is moved.

NOTE
Due to variations in individual idle stabilizer modules and in tachometers from different manufacturers, the engine speed at which timing advance occurs may vary slightly.

4. If the ignition timing rapidly advances as much as 9° as the engine speed falls below approximately 550 rpm, the idle stabilizer is operating properly. If timing does not advance, replace the idle stabilizer module.

Idle Stabilizer Shift System (XR6, Magnum III, 175 hp Carbureted, 150 hp EFI and 175 hp EFI Models)

The idle stabilizer shift system prevents stalling by advancing the ignition timing 3° when the outboard is shifted into forward gear.

When the outboard motor is running at idle speed in neutral, the shift switch (**Figure 38**) opens. When the motor is shifted into gear, the shift switch closes and completes the switch box bias circuit from each switch box to ground through a 6800 ohm resistor, resulting in a 3° timing advance. If the 6800 ohm resistor (**Figure 38**) opens or the shift switch remains open, the timing advance will not occur. Also, full-throttle timing is 3° retarded. If the resistor or the white/black wire between the resistor and the outer switch box short to ground, the timing will be excessively advanced causing serious power head damage.

CAUTION
If the idle stabilizer shift system is installed on models other than XR6, Mag III, 150 hp EFI, 175 hp carbureted and 175 hp EFI models as an accessory, the maximum ignition timing must be retarded 3°. Refer to Chapter Five for the timing procedure.

3

Idle stabilizer shift system troubleshooting

> *CAUTION*
> *Do not run the engine without an adequate water supply and do not exceed 3000 rpm without an adequate load. Refer to **Safety Precautions** at the beginning of this chapter.*

1. Connect a timing light to the No. 1 top starboard spark plug lead.

2. Start the engine and allow it to reach operating temperature. Reduce the engine speed to idle.

3. While observing the ignition timing, shift into forward gear. The idle stabilizer shift system is functioning properly if the timing advances 3° upon shifting into gear.

4. If the timing does not advance 3°, shut the engine off. Disconnect the white/black resistor wire from the shift switch bullet connector and the outer switch box white/black terminal stud.

5. Calibrate an ohmmeter to the appropriate scale to read 6800-7140 ohms. Connect one ohmmeter lead to each end of the resistor. If the reading is not within 6800-7140 ohms, replace the resistor and wire assembly. If the reading is within 6800-7140 ohms, go to Step 6.

6. Calibrate an ohmmeter to the R × 1 scale. Disconnect the shift switch wire from the white/black resistor wire bullet connector. Connect one ohmmeter lead to the shift switch ground lead terminal and the other ohmmeter lead to the shift switch bullet connector.

7. Position the gear shift mechanism in the NEUTRAL position. The ohmmeter should read no continuity. Position the gear shift mechanism into the FORWARD gear position. The ohmmeter should read continuity. Replace the shift switch if the readings are not as specified. If the shift switch and resistor test good and the timing is still not advancing 3° when shifting into gear, test the switch box bias circuit as previously described in this section.

Detonation Sensor and Module (200 hp EFI Models)

The 200 hp EFI models are equipped with a detonation sensor (A, **Figure 34**) and detonation sensor module (B). The detonation sensor detects the high-frequency vibration caused by pre-ignition or detonation. The detonation sensor creates a small voltage signal anytime the engine is running. The voltage signal increases dramatically if preignition or detonation is present. When the module detects the correct voltage signal from normal engine vibration at approximately 2500-3500 rpm, the module adds 6° spark advance. The module holds this advance as long as

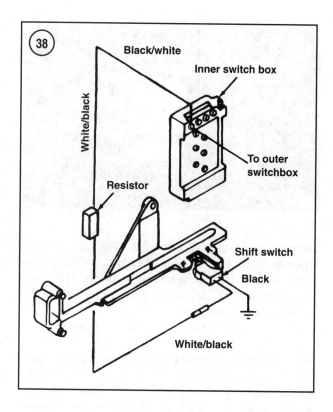

the voltage signal is in the normal range. If the module detects a voltage signal higher than normal from preignition or detonation, it removes added timing advance up to 6° and, if necessary, reduces timing advance up to an additional 2°.

The detonation sensor module also communicates with the ECM. If preignition or detonation is present, the ECM increases fuel flow through the fuel injector by up to 15 percent. The enriched air/fuel ratio along with the retarded spark advance helps cool the combustion chambers and eliminate detonation. The Quicksilver digital diagnostic terminal (DDT) is required to verify that the extra fuel is being added. The DDT allows verification of the increase in fuel injector pulse width.

Functional test

1. Connect a timing light to the No. 1 top starboard spark plug lead.

> *WARNING*
> *To prevent accidental starting, remove the spark plug leads from the spark plugs and install the spark gap tester (part No. 91-850439) to the spark plug leads. Connect the alligator clip of the spark tester to a clean engine ground. See **Figure 29**.*

2. Check the maximum timing at cranking speed as described in Chapter Five. Adjust the timing as necessary.

3. Remove the spark gap tester and reconnect the spark plug leads to the spark plugs.

CAUTION
*Do not run the engine without an adequate water supply and do not exceed 3000 rpm without an adequate load. Refer to **Safety Precautions** at the beginning of this chapter.*

4. Start the engine and allow it to reach operating temperature. Run the engine at 3500 rpm or higher in forward gear. Note the timing.

5. If the timing at 3500 rpm or higher is 6° more than the timing at cranking speed, the detonation sensor and detonation module are functioning correctly. If not, continue to troubleshooting.

Troubleshooting

Refer to the wiring diagrams at the end of this manual.

1. If the detonation sensor and module are not functioning as described, check the ground wire for secure attachment to the power head. Clean and tighten the connection as necessary.

2. Set the voltmeter to the 20-volt DC scale. Connect the positive voltmeter lead to the detonation sensor purple wire terminal at the power head terminal strip. Connect the negative voltmeter lead to a good engine ground. When the ignition key is ON, the voltmeter should read within 1 volt of battery voltage. When the key is OFF, the voltmeter should read 0 volts. If the meter reading is below specification, repair or replace the purple wire circuit from the key switch to the two-terminal, power head terminal strip.

3. Check the green detonation sensor module engine harness wire for continuity to the cylinder No. 2 ignition coil

primary positive terminal stud. Disconnect the engine harness green wire from the cylinder No. 2 ignition coil positive terminal stud and the detonation sensor module bullet connector. Set an ohmmeter to the R × 1 scale. Connect one ohmmeter lead to the ignition coil end of the engine harness green wire and the other ohmmeter lead to the detonation sensor module end of the engine harness green wire. If the ohmmeter does not read continuity, repair or replace the engine harness green wire.

4. Check the detonation sensor module gray/white wire and bullet connector for secure attachment to the ECM gray/white wire and bullet connector. Repair or replace the gray/white wire and connectors as necessary.

5. Check both white/black detonation sensor module wires for secure attachment to each switch box bias terminal stud.

6. If there is corrosion or sealant around the base of the sensor (**Figure 39**), remove the sensor and clean the threads of the sensor and cylinder head. Do not coat the threads of the sensor with sealant. Reinstall the sensor and torque it to 144 in.-lb. (16.3 N•m). Check the blue/white sensor wire for secure attachment. Clean and tighten the connection as necessary.

CAUTION
Use a digital voltmeter with an input impedance of 10 mega-ohms per volt for the following step. The incorrect meter could give inaccurate results and possibly damage electronic components.

7. Set a digital multimeter to the correct scale to read AC voltage in the 200 milli-volt range. Connect the meter negative lead to the detonation sensor housing. Connect the meter positive lead to the detonation sensor terminal white/blue wire.

CAUTION
*Do not run the engine without an adequate water supply and do not exceed 3000 rpm without an adequate load. Refer to **Safety Precautions** at the beginning of this chapter.*

8. Start the engine and allow it to reach operating temperature. Reduce the engine speed to idle.

9. Note the meter reading. The meter should read approximately 75-120 milli-volts AC (0.075-0.120 VAC) at idle speed. As engine speed increases, the voltage output also increases.

10. Replace the sensor if the voltage readings are not within specification.

11. To check the detonation sensor module voltage signal to the ECM, set the digital multimeter to the correct scale

to read 0-8 volts DC. Connect the meter negative lead to a good engine ground. Connect the meter positive lead to the gray/white wire bullet connector between the ECM and detonation sensor module. Do not disconnect the bullet connector.

CAUTION
Do not run the engine without an adequate water supply and do not exceed 3000 rpm without an adequate load. Refer to Safety Precautions at the beginning of this chapter.

12. Start the engine and allow it to reach operating temperature. Reduce the engine speed to idle. Note the meter reading. The meter should read 300-700 millivolts DC (0.30 to 0.70 VDC) at idle speed.

13. Increase engine speed to 3000-4000 rpm (in gear) while observing the meter. The meter reading should be approximately 10 millivolts DC (0.01 volt DC).

14. If the readings are within specification, the detonation sensor and module are functioning correctly. If the readings are higher than specification, preignition or detonation is occurring. If the reading stays constant at approximately 6.6 volts DC at all engine speeds, replace the detonation sensor module.

CAPACITOR DISCHARGE MODULE (CDM) IGNITION (2000-ON 105 JET AND 135-200 HP [EXCEPT OPTIMAX MODELS])

This CDM ignition is an alternator driven, capacitor discharge module system with mechanical spark advance. It is used on all 2000-on 105 jet and 135-200 hp models, except Optimax. Ignition test harness part No. 84-825207A2 is required to test the CDM system without damaging the wiring harness and connectors.

The major components (**Figure 40**) include:

1. *Flywheel*—The flywheel inner magnet is for the trigger coil and provides timing information. The outer magnets are for the ignition stator and battery charging stator.

2. *Ignition stator (charge) coils*—The stator (3, **Figure 40**) consists of one winding around three bobbins. The ignition stator is not grounded to the power head. The ignition stator provides power to the CDMs. Stator output is always AC (alternating current) voltage. The stator output circuit flows through multiple CDMs before returning to the stator.

    a. The return path for the No. 1, 2 and 3 CDM is through the No. 4, 5 or 6 CDM.

    b. The return path for the No. 4, 5 and 6 CDM is through the No. 1, 2 or 3 CDM.

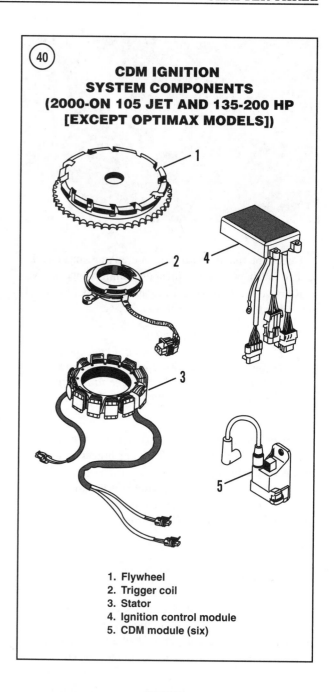

40

CDM IGNITION SYSTEM COMPONENTS (2000-ON 105 JET AND 135-200 HP [EXCEPT OPTIMAX MODELS])

1. Flywheel
2. Trigger coil
3. Stator
4. Ignition control module
5. CDM module (six)

NOTE
The ignition stator circuit must be complete from the stator to a CDM and back to the stator through a different CDM in order for the system to function.

3. *Trigger coil*—The trigger coil (2, **Figure 40**) signals the ignition control module when to trigger the individual CDMs. The trigger coil is rotated by mechanical linkage to change the trigger's position relative to the flywheel. This advances or retards the ignition spark timing. The trigger coil has three separate windings. Both wires for

each winding connect to the ignition control module. Failure of a trigger coil will result in no spark on two cylinders (one on each bank).

4. *CDMs*—There is one CDM (5, **Figure 40**) for each cylinder. The CDM is unique in that it integrates the CD module (switch box) and ignition coil into one unit. The rectifier in each CDM transforms the ignition stator AC voltage into DC voltage so it can be stored in the CDM capacitor. The capacitor holds the voltage until the silicon controlled rectifier (SCR), which is an electronic switch, releases the voltage to the integral ignition coil primary windings. The SCR is triggered by the ignition control module. The ignition coil transforms the relatively low voltage from the capacitor into voltage high enough (45,000 volts) to jump the spark plug gap and ignite the air/fuel mixture. Failure of a CDM results in no ignition on its cylinder.

5. *Ignition control module*—The ignition control module (**Figure 41**) monitors voltage pulses from the trigger coil to determine when to trigger the individual CDMs. The module also incorporates circuits to stabilize the idle control bias voltage and rev-limiting. If the engine speed exceeds approximately 5900 rpm, the module retards timing up to 30° on cylinder No. 2. If the engine continues to exceed the rpm limit, the module shuts off ignition on the cylinder. Continued excessive engine rpm results in retarded ignition timing and/or ignition interruption on additional cylinders until the engine drops below 5900 rpm.

6. *Spark plugs*—There is one spark plug for each cylinder. Only use the recommended spark plugs, or power head damage may occur. Resistor or suppressor plugs are designed to reduce radio frequency interference (RFI) emissions that can cause interference with electrical accessories. Use the recommended RFI spark plug if interference is causing a malfunction of electrical accessories.

7. *Stop circuit*—The stop circuit is connected to one end of the capacitor in each CDM. When the stop circuit is connected to ground, the capacitor is shorted out and can-

not store electricity. Therefore, no voltage is available to send to the ignition coil windings and the ignition system ceases producing spark. The stop circuit must have an open circuit to ground for the engine to run.

Troubleshooting

Refer to **Tables 8-10** for specifications and to the wiring diagrams at the end of the manual. Read *Troubleshooting Notes and Precautions (All Models)* at the beginning of the ignition section before continuing.

The recommended troubleshooting procedure is listed below.
1. Preliminary checks.
2. Ground circuit verification test.
3. Stop circuit isolation test.
4. Ignition stator output test.
5. Ignition stator resistance test.
6. CDM trigger input test.
7. Trigger resistance test.
8. Bias circuit test.
9. Idle stabilizer circuit test.
10. Idle stabilizing shift system.
11. CDM resistance test.

> *WARNING*
> *High voltage is present in the ignition system. **Never** touch or disconnect ignition components while the engine is running.*

> *CAUTION*
> *Do not run the engine without an adequate water supply and do not exceed 3000 rpm without an adequate load. Refer to **Safety Precautions** at the beginning of this chapter.*

Preliminary checks

1. Disconnect the spark plug leads from the spark plugs and install an air gap spark tester (part No. FT-11295 or an equivalent) to the spark plug leads. Connect the alligator clip of the spark tester to a clean engine ground. Set the spark tester air gap to 7/16 in. (11.1 mm). See **Figure 29**.
2. Make sure the safety lanyard is installed on the safety lanyard switch and the ignition switch is in the RUN position.
3. Crank the engine while observing the tester. If there is a crisp, blue spark at each air gap, the ignition system is functioning correctly. If the engine will not start or does not run correctly, check the spark plugs and ignition timing. If there is no spark, weak spark or erratic spark, continue with *Ground circuit verification* in the next section.

Ground circuit verification test

> *NOTE*
> *To prevent damage to the connector pins, use test harness adapter part No. 84-825207A2 for all tests involving connection to the CDMs and engine harness connectors (Figure 42).*

1. Disconnect all of the CDM plugs and connect the test harness adapter (part No. 84-825207A2) to the ignition wiring harness connector of the cylinder No. 1 CDM. Do not connect the test harness to the CDM. Calibrate the ohmmeter to the highest scale available. Connect one lead of the ohmmeter to a clean engine ground and connect the other ohmmeter lead to the black wire of the test harness. If the ohmmeter indicates high resistance or no continuity, repair or replace the engine harness black wire or CDM connector as necessary.

2. Repeat Step 1 for each of the remaining CDM harness connectors. Continue to Step 3 once all CDM grounds are verified.

3. Verify the grounding of the ignition component mounting plate by connecting one lead of the ohmmeter calibrated to the highest scale to a clean engine ground. Connect the other lead to the ground wire terminal(s) (A, **Figure 31**, typical) on the ignition component mounting plate. If the ohmmeter indicates high resistance or no continuity, tighten, repair or replace the ground path(s) (leads and ground stud) as required.

Stop circuit isolation test

> *WARNING*
> *To prevent accidental starting, remove the spark plug leads from the spark plugs and install the spark gap tester (part No. FT-11295 or an equivalent) to the spark plug leads. Connect the alligator clip of the spark tester to a clean engine ground.*

1. Isolate the stop circuit from the CDM ignition system by disconnecting the black/yellow bullet connector. This connector is in the tie-strapped bundle near the ignition control module (**Figure 41**). Make sure the black/yellow wire is not touching any other wire or ground.

2. Crank the motor and observe the spark tester. If there is now good spark, a short to ground is present in the key switch, safety lanyard switch or main engine harness black/yellow wire. Test, repair or replace the circuit or component as necessary.

Ignition stator output test

> *WARNING*
> *To prevent accidental starting, remove the spark plug leads from the spark plugs and install the spark gap tester part No. FT-11295 or an equivalent to the spark plug leads. Connect the alligator clip of the spark tester to a clean engine ground.*

1. Install the test harness (part No. 84-825207A2) between the cylinder No. 1 CDM and the ignition harness. Set the multimeter to the 400 DVA scale. Connect the meter positive lead to the test harness green wire and the meter negative lead to the test harness black wire.

2. Crank the engine while noting the meter reading. The meter should indicate at least the minimum specification in **Table 8**. Repeat the test for each remaining CDM. If only one CDM is below specification, replace that CDM and retest. If all stator voltage readings are below the specification, go to *Ignition stator resistance test*.

> *NOTE*
> *If all CDM ignition stator voltages are below specification and stator resistance tests are within specification, perform the Stop circuit output test in this section or replace each CDM one at a time with a known good CDM until the defective CDM is located.*

Ignition stator resistance test

1. To check the resistance of the stator windings, disconnect the plug with the green/white and white/green stator wires from the engine wire harness. Calibrate an ohmmeter to the appropriate scale to read 380-430 ohms. Connect the positive ohmmeter lead to the pin for the white/green stator wire and the negative ohmmeter lead to the pin for

the green/white stator wire. If the resistance is not within the specification in **Table 9**, the stator is defective and must be replaced. If the resistance is within specification, continue to Step 2.

2. To check the ignition stator windings for shorts to ground, calibrate an ohmmeter on the highest scale available. Connect one ohmmeter lead to a good engine ground and the other ohmmeter lead alternately to the pins for the ignition stator green/white and white/green wires while observing the meter. If the meter indicates continuity, the stator or stator wires are shorted to ground. Replace the stator if no faults are found with the wires.

CDM trigger input test

WARNING
To prevent accidental starting, remove the spark plug leads from the spark plugs and install the spark gap tester part No. FT-11295 or an equivalent to the spark plug leads. Connect the alligator clip of the spark tester to a clean engine ground.

NOTE
Pin C of the CDM connector is the trigger wire. The trigger wires on the ignition harness are color coded for each cylinder. Cylinder No. 1 uses a purple/white trigger wire, cylinder No. 2 uses a white/black trigger wire, cylinder No. 3 uses a brown/white trigger wire, cylinder No.4 uses a blue/white trigger wire, cylinder No. 5 uses a red/white trigger wire and cylinder No. 6 uses a white/yellow trigger wire. Connecting the wrong trigger wire to the wrong CDM will cause the engine to fire out of time.

1. Install the test harness part No. 84-825207A2 between the cylinder No. 1 CDM and the ignition harness.
2. Set the multimeter to the lowest DVA scale. Connect the meter positive lead to the test harness white wire and the meter negative lead to the test harness black wire. Crank the engine while noting the meter reading. The meter should indicate the trigger input specification in **Table 8**.
   a. If the trigger input voltage is below the specification, perform the trigger resistance test as described in this section. If the trigger resistance tests correctly, replace the CDM and retest. If the voltage remains below the specification, replace the ignition control module.
   b. If the trigger input voltage is above the specification, replace the cylinder No. 1 CDM.
3. Repeat the test for each remaining CDM.

Trigger coil resistance test

1. Disconnect the six wire trigger harness connector from the ignition control module.
2. Calibrate an ohmmeter on the appropriate scale to read the 1100-1400 ohms.
3. Connect one ohmmeter lead to the trigger coil brown wire and the other ohmmeter lead to the yellow trigger wire.
4. If the resistance reading is not 1100-1400 ohms, replace the trigger coil and retest the spark output.
5. Repeat the test for the next trigger coil winding. Connect one ohmmeter lead to the white trigger coil lead and the other ohmmeter lead to the yellow trigger coil wire.
6. If the resistance reading is not 1100-1400 ohms, replace the trigger coil and retest the spark output.
7. Repeat the test for the final trigger coil winding. Connect one ohmmeter lead to the trigger coil purple wire and the other ohmmeter lead to the trigger coil blue wire.
8. If the resistance reading is not 1100-1400 ohms, replace the trigger coil and retest the spark output.

Bias circuit test

Refer to **Table 8** and the wiring diagrams at the end of the manual.

CAUTION
The switch box bias circuit voltage output is DC (direct current). Do not use the DVA scale or adapter for this test.

1A. On carbureted models, disconnect the black/white wire from the shift switch, if so equipped. Locate the connector in the engine harness for models without the shift switch.
1B. On EFI models, disconnect the four wire connector from the detonation control module. Locate the pin for the black/white wire in the connector.
2. To check the switch box bias circuit output, connect the positive lead of a DC voltmeter, set to the 20 VDC scale.
3. Connect the positive test lead to a clean engine ground.
   a. On carbureted models, connect the negative test lead to the black/white wire described in Step 1A.
   b. On EFI models, use a paper clip and connect the negative test lead to the pin for the black/white engine harness wire described in Step 1B.
4. Crank the engine and observe the meter. If the bias circuit voltage is not within the specification in **Table 8**, replace the ignition control module.
5. Reconnect all wires when finished.

Idle stabilizer circuit test

An idle stabilizer circuit is integrated into the ignition control module. When engine speed drops below approximately 550 rpm, the idle stabilizer circuit electronically advances ignition timing through the bias circuit. The idle stabilizer can advance ignition timing a maximum of 9° above normal base timing. The additional timing advance raises the engine speed to 550 rpm and the ignition timing returns to normal operation.

CAUTION
*Do not run the engine without an adequate water supply and do not exceed 3000 rpm without an adequate load. Refer to **Safety Precautions** at the beginning of this chapter.*

Refer to the wiring diagrams at the end of the manual.
1. Connect a timing light to the No. 1 top starboard spark plug lead. Connect an accurate tachometer to the engine following its manufacturer's instructions.
2. Start the engine and allow it to warm to operating temperature. Reduce the engine speed to approximately 600-650 rpm.
3. Slowly, pull forward on the spark advance lever (**Figure 37**) to retard the timing and reduce the engine speed. Use the timing light to observe the timing as the spark advance lever is moved.
4. If the ignition timing rapidly advances as much as 9° as the engine speed falls below approximately 550 rpm, the idle stabilizer circuit is operating properly. If the timing does not advance, replace the ignition control module.

Idle Stabilizer Shift System (XR6, Magnum III, 175 hp Carbureted, 150 hp EFI and 175 hp EFI Models)

The idle stabilizer shift system prevents stalling by advancing the ignition timing 3° when the outboard motor is shifted into forward gear.

When the outboard motor is running at idle speed in neutral, the shift switch opens. When it is shifted into gear, the shift switch closes and completes the circuit to ground through the black/white ignition control module wire, resulting in a 3° timing advance. If the shift switch remains open, the timing advance will not occur. Also, full-throttle timing is 3° retarded. If the white/black wire between the resistor and the ignition control module shorts to ground, the timing will be excessively advanced and cause serious power head damage.

CAUTION
If the idle stabilizer shift system is installed on models other than XR6, Mag III, 150 hp EFI, 175 hp carbureted and 175 hp EFI models as an accessory, the maximum ignition timing must be retarded 3°. Refer to Chapter Five for the timing procedure.

Idle stabilizer shift system troubleshooting

CAUTION
*Do not run the engine without an adequate water supply and do not exceed 3000 rpm without an adequate load. Refer to **Safety Precautions** at the beginning of this chapter.*

1. Connect a timing light to the No. 1 top starboard spark plug lead.
2. Start the engine and allow it to reach operating temperature. Reduce the engine speed to idle.
3. While observing the ignition timing, shift into forward gear. The idle stabilizer shift system is functioning properly if the timing advances 3° when shifted into gear.
4. If the timing does not advance 3° when shifted into gear, shut the engine off. Disconnect the white/black wire from the shift switch bullet connector.
5. Calibrate an ohmmeter to the R × 1 scale. Connect one ohmmeter lead to the shift switch ground wire terminal and the other ohmmeter lead to the shift switch bullet connector.
6. Position the gear shift mechanism in the NEUTRAL position. The ohmmeter should read no continuity. Position the gear shift mechanism into FORWARD gear. The ohmmeter should read continuity. Replace the shift switch if the readings are not as specified. If the shift switch test correctly and the timing is still not advancing 3° when shifted into gear, replace the ignition control module.

Detonation Sensor and Module (200 hp EFI Models)

The 200 hp EFI models are equipped with a detonation sensor (A, **Figure 34**) and detonation sensor module (B). The detonation sensor is designed to detect the high-frequency vibration caused by preignition or detonation. The detonation sensor creates a small voltage signal when the engine is running. The voltage signal increases dramatically when preignition or detonation is present. When the module detects the correct voltage signal (from normal engine vibration at approximately 2500-3500 rpm, the module adds 6° spark advance. The module holds this advance as long as the voltage signal is in the

normal range. If the module detects a voltage signal higher than normal from preignition or detonation, it removes added timing advance up to 6° and, if necessary, reduces timing advance up to an additional 2°.

The detonation sensor module also communicates with the ECM. If preignition or detonation is present, the ECM increases fuel flow through the fuel injector by up to 15 percent. The enriched air/fuel ratio along with the retarded spark advance helps cool the combustion chambers and eliminate detonation. The Quicksilver digital diagnostic terminal (DDT) (**Figure 43**) is required to verify that the extra fuel is being added. The DDT also allows verification of the increase in fuel injector pulse width.

Functional test

1. Connect a timing light to the No. 1 top starboard spark plug lead.

> *WARNING*
> *To prevent accidental starting, remove the leads from the spark plugs and install the spark gap tester (part No. 91-850439) to the spark plug leads. Connect the alligator clip of the spark tester to a clean engine ground.*

2. Check the maximum timing at cranking speed as described in Chapter Five. Adjust the timing as necessary.
3. Remove the spark gap tester and reconnect the spark plug leads to the spark plugs.

> *CAUTION*
> *Do not run the engine without an adequate water supply and do not exceed 3000 rpm without an adequate load. Refer to **Safety Precautions** at the beginning of this chapter.*

4. Start the engine and allow it to reach operating temperature. Run the engine at 3500 rpm or higher in FORWARD gear. Note the timing.
5. If the timing at 3500 rpm or higher is 6° more than the timing at cranking speed, the detonation sensor and detonation module are functioning correctly. If not, continue to troubleshooting.

Troubleshooting

Refer to the wiring diagrams at the end of this manual.
1. If the detonation sensor and module are not functioning as described, check the ground wire for secure attachment to the power head. Clean and tighten the connection as necessary to assure a good ground path.
2. Set the voltmeter on the 20-volt DC scale. Connect the positive voltmeter lead to the detonation sensor purple wire terminal at the power head terminal strip. Connect the negative voltmeter lead to a good engine ground. When the ignition key is ON, the voltmeter should read within 1 volt of battery voltage. When the key is OFF, the voltmeter should read 0 volts. If the meter reading is below specification, repair or replace the purple wire circuit from the key switch to the two-terminal, power head terminal strip.
3. Check the green detonation sensor module engine harness wire for continuity to the ignition control harness connector. Disconnect the engine harness connector from the ignition control module. Calibrate an ohmmeter to the $R \times 1$ scale. Connect one ohmmeter lead to the ignition control module end of the engine harness green wire and the other ohmmeter lead to the detonation sensor module end of the engine harness green wire. If the ohmmeter does not read continuity, repair or replace the engine harness green wire.
4. Check the detonation sensor module gray/white wire and bullet connector for secure attachment to the ECM gray/white wire and bullet connector. Repair or replace the gray/white wire and connectors as necessary.
5. Check the white/black detonation sensor module wires for secure attachment to ignition control module connector.
6. If there is corrosion or sealant around the base of the sensor (**Figure 39**), remove the sensor and clean the threads of the sensor and cylinder head. Do not coat the threads of the sensor with sealant. Reinstall the sensor and torque it to 144 in.-lb. (16.3 N•m). Check the blue/white sensor wire for secure attachment. Clean and tighten the connection as necessary.
7. Further testing of the knock control circuit requires the Mercury/Mariner Quicksilver DDT system.

3

CDM resistance test

Refer to **Table 10** for specifications. Test harness part No. 84-825207A2 is required for this test.

1. Connect the test harness part No. 84-825207A2 to the CDM. Do not connect the test harness to the ignition harness. This test is for the CDM only.

2. Calibrate the ohmmeter to an appropriate scale to read the specifications in **Table 10**.

NOTE
The following test includes a diode test. The ohmmeter readings may be reversed depending on the polarity of the ohmmeter being used. If test results are incorrect, reverse the test lead connection points. If the test is correct with the leads reversed, the diode is probably functioning correctly.

3. Connect the meter test leads to the pins and terminals specified in **Table 10**. Record the resistance readings.

4. If the resistance is not within the specification in **Table 10** for each test, replace the CDM.

CAPACITOR DISCHARGE MODULE (CDM) IGNITION (225 AND 250 HP)

This CDM ignition is an alternator driven, capacitor discharge module system with electronic spark advance. It is used on 1998-on, 225 hp carbureted and EFI models and 250 hp EFI models. An ignition system test harness part No. 84-825207A2 is required to test the CDM system without damaging the wiring harness and connectors.

The following troubleshooting procedure requires a multimeter and adapter cables. However, the system is designed for easy troubleshooting diagnosis by using the Merc/Mariner Quicksilver Digital Diagnostic Terminal (DDT). This system displays sensor inputs and actuator outputs at the ECM.

The major components include:

1. *Flywheel*—The flywheel magnets are for the ignition stator. The outer diameter, lower edge of the flywheel contains cast-in encoding ribs (A, **Figure 44**) for the crankshaft position sensor (B).

2. *Crankshaft position sensor*—The crankshaft position sensor (CPS) detects the presence of the encoding ribs on the flywheel and sends a signal to the ECM. This signal tells the ECM the crankshaft position and engine rpm. The air gap between the flywheel encoding ribs and the CPS must be set correctly for proper ignition system operation. Position sensor adjustment is described in Chapter Five.

3. *Ignition stator coils*—The stator consists of six windings around six bobbins. The ignition stator provides

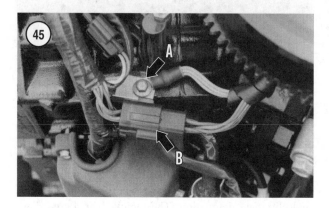

power to the CDMs. Stator output is always AC (alternating current) voltage. One lead from each bobbin is connected to engine ground (A, **Figure 45**). The six individual bobbin leads connect to the main engine harness through a quick-release connector (B, **Figure 45**). If the ignition ECM fails, the ignition system will not operate.

4. *CDMs*—There is one CDM for each cylinder. The CDM integrates the CD module (switch box) and ignition coil into one unit. The rectifier in each CDM transforms the ignition stator AC voltage into DC voltage so it can be stored in the CDM capacitor. The capacitor holds the voltage until the silicon controlled rectifier (SCR), which is an electronic switch, releases the voltage to the integral ignition coil primary windings. The SCR is triggered by the ignition ECM. The ignition coil transforms the relatively low voltage from the capacitor into voltage high enough (45,000 volts) to jump the spark plug gap and ignite the air/fuel mixture.

5. *Spark plugs*—There is one spark plug for each cylinder. Use only the recommended spark plugs or serious damage may occur. Resistor or suppressor plugs are designed to reduce radio frequency interference (RFI) emissions that can cause interference with electrical accessories. Use the recommended RFI spark plug if in-

terference is causing a malfunction of electrical accessories.

6. *Stop circuit*—The stop circuit is connected to one end of the capacitor in each CDM. When the stop circuit is connected to ground, the capacitor is shorted and cannot store electricity. Therefore no voltage available to send to the ignition coil windings and the ignition system ceases producing spark. The stop circuit must have an open circuit to ground for the engine to run.

7. *Ignition ECM*—The ignition ECM (**Figure 46**, typical) monitors input from the CPS, throttle position sensor (TPS) and engine coolant temperature sensor (ECT). The ECM then calculates the correct timing for each cylinder. On EFI models, the ignition ECM interfaces with the fuel ECM to coordinate the firing of the fuel injectors. The ignition ECM contains cold engine start, idle stabilizer, rpm limit, overheat protection, low oil level (carbureted models) and sensor failure warning programs.

NOTE
EFI models incorporate the low oil level and the water-in-fuel warning programs into the fuel ECM.

a. *Cold start program*—The cold engine start program advances the ignition timing when the engine is below operating temperature and below 3000 rpm.

The amount of timing advance is proportional to engine temperature and is added to normal spark advance. Once the engine reaches 146° Fahrenheit (63° Celsius) or 3000 rpm, the cold start timing advance is removed. On carbureted models, the fuel primer valve is also activated by the ECM during warm-up. On EFI models, all fuel injector pulse widths are increased by the fuel ECM to enrich the air/fuel mixture during warm-up.

b. *Idle stabilizer program*—The idle stabilizer program advances the ignition timing when the idle speed drops to 475 rpm or lower. At 475 rpm, 3° advance is added. If the idle speed drops below 450 rpm, 6° advance is added. This advance is added to the normal spark advance. Once idle speed exceeds 475 rpm, the idle stabilizer advance is removed.

c. *RPM limit program*—The rpm limit program retards ignition timing when engine speed exceeds 6000 rpm (carbureted models) or 6100 rpm (EFI models). Timing retard is gradual unless engine speed exceeds 6400 (carbureted models) or 6500 rpm (EFI models). If this occurs, the timing is immediately retarded to 2° ATDC. When engine speed drops below the preprogrammed limit, timing advance returns to normal. The low oil and overheat lamps alternately flash and the warning horn sounds when the rpm limit program is activated.

d. *Overheat warning program*—The overheat warning program retards ignition timing when the ECT indicates 200° F (93° C) or higher. Timing is retarded until engine speed is reduced to approximately 3000 rpm. Timing advance returns to normal when the ECT indicates 190° F (88° C) or lower. The overheat lamp flashes and the warning horns sound continuously when the overheat warning program is activated.

e. *Low oil warning program (carbureted models)*—The low oil warning program sounds the warning horn and illuminates the low oil warning light when the switch in the engine mounted oil tank closes. When the oil switch closes, the horn will beep four times in one second intervals, shut off for two minutes, then begin the warning cycle again. The warning light illuminates continuously until the ignition switch is turned off. This program does not affect ignition system operation.

f. *Sensor failure warning program*—The sensor warning program alerts the boat operator to a TPS or ECT sensor failure. If the ECM detects a failure in the TPS or ECT circuits, the low oil and overheat lamps of the dash-mounted warning panel flash alternately and the warning horn sounds. The warning continues until the faulty sensor is corrected or the ignition switch is turned off. The TPS and ECT sensors may be tested with a digital multimeter. The ignition ECM on EFI models incorporates the manifold absolute pressure (MAP) and intake air temperature (IAT) sensors into the sensor failure warning program. The IAT sensor may be tested with a digital multimeter; however, the MAP sensor can only be tested with the Quicksilver DDT. If the fuel ECM is disconnected, the warning horn sounds, the low-oil and overheat warning lamps flash alternately, and the engine will not run.

8. *Warning panel*—A multifunction warning panel (**Figure 47**) is recommended for all models. The EFI model has three lights for easy identification of low oil level, engine overheat, engine overspeed, sensor malfunction or water-in-fuel situations. The carbureted model does not include the water-in-fuel light.

9. *Shift switch*—The shift switch (**Figure 48**) is mounted underneath the shift cable on the port side of the engine. When shift loads exceed the spring force of the shift interrupt switch, the ignition ECM green/yellow lead is shorted to ground. The ignition ECM then retards spark advance to 20° ATDC. The retarded timing reduces engine speed, reducing shift effort. When the shift is completed, the shift interrupt switch opens and the ignition ECM returns spark advance to normal. If the shift interrupt switch stays closed for more than two seconds, the ignition ECM automatically returns spark advance to normal.

Troubleshooting

Refer to **Tables 8-10** for specifications and to the wiring diagrams at the end of the manual. Read *Troubleshooting Notes and Precautions (All Models)* at the beginning of the ignition section before continuing. When troubleshooting a timing control problem, go to the crankshaft position sensor tests and throttle position sensor tests. The recommended general troubleshooting procedure is listed below.

1. Preliminary checks.
2. Ground circuit verification test.
3. Stop circuit verification test.
4. Ignition ECM power test.
5. Tachometer circuit verification test.
6. Ignition stator output test.
7. Ignition stator resistance test.
8. ECM trigger signal output test.
9. Crankshaft position sensor test.
10. Throttle position sensor test.
11. Shift interrupt switch.

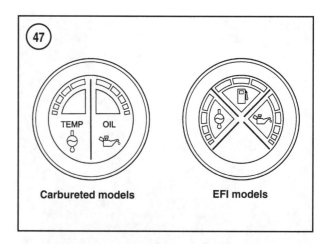

Carbureted models   **EFI models**

12. CDM module resistance test.

WARNING
*High voltage is present in the ignition system. **Never** touch or disconnect ignition components while the engine is running.*

CAUTION
Do not run the engine without an adequate water supply and do not exceed 3000 rpm without an adequate load. Refer to Safety precautions at the beginning of this chapter.

NOTE
Due to the ECM's idle stabilizer program, it is normal for timing to fluctuate at idle speed. Timing fluctuations at high speed could be caused by activation of the engine overheat or rpm limit programs. Make sure engine temperature is normal and wide-open throttle speed does not exceed the recommended range before attempting to troubleshoot a timing control problem.

Preliminary checks

1. Disconnect the spark plug leads from the spark plugs and install an air gap spark tester (part No. FT-11295 or an equivalent) to the spark plug leads. Connect the alligator clip of the spark tester to a clean engine ground. Set the spark tester air gap to 3/8 in. (9.5 mm).

2. Make sure the safety lanyard is installed on the safety lanyard switch and the ignition switch is in the RUN position.

3. Crank the engine while observing the tester. If there is a crisp, blue spark at each air gap, the ignition system is functioning correctly. If the engine will not start or does not run correctly, make sure the correct spark plugs are installed and in good condition. If the engine backfires or

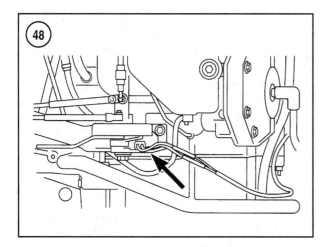

pops while attempting to start, remove the flywheel and check for a sheared flywheel key. If there is no spark, weak spark or erratic spark, continue with the ground circuit verification test in the next section.

NOTE
A CDM that has an internally shorted to ground stop circuit will disable all of the remaining CDMs. Disconnect each CDM one at a time and retest spark output. When a CDM is disconnected and the other CDMs start firing, the disconnected CDM is defective.

Ground circuit verification test

1. Disconnect all of the CDM plugs (**Figure 42**, typical) and connect the test harness adapter part No. 84-825207A2 to the ignition wiring harness connector of the cylinder No. 1 CDM. Do not connect the test harness to the CDM. Calibrate an ohmmeter to the highest scale available. Connect one lead of the ohmmeter to a clean engine ground. Connect the other ohmmeter lead to the black wire of the test harness. If the ohmmeter does not indicate continuity, repair or replace the engine harness black lead or CDM connector as necessary. Repeat this Step for each of the remaining CDM module harness connectors. Continue to Step 2 when all CDM grounds have been tested.

2. Trace the black ground wire from the ignition ECM main plug-in connector to its power head ground. Inspect all ground wires for a secure connection. Clean and tighten as necessary.

3. Inspect all ignition ECM ground connections on the ECM mounting plate. Clean and tighten as necessary. On EFI models, also check the fuel ECM ground.

Stop circuit verification test

1. Isolate the stop circuit from the CDM ignition modules by disconnecting all six CDM connectors (**Figure 42**, typical). Connect the test harness part No. 84-825207A 2 to the cylinder No. 1 CDM engine wiring harness connector. Do not connect the test harness to the CDM.

2. Calibrate an ohmmeter to the highest scale available. Connect one ohmmeter lead to a good engine ground and the other ohmmeter lead to the test harness stop circuit wire. The stop circuit wire is black/yellow on the test harness.

3. Make sure the safety lanyard is installed on the safety lanyard switch and the ignition switch is in the RUN position. Note the meter reading.

4. If the meter indicates continuity, there is a short to ground in the key switch, safety lanyard switch or the main engine harness black/yellow wire. Test, repair or replace the circuit or component as necessary.

5. Turn the ignition switch to the OFF position or pull the lanyard from the safety lanyard switch. Note the meter reading.

6. If the meter indicates no continuity, there is an open circuit in the key switch, safety lanyard switch or the main engine harness black/yellow wire. Test, repair or replace the circuit or component as necessary.

7. Repeat the test for the remaining CDM engine wiring harness connectors.

Ignition ECM power test

The ignition ECM needs key-switched, battery positive voltage to operate. The ignition ECM receives power through the purple wire connected to the power head mounted terminal block. Make sure the ignition ECM is receiving voltage as follows:

1. Set a multimeter to the 20 volts DC scale. Connect the negative meter lead to a good engine ground. Connect the positive meter lead to the purple wire stud of the single or double terminal block.

2. Turn the ignition switch to the ON position. If the meter indicates less than 1 volt of battery voltage, there is an open circuit or high resistance in the circuit from the ignition switch, boat wiring harness purple wire or the engine wiring harness purple wire. Isolate and repair or replace the defective circuit.

3. If the voltage reading is within 1 volt of battery voltage in Step 2, turn the ignition switch OFF and disconnect the engine wiring harness connector(s) from the ignition ECM.

4. Set the multimeter to the 20 volts DC scale. Connect the negative lead to a good engine ground. Connect the

positive lead to the purple wire pin of the ignition ECM engine harness connector. Do not damage the connector pin.

5. Turn the ignition switch to the ON position. If the meter indicates less than 1 volt of battery voltage, there is an open circuit or high resistance in the circuit from the purple wire stud of the single or double terminal block and the ignition ECM engine wiring harness connector. Repair or replace the circuit as necessary.

Tachometer circuit verification test

The tachometer signal is produced by the ignition ECM based on the crankshaft position sensor input. The tachometer signal is sent through the engine wiring harness to the main harness plug-in, through the boat wiring harness and into the dash mounted tachometer. On EFI models, the engine wiring harness also sends the tachometer signal to the fuel ECM. If the tachometer signal gray wire is shorted to ground, the engine will not run. Test the tachometer wire for continuity and short to ground as follows:

1. To check the engine wiring harness tachometer wire for continuity, disconnect the remote control harness from the main engine harness connector. Disconnect the main harness plug-in from the ignition ECM. On EFI models, also disconnect the main harness plug-in from the fuel ECM.

2. Calibrate an ohmmeter to the highest scale available. Connect one ohmmeter lead to the ignition ECM main harness connector gray wire. Connect the other ohmmeter lead to pin No. 5 of the main engine harness connector. If the meter does not indicate continuity, there is an open circuit in the engine wiring harness gray wire. Isolate and repair or replace the circuit as necessary.

3. On EFI models, repeat Step 2 for the fuel ECM gray wire.

4. To check the engine wiring harness tachometer wire for a short to ground, calibrate an ohmmeter to the highest scale available. Connect one ohmmeter lead to a good engine ground. Connect the other ohmmeter lead to pin No. 5 of the main engine harness connector. If the meter indicates continuity, there is a short to ground in the engine wiring harness gray wire. Isolate and repair or replace the circuit as necessary.

5. To check the boat wiring harness for a short to ground, disconnect the remote control harness from the main engine harness connector.

6. Disconnect and insulate the gray wire from the tachometer. If the gray wire is connected to any accessories, disconnect and insulate the gray wire from the accessories.

7. Calibrate an ohmmeter to the highest scale available. Connect one ohmmeter lead to pin No. 5 of the boat wiring harness main plug-in connector. Connect the other ohmmeter lead alternately to each of the remaining connector pins. If there is continuity at any connector pin, a short is present between the tachometer gray wire and the tested pin. Isolate and repair or replace the circuit or harness as necessary.

Ignition stator output test

> *WARNING*
> *To prevent accidental starting, remove the spark plug leads from the spark plugs and install the spark gap tester part No. FT-11295 or an equivalent to the spark plug leads. Connect the alligator clip of the spark tester to a clean engine ground.*

> *CAUTION*
> *To prevent damage to the connector pins, use the appropriate test harness adapter (part No. 84-825207A 2) for all tests involving connection to the CDMs and engine harness connectors.*

1. Install the test harness part No. 84-825207A 2 between the cylinder No. 1 CDM and the ignition harness. Set the multimeter to the 400 DVA scale.

2. Connect the meter positive lead to the test harness green wire and the meter negative lead to the test harness black wire.

3. Crank the engine while observing the meter reading. The meter should indicate at least the minimum stator output specification in **Table 8**. Repeat the test for each remaining CDM. If any or all ignition stator voltage readings at the CDM are below the specification, go to *Ignition stator resistance test*.

> *NOTE*
> *If one or more voltages in the preceding step are below the specification and all of the ignition stator resistance tests are satisfactory, replace the CDM(s) on the low reading ignition stator circuit(s). Retest ignition stator output after replacing the module.*

Ignition stator resistance test

1. To check the resistance of the ignition stator windings, disconnect the ignition stator-to-engine wiring harness connector (B, **Figure 45**).

2. Calibrate an ohmmeter to the appropriate scale to read 990-1210 ohms.

NOTE
*One wire from each of the ignition stators'
six bobbins is connected to engine ground.
The other wire from each of the ignition
stators' six bobbins is connected to the ignition stator quick-release connector. Test
each of the six bobbins.*

3. Connect one ohmmeter lead to a good engine ground
and the other ohmmeter lead to the ignition stator connector green wire. Note the meter reading. If the resistance
reading is not within the specification in Table 9, replace
the stator.

4. Repeat Step 3 for the green/red, green/orange,
green/blue, green/black and green/yellow ignition stator
connector wires.

ECM trigger output test

WARNING
*To prevent accidental starting, remove the
spark plug leads from the spark plugs and
install the spark gap tester part No.
FT-11295 or an equivalent to the spark plug
leads. Connect the alligator clip of the spark
tester to a clean engine ground.*

NOTE
*The trigger wires on the engine harness are
color coded for each cylinder. Cylinder No.
1 uses a white/blue trigger wire, cylinder
No. 2 uses a white/orange trigger wire, cylinder No. 3 uses a white/black trigger wire,
cylinder No. 4 uses a white/red trigger wire,
cylinder No. 5 uses a white/yellow trigger
wire and cylinder No. 6 uses a white/green
trigger wire. Connecting the wrong trigger
wire to the wrong CDM will cause the engine to fire out of time.*

1. Install the test harness part No. 84-825207A 2 between
the cylinder No. 1 CDM and the ignition harness. Set the
multimeter to the 20 DVA scale.

2. Connect the meter positive lead to the test harness
white wire and the meter negative lead to the test harness
black wire.

3. Make sure the safety lanyard is installed on the safety
lanyard switch and the ignition switch is in the RUN position.

4. Crank the engine while noting the meter reading. The
meter should indicate 2-10 DVA. If the trigger voltage is
below specification, note the cylinder number and voltage
reading. Repeat the test for each remaining CDM.

If trigger voltage is below specification on one CDM,
swap the wires with an adjoining CDM and retest. If the
low voltage reading follows the CDM, replace that CDM.
If the low voltage reading does not follow the CDM, verify the continuity of the trigger wire from the ECM to the
suspect CDM connector. If the trigger wire is good, replace the ECM.

If the trigger voltage is low or 0 on all CDMs, go to
Crankshaft position sensor test in the next section. If
the crankshaft position sensor tests good, replace the
ECM.

Crankshaft position sensor test

The crankshaft position sensor provides the ignition
ECM with engine speed and crankshaft position information. Its function is similar to the trigger coil of other ignition systems. The ignition ECM must know the precise
position of all pistons and how fast the engine is running
in order to fire the CDMs accurately. The crankshaft position sensor can cause erratic spark, no spark at all or erratic timing if it is incorrectly adjusted or faulty. If the
boat's tachometer is operating normally, the crankshaft
position sensor is functioning.

WARNING
*To prevent accidental starting, remove the
spark plug leads from the spark plugs and
install the spark gap tester part No.
FT-11295 or an equivalent to the spark plug
leads. Connect the alligator clip of the spark
tester to a clean engine ground.*

1. Disconnect the negative battery cable and remove the
flywheel cover.

2. Slightly rotate the flywheel to align an encoder rib (A,
Figure 44) with the crankshaft position sensor (B).

3. Check and adjust the sensor gap as described in Chapter Five. Do not continue with testing until verifying correct sensor adjustment.

4. Disconnect the two-pin crankshaft position sensor wiring harness connector. Calibrate an ohmmeter to the appropriate scale to read 900-1300 ohms. Connect one
ohmmeter lead to each of the crankshaft position sensor
wires. Replace the crankshaft position sensor if the reading is not within 900-1300 ohms. Sensor replacement is
described in Chapter Seven.

5. Reinstall the flywheel cover. Reconnect the negative
battery cable.

Throttle position sensor (TPS) test

Correct adjustment of the TPS is critical to correct ignition system operation. The TPS adjustment is made with the throttle at the idle position. The wide-open throttle TPS specification is not adjustable. If the wide-open throttle stop is correct, the TPS idle voltage reading is correct, and the TPS wide-open throttle voltage reading is incorrect, replace the TPS. To prevent damage to the throttle position sensor and wiring harness, test harness part No. 84-825207A1 is required. A digital multimeter is recommended for this procedure, as most analog meters will not accurately read the low voltages specified. Test and adjust the TPS as follows:

> *NOTE*
> *On EFI models, any change to the idle speed air flow screw will require the TPS setting to be rechecked and adjusted as necessary. On carbureted models, the TPS setting has a direct effect on idle timing and idle speed. On carbureted models, the TPS setting is changed within the specified range to obtain the specified idle speed.*

1. Disconnect the throttle cable from the engine throttle linkage.

2. Disconnect the engine wiring harness from the TPS. Connect test harness part No. 84-825207A1 (1, **Figure 49**) to the TPS and the engine wiring harness.

3. Set the multimeter to the 20 volt DC scale. Connect the negative meter lead to the test harness white wire. Connect the positive meter lead to the red test harness wire.

4. Make sure the throttle linkage is against the idle stop screw.

5. Turn the ignition switch to the ON position. The voltmeter should indicate 0.90-1.00 volts. If the reading is not as specified, loosen the two adjustment screws (2, **Figure 49**) slightly and rotate the sensor to obtain 0.90-1.00 volt DC. Tighten the screws while holding the sensor in position. Recheck the meter reading.

6. Slowly advance the throttle lever until it is against the wide-open throttle stop while observing the meter. The meter should indicate a smooth increase in voltage, without any sudden fluctuations. With the throttle lever held against the wide-open throttle stop, the meter should indicate 3.70-3.80 volts on carbureted models and 3.55-4.05 volts on EFI models. If the meter reading is not within specification, make sure the wide-open throttle stop is set correctly (Chapter 5). If the wide-open throttle stop is set correctly, but the wide-open throttle voltage is incorrect, replace the throttle position sensor. If the meter shows voltage fluctuations instead of a smooth voltage transition

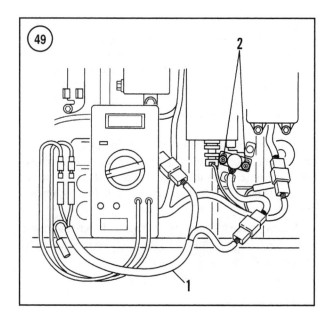

as the sensor is rotated, replace the throttle position sensor.

Shift interrupt switch (all models)

The shift switch connects to the ignition ECM. When the shift switch activates, the ignition ECM green/yellow wire is grounded. The ignition ECM then retards spark advance to 20° ATDC. The retarded timing reduces engine speed, reducing shift effort. As soon as the switch opens, the ignition ECM returns spark advance to normal. If the shift interrupt switch stays closed for more than two seconds, the ignition ECM automatically returns spark advance to normal. Test the shift interrupt switch as follows:

1. Calibrate an ohmmeter to the R × 1 scale. Disconnect both shift interrupt switch (**Figure 48**) bullet connectors from the engine harness black and green/yellow wires. Connect one ohmmeter lead to each of the shift interrupt switch wires.

2. Position the shift mechanism in the NEUTRAL position. The ohmmeter should read no continuity. Position the shift mechanism in the FORWARD gear position. The ohmmeter should read continuity. Replace the shift switch if the readings are not as specified.

CDM resistance test

Refer to **Table 10** for specifications. Test harness part No. 84-825207A2 is required for this test.

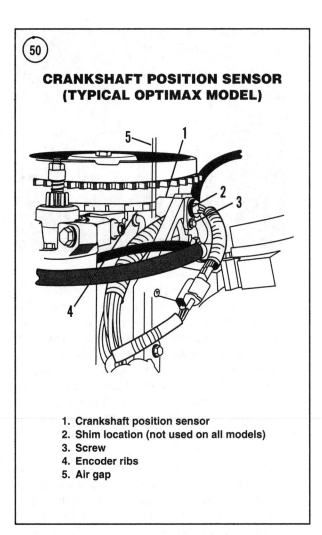

CRANKSHAFT POSITION SENSOR (TYPICAL OPTIMAX MODEL)

1. Crankshaft position sensor
2. Shim location (not used on all models)
3. Screw
4. Encoder ribs
5. Air gap

1. Connect the test harness (part No. 84-825207A2) to the CDM, but do not connect the test harness to the ignition harness. This test is for the CDM only.

2. Calibrate the ohmmeter on an appropriate scale to read the specifications in **Table 10**.

NOTE
The following test includes a diode test. The ohmmeter readings may be reversed depending on the polarity of the ohmmeter being used. If test results are incorrect, reverse the test lead connection points. If the test is correct with the leads reversed, the diode is probably functioning correctly.

3. Connect the meter test leads to the pins and terminals specified in **Table 10**. Record the resistance readings.

4. If the resistance is not within the specification in **Table 10** for each test, replace the CDM.

DIGITAL INDUCTIVE (DI [OPTIMAX MODELS])

The digital inductive ignition system is a battery driven, ECM controlled system with electronic spark advance. Once the engine starts, a 60 amp belt-driven alternator provides all operating voltage for the system. This system is used exclusively on Optimax models (direct fuel injection).

The following troubleshooting procedure requires a multimeter and adapter cables. However, the system is designed for easy troubleshooting diagnosis by using the Merc/Mariner Quicksilver Digital Diagnostic Terminal (DDT). This system displays sensor inputs and actuator outputs at the ECM.

The major components include:

1. *Flywheel*—The outer diameter, lower edge of the flywheel contains cast-in encoding ribs (4, **Figure 50**, typical) for the crankshaft position sensor (1).

2. *Crankshaft position sensor (CPS)*—The crankshaft position sensor (1, **Figure 50**) detects the presence of the encoding ribs on the flywheel and sends a signal to the ECM. This signal tells the ECM the crankshaft position and engine rpm. The air gap (5, **Figure 50**) between the flywheel encoding ribs and the CPS must be set correctly for proper engine operation.

3. *Ignition coils*—There is one ignition coil (A, **Figure 51**) for each cylinder. The ignition coil transforms the relatively low voltage from the battery into voltage high enough (50,000 volts) to jump the spark plug gap and ignite the air/fuel mixture. The ignition coils positive terminal has battery voltage present when the ignition switch is on.

   a. *1998-2000 models*—The ECM opens the ignition coil negative terminal to create spark.

   b. *2001-on models*—The ECM sends a signal to one of three coil driver modules. The coil driver (B, **Fig-**

ure 51) then opens the ignition coil negative terminal to create spark. Each coil driver controls two ignition coils.

4. *Spark plugs*—There is one spark plug for each cylinder. Use the recommended spark plugs (Chapter Four) or engine damage may occur.

5. *Stop circuit*—The stop circuit is connected to the ECM. When the stop circuit connects to ground the ECM shuts off the ignition coils. The stop circuit must have an open circuit to ground in order for the engine to run.

6. *ECM*—The ECM (A, **Figure 52**) monitors input from all of the sensors. The ECM then calculates the correct spark timing, fuel injector timing and direct injector timing for each cylinder. The ECM contains cold engine start, idle stabilizer, rpm limit, overheat protection, water in fuel, low oil level, no oil flow and sensor failure warning programs. The ECM receives power from a main power relay. The main power relay is activated by the ignition switch. On 2001-on models, the ECM provides signals to the Smart Craft gauges to provide troll speed control, fuel usage, boat speed and engine operation monitoring.

   a. *Cold start program*—The cold engine start program increases the fuel injector pulse width when the engine is below operating temperature. The amount of fuel injector pulse width increase is proportional to engine temperature.

   b. *Idle stabilizer program*—The idle stabilizer program controls the idle speed by advancing or retarding spark advance to maintain 525-675 rpm when the throttle position sensor (TPS) indicates that the throttle control is in the idle position. Idle speed is not adjustable.

   c. *RPM limit program*—The rpm limit program is activated when engine speed exceeds the maximum recommended rpm. If engine speed exceeds the limit, the ECM shuts the engine systems off until engine speed drops below the preprogrammed speed limit, at which point engine operation returns to normal. The warning horn sounds continuously when the rpm limit program is activated.

   d. *Overheat warning program*—The overheat warning program retards ignition timing and reduces engine power when the engine coolant temperature (ECT) sensor indicates overheating. On 1998-2000 models, the ECM reduces engine speed to a maximum of 3000 rpm. On 2001-on models, the ECM reduces engine speed as low as idle speed depending on engine temperature. Engine power returns to normal when the ECT indicates normal temperature. The overheat lamp flashes and the warning horn sounds continuously when the overheat warning program is activated.

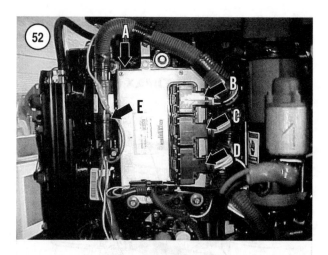

   e. *Water-in-fuel warning program*—The water-in-fuel warning program sounds the warning horn and illuminates the water-in-fuel warning light when the water separating fuel filter accumulates enough water to short the sensor to ground. When the water sensor shorts to ground, the horn beeps four times at one second intervals, shuts off for two minutes, then begins the warning cycle again. The warning light illuminates continuously until the ignition switch is turned off. This program does not affect ignition system operation.

   f. *Low oil warning program*—The low oil warning program sounds the warning horn and illuminates the oil warning light when the switch in the engine mounted oil tank closes. When the oil switch closes, the horn beeps four times at one second intervals, shuts off for two minutes, then begins the warning cycle again. The warning light illuminates continuously until the ignition switch is turned off. On 1998-2000 models, this program does not affect ignition system operation. On 2001-on models, the ECM computes the approximate amount of oil remaining in the reservoir. When the oil level reaches a critically low level, the ECM reduces the engine speed to idle rpm.

   g. *No oil flow warning program*—The no oil flow warning program sounds the warning horn, and illuminates the oil light and check engine light. On 1998-2000 models, the ECM reduces engine speed to a maximum of 3000 rpm. The ignition switch must be turned off to reset the warning program. On 2001-on models, the ECM reduces the engine speed to idle rpm. If the no oil flow warning program is activated, stop the engine as soon as possible and correct the defect. Operating the motor without oil flow will result in power head failure.

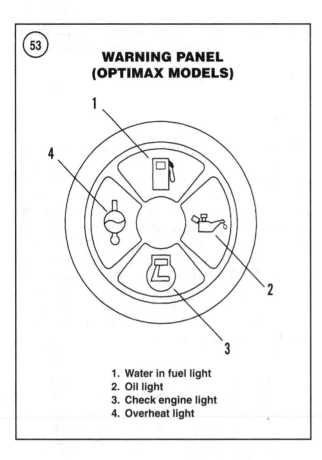

**WARNING PANEL
(OPTIMAX MODELS)**

1. Water in fuel light
2. Oil light
3. Check engine light
4. Overheat light

3

8. *Shift interrupt circuit*—All Optimax models use a shift interrupt circuit connected to the ECM. When shift load exceeds the spring force of the shift interrupt switch, the ECM black/red wire is grounded. The ECM reduces engine speed, reducing shift effort. As soon as the shift is completed, the shift interrupt switch opens and the ECM returns fuel delivery and engine speed to normal.

Troubleshooting

Refer to **Tables 8-11** for specifications and to the wiring diagrams at the end of the manual. Read *Troubleshooting Notes and Precautions (All Models)* at the beginning of the ignition section before continuing. The recommended troubleshooting procedure is listed below.

1. Preliminary check.
2. Ground circuit verification test.
3. Stop circuit verification test.
4. ECM power test.
5. Ignition coil power test.
6. Ignition coil resistance test.
7. Ignition driver power test.
8. Ignition driver resistance test.
9. Crankshaft position sensor check.

WARNING
High voltage is present in the ignition system. ***Never*** *touch or disconnect ignition system components while the engine is running.*

CAUTION
Do not run the engine without an adequate water supply and do not exceed 3000 rpm without an adequate load. Refer to ***Safety Precautions*** *at the beginning of this chapter.*

h. *Sensor failure warning program*—The sensor failure warning program is designed to alert the boat operator to a sensor, ignition coil or injector failure. If the ECM detects a failure in any of the sensor, ignition coil or injector circuits, the check engine lamp will illuminate. If one of the two throttle position sensors has failed, the warning horn will also sound. On 1998-2000 models, the engine will not run above idle speed if both throttle position sensors fail. On 2001-on models, the engine speed is reduced to a maximum of approximately 4500 if the single throttle position sensor fails. The ignition coils, injectors and ECT sensor can be tested with an ohmmeter. All other sensors require the DDT to determine if they are functioning correctly.

7. *Warning panel*—A multifunction warning panel is recommended for 2000-prior models. The warning panel has four lights that allow easy identification of low oil tank level, no oil flow, engine overheat, sensor malfunction, ignition coil or injector malfunction, and water-in-fuel conditions. See **Figure 53**. 2001-on models may be equipped with Smart Craft gauges. The LCD display on these gauges indicate which condition is activating the warning system.

Preliminary checks

NOTE
Air gap spark testers are not recommended as the resulting interference can cause the ECM to malfunction and produce incorrect results.

1. Install an inductive timing light to the cylinder No. 1 (top starboard) spark plug lead.
2. Make sure the safety lanyard is installed on the safety lanyard switch and the ignition switch is in the RUN position.
3. Crank the engine while observing the timing light. If the timing light flashes brightly and consistently, the igni-

tion coil is firing correctly. Repeat the test for each remaining ignition coil. If all ignition coils are firing correctly, but the engine will not start or does not run correctly, make sure the correct spark plugs are installed and in good condition. If the engine backfires or pops when attempting to start, remove the flywheel and check for a sheared flywheel key. If the timing light does not flash, flashes weakly or flashes erratically, continue with *Ground circuit verification* in the next section. If the light does not flash on one cylinder and flashes on others, check for power at the coil and check the coil resistance as described in this section.

On 2001-on models, if the light does not flash on two cylinders, and flashes on others, check for power at the ignition coil drivers and check the coil driver resistance as described in this chapter.

Ground circuit verification test

Trace the black and black/tan ground wires from each of the three ECM plug-in connectors (B, C and D, **Figure 52**) to the power head. Inspect all ground wires at these attachment points for a secure connection. Clean and tighten as necessary.

Stop circuit verification test

1. To check the engine wiring harness stop circuit wire for a short to ground, disconnect the remote control harness from the main engine harness connector (E, **Figure 52**). Then disconnect the engine harness plug-in from the lowest ECM plug-in connector (D, **Figure 52**).
2. Calibrate an ohmmeter to the highest scale available. Connect one ohmmeter lead to a good engine ground. Connect the other ohmmeter lead to the black/yellow lead pin of the ECM connector. If the meter does not indicate no continuity, there is a short to ground in the engine wiring harness black/yellow wire. Repair or replace the circuit as necessary.
3. To check the boat wiring harness for a short to ground, leave the remote control harness disconnected from the main engine harness connector (E, **Figure 52**).
4. Make sure the safety lanyard is installed on the safety lanyard switch and the ignition switch is in the RUN position.
5. Calibrate an ohmmeter to the highest scale available. Connect one ohmmeter lead to pin No. 1 of the boat wiring harness main connector. Connect the other ohmmeter lead alternately to each of the remaining connector pins. If the meter indicates continuity at a connector pin, there is a short between the boat harness black/yellow stop circuit

wire and the tested pin. Test, repair or replace the ignition switch, safety lanyard switch or wiring harness as necessary.
6. Reconnect all plugs and connectors.

ECM power test

The ECM is activated through the ignition switch purple wire. The ECM controls the main power relay by grounding the main power relay yellow/purple wire. When the main power relay activates, battery voltage from the starter solenoid positive terminal is relayed to the ignition coil, oil pump and fuel pump fuses. Power is also relayed back to the ECM through the ECM driver fuse. This fuse supplies protected working voltage and current to the ECM. The ECM shuts off the main power relay after three seconds if the engine is not cranked or started. When activated, the ECM continuously monitors the crankshaft position sensor signal to determine if the main power relay should be engaged.

> *CAUTION*
> *When measuring voltage or resistance at the ECM connectors, be careful not to damage the connector pins or sockets. Do not attempt to insert the meter probe into the socket. Simply hold the meter probe against the pin or socket.*

Determine if the ECM is receiving activation voltage, engaging the main power relay and receiving working voltage as follows:
1. Disconnect the engine harness from the lower ECM plug-in connector (D, **Figure 52**).
2. Set a multimeter to the 20 volt DC scale. Connect the negative meter lead to a good engine ground. Connect the positive meter lead to the purple wire (pin No. 1) of the engine harness ECM connector.
3. Turn the ignition switch to the ON position. If the meter reads less than 1 volt of battery voltage, there is an open circuit or high resistance in the purple wire from the ignition switch, remote control harness and the engine wiring harness. Isolate, repair or replace the purple wire circuit.
4. Reconnect the engine harness to the lower ECM connector.
5. Refer to the wiring diagrams at the end of the manual to locate the ECM fuse. Remove the fuse from its protective cover and disconnect the fuse from the fuse holder. Inspect the fuse for evidence of failure. Replace the fuse if there is any question of its integrity.
6. Set a multimeter to the 20 volt DC scale. Connect the negative meter lead to a good engine ground. Connect the

positive meter lead to the ECM fuse holder red/white wire.

NOTE
If the engine is not cranked or started, the ECM will turn the main power relay off after three seconds. The meter reading must be noted before this time elapses.

7. Turn the ignition switch to the ON position. If the meter indicates within 0.5 volt of battery voltage, proceed to Step 12. If the meter reading is less than specified, proceed to Step 8.

8. Refer to the wiring diagrams at the end of the manual to locate the main power relay. Unplug the main power relay from the engine wiring harness. Set a multimeter to the 20 volt DC scale. Connect the negative meter lead to a good engine ground. Connect the positive meter lead to the red wire of the engine wiring harness main power relay connector. If the meter indicates less than 0.5 volt of battery voltage, there is an open circuit or high resistance in the red wire from the starter solenoid battery positive terminal to the main power relay connector. If the meter shows the specified voltage, proceed with Step 9.

9. Move the positive meter lead to the purple wire terminal of the engine wiring harness main power relay connector. Turn the ignition switch to the ON position. If the meter indicates less than 1 volt of battery voltage, there is an open circuit or high resistance in the purple wire from the ignition switch to the main power relay connector. Isolate, repair or replace the circuit or component as necessary. If the meter shows the specified voltage, replace the main power relay and repeat Steps 5-7. If voltage is still below specification, continue with Step 10.

10. Unplug the main power relay from the main engine wiring harness. Calibrate an ohmmeter to the R × 1 scale. Connect one ohmmeter lead to the red/white wire of the ECM fuse holder and the other ohmmeter lead to the red/white wire of the main power relay connector. If the meter indicates no continuity, repair or replace the red/white wire from the main power relay connector to the ECM fuse holder.

11. If the voltage at the ECM fuse holder red/white wire is still not within specification, use an ohmmeter to test the yellow/purple wire from the main power relay connector to the lower ECM connector (D, **Figure 52**) for continuity. If the lead has no continuity, repair or replace the yellow/purple wire and repeat Steps 1-3. If the yellow/purple wire has continuity, the ECM has an internal defect and must be replaced. Consult a Mercury/Mariner dealership for ECM replacement policies and procedures. It is extremely rare for an ECM to fail. Usually the failure is the result of faulty wiring, terminals or fuses.

12. To check the continuity of the red/blue wires from the ECM fuse holder to the ECM connector, unplug the engine wiring harness from the lower ECM connector. Unplug the ECM fuse from the fuse holder. Calibrate an ohmmeter to the R × 1 scale.

13. Connect one ohmmeter lead to the red/blue wire of the ECM fuse holder and the other lead alternately to the ECM connector pin No. 1 and pin No. 2 (red/blue wires). If the meter indicates no continuity for either wire, repair or replace the circuit between the ECM fuse holder red/blue wire and the middle ECM plug-in connector pins No. 1 and No. 2.

Ignition coil power test

The ignition coils receive power from the main power relay. This circuit has a red/yellow wire for each ignition coil. When the ignition switch is on, battery voltage should be present at the red/yellow wire of each ignition coil connector. Do not test the ignition coil power unless the ECM power tests have been successfully completed.

Test the ignition coil power as follows:

1. Set a multimeter to the 20 volt DC scale. Connect the negative meter lead to a good engine ground.

2. Disconnect the cylinder No. 1 ignition coil wiring harness connector (C, **Figure 51**). Connect the positive meter lead to the red/yellow pin of the ignition coil lead harness connector. Be careful not to damage the wiring harness connector or pins.

3. Turn the ignition switch to the ON position. If the meter does not indicate within 1 volt of battery voltage, there is an open circuit or high resistance in the circuit from the main power relay red/white wire to the ignition coil. Repair the wire or terminal and retest.

4. Perform Steps 1-3 for the remaining five ignition coils.

Ignition coil resistance test

The ignition coil primary resistance can be tested with an ohmmeter. Failure of the ignition coil is extremely rare. Note that an internal short can allow a coil to pass a resistance test, but not create spark at the plug. If an ignition coil is not firing, swap the ignition coil with an ignition coil that is firing. If the problem follows the ignition coil, the coil is defective and must be replaced. If the problem stays at the original location, the problem is in the ECM or wiring harness. Test the coil resistance as follows:

1. Disconnect the wire harness connector (C, **Figure 51**) from the suspect ignition coil.

2. To check the primary resistance, calibrate an ohmmeter to the lowest scale available. Connect the ohmmeter leads to the pins that align with the green striped and black wire harness terminals. If the meter reading is not within the primary resistance specification in **Table 11**, the coil is defective and must be replaced.

3. To check the secondary resistance, calibrate an ohmmeter to the 1K scale. Connect one meter test lead to the spark plug wire terminal. Connect the other ohmmeter lead to the pin that aligns with the black wire harness terminal. If the meter reading is not within the secondary resistance specification in **Table 11**, the coil is defective and must be replaced.

Ignition coil driver power test

An ignition coil driver is used on 2001-on Optimax models. The ignition coils drivers receive power from the main power relay. This circuit is composed of a red/yellow wire for each driver. When the ignition switch is on, battery voltage should be present at the red/yellow wire of each driver. Do not test the ignition coil driver power unless the ECM power tests have been successfully completed.

Test the ignition coil power as follows:

1. Set a multimeter to the 20 volt DC scale. Connect the negative meter lead to a good engine ground.

2. Disconnect the wiring harness connector (E, **Figure 51**) from the top coil driver. Connect the positive meter lead to the red/yellow wire harness connector pin. Be careful not to damage the wiring harness connector or pins.

3. Turn the ignition switch to the ON position. If the meter does not indicate within 1 volt of battery voltage, there is an open circuit or high resistance in the circuit from the main power relay red/white wire to the ignition coil. Repair the wire or terminal and retest.

4. Perform Steps 1-3 for the remaining two ignition coil drivers.

Ignition coil driver resistance test

The ignition coil driver is used only on 2001-on Optimax models. Each coil driver fires two ignition coils. Switch a suspect ignition coil driver with another driver. If ignition is restored, replace the suspect driver. Test the ignition coil driver resistance as follows:

1. Disconnect the harness connectors (D and E, **Figure 51**) from the top ignition coil driver.

2. Calibrate an ohmmeter to the 10K scale. Touch one of the ohmmeter leads to the four-terminal connector pin that

aligns with the red/yellow wire harness terminal. Touch the other ohmmeter lead to the four-terminal connector pin that aligns with the black wire harness terminal. If the meter does not indicate the resistance specification in **Table 11**, replace the ignition coil driver.

3. Calibrate an ohmmeter to the R × 1 scale. Touch one of the ohmmeter leads to the four-terminal connector pin that aligns with the black wire harness terminal. Touch the other ohmmeter lead to the four-terminal connector pin that aligns with one of the green-stripe harness terminals. Note the meter reading and repeat the test using the four-terminal connector pin that aligns with the other green-stripe harness terminal. If either meter reading does not indicate the resistance specification in **Table 11**, replace the ignition coil driver.

4. Calibrate an ohmmeter to the R × 1 scale. Touch one of the ohmmeter leads to the four-terminal connector pin that aligns with the black wire harness terminal. Touch the other ohmmeter lead to the two-terminal connector pin that aligns with one of the green-stripe harness terminals. Note the meter reading and repeat the test using the two-terminal connector pin that aligns with the other green-stripe harness terminal. If either meter reading does not indicate the resistance specification in **Table 11**, replace the ignition coil driver.

Crankshaft position sensor check

The crankshaft position sensor provides the ECM with engine speed and crankshaft position information. Its function is similar to a trigger coil of other ignition systems. The ECM must know the precise position of all pistons and how fast the engine is running to fire the ignition coils accurately. The crankshaft position sensor can cause erratic spark, erratic timing or no spark if it has failed or is incorrectly adjusted. The DDT (Digital Diagnostic Terminal) is required to determine if the crankshaft position sensor is operating correctly. The manufacturer does not provide adaptors to check electrical output or resistance. If the boat's tachometer is operating normally, the crankshaft position sensor is functioning. Before replacing the sensor, adjust the sensor air gap as described in Chapter Five. If the tachometer does not operate and the air gap is correct, test the sensor using a DDT or replace the sensor.

FUEL SYSTEM

Outboard owners often assume the carburetor is out of adjustment if the engine does not run properly. While fuel system problems are not uncommon, carburetor adjustment is seldom the solution. In many cases, adjusting the carburetor only compounds the problem by making the engine run worse.

Never attempt to adjust the carburetor(s) idle speed and idle mixture unless:

1. The ignition timing is correctly adjusted.
2. The engine throttle and ignition linkage is correctly synchronized and adjusted.
3. The engine is running at normal operating temperature.
4. The outboard is in the water, running in FORWARD gear with the correct propeller installed.

If the engine appears to be running lean or starving for fuel, divide fuel system troubleshooting into determining whether the boat fuel system or the engine fuel system is causing the problem. Engines that appear to be running rich or receiving excessive fuel usually have a problem located in the engine fuel system, not the boat fuel system.

The boat fuel system consists of the fuel tank, fuel vent line and vent fitting, the fuel pickup tube and antisiphon valve, the fuel distribution lines, boat-mounted water separating fuel filter (recommended), and the primer bulb.

The typical carbureted engine fuel system consists of an engine fuel filter, crankcase pulse driven fuel pump, carburetor(s), primer valve, and the necessary lines and fittings.

An EFI engine's fuel system consists of a crankcase pulse driven fuel pump, a water separating fuel filter with water sensor, a vapor separator tank with integral final fuel filter and high pressure electric fuel pump, fuel rail(s) that house the six fuel injectors, a fuel pressure regulator on the return line to the vapor separator, and the necessary high and low pressure lines and fittings. Refer to the fuel flow diagrams in this chapter.

The Optimax (direct fuel injection) fuel system consists of a crankcase driven fuel pump, a water separating fuel filter with a water sensor, a vapor separator tank with integral final fuel filter and high-pressure electric fuel pump, a low pressure electric fuel pump, two air/fuel rails that house the six fuel injectors, a fuel pressure regulator in the port rail, a fuel cooler, and the necessary high- and low-pressure lines and fittings. A water screen is installed in the water outlet fitting at the power head adapter plate to filter the water going to the fuel cooler and air compressor. Remove and clean the screen every 100 hours of operation or once a season. Refer to the air and fuel flow diagrams in this chapter.

The Optimax (direct fuel injection) air system consists of a belt driven, water cooled air compressor with an air inlet filter in the flywheel cover, the air/fuel rails that also house the six direct injectors, an air pressure regulator in the port rail, a tracker diaphragm in the starboard rail that dampens pressure pulses between the air and fuel cham-

bers, and the necessary hoses, high-pressure lines and fittings. The excess air from the air pressure regulator is introduced into the exhaust at the power head adapter plate or the air plenum. Replace the compressor air inlet filter every 100 hours or once a season; the filter cannot be cleaned.

Preliminary Troubleshooting

Make sure fresh fuel is present in the fuel tank. If the fuel is stale or sour, drain the fuel tank and dispose of the fuel in an approved manner. Clean fuel filters and flush all fuel lines to remove traces of the stale or sour fuel. Inspect fuel lines for evidence of leaks or deterioration. Replace suspect components. Make sure the fuel tank vent is open and not restricted. Refer to Chapter Six for component removal, rebuilding and replacement procedures and component illustrations.

NOTE
When troubleshooting the fuel system, connect a substitute fuel tank and fuel line filled with fresh fuel to the engine. If the symptom is eliminated, the problem is in the original fuel tank and lines. If the symptom is still present, the problem is in the engine.

All models use a mechanical fuel pump driven by crankcase pressure and vacuum pulses. If the cylinder(s) that drives the fuel pump(s) fails, the fuel pump(s) cannot operate. Check the cranking compression before continuing. If the boat is equipped with a permanent fuel system, make sure the fuel tank vent line is not kinked or obstructed.

If all visual checks are satisfactory, continue with the mechanical fuel pump pressure and vacuum tests.

**Mechanical Fuel Pump
Pressure and Vacuum Tests**

CAUTION
*Do not run the engine without an adequate water supply and do not exceed 3000 rpm without an adequate load. Refer to **Safety Precautions** at the beginning of this chapter.*

1A. On permanent fuel tank models, make sure the fuel vent fitting and vent line are not obstructed.

1B. On portable fuel tank models, open the fuel tank vent to relieve pressure that may be present and make sure the tank is no more than 24 in. (61 cm) below the level of the fuel pump.

2. Disconnect the fuel inlet hose from the fuel pump (**Figure 54**).

3. Connect a combination vacuum and fuel pressure gauge between the fuel pump and the inlet line using a T-fitting, a short piece of clear vinyl hose, and the appropriate fittings and clamps. See **Figure 55**.

4A. On carbureted models, disconnect the fuel pump output hose that leads to the carburetor(s). See **Figure 55**.

4B. On EFI and Optimax models, disconnect the fuel pump output hose that leads to the engine mounted water separating fuel filter. See **Figure 54**.

5. Connect a fuel pressure gauge between the fuel pump and the output line using a T-fitting and appropriate fuel line and clamps. See **Figure 55**. Squeeze the primer bulb and check for leaks.

6. Start the engine and allow it to reach operating temperature. Refer to **Table 12** for fuel pump specifications. Run the engine in FORWARD gear to the speed in **Table 12**. Observe the fuel pressure gauge, vacuum gauge and clear hose at each engine speed.

7. If air bubbles are visible in the clear hose at any of the test speeds, check the fuel supply line back to the pickup tube in the fuel tank for loose fittings, loose clamps, a defective primer bulb, damaged filters or problems that would allow air to leak into the fuel line. The fuel pump cannot develop the specified pressure if air is present. Correct any problems and retest.

8. If no air bubbles are visible in the clear hose and the vacuum gauge reading does not exceed 4 in. Hg (13.5 kPa), the fuel supply system is in satisfactory condition. If the fuel pressure is below specification, repair or replace the fuel pump as described in Chapter Six.

9. If no air bubbles are visible in the clear hose, the vacuum did not exceed 4 in. Hg (13.5 kPa) and the fuel pressure is within specification, the problem is not in the mechanical fuel pump and fuel supply system.

10A. On carbureted models, inspect the fuel lines and fittings from the fuel pump(s) to the carburetor(s) for leaks, deterioration, kinks and blockages. Correct any problems found. If the lines and fittings are in satisfactory condition and the problem is still believed to be fuel related, rebuild and adjust the carburetor(s). On multi-carburetor engines, service all carburetors, even if only one is malfunctioning at this time.

10B. On EFI models, refer to *EFI fuel system troubleshooting* in this chapter.

10C. On Optimax, refer to *Optimax air/fuel system troubleshooting* in this chapter.

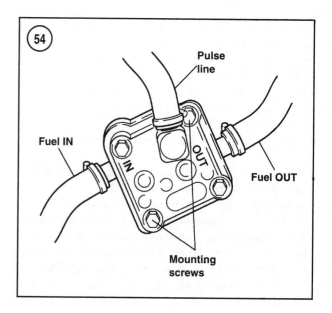

FUEL PRIMER AND ENRICHMENT SYSTEMS

Fuel Primer Valve (75-200 hp Carbureted Models)

Fuel primer valves (A, **Figure 56**) have replaced choke valves as the primary means of enriching the air/fuel mixture for cold starting. The fuel primer valve typically enriches the air/fuel mixture by sending fuel directly to the intake manifold or carburetor(s). If the fuel is injected into the carburetor(s), it is injected on the intake manifold side of the throttle plate(s). The fuel primer valve is an electrical solenoid valve that simply opens and closes. The fuel primer valve does not pump fuel; fuel must be supplied by the primer bulb or engine fuel pump.

When electricity is applied to the yellow/black wire, the solenoid energizes and the fuel valve opens. An internal spring forces the valve closed when the solenoid is not energized. The fuel primer valve is equipped with a button (B, **Figure 56**) to allow manual operation of the valve if the electrical circuit fails. Fuel will flow as long as the button is depressed.

Refer to Chapter Six for fuel primer valve hose routing diagrams and refer to the wiring diagrams at the end of the manual.

> *NOTE*
> *The ignition switch must be held in the CHOKE or PRIME position for all of the following tests.*

1. Check the fuel lines going to and from the fuel primer valve for deterioration and obstructions. Correct any problems found.

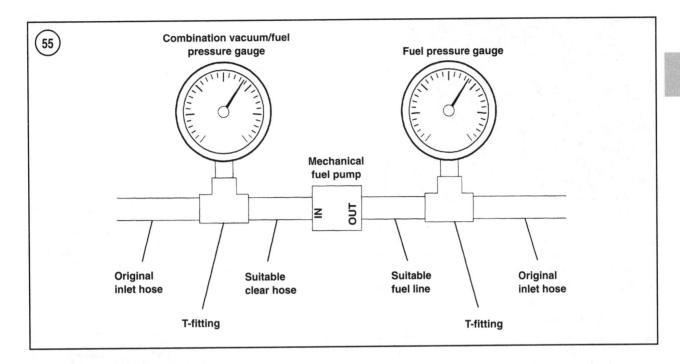

Figure 55. Combination vacuum/fuel pressure gauge — Fuel pressure gauge — Mechanical fuel pump (IN/OUT) — Original inlet hose — Suitable clear hose — Suitable fuel line — Original inlet hose — T-fitting — T-fitting

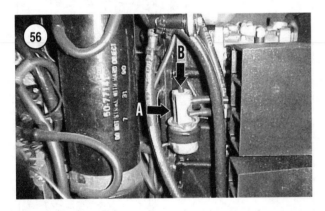

2. Make sure the black wire coming out of the fuel primer valve is connected to a good ground. Clean and tighten the connection as necessary.

3. Connect the test lamp lead to a good engine ground.

4. Access the ignition switch yellow/black wire (terminal C). Connect the test lamp probe to this wire. Turn the ignition switch to the CHOKE or PRIME position. If the test lamp lights, go to Step 6. If not, go to Step 5.

5. Connect the test lamp probe to the ignition switch red/purple wire (terminal B or BAT). The test lamp should light regardless of the ignition switch position. If the test lamp lights, replace the ignition switch and perform Step 4. If the test lamp does not light, repair or replace the red or red/purple wire from terminal B of the ignition switch back through the main 20 amp fuse to the starter solenoid.

6. Disconnect the yellow/black wire at the fuel primer valve. Connect the test lamp probe to the yellow/black wire on the engine harness side. Turn the ignition switch to the CHOKE or PRIME position. If the test lamp does not light, repair or replace the yellow/black wire from the fuel primer valve to the ignition switch.

7. Disconnect the yellow/black and black wires from the fuel primer valve. Connect an ohmmeter calibrated to the appropriate scale to read 10-12 ohms. Connect one meter lead to the fuel primer valve yellow/black wire and the other meter lead to the fuel primer valve black wire. If the resistance reading does not read 10-12 ohms, the fuel primer is defective and must be replaced.

8. Disconnect the fuel hoses from the fuel primer valve and connect a short length of hose to one of the valve ports. Blow into the hose while depressing the manual valve button on top of the valve. Air should flow through the valve when the button is depressed, but not flow when the button is released. Replace the valve if it does not perform as specified.

Thermal Enrichment Air Valve (105 Jet and 135-200 hp Carbureted Models)

The thermal air valve (**Figure 57**) is designed to enrich the idle circuits of WMV series of V-6 carburetors by restricting air flow to the idle circuits when the engine temperature is below 100° F (38° C). The thermal valve mounts in the starboard cylinder head just below the No. 3

spark plug. The valve has two ports. One is connected with hoses to each carburetor through a series of fittings on the carburetor bodies. The other port is open to the atmosphere (6, **Figure 58**). When the engine temperature is below 100° F (38° C), the valve is closed, preventing air from entering the idle circuits, causing a richer air/fuel mixture. When the temperature is above 100° F (38° C), the valve will be open, allowing air to enter the idle circuits, providing the normally calibrated air/fuel mixture.

1. Inspect the lines (5, **Figure 58**) from the thermal air valve to each carburetor fitting for kinks, blockages or deterioration. Inspect the fitting on each carburetor for debris or blockage. Clean any debris or blockage from the fittings and replace damaged or deteriorated lines.

CAUTION
*Do not run the engine without an adequate water supply and do not exceed 3000 rpm without an adequate load. Refer to **Safety Precautions** at the beginning of this chapter.*

NOTE
Run the engine to raise the temperature of the valve. Remove the valve and place the sensing element in a glass of ice water to lower the temperature of the valve. Test the valve above and below the specified temperature.

2. Disconnect the line from the thermal air valve. Attach a short piece of hose to either valve port. Blow into the valve. If the temperature is above 100° F (38° C), air should flow freely through the valve. If the temperature is below 100° F (38° C), air should not flow through the valve.

3. Replace the valve if it does not perform as specified.

Fuel Enrichment Valve
(225 hp Carbureted Models)

The fuel enrichment valve (1, **Figure 59**) on the 225 hp carbureted models is controlled by the ignition ECM,

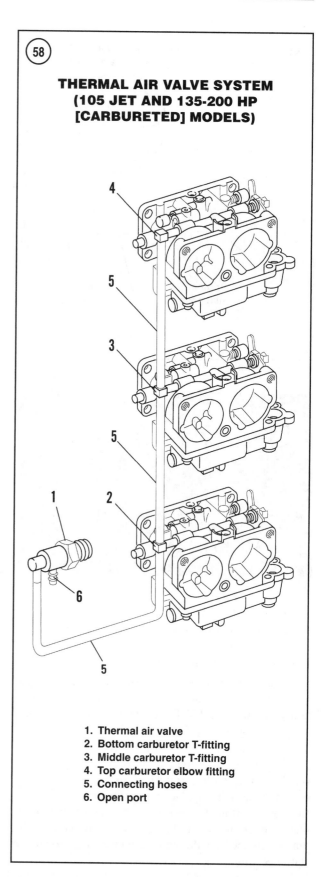

THERMAL AIR VALVE SYSTEM (105 JET AND 135-200 HP [CARBURETED] MODELS)

1. Thermal air valve
2. Bottom carburetor T-fitting
3. Middle carburetor T-fitting
4. Top carburetor elbow fitting
5. Connecting hoses
6. Open port

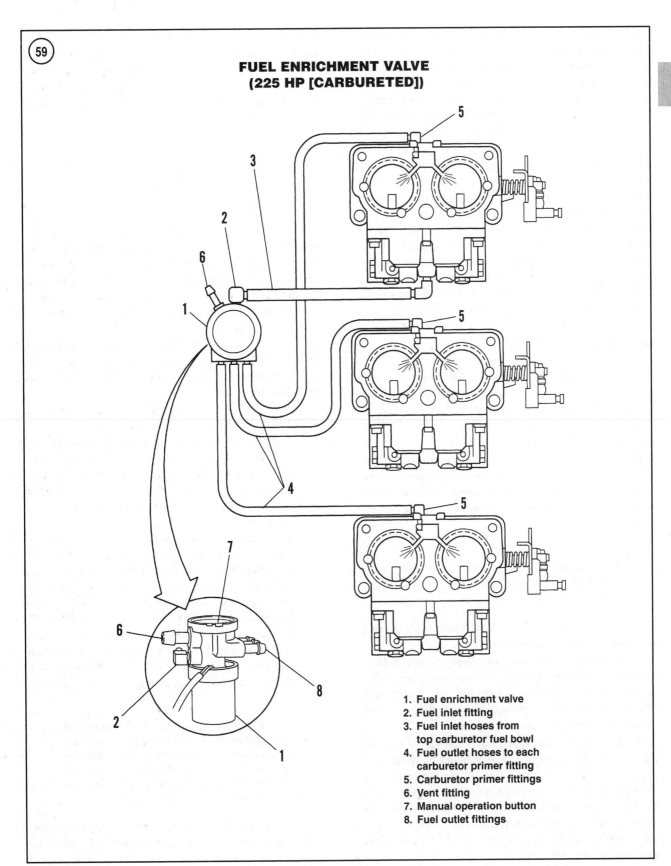

59

**FUEL ENRICHMENT VALVE
(225 HP [CARBURETED])**

1. Fuel enrichment valve
2. Fuel inlet fitting
3. Fuel inlet hoses from
   top carburetor fuel bowl
4. Fuel outlet hoses to each
   carburetor primer fitting
5. Carburetor primer fittings
6. Vent fitting
7. Manual operation button
8. Fuel outlet fittings

based on input from the engine coolant temperature (ECT) sensor. The fuel enrichment valve receives fuel gravity fed from the top carburetor float bowl through a fuel inlet hose (3, **Figure 59**). When activated, the valve delivers fuel to each carburetor's primer fitting located behind the throttle plates. The throttle plates must be fully closed for the system to function correctly.

The fuel enrichment valve is a simple open and close solenoid valve. A button (7, **Figure 59**) on the valve allows manual operation if the electrical portion of the valve fails. Fuel flows through the valve as long as the button is depressed. The valve has two wires: purple and yellow/black. The purple wire is battery voltage from the ignition switch. Battery voltage must be present at the purple wire connector when the ignition switch is on. The yellow/black wire is connected to the ignition ECM. The ECM grounds the yellow/black wire to activate the valve.

The ECM operates the valve in two modes: ECT indicates a temperature below 122° F (50° C) or ECT indicates a temperature above 122° F (50° C).

When the ECT indicates temperatures below 122° F (50° C), the ECM activates the valve for 2-3 seconds each time the ignition is switched on and the engine is not started. If the engine is cranking or running, the ECM re-opens the valve or keeps the valve open until the ECT indicates 122° F (50° C) or higher.

When the ECT indicates temperatures above 122° F (50° C), the ECM activates the valve for approximately 1/2 second each time the key is turned on, but does not activate the valve when the engine is cranking or running.

NOTE
If an ignition problem is present, correct it before attempting to diagnose the fuel enrichment valve system.

1. Squeeze the primer bulb until it is firm to ensure a good fuel supply to the top carburetor.

2. Pinch the fuel supply hose from the top carburetor float chamber (3, **Figure 59**) as close to the enrichment valve as possible. Remove the hose from the valve and place it in a suitable container. Release the pinch in the hose. Fuel should flow freely into the container.

3. If no fuel flows, check the fittings and supply hose on and from the top carburetor float chamber for debris and obstructions. If no fuel is present in the top carburetor float chamber, check the fuel hoses and fittings between the fuel pump and each carburetor for debris and obstructions. Correct any problems found. The enrichment system cannot operate unless the top carburetor float chamber is filled with fuel.

4. Disconnect each primer hose (4, **Figure 59**) from the valve. Use a small syringe filled with rubbing alcohol to make sure the primer line and primer fittings on each carburetor are open and fluid flows freely. Replace deteriorated or damaged primer hoses. Clean any blocked carburetor fittings.

NOTE
*Do not confuse the valve vent fitting (6, **Figure 59**) with the valve inlet fitting (2, **Figure 59**). If fuel leaks from the vent fitting, replace the valve.*

5. Connect a piece of hose to the enrichment valve inlet fitting. Blow into the hose while pressing and releasing the manual button. Air should blow out all three valve outlets when the button is depressed. Air should not blow out any of the three valve outlets when the manual button is released. Replace the enrichment valve if it does not perform as specified.

6. Set a multimeter to the 20 volt DC scale. Connect the negative meter lead to a good engine ground. Connect the positive meter lead to the enrichment valve purple wire at the bullet connector.

7. Turn the ignition switch to the ON position. The meter should read within 1 volt of battery voltage.

   a. If the meter reading is not within 1 volt of battery voltage, there is an open circuit or high resistance in the purple wire from (and including) the ignition switch, remote control harness and main engine harness. Test, isolate and repair the defective circuit or component.

   b. If the meter reading is within 1 volt of the battery voltage, disconnect the enrichment valve yellow/black bullet connector. With the ignition switch in the ON position, connect the valve yellow/black wire to ground. An audible click, indicating the valve is functioning correctly, should be heard. Retest the flow and no-flow capabilities of the valve as described in Step 5. Activate the valve by connecting and disconnecting the yellow/black wire to ground. Replace the valve if it does not perform as specified.

CAUTION
When measuring voltage or resistance at the ignition ECM connector, be careful not to damage the connector pins or sockets. Do not attempt to insert the test lead into the socket. Simply touch and hold the test lead against the pin or socket.

8. To test the yellow/black wire for continuity to the ignition ECM, calibrate an ohmmeter to the R × 1 scale. Disconnect the ignition ECM connector(s). Refer to the

wiring diagrams at the end of the manual. Connect one ohmmeter lead to the enrichment valve end of the engine wiring harness yellow/black bullet connector. Connect the other ohmmeter lead to the ignition ECM connector yellow/black terminal. If the meter does not indicate continuity, repair or replace the wiring harness.

9. If all tests are satisfactory to this point, test the ECT sensor as described in the *Capacitor Discharge Module Ignition (225 and 250 hp Models)*.

10. Test the ECT sensor tan/black engine harness wires for continuity. Refer to the wiring diagrams at the end of the manual. One tan/black wire should have continuity to the ignition ECM connector. The other tan/black wire should have continuity to engine ground. If the ECT sensor and wires test satisfactorily, the ignition ECM is defective and must be replaced.

EFI FUEL SYSTEM TROUBLESHOOTING

This section deals with troubleshooting the various EFI fuel systems used on Mercury and Mariner outboard motors. Once the defective component is identified, refer to the appropriate chapter for component removal and replacement procedures.

Troubleshooting Notes and Precautions (All Models)

Observe the following troubleshooting precautions to avoid damaging the ignition system or injury.

1. Do not reverse the battery connections. Reverse battery polarity will damage electronic components.

2. Do not *spark* the battery terminals with the battery cable connections to determine polarity.

3. Do not disconnect the battery cables with the engine running.

4. Do not crank or run the outboard if any electrical components are not grounded to the power head.

5. Do not disconnect the ECM when the outboard is running, while the ignition switch is on or while the battery cables are connected.

6. The EFI fuel system requires that the electric starter crank the engine at normal speed in order for the ignition system to produce adequate spark. All EFI fuel systems are triggered by the ignition system. If the starter motor cranks the engine slowly or not at all, refer to *Starting System* section and correct the problem before continuing.

7. Check the battery cable connections for secure attachment to both battery terminals and the engine. Clean corrosion from all connections. Discard wing nuts and install

corrosion resistant hex nuts at all battery cable connections. Place a corrosion resistant locking washer between the battery terminal stud and battery cable terminal end to ensure a positive connection. Loose battery connections can cause many different symptoms.

NOTE
All EFI engines are equipped with at least one ECM. EFI models cannot be started or operated without battery voltage.

8. Check all ECM and EFI component ground connections for secure attachments to the power head. Clean and tighten all ground leads, connections and fasteners as necessary. Loose ground connections and loose component mounting hardware can cause many different symptoms.

Resistance (Ohmmeter) Tests

The resistance values in the following test procedures are based on tests performed at room temperature. Actual resistance readings obtained during testing are generally slightly higher if components are hot. Also, resistance readings may vary depending on the manufacturer of the ohmmeter. Many ohmmeters have difficulty reading less than 1 ohm accurately. If this is the case, specifications of less than 1 ohm generally appear as a very low continuity reading. If possible, use a digital ohmmeter to measure circuits with less than 1 ohm resistance.

Due to these variables, use caution when considering the replacement of an electrical component that tests only slightly out of specification.

System Description (150-200 hp EFI Models)

The 150-200 hp EFI fuel system depends on the mechanical fuel pump to provide fuel to the vapor separator and high pressure electric fuel pump. The system also depends on the ignition system inner switch box primary circuit output to cylinders No. 1, No. 3 and No. 5 ignition coils to provide tachometer signals to the ECM so the ECM can calculate and activate the six fuel injectors at the correct time. The fuel injectors are activated in pairs. Cylinder No. 1 primary ignition circuit triggers cylinders No. 3 and No. 4 injectors, cylinder No. 3 primary ignition circuit triggers cylinders No. 5 and No. 6 injectors, and cylinder No. 5 primary ignition circuit triggers cylinders No. 1 and No. 2 injectors.

An ignition system failure that eliminates the switch box primary ignition voltage output to cylinders No. 1, No. 3 or No. 5 will prevent the ECM from activating the two fuel injectors triggered by that primary circuit.

The major components of the EFI fuel system include:
1. *ECM*—The electronic control module (ECM) is
mounted to the induction manifold assembly as shown in
Figure 60. A fault with the ECM is best diagnosed with the
DDT (**Figure 61**). The ECM may also be diagnosed with the
EFI tester (**Figure 62**) used on earlier models (1994-prior).
The ECM monitors engine coolant temperature, throttle
plate position, intake air temperature, manifold absolute
pressure, barometric pressure and engine speed data based
on signals from the various sensors and the ignition system.
The ECM processes this information and determines the
pulse width and injector timing necessary for optimum performance during all engine operating conditions.

2. *Vapor separator, final filter and high pressure fuel
pump*—The vapor separator (**Figure 63**) mounts on the
induction manifold and serves as a reservoir where fuel
from the diaphragm fuel pump and oil from the oil pump
are blended and circulated. Unused fuel from the fuel rail
bleed system returns to the vapor separator for
recirculation. The fuel level in the vapor separator is regulated by a float and needle, and seat valve assembly. If the
float sticks in the up position, fuel flow into the vapor separator is restricted. If the float sticks in the down position,
fuel overflows the vapor separator resulting in an excessively rich mixture. The electric fuel pump within the vapor separator tank delivers fuel under pressure to the fuel
rail. Any unused fuel returns to the vapor separator. When
the ignition switch is in the on position and the engine is
not running, the ECM activates the pump for approximately 30 seconds to pressurize the fuel system. The
ECM has an internal fuel pump driver circuit that controls
the pump. Battery voltage is always present at the pump
positive terminal. The ECM internally grounds the
red/purple wire to activate the pump. The pump operates
at two speeds, both controlled by the ECM. The pump
generally runs at the low speed below 2000 rpm. The final
fuel filter mounts on the bottom of the fuel pump, inside
the vapor separator. See Chapter Six.

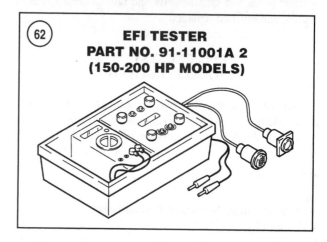

**EFI TESTER
PART NO. 91-11001A 2
(150-200 HP MODELS)**

3. *Fuel pressure regulator*—The electric fuel pump is capable of developing approximately 90 psi (621 kPa) fuel
pressure. The fuel pressure regulator (A, **Figure 64**) is
mounted on top of the vapor separator and regulates the
pressure to the fuel injectors to 36 psi (248 kPa) above
manifold pressure. The regulator has a vacuum line (B,

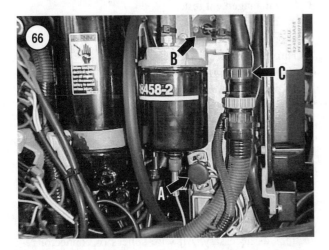

Figure 64) that goes to the induction manifold assembly. Fuel pressure varies as the manifold vacuum changes. Complete pressure specifications are in **Table 12**. If the fuel pressure is too low, the engine runs lean. If the fuel pressure is too high, the engine runs rich.

4. *Fuel filter, water sensor and module*—The water separating filter (A, **Figure 65**) helps prevents water contamination from damaging the fuel injection components. The water separating filter assembly is equipped with a water sensor (B, **Figure 65**) that activates a warning light (C) and horn if the water level in the filter canister reaches the level of the sensor probe. To determine if the water sensing system is functioning properly, place the ignition switch in the on position, disconnect the tan wire from the sensor probe (B, **Figure 65**) and connect it to a good engine ground for ten seconds. The warning light should glow and the horn should sound if the system is functioning properly.

5. *Induction manifold assembly*—The induction manifold assembly contains four throttle valves mounted on two throttle shafts. The manifold assembly contains the fuel rail, fuel injectors, throttle position sensor and intake air temperature sensor. The fuel injectors are connected to the fuel rail and are located inside the induction manifold assembly. Each injector consists of an electric solenoid that actuates a pintle valve assembly. The ECM determines when to activate the injectors by referencing the primary ignition circuits. The injectors are connected to the ECM by a four-wire harness. The red wire provides battery voltage to the injectors. The ECM actuates the injectors by grounding either the white (cylinders No. 1 and No. 2), blue (cylinders No. 3 and No. 4) or yellow (cylinders No. 5 and No. 6) wires.

> *NOTE*
> *The fuel injectors have a serviceable fuel filter in the inlet fitting of each injector. Clean or replace the filter when the injector is removed. See Chapter Six.*

6. *Throttle position sensor (TPS)*—The throttle position sensor (A, **Figure 66**) is a variable resistor that provides throttle position information to the ECM. The TPS mounts to the side of the induction manifold and is engaged with the lower throttle valve shaft. The sensor sends throttle position information to the ECM as a voltage signal and has a direct effect on the air/fuel ratio at lower engine speeds. The air/fuel mixture becomes richer as TPS resistance increases.

7. *Manifold absolute pressure sensor (MAP)*—When the ECM is first turned on, a barometric pressure reading is taken before the engine starts. The manifold absolute pressure sensor detects changes in manifold pressure via a vacuum hose connected to the intake manifold. The sensor is located inside the ECM and is non-serviceable. The ECM uses manifold pressure information from the MAP sensor to compensate for engine load conditions and changes in barometric pressure (altitude).

8. *Engine coolant temperature sensor (ECT)*—The engine coolant temperature sensor (**Figure 67**) provides the ECM with engine temperature information. The ECM uses this information to calculate the correct air/fuel enrichment during cold starts and engine warm up. The ECM stops the enrichment process when the engine temperature reaches 90° F (32° C). The sensor is located directly below the No. 2 (top port) spark plug. The sensor must have a clean, positive contact with the cylinder head or an overly-rich air/fuel mixture can occur.

9. *Intake air temperature sensor (IAT)*—The intake air temperature sensor (B, **Figure 66**) provides air temperature information to the ECM. As air temperature increases, the sensor resistance decreases, causing the ECM to lean the air/fuel mixture. If the sensor is disconnected (open circuit), the air/fuel mixture becomes richer by up to 10 percent. If the sensor is grounded (short circuit), the air/fuel mixture becomes leaner by up to 10 percent.

10. *Detonation sensor and module*—This system is used only on the 200 hp and 200 Magnum III models. System operation and troubleshooting are covered in *ADI 135-200 hp Ignition System Troubleshooting* in this chapter. When detonation occurs, the detonation sensor module sends signals to the ignition system bias circuit to retard spark timing and to the ECM to enrich the air/fuel mixture up to 15 percent. The detonation module gray/white wire transmits the signal to the ECM. Retarding ignition timing and enriching the air/fuel ratio are effective means of eliminating detonation.

11. *Bleed system*—At idle speed, some of the unusual fuel discharged by the fuel injectors pools in the crankcase. Through a series of check valves and hoses, the bleed system collects unburned fuel from the crankcase and pumps it to the vapor separator for recirculation. An inline bleed system filter (all models) prevents contamination from entering the vapor separator assembly. A plugged bleed system filter will cause an excessively rich mixture at idle and hesitation during acceleration. Refer to Chapter Six for bleed line routing and service. Refer to Chapter Four for filter service.

Troubleshooting (150-200 hp EFI Models)

Verify all synchronization and linkage adjustments (Chapter Five), and correct any ignition system problems *before* beginning EFI fuel system troubleshooting.

The following general EFI troubleshooting procedure requires a multimeter, jumper wires and a fuel pressure gauge.

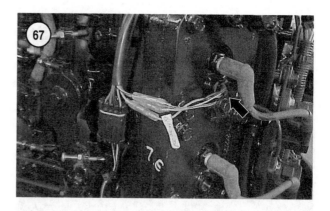

The system is designed so it can be diagnosed with the Quicksilver Digital Diagnostic Terminal (DDT) or the EFI tester (**Figure 62**). These systems display sensor inputs and actuator outputs at the ECM.

Troubleshooting without the DDT or EFI tester limits the components that can be tested. However, a significant amount of information can be obtained regarding system operation with basic resistance and voltage testing. If the following procedures do not isolate the failed system(s), have a Mercury/Mariner dealership diagnosis the system.

Read *Troubleshooting Notes and Precautions (All Models)* and *Safety Precautions* before continuing. Refer to **Figure 68** for a fuel flow diagram.

The recommended general EFI fuel system troubleshooting procedure is listed below.
1. Preliminary checks.
2. ECM power and ground test.
3. Fuel management test.
4. Injector and injector harness test.
5. Injector cylinder drop test.
6. Throttle position sensor test.
7. Manifold absolute pressure sensor test.
8. Engine coolant temperature sensor test.
9. Intake air temperature sensor test.
10. Water sensor and module test.

Preliminary checks

Perform a thorough visual inspection. Check all electrical connections for corrosion, mechanical damage, heat damage and loose connections. Clean and repair all connections as necessary. All wire splices or connector repairs must be made with waterproof marine grade connectors and heat shrink tubing. An electrical hardware repair kit and crimping pliers (part No. 86-813937A-1 and 91-808696) are available from Quicksilver. The Quicksilver dealer catalog also lists heat shrink connectors and heat shrink tubing for making other waterproof connec-

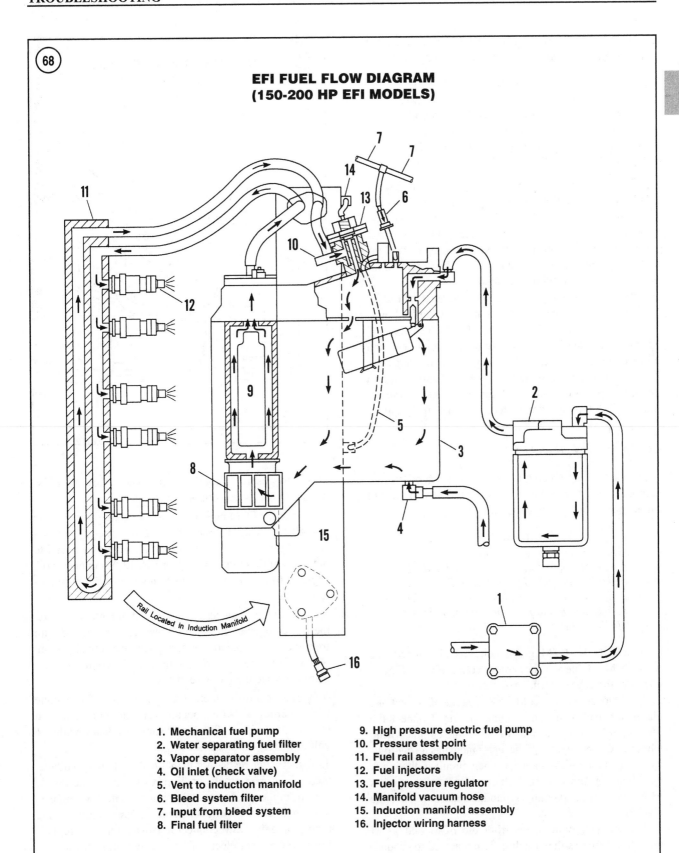

**EFI FUEL FLOW DIAGRAM
(150-200 HP EFI MODELS)**

Rail Located in Induction Manifold

1. Mechanical fuel pump
2. Water separating fuel filter
3. Vapor separator assembly
4. Oil inlet (check valve)
5. Vent to induction manifold
6. Bleed system filter
7. Input from bleed system
8. Final fuel filter
9. High pressure electric fuel pump
10. Pressure test point
11. Fuel rail assembly
12. Fuel injectors
13. Fuel pressure regulator
14. Manifold vacuum hose
15. Induction manifold assembly
16. Injector wiring harness

3

tions and repairs. Marine and industrial suppliers are other good sources for quality electrical repair equipment.

NOTE
Any electrical connection or repair that does not have perfect continuity affects the signal sent to or from the ECM, throwing the system out of calibration. This will have a detrimental effect on engine performance.

1. Check both battery cable connections at the battery and engine. Clean, tighten and repair the connections and terminals as necessary. Loose connections will cause erratic and intermittent symptoms. If the cranking speed is slower than normal, perform the voltage drop tests in the starting system troubleshooting section. The engine must crank at normal speed in order to start.

2. Check the mechanical integrity of the power head by performing a cranking compression test (Chapter Four). Correct any mechanical problems before proceeding.

3. Inspect the spark plugs for fouling, correct air gap and correct application. Replace any suspect spark plugs.

4. Perform an air gap spark test to verify that the ignition system is operating correctly. Refer to *Preliminary checks* in the 135-200 hp ignition system section of this chapter.

ECM power and ground test

The ECM must receive power and have good ground continuity in order to function correctly. Refer to the end of the manual for wiring diagrams.

CAUTION
When measuring voltage or resistance at the ECM connectors, be careful not to damage the connector pins or sockets. Do not attempt to insert the test lead into the socket. Simply touch and hold the lead against the pin or socket.

1. To check the ECM ground circuits, disconnect the main ECM engine wiring harness connector (C, **Figure 66**) from the engine wiring harness.

2. Calibrate an ohmmeter to the R × 1 scale. Connect one ohmmeter lead to a good engine ground. Connect the other ohmmeter lead to pin No. 16 of the engine wiring harness ECM connector. If the meter indicates no continuity, there is a high resistance or open circuit in the black wire between pin No. 16 of the engine wiring harness ECM connector and engine ground. Repair or replace the black wire as necessary.

3. Inspect all ground wires from the ECM and ECM mounting brackets that are directly connected to ground. Clean, tighten or repair connections and fasteners as nec-

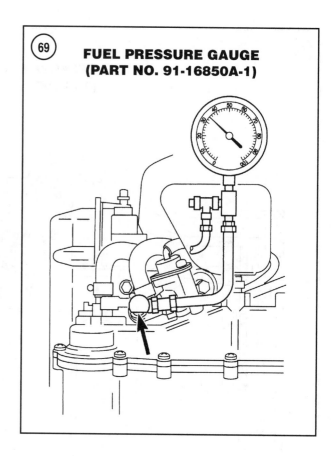

essary to ensure a good ground. Make sure all ECM mounting hardware is tightened securely.

4. To test the ECM power circuits, set a multimeter to the 20-volt DC scale. Connect the negative meter lead to a good engine ground. Connect the positive meter lead to pin No. 6 of the engine wiring harness ECM connector (C, **Figure 66**). The meter should read within 0.5 volt of battery voltage.

5. If the meter reads less than 0.5 volt of battery voltage, there is an open circuit or high resistance in the red wire from the starter solenoid battery positive terminal and pin No. 6 of the engine wiring harness ECM connector. Repair or replace the red wire as necessary.

6. Move the positive meter lead to pin No. 7 of the engine wiring harness ECM connector. Turn the ignition switch to the ON position. The meter should indicate within 1 volt of battery voltage.

7. If the meter reads less than 1 volt of battery voltage, there is an open circuit or high resistance in the purple wire from the ignition switch, remote control wiring harness, main engine harness connector, main engine wiring harness and the ECM connector. Isolate, repair or replace the purple wire or electrical components as necessary.

8. Reconnect all connectors.

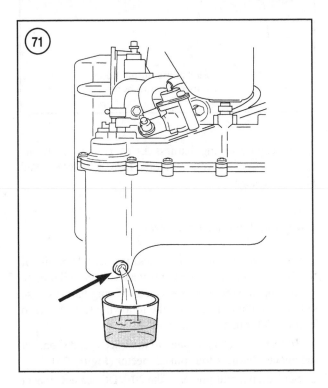

Fuel management test

CAUTION
*Do not run the engine without an adequate water supply and do not exceed 3000 rpm without an adequate load. Refer to **Safety Precautions** at the beginning of this chapter.*

NOTE
The fuel pressure at the high-pressure test point must be within specifications at all engine speeds. If the symptom occurs only at a certain engine speed, perform the test at the speed the symptom occurs.

1. Connect the fuel pressure test gauge (part No. 91-16850A-1) to the test port (C, **Figure 64**) at the top of the vapor separator tank, near the fuel pressure regulator. Make sure the gauge connections are secure.
2. Squeeze the primer bulb to ensure the fuel system is primed.

NOTE
If the engine is not cranked or started, the ECM will turn the fuel pump off after 30 seconds.

3. Turn the ignition switch to the ON position and observe the fuel pressure gauge (**Figure 69**). Fuel pressure should be 34-36 psi (234.4-248.2 kPa).
4. If the fuel pressure is above specification, replace the fuel pressure regulator and retest.
5. If the fuel pressure is below specification, determine if the electric fuel pump is running. Turn the ignition switch to the ON position and listen for pump operation. The pump should operate for approximately 30 seconds, then shut off. If necessary, use a mechanic's stethoscope to hear the pump. If the electric fuel pump does not operate, proceed to Step 12. If the electric fuel pump operates correctly, proceed to Step 6.
6. To make sure the electric fuel pump and vapor separator are receiving fuel, place a suitable container under the vapor separator drain plug (**Figure 70**). Remove the plug. Fuel should flow freely from the vapor separator (**Figure 71**). If fuel flows, proceed with Step 8. If not, check the engine mounted water separating fuel filter for water, debris or blockage. Check the fuel lines and fittings from the mechanical fuel pump to the vapor separator, including the vapor separator float and valve assembly, for deterioration, debris or blockage. Clean, repair or replace components as necessary. If no defects are noted, proceed with Step 7.
7. Test the mechanical fuel pump and boat fuel system for pressure and vacuum as described previously in this chapter.
8. If the electric fuel pump runs and the vapor separator is receiving fuel, but fuel pressure is still below specification, either the electric fuel pump or fuel pressure regulator is defective. Proceed with Step 9.
9. Remove the fuel pressure regulator from the vapor separator without disconnecting any vacuum or fuel lines. See Chapter Six. Hold the fuel pressure regulator over a suitable container. Turn the ignition switch to the ON position and note the fuel flow from the regulator.
10. If fuel flows freely from the regulator discharge port and fuel pressure is below specification, replace the fuel pressure regulator. If little or no fuel flows from the regulator discharge port, remove the vapor separator cover and

inspect the final filter. Replace the final filter if it is dirty or clogged and retest fuel pressure. If the final filter is clean, continue to Step 11.

> *WARNING*
> *EFI systems operate under high pressure. Do not remove the crimped stainless steel clamps unless absolutely necessary. Do not disconnect the rubber hoses from the electric fuel pump, fuel pressure regulator and fuel management adapter unless new clamps will be installed.*

11. Disconnect the electric fuel pump output hose (1, **Figure 72**) from the induction manifold fuel management adapter and the fuel rail return hose (2, **Figure 72**) from the fuel pressure regulator. Place a shop rag over the regulator hose to capture fuel that may be in the lines. Blow into the fuel pump output line with low pressure air. Air or fuel should exit freely from the regulator hose. If the air flow is restricted, disassembly and clean the induction manifold and fuel rail. If air flows freely, replace the electric fuel pump and final filter in the vapor separator and retest fuel pressure.

12. To check the electric fuel pump for power, set a multimeter to the 20-volt DC scale. Connect the negative lead to a good engine ground and the positive lead to the electric fuel pump positive terminal. The meter should indicate within 0.5 volt of battery voltage.

13. If the reading is less, check the red wire from the fuel pump positive terminal to the starter solenoid battery positive terminal for continuity. If no continuity is noted, repair or replace the red wire as necessary.

> *CAUTION*
> *When measuring voltage or resistance at the ECM connectors, be careful not to damage the connector pins or sockets. Do not attempt to insert the meter lead into the socket. Simply touch and hold the lead against the pin or socket.*

14. To check the electric fuel pump ground, disconnect the red/purple wire from the negative fuel pump terminal. Connect a suitable jumper wire to the fuel pump negative terminal and a good engine ground. If the fuel pump does not run, replace the electric fuel pump and final filter in the vapor separator and retest fuel pressure output. If the fuel pump now runs, disconnect the main ECM connector from the engine wiring harness and check the red/purple wire from the fuel pump negative terminal to pin No. 2 of the engine wiring harness ECM connector (C, **Figure 66**) for continuity. If no continuity is noted, repair or replace the red/purple wire from the fuel pump negative terminal

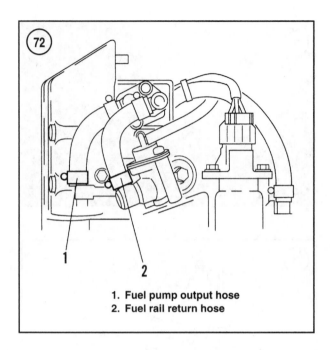

1. Fuel pump output hose
2. Fuel rail return hose

to the engine wiring harness ECM connector. If the red/purple wire has continuity, the ECM is defective and must be replaced.

Injector and injector harness test

The injector and injector harness test will determine if the fuel injectors are receiving battery voltage and if there are any open circuits in the injector wiring harness. Use only a digital multimeter for the following tests. Refer to **Figure 73** for this procedure.

1. To test the battery voltage to the injectors, disconnect the injector harness four-pin connector (**Figure 73**).

2. Set a digital multimeter to the 20-VDC scale. Connect the negative meter lead to a good engine ground. Connect the positive meter lead to pin No. 2 (red wire) of the engine harness side of the injector harness four-pin connector. The meter should indicate within 0.5 volt of battery voltage.

3. If the meter reads less than 0.5 volt of battery voltage, there is a high resistance or open circuit in the red wire from the starter solenoid battery positive terminal and pin No. 2 of the injector harness four-pin connector. Repair or replace the red wire as necessary.

4. To test the injector and injector harness resistance, set the digital ohmmeter to the 200 ohm scale.

5. Connect the positive ohmmeter lead to pin No. 2 of the injector harness side of the injector harness four-pin connector. Connect the negative ohmmeter lead alternately to

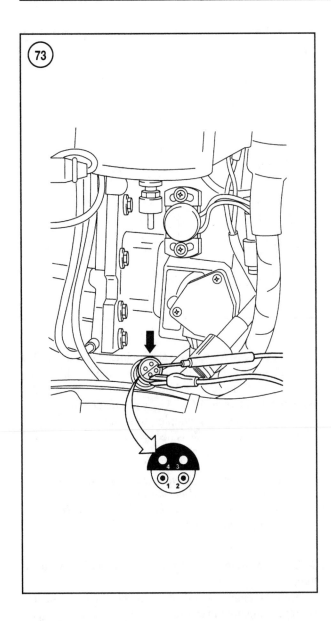

each of the following pins on the injector harness side of the four-pin injector harness connector:

   a. Pin No. 4 (white wire) for cylinders No. 1 and No. 2 injectors.

   b. Pin No. 3 (blue wire) for cylinders No. 3 and No. 4 injectors.

   c. Pin No. 1 (yellow wire) for cylinders No. 5 and No. 6 injectors.

6. The reading at each connection should be 0.9-1.3 ohms. If it is not, disassemble the induction manifold and test the resistance of each injector and check the continuity of each injector harness wire. If the measured resistance is 2.0-2.4 ohms at any connection, one injector or injector circuit has an open circuit.

Injector cylinder drop test

If the engine appears to be misfiring on one or more cylinders, perform a cylinder drop test to determine if each cylinder is firing normally. Before performing a cylinder drop test, make sure all previous tests have been performed with satisfactory results. Also make sure the compression is acceptable and the ignition system is functioning properly.

> *CAUTION*
> *Do not run the engine without an adequate water supply and do not exceed 3000 rpm without an adequate load. Refer to **Safety Precautions** at the beginning of this chapter.*

1. Start the engine and allow it to warm to operating temperature.
2. Adjust engine speed to approximately 1000-1500 rpm in neutral.

> *WARNING*
> *High voltage is present during ignition system operation. Do not touch ignition components, leads or test leads while cranking or running the engine.*

3. Using insulated spark plug pliers, disconnect the spark plug lead from each spark plug one at a time and note the resulting change in engine operation.
4. The engine speed should drop approximately the same amount as each spark plug lead is individually disconnected. If any cylinders do not produce a noticeable rpm drop or the same rpm drop as the majority of the cylinders, record the suspect cylinder numbers.
5. Remove the induction manifold and fuel rail. Inspect the reed valve for damage and repair it if needed. Refer to Chapter Six. If the reed valve tests correctly, remove the suspect injector(s) and inspect the injector inlet filter. If the filter is clean, replace the suspect injector. If the filter was dirty or clogged, clean or replace the filter, reassemble the induction manifold and retest the cylinder drop. If the cylinder drop is still unsatisfactory, replace the suspect injector.

Throttle position sensor (TPS) test

The correct operation and setting of the TPS is critical to achieving the correct air/fuel ratio. High TPS voltages provide a richer air/fuel ratio. Low TPS voltages provide a leaner air/fuel ratio. Adjustments, within specifications, to the TPS may be used to fine tune the idle air/fuel mixture. Never adjust the TPS out of the specified range. TPS adjustment is described in Chapter Five. Use only a digital multimeter for the following test. Test harness part No. 91-816085 (1, **Figure 74**) is required for this procedure.

NOTE
Verity the idle speed before adjusting the TPS. If idle speed is changed, readjust the TPS setting.

1. Disconnect the TPS from the engine wiring harness. Connect the test harness (part No. 91-816085) to the TPS and engine wiring harness. Connect the test harness meter leads to a digital multimeter. Set the multimeter to the 20-volt DC scale.
2. Disconnect both engine wiring harness tan/black wires from the engine coolant temperature (ECT) sensor (**Figure 67**).

NOTE
If the TPS cannot be correctly set or reads zero, check the continuity of the sensor wires from the TPS connector to the ECM connector. The orange wire goes to ECM connector pin No. 1, the light blue wire goes to pin ECM connector pin No. 15 and the tan/black wire goes to ECM connector pin No. 14.

3. Turn the ignition switch to the ON position. Make sure the throttle plates are against the idle stop. If the meter reading is 0.200-0.300 volts DC, continue to Step 5. If the reading is not within specification, loosen the two screws (2, **Figure 74**) securing the TPS to the induction manifold.
4. With the throttle shaft held against the idle stop screw, rotate the TPS to obtain 0.200-0.300 volts DC. While holding the TPS at the correct setting, tighten the screws securely. Recheck the voltage reading.
5. Disconnect the throttle cable and slowly move the throttle linkage to the full throttle position while noting the meter reading. The voltage should increase smoothly to 7.00-7.46 volts DC. If the meter reading fluctuates or is erratic as the throttle is advanced, replace the TPS sensor. If the meter reading is not within 7.00-7.46 volts DC at wide-open throttle, check the wide-open throttle stop for correct adjustment (Chapter Five).
6. Disconnect the test harness. Reconnect the TPS sensor harness and two ECT sensor leads.

Manifold absolute pressure (MAP) sensor test

The MAP sensor provides engine load and barometric pressure data to the ECM. The MAP sensor is mounted inside the ECM case and is not serviceable. The MAP sensor is best tested with the EFI tester or DDT.

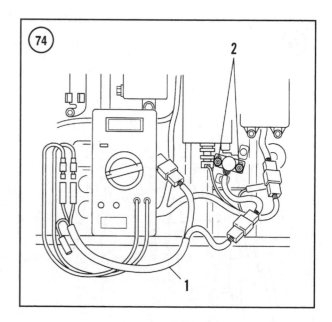

1. Inspect the MAP sensor vacuum line from the ECM to the induction manifold for secure attachment, kinks, deterioration or leakage. The line can be repaired up to the point that it enters the ECM. Use a plastic line fitting, such as a speedometer hose coupler, to repair or replace portions of the vacuum line as necessary.

CAUTION
*Do not run the engine without an adequate water supply and do not exceed 3000 rpm without an adequate load. Refer to **Safety Precautions** at the beginning of this chapter.*

2. Start the engine and let it warm to operating temperature.
3. Stop the engine and disconnect the MAP sensor line from the induction manifold.
4. Attach a hand vacuum pump to the MAP sensor line.
5. Run the engine at idle speed. Vary the vacuum applied to the MAP sensor line from zero to 10 in. Hg (34 kPa) of vacuum as the engine idles. Engine running quality should change noticeably. If running quality does not change, the MAP sensor is defective and the ECM will have to be replaced.

Engine coolant temperature (ECT) sensor test

The ECT sensor provides the ECM with coolant temperature data. The ECT sensor has four wires. The two tan/black wires are used by the ECM to sense engine temperature. The tan/blue and black wires are the temperature switch portion of the ECT sensor and are used to sound the warning horn whenever the temperature of the engine exceeds the switch rating. Refer to **Table 13** for ECT sensor resistance values and to the end of the manual for wiring diagrams. To test the ECT sensor and switch, refer to **Figure 67** and proceed as follows:

1. Disconnect the ECT sensor tan/blue and two tan/black wires from the engine wiring harness.

2. Calibrate an ohmmeter to the highest scale available. Connect one meter lead to the black sensor wire (ground) and the other meter lead to the tan/blue sensor lead. Replace the sensor assembly if continuity is noted.

CAUTION
*Do not run the engine without an adequate water supply and do not exceed 3000 rpm without an adequate load. Refer to **Safety Precautions** at the beginning of this chapter.*

3. Run the engine up to operating temperature as described in *Engine temperature check* in this chapter. Replace the sensor assembly if continuity is noted when the engine is at normal operating temperature. The only time the sensor should indicate continuity is if the engine is actually exceeding normal operating temperature.

4. Calibrate the ohmmeter on the appropriate scale to read the ECT sensor engine temperature data in **Table 13**.

NOTE
Determine the temperature of the engine accurately before the testing ECT sensor.

5. Measure the temperature of the cylinder head with a pyrometer or allow the engine to cool to ambient temperature. Connect one ohmmeter lead to each of the tan/black ECT sensor leads. Note the meter reading and compare it to the specification. If the reading is not within specification, replace the ECT sensor. If the reading is within specification, continue to Step 6.

6. Remove the sensor from the cylinder head with ohmmeter still connected and immerse the sensing element into a container of crushed ice and water while noting the meter reading. The reading should smoothly increase as the sensing element cools. If the reading does not increase to the specification in **Table 13**, replace the ECT sensor. If the reading is within specification, continue to Step 7.

7. Calibrate an ohmmeter to the highest scale available. Connect one ohmmeter lead to the black ECT sensor lead. Connect the other ohmmeter lead alternately to each of the tan/black ECT sensor leads. If the meter indicates continuity, replace the ECT sensor.

8. Disconnect the ECM connector (C, **Figure 66**) from the engine wiring harness. Calibrate an ohmmeter to the R × 1 scale. Connect one ohmmeter lead to the engine wir-

ing harness ECM connector pin No. 13 (orange lead) and the other ohmmeter lead to the engine wiring harness orange lead bullet connector at the ECT sensor. If the meter indicates no continuity, there is an open circuit or high resistance in the engine wiring harness orange lead. Repair or replace the orange lead as necessary.

9. Connect one ohmmeter lead, still calibrated on the R × 1 scale, to the engine wiring harness ECM connector pin No. 14 (tan/black lead). Connect the other ohmmeter lead to the engine wiring harness tan/black lead bullet connector at the ECT sensor. If the meter indicates no continuity, there is an open circuit or high resistance in the engine wiring harness tan/black lead. Repair or replace the tan/black lead as necessary.

Intake air temperature (IAT) sensor test

The intake air temperature (IAT) sensor provides the ECM with ambient temperature information. Cold air is denser and contains more oxygen, and requires a richer fuel delivery. Warm air is less dense and contains less oxygen, and requires a leaner fuel delivery. The ECM can compensate the normal air/fuel ratio a maximum of 10 percent richer or leaner. IAT sensor failure generally causes a running quality problem, but it will not normally cause a no-start condition. There are two brown leads coming from the IAT sensor (Figure B, **Figure 66**). One lead is connected to engine ground and the other lead is connected to the ECM connector pin No. 12. Refer to the end of the manual for wiring diagrams and **Table 14** for IAT sensor ohmmeter values. To test the IAT sensor, refer to **Figure 66** and proceed as follows:

1. Disconnect the IAT sensor brown leads from the engine wiring harness.

2. Calibrate the ohmmeter to the appropriate scale to read the IAT sensor temperature value in **Table 14**.

NOTE
Determine the ambient temperature accurately before testing the IAT sensor.

3. Allow the engine to cool to ambient temperature. Connect one ohmmeter lead to each of the brown IAT sensor wires. Note the meter reading and compare it to the specification. If the reading is not within specification, replace the IAT sensor. If the reading is within specification, continue to Step 6.

4. Remove the sensor from the induction manifold with ohmmeter still connected and immerse the sensing element into a container of crushed ice and water while noting the meter reading. The reading should smoothly increase as the sensing element cools. If the reading does

not increase to the specification in **Table 14**, replace the IAT sensor. If the reading is within specification, continue to Step 7.

5. Disconnect the ECM connector (C, **Figure 66**) from the engine wiring harness. Calibrate an ohmmeter to the R × 1 scale. Connect one ohmmeter lead to the engine wiring harness ECM connector pin No. 12 (brown wire) and the other ohmmeter lead to the engine wiring harness brown lead bullet connector at the IAT sensor. If the meter indicates no continuity, there is an open circuit or high resistance in the engine wiring harness brown wire. Repair or replace the brown wire as necessary.

6. Connect one ohmmeter lead, still calibrated on the R × 1 scale, to the engine wiring harness ECM connector pin No. 16 (black wire). Connect the other ohmmeter lead to the engine wiring harness black bullet connector at the IAT sensor. If the meter indicates continuity, there is an open circuit or high resistance in the engine wiring harness black wire. Repair or replace the black wire as necessary.

Water sensor and module test

The water sensor and module alert the boat operator to a buildup of water in the engine mounted water separating fuel filter. If the water level in the filter reaches potentially damaging levels, the light emitting diode (LED) on the warning module will illuminate and the warning horn will sound intermittently. There is a 5-10 second delay built into the warning module.

There are four wires used in the system. The purple wire indicates battery voltage when the ignition switch is in the ON position. The black wire should have continuity to ground at all times. The light blue wire should have continuity to the oil injection warning module (1998 and 1999) or ignition control module (2000-on). The oil injection warning module or ignition control module sounds the warning horn if it receives a signal from the water sensor module. The tan wire is connected to the sensing probe in the water separating fuel filter. If water submerges the sensing element, the tan wire shorts to ground. After a 5-10 second delay, the LED illuminates and the signal is sent to the oil injection warning module or ignition control module to sound the warning horn.

Refer to the end of the manual for wiring diagrams. To test the water sensor and module, refer to **Figure 65** and proceed as follows.

1. Disconnect the tan wire from the water sensor (B, **Figure 65**) at the base of the water separating fuel filter.

2. Turn the ignition switch to the ON position.

3. Connect the tan wire to a good engine ground.

4. After approximately 10 seconds, the LED on the water sensor module (C, **Figure 65**) should illuminate and the warning horn should sound. If the LED illuminates, but the warning horn does not sound, verify the continuity of the light blue wire to the oil injection warning module. Repair or replace the light blue wire as necessary. If the light blue wire has continuity to the oil injection warning module, test the oil injection warning module as described in Chapter Thirteen.

5. If the LED does not illuminate, test the power and ground to the water sensor module. If the water sensor module is receiving power and is grounded, but the LED does not illuminate when the tan wire is connected to ground for approximately 10 seconds, replace the water sensor module.

System Description (225-250 hp EFI Models)

The 225-250 hp EFI fuel system depends on the mechanical fuel pump to provide fuel to the vapor separator and on the ignition ECM to provide a reference tachometer signal to the fuel ECM.

Since the fuel and ignition ECMs are electrically connected and share many of the same sensors, refer to *Capacitor Discharge Module Ignition (225 and 250 hp)* in this chapter for an operational explanation and troubleshooting procedures on this ignition system.

The major components of the EFI fuel system include:

1. *Fuel ECM*—The fuel ECM (**Figure 75**) monitors engine coolant temperature, throttle plate position, intake air temperature, manifold absolute pressure, barometric pressure and engine speed data based on signals from the various sensors and the ignition ECM. The fuel ECM processes this information and determines the pulse width and injector timing necessary for optimum performance during all engine operating conditions. The fuel ECM is mounted at the rear of the engine, below the ignition ECM as shown in **Figure 75**. The fuel ECM incorporates a

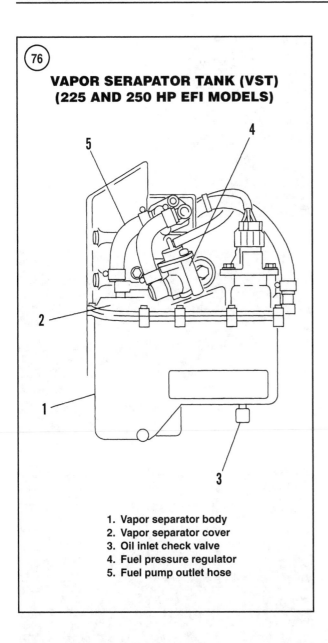

**VAPOR SERAPATOR TANK (VST)
(225 AND 250 HP EFI MODELS)**

1. Vapor separator body
2. Vapor separator cover
3. Oil inlet check valve
4. Fuel pressure regulator
5. Fuel pump outlet hose

the float sticks in the down position, fuel overflows the vapor separator resulting in an excessively rich mixture. The electric fuel pump within the tank delivers fuel under pressure to the fuel rail. Any unused fuel returns to the vapor separator. When the ignition switch is in the ON position with the engine not running, the fuel ECM activates the pump for approximately 30 seconds to pressurize the fuel system. The fuel ECM has an internal fuel pump driver circuit that controls the pump. Battery voltage is always present at the pump positive terminal. The fuel ECM internally grounds the red/purple wire to activate the pump. The pump operates at variable speeds, controlled by the fuel ECM. The pump generally runs at full speed above 2000 rpm. There is an internal final fuel filter mounted at the bottom of the fuel pump to prevent contamination from entering the fuel rail.

3. *Fuel pressure regulator*—The electric fuel pump is capable of developing approximately 90 psi (621 kPa) fuel pressure. The fuel pressure regulator (4, **Figure 76**) mounts on top of the vapor separator and regulates the pressure to the fuel injectors to approximately 36 psi (248 kPa). A hose connects the regulator to the induction manifold assembly. Fuel pressure varies as the manifold vacuum changes. Complete pressure specifications are in **Table 12**. If the fuel pressure is too low, the engine runs lean. If the fuel pressure is too high, the engine runs rich.

4. *Fuel filter and water sensor*—The water separating filter (A, **Figure 65**) helps prevent water contamination from damaging the fuel injection components. The water separating filter assembly is equipped with a sensor (B, **Figure 65**) that activates a warning light and horn at the control station if the water level in the filter canister reaches the level of the sensor probe.

5. *Induction manifold assembly*—There are two different induction manifold assemblies. The 225 hp uses two throttle valves mounted on one throttle shaft. The 250 hp induction manifold uses four throttle valves mounted on two throttle shafts. Some later 2001 225 hp models use the same four throttle valve manifold that is used on 250 hp models. The manifold assembly contains the fuel rail, fuel injectors, throttle position sensor and intake air temperature sensor. The fuel injectors connect to the fuel rail and are located inside the induction manifold assembly. Each injector consists of an electric solenoid that actuates a pintle valve assembly. The fuel ECM determines when to activate the injectors in pairs by referencing the primary ignition circuits. A four-wire harness connects the fuel ECM to the injectors. The red wire provides battery voltage to the injectors. The fuel ECM actuates the injectors by grounding either the white (cylinders No. 1 and No. 2), blue (cylinders No. 3 and No. 4) or yellow (cylinders No.

warning program for low-oil tank level and water-in-fuel situations. The fuel ECM sounds the warning horn and illuminates the appropriate warning panel light if the oil tank level becomes too low or the water separating fuel filter accumulates too much water.

2. *Vapor separator, final filter and high pressure fuel pump*—The vapor separator tank (**Figure 76**) is mounted on the induction manifold and serves as a reservoir where fuel from the diaphragm fuel pump and oil from the oil pump are blended and circulated. The bleed system does not return unused fuel to the vapor seperator. The fuel level in the vapor separator is regulated by a float and needle, and seat valve assembly. If the float sticks in the up position, fuel flow into the vapor separator is restricted. If

5 and No. 6) wires. Refer to Chapter Six for diagrams and repair instructions for the induction manifold assembly.

6. *Sensor input*—The fuel ECM relies on sensor input from the throttle position, manifold absolute pressure, engine coolant temperature, intake air temperature and the ignition ECM to provide detailed information about the engine operating conditions. Refer to *Capacitor Discharge Module Ignition System (225-250 hp)* in this chapter for more information about the ignition ECM and ignition sensors.

a. *Throttle position sensor (TPS)*—The throttle position sensor (**Figure 77**) is a variable resistor that provides throttle position information to the fuel and ignition ECMs. The TPS mounts to the side of the induction manifold and is engaged with the lower throttle valve shaft. The sensor inputs throttle position information to the ECM as a voltage signal and has a direct effect on the air/fuel ratio and ignition timing at lower engine speeds. The TPS adjustment is a critical engine adjustment.

b. *Manifold absolute pressure (MAP)*—The MAP sensor detects changes in manifold pressure and is connected to the intake manifold by a vacuum hose. The sensor (**Figure 78**) mounts on top of the vapor separator. The fuel ECM uses manifold pressure information from the MAP sensor to compensate for engine load conditions and changes in barometric pressure (altitude). When the fuel ECM is first turned on, a barometric pressure reading is taken before the engine starts.

c. *Engine coolant temperature (ECT)*—The ECT sensor provides the fuel and ignition ECMs with engine temperature information. The fuel ECM uses this information to calculate the correct air/fuel enrichment during cold starts and engine warm up. The fuel ECM stops the enrichment process when the engine temperature reaches 110° F (43° C). The sensor is located directly below the No. 1 top, starboard spark plug. The sensor must have a clean, positive contact with the cylinder head or an overly-rich air/fuel mixture can occur.

d. *Intake air temperature sensor (IAT)*—The IAT sensor (**Figure 79**) provides air temperature information to the ECM. As air temperature increases, the sensor resistance decreases, causing the ECM to lean the air/fuel mixture.

7. *Bleed system*—At idle speed, some of the fuel discharged by the fuel injectors pools in the crankcase. The bleed system collects the unburned fuel and returns it to a different cylinder's intake system for recirculation. Unlike the system used on 150-200 EFI models. This system does not return fuel to the vapor separator. Refer to Chapter Six for bleed system troubleshooting and hose routing information.

8. *Warning panel*—A multifunction warning panel is recommended. The warning panel (**Figure 80**) has three lights that allow easy identification of low oil tank level, engine overheat, engine over-speed, sensor malfunction or water-in-fuel situations.

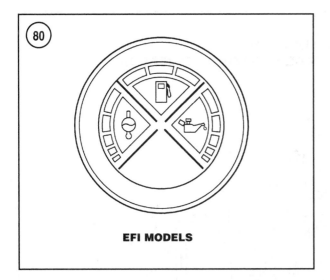

EFI MODELS

Troubleshooting (225 hp and 250 hp EFI Models)

Verify all synchronization and linkage adjustments (Chapter Five), and correct any ignition system problems *before* beginning EFI fuel system troubleshooting.

The following general EFI troubleshooting procedure requires a multimeter, jumper wires and a fuel pressure gauge.

The system is designed so it can be diagnosed with the Quicksilver Digital Diagnostic Terminal (DDT) or the EFI tester (**Figure 81**). These systems display sensor inputs and actuator outputs at the ECM.

Troubleshooting without the DDT or EFI tester limits the components that can be tested. However, a significant amount of information can be obtained regarding system operation with basic resistance and voltage testing. If the following procedures do not isolate the failed system(s), have a Mercury/Mariner dealership diagnosis the system.

Read *Troubleshooting Notes and Precautions (All Models)* and *Safety Precautions* before continuing. Refer to **Figure 82** for a fuel flow diagram.

The recommended general EFI fuel system troubleshooting procedure is listed below.

1. Preliminary checks.
2. Fuel ECM power and ground test.
3. Fuel management test.
4. Injector and injector harness test.
5. Injector cylinder drop test.
6. Throttle position sensor test.
7. Manifold absolute pressure sensor test.
8. Engine coolant temperature sensor test.
9. Intake air temperature sensor test.
10. Water sensor test.

Preliminary checks

Perform a thorough visual inspection. Check all electrical connections for corrosion, mechanical damage, heat damage and loose connections. Clean and repair all connections as necessary. Make all wire splices or connector repairs with waterproof marine grade connectors and heat shrink tubing. An electrical hardware repair kit and crimping pliers (part No. 86-813937A 1 and 91-808696) are available from Quicksilver to repair the serviceable connectors and make wire splices on the engine. The Quicksilver dealer catalog also lists heat shrink connectors and heat shrink tubing for making other waterproof connections and repairs. Marine and industrial suppliers are other good sources for quality electrical repair equipment.

> *NOTE*
> *Any electrical connection or repair that does not have perfect continuity affects the signal being sent to or from the ECM, throwing the system out of calibration. This has a detrimental effect on engine operating quality and performance.*

1. Check both cable connections at the battery and engine. Clean, tighten and repair the connections and terminals as necessary. Loose connections may cause erratic and intermittent symptoms. If the cranking speed is slower than normal, perform the *Voltage drop tests* in the starting system troubleshooting section. The engine must crank at normal speed in order to start.

2. Check the mechanical integrity of the power head by performing the cranking compression test in Chapter Four. Correct mechanical problems before proceeding.

3

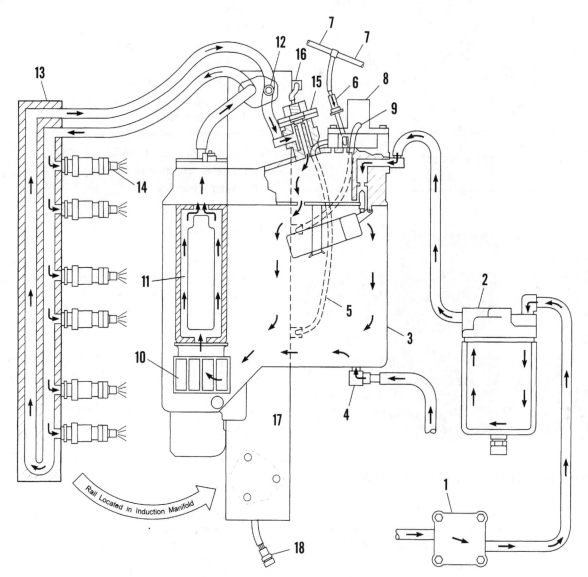

82

EFI FUEL FLOW DIAGRAM
(225 HP AND 250 HP MODELS [EXCEPT OPTIMAX MODELS])

Rail Located in Induction Manifold

1. Mechanical fuel pump
2. Water separating fuel filter
3. Vapor separator assembly
4. Oil inlet (check valve)
5. Vent to induction manifold
6. Bleed system filter
7. Input from bleed system
8. Manifold absolute pressure sensor (MAP)
9. Map vacuum hose

10. Final fuel filter
11. High pressure electric fuel pump
12. Test point
13. Fuel rail assembly
14. Fuel injectors
15. Fuel pressure regulator
16. Manifold vacuum hose
17. Induction manifold assembly
18. Injector wiring harness

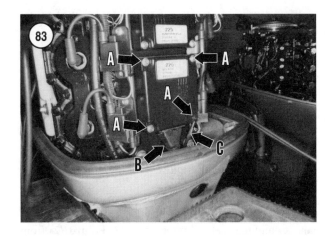

3. Inspect the spark plugs for fouling, correct air gap and correct application. Replace suspect spark plugs with the plugs recommended in Chapter Four.

4. Perform an air gap spark test to make sure the ignition system is operating correctly. Refer to *Preliminary checks* under *Capacitor Discharge Module Ignition (225-250 hp)* in this chapter. Correct ignition system problems before attempting to troubleshoot the EFI fuel system.

Fuel ECM power and ground tests

The fuel ECM must receive power and have good ground continuity in order to function correctly. If the fuel ECM is disconnected and the ignition ECM is functioning, the warning horn sounds intermittently and the low oil level and overheat lights on the warning panel alternately flash.

> *CAUTION*
> *When measuring voltage or resistance at the ECM connectors, be careful not to damage the connector pins or sockets. Do not attempt to insert the meter probe into the socket. Simply touch and hold the meter probe against the pin or socket.*

1. To test the fuel ECM ground circuits, disconnect the main fuel ECM engine wiring harness connector (B, **Figure 83**) from the fuel ECM.

2. Calibrate an ohmmeter to the R × 1 scale. Connect one ohmmeter lead to a good engine ground. Connect the other ohmmeter lead alternately to pin No. 1 (black/white) and pin No. 17 (black/white) of the engine wiring harness fuel ECM connector. If the meter indicates no continuity, there is a high resistance or open circuit in the black/white wires between pins No. 1 and No. 17 of the engine wiring harness fuel ECM connector and engine ground. Repair or replace the black/white wires as necessary.

3. Connect one ohmmeter lead calibrated to the R × 1 scale to a good engine ground. Connect the other ohmmeter lead alternately to pin No. 6 (black) and pin No. 21 (black) of the engine wiring harness fuel ECM connector. If the meter indicates no continuity, there is a high resistance or open circuit in the black wires between pins No. 6 and No. 21 of the engine wiring harness fuel ECM connector and engine ground. Repair or replace the black wires as necessary.

4. Inspect any other ground wires coming from the fuel ECM and fuel ECM mounting brackets that are directly connected to ground (C, **Figure 83**). Clean, tighten or repair all connections and fasteners as necessary to ensure a good ground. Make sure all ECM mounting hardware (A and C, **Figure 83**) is tightened securely.

5. To test the fuel ECM power circuits, set a multimeter to the 20-volt DC scale. Connect the negative meter lead to a good engine ground. Connect the positive meter lead to pin No. 4 (purple) of the engine wiring harness fuel ECM connector (B, **Figure 83**). The meter should indicate within 1.0 volt of battery voltage.

6. If the meter reads less than 1.0 volt of battery voltage, there is an open circuit or high resistance in the purple wire from (and including) the ignition switch, remote control wiring harness, main engine harness connector, main engine wiring harness, engine mounted terminal block and the fuel ECM connector. Isolate, repair or replace the purple wire or electrical components as necessary.

7. Refasten all connectors.

Fuel management test

> *NOTE*
> *The fuel pressure at the high-pressure test point must be within specification at all engine speeds. If the malfunction only occurs at a certain engine speed, perform the test at the speed the symptom occurs.*

> *CAUTION*
> *Do not run the engine without an adequate water supply and do not exceed 3000 rpm without an adequate load. Refer to **Safety Precautions** at the beginning of this chapter.*

> *NOTE*
> *If the engine is not cranked or started, the ECM will turn the fuel pump off after 30 seconds.*

1. Connect the fuel pressure test gauge (part No. 91-16850A-1) to the test port (C, **Figure 64**) at the top of

the vapor separator tank, near the fuel pressure regulator. Make sure the gauge connections are secure.

2. Squeeze the primer bulb to ensure the fuel system is primed.

NOTE
If the engine is not cranked or started, the ECM will turn the fuel pump off after 30 seconds.

3. Turn the ignition switch to the ON position and observe the fuel pressure gauge. Fuel pressure should be 34-36 psi (234.4-248.2 kPa).

4. If the pressure is above specification, replace the fuel pressure regulator and retest.

5. If the fuel pressure is below specification, determine if the electric fuel pump is running. Turn the ignition switch to the ON position while listening for pump operation. The pump should operate for approximately 30 seconds, then shut off. If necessary, use a mechanic's stethoscope to hear the pump. If the electric fuel pump does not operate, proceed to Step 12. If the electric fuel pump operates correctly, proceed to Step 6.

6. To make sure the electric fuel pump and vapor separator are receiving fuel, place a suitable container under the vapor separator drain plug (**Figure 70**). Remove the plug. Fuel should flow freely from the vapor separator (**Figure 71**). If fuel flows, proceed with Step 8. If not, check the engine mounted water separating fuel filter for water, debris or blockage. Check the fuel lines and fittings from the mechanical fuel pump to the vapor separator including the vapor separator float and valve assembly for deterioration, debris or blockage. Clean, repair or replace components as necessary. If no defects are noted, proceed with Step 7.

7. Test the mechanical fuel pump and fuel system for pressure and vacuum as described previously in this chapter.

8. If the electric fuel pump runs and the vapor separator is receiving fuel, but the fuel pressure is still below specification, either the electric fuel pump or fuel pressure regulator is defective. Proceed with Step 9.

9. Remove the fuel pressure regulator from the vapor separator without disconnecting any vacuum or fuel lines. See Chapter Six. Hold the fuel pressure regulator over a suitable container. Turn the ignition switch to the ON position and note the fuel flow from the regulator.

10. If fuel flows freely from the regulator discharge port and fuel pressure is below specification, replace the fuel pressure regulator. If little or no fuel flows from the regulator discharge port, remove the vapor separator cover and inspect the final filter. Replace the final filter if it is dirty

or clogged and retest fuel pressure. If the final filter is clean, continue to Step 11.

WARNING
EFI systems operate under high pressure. Do not remove the crimped stainless steel clamps unless absolutely necessary. Do not disconnect the rubber hoses from the electric fuel pump, fuel pressure regulator and fuel management adapter unless new clamps will be installed.

11. Disconnect the electric fuel pump output hose (1, **Figure 72**) to the induction manifold fuel management adapter and the fuel rail return hose (2, **Figure 72**) from the fuel pressure regulator. Place a shop rag over the regulator hose to capture fuel that may be present in the lines. Blow into the fuel pump output line with low pressure air. Air or fuel should exit freely from the regulator hose. If the air flow is restricted, the induction manifold and fuel rail must be disassembled and cleaned. If air flows freely, replace the electric fuel pump and final filter in the vapor separator and retest fuel pressure.

12. To test the electric fuel pump for power, set a multimeter to the 20-volt DC scale. Connect the negative lead to a good engine ground and the positive lead to the electric fuel pump positive terminal. The meter should indicate within 0.5 volt of battery voltage.

13. If the reading is less than 0.5 volt of battery voltage, check the red wire from the fuel pump positive terminal to the starter solenoid battery positive terminal for continuity. If there is no continuity, repair or replace the red wire as necessary.

CAUTION
When measuring voltage or resistance at the ECM connectors, be careful not to damage the connector pins or sockets. Do not attempt to insert the meter lead into the socket. Simply touch and hold the lead against the pin or socket.

14. To test the electric fuel pump ground, disconnect the red/purple wire from the negative fuel pump terminal. Connect a suitable jumper wire to the fuel pump negative terminal and a good engine ground. If the fuel pump does not run, replace the electric fuel pump and final filter in the vapor separator and retest fuel pressure output. If the fuel pump now runs, disconnect the main fuel ECM engine wiring harness connector from the ECM and test the red/purple wire from the fuel pump negative terminal to pin No. 9 of the engine wiring harness fuel ECM connector for continuity. If there is no continuity, repair or replace the red/purple wire from the fuel pump negative

terminal to the engine wiring harness fuel ECM connector. If the red/purple wire has continuity, the ECM is defective and must be replaced.

Injector and injector harness test

The injector and injector harness test determines if the fuel injectors are receiving battery voltage and if any open circuits are present in the injector wiring harness. Use only a digital multimeter for the following tests. Refer to **Figure 73** and proceed as follows:

1. To test the battery voltage to the injectors, disconnect the injector harness four-pin connector.

2. Set a digital multimeter to the 20-volt DC scale. Connect the negative meter lead to a good engine ground. Connect the positive meter lead to pin No. 2 (red wire) of the engine harness side of the injector harness four-pin connector. The meter should indicate within 0.5 volt of battery voltage.

3. If the meter reads less than 0.5 volt of battery voltage, there is a high resistance or open circuit in the red wire from the starter solenoid battery positive terminal and pin No. 2 of the injector harness four-pin connector. Repair or replace the red wire as necessary.

4. To test the injector and injector harness resistance, set the digital ohmmeter to the 200 ohm scale.

5. Connect the positive ohmmeter lead to pin No. 2 of the injector harness side of the injector harness four-pin connector. Connect the negative ohmmeter lead alternately to each of the following pins on the injector harness side of the four-pin injector harness connector:
   a. Pin No. 4 (white wire) for cylinders No. 1 and No. 2 injectors.
   b. Pin No. 3 (blue wire) for cylinders No. 3 and No. 4 injectors.
   c. Pin No. 1 (yellow wire) for cylinders No. 5 and No. 6 injectors.

6. The reading at each connection should be 5.0-7.0 ohms. If it is not, disassemble the induction manifold, test the resistance of each injector and verify the continuity of each injector harness. If the measured resistance is 11.0-13.0 ohms at one connection, one injector or injector circuit has an open circuit.

Injector cylinder drop test

If the engine appears to be misfiring on one or more cylinders, perform a cylinder drop test to determine if each cylinder is firing normally. Before performing a cylinder drop test, make sure all previous tests have been performed with satisfactory results. Also make sure compression is acceptable and the ignition system is functioning properly.

> *CAUTION*
> *Do not run the engine without an adequate water supply and do not exceed 3000 rpm without an adequate load. Refer to **Safety Precautions** at the beginning of this chapter.*

1. Start the engine and allow it to warm to operating temperature.

2. Adjust engine speed to approximately 1000-1500 rpm in neutral.

> *WARNING*
> *High voltage is present during ignition system operation. **Never** touch ignition components, leads or test leads while cranking or running the engine.*

3. Use insulated spark plug pliers to disconnect the spark plug lead from each spark plug one at a time. Note the resulting change in engine speed.

4. The engine speed should drop approximately the same amount as each spark plug lead is individually disconnected. If a cylinder does not produce a noticeable rpm drop or the same rpm drop as the majority of the cylinders, record the suspect cylinder numbers.

5. Remove the induction manifold and fuel rail. Remove the suspect injector(s) as described in Chapter Six and inspect the injector inlet filter. If the filter is clean, replace the suspect injector. If the filter is dirty or clogged, clean or replace the filter and reassemble the induction manifold and retest the cylinder drop. If the cylinder drop is still unsatisfactory, replace the suspect injector.

Throttle position sensor test (TPS)

The correct operation and setting of the TPS is critical to achieving the correct air/fuel ratio. High TPS voltages provide a richer air/fuel ratio. Low TPS voltages provide a leaner air/fuel ratio. Only use a digital multimeter for the following test. Test harness part No. 84-825207A-1 (1, **Figure 74**) is required for this procedure.

> *NOTE*
> *Make sure the idle speed is correct before adjusting the TPS sensor. If the idle speed is changed, the TPS setting must be readjusted.*

1. Disconnect the TPS from the engine wiring harness. Connect the test harness (part No. 84-825280A-1) to the

TPS sensor and engine wiring harness. Connect the test harness red wire to the positive meter lead. Connect the test harness white wire to the negative meter lead. Set the multimeter to the 20-volt DC scale.

NOTE
If the TPS sensor cannot be correctly set or reads zero, check the continuity of the sensor wires from the TPS connector to both the ignition and fuel ECM connectors and engine ground. The blue/yellow wire goes to both the ignition and fuel ECM connector pins No. 14 and the blue/red wire goes to both the ignition and fuel ECM connector pins No. 15. The black wire goes directly to engine ground.

2. Turn the ignition switch to the ON position. Make sure the throttle plates are against the idle stop. Note the meter reading. If the meter indicates 0.9-1.0 volt DC, continue to Step 4. If the reading is not within the specification, loosen the two screws (2, **Figure 74**) securing the TPS to the induction manifold.

3. With the throttle shaft held against the idle stop screw, rotate the TPS to obtain the desired specification. While holding the TPS at the correct setting, tighten the screws securely. Recheck the voltage reading.

4. Disconnect the throttle cable and slowly move the throttle linkage to the full-throttle position while noting the meter reading. The voltage should increase smoothly to 3.55-4.05 volts DC. If the meter reading fluctuates or is erratic as the throttle is advanced, replace the TPS. If the meter reading is not within the specification at wide-open throttle, check the wide-open throttle stop for correct adjustment as described in Chapter Five.

Manifold absolute pressure (MAP) sensor tests

The MAP sensor provides engine load and barometric pressure data to the ECM. The MAP sensor mounts on top of the vapor separator. A vacuum line connects the MAP sensor to the induction manifold. The MAP sensor is best tested with the DDT. If a sensor failure is detected, the warning horn will sound and the warning panel will alternately flash the low oil level and overheat lamps.

1. Inspect the MAP sensor vacuum line to the induction manifold for secure attachment, kinks, deterioration or leakage. Replace the line as necessary.

CAUTION
*Do not run the engine without an adequate water supply and do not exceed 3000 rpm without an adequate load. Refer to **Safety***

Precautions *at the beginning of this chapter.*

2. Start the engine and let it warm to operating temperature.

3. Stop the engine and disconnect the MAP sensor line from the induction manifold.

4. Attach a hand vacuum pump to the MAP sensor line.

5. Run the engine at idle speed. Vary the vacuum applied to the MAP sensor line from zero to 10 in. Hg (34 kPa) as the engine idles. A noticeable change in engine running quality should be noticed. If there is no change in running quality, test the wiring harness leads for continuity to the ECMs and engine ground.

6. To test the MAP sensor blue/yellow wire for continuity to the ignition and fuel ECMs, disconnect the map sensor from the engine wiring harness. Disconnect the fuel and ignition ECM engine wiring harness connectors from the ECMs.

7. Calibrate an ohmmeter to the R × 1 scale. Connect one ohmmeter lead to the engine wiring harness blue/yellow wire at the MAP sensor. Connect the other ohmmeter lead alternately to the fuel and ignition ECM connector pins No. 14 (blue/yellow). If the meter indicates no continuity, there is an open circuit or high resistance in the engine wiring harness blue/yellow wire. Repair or replace the blue/yellow wire if necessary.

8. Connect one ohmmeter lead calibrated to the R × 1 scale to the engine harness white/green wire at the MAP sensor connector. Connect the other ohmmeter lead to the fuel ECM connector pin No. 7 (white/green). If the meter indicates no continuity, an open circuit or high resistance in the engine wiring harness green/white lead. Repair or replace the green/white wire as necessary.

9. Connect one ohmmeter lead calibrated to the R × 1 scale to a good engine ground. Connect the other ohmmeter lead to the engine wiring harness black wire at the MAP sensor. If the meter indicates no continuity, there is an open circuit or high resistance in the engine wiring harness black wire. Repair or replace the black wire as necessary.

Engine coolant temperature (ECT) sensor test

The ECT sensor provides the ECM with coolant temperature data. The ECT data is primarily used for the cold start and engine overheat programs. The ECT sensor has four wires. The two tan/black wires are used by the ECM to sense engine temperature. The tan/blue and black wires are the temperature switch portion of the ECT sensor and are used to sound the warning horn when the temperature of the engine exceeds the switch rating. Refer to **Table 13** for ECT sensor resistance values and to the end of the manual for wiring diagrams. To test the ECT sensor and switch, refer to **Figure 67** and proceed as follows:

1. Disconnect the ECT sensor tan/blue and two tan/black wires from the engine wiring harness.

2. Calibrate an ohmmeter to the highest scale available. Connect one meter wire to the black (ground) sensor wire and the other ohmmeter lead to the tan/blue sensor wire. If the ohmmeter indicates continuity, replace the sensor assembly.

CAUTION
*Do not run the engine without an adequate water supply and do not exceed 3000 rpm without an adequate load. Refer to **Safety Precautions** at the beginning of this chapter.*

3. Run the engine to operating temperature as described in *Engine temperature check* in this chapter. The ohmmeter should continue to indicate no continuity when the engine is at normal operating temperature. Replace the sensor assembly if continuity is noted. The only time the sensor should indicate continuity is if the engine is actually exceeding normal operating temperature.

4. Calibrate the ohmmeter on the appropriate scale to read the ECT sensor engine temperature data in **Table 13**.

NOTE
Determine the temperature of the engine accurately before testing the ECT sensor.

5. Measure the temperature of the cylinder head with a pyrometer or allow the engine to cool to ambient temperature. Connect one ohmmeter lead to each of the tan/black ECT sensor wires. Note the meter reading and compare it to the specification. If the reading is not within specification, replace the ECT sensor. If the reading is within specification, continue to Step 6.

6. Remove the sensor from the cylinder head with the ohmmeter still connected and immerse the sensing element into a container of crushed ice and water while noting the meter reading. The reading should smoothly increase as the sensing element cools. If the reading does not increase to the specification in **Table 13**, replace the ECT sensor. If the reading is within specification, continue to Step 7.

7. Calibrate an ohmmeter to the highest scale available. Connect one ohmmeter lead to the black ECT sensor wire. Connect the other ohmmeter lead alternately to each of the tan/black ECT sensor wires. If the meter indicates continuity, replace the ECT sensor.

8. Disconnect the ignition (upper) and fuel (lower) ECM engine wiring harness connectors from the ECMs. Cali-

brate an ohmmeter to the R × 1 scale. Connect one ohmmeter lead to the engine wiring harness ignition ECM connector pin No. 16 brown lead and the other ohmmeter lead to the engine wiring harness brown or tan/black bullet connector at the ECT sensor. If the meter indicates no continuity, there is an open circuit or high resistance in the engine wiring harness brown wire. Repair or replace the brown wire as necessary.

9. Connect one ohmmeter lead, still calibrated to the R × 1 scale, to the engine wiring harness fuel ECM connector pin No. 16 tan/black lead. Connect the other ohmmeter lead to the engine wiring harness brown or tan/black bullet connector at the ECT sensor. If the meter indicates no continuity, there is an open circuit or high resistance in the engine wiring harness tan/black wire. Repair or replace the tan/black lead as necessary.

10. Connect one ohmmeter lead calibrated to the R × 1 scale to a good engine ground. Connect the other ohmmeter lead to the engine wiring harness black bullet connector at the ECT sensor. If the meter indicates no continuity, there is an open circuit or high resistance in the engine wiring harness black wire. Repair or replace the black wire as necessary.

Intake temperature (IAT) sensor test

The IAT sensor provides the ECM with ambient temperature information. Cold air is denser and contains more oxygen, and requires a richer fuel delivery. Warm air is less dense and contains less oxygen, and requires a leaner fuel delivery. The ECM can adjust the normal air/fuel ratio richer or leaner as IAT sensor data dictates. IAT sensor failure will generally cause a running quality problem, but it will normally not cause a no-start condition. There are two brown wires coming from the IAT sensor. One wire is connected to engine ground and the other is connected to the fuel ECM connector pin No. 22. Refer to the end of the manual for wiring diagrams and **Table 14** for IAT sensor resistance values. To test the IAT sensor, refer to **Figure 79** and proceed as follows:

1. Disconnect the IAT sensor brown wires from the engine wiring harness.

2. Calibrate the ohmmeter to the appropriate scale to read the appropriate IAT sensor temperature value in **Table 14**.

NOTE
Determine the ambient temperature accurately before testing the IAT sensor.

3. Allow the engine to cool to ambient temperature. Connect one ohmmeter lead to each of the brown IAT sensor wires. Note the meter reading and compare it to the speci-

fications. If the reading is not within specification, replace the IAT sensor. If the reading is within specification, continue to Step 6.

4. Remove the sensor from the induction manifold with the ohmmeter still connected and immerse the sensing element into a container of crushed ice and water while noting the meter reading. The reading should smoothly increase as the sensing element cools. If the reading does not increase, replace the IAT sensor. If the reading is within specification for the given temperature, continue to Step 7.

5. Disconnect the fuel ECM engine wiring harness connector from the fuel ECM. Calibrate an ohmmeter to the R × 1 scale. Connect one ohmmeter lead to the engine wiring harness fuel ECM connector pin No. 22 tan wire and connect the other ohmmeter lead to the engine wiring harness tan wire bullet connector at the IAT sensor. If the meter indicates no continuity, there is an open circuit or high resistance in the engine wiring harness brown wire. Repair or replace the tan wire as necessary.

6. Connect one ohmmeter lead calibrated to the R × 1 scale to a good engine ground. Connect the other ohmmeter lead to the engine wiring harness black bullet connector at the IAT sensor. If the meter indicates no continuity, there is an open circuit or high resistance in the engine wiring harness black wire. Repair or replace the black wire as necessary.

Water sensor test

The water sensor alerts the boat operator to a buildup of water in the engine mounted water separating fuel filter. When the water level in the filter reaches potentially damaging levels, the fuel ECM turns on the water-in-fuel light on the warning panel and activates the warning horn. The warning horn sounds four times, then is silent for two minutes. After two minutes, the cycle will repeat.

1. Disconnect the tan/blue wire from the water sensor at the base of the water separating fuel filter (B, **Figure 65**, typical).

2. Turn the ignition switch to the ON position.

3. Connect the tan/blue wire to a good engine ground.

4. The water-in-fuel light on the warning panel should illuminate and the warning horn should sound as described. If the lamp does not illuminate and the horn does not sound, check the tan/blue wire for continuity to the fuel ECM connector pin No. 12. Repair or replace the wire as necessary.

OPTIMAX 115-225 HP AIR/FUEL SYSTEM TROUBLESHOOTING

Troubleshooting Notes and Precautions

Strictly observe the following troubleshooting precautions to avoid damaging the system or injuring yourself.

1. Do not reverse the battery connections. Reverse battery polarity damages electronic components.

2. Do not spark the battery terminals with the battery cable connections to determine polarity.

3. Do not disconnect the battery cables with the engine running.

> *NOTE*
> *Optimax models (direct fuel injection) cannot be started or operated without battery voltage.*

4. Do not crank or run the outboard if any electrical components are not grounded to the power head.

5. Do not disconnect the ECM while the outboard is running, while the ignition switch is on or while the battery cables are connected.

6. The Optimax direct injection air/fuel system requires that the electric starter crank the engine at normal speed for the ignition system to produce adequate spark and the

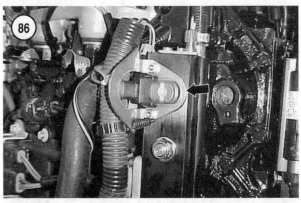

8. Check ECM and other component ground wires for secure attachment to the power head. Clean and tighten all ground connections and fasteners as necessary. Loose ground connections and loose component mounting hardware can cause many different symptoms.

Resistance (Ohm) Tests

The resistance values in the following test procedures are based on tests performed at room temperature. Actual resistance readings obtained during testing will generally be slightly higher if checked on hot components. Also, resistance readings may vary depending on the manufacturer of the ohmmeter. Many ohmmeters have difficulty reading less than 1 ohm accurately. If this is the case, specifications of less than 1 ohm generally appear as a very low (continuity) reading.

Due to these variables, use caution when considering the replacement of an electrical component that tests only slightly out of specification.

System Description

In addition to the normal EFI components, an Optimax outboard uses a belt-driven, water-cooled air compressor (A, **Figure 84**) with a port air/fuel rail (B, **Figure 84**) and a starboard air/fuel rail (A, **Figure 85**), a fuel pressure regulator (C, **Figure 84**), six direct injectors (C, **Figure 85**), a tracker diaphragm (B, **Figure 85**) in the starboard air/fuel rail and the necessary hoses, and high pressure lines and fittings.

The air compressor and air pressure regulator (D, **Figure 84**) maintain air pressure in the air portion of the air/fuel rails at approximately 80 psi (552 kPa). The fuel regulator maintains fuel pressure at 10 psi (69 kPa) over air pressure. If this 10 psi (69 kPa) difference is not maintained, the ECM calibrations will be incorrect. Fuel rail and fuel injector working pressure is approximately 90 psi (629 kPa). The fuel injectors (**Figure 86**) discharge into the passages in the fuel/air rail leading into the direct injectors which are pressurized at 80 psi (552 kPa). The direct injectors then fire this air/fuel mix directly into the combustion chamber at the precise time calculated by the ECM.

The tracker diaphragm dampens pressure fluctuations between the air and fuel passages. The diaphragm is positioned between the air and fuel passages, and flexes inward or outward depending on which chamber has the highest pressure at the moment.

NOTE
To help the motor start quickly, the ECM opens the direct injectors briefly during the

air system to produce adequate air rail pressure. If the starter motor cranks the engine slowly or not at all, refer to the *Starting System* section in this chapter and correct the starting system problem before continuing.

7. Check the battery cable connections for secure attachment to both battery terminals and the engine. Clean corrosion from all connections. Discard wing nuts and install corrosion resistant hex nuts at all battery cable connections. Place a corrosion resistant locking washer between the battery terminal stud and battery cable terminal end to ensure a positive connection. Loose battery connections can cause many different symptoms.

first moments of cranking. This allows combustion chamber compression to help charge the air rail faster than the air compressor would be able to.

The system injects the air/fuel charge into the combustion chamber after the intake and exhaust ports have closed, preventing leaking or dilution of the air/fuel charge with exhaust gases. The direct fuel injection system increases fuel economy and reduces exhaust emissions.

Optimax models depend on the following sensors and fuel system components for operation:

1. *Throttle position sensors (TPS)*—The throttle position sensor(s) (**Figure 87**) provides a varying voltage signal to the ECM indicating the exact amount of throttle plate opening.

   a. 1998-1999 models use two throttle position sensors. One sensor reads from low voltage to high voltage, and the other sensor reads from high voltage to low voltage. If one sensor fails, the check engine light illuminates and the warning horn will sound. If both sensors fail, the engine will not operate above idle speed. The sensors are mounted back-to-back and read throttle movement from a linkage connection to the throttle body. If a single sensor voltage output exceeds the preprogrammed limits, the ECM limits engine speed to a maximum of 3000 rpm. If both sensors exceed the limits, the ECM limits the engine to idle speed.

   b. 2000-on models use a single throttle position sensor. The sensor reads its highest voltage (4-4.7 volt DC) at idle position and its lowest voltage (0.4-1.3 volt DC) at wide-open throttle. If the sensor output voltage exceeds the preprogrammed limits, the ECM sounds the warning horn and illuminates the check engine light. The ECM then limits engine speed to a maximum of 4500 rpm.

2. *Crankshaft position sensor (CPS)*—The CPS (A, **Figure 88**) detects the presence of the encoding ribs (B) on the flywheel and sends a signal to the ECM. This signal tells the ECM crankshaft position and engine speed. 1998-2000 models have 24 encoding ribs, and 2001-on models have 54 ribs on the flywheel. The air gap between the flywheel encoding ribs and the CPS must be set correctly for proper engine operation. If the CPS fails, the engine will not run.

3. *Engine coolant temperature sensor (ECT)*—The ECT sensor provides the ECM with coolant temperature data. The ECM adjusts the fuel injector pulse width to compensate for different engine temperatures, such as cold starts. 1998-2000 models have a single engine coolant tempera-

ture sensor (**Figure 89**) mounted on the port cylinder head. The sensor is very similar to the component used on EFI models. 2001-on models have a engine coolant temperature sensor (**Figure 90**) on each cylinder head.

   a. On 1998-2000 models, if the ECT reads above 221° F (105° C), the ECM retards ignition timing to limit engine speed to approximately 3000 rpm. Refer to **Table 13** for ECT sensor resistance values.

   b. On 2000-on models, if the ECT reads above 221° F (105°C), the ECM gradually retards ignition timing to limit the engine speed. The limit depends on the

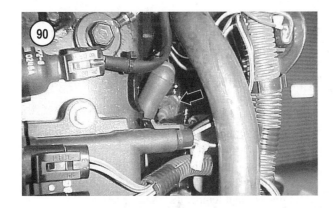

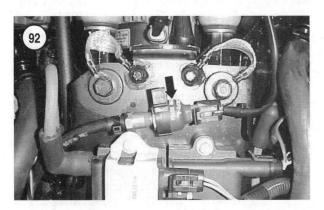

a. On 1998-2000 models, if the ECT reads above 221° F (105° C), the ECM retards ignition timing to limit engine speed to approximately 3000 rpm.

b. On 2001-on models, if the ECT reads above 221° F (105°C), the ECM gradually retards ignition timing to limit the engine speed. The limit depends on the engine temperature. The higher the temperature, the lower the limited speed.

5. *Manifold absolute pressure sensor (MAP)*—The output voltage from the MAP (**Figure 91**) indicates engine load to the ECM. This allows for subtle adjustments to the spark advance and air/fuel mixture as engine load changes, maintaining maximum combustion efficiency and minimum exhaust emissions.

6. *Intake air temperature sensor (IAT)*—The IAT sensor allows compensation for air temperature fluctuations. As air temperature changes, the density of the air changes, requiring subtle changes to the air/fuel ratio to maintain maximum combustion efficiency and minimum exhaust emissions.

7. *Water pressure sensor*—The water pressure sensor (**Figure 92**) is used on 2000-on Optimax models. Output from the sensor allows the ECM to determine and compensate for low cooling system pressure even before the engine overheats. If the water pressure drops below engine speed controlled limits for more than two seconds, the ECM sounds the warning horn and flashes the warning lights. If the pressure drops below the limit for more than five seconds, the ECM sounds the warning horn, flashes the warning lights and retards the timing to limit power output. Power is gradually reduced to idle speed if low water pressure persist. The pressure must be restored to normal readings and the throttle brought down to idle before the ECM allows full power output.

8. *Vapor separator tank (VST)*—The vapor separator tank (A, **Figure 93**) mounts onto the induction manifold and serves as a reservoir where fuel from the diaphragm fuel pump is supplied to the internal high pressure electric

engine temperature. The higher the temperature, the lower the limited speed.

4. *Air compressor temperature sensor*—The air compressor temperature sensor provides the ECM with the temperature of the cooling water for the air compressor. The ECM uses this input to determine if the compressor is overheating and determines the need for power reduction.

fuel pump. The low pressure electric fuel pump (B, **Figure 93**) moves fuel from the float chamber to a cavity just below the high pressure pump. The electric fuel pump within the vapor separator tank delivers fuel under pressure to the fuel rail. Unused fuel is cooled and returned to the vapor separator tank. The fuel level in the vapor separator is regulated by a float and needle, and seat valve assembly. If the float sticks in the up position, fuel flow into the vapor separator is restricted. If the float sticks in the down position, fuel overflows the vapor separator resulting in an excessively rich mixture. The vapor separator also serves as the mounting location for the water separating fuel filter (C, **Figure 93**).

The Optimax air/fuel system is integrated with the digital inductive (DI) ignition. Refer to the *Digital Inductive (DI [200 DFI])* section of this chapter for system description and components. If the ignition system is working correctly, the CPS is probably functional.

Troubleshooting

Verify all synchronization and linkage adjustments (Chapter Five), and correct any ignition system problems *before* beginning EFI fuel system troubleshooting.

The following general EFI troubleshooting procedure requires a multimeter, jumper wires and a fuel pressure gauge.

The system is designed so it can be diagnosed with the Quicksilver Digital Diagnostic Terminal (DDT) (**Figure 81**). These systems display sensor inputs and actuator outputs at the ECM.

Troubleshooting without the DDT tester limits the components that can be tested. However, a significant amount of information can be obtained regarding system operation with basic resistance and voltage testing. If the following procedures do not isolate the failed system(s), have a Mercury/Mariner dealership diagnosis the system.

Read *Troubleshooting Notes and Precautions (All Models)* and *Safety Precautions* before continuing.

Refer to **Figure 94**, typical, for air/fuel components and flow diagrams. Refer to the end of the manual for wiring diagrams.

Sensors and injectors can be disconnected and reconnected during engine operation without ECM damage. A noticeable change in engine performance will occur if the sensor or injector is functioning. If substitute direct and fuel injectors are available, plug them into each wiring harness connector to verify circuit operation while the engine is being cranked or run. The injectors audibly click when operating. A mechanic's stethoscope can also be used to listen for injector operation. If necessary, disconnect the other direct and fuel injectors in close proximity

to reduce background noise. Automotive Noid Lites or injector test lights with compatible connectors may also be used to check injector circuit operation. The recommended troubleshooting procedure is as follows:

1. Perform all of the ignition system checks in *Digital inductive (DI) ignition.*
2. Preliminary checks.
3. Fuel rail pressure test.
4. Air rail pressure test.
5. Fuel injector test.
6. Direct injector test.
7. Engine coolant temperature sensor test.
8. Air temperature sensor test.
9. Air compressor temperature sensor test.

> *CAUTION*
> *Do not run the engine without an adequate water supply and do not exceed 3000 rpm without an adequate load. Refer to **Safety Precautions** at the beginning of this chapter.*

Preliminary checks

Perform a thorough visual inspection of the engine. Check all electrical connections for corrosion, mechanical damage, heat damage and loose connections. Clean and repair all connections as necessary. Make all wire splices or connector repairs with waterproof marine grade connectors and heat shrink tubing. An electrical hardware repair kit and crimping pliers (part No. 86-813937A-1 and 91-808696) are available from Quicksilver to repair the serviceable connectors and make wire splices on the engine. The Quicksilver dealer catalog also lists heat shrink connectors and heat shrink tubing for making other waterproof connections and repairs. Marine and industrial suppliers are other good sources for quality electrical repair equipment.

> *NOTE*
> *An electrical connection or repair that does not have perfect continuity affects the signal being sent to or from the ECM, throwing the system out of calibration. This has a detrimental effect on engine performance.*

1. Inspect the battery. Make sure the battery rating is at least 750 cold cranking amps (CCA) or 1000 marine cranking amps (MCA). A smaller battery will not provide consistent starts.
2. Check both battery cable connections at the battery and engine. Clean, tighten and repair the connections and terminals as necessary. Loose connections cause erratic

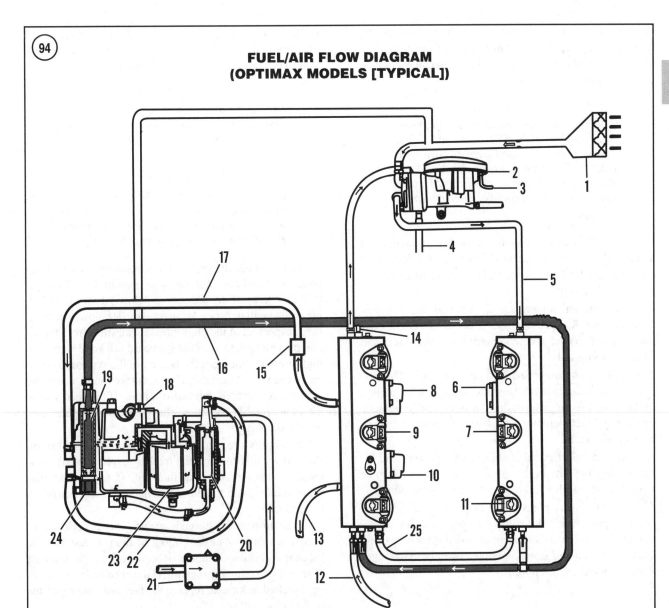

**FUEL/AIR FLOW DIAGRAM
(OPTIMAX MODELS [TYPICAL])**

3

1. Air filter (mounted in flywheel cover)
2. Air compressor oil inlet fitting
3. Excess oil outlet to intake plenum
4. Cooling water outlet to power head
   mounting adapter
5. Compressor air outlet hose
6. Tracker diaphragm
7. Starboard fuel/air rail
8. Fuel pressure regulator
9. Port fuel/air rail
10. Air pressure regulator
11. Fuel injector
12. Cooling water inlet from power head
    mounting adapter
13. Air outlet to drive shaft housing
    or intake plenum

14. Pressure test port
15. Check valve
16. High pressure fuel hose to air/fuel rails
17. Fuel return hose to
    vapor separator tank
18. Vent hose fitting (to air filter housing)
19. High pressure electric fuel pump
20. Low pressure electric fuel pump
21. Mechanical fuel pump
22. Low pressure pump outlet to
    high pressure pump inlet
23. Water separating fuel filter
24. Final fuel filter
25. Air line (port to starboard rail)

and intermittent symptoms. If the cranking rpm is slower than normal, perform the *Voltage drop tests* in the starting system troubleshooting section. The engine must crank at normal speed in order to start.

NOTE
If the recommended troubleshooting proce-dure is followed, the ECM and ignition coil and oil pump fuses and circuits have been tested in the DI ignition system section. If so, test only the remaining electric fuel pump and remote control harness fuses in the next section.

3. Refer to the wiring diagrams at the end of the manual and test all power head mounted fuses. Test the fuses with an ohmmeter set to the R × 1 scale. Replace fuses that do not read continuity.

4. Check the air compressor air filter as described in Chapter Four. Replace the filter if debris is visible, or if the filter is damaged or deteriorated. The white side of the filter must face out.

5. Check the air compressor and alternator belt. The belt is tensioned automatically by the floating idle pulley. Make sure the air compressor turns normally without binding and the alternator turns freely. Replace any damaged components.

6. Check the mechanical integrity of the power head by performing the cranking compression test in Chapter Four. Correct mechanical problems before proceeding.

7. Inspect the spark plugs for fouling, correct air gap and correct application. Only use the recommended spark plugs (Chapter Four). Non-recommended spark plugs will cause erratic operation and possible power head damage. Replace suspect spark plugs.

Air rail pressure test

WARNING
Optimax models use a high-pressure air sys-tem to inject the air/fuel charge into the combustion chamber. Do not attempt to check the air rail pressure unless a liquid filled gauge assembly capable of reading a minimum of 160 psi (1103 kPa) is used. Quicksilver test gauge part No. 91-852087A23 meets these requirements.

NOTE
The location of the fuel and air pressure test ports vary by model and year of production. Refer to the diagrams and information in Chapter Six to locate the test ports.

1. Remove the caps, then connect the test gauge to the test ports at the top (**Figure 95**) or sides of the air/fuel rail. Make sure the gauge connections are secure.

NOTE
Record the air pressure for later reference. The fuel pressure test results in the next sec-tion are dependent on the air pressure in the system.

CAUTION
*Do not run the engine without an adequate water supply and do not exceed 3000 rpm without an adequate load. Refer to **Safety Precautions** at the beginning of this chapter.*

2. Run or crank the engine for several seconds until air pressure stabilizes. Air pressure should be 77-81 psi (531-558 kPa). If the pressure is below 70 psi (483 kPa), the engine will not start. If the pressure is below specifica-tion, inspect all of the high- pressure air lines from the air compressor to the top of the starboard rail and inspect the high-pressure line from the bottom of the starboard rail to the bottom of the port rail. If no leaks are found, check the air compressor reed valves for failure. If the reed valves are in acceptable condition, the air pressure regulator or tracker diaphragm is faulty.

The air pressure regulator (10, **Figure 94**) is located on the port air/fuel rail and the tracker diaphragm (6) is lo-cated on the starboard air/fuel rail. If the tracker dia-phragm fails, there should be fuel in the air passages of the air/fuel rails.

3. If the air pressure exceeds specification, check the air regulator exit hose at the bottom of the port fuel rail for blockage or kinks. This hose connects to the exhaust adapter plate or intake plenum. If the hose and fittings are not blocked or kinked, replace the fuel pressure regulator or fuel rail.

Fuel rail pressure test

WARNING
Optimax models use a much higher fuel pressure system than traditional EFI en-gines. Do not attempt to check the fuel rail pressure unless a liquid filled gauge assem-bly capable of reading a minimum of 160 psi (1103 kPa) is used. Quicksilver test gauge part No. 91-852087A23 meets these re-quirements.

1. Connect the test gauge to the test port (**Figure 95**) at the top of the fuel rail. Make sure the gauge connections are secure.

3

NOTE
*The fuel pressure regulator (8, **Figure 94**) regulates fuel pressure at 10 psi (69 kPa) over air pressure. If there is no air pressure, the fuel pressure should be 10 psi (69 kPa). Do not check fuel pressure until air pressure is verified.*

CAUTION
*Do not run the engine without an adequate water supply and do not exceed 3000 rpm without an adequate load. Refer to **Safety Precautions** at the beginning of this chapter.*

2. Run or crank the engine for several seconds until fuel pressure stabilizes. Fuel pressure should be 10 psi (69 kPa) over the air rail test previously recorded. If the air pressure was within specification, fuel pressure should be within the specification in **Table 12**. If the fuel pressure is not 10 psi (69 kPa) over air pressure, the engine is out of calibration and will run poorly or not at all.

3. If the pressure is over specification, inspect the fuel return line and fittings from the port air/fuel rail to the fuel cooler assembly (1998 and 1999 models) and inspect the vapor separator tank for obstructions and kinks. Inspect the fuel cooler fuel passageways and fittings for debris or blockage. Inspect the fuel line and fittings from the fuel cooler to the vapor separator for obstructions, kinks and blockages. If there is no restriction to the fuel flow from the port rail to the vapor separator, replace the fuel pressure regulator or port fuel rail.

NOTE
If the engine is not cranked or started, the ECM will turn the main power relay and fuel pump off after 3 seconds.

4. If the fuel pressure is below specification, determine if both electric fuel pumps are running. Turn the ignition switch to the ON position while listening for pump opera-

tion. Both pumps should operate for approximately three seconds, then shut off. A mechanic's stethoscope can be used to better hear the pumps.

  a. If both pumps are operating, proceed to Step 7.

  b. If the low pressure pump does not operate, proceed to Step 5.

  c. If the high pressure pump within the VST does not operate, proceed to Step 6.

5. Disconnect the engine wire harness connector from the low pressure pump harness. The low pressure electric fuel pump (B, **Figure 93**) is located on the port side of the power head. Calibrate an ohmmeter to the 20-volt DC scale. Refer to the wiring diagrams at the end of the manual. Test the electrical current to the pump and wiring as follows:

  a. Touch the positive meter test lead to the red/black terminal in the disconnected engine harness connector. Touch the negative meter test lead to an engine ground. Observe the meter while turning the ignition switch to the ON position. If the meter does not indicate within 1 volt of battery voltage, test the system relay as described in this chapter under *ECM Power Test*. If the relay tests correctly, there is an open or shorted circuit in the red/black wire. Repair the wire if necessary.

  b. Calibrate an ohmmeter to the R × 1 scale. Touch one of the ohmmeter leads to an engine ground. Touch the other lead to the black terminal in the disconnected engine harness connector. If the ohmmeter indicates no continuity, check for a broken wire or a grounded terminal of the black wire.

  c. If the electrical supply and related wiring test correctly, but the pump does not operate, replace the low-pressure electric fuel pump as described in Chapter Six.

6. Disconnect the engine wire harness connector from the high pressure pump harness. The high pressure electric fuel pump is located in the vapor separator tank (A, **Figure 93**). Calibrate an ohmmeter to the 20-volt DC scale. Refer to the wiring diagrams at the end of the manual. Test the electrical current to the pump and wiring as follows:

  a. Touch the positive meter test lead to the red/black terminal in the disconnected engine harness connector. Touch the negative meter test lead to an engine ground. Observe the meter while turning the ignition switch to the ON position. If the meter does not indicate within 1 volt of battery voltage, test the system relay as described in this chapter under *ECM Power Test*. If the relay tests correctly, there is an open or shorted circuit in the red/black wire. Repair the wire if necessary.

b. Calibrate an ohmmeter to the R × 1 scale. Touch one of the ohmmeter leads to an engine ground. Touch the other lead to the black terminal in the disconnected engine harness connector. If the ohmmeter indicates no continuity, repair the broken wire or faulty ground terminal for the black wire.

c. If the electrical supply and related wiring test correctly, but the pump does not operate, replace the high pressure electric fuel pump as described in Chapter Six.

7. To make sure the electric fuel pump and vapor separator are receiving fuel, place a suitable container under the vapor separator drain plug (**Figure 96**). Remove the plug. Fuel should flow freely from the vapor separator. If fuel flows, proceed with Step 7. If fuel does not flow, check the engine mounted water separating fuel filter for water, debris or blockage. Check the fuel lines and fittings from the mechanical fuel pump to the vapor separator including the vapor separator float and valve for deterioration, debris or blockage. Clean, repair or replace components as necessary. If no defects are noted, proceed with Step 6.

8. Use suitable hoses clamps and fittings to connect a common fuel pressure test gauge to the outlet fitting (top) on the low pressure electric fuel pump (20, **Figure 94**). Observe the gauge while turning the ignition key switch to the ON position. The gauge should indicate the low pressure electric fuel pump pressure in **Table 12**. If not, replace the pump as described in Chapter Six.

9. Test the mechanical fuel pump and boat fuel system for pressure and vacuum as described previously in this chapter.

10. If the electric fuel pumps operate and the vapor separator is receiving fuel, but fuel pressure is still below specifications, disconnect the air line (25, **Figure 94**) from the bottom of both air/fuel rails. If fuel is present in the air chamber of either air/fuel rail, the tracker diaphragm or fuel pressure regulator diaphragm is faulty. Replace the suspect components as described in Chapter Six and retest fuel pressure. If no fuel flows from the air chamber of either air/fuel rail, either the electric fuel pump or fuel pressure regulator valve seat is defective. Replace the high pressure fuel pump and retest fuel pressure.

Fuel injector test

> *NOTE*
> *If the engine is not cranked or started, the ECM will turn the main power relay and fuel pump off after 3 seconds. The meter reading must be noted before this time elapses.*

The fuel injectors (11, **Figure 94**) are mounted in the air/fuel rails. There is one fuel injector for each cylinder.

The fuel injectors open and close under ECM control. The fuel injectors are normally closed. The period of time that the injectors are open is the pulse width. The longer the pulse width, the more fuel that is delivered to the direct injector air chamber. The power and ground wires for each injector are individually wired back to the ECM. There are a total of 12 injector wires.

1. To test the resistance of a fuel injector, disconnect the fuel injector wiring harness plug-in. Calibrate an ohmmeter to the appropriate scale to read 1.7-1.9 ohms. Connect one ohmmeter lead to each of the fuel injector terminals. If the reading is not 1.7-1.9 ohms, the fuel injector is defective.

2. Repeat Step 1 for the remaining fuel injectors.

> *CAUTION*
> *When measuring voltage or resistance at the ECM connectors, be careful not to damage the connector pins or sockets. Do not attempt to insert the test lead into the socket. Simply touch and hold the test lead against the pin or socket.*

3. If an injector with good resistance is not firing, check the continuity of the injector power and ground wires back to the appropriate ECM connector. Refer to the end of the manual for wiring diagrams. If a wire does not indicate continuity, repair or replace the defective wire or connector.

Direct injector tests

The direct fuel injectors are mounted between the air/fuel rails and the cylinder heads (**Figure 97**). The direct injector releases the air/fuel charge into the combustion chamber from the air chamber of the air/fuel rail. There is one direct injector for each cylinder. The injectors open and close under ECM control. The injectors are normally closed. The injectors must be precisely timed in

relation to piston position and ignition timing. Any miscalculations will cause a misfire. The power and ground wires for each injector are individually wired back to the ECM. There are a total of 12 injector wires.

1. To test the resistance of the direct injectors, disconnect each injector wiring harness plug-in. Calibrate an ohmmeter to the appropriate scale to read 1.0-1.6 ohms. Connect one ohmmeter lead to each of the DFI injector terminals. If the reading is not within 1.0-1.6 ohms, the direct injector is defective.

2. Repeat Step 1 for the remaining fuel injectors.

CAUTION
When measuring voltage or resistance at the ECM connectors, be careful not to damage the connector pins or sockets. Do not attempt to insert the test lead into the socket. Simply touch and hold the test lead against the pin or socket.

3. If an injector with good resistance is not firing, check the continuity of the injector power and ground wires back to the appropriate ECM connector. Refer to the end of the manual for wiring diagrams. If a wire does not indicate

continuity, repair or replace the defective wire or connector.

Engine coolant temperature (ECT) sensor resistance test

Refer to the wiring diagrams at the end of the manual and refer to **Table 13** for this procedure.

1A. On 1998-2000 models, disconnect the two tan/black ECT sensor wires (**Figure 89**) from the wiring harness. Calibrate an ohmmeter to the appropriate scale to read the engine temperature in **Table 13**.

1B. On 2001-on models, disconnect the port and starboard cylinder head mounted ECT sensor (**Figure 90**) harness connectors from the engine wire harness.

NOTE
Determine the temperature of the engine accurately before testing the ECT sensor.

2. Measure the temperature of the cylinder head with a pyrometer or allow the engine to cool to the ambient temperature.

  a. On 1998-2000 models, connect one ohmmeter lead to each of the tan/black ECT sensor wires. Note the meter reading and compare it to the specification in **Table 13**. If the reading is not within specification, replace the ECT sensor. If the reading is within specification, continue to Step 3.

  b. On 2001-on models, connect one ohmmeter lead to the tan wire terminal and the other lead to the orange wire terminal. Note the meter reading and compare to the specification in **Table 13**. If the reading is not within specification, replace the ECT sensor. If the reading is within specification, continue to Step 3.

3. Remove the sensor from the cylinder head with the ohmmeter connected and immerse the sensing element into a glass of crushed ice and water while noting the meter reading. The reading should smoothly increase as the sensing element cools. If the reading does not increase to the specifications in **Table 13** as the sensor cools, replace the ECT sensor.

4. Calibrate an ohmmeter to the appropriate ohms scale. Connect one ohmmeter lead to the black ECT sensor wire. Connect the other ohmmeter lead alternately to each of the tan/black ECT sensor wires. If the meter indicates continuity at any lead, replace the ECT sensor.

5. Disconnect the engine harness connectors from the ECM (**Figure 98**). Refer to the wiring diagrams at the end of the manual to identify the pins for the wires connecting the ECM to the ECT.

6. Calibrate an ohmmeter to the R × 1 scale. Touch one ohmmeter lead to one of the harness terminals at the ECT end. Touch the other ohmmeter lead to the corresponding pin in the engine harness connector at the ECM end. If the meter does not indicate continuity, repair the faulty wire or terminal. Repeat this step for all wires connecting the ECT to the ECM.

7. Reconnect all ECT and ECM connectors.

Air temperature (IAT) sensor test

The IAT sensor provides a varying resistance signal to the ECM, allowing precise calibration of fuel delivery for the ambient air temperature. Refer to Chapter Six to locate the sensor on the engine.

NOTE
Determine the ambient air temperature accurately before testing the IAT sensor.

Perform this test in the shade or preferably in a building. Sunlight can heat the intake plenum to temperatures far exceeding the ambient air temperature. Keep the engine in a shaded location until the entire engine is at ambient temperature.

1. Disconnect the two leads from the air temperature sensor. Calibrate an ohmmeter to read the approximate air temperature in **Table 14**.

2. Connect the ohmmeter leads to the two air temperature sensor leads and note the meter reading. The reading should be within the specification in **Table 14** for the ambient temperature. If not, the sensor is defective and must be replaced.

3. Disconnect the engine harness connectors from the ECM (**Figure 98**). Refer to the wiring diagrams at the end of the manual to identify the pins for the wires connecting the ECM to the IAT.

4. Calibrate an ohmmeter to the R × 1 scale. Touch one ohmmeter lead to one of the harness terminals at the IAT end. Touch the other ohmmeter lead to the corresponding pin in the engine harness connector at the ECM end. If the meter does not indicate continuity, repair the faulty wire or terminal. Repeat this step for all wires connecting the IAT to the ECM.

5. Reconnect all ECM and IAT wire connectors

Air compressor temperature sensor test

Refer to the wiring diagrams at the end of the manual and refer to **Table 13** for this procedure.

1. Disconnect the two tan/black compressor temperature sensor wires from the wiring harness. Calibrate an ohm-

meter to the appropriate scale to read the engine temperature in **Table 13**.

NOTE
Determine the temperature of the air compressor head before testing the air compressor temperature sensor.

2. Measure the temperature of the air compressor head with a pyrometer or allow the engine to cool to ambient temperature. On 1998-2000 models, connect one ohmmeter lead to each of the tan/black air compressor temperature sensor leads. Note the meter reading and compare it to the specification in **Table 13**. If the reading is not within specification, replace the sensor. If the reading is within specification, continue to Step 3.

3. Remove the sensor from the compressor as described in Chapter Six with ohmmeter still connected and immerse the sensing element into a glass of crushed ice and water while noting the meter reading. The reading should smoothly increase as the sensing element cools. If the reading does not increase to the specifications in **Table 13** as the sensor cools, replace the air compressor temperature sensor.

4. Disconnect the engine harness connectors from the ECM (**Figure 98**). Refer to the wiring diagrams at the end of the manual to identify the pins for the wires connecting the ECM to the air compressor temperature sensor.

5. Calibrate an ohmmeter to the R × 1 scale. Touch one ohmmeter lead to one of the harness terminals at the temperature sensor end. Touch the other ohmmeter lead to the corresponding pin in the engine harness connector at the ECM end. If the meter does not indicate continuity, repair the faulty wire or terminal. Repeat this Step for all wires connecting the sensor to the ECM.

6. Install the sensor into the air compressor as described in Chapter Six. Reconnect all sensor and ECM connectors.

ENGINE TEMPERATURE AND OVERHEATING

Proper temperature regulation is critical to good engine operation. Internal engine damage will occur if the engine is overheated. Engines that are overcooling will have fouled spark plugs, poor acceleration and idle quality, excessive carbon buildup in the combustion chamber, and reduced fuel economy. V-6 models use one thermostat in each cylinder head. Failure of a single thermostat would only cause one cylinder bank to overheat.

The thermostat(s) controls the flow of water leaving the cylinder block. Many engines with thermostat(s) also in-

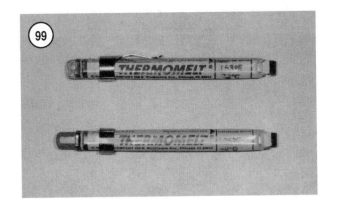

corporate a poppet or pressure relief valve. These valves may be mounted on the power head or in the power head adapter plate. These valves control the pressure in the cooling system. When water pressure exceeds the spring pressure of the valve, cooling water is bypassed out the water discharge on some models. This will have the same effect as bypassing the thermostats. On these models, thermostats control the water temperature at idle and low speeds. Once the engine speed has increased to the point that water pressure overcomes the poppet valve, the thermostats are no longer in primary control of engine temperature. Since an engine at high power settings is producing a lot of combustion chamber heat, this system helps keep the combustion chambers cool enough to prevent preignition and detonation. There is only one poppet valve on engines so equipped. Refer to the illustrations in Chapter Eight to locate the poppet valve and related components.

On all thermostat equipped engines, the thermostat always controls the minimum temperature that the engine can reach. The number stamped on the thermostat is the initial opening or *cracking* temperature. The thermostat will not reach full opening (full water flow) until 15-20° F (-9- -7°C) above the thermostat rated temperature. If the engine temperature drops at high engine speeds, but returns to thermostat controlled temperature at idle and low speeds, the system is working correctly. Engine temperature should not exceed the thermostat rated temperature by more than 20° F (-7°).

Troubleshooting

Engine temperature can be checked with thermomelt sticks. Thermomelt sticks (**Figure 99**) come in 100°, 125°, 131°, 163°, and 175° F ratings. The thermomelt sticks looks similar to a piece of chalk. When the engine is marked with the thermomelt sticks, the mark will stay dull and chalky until the temperature of the engine exceeds the rating of the stick, at which point the mark will become liquid and glossy.

The preferred and most accurate way to check engine temperature is with a pyrometer. A pyrometer is an electronic thermometer. Pyrometers come as a single instrument or as an adapter module designed to fit a standard digital multimeter. When using a pyrometer, a dab of silicone grease on the end of the probe will help to create a good thermal bond between the probe and the power head.

Measure the temperature on the cylinder block side of the thermostat housing. Measure the temperature just before the water reaches the thermostat.

Engine temperature check

To be accurate, the cooling water inlet temperature should be within 60-80° F (16-27° C). Extreme variation in water inlet temperature can affect engine operating temperature. Refer to cooling system specifications (**Table 15**). Engine temperature checks cannot be performed on an outboard running on a flushing device. The thermostat temperature rating is stamped on the body of the thermostat. Remove the thermostat(s) as described in Chapter Eight and check the rating before beginning this procedure.

> *CAUTION*
> *Do not run the engine without an adequate water supply and do not exceed 3000 rpm without an adequate load. Refer to **Safety Precautions** at the beginning of this chapter.*

1. Start the engine and run it at 2000-3000 rpm in forward for 5-10 minutes to allow it to reach operating temperature.
2. Reduce the speed to the specified idle speed, or a maximum of 900 rpm, for 5 minutes.
3A. If using thermomelt sticks, mark the cylinder block (both banks on a V-6) with the two thermomelt sticks that are just above and just below the thermostat(s) rated temperature.
3B. If using a pyrometer, note the temperature of the cylinder block (both banks on a V-6) and compare it to the thermostat rated temperature. The engine should operate within 5° F (-15°C) of the thermostat rated temperature at idle.
4A. If the lower temperature thermomelt sticks does not melt or the pyrometer reads more than 5° F (-15°C) below the thermostat rated temperature, the engine is overcooling. Check the thermostat(s) and poppet valve, if so equipped, for debris preventing the thermostat and poppet valve from closing. If the thermostat and poppet valve

pass a visual inspection, test the thermostat(s) as described in the following section.

4B. If the lower temperature thermomelt sticks melts or the pyrometer reads within 5° F (-15°C) of the thermostat rated temperature, the engine is at least reaching operating temperature and is not overcooling.

5A. If the higher temperature thermomelt sticks does not melt, or the pyrometer does not read more than 5° F (-15°C) above the thermostat rated temperature, the engine is not overheating.

5B. If the higher temperature thermomelt sticks melts, the engine is overheating. Test the thermostat(s) as described in the following section. Check the water inlet screens or cast inlet holes in the lower gearcase for blockage from debris or corrosion. Clean as necessary. Remove the lower gearcase and inspect the water pump assembly. Inspect the water tube from the water pump to the power head for damage or corrosion. If necessary, remove the cylinder head(s) or cylinder cover and check for debris and corrosion in the water jackets surrounding the cylinder(s).

CAUTION
It is normal for the engine to run cooler than the thermostat rated temperature at higher speeds if the engine is equipped with a poppet valve. However, regardless of whether the engine is equipped with poppet valve or not, engine temperature should not exceed the thermostat rated temperature by more than 20° F (-7°C).

6. Repeat the temperature test at 3000 rpm and wide-open throttle. It is acceptable for the pyrometer to read up to 15-20° F (-9- -7°C) above the thermostat rated temperature during the higher speed tests.

CAUTION
If the engine is run in a test tank, the 3000 rpm and wide open throttle tests may not accurate due to the aeration of the test tank water and subsequent overheating.

Thermostat test

1. Remove the screws securing the thermostat cover to the cylinder block or cylinder head(s). Carefully remove the thermostat cover(s).

2. Clean all gasket material from the thermostat cover(s) and cylinder block or cylinder head(s).

3. Check thermostat covers for cracks or corrosion damage and replace as necessary.

4. Wash the thermostat (**Figure 100**) with clean water. Remove the thermostat grommet, if so equipped, and dis-

card it. Read the thermostat rated opening temperature stamped on the thermostat.

NOTE
The thermostat and thermometer must not touch the sides or bottom of the container of water.

5. Manually open the thermostat and insert a thread or narrow feeler gauge through the valve and seat. Let the thermostat close, pinching the thread or feeler gauge in the valve.

6. Suspend the thermostat from the thread in a container of water that can be heated. Then suspend an accurate thermometer in the container of water. See **Figure 101**.

7. Heat the water and note the temperature at which the thermostat falls free from the thread or feeler gauge. The thermostat should begin to open within 5° F (-15°C) of the rated temperature.

8. Continue to heat the water until the thermostat fully opens. The thermostat must fully open within 15-20° F (-9- -7°C) above the rated temperature.

9. Replace the thermostat(s) if it fails to open at the specified temperature or if it does not open completely. Install a *new* gasket and grommet if so equipped.

CAUTION
If the engine is equipped with a poppet valve in the thermostat housing, make sure the poppet valve, spring and seat are correctly orientated and not damaged before reinstalling the thermostat cover. Replace damaged or worn parts (Chapter Eight).

Engine Temperature Switch

An engine temperature switch is used on all 75-125 and 135-200 hp models, except Optimax models. The switch is mounted on the rear and port side of the power head on 75-125 hp models, except 105 jet. The switch is mounted

on the starboard cylinder head on 105 jet and 135-200 hp models.

Engine temperature (overheat) switch circuit test

1. Disconnect the tan/blue wire from the switch. Turn the ignition switch to the ON position.

2. Use a jumper wire to connect the tan/blue wire (harness side) to an engine ground. If the warning horn does not sound, proceed to Step 3.

3. Check the voltage on the purple wire leading to the horn.

    a. If the voltage is less than 11.5 volt DC, repair the faulty wiring connecting the horn to the ignition key switch. If the wiring checks correctly, replace the ignition key switch.

    b. If the voltage is greater than 11.5 volt DC, the warning horn or related wiring is faulty. Replace the warning horn if no faults are found with the wiring.

Engine temperature (overheat) switch test

1. Remove the temperature switch from the power head.

2. Calibrate an ohmmeter to the R × 1 scale. Connect one ohmmeter lead to the tan/blue bullet connector. Connect the other lead to the metal disc at the other end of the switch.

3. Immerse the switch, but not the bullet connector end, into a container of water that can be heated. Place a liquid thermometer into the container.

4. With the water at room temperature, the ohmmeter should indicate an open circuit. If it does not, the switch is defective and must be replaced.

5. Observe the ohmmeter and begin heating the water. Note the temperature when the ohmmeter reading switches from no continuity to continuity. Stop the test and replace the switch if the water begins to boil before the ohmmeter reading changes.

6. The ohmmeter reading should switch at the temperature specification in **Table 15**. If it does not, replace the temperature switch.

ENGINE

Engine problems are generally cause by failure in another system, such as the ignition, fuel and lubrication, or cooling systems. If the power head is properly cooled, lubricated, timed correctly and given the correct air/fuel ratio, the engine should experience no mechanical problems other than normal wear. When a power head fails, determine why the power head failed. Replacing failed components will do no good if the cause of the failure is not corrected.

Overheating and Lack of Lubrication

Overheating and lack of lubrication cause the majority of engine mechanical problems. Anytime an outboard motor is run, adequate cooling water must be supplied by immersing the gearcase water inlets in test tank or lake, or using an approved flushing device. Only run the engine at low speeds on a flushing device. The motor must *never* be started without a water supply. Irreparable water pump damage will occur in seconds.

Carbon buildup in a two-stroke outboard motor *will* cause premature power head failure. Carbon buildup comes from the lubricating oil and fuel. Use a premium quality outboard motor power head lubricant. The current TCW-3 specification for power head lubricants ensures that maximum lubrication is delivered with minimal carbon deposit buildup. Using gasoline from a major brand manufacturer ensures that the fuel contains the detergents necessary to minimize carbon build-up. Fuels that contain alcohol tend to build carbon up at an accelerated rate. Avoid alcohol blended fuels whenever possible. Refer to Chapter Four for additional fuel and oil recommendations.

Use Quicksilver Power Tune (part No. 92-15104) periodically to remove carbon deposits from the combustion chamber and piston rings before they can contribute to high combustion chamber temperatures.

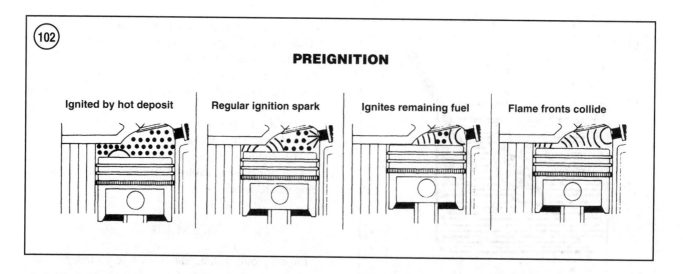

PREIGNITION

| Ignited by hot deposit | Regular ignition spark | Ignites remaining fuel | Flame fronts collide |

Preignition

Preignition is the premature ignition of the air/fuel charge in the combustion chamber. Preignition is caused by hot spots in the combustion chamber. See **Figure 102**. Anything in the combustion chamber that gets hot enough to ignite the air/fuel charge will cause preignition. Glowing carbon deposits, inadequate cooling, improperly installed thread inserts, incorrect head gaskets, sloppy machine work, previous combustion chamber damage, such as nicks and scratches, or overheated (incorrect) spark plugs can all cause preignition. Preignition is usually first noticed in the form of a power loss, but will eventually result in extensive damage to the internal engine components because of excessive combustion chamber pressure and temperature. Preignition damage typically looks like an acetylene torch was used to melt away the top of the piston, sometimes the piston will have a hole melted through the piston crown. Remember that preignition can lead to detonation and detonation can lead to preignition. Both types of damage may be evident when the engine is disassembled.

Detonation

Commonly referred to as *spark knock* or *fuel knock*, detonation is the violent, spontaneous explosion of fuel in the combustion chamber as opposed to the smooth, progressive burning of the air/fuel mixture that occurs during normal combustion. See **Figure 103**. If detonation occurs, combustion chamber pressure and temperature rise dramatically, creating severe shock waves in the engine. This will cause severe engine damage. It is not unusual for detonation to break a connecting rod or crankshaft.

Detonation occurs when the octane requirements of the engine exceed the octane of the fuel being used. It does not necessarily mean that the wrong fuel is being used. It means that at the time of detonation, the engine needed a higher octane fuel than is being used. All fuel will spontaneously explode when subjected to enough heat and pressure.

The fuel octane requirements of an engine are generally determined by:

1. *Compression ratio*—Higher compression ratios require higher octane fuel. It is important to note that carbon buildup raises compression ratios.

2. *Combustion chamber temperature*—Higher temperature requires higher octane fuel. Water pump and thermostat malfunctions typically raise the combustion chamber temperature.

3. *Air/fuel mixture*—Leaner mixtures require higher octane fuels. Richer mixtures require lower octane fuels.

4. *Spark advance*—Spark occurring too early causes excessive combustion chamber pressures, raising the octane requirements.

5. *Operating speed*—Propping an engine so it cannot reach the recommended operating speed range is considered *lugging* or *overpropping* the engine. When an engine is overpropped to the point that it cannot reach its recommended speed, combustion chamber temperatures skyrocket, increasing the octane requirement.

Fuel degrades over time in storage causing the actual octane rating of the fuel to drop. Even though the fuel may have exceeded the manufacturer's recommendations when the fuel was fresh, it may have dropped below recommendations over time. Use a fuel stabilizer, such as Quicksilver gasoline stabilizer to prevent octane deterioration. The fuel stabilizer must be added to fresh fuel. It will not raise the octane of stale or sour fuel.

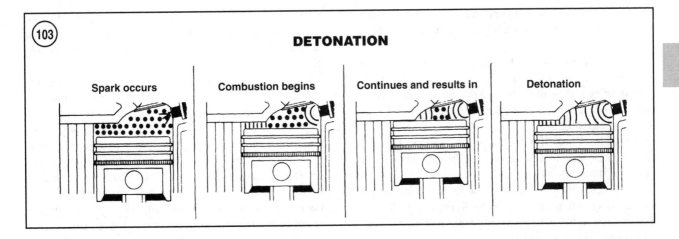

DETONATION

Spark occurs | Combustion begins | Continues and results in | Detonation

Properly dispose of questionable fuel and start with a fresh tank, rather than risk a power head failure. Catastrophic failure typically occurs in a few seconds or less when an engine is detonating. An operator can rarely detect detonation and reduce engine speed in time to save the power head. Detonation can lead to preignition and preignition can lead to detonation. Both types of damage may be evident when the engine is disassembled.

Poor Idle Quality

Poor idle quality can usually be attributed to one of the following conditions.

1. *Overcooling*—If the power head does not reach the recommended operating temperature, fuel tends to pool in the crankcase, resulting in a lean air/fuel ratio in the combustion chamber. This produces a lean spit or backfire through the carburetor at idle. Overheating is usually caused by debris caught in the thermostat(s) or poppet valve, if so equipped. A few models will not be equipped with thermostats. Refer to *Engine Temperature and Overheating* in this chapter for engine temperature checks.

2. *Crankcase seal failure*—A two-stroke engine cannot function unless the crankcase is adequately sealed. As the piston travels downward, the crankcase must pressurize and push the air/fuel mixture into the combustion chamber as the intake ports are uncovered. As the piston travels upward, the crankcase must create a vacuum to pull the air/fuel mixture into the crankcase from the carburetor in preparation for the next cycle. Leaks in the crankcase cause the air/fuel charge to leak into the atmosphere under crankcase compression. During the intake cycle, crankcase leaks will cause air from the atmosphere to be drawn into the crankcase, diluting the air/fuel charge. This causes inadequate fuel in the combustion chamber. On multiple cylinder engines, each crankcase must be sealed

from all other crankcases. Internal leaks will allow the air/fuel charge to leak to another cylinder's crankcase, rather than travel to the correct combustion chamber. Refer to *Starting Difficulties* at the beginning of this chapter for additional information.

3. *Crankcase bleed system failure*—Multiple cylinder motors are equipped with a fuel recirculation system designed to collect unburned fuel and oil from the low spots of the crankcase. Since the intake system used by a typical two-stroke engine does not completely transfer all of the fuel sent through the crankcase to the combustion chamber, especially during low-speed operation, the recirculation system collects the fuel and oil pooled in the low spots of the crankcase and transfers it to the intake ports or intake manifold where it can be burned. Correct recirculation system operation is important to efficient engine operation. If the system fails, excessive amounts of fuel and oil pool in the crankcase and do not reach the combustion chamber during low-speed operation, causing a lean mixture. When the engine is accelerated, the puddles of fuel and oil are drawn into the engine causing a temporary excessively rich mixture. This will result in poor low speed performance, poor acceleration, spark plug fouling, stalling or spitting at idle, and excessive smoke on acceleration. Refer to Chapter Six for bleed system service.

4. *Incorrect carburetor adjustments or carburetor malfunction*—The carburetor idle mixture screw must be correctly adjusted for the engine to idle and accelerate properly. An engine that is too lean at idle will spit or backfire through the carburetor and hesitate on acceleration. Refer to Chapter Six for carburetor adjustments.

Misfiring

True misfiring is an ignition system malfunction, generally caused by weak or erratic spark or defective spark plugs. The ignition system is not able to deliver enough spark energy to fire the spark plug at the time of the misfire.

Four-stroking is a form of misfire caused by an air/fuel ratio so rich it cannot consistently ignite. The term four-stroking comes from the fact that the engine is typically firing every other revolution, instead of every revolution. Four-stroking is caused by a fuel system malfunction. Check for excessive fuel pump pressure, carburetor(s) with a leaking inlet needle and seat or fuel primer systems stuck on.

Insufficient compression can cause a misfire at all speeds. It will often cause a cylinder to not fire at idle and low speed, and begin firing at mid-range and high speed. Always perform a compression test to verify the mechanical integrity of the combustion chamber.

Flat Spots and Hesitation During Acceleration

If the engine seems to hesitate or bog down when the throttle is opened, then recovers, check for a restricted main jet in the carburetor(s), water in the fuel, or an excessively lean fuel mixture. Faulty accelerator pump operation, on models so equipped, and incorrect synchronization of the spark advance to the throttle opening, on models with adjustments, can cause flat spots and hesitation on acceleration.

Water Leaking Into Cylinder(s)

Check for water leaking into a cylinder by checking the spark plugs. Water in the combustion chamber tends to clean the spark plug. If one spark plug in a multicylinder engine is clean and the others have normal deposits, a water leak is likely in the cylinder with the clean spark plug. A compression test can also be used to check the mechanical integrity of the combustion chamber. The piston crown can be visually inspected for the absence of carbon deposits. A cylinder crown that looks steam cleaned typically indicates water leaking into that combustion chamber. If the exhaust port area can be accessed, look for evidence of hard mineral deposits and the absence of soft, wet carbon deposits.

Water Damage in Power Head Lower Cylinder(s)

While water leaking into the combustion chambers is generally caused by defective or failed head gaskets, if so equipped, water can also enter the lower cylinder(s) of a power head through the exhaust ports and carburetor(s). When a steep unloading ramp or tilted trailer bed is used to launch the boat from a trailer and the boat enters the water too quickly, water can be forced into the drive shaft housing and up through the exhaust chamber into the cylinders if the pistons are not covering the exhaust ports.

Sudden deceleration with the engine shut off can cause a wave to swamp the engine and enter the exhaust ports or enter through the lower carburetor(s). This is most common in stern heavy boats. Operating a boat with twin engines with one engine shut off is considered hazardous because there is no exhaust back pressure to keep water out of the engine that is not running. Leave the engine that is not being used for docking or low speed maneuvering running at idle speed to reduce the risk of water entry.

Water entering a cylinder can result in a bent connecting rod, a broken piston and/or piston pin, a cracked cylinder and/or cylinder head, or any combination of these conditions. Even if no immediate physical damage is done to the power head, the entry of water will result in rust and corrosion of all internal surfaces, such as bearings, crankshaft, cylinder walls, connecting rods and piston rings.

Power Loss

Several factors can cause a loss of power. An engine needs three things to run properly: compression, fuel and ignition. Check the mechanical integrity of the combustion chamber by performing a cranking compression test. Test the ignition system with an air gap tester and verify ignition timing at wide-open throttle. Check the fuel system for air leaks into the fuel lines and fittings, and test the fuel pump for adequate output pressure at wide open throttle. Clean or replace all fuel filters. Remove a carburetor and inspect the float chamber for water in the fuel and gum or varnish buildup in the metering passages and jets. Clean all of the carburetors if any debris or buildup is found in one carburetor.

If the compression test reveals a mechanical defect in a combustion chamber, treat the engine with Quicksilver Power Tune Engine Cleaner (part No. 91-15104). Many times the piston rings are stuck to the piston and cannot adequately seal to the cylinder walls. Power Tune can free stuck piston rings and prevent unnecessary disassembly if no mechanical damage has occurred. Follow the instructions on the can and retest cranking compression after the treatment. If the compression is now within specification, consider changing lubricant and fuel to a higher quality brand. See Chapter Four.

If the compression is still not within specification after the Power Tune treatment, disassemble the motor and locate and repair the defect. After rebuilding the power head, make sure the carburetors and fuel pump are rebuilt, a new water pump and thermostat(s) are installed and all synchronization and linkage adjustments are made (Chapter Five).

Marine growth on the bottom of the hull and lower gearcase will reduce the top speed and fuel economy of a boat. If the motor is in a good state of tune and has no apparent malfunctions, but fuel economy and top speed have suffered, inspect the bottom of the hull and lower gearcase for marine growth and clean as necessary.

Piston Seizure

Piston seizure can be caused by insufficient piston-to-cylinder bore clearance, improper piston ring end gap, inadequate or inferior lubrication, cooling system failure (overheating), preignition or detonation.

Excessive Vibration

Excessive vibration can be caused by an engine misfiring on one or more cylinders, loose or broken motor mounts and worn or failed bearings. Gearcase problems that can cause excessive vibration are bent propeller shafts, damaged propellers or propellers with marine growth on the blades. A propeller ventilating because of damage or defects on the leading edge of the gearcase, an improperly mounted speedometer or depth finder sending unit, or any hull deformity that disturbs the water flow to the propeller can also cause excessive vibration.

Engine Noise

Experience is necessary to diagnose engine noises accurately. Noises are difficult to differentiate and hard to describe. Even a properly assembled two-stroke power head produces much more mechanical noise than a four-stroke. A two-stroke power head produces substantial intake (induction) noise. Deep knocking noises usually mean crankshaft main or rod bearing failure. A light slapping noise generally comes from a loose piston; however, some piston noise is normal, especially during warm-up. Any knocking noise during acceleration or at high speed could be preignition or detonation and should be investigated immediately.

Table 1 STARTING SYSTEM TROUBLESHOOTING

Symptom	Probable cause	Remedy
Low no-load speed with high current dray	Tight or dirty bushings Shorted armature	Clean and lubricate bushings Test armature (Chapter Seven)
Low no-load speed with low current dray	High resistance in the armature circuit	Check brushes and springs Test armature (Chapter Seven) Clean and inspect commutator
No rotation with high current draw	Stuck armature Internal short to ground	Clean and lubricate bushings Check brush leads for shorts
Starter continues after key is released	Starter solenoid stuck Key switch failure Yellow or yellow/red wire malfunction	Replace solenoid Test key switch Disconnect suspect wires
Starter turns motor over too slowly	High resistance in solenoid Mechanical failure of gearcase Mechanical failure of power head Battery cables too small	Measure voltage drop (Chapter Three) Check for debris on drain/fill plug Manually rotate flywheel Check battery cable size (Chapter Seven)
Starter spins but drive does not engage flywheel	Corroded starter drive Drive needs lubrication Faulty battery Faulty battery cables Faulty starter	Inspect starter drive (Chapter Seven) Lubricate starter drive Check battery (Chapter Seven) Check voltage drop (Chapter Three) Disassemble and inspect starter

Table 2 IGNITION SYSTEM TROUBLESHOOTING

Symptom	Probable cause	Remedy
Fails to start (spark test good)	Fouled spark plug(s)	Clean or replace spark plugs
	Incorrect timing	Check for sheared flywheel key
		Test ignition trigger
		Test crankshaft position sensor
	Low voltage to ECM	Test ECM voltage
Engine backfires	Incorrect timing	Check ignition timing (Chapter Five)
		Test ignition trigger
		Test crankshaft position sensor
	Incorrect firing order	Check primary and secondary coil winding
	Cracked spark plug insulator	Inspect spark plugs
High speed misfire	Insufficient spark	Check for strong blue spark
	Incorrect spark plug gap	Check spark plug gap (Chapter Four)
	Loose electrical connection	Check all wiring and terminals
	Low ignition stator voltage	Test ignition stator
	Faulty crankshaft position sensor	Test CPS sensor
	Faulty ignition coil	Test the ignition coil
Pre-ignition	Wrong type of spark plug	Check spark plugs (Chapter Four)
	High operating temperature	Check for overheating
	Incorrect ignition timing	Check ignition timing (Chapter Five)
	Lean fuel mixture	Check fuel system for blockage
Spark plug failure	Incorrect spark plug	Check spark plugs (Chapter Four)
	Loose spark plugs	Torque spark plugs
	Fuel system malfunction	Check for rich or lean condition
	High operating temperature	Check operating temperature
	Heavy carbon deposits	Clean carbon from engine
Ignition component failure	Loose electrical connection	Check wiring and terminals
	Loose mounting fasteners	Check component fasteners
	High operating temperature	Check for overheating
	Corrosion	Check for source of water

Table 3 FUEL SYSTEM TROUBLESHOOTING

Symptom	Probable cause	Remedy
Engine fails to start	No fuel to carburetor(s)	Verify fuel in tank
		Check fuel tank vent
		Check fuel tank pickup or filter
		Clean all fuel filters
		Verify primer bulb operation
	No fuel in VST (EFI and Optimax models)	Check for fuel in VST
	Electric fuel pump(s) not operating	Check for pump operation
	Carburetor(s) failure	Rebuild carburetor(s)
	Fuel injectors not operating	Check fuel injectors
Flooding at carburetor	Float or needle malfunction	Rebuild carburetor(s)
	Excessive fuel pump pressure	Check fuel pump pressure

(continued)

Table 3 FUEL SYSTEM TROUBLESHOOTING (continued)

Symptom	Probable cause	Remedy
Loss of power	Restricted fuel supply	Clean fuel filters
		Check fuel hoses
		Check hose connections
	Blocked carburetor passages	Rebuild carburetor(s)
	Air leakage in fuel supply	Check hoses and connections
	Low fuel pump pressure	Check fuel pump pressure
Hesitation on acceleration	Improper carburetor adjustment	Adjust carburetor
	Improper synchronization	Check carburetor synchronization
	Restricted fuel supply	Clean fuel filters
		Check fuel hoses
		Check hose connections
	Blocked carburetor passages	Rebuild carburetor(s)
	Air leakage in fuel supply	Check hoses and connections
	Low fuel pump pressure	Check fuel pump pressure
	Mis-adjusted TPS	Adjust throttle position sensor
	Faulty TPS	Test throttle position sensor
Excessive fuel consumption	Improper carburetor adjustment	Adjust carburetor
	Carburetor float malfunction	Rebuild carburetor(s)
	Blocked carburetor passages	Rebuild carburetor(s)
	High fuel pump pressure	Check fuel pump pressure
	Flooding VST	Check for fuel in vent hose
Spark plug fouling	Improper carburetor adjustment	Adjust carburetor
	Improper synchronization	Check carburetor synchronization
	Excessive oil in fuel	Adjust oil injection linkage
		Mix fuel at recommended ratio
	Wrong type of spark plug	Check spark plug No.
		(Chapter Four)
Engine detonation	Low fuel octane rating	Use higher octane fuel
	Carbon deposits	Remove deposits from engine
	Wrong type of spark plug	Check spark plug No.
		(Chapter Four)
Engine pre-ignition	Restricted fuel supply	Clean fuel filters
		Check fuel hoses
		Check hose connections
	Blocked carburetor passages	Rebuild carburetor(s)
	Air leakage in fuel supply	Check hoses and connections
	Low fuel pump pressure	Check fuel pump pressure
	Wrong type of spark plug	Check spark plug No.
		(Chapter Four)

Table 4 STARTER MOTOR CURRENT DRAW SPECIFICATIONS

Model	Load test 9	No load test
65 jet, 75 hp and 90 hp	120 amps	75 amps
80 jet and 100 hp	150	75
115 hp (except 115 hp Optimax) and 125 hp	150	75
135-200 hp (except Optimax models)	175	40
115-175 hp Optimax models		
1998-2000	165	30
2001-on	170	60
225 and 250 hp (except 225 hp Optimax)	165	25
225 hp Optimax		
1998-2000	210	30
2001-on	170	60

Table 5 CHARGING SYSTEM TROUBLESHOOTING

Symptom	Probable cause	Remedy
Battery overcharges	Regulator failure	Test sense circuit
Battery gasses excessively	Battery overcharging Faulty battery	Test sense circuit Substitute a different battery Test the battery
Battery looses charge (while running)	Alternator failure Loose drive belt Excess accessory load	Test alternator Adjust belt tension Perform current draw test
Battery looses charge (during storage)	Current drain from accessories Defective battery	Turn all accessories off Substitute a different battery

Table 6 CHARGING SYSTEM AMPERAGE

Model	Maximum output rating
65 jet and 75-125 hp (except 105 jet and 115 Optimax)	16 amps at 2000 rpm
105 jet and 135-200 hp (except Optimax models)	40 amps at 5000 rpm
115-175 hp Optimax models	60 amps at 2000 rpm
200 hp Optimax, 225 hp and 250 hp	60 amps at 2000 rpm

Table 7 BATTERY CHARGING COIL (STATOR)
RESISTANCE SPECIFICATIONS (EXCEPT BELT-DRIVEN) SYSTEM

Model	Specification (ohms)
65 jet and 75-125 hp (except 105 jet and 115 Optimax)	0.16-0.19
105 jet and 135-200 hp (except Optimax models)	
1998 and 1999 models	
Long yellow lead to long yellow wire	0.25-0.45
Short yellow lead to short yellow wire	0.25-0.45
Yellow wire to engine ground	No continuity
2000-on	
Yellow terminals in either connector	0.18-0.45
Yellow terminals in each connector to engine ground	No continuity

Table 8 IGNITION SYSTEM VOLTAGE OUTPUT SPECIFICATIONS

Model	Specification (DVA)
65 jet and 75-125 hp (except 105 jet and 115 Optimax)	
Stator output	
At cranking speed	100-350
At idle speed	200-350
Trigger output	
At cranking speed	0.2-2.0
At idle speed	2-8
Stop circuit output	
At cranking speed	100-350
At idle speed	200-350

(continued)

Table 8 IGNITION SYSTEM VOLTAGE OUTPUT SPECIFICATIONS (continued)

Model	Specification (DVA)
105 jet and 135-200 hp (except Optimax models)	
1998 and 1999	
Low speed stator	
At cranking speed	100-265
At 1000 rpm	195-265
At 4000 rpm	255-345
High speed stator	
At cranking speed	25-50
At 1000 rpm	120-160
At 4000 rpm	230-320
Switch box stop circuit	
At cranking speed	200-300
At 1000-4000 rpm	225-400
Switch box output (to ignition coils)	
At cranking speed	90-145
At 1000 rpm	125-175
At 4000 rpm	175-240
Switch box bias circuit output	
At cranking speed	1-6 DC volts
At 1000 rpm	3-15 DC volts
At 4000 rpm	10-30 DC volts
2000-on	
Stator output	160-320
Trigger input to CDM	
Cranking speed	0.2-2
At idle to 2500 rpm	2-8
Bias circuit voltage	25-40
225 hp and 250 hp (except Optimax models)	
Stator output	
At cranking speed	100-225
At 650-3000 rpm	250-300
At 4000-5500 rpm	230-300

Table 9 IGNITION STATOR RESISTANCE SPECIFICATION

Model	Specification (ohms)
65 jet and 75-125 hp (except 105 jet and 115 Optimax)	
White/green to green white wires	660-710
White/green to engine ground	No continuity
Green/white to engine ground	No continuity
105 jet and 135-200 hp (except Optimax models)	
1998 and 1999	
Blue/white to red white wires (low speed winding)	3500-4200
Blue to red wires (low speed winding)	3500-4200
Red/white to black ground wires (high speed winding)	90-140
Red to black ground wires (high speed winding)	90-140
2000-on	
White/green to green white wires	380-430
White green to engine ground	No continuity
Green/white to engine ground	No continuity
225 hp and 250 hp (except Optimax models)	
Green/red to stator ground terminal	990-1210
Green/yellow to stator ground terminal	990-1210
Green to stator ground terminal	990-1210
Green/blue to stator ground terminal	990-1210
Green/orange to stator ground terminal	990-1210
Green/black to stator ground terminal	990-1210

Table 10 CAPACITOR DISCHARGE MODULE (CDM) RESISTANCE SPECIFICATIONS

Positive test lead connection	Negative test lead connection	Scale	Specification
Terminal C	Terminal A	R × 100	1000-1250 (ohms)
Terminal B	Terminal D	R × 100	Continuity
Terminal D	Terminal B	R × 100	No continuity
Terminal D	Terminal A	R × 100	Continuity
Terminal A	Terminal D	R × 100	No continuity
Spark plug lead	Terminal A	R × 100	900-1200 (ohms)

TABLE 11 IGNITION COIL RESISTANCE SPECIFICATIONS

Model	Specification
1998 and 1999 105 jet and 135-200 hp	
(except Optimax models)	
Primary resistance	0.02-0.04
Secondary resistance	800-1100
115-225 hp Optimax models	
Primary resistance	0.38-0.78
Secondary resistance	8100-8900
Coil driver	
Red/yellow to black terminals	76,500-93,500
Black to each green/stripe (four-pin connector)	9-11
Black to each green/stripe (four-pin connector)	No continuity

Table 12 FUEL PUMP PRESSURE SPECIFICATIONS

Fuel pump type	Specification
Mechanical fuel pump	
75-125 hp (except 105 jet and 115 Optimax)	
Idle speed	3.5 psi (24.1 kPa)*
At 5000 rpm	6 psi (41.4 kPa)*
105 jet and 135-200 hp (except Optimax models)	
1998 and 1999	
Idle speed	2 psi (13.8 kPa)*
At 5000 rpm	8 psi (55.2 kPa)*
2000-on	
Idle speed	1-3 psi (6.9-20.7 kPa)
At 5000 rpm	12 psi (82.7 kPa)*
135 and 150 Optimax (1998 and 1999)	
Idle speed	2 psi (13.8 kPa)*
At 5000 rpm	8 psi (55.2 kPa)*
115-175 hp Optimax models (2000-on)	
Idle speed	
Normal pressure	2-3 psi (13.8-20.7 kPa)
Minimum pressure	1 psi (6.9 kPa)*
At 5000 rpm	
Normal pressure	8-10 (55.2 kPa-69.0 kPa)
Minimum pressure	3 psi (20.7 kPa)*
200 hp and 225 hp Optimax models	
1998 and 1999	
Idle speed	2 psi (13.8 kPa)*
At 5000 rpm	8 psi (55.2 kPa)*
	(continued)

Table 12 FUEL PUMP PRESSURE SPECIFICATIONS (continued)

Fuel pump type	Specification
Mechanical fuel pump (cont.)	
200 hp and 225 hp Optimax models	
2000-on	
Idle speed	
Normal pressure	2-3 psi (13.8-20.7 kPa)
Minimum pressure	1 psi (6.9 kPa)*
At 5000 rpm	
Normal pressure	8-10 (55.2 kPa-69.0 kPa)
Minimum pressure	4 psi (27.6 kPa)*
Maximum pressure	10 psi (69.0 kPa)
225 hp and 250 hp (except Optimax models)	
Idle speed	2 psi (13.8 kPa)*
At 5000 rpm	8 psi (55.2 kPa)*
Low pressure electric fuel pump	
All Optimax models	6-9 psi (41.4-62.1 kPa)
High pressure electric fuel pump	
150-200 hp EFI models	34-36 psi (234.4-248.2 kPa)
115-225 hp Optimax models	87-91 psi (599.9-627.4 kPa)
*Minimum fuel pump pressure specification.	

**Table 13 ENGINE COOLANT TEMPERATURE (ECT)
AND COMPRESSOR TEMPERATURE SENSOR SPECIFICATIONS**

Model	Temperature °F (°C)	Specification (ohms)
150-250 hp (except Optimax)	14 (-10)	5073-6199
	32 (0)	2959-3615
	50 (10)	1797-2195
	68 (20)	1125-1375
	86 (30)	725-885
	104 (40)	479-585
	122 (50)	324-396
	140 (60)	224-272
	158 (70)	158-192
	176 (80)	114-128
	194 (90)	83-101
	212 (100)	62-74
	230 (110)	46-56
	248 (120)	35-41
115-225 Optimax models		
1998-2000	5 (-15)	6565-8023
	14 (-10)	4979-6085
	32 (0)	2939-3592
	41 (5)	2286-2794
	50 (10)	1791-2189
	59 (15)	1414-1729
	68 (20)	1124-1374
	77 (25)	900-1100
	86 (30)	725-886
	95 (35)	588-718
	104 (40)	479-586
	113 (45)	393-481
	122 (50)	324-396
	131 (55)	269-329
	140 (60)	224-274
	(continued)	

3

**Table 13 ENGINE COOLANT TEMPERATURE (ECT)
AND AIR COMPRESSOR TEMPERATURE SENSOR SPECIFICATIONS (continued)**

Model	Temperature °F (°C)	Specification (ohms)
115-225 Optimax models		
1998-2000	149 (65)	188-229
	158 (70)	158-193
	167 (75)	133-163
	176 (80)	113-138
	185 (85)	96-118
	194 (90)	82-100
	203 (95)	71-87
	212 (100)	61-75
	221 (105)	53-65
	230 (110)	47-57
	239 (115)	41-50
	248 (120)	35-43
	257 (125)	30-37
2001-on	5 (-15)	65,646-80,234
	14 (-10)	49,787-60,851
	32 (0)	29,387-35,919
	41 (5)	22,856-27,936
	50 (10)	17,913-21,893
	59 (15)	14,143-17,285
	68 (20)	11,244-13,742
	77 (25)	9000-11,000
	86 (30)	7250-8862
	95 (35)	5877-7183
	104 (40)	4794-5860
	113 (45)	3933-4807
	122 (50)	3243-3963
	131 (55)	2687-3285
	140 (60)	2239-2737
	149 (65)	1875-2291
	158 (70)	1577-1927
	167 (75)	1332-1628
	176 (80)	1130-1381
	185 (85)	963-1177
	194 (90)	824-1007
	203 (95)	708-866
	212 (100)	612-748
	221 (105)	533-651
	230 (110)	465-569
	239 (115)	405-495
	248 (120)	351-429
	257 (125)	306-374

Table 14 AIR TEMPERATURE (IAT) SENSOR SPECIFICATIONS

Temperature °F (°C)	Specification (ohms)
41 (5)	12,600-15,400
50 (10)	10,980-13,420
68 (20)	7650-9350
77 (25)	6750-8250
86 (30)	5850-7150
104 (40)	4500-5500
113 (45)	360-440

Table 15 COOLING SYSTEM SPECIFICATIONS

Water pressure	
75-125 hp (except 105 jet and 115 Optimax)	
At 5250 rpm	10-15 psi (69.0-103.4 kPa)
105 jet and 135-200 hp (except Optimax models)	
At idle speed	1-3 psi (6.9-20.6 kPa)
At 5500 rpm	12 psi (82.7 kPa)*
115-175 hp (Optimax models)	
At 5000 rpm	12 psi (82.7 kPa)*
200 and 225 hp (Optimax models)	
At 5000 rpm	8-10 psi (55-69 kPa)*
225 and 250 hp (except Optimax)	
At 5000 rpm	8-10 psi (55-69 kPa)*
Engine temperature switch	
switches to continuity	182°-198° F (83°-92° C)
*Minimum water pressure.	

3

Chapter Four

Lubrication, Maintenance and Tune-Up

Modern outboard motors deliver more power and performance than ever before due to the higher compression ratios, improved electrical systems and other design advances. Proper lubrication, maintenance and tune-ups are increasingly important to maintain a high level of performance, extend engine life and extract the maximum economy of operation.

The owner's operation and maintenance manual is a helpful supplement to this service manual and a valuable resource for anyone operating or maintaining an outboard engine. If it is missing, purchase a new owner's manual through a Mercury or Mariner dealership. The complete serial number of the outboard motor is required to obtain the correct owner's manual.

Tables 1-5 (located at the end of this chapter) are based on recommendations from Mercury/Mariner that will help keep the Mercury or Mariner outboard motor operating at its peak performance level. **Table 1** provides specific application torque specifications. **Table 2** provides general torque specifications. Use the general torque specification for fasteners not in **Table 1**. **Table 3** provides the recommended preventive maintenance schedule. **Table 4** lists spark plug recommendations and **Table 5** lists lubricant capacity.

HOUR METER

Service schedules for outboard motors are based on hours of engine operation. An engine hour meter (**Figure 1**) is highly recommended to help keep track of the actual hours of engine operation. Many types of hour meters are available. The most accurate type for maintenance purposes is triggered by a spark plug lead. This type makes sure that only actual running time is recorded. If an hour meter is operated by the key switch, any time the key is on, hours are recorded.

The Quicksilver Service Monitor (part No. 79-828010A-1) is a spark plug wire driven hour meter that can also be set to flash an alarm at a time interval set by the operator. Quicksilver also offers many models of ignition switch operated hour meters.

Record service performed in the maintenance log at the back of this manual.

FUELS AND LUBRICATION

Proper Fuel Selection

Two-stroke engines are lubricated by mixing oil with the fuel. The oil is either automatically mixed with the fuel or injected directly into the crankcase by an oil injection system. Oil injection systems are described in Chapter Thirteen. The various components of the engine are lubricated as the fuel or fuel/oil mixture passes through the crankcase and cylinders. Since two-stroke fuel serves the dual function of producing combustion and distributing the lubrication, except on Optimax models, never use marine white gasoline or any other fuel that is not intended to be used in modern gasoline powered engines. A substandard fuel and lubricating oil will aggravate combustion chamber deposits, which leads to piston ring sticking, exhaust port blockage, and preignition and detonation.

NOTE
The simplest way to reduce combustion chamber deposits is to use the highest qual-
ity fuel without alcohol and lubricating oil available.

The recommended fuel is regular unleaded gasoline from a major supplier with a minimum pump posted octane rating of 87 with no alcohol. The minimum fuel requirements are regular unleaded gasoline with a minimum pump posted octane rating of 87 with no more than 10% ethanol. The use of methanol is not recommended.

Currently reformulated fuels have not achieved federally mandated reductions in emissions. Reformulated fuels are specifically blended to reduce emissions. Reformulated fuels normally contain oxygenates, such as ethanol, methanol or MTBE (methyl tertiary butyl ether). Reformulated fuels may be used as long as they do not contain methanol and normal precautions for alcohol (ethanol) extended fuels are taken. See *Alcohol Extended Gasoline* in this chapter.

Mid-grade or premium fuel typically has an octane rating or 89 (mid-grade) or 93 (premium). These higher octane fuels are not required under normal operating conditions. Consider using a higher octane fuel only if the engine is subjected to heavy duty use, such as a work or commercial fishing boat, or if low octane fuel is suspected of causing preignition or detonation damage to the piston (**Figure 2**).

The installation of a Quicksilver Water Separating Fuel Filter is recommended as a preventive measure on all permanently installed fuel systems. The manufacturer recommends the installation of the Quicksilver water separating fuel filter if any alcohol blended or alcohol extended gasoline is used.

Sour Fuel

Avoid storing fuel for more than 60 days even under ideal conditions. As gasoline ages, it forms gum and varnish deposits that restrict carburetor and fuel system passages, causing the engine to starve for fuel. The octane rating of the fuel also deteriorates over time, increasing the likelihood of preignition or detonation. Use a fuel additive, such as Quicksilver Gasoline Stabilizer, on a regular basis to stabilize the octane rating and prevent gum and varnish formation. All gasoline stabilizers must be added to fresh fuel. Gasoline stabilizers cannot rejuvenate fuel. If the fuel is sour or stale, drain the tank and refill it with fresh gasoline. Dispose of the sour fuel in an approved manner. Always use fresh gasoline when mixing fuel for outboard motors.

Alcohol Extended Gasoline

Although the manufacturer does not recommend the use of gasoline that contains alcohol, the minimum gasoline specification allows for a maximum of 10% ethanol to be used. Methanol is not recommended since the detrimental effects of methanol are more extreme than ethanol. If alcohol extended gasoline is being used, consider the following.

1. Alcohol extended gasoline promotes leaner air/fuel ratios, which can:
    a. Raise combustion chamber temperatures, leading to preignition and/or detonation.
    b. Cause hesitation or stumbling on acceleration.
    c. Cause hard starting when the engine is hot and cold.
    d. Cause the engine to produce slightly less horsepower.
2. Alcohol extended gasoline attracts moisture, which can:
    a. Cause a water buildup in the fuel system.
    b. Block fuel filters.
    c. Block fuel metering components.
    d. Cause corrosion of metallic components in the fuel system and power head.
3. Alcohol extended gasoline deteriorates nonmetallic components, such as:
    a. Rubber fuel lines.
    b. Primer bulbs.
    c. Fuel pump internal components.
    d. Carburetor internal components.
    e. Fuel recirculation components.
4. Alcohol extended gasoline promotes vapor lock and hot soak problems.
5. Alcohol extended fuel tends to build up combustion chamber deposits more quickly, which leads to:
    a. Higher compression ratios, increasing the likelihood of preignition or detonation.
    b. Piston ring sticking, which causes elevated piston temperatures, loss of power and ultimately preignition or detonation.
    c. Exhaust port blockage or obstruction on engines with small or multiple exhaust ports.

NOTE
When the moisture content of the fuel reaches 0.5%, the water separates from the fuel and settles to the low points of the fuel system. This includes the fuel tank, fuel filters and carburetor float chambers. Alcohol extended fuels aggravate this situation.

If any or all of these symptoms regularly occur, consider testing the fuel for alcohol or simply changing to a different gasoline supplier. If the symptoms are no longer present after the change, continue using the gasoline from the new supplier.

If the use of alcohol extended fuel is unavoidable, perform regular maintenance and inspections more often than normal recommendations. Pay special attention to changing or cleaning the fuel filters, inspecting rubber fuel system components for deterioration, inspecting metallic fuel system components for corrosion and monitoring the power head for warning signs of preignition and/or detonation. It is sometimes necessary to enrich the carburetors metering circuits to compensate for the leaning effect of these gasolines.

Reformulated gasolines that contain MTBE (methyl tertiary butyl ether) in normal concentrations have no side effects other than those listed previously. This does not apply to reformulated gasoline that contains ethanol or methanol.

Alcohol Test

The following procedure is an accepted procedure for detecting alcohol in gasoline. Check the gasoline before mixing it with oil. Use a small transparent bottle or tube that can be capped and has graduations, or mark it at approximately 1/3 full. A pencil mark on a piece of adhesive tape is sufficient.

1. Fill the container with water to the 1/3 full mark.
2. Add gasoline until the container is almost full. Leave a small air space at the top.
3. Shake the container vigorously, then allow it to sit for 3-5 minutes. If the volume of water appears to have increased, alcohol is present. If the dividing line between the water and gasoline becomes cloudy, reference from the center of the cloudy band.

This procedure cannot differentiate between types of alcohol (ethanol or methanol), but it is accurate enough to determine if sufficient alcohol is present to cause the user to take precautions.

Gasoline Additives

The only recommended fuel additives and the benefits from their use are:

1. *Quicksilver Fuel System Treatment and Stabilizer*—When added to *fresh* fuel, this additive stabilizes the octane rating, preventing fuel degradation and oxidation, prevents the formation of gum and varnish in the fuel system components, and prevents moisture buildup in the fuel tank, fuel system and carburetors.
2. *Quicksilver Gasoline Stabilizer*—This additives provides the same benefits as Quicksilver Fuel System Treatment and Stabilizer, but is much more concentrated and is used to treat large quantities of fuel.

3. *Quicksilver QuicKleen Fuel Treatment*—QuicKleen helps prevent combustion chamber deposits and protects the internal fuel system and power head mechanical surfaces against corrosion. Use QuicKleen if substandard or questionable fuels or oils are being used, or if combustion chamber deposits are a continual problem.

Unless the boat is consistently operated with fresh fuel in the fuel tank, a fuel stabilizer is recommended.

CAUTION
Some marinas are blending valve recession additives into their fuel to accommodate owners of older four-stroke marine engines. Valve recession additives help prevent premature valve seat wear on older four-stroke engines. The valve recession additives may react with some outboard motor oils causing certain two-stroke oil additives to precipitate (gel). This precipitation can plug fuel system filters and smaller passages; therefore, avoid using any fuel containing valve recession additives in an outboard motor.

Recommended Fuel/Oil Mixtures

The recommended oil for all Mercury/Mariner outboard motors, except Optimax models, is Quicksilver Premium or Premium Plus, Two-Cycle Outboard Oil. This oil meets or exceeds TCW-3 (two-cycle, water cooled) standards set by the NMMA (National Marine Manufacturers Association). If Quicksilver Premium Blend is not available, use a NMMA certified TCW-3 outboard oil from another engine manufacturer. The only recommended oil for Optimax models is Quicksilver Premium Plus Outboard Oil.

TCW-3 oils are designed to improve lubrication over previous standards (TCW and TCW-II), and reduce combustion chamber deposits caused by the lubricating oil. Do not use an oil other than a NMMA approved TCW-3 outboard motor oil.

CAUTION
Never use automotive four-cycle crankcase oil in a two-cycle outboard motor. These types of lubricants cause serious power head damage.

All models covered in this manual are equipped with an engine mounted oil injection system. Oil injection equipped models can be readily identified by the presence of an engine mounted oil reservoir. The oil injection systems are described in Chapter Thirteen.

Optimax models are equipped with an electric oil pump controlled by the ECM (electronic control module). The ECM controls the fuel/oil ratio for all operating modes, including break-in. Never mix oil with the fuel on an Optimax engine.

Filling the oil tank/reservoir

Oil tank/reservoir mounting locations and fill procedures vary by model.

On 75-125 hp (except 115 Optimax), 65 jet and 80 jet models, the engine-mounted oil reservoir is mounted under the engine cover. The oil fill cap is equipped with a dipstick to determine the remaining oil level. Do not remove the engine cover to fill the reservoir or check the oil level, simply remove the fill cap and dipstick and fill the reservoir with the recommended oil.

On 135-250 hp, 105 jet and 115 Optimax models, refill the boat mounted remote oil tank by removing the fill cap and adding the recommended oil until it reaches the full marking on the side of the tank. Install and securely tighten the fill cap. To refill the engine mounted oil reservoir, make sure the remote oil tank is full and the fill cap is securely tightened. With the engine running at idle speed, loosen the engine oil reservoir fill cap to allow air to escape and oil to enter. Tighten the filler cap when the tank is full. Avoid twisting the wires on models that have the oil level switch integrated into the filler cap.

Power head break-in procedure

Operate a new outboard motor, rebuilt power head or replacement power head in accordance with the manufacturer's recommended break-in procedure. During the first hour of engine operation, change the engine speed frequently and avoid extended full-throttle operation. After the first hour of operation, the engine can be operated as desired within normal operating guidelines.

Mercury/Mariner also requires that a new motor, rebuilt power head or replacement power head be operated on a 25:1 fuel/oil mixture, for the first tank of fuel or a number of tanks calculated based on the engine's horsepower.

The formula is 1 gal. (3.8 L) of 25:1 fuel/oil mix for every 10 hp, rounded to the nearest gallon (liter). For example, a 150 hp outboard motor should be operated on the 25:1 mixture for the first 15 gal. (56.8 L) of fuel. It is acceptable to exceed the amount of fuel/oil mix in order to accommodate the fuel tank size, especially on mid-size motors, but the amount of 25:1 fuel/oil mix should not be less than the formula recommends.

To provide the required 25:1 fuel/oil mixture during the engine break-in period, mix 8 fl. oz. (236.6 mL) of the recommended outboard oil for every 3 gal. (11.4 L) of the recommended fuel. This will provide a 50:1 fuel/oil mixture in the fuel tank that will be supplemented by the engine mounted oil injection system. The final result will be a 25:1 fuel/oil mixture to the engine.

CAUTION
All Optimax models use an electric oil pump controlled by the ECM. The ECM controls the fuel/oil ratio for all operating conditions, including break-in. Never mix oil with the fuel in an Optimax engine.

To provide the required fuel/oil mixture after break-in and for all normal operation, do not mix oil in the fuel tank. The engine mounted oil injection system provides the engine with the required fuel/oil mixture. Monitor the engine mounted oil tank (reservoir) and the boat mounted oil tank, if so equipped, and keep the tank(s) filled with the recommended outboard oil.

Fuel Mixing Procedure

WARNING
Gasoline is an extreme fire hazard. Never use gasoline near heat, a spark or a flame.

Mix the fuel and oil outside or in a well-ventilated area. Mix the fuel and oil to the recommended fuel/oil ratio. Using less than the specified amount of oil can result in insufficient lubrication and serious engine damage. Using more oil than specified causes spark plug fouling, erratic fuel metering, excessive smoke and accelerated carbon accumulation.

CAUTION
All Optimax models use an electric oil pump controlled by the ECM. The ECM controls the fuel/oil ratio for all operating conditions, including break-in. Never mix oil with the fuel in an Optimax engine.

Cleanliness is very important when mixing fuel. Even a very small particle of dirt can restrict fuel metering passages.

Only use fresh fuel. If the fuel is sour, dispose of the fuel in an approved manner and start over with fresh fuel. If the fuel mix is not going to be used immediately, add a fuel stabilizer to the fuel mix.

For temperatures above 32° F (0° C), measure the required amount of gasoline and recommended outboard oil accurately. Pour the oil into a portable tank and add the fuel. Install the tank fill cap and mix the fuel by tipping the tank from side-to-side several times. See **Figure 3**.

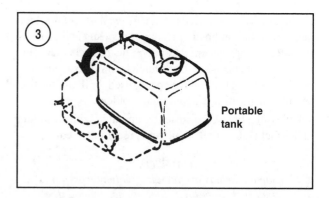

Portable tank

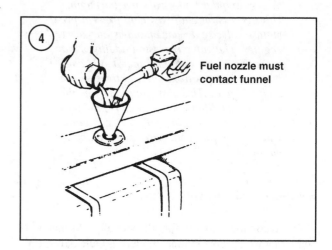

Fuel nozzle must contact funnel

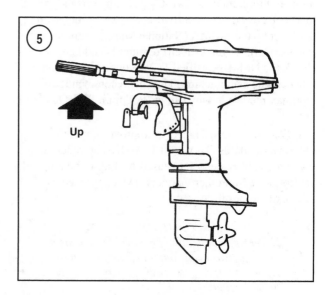

Up

If a built-in tank is used, insert a large filter-type funnel into the tank fill neck. Carefully pour the specified oil and gasoline into the funnel at the same time. See **Figure 4**.

For temperatures below 32° F (0° C), measure the required amount of gasoline and the recommended out-

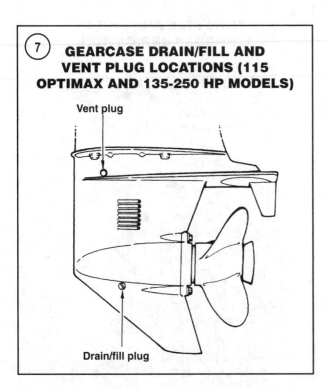

6 GEARCASE DRAIN/FILL AND VENT PLUG LOCATIONS (75-125 HP [EXCEPT 115 OPTIMAX MODELS])

Rear vent plug

Front vent plug

Drain/fill plug

7 GEARCASE DRAIN/FILL AND VENT PLUG LOCATIONS (115 OPTIMAX AND 135-250 HP MODELS)

Vent plug

Drain/fill plug

board oil accurately. Pour approximately 1 gal. (3.8 L) of gasoline into the tank, then add the required amount of oil. Install the tank fill cap and shake the tank vigorously to mix the fuel and oil. Remove the cap, add the balance of the gasoline and shake the tank again. If a built-in tank is

used, insert a large filter-type funnel into the tank fill neck. Mix the required amount of oil with one gallon of gasoline in a separate container. Carefully pour the mixture into the funnel at the same time the tank is being filled with gasoline.

Consistent Fuel Mixtures

The carburetor idle mixture adjustment is sensitive to fuel mixture variations which result from the use of different oils and gasolines, or inaccurate measuring and mixing. Constant readjustment of the idle mixture screw(s) may be necessary. To prevent the necessity of carburetor readjustment or erratic running qualities from one fuel batch to another, always be consistent when mixing fuel. Prepare each batch of fuel exactly the same as previous batches.

Use caution when considering using premixed fuel sold at some on-water locations, such as marinas. The quality and consistency of premixed fuel can vary greatly. The possibility of engine damage resulting from an incorrect or substandard fuel/oil mixture often outweighs the convenience of premixed fuel. Consult with the operator of the marina or fuel supply station about the specifications for the oil and fuel being used in the advertised premix. Do not use the fuel if the fuel does not meet or exceed the engine fuel and oil requirements as previously stated in this chapter.

Checking Gearcase Lubricant Level

Check the gearcase lubricant level at the intervals specified in **Table 3**. The recommended lubricant is Quicksilver Premium Blend Gear Lube. If the gearcase is subjected to heavy duty use, consider using Quicksilver High Performance Gear Lube.

CAUTION
Do not use regular automotive gear lubricant in the gear housing. The expansion and foam characteristics and water tolerance of automotive gear lubricant are not suitable for marine use.

1. Place the outboard motor in an upright position (**Figure 5**). Place a suitable container under the gear housing. Loosen the gearcase drain/fill plug (**Figure 6** or **Figure 7**). Allow a small amount of lubricant to drain. If water is present inside the gear housing, it will drain before the lubricant, or the lubricant will have a white or cream tint to the normal lubricant color. If the lubricant looks satisfactory, retighten the drain/fill plug securely. If water was present in the lubricant, or if the lubricant is dirty, is

fouled or contains substantial metal shavings, allow the remaining lubricant to drain completely from the gearcase.

> *NOTE*
> *The presence of a small amount of metal filings and fine metal particles in the lubricant is normal, while an excessive amount of metal filings and larger chips indicates a problem. Remove and disassemble the gearcase to determine the source and cause of the metal filings and chips. Replace damaged or worn parts. See Chapter Nine.*

> *CAUTION*
> *If water is present in the gearcase and it is not possible to repair it at the time, completely drain the contaminated lubricant and refill the gearcase with fresh lubricant. Crank the engine through several revolutions and spin the propeller shaft several turns to spread the fresh lubricant throughout the gearcase.*

2. Remove the gearcase vent plug(s) (**Figure 6** or **Figure 7**). Replace the sealing washer on each plug. Make sure the lubricant level is as follows:
   a. On 75-125 hp models (except 115 hp Optimax), the fluid must be level with the bottom of the rear vent plug hole (**Figure 6**).
   b. On 115 hp Optimax and 135-250 hp models, the fluid must be level with the vent plug hole (**Figure 7**).

> *CAUTION*
> *The vent plug(s) expels displaced air while lubricant is added to the gearcase. Never attempt to fill or add lubricant to the gearcase without first removing the vent plug(s).*

3. If the lubricant level is low, temporarily reinstall the vent plug(s) and remove the drain/fill plug. Insert the gearcase filling tube into the drain/fill plug hole, then remove the vent plug(s) again.

4. Replace the sealing washer on the drain plug.

5A. On 75-125 hp models (except 115 Optimax), inject the recommended lubricant into the drain/fill plug hole until lubricant flows from the front vent plug hole (**Figure 6**). Install and tighten the front vent plug. Continue adding lubricant until the lubricant flows from the rear vent plug hole. Without removing the filling tube from the drain/fill plug hole, install and tighten the rear vent plug. Remove the gearcase filling tube, and quickly install and tighten the drain/fill plug

5B. On 115 Optimax and 135-250 hp models, inject the recommended lubricant into the drain/fill plug hole until

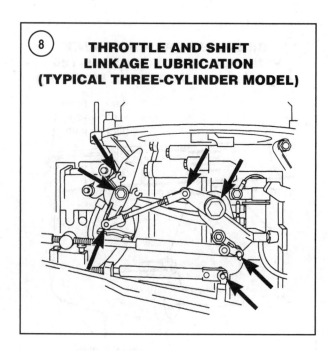

(8) **THROTTLE AND SHIFT LINKAGE LUBRICATION (TYPICAL THREE-CYLINDER MODEL)**

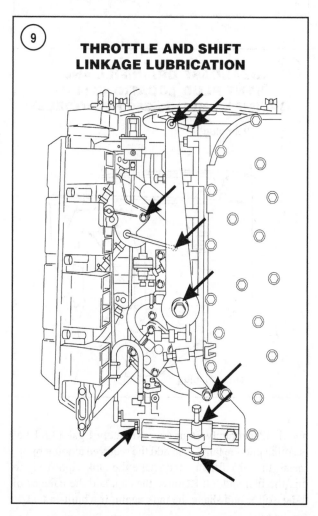

(9) **THROTTLE AND SHIFT LINKAGE LUBRICATION**

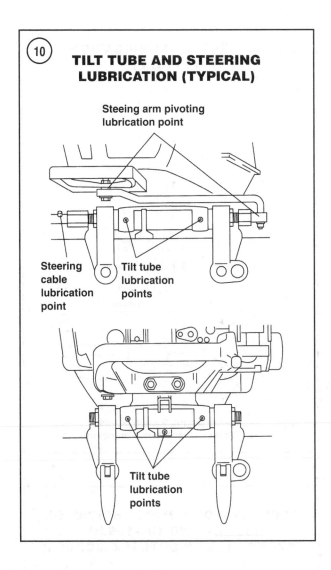

TILT TUBE AND STEERING LUBRICATION (TYPICAL)

Steering arm pivoting lubrication point

Steering cable lubrication point

Tilt tube lubrication points

Tilt tube lubrication points

excess lubricant flows from the vent plug hole (**Figure 7**). Install and tighten the vent plug. Remove the gearcase filling tube, and quickly install and tighten the drain/fill plug.

Changing Lower Gearcase Lubricant

Change the lower gearcase lubricant after the first 20 hours of operation and every 100 hours or seasonally thereafter. Refer to **Table 5** for gearcase capacities.

Refer to **Figure 6** for 75-125 hp models, except 115 Optimax, and **Figure 7** for 115 Optimax and 135-250 hp models.

1. Remove the engine cover. Disconnect and ground the spark plug leads to the power head to prevent accidental starting.

2. Place the outboard motor in an upright position (Figure 5). Place a suitable container under the lower gearcase.

3. Remove the drain/fill plug, then the vent plug(s). Allow the lubricant to drain fully into the container.

4. Inspect the drained lubricant. Lubricant contaminated with water will have a white or cream tint to the normal lubricant color. The presence of a small amount of metal filings and fine metal particles in the lubricant is normal, while an excessive amount of metal filings and larger chips indicates a problem.

NOTE
If there are excessive metal filings and larger chips, remove and disassemble the gearcase to determine the cause of the metal filings and chips. Replace damaged or worn parts. See Chapter Nine.

CAUTION
If water is present in the gearcase and it is not possible to repair it at this time, completely drain the contaminated lubricant and refill the gearcase with fresh lubricant. Crank the engine through several revolutions and spin the propeller shaft several turns to spread the fresh lubricant throughout the gearcase.

5. Refill the gearcase with the recommended lubricant as described under *Checking Lower Gearcase Lubricant* in this chapter. Refer to **Table 5** for lower gearcase lubricant capacities.

Jet Pump Maintenance

Jet pump maintenance is described in Chapter Ten.

Propeller Shaft

To prevent corrosion and to ease the future removal of the propeller, lubricate the propeller shaft at least once each season during freshwater operation and more often in saltwater operation. Remove the propeller as described in Chapter Nine and thoroughly remove corrosion or dried grease, then coat the propeller shaft splines with Quicksilver Special Lubricant 101 (part No. 92-13872A 1), Quicksilver 2-4-C Marine Lubricant (part No. 92-825407) or a suitable waterproof anticorrosion grease.

Recommended Preventive Maintenance and Lubrication

Refer to **Table 3** for recommended preventive maintenance intervals. Typical lubrication points for the more common engines are shown in **Figures 8-17**.

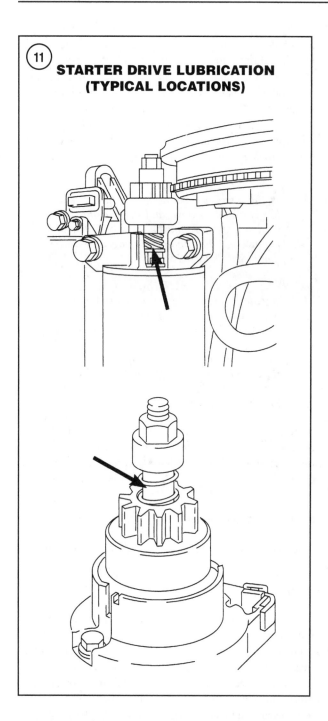

11 STARTER DRIVE LUBRICATION (TYPICAL LOCATIONS)

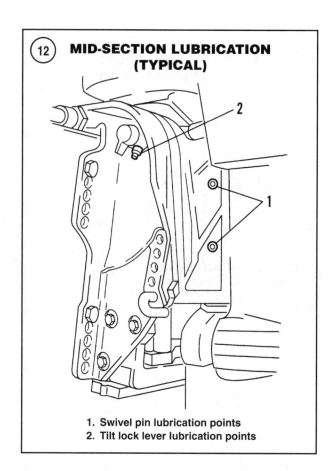

12 MID-SECTION LUBRICATION (TYPICAL)

1. Swivel pin lubrication points
2. Tilt lock lever lubrication points

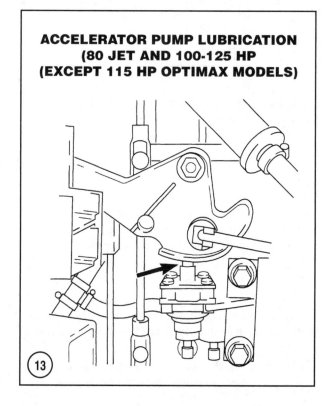

ACCELERATOR PUMP LUBRICATION (80 JET AND 100-125 HP (EXCEPT 115 HP OPTIMAX MODELS)

13

Lubricate every grease fitting on the midsection with 2-4-C grease (part No. 92-825407). Lubricate all pivoting or sliding throttle, shift and ignition linkages with 2-4-C grease. Lubricate the steering arm pivot points on remote control models with SAE 30 engine oil. Lubricate the steering cable sliding surfaces with 2-4-C grease.

The operation and maintenance manual that comes with each engine from Mercury/Mariner is an excellent source for detailed pictures of the lubrication points for a specific

4

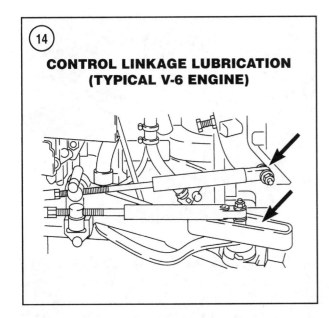

**CONTROL LINKAGE LUBRICATION
(TYPICAL V-6 ENGINE)**

⑭

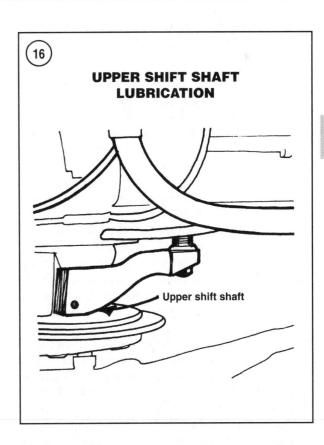

⑯

**UPPER SHIFT SHAFT
LUBRICATION**

Upper shift shaft

⑮

**UPPER SHIFT SHAFT
LUBRICATION POINTS
(TYPICAL THREE- AND
FOUR-CYLINDER MODELS)**

1. **Shift linkage**
2. **Upper shift shaft**

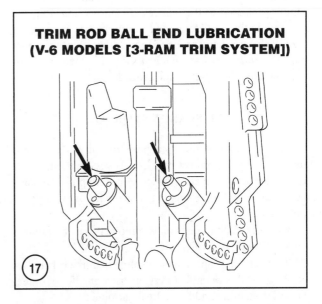

**TRIM ROD BALL END LUBRICATION
(V-6 MODELS [3-RAM TRIM SYSTEM])**

⑰

engine. If the operation and maintenance manual is missing, one can be ordered from any Mercury/Mariner dealership. Have the complete engine serial number before attempting to order the manual.

WARNING
When lubricating the steering cable, make sure its core is fully retracted into the cable housing. Lubricating the cable while extended can cause a hydraulic lock to occur that could result in hard turning or loss of steering control.

Corrosion of the Propeller Shaft
Bearing Carrier

Saltwater corrosion that accumulates between the propeller shaft bearing carrier and gearcase housing can eventually split the housing and destroy the lower gearcase assembly. If the outboard motor is operated in saltwater, remove the bearing carrier retaining ring or bearing carrier attachment hardware and the propeller shaft bearing carrier (**Figure 18**, typical) at least once per season. Refer to Chapter Nine for bearing carrier removal procedures for all models.

Thoroughly clean corrosion and dried lubricant from each end of the propeller shaft bearing carrier.

Clean the gear housing internal threads and retaining ring external threads on models so equipped. Replace the bearing carrier O-rings and propeller shaft seals if the carrier is removed. Apply a liberal coat of Quicksilver Perfect Seal (part No. 92-34227-1), Special Lubricant 101 (part No. 92-13872A1) or 2-4-C Marine Lubricant (part No. 92-825407) to each end of the carrier and to the gear housing and cover nut threads, if so equipped. If Quicksilver Perfect Seal is used, do not allow any Perfect Seal into the propeller shaft bearings. Reinstall the bearing carrier and retaining ring as described in Chapter Nine.

Make sure all available anodes are installed and securely grounded to the gearcase or midsection. Replace any anode that is deteriorated to one half of its original size. Refer to Chapter One for anode theory information. Refer to *Anticorrosion maintenance* in this chapter for additional corrosion prevention procedures.

OFF-SEASON STORAGE

The major considerations in preparing an outboard motor for storage are protecting it from rust, corrosion, dirt or other contamination and protecting it from physical damage. Mercury/Mariner recommends the following storage procedure.

1. On carbureted models only, remove the air box intake cover (**Figure 19**, typical).

2. Treat all fuel tanks with gasoline stabilizer. Mix according to the manufacturers instructions for storage. Gasoline stabilizer added to fresh gasoline:

   a. Prevents gum and varnish from forming in the fuel system.

   b. Controls moisture in the fuel system.

   c. Prevents modern fuels from reacting with brass and copper fuel system components.

   d. Stabilizes the fuel to prevent octane loss and prevents the fuel from going sour.

CAUTION
*Do not run the engine without an adequate water supply and do not exceed 3000 rpm without an adequate load. Refer to **Safety Precautions** in Chapter Three.*

3. Start the engine and run it at fast idle at least 15 minutes until it is warmed up to operating temperature. This ensures that the gasoline stabilizer has had time to reach the carburetor(s) or the fuel injection system.

NOTE
If the fuel in the fuel tank is fresh and properly stabilized, it is not necessary to run the engine fuel system dry. However, it may be desirable on small, portable engines that will be transported or stored in a position that could cause spilling. Engines permanently mounted to the transom and connected to permanently installed fuel tanks gain no benefit from running the engine fuel system dry.

4. On carbureted models, with the engine running at fast idle and at operating temperature, spray the recommended quantity of Quicksilver Storage Seal or an equivalent into each carburetor throat, following the manufacturer's instructions.

5A. On EFI models, prepare a 50:1 fuel/oil mixture in a portable fuel tank using the recommended oil, fresh gasoline and a gasoline stabilizer. Connect the portable fuel tank to the engine fuel inlet connector.

5B. On Optimax models, prepare a mixture of fresh gasoline and gasoline stabilizer in a portable fuel tank. Connect the portable fuel tank to the engine fuel inlet connector.

6. On EFI and Optimax models, start the engine and allow it to run at approximately 1000 rpm for 15 minutes. After 15 minutes, shut off the engine and disconnect the portable fuel tank from the engine.

7A. On carbureted and EFI models, remove the spark plugs as described in this chapter. Spray about 1 oz. (30

mL) of Quicksilver Storage Seal (part No. 92-86145) into each spark plug hole. Crank the engine clockwise by hand several revolutions to distribute the Storage Seal throughout the cylinders. Reinstall the spark plugs.

7B. On Optimax models, remove the spark plugs as described in this chapter. Pour about 1 oz. (30 mL) of Quicksilver Premium TCW-3 engine oil into each spark plug hole. Crank the engine clockwise by hand several revolutions to distribute the oil throughout the cylinders. Reinstall the spark plugs.

8. For portable fuel tanks, service the portable fuel tank filter by detaching the fuel hose from the tank. Unthread the pickup tube assembly or pickup tube retaining ring from the tank. Remove the pickup tube assembly. Clean or replace the fine mesh filter as necessary. Replace any gaskets, seals or O-rings. Thread the pickup assembly into the tank and tighten it or the retaining ring securely.

NOTE
Carbureted models use an inline filter. EFI and Optimax models use a spin-on water separating filter and one of two types of a final filter. EFI models normally have a small inline fuel filter in the bleed system return to the vapor separator. Optimax models have a small inline fuel filter in the vent line connecting the vapor separator tank to the flywheel cover.

9. Service the inline fuel filter (**Figure 20**) as follows:
   a. Carefully compress the spring clamps or cut the tie-strap clamps from each end of the filter.
   b. Disconnect the fuel lines from the filter. Discard the filter and replace fuel lines damaged in the filter removal process.
   c. Connect the fuel lines to the new filter. Make sure the arrow is pointing in the direction of fuel flow toward the carburetor. Fasten the hoses to the filter securely with new tie-straps.
   d. Test the installation by squeezing the primer bulb and checking for leaks.

10. Service the water separating fuel filter (A, **Figure 21**, typical) on EFI and Optimax models as follows:
   a. Disconnect the water sensor lead (B, **Figure 21**) from the bottom of the filter canister (A).
   b. Remove the water separating fuel filter by unscrewing the filter from the filter base. Empty the contents of the filter into a suitable container for inspection.
   c. If there is excessive debris or water accumulation, inspect the fuel tanks for water contamination and other debris.
   d. Remove the water sensing probe from the bottom of the filter and discard the filter.

e. Install the water sensing probe into a new filter. Lubricate the filter seal with a light coat of outboard motor oil.

f. Install the filter onto the filter base and tighten it securely *by hand*. Reconnect the water sensor probe lead. Coat the sensor lead connection with Quicksilver Liquid Neoprene (part No. 92-25711-2).

g. Test the installation by squeezing the primer bulb and checking for leaks.

11. To service the final fuel filter (**Figure 22**) on EFI models, refer to Chapter Six. The final filter is mounted between the electric fuel pump outlet and the fuel rail. Relieve fuel rail pressure before servicing the final fuel filter.

12. Replace the bleed system filter on EFI models (**Figure 23**).

13. Drain and refill the lower gearcase with the recommended lubricant as described in this chapter. Install new sealing washers on all drain and vent plugs.

14. For jet pump models, refer to *Jet pump maintenance* in Chapter Ten for drive shaft bearing lubrication.

15. Refer to **Figures 8-17** and **Table 1** as necessary, for preventive maintenance and general lubrication recommendations.

16. Clean all exterior areas of the outboard motor, including all accessible power head parts. Spray the entire power head, including all electrical connections, with Quicksilver Corrosion Guard (part No. 92-815869). Install the engine cowling and spray a thin film of Quicksilver Corrosion Guard on all remaining metal painted surfaces of the midsection and lower gearcase.

17. Remove the propeller as described in Chapter Nine. Lubricate the propeller shaft with Quicksilver Special Lubricant 101 (92-13872 A1) or Quicksilver 2-4-C Marine Lubricant (92-825407) and reinstall the propeller.

CAUTION
Make sure all water drain holes in the gear housing are open to allow water to drain. Water expands as it freezes and can crack the gear housing or water pump. If the boat is equipped with a speedometer, disconnect the pickup tube and allow it to drain completely, then reconnect the tube.

18. Drain the cooling system completely to prevent freeze damage by positioning the motor in a vertical position. Check all water drain holes for blockage.

19. On Optimax models, remove the compressor cooling water strainer (**Figure 24**) from the power head adapter plate. Remove the split lower cowl panels to gain access to the strainer. Clean the strainer and allow water to drain from the hose and adapter plate. Coat the threads of the

water strainer with Loctite 567 PST pipe sealant (part No. 92-809822). Install and tighten the strainer securely.

20. On Optimax models, inspect the air compressor inlet filter (**Figure 25**). Replace the filter if it is obstructed. Replace the filter at least once a year.

a. Remove the flywheel cover.

b. Remove the four screws from the filter retainer. Lift the retainer and filter from the flywheel cover.

c. Fit the new filter into the recess. Place the retainer over the filter and align the screw holes.

d. Apply Loctite 271 (part No. 92-80819) to the screw threads. Install and securely tighten the screws.

21. Store the motor in a vertical position. Never store an outboard motor with the power head below the lower gearcase. The power head must be higher than the lower gearcase to prevent water from entering the engine through the exhaust ports.

22. Prepare the battery for storage as follows:

a. Disconnect the negative, then the positive, battery cables.

b. Clean all grease, sulfate or other contamination from the battery case and terminals.

c. Remove the vent caps, if possible, and check the electrolyte level of each cell. Add distilled water to

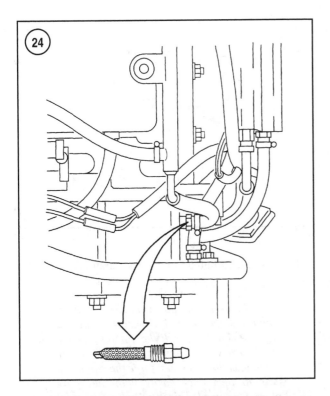

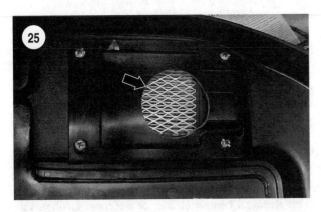

e. With the battery in a fully-charged condition (specific gravity at 1.260-1.280), store the battery in a cool, dry location where the temperature will not drop below freezing.

f. Recharge the battery every 45 days or whenever the specific gravity drops below 1.230. Maintain the recommended electrolyte level at all times. Add distilled water as necessary to maintain the level recommended by the battery manufacturer. For maximum battery life, avoid charge rates exceeding 6 amps. Discontinue charging when the specific gravity reaches 1.260 at 80° F (27° C).

g. Remove the grease on the battery terminals prior to returning the battery to service. Make sure the battery is installed in a fully-charged state.

ANTICORROSION MAINTENANCE

NOTE
Magnesium anodes are available for extra corrosion protection in freshwater. Do not use magnesium anodes in saltwater. The unit will be overprotected, causing the paint to blister and peel off.

1. Flush the cooling system with freshwater as described in this chapter after each outing in saltwater. Wash the exterior with freshwater.

2. Dry the exterior of the outboard and apply primer over any paint nicks and scratches. Use only Mercury/Mariner recommended touch-up paint. Do not use paints containing mercury or copper. Do not paint sacrificial anodes or the trim tab, if it is anodic.

3. Spray the power head and all electrical connections with Quicksilver corrosion guard.

4. Inspect all of the sacrificial anodes and trim tab, if it is anodic. Replace any that are deteriorated to less than one-half their original size.

   a. To check for proper anode grounding, calibrate an ohmmeter on the highest scale available.

   b. Connect one meter lead to a power head ground. Connect the other meter lead to the anode. The ohmmeter should indicate continuity or a very low reading.

   c. If any other reading is noted, remove the anode and thoroughly clean the mounting surfaces of the anode and the motor. Wire brush the threads of the mounting hardware and run a thread chaser into the mounting holes.

   d. Reinstall the anode and retest as previously described. If the meter reading is still unsatisfactory, replace the anode and inspect the gearcase to

the level recommended by the battery manufacturer. Do not overfill.

d. Lubricate the terminals and terminal fasteners with Quicksilver corrosion guard (part No. 92-815869).

CAUTION
*A discharged battery can be damaged by freezing. Consider using a battery **float** style charger to maintain the battery charge. A float charger is an inexpensive way to keep the battery at peak charge without causing excessive venting or gassing and subsequent water loss. Float chargers are available from most marine dealerships and marine supply outlets.*

midsection and midsection to power head mounting hardware for corrosion and high resistance.

5. If the outboard motor is operated consistently in saltwater, polluted or brackish water, shorten the lubrication intervals in **Table 3** by one-half.

ENGINE SUBMERSION

An outboard motor which has been lost overboard should be recovered and attended to as quickly as possible. A delay will cause irreparable rust and corrosion damage to internal components. The following emergency steps should be attempted immediately if the motor is submerged in freshwater.

> *NOTE*
> *If the outboard motor falls overboard in saltwater, completely disassemble and clean the motor before attempting to start the engine. If it is not possible to disassemble and clean the motor immediately, flush and re-submerge the outboard in freshwater to minimize rust and corrosion until it can be properly attended to.*

1. Wash the outside of the motor with clean water to remove weeds, mud and other debris.
2. Remove the engine cowling.
3. Rinse the power head clean of all weeds, mud and other debris with freshwater.
4. Remove, clean and dry the spark plug(s).
5A. On EFI and Optimax models, drain the vapor separator assembly. Do not reinstall the drain plug. See Chapter Six.
5B. On carbureted models, drain the carburetor float bowl(s). Do not reinstall the float chamber plugs. See Chapter Six.
6. Drain and clean all oil tanks (reservoirs). Flush out all lines. Refill the system with the recommended oil. Bleed as much air out of the system as possible at this time. See Chapter Thirteen.
7. Connect a clean fuel tank to the engine fuel line connector. Squeeze the primer bulb repeatedly to flush fresh fuel through the entire fuel system and purge the system of water.

> *NOTE*
> *If a boat with a permanent fuel system and remote controls was submerged, service the boat's fuel system and electrical system in the same manner as the engine's fuel and electrical systems.*

8. Replace *all* fuel filters.

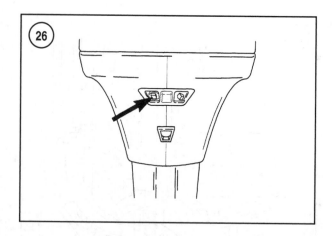

9. Reinstall the carburetor or vapor separator drain plugs.

> *CAUTION*
> *If sand entered the power head, do not attempt to start the engine or severe internal damage could occur. If the outboard is lost overboard while running, internal engine damage is likely. Do not force the motor if it fails to turn over easily with the spark plug(s) removed. This is an indication of internal damage, such as a bent connecting rod or broken piston.*

10. Drain as much water as possible from the power head by placing the motor in a horizontal position. Position the spark plugs facing downward and manually rotate the flywheel to expel water from the cylinder(s).
11. Pour liberal amounts of isopropyl (rubbing) alcohol into each carburetor or throttle body throat while rotating the flywheel to help absorb any remaining water or moisture.
12. Disconnect all electrical connectors and dry them with electrical contact cleaner or isopropyl alcohol. Lubricate all electrical connectors with Quicksilver dielectric silicone grease (part No. 92-823506-1).
13. Remove the electric starter motor. Disassemble the starter motor and dry all components with electrical contact cleaner or isopropyl alcohol. Reassemble and install the starter (Chapter Seven).
14. If the alternator, on 225-250 hp and all Optimax models, can be disassembled, cleaned and dried without damaging any parts, it is acceptable to do so. However, if any parts are damaged, replace the alternator as an assembly.
15. 150-200 hp EFI models:
   a. Remove the ECU from the power head. Drain as much water as possible from the manifold absolute pressure (MAP) sensor tube. Do not attempt to remove the MAP sensor hose from the ECU.

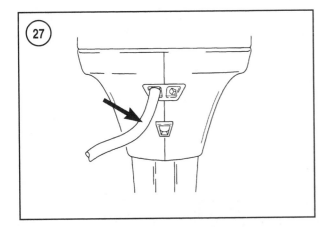

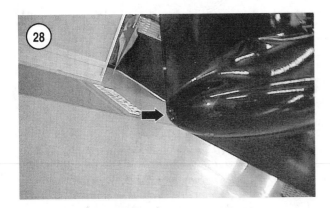

b. Place the ECU assembly in an oven and heat it at 120° F (50° C) for approximately 2 hours to dry the ECU assembly. Remove the ECU from the oven and have it tested with the Mercury/Mariner tester (part No. 91-11011A2 EFI).

16. On 225-250 EFI and all Optimax models, remove and replace the MAP sensor. Make sure the map sensor vacuum line to the induction manifold is completely free of water and moisture before reconnection.

17. Pour approximately one teaspoon of engine oil into each cylinder through the spark plug hole(s). Rotate the flywheel by hand to distribute the oil.

18. Position the outboard with the induction system facing upward. Pour engine oil into each carburetor or throttle body throat while rotating the flywheel by hand to distribute the oil.

19. Reinstall the spark plug(s).

20. Attempt to start the engine using a fresh tank of 50:1 fuel/oil mixture. Use only fuel on Optimax models. If the outboard motor will start, allow it to run at least one hour to evaporate any remaining water inside the engine. Purge any remaining air from the oil injection system on models so equipped.

21. If the motor will not start, attempt to diagnose the cause as fuel, electrical or mechanical and repair as necessary. If the engine cannot be started within two hours, completely disassemble, clean and oil all internal components as soon as possible.

COOLING SYSTEM FLUSHING

Periodic flushing with clean freshwater prevents excessive salt or silt deposits from accumulating in the cooling system passageways. Perform the flushing procedure after each outing. Flushing is especially important if the engine is operated in salt, brackish or polluted water.

Keep the motor in an upright position during and after flushing. This prevents water from passing into the power head through the drive shaft housing and exhaust ports during the flushing procedure. It also eliminates the possibility of residual water being trapped in the drive shaft housing or other passages.

The engine can be flushed with the engine running on all models. All V-6 models (115-250 hp) incorporate a static flush port (**Figure 26**) that allows flushing of the power head without running the engine.

Flushing Without Running the Engine (135-250 hp and 115 hp Optimax)

Some 135-250 hp models are equipped with a built-in static flushing port. This port can only be used for static flushing. Any attempt to operate the engine while it is attached to the static flushing port will result in water pump failure and subsequent engine overheat.

1. Position the engine in a vertical position, remove the plug from the port.

2. Connect a garden hose to the port (**Figure 27**). Run water into the port for 3-5 minutes.

3. Disconnect the garden hose. Make sure to reinstall the plug when finished.

Flushing With the Engine Running (All Models)

CAUTION
*All 2000-on 200 Optimax, 225 hp and 250 hp models have water inlet openings at the front of the gearcase (**Figure 28**). Since the flushing adapter does not cover these openings, air may be drawn into the cooling system through these openings, preventing adequate water flow and subsequently overheating the engine. Always monitor the tell-tale stream and the engine temperature*

while flushing the engine while running. If overheating or a weak tell-tale stream occur, temporarily cover the front water inlets with duct tape. Remove the tape after flushing the engine.

This method is required on 75-125 hp, except 115 hp Optimax, models and can be performed on all models. Use flushing adapter Quicksilver part No. 44357A-2 (**Figure 29**) or an equivalent.

1. Remove the propeller as described in Chapter Nine.

2. Position the outboard in the normal operating position.

3. Attach the flushing device to the lower gearcase as shown in **Figure 29**.

4. Connect a garden hose (1/2 in. or larger) between a water tap and the flushing device.

5. Open the water tap partially. Adjust the water pressure until a significant amount of water escapes from around the flushing cups, but do not apply full pressure.

6. Shift the outboard into NEUTRAL and start the engine. Adjust the engine speed to approximately 1000-1500 rpm.

7. Adjust the water flow to maintain a slight loss of water around the rubber cups of the flushing device.

8. Check the motor to be certain that water is being discharged from the water pump indicator hose or fitting (**Figure 30**). If not, stop the motor immediately and determine the cause of the problem.

9. Flush the motor for 5-10 minutes or until the discharged water is clear. If the outboard was last used in saltwater, flush for 10 minutes minimum.

10. Stop the engine, then shut off the water supply. Remove the flushing device from the outboard.

11. Keep the outboard in the normal operating position to allow all water to drain from the drive shaft housing. If this is not done, water can enter the power head through the exhaust ports.

12. Reinstall the propeller as described in Chapter Nine.

65-140 Jet Models

The 65-140 jet models have a flushing port built into the jet pump unit. A flushing adaptor is available from Quicksilver Parts and Accessories (part No. 24789A-1). The flushing procedure is outlined in the following sections.

Rinse the water intake grate area, impeller and the entire outside surface of all jet pump units with freshwater. Direct a garden hose into the grate area and over the outer surfaces of the pump unit *after* the recommended flushing procedure has been completed.

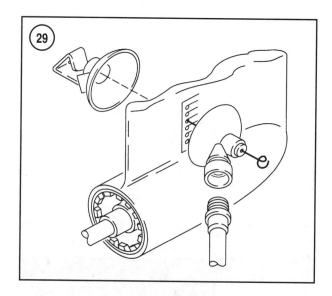

105 jet and 140 jet models incorporate a static flush port (**Figure 26**) that allows flushing of the power head without running the engine.

> *CAUTION*
> *105 and 140 jet models are equipped with a built-in static flushing port (**Figure 26**). This port can only be used for static flushing. Any attempt to operate the engine while it is attached to the static flushing port will cause water pump failure and subsequent engine overheat.*

To use the static flush port, position the engine in a vertical position, remove the plug from the port and connect a garden hose to the port (**Figure 27**). Run water into the port for 3-5 minutes. Reinstall the plug when finished.

Flushing without running the engine (105 jet and 140 jet models)

1. Position the engine in a vertical position, remove the plug from the port.

2. Connect a garden hose to the port (**Figure 27**). Run water into the port for 3-5 minutes.

3. Disconnect the garden hose. Reinstall the plug.

Flushing with the engine running (all jet models)

1. Position the outboard in the vertical position.

2. Remove the flushing port plug and washer (**Figure 31**), install the flushing adapter and connect a 1/2 in. or larger garden hose to the flushing adapter.

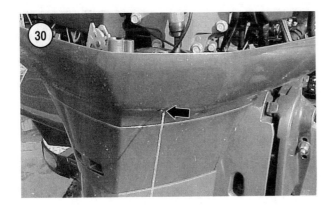

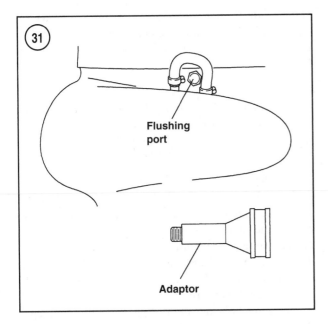

Flushing port

Adaptor

3. Open the water tap approximately halfway. It is not necessary to use full water pressure.

4. Shift the outboard into neutral and start the engine. Adjust the engine speed to approximately 1000 rpm.

5. Check the motor to make sure water is being discharged from the water pump indicator hose or fitting (**Figure 30**). Adjust the water tap as necessary. If no water is being discharged, stop the motor immediately and determine the cause of the problem.

6. Flush the motor for 5-10 minutes or until the discharged water is clear. If the outboard was last used in saltwater, flush for 10 minutes minimum.

7. Stop the engine, then shut off the water supply. Remove the flushing device from the outboard and reinstall the plug and washer in the flushing port (**Figure 31**). Tighten the plug securely.

8. Thoroughly rinse the intake grate area and all outer surfaces of the pump unit with the garden hose.

9. Keep the outboard in the vertical position to allow all water to drain from the drive shaft housing. If this is not done, water can enter the power head through the exhaust ports.

TUNE-UP

4

A tune-up consists of a series of inspections, adjustments and parts replacement to compensate for normal wear and deterioration of the outboard motor components. Regular tune-ups are important to maintain performance. Mercury/Mariner recommends that tune-up procedures be performed at least once a season or every 100 hours of operation. Individual operating conditions may dictate that a tune-up be performed more often. Also perform a tune-up when the outboard exhibits a substantial performance loss.

Since proper outboard motor operation depends upon a number of interrelated system functions, a tune-up consisting of only one or two of the recommended procedures will seldom provide satisfactory results. For best results, a thorough and systematic procedure of analysis and correction is necessary.

Prior to performing a tune-up, flush the outboard cooling system as described in this chapter to check for proper water pump operation.

The recommended tune-up procedure is listed below. Any procedure not covered in this chapter or section is so identified.

1. Quicksilver Power Tune treatment which is listed under *Removing Combustion Chamber Deposits.*

2. Compression test.

3. Electrical wiring harness inspection.

4. Spark plug service.

5. Gearcase lubricant change and propeller shaft spline lubrication.

6. General engine lubrication at all applicable lubrication points. See **Table 3**.

7. Fuel, air, water and bleed filter service as applicable.

8. Lower gearcase water pump service.

9. Fuel system and oil injection system service.

10. Ignition system service.

11. Charging system service.

12. Battery and starter system service.

13. All synchronization and linkage adjustments (Chapter Five).

14. On-water performance test.

When the fuel or ignition system is adjusted or defective parts are replaced, verify all engine synchronization and linkage adjustments. These procedures are described in Chapter Five. Perform all synchronization and linkage adjustments *before* running the on-water performance test.

Removing Combustion Chamber Deposits

During operation, carbon deposits will accumulate on the piston(s), rings, cylinder head(s) and exhaust ports. If the carbon is allowed to build up unchecked, the effective compression ratio will increase, raising the fuel octane requirements of the power head.

If the carbon builds up in the piston ring area, the piston rings eventually stick in the piston ring grooves causing a loss of compression and the loss of heat transfer to the cylinder walls and water passages. When the piston rings stick, performance suffers and combustion chamber temperatures increase dramatically, leading to preignition and detonation. All of these situations eventually lead to power head failure.

Quicksilver Power Tune (part No. 92-15104) is designed to remove combustion chamber deposits and free stuck piston rings, restoring engine performance and lowering the risk of power head failure.

> *NOTE*
> *A quality gasoline and an NMMA approved TCW-3 outboard oil will minimize combustion chamber deposits and piston ring sticking. If the use of poor quality gasoline and outboard oil is unavoidable, or if combustion chamber deposits are a continual problem, use Quicksilver QuicKleen Fuel Treatment regularly.*

For effective preventive maintenance, all engines should have Quicksilver Power Tune Engine Cleaner applications performed every 100 hours of operation or as required. Follow the manufacturer's instructions on the Quicksilver Power Tune container.

Compression Test

An accurate cylinder cranking compression check provides an indication of the mechanical condition of the combustion chamber. An engine with low or unequal compression between cylinders *cannot* be satisfactorily tuned. Correct any compression problem discovered during this test before continuing with the tune-up procedure. A thread-in compression tester is recommended for best results.

A variation of more than 15 psi (103.4 kPa) between any two cylinders indicates a problem. If the compression is unacceptable, remove the cylinder head, if applicable, and inspect the cylinder wall(s), piston(s) and head gas-

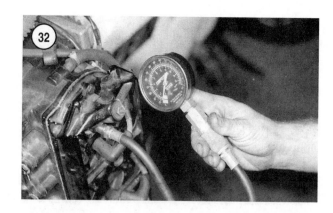

ket(s) condition. If the cylinder wall(s), piston(s) and head gasket show no evidence of damage or failure, the piston rings are stuck, worn or damaged, and the power head will have to be repaired.

> *CAUTION*
> *Do not run the engine without an adequate water supply and do not exceed 3000 rpm without an adequate load. Refer to **Safety Precautions** at the beginning of Chapter Three.*

1. Run the engine to operating temperature.
2. Remove the spark plug(s) as described in this chapter.
3. Securely ground the spark plug lead(s) to the engine to disable the ignition system, prevent accidental starting and prevent possible ignition system damage.
4. Following the compression gauge manufacturer's instructions, connect the gauge to the No. 1 cylinder (top) spark plug hole (**Figure 32**, typical).
5. Manually hold the throttle plates in the wide-open throttle position. Crank the engine through at least four compression strokes and record the gauge reading.
6. Repeat Step 4 and Step 5 for all remaining cylinders. A variation of more than 15 psi (103.4 kPa) between two cylinders indicates a problem with the low reading cylinder, such as worn or sticking piston rings and/or scored pistons or cylinder walls. In these cases, pour a tablespoon of engine oil into the suspect cylinder and repeat Step 4 and Step 5. If the compression increases by 10 psi (69 kPa) or more, the rings are worn or damaged and the power head must be disassembled and repaired.
7. If the compression is within specification, but the outboard motor is difficult to start or has poor idle quality, refer to *Starting Difficulties* in Chapter Three.

Electrical Wiring Harness Inspection

Inspect all harnesses, leads, connectors and terminals for loose connection, corrosion, mechanical damage,

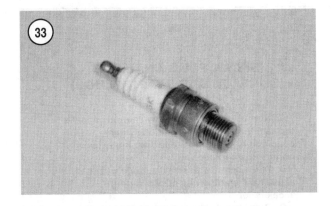

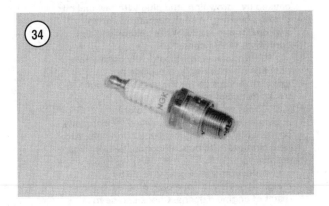

damaged insulation and improper routing. Check harnesses that are close to moving components for chafing or rubbing damage. Reroute, retape and secure harnesses as necessary. Inspect all harnesses, leads and components on or near the cylinder head and exhaust passages for heat damage. Repair any damage found. Refer to Chapter Three for recommended tools and repair kits.

Spark Plug Replacement

Improper installation and incorrect application are common causes of poor spark plug performance in outboard motors. The gasket on the plug must be fully compressed against a clean plug seat for effective heat transfer. If heat transfer cannot take place, the spark plug will overheat and fail. This may also lead to preignition and detonation. Make sure the spark plugs are correctly torqued.

Incorrect application can cause not only spark plug problems, but can also lead to ignition system symptoms or failure from radio frequency interference (RFI). Most engines with an ECM require suppression or inductor spark plugs that reduce the RFI caused by the spark jumping the air gap of the spark plug. Always use the recommended spark plugs.

If the engine does not require inductor or suppression spark plugs, yet there is ignition interference with onboard accessories, install the recommended inductor or suppression spark plug as recommended in **Table 4**.

CAUTION
When the spark plug(s) are removed, dirt or other debris surrounding the spark plug hole(s) can fall into the cylinder(s). Debris inside the cylinders can cause engine damage when the engine is started.

1. Clean the area around the spark plug(s) using compressed air or an appropriate brush.
2. Disconnect the spark plug lead(s) by twisting the boot back and forth on the spark plug insulator while pulling outward. Pulling on the lead instead of the boot can cause internal damage to the lead.
3. Remove the spark plugs using an appropriate size spark plug socket. Arrange the spark plugs in order of the cylinder from which they were removed.
4. Examine each spark plug. See **Figure 33** for surface gap plugs and **Figure 34** for conventional gap plugs. Compare the spark plug condition to **Figure 35** (surface gap) or **Figure 36** (conventional gap). Spark plug condition is a good indicator of piston, rings and cylinder condition, and it can provide a warning of developing trouble.
5. Check each plug for make and heat range. All spark plugs should be identical. Refer to **Table 4** and make sure the spark plugs are correct for the application.
6. If the spark plugs are in good condition, they can be cleaned and regapped, if applicable. Install new spark plugs if there is any question about the condition of the spark plugs.
7. Inspect the spark plug threads in the engine and clean them with a thread chaser (**Figure 37**) if necessary. Wipe the spark plug seats clean before installing new spark plugs.
8. Install the spark plugs with new gaskets and tighten them to the specification in **Table 1**. If a torque wrench is not available, seat the plugs finger tight, then tighten them an additional 1/4 turn with a wrench.
9. Inspect each spark plug lead before reconnecting it to its spark plug. If the insulation is damaged or deteriorated, install a new plug lead. Push the boot onto the plug terminal making sure it is fully seated.

Spark Plug Gap Adjustment
(Conventional Gap Only)

Carefully set the electrode gap on new spark plugs to ensure a reliable, consistent spark. Use a special spark

4

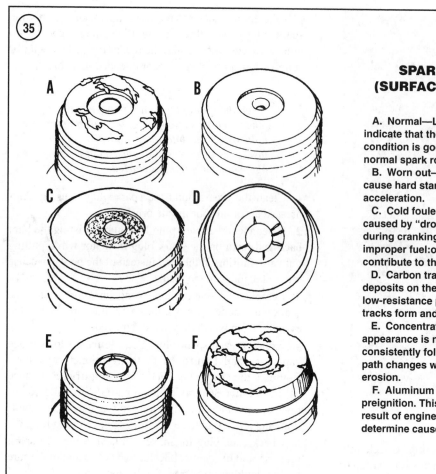

**SPARK PLUG ANALYSIS
(SURFACE GAP SPARK PLUGS)**

A. Normal—Light tan or gray colored deposits indicate that the engine/ignition system condition is good. Electrode wear indicates normal spark rotation.

B. Worn out—Excessive electrode wear can cause hard starting or a misfire during acceleration.

C. Cold fouled—Wet oil or fuel deposits are caused by "drowning" the plug with raw fuel mix during cranking, overich carburetion or an improper fuel:oil ratio. Weak ignition will also contribute to this condition.

D. Carbon tracking—Electrically conductive deposits on the firing end provide a low-resistance path for the voltage. Carbon tracks form and can cause misfires.

E. Concentrated arc—Multi-colored appearance is normal. It is caused by electricity consistently following the same firing path. Arc path changes with deposit conductivity and gap erosion.

F. Aluminum throw off—Caused by preignition. This is not a plug problem but the result of engine damage. Check engine to determine cause and extent of damage.

---

plug gapping tool with wire gauges. **Figure 38** shows a common type of gapping tool.

> *NOTE*
> *Some spark plug brands require that the terminal nut (**Figure 39**) be screwed on the plug before installation.*

1. Make sure the gaskets are installed on the spark plugs.

> *CAUTION*
> *Never attempt to close the gap by tapping the spark plug on a solid surface. This can damage the spark plug. Always use the proper adjusting tool to open or close the gap.*

2. Insert the appropriate size wire gauge (**Table 4**) between the electrodes (**Figure 40**). If the gap is correct, there will be a slight drag as the wire is pulled through. To adjust the gap, bend the side electrode with the gapping tool (**Figure 41**), then remeasure the gap.

**Lower Gearcase and
Jet Pump Unit Water Pump**

Overheating and extensive power head damage can result from a faulty water pump. Replace the water pump impeller, seals and gaskets at the following intervals:

> *NOTE*
> *Individual operating conditions may dictate that the pump be serviced more often. Also service the water pump anytime the lower gearcase or jet pump assembly is removed for service.*

1. On 115 Optimax, 135-175 hp and 200 hp (except 200 Optimax) models, replace the water pump after every 100 hours of operation or once per year. Refer to Chapter Nine for pump identification and service procedures.

2. On 75-125 hp (except 115 Optimax), 200 hp Optimax, 225 hp and 250 hp models, replace the water pump after every 300 hours of operation or every 3 years. Refer to

4

CONVENTIONAL SPARK PLUG CONDITION

NORMAL
- Identified by light tan or gray deposits on the firing tip.
- Can be cleaned.

GAP BRIDGED
- Identified by deposit buildup closing gap between electrodes.

OIL FOULED
- Identified by wet black deposits on the insulator shell bore and electrodes.
- Caused by excessive oil entering combustion chamber through worn rings and pistons, excessive clearance between valve guides and stems or worn or loose bearings. Can be cleaned. If engine is not repaired, use a hotter plug.

CARBON FOULED
- Identified by black, dry fluffy carbon deposits on insulator tips, exposed shell surfaces and electrodes.
- Caused by too cold a plug, weak ignition, dirty air cleaner, too rich fuel mixture or excessive idling. Can be cleaned.

ADDITIVE FOULED
- Identified by dark gray, black, yellow or tan deposits or a fused glazed coating on the insulator tip.
- Caused by using gasoline additives. Can be cleaned.

WORN
- Identified by severely eroded or worn electrodes.
- Caused by normal wear. Should be replaced.

FUSED SPOT DEPOSIT
- Identified by melted or spotty deposits resembling bubbles or blisters.
- Caused by sudden acceleration. Can be cleaned.

OVERHEATING
- Identified by a white or light gray insulator with small black or gray brown spots with bluish-burnt appearance of electrodes.
- Caused by engine overheating, wrong type of fuel, loose spark plugs, too hot a plug or incorrect ignition timing. Replace the plug.

PREIGNITION
- Identified by melted electrodes and possibly blistered insulator. Metallic deposits on insulator indicate engine damage.
- Caused by wrong type of fuel, incorrect ignition timing or advance, too hot a plug, burned valves or engine overheating. Replace the plug.

Chapter Nine for pump identification and service procedures.

> *NOTE*
> *Anytime the lower gearcase is removed, clean and lubricate the drive shaft splines with 2-4-C (part No. 92-825407) or Special Lube 101 lubricant (part No. 92-13872A1). Do not apply lubricant to the top drive shaft surface as this may prevent the drive shaft from fully seating into the crankshaft.*

Many outboard owners depend on the water pump indicator hose or *tell tale* as the sole indicator of water pump performance. While monitoring the water pump indicator hose is important, a water pressure gauge kit available from a Mercury/Mariner dealership is a more effective method to ensure the pump is operating correctly. The kit contains a fitting and hose that attaches to the power head and a water pressure gauge that is mounted in the boat.

Water pressure specifications are listed in the appropriate engine's general specification table at the end of Chapter Five. After installing the pressure gauge kit and every time the water pump is serviced, note the normal water pressure readings at various speeds for the engine. If the pressure readings show a gradual drop from the normal readings, the impeller is worn and impeller replacement should be planned in the near future. If the pressure readings show a sudden drop, the water pump is damaged and the pump must be serviced immediately (Chapter Nine).

Fuel and Oil Injection Systems

During a tune-up, verify all synchronization and linkage adjustments as described in Chapter Five. Clean or replace all fuel, bleed and air filters. Inspect all fuel lines, fuel system components and spring clamps, worm clamps or tie-straps for leaks, deterioration, mechanical damage and secure mounting. Replacement fuel lines must be alcohol resistant. If the fuel system is suspected of not functioning correctly, refer to Chapter Three for troubleshooting procedures.

Refer to *Fuel and Lubrication* in this chapter for basic oil injection system description and component function. Check the oil injection system, if so equipped, for leaks, loose lines and fittings, and deterioration. Synchronize the oil pump linkage with the throttle linkage (Chapter Five). Inspect the warning module and sensor wiring, if so equipped, as described under *Electrical Wiring Harness Inspection* in this chapter. If the oil injection system is suspected of not functioning correctly, refer to Chapter Thirteen for oil injection system troubleshooting and service procedures.

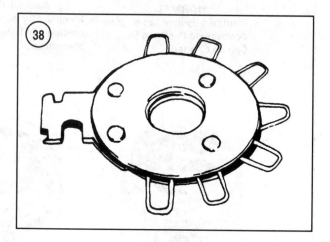

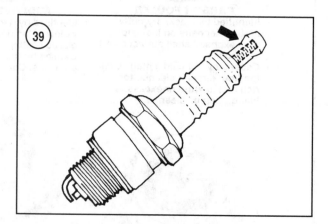

Fuel, bleed, air and water filters

1. Service the portable fuel tank filter by detaching the fuel hose from the tank. Unthread the pickup tube assembly or pickup tube retaining ring from the tank. Remove the pickup tube assembly. Clean or replace the fine mesh filter as necessary. Replace any gaskets, seals or O-rings. Thread the pickup assembly into the tank and tighten it or the retaining ring securely.

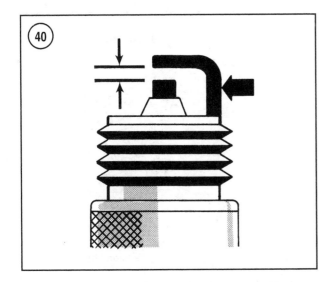

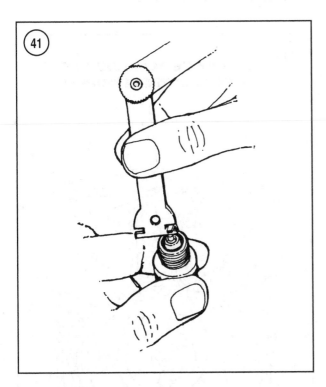

2. Service the inline fuel filter (**Figure 20**) as follows:

   a. Carefully compress the spring clamps or cut the tie-strap clamps from each end of the filter.

   b. Disconnect the fuel lines from the filter. Discard the filter and replace any fuel lines damaged in the filter removal process.

   c. Connect the fuel lines to the new filter. Make sure the arrow is pointing in the direction of fuel flow toward the carburetor. Fasten the hoses to the filter securely with new tie-straps.

   d. Test the installation by squeezing the primer bulb and checking for leaks.

3. Service the water separating fuel filter (A, **Figure 21**, typical) on EFI and Optimax models as follows:

   a. Disconnect the water sensor lead (B, **Figure 21**) from the bottom of the filter canister (A).

   b. Remove the water separating fuel filter by unscrewing the filter from the filter base. Empty the contents of the filter into a suitable container for inspection.

   c. If there is excessive debris or water accumulation, inspect the fuel tanks for water contamination and other debris.

   d. Remove the water sensing probe from the bottom of the filter and discard the filter.

   e. Install the water sensing probe into a new filter. Lubricate the filter seal with a light coat of outboard motor oil.

   f. Install the filter onto the filter base and tighten it securely *by hand*. Reconnect the water sensor probe lead. Coat the sensor lead connection with Quicksilver Liquid Neoprene (part No. 92-25711-2).

   g. Test the installation by squeezing the primer bulb and checking for leaks.

4. To service the final fuel filter (**Figure 22**) on EFI models, refer to Chapter Six. The final filter is mounted between the electric fuel pump outlet and the fuel rail. Relieve fuel rail pressure *before* servicing the final fuel filter.

5. Replace the bleed system filter on EFI models (**Figure 23**).

6. On Optimax models, remove the compressor cooling water strainer (**Figure 24**) from the power head adapter plate. Remove the split lower cowl panels to gain access to the strainer. Clean the strainer and allow water to drain from the hose and adapter plate. Coat the threads of the water strainer with Loctite 567 PST pipe sealant (part No. 92-809822). Install and tighten the strainer securely.

7. On Optimax models, inspect the air compressor inlet filter (**Figure 25**). Replace the filter if it is obstructed. Replace the filter at least once a year.

   a. Remove the flywheel cover.

   b. Remove the four screws from the filter retainer. Lift the retainer and filter from the flywheel cover.

   c. Fit the new filter into the recess. Place the retainer over the filter and align the screw holes.

   d. Apply Loctite 271 (part No. 92-80819) to the screw threads. Install, then securely tighten the screws.

Fuel pump

The fuel pump does not generally require service during a tune-up. However, conduct a visual inspection of the fuel pump, pump mounting hardware, all fuel and crank-case pulse hoses, and all spring clamps, worm clamps or tie-straps. Replace damaged or deteriorated components. If the fuel pump or fuel system is suspected of not functioning correctly, refer to Chapter Three for troubleshooting procedures.

Ignition System Service

Other than inspecting or replacing the spark plugs, the ignition system is relatively maintenance free. During a tune-up, verify all synchronization and linkage adjustments as described in Chapter Five. If the ignition system is suspected of not functioning correctly, refer to Chapter Three for troubleshooting procedures.

Charging System Service

Other than inspecting the belt and belt tension on 225-250 hp and all Optimax models, no maintenance is required on the charging system. If the charging system is suspected of not functioning correctly, refer to Chapter Three for troubleshooting procedures.

Alternator Belt (225 and 250 hp Except Optimax Models)

The 225 and 250 hp models use a V-belt to drive the alternator off the crank pulley. Adjust belt tension by rotating the alternator away from or towards the flywheel pulley. Belt tension should be 1/4-1/2 in. (6.3-12.7 mm) deflection under moderate thumb pressure at the point shown in **Figure 42**. Inspect the belt for deterioration, wear and fraying. Tension or replace the belt as follows.

1. Remove and ground the spark plug leads to the power head to prevent accidental starting.

2. Remove the flywheel cover.

3. Loosen the pivot bolt and the tension bolt (**Figure 42**). Rotate the alternator toward the flywheel and slip the belt off of both pulleys.

4. Install a new belt over both pulleys. Rotate the alternator away from the flywheel until the belt is properly tensioned (1/4-1/2 in. [6.3-12.7 mm] deflection under moderate thumb pressure). Tighten the tension bolt to hold the alternator in place.

5. Recheck belt tension, repeating Step 4 as necessary. When the tension is correct, tighten both the pivot bolt and tension bolt to the specification in **Table 1**.

6. Reinstall the flywheel cover.

7. Reconnect the spark plug leads to the spark plugs.

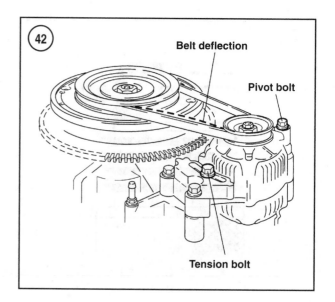

Belt deflection

Pivot bolt

Tension bolt

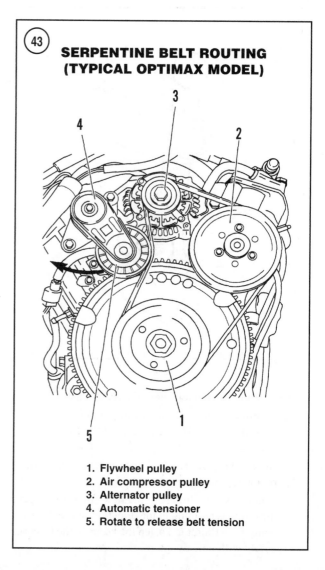

SERPENTINE BELT ROUTING (TYPICAL OPTIMAX MODEL)

1. Flywheel pulley
2. Air compressor pulley
3. Alternator pulley
4. Automatic tensioner
5. Rotate to release belt tension

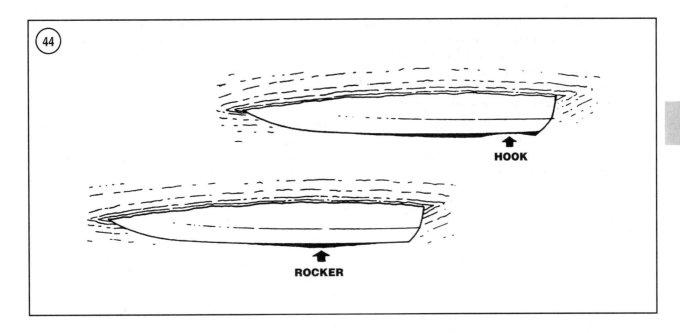

8. Recheck belt tension and condition after the first 10 hours of new belt operation and every 50 hours thereafter.

Alternator Belt (Optimax models)

Optimax models use a serpentine belt and automatic tensioner system. While no adjustments are required with this system, inspect the belt and belt tensioner assembly for deterioration, wear, fraying and mechanical damage or failure. Replace the belt as follows:

1. Remove and ground the spark plug leads to the power head to prevent accidental starting.
2. Remove the flywheel cover. Disconnect the air compressor inlet at the rear and the vent line at the front.
3. Manually rotate the automatic tensioner (4, **Figure 43** typical) away from the belt (5) and slip the belt off the pulleys.
4. Install a new belt while holding the tensioner fully open. Route the belt around the pulleys.
5. Release the tensioner against the belt. Make sure the belt is tracking on each pulley correctly.
6. Reinstall the flywheel cover.
7. Reconnect the spark plug leads to the spark plug.

Battery and Electric Starter System

During a tune-up, the electric starter system requires minimal maintenance. Lubricate the starter pinion as described previously in this chapter.

Inspect the battery cable connections for corrosion, loose connections or mechanical damage. If wing-nuts are present, discard them and replace them with corrosion re-sistant hex nuts and lock washers. Place a lockwasher under each battery cable to ensure positive contact with the battery terminal. Tighten the battery connections securely. Loose battery connections can cause many different symptoms. Verify correct operation of the electric starter system as follows:

1. Check the battery state of charge. See Chapter Seven.
2. Disable the ignition system by removing the spark plug lead from each spark plug and securing the spark plug leads to the power head (electrical ground).
3. Connect a multimeter set to the 20-volt DC scale to the battery positive and negative terminals.
4. Turn the ignition switch to the start position and note the meter reading while the engine is cranking for several seconds.

    a. If the voltage is 9.5 volts or higher and the cranking speed is normal, the starting system is functioning normally and the battery is at sufficient capacity for the engine.

    b. If the voltage is below 9.5 volts and/or the cranking speed is below normal, the starting system is malfunctioning. Refer to Chapter Three for troubleshooting procedures.

5. Reconnect the spark plug leads when finished.

On-Water Performance Testing

Before performance testing the outboard motor, make sure there is no marine growth and that no *hook* or *rocker* in the boat bottom (**Figure 44**). These conditions reduce the boat performance.

Test the boat performance with an average load on board. Tilt or trim the outboard motor at an angle that will produce optimum performance and balanced steering control. The adjustable trim tab, if equipped, should be properly adjusted to allow the boat to steer in either direction with equal ease at the boat's normal cruising speed.

CAUTION
Mercury/Mariner outboard motors tend to perform best when propped toward the up-

per limit of the recommended rpm range. Do not allow the engine to operate above or below the recommended speed range at wide-open throttle or engine damage will eventually occur.

Check the engine speed at wide-open throttle. If engine speed is not within the specified range (Chapter Five) and the engine is in a proper state of tune, change the propeller. Use a higher pitch propeller to reduce engine speed or a lower pitch propeller to increase engine speed.

Table 1 MAINTENANCE TORQUE SPECIFICATIONS

Fastener	in.-lb.	ft.-lb.	N•m
Alternator bolt			
225 and 250 hp (except Optimax)			
Tension bolt	–	40	54
Pivot bolt	–	40	54
Gearcase drain/fill/vent plugs	60	–	7
Spark plug	–	20	27

Table 2 GENERAL TORQUE SPECIFICATIONS

Screw or nut size	in.-lb.	ft.-lb.	N•m
U.S. Standard			
6-32	9	–	1.0
8-32	20	–	2.3
10-24	30	–	3.4
10-32	35	–	4.0
12-24	45	–	5.1
1/4-20	70	–	7.9
1/4-28	84	–	9.5
5/16-18	160	13	18
5/16-24	168	14	19
3/8-16	–	23	31
3/8-24	–	25	34
7/16-14	–	36	49
7/16-20	–	40	54
1/2-13	–	50	68
1/2-20	–	60	81
Metric			
M5	36	–	4
M6	70	–	8
M8	156	13	18
M10	–	26	35
M12	–	35	48
M14	–	60	81

Table 3 MAINTENANCE SCHEDULE

Maintenance interval	Maintenance required
Before each use	Check the lanyard switch operation*
	Inspect the propeller for damage
	Check the propeller nut tightness
	Inspect the fuel system for leakage
	Check the outboard mounting bolt tightness
	Check the steering for binding or looseness
	Check the shift and throttle control
After each use	Flush the cooling system
	Wash debris from the gearcase
After the first 10 days of operation	Check the gearcase lubricant level
Every 30 day or 50 hours of usage	Check the gearcase lubricant level
Once a season or 100 hours of usage	Lubricate the steering system
	Lubricate tiller control pivots*
	Lubricate the tilt and swivel shaft
	Lubricate the shift and throttle linkages/cables
	Check the tightness of all accessible fasteners
	Clean and inspect the spark plugs
	Remove carbon from the combustion chambers
	Inspect fuel filters for contamination
	Check control cable adjustments
	Adjust the carburetors*
	Test and inspect the battery
	Check ignition timing
	Check trim/tilt fluid level (Chapter Eleven)
	Clean and inspect sacrificial anodes
	Lubricate the drive shaft splines
	Lubricate the propeller shaft splines
	Change the gearcase lubricant
	Lubricate the starter motor pinion
	Clean remote fuel tank filter*
	Change the water separating filter (EFI)*
	Inspect or replace the water pump impeller
	Replace the compressor air filter (Optimax)*
	Clean the compressor cooling water strainer*
	Replace high-pressure water impeller pump
Before long term storage	Drain and refill the gearcase lubricant

*This maintenance item does not apply to all models.

Table 4 SPARK PLUG RECOMMENDATIONS

Model	Recommended plug	Spark plug gap
65 jet, 75 hp and 90 hp	NGK BUHW-2	Surface gap plug
Alternate plug (resistor type)	NGK BUZHW-2	Surface gap plug
80 jet, 100 hp, 115 hp and 125 hp	NGK BP8H-N-10	0.040 in. (1.0 mm)
Alternate plug (resistor type)	NGK-BPZ8H-N-10	0.040 in. (1.0 mm)
105 jet and 140 jet		
1998 and 1999	NGK BU8H	Surface gap plug
2000-on	NGK BPZ8HS-10	0.040 in. (1.0 mm)
135-200 hp (except Optimax)		
1998 and 1999	NGK BU8H	Surface gap plug
2000-on	NGK BPZ8HS-10	0.040 in. (1.0 mm)
115-150 hp (Optimax models)	NGK PZFR5F-11	0.040 in. (1.0 mm)
Alternate plug	NGK ZFR5F-11	0.040 in. (1.0 mm)
Alternate plug	Champion RC12MC4	0.040 in. (1.0 mm)
	(continued)	

Table 4 SPARK PLUG RECOMMENDATIONS (continued)

Model	Recommended plug	Spark plug gap
200 and 225 hp (Optimax models)		
1998 and 1999	NGK PZFR5F-11	0.040 in. (1.0 mm)
Alternate plug	NGK ZFR5F-11	0.040 in. (1.0 mm)
2000	Champion QC12GMC	0.040 in. (1.0 mm)
2001-on	NGK PZFR5F-11	0.040 in. (1.0 mm)
225 and 250 hp (except Optimax)	Champion QL77CC	0.035 in. (0.9 mm)

Table 5 LUBRICANT CAPACITIES

Model	Oil capacity	Gearcase capacity
65 jet, 75 hp and 90 hp	1 gal. (3.8 liter)*	22.5 oz. (665 ml)*
80 jet and 100-125 hp (except 115 Optimax)	1.4 gal. (5.3 liter)*	22.5 oz. (665 ml)*
105 jet and 140 jet	12.9 qt. (12.2 liter)	–
135-200 hp (except Optimax)	12.9 qt. (12.2 liter)*	22.5 oz. (665 ml)*
115-175 hp Optimax models	13.5 qt. (12.8 liter)*	22.5 oz. (665 ml)*
200/225 Optimax, 225 hp and 250 hp	13.5 qt. (12.8 liter)*	28.0 oz. (828 ml)*

*Approximate capacity. Always add lubricant until it reaches the full level.

Chapter Five

Synchronization and Linkage Adjustments

For an outboard motor to deliver maximum performance and reliability, the ignition and fuel systems must be correctly adjusted. This adjustment procedure is referred to as *synch and link*.

Failure to properly adjust an engine will cause a loss of engine performance and efficiency, and can lead to power head damage. Perform all synchronization and linkage adjustments during a tune-up or when replacing, servicing or adjusting ignition or fuel system components.

On a typical larger engine, a synch and link procedure will generally involve the following:
1. Synchronizing and adjusting the ignition and fuel systems linkages.
2. Making sure the fuel system throttle plate(s) fully open and close, and all throttle plates are synchronized to open and close at exactly the same time.
3. Synchronizing the ignition system spark advance with throttle plate(s) operation to provide optimum off-idle acceleration and smooth part-throttle operation.
4. Adjusting the ignition timing at idle and wide-open throttle engine speeds.
5. Setting the idle speed correctly and verifying the wide-open throttle rpm.

Adjustment procedures for Mercury/Mariner outboard motors differ according to engine model and the specific ignition and fuel systems used. This chapter is divided into self-contained sections for fast and easy reference. Each section specifies the appropriate procedure and sequence to be followed. **Tables 1-7** provide the necessary general specifications. **Table 8** provides specific application torque specifications. **Table 9** provides general torque specifications. Use the general torque specifications for fasteners not listed in **Table 8**. **Tables 1-9** are located at the end of the chapter.

Read the safety precaution and general information in the next two sections, then proceed directly to the section pertaining to the particular outboard motor.

SAFETY PRECAUTIONS

Wear approved eye protection at all times, especially when machinery is in operation. Wear approved ear protection during all running tests and in the presence of noisy machinery. Keep loose clothing tucked in and long hair tied back. Refer to *Safety* in Chapter 2 for additional safety guidelines.

When making or breaking any electrical connection, always disconnect the negative battery cable. When performing tests that require cranking the engine without starting, disconnect and ground the spark plug leads to prevent accidental starts and sparks.

Securely cap or plug all disconnected fuel lines to prevent fuel discharge when the motor is cranked or the primer bulb is squeezed.

Thoroughly read all manufacturer's instructions and safety sheets for test equipment and special tools being used.

Do not substitute parts unless they meet or exceed the original manufacturer's specifications.

Never run an outboard motor without an adequate water supply. Never run an outboard motor at wide-open throttle without an adequate load. Never exceed 3000 rpm in neutral (no load).

Safely performing on-water tests requires two people; one person to operate the boat, the other to monitor the gauges or test instruments. All personnel must remain seated inside the boat at all times. Do not lean over the transom while the boat is under way. Use extensions to allow gauges and meters to be in the normal seating area.

TEST PROPELLER

A test propeller is an economical alternative to the dynometer. A test propeller is also a convenient alternative to on-water testing. Test propellers are made by modifying (turning down) the diameter of a standard low pitch aluminum propeller until the recommended wide-open throttle speed can be obtained with the motor in a test tank or on the trailer backed into the water. Be careful when tying the boat to a dock as considerable thrust is developed by the test propeller. Some docks may not be able to withstand the load.

Propeller repair stations can provide the modification service. Normally, approximately 1/3 to 1/2 of the outer blade surface is removed. However, it is better to remove too little, than too much. It may take several tries to achieve the correct full throttle speed, but once achieved, no further modifications will be required. Many propeller repair stations have experience with this type of modification and may be able to recommend a starting point.

Test propellers also allow simple tracking of engine performance. The full-throttle test speed of an engine fitted with a correctly modified test propeller can be tracked from season to season. It is not unusual for a new or rebuilt engine to show a slight increase in test propeller speed as complete break-in is achieved and then to hold that speed over the normal service life of the engine. As the engine begins to wear out, the test propeller speed will show a gradual decrease that becomes a marked or drastic decrease as the point of engine failure is reached.

GENERAL INFORMATION

Perform adjustments with the engine running under actual operating conditions to be as accurate as possible. Carburetor idle speed adjustments are very sensitive to engine load and exhaust system back pressure. If the adjustments are made with the engine running on a flushing device, the adjustments will not be correct when the motor is operated in the water under load.

> *CAUTION*
> *Do not run the engine without an adequate water supply and do not exceed 3000 rpm without an adequate load. Refer to **Safety Precautions** at the beginning of this chapter.*

Ignition Timing

All models use timing marks that allow the ignition timing to be checked using a suitable stroboscopic timing light. On models with adjustable timing, a linkage adjustment is made to bring the timing into specification. If the timing is not within specification on models with nonadjustable timing, there is either a mechanical or electrical defect in the system. Chapter Three covers ignition troubleshooting for all models.

The maximum timing specification is best checked at wide-open throttle. This method is not always practical, however, as the outboard must be operated at full throttle in FORWARD gear under load to verify maximum timing advance. This requires the use of a test tank or test propeller, as timing an engine while speeding across open water is not safe and is not recommended. Refer to *Safety Precautions* in the previous section.

The maximum timing advance on some models can be set by holding the ignition linkage in the full-throttle position while the engine is being cranked. While acceptable where noted, this procedure is not considered as accurate as the wide-open throttle check. Whenever possible, check the maximum timing specification at wide-open throttle with a test propeller.

Wide-Open Throttle Speed Verification

All outboard motors have a specified wide-open throttle (W.O.T.) speed range (**Tables 1-6**). This means that when the engine is mounted on a boat and run at wide-open throttle, the engine speed must be within the specified

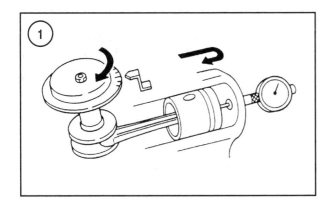

range. If the engine is run above or below the specified range for an extended period of time, the engine will be damaged.

NOTE
Use an accurate shop tachometer for checking W.O.T. speed. Do not use the boat's tachometer for W.O.T. verification.

Operating an engine with a propeller that will not allow the engine to reach its specified range is called over-propping. This causes the combustion chamber temperature to rise dramatically, leading to preignition and detonation (Chapter Three).

Operating an engine with a propeller that allows an engine to exceed its specified range is called over-speeding. Over-speeding an engine will lead to mechanical failure of the reciprocating engine components. Some engines are equipped with an rpm limit module that shorts out the ignition system to limit engine speed. Over-speeding these engines can cause ignition misfire symptoms that can cause troubleshooting difficulty.

Changing the propeller's pitch, diameter or style changes the load on the engine and the resulting W.O.T. engine speed. If the W.O.T. engine speed exceeds the specified range, install a propeller with more pitch or a larger diameter and recheck engine speed. If the W.O.T. engine speed is below the specified range, install a propeller with less pitch or smaller diameter and retest engine speed.

Required Equipment

Static adjustment of the ignition timing and/or verification of the timing pointer requires the use of a suitable dial indicator to position the No. 1 piston at top dead center (TDC) accurately before making timing adjustments. This procedure requires the removal of the No. 1 spark plug. The dial indicator is threaded into the spark plug opening. Adjustments to the timing pointer synchronize the pointer

to the actual piston position relative to TDC. See **Figure 1**.

All ignition timing checks and adjustments require the use of a stroboscopic timing light connected to the No. 1 spark plug lead. As the engine is cranked or operated, the light flashes each time the spark plug fires. When the light is pointed at the moving flywheel, the mark on the flywheel appears to stand still. The appropriate timing marks will be aligned if the timing is correctly adjusted.

CAUTION
*Timing specifications provided by Mercury/Mariner are in **Tables 1-7** at the end of the chapter. However, Mercury/Mariner has occasionally modified their specifications during production. If the engine has a decal attached to the power head or air box, always follow the specification on the decal, instead of the specification in **Tables 1-7**.*

NOTE
Timing lights with built-in features, such as a timing advance function, are not recommended for use on outboard motors. A basic high-speed timing light with an inductive pickup is recommended. Mercury/Mariner timing light (part No. 91-99379) fulfills these requirements.

Use an accurate shop tachometer to determine engine speed during timing adjustment. Do not rely on the tachometer installed in a boat to provide accurate engine speed readings.

65 JET, 75 HP AND 90 HP MODELS

The ignition timing is mechanically advanced and requires adjustment of the idle and maximum timing. Timing can be set at cranking speed or while running. Setting the timing while running is more accurate.

Refer to **Table 1** for general specifications. The recommended synch and link procedure is as follows:

1. Preliminary adjustments.
2. Throttle plate synchronization.
3. Throttle cam adjustment.
4. Wide-open throttle stop adjustment.
5. Timing adjustments.
6. Idle speed and idle mixture adjustments.
7. Oil pump linkage adjustment.
8. Shift and throttle cable adjustments remote control models.
9. Wide-open throttle speed verification.

Preliminary Adjustments

1. Disconnect the remote control throttle cable from the throttle lever arm.

2. Remove the screws from the carburetor air box cover. Remove the air box cover.

3. Turn the idle mixture screw (**Figure 2**) on each carburetor clockwise until it is lightly seated. Do not force the screws tightly into the carburetors or the tips of the screws and the carburetors will be damaged. Back out each mixture screw to specification in **Table 1**.

Throttle Plate Synchronization

1. Loosen the cam follower screw (**Figure 3**).

2. Loosen the two throttle shaft synchronizing screws on the upper and lower carburetor throttle shafts (5, **Figure 4**, similar).

3. Make sure the throttle valves in all three carburetors are fully closed, then retighten the screws (5, **Figure 4**). Do not tighten the cam follower screw at this time.

4. Make sure all throttle plates open and close together. Readjust as necessary.

Throttle Cam Adjustments

1. Hold the idle stop screw (1, **Figure 5**) against its stop on the cylinder block.

2. Position the cam follower roller (2, **Figure 5**) against the throttle cam. Adjust the idle stop screw (1, **Figure 5**) to align the throttle cam mark (3) with the center of the follower roller (2), then tighten the idle stop screw locknut.

3. While holding the throttle arm in the idle position, adjust the cam follower to set a 0.005-0.020 in. (0.13-0.51 mm) clearance between the cam follower roller and throttle cam. See **Figure 3**. Make sure the throttle cam mark is aligned with the center of the roller, then securely tighten the cam follower screw (**Figure 3**).

4. Hold the throttle arm so the wide-open throttle stop screw (4, **Figure 5**) is against its stop on the throttle arm. Adjust the wide-open throttle stop screw so the carburetor throttle valves are fully open at wide-open throttle while allowing for approximately 0.015 in. (0.38 mm) play in the throttle linkage. Make sure the throttle valves do not bottom out at wide-open throttle.

> *CAUTION*
> *The carburetors can be damaged if the throttle valves serve as throttle stops during full throttle operation.*

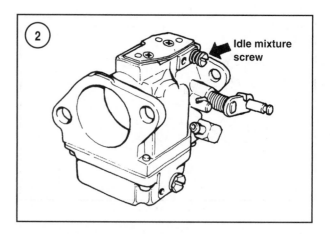

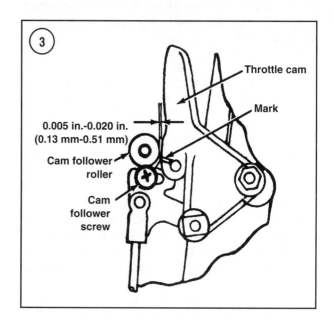

5. Reinstall the carburetor air box cover.

Timing Adjustments

Running adjustment

1. Connect a suitable timing light to the top, cylinder No. 1 spark plug lead.

> *CAUTION*
> *Do not run the engine without an adequate water supply and do not exceed 3000 rpm without an adequate load. Refer to **Safety Precautions** at the beginning of this chapter.*

2. Start the engine and allow it to warm to normal operating temperature.

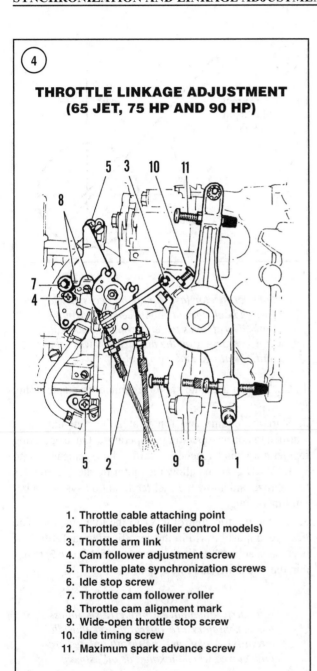

④

THROTTLE LINKAGE ADJUSTMENT
(65 JET, 75 HP AND 90 HP)

1. Throttle cable attaching point
2. Throttle cables (tiller control models)
3. Throttle arm link
4. Cam follower adjustment screw
5. Throttle plate synchronization screws
6. Idle stop screw
7. Throttle cam follower roller
8. Throttle cam alignment mark
9. Wide-open throttle stop screw
10. Idle timing screw
11. Maximum spark advance screw

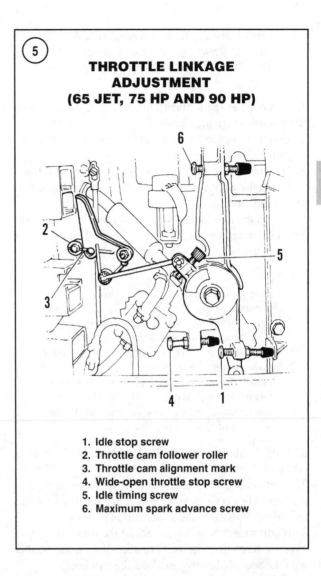

⑤

THROTTLE LINKAGE
ADJUSTMENT
(65 JET, 75 HP AND 90 HP)

1. Idle stop screw
2. Throttle cam follower roller
3. Throttle cam alignment mark
4. Wide-open throttle stop screw
5. Idle timing screw
6. Maximum spark advance screw

3. Reduce the engine speed to idle and shift the gearcase into FORWARD gear.

4. Point the timing light at the flywheel and timing pointer. Note the reading. The timing should be 5° BTDC at idle speed at this time. Adjust the idle timing as follows:

   a. Hold the idle stop screw (1, **Figure 5**) against the stop.

   b. Rotate the idle timing screw (5, **Figure 5**) to obtain a 5° BTDC idle timing.

5. Point the timing light at the flywheel and timing pointer. Advance the throttle arm to position the maximum spark advance screw (6, **Figure 5**) against its stop. Note the timing reading.

6. The maximum timing advance while running should be adjusted to the specification in **Table 1**. If adjustment is needed, stop the engine and loosen the maximum spark advance adjustment jam nut.

7. Turn the adjustment screw clockwise to retard timing or counterclockwise to advance timing. Tighten the jam nut securely. Recheck the timing.

Cranking speed adjustment

NOTE
The battery must be fully charged and the starting system must be functioning prop-

erly for this adjustment procedure to be accurate. Removing the spark plugs helps increase cranking speed and timing accuracy.

1. Remove the spark plugs and connect an air gap spark tester to the spark plug leads.
2. Connect a suitable timing light to the top, cylinder No. 1 spark plug lead.
3. Hold the idle stop screw (1, **Figure 5**) against its stop.
4. Crank the engine with the electric starter while noting the ignition timing.
5. Adjust the idle timing screw (5, **Figure 5**) to align the 5° BTDC mark on the flywheel with the V-notch in the timing window.

NOTE
Due to the electronic spark advance characteristics of this ignition system, the timing will retard slightly when running at wide-open throttle (3000 rpm or higher). Therefore, the maximum timing must be adjusted to the cranking speed specification to obtain the desired wide-open throttle timing when running above 3000 rpm. Verify all timing adjustments made at cranking speed with the outboard running.

6. Hold the throttle arm so the maximum spark advance screw (6, **Figure 5**) is against its stop.
7. Crank the engine while noting the timing with the timing light. The maximum timing advance at cranking speed should be adjusted to the specification in **Table 1**.
8. If adjustment is necessary, adjust the maximum spark advance screw (6, **Figure 5**) to align the timing pointer with the specified timing mark on the flywheel.
9. Tighten the maximum spark advance screw jam nut when finished.
10. Remove the timing light and the air gap spark tester. Reinstall the spark plugs and reconnect the spark plug leads.

Idle Mixture and Idle Speed Adjustments

NOTE
Never adjust the idle mixture or idle speed beyond the manufacturer's specification. Adjustment beyond the specified range can compromise engine durability, cause hard starting and increase exhaust emissions.

NOTE
The idle mixture must be properly set on all carburetors. Adjust the top carburetor first, the middle carburetor second and the bot-

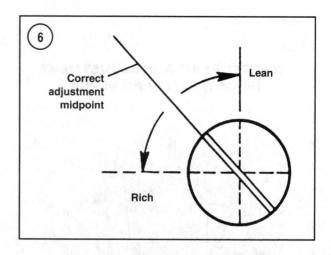

tom carburetor last. It may be necessary to switch back and forth between the carburetors several times to get the mixture correct. If necessary, reset the mixture screws to the initial settings and try again.

1. Connect an accurate shop tachometer to a spark plug lead.
2. Start the engine and run it at 2000 rpm until it is warmed to normal operating temperature. Once operating temperature is reached, shift the gearcase into FORWARD gear and allow the motor to idle 1-2 minutes to stabilize and allow the fuel recirculation system to begin functioning.
3. Set the throttle control lever to the idle position. The idle speed must be within the specification in **Table 1**. If necessary, adjust the idle timing screw (5, **Figure 5**) to obtain the recommended idle speed.

NOTE
Idle mixture cannot be properly set unless the carburetors are operating on the idle circuit(s). Make sure the throttle plates are fully closed when making this adjustment.

4. Slowly turn the idle mixture screw counterclockwise in 1/8 turn increments, pausing at least 10 seconds between turns. Continue this step until the idle speed decreases and idle becomes rough due to an excessively rich mixture. Note the position of the mixture screw slot.
5. Slowly turn the idle mixture screw clockwise in 1/8 turn increments, pausing at least 10 seconds between turns. The idle speed will gradually become smooth and speed will increase. Continue this step until the engine speed begins to slow again and/or misfires due to the excessively lean mixture. Note the position of the mixture screw slot.

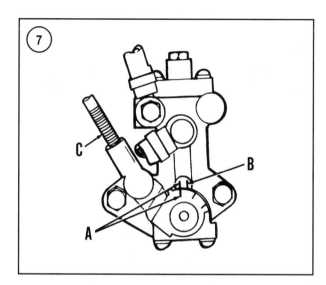

6. Position the mixture screw at a midpoint between the settings of Step 4 and Step 5. See **Figure 6**. Repeat Steps 4-6 for the remaining carburetors. Do not adjust the idle mixture screws beyond the turns out specification in **Table 1**.

7. Quickly accelerate the engine to wide-open throttle, then throttle back to idle. The engine will accelerate cleanly and without hesitation if the mixture is adjusted correctly. Readjust as necessary.

8. Remove the throttle cable barrel from the barrel retainer on the cable anchor bracket.

9. Adjust the idle timing screw (5, **Figure 5**) to obtain the idle speed in FORWARD gear specified in **Table 1**.

10. Hold the throttle lever against the idle stop. Adjust the cable barrel to slip into the retainer with a very light preload of the throttle lever against the idle stop. Fasten the barrel in the retainer.

NOTE
Excessive preload in Step 10 will result in difficult shifting from forward or reverse into neutral gear.

11. Check the throttle cable preload by inserting a thin piece of paper, such as a matchbook cover between the cylinder block idle stop and stop screw. If the preload is correct, a slight drag without tearing will be noted when the paper is removed. Readjust the cable as required to obtain the desired preload.

Oil Pump Linkage Adjustment

When the throttle linkage is adjusted, the oil pump linkage must be synchronized to the throttle linkage.

1. Hold the throttle arm against the idle stop.

2. The mark stamped in the oil pump control lever should be aligned with the mark stamped in the oil pump body. See A, **Figure 7**. A second mark (B, **Figure 7**) is stamped in the oil pump body on some models. *Do not* use this mark for oil pump synchronization.

3. If adjustment is necessary, disconnect the oil pump control rod (C, **Figure 7**) and adjust the length of the rod to align the marks.

Shift and Throttle Cable Adjustments (Remote Control Models)

Refer to Chapter Fourteen for additional information on remote control cable adjustments.

Wide-Open Throttle Speed Verification

1. Connect an accurate shop tachometer to a spark plug lead.

2. With the engine mounted on a boat, the boat unrestrained in the water and the engine running at wide-open throttle in FORWARD gear, record the maximum rpm noted on the tachometer.

3. If the maximum rpm exceeds the recommended speed range in **Table 1**, check the propeller for damage. Repair or replace the propeller as necessary. If the propeller is in good condition, install a propeller with more pitch or a larger diameter and the wide-open throttle speed.

4. If the maximum rpm does not reach the recommended speed range in **Table 1**, install a propeller with less pitch or a smaller diameter and recheck the wide-open speed.

80 JET AND 100-125 HP MODELS (EXCEPT 115 HP OPTIMAX)

The ignition timing is mechanically advanced and requires adjustment of the idle and maximum timing. Timing can be set at cranking speed or while running. Setting the timing while running is more accurate.

These engines idle on the top two cylinders only. The top two carburetors are different from the bottom two in that only the top two carburetors have idle mixture adjustment screws. These engines are also equipped with a mechanical accelerator pump system that injects fuel into the bottom two cylinders on acceleration as the throttle linkage is advanced.

Refer to **Table 2** for general specifications. The recommended synch and link procedure is as follows:

1. Preliminary adjustments.

2. Throttle plate synchronization.

5

3. Throttle cam adjustment.

4. Wide-open throttle stop adjustment.

5. Accelerator pump clearance adjustment.

6. Timing adjustments.

7. Idle speed and idle mixture adjustments.

8. Oil pump linkage adjustment.

9. Shift and throttle cable adjustments (remote control models).

10. Wide-open throttle verification.

Preliminary Adjustments

1. Disconnect the remote control throttle cable from the throttle lever arm.

2. Remove the screws from the carburetor air box cover. Remove the air box cover.

3. Turn the idle mixture screws (**Figure 2**) on the top two carburetors clockwise until each is *lightly* seated. Do not force the screws tightly into the carburetors or the tips of the screws and the carburetors will be damaged. Back out each mixture screw to the turns out specification in **Table 2**.

Throttle Plate Synchronization

1. Loosen the cam follower screw (**Figure 3**).

2. Loosen the three throttle shaft synchronizing screws (1, **Figure 8**) on the cylinders No. 1, 3 and 4 carburetor throttle shafts.

3. Make sure the throttle valves in all four carburetors are fully closed, then retighten the screws. **Do not** tighten the cam follower screw (**Figure 3**) at this time.

4. Make sure all throttle plates open and close together. Readjust as necessary.

Throttle Cam Adjustments

1. Hold the idle stop screw (2, **Figure 8**) against its cylinder block stop.

2. Position the cam follower roller (3, **Figure 8**) against the throttle cam. Adjust the idle stop screw (2, **Figure 8**) to align the throttle cam alignment mark (4) with the center of the follower roller (3), then tighten the idle stop screw locknut.

3. While holding the throttle arm in the idle position, adjust the cam follower to set a 0.005-0.020 in. (0.13-0.51 mm) clearance between the cam follower roller and throttle cam. See **Figure 3**. Make sure the throttle cam mark is aligned with the center of the roller. Tighten the cam follower screw (**Figure 3**).

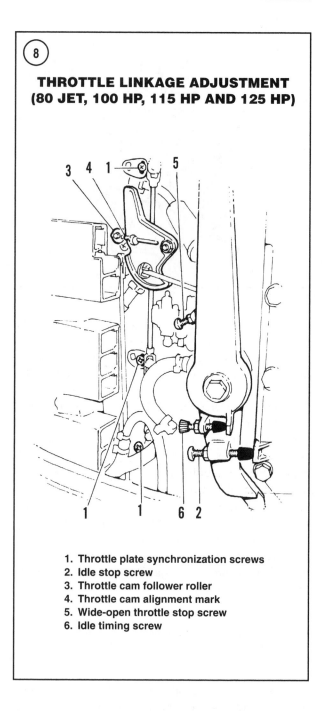

THROTTLE LINKAGE ADJUSTMENT (80 JET, 100 HP, 115 HP AND 125 HP)

1. Throttle plate synchronization screws
2. Idle stop screw
3. Throttle cam follower roller
4. Throttle cam alignment mark
5. Wide-open throttle stop screw
6. Idle timing screw

CAUTION
The carburetors can be damaged if the throttle valves serve as throttle stops during full throttle operation.

4. Hold the throttle arm so the wide-open throttle stop screw (5, **Figure 8**) is against its cylinder block stop. Adjust the wide-open throttle stop screw so the carburetor throttle valves are fully open at wide-open throttle while allowing for approximately 0.015 in. (0.38 mm) play in

9

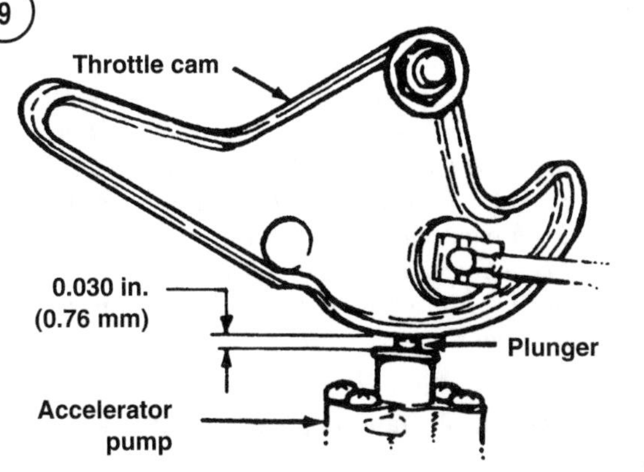

10

ACCELERATOR PUMP ADJUSTMENT (80 JET, 100 HP, 115 HP AND 125 HP)

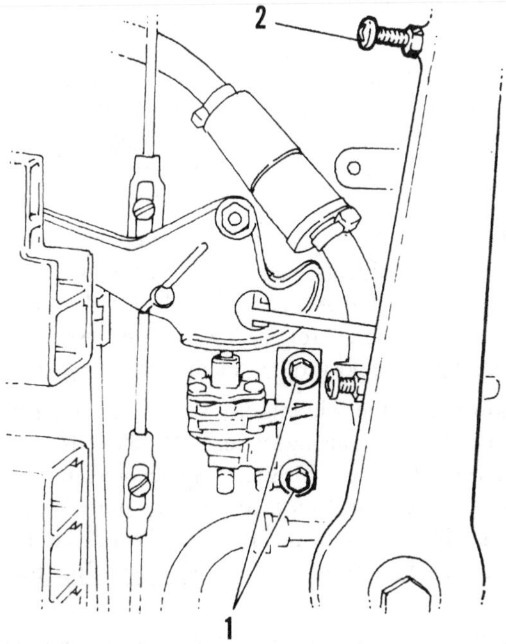

1. Accellerator pump mounting screws
2. Maximum timing advance adjusting screw

the throttle linkage. Make sure the throttle valves **do not** bottom out at wide-open throttle.

5. Reinstall the carburetor air box cover.

Accelerator Pump Adjustment

1. Move the throttle arm against the wide-open throttle stop. The tip of the stop screw (5, **Figure 8**) must contact the cylinder block stop.
2. Check for a 0.030 in. (0.76 mm) clearance between the throttle cam and the top of the pump casting as shown in **Figure 9**.
3. If adjustment is required, loosen the two pump mounting screws (1, **Figure 10**) and adjust the pump position to obtain the specified clearance.
4. Tighten the pump mounting screws.

Timing Adjustments

Running adjustment

1. Connect a suitable timing light to the top, cylinder No. 1 spark plug lead.

CAUTION

*Do not run the engine without an adequate water supply and do not exceed 3000 rpm without an adequate load. Refer to **Safety Precautions** at the beginning of this chapter.*

2. Start the engine and allow it to warm to normal operating temperature.
3. Reduce the engine speed to idle and shift the gearcase into FORWARD gear.
4. Point the timing light at the flywheel and timing pointer. Note the reading. Timing should be 2° BTDC at idle speed at this time.
5. If adjustment is needed, move the throttle arm to position the idle stop screw (2, **Figure 8**) against its cylinder block stop. Adjust the idle timing screw (6, **Figure 8**) to obtain a 2° BTDC timing reading. Tighten the idle timing screw jam nut when finished.
6. Point the timing light at the flywheel and timing pointer.
7. Advance the throttle to position the maximum timing advance adjusting screw (2, **Figure 10**) against its cylinder block stop. Note the timing reading.
8. The maximum timing advance while running should be adjusted to the specification in **Table 2**. If adjustment is needed, stop the engine and loosen the maximum timing advance adjustment jam nut.

5

9. Turn the adjustment screw clockwise to retard timing or counterclockwise to advance timing. Tighten the jam nut securely. Recheck the timing.

Cranking speed adjustment

NOTE
The battery must be fully charged and the starting system must be functioning properly for this adjustment procedure to be accurate. Removing the spark plugs helps increase cranking speed and timing accuracy.

1. Remove the spark plugs and connect an air gap spark tester to the spark plug leads.
2. Connect a suitable timing light to the top, cylinder No. 1 spark plug lead.
3. Hold the idle stop screw (2, **Figure 8**) against its cylinder block stop.
4. Crank the engine with the electric starter while noting the timing with the timing light.
5. Adjust the idle timing screw (6, **Figure 8**) to align the 2° BTDC mark on the flywheel with the V-notch in the timing window.

NOTE
Due to the electronic spark advance characteristics of this ignition system, the timing will retard slightly when running at wide-open throttle (3000 rpm or higher). Therefore, adjust the maximum timing to the cranking speed specification to obtain the desired wide-open throttle timing when running above 3000 rpm. Verify all timing adjustments made at cranking speed with the outboard running and readjust them if necessary.

6. Hold the throttle arm so the maximum timing advance adjusting screw (2, **Figure 10**) is against its cylinder block stop.
7. Crank the engine while noting the timing with the timing light. The maximum timing advance at cranking speed should be adjusted to the specification in **Table 2**.
8. If adjustment is necessary, adjust the maximum timing advance adjusting screw (2, **Figure 10**) to align the timing pointer with the specified timing mark on the flywheel.
9. Tighten the maximum timing advance adjusting screw jam nut when finished.
10. Remove the timing light and the air gap spark tester. Reinstall the spark plugs and reconnect the spark plug leads.

Idle Mixture and Idle Speed Adjustments

NOTE
The idle mixture can only be set on the top two carburetors. Adjust the top carburetor first and the cylinder No. 2 carburetor last. It might be necessary to switch back and forth between the carburetors several times to get the mixture correct. If necessary, reset the mixture screws to the initial settings and try again.

1. Connect an accurate shop tachometer to a spark plug lead.
2. Start the engine and run it at 2000 rpm until it is warmed to normal operating temperature. Once operating temperature is reached, shift the gearcase into FORWARD gear and allow the motor to idle 1-2 minutes to stabilize the motor and allow the fuel recirculation system to begin functioning.
3. Set the throttle lever control to the idle position. The idle speed should be within the specification in **Table 2**. If necessary, adjust the idle timing screw (6, **Figure 8**) to obtain the specified idle speed in FORWARD gear.

NOTE
Idle mixture cannot be properly set unless the carburetors are operating on the idle circuit(s). Make sure the throttle plates are fully closed when making this adjustment.

4. Slowly turn the idle mixture screw counterclockwise in 1/8 turn increments, pausing at least 10 seconds between turns. Continue this step until the idle speed decreases and becomes rough due to an excessively rich mixture. Note the position of the mixture screw slot.
5. Slowly turn the idle mixture screw clockwise in 1/8 turn increments, pausing at least 10 seconds between turns. The idle speed will gradually become smooth and speed will increase. Continue this step until the engine speed begins to slow again and/or misfires due to the excessively lean mixture. Note the position of the mixture screw slot.
6. Position the mixture screw at a midpoint between the settings of Step 4 and Step 5. See **Figure 6**. Do not adjust the idle mixture outside of the *turns out* range in **Table 2**. Repeat Steps 4-6 for the remaining carburetor.
7. Quickly accelerate the engine to wide-open throttle, then throttle back to idle. The engine will accelerate cleanly and without hesitation if the mixture is adjusted correctly. Readjust as necessary.

NOTE
If the accelerator pump circuit to cylinders No. 3 and No. 4 is malfunctioning, the engine will hesitate on acceleration. Adjustments to the idle mixture of cylinders No. 1 and No. 2 will not correct this problem. Verify accelerator pump operation (Chapter Six) if the hesitation persists.

8. Remove the throttle cable barrel from the barrel retainer on the cable anchor bracket.

9. Adjust the idle timing screw (6, **Figure 8**) to obtain the idle speed in FORWARD gear specified in **Table 2**.

10. Move the throttle lever until the idle stop screw contacts its cylinder block stop. Adjust the cable barrel to slip into the retainer with a very light preload of the throttle lever against the idle stop. Fasten the barrel in the retainer.

NOTE
Excessive preload in Step 10 will result in difficult shifting from forward or reverse gear into neutral.

11. Check the throttle cable preload by inserting a thin piece of paper, such as a matchbook cover, between the cylinder block idle stop and stop screw. If the preload is correct, a slight drag without tearing will be noted when the paper is removed. Readjust the cable as required to obtain the desired preload.

Oil Pump Linkage Adjustment

When the throttle linkage is adjusted, the oil pump linkage must be synchronized to the throttle linkage.

1. Move the throttle arm until the idle stop screw (2, **Figure 8**) contacts its cylinder block stop.

2. The mark stamped in the oil pump control lever should align with the mark stamped in the oil pump body. See A, **Figure 7**. A second mark (B, **Figure 7**) is stamped in the oil pump body on some models. Do not use this mark for oil pump synchronization.

3. If adjustment is necessary, disconnect the oil pump control rod (C, **Figure 7**) and adjust the length of rod to align the marks.

Shift and Throttle Cable Adjustments (Remote Control Models)

Refer to Chapter Fourteen for additional information on remote control cable adjustments.

Wide-Open Throttle Verification

1. Connect an accurate shop tachometer to a spark plug lead.

2. With the engine mounted on a boat, the boat unrestrained in the water and the engine running at wide-open throttle in forward gear, record the maximum rpm noted on the tachometer.

3. If the maximum rpm exceeds the recommended speed range in **Table 2**, check the propeller for damage. Repair or replace the propeller as necessary. If the propeller is in good condition, install a propeller with more pitch or a larger diameter and recheck the wide-open throttle.

4. If the maximum rpm does not reach the recommended speed range in **Table 2**, install a propeller with less pitch or a smaller diameter and recheck the wide-open throttle.

105 JET, 140 JET AND 135-200 HP CARBURETED MODELS

The ignition timing is mechanically advanced and requires adjustment of the idle (primary pickup) and maximum timing. Timing can be set at cranking speed or while running. Setting the timing while running is more accurate.

CAUTION
Idle stabilizer modules used on some 1998 and 1999 models must be disconnected during timing adjustments.

Refer to **Table 3** for general specifications. The recommended synch and link procedure is as follows:
1. Preliminary adjustments.
2. Timing pointer adjustment.
3. Throttle cam adjustment.
4. Throttle plate synchronization.
5. Wide-open throttle stop adjustment.
6. Oil pump linkage adjustment.
7. Timing adjustments.
8. Idle speed and idle mixture adjustments.
9. Shift and throttle cable adjustments.
10. Wide-open throttle speed verification.

Preliminary Adjustments

1. Disconnect the remote control throttle cable from the throttle lever arm.

2. Remove the screws from the carburetor air box cover. Remove the air box cover.

3. Remove the spark plugs and ground the spark plug leads to the power head to prevent accidental starting during the timing pointer adjustment.

Timing Pointer Adjustment

1. Install a dial indicator (part No. 91-58222A1 or an equivalent) into the top starboard, cylinder No. 1 spark plug hole. See **Figure 11**.

2. Rotate the flywheel clockwise until the top starboard, cylinder No. 1 piston is at TDC, then zero the indicator.

3. Rotate the flywheel counterclockwise until the dial indicator needle is approximately 1/4 turn past the 0.462 in. (11.73 mm) BTDC reading on the indicator dial.

4. Rotate the flywheel clockwise until the dial indicator reads exactly 0.462 in. (11.73 mm) BTDC. If the timing pointer (A, **Figure 12**) is not aligned with the 0.462 mark on the flywheel, loosen the two timing pointer adjustment screws (B) and reposition the timing pointer as required. Retighten the timing pointer screws securely.

5. Remove the dial indicator.

6. Reinstall the spark plugs if the timing adjustments will be made with the engine running. If the timing adjustments will be made with the engine cranking, leave the spark plugs removed.

Throttle Cam Adjustment

1. Loosen the throttle cam follower adjusting screw (1, **Figure 13**) on the lower carburetor to allow the cam follower to move freely.

2. With the cam follower roller resting on the throttle cam, adjust the idle stop screw (2, **Figure 13**) so the throttle cam alignment mark (3) aligns with the center of the cam follower roller. **Do not** tighten the cam follower screw at this point.

3. Tighten the idle stop screw (2, **Figure 13**) jam nut when finished.

Throttle Plate Synchronization

1. Loosen the two throttle plate synchronizing screws (4, **Figure 13**) on the middle and upper carburetors, allowing the carburetor throttle plates to fully close.

2. Move the throttle arm until the idle stop screw (2, **Figure 13**) contacts the stop cast into the cylinder block. Move the throttle cam follower so the follower roller just contacts the throttle cam. While holding the roller in this position, securely tighten the throttle cam follower screw (1, **Figure 13**) and the two carburetor synchronizing screws (4).

3. Make sure all carburetor throttle plates open and close simultaneously during throttle operation. Readjust the carburetor synchronization as necessary.

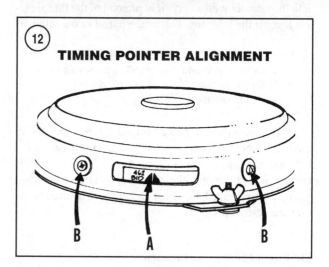

Wide-Open Throttle Stop Adjustment

1. Move the throttle arm until it contacts the wide-open throttle stop screw (5, **Figure 13**). Hold the throttle arm in this position.

2. Adjust the wide-open throttle stop screw (5, **Figure 13**) to position the carburetor throttle valves in the wide-open position while allowing for 0.010-0.015 in. (0.25-0.38 mm) free play between the throttle shaft arms and the cast-in stop (6) on the carburetor bodies.

3. Tighten the wide-open throttle stop screw jam nut.

> *CAUTION*
> *The carburetors can be damaged if the throttle plates bottom out at wide-open throttle.*

4. Reinstall the carburetor air box cover.

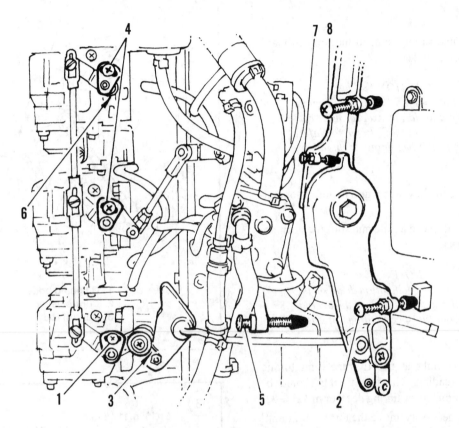

13

THROTTLE LINKAGE ADJUSTMENT
(105 JET, 140 JET AND 135-200 HP CARBURETOR EQUIPPED ENGINES)

1. Throttle cam follower adjusting screw
2. Idle stop screw
3. Throttle cam alignment mark
4. Throttle plate synchronization screws
5. Wide-open throttle stop screw
6. Cast-in throttle stop (each carburetor)
7. Idle timing (pickup timing) adjustment screw
8. Maximum timing advancement screw

5

Oil Pump Linkage Adjustment

If the throttle linkage is adjusted, the oil pump linkage must be synchronized to the throttle linkage.

1. Move the throttle arm until the idle stop screw (2, **Figure 13**) contacts the cylinder block stop.

2. With the throttle in the idle position, the stamped mark on the oil pump body (1, **Figure 14**) should align with the stamped mark on the control lever (2).

3. If adjustment is necessary, disconnect the pump control rod (3, **Figure 14**) from the pump control lever and adjust the length of the rod to align the marks.

Timing Adjustments

Preliminary adjustments

Perform these steps whether the engine is being timed while running or at cranking speed.

1. Check the trigger link rod length from the end of the rod to the locknut as shown in **Figure 15**. The length should be 11/16 in. (17.5 mm). If the length is incorrect, disconnect the link rod and adjust the length as necessary.

2. On 1998 and 1999 models, disconnect the idle stabilizer module white/black wire bullet connector located on

the starboard side of the engine. Insulate the disconnected wires with electrical tape.

Running adjustment

1. Connect a suitable timing light to the top starboard, cylinder No. 1 spark plug lead.

> *CAUTION*
> *Do not run the engine without an adequate water supply and do not exceed 3000 rpm without an adequate load. Refer to* **Safety Precautions** *at the beginning of this chapter.*

2. Start the engine and allow it to warm to normal operating temperature.

3. Reduce the engine speed to idle and shift the gearcase into FORWARD gear.

> *NOTE*
> *If there is a timing specification decal on the engine, use the specifications on the decal if they differ from the specifications in* **Table 3**.

4. Point the timing light at the flywheel and timing pointer. Note the reading. The idle timing should be within the specification on the timing decal or in **Table 3**.

5. If adjustment is necessary, move the throttle arm until the idle stop screw (2, **Figure 13**) contacts the cylinder block stop. Then adjust the idle timing (pickup timing) screw (7, **Figure 13**) to obtain the specified timing. Adjust the timing to the middle of the range. Tighten the idle timing (pickup timing) screw jam nut when finished.

6. Point the timing light at the flywheel and timing pointer.

7. Advance the throttle to position the maximum timing advance adjusting screw (**Figure 16**) against its stop on the cylinder block. Note the timing reading.

8. The timing should equal the specification on the decal or in **Table 3**. If adjustment is necessary, stop the engine and loosen the maximum timing advance adjustment jam nut.

9. Turn the maximum advance adjustment screw (8, **Figure 13**) clockwise to retard timing or counterclockwise to advance timing. Tighten the jam nut securely. Recheck the timing and adjust as necessary.

10. When timing is correct, reconnect the idle stabilizer module white/black wire bullet connector located on the starboard side of the engine.

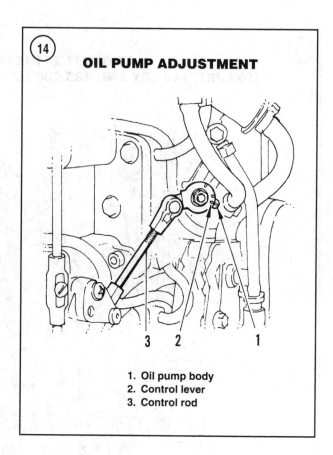

14

OIL PUMP ADJUSTMENT

3   2   1

1. Oil pump body
2. Control lever
3. Control rod

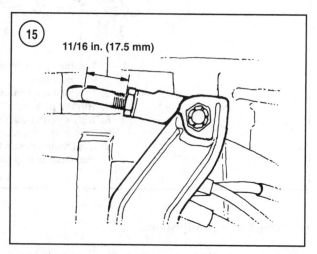

15

11/16 in. (17.5 mm)

Cranking speed adjustment

> *CAUTION*
> *Perform all cranking timing adjustments in NEUTRAL.*

> *NOTE*
> *The battery must be fully charged and the starting system must be functioning prop-*

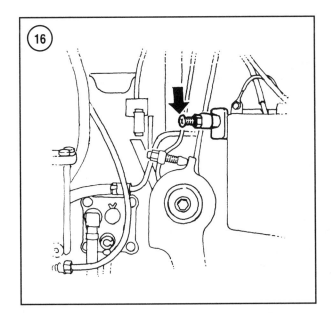

erly for this adjustment procedure to be accurate. Removing the spark plugs helps increase cranking speed and timing accuracy.

1. Remove the spark plugs and connect an air gap spark tester to the spark plug leads.

2. Connect a suitable timing light to the top starboard, cylinder No. 1 spark plug lead.

3. Move the throttle arm to position the idle stop screw (2, **Figure 13**) against its stop on the cylinder block.

4. Crank the engine with the electric starter while noting the timing with the timing light.

NOTE
*If there is a timing specification decal on the engine, use the specifications on the decal if they differ from the specifications in **Table 3**.*

5. The idle timing should be within the specification on the timing decal or in **Table 3**.

6. If adjustment is necessary, move the throttle arm until the idle stop screw (2, **Figure 13**) contacts the cylinder block stop. Then adjust the idle timing (pickup timing) adjustment screw (7, **Figure 13**) to obtain the specified timing. Adjust the timing to the middle of the range. Tighten the idle timing (pickup timing) screw jam nut when finished.

NOTE
Due to the electronic spark advance characteristics of this ignition system, the timing will retard slightly when running at wide-open throttle. Therefore, adjust the maximum timing to the cranking speed specification to obtain the desired wide-open throttle timing when running at wide-open throttle. Check all timing adjustments made at cranking speed with the outboard running and readjust if necessary.

7. Move the throttle arm until the maximum advance screw (**Figure 16**) contacts its stop on the cylinder block.

8. Crank the engine while noting the timing with the timing light.

9. The maximum timing advance should equal the specification on the engine timing decal or **Table 3**. If adjustment is necessary, stop the engine and loosen the maximum spark advance adjustment jam nut.

10. Adjust the maximum timing advance adjustment screw (8, **Figure 13**) to align the timing pointer with the specified timing mark on the flywheel.

11. Tighten the maximum spark advance screw jam nut when finished.

12. Remove the timing light and the air gap spark tester. Reinstall the spark plugs and reconnect the spark plug leads. Reconnect the idle stabilizer module white/black wire bullet connector located on the starboard side of the engine.

Idle Speed and Idle Mixture Adjustments

Each carburetor is equipped with two idle mixture screws (**Figure 17**). The idle mixture screws have plastic limiter caps installed on each screw to limit adjustment range. When adjusting the idle mixture, make sure all mixture screws are turned equal amounts in the same direction; clockwise rotation leans the air/fuel mixture and counterclockwise rotation enriches the air/fuel mixture. Do not remove the limiter caps to increase the adjustment range. If the limiter caps are missing, refer to *Idle mixture adjustment (limiter cap missing).*

5

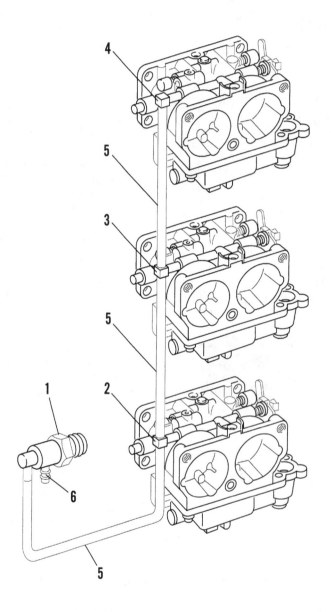

(18)

**THERMAL AIR VALVE ENRICHMENT SYSTEM
(105 JET, 140 JET AND 135-200 HP CARBUERTOR EQUIPPED MODELS)**

1. Thermal air valve
2. Bottom carburetor T-fitting
3. Middle carburetor T-fitting
4. Top carburetor elbow fitting
5. Connecting hoses
6. Open port

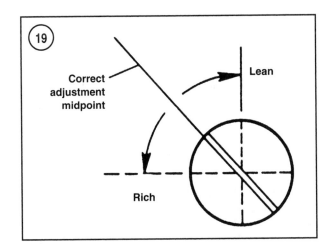

These engines are equipped with a thermal air valve enrichment system (**Figure 18**). The thermal valve is mounted in the starboard cylinder head near the No. 3 spark plug. The thermal air valve restricts air flow into the carburetors when the engine is cold, enriching the air/fuel mixture. When the engine is warm, the valve opens, letting air flow into the carburetors and normalizing the air/fuel mixtures. The valve must be open for the idle mixture to be set properly.

To make sure the thermal air valve is open, warm the engine to operating temperature. Reduce the engine speed to idle and cover the valve's open port (6, **Figure 18**) with your finger. The engine should slow slightly and run rough as the air/fuel mixture is enriched. If there is no change to engine operation, refer to Chapter Three for troubleshooting procedures. Carburetor idle mixture cannot be adjusted until the thermal air valve is open.

NOTE
The idle mixture must be properly set on all carburetors (total of six mixture screws). Note the original position of each mixture screw before starting. If the mixture adjustment procedure is difficult, reposition the screws to their original positions and try again.

1. Connect an accurate shop tachometer to a spark plug lead.
2. Start the engine and run it at 2000 rpm until it is warmed to normal operating temperature. Shift the gearcase into FORWARD gear and allow the motor to idle 1-2 minutes to stabilize the motor and allow the fuel recirculation system to begin functioning.
3. Set the throttle lever control to the idle position. If necessary, adjust the idle timing adjustment screw (7, **Figure 13**) to obtain the idle speed in forward gear in **Table 3**.

NOTE
The idle mixture cannot be properly set unless the carburetors are operating on the idle circuit(s). Make sure the throttle plates are fully closed when making this adjustment.

4. Turn all idle mixture screws counterclockwise in 1/8 turn increments, pausing at least 10 seconds between turns. Repeat this step until the idle speed decreases and becomes rough due to an excessively rich mixture or until the plastic cap limits movement. Note the position of each mixture screw limiting cap.
5. Turn all of the idle mixture screws clockwise in 1/8 turn increments, pausing at least 10 seconds between turns. The idle speed will gradually become smooth and speed will increase. Repeat this step until the engine speed begins to slow again and/or misfires due to the excessively lean mixture or until the plastic caps limit movement. Note the position of each mixture screw limiting cap.
6. Position the mixture screw at a midpoint (**Figure 19**) between the settings of Step 4 and Step 5. Do not adjust the screws beyond the turns out specification in **Table 3**.
7. Quickly accelerate the engine to wide-open throttle, then back to idle. The engine will accelerate cleanly without hesitation if the mixture is adjusted correctly. Readjust all mixture screws together as necessary.
8. Remove the throttle cable barrel from the barrel retainer on the cable anchor bracket.
9. Adjust the idle timing adjustment screw (7, **Figure 13**) to obtain the idle speed in **Table 3** in FORWARD gear. Do not adjust the screws beyond the idle timing specification in **Table 3**.

CAUTION
Idle speed must never exceed 750 rpm in forward gear.

10. Hold the throttle lever against the idle stop. Adjust the cable barrel to slip into the retainer with a very light preload of the throttle lever against the idle stop. Fasten the barrel in the retainer.

NOTE
Excessive preload in Step 10 will result in difficult shifting from forward gear or reverse gear into neutral.

11. Check the throttle cable preload by inserting a thin piece of paper such as a matchbook cover between the idle stop screw (2, **Figure 13**) and the cylinder block stop. If the preload is correct, a slight drag without tearing will be

noted when removing the paper. Readjust the cable as required to obtain the desired preload.

Idle mixture adjustment (limiter caps missing)

NOTE
This procedure is only necessary if the carburetors are missing the limit caps (the carburetor mixture screw factory adjustment has been tampered with, or the carburetor has been repaired or rebuilt and the factory position was not noted).

1. Turn each idle mixture screw on all the carburetors clockwise until each is lightly seated. Do not force the screws tightly into the carburetors or the tips of the screws and the carburetors will be damaged. Back each mixture screw to the turns out specification in **Table 3**.
2. Connect an accurate shop tachometer to a spark plug lead.
3. Start the engine and run it at 2000 rpm until it is warmed to normal operating temperature. Shift the gearcase into FORWARD gear and allow the motor to idle 1-2 minutes to stabilize the motor and to allow the fuel recirculation system to begin functioning.
4. Set the throttle lever control to the idle position. If necessary, adjust the idle timing screw (7, **Figure 13**) to obtain the idle speed in **Table 3** in FORWARD gear.

NOTE
The idle mixture cannot be properly set unless the carburetors are operating on the idle circuit(s). Make sure the throttle plates are fully closed when making this adjustment. Each adjustment screw affects only one cylinder. Changes in the idle mixture on only one cylinder of a six-cylinder engine will produce subtle changes to engine running quality. Take your time and listen to the engine carefully.

5. Slowly turn the first idle mixture screw counterclockwise in 1/8 turn increments, pausing at least 10 seconds between turns. Continue this step until the idle speed decreases and idle becomes rough due to an excessively rich mixture. Note the position of the mixture screw slot.
6. Slowly turn the idle mixture screw clockwise in 1/8 turn increments, pausing at least 10 seconds between turns. Do not adjust the mixture screws beyond the turns out specification in **Table 3**. The idle speed will gradually become smooth and speed will increase. Continue this step until the engine speed begins to slow again and/or misfires due to the excessively lean mixture. Note the position of the mixture screw slot.

7. Position the mixture screw at a midpoint between the settings of Step 4 and Step 5. See **Figure 19**. Repeat Steps 5-7 for the remaining mixture screws.
8. Quickly accelerate the engine to wide-open throttle and back to idle. The engine will accelerate cleanly without hesitation if the mixture is adjusted correctly. Readjust as necessary.
9. Follow Steps 8-11 in the preceding section for throttle cable and final idle speed adjustments.

Shift and Throttle Remote Control Cable Adjustments

Refer to Chapter Fourteen for additional information on remote control cable adjustments.

Wide-Open Throttle Speed Verification

1. Connect an accurate shop tachometer to a spark plug lead.
2. With the engine mounted on a boat, the boat unrestrained in the water and the engine running at wide-open throttle in forward gear, record the maximum rpm on the tachometer.
3. If the maximum rpm exceeds the recommended speed range in **Table 3**, check the propeller for damage. Repair or replace the propeller as necessary. If the propeller is in good condition, install a propeller with more pitch or a larger diameter and recheck the wide-open throttle speed.
4. If the maximum rpm does not reach the recommended speed range in **Table 3**, install a propeller with less pitch or a smaller diameter and recheck the wide-open throttle speed.

150-200 HP ELECTRONIC FUEL INJECTION (EFI) MODELS

The ignition timing is mechanically advanced and requires adjustment of the idle (primary pickup) and maximum timing. Timing may be set at cranking speed with the ECM and idle stabilizer module disconnected or while the engine is running with only the idle stabilizer disconnected.

The 200 hp models are equipped with a detonation sensor and module that advances the ignition timing 6° at high speed (beginning at approximately 2500-3000 rpm) if detonation is not present.

The setting of the throttle position sensor (TPS) has a direct effect on air/fuel mixture. Setting the TPS requires a test harness (part No. 91-816085) and a digital multimeter. The engine coolant temperature (ECT) sensor

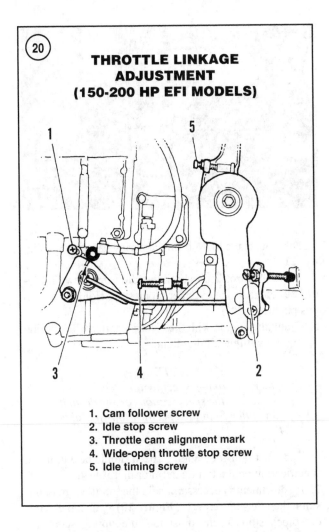

THROTTLE LINKAGE ADJUSTMENT (150-200 HP EFI MODELS)

1. Cam follower screw
2. Idle stop screw
3. Throttle cam alignment mark
4. Wide-open throttle stop screw
5. Idle timing screw

5

2. Remove the spark plugs and ground the spark plug leads to the power head to prevent accidental starting during the timing pointer adjustment.

Timing Pointer Adjustment

1. Install a dial indicator (part No. 91-58222A1 or an equivalent) into the top starboard, cylinder No. 1 spark plug hole. See **Figure 11**.
2. Rotate the flywheel clockwise until the top starboard, cylinder No. 1 piston is positioned at TDC, then zero the indicator.
3. Rotate the flywheel counterclockwise until the dial indicator needle is approximately 1/4 turn past the 0.462 in. (11.73 mm) BTDC reading on the indicator dial.
4. Rotate the flywheel clockwise until the dial indicator reads exactly 0.462 in. (11.73 mm) BTDC. If the timing pointer (A, **Figure 12**) is not aligned with the 0.462 mark on the flywheel, loosen the two timing pointer adjustment screws (B) and reposition the timing pointer as required. Retighten the timing pointer screws securely.
5. Remove the dial indicator.
6. Reinstall the spark plugs if the timing adjustments will be made with the engine running. If the timing adjustments will be made with the engine cranking, do not reinstall the spark plugs.

Throttle Cam Adjustment

1. Loosen the throttle cam follower screw (1, **Figure 20**) and allow the cam follower roller to rest against the throttle cam.
2. Adjust the idle stop screw (2, **Figure 20**) so the throttle cam mark (3) aligns with the center of the cam follower roller. Tighten the idle stop jam nut securely.
3. Hold the throttle arm against the idle stop, then tighten the cam follower screw securely.

Wide-Open Throttle Stop Adjustment

1. Move the throttle arm until it contacts the wide-open throttle stop screw (4, **Figure 20**). Hold the arm in this position.
2. Adjust the wide-open throttle stop screw so the induction chamber throttle plates are fully open. Allow for slight free play in the throttle linkage between the throttle shaft arm and the stop on the induction chamber.

CAUTION
To prevent the throttle linkage from binding at full throttle, make sure 0.010-0.015 in. (0.25-0.38 mm) clearance is present be-

tan/black leads must also be disconnected during TPS adjustment.

Refer to **Table 4** for general specifications. The recommended synch and link procedure is as follows:
1. Preliminary adjustments.
2. Timing pointer adjustment.
3. Throttle cam adjustment.
4. Wide-open throttle stop adjustment.
5. Oil pump linkage adjustment.
6. Timing adjustments.
7. Idle speed adjustment.
8. Throttle position sensor adjustment.
9. Shift and throttle cable adjustments.
10. Wide-open throttle speed verification.

Preliminary Adjustments

1. Disconnect the remote control throttle cable from the throttle lever arm.

tween the throttle cam and cam follower roller at wide-open throttle. Readjust the wide-open throttle stop screw as necessary to provide clearance.

Oil Pump Linkage Adjustment

Synchronize the oil pump linkage with the throttle linkage when adjusting the throttle linkage.

1. Move the throttle arm until the idle stop screw (2, **Figure 20**) contacts the cylinder block stop. Hold the arm in this position.

2. While the throttle in the idle position, the stamped mark on the oil pump body (1, **Figure 14**) should align with the stamped mark on the control lever (2).

3. If adjustment is necessary, disconnect the pump control rod (3, **Figure 14**) from the pump control lever and adjust the length of the rod as required to align the marks.

Timing Adjustments

Preliminary adjustments

Perform these steps while the engine is running or at cranking speed.

1. Check the trigger link rod length from the end of the rod to the locknut as shown in **Figure 15**. If the length is incorrect, disconnect the link rod and adjust the length as necessary.

2. On 1998 and 1999 models, disconnect the idle stabilizer module white/black wire bullet connector located on the starboard side of the engine. Insulate the disconnected wires with electrical tape.

Cranking speed adjustment

> *NOTE*
> *The battery must be fully charged and the starting system must be functioning properly for this adjustment procedure to be accurate. Remove the spark plugs to increase cranking speed and timing accuracy.*

> *CAUTION*
> *Perform all cranking timing adjustments in NEUTRAL.*

1. Remove the spark plugs and connect an air gap spark tester (part No. FT-11295) to the spark plug leads.

2. Connect a suitable timing light to the top starboard, cylinder No. 1 spark plug lead.

3. Disconnect the ECM from the wiring harness. See **Figure 21**.

4. Move the throttle arm until the idle stop screw (2, **Figure 20**) contacts the cylinder block stop. Hold the arm in this position.

5. Crank the engine with the electric starter while noting the timing with the timing light.

> *NOTE*
> *If there is a timing specification decal on the engine, use the specifications on the decal if they differ from the specifications in **Table 4**.*

6. The idle timing at cranking speed should be within the specification on the timing decal or in **Table 4**.

7. If adjustment is necessary, hold the throttle arm to position the idle stop screw (2, **Figure 20**) against the cylinder block stop. Then adjust the idle timing screw (5, **Figure 20**) to obtain the specified idle timing. Adjust the timing to the middle of the range. Tighten the idle timing screw jam nut when finished.

> *NOTE*
> *Due to the electronic spark advance characteristics of this ignition system, the timing will change slightly when running at wide-open throttle. Therefore, adjust the maximum timing to the cranking speed specification to obtain the desired wide-open throttle timing when running at wide-open throttle. Check all timing adjustments made at cranking speed with the outboard running and readjust if necessary.*

8. Move the throttle arm to position the maximum advance screw (**Figure 16**) against its cylinder block stop.

9. Crank the engine while noting the timing with the timing light.

10. The maximum timing advance at cranking speed should equal the specification in **Table 4**. If adjustment is

22

Idle speed screw

necessary, stop the engine and loosen the maximum spark advance adjustment jam nut.

11. Adjust the maximum spark advance screw (**Figure 16**) to align the timing pointer with the timing mark on the flywheel.

12. Tighten the maximum spark advance screw jam nut when finished.

13. Remove the timing light and the air gap spark tester. Reinstall the spark plugs and reconnect the spark plug leads.

14. Reconnect the idle stabilizer module white/black wire bullet connector located on the starboard side of the engine.

15. Reconnect the ECM to the engine wiring harness (**Figure 21**).

Running adjustment

1. Connect a suitable timing light to the top starboard, cylinder No. 1 spark plug lead.

CAUTION
Do not run the engine without an adequate water supply and do not exceed 3000 rpm without an adequate load. Refer to Safety Precautions at the beginning of this chapter.

2. Start the engine and allow it to warm to normal operating temperature.

3. Reduce the engine speed to idle and shift the gearcase into FORWARD gear.

NOTE
If there is a timing specification decal on the engine, use the specifications on the decal if they differ from the specifications in Table 4.

4. Point the timing light at the flywheel and timing pointer. Note the reading. The idle timing should be within the specification on the timing decal or in **Table 4**.

5. If adjustment is necessary, hold the throttle arm to position the idle stop screw (2, **Figure 20**) against the cylinder block stop. Then adjust the idle timing screw (5, **Figure 20**) to obtain the specified idle timing. Adjust the timing to the middle of the range. Tighten the idle timing screw jam nut when finished.

NOTE
*The 200 XRI and 200 Magnum models are equipped with a detonation sensor and module that advances the ignition timing 6° at high speed (beginning at approximately 2500-3000 rpm) if detonation is **not** present. If the maximum timing reading is approximately 6°-8° out of specification, refer to Chapter Three for detonation sensor and module troubleshooting procedures.*

6. Point the timing light at the flywheel and timing pointer.

7. Advance the throttle to position the maximum spark advance screw against its stop (**Figure 16**). Note the timing reading.

8. The maximum timing advance should equal the specification on the engine timing decal or in **Table 4**. If adjustment is necessary, stop the engine and loosen the maximum timing advance adjustment jam nut.

9. Turn the adjustment screw clockwise to retard timing or counterclockwise to advance timing. Tighten the jam nut securely. Recheck the timing and adjust as necessary.

10. When timing is correct, reconnect the idle stabilizer module white/black wire bullet connector located on the starboard side of the engine.

Idle Speed Adjustment

1. Connect an accurate shop tachometer to a spark plug lead.

2. Start the engine and warm it to normal operating temperature.

3. Position the throttle lever against the idle stop and shift the gearcase into FORWARD gear.

4. Loosen the cam follower screw (1, **Figure 20**).

5. While holding the throttle arm against the idle stop, adjust the idle speed screw (**Figure 22**) to obtain the idle speed specified in **Table 4**.

6. Retighten the cam follower screw.

7. Connect the throttle cable to the throttle arm.

8. While holding the throttle arm against the idle stop, adjust the throttle cable barrel to slip into the barrel retainer

5

on the cable anchor bracket with a slight preload of the throttle arm against the idle stop.

9. Lock the throttle cable barrel in place.

NOTE
Excessive preload in Step 8 will result in difficult shifting from forward gear and reverse gear into neutral.

10. Check the throttle cable preload by inserting a thin piece of paper such as a matchbook cover between the idle stop and stop screw. If the preload is correct, there will be a slight drag without tearing when the paper is removed. Readjust the cable as required to obtain the desired preload.

Throttle Position Sensor (TPS) Adjustment

The correct operation and setting of the TPS is critical to achieving the correct air/fuel ratio. High TPS voltage provides a richer air/fuel ratio. Low TPS voltage provides a leaner air/fuel ratio. Adjustments to the TPS within the specification may be used to fine tune the idle air/fuel mixture. Never adjust the TPS out of the specified range. Only use a digital multimeter for the following test. A test harness is required for this procedure.

Use test harness part No. 91-816085 for 1998 and 1999 models.

Use test harness part No. 91-859199 for 2000-on models.

NOTE
Verify the correct idle speed before adjusting the TPS. If the idle speed is changed, readjust the TPS setting. It may be necessary to go back and forth between idle speed and TPS adjustment more than once to get both systems correctly adjusted.

1. Disconnect the TPS harness (A, **Figure 23**) from the engine wiring connector (B). Connect the test harness to the TPS and engine wiring harness. Connect the test harness meter leads to a digital multimeter. Set the multimeter to the DC voltage scale.

2. Disconnect both engine wiring harness tan/black leads from the engine coolant temperature sensor (ECT) (**Figure 24**).

NOTE
If the TPS cannot be correctly set or reads zero, refer to Chapter Three for troubleshooting procedures.

3. Turn the ignition switch to the ON position. Make sure the throttle arm is against the idle stop. If the voltage read-

ing is within .2-.3 volts, continue to Step 5. If the reading is not within the specification, loosen the two screws securing the TPS to the induction manifold.

4. With the throttle arm held against the idle stop screw, rotate the TPS to obtain the voltage reading of .2-.3 volts. Adjust the sensor to the middle of the voltage range. While holding the TPS at the correct setting, tighten the screws securely. Recheck the voltage reading.

5. Slowly move the throttle linkage to the full-throttle position while noting the meter reading. The voltage should increase smoothly to 7.00-7.46 volts DC. If the meter reading fluctuates or is erratic as the throttle is advanced, replace the TPS. If the meter reading is not within 7.00-7.46 volts DC at wide-open throttle, recheck the wide-open throttle stop for correct adjustment.

6. Remove the TPS test harness. Reconnect the TPS lead to the wiring harness. Reconnect the ECT leads to the wiring harness.

Shift and Throttle Remote Control
Cable Adjustments

Refer to Chapter Fourteen for additional information on remote control cable adjustments.

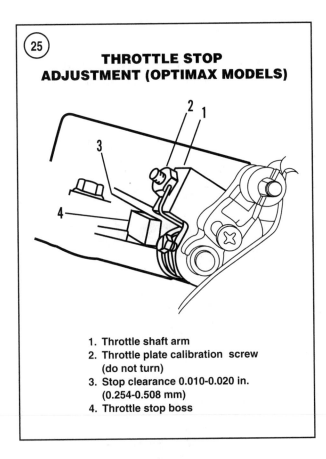

**THROTTLE STOP
ADJUSTMENT (OPTIMAX MODELS)**

1. Throttle shaft arm
2. Throttle plate calibration screw
   (do not turn)
3. Stop clearance 0.010-0.020 in.
   (0.254-0.508 mm)
4. Throttle stop boss

Wide-Open Throttle Speed Verification

1. Connect an accurate shop tachometer to a spark plug lead.

2. With the engine mounted on a boat, the boat unrestrained in the water and the engine running at wide-open throttle in forward gear, record the maximum rpm noted on the tachometer.

3. If the maximum speed exceeds the recommended range in **Table 4**, check the propeller for damage. Repair or replace the propeller as necessary. If the propeller is in good condition, install a propeller with more pitch or a larger diameter and the wide-open throttle speed.

4. If the maximum speed does not reach the recommended range in **Table 4**, install a propeller with less pitch or a smaller diameter and recheck the wide-open throttle speed.

115-225 HP OPTIMAX (DIRECT FUEL INJECTION) MODELS

The ignition timing is controlled by the ECM and is not adjustable. Refer to the timing decal on the engine for specifications if timing verification is desired.

The oil injection system is controlled by the ECM and does not require adjustment.

CAUTION
The throttle plate calibrations screw (2, Figure 25) is preset at the factory and must not be adjusted. Tampering with these screws can cause a serious engine malfunction. If the screw has been tampered with, contact a Mercury/Mariner dealership or Mercury/Mariner Customer Support for adjustment procedures.

Refer to **Table 5** for general specifications. The recommended synch and link procedure is as follows:
1. Preliminary adjustments.
2. Crankshaft position sensor adjustment.
3. Throttle cam adjustment.
4. Wide-open throttle stop screw adjustment.
5. Shift and throttle cable adjustments.
6. Wide-open throttle speed verification.

Preliminary Adjustments

1. Disconnect the negative battery cable and remove the flywheel cover.
2. Remove the spark plugs and ground the spark plug leads to the power head to prevent accidental starting during the following adjustments.
3. Disconnect the throttle cable from the throttle arm.
4. Refer to *Tune-up, Charging System Service* in Chapter Four and inspect the serpentine belt and tensioner that runs the air compressor and alternator.

Crankshaft Position Sensor (CPS) Adjustment

The crankshaft position sensor (1, **Figure 26**) provides the ECM with engine speed and crankshaft position information. Its function is similar to the trigger coil used on a conventional CDI ignition system. The ECM must know the precise position of all the pistons and how fast the engine is running to fire the ignition coils accurately. If the crankshaft position sensor fails or is incorrectly adjusted, it can cause erratic spark, erratic timing or no spark at all.

On 115-175 hp models, the crankshaft position sensor is mounted in a fixed location on the power head and does not normally require adjustment. See **Figure 26**. On 1998-2000 model engines, adjustment may be required after replacing the sensor, cylinder block, or flywheel. Shims are available to move the sensor if it is too close to the flywheel. Shims are not required on 2001-on model engines.

5

On 200 and 225 hp models, two screws retain the sensor to the cylinder block. See **Figure 27**. Adjustment slots in the sensor bracket allow positioning of the sensor relative to the flywheel.

1. Slightly rotate the flywheel to align an encoder rib with the crankshaft position sensor.

2. Measure the gap between the flywheel encoder rib and the crankshaft position sensor (5, **Figure 26**) with a feeler gauge. The gap should be 0.025-0.040 in. (0.635-1.02 mm). If it is not, adjust it as follows:

   a. On 115-175 hp models, loosen the screw (3, **Figure 26**) and pull the sensor (1) from its opening. Insert the appropriate size shim between the sensor and the opening, then install the sensor. Tighten the screw and recheck the clearance. Correct the clearance as required.

   b. On 200 and 225 hp models, loosen the screw (**Figure 27**) and set the gap to the specification in **Table 5**. Tighten the screws to the specification in **Table 8**.

3. Reinstall the flywheel cover.

Throttle Cam Adjustment

1. Loosen the throttle cam follower screw (1, **Figure 28**). The roller must rest freely on the throttle cam (3, **Figure 28**).

2. Adjust the idle stop screw (4, **Figure 28**) so the throttle shaft roller (2) rests in the pocket on the throttle cam (3).

3. Move the roller up to obtain a clearance of approximately 0.005 in. (0.127 mm) between the roller and the throttle cam. The roller must remain in the pocket.

4. Hold the throttle shaft roller (2, **Figure 28**) in position, then securely tighten the cam follower screw (1). Check the roller to cam clearance and readjust as needed.

5. Verify correct alignment of the roller with the pocket in the cam. Then tighten the jam nut on the idle stop screw (4, **Figure 28**).

Wide-Open Throttle Stop Screw Adjustment

1. Move the throttle arm until it contacts the wide-open throttle stop screw (5, **Figure 28**).

2. Hold the throttle arm in position and measure the clearance (3, **Figure 25**) between the throttle shaft arm and the stop on the throttle body. The clearance should be within the specification in **Table 5**.

3. If adjustment is needed, loosen the jam nut and adjust the wide-open stop screw (5, **Figure 28**) to obtain the correct clearance.

4. Tighten the wide-open throttle stop screw when finished.

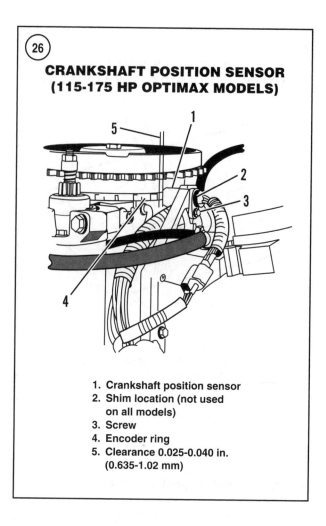

26

CRANKSHAFT POSITION SENSOR (115-175 HP OPTIMAX MODELS)

1. Crankshaft position sensor
2. Shim location (not used on all models)
3. Screw
4. Encoder ring
5. Clearance 0.025-0.040 in. (0.635-1.02 mm)

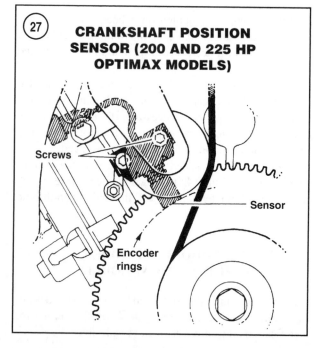

27

CRANKSHAFT POSITION SENSOR (200 AND 225 HP OPTIMAX MODELS)

Screws

Sensor

Encoder rings

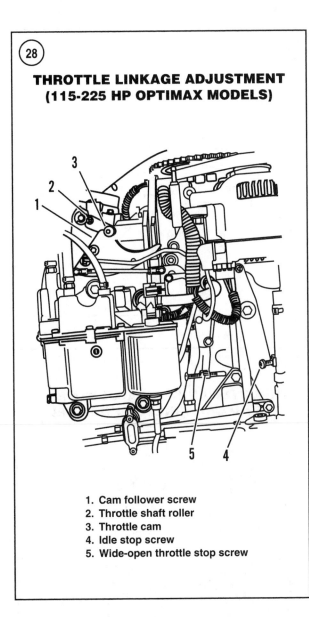

(28)

THROTTLE LINKAGE ADJUSTMENT (115-225 HP OPTIMAX MODELS)

1. Cam follower screw
2. Throttle shaft roller
3. Throttle cam
4. Idle stop screw
5. Wide-open throttle stop screw

Shift and Throttle Cable Adjustments

Refer to Chapter Fourteen for additional information on remote control cable adjustments.

1. Connect the throttle cable to the throttle arm.
2. While holding the throttle arm against the idle stop, adjust the throttle cable barrel to slip into the barrel retainer on the cable anchor bracket with a slight preload of the throttle arm against the idle stop.
3. Lock the throttle cable barrel in place.

NOTE
Excessive preload in Step 3 will result in difficult shifting from forward gear and reverse gear into neutral.

4. Check the throttle cable preload by inserting a thin piece of paper such as a matchbook cover between the idle stop and stop screw. If the preload is correct, there will be a slight drag without tearing when the paper is removed. Readjust the cable as required to obtain the desired preload.
5. Reinstall the spark plugs and reconnect the spark plug leads.
6. Reconnect the negative battery cable.

Wide-Open Throttle Speed Verification

1. Connect an accurate shop tachometer to a spark plug lead.
2. While the engine mounted on a boat, the boat unrestrained in the water and the engine running at wide-open throttle in forward gear, record the maximum rpm noted on the tachometer.
3. If the maximum rpm exceeds the recommended speed range in **Table 5**, check the propeller for damage. Repair or replace the propeller as necessary. If the propeller is in good condition, install a propeller with more pitch or a larger diameter and recheck the wide-open throttle speed.
4. If the recorded maximum rpm does not reach the recommended speed range in **Table 5**, install a propeller with less pitch or a smaller diameter and recheck the wide-open throttle speed.

225 HP CARBURETED MODELS

The ignition timing is controlled by the ECM and is not adjustable. Ignition timing depends on the crankshaft position sensor and throttle position sensor signals. As long as the crankshaft position sensor and throttle position sensor are correctly adjusted, the ECM will correctly calculate timing. If timing verification is desired, timing specifications are in **Table 6**.

The throttle position sensor is adjusted within the specification to set the idle speed. A test harness (part No. 84-825207A1) and a digital multimeter are required for throttle position sensor adjustment.

These models are not equipped with a throttle cam and do not require throttle cam adjustment.

Remove the shift rail assembly to see the oil pump alignment marks and adjust the oil pump linkage.

Refer to **Table 6** for general specifications. The recommended synch and link procedure is as follows:

1. Preliminary adjustments.
2. Timing pointer adjustment.
3. Throttle plate synchronization.
4. Wide-open throttle stop adjustment

5

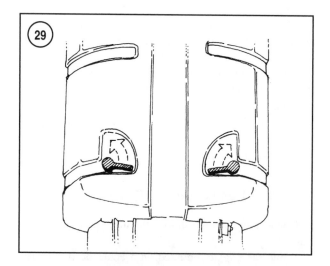

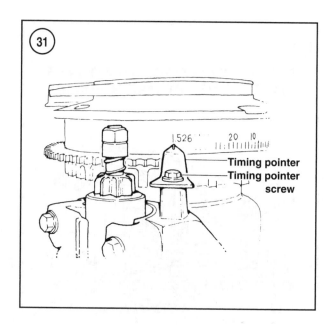

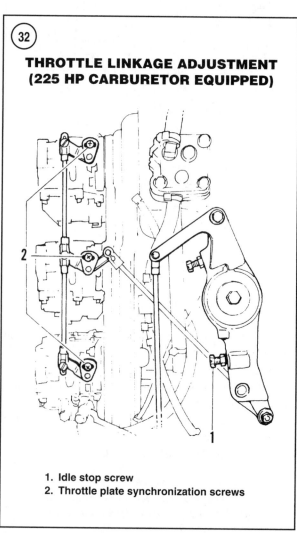

5. Oil pump linkage adjustment.

6. Crankshaft position sensor adjustment.

7. Throttle position sensor adjustment.

8. Idle mixture and idle speed adjustments.

9. Shift and throttle cable adjustments.

10. Wide-open throttle speed verification.

Preliminary Adjustments

1. Disconnect the negative battery cable and remove the flywheel cover.

2. Release the two carburetor air box latches (**Figure 29**) and remove the carburetor air box.

3. Remove the spark plugs and ground the spark plug leads to the power head to prevent accidental starting during the following adjustments.

4. Disconnect the throttle cable from the throttle arm.

5. Refer to *Tune-up, Charging System Service* in Chapter Four and inspect the alternator belt as instructed.

THROTTLE LINKAGE ADJUSTMENT (225 HP CARBURETOR EQUIPPED)

1. Idle stop screw
2. Throttle plate synchronization screws

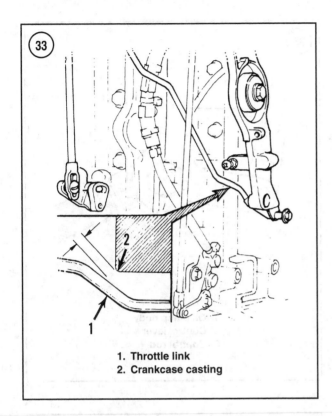

1. Throttle link
2. Crankcase casting

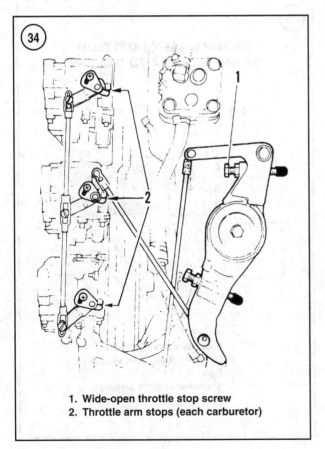

1. Wide-open throttle stop screw
2. Throttle arm stops (each carburetor)

Timing Pointer Adjustment

Adjust the timing pointer before making timing checks.

1. Install a dial indicator (part No. 91-58222A1 or an equivalent) into the top starboard, cylinder No.1 spark plug hole (**Figure 30**).

2. Rotate the flywheel clockwise until the top starboard, cylinder No. 1 piston is positioned at TDC, then zero the indicator.

3. Rotate the flywheel counterclockwise until the dial indicator needle is approximately 1/4 turn past the 0.526 in. (13.36 mm) BTDC reading on the indicator dial.

4. Rotate the flywheel clockwise until the dial indicator reads exactly 0.526 in. (13.36 mm) BTDC. The timing pointer should be aligned with the 0.526 mark on the flywheel (**Figure 31**). If adjustment is necessary, loosen the timing pointer adjustment screw and reposition the timing pointer as required. Retighten the timing pointer screw to the specification in **Table 8**.

5. Remove the dial indicator.

Throttle Plate Synchronization

1. Move the throttle arm until the idle stop screw (1, **Figure 32**) contacts the stop on the cylinder block.

2. Adjust the idle stop screw until the bend in the carburetor linkage (1, **Figure 33**) is 1/4 in. (6.4 mm) from the crankcase casting (2). The idle stop screw should be approximately in the middle of its adjustment range.

3. Loosen the three throttle plate synchronizing screws (2, **Figure 32**) on the carburetors, allowing the carburetor throttle valves to fully close.

4. Hold the throttle arm firmly against the idle stop. While holding the throttle arm in this position, securely tighten the center carburetor synchronizing screw first, then tighten the upper and lower carburetor synchronizing screws.

5. Make sure all carburetor throttle plates open and close simultaneously during throttle operation. Readjust the carburetor synchronization as necessary.

Wide-Open Throttle Stop Adjustment

1. Move the throttle arm until the wide-open throttle stop screw (1, **Figure 34**) contacts the stop on the cylinder block. Hold the throttle arm in this position.

2. Adjust the wide-open throttle stop screw (1, **Figure 34**) to position the carburetor throttle valves in the wide-open position while allowing for 0.010-0.015 in. (0.25-0.38 mm) clearance between the carburetor throttle arms and the carburetor body cast throttle arm stops (2, **Figure 34**).

3. Tighten the wide-open throttle stop screw jam nut securely.

CAUTION
The carburetors can be damaged if the throttle plates bottom out at wide-open throttle.

4. Reinstall the carburetor air box cover.

Oil Pump Linkage Adjustment

Adjust the pump when the idle stop position is changed. Remove the shift rail assembly to see the oil pump alignment marks and adjust the oil pump linkage.
1. Move the throttle arm until the idle stop screw (1, **Figure 32**) contacts the stop on the cylinder block. Hold the arm in this position.
2. The stamped mark on the oil pump body (1, **Figure 35**) should align with the lower stamped marking on the control lever (2).
3. If adjustment is necessary, disconnect the pump control rod (3, **Figure 35**) from the pump control lever and adjust the length of the rod as required to align the marks.

Crankshaft Position Sensor (CPS) Adjustment

The crankshaft position sensor provides the ignition ECM with engine speed and crankshaft position information. Its function is similar to a trigger coil on a conventional CDI ignition system. The ignition ECM must know the precise position of the pistons and how fast the engine is running in order to fire the CDMs accurately.
1. Slightly rotate the flywheel to align an encoder rib (1, **Figure 36**) with the crankshaft position sensor (2).
2. Measure the gap (3, **Figure 36**) between the flywheel encoder rib and the crankshaft position sensor with a feeler gauge. If the gap is not within the specification in **Table 6**, loosen the two sensor mounting screws (4, **Figure 36**) slightly and reset the gap to specifications.
3. Tighten the screws to the specification in **Table 8** and recheck the sensor air gap.
4. Reinstall the flywheel cover. Reconnect the negative battery cable.
5. Reinstall the spark plugs and reconnect the spark plug leads.

Throttle Position Sensor (TPS) Adjustment

Correct adjustment and function of the TPS is critical to correct ignition system operation. The TPS adjustment is made with the throttle against the idle stop. The wide-

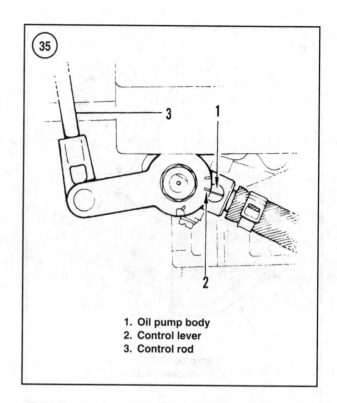

1. Oil pump body
2. Control lever
3. Control rod

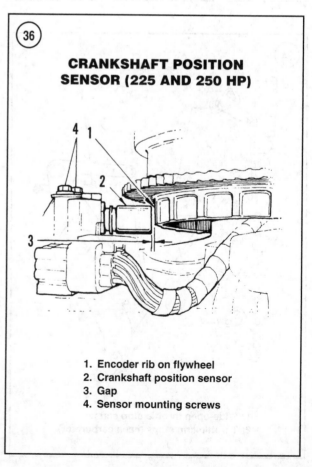

CRANKSHAFT POSITION SENSOR (225 AND 250 HP)

1. Encoder rib on flywheel
2. Crankshaft position sensor
3. Gap
4. Sensor mounting screws

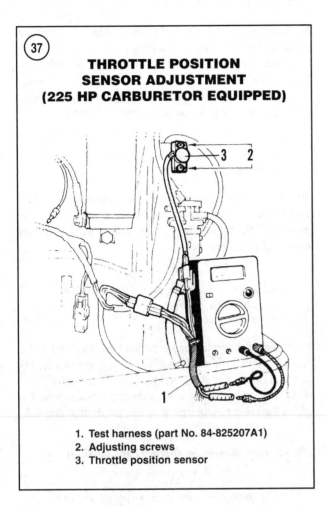

**THROTTLE POSITION
SENSOR ADJUSTMENT
(225 HP CARBURETOR EQUIPPED)**

1. Test harness (part No. 84-825207A1)
2. Adjusting screws
3. Throttle position sensor

3. Move the throttle arm until the idle stop screw (1, **Figure 32**) contacts the cylinder block stop.

4. Turn the ignition switch to the ON position. If the voltmeter does not indicate the idle position voltage specified in **Table 6**, loosen the two adjustment screws (2, **Figure 37**) slightly and rotate the sensor to the middle of the specified voltage range. Tighten the screws while holding the sensor in position. Recheck the meter reading. Readjust the throttle position sensor as needed.

5. Slowly advance the throttle lever until the stop screw (1, **Figure 34**) contacts the stop while noting the meter. The meter should indicate a smooth increase in voltage without sudden fluctuations. With the throttle lever held against the wide-open throttle stop, the meter should indicate the wide-open throttle position voltage specified in **Table 6**. If not, make sure the wide-open throttle stop is correctly set. If the wide-open throttle stop is correctly set, but the wide-open throttle voltage is not correct, replace the TPS. If the meter shows voltage fluctuations, instead of a smooth voltage transition as the sensor is rotated, replace the TPS.

6. Turn the ignition switch OFF. Disconnect the test harness and reconnect the TPS harness to the engine wire harness.

Idle Mixture and Idle Speed Adjustments

Each carburetor is equipped with two idle mixture screws (**Figure 38**), one on each side of the carburetor. The idle mixture screws are set at the factory and plastic limiter caps are installed on each screw to limit adjustment range. When adjusting the idle mixture, make sure all mixture screws are turned equal amounts in the same direction; clockwise rotation leans the air/fuel mixture and counterclockwise rotation enriches the air/fuel mixture. Do not remove the limiter caps to increase the adjustment range. If the limiter caps are missing, proceed to *Idle mixture adjustments (limiter cap missing)*.

open throttle TPS specification is not adjustable. If the wide-open throttle stop is correctly set and the TPS idle voltage setting is correct, but the TPS wide-open throttle voltage reading is incorrect, replace the TPS sensor. To prevent damage to the throttle position sensor and wiring harness, adjust the TPS using test harness 84-825207A1. A digital multimeter is recommended for this procedure, as most analog meters will not accurately read the low voltage specified. Adjust the TPS as follows:

NOTE
The TPS setting has a direct effect on idle timing and idle speed. The TPS setting can be changed within the specified range to obtain the specified idle speed.

1. Disconnect the engine wiring harness from the TPS. Connect test harness part No. 84-825207A1 (1, **Figure 37**) to the TPS and the engine wiring harness.

2. Set the multimeter to the 20-volt DC scale. Connect the meter negative lead to the test harness white lead. Connect the meter positive lead to the red test harness lead.

These engines are equipped with an electronic fuel enrichment valve. The ignition ECM opens the enrichment valve for varying lengths of time based on the engine temperature signal from the engine coolant temperature (ECT) sensor. Refer to Chapter Three for a functional description and troubleshooting procedures. The carburetor idle mixture cannot be adjusted if the enrichment valve is open.

NOTE
The idle mixture must be properly set on all carburetors (total of six mixture screws). Note the original position of each mixture screw before starting. If the mixture adjustment procedure goes poorly, reposition the screws to their original positions and try again.

1. Connect an accurate shop tachometer to a spark plug lead.
2. Start the engine and run it at 2000 rpm until it is warmed to normal operating temperature. Shift the gearcase into FORWARD gear and allow the motor to idle 1-2 minutes to stabilize the motor and allow the fuel recirculation system to begin functioning.
3. Set the throttle lever control to the idle position.

NOTE
Idle mixture cannot be properly set unless the carburetors are operating on the idle circuit(s). Make sure the throttle plates are fully closed when making this adjustment.

4. Turn all idle mixture screws counterclockwise in 1/8 turn increments, pausing at least 10 seconds between turns. Repeat this step until the idle speed decreases and becomes rough due to an excessively rich mixture or until the plastic caps limit movement. Note the position of each mixture screw limiting cap.
5. Turn all of the idle mixture screws clockwise in 1/8 turn increments, pausing at least 10 seconds between turns. The idle speed will gradually become smoother and the speed will increase. Repeat this step until the engine speed begins to slow again and/or misfires due to the excessively lean mixture or until the plastic caps limit movement. Note the position of each mixture screw limiting cap.
6. Position the mixture screw at a midpoint between the settings of Step 4 and Step 5.
7. Quickly accelerate the engine to wide-open throttle, then throttle back to idle. The engine will accelerate cleanly without hesitation if the mixture is adjusted correctly. Readjust all mixture screws together as necessary.

8. Remove the throttle cable barrel from the barrel retainer on the cable anchor bracket.
9. Check the idle speed in FORWARD gear. Make sure the throttle lever is held against the idle stop. If necessary, adjust the throttle position sensor within the specification to obtain the forward gear idle speed in **Table 6**.

CAUTION
Idle speed must never exceed 700 rpm in forward gear.

10. Hold the throttle lever against the idle stop. Adjust the cable barrel to slip into the retainer with a very light preload of the throttle lever against the idle stop. Fasten the barrel in the retainer.

NOTE
Excessive preload in Step 10 will result in difficult shifting from forward gear or reverse gear into neutral.

11. Check the throttle cable preload by inserting a thin piece of paper such as a matchbook cover between the idle stop and stop screw. If the preload is correct, there will be a slight drag without tearing when the paper is removed. Readjust the cable as required to obtain the desired preload.

Idle mixture adjustment (limiter caps missing)

NOTE
This procedure is necessary only if the carburetors are missing the limit caps or if the carburetor mixture screw factory adjustment has been tampered with, or the carburetor has been repaired or rebuilt and the factory position was not noted.

1. Turn each idle mixture screw on all of the carburetors clockwise until each is lightly seated. Do not force the screws tightly into the carburetors or the tips of the screws and the carburetors will be damaged. Back each mixture screw to the middle of the turns out range in **Table 6**.
2. Connect an accurate shop tachometer to a spark plug lead.
3. Start the engine and run it at 2000 rpm until it is warmed to normal operating temperature. Shift the gearcase into FORWARD gear and allow the motor to idle 1-2 minutes to stabilize the motor and to allow the fuel recirculation system to begin functioning.
4. Set the throttle lever control to the idle position.

NOTE
Idle mixture cannot be properly set unless the carburetors are operating on the idle

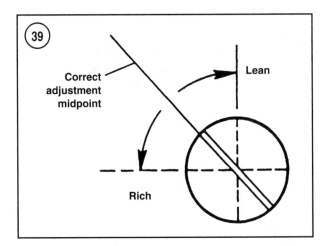

circuit(s). Make sure the throttle plates are fully closed when making this adjustment. Each adjustment screw affects only one cylinder. Changes in the idle mixture on only one cylinder of a six-cylinder engine will produce subtle changes to engine running quality. Take your time and listen to the engine carefully.

5. Slowly turn the first idle mixture screw counterclockwise in 1/8 turn increments, pausing at least 10 seconds between turns. Continue this step until the idle speed decreases and idle becomes rough due to an excessively rich mixture. Note the position of the mixture screw slot.

6. Slowly turn the idle mixture screw clockwise in 1/8 turn increments, pausing at least 10 seconds between turns. The idle speed will gradually become smooth and speed will increase. Continue this step until the engine speed begins to slow again and/or misfires due to the excessively lean mixture. Note the position of the mixture screw slot.

7. Position the mixture screw at a midpoint between the settings of Step 4 and Step 5. See **Figure 39**. Do not adjust the screw beyond the turns out range in **Table 6**. Repeat Steps 5-7 for the remaining mixture screws.

8. Quickly accelerate the engine to wide-open throttle, then throttle back to idle. The engine will accelerate cleanly without hesitation if the mixture is adjusted correctly. Readjust as necessary.

9. Refer to Steps 8-11 in the preceding section for throttle cable and final idle speed adjustments.

Shift and Throttle Cable Adjustments

Refer to Chapter Fourteen for additional information on remote control cable adjustments.

Wide-Open Throttle Speed Verification

1. Connect an accurate shop tachometer to a spark plug lead.

2. With the engine mounted on a boat, the boat unrestrained in the water and the engine running at wide-open throttle in forward gear, record the maximum rpm on the tachometer.

3. If the maximum rpm exceeds the recommended speed range in **Table 6**, check the propeller for damage. Repair or replace the propeller as necessary. If the propeller is in good condition, install a propeller with more pitch or a larger diameter and recheck the wide-open throttle speed.

4. If the recorded maximum rpm does not reach the recommended rpm range in **Table 6**, install a propeller with less pitch or a smaller diameter and recheck the rpm.

225 AND 250 HP EFI MODELS

The ignition timing is controlled by the ECM and is not adjustable. Ignition timing depends on the crankshaft position sensor and throttle position sensor signals. As long as the crankshaft position sensor and throttle position sensor are correctly adjusted, the ECM will correctly calculate timing.

Throttle position sensor adjustment requires a test harness (part No. 84-825207A1) and a digital multimeter.

Remove the shift rail assembly to see the oil pump alignment marks and adjust the oil pump linkage.

Refer to **Table 7** for general specifications. The recommended synch and link procedure is as follows:
1. Preliminary adjustments.
2. Timing pointer adjustment.
3. Throttle cam adjustment.
4. Wide-open throttle stop adjustment.
5. Oil pump linkage adjustment.
6. Crankshaft position sensor adjustment.
7. Throttle position sensor adjustment.
8. Idle speed adjustment.
9. Shift and throttle cable adjustments.
10. Wide-open throttle speed verification.

Preliminary Adjustments

1. Disconnect the negative battery cable and remove the flywheel cover.

2. Remove the spark plugs and ground the spark plug leads to the power head to prevent accidental starting during the following adjustments.

3. Disconnect the throttle cable from the throttle arm.

4. Refer to *Tune-up, Charging System Service* in Chapter Four and inspect the alternator belt.

Timing Pointer Adjustment

Adjust the timing pointer before making timing checks.
1. Install a dial indicator (part No. 91-58222A1 or an equivalent) into the top starboard, cylinder No. 1 spark plug hole (**Figure 30**).
2. Rotate the flywheel clockwise until the top starboard, cylinder No. 1 piston is positioned at TDC, then zero the indicator.
3. Rotate the flywheel counterclockwise until the dial indicator needle is approximately 1/4 turn past the 0.526 in. (13.36 mm) BTDC reading on the indicator dial.
4. Rotate the flywheel clockwise until the dial indicator reads exactly 0.526 in. (13.36 mm) BTDC. If the timing pointer is not aligned with the 0.526 mark on the flywheel (**Figure 31**), loosen the timing pointer adjustment screw and reposition the timing pointer as required. Retighten the timing pointer screw (**Figure 31**) to the specification in **Table 8**.
5. Remove the dial indicator.

Throttle Cam Adjustment

1. Loosen the throttle cam follower screw (1, **Figure 40**), allowing the cam follower roller (4) to rest on the throttle cam.
2. Move the throttle arm until the idle stop screw (2, **Figure 40**) contacts the stop on the cylinder block. Hold the throttle arm against the stop.
3. Adjust the idle stop screw (2, **Figure 40**) until the throttle cam marking (3) aligns with the center of the cam follower roller (4). Tighten the idle stop jam nut securely.
4. Move the cam follower away from the throttle cam to obtain a clearance of 0.005 in. (0.13 mm). Then tighten the cam follower screw. Check the clearance (5, **Figure 40**) between the throttle cam and the throttle cam follower roller after tightening the screw and readjust as needed.

Wide-Open Throttle Stop Adjustment

1. Move the throttle arm until the wide-open stop screw (6, **Figure 40**) contacts the stop on the cylinder block. Hold the throttle arm against the stop.
2. Adjust the wide-open throttle stop screw (6, **Figure 40**) to position the induction manifold throttle plates in the wide-open position while allowing for 0.010 in. (0.25 mm) free play between the throttle cam follower roller and throttle cam.

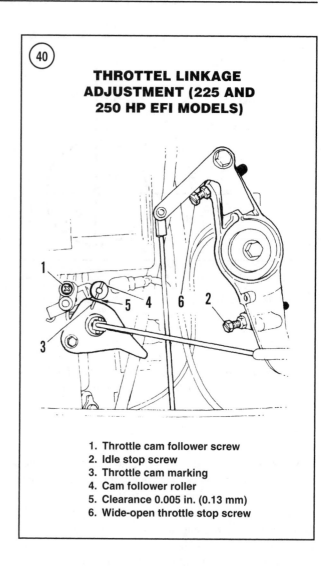

40

THROTTEL LINKAGE ADJUSTMENT (225 AND 250 HP EFI MODELS)

1. Throttle cam follower screw
2. Idle stop screw
3. Throttle cam marking
4. Cam follower roller
5. Clearance 0.005 in. (0.13 mm)
6. Wide-open throttle stop screw

3. Tighten the wide-open throttle stop screw jam nut securely.

> *CAUTION*
> *The induction manifold can be damaged if the throttle linkage bottoms out at wide-open throttle.*

Oil Pump Linkage Adjustment

Adjust the pump, if possible, when the idle stop position is changed. Remove the shift rail assembly to see the oil pump alignment marks and adjust the oil pump linkage.
1. Move the throttle arm until the idle stop screw (2, **Figure 40**) contacts the stop on the cylinder block. Hold the arm in this position.
2. The stamped mark on the oil pump body (1, **Figure 35**) and the lower stamped mark on the control lever (2)

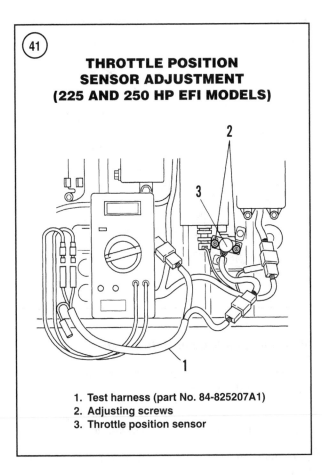

THROTTLE POSITION SENSOR ADJUSTMENT (225 AND 250 HP EFI MODELS)

1. Test harness (part No. 84-825207A1)
2. Adjusting screws
3. Throttle position sensor

should align. If not, disconnect the pump control rod (3, **Figure 35**) from the pump control lever and adjust the length of the rod as required to align the marks.

Crankshaft Position Sensor (CPS) Adjustment

The crankshaft position sensor provides the ignition ECM with engine speed and crankshaft position information. Its function is similar to a trigger coil used on a conventional CDI ignition system. The ignition ECM must know the precise position of all the pistons and how fast the engine is running in order to fire the CDMs accurately.

1. Slightly rotate the flywheel to align an encoder rib (1, **Figure 36**) with the crankshaft position sensor (2).
2. Measure the gap (3, **Figure 36**) between the flywheel encoder rib and the crankshaft position sensor with a feeler gauge. If the gap is not within the specification in **Table 7**, loosen the two sensor mounting screws (4, **Figure 36**) slightly and reset the gap to specifications.
3. Tighten the screws to the specification in **Table 8** and recheck the sensor air gap.
4. Reinstall the flywheel cover. Reconnect the negative battery cable.

5. Reinstall the spark plugs and reconnect the spark plug leads.

Throttle Position Sensor (TPS) Adjustment

Correct adjustment and function of the TPS is critical to correct ignition system operation. The TPS adjustment is made with the throttle against the idle stop. The wide-open throttle TPS specification is not adjustable. If the wide-open throttle stop is correctly set and the TPS sensor idle voltage setting is correct, but the TPS wide-open throttle voltage reading is incorrect, replace the TPS. To prevent damage to the throttle position sensor and wiring harness, adjust the TPS using test harness part No. 84-825207A1. A digital multimeter is recommended for this procedure, as most analog meters will not accurately read the low voltages specified. Adjust the TPS as follows:

NOTE
Any change to the idle speed air flow screw will require the TPS setting to be rechecked and readjusted as necessary. It might be necessary to go back and forth between idle speed and TPS adjustment more than once to get both systems correctly adjusted.

1. Disconnect the engine wiring harness from the TPS. Connect test harness part No. 84-825207A1 (1, **Figure 41**) to the TPS and the engine wiring harness.
2. Set the multimeter to the 20-volt DC scale. Connect the meter negative lead to the test harness white lead. Connect the meter positive lead to the red test harness lead.
3. Move the throttle arm until the idle stop screw (2, **Figure 40**) contacts the cylinder block stop.
4. Turn the ignition switch to the ON position. If the voltmeter does not indicate the idle position voltage specified in **Table 7**, loosen the two adjustment screws (2, **Figure 41**) slightly and rotate the sensor to the middle of the specified voltage range. Tighten the screws while holding the sensor in position. Recheck the meter reading. Readjust the throttle position sensor as needed.
5. Slowly advance the throttle lever until the stop screw (6, **Figure 40**) contacts the stop, while noting the meter. The meter should indicate a smooth increase in voltage, without sudden fluctuations. With the throttle lever held against the wide-open throttle stop, the meter should indicate the wide-open throttle position voltage specified in **Table 7**. If not, make sure the wide-open throttle stop is correctly set. If the wide-open throttle stop is correctly set, but the wide-open throttle voltage is not correct, replace the TPS. If the meter shows voltage fluctuations, instead

5

of a smooth voltage transition as the sensor is rotated, replace the TPS.

6. Turn the ignition switch OFF. Disconnect the test harness and reconnect the TPS harness to the engine wire harness.

Idle Speed Adjustment

1. Remove the throttle cable barrel from the barrel retainer on the cable anchor bracket.

2. Check the idle speed in FORWARD gear. Make sure the throttle lever is held against the idle stop. The idle speed should be within the specification in **Table 7**.

3. If necessary, adjust the idle air flow screw (**Figure 42**) on the lower throttle shaft on the port side of the induction manifold. Tighten the idle air flow screw jam nut securely when finished.

4. Recheck the throttle position sensor setting and readjust as necessary as described in the previous section.

> *CAUTION*
> *Idle speed must never exceed 700 rpm in forward gear.*

5. Attach the throttle cable to the throttle arm.

6. Hold the throttle lever against the idle stop. Adjust the cable barrel to slip into the retainer with a very light preload of the throttle lever against the idle stop. Fasten the barrel in the retainer.

> *NOTE*
> *Excessive preload in Step 6 will result in difficult shifting from forward gear or reverse gear into neutral.*

7. Check the throttle cable preload by inserting a thin piece of paper such as a matchbook cover between the idle stop and stop screw. If the preload is correct, there will be a slight drag without tearing when the paper is removed. Readjust the cable as required to obtain the desired preload.

Shift and Throttle Cable Adjustments

Refer to Chapter Fourteen for additional information on remote control cable adjustments.

Wide-Open Throttle Speed Verification

1. Connect an accurate shop tachometer to a spark plug lead.

2. With the engine mounted on a boat, the boat unrestrained in the water and the engine running at wide-open throttle in forward gear, record the maximum rpm on the tachometer.

3. If the maximum rpm exceeds the recommended speed range in **Table 7**, check the propeller for damage. Repair or replace the propeller as necessary. If the propeller is in good condition, install a propeller with more pitch or a larger diameter and recheck the wide-open throttle speed.

4. If the maximum rpm does not reach the recommended speed range in **Table 7**, install a propeller with less pitch or a smaller diameter and recheck the wide-open throttle speed.

Table 1 GENERAL SPECIFICATIONS (65 JET, 75 HP AND 90 HP)

Cylinder displacement	84.6 cu. in. (1387 cc)
Engine type	In-line three-cylinder
Firing order	1-2-3
Fuel pressure	
Idle speed	3.5 psi (24.1 kPa)
W.O.T. speed	6 psi (41.4 kPa)
(continued)	

Table 1 GENERAL SPECIFICATIONS (65 JET, 75 HP AND 90 HP) (continued)

Gear ratio (standard)	2.3:1
Idle mixture screw adjustment	
65 jet	1 1/2 turns out
75 hp	7/8 - 1 3/8 turns out
90 hp	1 1/2 turns out
Idle speed (in FORWARD gear)	650-700 rpm
Ignition timing	
65 jet	
Maximum timing advance	
Cranking speed	22° BTDC
Running at 3000 rpm	20° BTDC
Idle timing (running)	2° ATDC-6° BTDC
75 hp	
Maximum timing advance	
Cranking speed	20° BTDC
Running at 3000 rpm	18° BTDC
Idle timing (running)	2° ATDC-6° BTDC
90 hp	
Maximum timing advance	
Cranking speed	22° BTDC
Running at 3000 rpm	20° BTDC
Idle timing (running)	2° ATDC-6° BTDC
Rated power	
65 jet	90 hp (67.1 kW)
75 hp	75 hp (55.9 kW)
90 hp	90 hp (67.1 kW)
Water pressure	10-15 psi (69-103 kPa)*
Weight	
65 jet	315 lb. (143 kg)
75 hp, 90 hp	305 lb. (139 kg)
W.O.T speed	
65 jet	5000-5500 rpm
75 hp	4750-5250 rpm
90 hp	5000-5500 rpm

*Measure at 5250 rpm engine speed.

Table 2 GENERAL SPECIFICATIONS (80 JET AND 100-125 HP
[EXCEPT 105 JET AND 115 HP OPTIMAX] MODELS)

Cylinder displacement	112.8 cu. in. (1848.5 cc)
Engine type	In-line four-cylinder
Firing order	1-3-4-2
Fuel pressure	
Idle speed	3.5 psi (24.1 kPa)
W.O.T. speed	6 psi (41.4 kPa)
Gear ratio (standard)	2.07:1
Idle mixture screw adjustment	1–1 1/2 turns out
Idle speed (in FORWARD gear)	650-700 rpm
Ignition timing	
Maximum timing advance	
Cranking speed	25° BTDC
Running at 3000 rpm	23° BTDC
Idle timing (running)	4° ATDC-2° BTDC
Rated power	
80 jet	115 hp (85.8 kW)
100 hp	100 hp (74.6 kW)
115 hp	115 hp (85.8 kW)
125 hp	125 hp (93.3 kW)

(continued)

5

**Table 2 GENERAL SPECIFICATIONS (80 JET AND 100-125 HP
[EXCEPT 105 JET AND 115 HP OPTIMAX] MODELS) (continued)**

Water pressure	10-15 psi (69-103 kPa)*
Weight	
80 jet	357 lb. (162 kg)
100-125 hp	348 lb. (158 kg)
W.O.T speed	4750-5250 rpm

*Measure at 5250 rpm engine speed.

**Table 3 GENERAL SPECIFICATIONS (105 JET, 140 JET
AND 135-200 HP CARBURETOR MODELS)**

Cylinder displacement	
105 jet, 135 hp and 150 hp (except XR6 and Mag III)	121.9 cu. in. (1998 cc)
140 jet, 150 XR6, 150 Mag III, 175 hp and 200 hp	153 cu. in. (2507 cc)
Engine type	V-6
Firing order	1-2-3-4-5-6
Fuel pressure	
Idle speed	2 psi (13.8 kPa)
W.O.T. speed	8 psi (55.2 kPa)
Gear ratio (standard)	
135 hp and 150 hp (except XR6 and Mag III)	2.0:1
150 XR6, 150 Mag III, 175 hp and 200 hp	1.87:1
Idle mixture screw adjustment	
1998 and 1999	1 3/8–1 5/8 turns out
2000-on	
135 hp	1 3/8–1 5/8 turns out
105 jet, 140 jet, 150 hp, XR6, Mag III and 200 hp	1 1/8–1 3/8 turns out
Idle speed	
105 jet, 140 jet, 150 hp (except XR6 and Mag III),	
175 hp and 200 hp	600-700 rpm
150 XR6 and 150 Mag III	625-725
Ignition timing	
105 jet, 135 hp and 150 hp (except XR6 and Mag III)	
Maximum timing advance	
Cranking speed	
1998 and 1999	21° BTDC
2000-on	25° BTDC
Running at W.O.T.	19° BTDC
Idle timing	
1998 and 1999	2°-9° ATDC
2000-on	0°-9° ATDC
150 XR6, 150 Mag III, 175 hp	
Maximum timing advance	
Cranking speed	
1998 and 1999	20° BTDC
2000-on	26° BTDC
Running at W.O.T.	
1998 and 1999	19° BTDC
2000-on	20° BTDC
Idle timing	0°-9° ATDC
140 jet and 200 hp	
Maximum timing advance	
Cranking speed	
1998 and 1999	22° BTDC
2000-on	20° BTDC
Running at W.O.T.	
1998 and 1999	20° BTDC
2000-on	18° BTDC
Idle timing	0°-9° ATDC

(continued)

**Table 3 GENERAL SPECIFICATIONS (105 JET, 140 JET
AND 135-200 HP CARBURETOR MODELS) (continued)**

Rated power	
105 jet	150 hp (111.9 kW)
135 hp	135 hp (100.7 kW)
140 jet	200 hp (149.2 kW)
150 hp, 150 XR6, 150 Mag III	150 hp (111.9 kW)
175 hp	175 hp (130.6 kW)
200 hp	200 hp (149.2 kW)
Water pressure	12 psi (83 kPa)*
Weight	
105 jet	428 lb. (194 kg)
135 hp and 150 hp (except XR6 and Mag III)	
1998 and 1999	404 lb. (183 kg)
2000-on	413 lb. (187 kg)
140 jet	408 lb. (185 kg)
150 XR6, 150 Mag III, 175 hp and 200 hp	
1998 and 1999	395 lb. (179 kg)
2000-on	406 lb. (184 kg)
W.O.T speed	
105 jet and 140 jet	5000-5600 rpm
135 hp, 150 hp, XR6 and Mag III	5000-5500 rpm
175 hp and 200 hp	5000-5500 rpm
*Minimum water pressure at 5500 rpm.	

Table 4 GENERAL SPECIFICATIONS (150-200 HP EFI MODELS)

Cylinder displacement	153 cu. in. (2507 cc)
Engine type	V-6
Firing order	1-2-3-4-5-6
Fuel pressure	
Low pressure mechanical pump	
Idle speed	2 psi (13.8 kPa)
W.O.T. speed	8 psi (55.2 kPa)
High pressure electric pump	34-36 psi (234-248 kPa)
Gear ratio (standard)	1.87:1
Idle speed	600-700 rpm
Ignition timing	
150 hp	
Maximum timing advance	
Cranking speed	
1998 and 1999	15° BTDC
2000-on	22° BTDC
Running at W.O.T.	16° BTDC
Idle timing	0°-9° ATDC
175 hp	
Maximum timing advance	
Cranking speed	
1998 and 1999	20° BTDC
2000-on	26° BTDC
Running at W.O.T.	
1998 and 1999	19° BTDC
2000-on	20° BTDC
Idle timing	0°-9° ATDC

(continued)

5

Table 4 GENERAL SPECIFICATIONS (150-200 HP EFI MODELS) (continued)

Ignition timing (cont.)	
200 hp	
Maximum timing advance	
Cranking speed	
1998 and 1999	16° BTDC
2000-on	24° BTDC
Running at W.O.T.	
1998 and 1999	22° BTDC
2000-on	18° BTDC
Idle timing	0°-9° ATDC
Rated power	
150 hp	150 hp (111.9 kW)
175 hp	175 hp (130.6 kW)
200 hp	200 hp (149.2 kW)
Water pressure	12 psi (83 kPa) *
Weight	
1998 and 1999	410 lb. (186 kg)
2000-on	416 lb. (189 kg)
W.O.T speed	
150 hp and 175 hp	5000-5600 rpm
200 hp	5000-5800 rpm

*Minimum water pressure at 5500 rpm.

Table 5 GENERAL SPECIFICATIONS (115-225 HP OPTIMAX MODELS)

Air compressor pressure	77-81 psi (531-558 kPa)
Crankshaft position sensor air gap	0.025-0.040 in. (0.635-1.02 mm)
Cylinder displacement	
115-175 hp	153 cu. in. (2507 cc)
200 and 225 hp	185.9 cu. in. (3046 cc)
Engine type	V-6
Firing order	1-2-3-4-5-6
Fuel pressure	
Low pressure mechanical pump	
Idle speed	1-3 psi (6.9-20.7 kPa)
W.O.T. speed	8-10 psi (55.3-68.9 kPa)
Low pressure electric pump	6-9 psi (41.4-62 kPa)
High pressure electric pump	87-91 psi (599.9-627.4 kPa)
Gear ratio (standard)	
115 and 135 hp	2.0:1
150 and 175 hp	1.87:1
200 and 225 hp	1.75: 1
Idle speed	525-575 rpm
Rated power	
115 hp	115 hp (85.8 kW)
135 hp	135 hp (100.7 kW)
150 hp	150 hp (111.9 kW)
175 hp	175 hp (130.6 kW)
200 hp	200 hp (149.2 kW)
225 hp	225 hp (167.9 kW)
Water pressure	
115-175 hp	12 psi (83 kPa)*
200 and 225 hp	8-10 psi (55-69 kPa)*

(continued)

Table 5 GENERAL SPECIFICATIONS (115-225 HP OPTIMAX MODELS) (continued)

Weight	
115-175 hp (1998 and 1999)	
20 in. (50.8 cm) shaft	440 lb. (199.6 kg)
25 in. (63.5 cm) shaft	452 lb. (205.0 kg)
115-175 hp (2000-on)	
20 in. (50.8 cm) shaft	453 lb. (205.5 kg)
25 in. (63.5 cm) shaft	462 lb. (209.6 kg)
200 and 225 hp (1998 and 1999)	
20 in. (50.8 cm) shaft	507 lb. (230.0 kg)
25 in. (63.5 cm) shaft	512 lb. (232.2 kg)
200 and 225 hp (2000-on)	
20 in. (50.8 cm) shaft	516 lb. (234.1 kg)
25 in. (63.5 cm) shaft	528 lb. (239.5 kg)
30 in. (76.2 cm) shaft	544 lb. (246.8 kg)
W.O.T speed	
115 hp and 135 hp	5000-5500 rpm
150 and 175 hp	5250-5750 rpm
200 and 225 hp	5000-5750 rpm
Wide-open throttle stop clearance	0.010-0.020 in. (0.254-0.508 mm)

*Minimum water pressure at 5500 rpm.

Table 6 GENERAL SPECIFICATIONS (225 HP CARBURETOR EQUIPPED)

Crankshaft position sensor gap	0.020-0.040 in. (0.51-1.52 mm)
Cylinder displacement	185.9 cu. in. (3047 cc)
Engine type	V-6
Firing order	1-2-3-4-5-6
Fuel pressure	
Idle speed	2 psi (13.7 kPa)
W.O.T. speed	8 psi (55.1 kPa)
Gear ratio (standard)	1.75:1
Idle mixture screw adjustment	1 1/4–1 3/4 turns out
Idle speed	600-700
Ignition timing	Non-adjustable
Rated power	
225 hp	225 hp (167.8 kW)
Throttle position sensor adjustment	
Idle position	0.9-1.0 VDC
W.O.T. position	3.7-3.9 VDC
Water pressure	8-10 psi (55-69 kPa)*
Weight	
20 in. (50.8 cm) shaft	440 lb. (199.8 kg)
25 in. (63.5 cm) shaft	445 lb. (202 kg)
30 in. (76.2 cm) shaft	461 lb. (209.8 kg)
W.O.T speed	5000-5500 rpm
Wide-open throttle stop clearance	0.010-0.015 in. (0.25-0.38 mm)

*Minimum water pressure at 5500 rpm.

Table 7 GENERAL SPECIFICATIONS (225-250 HP EFI MODELS)

Crankshaft position sensor gap	0.020-0.040 in. (0.51-1.02 mm)
Cylinder displacement	185.9 cu. in. (3046 cc)
Engine type	V-6
Firing order	1-2-3-4-5-6
Fuel pressure	
Low pressure mechanical fuel pump	
Idle speed	2 psi (13.8 kPa)
W.O.T. speed	8 psi (55.2 kPa)
High pressure electric fuel pump	34-36 psi (234-248 kPa)

(continued)

Table 7 GENERAL SPECIFICATIONS (225-250 HP EFI MODELS) (continued)

Gear ratio (standard)	1.75:1
Idle speed	600-700
Ignition timing**	Non-adjustable
Rated power	
225 hp	225 hp (167.9 kW)
250 hp	250 hp (186.5 kW)
Throttle cam to roller clearance	0.005 in. (0.13 mm)
Throttle position sensor adjustment	
Idle position	0.9-1.0 VDC
W.O.T. position	3.55-4.05 VDC
Water pressure	8-10 psi (55-69 kPa)*
Weight	
20 in. (50.8 cm) shaft	450 lb. (204 kg)
25 in. (63.5 cm) shaft	455 lb. (206 kg)
30 in. (76.2 cm) shaft	471 lb. (214 kg)
W.O.T speed	5000-5800 rpm
Wide-open throttle stop clearance	0.010 in. (0.25 mm)

*Minimum water pressure at 5000 rpm.
**Refer to specification decal on the engine.

Table 8 SYNCHRONIZATION AND LINKAGE TORQUE SPECIFICATIONS

Fastener	in.-lb.	ft.-lb.	N•m
Crankshaft position sensor			
115-175 hp Optimax	50	–	5.6
200-225 hp Optimax	105	–	11.9
225-250 hp (Carburetor and EFI)	100	–	11.3
Spark plugs	–	20	27
Throttle position sensor			
225-250 hp (carburetor and EFI)	20	–	2.3
Timing pointer screw			
225-250 hp (carburetor and EFI)	105	–	11.9

Table 9 GENERAL TORQUE SPECIFICATIONS

Screw or nut size	in.-lb.	ft.-lb.	N•m
U.S. Standard			
6-32	9	–	1.0
8-32	20	–	2.3
10-24	30	–	3.4
10-32	35	–	4.0
12-24	45	–	5.1
1/4-20	70	–	7.9
1/4-28	84	–	9.5
5/16-18	160	13	18
5/16-24	168	14	19
3/8-16	–	23	31
3/8-24	–	25	34
7/16-14	–	36	49
7/16-20	–	40	54
1/2-13	–	50	68
1/2-20	–	60	81
Metric			
M5	36	–	4
M6	70	–	8
M8	156	13	18
M10	–	26	35
M12	–	35	48
M14	–	60	81

Chapter Six

Fuel System

This chapter contains removal, overhaul, installation and adjustment procedures for all fuel system components used with the Mercury/Mariner outboard motors covered in this manual.

Specific application torque specifications are in **Table 1**. General torque specifications are in **Table 2**. Use the general torque specification for fasteners not in **Table 1**. Carburetor specifications are in **Table 3**. All tables are at the end of this chapter.

CAUTION
Metric and U.S. standard fasteners are used on newer model outboards. Always match a replacement fastener to the original. Do not run a tap or thread chaser into a hole or over a bolt without first verifying the thread size and pitch. Newer manufacturer's parts catalogs list every standard fastener by diameter, length and pitch. Always have the engine model and serial numbers when ordering a parts catalog from a dealership.

FUEL PUMP

All models are equipped with a mechanical diaphragm-type fuel pump operated by crankcase pressure and vacuum pulses. All EFI and Optimax direct fuel injection models use a mechanical fuel pump to supply fuel to the vapor separator/fuel reservoir. An electric fuel pump in the vapor separator provides the high fuel pressure necessary for correct fuel injector operation. All Optimax models use a low pressure electric fuel pump in addition to the high pressure pump. The low pressure pump moves fuel through the fuel cooling passages to prevent vapor bubbles from forming in the fuel lines during warm weather operation.

These types of mechanical fuel pumps cannot move large quantities of fuel at cranking rpm; therefore, fuel must be transferred to the carburetor or vapor separator by manually operating the primer bulb installed in the fuel supply hose.

Mechanical fuel pumps are operated by crankcase pressure and vacuum pulses created by movement of the pistons. The pulses reach the fuel pump through either an external hose or internal passage into the crankcase.

Upward piston movement creates low pressure in the crankcase and against the pump diaphragm. This low pressure opens the inlet check valve in the pump, drawing fuel from the supply line into the pump.

Downward piston movement creates a high pressure in the crankcase and against the pump diaphragm. This pressure closes the inlet check valve and opens the outlet check valve, forcing the fuel out of the fuel pump and into

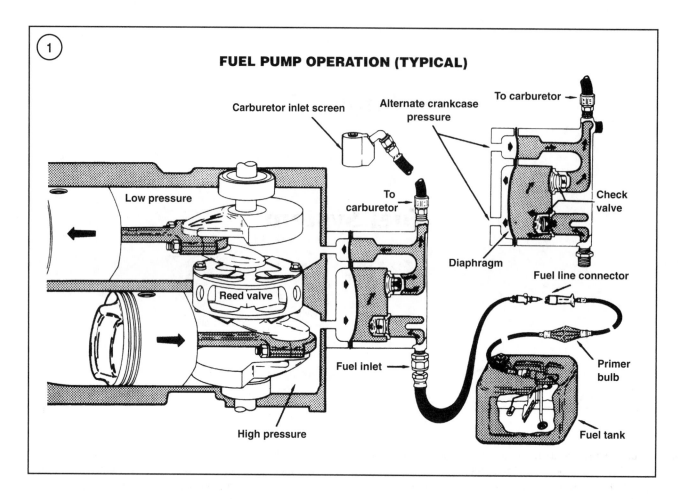

FUEL PUMP OPERATION (TYPICAL)

Carburetor inlet screen

Alternate crankcase pressure

To carburetor

Low pressure

To carburetor

Check valve

Reed valve

Diaphragm

Fuel line connector

Fuel inlet

Primer bulb

Fuel tank

High pressure

the carburetor(s) or vapor separator. **Figure 1** shows the general operating principles of a pulse driven, mechanical fuel pump.

> *NOTE*
> *If the cylinder(s) that supplies crankcase pressure and vacuum to a fuel pump mechanically fails, all of the cylinders starve for fuel. Check the compression of the engine before failing the fuel pump. See Chapter Four.*

Mercury/Mariner fuel pumps are simple in design and reliable in operation. Diaphragm failures are the most common problem, although sour fuel or fuel with excessive alcohol or other additives can cause check valve failure. Refer to Chapter Four for fuel recommendations.

If the fuel pump is suspected of not functioning correctly, refer to Chapter Three for fuel system troubleshooting.

Test the mechanical fuel pump as described in Chapter Three. Also check the fuel delivery hose for restrictions

and air leakage by connecting a vacuum gauge and a piece of clear hose to the fuel pump inlet using a T-fitting. Check fuel pump output by connecting a pressure gauge to the fuel pump outlet using a T-fitting.

> *CAUTION*
> *Fuel pump assemblies and internal fuel pump components vary between earlier and later models. Make sure the correct fuel pump or fuel pump components are used when replacing or rebuilding the fuel pump. An incorrect fuel pump or internal component can cause reduced fuel flow, resulting in poor performance or power head damage.*

Mechanical Fuel Pump Removal/Installation

Refer to **Figure 2** for this procedure.
1. Remove and discard the tie-strap clamps from the hoses at the fuel pump.
2. Label the hoses at the pump for correct reinstallation. The inlet and outlet fittings of the fuel pump are marked

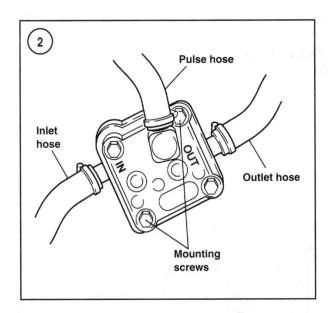

on the fuel pump cover plate. If a hose connects directly to the cover plate through a 90° fitting, it is a pulse hose for the boost diaphragm. Disconnect all hoses from the pump assembly.

> *NOTE*
> *If two of the fuel pump screws are slotted or Phillips head, they are the mounting screws. The two screws that hold the fuel pump components together are always hex-head screws. If all four fuel pump screws are hex-head, look at the rear of the pump to determine which two screws go through the mounting gasket and into the power head.*

3. Remove the two screws securing the fuel pump assembly to the power head and remove the pump.
4. Carefully clean the fuel pump-to-power head gasket off the power head and fuel pump.
5. Install a new gasket between the fuel pump and power head.
6. Install the pump to the power head and secure it with the two screws. Tighten the pump mounting screws to the specification in **Table 1**.
7. Reconnect the fuel inlet and outlet hoses. Secure the hoses with new tie-strap clamps.
8. On models so equipped, install and secure the pulse hose to the fuel pump cover fitting with a new tie-strap clamp.

Mechanical Pump Disassembly/Reassembly

Replace all fuel pump gaskets and diaphragms when the pump is disassembled. If the check valves are removed,

replace them. Refer to **Figure 3** for the following procedures.

Disassembly

1. Remove the hex-head screws holding the pump assembly together.
2. Separate the pump cover, gaskets and diaphragms from the pump body and base. Discard the gaskets and diaphragms.
3. Use needlenose pliers to remove the inner check valve retainer (4, **Figure 3**) from the fuel pump body (1). Remove the plastic disc and check valve from the retainer.
4. Remove the boost spring cap (9, **Figure 3**) and boost spring (10) from the pump cover (11).
5. Remove the main spring cap (5, **Figure 3**) and main spring (6) from the pump body (1).
6. Use needlenose pliers to remove the outer check valve retainer from the pump body. Remove the plastic disc and check valve from the retainer. Discard the check valves and check valve retainers. *Do not* discard the plastic discs.

Cleaning and inspection

1. Clean the pump components in a suitable solvent and dry them with compressed air.
2. Inspect the plastic discs for cracks, holes or other damage. Replace as required.
3. Inspect the pump base, pump body and pump cover for cracks, distortion, deterioration or other damage. Replace as required.

Check valve installation

1. Insert a new check valve retainer into the plastic disc, then insert the new check valve. See **Figure 4**. Repeat this step for the other check valve assembly.
2. Lubricate the check valve retainers with motor oil. Insert the check valve and retainer assemblies into the pump body. See **Figure 4**.
3. Bend the check valve retainer stem from side to side, until the stem breaks off flush with the retainer cap. See **Figure 5**. Repeat this step for the other retainer.
4. Insert the broken retainer stem into the retainer as shown in **Figure 6**. Use a small hammer and punch to tap the stem into the retainer until it is flush with the retainer cap.

6

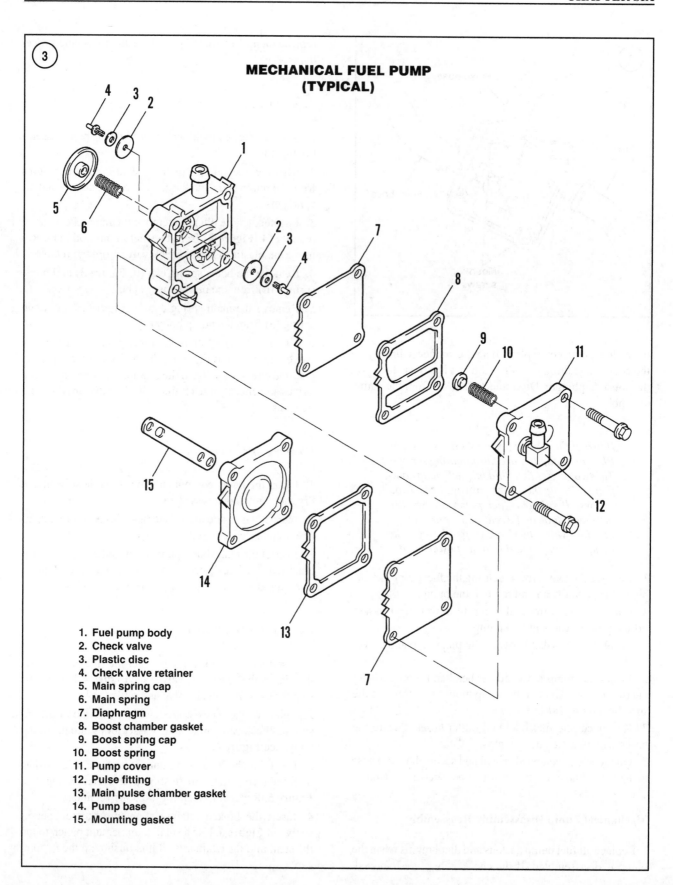

**MECHANICAL FUEL PUMP
(TYPICAL)**

1. Fuel pump body
2. Check valve
3. Plastic disc
4. Check valve retainer
5. Main spring cap
6. Main spring
7. Diaphragm
8. Boost chamber gasket
9. Boost spring cap
10. Boost spring
11. Pump cover
12. Pulse fitting
13. Main pulse chamber gasket
14. Pump base
15. Mounting gasket

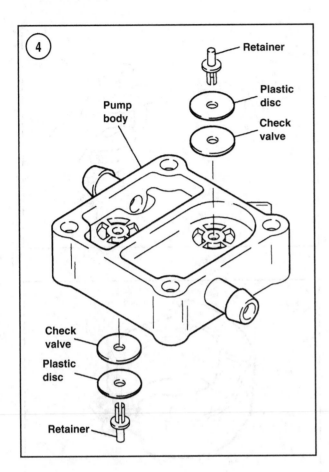

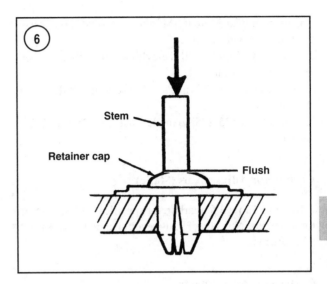

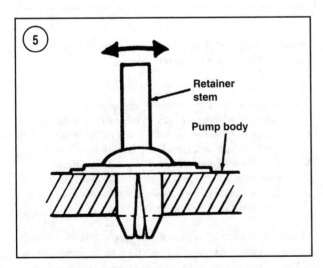

Reassembly

NOTE
Fuel pump components have one or more V tabs on one side for directional reference during assembly. Make sure the V tabs on all components are aligned. To ensure the cor-

rect alignment of pump components, use 1/4 in. bolts or dowels as guides. Insert the guides through the pump mounting screw holes.

1. Refer to **Figure 3** to reassemble the pump. Do not use gasket sealer on the pump gaskets or diaphragms. Spring caps should always push against the diaphragm. Make sure all pump components are properly aligned, and the springs and spring caps are properly assembled.

2. Remove one of the alignment bolts or dowels and install a hex-head screw finger-tight. Remove the other alignment bolt or dowel and install the other hex-head screw finger-tight.

3. Tighten both hex head cover screws to the specification in **Table 1**.

CARBURETORS

Carburetor Identification

All Mercury/Mariner carburetors have a carburetor series identification number cast into the carburetor body and a carburetor model identification number stamped into the front or rear flange. The stamped model identification number is in the following format: model number, carburetor location (on multi-carburetor models) and Julian date code.

For example, a WMV-7-3-3246 is a WMV series carburetor, model No. 7, mounted in the third carburetor location from the top, built on the 324th day of 1996. Carburetor location refers to the position of the carburetor on the power head. This is not always the same as the cylinder number.

Current model Mercury/Mariner outboard motors use the following carburetors:

1. 65 jet and 75-90 hp (three-cylinder) models use three WME series carburetors.

2. 80 jet and 100-125 hp models use tour WME series carburetors.

3. 105 jet and 135-225 hp models use three WMV series carburetors.

Carburetor Adjustments (Static)

Refer to **Table 3** for carburetor specifications. Carburetor scale part No. 91-36392 is recommended for all float adjustments.

Carburetor Adjustments (Engine Running)

NOTE
When service or repair has been performed on the carburetor(s), perform the synchronization and linkage adjustments procedures in Chapter Five.

All running adjustments are described in Chapter Five. Always supply the engine with an adequate supply of cooling water before starting and running. Refer to *Safety Precautions* at the beginning of Chapter Three.

NOTE
Idle speed and idle mixture adjustments cannot be satisfactorily performed with the engine running on a cooling system flushing device.

When performing idle speed and idle mixture adjustments, the outboard must be running in FORWARD gear at normal operating temperature with the correct propeller installed. The best results will be obtained if the motor is operated in the normal operating environment: mounted on a boat in the water and running in FORWARD gear with boat movement unrestrained.

High Altitude Compensation

If an outboard motor is operated at higher altitudes, several factors affect how the engine must be adjusted and operated. As the altitude increases, the air becomes less dense. Since a two-stroke outboard motor is essentially an air pump, the less dense air will reduce the efficiency of the engine, reducing the horsepower output proportionally to the air density. The loss of horsepower requires a

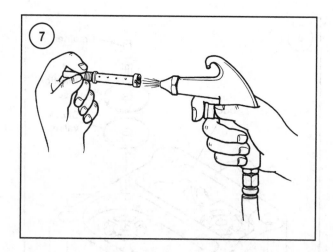

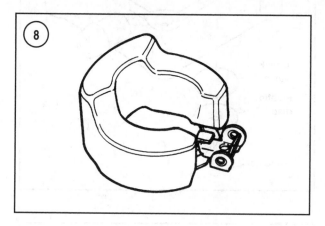

propeller pitch and diameter change to maintain the recommended full-throttle operating speed.

CAUTION
*Regardless of the altitude, the engine must operate within, and preferably toward the upper limit of the recommended full-throttle speed range described in Chapter Five under **Wide-Open Throttle Speed Verification**. Change the propeller pitch and diameter as necessary to maintain the specified full-throttle engine speed.*

Less dense air also affects the engine's carburetor calibration, causing the air/fuel mixture to become richer. Richer mixtures cause the engine to produce less horsepower and lead to fouled spark plugs, reduced fuel economy and accelerated carbon buildup in the combustion chamber.

All Mercury/Mariner carbureted engines are calibrated to operate efficiently between sea level and 2500 ft. (762 m). Mercury/Mariner recommends rejetting the main jet (high speed jet) at altitudes of 5000 ft. (1524 m) or higher.

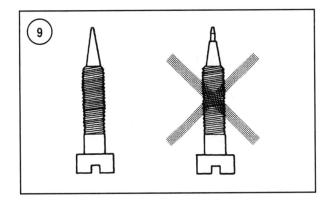

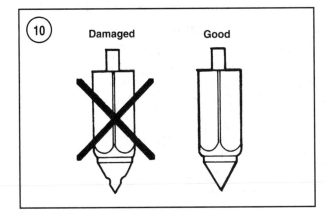

High altitude main jets are smaller than the standard main jets and will correct the air/fuel ratio for the specified altitude. The engine will still produce less power than it would at a low altitude, but the running quality will be restored and the rich air/fuel mixture problems will be eliminated. If possible, have the rejetting performed by a dealership in the area where the engine is to be operated.

CAUTION
If an engine has been rejetted for high altitude, rejet it again before operating at a lower altitude or serious power head damage will occur from the engine operating on an excessively lean air/fuel mixture.

Mercury/Mariner also recommends re-gearing the lower gearcase on larger engines at altitudes of 5000 ft. (1524 m) or higher. The new gear ratio will be a higher number ratio that will allow more gear reduction between the power head and the propeller shaft. This increases the torque at the propeller shaft, increasing the engine's efficiency at high altitudes. Verify the wide-open throttle speed as described in Chapter Five after any altitude or gear ratio change. Refer to Chapter Nine for gearcase and gear ratio information.

Cleaning and Inspection (All Models)

CAUTION
Do not remove the throttle plate(s) and throttle shaft unless absolutely necessary and unless parts are available. Reinstall each throttle plate in its original bore and orientation. Make sure the throttle plate(s) will open and close fully before torquing the screws. Use Loctite 271 threadlocking adhesive (part No. 82-809819) on the throttle plate screws. Throttle shafts and throttle plates are not serviceable on WMV series carburetors.

1. Thoroughly and carefully remove gasket material from all mating surfaces. Do not nick, scratch or damage the mating surfaces.
2. Clean the carburetor body and metal parts using an aerosol carburetor and choke cleaning solvent, available at any automotive parts store, to remove gum, dirt and varnish.
3. Rinse the carburetor components in clean solvent and dry them with compressed air. Blow out all orifices, nozzles and passages thoroughly (**Figure 7**).

CAUTION
Do not use wire or drill bits to clean carburetor passages. Doing so will alter calibration and ruin the carburetor.

4. Check the carburetor body casting for stripped threads, cracks or other damage. Replace the body if it is damaged.
5. Check the fuel bowl for distortion, corrosion, cracks, blocked passages or other damage.
6. Check the float (**Figure 8**) for fuel absorption, deterioration or other damage. Check the float arm for wear in the hinge pin and inlet needle contact areas. Replace the float as necessary. The float is made of a translucent material, allowing it to be easily inspected for fuel absorption.
7. Check the idle mixture screw(s) tip for wear grooves, nicks or other damage (**Figure 9**). Replace the idle mixture screw(s) as necessary.
8. Check the inlet needle and seat for excessive wear (**Figure 10**). Some carburetors do not have a replaceable inlet needle seat. Replace the needle and seat as an assembly if both parts are serviceable.

WME Series Carburetor
(65 Jet, 80 Jet and 75-125 hp
[Except 105 Jet and 115 Optimax] Models)

An electric fuel primer valve enriches the air/fuel mixture for cold engine starting. The throttle plates must be fully closed to develop the most vacuum for the system to function correctly. Refer to Chapter Three for operational

6

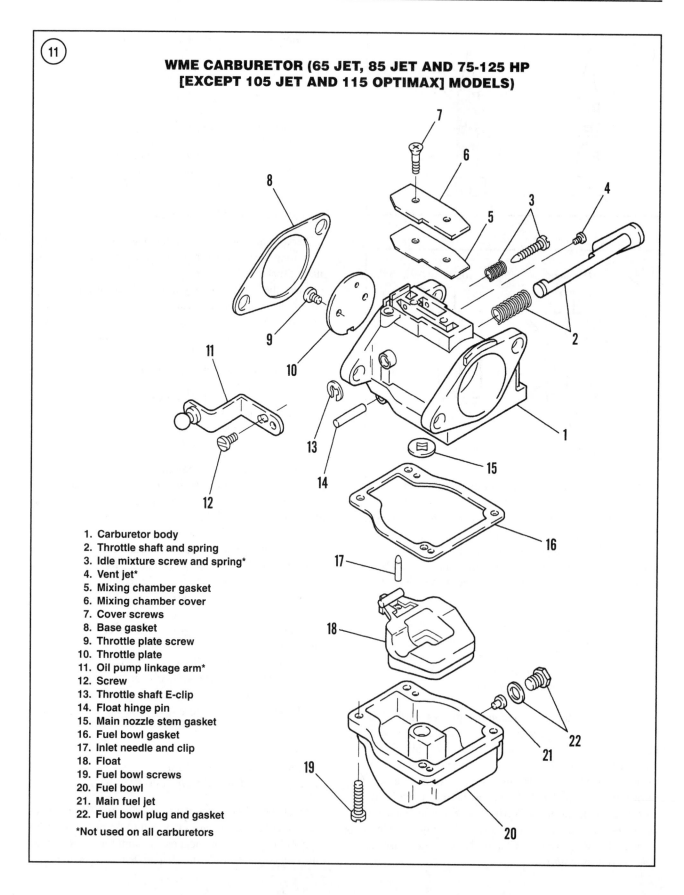

11

WME CARBURETOR (65 JET, 85 JET AND 75-125 HP [EXCEPT 105 JET AND 115 OPTIMAX] MODELS)

1. Carburetor body
2. Throttle shaft and spring
3. Idle mixture screw and spring*
4. Vent jet*
5. Mixing chamber gasket
6. Mixing chamber cover
7. Cover screws
8. Base gasket
9. Throttle plate screw
10. Throttle plate
11. Oil pump linkage arm*
12. Screw
13. Throttle shaft E-clip
14. Float hinge pin
15. Main nozzle stem gasket
16. Fuel bowl gasket
17. Inlet needle and clip
18. Float
19. Fuel bowl screws
20. Fuel bowl
21. Main fuel jet
22. Fuel bowl plug and gasket

*Not used on all carburetors

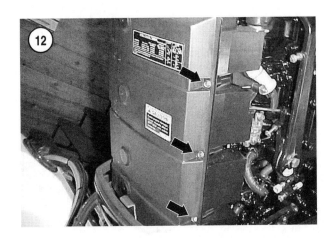

information and troubleshooting procedures on the electric fuel primer valve.

NOTE
*Install each carburetor in the correct location according to its identification number. See **Carburetor Identification** at the beginning of this section.*

On four-cylinder models, the carburetors for cylinders No. 3 and No. 4 do not have an idle mixture adjustment screw. These engines idle on cylinders No. 1 and No. 2 only. Cylinders No. 3 and No. 4 provide an air/fuel mixture at idle and off-idle speeds that is too lean for combustion to occur, yet adequate for proper engine lubrication. As the engine speed reaches approximately 1600-2000 rpm, depending on engine load, the air/fuel mixture to cylinders No. 3 and No. 4 becomes sufficient to support combustion and all four cylinders become operational.

An accelerator pump system injects fuel into the intake manifold of cylinders No. 3 and No. 4 during acceleration to prevent hesitation during the transition from two-cylinder to four-cylinder operation.

Figure 11 shows a typical WME carburetor.

Carburetor removal/installation

These models use three or four carburetors. Do not intermix components. Install each carburetor in its original location. Refer to **Figure 11** for this procedure.

1. Disconnect the negative battery cable.

2. Disconnect and ground the spark plug leads to the power head.

3A. On 65 jet, 75 hp and 90 hp models, remove the six screws retaining the air intake cover. Remove the air intake cover.

3B. On 80 jet and 100 hp, 115 hp and 125 hp models, remove the eight screws retaining the air intake cover (**Figure 12**). Remove the air intake cover.

4A. On 65 jet, 75 hp and 90 hp models, remove the two air intake plate/carburetor mounting nuts and four bolts. Remove the air intake plate.

4B. On 80 jet and 100 hp, 115 hp and 125 hp models, remove the two air intake plate/carburetor mounting nuts and six bolts. Remove the air intake plate.

5A. On 65 jet, 75 hp and 90 hp models, disconnect the oil pump linkage from the center carburetor ball socket.

5B. On 80 jet and 100 hp, 115 hp and 125 hp models, disconnect the oil pump linkage from the cylinder No. 2 carburetor ball socket.

6. Disconnect the fuel supply line from the top carburetor.

7. Disconnect the primer line from the top carburetor fuel bowl or T-fitting between the upper two carburetors.

8. On 80 jet and 100 hp, 115 hp and 125 hp models, disconnect the accelerator pump fuel supply line from the T-fitting between the middle two carburetors.

9. Remove the carburetors as an assembly. Discard the carburetor base gaskets.

10. Separate the carburetors by disconnecting the fuel lines and throttle linkage from each carburetor.

11. To install the carburetors, connect the fuel lines and throttle linkages to each carburetor. Secure the fuel lines with new tie-straps.

12. Install new base gaskets over the carburetor mounting studs. The lowest cylinder uses bolts to secure the carburetor. Insert the gasket when the air intake plate and lower carburetor mounting bolts are installed.

13. Install the carburetors as an assembly. Install the air intake plate. Install the six or eight carburetor/air intake plate mounting nuts finger-tight.

14. Position the lower carburetor base gasket in place between the carburetor and intake manifold. Insert the lower carburetor mounting bolts through the air intake plate and lower carburetor. Make sure the bolts go through the gasket and the gasket is properly positioned.

15. Tighten the air intake plate mounting hardware evenly to the specification in **Table 1**.

16. Reconnect the fuel supply and primer lines. Secure the lines with new tie-straps.

17. On 80 jet and 100 hp, 115 hp and 125 hp models, reconnect the accelerator pump fuel supply line. Secure the line with a new tie-strap.

18. Reconnect the oil pump linkage to the appropriate carburetor throttle arm.

19. Reinstall the air intake cover. Tighten the six or eight screws securely.

20. Reconnect the spark plug leads to the spark plugs.

6

21. Reconnect the negative battery cable.

22. Refer to Chapter Five for carburetor and linkage adjustment procedures.

Disassembly

Refer to **Figure 11** for this procedure. On models with multiple carburetors, do not intermix components. Install each carburetor in its original location.

CAUTION
*Do not remove or attempt to adjust the air correction screw (**Figure 13**). This screw is preset by the manufacturer and never requires adjustment. Conventional carburetor cleaning solvents will not affect the sealant securing the screw adjustment. If the air correction screw has been tampered with, seal the threads with Loctite 271 threadlocking adhesive (part No. 92-809819). Seat the screw lightly into the carburetor body, then back out the screw 1/4 turn.*

1. Remove the four screws (19, **Figure 11**) securing the fuel bowl (20) to the carburetor body (1). Remove the fuel bowl. Discard the fuel bowl gasket (16, **Figure 11**).

2. Remove the float hinge pin (14, **Figure 11**), float (18) and inlet needle (17).

3. Remove the main nozzle stem gasket (15, **Figure 11**).

4. Remove the two screws securing the mixing chamber cover (**Figure 14**) to the carburetor body. Discard the gasket.

NOTE
On four-cylinder models, only cylinders No. 1 and No. 2 are equipped with idle speed mixture screws. The bottom two carburetors have plugs installed in place of mixture screws. Remove the plugs to clean the passages.

5. Remove the idle speed mixture screw and spring (**Figure 14**).

6. Remove the main jet plug and gasket from the fuel bowl, then remove the main jet from the fuel bowl. Discard the gasket. See **Figure 15**.

CAUTION
Further disassembly is not necessary for normal cleaning and inspection. Proceed to Step 7 only if the throttle shaft or throttle valve requires replacement and parts are available. If the throttle shaft is not being removed, proceed to Step 9.

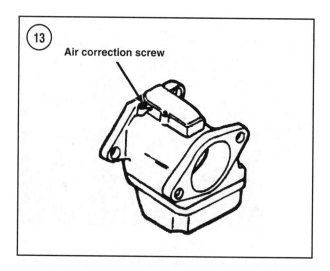

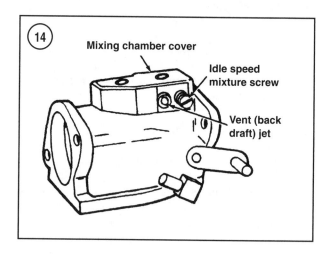

7. Inspect the throttle shaft (2, **Figure 11**) and plate (10) for excessive wear or damage. If throttle shaft or valve removal is necessary, remove the oil pump linkage arm on models so equipped.

8. Remove the E-clip (13, **Figure 11**) from the end of the throttle shaft, then remove the two screws securing the throttle valve to the shaft. Remove the throttle valve, then pull the shaft from the carburetor body.

9. Refer to *Cleaning and Inspection (All Models)* in this chapter.

Reassembly

Refer to **Figure 11** for this procedure. On models with multiple carburetors, do not intermix components. Install each carburetor in its original location.

1. If the throttle shaft was removed, insert it into the carburetor body. Make sure the throttle shaft return spring is properly engaged with the throttle lever and the boss on

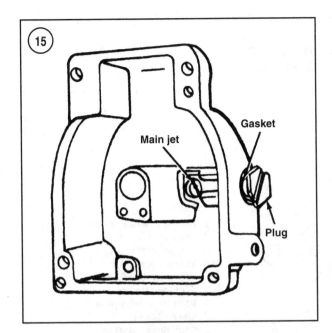

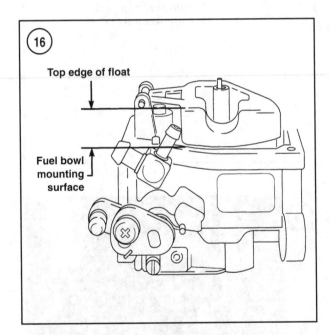

4. If so equipped, install the oil pump linkage arm. Tighten the retaining screw securely.

5. Install the main jet into the fuel bowl. Using a new gasket, install the fuel bowl plug (**Figure 15**). Tighten the fuel bowl plug to the specification in **Table 1**.

NOTE
On four-cylinder models, carburetors No. 3 and No. 4 do not have idle mixture screws. Install the plugs into the idle mixture screw holes.

6. Install the idle speed mixture screw and spring. Turn the screw in until it is lightly seated, then back it out to the specification in **Table 3**.

7. Install the mixing chamber cover using a new gasket. Tighten the cover screws to the specification in **Table 1**.

8. Install a new main nozzle stem gasket (15, **Figure 11**).

9. Attach the inlet needle wire clip over the float's metal tab. Install the float. Make sure the inlet needle properly enters the inlet valve seat. Install the float pin.

10. With the float bowl removed and the carburetor inverted, measure the float height at the points indicated in **Figure 16**. The float height measurement should equal the specification in **Table 3**. If adjustment is necessary, carefully bend the float's metal tab.

11. Install the fuel bowl using a new gasket. Tighten the fuel bowl screws evenly to the specification in **Table 1**.

WMV Series Carburetor (105 Jet and 135-225 hp)

WMV carburetors are two-barrel, single fuel bowl carburetors used on all V6 models. The intake manifolds on these engines *crosses* the air/fuel charge coming from the carburetor. The starboard side of the carburetor meters fuel to the port cylinders and the port side of the carburetor meters fuel to the starboard cylinders.

The throttle plates and the throttle shaft are not serviceable on WMV carburetors. Do not attempt to remove them.

NOTE
*Install each carburetor in the correct location according to its identification number. See **Carburetor Identification** at the beginning of this section.*

WMV carburetors incorporate two main fuel jets, two idle air bleeds, two off-idle fuel jets, one back draft (vent) jet and two adjustable idle mixture screws with limit caps. WMV carburetors have removable top covers that allow easy cleaning and inspection of the metering

the carburetor body. Position the throttle plate in its original orientation in the throttle bore.

2. Apply Loctite 271 threadlocking adhesive (part No. 92-809819) to the threads of the throttle valve screws, then install the screws finger-tight.

3. Install the E-clip onto the end of the throttle shaft. Check the alignment of the throttle plate. Make sure the throttle plate opens and closes fully without binding. Adjust throttle plate position as necessary and tighten the throttle plate screws to the specification in **Table 1**.

6

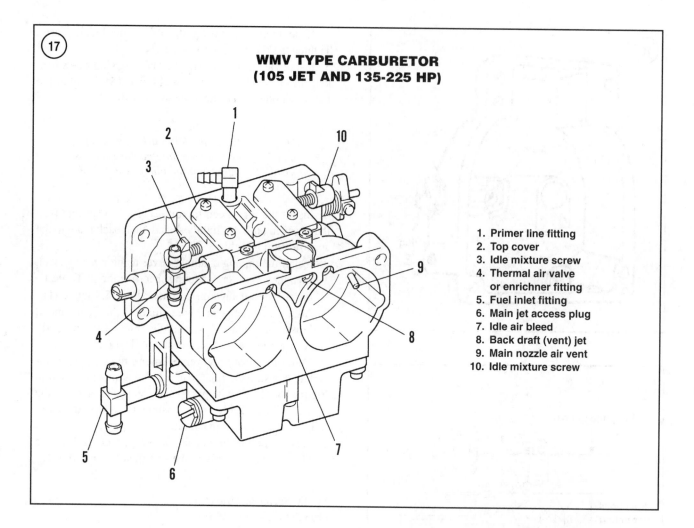

**WMV TYPE CARBURETOR
(105 JET AND 135-225 HP)**

1. Primer line fitting
2. Top cover
3. Idle mixture screw
4. Thermal air valve
   or enrichner fitting
5. Fuel inlet fitting
6. Main jet access plug
7. Idle air bleed
8. Back draft (vent) jet
9. Main nozzle air vent
10. Idle mixture screw

circuits. **Figure 17** shows an external view of a typical WMV carburetor.

Main jets always meter fuel flow. Decreasing the main jet size leans the air/fuel mixture and increasing the main jet size enriches the air/fuel mixture.

Off-idle fuel jets meter fuel flow. Decreasing the jet size will lean the off-idle air/fuel mixture and increasing the jet size enriches the off-idle air/fuel mixture.

Air bleeds meter air flow. Decreasing the air bleed size enriches the air/fuel mixture and increasing the air bleed jet size leans the air/fuel mixture for the circuit the air bleed or vent on which it is located.

Back draft (vent) jets control air pressure in the fuel bowl. Decreasing the back draft jet size leans the air fuel mixture at mid-range engine speeds. Increasing the back draft jet size enriches the air fuel mixture.

A thermal air valve is used on 105 jet and 135-200 hp models to automatically enrich the idle circuits of the carburetors whenever the engine temperature is below 100° F (38° C). The thermal valve (**Figure 18**) is mounted in the

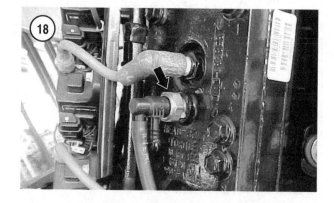

starboard cylinder head just below the No. 3 spark plug. The valve has two ports. One is connected to each carburetor through a series of fittings on the carburetor bodies. The other port is open to the atmosphere. When the engine temperature is below 100° F (38° C), the valve closes preventing air from entering the idle circuits and causing a rich air/fuel mixture. When the engine temperature ex-

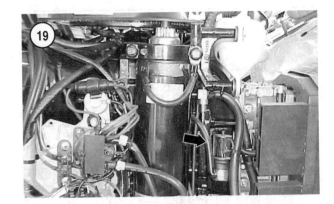

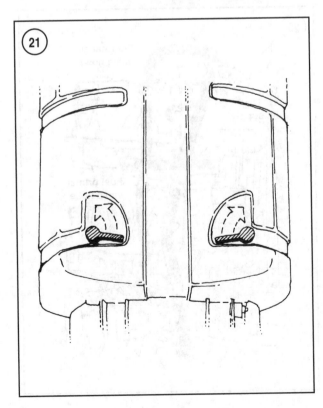

6

ceeds 100° F (38° C), the valve opens, allowing air to enter the idle circuits, providing the normally calibrated air/fuel mixture. Refer to Chapter Three for troubleshooting procedures.

All 105 jet and 135-200 hp models use an electric fuel primer valve (**Figure 19**) to enrich the air/fuel mixture whenever the fuel primer valve is engaged by the operator. This system delivers fuel to the middle and lower carburetors only. The throttle plates must be fully closed to develop the most vacuum for the system to function correctly. Refer to Chapter Three for operational information and troubleshooting procedures on the electric fuel primer valve.

A fuel enrichment valve is used on 225 hp models to enrich the air/fuel mixture during cold starts. The fuel enrichment valve is automatically controlled by the ignition ECM, based on input from the engine coolant temperature (ECT) sensor. The fuel enrichment valve receives fuel gravity fed from the top carburetor float chamber. When activated, the valve delivers fuel to each carburetor's primer fitting located behind the throttle plates. The throttle plates must be fully closed to develop the most vacuum for the system to function correctly. Refer to Chapter Three for troubleshooting procedures.

Carburetor removal/installation

These models are equipped with three carburetors. Do not intermix components. Install each carburetor in its original location.

1. Disconnect the negative battery cable.

2. Disconnect and ground the spark plug leads to the power head.

3A. On 105 jet and 135-200 hp models, remove the six bolts securing the air intake cover (**Figure 20**) to the carburetors. Remove the air intake cover.

3B. On 225 hp models, remove the flywheel cover. Release the two latches (**Figure 21**). Then, remove the air box cover.

4. On 225 hp models, remove the six screws securing the air intake plate to the carburetors. Remove the air intake plate.

5. Remove the three linkage synchronization screws, then carefully pry the throttle linkage away from the throttle lever at each carburetor (**Figure 22**, typical).

6. Disconnect the oil pump control rod (**Figure 22**, typical) from the carburetor throttle lever.

7. Disconnect the fuel supply hose from the top carburetor. Disconnect the upper and lower fuel supply hoses interconnecting all three carburetors.

8A. On 105 jet and 135-200 hp models, disconnect the fuel primer valve hose and thermal air valve hoses from the carburetors. See **Figure 23**.

8B. On 225 hp models, disconnect the three enrichment valve delivery hoses from the primer fitting (1, **Figure 24**) on the top of each carburetor mounting flange. Disconnect the fuel supply hose (2, **Figure 24**) from the top carburetor's float chamber.

9. Remove the two nuts and two Allen screws from each carburetor to be removed. Remove the carburetor(s). Remove and discard the carburetor base gasket(s).

10. To reinstall the carburetor(s), place new carburetor gaskets onto the mounting studs and install the carburetor(s) in their original locations.

11. Install the nuts and Allen screws, and tighten them evenly to the specification in **Table 1**.

12. Reconnect the fuel supply hose to the top carburetor. Reconnect the upper and lower fuel supply hoses interconnecting all three carburetors. Secure all connections with new tie-straps.

13A. On 105 jet and 135-200 hp models, connect the fuel primer valve hose and thermal air valve hoses to the carburetors as shown in **Figure 23**. Secure all connections with new tie-straps.

13B. On 225 hp models, connect the enrichment valve supply hose to the top carburetor's float chamber. Connect the three enrichment valve delivery hoses to the primer fittings on top of each carburetor mounting flange. See **Figure 24**. Secure the supply hose connection (2, **Figure 24**) with a new tie-strap.

14. Install the throttle linkage (**Figure 22**, typical).

15. Reconnect the oil pump control rod (**Figure 22**) to the carburetor throttle lever.

16A. On 105 jet and 135-200 hp models, install the air intake cover to the carburetors and secure the cover with six screws. Tighten the screws to the specification in **Table 1**.

16B. On 225 hp models, install the air intake plate to the carburetors and secure the plate with six screws. Tighten the screws to the specification in **Table 1**.

17. On 225 hp models, install the air box cover. Secure the two latches on the air box cover (**Figure 21**).

18. Reconnect the spark plug leads to the spark plugs.

19. Reconnect the negative battery cable.

20. Refer to Chapter Five for carburetor and linkage adjustment procedures.

Disassembly

Refer to **Figure 25** for this procedure. When disassembling two or more carburetors, keep individual components with their respective carburetors. Do not interchange parts between carburetor assemblies.

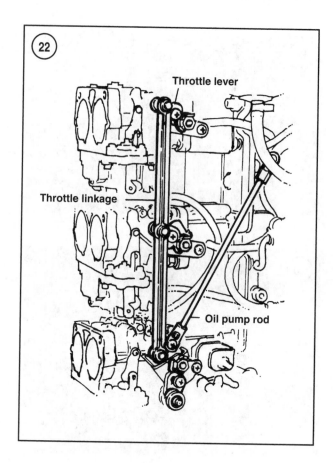

Throttle lever

Throttle linkage

Oil pump rod

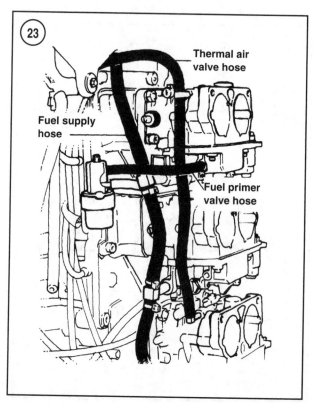

Thermal air valve hose

Fuel supply hose

Fuel primer valve hose

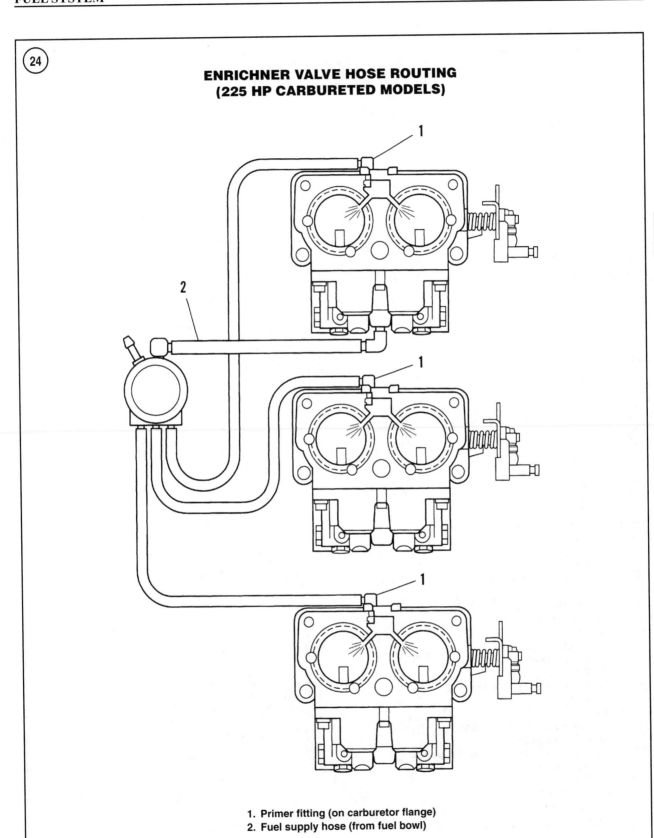

**ENRICHNER VALVE HOSE ROUTING
(225 HP CARBURETED MODELS)**

1. Primer fitting (on carburetor flange)
2. Fuel supply hose (from fuel bowl)

6

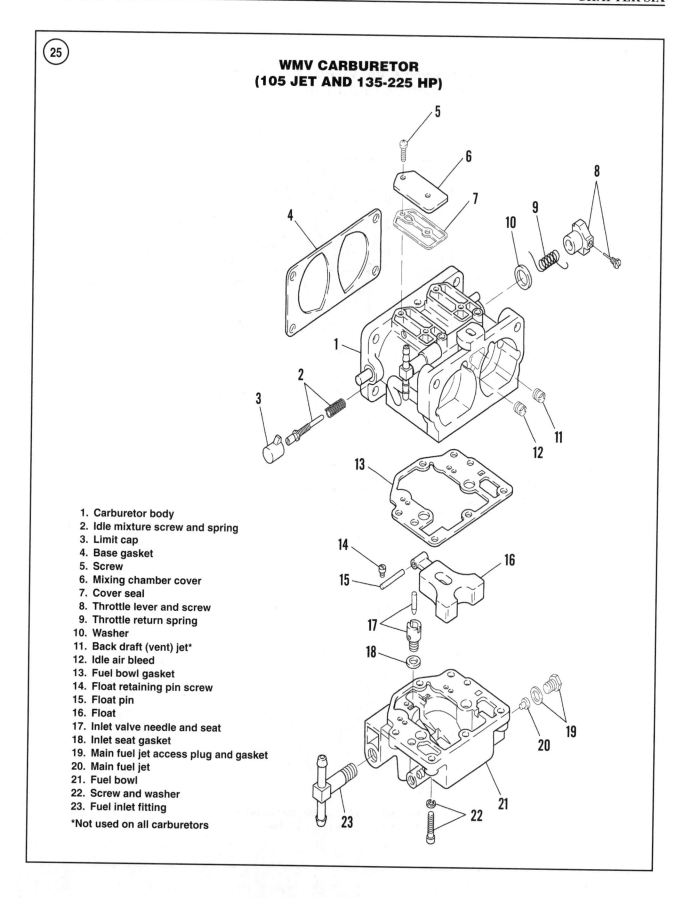

㉕

**WMV CARBURETOR
(105 JET AND 135-225 HP)**

1. Carburetor body
2. Idle mixture screw and spring
3. Limit cap
4. Base gasket
5. Screw
6. Mixing chamber cover
7. Cover seal
8. Throttle lever and screw
9. Throttle return spring
10. Washer
11. Back draft (vent) jet*
12. Idle air bleed
13. Fuel bowl gasket
14. Float retaining pin screw
15. Float pin
16. Float
17. Inlet valve needle and seat
18. Inlet seat gasket
19. Main fuel jet access plug and gasket
20. Main fuel jet
21. Fuel bowl
22. Screw and washer
23. Fuel inlet fitting

*Not used on all carburetors

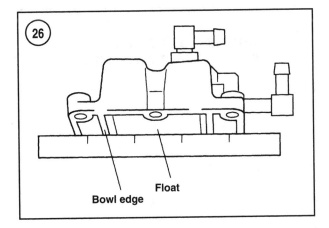

Float

Bowl edge

1. Remove the four mixing chamber cover screws (5, **Figure 25**). Remove both covers and the seals. Discard the seals.

2. Carefully pry off the idle mixture limit caps (3, **Figure 25**). Count the turns required to seat each idle mixture needle *lightly* in the carburetor body. Record the figures for reassembly.

3. Remove the idle mixture screws and springs (2, **Figure 25**). Mark the components for reassembly in their original locations.

4. Remove the main jet access plugs and gaskets (19, **Figure 25**), then remove the main fuel jets (20). Discard the gaskets. Note the mounting location for each jet upon removal.

5. Remove the idle air bleeds (12, **Figure 25**) and the back draft (vent) jet (11).

6. Remove the six screws securing the fuel bowl (21, **Figure 25**) to the carburetor body (1). Separate the fuel bowl from the body. Remove and discard the fuel bowl gasket (13, **Figure 25**).

7. Remove the float pin retaining screw (14, **Figure 25**). Lift the float (16, **Figure 25**) and float pin (15) out of the float bowl.

8. Remove the inlet needle. Remove the inlet valve seat (17, **Figure 25**) using a wide-blade screwdriver. Remove and discard the inlet seat gasket (18, **Figure 25**).

9. Refer to *Cleaning and Inspection (All Models)* at the beginning of the carburetor section.

Reassembly

Refer to **Figure 25** for this procedure.

1. Using a new inlet seal gasket (18, **Figure 25**), install the inlet valve seat (17) into the float bowl with a wide blade screwdriver. Be careful not to damage the inlet valve seat.

2. Place the inlet valve needle into the valve seat.

3. Insert the float pin into the float. Install the float and pin assembly into the fuel bowl and secure it with the float retaining pin screw (14, **Figure 25**). Tighten the screw to the specification in **Table 1**.

4. Invert the fuel bowl and place a machinist's scale or a straightedge across the fuel bowl as shown in **Figure 26**. The float must be flush with the fuel bowl mating surface.

5. If adjustment is necessary, carefully bend the float's metal tab.

6. Invert the carburetor body (1, **Figure 25**) and place a new fuel bowl gasket (13) onto the body. Install the fuel bowl (21, **Figure 25**) and the six fuel bowl screws (22). Tighten the screws evenly to the specification in **Table 1**.

7. Install the main fuel jets (20, **Figure 25**) into their respective position in the fuel bowl. Tighten the jets to the specification in **Table 1**. Install the main jet access plugs (19, **Figure 25**) using new gaskets. Tighten the access plugs to the specification in **Table 1**.

8. Install the idle air bleeds and the vent jet. See **Figure 17**.

9. Install the idle mixture screws and springs. Turn the screws inward until they are lightly seated. Back out the screws to the setting noted on disassembly, or to the specification in **Table 3**.

10. Install the idle mixture screw (2, **Figure 25**) limit caps (3) with the tabs pointing straight up.

11. Install both mixing chamber covers (6, **Figure 25**) using new seals. Tighten the top cover screws to the specification in **Table 1**.

FUEL PRIMER VALVE (65 JET AND 75-200 HP [REMOTE CONTROL MODELS])

The electrically operated fuel primer valve provides additional fuel for easier cold starts. Fuel is gravity fed from the top carburetor, or pressure fed from the fuel pump, to the fuel primer valve. When the ignition switch is held in the choke or prime position, the valve opens and allows fuel to flow to the carburetor(s), intake manifold fitting(s) or balance tube(s) (depending on the model). The valve can be operated manually by depressing and holding the button on the valve. Typical fuel primer valve system hose routing is shown in **Figures 27-29**.

Refer to Chapter Three for electrical troubleshooting procedures.

Fuel Primer Valve Replacement

1. Disconnect the negative battery cable. Disconnect and ground the spark plug leads to the power head.

6

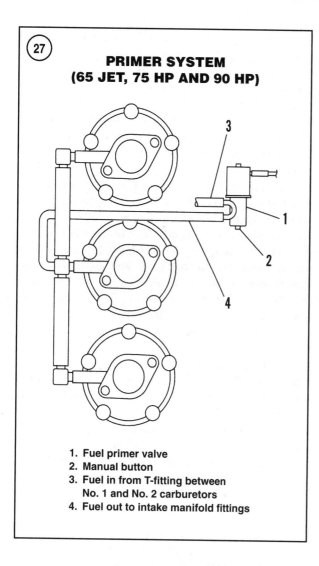

27

**PRIMER SYSTEM
(65 JET, 75 HP AND 90 HP)**

1. Fuel primer valve
2. Manual button
3. Fuel in from T-fitting between
   No. 1 and No. 2 carburetors
4. Fuel out to intake manifold fittings

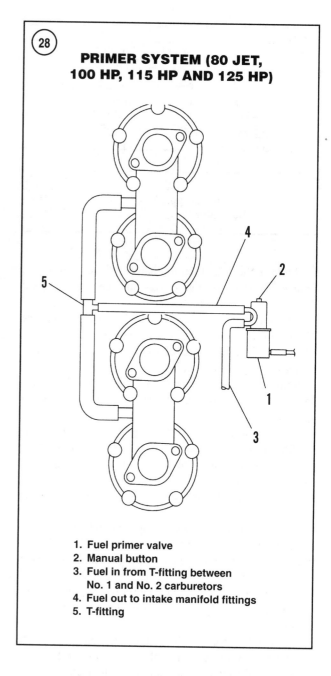

28

**PRIMER SYSTEM (80 JET,
100 HP, 115 HP AND 125 HP)**

1. Fuel primer valve
2. Manual button
3. Fuel in from T-fitting between
   No. 1 and No. 2 carburetors
4. Fuel out to intake manifold fittings
5. T-fitting

2. Disconnect the fuel primer valve yellow/black lead at the engine wiring harness bullet connector.

3. Disconnect the two fuel lines from the valve.

4. Remove the bolt holding the clamp around the valve and the black ground wire. Remove the valve from the clamp.

5. To install the fuel primer valve, position the clamp around the fuel primer valve. Apply Loctite 271 threadlocking adhesive (92-809819) to the mounting clamp bolt. Install the bolt through the clamp and ground wire. Secure the clamp, ground wire and valve assembly to the power head. Tighten the bolt securely.

6. Reconnect the two fuel lines to the valve. Secure the fuel lines with new tie-straps.

7. Reconnect the fuel primer valve yellow/black leads to the engine wiring harness bullet connector.

8. Reconnect the spark plug lead and the negative battery cable.

THERMAL AIR VALVE (105 JET AND 135-200 HP CARBURETED MODELS)

The thermal air valve is installed in the starboard cylinder below the No. 3 spark plug. See **Figure 30**. During cold engine operation (below 100° F), the thermal air valve closes, causing an air restriction to the idle circuits of all three carburetors. This restriction results in a richer mixture, eliminating the need to activate the enrichment circuit periodically to keep the engine running. When the engine warms up, the thermal air valve opens, permitting

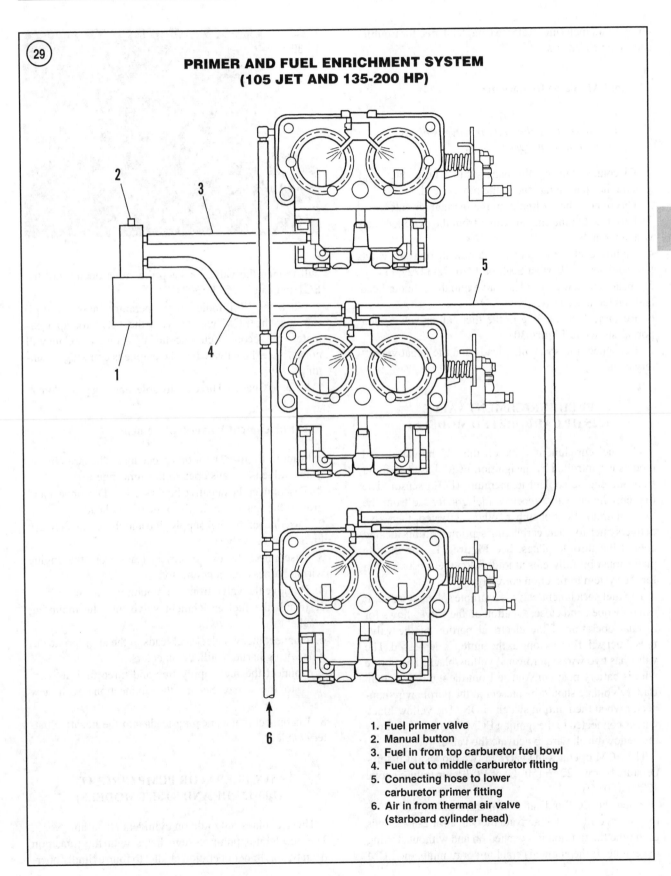

29

**PRIMER AND FUEL ENRICHMENT SYSTEM
(105 JET AND 135-200 HP)**

6

1. Fuel primer valve
2. Manual button
3. Fuel in from top carburetor fuel bowl
4. Fuel out to middle carburetor fitting
5. Connecting hose to lower
   carburetor primer fitting
6. Air in from thermal air valve
   (starboard cylinder head)

normal fuel metering. Refer to Chapter Three for trouble-shooting procedures.

Thermal Air Valve Replacement

NOTE
One port of the thermal air valve is always
open to the atmosphere.

1. Disconnect the negative battery cable. Disconnect and ground the spark plug lead to the power head.
2. Disconnect the air line from the thermal air valve.
3. Unscrew the thermal air valve from the cylinder head with a wrench.
4. Lightly coat the threads of the new thermal air valve with Quicksilver Perfect Seal (part No. 92-34227-1).
5. Install the new thermal air valve into the cylinder head and tighten it securely.
6. Reconnect the air line to the thermal air valve outer port as shown in **Figure 30**.
7. Reconnect the spark plug leads and the negative battery cable.

FUEL ENRICHMENT VALVE
(225 HP CARBURETED MODELS)

The fuel enrichment valve on the 225 hp carbureted models is controlled by the ignition ECM, based on input from the engine coolant temperature (ECT) sensor. The fuel enrichment valve receives fuel gravity fed from the top carburetor float chamber. When activated, the valve delivers fuel to each carburetor's primer fitting located behind the throttle plates. See **Figure 31**. The throttle plates must be fully closed to develop the most vacuum for the system to function correctly.

The fuel enrichment valve is a simple solenoid valve. It can only open and close. A button on the valve allows for manual operation if the electrical portion of the valve fails. Fuel will flow as long as the button is depressed. The valve has two wires: purple and yellow/black. The purple wire is battery positive voltage from the ignition switch. Battery voltage should be present at the purple wire connector when the ignition switch is ON. The yellow/black wire is connected to the ignition ECM. The ECM grounds the yellow/black wire to activate the valve.

The ECM operates the valve in two modes: ECT temperature below 122° F (50° C) or ECT temperature above 122° F (50° C).

When the ECT indicates temperatures below 122° F (50° C), the ECM will activate the valve for 2-3 seconds each time the ignition is switched on and without starting the engine. If the engine is cranking or running, the ECM

will reopen the valve, or keep the valve open, until the ECT indicates 122° F (50° C).

When the ECT indicates temperatures above 122° F (50° C), the ECM will activate the valve for approximately 1/2 second each time the key is turned on, but will not activate the valve when the engine is cranking or running.

Refer to Chapter Three for troubleshooting procedures.

Fuel Enrichment Valve Replacement

Refer to **Figure 31** for this procedure. The large fitting of the valve is always open to the atmosphere.
1. Disconnect the negative battery cable. Disconnect and ground the spark plug leads to the power head.
2. Disconnect the fuel supply line and three fuel delivery lines from the valve.
3. Disconnect the two electrical leads from the engine wiring harness bullet connectors.
4. Remove the valve from the mounting bracket.
5. Install the fuel enrichment valve into the mounting bracket.
6. Connect the two electrical leads to the appropriate engine wiring harness bullet connectors.
7. Connect the fuel supply line and three fuel delivery lines to the valve. Secure the connections with new tie-straps.
8. Reconnect the spark plug leads and the negative battery cable.

ACCELERATOR PUMP CIRCUIT
(100-125 HP AND 80 JET MODELS)

These engines only idle on cylinders No. 1 and No. 2. The accelerator pump system helps with the transition from two-cylinder operation at idle, to four-cylinder oper-

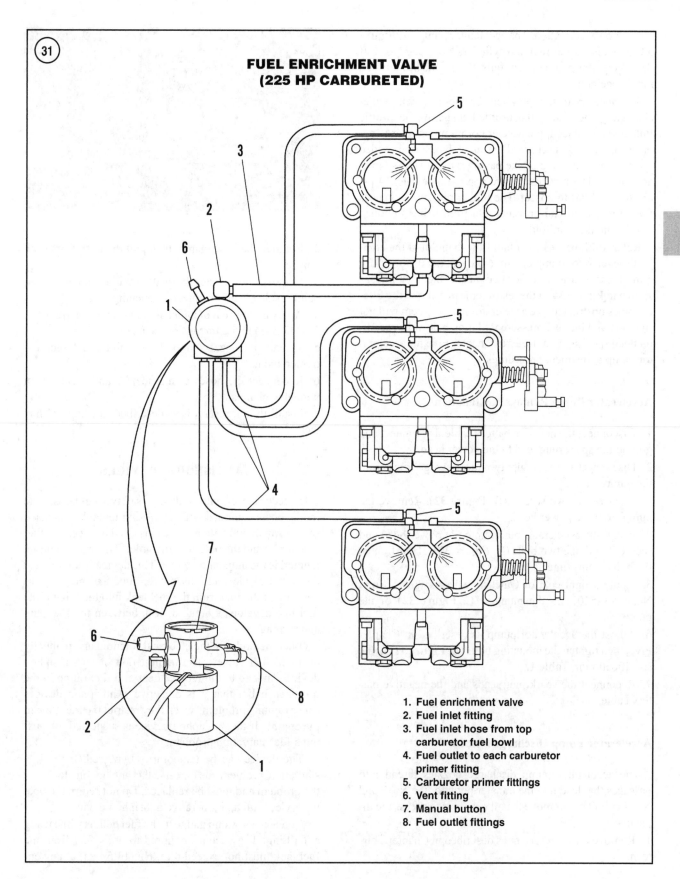

**FUEL ENRICHMENT VALVE
(225 HP CARBURETED)**

1. Fuel enrichment valve
2. Fuel inlet fitting
3. Fuel inlet hose from top carburetor fuel bowl
4. Fuel outlet to each carburetor primer fitting
5. Carburetor primer fittings
6. Vent fitting
7. Manual button
8. Fuel outlet fittings

ation upon acceleration. The accelerator pump (A, **Figure 32**) only discharges fuel into cylinders No. 3 and No. 4. If the accelerator pump system fails, the engine hesitates on rapid acceleration.

The accelerator pump system on these models is mechanically operated by the throttle linkage. As the throttle linkage is advanced, the accelerator pump plunger is depressed. Fuel is discharged through two spring-loaded nozzles located in the intake passages of cylinders No. 3 and No. 4. The nozzles require approximately 11-14 psi (75.8-96.5 kPa) to unseat. The higher pressure enhances fuel atomization and prevents fuel from being siphoned into the intake manifold.

Refer to **Figure 33** for a fuel flow diagram of the complete accelerator pump circuit. Note that a 0.014 in. (0.36 mm) brass restrictor is located inside the fuel line as shown in **Figure 34**. If the restrictor is missing or the filter becomes obstructed, the accelerator pump system will not function and the fuel pressure will drop below the recommended specification. Refer to Chapter Five for accelerator pump adjustment procedures.

Accelerator Pump Removal/Installation

1. Disconnect the negative battery cable. Disconnect and ground the spark plug lead to the power head.
2. Disconnect the fuel supply and discharge lines from the pump.
3. Remove the two screws (B, **Figure 32**). Remove the pump from the power head.
4. Install the accelerator pump onto the power head and secure it with the two bolts (B, **Figure 32**). Hand-tighten the bolts at this time.
5. Apply a light coat of Quicksilver 2-4-C grease (part No. 92-825407) to the plunger (C, **Figure 32**) of the pump.
6. Adjust the accelerator pump as described in Chapter Five, then tighten the mounting bolts (B, **Figure 32**) to the specification in **Table 1**.
7. Reconnect the spark plug leads and the negative battery cable.

Accelerator Pump Discharge Nozzles

The accelerator pump discharge nozzles thread into passages that lead into the transfer ports for the No. 3 and No. 4 cylinders. Remove the oil reservoir to access the injectors.
1. Remove the oil reservoir as described in Chapter Thirteen.

2. Remove the hose clamp, then pull the hose from each nozzle.
3. Remove the nozzles from the cylinder block. Clean paint residue from the threaded openings.
4. Apply a light coat of Quicksilver Perfect Seal (part No. 92-34227-1) to the threads of the nozzles.
5. Thread the nozzles into the openings and securely tighten them.
6. Reconnect the hoses to the nozzles and secure them with new clamps.
7. Install the oil reservoir as described in Chapter Thirteen.

ANTISIPHON DEVICES

In accordance with industry safety standards, late model boats equipped with a built-in fuel tank must have some form of antisiphon device installed between the fuel tank outlet and the outboard fuel inlet. The most common method is the antisiphon valve. This device is mounted at the outlet of the fuel tank pickup tube and prevents siphoning of the fuel from the fuel tank into the bilge if the fuel line develops a break or leak between the fuel tank and the engine.

Other methods are the electrical solenoid and manually operated fuel valves. The malfunction of an antisiphon device can lead to the replacement of a fuel pump in the mistaken belief that it is defective. Antisiphon devices cause running problems when they restrict the fuel flow to the engine. If the antisiphon device is suspected of causing a fuel starvation problem:
1. The device can be temporarily bypassed. If the fuel starvation problem disappears, the antisiphon device is the problem and must be replaced. Do not return the boat to service with an inoperative antisiphon device.
2. Connect a vacuum gauge to the fuel delivery line using a T-fitting. The vacuum required to draw fuel from the fuel tank must not exceed 4 in. Hg (13.5 kPa) at any en-

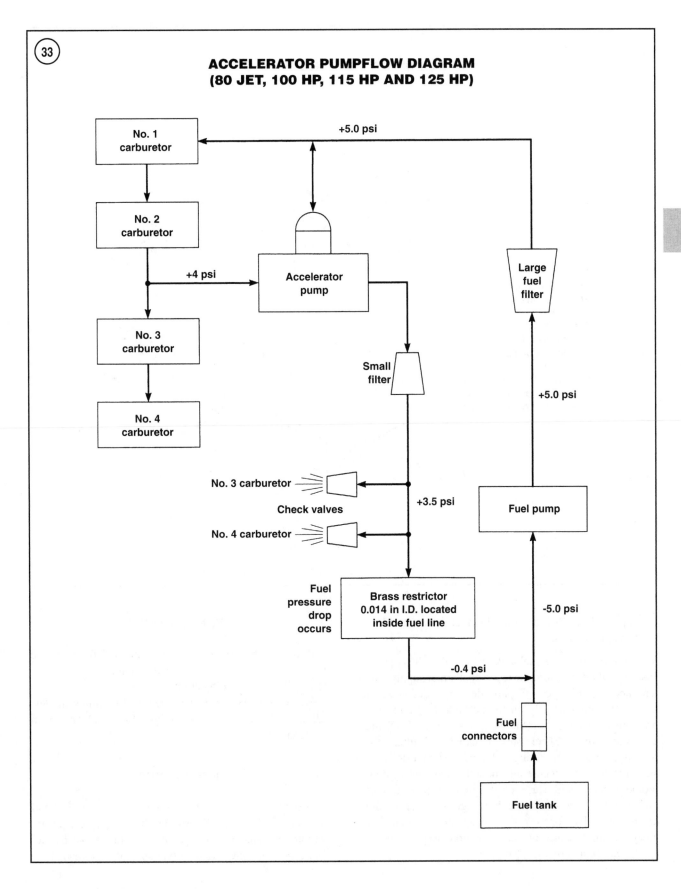

33

ACCELERATOR PUMPFLOW DIAGRAM
(80 JET, 100 HP, 115 HP AND 125 HP)

No. 1 carburetor

No. 2 carburetor

No. 3 carburetor

No. 4 carburetor

+5.0 psi

+4 psi

Accelerator pump

Large fuel filter

Small filter

No. 3 carburetor

Check valves

No. 4 carburetor

+3.5 psi

+5.0 psi

Fuel pump

Fuel pressure drop occurs

Brass restrictor 0.014 in I.D. located inside fuel line

-5.0 psi

-0.4 psi

Fuel connectors

Fuel tank

6

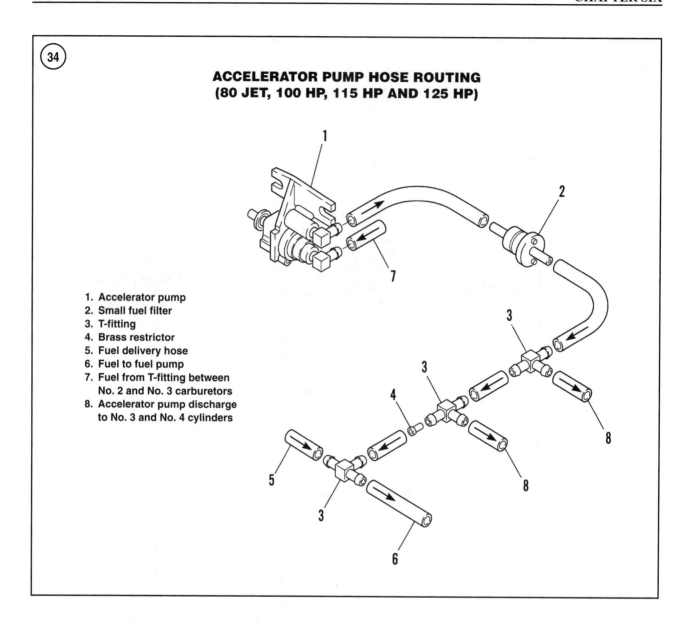

ACCELERATOR PUMP HOSE ROUTING (80 JET, 100 HP, 115 HP AND 125 HP)

1. Accelerator pump
2. Small fuel filter
3. T-fitting
4. Brass restrictor
5. Fuel delivery hose
6. Fuel to fuel pump
7. Fuel from T-fitting between No. 2 and No. 3 carburetors
8. Accelerator pump discharge to No. 3 and No. 4 cylinders

gine speed. See Chapter Three for fuel system trouble-shooting procedures.

3. Connect a portable fuel tank to the motor. This is the easiest method to determine if the boat's fuel supply system, and possibly the antisiphon device, is defective. If the motor runs correctly on the portable fuel tank, the problem is in the boat's fuel supply system. Check the easy things first. Check boat mounted fuel filters for blockage. Inspect all fittings, clamps, and fuel delivery and vent lines for secure attachment, leaks and routing problems that could cause a restriction. Inspect the fuel pickup tube filter screen for blockage and inspect the antisiphon valve for corrosion, mechanical damage or blockage from debris or contamination. Replace damaged, deteriorated or corroded parts.

FUEL FILTERS

Refer to Chapter Four for standard fuel filter service procedures on all models *except* the final fuel filter on EFI and DFI (direct fuel injection) models.

For all 150-250 hp EFI models and Optimax models (direct fuel injection), refer to *Vapor Separator Service* in this chapter.

FUEL TANKS

Portable (remote) fuel tanks come in 3.2 gal. (12 L) and 6.6 gal. (25 L) sizes. **Figure 35** shows a typical plastic remote fuel tank and components. Late model plastic fuel tanks use a simple threaded pickup tube or threaded re-

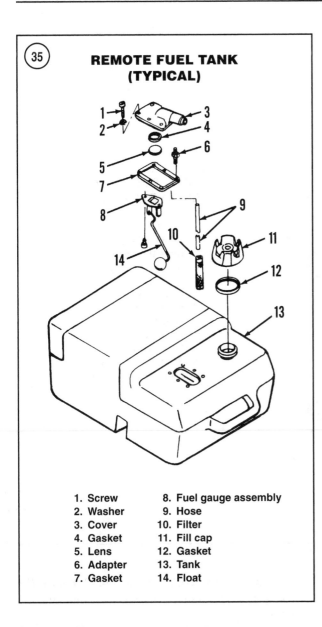

REMOTE FUEL TANK (TYPICAL)

1. Screw
2. Washer
3. Cover
4. Gasket
5. Lens
6. Adapter
7. Gasket
8. Fuel gauge assembly
9. Hose
10. Filter
11. Fill cap
12. Gasket
13. Tank
14. Float

taining nut. Unscrew the tube or nut to remove the pickup tube and clean the filter. Replace the O-ring or seal each time the pickup assembly is removed.

Inspect and clean, if necessary, the portable fuel tank and pickup tube fuel filter at least once a season and during each tune-up or major repair procedure.

Inspect the portable fuel tank, pickup assembly, fuel lines, fittings, connectors, and the fill cap and vent assembly for leaks, loose connections, deterioration, corrosion and contamination. Replace suspect parts and secure fuel line connections with new tie-straps.

NOTE
All integral and portable fuel tanks contain an air vent to allow air into the tank as the

fuel is consumed. A plugged or blocked air vent will create a vacuum in the tank and the engine will eventually starve for fuel. Always inspect the tank vent and make sure it will allow air to enter the tank.

FUEL HOSE AND PRIMER BULB

Figure 36 shows a typical fuel hose and primer bulb components. Current fuel line connectors are called *Quick Connect* snap lock connectors. These connectors come in two different hose inside diameter sizes: 1/4 in. (6.3 mm) for smaller engines and 5/16 in. (7.9 mm) for larger engines. Quick Connect connectors are replaced as assemblies, no internal components are available for the engine or fuel tank ends.

On large engines, such as V-6 models, avoid using Quick Connect connectors as they can restrict fuel flow at high speed. Use a permanently mounted fuel tank with the fuel supply line connected directly to the fuel pump inlet line eliminating the quick connectors on these engines.

On all engines with permanent mounted fuel tanks, consider connecting the fuel supply line directly to the fuel pump inlet line, eliminating the quick connectors, to minimize all possible fuel restrictions and ensure adequate fuel supply to the engine.

Inspect the fuel hose and primer bulb periodically for leaks, deterioration, loose clamps, kinked or pinched lines and other damage. Make sure fuel hose connections are tight and securely clamped. Replace the fuel supply line and primer bulb as an assembly if there are any doubts as to its integrity.

ELECTRONIC FUEL INJECTION (EFI) AND DIRECT FUEL INJECTION (DFI)

This section covers component removal and replacement for the fuel related components on the 150-250 hp EFI and 115-225 hp Optimax (direct fuel injection) models.

WARNING
Make sure the ignition switch is in the OFF position and the negative battery cable is disconnected before beginning service on EFI or Optimax models.

Air Compressor Removal/Installation (115-225 hp Optimax models)

115-175 hp models

1. Disconnect the negative battery cable.

6

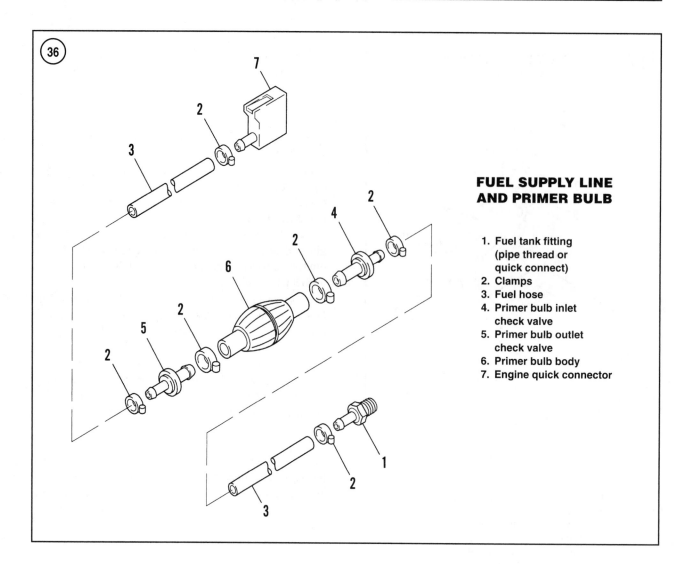

FUEL SUPPLY LINE AND PRIMER BULB

1. Fuel tank fitting (pipe thread or quick connect)
2. Clamps
3. Fuel hose
4. Primer bulb inlet check valve
5. Primer bulb outlet check valve
6. Primer bulb body
7. Engine quick connector

2. Remove the drive belt as described in Chapter Seven under *Alternator Removal/Installation*.

3. Disconnect the air outlet hose (1, **Figure 37**) from the starboard side fuel/air rail. Remove and discard the crimp type hose clamp.

4. Disconnect the cooling water inlet hose. Remove and discard the hose clamp.

   a. On 1998 and 1999 models, the inlet hose (2, **Figure 37**) connects to the fitting on the bottom of the compressor.

   b. On 2000-on models, the inlet hose (3, **Figure 37**) connects to the fitting on the top of the compressor.

5. Disconnect the cooling water outlet hose. Remove and discard the hose clamp.

   a. On 1998 and 1999 models, the outlet hose (3, **Figure 37**) connects to the fitting on the top of the compressor.

   b. On 2000-on models, the outlet hose (2, **Figure 37**) connects to the fitting on the bottom of the compressor.

6. Disconnect the oil inlet hose (4, **Figure 37**) from the fitting beneath the compressor pulley.

7. Disconnect the oil return hose(s) from the compressor.

   a. On 1998 and 1999 models, a single hose (5, **Figure 37**) connects the fitting on the starboard side of the compressor.

   b. On 2000-on models, two hoses (5 and 6, **Figure 37**) connect to fittings on the starboard side of the compressor.

8. Disconnect the compressor temperature sensor leads from the engine wire harness.

9. Remove the fasteners and lift the compressor from the power head.

   a. On 1998 and 1999 models, four bolts secure the compressor to the power head.

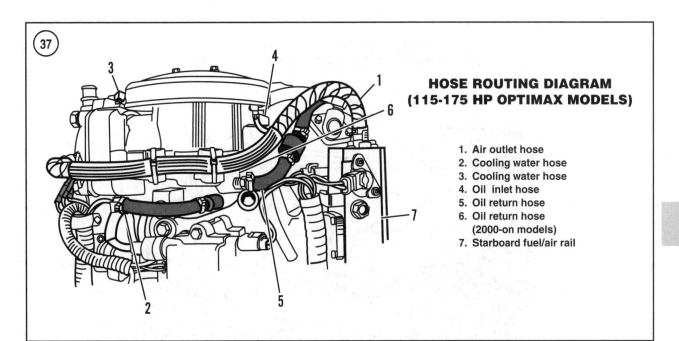

HOSE ROUTING DIAGRAM (115-175 HP OPTIMAX MODELS)

1. Air outlet hose
2. Cooling water hose
3. Cooling water hose
4. Oil inlet hose
5. Oil return hose
6. Oil return hose (2000-on models)
7. Starboard fuel/air rail

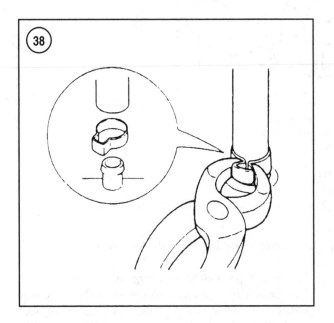

b. On 2000-on models, two bolts and one nut secure the compressor to the power head.

10. Install the compressor by placing the compressor on the power head. Secure the compressor with the fasteners. Tighten the fasteners to the specification in **Table 1**.

11. Reconnect all air, cooling water and oil hoses at the points described in Steps 3-7. Use new hose clamps in all locations. Use nipping pliers to tighten the new crimp type hose clamps as shown in **Figure 38**. Avoid using excessive force, otherwise the clamp may be damaged.

12. Install the drive belt as described in Chapter Seven (see *Alternator Removal/Installation*).

13. Reconnect the compressor temperature sensor leads to the engine wire harness.

14. Reconnect the negative battery cable. Prime the oiling system as described in Chapter Thirteen.

15. Start the engine and immediately check for water, air or fuel leaks.

200 and 225 hp models

1. Disconnect the negative battery cable.

2. Remove the drive belt as described in Chapter Seven under *Alternator Removal/Installation*.

3. Remove the clamp, then pull the outlet hose fitting from the compressor head.

4. Disconnect the cooling water inlet hose (1, **Figure 39**) from the compressor fitting.

5. Disconnect the cooling water outlet hose from the compressor fitting (2, **Figure 39**).

6. Disconnect the oil inlet hose from the fitting (3, **Figure 39**) beneath the compressor pulley.

7. Disconnect the oil return hoses (4 and 5, **Figure 39**) from the compressor fittings.

8. Disconnect the compressor temperature sensor leads from the engine wire harness.

9. Remove the four bolts and lift the compressor from the power head.

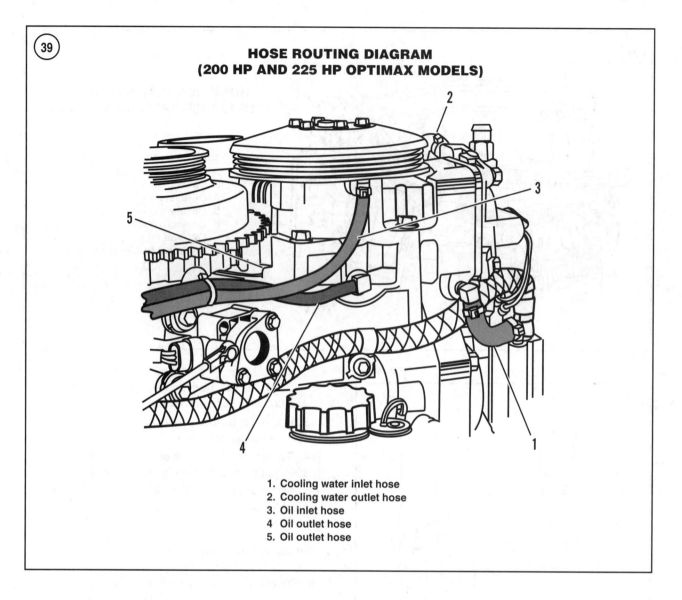

**HOSE ROUTING DIAGRAM
(200 HP AND 225 HP OPTIMAX MODELS)**

1. Cooling water inlet hose
2. Cooling water outlet hose
3. Oil inlet hose
4. Oil outlet hose
5. Oil outlet hose

10. Install the compressor by placing the compressor on the power head. Secure the compressor with the four mounting bolts. Tighten the bolts to the specification in **Table 1**.

11. Reconnect all air, cooling water and oil hoses at the points described in Steps 3-7. Use new hose clamps in all locations. Use nipping pliers to tighten the new crimp type hose clamps as shown in **Figure 38**. Avoid using excessive force, otherwise the hose can be damaged.

12. Install the drive belt as described in Chapter Seven under *Alternator Removal/Installation*.

13. Reconnect the compressor temperature sensor leads to the engine wire harness.

14. Reconnect the negative battery cable. Prime the oiling system as described in Chapter Thirteen.

15. Start the engine and immediately check for water, air or fuel leaks.

Air Compressor Disassembly/Assembly

Refer to **Figure 40** for this procedure. The piston and rings, connecting rod and bearings, and end cap are only sold as an assembly. The compressor block is not sold separately. If the block or cylinder bore is faulty, replace the compressor. Replace O-rings if they are removed. Apply a coat of outboard oil to all internal surfaces during assembly.

1. Remove the bolts, then lift the pulley from the crankshaft flange.

2. Remove the four bolts (16, **Figure 40**), then carefully pull the crankshaft and bearing assembly (17) from the compressor block (20). Remove and discard the O-rings (18 and 19, **Figure 40**). Rotate the assembly back and forth 1/4 turn to assist with removal.

(40)

AIR COMPRESSOR COMPONENTS

1. Bolt
2. Compressor temperature sensor
3. Compressor head
4. Fitting
5. O-ring
6. O-ring
7. Reed plate
8. O-ring
9. O-ring
10. Piston and ring assembly
11. Fitting
12. Cylinder bore
13. Fitting
14. Fitting
15. Snap ring
16. Bolt
17. Crankshaft and bearing assembly
18. O-ring
19. O-ring
20. Compressor block
21. Decal
22. Lock ring
23. Piston pin
24. Connecting rod
25. Lock ring
26. Grommet
27. Air inlet fitting
28. Plug
29. Seal
30. Air outlet fitting
31. Retainer
32. Screw

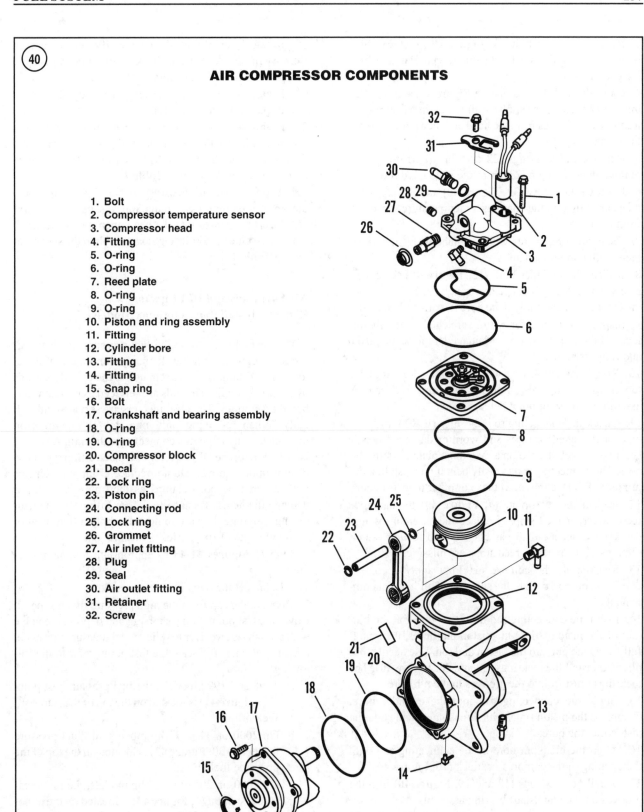

3. Remove the four bolts (1, **Figure 40**), then carefully remove the compressor head (3) and reed plate (7) from the compressor.

4. Carefully slide the piston (10, **Figure 40**) and connecting rod (24) as an assembly from the cylinder bore (12). Remove the O-rings from the head and reed plate. Discard the O-rings.

5. Remove the lockrings (22 and 25, **Figure 40**), then remove the piston pin (23) from the piston and rod.

6. Remove the screw (32, **Figure 40**) and retainer (31), then carefully pull the compressor temperature sensor (2) from the head.

7. Clean all components with a suitable solvent and dry them with compressed air.

8. Inspect the cylinder bore (12, **Figure 40**) for excessively worn, deeply scratched or rough surfaces. Replace the compressor assembly if the bore is worn or damaged.

9. Inspect the piston for worn, scratched or rough surfaces. If the piston is worn or damaged, replace the piston and ring assembly.

10. Rotate the crankshaft while checking for excessive looseness or roughness. Replace the crankshaft/bearing assembly if these or other defects occur.

11. Check the connecting rod (24, **Figure 40**) for discolored or damaged surfaces and worn or damaged needle bearings. Check the rod on a machinist plate for straightness. The connecting rod is easily bent if it is installed improperly. Replace the rod if these or other defects occur.

12. Inspect the reed plate (7, **Figure 40**) for damaged reed valves or reed stops. Replace the assembly if it is damaged. Inspect the air passages in both fuel/air rails if sections of the reeds or reed stops are missing.

13. Reassemble the compressor. First apply a coat of two-cycle outboard oil to the surfaces of all internal components.

14. Insert the connecting rod into its opening at the bottom of the piston. Align the piston pin bores, then carefully slide the pin into the piston and rod. Use needlenose pliers to install the lockrings (22 and 25, **Figure 40**). The lockrings must fit into the grooves in the pin bore.

15. Guide the connecting rod into the cylinder bore. Compress the piston rings with your fingers and slide the piston into the bore.

16. Align the crankpin bore in the connecting rod with the opening in the compressor block (20, **Figure 40**).

17. Install new O-rings (18 and 19, **Figure 40**) into the grooves on the crankshaft/bearing assembly.

18. Align the crankpin of the crankshaft with the crankpin bore in the connecting rod. Then carefully insert the crankshaft /bearing assembly into the block. Seat the crankshaft/bearing against the block.

19. Rotate the crankshaft flange to verify free movement. Remove the crankshaft and check for improperly installed components if binding occurs.

20. Install the four bolts (16, **Figure 40**) and tighten them to the specification in **Table 1**.

21. Install new O-rings onto the head and reed plate as shown in **Figure 40**. Install the reed plate and head onto the block. Install the four bolts (1, **Figure 40**) and tighten them to the specification in **Table 1**.

22. Apply Dielectric grease (part No. 92-823506) onto the tip of the compressor temperature sensor (2, **Figure 40**). Insert the sensor into the head opening and secure it with the retainer and bolt. Tighten the bolt to the specification in **Table 1**.

Air/Fuel Rails and DFI Injector Removal/Installation (Optimax Models)

The air/fuel rails house the fuel pressure regulator, air pressure regulator, tracker diaphragm and the fuel injectors. The DFI injectors are retained to the cylinders heads by the air/fuel rails. The rails are serviced as port and starboard assemblies. The DFI injectors are serviced individually. When removing only one rail or one injector, disconnect only the items connected to that rail. A seal kit is available for the DFI injectors. Replace crimp type hose clamps upon removal. Do not replace crimp type clamps with worm type hose clamps as they may leak and/or damage the hoses. Replace fuel hose fittings, or injector O-rings anytime they are removed. Apply a light coat of soapy water to O-rings prior to installation.

Refer to **Figures 41-43** as appropriate for this procedure.

1. Disconnect the negative battery cable.

2. Remove the cap from the high pressure fuel test point. Cover the test point with a shop rag and depress the valve with a small screwdriver to relieve fuel pressure present in the air/fuel rails. To locate the test point, refer to the following:

    a. 1998 and 1999 models, the fuel pressure test point (27, **Figure 41**) is located on the top of the starboard fuel/air rail.

    b. On 2000-on 115-175 hp models, the fuel pressure test point (30, **Figure 42**) is located on the top of the port side fuel/air rail.

    c. On 2000-on 200 and 225 hp models, the fuel pressure test point (1, **Figure 43**) is located on the top of the starboard side fuel/air rail.

3. Disconnect the six fuel injector and six direct fuel injector harness connectors. Carefully lift both tabs of the injector harness connectors during removal.

4. Disconnect the air supply line to the fuel, air and cooling water hoses from the rails. Discard the crimp type clamps upon removal.

5. Remove the locknuts (40, **Figure 41** typical) holding each air/fuel rail to the cylinder head. Carefully slide each air/fuel rail from the mounting studs. The direct injectors may come off with the air/fuel rail or remain in the cylinder head. Carefully pull the direct injectors from the cylinder heads or air/fuel rails. Remove the teflon seals and O-rings from each injector. Discard the seals and O-rings.

6. Only remove the fuel injector(s) if replacement is necessary. Remove the screws and retaining clamps. Use a blunt tip screwdriver to carefully pry the injector from the rail. Remove the O-rings from the injector. Discard the O-rings.

7. Only remove the tracker valve, fuel pressure regulator or air pressure regulator if replacement is necessary. Carefully and evenly loosen the cover retaining screws. The spring tension is quite high and the cap may unexpectedly spring free, damaging the threads in the rail. Have an assistant hold the cover in position until all of the cover screws are removed.

8. Inspect the diaphragm from the fuel pressure regulator, air pressure regulator or tracker valve for tears or deteriorated surfaces. Replace as needed.

9. Clean the empty fuel rails with a suitable solvent and dry them with compressed air. Cover all openings to prevent contamination during the repair.

10. Reinstall the diaphragm and spring from the regulators or tracker valve as shown in **Figures 41-43**. Tighten the cover screws to the specification in **Table 1**.

11. To reassemble the air/fuel rails and injectors, install new O-rings onto the grooves in the direct and fuel injectors. Insert the fuel injectors into their respective openings in the rails. Install the retainer and screws. Tighten the screws to the specification in **Table 1**.

12. Carefully slip the teflon sealing rings onto each direct injector. Push the compressor cap (**Figure 44**) over the injector to compress the seals. The compressor cap is usually included with the seal kit. Leave the cap on the injector a minimum of 5 minutes to fully compress the seals.

13. Make sure the stainless steel washer is present in the cylinder head opening for each direct injector. Replace the washer if it is damaged or if replacing the cylinder head. To remove the washer, pry the washer out with a screwdriver tip.

14. Remove the compressor cap and quickly insert the injector into its respective cylinder head opening. Seat the injector against the washer. Repeat Steps 12-14 for each direct injector.

15. Apply a light coat of outboard engine oil to the exposed O-rings of the direct injectors. Align the rail openings with the direct injectors and carefully press the rail onto the injectors. Work carefully to avoid damaging the injector O-rings.

16. Secure the fuel rails to the cylinder head studs with the nuts. Tighten the nuts to the specification in **Table 1**.

17. Install new O-rings, where applicable, onto the fuel and air hose fittings. Use new hose clamps in all locations.

18. Use nipping pliers to tighten the new crimp type hose clamps as shown in **Figure 38**. Avoid using excessive force, otherwise the hose may be damaged. Reconnect all fuel, air and cooling water hoses.

WARINING
The fuel return line is under high pressure (20 psi [138 kPa] or greater) at all times. Use a new clamp to ensure a leak-free seal. Do not use tie-straps or attempt to reuse the old clamp.

19. Reconnect the six fuel injector harness connectors and the six direct injector harness connectors.

20. Reconnect the negative battery cable.

21. Start the engine and check for fuel, air and water leaks. Perform visual checks for fuel leaks. Spray soapy water on all of the air connections to check for air leaks. Correct any problems found.

Fuel Cooler Removal/Installation (Optimax Models)

A separate fuel cooler is used on 1998 and 1999 models. The cooler is located on the port side of the power head and is mounted vertically next to the oil reservoir. On 2000-on models, the fuel cooler is integrated into the port side fuel rail.

The fuel cooler receives water from the adapter plate fitting. This fitting has a strainer that needs to be cleaned annually. See off season storage in Chapter Four. The water flows through the fuel cooler and to the air compressor. The fuel flowing through the fuel cooler is returning from the port air/fuel rail and is under approximately 20 psi (138 kPa). After passing through the fuel cooler, the fuel returns to the vapor separator.

1. Disconnect the negative battery cable.

2. Relieve fuel pressure in the fuel rail as described under *Fuel/Air Rails and DFI Injector Removal/Installation (Optimax Models)*.

3. Disconnect the water supply hoses from the top and bottom fittings on the cooler.

4. Disconnect the upper and lower fuel hoses from the fuel cooler. Discard the crimp type clamps.

5. Remove the two mounting bolts and remove the fuel cooler from the power head.

6. Remove the grommets from the fuel cooler.

6

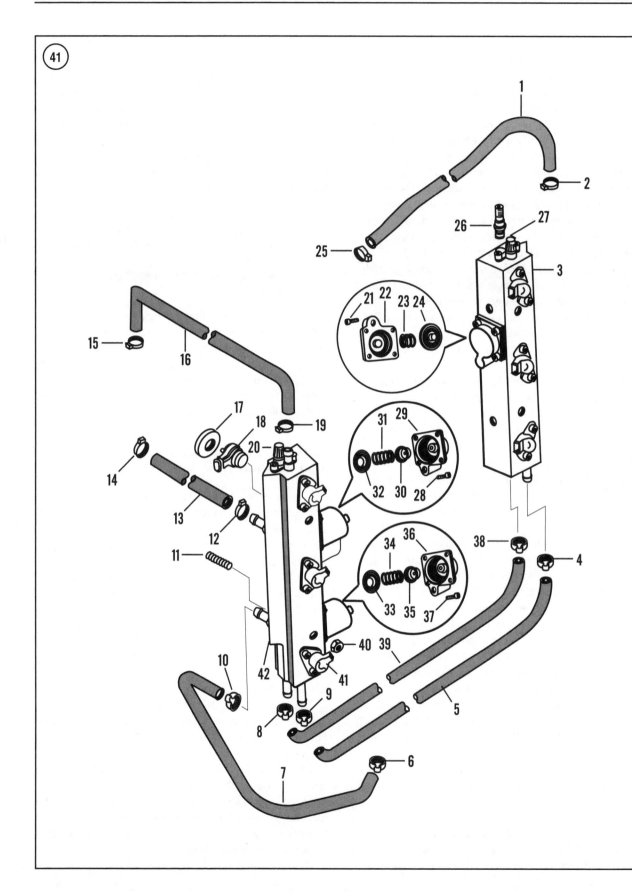

FUEL/AIR RAILS
(1998-1999 115-225 HP
OPTIMAX MODELS)

1. Air hose (from air compressor)
2. Crimp clamp
3. Starboard fuel/air rail
4. Crimp clamp
5. Fuel hose (port to starboard rail)
6. Crimp clamp
7. Air return hose (to drive shaft housing fitting)
8. Crimp clamp
9. Crimp clamp
10. Crimp clamp
11. Stud
12. Crimp clamp
13. Fuel return hose (to fuel/cooler and vapor separator tank)
14. Crimp clamp
15. Crimp clamp
16. Fuel supply hose (from vapor separator tank)
17. Stainless steel washer
18. Direct fuel injector
19. Crimp clamp
20. Air pressure test port
21. Screw
22. Tracker valve cover
23. Spring
24. Diaphragm
25. Crimp clamp
26. Fitting
27. Fuel pressure test point
28. Screw
29. Cover (fuel pressure regulator)
30. Cup
31. Spring
32. Diaphragm
33. Diaphragm
34. Spring
35. Cup
36. Cover (air pressure regulator)
37. Screw
38. Crimp clamp
39. Air hose (starboard to port rail)
40. Locknuts
41. Fuel injector
42. Port fuel/air rail

7. To install the fuel cooler, install the two grommets into the fuel cooler mounting tabs.

8. Position the fuel cooler onto the power head. Install the two mounting bolts and tighten them to the specification in **Table 1**.

WARNING
The fuel return lines are under high pressure (20 psi [138 kPa] or greater) at all times. Use the correct new clamps to ensure leak-free seals. Do not use tie-straps or attempt to reuse the old clamps.

9. Reconnect the upper and lower fuel lines to the fuel cooler. Use new hose clamps in all locations. Use nipping pliers to tighten the new crimp type hose clamps as shown in **Figure 38**. Avoid using excessive force, otherwise the hose may be damaged.

10. Reconnect the upper and lower water lines and secure the connections with new tie-straps.

11. Reconnect the negative battery cable.

12. Start the engine, and check for fuel and water leaks. Correct any problems found.

Engine Coolant Temperature (ECT)
Sensor Removal/Installation

The ECT sensor is mounted on the port cylinder head on 150-200 hp EFI models and is mounted on the starboard cylinder head on 1998-2000 115-150 hp, and 1998 and 1999 200 and 225 hp Optimax models. Both port and starboard sensors are used on 2001-on 115-175 hp and 2000-on 200 and 225 hp Optimax models. On EFI and 1998-2000 Optimax models, the sensor is grounded with a ring terminal secured by the sensor mounting bolt. **Figure 45** shows a typical ECT sensor installation. The sensor simply threads into the cylinder head on 2001-on Optimax models.

1. Disconnect the negative battery cable.

2A. On all models (except 2001-on Optimax), remove the sensor as follows:

   a. Remove the screw and retainer (1 and 2, **Figure 45**) securing the sensor to the appropriate cylinder head.

   b. Disconnect the three sensor wires (two tan/black and one tan/blue) at the engine harness bullet connectors.

   c. Remove the sensor from the cylinder head.

2B. On 2001-on Optimax models, unplug the sensor harness from the engine wire harness. Then unthread the sensor from the cylinder head(s).

3. Thoroughly clean the cylinder head sensor bore.

4. On all models (except 2001-Optimax), install the sensor as follows:

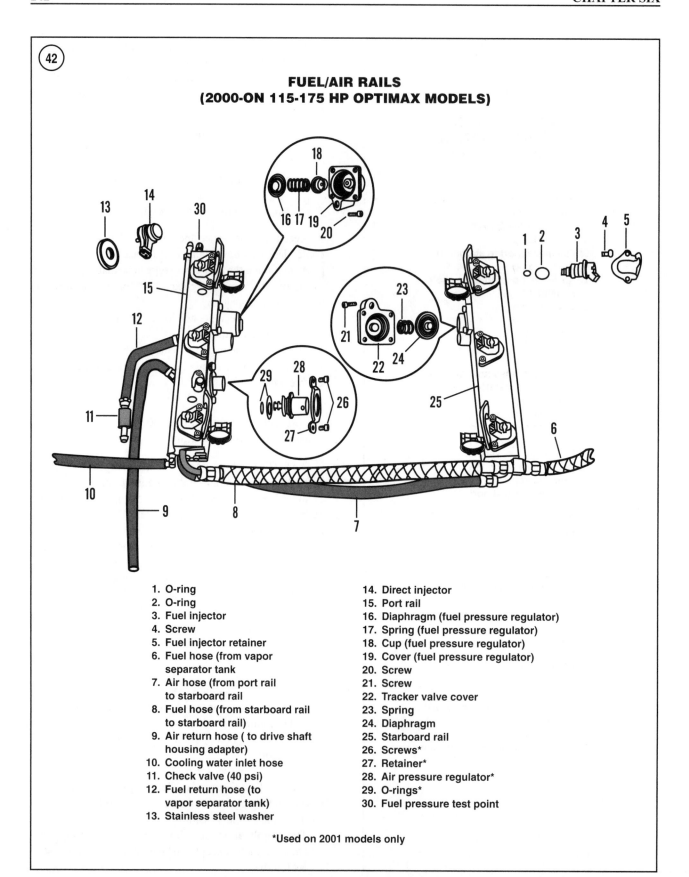

FUEL/AIR RAILS
(2000-ON 115-175 HP OPTIMAX MODELS)

1. O-ring
2. O-ring
3. Fuel injector
4. Screw
5. Fuel injector retainer
6. Fuel hose (from vapor
   separator tank
7. Air hose (from port rail
   to starboard rail)
8. Fuel hose (from starboard rail
   to starboard rail)
9. Air return hose (to drive shaft
   housing adapter)
10. Cooling water inlet hose
11. Check valve (40 psi)
12. Fuel return hose (to
   vapor separator tank)
13. Stainless steel washer
14. Direct injector
15. Port rail
16. Diaphragm (fuel pressure regulator)
17. Spring (fuel pressure regulator)
18. Cup (fuel pressure regulator)
19. Cover (fuel pressure regulator)
20. Screw
21. Screw
22. Tracker valve cover
23. Spring
24. Diaphragm
25. Starboard rail
26. Screws*
27. Retainer*
28. Air pressure regulator*
29. O-rings*
30. Fuel pressure test point

*Used on 2001 models only

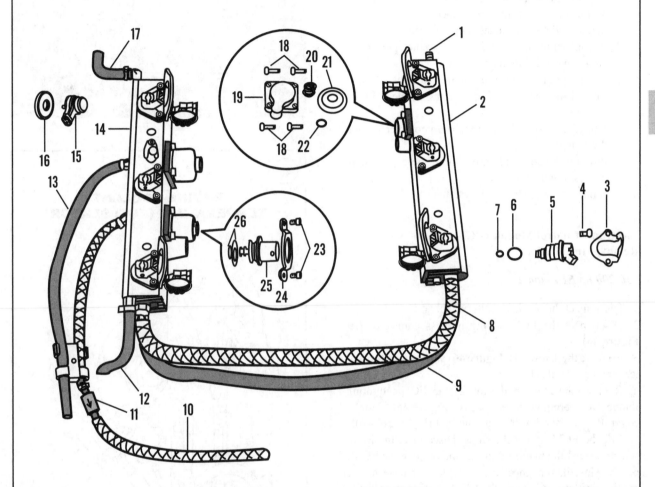

**FUEL/AIR RAILS
(2000-ON 200 HP AND 225 HP OPTIMAX MODELS)**

1. Fuel pressure test point
2. Starboard fuel/air rail
3. Fuel injector retainer
4. Screw
5. Fuel injector
6. O-ring
7. O-ring
8. Fuel hose
9. Air hose
10. Fuel return hose (to vapor separator tank
11. Check valve (40 psi)
12. Cooling water inlet hose
13. Air return hose (to intake plenum)
14. Port fuel rail
15. Direct fuel injector
16. Stainless steel washer
17. Cooling water outlet hose (to air compressor water inlet fitting)
18. Screws
19. Tracker valve cover
20. Spring
21. Diaphragm
22. O-ring
23. Screws*
24. Retainer*
25. Air pressure regulator*
26. O-rings*

*Used on 2001 models only

6

a. Install the sensor into the cylinder head bore. Seat the sensor in the bore.

b. Place the ground terminal, followed by the retaining plate, over the sensor screw and install the assembly over the ECT sensor and the cylinder head.

c. Tighten the screw to the specification in **Table 1**. Make sure the retainer is properly positioned and the ground wire terminal is not twisted.

d. Reconnect the three sensor wires to the appropriate engine harness bullet connectors.

5. On 2001-Optimax models, install the sensor as follows:

a. Thread the sensor into its opening in the cylinder head(s).

b. Snug the sensor with a wrench. Do not over-tighten the sensor.

c. Plug the sensor wire harness into the engine wire harness connector.

6. Reconnect the negative battery cable.

Electronic Control Module (ECM)
Removal/Installation

150-200 hp EFI models

1. Disconnect the negative battery cable.

2. Disconnect the ECM wiring harness connector (A, **Figure 46**).

3. Remove the screws (B, **Figure 46**) and remove the water sensing module (E).

4. Remove the nuts on the top of the ECU mounting flange. Do not remove the screws (C, **Figure 46**) from the cover. Remove the lower mounting bolt (D, **Figure 46**).

5. Lift the ECM up off the studs. Disconnect the MAP sensor hose at the manifold fitting and remove the ECM.

6. To reinstall, reconnect the MAP sensor hose to the manifold fitting and mount the ECM on the power head.

7. Secure the ECM to the power head with the two nuts and one bolt. Tighten the fasteners to the specification in **Table 1**.

8. Install the water sensing module. Make sure the two ground wires are installed under the outer module screw. Tighten the mounting screws to the specification in **Table 1**.

9. Reconnect the ECM wiring harness connector.

10. Reconnect the negative battery cable.

225 and 250 hp EFI models—fuel ECM

The fuel ECM is the lower of the two ECMs mounted on the rear of the power head. The upper ECM is the ignition ECM. Refer to **Figure 47** for this procedure.

1. Disconnect the negative battery cable.

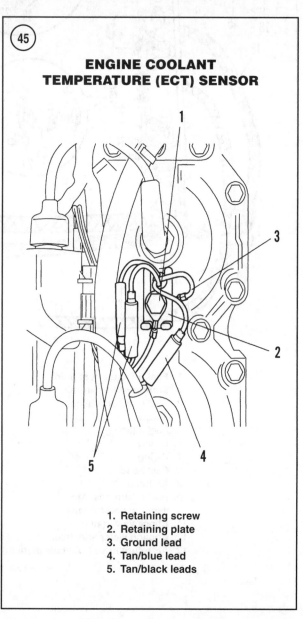

ENGINE COOLANT
TEMPERATURE (ECT) SENSOR

1. Retaining screw
2. Retaining plate
3. Ground lead
4. Tan/blue lead
5. Tan/black leads

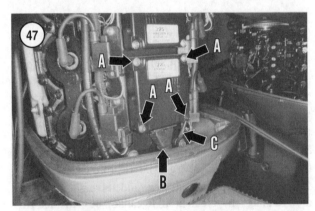

2. Disconnect the main engine wiring harness ECM connector (B, **Figure 47**) from the bottom of the fuel ECM. Squeeze the rubber boot tab to unlock the connector.

3. Remove the four fuel ECM mounting bolts (A, **Figure 47**). Remove the fuel ECM.

4. To install the fuel ECM, position the ECM on the power head mounting plate.

5. Install the four mounting screws, making sure to connect the ground lead (C, **Figure 47**) to the lower starboard mounting screw. Tighten the four mounting screws to the specification in **Table 1**.

6. Reconnect the main engine wiring harness to the fuel ECM.

7. Reconnect the negative battery cable.

Optimax models

1. Disconnect the negative battery cable.

2. Carefully unplug the three wire harness connectors from the side of module. See **Figure 48**.

3. Remove the screw and the fuse bracket from the ECM.

4. Remove the three bolts securing the ECM to the starboard side of the power head.

5. Remove the ECM. Remove the sleeves and grommets from the ECM.

6. Install the ECM by first fitting the three grommets into the opening in the ECM.

7. Install the ECM onto the power head. Secure the ECM with the three bolts and sleeves. Tighten the bolts to the specification in **Table 1**.

8. Install the fuse bracket onto power head. Tighten the bracket screws to the specification in **Table 2**. The rubber cushion must fit between the bracket and ECM.

9. Carefully plug the three connectors into the ECM.

10. Reconnect the negative battery cable.

Electric Fuel Pump Removal/Installation

The electric fuel pump is internally mounted inside the vapor separator on all 150-250 hp EFI and all Optimax models. An additional external electric fuel pump is used on Optimax models. Refer to *Vapor Separator Service* in this section for service on the internally mounted electric fuel pump.

WARNING
EFI systems operate under high pressure. Do not remove the crimped stainless steel clamps unless absolutely necessary. Do not disconnect the rubber lines from the electric fuel pump, fuel pressure regulator and fuel management adapter unless new hoses and

6

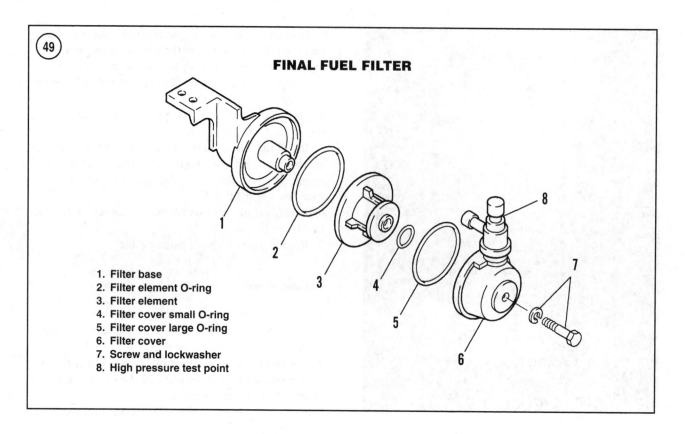

FINAL FUEL FILTER

1. Filter base
2. Filter element O-ring
3. Filter element
4. Filter cover small O-ring
5. Filter cover large O-ring
6. Filter cover
7. Screw and lockwasher
8. High pressure test point

clamps will be installed. Always replace O-rings and seals when servicing EFI systems.

WARNING
The output of the electric fuel pump is considered high pressure. Only use the recommended clamps on all high-pressure hoses.

Final Fuel Filter Service (Earlier EFI Models)

This procedure covers 150-200 hp EFI models with an externally mounted final fuel filter located above the vapor separator and electric fuel pump. The filter cover also contains the high pressure test point (8, **Figure 49**).

To service the final fuel filter on all other EFI and Optimax models, refer to *Vapor Separator Service* later in this section.

WARNING
The final fuel filter is under high fuel pressure. Replace all O-rings each time the filter is disassembled. Do not disconnect the fuel lines from the filter cover and base unless parts replacement is required. Only use the recommended clamps on high pressure fuel lines.

1. Remove the cap from the high pressure fuel test point (8, **Figure 49**). Cover the test point with a shop rag and depress the valve with a small screwdriver to relieve fuel pressure present in the air/fuel rails. Reinstall the cap after the pressure has been relieved.

2. Remove the screw and lock washer (7, **Figure 49**).

3. Separate the fuel filter cover (6, **Figure 49**) from the filter base.

4. Remove the filter element (3, **Figure 49**) and the three O-rings (2, 4 and 5, **Figure 49**). Discard the O-rings.

5. Clean the filter element in a mild solvent and blow it dry. Replace the element if it cannot be satisfactorily cleaned.

6. To reassemble the filter, install new O-rings (4 and 5, **Figure 49**) into the filter cover.

7. Install a new O-ring (2, **Figure 49**) into the filter element.

8. Carefully assemble the filter cover to the base. Be careful not to displace any of the O-rings. Make sure the high-pressure test point is pointing straight up.

9. Install the screw and lock washer and tighten the screw securely.

10. Reconnect the negative battery cable.

11. Start the engine and check for fuel leaks. Correct any problem found.

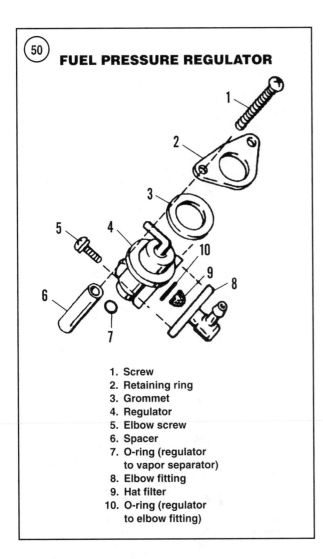

FUEL PRESSURE REGULATOR

1. Screw
2. Retaining ring
3. Grommet
4. Regulator
5. Elbow screw
6. Spacer
7. O-ring (regulator to vapor separator)
8. Elbow fitting
9. Hat filter
10. O-ring (regulator to elbow fitting)

Fuel Pressure Regulator Removal/Installation (EFI models)

The fuel regulator controls the fuel pressure by dumping excess fuel into the vapor separator when fuel pressure exceeds the regulator's preset value. Fuel pressure will vary with engine load based on the vacuum signal to the pressure regulator.

> *WARNING*
> *EFI systems operate under high pressure. Do not remove the crimped stainless steel clamps unless absolutely necessary. Do not disconnect the rubber lines from the electric fuel pump, fuel pressure regulator and fuel management adapter unless new hoses and clamps will be installed. Always replace the O-rings and seals when servicing EFI systems.*

150-250 hp EFI models

Refer to **Figure 50** for this procedure.

1. Disconnect the negative battery cable.

2. Remove the cap from the high-pressure fuel test point on the side of the elbow fitting (8, **Figure 50**). Cover the test point with a shop rag and depress the valve with a small screwdriver to relieve fuel pressure present in the air/fuel rails. Reinstall the cap after the pressure has been relieved.

3. Disconnect the vacuum line from the pressure regulator (4, **Figure 50**).

4. Remove the two regulator mounting screws. Remove the regulator retaining plate, grommet and two spacer tubes. See **Figure 50**.

5. Lift the regulator from the vapor separator. Remove and discard the O-ring from the vapor separator.

6. Remove the two screws from the regulator elbow fitting (8, **Figure 50**). Remove the elbow fitting from the regulator. Remove the hat filter (9, **Figure 50**) from the elbow fitting. Remove and discard the elbow fitting O-ring.

7. To reinstall the regulator, clean the hat filter. Replace the filter if it cannot be satisfactorily cleaned.

8. Install a new elbow fitting O-ring into the regulator groove. Install the hat filter into the regulator elbow. Install the regulator to the elbow and secure it with two screws (1, **Figure 50**). Tighten the screws to the specification in **Table 1**.

9. Install a new O-ring into the vapor separator groove.

10. Install the regulator onto the vapor separator and seat it against the vapor separator.

11. Slide the grommet and regulator retaining plate over the pressure regulator. Secure the plate with the two regulator mounting screws and spacers. Tighten the screws evenly to the specification in **Table 1**.

12. Reconnect the vacuum line to the regulator.

13. Reconnect the negative battery cable.

14. Start the engine and check for fuel leaks. Correct any problems found.

Induction Manifold Removal/Installation

> *WARNING*
> *EFI systems operate under high pressure. Do not remove the crimped stainless steel clamps unless absolutely necessary. Do not disconnect the rubber lines from the electric fuel pump, fuel pressure regulator and fuel management adapter unless new hoses and clamps will be installed. Always replace all O-rings and seals when servicing EFI systems.*

6

150-250 hp EFI models

1. Disconnect the negative battery cable.

2. Remove the cap from the high pressure fuel test point on the side of the fuel pressure regulator elbow fitting (8, **Figure 50**). Cover the test point with a shop rag and depress the valve with a small screwdriver to relieve fuel pressure present in the air/fuel rails. Reinstall the cap after the pressure has been relieved.

3. Remove the ECM assembly as described previously in this section.

4. Remove the oil reservoir as described in Chapter Thirteen.

5. Remove the two screws securing the water separating fuel filter assembly to the induction manifold. Lay the filter to one side. Do not disconnect the fuel lines.

6. Disconnect the vacuum line from the fuel pressure regulator (4, **Figure 50**).

7. Disconnect the vent line from the vapor separator fitting. It is not necessary to disconnect the bleed return line with the small filter from the vapor separator at this time.

8. Remove the two screws (**Figure 51**) securing the fuel management adapter to the top port side of the induction manifold.

9. Remove the three screws securing the vapor separator assembly to the induction manifold. Pull the fuel management adapter and the vapor separator away from the induction manifold, and lay the vapor separator and fuel management adapter to one side. Do not disconnect any additional lines.

10. Disconnect the throttle position sensor from the engine harness three-pin connector.

11. Disconnect the two intake air temperature sensor leads from the engine harness bullet connectors.

12. Disconnect the fuel injector harness from the engine harness four-pin connector.

13. Disconnect the throttle link rod from the throttle cam.

14. Disconnect the oil injection control rod from the oil injection pump control arm.

15. Note the location of the ground wires for reference during installation.

NOTE
The manifold cover and the manifold body are held together by the 12 mounting screws. Support the manifold as the last screws are removed.

16. Remove the 12 manifold cover screws and remove the manifold cover (**Figure 52**).

17. Disconnect the bleed hose from the bleed shutoff valve on the port side of the induction manifold.

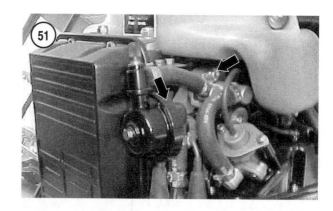

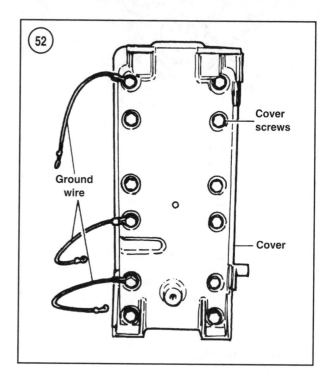

18. Pull the manifold away from the power head enough to disconnect the bleed hoses from the fittings at the bottom of the manifold assembly.

19. Remove the induction manifold assembly from the power head.

20. Carefully remove gasket material from the intake and induction manifolds.

21. To reinstall the induction manifold, first place a new gasket onto the manifold-to-engine mating surface.

22. Hold the manifold in position while connecting the bleed hoses to the bleed fittings at the bottom of the manifold. Install the manifold onto the power head and secure it with the 12 screws.

23. Tighten the manifold screws to the specification in **Table 1** and in the sequence shown in **Figure 53**. Remove

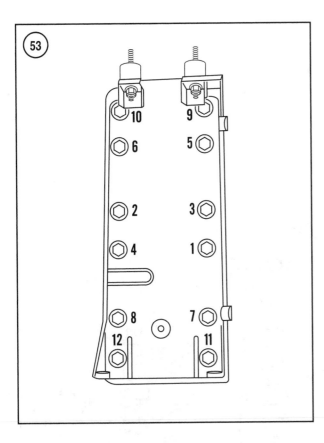

the excess gasket material from the area adjacent to each throttle plate. Remove only excess gasket material.

24. Rotate the oil injection pump control arm clockwise until the arm is facing aft, then connect the oil pump control rod to the pump arm.

25. Connect the throttle link rod to the throttle cam.

26. Install new O-rings on the fuel management adapter. Position the vapor separator and install the fuel management adapter to the induction manifold. Tighten the two retaining bolts (**Figure 51**) to the specification in **Table 1**.

27. Reconnect the vacuum line from the fuel pressure regulator.

28. Reconnect the vent line from the vapor separator fitting.

29. Position the vapor separator and install the three screws securing the vapor separator assembly to the induction manifold. Tighten the screws to the specification in **Table 1**.

30. Install the oil reservoir as described in Chapter Thirteen.

31. Reconnect the throttle position sensor, intake air temperature sensor and fuel injector wiring harnesses to the appropriate engine wiring harness connectors.

32. Install the water separating filter assembly and the ECM.

33. Reconnect the negative battery cable.

34. Start the engine and check for fuel leaks. Correct any problems found.

35. Refer to Chapter Five for synchronization and linkage adjustments.

Optimax models

Refer to **Figure 54** for this procedure.

1. Disconnect the negative battery cable.

2. Relieve the system pressure as described in this chapter under *Fuel/Air Rails*.

3. Remove the electric oil pump (23, **Figure 54**) from the intake manifold as described in Chapter Thirteen.

4. Place a container suitable for holding fuel under the vapor separator tank (12, **Figure 54**). Remove the brass screw from the front of the vapor separator tank and drain the fuel from the tank. Disconnect the fuel pump harness on the vapor separator tank from the engine wire harness. Two connectors are used.

5. Mark all hose connection points to the vapor separator tank for reference during assembly. Remove the hose clamps and carefully disconnect all hoses from the tank. Disconnect the water sensor lead from the connection on the bottom of the vapor separator tank.

6. Remove the three mounting bolts and washers (13 and 14, **Figure 54**), and carefully remove the vapor separator tank.

7. Disconnect the throttle linkages from the lever on the throttle body (10, **Figure 54**).

8A. On 1998 and 1999 models, disconnect the two engine wire harness connectors from the air temperature sensor. The sensor mounts onto the induction manifold at the point shown (24, **Figure 54**).

8B. On 2000-on models, disconnect the engine wire harness from the manifold pressure sensor (5, **Figure 54**) and air temperature sensor (6).

9. Remove the bolts (18, **Figure 54**) securing the induction manifold to the power head. Carefully remove the manifold. Remove and discard the gasket (2, **Figure 54**) from between the manifold and reed plate.

10. Remove the throttle body (10, **Figure 54**) only if replacement is necessary. Remove it as follows:

    a. Remove the four screws (11, **Figure 54**) and carefully pull the throttle body from the manifold.

    b. Remove and discard the throttle body O-ring.

11. Reinstall the throttle body, if it was removed, onto the manifold as follows:

    a. Fit a new O-ring onto the throttle body.

6

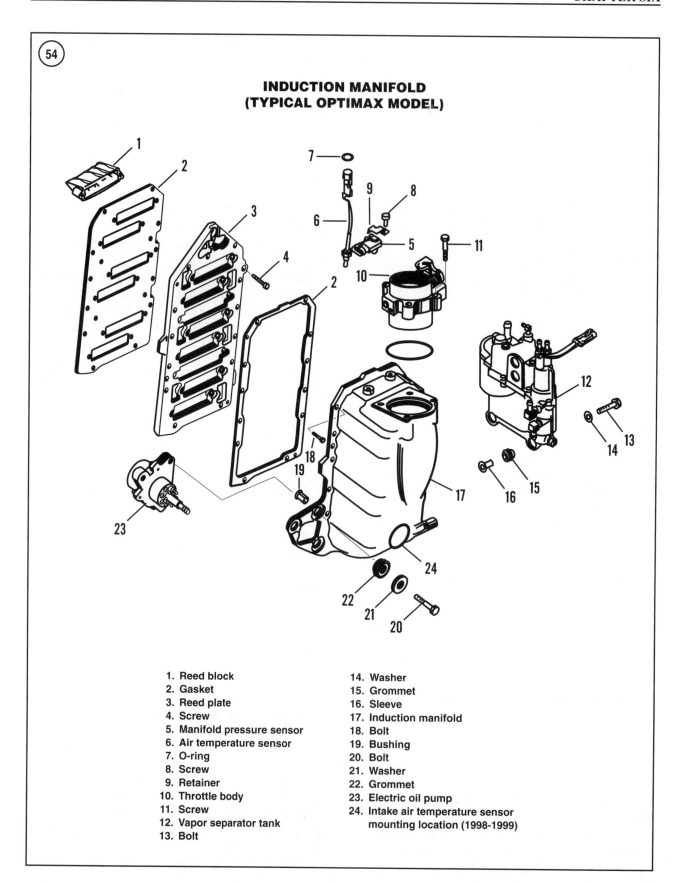

54

**INDUCTION MANIFOLD
(TYPICAL OPTIMAX MODEL)**

1. Reed block
2. Gasket
3. Reed plate
4. Screw
5. Manifold pressure sensor
6. Air temperature sensor
7. O-ring
8. Screw
9. Retainer
10. Throttle body
11. Screw
12. Vapor separator tank
13. Bolt
14. Washer
15. Grommet
16. Sleeve
17. Induction manifold
18. Bolt
19. Bushing
20. Bolt
21. Washer
22. Grommet
23. Electric oil pump
24. Intake air temperature sensor
    mounting location (1998-1999)

b. Carefully slide the throttle body into its bore in the manifold.

c. Align the hole, then install the four screws (11, **Figure 54**). Tighten the screws to the specification in **Table 1**.

12. Install a new gasket onto the induction manifold. Align the openings, then install the bolts (18, **Figure 54**). Tighten the induction manifold bolts in a crossing pattern to the specification in **Table 1**.

13. Install the vapor separator tank onto the induction manifold. Secure the tank with the bolts, washers, grommets and sleeves as shown in **Figure 54**. Tighten the bolts to the specification in **Table 1**.

14. Install the fuel hoses onto the vapor separator tank. Use new hose clamps in all locations. Use nipping pliers to tighten the new crimp type hose clamps as shown in **Figure 38**. Avoid using excessive force, otherwise the clamp may be damaged.

15. Reconnect the wire harness plugs to the fuel pump connection on the vapor separator tank.

16. Reconnect all vent hoses to their respective fittings on the vapor separator tank. Reconnect the water sensor lead to its connection on the bottom of the vapor separator tank.

17. Reattach the throttle linkages to the throttle lever on the throttle body.

18. Reconnect the air temperature sensor and manifold pressure sensor lead at the points described in Step 8.

19. Install the electric oil pump to the induction manifold as described in Chapter Thirteen.

20. Reconnect the negative battery cable.

21. Refer to Chapter Five for synchronization and linkage adjustments.

Induction Manifold Disassembly/Reassembly (EFI Models)

The induction manifold on the 150-200 hp and 250 hp models (except Optimax) uses four throttle plates mounted on two separate shafts. The earlier 225 hp models use two throttle plates mounted on a single shaft. The service procedures between the 150-200 hp and 225-250 hp induction manifolds are very similar, with only minor differences in the number of fasteners. The following procedure focuses mainly on fuel injector and fuel injector harness replacement for EFI models.

Replace all O-rings and seals. Seal and O-ring kits are available from Mercury/Mariner dealerships. Lubricate all O-rings and seals with outboard motor oil.

Refer to **Figure 55** for this procedure.

1. Place the induction manifold assembly on a clean work surface.

2. Remove the induction manifold cover seal (13, **Figure 55**).

3. Remove the screw and washer (4, **Figure 44**) securing the adapter (5) to the fuel rail.

4. Remove the adapter from the manifold. Remove the tube (7, **Figure 55**) from the adapter (5) or fuel rail (8). Remove and discard the O-ring (6, **Figure 55**).

5. Remove the fuel rail mounting screws (**Figure 56**) and remove the fuel rail from the manifold. Do not lose the two fuel rail locating guides in the two fuel rail mounting bolt bores.

6. Lift the wire clip that secures the injector harness connectors to the injectors from its groove. Disconnect the injector connectors. See **Figure 57**.

7. Remove the injectors by lifting them straight up from the manifold.

8. Remove the upper and lower seal, the O-ring, and the filter from each injector (**Figure 58**). Discard the O-ring and seals. Clean the filter in mild solvent and blow it dry. Replace any filter that cannot be satisfactorily cleaned.

NOTE
The following steps deal with injector harness replacement. If injector harness replacement is not required, go to Step 16 for reassembly.

9. Note the position of the injector harness (18, **Figure 55**) and protective casing for reassembly. Remove the protective casing covering the injector harness. See **Figure 59**.

10. Remove the three screws (17, **Figure 55**) securing the injector harness plate (16). Remove the injector harness plate.

11. Remove the injector harness from the induction manifold. Discard the injector harness plug O-ring.

12. To reassemble, install a new O-ring (14, **Figure 55**) onto the injector harness plug. Insert the injector lead and harness assembly through the induction manifold bore.

13. Seat the harness plug in the induction manifold. Install the injector harness plate and secure it with three screws. Tighten the screws securely.

14. Position the injector leads as noted on disassembly. Install the protective cover. See **Figure 59**.

15. Install the filter, new O-ring, and new upper and lower seals on each injector. See **Figure 58**.

16. Install the injectors into the manifold. Attach the injector connectors to the injectors and install the wire clips (1, **Figure 57**) to secure the connectors.

17. Install new O-rings onto the inner fuel rail adapter and fuel tubes. Install the adapter onto the fuel rail and secure it with the screws. Tighten the bolts to the specification in **Table 1**.

6

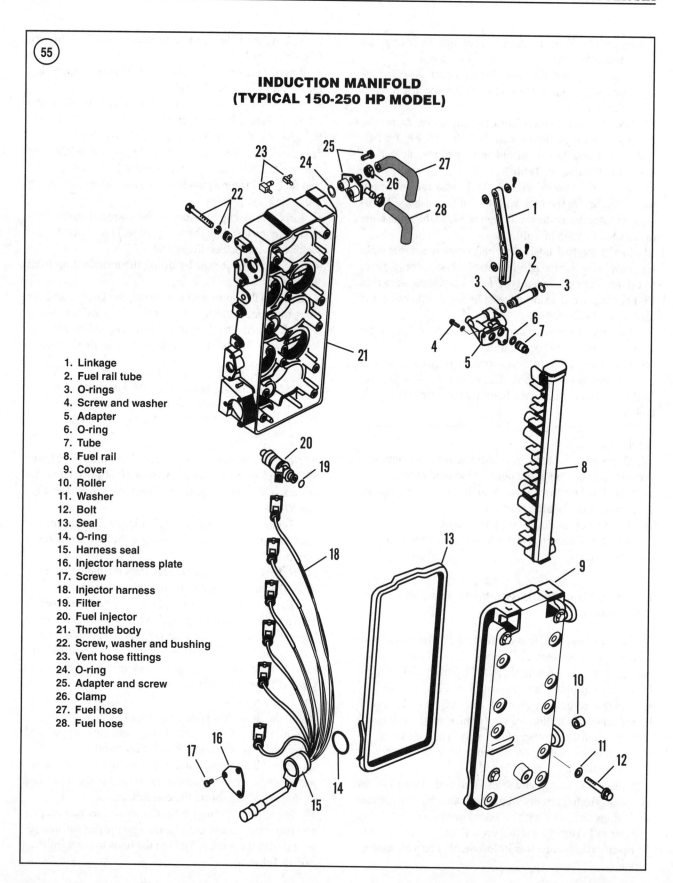

**INDUCTION MANIFOLD
(TYPICAL 150-250 HP MODEL)**

1. Linkage
2. Fuel rail tube
3. O-rings
4. Screw and washer
5. Adapter
6. O-ring
7. Tube
8. Fuel rail
9. Cover
10. Roller
11. Washer
12. Bolt
13. Seal
14. O-ring
15. Harness seal
16. Injector harness plate
17. Screw
18. Injector harness
19. Filter
20. Fuel injector
21. Throttle body
22. Screw, washer and bushing
23. Vent hose fittings
24. O-ring
25. Adapter and screw
26. Clamp
27. Fuel hose
28. Fuel hose

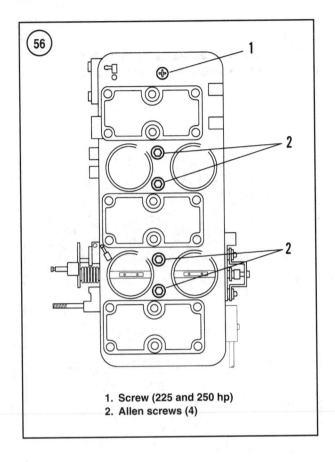

1. Screw (225 and 250 hp)
2. Allen screws (4)

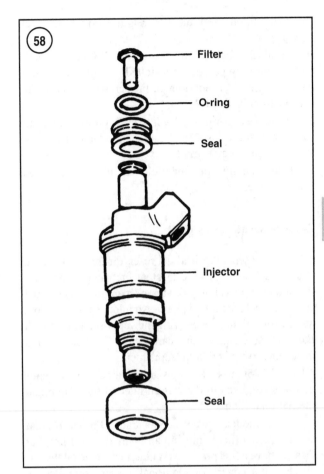

- Filter
- O-ring
- Seal
- Injector
- Seal

6

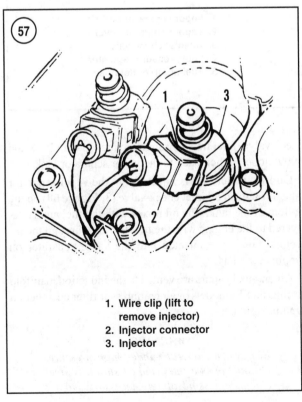

1. Wire clip (lift to
   remove injector)
2. Injector connector
3. Injector

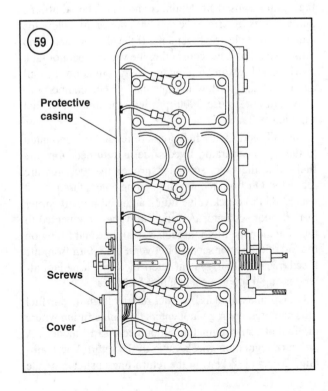

- Protective
  casing
- Screws
- Cover

18. Install the fuel rail tubes (2, **Figure 55**) into the fuel rail adapter.

19. Install the fuel rail to the manifold. Make sure both fuel rail locating guides are installed. Install the fuel rail screws (**Figure 56**) and tighten the screws evenly to the specification in **Table 1**.

20. Install new O-rings (24, **Figure 55**) onto the fuel rail hose adapter (25). Install and tighten the adapter screws to the specification in **Table 1**.

21. Install the induction manifold assembly as described in this chapter.

Vapor Separator Service

The vapor separator is a fuel reservoir that ensures the electric fuel pump has a consistent fuel supply and does not take in air or vapor. The vapor separator receives fuel from the mechanical fuel pump. An inlet needle and float system control the fuel entering the vapor separator much like the float chamber on a carburetor. The float level is preset and does not require adjustment.

The 150-250 hp EFI models are equipped with a vapor separator (**Figure 60**) that has an internal fuel pump and internal final filter.

Optimax models use a vapor separator (**Figure 61**) that has an internal fuel pump and an internal final filter, but does not have a fuel pressure regulator mounted on the vapor separator cover. An additional low pressure electric fuel pump is used on Optimax models. The additional pump moves fuel from the tank into the cavity below the high pressure electric fuel pump. If the electric fuel pump fails, a small passage connecting the vapor separator tank bowl to the high pressure pump cavity will allow a small amount of fuel to flow into the cavity. The engine typically will not exceed 3000 rpm with the amount of fuel supplied.

On EFI models, the fuel pressure regulator is mounted to the vapor separator. Excess fuel is returned from the fuel rail to the vapor separator through the fuel pressure regulator. Oil from the injection pump enters through a 2 psi (13.8 kPa) check valve fitting at the bottom aft corner of the vapor separator. Air and fuel vapors are vented to the induction manifold through a small line and fitting on the top of the vapor separator cover. Fuel return from the bleed (recirculation) system enters the vapor separator after passing through a small inline fuel filter.

On Optimax models, the fuel returns from the air/fuel rails and pressure regulator enters through a fitting where the fuel pressure regulator is mounted on EFI models. A pressure regulation check valve in the return line maintains 20 psi (138 kPa) in the return line upstream of the

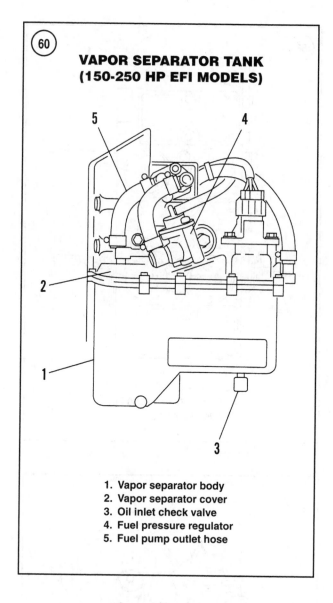

60

VAPOR SEPARATOR TANK (150-250 HP EFI MODELS)

1. Vapor separator body
2. Vapor separator cover
3. Oil inlet check valve
4. Fuel pressure regulator
5. Fuel pump outlet hose

check valve. Fuel flows through the fuel cooler (1998 and 1999 models), then back to the vapor separator tank.

On EFI models, oil is injected into the vapor separator tank through an oil inlet check valve (3, **Figure 60**) on the bottom of the tank. The oil mixes with the fuel and is delivered to the engine with the fuel flowing through the injectors. Oil is not injected into the vapor separator on Optimax models.

Air and fuel vapors are vented to the induction manifold fittings on EFI models or air compressor filter chamber on Optimax models.

> *WARNING*
> *EFI systems operate under high pressure. Do not remove the crimped stainless steel clamps unless absolutely necessary. Do not*

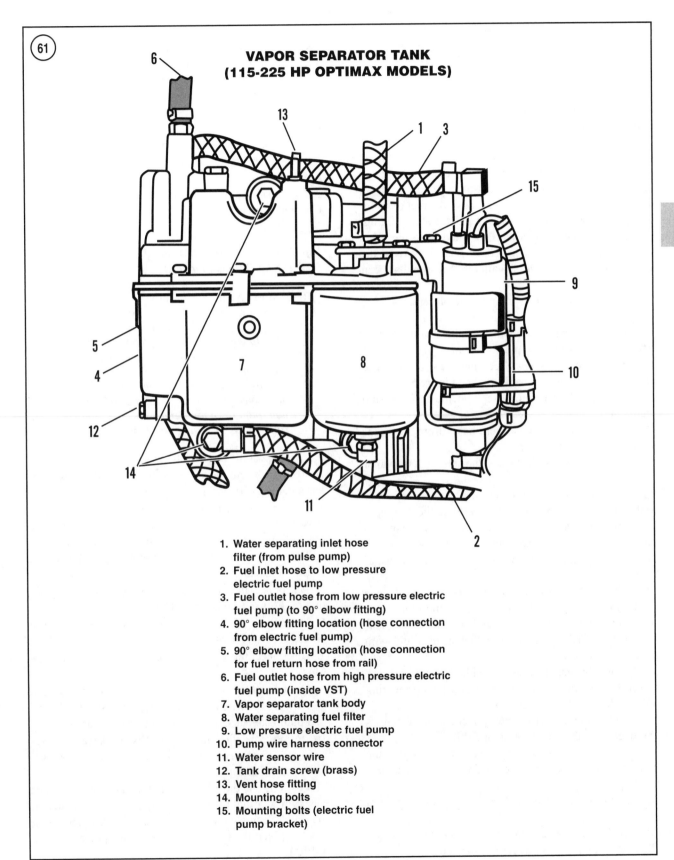

61

**VAPOR SEPARATOR TANK
(115-225 HP OPTIMAX MODELS)**

1. Water separating inlet hose
   filter (from pulse pump)
2. Fuel inlet hose to low pressure
   electric fuel pump
3. Fuel outlet hose from low pressure electric
   fuel pump (to 90° elbow fitting)
4. 90° elbow fitting location (hose connection
   from electric fuel pump)
5. 90° elbow fitting location (hose connection
   for fuel return hose from rail)
6. Fuel outlet hose from high pressure electric
   fuel pump (inside VST)
7. Vapor separator tank body
8. Water separating fuel filter
9. Low pressure electric fuel pump
10. Pump wire harness connector
11. Water sensor wire
12. Tank drain screw (brass)
13. Vent hose fitting
14. Mounting bolts
15. Mounting bolts (electric fuel
    pump bracket)

disconnect the rubber lines from the electric fuel pump, fuel pressure regulator and fuel management adapter unless new hoses and clamps will be installed.

Vapor separator removal/installation (150-250 hp EFI models)

Refer to **Figure 60** for this procedure.

1. Disconnect the negative battery cable.
2. Remove the cap from the high-pressure test point on the fuel management adapter just above the fuel pressure regulator or on the fuel pressure regulator elbow fitting. Cover the test point with a shop rag and depress the valve with a small screwdriver to relieve fuel pressure in the air/fuel rails. Reinstall the cap after the pressure has been relieved.
3. On 150-200 hp models, remove the oil reservoir. See Chapter Thirteen.
4. On 225-250 hp models, disconnect the manifold absolute pressure sensor three-pin connector.
5. Remove the two screws securing the fuel rail hose adapter to the induction manifold. See **Figure 51**.
6. Disconnect the vacuum hose from the fuel pressure regulator.
7. Disconnect the bleed and vent hoses from the vapor separator top cover fittings.
8. Disconnect the oil inlet hose at the bottom of the vapor separator assembly.
9. Remove the three screws securing the vapor separator to the induction manifold. Pull outward on the fuel management adapter and the vapor separator. Remove the vapor separator and fuel management adapter assembly.
10. Remove and discard the O-rings on the fuel management adapter.
11. To reinstall the vapor separator, install new O-rings on the fuel management adapter and position the vapor separator and fuel rail hose adapter on the induction manifold. Seat the adapter into the induction manifold with hand pressure.
12. Secure the vapor separator with the three screws, washers, grommets and sleeves. Tighten the mounting bolts to the specification in **Table 1**.
13. Tighten the two fuel management adapter screws (**Figure 51**) to the specification in **Table 1**.
14. Reconnect the oil delivery hose to the fitting on the bottom of the separator. Secure the hose with a new tie-strap.
15. Reconnect the bleed and vacuum hoses to the top cover.
16. On 225 and 250 hp models, reconnect the manifold absolute pressure sensor three-pin connector.

17. On 150-200 hp models, reinstall the oil tank and bleed the system as described in Chapter Thirteen.
18. Reconnect all air, cooling water and oil hoses at the points described in Steps 6-8. Use new hose clamps in all locations. Use nipping pliers to tighten the new crimp type hose clamps. Avoid using excessive force, otherwise the clamp may be damaged.
19. Reconnect the negative battery cable.
20. Start the engine and check for fuel leaks. Correct any problems found.
21. Bleed air from the oil injection system as described in Chapter Thirteen.

Vapor separator removal/installation (115-225 hp Optimax models)

Refer to **Figure 61** for this procedure.

> *WARNING*
> *The Optimax direct fuel injection system operates under extremely high pressure. Do not remove the crimped stainless steel clamps unless absolutely necessary. Do not disconnect the rubber lines from the electric fuel pump, vapor separator and air/fuel rails unless installing new clamps.*

1. Disconnect the negative battery cable.
2. Relieve system fuel pressure as described in this chapter under *Fuel/Air Rail*.
3. Place a container suitable for holding fuel under the tank drain screw (12, **Figure 61**). Remove the screw and drain all fuel from the tank. Reinstall the drain screw.
4. Disconnect the fuel pump outlet hose (6, **Figure 61**). Discard the clamp.
5. Disconnect the fuel return line from the 90° elbow fitting (5, **Figure 61**). Discard the clamp.
6. Disconnect the water separating fuel filter inlet hose (1, **Figure 61**). Discard the clamp.
7. Disconnect the vent hose from the fitting (13, **Figure 61**).
8. Disconnect the water sensor wire (11, **Figure 61**).
9. Remove the wire tie clamps, then unplug both electric fuel pump connectors from the engine wire harness.
10. Remove the three mounting bolts (14, **Figure 61**) securing the vapor separator to the induction manifold. Remove the vapor separator assembly.
11. To reinstall the vapor separator, position the vapor separator and fuel management adapter on the induction manifold. Secure the vapor separator with three mounting bolts. Tighten the mounting bolts to the specification in **Table 1**.

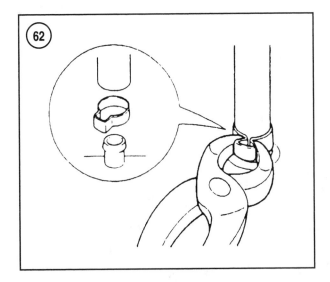

12. Reconnect the water separating fuel filter inlet hose (1, **Figure 61**) and secure the connection with a new clamp. Crimp the clamp securely.

13. Reconnect the vent hose to the fitting (13, **Figure 61**) and secure it with a new tie-strap.

14. Reconnect the fuel return hose to the upper 90° elbow fitting (5, **Figure 61**) and secure the connection with a new clamp. Crimp the clamp securely.

15. Reconnect the high pressure electric fuel pump outlet hose (6, **Figure 61**) and secure the connection with a new clamp.

16. Reconnect both electric fuel pump connectors to the engine wire harness. Secure the harnesses with new wire tie clamps.

17. Reconnect the water sensor (11, **Figure 61**) wire to the terminal on the bottom of the filter.

18. Reconnect the negative battery cable.

19. Start the engine and check for fuel leaks. Correct any problems found.

Low pressure electric fuel pump removal/installation

It is not necessary to remove the vapor separator tank when replacing the low pressure electric fuel pump.

1. Disconnect the negative battery cable.

2. Relieve system fuel pressure as described in this chapter under *Fuel/Air Rail*.

3. Place a container suitable for holding fuel under the tank drain screw (12, **Figure 61**). Remove the screw and drain all fuel from the tank. Reinstall the drain screw.

4. Remove the clamps, then disconnect the fuel inlet hose (2, **Figure 61**) and fuel outlet hose (3). Drain residual fuel from the hoses.

5. Disconnect the pump wire harness connector (10, **Figure 61**) from the engine wire harness.

6. Cut the plastic wire tie clamps and remove the pump from the bracket.

7. Install the pump by first placing the sleeve and grommet onto the pump. Earlier production engines were not originally equipped with these components. Install them onto the replacement pump.

8. Install the pump onto the bracket. Secure the pump with a plastic wire tie clamp.

9. Using new crimp type hose clamps, connect the fuel inlet and outlet hoses onto the pump fittings. Use nipping pliers to tighten the new crimp type hose clamps as shown in **Figure 62**. Avoid using excessive force, otherwise the clamp or hose may be damaged.

10. Connect the pump wire harness to the engine wire harness connector (10, **Figure 61**). Use a plastic wire tie clamp to secure the connector to the pump and bracket.

Vapor separator disassembly/reassembly (150-250 hp EFI models)

Refer to **Figure 63** for this procedure. The final filter on some models can be serviced without removing the vapor separator from the engine. If the nine cover screws can be accessed, it is not necessary to remove the vapor separator from the engine. The electric fuel pump is not serviceable. If the pump malfunctions, replace it.

1. Remove the fuel pressure regulator as described in this chapter.

2. Remove the nine vapor separator cover screws (7, **Figure 63**) and lock washers. Lift off the cover assembly. Discard the cover seal.

3. Grasp the final filter (33, **Figure 63**) on the end of the fuel pump and pull down while rotating the filter counterclockwise. Remove and inspect the final filter. Discard the filter if it is not clean. Remove the stabilizing ring (32, **Figure 63**) and the rubber grommet (31).

NOTE
The float level is preset by the manufacturer.
Do not *bend the float arm or the float drop limit bracket.*

4. Remove the float pin using needlenose pliers. Remove the float and inlet needle.

NOTE
If fuel pump replacement is not required, go to Step 6. If fuel pump replacement is required, go to Step 5.

6

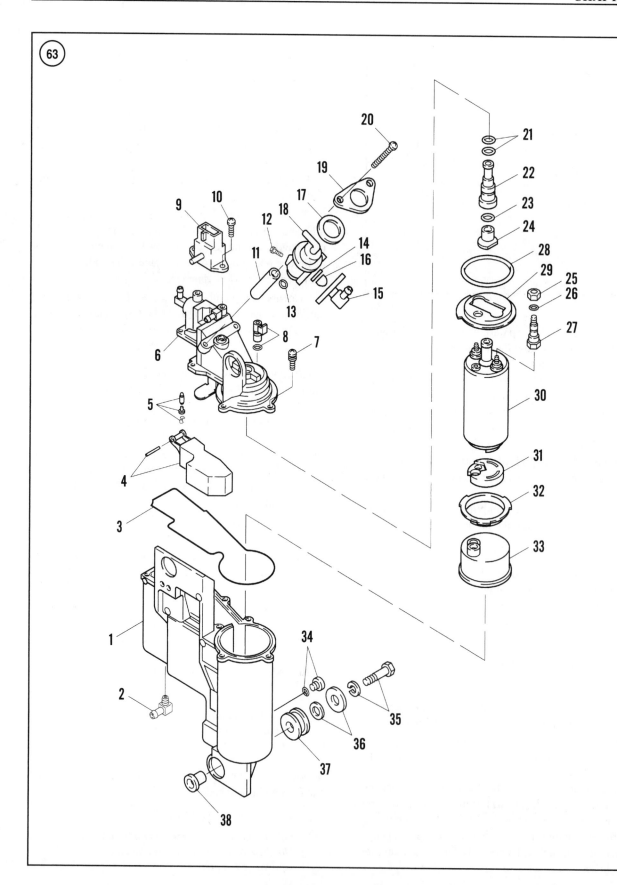

VAPOR SEPARATOR TANK COMPONENTS (150-250 HP EFI MODELS)

1. Vapor separator tank body
2. Oil inlet check valve
3. Top cover seal
4. Float and float pin
5. Inlet needle and spring clip
6. Top cover
7. Cover screws
8. Insulator and O-ring
9. Manifold air pressure sensor (225 and 250 hp)
10. Screw
11. Spacer
12. Screw
13. O-ring
14. O-ring
15. Elbow fitting
16. Hat filter
17. Grommet
18. Fuel pressure regulator
19. Regulator retaining plate
20. Screw
21. O-ring
22. Fuel pump outlet fitting
23. O-ring
24. Fuel pump adapter fitting
25. Terminal nut
26. O-ring
27. Terminal stud
28. O-ring
29. Plate
30. Electric fuel pump
31. Rubber grommet
32. Stabilizing ring
33. Final fuel filter
34. Drain plug and sealing washer
35. Bolt and lockwasher
36. Flat washer
37. Grommet
38. Sleeve collar

5. To replace the fuel pump, remove the nuts from the negative and positive fuel pump terminal. Pull the pump out of the vapor separator top cover. Remove the pump adapter. Remove both terminal insulators from the pump cover. Discard all O-rings and seals. See **Figure 63**.

6. Clean and inspect all components. Replace suspect parts.

7. Install the fuel pump as shown in **Figure 63**, using all new O-rings and seals. Seat the fuel pump assembly in the top cover. Install the terminal insulators and O-rings into the cover and over the terminal studs. Tighten each terminal stud nut securely

8. Attach the inlet needle to the float with the wire clip. Install the float, making sure the inlet needle enters the seat, then install the float hinge pin.

9. Install a new top cover seal (3, **Figure 63**) into the vapor separator body.

10. Install the stabilizing ring (32, **Figure 63**) and rubber grommet (31) onto the end of the fuel pump. Install the final filter to the fuel pump. Press the filter onto the fuel pump while rotating the filter clockwise. Make sure the filter has locked in place.

NOTE
*There are two sizes of cover screws. Tighten each to the appropriate specification in **Table 1**.*

11. Install the cover assembly onto the body. Secure the cover with the nine screws and lock washers. Tighten the screws evenly to the specification in **Table 1**.

12. Install the fuel pressure regulator as described previously in this section.

Vapor separator disassembly/reassembly (115-225 hp Optimax models)

Refer to **Figure 64** for this procedure.

1. Remove the vapor separator tank as described in this chapter.

2. Remove the seven cover screws and lockwashers (6, **Figure 64**). Lift off the cover (5, **Figure 64**). Discard the gasket (7, **Figure 64**).

3. Carefully pull the high pressure electric fuel pump (10, **Figure 64**) from the cover (5). Remove the sealing grommets (8 and 11, **Figure 64**) from the cover or from the fuel pump and tank body. Inspect the sealing grommet (8, **Figure 64**) for torn or damaged surfaces and replace it if necessary.

4. Inspect the fuel filter in the lower opening of the electric fuel pump. Carefully pry the filter from the opening with a screwdriver and replace it if it is damaged or dirty.

6

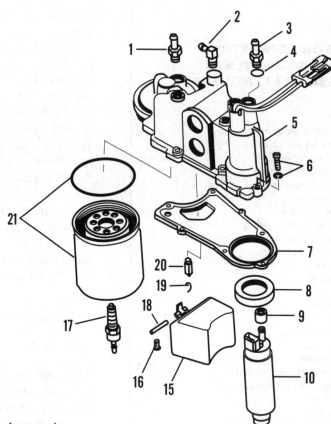

VAPOR SEPARATOR TANK COMPONENTS
(115-225 HP OPTIMAX MODELS)

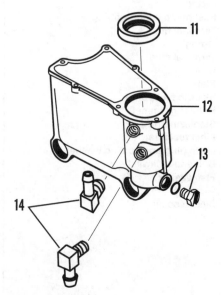

1. Fuel inlet fitting (from pulse pump)
2. Vent fitting (to flywheel cover)
3. Fuel outlet fitting (to fuel rail)
4. O-ring
5. Cover
6. Cover screw and washer
7. Gasket
8. Sealing grommet
9. Sleeve
10. High pressure electric fuel pump
11. Sealing grommet
12. Vapor separator tank body
13. Drain screw and O-ring
14. Elbow fittings
15. Float
16. Screw
17. Water sensor
18. Float pin
19. Spring clip
20. Inlet needle
21. Water separating fuel filter

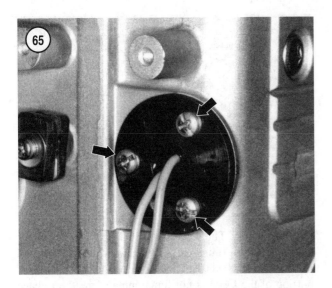

5. Loosen the screw (16, **Figure 64**) and remove the float pin and float from the cover. Remove the inlet needle (20, **Figure 64**) and spring clip (19) from the cover. Inspect the inlet needle as described earlier in this chapter. Replace the needle and clip if it is worn or damaged.

6. Clean all components in a suitable solvent. Do not use solvents that are not suited for plastic or composite material.

7. Assemble the vapor separator tank by first applying a light coat of 2-4-C grease (part No. 92-825407) to the sealing surfaces of the sealing grommets (8 and 11, **Figure 64**). Slip the sealing grommets over the ends of the fuel pump.

8. Install the sleeve (9, **Figure 64**) over the outlet fitting on the electric fuel pump. Carefully insert the electric fuel pump (10, **Figure 64**) into the cover (5). Plug the pump terminal connectors onto the connector in the cover. Seat the pump into the cover.

9. Install the inlet needle and spring clip into the needle seat. Install the float and float pin, and secure them with the screw (16, **Figure 64**). The spring clip must fit over the tab on the float. Tighten the float pin screw to the specification in **Table 1**.

10. Install a new gasket (7, **Figure 64**) onto the cover. Align the lower end of the electric fuel pump with the opening in the body while installing the cover into the tank body. Carefully seat the cover against the body.

11. Install the seven screws (6, **Figure 64**) and lockwashers. Evenly tighten the screws to the specification in **Table 1**.

Intake Air Temperature (IAT) Sensor Removal/Installation

1. Disconnect the negative battery cable.

2. Locate the sensor on the engine as follows:
   a. On 150-250 hp EFI models, the sensor mounts to the starboard side of the induction manifold.
   b. On 135 hp and 150 hp Optimax models (1998 and 1999), the sensor mounts to the lower front side of the induction manifold. See **Figure 65**.
   c. On 115-175 hp (2000-on), 200 hp and 225 hp Optimax models, the sensor mounts to the top side of the induction manifold near the throttle body. See 24, **Figure 54**.

3A. On 150-250 hp EFI models, remove the intake air temperature sensor as follows:
   a. Remove the two screws securing the water separating fuel filter bracket to the induction manifold. Lay the filter on one side.
   b. Disconnect the two sensor leads from the engine harness bullet connectors.
   c. Remove the three screws securing the sensor (**Figure 65**, typical) to the induction manifold.
   d. Remove and discard the O-ring from the inner surface of the sensor.

3B. On 135 hp and 150 hp EFI models, remove the sensor as follows:
   a. Disconnect the two sensor leads from the engine wire harness connectors.
   b. Remove the three screws, then carefully pull the sensor from the manifold.
   c. Remove the O-ring from the sensor body or induction manifold. Discard the O-ring.

3C. On 115-175 hp (2000-on), 200 hp and 225 hp Optimax models, remove the sensor as follows:
   a. Disconnect the two-pin harness sensor harness connector from the engine harness connector.
   b. Carefully unthread the sensor from the induction manifold. Remove the O-ring from the sensor or manifold opening. Discard the O-ring.

4. To install the sensor, install a new O-ring to the sensor.

5A. On 150-250 hp EFI models and 1998 and 1999 135-150 hp Optimax models, install the sensor as follows:
   a. Insert the sensor into the induction manifold and seat it with hand pressure.
   b. Install the three retaining screws (**Figure 65**). Tighten the screws securely. Do not over tighten.
   c. Reconnect the two sensor leads to the engine wiring harness bullet connectors.
   d. On 150-200 hp EFI models, place the fuel filter on the induction manifold. Install the two screws securing the water separating fuel filter bracket to the induction manifold. Tighten the screws to the specification in **Table 2**.

5B. On 115-175 hp (2000-on), 200 hp and 225 hp Optimax models, install the sensor as follows:

6

a. Carefully thread the sensor into the opening on the induction manifold. Tighten the sensor snugly. Do not over tighten.

b. Plug the two-pin connector into the engine wire harness. Secure the sensor wire harness to the engine wire harness with a plastic wire tie clamp.

6. Reconnect the negative battery cable.

Air Compressor Temperature Sensor

Replacement instructions for this sensor are in the compressor disassembly/assembly procedures in this chapter.

Water Pressure Sensor

This sensor (**Figure 66**) is only used on Optimax models. The sensor mounts to the upper rear of the power head. On most models, a water hose connects to the sensor fitting. On later models, the sensor threads into a fitting on the rear of the power head. A three-pin connector connects the sensor to the engine wire harness. It provides a varying voltage signal corresponding to the water pressure in the cooling system. The ECM uses this signal to activate the low water pressure warning system.

Replace the sensor as follows:

1. Disconnect the negative battery cable.

2. Unplug the three-pin connector from the sensor. Do not disconnect the sensor harness from the engine wire harness.

3A. If the hose is connected to the sensor, remove the hose clamp, then remove the water hose from the sensor fitting.

3B. If the sensor threads into the block, carefully unthread the sensor from the block fitting.

4A. If the hose is connected to the sensor, connect the hose onto the sensor fitting and secure it with a plastic wire tie clamp.

4B. If the sensor threads into the block, carefully thread the sensor into the block. Do not over tighten the sensor.

5. Plug the three-pin harness connector into the sensor. Secure the wire harness with a plastic wire tie clamp.

6. Reconnect the negative battery cable.

Manifold Air Pressure (MAP) Sensor Removal/Installation

150-200 hp EFI models

The manifold air pressure sensor is an integral part of the ECM on 150-200 hp EFI models. If the sensor is not functioning correctly, make sure the vacuum line is not damaged or deteriorated, and is securely connected to the

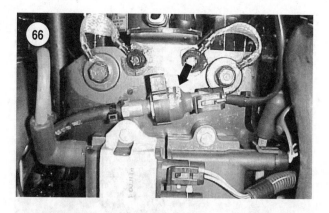

intake manifold. The line can be repaired up to the point it enters the ECM. If the line is in satisfactory condition and is securely attached to the intake manifold, but the sensor portion of the ECM is not functioning correctly, replace the ECM.

115-225 hp Optimax and 225-250 hp EFI models

The mounting locations for this sensor vary by model.

On 225 hp and 250 hp EFI models, two screws (10, **Figure 63**) retain the sensor to the top of the vapor separator. The sensor is connected to the intake manifold by a vacuum line.

On 135 and 150 hp Optimax models (1998 and 1999), two screws retain the sensor to the coil mounting plate on the rear of the power head. A hose connects the sensor to a fitting on the induction manifold.

On 115-175 hp (2000-on), 200 hp and 225 hp Optimax models, a single screw and bracket secure the sensor to the top of the induction manifold.

1. Disconnect the negative battery cable.

2. Disconnect the MAP sensor three-pin electrical connector.

3. Disconnect the MAP sensor vacuum line from the sensor, if so equipped.

4. Remove the screw(s) and bracket, if used, securing the sensor to the vapor separator, induction manifold or coil mounting plate. Remove the sensor.

5. On 115-175 hp (2000-on), 200 hp and 225 hp Optimax models, inspect the sealing grommet on the bottom side of the sensor for torn or deteriorated surfaces and replace it if necessary.

6A. On 225 hp and 250 hp EFI models, to install the sensor, position the sensor on the vapor separator and install the retaining screws. Tighten the retaining screws securely.

6B. On 135 hp and 150 hp Optimax models (1998 and 1999), attach the sensor to the coil mounting plate with the two screws. Securely tighten the screws.

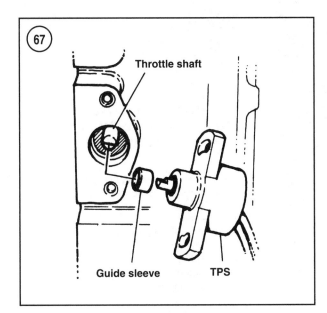

Throttle shaft

Guide sleeve   TPS

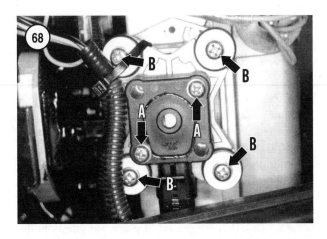

6C. On 115-175 hp (2000-on), 200 hp and 225 hp Optimax models, insert the lower fitting of the sensor into the opening in the induction manifold. Secure the sensor with the bracket and screw. Tighten the bracket screws securely.

7. Connect the three-pin electrical connector and the vacuum hose to the sensor. Secure the vacuum hose, if so equipped, with a new tie-strap.

8. Reconnect the negative battery cable.

Throttle Position Sensor (TPS) Removal/Installation

The TPS on all EFI models requires readjustment any time it is removed or the mounting screws are turned. Refer to Chapter Five for adjustment procedures.

All 1998 and 1999 Optimax models use two throttle position sensors. Both sensors are automatically calibrated by the ECM during start-up. If one sensor fails, the warning panel will illuminate and the warning horn will sound. If both sensors fail, the engine will not run above idle.

All 2000-on Optimax models use a single throttle position sensor. The sensor is automatically calibrated by the ECM during start-up. If the sensor fails the warning panel illuminates and engine speed is reduced to a maximum of approximately 4500 rpm.

150-200 hp EFI models

1. Disconnect the negative battery cable.
2. If the same sensor will be reinstalled, place match marks on the sensor base and induction manifold for reference during reinstallation.
3. Disconnect the sensor three-pin connector from the engine harness.
4. Remove the two mounting screws and remove the sensor and guide sleeve (**Figure 67**).
5. To reinstall the sensor, place the guide sleeve onto the sensor shaft.
6. Install the sensor onto the induction manifold. Make sure the shaft properly aligns with and engages the throttle shaft.
7. If applicable, align the match marks made during removal. Lightly tighten the mounting screws.
8. Reconnect the negative battery cable.
9. Adjust the sensor as described in Chapter Five. Then tighten the screws to the specification in **Table 1**.

115-225 hp Optimax models (1998 and 1999)

The sensor mounts onto a bracket on the port side of the power head. A linkage connects the sensor shaft to the throttle lever on the throttle body.
1. Disconnect the negative battery cable.
2. Disconnect the outer sensor three-pin connector.
3. Remove the outer sensor mounting screws (A, **Figure 68**) and remove the outer sensor.

NOTE
If the inner sensor does not require replacement, go to Step 13.

4. Remove the tie-strap from the upper aft sensor mounting plate screw.
5. Remove the four inner sensor mounting plate screws (B, **Figure 68**).
6. Remove the inner sensor and mounting plate assembly.
7. Disconnect the inner sensor three-pin connector.

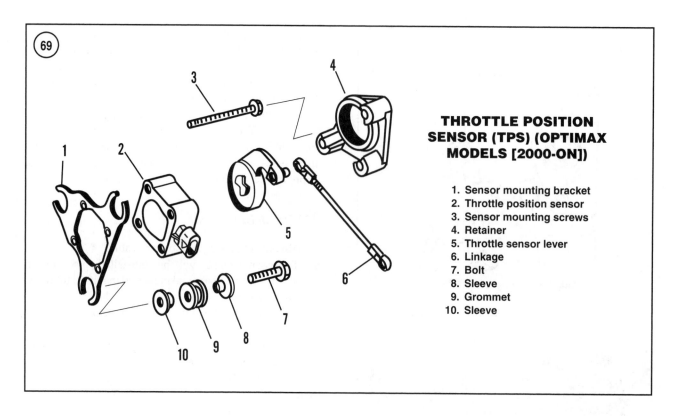

**THROTTLE POSITION
SENSOR (TPS) (OPTIMAX
MODELS [2000-ON])**

1. Sensor mounting bracket
2. Throttle position sensor
3. Sensor mounting screws
4. Retainer
5. Throttle sensor lever
6. Linkage
7. Bolt
8. Sleeve
9. Grommet
10. Sleeve

8. Remove the two inner sensor mounting screws and re-move the inner sensor from the mounting plate.

9. To reinstall the inner sensor, position the sensor on the mounting plate with the connector facing down. Install the screws and tighten them to the specification in **Table 1**.

10. Reconnect the engine harness three-pin connector to the inner sensor.

11. Carefully slide the inner sensor and mounting plate over the throttle shaft. Make sure the sensor aligns with and engages the throttle shaft.

12. Install and tighten the four mounting plate screws to the specification in **Table 1**.

13. Carefully position the outer sensor on the mounting plate. Make sure the sensor aligns with and engages the throttle shaft.

14. Install and tighten the two outer sensor screws to the specification in **Table 1**.

15. Reconnect the engine harness three-pin connector to the outer sensor.

16. Reconnect the negative battery cable.

115-225 hp Optimax models (2000-on)

Refer to **Figure 69** for this procedure.

1. Disconnect the negative battery cable.

2. Disconnect the three-pin connector from the throttle position sensor (2, **Figure 69**).

3. Remove the three bolts (7, **Figure 69**) from the retainer (4). Pull the retainer and throttle sensor lever (5) from the sensor.

4. Remove the four sensor mounting screws (3, **Figure 69**). Pull the sensor from the mounting plate.

5. To install the sensor, fit the sensor onto the plate and secure it with the four screws. Tighten the screws to the specification in **Table 1**.

6. Align the throttle lever opening with the shaft of the sensor. Seat the lever against the plate. Align the bolt openings and fit the retainer (4, **Figure 69**) onto the plate. Insert the sleeves into the mounting plate grommets as shown in **Figure 69**. Install the sensor and mounting plate onto the power head. Tighten the mounting plate bolts to the specification in **Table 1**.

7. Reconnect the three-pin connector onto the sensor.

8. Reconnect the negative battery cable.

225-250 hp models

Refer to **Figure 70** for this procedure.

1. Disconnect the negative battery cable.

2. If the same sensor will be reinstalled, place match marks on the sensor base and induction manifold for refer-ence during reinstallation.

4. Remove the two mounting screws and remove the module.

5. To install the module, position the engine and module ground wires under the mounting screw as shown in **Figure 71**. Install and tighten both screws to the specification in **Table 1**.

6. Reconnect the tan wire to the water separating fuel filter sensor.

7. Reconnect the light blue wire to the engine harness bullet connector and the purple wire to the terminal block or engine harness bullet connector.

8. Reconnect the negative battery cable.

Water Separating Filter Assembly Removal/Installation

1. Disconnect the negative battery cable.

2. Remove the two fuel lines from the water separator fuel filter bracket. Label each hose for reassembly.

3. Remove the tan wire from the water sensor probe at the bottom of the filter canister.

4. Remove the two screws securing the filter bracket to the induction manifold and remove the filter assembly.

5. If necessary, service the filter assembly as described in Chapter Four.

6. To reinstall the filter assembly, position the filter bracket on the induction manifold.

7. Install and securely tighten the two retaining screws.

8. Reconnect the two fuel lines to the appropriate fittings on the filter bracket. Secure the connections with new tie-straps.

9. Reconnect the tan wire to the water sensor probe at the bottom of the filter canister.

10. Reconnect the negative battery cable.

REED VALVE SERVICE

All Mercury/Mariner two-stroke outboard motors are equipped with one set of reed valves per cylinder. The reed valves allow the air/fuel mixture from the carburetor to enter the crankcase, but not exit. They are one-way check valves.

Reed valves are essentially maintenance-free and cause very few problems. However, if a reed valve does not seal, the air/fuel mixture will escape the crankcase and not be transported to the combustion chamber. Some slight spitting of fuel out of the carburetor throat at idle can be considered normal, but a substantial discharge of fuel from the carburetor throat indicates reed valve failure.

On most models, the reeds can be inspected with the carburetor removed. Use a small flashlight and inspection

3. Disconnect the sensor three-pin connector from the engine harness.

4. Remove the two mounting screws and remove the sensor.

5. To reinstall the sensor, make sure the coupler is present in the induction manifold.

6. Install the sensor on the induction manifold. Make sure the shaft properly aligns with and engages the throttle shaft coupler.

7. If applicable, align the match marks made during removal. Lightly tighten the mounting screws.

8. Reconnect the negative battery cable.

9. Adjust the sensor as described in Chapter Five. Then tighten the mounting screws to the specification in **Table 1**.

Water Sensing Warning Module Removal/Installation (150-200 hp EFI models)

Refer to **Figure 71** for this procedure.

1. Disconnect the negative battery cable.

2. Disconnect the tan wire from the water separating fuel filter sensor.

3. Disconnect the light blue wire from the engine harness bullet connector and the purple wire from the terminal block or engine harness bullet connector.

6

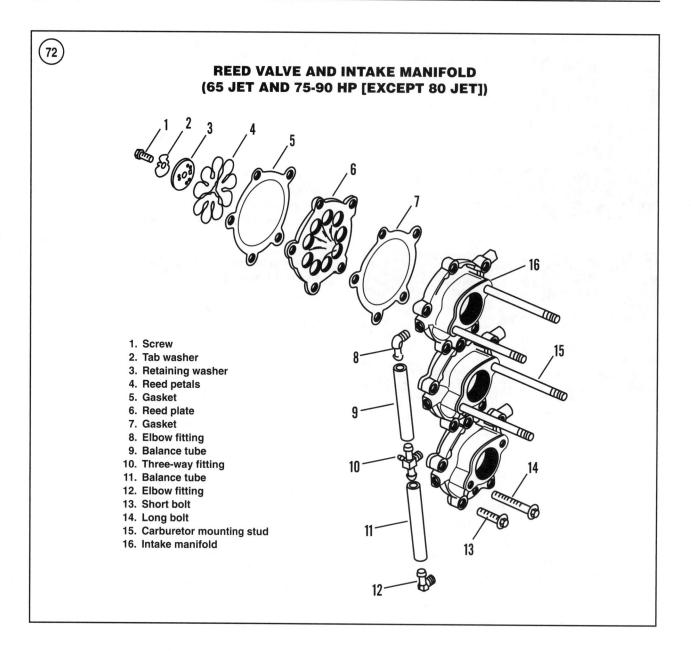

**REED VALVE AND INTAKE MANIFOLD
(65 JET AND 75-90 HP [EXCEPT 80 JET])**

1. Screw
2. Tab washer
3. Retaining washer
4. Reed petals
5. Gasket
6. Reed plate
7. Gasket
8. Elbow fitting
9. Balance tube
10. Three-way fitting
11. Balance tube
12. Elbow fitting
13. Short bolt
14. Long bolt
15. Carburetor mounting stud
16. Intake manifold

mirror to check for broken, cracked or chipped reeds. If reed damage is discovered, attempt to locate the missing pieces of the reed petal. The reed petals are made of stainless steel and will cause internal engine damage if they pass through the crankcase and combustion chamber.

When the reed valves are removed from the power head, inspect the reeds for excessive stand-open.

Never turn over and reinstall reed petals. This can lead to a preloaded condition. Preloaded reeds require a higher crankcase vacuum level to open. This causes acceleration and carburetor calibration problems. The reed petals should be flush to nearly flush along the entire length of the reed block mating surface with no preload. All models

covered in this manual have a maximum stand-open specification of 0.020 in. (0.51 mm).

Many new models use rubber coated reed blocks. These reed blocks cushion the impact as the reed closes and improves sealing. Reed block assembly part numbers automatically supersede where applicable. Rubber coated reed blocks are serviced as assemblies only.

65 Jet and 75-125 hp (Except 105 Jet and 115 Optimax) Models

Three individual reed plates and intake manifolds are used on 75-90 hp and 65 jet models. Four individual reed

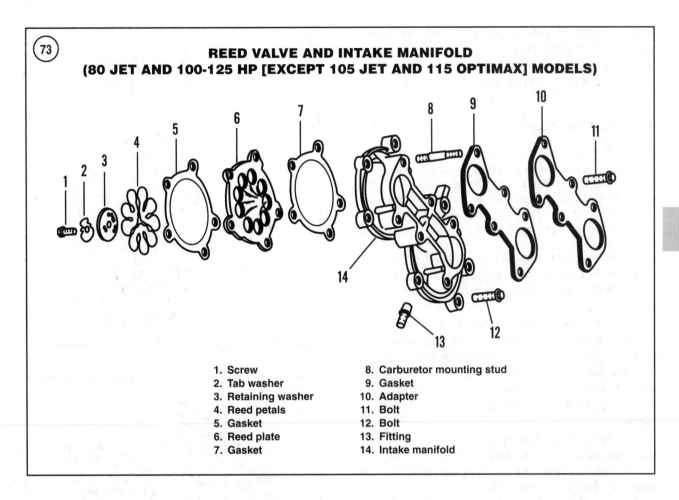

73 **REED VALVE AND INTAKE MANIFOLD (80 JET AND 100-125 HP [EXCEPT 105 JET AND 115 OPTIMAX] MODELS)**

1. Screw
2. Tab washer
3. Retaining washer
4. Reed petals
5. Gasket
6. Reed plate
7. Gasket
8. Carburetor mounting stud
9. Gasket
10. Adapter
11. Bolt
12. Bolt
13. Fitting
14. Intake manifold

6

plates and two intake manifolds are used on 80 jet and 100-125 hp models.

CAUTION
*Do not allow the internal bleed (recirculation) system check valves to fall out or become misplaced while the intake manifolds are removed. Refer to **Fuel Bleed System Service** in this chapter for additional information.*

Reed valve removal/installation

Refer to **Figure 72** or **Figure 73** for this procedure.

1. Disconnect the negative battery cable.

2. Remove the carburetors as described previously in this chapter.

3A. On 65 jet and 75-90 hp models, remove the 15 screws (five on each manifold) securing the three intake manifolds and reed plates to the power head. Disconnect the fuel primer valve line from the balance tubes at the fuel primer valve.

3B. On 80 jet and 100-125 hp models, remove the 18 screws (nine on each manifold) securing the two intake manifolds and four reed plates to the power head.

4. Carefully remove the intake manifolds and reed plates from the power head. Do not scratch, warp or gouge the reed plate, intake manifold or crankcase cover. Separate the reed plates from the intake manifolds. Remove all gasket material from the reed plates, intake manifolds and crankcase cover.

5. Clean and inspect the intake manifolds and reed plates as described in this chapter. Do not remove the reed valves from the reed plates unless replacement is necessary.

6. Using new gaskets, install the reed plates and intake manifolds to the power head. Install the retaining screws finger-tight.

7A. On 65 jet and 75-90 hp models, tighten the 15 screws (five on each manifold) evenly and in a crossing pattern to the specification in **Table 1**. Reconnect the fuel primer valve hose from the balance tubes to the fuel primer valve. Secure the connection using a new tie-strap clamp.

7B. On 100-125 hp and 80 jet models, tighten the 18 screws (nine each manifold) to the specification in **Table**

1 and in a circular pattern starting with the two middle screws in each manifold.

8. Install the carburetors as described in this chapter.

9. Reconnect the negative battery cable.

Cleaning and inspection

> *CAUTION*
> *Do not remove the reed petals from the reed plate unless replacement is necessary. Always replace reed petals in complete sets. Never turn a reed over for reuse or attempt to straighten a damaged reed.*

1. Thoroughly clean the reed plates using clean solvent.

2. Check for excessive wear, cracks or grooves in the seat area of the reed plate. Replace the reed plate if damaged is found.

3. Check the reed petals for cracks, chips or evidence of fatigue. Replace the reed petals if damage is found.

4. Check the stand-open gap between the reed petals and the reed plate mating surface. See **Figure 74**, typical. Replace the reed petals if they are preloaded (stick tightly to the reed plate) or stand open more than 0.020 in. (0.51 mm).

5. To replace the reed petals, bend the lockwasher lock tabs away from the screw heads. Remove the screws attaching the reed petals and retaining washer to the reed plate. Discard the lock tab washers.

6. To reinstall, apply Loctite 271 threadlocking adhesive to the threads of the screws. Position the new reed petals, the original retaining washers and new lock tab washers on the intake manifold. Make sure all components are aligned with the alignment pins in the intake manifold.

7. Tighten the screws to the specification in **Table 1** and check the alignment of the screw head to the lock tab washer. If necessary, continue to tighten it to a maximum of 100 in.-lb. (11.3 N•m) to align the screw head with the lock tab washer.

8. Bend the lock tab washer of each washer against each screw head.

V6 Models

All models from 1998-on use a one-piece manifold with six reed blocks. The reed blocks are rubber coated and have square-tipped reeds. Only service the reed blocks as an assembly.

The rubber coated reed blocks offer a significant improvement over previous Mercury/Mariner designs. Rubber coated reed blocks can be retrofitted to older models.

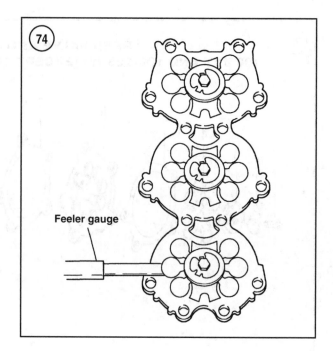

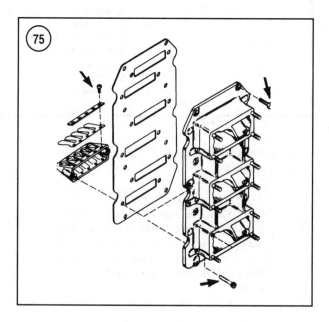

Check with a Mercury/Mariner dealership for applications on models prior to 1998.

On Optimax models the manifold incorporates oil passages. An electric oil pump moves oil through hoses to an individual passage for each cylinder.

Removal/installation (105 jet and 135-200 hp models [carbureted and EFI])

1. Disconnect the negative battery cable.

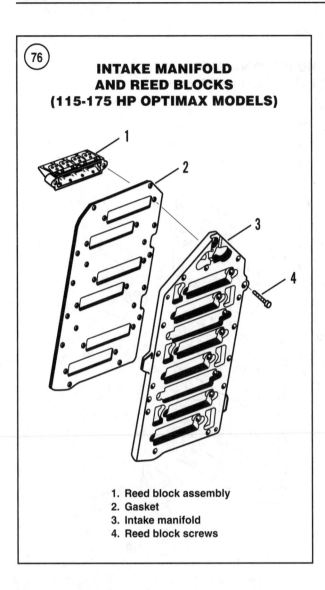

(76) INTAKE MANIFOLD AND REED BLOCKS (115-175 HP OPTIMAX MODELS)

1. Reed block assembly
2. Gasket
3. Intake manifold
4. Reed block screws

2A. On carbureted models, remove the carburetors as described previously in this chapter.

2B. On EFI models, remove the induction manifold as described previously in this chapter.

3. Remove the eight screws securing the intake manifold assembly to the power head. See **Figure 75**. If unsure which screws to remove, remove all 20 intake manifold screws at this time.

4. Note the position and routing of all bleed (recirculation) lines on the intake manifold. Disconnect all bleed lines from the intake manifold.

5. Carefully remove the intake manifold assembly from the power head. Do not scratch, warp or gouge the intake manifold or crankcase cover.

6. Remove the 12 screws (two on each reed block) securing the six reed blocks to the intake manifold. Separate the reed blocks from the intake manifold. Remove all gasket

material from the reed blocks, intake manifold and crankcase cover.

7. Clean and inspect the reed blocks and intake manifold as described in the next section. On models with serviceable reeds, do not remove the reed petals from the reed plate(s) unless they will be replaced.

8. Using a new gasket, install the reed blocks to the intake manifold. Install the 12 retaining screws (two on each reed block) finger-tight.

9. Make sure the gasket is properly positioned and all holes align correctly. Tighten the 12 reed block retaining screws evenly to the specification in **Table 1**.

10. Position the intake manifold against the crankcase cover and install the eight retaining screws. Tighten the retaining screws evenly to the specification in **Table 1**.

11. Reconnect all bleed lines to their original positions.

12A. On carbureted models, install the carburetors as described previously in this chapter.

12B. On EFI models, install the induction manifold as described previously in this chapter.

13. Reconnect the negative battery cable on electric start models.

14. Check for fuel and oil leaks and repair as necessary.

Removal/installation
(115-175 hp Optimax models)

Refer to **Figure 76** for this procedure.

1. Disconnect the negative battery cable.

2. Remove the oil pump and hoses as described in Chapter Thirteen.

3. Remove the induction manifold as described in this chapter.

4. Carefully remove the intake manifold from the power head. Do not scratch, warp or gouge the intake manifold or crankcase cover.

5. Remove the 12 screws (two per reed block) securing the six reed blocks to the intake manifold. Separate the reed block from the intake manifold. Remove all gasket material from the reed block, intake manifold and crankcase cover.

6. Using a new gasket, install the reed blocks to the intake manifold. Install the 12 retaining screws (two per reed block) finger-tight.

7. Make sure the gasket is properly positioned and all holes align correctly. Tighten the 12 reed block retaining screws evenly to the specification in **Table 1**.

8. Install the intake manifold onto the crankcase cover.

9. Install the induction manifold as described in this chapter. The induction manifold bolts retain the intake manifold to the crankcase cover.

6

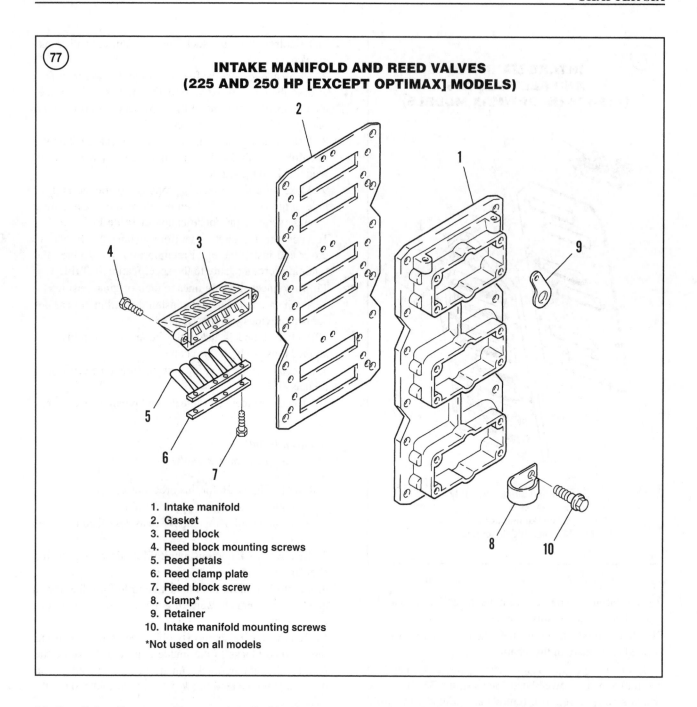

**INTAKE MANIFOLD AND REED VALVES
(225 AND 250 HP [EXCEPT OPTIMAX] MODELS)**

1. Intake manifold
2. Gasket
3. Reed block
4. Reed block mounting screws
5. Reed petals
6. Reed clamp plate
7. Reed block screw
8. Clamp*
9. Retainer
10. Intake manifold mounting screws

*Not used on all models

10. Install the oil pump and hoses as described in Chapter Thirteen.

11. Connect the negative battery cable.

12. Check for fuel and oil leaks and repair as necessary.

***Removal/installation (225-250 hp
carbureted and EFI models)***

Refer to **Figure 77** for this procedure.

1. Disconnect the negative battery cable.

2A. On carbureted models, remove the carburetors as described previously in this chapter.

2B. On EFI models, remove the induction manifold as described previously in this chapter.

3. Remove the 12 mounting screws (10, **Figure 77**) securing the intake manifold assembly to the power head.

4. Note the position and routing of all bleed (recirculation) lines on or over the intake manifold. Disconnect all bleed lines that interfere with manifold removal.

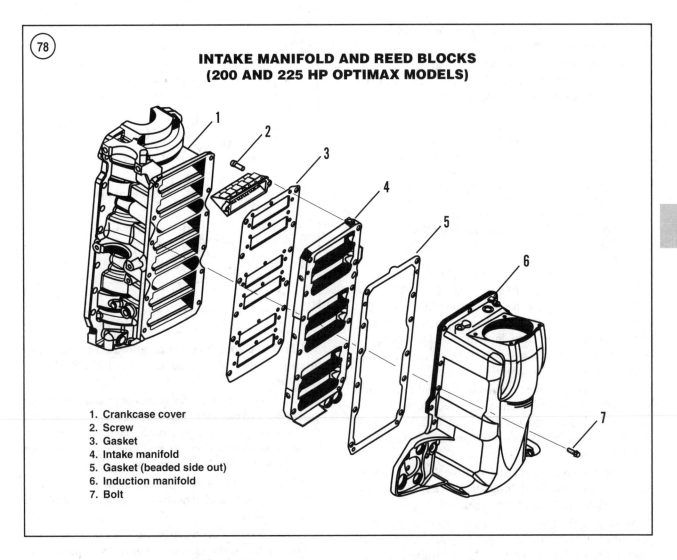

**INTAKE MANIFOLD AND REED BLOCKS
(200 AND 225 HP OPTIMAX MODELS)**

1. Crankcase cover
2. Screw
3. Gasket
4. Intake manifold
5. Gasket (beaded side out)
6. Induction manifold
7. Bolt

6

5. Carefully remove the intake manifold assembly from the power head. Do not scratch, warp or gouge the intake manifold or crankcase cover.

6. Remove the 12 mounting screws (two on each reed block) securing the six reed blocks to the intake manifold (4, **Figure 77**). Separate the reed blocks from the intake manifold. Remove all gasket material from the reed blocks, intake manifold and crankcase cover.

7. Clean and inspect the reed blocks and intake manifold as described in this chapter.

8. Using a new gasket, install the reed blocks to the intake manifold. Coat the threads of the reed block retaining screws with Loctite 271 threadlocking adhesive (part No. 92-809819). Install the 12 retaining screws (two on each reed block) finger-tight.

9. Make sure the gasket is properly positioned and all holes are aligned. Tighten the 12 reed block retaining screws evenly to the specification in **Table 1**.

10. Position the intake manifold against the crankcase cover and install the 12 retaining screws. Tighten the retaining screws evenly to the specification in **Table 1**.

11. Reconnect all bleed lines to their original positions.

12A. On carbureted models, install the carburetors as described previously in this chapter.

12B. On EFI models, install the induction manifold as described previously in this chapter.

13. Reconnect the negative battery cable on electric start models.

14. Check for fuel and oil leaks and repair as necessary.

*Removal/installation
(200 and 225 hp Optimax models)*

Refer to **Figure 78** for this procedure.

1. Disconnect the negative battery cable.

2. Remove the induction manifold (6, **Figure 78**) as described previously in this chapter.

3. Carefully remove the intake manifold assembly (4, **Figure 78**) from the power head. Do not scratch, warp or gouge the intake manifold or crankcase cover.

NOTE
*Internal recirculation valves are used on this engine. The six valves fit into machined grooves on the mating surface of the crankcase cover to intake manifold. The valves are installed in rubber carriers. Do not lose or misplace the check valves and carriers. See **Fuel Bleed (Recirculation) System Service** in this chapter for more information.*

4. Remove the 12 screws (two on each reed block) securing the six reed blocks to the intake manifold Separate the reed blocks from the spacer plate. Separate the spacer plate from the intake manifold. Remove all gasket material from the reed blocks, spacer plate, oil pump, intake manifold and crankcase cover.

5. Clean and inspect the reed blocks and intake manifold as described in the next section. The reed blocks are not serviceable. If there are any defects, replace the suspect reed block. Make sure all machined passages in the intake manifold are clean.

6. Using new gaskets, install the reed blocks to the spacer plate and intake manifold. Install the 12 retaining screws (two on each reed block) finger-tight.

7. Make sure the gaskets and spacer plate are properly positioned and all holes are aligned. Tighten the 12 reed block retaining screws evenly to the specification in **Table 1**.

8. Install the induction manifold (6, **Figure 78**) onto the intake manifold. The induction manifold bolts (7, **Figure 78**) retain the intake manifold onto the crankcase cover.

9. Reconnect the negative battery cable. Bleed the air from the oil injection system as described in Chapter Thirteen.

10. Check for fuel and oil leaks and repair as necessary.

Cleaning and inspection (all V-6 models)

1. Clean the reed blocks gasket surfaces thoroughly. Wash the reed blocks, intake manifold, reed mounting blocks and spacer plates, if equipped, in clean solvent.

2. Inspect the intake manifold, reed mounting blocks and spacer plates, if equipped, for distortion, cracks and blocked passages and fittings.

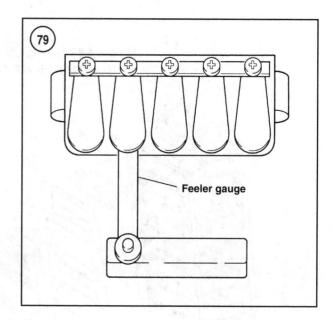

Feeler gauge

3. Check the reed blocks for distortion, cracks, deep grooves or other damage that may cause leaks. Replace as necessary.

4. Check for excessive wear, cracks or grooves in the seat area of the reed blocks. Replace the reed block assembly if there is damage. On rubber coated reed blocks, check for rubber delamination from the reed block casting. Replace any reed block showing rubber delamination.

5. Check the reed petals for cracks, chips or evidence of fatigue. Replace the reed petals or reed block assembly if there is damage.

6. Check the stand-open gap between the reed petals and the reed plate mating surface (**Figure 79**, typical). Replace the reed petals or reed block assembly if any are preloaded (stick tightly to the reed plate) or stand open more than 0.020 in. (0.51 mm).

FUEL BLEED (RECIRCULATION) SYSTEM

Multiple cylinder motors are equipped with a fuel bleed (recirculation) system designed to collect unburned fuel and oil from the low spots of the individual crankcase areas. Since the intake system used by two-stroke engines does not completely transfer all of the fuel sent through the crankcase to the combustion chamber, especially during low-speed operation, the recirculation collects the fuel and oil pooled in the low spots of the crankcase. The bleed system pumps the fuel/oil to the intake ports or intake manifold where it can be transferred to the combustion chamber and burned.

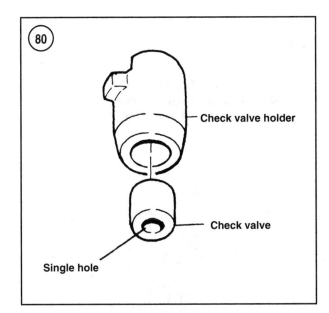

Check valve holder

Check valve

Single hole

Many recirculation systems also collect the fuel and oil pooled in the lower crankshaft bearing area and pump it to the upper crankshaft bearing to ensure proper upper crankshaft bearing lubrication. These models can suffer an upper crankshaft bearing failure if the system malfunctions and does not pump fuel and oil to the upper bearing carrier.

Correct recirculation system operation is important for efficient engine operation. If the system fails, excessive amounts of fuel and oil will puddle in the crankcase and not reach the combustion chamber during low-speed operation, causing a lean mixture. When the engine is accelerated, the puddles of fuel and oil are quickly drawn into the engine causing a temporary excessively rich mixture. This will cause the following symptoms:

1. Poor low-speed performance.
2. Poor acceleration.
3. Spark plug fouling.
4. Stalling or spitting at idle.
5. Excessive smoke on acceleration.

Recirculation System Service

All recirculation systems require one-way check valves for operation. External check valves are either mounted directly to the crankcase or intake manifold, or are mounted in the recirculation lines.

On many models, internal check valves are mounted in the crankcase cover (**Figure 80**, typical) behind the intake manifolds. Refer to Chapter Eight for additional power head illustrations.

Inspect the internal check valves by removing them from their holder/carrier and looking into the check valve assembly. If light is visible, the nylon check ball has melted and the check valve must be replaced. If light is not visible, insert a fine wire into the valve to check for slight movement of the check ball. Replace the check valve if movement is not possible. Replace the check valve holder/carrier if it is burned or damaged.

The end of the check valve with one hole is the inlet side. Fluid should flow into this hole, but not back out. The end of the check valve with two or more holes is the outlet side. Fluid should exit these holes, but not enter. On inline models, the internal valves are always installed so fluid flows towards the intake manifold, but not towards the crankshaft.

All check valves should flow in the direction of the arrow on the appropriate diagram, but not flow in the opposite direction. Fittings should flow in both directions. A small syringe and a piece of recirculation line can be used to quickly test the system. Replace or clean fittings that will not flow in both directions. Replace check valves that flow in both directions or will not flow in either direction. Push on the syringe plunger to check the flow into a fitting or check valve. Pull on the syringe plunger to check flow out of a fitting or check valve. Also inspect and replace recirculation lines that are damaged or deteriorated.

When replacing fittings or check valves, coat pipe thread fittings with Loctite PST pipe sealant (part No. 92-80822). Coat check valves that are press fit lightly with Loctite 271 threadlocking adhesive (part No. 92-809819) prior to installation.

65 jet and 75-125 hp (except 105 jet and 115 Optimax) models

These models use internal and external systems. The internal system consists of two check valves and carriers (**Figure 80**) on three-cylinder models and three check valves and carriers on four-cylinder models. The check valve end with a single hole must face the crankshaft when installed. The check valve end with double holes must face the carburetors when installed. The check valve must flow from the single hole end to the double hole end, but not flow from the double hole end to the single hole end. The check valves are mounted in the crankcase cover intake passages, directly behind the reed plate(s).

The external system on three-cylinder models is shown in **Figure 81**. The valves at the top and bottom of the crankcase cover must allow fluid to travel to the upper crankshaft bearing, but not back down. The inline check valves are marked with an arrow showing the normal direction of flow.

6

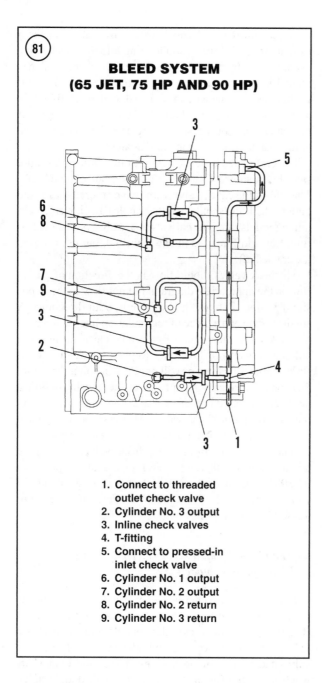

**BLEED SYSTEM
(65 JET, 75 HP AND 90 HP)**

1. Connect to threaded outlet check valve
2. Cylinder No. 3 output
3. Inline check valves
4. T-fitting
5. Connect to pressed-in inlet check valve
6. Cylinder No. 1 output
7. Cylinder No. 2 output
8. Cylinder No. 2 return
9. Cylinder No. 3 return

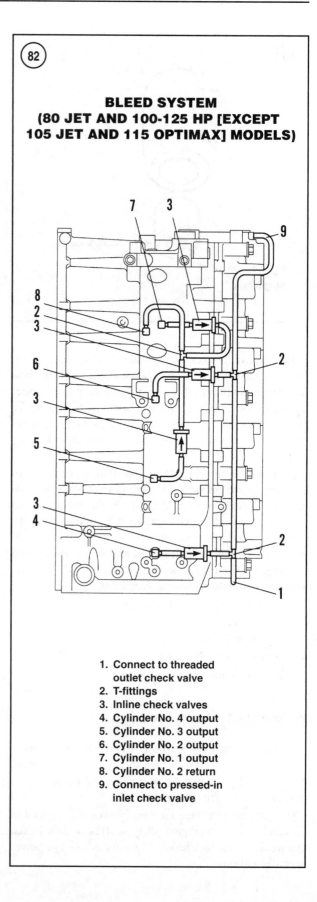

**BLEED SYSTEM
(80 JET AND 100-125 HP [EXCEPT
105 JET AND 115 OPTIMAX] MODELS)**

1. Connect to threaded outlet check valve
2. T-fittings
3. Inline check valves
4. Cylinder No. 4 output
5. Cylinder No. 3 output
6. Cylinder No. 2 output
7. Cylinder No. 1 output
8. Cylinder No. 2 return
9. Connect to pressed-in inlet check valve

The external system on four-cylinder models is shown in **Figure 82**. The output from all three check valves comes together and enters the top of the crankcase cover through a pressed-in check valve. Two additional inline check valves mounted on cylinders No. 1 and No. 3 and are connected together and discharge into cylinder No. 2 intake transfer passages. The valves at the top and bottom of the crankcase cover must allow fluid to travel to the upper crankshaft bearing, but not back down. The inline check valves are marked with an arrow showing the normal direction of flow.

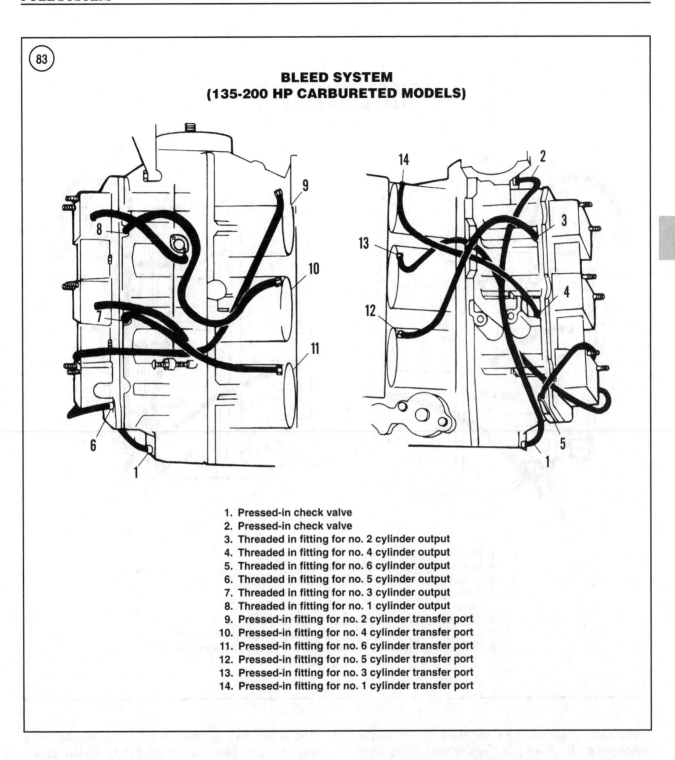

**BLEED SYSTEM
(135-200 HP CARBURETED MODELS)**

1. Pressed-in check valve
2. Pressed-in check valve
3. Threaded in fitting for no. 2 cylinder output
4. Threaded in fitting for no. 4 cylinder output
5. Threaded in fitting for no. 6 cylinder output
6. Threaded in fitting for no. 5 cylinder output
7. Threaded in fitting for no. 3 cylinder output
8. Threaded in fitting for no. 1 cylinder output
9. Pressed-in fitting for no. 2 cylinder transfer port
10. Pressed-in fitting for no. 4 cylinder transfer port
11. Pressed-in fitting for no. 6 cylinder transfer port
12. Pressed-in fitting for no. 5 cylinder transfer port
13. Pressed-in fitting for no. 3 cylinder transfer port
14. Pressed-in fitting for no. 1 cylinder transfer port

135-200 hp models except Optimax

These models only use external systems. Both carbureted and EFI models use a check valve at the bottom of the crankcase cover that is connected by a flexible line to the fitting or check valve at the top of the crankcase cover. This line lubricates the crankshaft upper bearing.

Refer to **Figure 83** for carbureted models and **Figure 84** for EFI models.

Carbureted models use six check valves pressed into the crankcase cover at the bottom of each reed block area. Six fittings (one for each cylinder) are threaded into the intake transfer passages on the sides of the crankcase. No T-fittings are used on carbureted models.

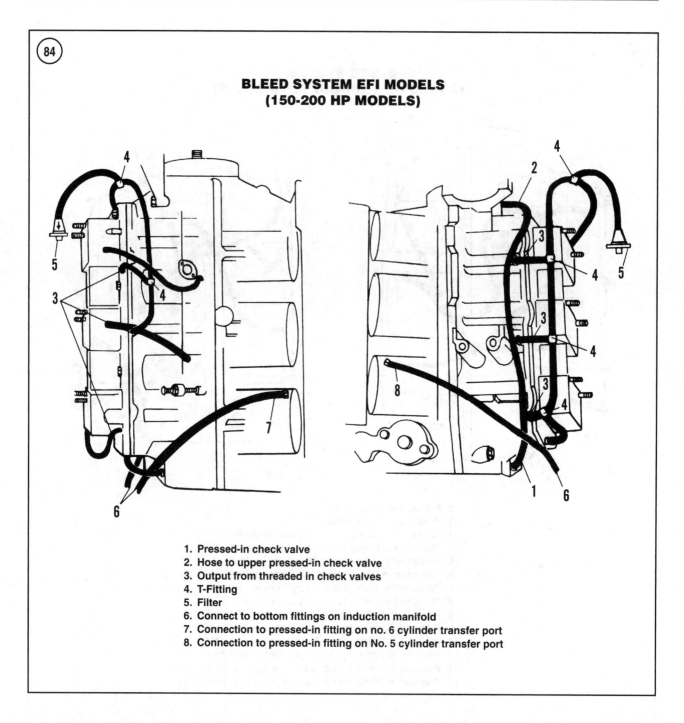

84

BLEED SYSTEM EFI MODELS
(150-200 HP MODELS)

1. Pressed-in check valve
2. Hose to upper pressed-in check valve
3. Output from threaded in check valves
4. T-Fitting
5. Filter
6. Connect to bottom fittings on induction manifold
7. Connection to pressed-in fitting on no. 6 cylinder transfer port
8. Connection to pressed-in fitting on No. 5 cylinder transfer port

EFI models use the same six check valves as the carbureted models, but all six check valves are ultimately connected into one line. This line returns all bleed fluid to the vapor separator through a small inline fuel filter.

Optimax models

The Optimax (direct fuel injection) system only recirculates oil. Since the fuel is injected directly into the combustion chamber, there is no fuel to puddle in the crankcase chambers. On 200 and 225 hp models, excess oil from the oil injection system is collected in the reed block area of each crankcase and pumped out through a series of one-way check valves and fittings to the air compressor crankcase. The oil passes through a small filter before entering the air compressor. Excess oil from the compressor is directed to a fitting on the intake manifold for recirculation.

Excess oil from the lower crankshaft bearing is collected and pumped through a check valve to the upper main bearing. Refer to Chapter Thirteen for additional information on oil hose routing.

225-250 hp models

All 225-250 hp models use an external bleed system. Blocking plugs are mounted in the grooved cavities on the crankcase cover to the intake manifold mating surface.

The external bleed systems used on 225-250 hp carbureted and EFI models have undergone numerous major revisions. It is very important to note the original position of the lines and valves before removal. An instant camera is definitely warranted for these systems. Also, consider using color-coded tape or tie-straps to identify the lines.

The upper crankshaft bearing lubrication system and port side mounted check valves with 4 in. (102 mm) hose are common to all 225-250 hp models.

Table 1 FUEL SYSTEM TORQUE SPECIFICATIONS

Fastener	in.-lb.	ft.-lb.	N•m
Acccerator pump mounting bolts	130	–	14.7
Air compressor (Optimax models)			
Mounting			
115-175 hp			
1998 and 1999			
Bolts	–	40	54.2
Nut	–	25	33.9
2000-on	–	42	56.9
200 and 225 hp	–	20	27.1
Pulley			
115-175 hp	100	–	11.3
200 and 225 hp			
1998 and 1999	100	–	11.3
2000-on			
Gold color pulley	192	16	21.7
Black color pulley	170	–	19.2
Crankshaft/bearing assembly	100	–	11.3
Head/reed plate bolts	–	20	27.1
Temperature sensor bolt	–	20	27.1
Air intake cover			
105 jet and 125-200 hp	60	–	6.8
Air intake plate			
65 jet and 75-125 hp	100	–	11.3
(except 105 jet and 115)			
225 hp	70	–	7.9
Air pressure regulator (Optimax models)	70	–	7.9
Carburetor mounting bolts/nuts			
65 jet and 75-125 hp (except 105 jet)	100	–	11.3
105 jet and 135-225 hp	70	–	7.9
Engine coolant temperature sensor			
All models except 2001-on Optimax	–	17	23.0
Engine control module			
150-200 hp (EFI models)			
225 and 250 hp (except Optimax)	80	–	9.0
Float retaining pin screw			
105 jet and 135-225 hp	10	–	1.1
Fuel bowl plug	33	–	3.7
Fuel bowl screws			
65 jet and 75-125 hp (except 105 jet)	18	–	2.0
105 jet and 135-200 hp	26	–	2.9
Fuel and air jets	14	–	1.6
Fuel cooler (1998 and 1999 Optimax)	170	–	19.2
Fuel injector retainers (2000-on Optimax)	70	–	7.9
Fuel management adapter (fitting)	45	–	5.1
	(continued)		

6

Table 1 FUEL SYSTEM TORQUE SPECIFICATIONS (continued)

Fastener	in.-lb.	ft.-lb.	N•m
Fuel pressure regulator			
150-250 hp EFI models	30	–	3.4
Optimax models	70	–	7.9
Fuel pressure regulator (elbow fitting)	45	–	5.1
Fuel pump (mechanical)			
Mounting screws	60	–	6.8
Fuel pump cover screws	60	–	6.8
Fuel/air rail nuts (Optimax)	–	33	44.7
Fuel rail screws (EFI models)			
150-200 hp	35	–	4.0
225 and 250 hp	45	–	5.1
Fuel rail hose adapter (outer) screws	45	–	5.1
Fuel rail adapter (inner) screws	18	–	2.0
High-pressure electric fuel pump			
Positive terminal nut	6	–	0.7
Negative terminal nut	16	–	1.8
Induction manifold bolts			
150-200 hp (EFI models)	90	–	10.2
225 and 250 hp (EFI models)	–	19	25.7
115-225 hp (Optimax models)	175	–	19.8
Intake manifold screws			
105 jet and 135-200 hp (except Optimax models)	105	–	11.9
225 and 250 hp (except Optimax models)	100	–	11.3
Mixing chamber cover	18	–	2.0
Reed plate/intake manifold			
65 jet and 75-90 hp	–	18	24.4
80 jet and 100-125 hp	–	18	24.4
(except 105 jet and 115 Optimax)			
150-200 hp (except Optimax models)			
Reed block retaining screws			
105 jet and 135-200 hp (except Optimax)	80	–	9.0
115-175 hp Optimax models	105	–	11.9
225 and 250 hp (except Optimax)	90	–	10.2
200 and 225 Optimax	90	–	10.2
Reed petal retaining screws			
65 jet and 75-125 hp			
(except 105 jet and 115 Optimax models)	80	–	9.0
T-fitting and elbow fitting			
105 jet and 135-225 hp	45	–	5.1
Throttle body (Optimax) screws	100	–	11.3
Throttle plate screws			
65 jet and 75-125 hp	6	–	0.7
(except 105 jet and 115 Optimax)			
Throttle position sensor	20	–	2.3
Throttle position sensor mounting plate	70	–	7.9
(Optimax models)			
Tracker valve cover	70	–	7.9
Vapor separator tank			
Mounting bolts			
150-250 hp EFI models	45	–	5.1
115-225 hp Optimax models)	140	–	15.8
Cover screws			
EFI models			
Large screws	30	–	3.4
Small screws	20	–	2.3
Optimax models	30	–	3.4
Float pin screw (Optimax models)	10	–	1.1
Water sensor module (150-200 hp EFI models)	25	–	2.8

Table 2 GENERAL TORQUE SPECIFICATIONS

Screw or nut size	in.-lb.	ft.-lb.	N•m
U.S. Standard			
6-32	9	–	1.0
8-32	20	–	2.3
10-24	30	–	3.4
10-32	35	–	4.0
12-24	45	–	5.1
1/4-20	70	–	7.9
1/4-28	84	–	9.5
5/16-18	160	13	18
5/16-24	168	14	19
3/8-16	–	23	31
3/8-24	–	25	34
7/16-14	–	36	49
7/16-20	–	40	54
1/2-13	–	50	68
1/2-20	–	60	81
Metric			
M5	36	–	4
M6	70	–	8
M8	156	13	18
M10	–	26	35
M12	–	35	48
M14	–	60	81

6

Table 3 CARBURETOR SPECIFICATIONS

Model	Specification
65 jet	
Carburetor type	WME
Carburetor ID No.	WME-78
Float height	9/16 in. (14.3 mm)
Idle mixture screw adjustment	1 1/4 turns out
Main fuel jet size	
No. 1 carburetor (top)	0.062 in.
No. 2 carburetor (middle)	0.064 in.
No. 3 carburetor (bottom)	0.064 in.
75 hp	
Carburetor type	WME
Carburetor ID No.	
Remote control	WME-75
Tiller control	WME-77
Float height	9/16 in. (14.3 mm)
Idle mixture screw adjustment	7/8–1 3/8 turns out
Main fuel jet size	
Remote control	
No. 1 carburetor (top)	0.052 in.
No. 2 carburetor (middle)	0.054 in.
No. 3 carburetor (bottom)	0.054 in.
Tiller control (electric start)	
No. 1 carburetor (top)	0.054 in.
No. 2 carburetor (middle)	0.054 in.
No. 3 carburetor (bottom)	0.054 in.
80 jet	
Carburetor type	WME
Carburetor ID No.	WME-80
Float height	9/16 in. (14.3 mm)

(continued)

Table 3 CARBURETOR SPECIFICATIONS (continued)

Model	Specification
80 jet (cont.)	
Idle mixture screw adjustment	1–1 1/2 turns out
Main fuel jet size	
No. 1 carburetor (top)	0.060 in.
No. 2 carburetor (second from top)	0.064 in.
No. 3 carburetor (second from bottom)	0.062 in.
No. 4 carburetor (bottom)	0.064 in.
90 hp	
Carburetor type	WME
Carburetor ID No.	WME-78
Float height	9/16 in. (14.3 mm)
Idle mixture screw adjustment	1 1/2 turns out
Main fuel jet size	
No. 1 carburetor (top)	0.062 in.
No. 2 carburetor (middle)	0.064 in.
No. 3 carburetor (bottom)	0.064 in.
100 hp	
Carburetor type	WME
Carburetor ID No.	WME-79
Float height	9/16 in. (14.3 mm)
Idle mixture screw adjustment	1–1 1/2 turns out
Main fuel jet size	
No. 1 carburetor (top)	0.048 in.
No. 2 carburetor (second from top)	0.050 in.
No. 3 carburetor (second from bottom)	0.050 in.
No. 4 carburetor (bottom)	0.052 in.
115 hp	
Carburetor type	WME
Carburetor ID No.	WME-80
Float height	9/16 in. (14.3 mm)
Idle mixture screw adjustment	1–1 1/2 turns out
Main fuel jet size	
No. 1 carburetor (top)	0.060 in.
No. 2 carburetor (second from top)	0.064 in.
No. 3 carburetor (second from bottom)	0.062 in.
No. 4 carburetor (bottom)	0.064 in.
125 hp	
Carburetor type	WME
Carburetor ID No.	WME-81
Float height	9/16 in. (14.3 mm)
Idle mixture screw adjustment	1–1 1/2 turns out
Main fuel jet size	
No. 1 carburetor (top)	0.070 in.
No. 2 carburetor (second from top)	0.080 in.
No. 3 carburetor (second from bottom)	0.080 in.
No. 4 carburetor (bottom)	0.082 in.
105 jet	
Carburetor type	WMV
Carburetor ID No.	WMV-2A or WMV-16
Float height	Flush with bowl edge
Idle mixture screw adjustment	1 1/8–1 3/8 turns out
Main fuel jet size	0.074 in.
Idle air jet	
WMV-2A	
Cylinders No. 1, 2, 3, 4, 6	0.034 in.
Cylinder No. 5	0.038 in.
WMV-16	
Cylinders No. 1, 2, 3, 4, 6	0.044 in.
Cylinder No. 5	0.048 in.

(continued)

Table 3 CARBURETOR SPECIFICATIONS (continued)

Model	Specification
105 jet (cont.)	
Back draft jet (vent jet)	
WMV-2A	0.086 in.
WMV-16	0.082 in.
135 hp	
Carburetor type	WMV
Carburetor ID No.	WMV-1A or WMV-15
Float height	Flush with bowl edge
Idle mixture screw adjustment	1 3/8–1 5/8 turns out
Main fuel jet size	0.072 in.
Idle air jet	
WMV-1A	
Cylinders No. 1, 2, 3, 4, 6	0.036 in.
Cylinder No. 5	0.040 in.
WMV-15	
Cylinder No. 1	0.036 in.
Cylinders No. 2 and 3	0.040 in.
Cylinder No. 4	0.030 in.
Cylinder No. 6	0.038 in.
Cylinder No. 5	0.048 in.
Back draft jet (vent jet)	0.086 in.
140 jet	
Carburetor type	WMV
Carburetor ID No.	WMV-5A
Float height	Flush with bowl edge
Idle mixture screw adjustment	1 1/8–1 3/8 turns out
Main fuel jet size	
Cylinders No. 1, 2	0.082 in.
Cylinders No. 3, 4, 5, 6	0.080 in.
Idle air jet	
Cylinders No. 1, 2	0.052 in.
Cylinders No. 3, 4, 6	0.028 in.
Cylinder No. 5	0.032 in.
Back draft jet (vent jet)	0.096 in.
150 hp (except XR6 and Mag III)	
Carburetor type	WMV
Carburetor ID No.	WMV-2A or WMV-16
Float height	Flush with bowl edge
Idle mixture screw adjustment	1 1/8–1 3/8 turns out
Main fuel jet size	0.074 in.
Idle air jet	
WMV-2A	
Cylinders No. 1, 2, 3, 4, 6	0.034 in.
Cylinder No. 5	0.038 in.
WMV-16	
Cylinders No. 1, 2, 3, 4, 6	0.044 in.
Cylinder No. 5	0.048 in.
Back draft jet (vent jet)	
WMV-2A	0.086 in.
WMV-16	0.082 in.
150 XR6 and MAG III	
Carburetor type	WMV
Carburetor ID No.	WMV-3A or WMV-16
Float height	Flush with bowl edge
Idle mixture screw adjustment	1 1/8–1 3/8 turns out
Main fuel jet size	0.074 in.

(continued)

6

Table 3 CARBURETOR SPECIFICATIONS (continued)

Model	Specification
150 XR6 and MAG III (cont.)	
Idle air jet	
WMV-3A	
Cylinders No. 1, 2, 3, 4, 6	0.044 in.
Cylinder No. 5	0.048 in.
WMV-16	
Cylinders No. 1, 2, 3, 4, 6	0.044 in.
Cylinder No. 5	0.048 in.
Back draft jet (vent jet)	0.082 in.
175 hp	
Carburetor type	WMV
Carburetor ID No.	WMV-4A
Float height	Flush with bowl edge
Idle mixture screw adjustment	1 1/8–1 3/8 turns out
Main fuel jet size	0.078 in.
Idle air jet	
Cylinders No. 1, 2, 3, 4, 6	0.030 in.
Cylinder No. 5	0.034 in.
Back draft jet (vent jet)	0.086 in.
200 hp	
Carburetor type	WMV
Carburetor ID No.	WMV-5A or WMV-18
Float height	Flush with bowl edge
Idle mixture screw adjustment	1 1/8–1 3/8 turns out
Main fuel jet size	
WMV-5A	
Cylinders No. 1, 2	0.082 in.
Cylinders No. 3, 4, 5, 6	0.080 in.
WMV-18	
Cylinders No. 1, 4	0.080 in.
Cylinders No. 2, 3	0.082 in.
Cylinder No. 5	0.084 in.
Cylinder No. 6	0.078 in.
Idle air jet	
WMV-5A	
Cylinders No. 1, 2	0.052 in.
Cylinders No. 3, 4, 6	0.028 in.
Cylinder No. 5	0.032 in.
WMV-18	
Cylinder No. 1	0.042 in.
Cylinder No. 2	0.038 in.
Cylinders No. 3-6	0.028 in.
Back draft jet (vent jet)	
WMV-5A	0.096 in.
WMV-18	0.086 in.
225 hp	
Carburetor type	WMV
Carburetor ID No.	WMV-13
Float height	Flush with bowl edge
Idle mixture screw adjustment	1 1/4–1 3/4 turns out
Main fuel jet size	
Cylinders No. 1, 3, 5	0.084 in.
Cylinders No. 2, 6	0.082 in.
Cylinder No. 4	0.086 in.
Idle air jet	
Cylinder No. 1	0.046 in.
Cylinder No. 2	0.060 in.
Cylinder No. 3	0.054 in.

(continued)

Table 3 CARBURETOR SPECIFICATIONS (continued)

Model	Specification
225 hp (cont.)	
Idle air jet	
Cylinders No. 4, 6	0.052 in.
Cylinder No. 5	0.058 in.
Back draft jet (vent jet)	
Cylinders No. 1, 2, 5, 6	0.082 in.
Cylinders No. 3, 4	0.086 in.

6

Chapter Seven

Electrical System

This chapter provides service procedures for the battery, starter motor, charging system and ignition system used on outboard motors covered in this manual. Wiring diagrams are located at the end of the manual.

Table 1 provides specific application torque specifications. **Table 2** provides general torque specifications. Use the general torque specifications for fasteners not in **Table 1**. **Tables 3-6** provide battery charge percentage, battery capacity, and battery and battery cable size requirements. All tables are at the end of the chapter.

BATTERY

Batteries used in marine applications endure far more rigorous treatment than those used in automotive applications. Marine batteries (**Figure 1**) generally have a thicker exterior case to cushion the plates during tight turns and rough water. Thicker plates are also used. Each plate is fastened in the case to help prevent premature failure. Spill-resistant caps on the battery cells help prevent electrolyte from spilling into the bilge. Automotive batteries should be used in a boat *only* during an emergency when a suitable marine battery is not available.

CAUTION
Sealed or maintenance-free batteries are not recommended for use with unregulated charging systems. Excessive charging during continued high-speed operation will cause the electrolyte to boil, resulting in its loss. Since water cannot be added to sealed batteries, prolonged overcharging damages the battery. All models covered in this manual use a regulated charging system.

Battery Rating Methods

The battery industry has developed specifications and performance standards to evaluate batteries and their energy potential. Several rating methods are used.

Cold cranking amps (CCA)

Cold cranking amps represents in amps the current flow the battery can deliver for 30 seconds at 0° F (-17.8° C) without dropping below 1.2 volts per cell (7.2 volts on a standard 12-volt battery). The higher the number, the more amps it can deliver to crank the engine. CCA times 1.3 equals marine cranking amps (MCA).

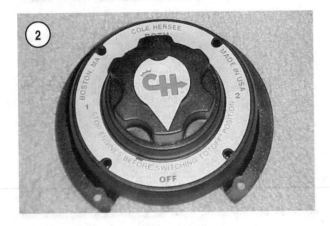

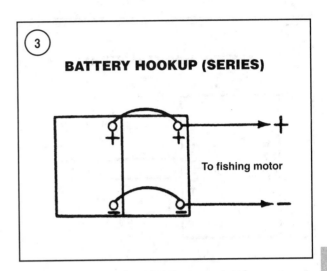

flow that the battery will deliver for 20 hours while at 80° F (26.7° C) without dropping below 1.75 volts per cell (10.5 volts on a standard 12 volt battery). The rating is actually the steady current flow times the 20 hours. Example: A 60 amp-hour battery will deliver 3 amps continuously for 20 hours. This rating method has been largely discontinued by the battery industry. Cold cranking amps or marine cranking amps and reserve capacity ratings are now the most common battery rating methods.

Battery Recommendations

A battery with inadequate capacity can cause hard starting or an inability to start the engine. Battery recommendations are in **Table 5**. A battery with a capacity exceeding the minimum requirement, is acceptable and is highly recommended if the boat is equipped with numerous electrical accessories. Consider adding an additional battery and installing a battery switch (**Figure 2**) on such applications. The switch allows starting and charging operations to use one or both batteries. The switch can be turned off if the boat is at rest or in storage to prevent discharge that occurs from some on-board accessories.

Battery Installation

Separate batteries may be used to provide power for accessories such as lighting, fish finders and depth finders. To determine the required capacity of such batteries, calculate the accessory current (amperage) draw rate of the accessory and refer to **Table 4**.

Two batteries may be connected in parallel to double the ampere-hour capacity while maintaining the required 12 volts. See **Figure 3**. For accessories that require 24

Marine cranking amps (MCA)

MCA is similar to the CCA except the battery is run at 32° F (0° C) instead of 0° F (-17.8° C). This is closer to actual boat operating environments. MCA times 0.77 equals CCA.

Reserve capacity

Reserve capacity represents the time in minutes that a fully charged battery at 80° F (26.7° C) can deliver 25 amps without dropping below 1.75 volts per cell (10.5 volts on a standard 12 volt battery). The reserve capacity rating defines the length of time that a typical vehicle can be driven after the charging system fails. The 25 amp figure takes into account the power required by the ignition, lighting and other accessories. The higher the reserve capacity rating, the longer the vehicle could be operated after a charging system failure.

Amp-hour rating

The amp-hour rating method is also called the 20-hour rating method. This rating represents the steady current

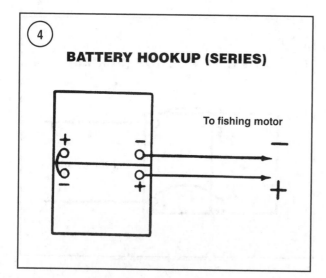

BATTERY HOOKUP (SERIES)

To fishing motor

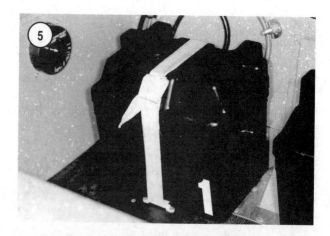

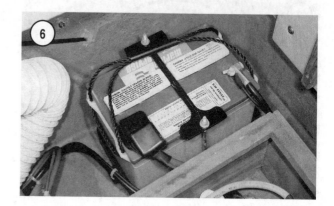

volts, batteries may be connected in series (**Figure 4**), but only accessories specifically requiring 24 volts should be connected to the system. If charging becomes necessary, individually disconnect and charge batteries connected in a parallel or series circuit.

Safety

The battery must be securely fastened in the boat to prevent the battery from shifting or moving in the bilge area. The positive battery terminal or the entire top of the battery must also be covered with a nonconductive shield or boot.

If the battery is not properly secured, it can contact the hull or metal fuel tank in rough water or while being transported. If the battery shorts against the metal hull or fuel tank, it can cause sparks and cause an electrical fire. An explosion could occur if the fuel tank or battery case is compromised.

If the battery is not properly grounded and the battery contacts the metal hull, the battery will try to ground through the control cables or the boat's wiring harness. Again, the short circuit can cause sparks and an electrical fire. The control cables and boat wiring harness can be irreparably damaged.

Observe the following preventive steps when installing a battery in a boat, especially a metal boat or a boat with a metal fuel tank.

1. Choose a location that is as far as is practical from the fuel tank while still providing access for maintenance.
2. Secure the battery to the hull with a plastic battery box and tie-down strap (**Figure 5**), or a battery tray (**Figure 6**) with a nonconductive shield or boot covering the positive battery terminal.

3. Make sure all battery cable connections (two at the battery and two at the engine) are clean and tight. Do *not* use wing nuts to secure battery cables. If wing nuts are present, discard them and replace them with corrosion resistant hex nuts and lock washers to ensure positive electrical connections. Loose battery connections can cause engine malfunction and failure of expensive components.
4. Periodically inspect the installation to make sure the battery is physically secured to the hull and the battery cable connections are clean and tight.

Care and Inspection

1. Remove the battery tray top or battery box cover. See **Figure 5** or **Figure 6**.
2. Disconnect the negative battery cable, then the positive battery cable.

NOTE
Some batteries have a built-in carry strap (Figure 1).

3. Attach a battery carry strap to the terminal posts. Remove the battery from the boat.

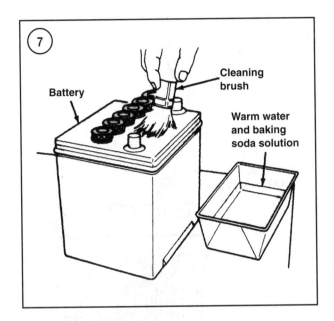

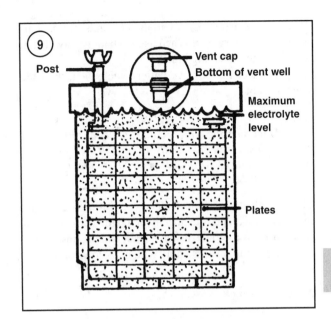

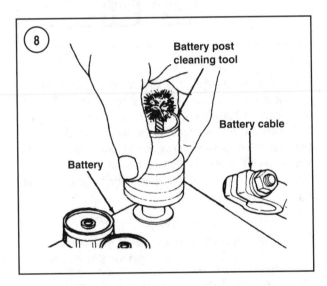

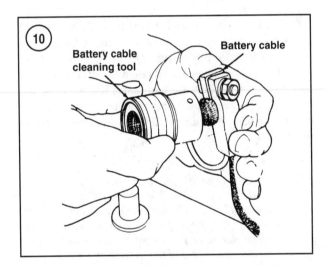

7

4. Inspect the entire battery case for cracks, holes or other damage.

5. Inspect the battery tray or battery box for corrosion or deterioration. Clean as necessary with a solution of baking soda and water.

NOTE
Do not allow the baking soda cleaning solution to enter the battery cells in Step 6 or the electrolyte will be severely weakened.

6. Clean the top of the battery with a stiff bristle brush using the baking soda and water solution (**Figure 7**). Rinse the battery case with clear water and wipe it dry with a clean cloth or paper towel.

7. Clean the battery terminal posts with a stiff wire brush or battery terminal cleaning tool (**Figure 8**).

NOTE
Do not overfill the battery cells in Step 8. The electrolyte expands due to heat from the charging system and will overflow if the level is more than 3/16 in. (4.8 mm) above the battery plates.

8. Remove the filler caps and check the electrolyte level. Add distilled water, if necessary, to bring the level up to 3/16 in. (4.8 mm) above the plates in the battery case. See **Figure 9**.

9. Clean the battery cable clamps with a stiff wire brush (**Figure 10**).

10. Place the battery back into the boat and into the battery tray or battery box. When using a battery tray, install and secure the retaining bracket.

11. Reconnect the positive battery cable first, then the negative cable.

> *CAUTION*
> *Make sure the battery cables are connected to their proper terminals. Reversing the battery polarity will result in electrical and ignition system damage.*

12. Securely tighten the battery connections. Coat the connections with petroleum jelly or a light grease to minimize corrosion. When using a battery box, install the cover and secure the assembly with a tie-down strap.

Battery Testing

Hydrometer testing

On batteries with removable vent caps, the best way to check the battery state of charge is to check the specific gravity of the electrolyte with a hydrometer. Use a hydrometer with numbered graduations from 1.100-1.300 points rather than one with color-coded bands. To use the hydrometer, squeeze the rubber bulb, insert the tip into a cell, then release the bulb to fill the hydrometer. See **Figure 11**.

> *NOTE*
> *Do not test specific gravity immediately after adding water to the battery cells, as the water will dilute the electrolyte and lower the specific gravity. To obtain an accurate hydrometer reading, charge the battery after adding water and before testing with a hydrometer.*

Draw enough electrolyte to raise the float inside the hydrometer. When using a temperature-compensated hydrometer, discharge the electrolyte back into the battery cell and repeat the process several times to adjust the temperature of the hydrometer to the electrolyte.

Hold the hydrometer upright and note the number on the float that is even with the surface of the electrolyte (**Figure 12**). This number is the specific gravity for the cell. Discharge the electrolyte into the cell from which it came.

The specific gravity of a cell is the indicator of the cell's state of charge. A fully charged cell will read 1.260 or more at 80° F (26.7° C). A cell that is 75 percent charged will read from 1.220-1.230 while a cell with a 50 percent charge will read from 1.170-1.180. A cell reading 1.120 or

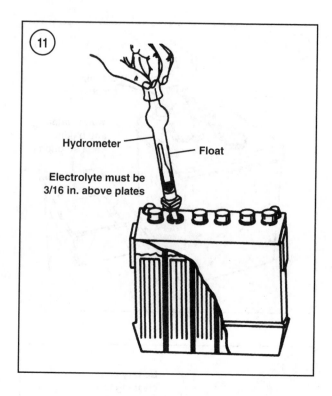

11

Hydrometer — Float

Electrolyte must be
3/16 in. above plates

less is discharged. All cells should be within 30 points specific gravity of each other. If there is over 30 points variation, the battery condition is questionable. Charge the battery and recheck the specific gravity. If 30 points or more variation remains between cells after charging, the battery has failed and should be replaced. Refer to **Table 3** for battery charge level based on specific gravity readings.

> *NOTE*
> *If a temperature-compensated hydrometer is **not** used, add 4 points specific gravity to the actual reading for every 10° above 80° F (26.7° C). Subtract 4 points specific gravity for every 10° below 80° F (26.7° C).*

Open-circuit voltage test

On sealed or maintenance-free batteries, check the state of charge by measuring the open-circuit (no load) voltage of the battery. Use a digital voltmeter for best results. For the most accurate results, allow the battery to set at rest for at least 30 minutes to allow the battery to stabilize. Then, observing the correct polarity, connect the voltmeter to the battery and note the meter reading. If the open-circuit voltage is 12.7 volts or higher, the battery is fully charged. A reading of 12.4 volts means the battery is approximately 75 percent charged, a reading of 12.2 means the battery is

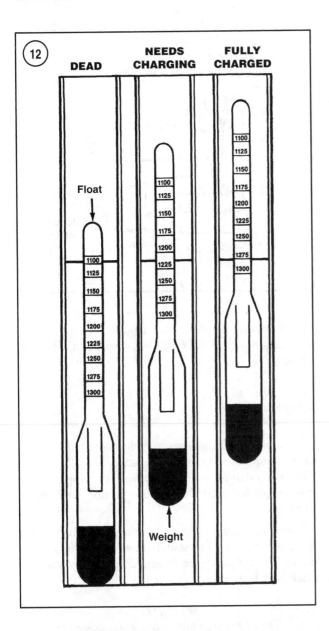

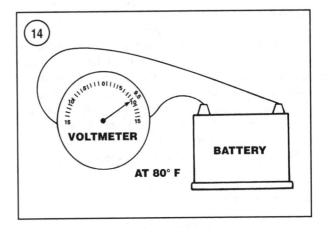

approximately 50 percent charged and a reading of 12.1 volts means that the battery is approximately 25 percent charged.

Load testing

Two common methods are used to load test batteries. A commercially available load tester (**Figure 13**) measures the battery voltage as it applies a load across the terminal. Measure the cranking voltage following the instructions in this section if a load tester is not available.

1. Attach a voltmeter across the battery as shown in **Figure 14**.

2. Remove and ground the spark plug leads to the power head to prevent accidental starting.

3. Crank the engine for approximately 15 seconds while noting the voltmeter reading. Note the voltage at the end of the 15 second period.

4A. If the voltage is 9.5 volts or higher, the battery is sufficiently charged and of sufficient capacity for the outboard motor.

4B. If the voltage is below 9.5 volts, one of the following conditions is present:

    a. The battery is discharged or defective. Charge the battery and retest.

    b. The battery capacity is too small for the outboard motor. Refer to *Battery Recommendations* in this chapter.

    c. The starting system is drawing excessive current causing the battery voltage to drop. Refer to Chapter Three for starting system troubleshooting procedures.

    d. A mechanical defect is present in the power head or gearcase creating excessive load and current draw on the starting system. Inspect the power head and gearcase for mechanical defects.

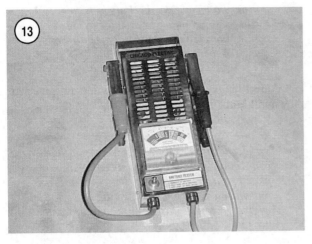

Battery Storage

Wet cell batteries slowly discharge when stored. Before storing a battery, clean the case with a solution of baking soda and water. Rinse it with clear water and wipe it dry. Fully charge the battery, then store it in a cool, dry location. Check electrolyte level and state of charge frequently during storage. If the specific gravity falls to 40 points or more below full charge (1.260), or the open circuit voltage falls below 12.4 volts, recharge the battery.

Battery Charging

Check the state of charge with a hydrometer or digital voltmeter as described in the previous section.

Remove the battery from the boat for charging. A charging battery releases highly explosive hydrogen gas. In many boats, the area around the battery is not well ventilated and the gas may remain in the area for hours after the charging process has been completed. Sparks or flames occurring near the battery can cause it to explode and spray battery acid over a wide area.

If the battery cannot be removed for charging, make sure the bilge access hatches, doors or vents are fully open to allow adequate ventilation. Observe the following precautions when charging batteries:

1. Never smoke in close proximity to a battery.
2. Make sure all accessories are turned off before disconnecting the battery cables. Disconnecting a circuit that is electrically active will create a spark that can ignite explosive gas that may be present.
3. Always disconnect the negative battery cable first, then the positive cable.
4. On batteries with removable vent caps, always check the electrolyte level before charging the battery. Maintain the correct electrolyte level throughout the charging process.
5. Never attempt to charge a battery that is frozen.

WARNING
Be extremely careful not to create any sparks around the battery when connecting the battery charger.

6. Connect the negative charger lead to the negative battery terminal and the positive charger lead to the positive battery terminal. If the charger output is variable, select a setting of approximately 4 amps. Charge the battery slowly at low amp settings, rather than quickly at high amp settings.
7. If the charger has a dual voltage setting, set the voltage switch to 12 volts, then switch the charger ON.

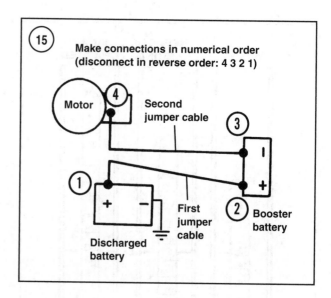

Make connections in numerical order (disconnect in reverse order: 4 3 2 1)

8. If the battery is severely discharged, allow it to charge for at least 8 hours. Check the charging process with a hydrometer.

Jump Starting

If the battery becomes severely discharged, the engine can be jump started from another battery in or out of a vehicle. Jump starting can be dangerous if the proper procedure is not followed. Always use caution when jump starting.

Check the electrolyte level of the discharged battery before attempting the jump start. If the electrolyte is not visible or if it appears to be frozen, do not jump start the discharged battery.

WARNING
Use extreme caution when connecting the booster battery to the discharged battery to avoid personal injury or damage to the system. **Make sure** *the jumper cables are connected to the correct polarity.*

1. Connect the jumper cables in the order and sequence shown in **Figure 15**.

WARNING
An electrical arc can occur when the final connection is made. This could cause an explosion if it occurs near the battery. For this reason, make the final connection to a good engine ground, away from the battery and not to the battery itself.

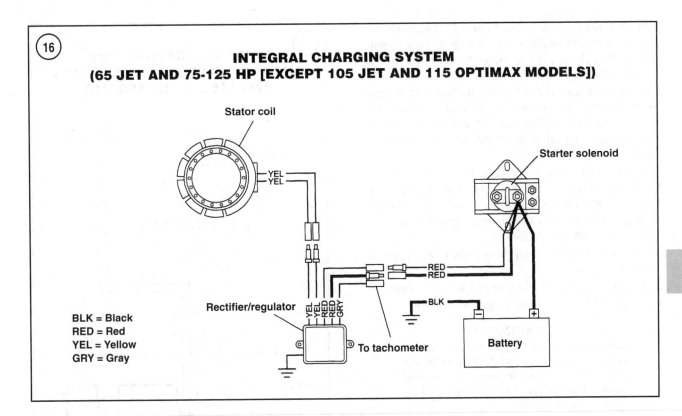

INTEGRAL CHARGING SYSTEM
(65 JET AND 75-125 HP [EXCEPT 105 JET AND 115 OPTIMAX MODELS])

Stator coil

Starter solenoid

YEL
YEL

RED
RED

BLK

Rectifier/regulator

BLK = Black
RED = Red
YEL = Yellow
GRY = Gray

YEL
YEL
RED
RED
GRY

To tachometer

Battery

7

2. Make sure all jumper cables are out of the way of moving engine parts.

CAUTION
*Do not run the engine without an adequate water supply and do not exceed 3000 rpm without an adequate load. Refer to **Safety Precautions** in Chapter Three.*

3. Start the engine. Once it starts, run it at a moderate speed (fast idle).

CAUTION
Running the engine at high speed with a discharged battery can damage the charging system.

4. Remove the jumper cables in the exact reverse of the order shown in **Figure 15**.

CHARGING SYSTEM

A fully regulated charging system is used on all models covered in this manual. The charging system keeps the battery fully charged and supplies current to run accessories. Charging systems can be divided into two basic designs: integral regulated and external (belt-driven) regulated. All Optimax and 225-250 hp models use a belt driven external alternator. All other models use an integral regulated system.

Integral systems use permanent magnets mounted in the flywheel and a stator coil winding mounted to the power head. As the flywheel rotates, the magnetic fields in the flywheel pass through the stator coil windings, inducing AC (alternating current). The rectifier portion of the rectifier/regulator changes the AC current to DC current, while the regulator portion monitors system voltage and controls the charging system output accordingly. Batteries that are maintained at 13-15 volts will stay fully charged without excessive venting. The regulator controls the output of the charging system to keep system voltage at approximately 14.5 volts or lower. The large red cable of the rectifier/regulator is DC output. The small red wire is the sense terminal which allows the regulator portion to monitor system voltage. See **Figure 16**.

Another function of the integral charging system is to provide the signal for the tachometer. The tachometer counts AC voltage pulses coming from the stator before the AC voltage is rectified to DC. Tachometer failure on models with integral charging systems is related to the charging system, not the ignition system. The tachometer connects to the gray wire. See **Figure 16**.

External regulated systems use a belt-driven, excited rotor, internally regulated 60 amp alternator, similar to many automotive designs. See **Figure 17**. The alternator has no permanent magnets. The voltage regulator sends current through the rotor windings to create a magnetic field. By changing the strength of the rotor magnetic field, the output of the alternator can be controlled. The alternator is not serviceable and is only sold as an assembly. This system is used on all Optimax, 225 and 250 hp models. The tachometer signal on these models is produced by the ECM.

A malfunction in the charging system generally causes the battery to be undercharged, and on integral systems, the tachometer will read erratically or totally fail. The following conditions will cause charging system failure.

1. Reversing the battery leads.

2. Disconnecting the battery leads while the engine is running.

3. Loose connections in the charging system circuits, including battery connections and ground circuits.

CAUTION
Never operate the engine with the battery disconnected. The charging system or engine control system can suffer serious and often costly damage if it is operated with the battery disconnected.

NOTE
The 40 amp (integral regulated) charging system used on the 135-200 hp, 275 hp and 105-140 jet models is basically two separate 20 amp charging systems. Half of the stator windings are connected to the upper regulator/rectifier assembly and the remaining stator windings are connected to the lower regulator/rectifier. If one regulator/rectifier fails, the charging system will still function, but at only half of its rated output. See Figure 18.

Perform the following visual inspection prior to troubleshooting the charging system. If the visual inspection does not locate the problem, refer to Chapter Three for complete charging system troubleshooting procedures.

1. Make sure the battery cables are connected properly. Connect the positive cable to the positive battery terminal. If the polarity is reversed, check for a damaged rectifier (or rectifier/regulator). See Chapter Three.

2. Inspect the battery terminals for loose or corroded connections. Tighten or clean them as necessary. Replace wing nuts with corrosion resistant hex nuts and lock washers.

3. Inspect the physical condition of the battery. Look for bulges or cracks in the case, leaking electrolyte and corrosion build-up. Clean, refill or replace the battery as necessary.

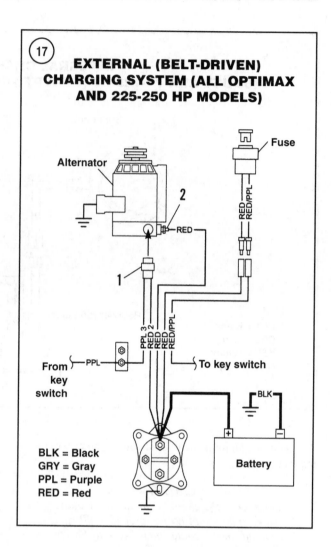

EXTERNAL (BELT-DRIVEN) CHARGING SYSTEM (ALL OPTIMAX AND 225-250 HP MODELS)

BLK = Black
GRY = Gray
PPL = Purple
RED = Red

4. Carefully check the wiring between the stator coil and the battery for damage or deterioration. Refer to the end of the manual for wiring diagrams. Repair or replace wires and connectors as necessary.

5. Check all accessory circuits and associated wiring for corroded, loose or disconnected connections. Clean, tighten or reconnect as necessary.

6. Determine if the accessory load on the battery is greater than the charging system's capacity by performing the *Current draw* test in Chapter Three.

Alternator Removal/Installation (External Belt-Driven Models)

225-250 hp models except Optimax models

The 225 and 250 hp models use a V-belt to drive the alternator off the crank pulley. Belt tension must be 1/4-1/2 in. (6.4-12.7 mm) deflection under moderate thumb pres-

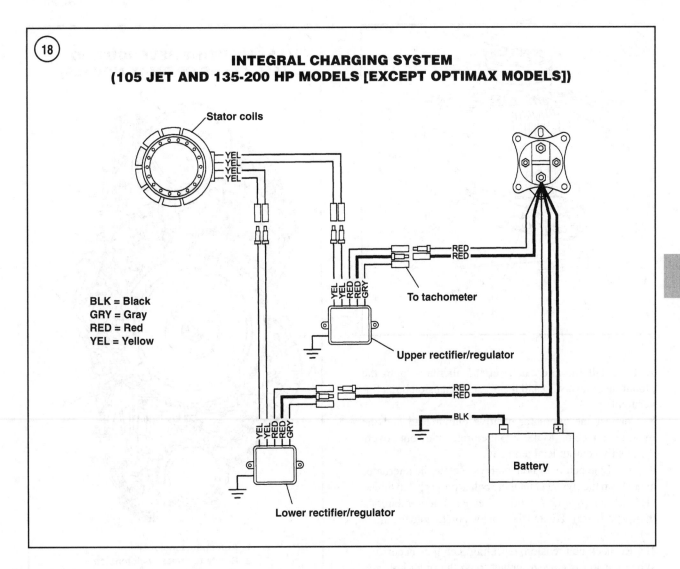

**INTEGRAL CHARGING SYSTEM
(105 JET AND 135-200 HP MODELS [EXCEPT OPTIMAX MODELS])**

7

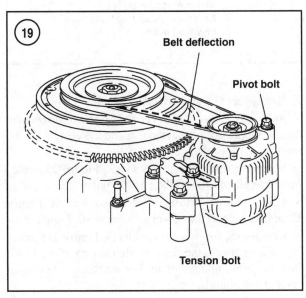

sure at the point shown in **Figure 19**. Adjust the belt tension by rotating the alternator away or toward the flywheel pulley. Always inspect the belt for deterioration, wear and fraying when servicing or replacing the alternator.

Replace the alternator as follows:

1. Disconnect and ground the spark plug leads to the power head to prevent accidental starting.

2. Disconnect the negative battery cable.

3. Remove the flywheel cover.

4. Loosen the pivot and tension bolts (**Figure 19**). Rotate the alternator toward the flywheel and slip the belt off both pulleys.

5. Remove the alternator positive output lead (A, **Figure 20**) and disconnect the two-pin connector (B, **Figure 20**).

6. Remove the pivot and tension bolts. Remove the alternator from the engine.

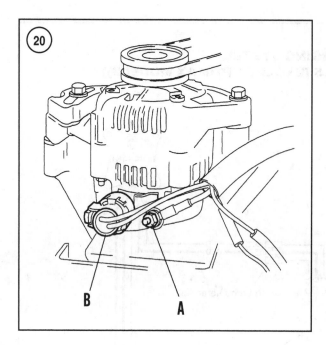

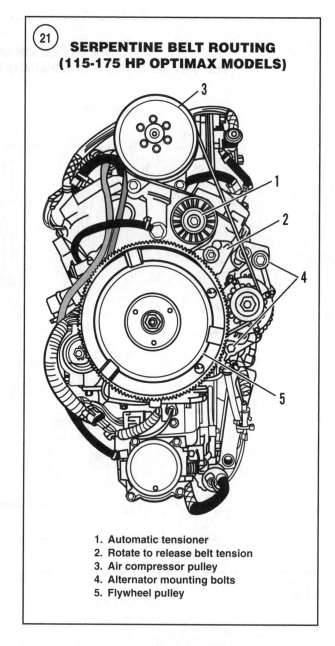

**SERPENTINE BELT ROUTING
(115-175 HP OPTIMAX MODELS)**

1. Automatic tensioner
2. Rotate to release belt tension
3. Air compressor pulley
4. Alternator mounting bolts
5. Flywheel pulley

7. To install the alternator, set the alternator onto the mounting brackets. Install the pivot and tension bolts finger-tight.

8. Connect the alternator positive output lead and the two-pin connector. Make sure the protective boot covers the positive output lead terminal.

9. Install the belt over both pulleys. Rotate the alternator away from the flywheel until the belt is properly tensioned (1/4-1/2 in. [6.4-12.7 mm] deflection under moderate thumb pressure). Tighten the tension bolt to hold the alternator in place.

10. Recheck belt tension, repeating Step 9 as necessary. When tension is correct, tighten both the pivot bolt and tension bolt to the specification in **Table 1**.

11. Reinstall the flywheel cover.

12. Reconnect the spark plug leads to the spark plugs.

13. Reconnect the negative battery cable.

14. Recheck belt tension and condition after the first 10 hours of new belt operation and every 50 hours thereafter.

115-175 hp (Optimax) models

These models use a serpentine belt and automatic tensioner system very similar to current automotive designs. While no adjustments are required with this system, inspect the belt and belt tensioner assembly for deterioration, wear, fraying and mechanical damage or failure.

Replace the alternator as follows:

1. Disconnect and ground the spark plug leads to the power head to prevent accidental starting.

2. Disconnect the negative battery cable.

3. Remove the flywheel cover. Be careful to disconnect the air compressor inlet at the rear and the vent line at the front.

4. Manually rotate the tensioner (2, **Figure 21**) away from the belt and slip the belt off the pulleys.

5. Remove the alternator positive output lead (A, **Figure 20**) and disconnect the two-pin connector (B, **Figure 20**).

6. Remove the two mounting bolts (4, **Figure 21**) securing the alternator to the brackets. Remove the ground wire from the front mounting bolt. Loosen the rear mounting bracket bolt slightly.

22

SERPENTINE BELT ROUTING
(200 AND 225 HP OPTIMAX MODELS)

3

4

2

5

1

1. Flywheel pulley
2. Air compressor pulley
3. Alternator pulley
4. Automatic tensioner
5. Rotate to release belt tension

23

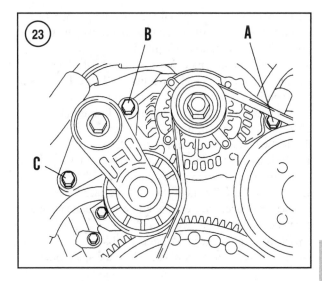

11. Release the tensioner against the belt. Make sure the belt is tracking on each pulley correctly.

12. Reinstall the flywheel cover. Make sure the air compressor inlet is connected at the rear and the vent line is connected at the front.

13. Reconnect the negative battery cable.

14. Reconnect the spark plug leads to the spark plug.

200 and 225 hp (Optimax) models

These models use a serpentine belt and automatic tensioner system. While no adjustments are required with this system, inspect the belt and belt tensioner assembly for deterioration, wear, fraying and mechanical damage or failure.

Replace the alternator as follows:

1. Disconnect and ground the spark plug leads to the power head to prevent accidental starting.

2. Disconnect the negative battery cable.

3. Remove the flywheel cover. Be careful to disconnect the air compressor inlet at the rear and the vent line at the front.

4. Manually rotate the tensioner (5, **Figure 22**) away from the belt and slip the belt off the pulleys.

5. Remove the alternator positive output lead (A, **Figure 20**) and disconnect the two-pin connector (B, **Figure 20**).

6. Remove the two mounting bolts (A and B, **Figure 23**) securing the alternator to the brackets. Remove the grounding wire from the port mounting bolt. Loosen the tensioner bracket bolt (C, **Figure 23**) slightly.

7. Remove the alternator from the engine.

8. To install the alternator, set the alternator onto the mounting brackets. Install the two alternator mounting bolts (A and B, **Figure 23**). Connect the ground wire to the

7. Remove the alternator from the engine.

8. To install the alternator, set the alternator onto the mounting brackets. Install the two alternator mounting bolts (4, **Figure 21**). Connect the grounding wire to the front mounting bolt. Tighten the upper and lower bolts/nuts to the specification in **Table 1**. Tighten the tensioner bracket bolt to the specification in **Table 1**.

9. Connect the alternator positive output lead/insulator. Tighten the nut to the specification in **Table 1**. Connect the two-pin connector to the alternator. Make sure the protective boot covers the positive output lead terminal.

10. Install the belt while holding the tensioner fully open. Route the belt as shown in **Figure 21**.

7

port mounting bolt. Tighten the mounting bolts to the specification in **Table 1**. Tighten the tensioner bracket bolt to the specification in **Table 1**.

9. Connect the alternator positive output lead/insulator. Tighten the nut to the specification in **Table 1**. Connect the two-pin connector to the alternator. Make sure the protective boot covers the positive output lead terminal.

10. Install the belt while holding the tensioner fully open. Route the belt as shown in **Figure 22**.

11. Release the tensioner against the belt. Make sure the belt is tracking on each pulley correctly.

12. Reinstall the flywheel cover. Make sure the air compressor inlet is connected at the rear and the vent line is connected at the front.

13. Reconnect the negative battery cable.

14. Reconnect the spark plug leads to the spark plug.

Rectifier/Regulator Removal/Installation (Internal Regulated Models)

The rectifier/regulators used on all internal models are of the same basic construction. See **Figure 24**.

The 40 amp charging system on 135-200 hp (except Optimax), 105 and 140 jet models uses two voltage rectifier/regulators (**Figure 18**).

1. Disconnect and ground the spark plug leads to the power head to prevent accidental starting.

2. Disconnect the negative battery cable.

3A. On 65 jet and 75-125 hp (except 105 jet) models, locate the rectifier/regulator (**Figure 25**, typical) on the electrical plate on the rear starboard side of the power head. The rectifier/regulator mounts directly above the DCM ignition modules.

3B. On 1998 and 1999 105 jet and 135-200 hp models, remove the four locknuts and spacers from the ignition coil mounting plate. The plate is located on the rear of the power head. Slide the plate from the stud and move it to one side to access the two rectifier/regulators. Remove the four spacers from the plate mounting studs.

3C. On 2000-on 105 jet and 135-200 hp models, locate the two voltage rectifier/regulator(s) on the rear starboard side of the power head and next to the starter motor.

4. Cut the tie-strap(s) and/or loosen the clamps securing the wires and bullet connectors of each regulator to the power head or electrical/ignition bracket. Discard the tie-strap(s).

5. Disconnect the two yellow, two red (or red and red/gray) and one gray wire bullet connectors of each regulator from the engine wiring harness. Be careful not to damage the connector terminals or insulating sleeve.

6A. On 65 jet and 75-125 hp (except 105 jet) models, remove the two screws and the J-clamp securing the recti-

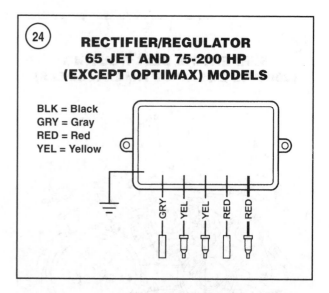

fier/regulator to the electrical/ignition bracket. Remove the rectifier/regulator.

6B. On 1998 and 1999 105 jet and 135-200 hp models, slide the voltage regulators off the plate mounting studs. Disconnect the trim solenoid and rectifier/regulator grounds from the ignition coil mounting plate. Then remove the regulators.

6C. On 2000-on 105 jet and 135-200 hp models, remove the two screws from each rectifier/regulator. Then remove the regulators.

7. Clean all corrosion from the rectifier/regulator mounting surface. The surfaces must be clean for proper cooling of the rectifier/regulator(s).

8A. On 65 jet and 75-125 hp (except 105 jet) models, mount the replacement rectifier/regulator onto the electrical plate. The flat metal side must make good contact with the plate. Install the mounting screws with the J-clamp over the upper screw. Tighten the screws to the specification in **Table 1**.

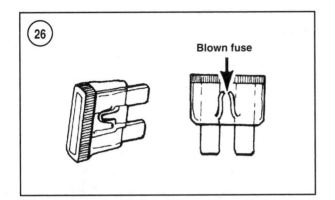

Blown fuse

8B. On 1998 and 1999 105 jet and 135-200 hp models, install the rectifier/regulator(s) as follows:

a. Slide the rectifier/regulator(s) over the mounting studs and against the power head. Make sure the solid metal side of the rectifier/regulator(s) contacts the power head.

b. Slide a spacer collar over each mounting stud.

c. Position the ignition coil bracket over the mounting studs.

d. Install the four locknuts and washers. Tighten the nuts to the specification in **Table 1**.

e. Attach the rectifier/regulator and trim solenoid ground wires to the coil mounting plate.

8C. On 2000-on 105 jet and 135-200 hp models, mount the replacement rectifier/regulator onto the electrical plate. The flat metal side must make good contact with the plate. Install the mounting screws and straps and tighten them to the specification in **Table 1**.

9A. On 65 jet and 75-125 hp (except 105 jet) models, connect the two red, two yellow and one gray rectifier/regulator bullet connectors to the engine wire harness.

9B. On 1998 and 1999 105 jet and 135-200 hp models, connect the two long yellow stator wires and one long red wire to the lower rectifier/regulator. The gray wire is normally not used on the lower rectifier/regulator. Connect the two short yellow stator wires, one short red wire and one gray wire to the upper rectifier/regulator.

9C. On 2000-on 105 jet and 135-200 hp models, connect the yellow wire plug, red wire and red/blue wire to each regulator. Connect the gray wire to the lower rectifier/regulator. Install the plug onto the gray wire of the upper rectifier/regulator.

10. Secure the wires to the power head or ignition coil bracket using original clamps or new tie-straps.

11. Reconnect the spark plug leads.

12. Reconnect the negative battery cable.

Stator Removal/Installation (All Integral Models)

The alternator and ignition windings of the stator are integrated into one assembly on all models.

Removal and installation procedures for all stator windings on charging, ignition and integrated models are covered under *Ignition Systems* later in this chapter.

FUSES

Fuses protect wire and electrical components from damage due to excessive current (amp) flow. A fuse that repeatedly blows indicates a problem with the circuit or component that the fuse protects.

Never install a larger fuse in an attempt to remedy the problem. Refer to Chapter Three to locate the defect causing excessive current flow in the suspect circuit.

While a visual inspection (**Figure 26**) can quickly determine if a fuse is bad, do not trust a visual inspection alone to determine if a fuse is good. Fuses can be quickly and accurately tested using an ohmmeter. A good fuse indicates continuity across the terminals. When testing fuses, do not touch both ohmmeter probes at the same time with your hands. Ohmmeters set to higher scales will typically show a false continuity reading through your body.

Fuse Locations

Fuse locations vary by model and type of fuel system. Refer to the wiring diagrams at the end of the manual and the following to locate the fuse(s).

1. On 75-125 hp (except 105 jet and 115 Optimax) models, a single 20-amp blade type fuse (**Figure 26**) is used. This fuse protects the trim switches and instruments. The fuse plugs into the holder (**Figure 27**) mounted at the top of the electrical plate on the rear starboard side of the power head.

2. On 1998 and 1999 105 jet and 135-200 hp (except Optimax) models, a single 20-amp glass cartridge fuse is used. This fuse protects the trim switches and instruments. The fuse fits within the inline holder (**Figure 28**) on the starboard side of the power head. A J-clamp retains the holder to the electrical plate.

3. On 2000-on 105 jet and 135-200 hp (except Optimax) models, three 20-amp blade type fuses (**Figure 26**) are used. The fuses fit into the holder (**Figure 29**) on the starboard side of the power head. One fuse protects the trim system switches and instruments. The other fuses protect the individual voltage rectifier/regulators.

4. On 1998-2000 135-225 hp (Optimax) models, four 20-amp blade type fuses (**Figure 26**) are used. The fuses plug into the holders on the upper rear and starboard side of the power head (**Figure 30**). One fuse protects the electric fuel pumps. One fuse protects the fuel and direct injectors. One fuse protects the trim switches and instruments. The fourth fuse protects the ignition coils and oil pump.

5. On 2001-on 115-125 hp (Optimax) models, four blade type fuses (**Figure 26**) are used. The fuses plug into a single holder on the lower rear and starboard side of the power head. A 20-amp fuse protects the trim switches and starting circuit. A 20-amp fuse protects the ignition coils. A 20-amp fuse protects the electric fuel pump, ECM and oil pump. A 15-amp fuse protects the Smart Craft gauges.

6. On 225 and 250 hp (except Optimax) models, a single 20-amp blade type fuse (**Figure 26**) is used. This fuse protects the trim switches and instruments. The fuse plugs into the holder mounted at the top of the electrical plate on the rear starboard side of the power head.

STARTING SYSTEMS

A typical electric starter system consists of the battery, starter solenoid, neutral safety switch, starter motor, starter or ignition switch and the associated wiring. On tiller models, the neutral safety switch is mounted on the engine shift linkage. On remote control models, the neutral safety switch is mounted in the remote control box. Troubleshooting of the electric starter system is covered in Chapter Three.

Starter Motor Description

Marine starter motors are very similar to those found on automotive engines. The starter motors on outboards covered in this manual (except 2001-on Optimax models) have an inertia-type drive in which external spiral splines on the armature shaft mate with internal splines on the

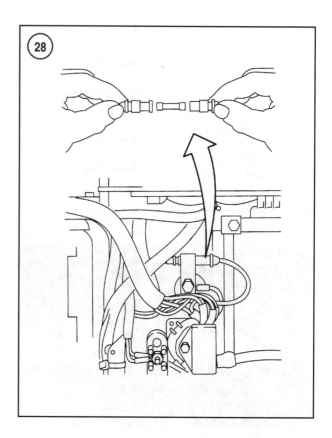

drive or bendix assembly. All 2001-on Optimax models use a starter solenoid driven bendix.

The starter motor is an intermittent duty electric motor, capable of producing a very high torque, but only for a brief time. The high amperage flow through the starter motor causes the starter motor to overheat very quickly. To prevent overheating, never operate the starter motor continuously for more than 10-15 seconds. Allow the starter motor to cool 2-3 minutes before cranking the engine again.

If the starter motor does not crank the engine, check the battery cables and terminals for loose or corroded connec-

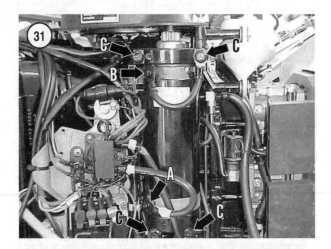

tions. Correct any problems found. If this does not solve the starting problem, refer to Chapter Three for starting system troubleshooting procedures.

CAUTION
Mercury and Mariner electric starter motors use permanent magnets glued to the main housing. Never strike a starter as this will damage the magnets, leading to total starter failure. Inspect the magnets anytime the starter is disassembled.

Replace the housing if the magnets are cracked, damaged or loose.

Starter Motor Removal/Installation
(65 Jet and 75-200 hp Except Optimax Models)

1. Disconnect the negative battery cable from the battery.
2. Disconnect and ground the spark plug leads to the power head to prevent accidental starting.
3. Disconnect the black ground cable (B, **Figure 31**, typical) from the starter motor.

4. Remove the positive cable (A, **Figure 31**, typical) from the starter motor terminal stud. This is the cable from the starter solenoid to the starter motor. The cable is normally black with yellow ends.
5. Remove the four starter motor mounting bolts (C, **Figure 31**, typical). Note the position of any additional ground cables or straps.
6. Remove the starter motor along with the upper and lower mounting clamps.
7. Remove the upper and lower mounting clamps from the starter motor.
8. Remove the rubber collars from each end of the starter motor. If present, remove the spacer from the drive end frame of the starter motor.
9. To install the starter, install the spacer over the drive end frame, if so equipped.
10. Install the rubber collars over each end of the starter motor.
11. Position the starter motor in the power head brackets. Make sure the starter cable terminal stud and ground cable bolt hole are positioned as shown in **Figure 31**.
12. Position the upper and lower mounting clamps over the starter, one at a time. Secure each bracket with two bolts. Tighten the bolts finger-tight at this time.
13. Make sure all ground cables and straps are reconnected to the starter mounting bolts and that the starter motor is correctly positioned in the mounting clamps. Tighten the mounting bolts to the specification in **Table 1**.
14. Connect the positive cable (A, **Figure 31**, typical) and the ground cable (C) to the starter motor. Tighten the cable terminal nut to the specification in **Table 1**.
15. Reconnect the spark plug leads and the negative battery cable.

Starter Motor Removal/Installation
(135-225 hp Optimax [1998-2000] and 225-250 hp
EFI and Carburetor Equipped Models)

1. Disconnect the negative battery cable.
2. Disconnect and ground the spark plug leads to the power head to prevent accidental starting.
3. Remove the positive cable (1, **Figure 32**, typical) from the starter motor terminal stud. This is the cable from the starter solenoid to the starter motor. The cable is normally black with yellow ends.
4. Remove the two starter motor mounting bolts from the top of the starter (2, **Figure 32**) and the one bolt from the bottom of the starter (3).
5. Remove the starter from the power head.
6. To install the starter, position the starter motor to the power head brackets. Install the three mounting bolts hand-tight. If the battery ground cable, other ground ca-

7

bles or ground straps are attached to one or more of the mounting bolts, reconnect the ground cable(s) at this time.

7. Tighten the three starter mounting bolts to the specification in **Table 1**.

8. Connect the positive cable to the starter motor terminal stud and tighten it to the specification in **Table 1**.

9. Reconnect the spark plug leads.

10. Reconnect the negative battery cable.

Starter Motor Removal/Installation (115-225 Optimax 2001-On Models)

1. Disconnect the negative battery cable

2. Disconnect and ground the spark plug leads to the power head to prevent accidental starting.

3. Disconnect the red or black with red sleeve, black and yellow/red wires from the starter solenoid (B, **Figure 33**).

4. Remove the four starter mounting bolts (A, **Figure 33**).

5. Remove the starter from the power head.

6. To install the starter, position the starter motor onto the power head brackets. Install the four mounting bolts hand-tight. Install the large diameter grounding wire to the upper forward mounting bolts.

7. Tighten the four mounting bolts to the specification in **Table 1**.

8. Connect the large diameter red or black with red sleeve wire to the larger diameter terminal on the solenoid (B, **Figure 33**). Tighten the cable terminal to the specification in **Table 1**. Connect the yellow/red and black wires to their respective smaller terminals on the solenoid.

9. Reconnect the spark plug leads.

10. Reconnect the negative battery cable.

Starter Motor Disassembly/Reassembly (65 Jet and 75-250 hp [Except 2001-On Optimax] Models)

Fabricate a brush retaining tool from 18-gauge sheet metal to the dimensions shown in **Figure 34**. This tool is necessary to position the brushes properly and to prevent damaging them when installing the starter end cap to the housing.

Refer to *Cleaning and Inspection* before reassembly.

1. Remove the starter motor as described previously in this chapter.

2. Place match marks on the drive end frame and end cap (**Figure 35**) for alignment reference during reassembly.

3. Remove the two through-bolts, then lightly tap on the drive end frame and lower end cap with a rubber mallet until they are both loosened.

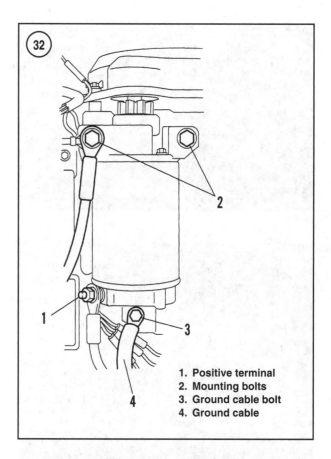

1. Positive terminal
2. Mounting bolts
3. Ground cable bolt
4. Ground cable

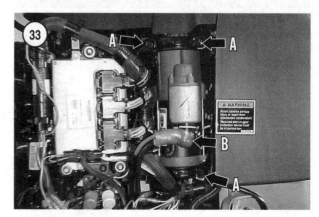

4. Remove the end cap. Do not lose the brush springs.

5. Lift the armature and drive end frame assembly from the starter housing.

NOTE
Do not remove the drive assembly in Step 6 and Step 7 unless the drive assembly or end frame requires replacement.

6. Place an appropriate size wrench on the hex area located on the back side of the drive gear. See **Figure 36**.

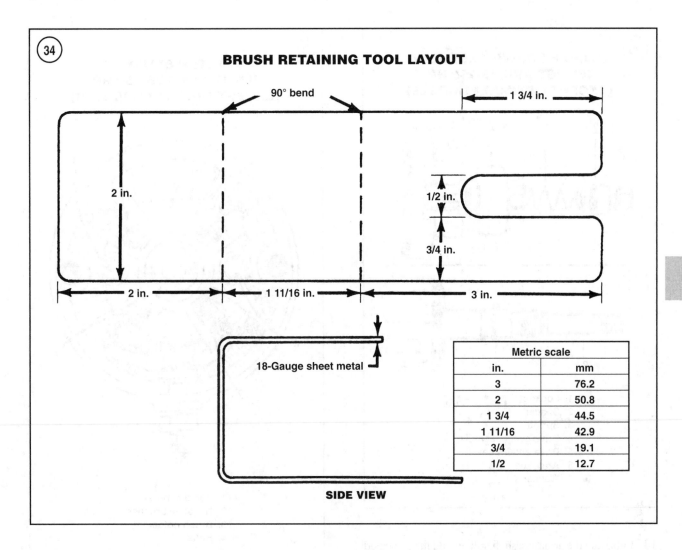

BRUSH RETAINING TOOL LAYOUT

90° bend

1 3/4 in.

2 in.

1/2 in.

3/4 in.

2 in.   1 11/16 in.   3 in.

18-Gauge sheet metal

SIDE VIEW

Metric scale	
in.	mm
3	76.2
2	50.8
1 3/4	44.5
1 11/16	42.9
3/4	19.1
1/2	12.7

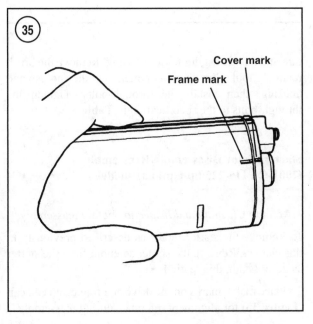

Cover mark

Frame mark

7. Remove the drive assembly lock nut and slide the drive components and drive end frame off the armature shaft.

8. Remove the screws securing the brush holder and negative brushes to the end cap. Lift the brush holder from the end cap. See **Figure 37**.

9. Remove the negative brushes from the brush holder.

10. Remove the hex nut and washers from the positive terminal. Remove the positive terminal and positive brushes from the end cap as an assembly.

11. To reassemble, install new positive brushes and the terminal assembly into the end cap. Locate the longest brush lead as shown in **Figure 38**.

12. Install the negative brushes into the brush holder. Install the brush holder into the end cap. Tighten the fasteners securely.

13. Fit the springs and brushes into the brush holder. Hold the brushes in place with the brush retaining tool (**Figure 39**).

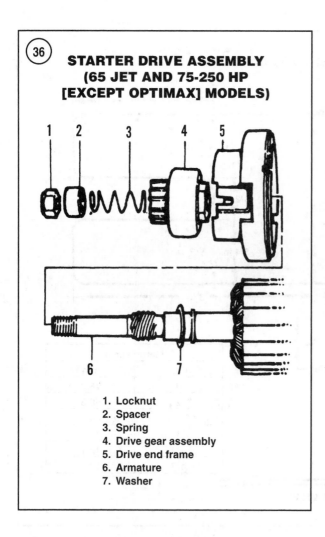

36 **STARTER DRIVE ASSEMBLY (65 JET AND 75-250 HP [EXCEPT OPTIMAX] MODELS)**

1. Locknut
2. Spacer
3. Spring
4. Drive gear assembly
5. Drive end frame
6. Armature
7. Washer

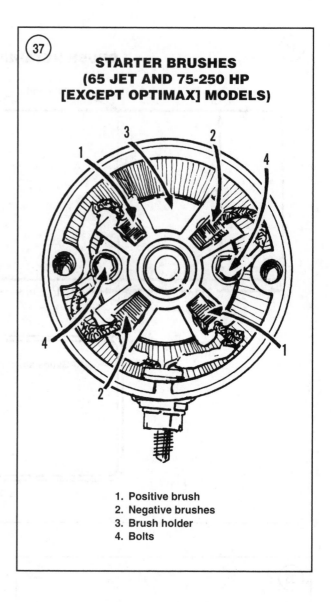

37 **STARTER BRUSHES (65 JET AND 75-250 HP [EXCEPT OPTIMAX] MODELS)**

1. Positive brush
2. Negative brushes
3. Brush holder
4. Bolts

14. Lubricate the armature shaft splines and the drive end frame bushing with one drop of SAE 10W oil each.

15. Install the drive components (**Figure 36**) onto the armature shaft. Tighten the locknut securely while holding the drive gear with an appropriate size wrench.

16. Place the armature and end frame assembly into the starter housing. Make sure the commutator end of the armature is located at the end of the housing with the magnets recessed 1 in. (25.4 mm). Align the match marks on the frame and end cap (**Figure 35**).

CAUTION
Do not over lubricate the starter bushing in Step 17. The starter will not operate properly and can be ruined if oil contaminates the commutator and brushes.

17. Lubricate the lower end cap bushing with a single drop of SAE 10W motor oil. Do not over lubricate.

18. With the brushes held in position with the brush retaining tool (**Figure 39**), install the end cap onto the arma-

ture and up against the starter housing. Remove the brush retaining tool, align the match marks on the end cap and housing, then install the through-bolts. Tighten the through-bolts to the specification in **Table 1**.

Starter Motor Disassembly/Reassembly (2001-On 115-225 hp Optimax models)

Refer to *Cleaning and Inspection* before reassembly.

1. Remove the starter motor as described previously in this chapter. Remove the starter solenoid from the starter as described in this section

2. Place match marks on the drive end frame and end cap (**Figure 35**) for alignment reference during reassembly.

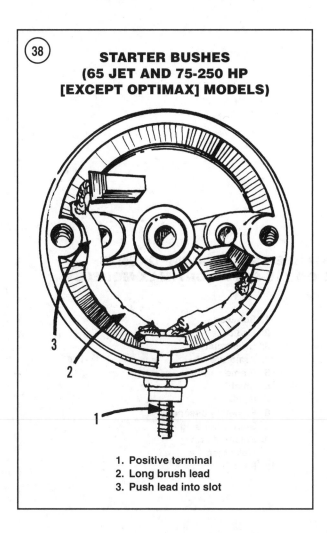

STARTER BUSHES
(65 JET AND 75-250 HP
[EXCEPT OPTIMAX] MODELS)

1. Positive terminal
2. Long brush lead
3. Push lead into slot

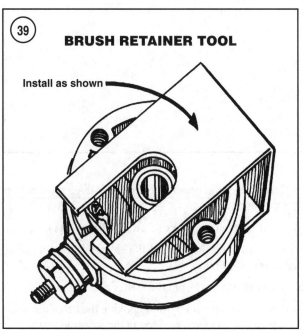

BRUSH RETAINER TOOL

Install as shown

7

3. Remove the two through-bolts, then lightly tap on the lower end cap (2, **Figure 40**) with a rubber mallet until it is loose from the frame (5).

4. Carefully remove the end cap from the frame. Pull the frame (5, **Figure 40**) and armature (4) as an assembly from the starter housing (9). Pull the armature from the frame. Grip the armature tightly to overcome the magnets in the frame.

5. Remove the shield (6, **Figure 40**) and guide (7) from the starter housing.

6. Remove the snap ring (1, **Figure 41**), then pull the drive gear (2) from the planetary shaft. Remove the planetary assembly (8, **Figure 40**) from the starter housing (9). Remove the three small gears from the planetary housing.

7. Grip the plug (12, **Figure 40**) with needlenose pliers, then pull the plug and metal disc (11) from the housing. Remove the solenoid arm (10, **Figure 40**) from the housing.

8. Remove the screws (1, **Figure 40**), then lift the brush plate (3) from the end cap (2).

9. Fit the solenoid arm (10, **Figure 40**) into the collar of the planetary shaft. Insert the planetary assembly and arm as an assembly into the starter housing. The solenoid arm must fit into the slot provided in the housing. Align the protrusions on the planetary assembly with the slots in the housing, then seat the assembly into the housing.

10. Install the metal disc (11, **Figure 40**), then plug (12), into the starter housing (9).

11. Align the splines, then fit the drive gear (2, **Figure 41**) over the planetary shaft. Install the snap ring (1, **Figure 41**) to secure the shaft and gear. The snap ring must fit into the groove on the planetary shaft.

12. Install the three gears into the planetary assembly. The gear teeth must mesh with the outer gear.

13. Align the grooves and protrusion, then insert the guide (7, **Figure 40**) into the starter housing. Install the shield (6, **Figure 40**) into the housing. The open side of the shield must face outward.

14. Carefully insert the armature (4, **Figure 40**) into the frame (5). The splined end of the armature must exit the side of the frame opposite the notch for the brush lead. Use gloves and be careful as the magnets are very powerful.

15. Carefully compress the brush springs while fitting the brush plate (3, **Figure 40**) over the commutator. Align the brush lead with the notch in the armature. Then seat the brush plate against the frame.

16. Install the end cap (2, **Figure 40**) onto the brush plate. Align the opening, then install the screws (1, **Figure 40**). Tighten the screws to the specification in **Table 1**.

17. Align the splined end of the armature shaft with the three planetary gears while installing the frame assembly.

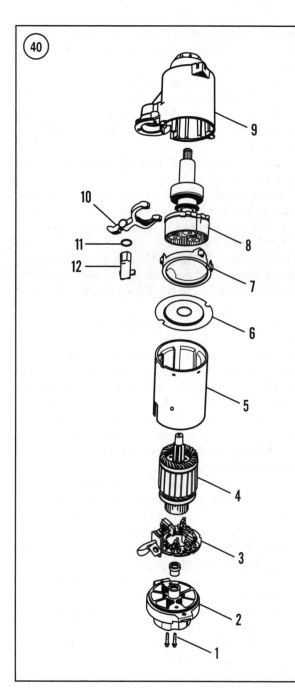

**STARTER MOTOR COMPONENTS
(2001-ON 115-225 HP OPTIMAX MODELS)**

1. Screws
2. End cap
3. Brush plate
4. Armature
5. Frame
6. Shield
7. Guide
8. Planetary assembly
9. Starter housing
10. Solenoid arm
11. Metal disc
12. Plug

18. Align the match marks (**Figure 35**), then install the through-bolts. Tighten the through-bolts to the specification in **Table 1**.

19. Install the starter solenoid as described in this section.

Starter solenoid removal/installation
(2001-on 115-225 Optimax models)

1. Remove the starter motor as described in this chapter.

2. Disconnect the brush lead from the large terminal on the solenoid.

3. Remove the three Torx screws (3, **Figure 41**).

4. Carefully slip the shaft of the solenoid from the solenoid arm (10, **Figure 40**).

5. Pull the solenoid from the starter housing.

6. Install the solenoid by first hooking the tip of the solenoid arm into the slot provided in the solenoid arm.

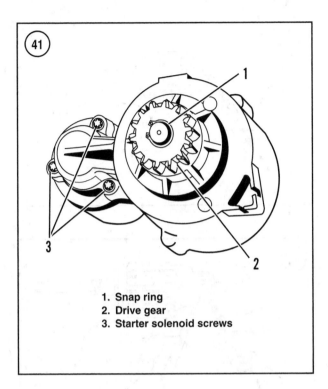

1. Snap ring
2. Drive gear
3. Starter solenoid screws

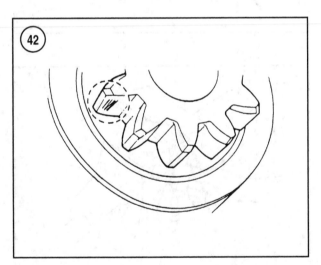

7. Move the solenoid toward and away from the starter housing. If the drive gear does not move with the solenoid, the solenoid shaft is not properly engaging the solenoid arm. Correct as needed.

8. Seat the solenoid against the starter housing. Align the brush lead terminal with the bush lead. Align the openings, then install the three Torx screws. Tighten the solenoid screws to the specification in **Table 1**.

9. Connect the brush lead to the corresponding terminal on the solenoid. Tighten the terminal nut to the specification in **Table 1**.

Cleaning and Inspection
(Except 2001-On Optimax Models)

1. Thoroughly clean all starter motor components with clean solvent, then dry them with compressed air.

2. Check the starter drive gear for chipped teeth, cracks or excessive wear. Replace drive components as necessary.

3. Inspect the brushes. Replace all brushes if any are chipped, pitted, oil soaked or worn to 1/4 in. (6.4 mm) or less.

4. Use an ohmmeter to check for continuity between each commutator segment and the armature shaft. Replace the armature if there is continuity.

5. Inspect the armature shaft bushings in the drive end frame and lower end cap for excessive wear or other damage. Replace the bushings, end frame or end cap as necessary.

6. Clean the commutator using 00 sandpaper. Clean copper particles or other contamination from between the commutator segments.

7. If the commutator is pitted, rough or worn unevenly, resurface and undercut it, or replaced it. If the armature shows water or overheat damage, check it for shorted windings using an armature growler. Most automotive electrical shops can perform commutator resurfacing and undercutting, and armature testing.

NOTE
If the armature is resurfaced, the insulation between the commutator segments must be undercut. Undercut the insulation between the commutator segments using a broken hacksaw blade or similar tool. The undercut should be the full width of the insulation and 1/32 in. (0.8 mm) deep. Do not damage the commutator segments during the process. Thoroughly clean copper particles from between the segments after undercutting. Clean and smooth the commutator after undercutting using 00 sandpaper to remove all burrs.

Cleaning and Inspection
(2001-On Optimax models)

1. Use compressed air and clean shop towels to clean the starter components. Do not use solvent. Solvent may damage the components.

2. Check the starter drive gear (**Figure 42**) for chipped teeth, cracks or excessive wear. Replace drive components as necessary.

3. Inspect the brushes. Replace all brushes if any are chipped, pitted, oil soaked or worn to 1/4 in. (6.4 mm) or less.

4. Use an ohmmeter to check for continuity between each commutator segment and the armature shaft (**Figure 43**). Check for continuity between the commutator and the armature laminations (**Figure 43**). Replace the armature if there is continuity in either test.

5. Use an ohmmeter to check for continuity between each pair of commutator segments (**Figure 44**). If the meter does not indicate continuity for each pair, the armature is electrically open and must be replaced.

6. Inspect the armature and planetary shaft bearing in the drive end frame and lower end cap for excessive wear or other damage. Replace the bearings, frame or end cap as necessary.

7. Clean the commutator using 00 sandpaper (**Figure 45**). Clean copper particles or other contamination from between the commutator segments.

8. If the commutator is pitted, rough or worn unevenly, resurface and undercut it, or replace it. If the armature shows water or overheat damage, check it for shorted windings using an armature growler. Most automotive electrical shops can perform commutator resurfacing and undercutting, and armature testing.

Starter Solenoid

Two types of starter solenoids are used on Mercury and Mariner outboard motors. See **Figure 46**. Both types of solenoids use two mounting screws, use the same type and quantity of electrical connections, and are serviced in the same manner, but they are not interchangeable.

The large terminals (**Figure 46**) always carry the electrical load from the battery to the starter motor. The large terminals have an open circuit across them when the solenoid is not energized. The large cable from the battery is usually black with red ends. The large cable from the solenoid to the starter motor is usually yellow or black with yellow ends.

The small terminals (**Figure 46**) are control circuits of the solenoid. When battery voltage is applied to these terminals, the solenoid is energized and the large terminals (**Figure 46**) have a closed circuit across them, allowing electricity to flow from the battery to the starter motor. The polarity of the small terminals is not important as long as one is positive and one is negative. One small wire is always yellow/red, the other small wire is black.

The starter solenoid is always located near the starter motor and, depending on the model, it may or may not be behind an electrical/ignition component access cover.

Refer to Chapter Three for troubleshooting procedures.

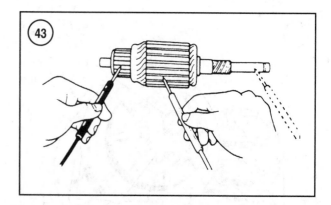

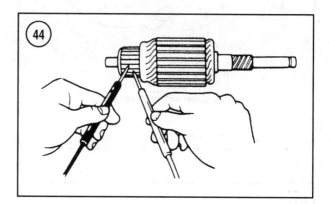

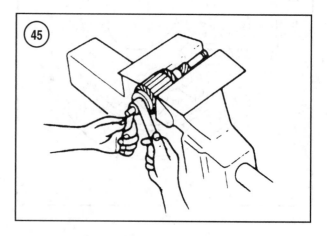

Starter solenoid removal/installation

Refer to **Figure 47** and replace the starter solenoid as follows:

1. Disconnect the negative battery cable.

2. Disconnect and ground the spark plug leads to the power head to prevent accidental starting.

3. Locate the starter solenoid on the power head. Remove the electrical/ignition component access cover, if so equipped.

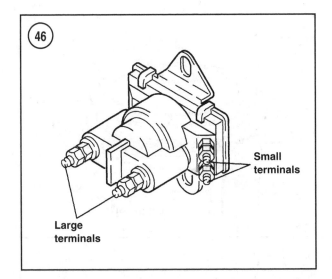

4. Note the location and position of all wires on the starter solenoid and mounting screws.

5. Remove the nuts, lock washers and electrical cables from the two large solenoid terminals.

6. Remove the nuts, lock washers and electrical leads from the two small solenoid terminals.

7. Remove the two solenoid mounting screws, then remove the solenoid from the power head or electrical bracket.

8. To install the solenoid, position the solenoid on the power head or electrical bracket. Make sure ground leads or ground straps are reconnected to the mounting screws as noted on removal. Tighten both mounting screws securely.

9. Install the small wires, lock washers and nuts. Tighten the nuts securely.

10. Install the large cables, lock washers and nuts. Tighten the nuts securely. Make sure the positive battery cable is covered with a protective boot as shown in **Figure 47** unless the engine is equipped with a plastic electrical/ignition component access cover.

11. Reinstall the electrical/ignition component access cover, if so equipped.

12. Reconnect the spark plug leads.

13. Reconnect the negative battery cable.

Neutral Safety Switch

On tiller models, the neutral safety switch is mounted on the engine shift linkage. On remote control models, the neutral safety switch is mounted in the remote control box. Refer to Chapter Fourteen for Mercury/Mariner remote control box service procedures. If the boat is equipped with an aftermarket control box, consult with the control box manufacturer for service procedures.

The neutral safety switch prevents the engine from starting in gear. The electric starter can only engage when the engine shift linkage is in neutral. A neutral safety switch should have continuity across its two terminals when the shift linkage is in neutral. The switch should indicate no continuity when the shift linkage is in gear.

IGNITION SYSTEMS

This section describes operating theory, and component removal and replacement. Refer to Chapter Three for ignition system troubleshooting procedures.

Alternator Driven Capacitor Discharge Ignition (1998 and 1999 105 Jet and 135-200 hp Except Optimax Models)

This section covers all models equipped with an alternator driven capacitor discharge ignition (ADI). Major components of the ADI system include the flywheel, stator assembly with low- and high-speed charge coils, trigger coil assembly, switch box(es), ignition coils, spark plugs and related wiring. There is one low-speed and one high-speed charge coil winding for each switch box. All 1998 and 1999 V6 models use two switch boxes. One ignition coil and one spark plug are required for each cylinder.

A series of permanent magnets are located along the inner diameter of the outer rim of the flywheel. As the flywheel rotates, alternating current (AC) is induced into the low- and high-speed charge coil windings. The low-speed windings provide the majority of the voltage required for starting and low-speed operation. The high-speed windings provide the majority of the voltage required for high-speed operation. However, the low- and high-speed winding outputs are combined in the switch box. The switch box contains a rectifier to convert the AC voltage into direct current (DC) so it can be stored in the switch box capacitor. The capacitor holds this voltage until it is released by a signal from the trigger coil(s).

Another set of permanent magnets is located along the outer diameter of the flywheel inner hub. As the flywheel rotates, low-voltage signals are induced in the trigger coil windings. This low voltage pulse is sent to the switch box where it causes an electronic switch or silicon controlled rectifier (SCR) to close, allowing the stored voltage in the capacitor to discharge to the appropriate ignition coil. The ignition coil amplifies the voltage and discharges it into the spark plug lead.

This sequence of events is duplicated for each cylinder of the engine, and is repeated with each revolution of the flywheel. One spark occurs for each cylinder for each complete flywheel rotation.

All models are equipped with mechanical spark advance. The spark advance is controlled by the rotation of the position of the trigger coil assembly in relation to the magnets on the flywheel inner hub. The trigger coil rotation is based on throttle lever position.

Component wiring

Modern outboard motor electrical systems are complex, especially on the higher output engines. For this reason, electrical wiring is color-coded, and the terminals on the components to which each wire connects are embossed with the correct wire color. Follow these identifications and the correct electrical diagram to avoid incorrect wire connections.

In addition, the routing of the wiring harness and individual wires is very important to prevent possible electrical interference and/or physical damage to the wiring harnesses from moving engine parts or vibration. Mercury outboards come from the factory with all wiring harnesses and leads properly positioned and secured with the appropriate clamps and tie-straps.

If component replacement is necessary, either carefully draw a sketch of the area to be serviced, noting the positioning of all wire harnesses involved, or photograph the area to be serviced. Either method can be invaluable for rerouting the harnesses during reassembly. Reinstall all clamps and new tie-straps where necessary to maintain the correct wire routing.

Flywheel

Never strike the flywheel with a hammer. Striking the flywheel and magnets can cause the magnets to lose their charge. Repeatedly striking a flywheel can lead to a weak,

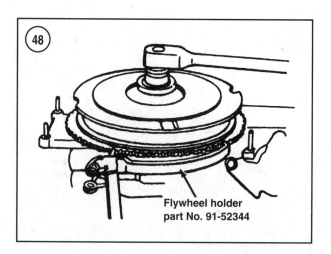

Flywheel holder
part No. 91-52344

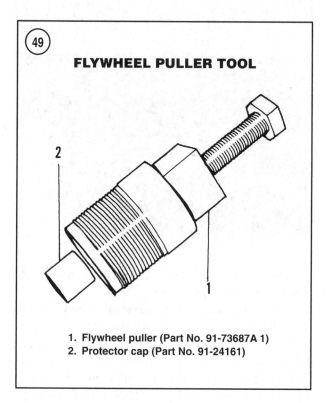

FLYWHEEL PULLER TOOL

1. Flywheel puller (Part No. 91-73687A 1)
2. Protector cap (Part No. 91-24161)

erratic spark. Crankshafts are made of hardened steel, striking the flywheel or crankshaft can also permanently damage the crankshaft. Use only the recommended flywheel puller tools or their equivalents.

**Flywheel Removal/Installation
(1998 and 1999 105 Jet and 135-200 hp
Except Optimax Models)**

1. Disconnect and ground the spark plug leads to the power head to prevent accidental starting.

hammering can damage the ignition compo-nents, the crankshaft or flywheel.

5. Install flywheel puller (part No. 91-849154T1) (1, **Figure 49**) into the flywheel. Hold the puller with a wrench and tighten the puller screw until the flywheel dislodges from the crankshaft taper. See **Figure 50**.

6. Lift the flywheel off the crankshaft.

7. Inspect and clean the flywheel and crankshaft as described in this chapter.

8. To reinstall the flywheel, place the flywheel onto the crankshaft while aligning the splines in the flywheel with the crankshaft splines.

9. Install the flywheel nut and washer. Hold the flywheel using the flywheel holder and tighten the flywheel nut to the specification in **Table 1**.

10. Install the flywheel cover, reconnect the negative battery cable and reconnect the spark plug leads.

Flywheel Inspection

1. Inspect the entire flywheel for cracks, chips, mechanical damage, wear and corrosion.

2. Carefully inspect the flywheel and crankshaft tapers for cracks, wear, corrosion and metal transfer.

3. Inspect the flywheel and crankshaft key slots for wear or damage.

4. Inspect the flywheel for loose, cracked or damaged magnets (**Figure 51**). Replace the flywheel if the magnets are loose, cracked or damaged.

> *WARNING*
> *Replace defective flywheels. A defective fly-wheel can fly apart at high engine speed, throwing fragments over a large area. Do not attempt to use or repair a defective fly-wheel.*

5. Clean the flywheel and crankshaft tapers with a suitable solvent and blow them dry with compressed air. The tapers must be clean, dry and free of oil or other contamination.

Stator Assembly Removal/Installation (1998 and 1999 105 Jet and 135-200 hp Except Optimax Models)

The stator assembly is a one-piece integrated unit, containing both the ignition stator windings and the alternator coils. **Figure 52** shows a typical stator. All stator assemblies are mounted under the flywheel.

All 1998 and 1999 models use a unique black stator assembly that has two sets of ignition stator windings (two

2. Disconnect the negative battery cable and remove the flywheel cover.

3. Hold the flywheel using flywheel holder (**Figure 48**) part No. 91-52344 or an equivalent. Remove the flywheel nut and washer.

> *CAUTION*
> *Do not remove the flywheel without using a protector cap (2, **Figure 49**) or crankshaft damage can occur.*

4. Install crankshaft protector cap (2, **Figure 49**) onto the end of the crankshaft. Use a small amount of cold grease to hold the protector cap in position.

> *CAUTION*
> *Do not apply heat to or strike the puller screw with a hammer in Step 5. Heat and/or*

7

low-speed and two high-speed windings) and two sets of alternator coil windings. The ignition windings are separated by a yellow band on one set of ignition stator wires. All the yellow banded wires must be routed to the outer switch box. The alternator coil wires are identified by wire length. The two long wires go to the lower rectifier/regulator and the two short wires go to the upper rectifier/regulator.

This section covers stator replacement. Refer to the end of the manual for wiring diagrams.

1. Remove the flywheel as described in this chapter.

2. Note the orientation of the stator assembly and stator leads before proceeding.

3. Remove the four stator mounting screws.

NOTE
A yellow band separates the two ignition stator windings. All yellow banded wires must go to the outer switch box.

4. Remove the switch box mounting screws. Separate the outer and inner switch boxes. Do not lose the spacers located between the switch boxes (**Figure 53**).

5. Disconnect the four ignition stator wires. Then disconnect the stator ground (black) wires from the switch box mounting screws or power head.

6. Disconnect the two yellow alternator wires from each rectifier/regulator bullet connector (a total of four yellow wires).

7. Remove clamps or tie-straps securing the stator wires to the power head or wiring harness. Then remove the stator assembly from the engine.

CAUTION
Stator mounting position is critical on most models. Make sure the stator is in its original position unless instructions or decals included with the replacement stator show otherwise. All stator positions described are referenced by clock position with the front of the engine being 12 o'clock. Also make sure the stator wiring is not pinched between the stator and power head during installation.

8. To install the stator, position the stator as noted on removal. Make sure none of the stator windings or harnesses are contacting the power head.

9. Clean the stator mounting screws with Locquic Primer (part No. 92-59327-1) and allow them to air dry. Apply Loctite 271 threadlocking compound (part No. 92-809819) to the threads of the screws.

10. Install the stator screws and tighten them evenly to the specification in **Table 1**.

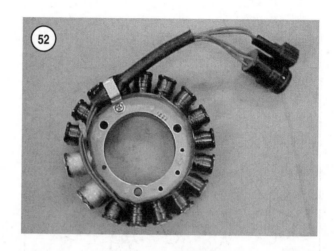

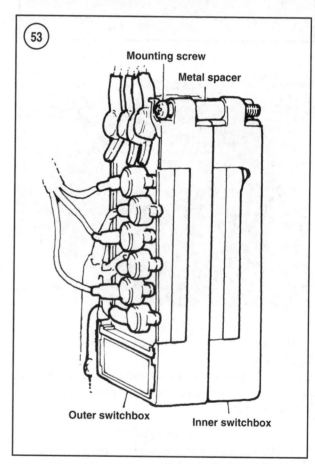

11. Route the stator wiring harness as noted during removal. Secure the harness to the power head or other harnesses with clamps and/or new tie-straps.

12. Connect all stator wires to their respective connectors or terminals on the switch box and rectifier/regulators.

13. Install the outer switch box over the inner switch box. Make sure the spacers are properly located and install the

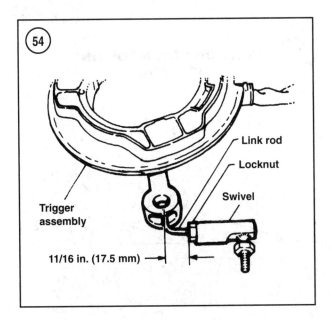

Figure 54
Link rod
Locknut
Swivel
Trigger assembly
11/16 in. (17.5 mm)

8. Verify the link rod dimension as shown in **Figure 54**. Position the swivel to provide 11/16 in. (17.5 mm) between the lock nut and the center of the trigger pivot as shown in **Figure 54**, then tighten the locknut securely.

9. Connect the link rod swivel to the spark advance lever. Install the lock nut and tighten securely.

NOTE
A yellow band separates the two trigger coil harnesses. All yellow-banded wires must go to the outer switch box.

10. Route both trigger wiring harnesses as noted during removal. Install the necessary clamps and/or tie-straps to secure the harness.

NOTE
Make sure the trigger coil rotates freely with the control linkage after installation is complete.

11. Connect the trigger wires to their respective switch box terminal studs. The trigger wires with the yellow band must be connected to the outer switch box.

12. Reinstall the stator assembly as described previously in this section. Make sure all stator wires are clamped and/or tie-strapped in place.

13. Install the outer switch box over the inner switch box. Make sure all the spacers are properly located and install the two switch boxes as described in this section. Make sure all ground wires are reconnected to the switch boxes.

CAUTION
The switch boxes must be grounded to the power head or switch box damage will occur when the engine is cranked or started.

14. Reinstall the flywheel as described previously in this section.

15. Refer to Chapter Five and perform the synchronization and linkage adjustments.

switch boxes as described in this section. Make sure all ground wires are connected to the switch boxes.

14. Install the flywheel as described in this chapter.

Trigger Coil Removal/Installation (1998 and 1999 105 Jet and 135-200 hp Except Optimax Models)

The trigger coil assembly is mounted under the flywheel. Note the trigger wiring harness routing for reference during installation. After trigger coil installation, refer to Chapter Five and perform the synchronization and linkage adjustments.

1. Remove the flywheel as described in this chapter.

2. Remove the stator as described in this section, but do not disconnect the stator electrical wires. Lift the stator off the power head and set it to one side.

3. Remove the lock nut securing the link rod to the spark advance lever, then pull the link rod from the arm.

4. Remove the switch box mounting screws. Separate the outer and inner switch boxes. Do not lose the spacers located between the switch boxes. See **Figure 53**.

5. Disconnect the three trigger wires (white, brown and purple) from each switch box. Remove clamps and tie-straps securing the trigger coil wiring harness. Remove the trigger coil assembly from the power head.

6. If necessary, transfer the link rod and swivel assembly to the new trigger assembly.

7. To install the trigger, lubricate the trigger bearing surfaces with 2-4-C Multi-Lube (part No. 92-825407). Then position the trigger assembly on the power head boss.

Ignition Coil Removal/Installation (1998 and 1999 105 Jet and 135-200 hp Except Optimax Models)

The six ignition coils are mounted on the electrical plate on the rear of the power head. Each ignition coil primary wire is green, with or without a colored stripe. The color of the green primary wire determines the engine firing order. Each switch box primary wire must be connected to the correct ignition coil. Note the primary wire color on all cylinders before disconnecting any wires.

7

Refer to the end of the manual for wiring diagrams and refer to **Figure 55** for a typical ignition coil installation.

1. Disconnect the spark plug leads from the spark plugs.

2. Disconnect the green primary wire from the each ignition coil positive terminal. Disconnect the black ground wire from each coil negative terminal.

3. Remove the screws (2, **Figure 55**) and washers holding each coil cover and coil in place. Remove the covers and coils from the engine.

4. If necessary, cut the tie-strap securing the spark plug boot to each ignition coil. Remove the spark plug lead from the coil.

5. To install the coils, connect the spark plug lead to each ignition coil. Apply Quicksilver Ignition Coil Insulating Compound (part No. 92-41669) to the boots to create a water-tight seal. Secure each boot to the coil using a new tie-strap.

6. Fit the ignition coils into the cover. Position the coil and cover onto the power head, and secure them with the screws and washers. Tighten the screws to the specification in **Table 1**.

7. Connect the switch box green primary wire to each coil positive terminal. Connect the black ground wire to each coil negative terminal. Tighten the screws to the specification in **Table 1**.

8. Coat the coil primary terminal connections with Quicksilver Liquid Neoprene (part no. 92-25711-2). Reconnect the spark plug leads to the spark plugs.

Switch Box Removal/Installation (105 Jet and 135-200 hp Except Optimax Models)

All terminal stud style switch boxes have the wire color code for each stud embossed into the switch box body. All bullet connector style switch boxes use wires that are always connected to another wire with the exact same color code. It is still a good practice to note the wire routing and terminal connections before disconnecting any wires. Correct wire routing is very important to prevent insulation and wire damage from heat, vibration or interference with moving parts.

The dual switch box arrangement can be especially confusing. Trigger coils and stator coils use wires that have yellow bands on one set of wires. The yellow banded wires always attach to the outer switch box.

Refer to the end of the manual for wiring diagrams.

Terminal stud switch boxes use leads with rubber boots to protect the terminal connection. Pull the rubber boot away from the switch boxes to access the terminal nut.

1. Disconnect the negative battery cable.

2. Disconnect and ground the spark plug leads to the power head to prevent accidental starting.

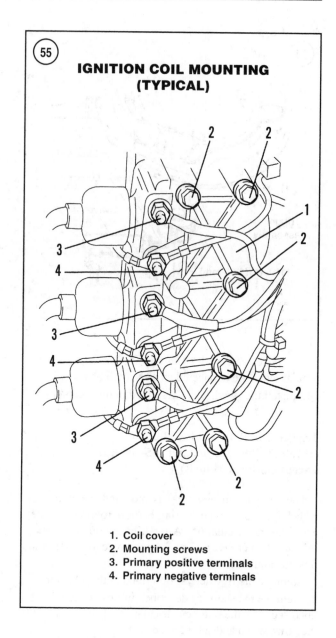

55

IGNITION COIL MOUNTING (TYPICAL)

1. Coil cover
2. Mounting screws
3. Primary positive terminals
4. Primary negative terminals

3. Remove the two switch box mounting screws (**Figure 53**). Separate the inner and outer switch boxes and remove the metal spacers between the switch boxes (**Figure 53**).

4. Note the position and routing of each switch box wire. The color code for each terminal is embossed in the switch box body. The outer switch box stator wires are shown as blue and red even though they are actually red/white and blue/white.

5. Unsnap the neoprene cap on each wire terminal. Pull the caps back and remove the terminal nuts. Disconnect the wires from the terminals and remove the switch boxes.

6. To install the switch boxes, reconnect the wires to the appropriate switch box terminals. The yellow banded wires must be connected to the outer switch box.

7. Connect the ground wire to each switch box. Tighten the ground screws securely.

8. Apply Loctite 242 threadlocking adhesive (part No. 92-809821) to the threads of the switch box mounting screws. Install the switch boxes to the power head using the mounting screws and spacers. Make sure *both* switch boxes are properly grounded to the power head or the switch boxes will be damaged when the engine is cranked or started.

9. Tighten the switch box mounting screws to the specification in **Table 1**.

10. Reconnect the spark plug leads and the negative battery cable.

Rpm Limit Module Removal/Installation

The 105 and 140 jet models are equipped with a rpm limit module. The rpm limit module is connected to the switch box stop circuit (black/yellow). If engine speed exceeds the preprogrammed limit, the rpm limit module momentarily shorts the black/yellow wire to ground, limiting engine speed. There are four wires on the rpm limit module. The purple wire is power for the module from the key switch. The brown wire is connected to the brown trigger coil wire and is an engine speed signal for the module. The black/yellow wire is connected to the switch box stop circuit and is shorted to ground by the module to control engine speed by switching the ignition system on and off. The black wire is the ground path for the module.

1. Disconnect the negative battery cable.

2. Disconnect the spark plug leads and ground them to the power head to prevent accidental starting.

3. Remove the three limit mounting screws.

4. Note the position and routing of each limit module lead. Disconnect the black/yellow and brown leads from the switch box. Disconnect the purple lead from the terminal on the starboard side of the power head.

5. Remove the limit module from the power head. Clean corrosion from the mounting screw holes.

6. To install the limit module, reconnect the black/yellow and brown wires to the appropriate switch box terminals. Connect the purple wire to the terminal on the starboard side of the power head. Slip one of the mounting screws through the black module lead.

7. Install the module to the power head and secure it with the three screws. One of the mounting screws must pass through the terminal for the black module lead. Securely tighten the mounting screws.

8. Reconnect the spark plug leads and the negative battery cable.

Detonation Control Module Removal/Installation

The detonation control module is only used on 200 hp (except Optimax) models with electronic fuel injection. The module monitors electrical impulses produced by the detonation sensor. The module is mounted on top of the power head and to the rear of the flywheel. The detonation sensor is mounted near the No. 2 spark plug.

1. Disconnect the negative battery cable.

2. Disconnect the spark plug leads and ground them to the power head to prevent accidental starting.

3. Remove the three mounting screws.

4. Note the position and routing of each limit module wire.

   a. Disconnect the white/blue wire from the detonation sensor.

   b. Disconnect the purple wire from the terminal block on the starboard side of the power head.

   c. Disconnect the white/black wire from its connection to the engine wire harness. Disconnect the white/black, gray/white and green wires from the bullet connectors to the engine wire harness.

5. Remove the module from the power head. Clean corrosion from the mounting screw holes.

6. To install the limit module, reconnect the wires to their respective terminals as described in Step 4.

7. Slip one of the mounting screws through the black module wire. Install the module to the power head and secure it with the three screws. One of the mounting screws must pass through the terminal for the black module wire. Tighten the mounting screws to the specification in **Table 1**.

8. Reconnect the spark plug leads and the negative battery cable.

CAPACITOR DISCHARGE MODULE (CDM) IGNITION

CDM ignition systems combine the switch box and ignition coil functions into one module, called the CDM. There is one CDM for each cylinder. A rectifier in each CDM transforms the ignition stator AC voltage into DC voltage so it can be stored in the CDM capacitor. The capacitor holds the voltage until the silicon controlled rectifier (SCR), which is an electronic switch, releases the voltage to the integral ignition coil primary windings. Depending on the engine model, the SCR is triggered by either a conventional trigger coil, ignition control module or an electronic control module (ECM). The ignition coil transforms the relatively low voltage from the capacitor into voltage high enough (45,000 volts) to jump the spark plug gap and ignite the air/fuel mixture.

7

The CDM ignition system is used on the following models:

1. 65 jet and 75-123 hp (except 1998 and 1999 105 jet and 115 Optimax) models.
2. 2000-on 105 jet and 135-200 hp (except Optimax) models.
3. 225 and 250 hp (except Optimax models).

Refer to Chapter Three for troubleshooting procedures on all CDM ignition systems. Refer to the end of the manual for wiring diagrams.

Spark Plugs

There is one spark plug for each cylinder. Only use the recommended spark plugs or engine damage may occur. Resistor or suppressor plugs reduce radio frequency interference (RFI) emissions that can cause interference with electrical accessories. Use the recommended RFI spark plug if RFI is suspected of causing interference or malfunction of electrical accessories.

Stop Circuit

The stop circuit is connected to one end of the capacitor in each CDM. When the stop circuit is connected to ground, the capacitor is shorted and cannot store electricity. At this point there is no voltage available to send to the ignition coil windings and the ignition system ceases producing spark. The stop circuit must have an open circuit to ground for the engine to run. The stop circuit wires are black/yellow.

The 65 jet, 60 jet and 100-125 hp models are equipped with an rpm limit module. The rpm limit module is connected to the CDM's stop circuit (black/yellow). When engine speed exceeds the preprogrammed limit, the rpm limit module momentarily shorts the black/yellow wire to ground, limiting engine speed.

Component Wiring

Modern outboard motor electrical systems are complex, especially on the higher output engines. For this reason, electrical wiring is color coded, and the terminals on the components to which each wire connects are embossed with the correct wire color. When used with the correct electrical diagram, incorrect wire connections should be eliminated.

The routing of the wiring harness and individual wires is very important to prevent possible electrical interference and/or physical damage to the wiring harnesses from moving engine parts or vibration. Mercury/Mariner out-

boards come from the factory with all wiring harnesses and wires properly positioned and secured with the appropriate clamps and tie-straps.

If component replacement is necessary, carefully draw a sketch of the area to be serviced, noting the positioning of all wire harnesses involved, or photograph the area to be serviced. Either method is invaluable when rerouting the harnesses for reassembly. Reinstall all clamps and new tie-straps where necessary to maintain the correct wire routing.

Flywheel

Never strike the flywheel with a hammer. Striking the flywheel and magnets can cause the magnets to lose their magnetism. Repeatedly striking a flywheel can lead to a weak, erratic spark. Crankshafts are made of hardened steel; therefore, striking the flywheel or crankshaft can also permanently damage the crankshaft. Only use the recommended flywheel puller tools or their equivalents.

Removal/installation

1. Disconnect and ground the spark plug leads to the power head to prevent accidental starting.
2. Remove the flywheel cover.
3. On 225 and 250 hp (except Optimax) models, remove the timing pointer from the top of the starter motor drive end frame. Remove the alternator belt as described in this chapter under *Alternator removal/installation*.
4. Hold the flywheel using a flywheel holder (part No. 91-52344 or an equivalent). See **Figure 48**.

CAUTION
*To prevent crankshaft damage, do not remove the flywheel without using a crankshaft protector cap (2, **Figure 49**).*

5. Install the crankshaft protective cap (2, **Figure 49**) onto the end of the crankshaft. Use cold grease to hold the protective cap in place.

CAUTION
Never apply heat or strike the puller screw with a hammer during flywheel removal. Heat and/or hammering can damage the ignition components, flywheel and crankshaft.

6. Install the recommended flywheel puller into the flywheel.

    a. On 65 jet and 75-125 hp (except 105 jet) models, use puller part No. 91-73687A1.

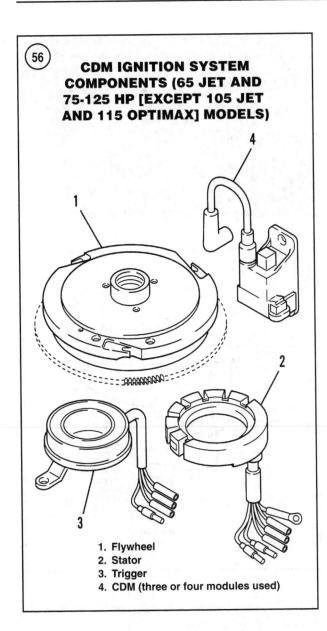

56

CDM IGNITION SYSTEM COMPONENTS (65 JET AND 75-125 HP [EXCEPT 105 JET AND 115 OPTIMAX] MODELS)

1. Flywheel
2. Stator
3. Trigger
4. CDM (three or four modules used)

b. On 105 jet and 135-200 hp (except Optimax) models, use puller part No. 91-849154T.

c. On 225 and 250 hp (except Optimax) models, use puller part No. 91-73687A1.

7. Hold the puller with one wrench and tighten the puller screw (**Figure 50**) until the flywheel dislodges from the crankshaft taper.

8. Lift the flywheel off the crankshaft. Remove the flywheel key, if so equipped, from the crankshaft slot.

9. Inspect and clean the flywheel key, if so equipped, and crankshaft as described in this chapter.

10. To install the flywheel, insert the flywheel key, if so equipped, into the crankshaft keyslot.

11A. On models with a flywheel key, align the flywheel key slot with the flywheel key and place the flywheel onto the crankshaft.

11B. On models without a flywheel key, align the splines in the flywheel with the splines on the crankshaft taper.

12. Install the flywheel nut and washer. Hold the flywheel with a flywheel holder and tighten the flywheel nut to the specification in **Table 1**.

13. On 225 and 250 hp (except Optimax) models, install the timing pointer. Refer to Chapter Five for timing pointer adjustment. Install the alternator belt as described in this chapter under *Alternator removal/installation*.

14. Install the flywheel cover.

15. Reconnect the spark plug leads to the spark plugs.

Flywheel inspection

1. Inspect the entire flywheel for cracks, chips, mechanical damage, wear and corrosion.

2. Carefully inspect the flywheel and crankshaft tapers for cracks, wear, corrosion and metal transfer.

3. Inspect the flywheel and crankshaft key slots for wear or damage.

4. Carefully inspect the flywheel key, if so equipped. Replace the key if it is in questionable condition.

5. Inspect the flywheel for loose, cracked or damaged magnets (**Figure 51**). Replace the flywheel if the magnets are loose, cracked or damaged.

> *WARNING*
> *Replace a defective flywheel. A defective flywheel may fly apart at high engine speed, throwing fragments over a large area. Do not attempt to use or repair a defective flywheel.*

6. Clean the flywheel and crankshaft tapers with a suitable solvent and blow them dry with compressed air. The tapers must be clean, dry and free of oil or other contamination.

CDM Ignition (65 Jet and 75-125 hp [Except 105 Jet and 115 Optimax] Models)

This CDM ignition system is an alternator driven, capacitor discharge module system with mechanical spark advance.

The major components include:

1. *Flywheel*—The flywheel (1, **Figure 56**) inner magnet is for the trigger coil timing information. The outer magnets are for the ignition stator and battery charging stator.

7

2. *Ignition stator (charge) coils*—The stator (2, **Figure 56**, typical) consists of one winding around three bobbins. The ignition stator windings are not grounded to the power head. The ignition stator provides power to the CDMs. Stator output is always AC (alternating current) voltage.

NOTE
The ignition stator circuit must be complete from the stator to a CDM and back to the stator through a different CDM for the system to function. See Chapter Three for troublshooting procedures.

3. *Trigger coil*—The trigger coil (3, **Figure 56**) tells the CDMs (4, **Figure 56**) when to fire. The trigger coil is rotated by mechanical linkage to change the trigger's position relative to the flywheel. This movement advances or retards the ignition spark timing.

4. *CDMs, spark plugs and stop circuit*—All of these components function as described at the beginning of this section.

Stator removal/installation

The stator assembly is a one-piece integrated unit, containing both the ignition stator windings and the alternator coils. The stator assembly is mounted under the flywheel. Alternator coil leads are always yellow. Ignition stator wires are green/white and white/green.

1. Remove the flywheel as described in this chapter.

2. Note the orientation of the stator assembly and all stator wires before proceeding.

3. Remove the stator assembly mounting screws.

4. Disconnect the green/white and white/green ignition stator wires from the wiring harness bullet connectors. Then disconnect the two yellow alternator coil wires from the rectifier/regulator bullet connectors (**Figure 57**).

5. Remove any clamps or tie-straps securing the stator wires to the power head, electrical bracket or wiring harness. Then remove the stator assembly from the engine.

CAUTION
Make sure the stator is repositioned in its original position unless instructions or decals included with the replacement stator show otherwise. The stator windings and wiring harness must not be crushed between the stator and the power head.

6. To install the stator, position the stator on the power head as noted on removal. Make sure none of the stator windings or harnesses are contacting the power head.

7. Clean the stator mounting screws with Locquic Primer (part No. 92-59327-1) and allow them to air dry. Apply

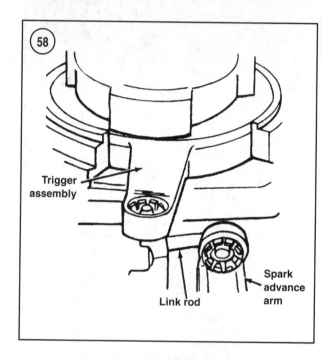

Loctite 222 threadlocking adhesive (part No. 92-809818) to the threads of the screws.

8. Install the stator screws and tighten them evenly to the specification in **Table 1**.

9. Route the stator wiring harness as noted on removal. Secure the harness to the power head, electrical bracket or other harnesses with clamps and/or new tie-straps.

10. Connect all stator wires disconnected in Step 4 to their respective bullet connectors.

11. Reinstall the flywheel as described previously in this section.

Trigger coil removal/installation

The trigger coil assembly is mounted under the flywheel. Note the trigger wiring harness routing for refer-

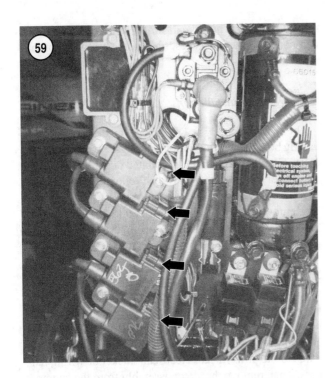

ence during installation. After trigger coil installation, refer to Chapter Five and perform the synchronization and linkage adjustments.

1. Remove the flywheel as described previously in this section.

2. Remove the stator as described previously in this section, but do not disconnect the stator electrical leads. Lift the stator off the power head and set it to one side.

3. Disconnect the trigger link rod ball and socket connector from the spark control arm. See **Figure 58**.

4. Disconnect the trigger wires from the wiring harness bullet connectors. If so equipped, remove the screw securing the trigger coil ground wire to the power head or electrical bracket.

5. If necessary, transfer the link rod assembly to the new trigger coil assembly.

6. To install the trigger, lubricate the trigger bearing surfaces with 2-4-C Multi-Lube (part No. 92-825407). Then position the trigger assembly on the power head boss.

7. Connect the trigger link rod ball and socket connector to the spark control arm.

8. Route the trigger wires as noted during removal. Install the necessary clamps and/or tie-straps to secure the harness.

NOTE
Make sure the trigger coil rotates freely with the control linkage after the installation is complete.

9. Connect the trigger wires to the appropriate wiring harness bullet connectors. If so equipped, secure the trigger coil ground wire to the power head or electrical bracket. Tighten the ground screw securely.

10. Reinstall the stator assembly as described previously in this section. Make sure all stator wires are clamped and/or tie-strapped in place.

11. Reinstall the flywheel as described previously in this section.

12. Refer to Chapter Five and perform the synchronization and linkage adjustments.

CDMs removal/installation

The CDMs are mounted to the electrical plate on the rear and starboard side of the power head. Refer to **Figure 59** for this procedure.

1. Disconnect and ground the spark plug leads connected to the power head to prevent accidental starting.

2. Disconnect the four-pin connector (**Figure 59**) from each CDM to be removed.

3. Remove the two CDM mounting bolts from each module. Then remove the module(s) from the engine.

4. To install the CDM(s), position each module in its mounted position and secure it with two screws. Tighten both mounting screws to the specification in **Table 1**.

5. Reconnect the four-pin connector to each module.

6. Reconnect the spark plug leads.

Rpm limit module removal/installation

All 65 jet, 80 jet and 100-125 hp models are equipped with an rpm limit module. The rpm limit module is connected to the CDM stop circuit black/yellow wire. When engine speed exceeds the preprogrammed limit, the rpm limit module momentarily shorts the black/yellow wire to ground, limiting engine speed. There are four wires on the rpm limit module. The purple wire is power for the module from the key switch. The brown wire is connected to the brown trigger coil wire and is an engine speed signal for the module. The black/yellow wire is connected to the CDM stop circuit and is shorted to ground by the module to control engine speed by switching the ignition system on and off. The black wire is the ground path for the module.

Locate the rpm limit module on the power head. The module is typically mounted in the lower cowl area on the starboard side of the engine. Verify the location by matching the color of the wires. It may be necessary to split the lower cowl to access the module.

1. Disconnect the negative battery cable.

2. Disconnect and ground the spark plug leads to the power head to prevent accidental starting.

3. Disconnect the brown, purple and black/yellow wires at the module bullet connectors. If necessary, cut any tie-straps securing the module wires.

4. Remove the screw securing the black ground wire to the power head.

5. Remove the two module mounting screws, then remove the module from the power head or electrical bracket.

6. To install the module, position the module on the power head or electrical bracket and secure it with two screws. Tighten the screws securely.

7. Connect the module ground wire to the power head. Tighten the ground screw securely.

8. Connect the brown, purple and black/yellow wires to the module bullet connectors. If necessary, secure the wires with a new tie-strap.

9. Reconnect the spark plug leads and the negative battery cable.

CDM ignition (2000-on 105 Jet and 135-200 hp [Except Optimax] Models)

This CDM ignition system is an alternator driven, capacitor discharge module system with mechanical spark advance.

The major components include:

1. *Flywheel*—The flywheel (1, **Figure 60**) inner magnet is for the trigger coil timing information. The outer magnets are for the ignition stator and battery charging stator.

2. *Ignition stator (charge) coils*—The stator (3, **Figure 60**) consists of one winding around three bobbins. The ignition stator windings are not grounded to the power head. The ignition stator provides power to the CDMs. Stator output is always AC (alternating current) voltage.

> *NOTE*
> *The ignition stator circuit must be complete from the stator to a CDM and back to the stator through a different CDM for the system to function. See Chapter Three for troubleshooting procedures.*

3. *Trigger coil*—The trigger coil (2, **Figure 60**) tells the ignition control module (4) when to fire the individual CDMs (5). The trigger coil is rotated by mechanical linkage to change the trigger's position relative to the flywheel. This movement advances or retards the ignition spark timing.

4. *CDMs, spark plugs and stop circuit*—All of these components function as described at the beginning of this section.

Stator removal/installation

The stator assembly is a one-piece integrated unit, containing both the ignition stator windings and the alternator coils. The stator assembly is mounted under the flywheel. Alternator coil wires are always yellow. Ignition stator wires are green/white and white/green.

1. Remove the flywheel as described in this chapter.

2. Note the orientation of the stator assembly and all stator wires before proceeding.

3. Remove the stator assembly mounting screws.

4. Disconnect the green/white and white/green ignition stator wires from the wiring harness connectors (**Figure 61**). Then disconnect the yellow alternator coil wire connectors from the rectifier/regulator bullet connectors.

5. Remove any clamps or tie-straps securing the stator wires to the power head, electrical bracket or wiring harness. Then remove the stator assembly from the engine.

> *CAUTION*
> *Make sure the stator is repositioned in its original position unless instructions or decals included with the replacement stator show otherwise. The stator windings and wiring harness must not be crushed between the stator and the power head.*

6. To install the stator, position the stator on the power head as noted on removal. Make sure none of the stator windings or harnesses are contacting the power head.

7. Clean the stator mounting screws with Locquic Primer (part No. 92-59327-1) and allow them to air dry. Apply Loctite 222 threadlocking adhesive (part No. 92-809818) to the threads of the screws.

8. Install the stator screws and tighten them evenly to the specification in **Table 1**.

9. Route the stator wiring harness as noted on removal. Secure the harness to the power head, electrical bracket or other harnesses with clamps and/or new tie-straps.

10. Connect all stator wires disconnected in Step 4 to their respective bullet connectors.

11. Reinstall the flywheel as described previously in this section.

Trigger coil removal/installation

The trigger coil assembly is mounted under the flywheel. Note the trigger wiring harness routing for refer-

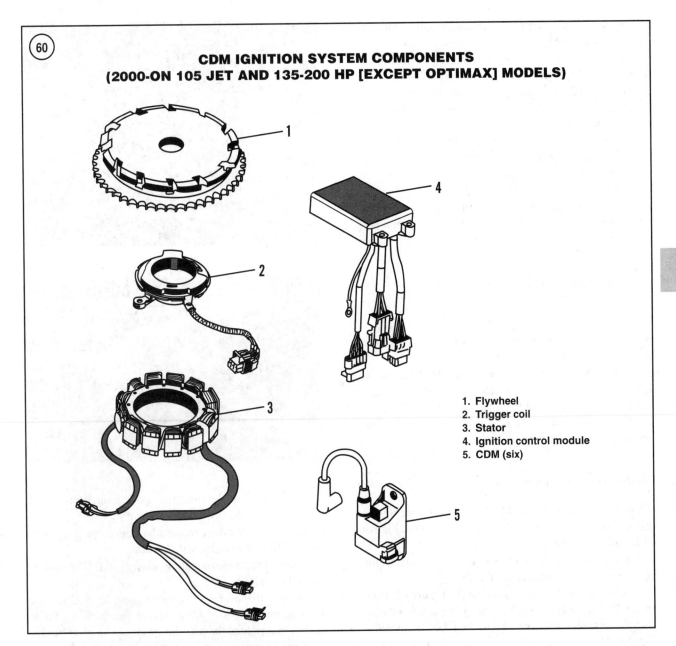

**CDM IGNITION SYSTEM COMPONENTS
(2000-ON 105 JET AND 135-200 HP [EXCEPT OPTIMAX] MODELS)**

1. Flywheel
2. Trigger coil
3. Stator
4. Ignition control module
5. CDM (six)

ence during installation. After trigger coil installation, refer to Chapter Five and perform the synchronization and linkage adjustments.

1. Remove the flywheel as described previously in this section.

2. Remove the stator as described previously in this section, but do not disconnect the stator electrical wires. Lift the stator off the power head and set it to one side.

3. Disconnect the trigger link rod ball and socket connector from the spark control arm. See **Figure 54**.

4. Disconnect the trigger coil harness from the wiring harness bullet connectors (**Figure 61**).

5. If necessary, transfer the link rod assembly to the new trigger coil assembly.

6. To install the trigger, lubricate the trigger bearing surfaces with 2-4-C Multi-Lube (part No. 92-825407). Then position the trigger assembly on the power head boss.

7. Verify the link rod dimension as shown in **Figure 54**. Position the swivel to provide 11/16 in. (17.5 mm) between the lock nut and the center of the trigger pivot as shown in **Figure 54**, then tighten the locknut securely.

8. Connect the link rod swivel to the spark advance lever. Install the lock nut and tighten it securely.

9. Route the trigger wires as noted during removal. Install the necessary clamps and/or tie-straps to secure the harness.

NOTE
Make sure the trigger coil rotates freely with the control linkage after the installation is complete.

10. Connect the trigger coil harness to the engine wire harness connectors.

11. Reinstall the stator assembly and flywheel as described previously in this section. Make sure all stator wires are clamped and/or tie-strapped in place.

12. Refer to Chapter Five and perform the synchronization and linkage adjustments.

CDMs removal/installation

The CDMs are mounted to the electrical plate on the rear and starboard side of the power head. Refer to **Figure 62** for this procedure.

1. Disconnect and ground the spark plug leads to the power head to prevent accidental starting.

2. Disconnect the four-pin connector (B, **Figure 62**) from each CDM to be removed. It is not necessary to disconnect the engine wire harness from the CDM harness (A, **Figure 62**).

3. Remove the two CDM mounting bolts from each module. Then remove the module(s) from the engine.

4. To install the CDM(s), position each module in its mounted position and secure it with two screws. Tighten both mounting screws to the specification in **Table 1**.

5. Reconnect the four-pin connector to each module.

6. Reconnect the spark plug leads.

Ignition control module removal/installation

The ignition control module is mounted to the top of the power head and to the rear of the flywheel (**Figure 63**).

1. Disconnect and ground the spark plug leads to the power head to prevent accidental starting.

2. Disconnect the three module harness connectors (**Figure 61**) from the engine wire harness.

3. Remove the three mounting screws and lift the module from the power head.

4. To install the ignition control module, position the module on the power head. Install the three mounting screws and tighten them to the specification in **Table 1**.

5. Connect the three module harness connectors to the engine wire harness. Secure the harness to the power head, electrical bracket or other harnesses with clamps and/or new tie-straps.

6. Reconnect the spark plug leads.

Detonation control module removal/installation

The detonation control module is only used on 200 hp (except Optimax) models with electronic fuel injection. The module interprets if detonation is occurring by monitoring electrical impulses produced by the detonation sensor. The module directs the ECU to retard the ignition

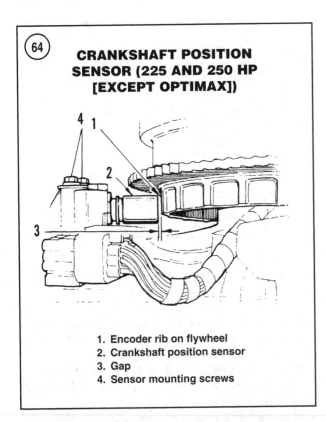

CRANKSHAFT POSITION SENSOR (225 AND 250 HP [EXCEPT OPTIMAX])

1. Encoder rib on flywheel
2. Crankshaft position sensor
3. Gap
4. Sensor mounting screws

timing and increase fuel delivery to stop detonation. The detonation control module is mounted on the port side of the power head. The detonation sensor is mounted near the No. 2 spark plug.

1. Disconnect the negative battery cable.

2. Disconnect and ground the spark plug leads to the power head to prevent accidental starting.

3. Remove the three mounting screws.

4. Note the position and routing of each limit module lead. Disconnect the module harness from the engine wire harness. The plug connector is located next to the module. Disconnect the white/blue wire from the detonation sensor.

5. Remove the module from the power head. Clean corrosion from the mounting screw holes.

6. To install the limit module, reconnect the wires to their respective terminals as described in Step 4.

7. Slip one of the mounting screws through the black module wire. Install the module to the power head and secure it with the three screws. Tighten the mounting screws to the specification in **Table 1**.

8. Reconnect the spark plug leads and the negative battery cable.

CDM Ignition (225 and 250 hp [Except Optimax] Models)

This CDM ignition is an alternator driven, capacitor discharge module system with electronic spark advance.

Refer to Chapter Three for troubleshooting.

The major components include:

1. *Flywheel*—The magnets are for the ignition stator. The outer diameter, lower edge of the flywheel contains cast-in encoding ribs (1, **Figure 64**) for the crankshaft position sensor (2).

2. *Crankshaft position sensor (CPS)*—The CPS detects the presence of the encoding ribs on the flywheel and sends a signal to the ECM. This signal tells the ECM crankshaft position and engine rpm. The air gap between the flywheel encoding ribs and the CPS must be set correctly for proper operation of the ignition system.

3. *Ignition stator (charge) coils*—The stator consists of six windings around six bobbins. The ignition stator provides power to the CDMs. Stator output is always AC (alternating current) voltage.

4. *CDMs, spark plugs and stop circuit*—These components function as described at the beginning of this section.

5. *Ignition ECM*—The ignition ECM (**Figure 65**, typical) monitors input from the CPS, throttle position sensor (TPS) and engine coolant temperature sensor (ECT). The ECM then calculates the correct timing for each cylinder. On EFI models, the ignition ECM interfaces with the fuel ECM to coordinate the firing of the fuel injectors. The ignition ECM contains a cold engine start, idle stabilizer, rpm limit, overheat protection, low oil level (carbureted models) and sensor failure warning programs all described in Chapter Three. The shift interrupt circuit connects to the ignition ECM. When shift load exceeds the spring force of the shift interrupt switch, the ignition ECM

7

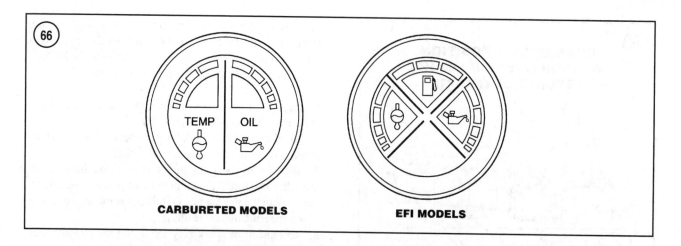

CARBURETED MODELS   **EFI MODELS**

green/yellow lead shorts to ground. The ignition ECM then retards spark advance to 20° ATDC. The retarded timing reduces engine speed, reducing shift effort. As soon as the shift is completed, the shift interrupt switch opens and the ignition ECM returns spark advance to normal. If the shift interrupt switch stays closed for more than two seconds, the ignition ECM automatically returns spark advance to normal.

NOTE
EFI models incorporate the low oil level and the water-in-fuel warning programs into the fuel ECM.

6. *Warning panel*—A multifunction warning panel is recommended for all models. The EFI model has three lights for easy identification of low oil tank level, engine overheat, engine over-speed, sensor malfunction or water-in-fuel situations. The carbureted model does not include the water-in-fuel light. See **Figure 66**.

Component removal/installation

Flywheel removal and installation is covered at the beginning of the *Capacitor Discharge Module (CDM) Ignition* section.

Replacement of the engine coolant temperature (ECT) sensor, intake air temperature (IAT) sensor, manifold absolute pressure (MAP) sensor and throttle position sensor (TPS) is covered in Chapter Six under *EFI Fuel Systems*.

Refer to Chapter Three for troubleshooting procedures and the end of the manual for wiring diagrams.

Ignition stator removal/installation

The ignition stator assembly is a one-piece unit containing only ignition stator windings. The stator assembly is

mounted under the flywheel. An external, belt-driven alternator is used on these engines.

One wire from each bobbin (six total) connects to engine ground (A, **Figure 67**). The six individual bobbin wires connect to the main engine harness through a quick-disconnect connector (B, **Figure 67**).
1. Remove the flywheel as described in this chapter.
2. Note the orientation of the stator assembly and all stator wires before proceeding.
3. Remove the four stator assembly mounting screws.
4. Disconnect the six wire stator connector (B, **Figure 67**) from the engine wiring harness. Then remove the screw securing the stator ground wires (A, **Figure 67**) to the power head.
5. Remove any clamps or tie-straps securing the stator wires to the power head. Then remove the stator assembly from the engine.

CAUTION
Make sure the stator is in its original position unless instructions or decals included with the replacement stator show otherwise. The stator windings and wiring harness must not be crushed between the stator and the power head.

6. To install the stator, position the stator on the power head as noted on removal. Make sure none of the stator windings or harnesses are contacting the power head.
7. Clean the stator mounting screws with Locquic Primer and allow them to air dry. Apply Loctite 271 threadlocking adhesive (part No. 92-809819) to the threads of the screws.
8. Install the stator screws and tighten them evenly to the specification in **Table 1**.
9. Route the stator wiring harness as noted on removal. Secure the harness to the power head with clamps and/or new tie-straps.

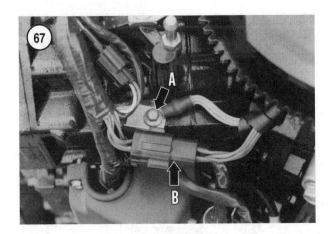

10. Connect all stator wires disconnected in Step 4 to their respective connectors or grounds.

11. Reinstall the flywheel as described previously in this section.

Ignition ECM removal/installation

The ignition ECM is the only ECM on the 225 hp carbureted models. On 225 and 250 hp EFI models, the ignition ECM is mounted above the fuel ECM . The ECMs are mounted on the rear of the power head. The lower ECM is the fuel ECM.

1. Disconnect the negative battery cable.

2. Disconnect the main engine wiring harness ECM connector from the top of the ignition ECM. Squeeze the rubber boot tab to unlock the connector.

3. Note the position of the ground wires, then remove the four ignition ECM mounting bolts. Remove the ignition ECM.

4. To install the ignition ECM, position the ECM on the power head mounting plate.

5. Install the four mounting screws, making sure to reconnect the ground wires to the appropriate mounting screws. Tighten the four mounting screws to the specification in **Table 1**.

6. Reconnect the main engine wiring harness to the ignition ECM.

7. Reconnect the negative battery cable.

Crankshaft position sensor removal/installation

1. Disconnect and ground the spark plug leads to the power head to prevent accidental starting.

2. Disconnect the negative battery cable.

3. Remove the flywheel cover.

4. Remove the two screws (4, **Figure 64**) securing the crankshaft position sensor (2) to the power head.

5. Disconnect the sensor two-wire connector from the engine wiring harness.

6. Remove any tie-straps securing the sensor wires to the power head or wiring harness and remove the sensor from the power head.

7. If necessary, transfer the sensor bracket to the new sensor. Tighten the sender screw to the specification in **Table 1**.

8. To install the sensor, position the sensor on the power head mounting bosses and secure the sensor with the two screws. Tighten the screws hand tight at this time.

9. Reconnect the sensor connector to the engine wiring harness.

10. Secure the sensor wires to the power head and/or engine wiring harness with new tie-strap(s).

11. Adjust the sensor air gap as described in Chapter Five.

12. Tighten the screws (4, **Figure 64**) to the specification in **Table 1** and recheck the sensor air gap.

13. Install the flywheel cover.

14. Reconnect the negative battery cable and the spark plug leads.

CDMs removal/installation

1. Disconnect and ground the spark plug leads to the power head to prevent accidental starting.

2. Disconnect the four-pin connector from each CDM to be removed.

3. Remove the two CDM mounting bolts from each module. Then remove the module(s) from the engine.

4. To install the CDM(s), position each module in its mounted position and secure it with two screws. Tighten both mounting screws to the specification in **Table 1**.

5. Reconnect the four-pin connector to each module.

6. Reconnect the spark plug leads.

DIGITAL INDUCTIVE IGNITION (115-225 HP OPTIMAX MODELS)

Refer to Chapter Three for troubleshooting.

The digital inductive ignition system is a battery driven, ECM controlled system with electronic spark advance. Once the engine starts, a 60 amp belt-driven alternator provides all operating voltage for the system. This system is used exclusively on 115-225 hp Optimax models (direct fuel injection).

The major components includes:

7

1. *Flywheel*—The outer diameter, lower edge of the flywheel contains cast-in encoding ribs (4, **Figure 68**, typical) for the crankshaft position sensor (1).

2. *Crankshaft position sensor (CPS)*—The crankshaft position sensor detects the presence of the encoding ribs on the flywheel and sends a signal to the ECM. This signal tells the ECM crankshaft position and engine rpm. The air gap between the flywheel encoding ribs and the CPS must be set correctly for proper engine operation.

3. *Ignition coils*—There is one ignition coil (**Figure 69**) for each cylinder. The ignition coil transforms the relatively low voltage from the battery into voltage high enough (50,000 volts) to jump the spark plug gap and ignite the air/fuel mixture. The ignition coils positive terminal has battery voltage present when the ignition switch is on.

   a. On 1998-2000 models, the ECM opens the ignition coil negative terminal to create spark.

   b. On 2001-on models, the ECM sends a signal to one of three coil driver modules. The coil driver then opens the ignition coil negative to create spark. Each coil driver controls two ignition coils.

4. *Spark plugs*—There is one spark plug for each cylinder. Only use the recommended spark plugs or engine damage may occur. The only recommended spark plug for the 200 DFI is the Champion RC10ECC.

5. *Stop circuit*—The stop circuit is connected to the ECM. When the stop circuit connects to ground, the ECM shuts off the ignition coils. The stop circuit must have an open circuit to ground in order for the engine to run.

6. *ECM*—The ECM (**Figure 70**) monitors input from all of the sensors. The ECM then calculates the correct spark timing, fuel injector timing and direct injector timing for each cylinder. The ECM contains a cold engine start, idle stabilizer, rpm limit, overheat protection, water-in-fuel, low oil level, no oil flow and sensor failure warning programs. The ECM receives power from a main power relay. The main power relay is activated by the ignition switch. On 2001 models, the ECM provides signals to the Smart Craft gauges to provide troll speed control, fuel usage, boat speed and engine operation monitoring.

   a. *Cold start program*—The cold engine start program increases the fuel injector pulse width when the engine is below operating temperature. The amount of fuel injector pulse width increase is proportional to engine temperature.

   b. *Idle stabilizer program*—The idle stabilizer program controls the idle speed by advancing or retarding spark advance to maintain 525-675 rpm when the TPS (throttle position sensor) indicates that the throttle control is in the idle position. Idle speed is not adjustable.

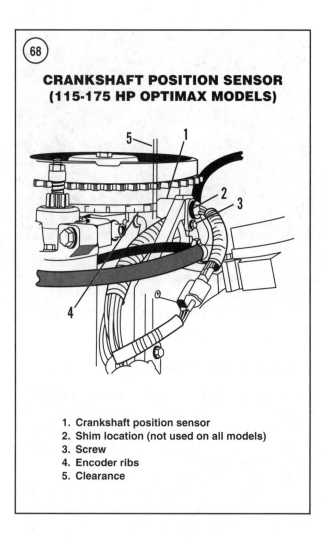

(68)

CRANKSHAFT POSITION SENSOR (115-175 HP OPTIMAX MODELS)

1. Crankshaft position sensor
2. Shim location (not used on all models)
3. Screw
4. Encoder ribs
5. Clearance

   c. *Rpm limit program*—The rpm limit program is activated when engine speed exceeds the maximum recommended rpm. If engine speed exceeds the limit, the ECM shuts the engine systems off until engine speed drops below the preprogrammed speed limit, at which point engine operation returns to normal. The warning horn sounds continuously when the rpm limit program is activated.

   d. *Overheat warning program*—The overheat warning program retards ignition timing and reduces engine power when the engine coolant temperature (ECT) sensor indicates overheating. On 1998-2000 models, the ECM reduces engine speed to a maximum of 3000 rpm. On 2001-on models, the ECM reduces engine speed as low as idle speed depending on engine temperature. Engine power returns to normal when the ECT indicates normal temperature. The overheat lamp flashes and the warning horn sounds continuously when the overheat warning program is activated.

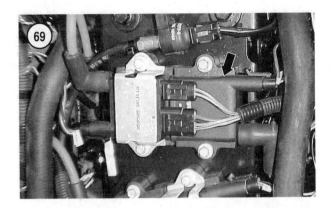

g. *No oil flow warning program*—The no oil flow warning program sounds the warning horn and illuminates the oil light and check engine light. On 1998-2000 models, the ECM reduces engine speed to a maximum of 3000 rpm. The ignition switch must be turned off to reset the warning program. On 2001-on models, the ECM reduces the engine speed to idle rpm. If the no oil flow warning program is activated, stop the engine as soon as possible and correct the defect. Operating the motor without oil flow will result in power head failure.

h. *Sensor failure warning program*—The sensor warning program is designed to alert the boat operator to a sensor, ignition coil or injector failure. This is similar to the check engine light on a modern fuel injected car. If the ECM detects a failure in any of the sensor, ignition coil or injector circuits, the check engine lamp will illuminate. If one of the two TPS sensors has failed, the warning horn also sounds. On 1998-2000 models, the engine will not run above idle speed if both throttle position sensors fail. On 2001-on models, the engine speed is reduced to a maximum of approximately 4500 if the single throttle position sensor fails.

7. *Warning panel*—A multifunction warning panel is recommended for 1998-2000 models. The warning panel has four lights that allow easy identification of low oil tank level, no oil flow, engine overheat, sensor malfunction, ignition coil or injector malfunction and water-in-fuel situations. 2001-on models may be equipped with Smart Craft gauges. The LCD display on these gauges indicates which condition is activating the warning system.

All Optimax models use a shift interrupt circuit connected to the ECM. When shift load exceeds the spring force of the shift interrupt switch, the ECM black/red wire shorts to ground. The ECM then reduces engine speed, reducing shift effort. As soon as the shift is completed, the shift interrupt switch opens and the ECM returns fuel delivery and engine speed to normal.

Component Removal/Installation

Replacement of the engine coolant temperature (ECT) sensor, intake air temperature (IAT) sensor, manifold absolute pressure (MAP) sensor, throttle position sensor (TPS) are covered in Chapter Six under *Optimax Air/Fuel Systems*.

Refer to Chapter Three for troubleshooting procedures and the end of the manual for wiring diagrams.

e. *Water-in-fuel warning program*—The water-in-fuel warning program sounds the warning horn and illuminates the water-in-fuel warning light when the water separating fuel filter accumulates enough water to short the sensor to ground. When the water sensor shorts to ground, the horn beeps four times at one second intervals, shuts off for two minutes, then begins the warning cycle again. The warning light illuminates continuously until the ignition switch is turned off. This program does not affect ignition system operation.

f. *Low-oil warning program*—The low-oil warning program sounds the warning horn and illuminates the oil warning light when the switch in the engine mounted oil tank closes. When the oil switch closes, the horn beeps four times at one second intervals, shuts off for two minutes, then begins the warning cycle again. The warning light illuminates continuously until the ignition switch is turned off. On 1998-2000 models, this program does not affect ignition system operation. On 2001-on models, the ECM computes the approximate amount of oil remaining in the reservoir. When the oil level reaches a critically low level, the ECM reduces the engine speed to idle rpm.

7

Flywheel removal/installation

1. Disconnect and ground the spark plug leads to the power head to prevent accidental starting.

2. Remove the flywheel cover.

3. Remove the alternator/compressor drive belt as described in this chapter. See *Alternator removal/installation*.

4. Hold the flywheel using flywheel holder part No. 91-52344 or an equivalent. See **Figure 48**.

> *CAUTION*
> *To prevent crankshaft damage, do not remove the flywheel without using a crankshaft protector cap (2, **Figure 49**).*

5. Install the crankshaft protective cap (2, **Figure 49**) to the end of the crankshaft. Use cold grease to hold the protective cap in place.

> *CAUTION*
> *Never apply heat or strike the puller screw with a hammer during flywheel removal. Heat and/or hammering can damage the ignition components, flywheel and crankshaft.*

6. Install the recommended flywheel puller (part No. 91-73687A1) into the flywheel (**Figure 49**, typical).

7. Hold the puller with one wrench and tighten the puller screw (**Figure 50**) until the flywheel dislodges from the crankshaft taper.

8. Lift the flywheel off the crankshaft. Remove the flywheel key, if so equipped, from the crankshaft slot.

9. Inspect and clean the flywheel key, if so equipped, and crankshaft as described in this chapter.

10. To install the flywheel, insert the flywheel key, if so equipped, into the slot in the crankshaft.

11A. On 115-175 hp models, align the splines in the flywheel with the splines on the crankshaft taper.

11B. On 200 and 225 hp models, align the flywheel key slot with the flywheel key and place the flywheel onto the crankshaft.

12. Install the flywheel nut and washer. Hold the flywheel with a flywheel holder and tighten the flywheel nut to specification in **Table 1**.

13. Install the alternator/compressor drive belt as described in this chapter. See *Alternator removal/installation*.

14. Install the flywheel cover.

15. Reconnect the spark plug leads to the spark plugs.

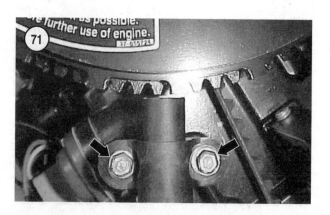

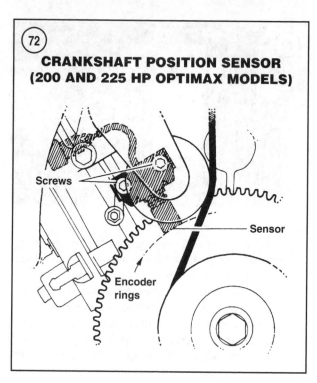

CRANKSHAFT POSITION SENSOR (200 AND 225 HP OPTIMAX MODELS)

Screws

Sensor

Encoder rings

Crankshaft position sensor removal/installation

1. Disconnect and ground the spark plug leads to the power head to prevent accidental starting.

2. Disconnect the negative battery cable.

3. Remove the flywheel cover.

4A. On 1998-2000 115-150 hp models, remove the single screw (3, **Figure 68**) and remove the sensor (1) and shim, if so equipped, from the power head.

4B. On 2001-on 115-175 hp models, remove the two screws (**Figure 71**) and remove the crankshaft position sensor from the power head.

4C. On 200 and 225 hp models, remove the two screws (**Figure 72**) and remove the crankshaft position sensor from the power head.

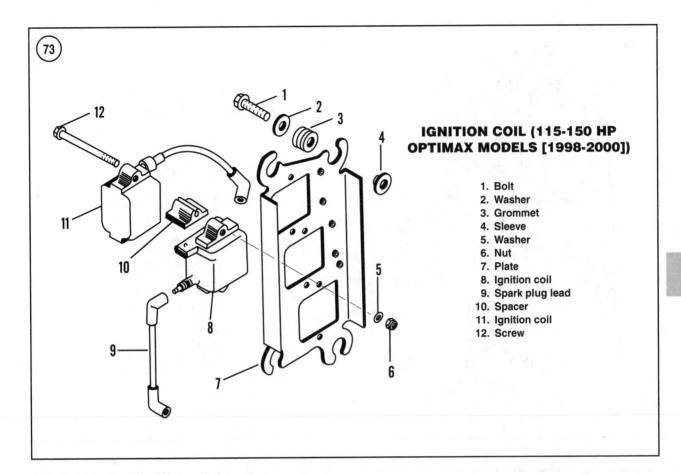

IGNITION COIL (115-150 HP OPTIMAX MODELS [1998-2000])

1. Bolt
2. Washer
3. Grommet
4. Sleeve
5. Washer
6. Nut
7. Plate
8. Ignition coil
9. Spark plug lead
10. Spacer
11. Ignition coil
12. Screw

5. Disconnect the sensor wire connector from the engine wiring harness and remove the sensor from the power head.

6. If necessary, transfer the sensor bracket to the new sensor. Tighten the screw that holds the sensor to the bracket to the specification in **Table 1**.

7. To install the sensor, position the sensor on the power head mounting bosses and secure the sensor with screws. Do not forget to install the shim, if so equipped, between the sensor and the power head boss. Tighten the screw(s) hand tight at this time.

8. Reconnect the sensor connector to the engine wiring harness.

9. Adjust the sensor air gap as described in Chapter Five. Then tighten the screw(s) to the specification in **Table 1**.

10. Install the flywheel cover.

11. Reconnect the negative battery cable and the spark plug leads.

Coil removal/installation

Each coil's primary wires are connected through a three-pin connector. A red/yellow wire carries battery voltage to each ignition coil positive terminal. A different color coded wire connects each coil's negative terminal to the ECM or coil driver (2001-on). The color coding of this wire determines the engine's firing order. Each coil connector must be connected to the correct ignition coil. Note the coil primary negative wire color code of all cylinders before disconnecting any wires.

Ignition coil mounting varies by model and model year. On all models, the coil mount in pairs to a bracket on the rear of the power head. Refer to the back of the manual for wiring diagrams and **Figures 73-76** for ignition coil removal/installation. Remove the ignition coil mounting plate from the power head as necessary to access the coil mounting fasteners.

1. Disconnect the spark plug leads from all of the spark plugs.

2. Disconnect the primary wire connector from the coil(s).

3. Note the position of any harness clamps and/or ground straps. See **Figures 73-76** as appropriate. Remove the screws securing the coil(s) or coil(s) and driver(s) to the plate.

4. To install the coils, position the coils into the coil plate. Secure the coils with the screws and nuts. Make sure elec-

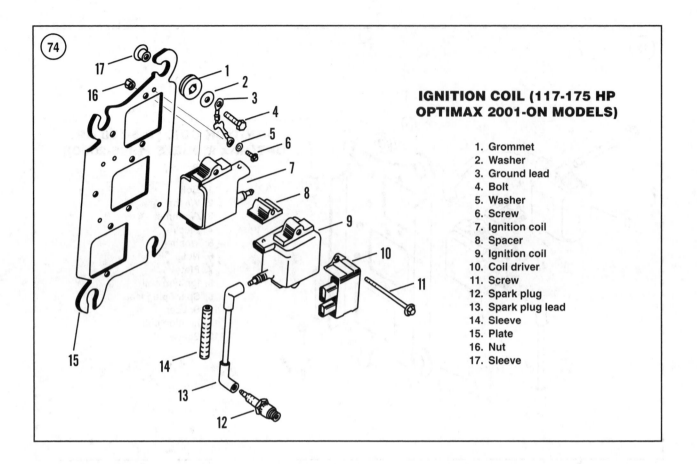

IGNITION COIL (117-175 HP OPTIMAX 2001-ON MODELS)

1. Grommet
2. Washer
3. Ground lead
4. Bolt
5. Washer
6. Screw
7. Ignition coil
8. Spacer
9. Ignition coil
10. Coil driver
11. Screw
12. Spark plug
13. Spark plug lead
14. Sleeve
15. Plate
16. Nut
17. Sleeve

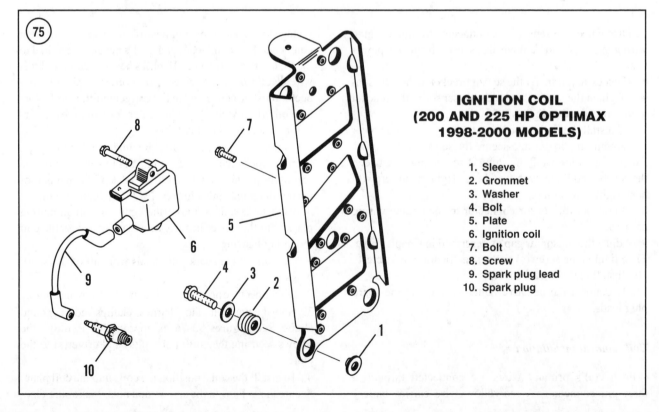

IGNITION COIL (200 AND 225 HP OPTIMAX 1998-2000 MODELS)

1. Sleeve
2. Grommet
3. Washer
4. Bolt
5. Plate
6. Ignition coil
7. Bolt
8. Screw
9. Spark plug lead
10. Spark plug

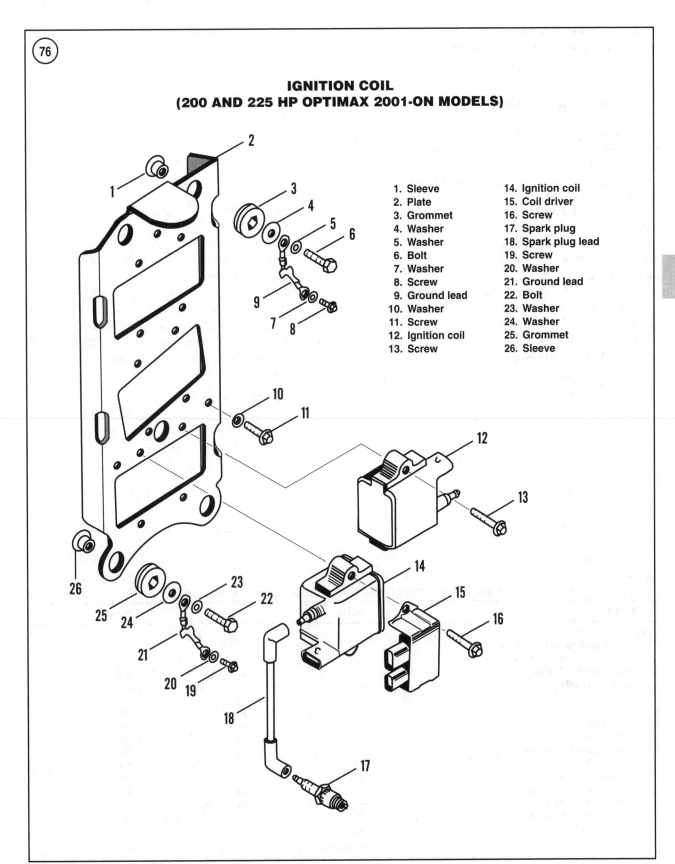

**IGNITION COIL
(200 AND 225 HP OPTIMAX 2001-ON MODELS)**

1. Sleeve
2. Plate
3. Grommet
4. Washer
5. Washer
6. Bolt
7. Washer
8. Screw
9. Ground lead
10. Washer
11. Screw
12. Ignition coil
13. Screw
14. Ignition coil
15. Coil driver
16. Screw
17. Spark plug
18. Spark plug lead
19. Screw
20. Washer
21. Ground lead
22. Bolt
23. Washer
24. Washer
25. Grommet
26. Sleeve

7

trical clamps and/or ground straps are reattached. Tighten the screws to the specification in **Table 1**.

5. Reconnect all spark plug leads.

Coil driver removal/installation

The coil driver is used on 2001-on 115-225 hp Optimax models. The same screws that retain the coils to the plate retain the driver to the coil. Refer to the end of the manual for wiring diagrams, and to **Figure 74** or **Figure 76** as appropriate for coil drive removal/installation.

1. Disconnect the spark plug leads from all of the spark plugs.

2. Disconnect the two connectors from the coil driver(s). Remove the screws (11, **Figure 74** or 16, **Figure 76**) and remove the coil driver.

3. To install the coil driver, position the coil driver on the ignition coil. Install the screws to secure the coil driver and coil to the plate. Tighten the coil mounting screws to the specification in **Table 1**.

4. Reconnect all spark plug leads.

Engine control module (ECM) removal/installation

1. Disconnect the negative battery cable.

2. Carefully unplug the three wire harness connectors from the side of the module.

3. Remove the screw and the fuse bracket from the ECM.

4. Remove the three bolts securing the ECM to the starboard side of the power head.

5. Remove the ECM. Remove the sleeves and grommets from the ECM.

6. Install the ECM by first fitting the three grommets into the opening in the ECM.

7. Install the ECM onto the power head. Secure the ECM with the three bolts and sleeves. Tighten the bolts to the specification in **Table 1**.

8. Install the fuse bracket onto the power head. Tighten the bracket screws to the specification in **Table 1**. The rubber cushion must fit between the bracket and the ECM.

9. Carefully plug the three connectors into the ECM.

10. Reconnect the negative battery cable.

Table 1 ELECTRICAL SYSTEM TORQUE SPECIFICATIONS

Fastener	in.-lb	ft.-lb.	N•m
Alternator			
115-175 hp (Optimax models)			
Forward mounting bracket	–	16	22
Housing cover bolts	23	–	2.6
Mounting bolts			
Upper	–	40	54
Lower	–	35	47.5
Pivot bolt	–	40	54
Pulley nut	–	50	68
Rear mounting bracket bolt	–	40	54
Rectifier bolts	17	–	1.9
Regulator bolts	17	–	1.9
Tensioner bracket (pivot) bolt	–	15	20
Tensioner pulley bolt	–	25	34
Terminal/insulator nut	36	–	4.1
Through bolts	40	–	4.5
(continued)			

Table 1 ELECTRICAL SYSTEM TORQUE SPECIFICATIONS (continued)

Fastener	in.-lb	ft.-lb.	N•m
Alternator (cont.)			
200 and 200 hp (Optimax models)			
Housing cover	23	–	2.6
Mounting bolts	–	40	54
Output lead/insulator nut	36	–	4.1
Pulley nut	–	50	68
Rectifier	17	–	1.9
Regulator	17	–	1.9
Tensioner pulley	–	25	34
Tensioner bracket (pivot) bolt	–	17	23
Through bolts	40	–	4.5
225-250 hp (except Optimax models)			
Housing cover	23	–	2.6
Output lead/insulator nut	36	–	4.1
Pivot bolt	–	40	54
Pulley nut	–	50	68
Rectifier	17	–	1.9
Regulator	17	–	1.9
Tension bolt	–	40	54
Through bolts	40	–	4.5
CDM mounting screws			
65 jet and 75-125 hp			
(except 105 jet and 115 Optimax)	60	–	6.8
105 jet and 135-200 hp (except Optimax)	70	–	7.9
225 and 250 hp (except Optimax)	80	–	9
Crankshaft position sensor			
115-175 hp (Optimax)	50	–	5.6
200 and 225 hp (Optimax)			
Sender to bracket	50	–	5.6
Bracket to power head	100	–	11.3
225 and 250 hp (except Optimax)			
Sender to bracket	50	–	5.6
Bracket to power head	105	–	11.9
Detonation control module mounting screws			
200 hp (except Optimax models)	30	–	3.4
Engine control module			
225 an 250 hp	80	–	9
115-225 hp (Optimax models)			
Mounting screws	80	–	9
Flywheel nut			
65 jet and 75-125 hp			
(except 105 jet and 115 Optimax)	–	100	136
105 jet and 135-200 hp (except Optimax)	–	120	163
115-255 hp Optimax	–	125	169
225 and 250 hp (except Optimax)	–	125	169
Fuse bracket (Optimax models)	80	–	9
Ignition coil			
105 jet and 135-200 hp (except Optimax)			
Mounting screws	20	–	2.3
Primary terminal nuts	30	–	3.4
115-225 hp Optimax			
Mounting plate to power head	–	20	27
Coil mounting bolts/nuts			
115-175 hp	80	–	9
200 and 225 hp	60	–	6.8
Ignition control module			
2000-on 105 jet and 135-200 hp			
(except Optimax)	30	–	3.4

(continued)

Table 1 ELECTRICAL SYSTEM TORQUE SPECIFICATIONS (continued)

Fastener	in.-lb	ft.-lb.	N•m
Starter motor			
Cable terminal nut	60	–	6.8
Brush plate screws	30	–	3.4
Mounting bolts			
65 jet and 75-125 hp			
(except 105 jet and 115 Optimax)	–	15	20.3
105 jet and 135-200 hp (except Optimax)	–	17.5	23.7
115-225 hp Optimax			
Upper bolts	–	23	31
Lower bolt(s)	–	21	28.5
225-250 hp (except Optimax)			
Upper bolts	–	23	31
Lower bolt	–	21	28.5
Solenoid mounting (2001-on Optimax)	40	–	4.5
Through bolts			
All models (except 2001-on Optimax)	70	–	7.9
2001-on Optimax	110	–	12.4
Stator screws			
65 jet and 75-125 hp			
(except 105 jet and 115 Optimax)	60	–	6.8
105 jet and 135-200 hp (except Optimax)	50	–	5.6
225 and 250 hp (except Optimax)	100	–	11.3
Switch box mounting screws			
105 jet and 135-200 hp (except Optimax)	3	–	0.3
Rectifier/regulator			
65 jet and 75-125 hp			
(except 105 jet and 115 Optimax) screws	70	–	7.9
1998 and 1999 105 jet and 135-200 hp			
(except Optimax) screws	80	–	9
2000-on 105 jet and 135-200 hp			
(except Optimax) nuts	70	–	7.9

Table 2 GENERAL TORQUE SPECIFICATIONS

Screw or nut size	in.-lb.	ft.-lb.	N•m
U.S. Standard			
6-32	9	–	1.0
8-32	20	–	2.3
10-24	30	–	3.4
10-32	35	–	4.0
12-24	45	–	5.1
1/4-20	70	–	7.9
1/4-28	84	–	9.5
5/16-18	160	13	18
5/16-24	168	14	19
3/8-16	–	23	31
3/8-24	–	25	34
7/16-14	–	36	49
7/16-20	–	40	54
1/2-13	–	50	68
1/2-20	–	60	81
Metric			
M5	36	–	4
M6	70	–	8
M8	156	13	18
M10	–	26	35
M12	–	35	48
M14	–	60	81

Table 3 BATTERY CHARGE PERCENTAGE

Specific gravity reading	Percentage of charge remaining
1.120-1.140	0
1.135-1.155	10
1.150-1.170	20
1.160-1.180	30
1.175-1.195	40
1.190-1.210	50
1.205-1.225	60
1.215-1.235	70
1.230-1.250	80
1.245-1.265	90
1.260-1.280	100

Table 4 BATTERY CAPACITY

Accessory draw	Provides continuous power for:	Approximate recharge time
80 amp-hour battery		
5 amps	13.5 hours	16 hours
15 amps	3.5 hours	13 hours
25 amps	1.6 hours	12 hours
105 amp-hour battery		
5 amps	15.8 hours	16 hours
15 amps	4.2 hours	13 hours
25 amps	2.4 hours	12 hours

Table 5 BATTERY REQUIREMENTS (MINIMUM)

Model	CCA rating	MCA rating	Reserve capacity	Amp hour
65 jet and 75-125 hp (except 105 jet and 115 Optimax)	350	–	100 minutes	–
1998 and 1999 105 jet and 135-200 hp (except Optimax models)	350	–	100 minutes	–
2000-on 105 jet and 135-250 hp (except Optimax models)	490	630	–	–
115-225 hp (Optimax models)	750	1000	–	105

Table 6 BATTERY CABLE REQUIREMENTS

Cable length	Minimum cable gauge size (AWG)
To 3 1/2 ft.	4
3 1/2 to 6 ft.	2
6 to 7 1/2 ft.	1
7 1/2 to 9 1/2 ft.	0
9 1/2 to 12 ft.	00
12 to 15 ft.	000
15 to 19 ft.	0000

7

Chapter Eight

Power Head

This chapter provides power head removal/installation, disassembly/reassembly, and cleaning and inspection procedures for all models. The power head can be removed from the outboard motor without removing the entire outboard motor from the boat.

Since this chapter covers a large range of models, spanning several model years, the power heads from different models will differ in construction and require different service procedures. When possible, engines with similar service procedures have been grouped together.

The components shown in the accompanying illustrations are generally from the most common models. While the components shown in the illustrations may not be identical to those being serviced, the step-by-step procedures cover each model in this manual. Exploded illustrations, typical of each power head model group are located in the appropriate *Disassembly* section and are helpful references for many service procedures.

This chapter is arranged in a normal disassembly/assembly sequence. When only a partial repair is required, follow the procedure(s) to the point where the faulty parts

can be replaced, then jump ahead to reassemble the unit. Many procedures require manufacturer recommended special tools, which can be purchased from a Mercury or Mariner outboard dealership.

Power head work stands and holding fixtures are available from specialty shops or marine and industrial product distributors.

Make sure the work bench, work station, engine stand or holding fixture is of sufficient capacity to support the size and weight of the power head. This is especially important when working on larger engines, such as V-6 models.

SERVICE CONSIDERATIONS

Performing internal service procedures on the power head requires considerable mechanical ability. Carefully consider your capabilities before attempting an operation involving major disassembly of the engine.

If, after studying the text and illustrations in this chapter, you decide not to attempt a major power head disas-

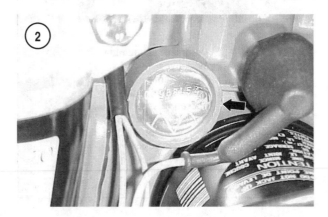

sembly or repair, it may be financially beneficial to perform certain preliminary operations yourself. Consider separating the power head from the outboard motor and removing the fuel, ignition and electrical systems and all accessories, taking only the basic power head to the dealership for the actual overhaul or major repair.

Since marine dealerships often have lengthy waiting lists for service, this practice can reduce the time the unit is in the shop. If the preliminary work is done, repairs can be scheduled and performed much quicker. Always discuss your options with the dealership before taking a disassembled engine to the dealership. Dealerships will often want to install, adjust and test run the engine in order to provide warranty coverage for the overhaul or repair.

Repair will be quicker and easier if the motor is clean before any service procedure is started. There are many special cleaners available from automotive supply stores. Most of these cleaners are simply sprayed on, then rinsed off with a garden hose after the recommended time period. Always follow the instructions provided by the manufacturer. Do not apply cleaning solvent to electrical and ignition components, and never spray it into the induction system.

WARNING
Never use gasoline as a cleaning agent. Gasoline presents an extreme fire and explosion hazard. Work in a well-ventilated area when using cleaning solvent. Keep a large fire extinguisher rated for gasoline and oil fires nearby in case of an emergency.

Before starting repairs, thoroughly read this chapter to understand what is involved in completing the repair satisfactorily. Make arrangements to buy or rent the necessary special tools and obtain a source for replacement parts *before* starting. It is frustrating and time-consuming to start a major repair, then be unable to finish because the necessary tools or parts are not available.

NOTE
A series of photographs, taken from the front, rear, top and both sides of the power head before removal will be very helpful during reassembly and installation. The photographs are especially useful when rerouting electrical harnesses, and fuel, primer and recirculation lines. They will also be helpful during the installation of accessories, control linkages and brackets.

Before beginning the job, review Chapter One and Chapter Two of this manual.

Table 1 lists specific application torque specifications for most power head fasteners. **Table 2** lists general torque specifications for both American standard and Metric fasteners. Use the general torque specification for fasteners not listed in **Table 1**. **Table 3** and **Table 4** list power head dimensional specifications. **Table 5** lists model number codes. All tables are located at the end of this chapter.

MERCURY/MARINER MODEL IDENTIFICATION

All Mercury/Mariner outboard models use an individual, unique serial number for the primary means of identification. The serial number plate is located on the midsection (**Figure 1**) of the outboard motor and is usually attached to the starboard stern bracket. If the engine is still equipped with its original power head, the serial number is also stamped on a welch plug attached the power head (**Figure 2**, typical).

Unique Serial Number

The engine's unique serial number is listed on the serial number tag (1, **Figure 3**). Serial numbers are never duplicated. In many states this number is used to register or title the outboard. Record this number and place it in a safe place. If the outboard is lost or stolen, this number will accurately identify the outboard.

In the example in **Figure 3**, the first digit, 0, is followed by a letter code, then six numbers. The numbers increase sequentially as engines are produced. The letter code increases alphabetically when all number combinations are used. The serial number following 0G999999 would be 0H000000, then 0H000001 and so on. Because the serial number identifies the outboard motor, always supply it when purchasing replacement parts.

Model Name

The serial number tag list the model's name (3, **Figure 3**). In **Figure 3**, the engine is a 9.9 EL. The model name usually describes the actual rated horsepower output of the engine. Many engines are produced in different versions for a given horsepower. Variations include the type of starting system, drive shaft length, tiller or remote control and power trim or manual tilt system. Refer to *Engine Characteristics* in this chapter for additional information.

On all 1998-on models, the horsepower or kilowatt rating is listed on the serial number tag (5 and 9, **Figure 3**).

Year of Production

The year of production is listed at the lower right of the serial number tag (7, **Figure 3**). Do not assume the year model and year of production are the same.

Engine Weight

All boats have a maximum weight carrying capacity listed on the boat rating tag. Consider the weight of all passengers, gear fuel, tanks and the engine before loading or operating the boat. Never load the boat beyond its rated capacity. To determine the total weight, refer to the engine weight on the serial number tag. The engine weight without fuel, oil or tanks is listed in both pounds (6, **Figure 3**) and kilograms (8).

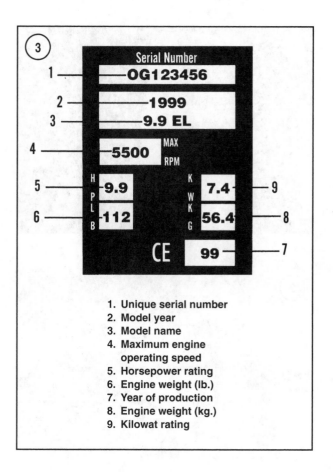

1. Unique serial number
2. Model year
3. Model name
4. Maximum engine operating speed
5. Horsepower rating
6. Engine weight (lb.)
7. Year of production
8. Engine weight (kg.)
9. Kilowat rating

Engine Characteristics

NOTE
Tiller control kits and drive shaft length extension kits may be installed on the outboard. If testing or repair is required on these add-on kits, refer to the specifications and instructions for similar models with the selected equipment factory installed.

Mercury and Mariner outboards are produced with many variations of each horsepower rating. Variations exist in drive shaft length, starting system used, type of control system and trim or manual tilt system. The test and repair requirement may also vary with the engine characteristics.

Refer to the model name portion of the serial number tag (3, **Figure 3**) for engine characteristic identification. In **Figure 3**, the engine is a 9.9 EL. The 9.9 indicates the approximate horsepower of the engine. The letter code(s) to the right of the horsepower indicates the characteristics or version of the engine. The EL (3, **Figure 3**) in this example indicates the engine is equipped with electric starting and a long drive shaft. Refer to **Table 5** to match the model code(s) to the outboard's version or characteristics.

POWER HEAD BREAK-IN

When a power head has been rebuilt or replaced, or if *any* new internal parts have been installed, treat it as a new engine. Run the engine on the specified fuel/oil mixture and operate it in accordance with the recommended break-in procedure described in Chapter Four.

CAUTION
Failure to follow the recommended break-in procedure will result in premature power head failure.

SERVICE RECOMMENDATIONS

If the engine has experienced a power head failure, attempt to determine the cause of the failure. Refer to *Engine* in Chapter Three for troubleshooting procedures.

Many failures are caused by the incorrect or stale fuel and lubricating oil. Refer to Chapter Four for all fuel and oil recommendations.

When rebuilding or performing a major repair on the power head, consider performing the following steps to prevent the failure from reoccurring.

1. Service the water pump. Replace the impeller and all seals and gaskets. See Chapter Nine.

2. Replace the thermostat(s), and remove and inspect the poppet valve assembly, on models so equipped, as described in this chapter. Replace any suspect components.

3. Drain the fuel tank(s) and dispose of the old fuel in an approved manner.

4. Fill the fuel tank with fresh fuel and add the recommended oil to the fuel tank (except Optimax models) at the *break-in* ratio described in Chapter Four.

5. Replace or clean all fuel filters. See Chapter Four.

6. Clean and adjust the carburetors on carbureted models or drain the vapor separator on EFI or Optimax models. See Chapter Six.

7. Drain and clean the oil reservoir(s). Dispose of the old oil in an approved manner. Then refill the oil system with the specified oil (Chapter Four) and bleed the oil system as described in Chapter Thirteen.

8. Install new spark plugs. Only use the recommended spark plugs listed in Chapter Four. Make sure the spark plugs are correctly torqued as described in Chapter Four.

9. Perform *all* of the synchronization and linkage adjustments as described in Chapter Five before returning the motor to operation.

LUBRICANTS, SEALANTS AND ADHESIVES

The part numbers for the lubricants, sealants and adhesives specified in this chapter are all listed in the repair instructions. Equivalent products are acceptable for use, as long as they meet or exceed the original manufacturer's specifications.

During power head assembly, lubricate all internal engine components with Quicksilver two-cycle (TCW-3) outboard motor oil. Do not assemble any components *dry*. Lubricate all seal lips and O-rings with Quicksilver 2-4-C Multi-Lube grease (part No. 92-825407). Lubricate and hold all needle and roller bearings in place with Quicksilver Needle Bearing Assembly Grease (part No. 92-825265A-1).

To efficiently remove the carbon from the pistons and combustion chambers, use Quicksilver Power Tune Engine Cleaner (part No. 92-15104). Allow ample time for the cleaner to soak into and soften carbon deposits.

When no other sealant or adhesive is specified, coat all gaskets with Quicksilver Perfect Seal (part No. 92-34227-1). Coat the threads of all external fasteners (when no other sealant or adhesive is specified) with Quicksilver Perfect Seal to help prevent corrosion and ease future removal.

Before sealing the crankcase cover/cylinder block, make sure both mating surfaces are free of all sealant residue, dirt, oil or other contamination. Locquic Primer (part No. 92-809824), lacquer thinner, acetone or similar solvents work well when used with a plastic scraper. Never use solvents with an oil, wax or petroleum base.

CAUTION
*Clean all mating surfaces carefully to avoid nicks and gouges. A plastic scraper can be improvised from a common household electrical outlet cover or a piece of Lucite with one edge ground to a 45° angle. Be careful when using a metal scraper, such as a putty knife. Nicks and gouges may prevent the sealant from curing. The crankcase cover-to-cylinder block surface must **not** be lapped or machined.*

Use Loctite Master Gasket Sealant (part No. 92-12564-2) to seal the crankcase cover-to-cylinder block mating surfaces on models without a gasket. The sealant comes in a kit that includes a special primer. Follow the instructions included in the kit for preparing the surfaces and applying the sealant. Apply the sealant bead to the inside (crankshaft side) of all crankcase cover bolt holes.

8

Apply Loctite 271 threadlocking adhesive (part No. 92-809819) to the outer diameter of all seals before pressing the seals into place. Also apply this adhesive to the threads of all internal fasteners if no other adhesive is specified.

Before using a Loctite product, always clean the surface to be sealed or threads to be secured with Locquic Primer (part No. 92-809824). Locquic Primer cleans and primes the surface and ensures a quick secure bond by leaving a thin film of catalyst on the surface or threads. Allow the primer to air dry, as blow drying disables the catalyst.

SEALING SURFACES

Clean all sealing surfaces carefully to prevent nicks and gouges. Often a shop towel soaked in solvent can be used to rub gasket material and/or sealant from a mating surface. If a scraper must be used, try using a plastic scraper, such as a household electrical outlet cover, or a piece of Lucite with one edge ground to a 45° angle to prevent damage to the sealing surfaces. When using a metal scraper or putty knife, be very careful to prevent destroying the component being cleaned.

> *NOTE*
> *Use plate glass or a machinist's surface plate or straightedge to check surfaces. Ordinary window glass does not have a uniform surface and will give false readings. Plate glass has a uniform surface.*

Once the surfaces are clean, check the component for warp by placing the component on a piece of plate glass or a machinist's surface plate. Apply uniform downward pressure and try to insert a selection of feeler gauges between the plate and the component. Specifications for maximum cylinder head warp are in **Table 3**. On other components, remove minor warp by lapping, replace or the component.

> *CAUTION*
> *Do not lap the cylinder block-to-crankcase cover (all models). In addition, do not lap the cylinder heads on the following models:*

1. 2000-on 115-175 hp Optimax models.
2. 2000-on XR6, Mag III, 175 hp and 200 hp.
3. All 200 hp and 225 hp Optimax models.
4. All 225 hp and 250 hp (carburetor and EFI) models.

To remove minor warpage, minor nicks or scratches, or traces of sealant or gasket material, place a large sheet of 320-400 grit wet sandpaper on the plate glass or surface plate. Apply light downward pressure and move the com-

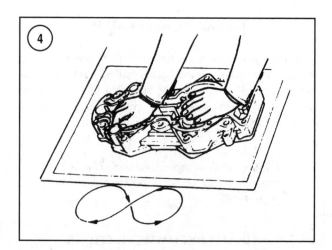

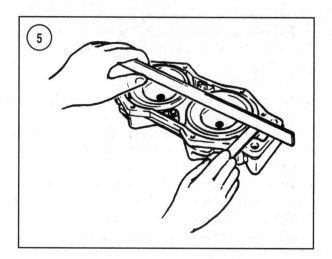

ponent in a figure-eight pattern as shown in **Figure 4**. Use a light oil, such as WD-40, to keep the sandpaper from loading up. Remove the component from the sandpaper and recheck the sealing surface. Use a machinist's straightedge to check areas that cannot be accessed using the glass or surface plate. See **Figure 5**.

It may be necessary to repeat the lapping process several times to achieve the desired results. Never remove more material than is absolutely necessary. Make sure the component is thoroughly washed to remove all grit before reassembly.

FASTENERS AND TORQUE

Always replace a worn or damaged fastener with one of equal size, type and torque requirement. Power head torque specifications are in **Table 1**. If a specification is not provided for a fastener, use the general torque specifications in **Table 2** according to fastener size.

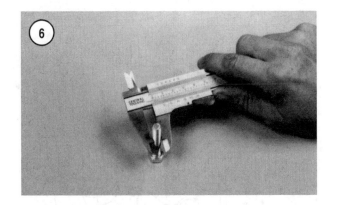

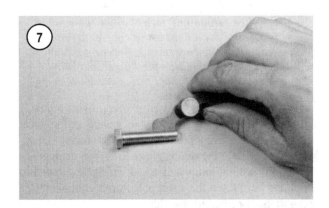

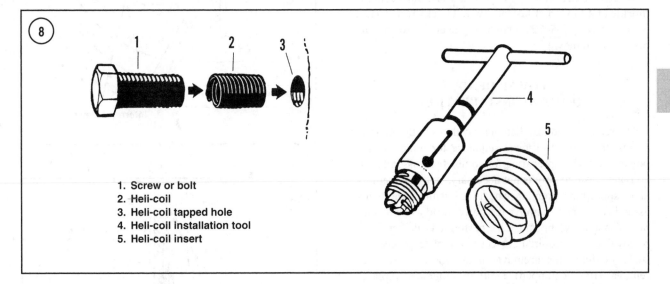

1. Screw or bolt
2. Heli-coil
3. Heli-coil tapped hole
4. Heli-coil installation tool
5. Heli-coil insert

8

Determine the fastener size by measuring the shank of the screw or bolt as shown in **Figure 6**. Determine the thread pitch using the appropriate metric or American thread pitch gauge as shown in **Figure 7**.

Damaged threads in components and castings may be repaired using a Heli-coil or an equivalent stainless steel threaded insert (**Figure 8**, typical). Heli-coil kits are available at automotive or marine and industrial supply stores. Never run a thread tap or thread chaser into a hole equipped with a Heli-coil. Replace damaged Heli-coils by gripping the outermost coil with needlenose pliers and unthreading the coil from the hole. Do not pull the coil straight out or the threads in the hole will be damaged.

CAUTION
Metric and American fasteners are used on these engines. Always match a replacement fastener to the original. Do not run a tap or thread chaser into a hole or over a bolt without first verifying the thread size and pitch. Newer model manufacturer's parts catalogs

will list every standard fastener by diameter, length and pitch. Always have the engine model and serial numbers when ordering a parts catalog from a dealership.

Unless otherwise specified, tighten components secured by more than one fastener in a minimum of three steps. First, evenly tighten all fasteners hand-tight. Then evenly tighten all fasteners to 50% of the torque specification. Finally, evenly tighten all fasteners to 100% of the specification.

Follow torque sequences as directed. If a sequence is not specified, start at the center of the component and tighten in a circular pattern, working outward. All torque sequences are in the appropriate *Assembly* section of this chapter.

CAUTION
Many models use a new torque process for the connecting rod bolts, cylinder head bolts and crankcase cover bolts. This procedure

*is called **torque and turn**. Follow the new procedure as outlined in this chapter to prevent damaging components. Never retorque a fastener secured by the torque and turn method. Refer to **Table 1** to determine which models use this process.*

Always retorque spark plugs to ensure proper heat transfer and to prevent preignition and detonation (Chapter Three). Retorque spark plugs after the engine has reached operating temperature and has been allowed to cool. Do not loosen the spark plug; simply retighten the plug to the specified torque value.

When no other sealant or adhesive is specified, coat the threads of all external fasteners with Quicksilver Perfect Seal (part No. 92-34227-1) to help prevent corrosion and ease future removal.

POWER HEAD
REMOVAL/INSTALLATION

The removal and installation procedures in this chapter represent the most efficient sequence for removing the power head while preparing for complete disassembly. If complete disassembly is not necessary, stop disassembly at the appropriate point, then begin reassembly where disassembly stopped. Remove the power head as an assembly if major repair must be performed. Power head removal is not required for certain service procedures such as cylinder head removal, intake and exhaust cover removal (if so equipped), ignition component replacement, fuel system component replacement and reed block/intake manifold removal.

Removal/Installation (65 Jet and 75-125 hp [Except 105 Jet and 115 hp Optimax] Models)

These models are equipped with the CDM (capacitor discharge module) ignition system. The electrical/ignition components are mounted on a metal plate that is grounded to the power head. There is no access cover. Power head mounted relays control a two-wire trim/tilt motor.

Remove the power head with most of the accessories and systems still installed. Remove these items after the power head is separated from the drive shaft housing. Refer to the end of the manual for wiring diagrams. Reinstall all cable clamps in their original positions and replace any tie-straps that were removed with new tie-straps.

1. Disconnect the spark plug leads and remove all spark plugs.

2. Disconnect both battery cables from the battery.

3. Remove the split lower covers as follows:

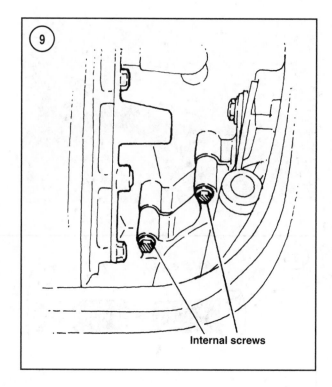

Internal screws

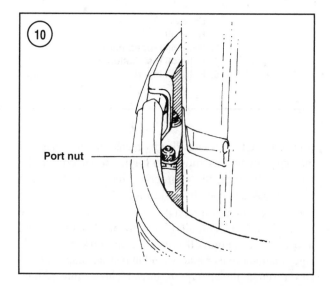

Port nut

a. Remove the two aft internal screws (**Figure 9**) and the one front external screw (just above the steering arm). Then, loosen the port nut (**Figure 10**) securing the front latch plate to both lower covers.

b. Disconnect the lower cover mounted trim switch wires at their bullet connectors and disconnect the water (tell-tale) discharge hose from the top of the exhaust cover.

c. Remove the starboard and port lower covers. Pull the fuel line connector and grommet free from the

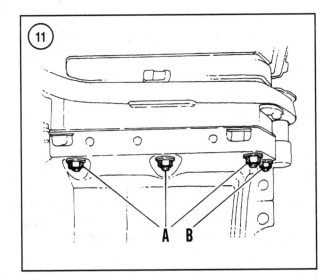

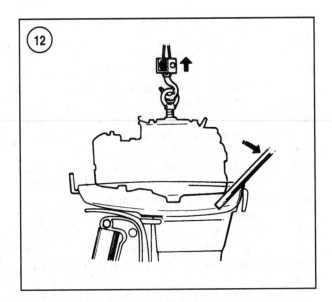

starboard cover. Lift the electrical harnesses, and control cables and grommets from each cover as it is removed.

4. Remove the battery cables from the power head. Note each connection's location and the cable routing for reassembly.

5. Disconnect the power trim motor blue and green wires from the main engine harness bullet connectors.

6. Disconnect the remote control harness from the engine harness at the main harness connector. Then disconnect the remote control harness blue/white and green/white power trim/tilt wires at their bullet connectors. If an engine temperature switch or trim indicator gauge is installed, disconnect the remote control harness tan and/or brown/white wires at their bullet connectors.

NOTE
The 65 and 80 jet models do not require the shift cable or shift linkage to be disconnected to remove the power head.

7. Disconnect and remove the remote control throttle and shift cables as described in Chapter Fourteen.

8. Remove the locknut securing the shift link arm to the bottom of the shift slide located on the shift rail. Disengage the link arm from the shift slide. Locate and secure the bushing. If any washers are present, note their positions and secure them for reassembly.

9. Remove the flywheel cover and the plastic protective cap from the center of the flywheel. Install the lifting eye (part No. 91-90455) or an equivalent into the flywheel a minimum of five full turns.

10. Remove the eight power head mounting nuts and washers. There are three nuts on each side (A, **Figure 11**) and two nuts across the rear (B) of the drive shaft housing.

CAUTION
Make sure there are no hoses, wires or linkages connecting the power head to the drive shaft housing.

11. Apply upward pressure with a suitable hoist while rocking the power head to break the gasket seal between the drive shaft housing and power head. Use a blunt tip pry bar to break the power head loose from the drive shaft housing. See **Figure 12**. Then, continue lifting the power head until the mounting studs are free of the drive shaft housing.

12. Place the power head on a clean workbench or on a power head (crankshaft) stand (part No. 91-812549). Securely clamp the power head stand in a vise.

13. Thoroughly clean all gasket material from the drive shaft housing and power head mating surfaces.

14. To install the power head, lubricate the drive shaft splines with Quicksilver Special Lubricant 101 (part No. 92-13872A 1) or 2-4-C Multi-Lube (part No. 92-825407). Wipe excess lubricant from the top of the drive shaft.

15. Place a new gasket onto the drive shaft housing.

16. Thread the lifting eye (part No. 91-90455) into the flywheel a minimum of five full turns. Support the power head with a suitable hoist.

17. Coat the threads of the eight power head mounting studs with Loctite 271 threadlocking adhesive (part No. 92-809819). Then, position the power head over the drive shaft housing and lower it into position. Rotate the crankshaft as necessary to align the drive shaft splines.

18. Install the eight nuts and washers (A and B, **Figure 11**) to the power head mounting studs. Evenly tighten the

nuts in three progressive steps to the specification in **Table 1**.

19. Remove the lifting eye and reinstall the flywheel plastic plug and the flywheel cover.

20. Install the shift bushing over the stud on the bottom of the shift slide. Then engage the shift link arm to the stud and bushing. If any washers were present on removal, reinstall them as noted. Secure the link arm with a locknut. Tighten the nut securely, then back it off 1/4 turn to allow free linkage movement.

21. Install and adjust the remote control throttle and shift cables as described in Chapter Fourteen.

22. Connect the remote control harness to the engine harness at the main harness connector. Position the connector in its bracket or spring clamp. Then connect the remote control harness blue/white and green/white power trim/tilt wires to the engine harness bullet connectors. If an engine temperature switch or trim indicator gauge is installed, reconnect the remote control harness tan and/or brown/white wires to the appropriate engine harness bullet connectors.

23. Connect the power trim motor blue and green wires to the main engine harness bullet connectors.

24. Connect the battery cables to the power head. Position them as noted on removal. Tighten the connection securely.

25. Install the split lower covers as follows:

    a. Position the starboard and port lower covers on the power head and drive shaft housing. Push the fuel line connector and grommet into the starboard cover. Slide the electrical harnesses, and control cables and grommets into each cover as it is installed.

    b. Connect the lower cover mounted trim switch leads to the engine harness bullet connectors and connect the tell-tale water discharge hose to the exhaust cover. Secure the hose connection with a new tie-strap.

    c. Install the two aft internal screws (**Figure 9**) and the one front external screw. Tighten these screws hand-tight at this time.

    d. Tighten the port nut (**Figure 10**) securing the front latch plate to both lower covers. Tighten the nut securely. Then, tighten the two aft internal screws (**Figure 9**) and one front external screw securely.

26. Install the spark plugs and reconnect the spark plug leads. Tighten the spark plugs to the specification in **Table 1**.

27. Connect both battery cables to the battery. Tighten the connections securely.

28. Bleed the oil system as described in Chapter Thirteen.

29. Refer to Chapter Four as needed for fuel and oil recommendations and break-in procedures. Then refer to Chapter Five and perform the synchronization and linkage adjustments.

Removal/Installation (105 Jet and 135-200 hp [Except 200 hp Optimax] Models)

Remove the power head with most of the accessories and systems still installed. Remove these items after the power head is separated from the drive shaft housing. Refer to the end of the manual for wiring diagrams. Reinstall all cable clamps in their original positions and replace any tie-straps that were removed with new tie-straps.

Removal

1. Disconnect the spark plug leads and remove all spark plugs.

2. Disconnect both battery cables from the battery, then disconnect the battery cables from the power head. Note each cable's location and routing for reassembly.

3. Remove the two screws securing the split harness clamp, that holds the remote control harness, to the starboard side of the split lower cover. Remove the upper and lower halves of the clamp from the lower cover.

4. Disconnect the remote control harness from the engine harness at the main harness connector located near the starter motor. Then disconnect the remote control harness blue/white and green/white power trim/tilt wires at their bullet connectors. If an engine temperature switch or trim indicator gauge is installed, disconnect the remote control harness tan and/or brown/white wires at their bullet connectors.

5. Disconnect the power trim motor blue and green wires from the main engine harness bullet connectors.

> *NOTE*
> *The shift cable or shift linkage does not have to be disconnected on 105 and 140 jet models in order for the power head to be removed.*

6. Disconnect and remove the remote control throttle and shift cables as described in Chapter Fourteen.

7A. On carbureted models, disconnect the fuel supply hose from the fitting just before the fuel pump. Plug the line and cap the fitting to prevent contamination and leaks. On some later models, the fuel supply hose connects to a fitting near the front of the lower cover.

7B. On EFI and Optimax models, disconnect the fuel supply hose from the inline fuel fitting just inside the front of

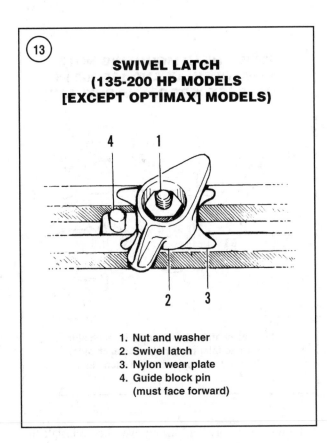

**SWIVEL LATCH
(135-200 HP MODELS
[EXCEPT OPTIMAX] MODELS)**

1. **Nut and washer**
2. **Swivel latch**
3. **Nylon wear plate**
4. **Guide block pin
   (must face forward)**

the lower cover. Plug the line and cap the fitting to prevent contamination and leaks.

8. On Optimax models, disconnect the warning gauge wire harness from the engine wire harness. The connectors are located on the front and starboard side of the power head.

9. On 2001-on Optimax models with Smart Craft gauges, disconnect the Smart Craft gauge harness as follows:

   a. Disconnect the gauge harness from the engine wire harness. The plug is located on the lower starboard and front side of the power head near the oil pump hoses.

   b. Disconnect the water pressure sensor harness (speedometer) from the engine wire harness. The connector is located on the rear port side of the power head and near the No. 4 cylinder ignition coil.

10. Remove the split lower covers as follows:

   a. Disconnect the cover-mounted trim/tilt switch wires from the engine wiring harness bullet connectors.

   b. Disconnect the water (tell-tale) discharge hose from the fitting at the rear of the starboard lower cover.

   c. Remove the three internal and one external screws securing the lower cover halves to each other. The

screws are accessed from the port side of the motor. There are two internal screws at the rear and one internal screw at the front. The external screw is just above the steering arm.

   d. Remove the starboard and port lower covers.

11. Disconnect the oil line with the blue stripe from the fitting just below or on the engine-mounted oil reservoir. Then disconnect the vent line from the crankcase fitting on the starboard side, below the starter motor. Plug the lines and cap the fittings to prevent contamination and leaks.

12. Position the outboard shift linkage in the NEUTRAL position. This is the midpoint of the total shift linkage travel. Rotate the propeller when moving the shift linkage to prevent gearcase damage.

13. On all models, except Optimax, remove the locknut holding the shift cable swivel latch assembly to the shift slide rail. Then, remove the washer, swivel latch and nylon wear plate from the control cable anchor bracket. See **Figure 13**.

14. On Optimax models, disconnect the following cooling water and air hoses:

   a. Mark the hose and fitting, then disconnect the fuel rail/cooler inlet cooling hose from the upper fitting on the port side of the power head adapter plate. See Chapter Six. Mark the hose and fittings to ensure proper connections after power head installation.

   b. On 1998-2000 models, mark the hose and fitting, then disconnect the air outlet hose from the lower fitting on the port side of the adapter plate. The hose connects to the fuel/air rail. See Chapter Six.

15. Disconnect the thermostat cover hose from the adapter plate. The fitting is just below the rear of the power head.

16. Remove the ten nuts and washers holding the power head to the adapter plate and drive shaft housing. See **Figure 14**.

17. Remove the flywheel cover access plug and the plastic cap from the center of the flywheel. Thread the lifting eye (part No. 91-90455 or an equivalent) into the flywheel a minimum of five full turns.

CAUTION
Make sure there are no hoses, wires or linkages connecting the power head to the drive shaft housing.

18. Apply upward pressure with a suitable hoist while rocking the power head to break the gasket seal between the drive shaft housing and power head. Use a blunt tip pry bar to break the power head loose from the drive shaft housing. See **Figure 12**. Then continue lifting the power

8

head until the mounting studs are free of the power head adapter.

> *CAUTION*
> *When using a power head (crankshaft) stand (part No. 91-30591A-1) **securely** clamp it in a vise large enough to support the weight of the power head. Fasten the vise to a workbench or support stand that can support the weight of the power head and the stresses of disassembly and reassembly.*

19. Place the power head on a clean workbench or on a power head (crankshaft) stand (part No. 91-30591A-1). Clamp the power head stand securely in a vise.

20. Thoroughly clean all gasket material from the drive shaft housing and power head mating surfaces.

21. On 135-200 hp (except Optimax) models, remove the guide block and spring from the shift linkage arm on the drive shaft housing.

Installation

1. Lubricate the drive shaft splines with Quicksilver Special Lubricant 101 (part No. 92-13872A1) or 2-4-C Multi-Lube (part No. 92-825407). Wipe excess lubricant from the top of the drive shaft.

2. Place a new gasket over the power head studs and against the power head mating surface. A *small* amount of contact adhesive may be used to hold the gasket in place.

3. On 135-200 hp (except Optimax) models, lubricate the spring and guide block with Quicksilver 2-4-C Multi-Lube. Install the spring and guide block onto the shift linkage arm on the drive shaft housing. Position the guide block with the anchor pin facing forward (**Figure 13**).

4. Thread the lifting eye (part No. 91-90455) into the flywheel a minimum of five full turns. Support the power head with a suitable hoist.

5. Coat the shanks and threads of the power head mounting studs with Quicksilver Perfect Seal (part No. 92-34227-1).

6. Position the power head over the drive shaft housing and carefully lower the power head onto the drive shaft housing. Make sure the shift linkage guide block is piloted in the shift slide rail with the guide block anchor pin facing forward. Then rotate the flywheel to align the crankshaft and drive shaft splines and seat the power head to the drive shaft housing.

7. Install the power head mounting nuts and flat washers (**Figure 14**). Evenly tighten the nuts in three progressive steps to the specification in **Table 1**.

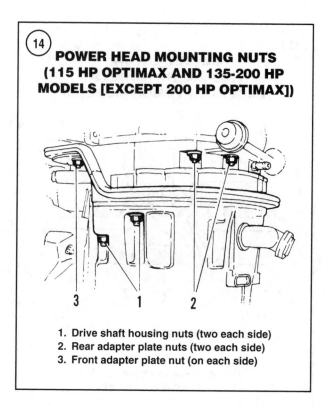

POWER HEAD MOUNTING NUTS (115 HP OPTIMAX AND 135-200 HP MODELS [EXCEPT 200 HP OPTIMAX])

1. Drive shaft housing nuts (two each side)
2. Rear adapter plate nuts (two each side)
3. Front adapter plate nut (on each side)

8. Remove the hoist and lifting eye, then reinstall the plastic cap in the center of the flywheel and the access plug in the flywheel cover.

9. On 135-200 hp (except Optimax) models, install the nylon wear plate, swivel latch, flat washer and locknut onto the shift linkage arm. Tighten the locknut until two or three threads are exposed beyond the top of the nut. See **Figure 13**.

10. Connect the oil line with the blue stripe to the T-fitting located just below or on the engine-mounted oil reservoir. Then connect the vent line to the crankcase fitting on the starboard side of the power head, below the starter motor. Secure both connections with new tie-straps.

11. On all models, except Optimax, install the swivel latch assembly onto the shift slide rail. Secure the assembly with the locknut. Then install the washer, swivel latch and nylon wear plate onto the control cable anchor bracket. See **Figure 13**.

12. On Optimax models, connect the following cooling water and air hoses:

   a. Connect the fuel rail/cooler inlet cooling hose from the upper fitting on the port side of the power head adapter plate as described in *Air/Fuel Rails and DFI Injector* in Chapter Six. Compare the markings made on the hose and fittings prior to removal to ensure proper connections. Secure all hoses with suitable clamps.

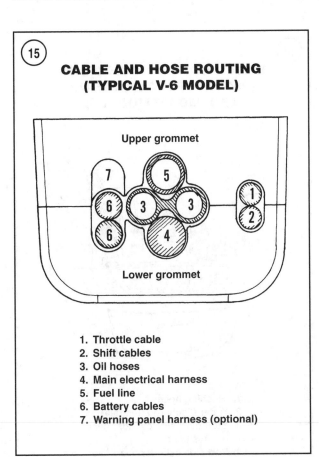

(15)

CABLE AND HOSE ROUTING (TYPICAL V-6 MODEL)

Upper grommet

7 5 1 2

6 3 3

6 4

Lower grommet

1. **Throttle cable**
2. **Shift cables**
3. **Oil hoses**
4. **Main electrical harness**
5. **Fuel line**
6. **Battery cables**
7. **Warning panel harness (optional)**

b. Connect the air outlet hose onto the lower fitting on the port side of the adapter plate. The other end of the hose connects to the fuel/air rail. Install the hoses and clamps as described in Chapter Six.

13. Connect the thermostat cover hose to the adapter plate fitting. The fitting is just below the rear of the power head. Secure the hose to the fitting with a suitable clamp.

14. Install the split lower covers as follows:

a. Position the starboard and port lower covers on the power head and the drive shaft housing.

b. Secure the covers to each other with three internal screws and one external screw. Make sure no hoses, wiring or other engine components are pinched between the covers, then tighten the screws securely.

c. Connect the cover-mounted trim/tilt switch leads to the engine wiring harness bullet connectors.

d. Connect the water (tell-tale) discharge hose to the fitting at the rear of the starboard lower cover. Secure the connection with a new tie-strap.

15A. On carbureted models, connect the fuel supply hose to the fitting just before the fuel pump. On some later models, the fuel supply hose connects to a fitting near the

front of the lower cover. Secure the fuel supply hose to the fitting with a suitable clamp.

15B. On EFI and Optimax models, connect the fuel supply hose from the inline fuel fitting just inside the front of the lower cover. Secure the fuel supply hose to the fitting with a suitable clamp.

16. On Optimax models, connect the warning gauge wire harness to the engine wire harness. The connectors are located on the front starboard side of the power head.

17. On 2001-on Optimax with Smart Craft gauges, reconnect the Smart Craft gauge harnesses as follows:

a. Connect the gauge harness to the engine wire harness. The plug is located on the lower starboard front side of the power head near the oil pump hoses.

b. Connect the water pressure sensor harness (speedometer) to the engine wire harness. The connector is located on the rear port side of the power head and near the No. 4 cylinder ignition coil.

18. Install the remote control throttle and shift cables as described in Chapter Fourteen.

19. Connect the power trim motor blue and green wires to the main engine harness bullet connectors.

20. Connect the remote control harness to the engine harness at the main harness connector. Then connect the remote control harness blue/white and green/white power trim/tilt wires to the engine harness bullet connectors. If an engine temperature switch or trim indicator gauge is installed, connect the remote control harness tan and/or brown/white wires to their bullet connectors.

21. Connect the battery cables to the engine. Position them as noted on removal. Tighten the connections securely.

> *CAUTION*
> *The split clamp hose routing shown in **Figure 15**, typical does not apply to all models. To prevent damaged hoses or cables and fuel/oil starvation problems, route the hoses through the clamp as described in Chapter Fourteen.*

22. Route the hoses and cables through the split clamp grommet (**Figure 15**, typical) as described in Chapter Fourteen.

23. Install the spark plugs and reconnect the spark plug leads. Tighten the spark plugs to the specification in **Table 1**.

24. Connect the battery cables to the battery. Tighten the connections securely.

25. Bleed the oil injection system as described in Chapter Thirteen.

8

26. Refer to Chapter Four as needed for fuel and oil recommendations and break-in procedures. Then refer to Chapter Five and perform synchronization and linkage adjustments.

Removal/Installation (200 Optimax, 225 hp and 250 hp Models)

The power head is best removed with most of the accessories and systems left installed. These items can be removed after the power head is separated from the drive shaft housing. Refer to the back of the manual for wiring diagrams. Make sure all cable clamps are reinstalled in their original positions and new tie-straps are installed to replace any that were removed.

Removal

1. Disconnect the spark plug leads and remove all spark plugs.

2. Disconnect both battery cables at the battery, then remove the electrical/ignition component access cover located on the starboard side of the power head. Disconnect the battery cables from the power head after noting each cable's location and the routing for reassembly.

3. Remove the two screws securing the split harness clamp (**Figure 15**, typical) to the starboard side of the split lower cover. Remove the upper and lower halves of the clamp from the lower cover.

4. Disconnect the remote control harness from the engine harness at the main harness connector located at the rear of the starter motor. Then disconnect the remote control harness blue/white and green/white power trim/tilt wires at their bullet connectors. If an engine temperature switch or trim indicator gauge is installed, disconnect the remote control harness tan and/or brown/white wires at their bullet connectors.

5A. On carbureted and EFI models, if the engine is equipped with the factory warning panel (gauge), disconnect the warning panel harness wires from the appropriate engine wiring harness bullet connectors. Refer to the end of the manual for specific wiring diagrams.

5B. On Optimax models, disconnect the warning gauge or Smart Craft harness from the engine wire harness. The connectors are on the lower starboard side of the power head and near the oil pump hoses. Refer to the wiring diagrams at the end of the manual and to the following to identify the wire harness.

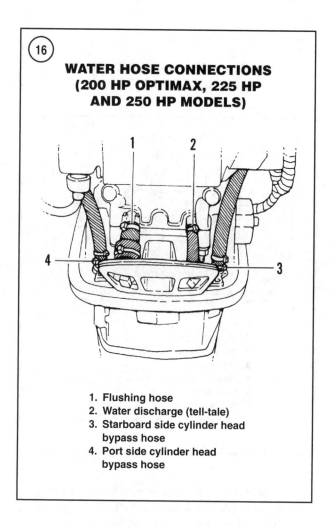

WATER HOSE CONNECTIONS (200 HP OPTIMAX, 225 HP AND 250 HP MODELS)

1. Flushing hose
2. Water discharge (tell-tale)
3. Starboard side cylinder head bypass hose
4. Port side cylinder head bypass hose

a. On 1998-2000 models, four wires (tan/black, tan/white, pink/light blue and orange) connect the gauge to the engine harness.

b. On 2001-on, a single plug connects the Smart Craft gauges to the engine wire harness. Disconnect the water pressure sensor harness (speedometer) from the engine wire harness. The sensor and harness connector is on the lower starboard side of the power head below the starter motor.

6. Disconnect the power trim motor blue and green wires from the main engine harness bullet connectors located on or near the electrical component plate. Remove clamps or tie-straps securing the trim motor harness to the power head.

7. Disconnect and remove the remote control throttle and shift cables as described in Chapter Fourteen.

8. Disconnect the fuel supply hose from the inline fuel fitting just inside the front of the lower cover. Plug the line and cap the fitting to prevent contamination and leaks.

9. Remove the split lower covers as follows:

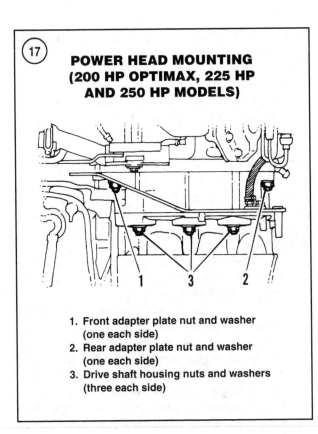

⑰ POWER HEAD MOUNTING (200 HP OPTIMAX, 225 HP AND 250 HP MODELS)

1. Front adapter plate nut and washer (one each side)
2. Rear adapter plate nut and washer (one each side)
3. Drive shaft housing nuts and washers (three each side)

a. Disconnect the cover-mounted trim/tilt switch leads from the engine wiring harness bullet connectors.

b. Remove the three internal and one external screws securing the lower cover halves to each other. Access the screws from the port side of the motor. There are two internal screws at the rear and one internal screw at the front. The external screw is just above the steering arm.

c. Remove the starboard and port lower covers.

10. Disconnect the water discharge (2, **Figure 16**) and water flushing hose (1) from the fittings at the rear of the power head.

11. Locate the water bypass hoses that connect each cylinder head's thermostat housing to an adapter plate fitting. Disconnect the hoses (3 and 4, **Figure 16**) from the adapter plate fittings.

12. On Optimax models, mark the hose and fitting, then disconnect the fuel cooler/rail water hose from the upper fitting on the starboard rear corner of the adapter plate.

13. On 1998-2000 Optimax models, mark the hose and fitting, then disconnect the air discharge hose from the lower fitting on the starboard rear corner of the adapter plate.

14. Disconnect the oil line with the blue stripe from the T-fitting located just below the engine-mounted oil reser-

voir. Then, disconnect the vent line from the crankcase fitting on the starboard side, far below the starter motor. Plug the lines and cap the fittings to prevent contamination and leaks.

15. Remove the ten nuts and washers holding the power head to the adapter plate and drive shaft housing. See **Figure 17**.

16. Remove the flywheel cover and the plastic cap from the center of the flywheel. Thread the lifting eye (part No. 91-90455 or an equivalent) into the flywheel a minimum of five full turns.

CAUTION
Make sure there are no hoses, wires or linkages connecting the power head to the drive shaft housing.

17. Apply upward pressure with a suitable hoist while rocking the power head to break the gasket seal between the drive shaft housing and power head. Use a blunt tip pry bar to break the power head loose from the drive shaft housing. See **Figure 12**. Then continue lifting the power head until the mounting studs are free of the power head adapter.

CAUTION
When using the power head (crankshaft) stand (part No. 91-30591A-1 [eight-spline] or part No. 91-812549 [13-spline]), securely clamp it in a vise large enough to support the power head's weight. Fasten the vise to a workbench or support stand that can support the weight of the power head, and the stresses of disassembly and reassembly.

18. Place the power head on a clean workbench or on the appropriate power head (crankshaft) stand. Securely clamp the power head stand in a vise.

19. Thoroughly clean all gasket material from the drive shaft housing and power head mating surfaces.

Installation

1. Lubricate the drive shaft splines with Quicksilver Special Lubricant 101 (part No. 92-13872A1) or 2-4-C Multi-Lube (part No. 92-825407). Wipe excess lubricant from the top of the drive shaft.

2. Place a new gasket over the power head studs and against the power head mating surface. A *small* amount of contact adhesive may be used to hold the gasket in place.

3. Thread the lifting eye (part No. 91-90455) into the flywheel a minimum of five full turns. Support the power head with a suitable hoist.

8

4. Coat the shanks and threads of the power head mounting studs with Quicksilver Perfect Seal (part No. 92-34227-1).

5. Position the power head over the drive shaft housing and carefully lower the power head onto the drive shaft housing. Rotate the shift slide as necessary to allow the shift link arm roller to pilot into the shift slide. Then rotate the flywheel to align the crankshaft and drive shaft splines, and seat the power head to the drive shaft housing.

6. Install the power head mounting nuts and flat washers (**Figure 17**). Evenly tighten the nuts in three progressive steps to the specification in **Table 1**.

7. Remove the hoist and lifting eye, then reinstall the plastic cap in the center of the flywheel.

8. Connect the oil line with the blue stripe to the T-fitting located just below the engine-mounted oil reservoir. Then connect the vent line to the crankcase fitting on the starboard side of the power head, below the starter motor. Secure both connections with new tie-straps.

9. Connect the water (tell-tale) discharge and water flushing hoses to appropriate fittings at the rear of the power head. See **Figure 16**.

10. Connect the water bypass hoses from each cylinder head's thermostat housing to the appropriate adapter plate fittings. See **Figure 16**. Secure each connection with a new tie-strap.

11. On Optimax models, connect the fuel cooler/rail water hose onto the upper fitting on the starboard rear corner of the adapter plate. Secure the hose to the fitting with a suitable clamp. Check the connections using the markings made on the hoses and fittings prior to removal.

12. On 1998-2000 Optimax models, connect the air discharge hose onto the lower fitting on the starboard rear corner of the adapter plate. Secure the hose to the fitting with a suitable clamp. Check the connections using the markings made on the hoses and fittings prior to removal.

13. Install the split lower covers as follows:
   a. Position the starboard and port lower covers to the power head and the drive shaft housing.
   b. Secure the covers to each other with three internal screws and one external screw. Make sure no hose or wiring is pinched between the covers, then tighten the four screws to the specification in **Table 1**.
   c. Connect the cover-mounted trim/tilt switch leads to the engine wiring harness bullet connectors.

14. Connect the fuel supply hose to the inline fuel fitting just inside the front of the lower cover. Secure the connection with a suitable clamp.

15. Install the remote control throttle and shift cables as described in Chapter Fourteen.

16. Connect the power trim motor blue and green leads to the main engine harness bullet connectors.

17A. On carbureted and EFI models, if the engine is equipped with the factory warning panel (gauge), connect the warning panel harness leads to the appropriate engine wiring harness bullet connectors. Refer to the end of the manual for specific wiring diagrams. The color codes are typically as follows:

17B. On Optimax models, connect the warning gauge or Smart Craft harness to the engine wire harness. The connectors are located on the lower starboard side of the power head near the oil pump hoses. Refer to the wiring diagrams at the end of the manual and the following to identify the wire harness.
   a. On 1998-2000 models, four wires (tan/black, tan/white, pink/light blue and orange) connect the gauge to the engine harness.
   b. On 2001-on models, a single plug connects the Smart Craft gauges to the engine wire harness. Connect the water pressure sensor harness (speedometer) to the engine wire harness. The sensor and harness connector is located on the lower starboard side of the power head below the starter motor.

18. Connect the remote control harness to the engine harness at the main harness connector located to the rear of the starter motor. Then connect the remote control harness blue/white and green/white power trim/tilt wires to the engine harness bullet connectors. If an engine temperature switch or trim indicator gauge is installed, connect the remote control harness tan and/or brown/white wires to the engine harness bullet connectors.

19. Connect the battery cables to the engine. Position them as noted on removal. Tighten the connections securely. Then install the electrical/ignition component access cover, if so equipped. Tighten the cover screws securely.

CAUTION
*The split clamp hose routing shown in **Figure 15**, typical does not apply to all models. To prevent damaged hoses or cables and fuel/oil starvation problems, route the hoses through the clamp as described in Chapter Fourteen.*

20. Route the hoses and cables through the split clamp grommet (**Figure 15**, typical) as described in Chapter Fourteen.

21. Install the spark plugs and reconnect the spark plug leads. Tighten the spark plugs to the specification in **Table 1**.

22. Connect the battery cables to the battery. Tighten the connections securely.

23. Bleed the oil injection system as described in Chapter Thirteen.

24. Refer to Chapter Four as needed for fuel and oil recommendations and break-in procedures. Then refer to Chapter Five and perform all synchronization and linkage adjustments.

POWER HEAD DISASSEMBLY

Power head gasket sets are available for all models. It is often more economical and always simpler to order the gasket set instead of ordering each component individually. Replace *every* gasket, seal and O-ring during a power head reassembly. Replace the piston rings if the piston(s) are taken out of the cylinder bore.

Dowel pins position the crankcase halves to each other and position some crankshaft bearings. The dowel pins do not have to be removed if they are securely seated in a bore on either side of the crankcase halves or in the bearing. However, they must be located during disassembly and reassembly. If a dowel pin can be readily removed from its bore, remove it and store it with the other internal components until reassembly begins.

The connecting rods on all models are the fractured cap design. The cap is broken from the rod during the manufacturing process, leaving a jagged mating surface that will mate perfectly when installed in its original orientation. If the cap is reversed and the rod bolts are tightened, the rod will be distorted and must be discarded. While alignment marks are provided, always mark the rod and cap with a permanent marker. Correct orientation is obvious if the time is taken to examine the mating surfaces of the rod and cap.

Clean and inspect all power head components before reassembly. If the power head has had a major failure, it may be more economical to replace the basic power head as an assembly.

Special tools are required for power head repair. The part numbers are listed in the repair instructions. Remember that parts damaged by not using the correct tool can often be more expensive than the original cost of the tool.

A large number of fasteners of different lengths and sizes are used in a power head. Plastic sandwich bags and/or cupcake tins are excellent methods of keeping small parts organized. Tag all larger internal parts for location and orientation. Use a felt-tipped permanent marker to mark components after they have been cleaned. Avoid scribing or stamping internal components as the marking process may damage or weaken the component.

NOTE
Take a series of photographs from the front, rear, top, bottom and both sides of the power head after removal and before disassembly for help during reassembly. The photographs are especially useful when trying to route electrical harnesses, fuel, primer and recirculation lines, and installing accessories and control linkages.

Disassembly (65 Jet and 75-125 hp [Except 105 Jet and 115 Optimax] Models)

Refer to **Figure 18** and **Figure 19** for this procedure. Since the power head is removed with most of the accessories installed, all accessories and systems must first be removed from the power head.

Because this section covers three- and four-cylinder models, and since the three-cylinder models are essentially a shortened version of a four-cylinder model, the exploded illustrations are of a four-cylinder model. Any procedures specific to one model are described in the text.

After power head disassembly, refer to *Cleaning and Inspection* in this chapter and clean and inspect all components before reassembling the power head.

1. Remove the flywheel and electric starter as described in Chapter Seven.

2. Remove the oil reservoir (if not already removed), oil pump, oil warning module and all oil lines as described in Chapter Thirteen.

3. Remove the carburetors, fuel pump, fuel filter, fuel primer valve, intake manifold(s) and reed block(s), and all fuel, primer and fuel bleed (recirculation) lines as described in Chapter Six.

4. On four-cylinder models, remove the accelerator pump, the two check valves, filter and all associated fuel lines. See Chapter Six.

5. Remove the internal fuel bleed (recirculation) valves and carriers from the crankcase cover openings for cylinders No. 2, 3 and 4. See 8 and 9, **Figure 18**.

6. Remove the remaining ignition and electrical components as an assembly. This includes the stator assembly, trigger coil, trim/tilt relays and the electrical/ignition plate containing the CDMs, voltage regulator and starter solenoid. If equipped with an rpm limit module, remove it with the other components. Do not disconnect electrical components from each other unless absolutely necessary; simply remove the mounting screws, cable clamps and tie-straps. See Chapter Seven.

7. Remove the bolt at the center of the main throttle and spark control arm located on the port side of the power head. Then remove the control arm and any remaining

8

18

CYLINDER BLOCK (65 JET AND 75-125 HP [EXCEPT 105 JET AND 115 HP OPTIMAX] MODELS) (FOUR-CYLINDER SHOWN)

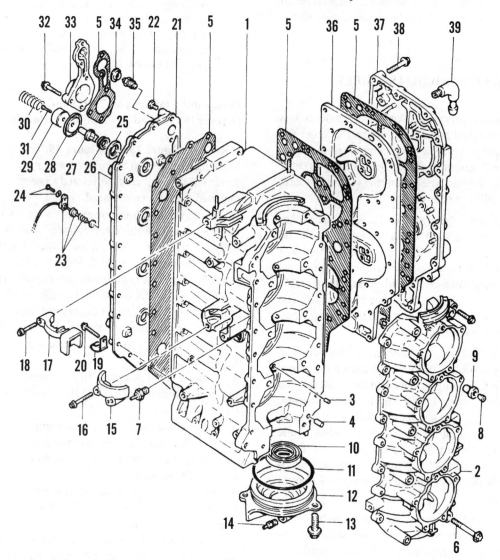

1. Cylinder block	14. Check valve	28. Diaphragm
2. Crankcase cover	15. Lower starter bracket	29. Cup
3. Bearing locating dowel	16. Bolt	30. Spring
4. Crankcase cover dowel	17. Upper starter bracket	31. Screw
5. Gaskets	18. Bolt	32. Screw
6. Crankcase cover bolts	19. Clamp	33. Thermostat cover
7. Accelerator pump discharge nozzle	20. Screw	34. Grommet
8. Fuel bleed check valve	21. Cylinder block cover	35. Thermostat
9. Fuel bleed check valve carrier	22. Brass pipe plug	36. Exhaust manifold
10. Crankshaft lower seal	23. Engine temperature switch	37. Exhaust cover
11. O-ring	24. Screw and washer	38. Bolt
12. Lower end cap	25. Carrier	39. Water discharge (tell-tale) fitting
13. Bolt	26. Grommet	
	27. Poppet valve	

CRANKSHAFT ASSEMBLY (65 JET AND 75-125 HP [EXCEPT 105 JET AND 115 HP OPTIMAX] MODELS) (FOUR CYLINDER SHOWN)

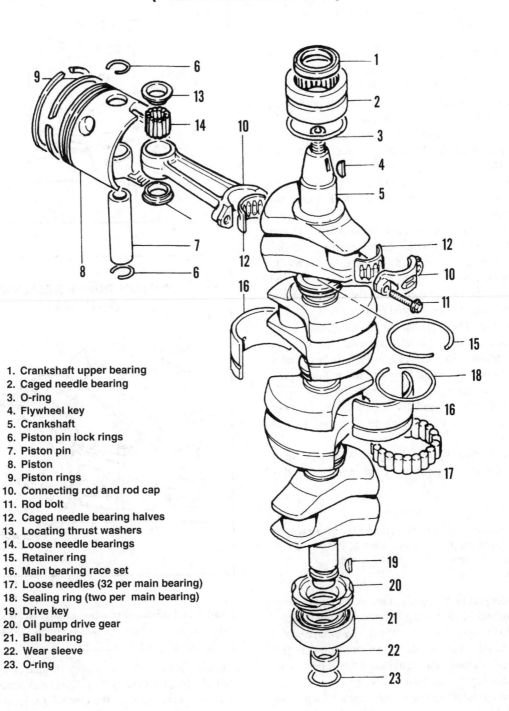

1. Crankshaft upper bearing
2. Caged needle bearing
3. O-ring
4. Flywheel key
5. Crankshaft
6. Piston pin lock rings
7. Piston pin
8. Piston
9. Piston rings
10. Connecting rod and rod cap
11. Rod bolt
12. Caged needle bearing halves
13. Locating thrust washers
14. Loose needle bearings
15. Retainer ring
16. Main bearing race set
17. Loose needles (32 per main bearing)
18. Sealing ring (two per main bearing)
19. Drive key
20. Oil pump drive gear
21. Ball bearing
22. Wear sleeve
23. O-ring

8

control linkage as an assembly. Position the bolt through the control arm, then install a suitable nut to keep the control arm components together.

NOTE
Three-cylinder models have a washer that fits between the thermostat cover, and the thermostat and grommet assembly. Do not lose the washer.

8. Remove the five screws securing the thermostat cover (33, **Figure 18**) to the rear of the power head at the top of the crankcase cover. Remove the thermostat cover and discard the gasket. Then remove thermostat and grommet, and the poppet valve and spring assembly.

9. Reach into the cylinder block's poppet valve cavity and retrieve the grommet from the grommet carrier. See 26, **Figure 18**. Discard the grommet.

10. Remove the screw and washer securing the engine temperature switch to the cylinder block. Remove the switch assembly.

11. Remove the 14 (on three-cylinder models) or 18 (on four-cylinder models) remaining bolts securing the cylinder block cover (21, **Figure 18**) to the cylinder block. Carefully pry the cover from the block, then remove and discard the gasket. Do not damage or distort the cover or cylinder block during the removal process.

12. Remove the 24 bolts (on three-cylinder models) or 35 bolts (on four-cylinder models) securing the exhaust cover and manifold (36 and 37, **Figure 18**) to the cylinder block. Carefully pry the tabs provided to remove the assembly from the block, then separate the manifold from the cover plate. Remove and discard the gaskets. Do not damage or distort the cover or manifold during the removal process.

13. Remove the three bolts securing the lower end cap to the power head. Do not remove the lower end cap at this time.

CAUTION
The crankcase cover and cylinder block are a matched, align-bored unit. Do not scratch, nick or damage the machined mating surfaces.

14A. On three-cylinder models, remove the eight long main bearing and 12 short outer bolts securing the crankcase cover to the cylinder block. Tap the crankcase cover with a soft-faced rubber or plastic hammer to break the crankcase seal. Remove the crankcase cover. Locate and secure the locating dowel as necessary.

14B. On four-cylinder models, remove the ten long main bearing and 16 short outer bolts securing the crankcase cover to the cylinder block. Tap the crankcase cover with

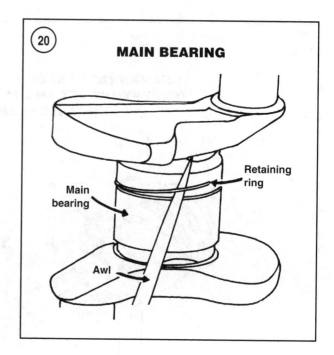

MAIN BEARING

Main bearing

Retaining ring

Awl

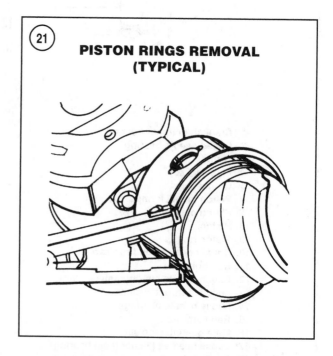

PISTON RINGS REMOVAL (TYPICAL)

a soft-faced rubber or plastic hammer to break the crankcase seal. Remove the crankcase cover. Locate and secure the locating dowel as necessary.

15. Lift the crankshaft assembly straight up and out of the cylinder block and set it on a clean workbench. Then pull the lower end cap from the crankshaft. Remove and discard the O-ring and crankshaft seal. Do not damage the end cap when removing the seal.

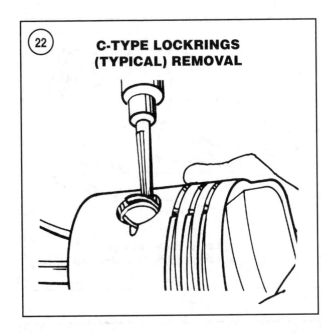

C-TYPE LOCKRINGS (TYPICAL) REMOVAL

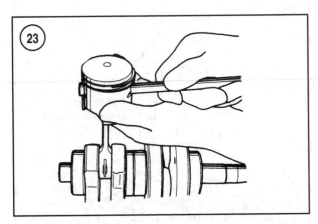

16. Mount the crankshaft vertically in a power head (crankshaft) stand (part No. 91-812549 or on equivalent). Make sure the stand is securely clamped in a vise.

17. Locate and secure the crankshaft center main bearing locating dowel (3, **Figure 18**) as necessary. There are three dowels on a three-cylinder model and four dowels on a four-cylinder model.

18. Slide the upper crankshaft seal and caged roller bearing assembly from the crankshaft. Remove the seal from the bearing, then discard the seal.

NOTE
There are two center main bearing assemblies on a three-cylinder model and three center main bearing assemblies on a four-cylinder model. Each center main bearing consists of a retainer ring, two bearing race halves, 32 loose needle bear-

ings and two seal rings mounted in one groove with the open ends 180° apart.

19. Remove the retaining ring from around a center main bearing. See **Figure 20**. Then remove the outer race halves, 32 loose rollers and the two crankshaft seal rings. Store the bearing components in marked containers to allow reassembly in their original locations. Repeat the procedure for the remaining center main bearing(s).

20. Mark the corresponding cylinder number on the pistons and connecting rods with a felt-tipped permanent marker. Mark the connecting rods and rod caps so the rod caps can be reinstalled in their original orientation.

NOTE
*Always store **all** components from each connecting rod and piston assembly together. They must be reinstalled in their original locations.*

CAUTION
Wear suitable eye protection for piston ring and piston pin retainer removal procedures.

21. Remove the piston rings from all of the pistons using a piston ring expander (part No. 91-24697 or an equivalent). See **Figure 21**, typical. Keep the rings to clean the piston's ring grooves.

22. Remove each connecting rod and piston assembly as follows:
   a. Remove the connecting rod bolts from the upper, cylinder No. 1 connecting rod. Alternately loosen each bolt a small amount until all tension is off both bolts.
   b. Tap the rod cap with a soft metal (brass) mallet to separate the cap from the rod.
   c. Remove the cap and rod from the crankshaft, then remove the two caged roller bearing halves from the crankshaft.
   d. Reinstall the rod cap to the connecting rod in its original orientation. Tighten the rod cap bolts finger-tight.
   e. Store the caged roller bearing assemblies in clean, numbered containers, corresponding to the cylinder number.
   f. Repeat this procedure to remove the cylinders No. 2-4 connecting rods.

23. Use a lock ring remover (part No. 91-52952A-1) or a suitable awl to remove all piston pin lock rings. See **Figure 22**.

24. Place the piston pin tool (part No. 91-76160A-2 or an equivalent) into one end of the cylinder No. 1 piston pin bore. Support the bottom of the piston with one hand and drive the pin tool and pin from the piston. See **Figure 23**.

8

25. Remove the piston from the connecting rod. Remove the locating (thrust) washers and the 29 loose needle bearings (**Figure 24**). Store the components in clean, numbered containers corresponding to the cylinder number.

26. Repeat Steps 24 and 25 to separate the pistons from cylinders No. 2-4 from their connecting rods.

27. If the crankshaft ball bearing and/or the oil pump drive gear requires replacement, replace them as follows:

    a. Support the ball bearing in a knife-edged bearing separator and press against the crankshaft using the power head stand as a mandrel until the bearing is free from the crankshaft. See **Figure 25**. Discard the bearing.

    b. If necessary, pull the oil pump gear from the crankshaft and discard it.

    c. Locate and secure the oil pump gear drive key (19, **Figure 19**).

28. Remove and discard the O-ring (23, **Figure 19**) inside the splined bore of the crankshaft. Use a dental pick or similar instrument to hook the O-ring and pull it from the bore.

29. If the wear sleeve is damaged, pull it from the crankshaft with a pair of pliers. Do not damage the crankshaft surface during removal. Discard the sleeve. If necessary, apply mild heat with a heat light (part No. 91-63209) or an equivalent to the sleeve to loosen the Loctite bond.

30. Refer to *Cleaning and Inspection* in this chapter before beginning the reassembly procedure.

Disassembly (105 Jet, 115 Optimax and 135-200 hp [Except 200 Optimax] Models)

Refer to **Figure 26** and **Figure 27** for this procedure. Since the power head is removed with most of the accessories installed, all accessories and systems must first be removed from the power head.

1. Remove the flywheel and electric starter as described in Chapter Seven.

2. Remove the oil reservoir, oil pump, oil warning module and all oil lines as described in Chapter Thirteen.

3A. On carbureted models, remove the carburetors, fuel pump, fuel filter, fuel primer valve, intake manifold and reed blocks, and all fuel, primer and fuel bleed (recirculation) lines as described in Chapter Six.

3B. On EFI models, remove the induction manifold assembly including the ECM, mechanical fuel pump, vapor separator assembly, water separating fuel filter, water warning module, intake manifold and reed blocks, and all fuel and fuel bleed (recirculation) lines as described in Chapter Six.

3C. On Optimax models, remove the induction manifold, ECM, mechanical fuel pump, fuel/air rails, air compres-

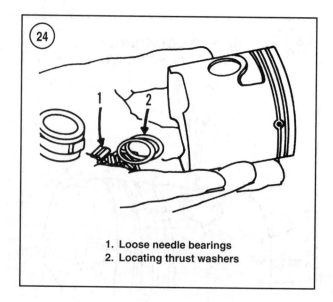

1. Loose needle bearings
2. Locating thrust washers

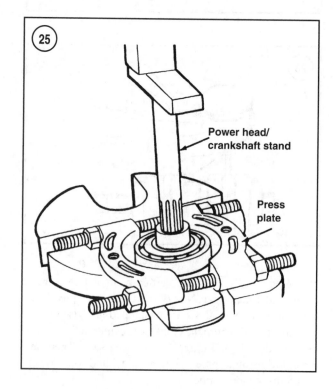

Power head/crankshaft stand

Press plate

sor, intake manifold, and all fuel and fuel bleed (recirculation) lines as described in Chapter Six.

4. On 200 hp EFI models, remove the detonation sensor and module as described in Chapter Six.

5. On models equipped with a shift switch, such as XR6, Mag III, Optimax models and engines with this system added as an accessory, disconnect the shift switch leads from the engine harness bullet connector and the ring terminal from engine ground.

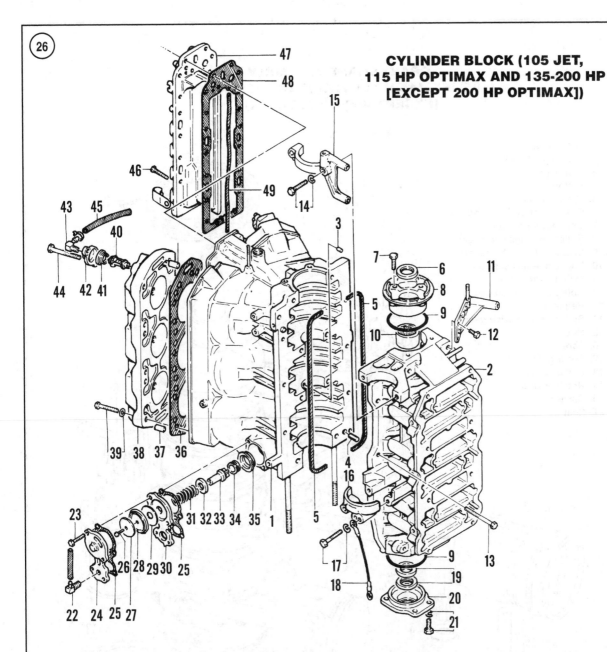

CYLINDER BLOCK (105 JET, 115 HP OPTIMAX AND 135-200 HP [EXCEPT 200 HP OPTIMAX])

8

1. Cylinder block
2. Crankcase cover
3. Bearing locating dowel
4. Crankcase cover dowel pin
5. Crankcase sealing ring
6. Crankshaft upper seal
7. Bolt
8. Upper end cap
9. O-ring
10. Caged needle bearing
11. Bracket
12. Bolt
13. Crankcase cover bolt

14. Bolt and washer
15. Upper starter bracket
16. Lower starter bracket
17. Bolt and washer
18. Ground strap
19. Crankshaft lower seals
20. Lower end cap
21. Bolt and washer
22. Fitting (water discharge)*
23. Screw
24. Outer plate
25. Gaskets

26. Screw
27. Washer
28. Diaphragm
29. Water deflector
30. Inner plate
31. Spring
32. Washer
33. Poppet valve
34. Grommet
35. Carrier
36. Head gasket*
37. Dowel pins

38. Cylinder head
39. Bolt and washer
40. Thermostat
41. Grommet
42. Thermostat housing
43. Fitting
44. Bolt
45. Hose (water discharge)
46. Bolt
47. Exhaust divider plate
48. Gasket
49. Sealing strip

*Not used on all models.

(27)

**CRANKSHAFT ASSEMBLY
(105 JET, 115 HP OPTIMAX AND 135-200 HP
[EXCEPT 200 HP OPTIMAX])**

1. Crankshaft
2. Piston pin lock rings
3. Piston pin
4. Piston
5. Piston rings
6. Connecting rod and rod cap
7. Connecting rod bolt
8. Roller bearings and cages
9. Locating (thrust) washers
10. Loose needle bearings
11. Main bearing race
12. Roller bearings an cages
13. Retainer ring
14. Split oil pump drive gear
15. Nut
16. Screw
17. Sealing ring
18. Ball bearing
19. Retainer ring
20. Carrier
21. Seal

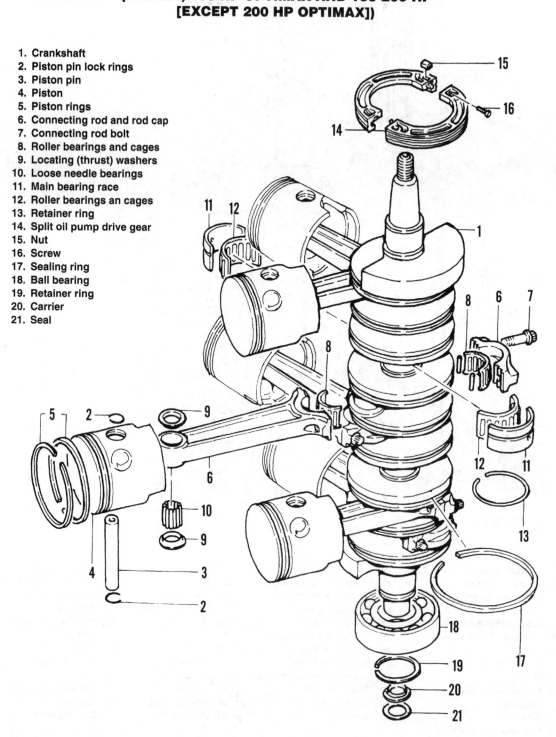

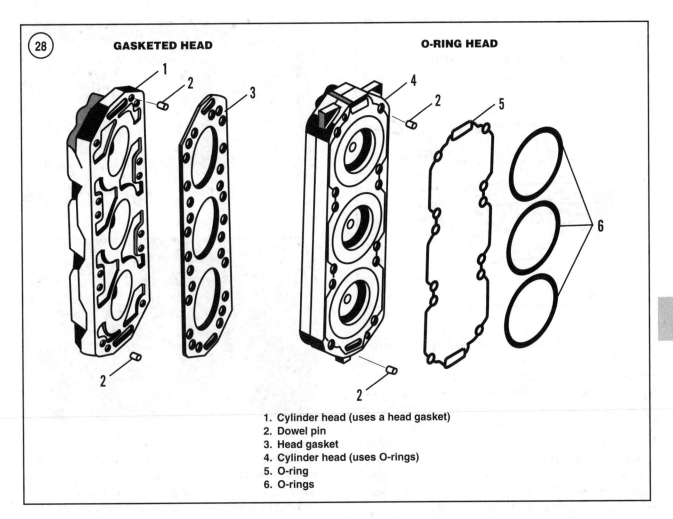

1. **Cylinder head (uses a head gasket)**
2. **Dowel pin**
3. **Head gasket**
4. **Cylinder head (uses O-rings)**
5. **O-ring**
6. **O-rings**

6. Remove the remaining ignition and electrical components as an assembly. This includes the stator assembly, trigger coil, both switch boxes, starter solenoid, idle stabilizer module, oil and overheat warning module, and the electrical/ignition plate containing the ignition coils, voltage regulators and trim relays. If equipped with an rpm limit module, remove it with the other components. Do not disconnect electrical components from each other unless absolutely necessary; simply remove the mounting screws, cable clamps and tie-straps. See Chapter Seven.

7. Remove the bolt from the center of the throttle and spark control arm located on the port side of the power head. Then remove the control arm and any remaining control linkage as an assembly. Position the bolt through the control arm, then install a suitable nut to keep the control arm components together.

8. Remove the shift and throttle cable anchor bracket from the port lower side of the power head.

9. Disconnect the water discharge hose(s) from both thermostat housings. Then remove the two screws securing

the thermostat housing (42, **Figure 26**) to the top of each cylinder head. Remove both thermostat covers, grommets and thermostats. Discard both grommets.

10. Remove the water discharge hose from the poppet valve fitting (22, **Figure 26**). Then remove the four screws securing the poppet valve assembly to the power head. Remove the valve assembly from the power head. Separate the inner and outer plates, then remove and discard both gaskets.

11. Reach into the cylinder block's poppet valve cavity and retrieve the grommet (34, **Figure 26**) from the carrier in the cavity. Discard the grommet.

NOTE
*All 2000-on 105 jet, 115 Optimax, 135 Optimax and 150-200 hp models use O-rings to seal the cylinder heads. All 1998 and 1999 models and 2000-on 135 hp (except Optimax) models use gaskets to seal the cylinder heads. See **Figure 28**.*

8

CRANKCASE COVER
REMOVAL

12. Remove the 12 bolts securing each cylinder head to the cylinder block. Carefully pull each head from the block, then remove and discard the gaskets or O-rings. If necessary, tap each cylinder head with a soft-faced rubber or plastic hammer to break the gasket seal. Do not damage the sealing surfaces during the removal process.

13. Remove the 20 bolts securing the exhaust divider plate to the cylinder block. Carefully pry the divider from the block, then remove and discard the gasket. Do not damage or distort the divider plate, or damage the cylinder block sealing surfaces during the removal process.

14. Remove and discard the strip seal (49, **Figure 26**) from the exhaust cavity.

15. Remove the four bolts (21, **Figure 26**) securing the lower end cap (20) to the power head. Do not remove the lower end cap at this time.

16. Remove the four bolts (7, **Figure 26**) securing the upper end cap (8) to the power head. Do not remove the upper end cap at this time.

CAUTION
The crankcase cover and cylinder block are a matched, align-bored unit. Do not scratch, nick or damage the machined mating surfaces.

17. Remove the eight large main bearing and six small outer bolts securing the crankcase cover to the cylinder block. Carefully pry the crankcase cover at the points shown in **Figure 29** to break the crankcase seal. Then remove the crankcase cover. Locate and secure the locating dowels as necessary.

18. Mark the corresponding cylinder number on the pistons and connecting rods with a felt-tipped permanent marker. Mark the connecting rods and rod caps so the rod caps can be reinstalled in their original orientation.

NOTE
*Always store **all** components from each connecting rod and piston assembly together. They must be reinstalled in their original locations.*

19. Remove each connecting rod and piston assembly as follows:
   a. Manually rotate the crankshaft to position the upper, cylinder No. 1 piston at the bottom of its cylinder bore. This will expose the connecting rod bolts (**Figure 30**, typical) for easy removal.
   b. Use a 12-point socket to remove the connecting rod bolts from the upper, cylinder No. 1 connecting rod. Alternately loosen each bolt a small amount until all tension is off both bolts.
   c. Tap the rod cap with a soft metal (brass) mallet to separate the cap from the rod.
   d. Remove the cap and rod from the crankshaft, then remove the roller bearings and cages from the crankshaft.

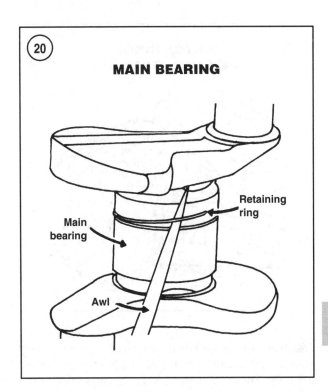

MAIN BEARING

Retaining ring

Main bearing

Awl

8

e. Carefully slide the piston and rod assembly from its cylinder bore. Be ready to catch the assembly as it leaves the cylinder bore (**Figure 31**).

CAUTION
Each connecting rod and cap is a matched assembly and must not be mismatched. The cap must be installed in its original orientation.

f. Reinstall the rod cap to the connecting rod in its original orientation. Tighten the rod cap bolts finger-tight.

g. Store the roller bearings and cages in clean, numbered containers, corresponding to the cylinder number.

h. Repeat this procedure to remove the cylinders No. 2-6 connecting rod assemblies.

20. Remove the upper end cap from the crankshaft. See **Figure 32**. Then remove the lower end cap. If the lower end cap sticks, tap it *gently* with a soft-faced rubber or plastic hammer to free it from the ball bearing. Rotate the end cap and tap around the entire outer diameter or it will cock and be damaged.

NOTE
If the caged roller bearing in the upper end cap requires replacement, replace the end cap and bearing as an assembly. The cap will be damaged if the engine is operated with a worn or damaged bearing.

21. Remove and discard the O-ring from each end cap. Then drive the seal(s) from each end cap with a suitable punch and hammer. Do not damage either end cap's seal bore during removal. Discard all seals.

22. Lift the crankshaft assembly straight up and out of the cylinder block (**Figure 33**) and mount it vertically in a power head (crankshaft) stand (part No. 91-30591A-1 or an equivalent). Make sure the stand is securely clamped in a vise.

23. Locate and secure the crankshaft center main bearing locating dowels (3, **Figure 26**) as necessary. There are two pins on these models.

24. Remove the retaining ring from around a center main bearing. See **Figure 34**, typical. Then remove the outer race halves and the roller bearings and cages. Store the bearing components in marked containers to allow reassembly in their original location. Repeat the procedure for the remaining center main bearing.

CAUTION
Wear suitable eye protection for piston ring and piston pin retainer removal procedures.

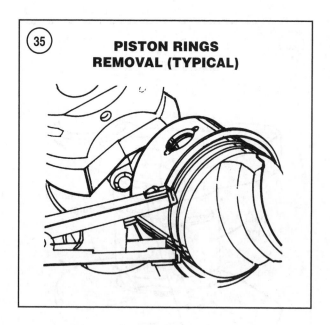

**PISTON RINGS
REMOVAL (TYPICAL)**

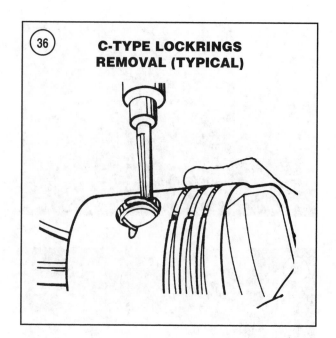

**C-TYPE LOCKRINGS
REMOVAL (TYPICAL)**

25. Remove the piston rings from all of the pistons using a piston ring expander (part No. 91-24697 or an equivalent). See **Figure 35**, typical. Keep the rings to clean the piston ring grooves.

26. Use a lock ring remover (part No. 91-52952A-1) or a suitable awl to remove and discard all piston pin lock rings. See **Figure 36**, typical.

27. Place the piston pin tool (part No. 91-76159A-2 or an equivalent) into one end of the cylinder No. 1 piston pin bore. Support the bottom of the piston with one hand and drive the pin tool and pin from the piston. See **Figure 37**.

28. Remove the piston from the connecting rod. Remove the locating (thrust) washers and the 29 loose needle bearings (**Figure 38**). Store the components in clean, numbered containers corresponding to the cylinder number.

29. Repeat Steps 27 and 28 to separate the cylinders No. 2-6 pistons from their connecting rod.

30. If the crankshaft ball bearing requires replacement, replace it as follows:

    a. Remove the retainer ring with pliers (part No. 91-822778A-3) or Sears Craftsman part No. 4735.

    b. Support the ball bearing in a knife-edged bearing separator, such as part No. 91-37241.

    c. Press against the crankshaft using the power head stand as a mandrel until the bearing is free from the crankshaft. See **Figure 39**.

    d. Discard the bearing.

31. Remove and discard the seal and seal carrier from the drive shaft end of the crankshaft. See **Figure 40**, typical.

32. If the oil pump drive gear (**Figure 41**) requires replacement, remove the two screws (16, **Figure 27**) secur-

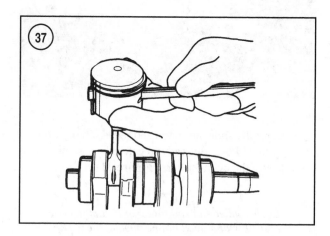

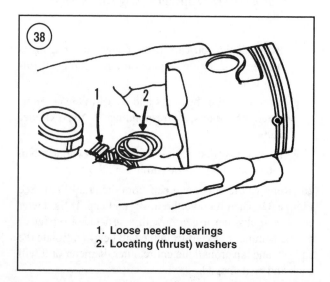

1. Loose needle bearings
2. Locating (thrust) washers

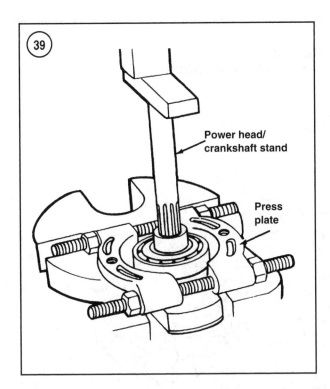

Power head/crankshaft stand

Press plate

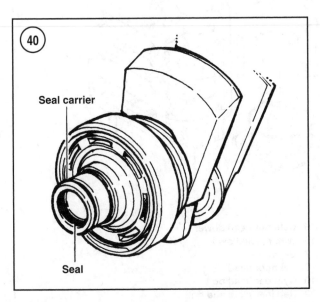

Seal carrier

Seal

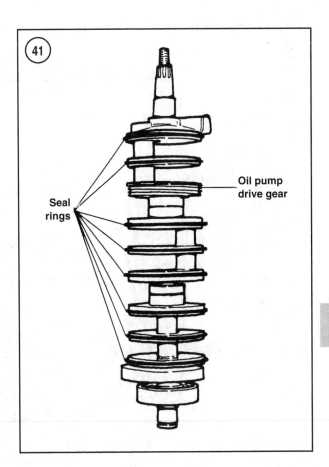

Seal rings

Oil pump drive gear

ing the gear. Then remove and discard the drive gear halves and the two screws.

CAUTION
There are seven sealing rings (Figure 41) that seal each crankcase chamber from the adjacent chamber(s). If the rings are damaged or broken, replace them. Do not remove any seal ring unless it must be replaced.

33. If the crankshaft seal ring(s) must be replaced, remove the ring(s) using a piston ring expander (part No. 91-24697 or an equivalent).

34. Refer to *Cleaning and Inspection* in this chapter before beginning the reassembly procedure.

Disassembly (200 Optimax, 225 hp and 250 hp Models)

Refer to **Figure 42** and **Figure 43** for this procedure. Since the power head is removed with most of the accessories installed, all accessories and systems must first be removed from the power head.

CAUTION
These are complex power heads. Take pictures or draw sketches of component locations, hose and harness routing, and linkage assemblies. Label components and connections as necessary. The fuel bleed (recirculation) system is particularly difficult to reroute. Refer to Chapter Six for fuel bleed system service.

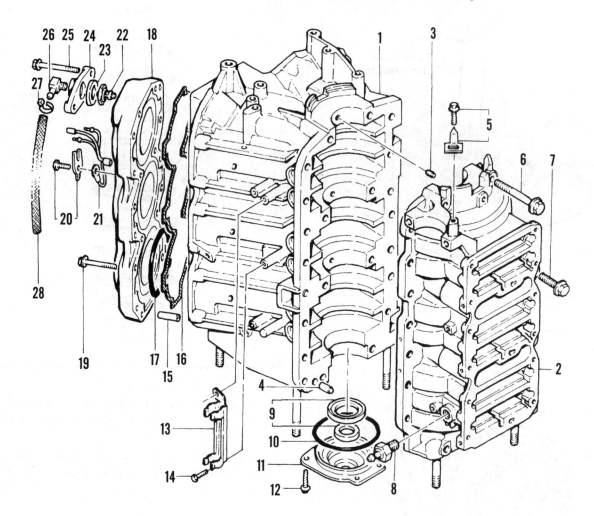

**CYLINDER BLOCK
(200 HP OPTIMAX, 225 HP AND 250 HP MODELS)**

1. Cylinder block
2. Crankcase cover
3. Bearing locating dowel
4. Crankcase dowel pin
5. Timing pointer*
6. Main bearing bolt (large)
7. Outer crankcase bolt (small)
8. Pulse fitting (remote oil tank)
9. Crankshaft lower seals
10. O-ring
11. Lower end cap
12. Bolt
13. Main harness connector bracket
14. Screw
15. Cylinder head dowel
16. Water jacket seal
17. O-ring
18. Cylinder head
19. Cylinder head bolt
20. Retainer plate and bolt
21. ECT sensor
22. Thermostat
23. Gasket
24. Thermostat housing
25. Thermostat housing/cylinder head bolt
26. Water discharge fitting*
27. Tie-strap
28. Water discharge hose

*Not used on all models

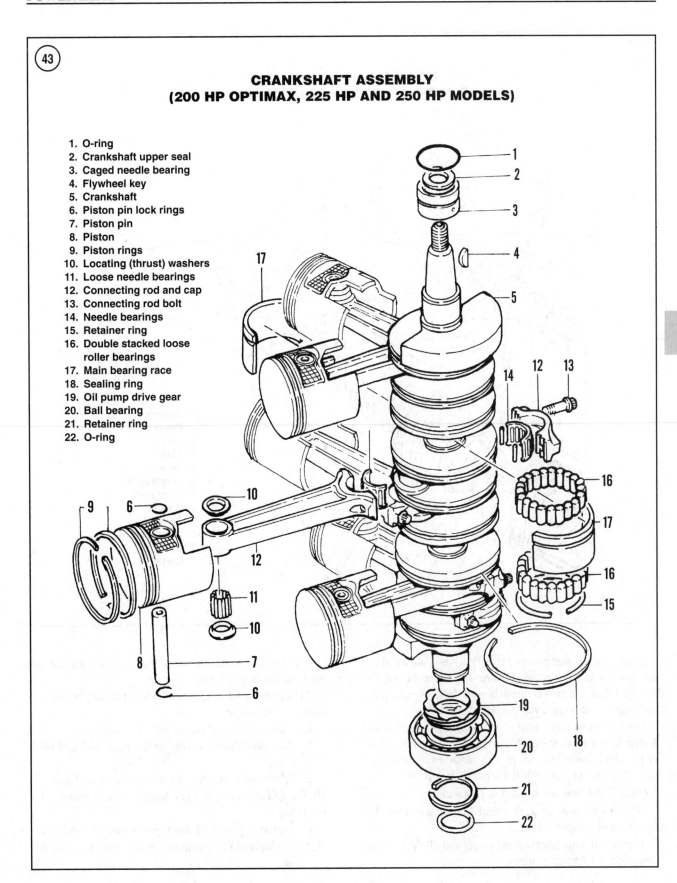

43

CRANKSHAFT ASSEMBLY
(200 HP OPTIMAX, 225 HP AND 250 HP MODELS)

1. O-ring
2. Crankshaft upper seal
3. Caged needle bearing
4. Flywheel key
5. Crankshaft
6. Piston pin lock rings
7. Piston pin
8. Piston
9. Piston rings
10. Locating (thrust) washers
11. Loose needle bearings
12. Connecting rod and cap
13. Connecting rod bolt
14. Needle bearings
15. Retainer ring
16. Double stacked loose
    roller bearings
17. Main bearing race
18. Sealing ring
19. Oil pump drive gear
20. Ball bearing
21. Retainer ring
22. O-ring

8

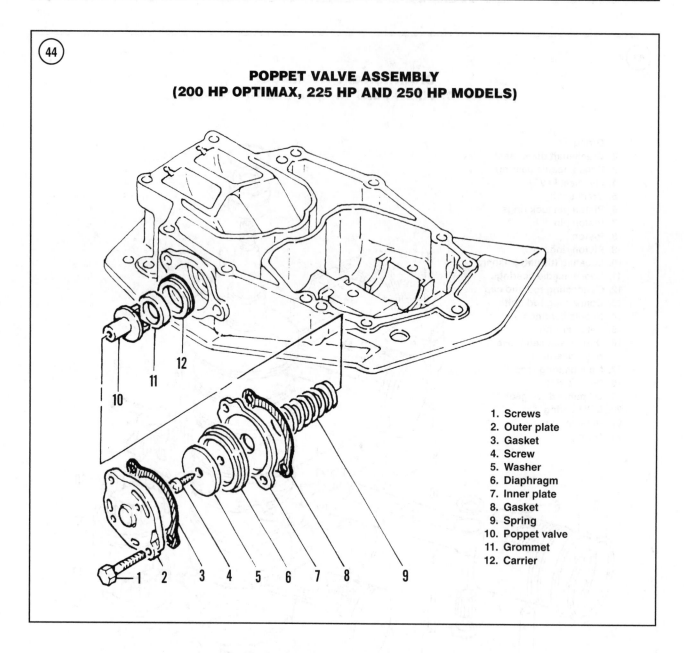

POPPET VALVE ASSEMBLY
(200 HP OPTIMAX, 225 HP AND 250 HP MODELS)

1. Screws
2. Outer plate
3. Gasket
4. Screw
5. Washer
6. Diaphragm
7. Inner plate
8. Gasket
9. Spring
10. Poppet valve
11. Grommet
12. Carrier

The poppet (water pressure relief) valve is mounted on the exhaust adapter plate (**Figure 44**) which is not removed when the power head is removed. Disassemble and inspect the poppet valve when instructed.

The lower end cap contains two large crankshaft seals. A stainless steel wear sleeve is pressed onto the lower end of the crankshaft. The sleeve also holds an internal, replaceable O-ring that seals the drive shaft splines.

Disassemble the power head as follows:

1. Remove the alternator, flywheel and electric starter as described in Chapter Seven.

2. Remove the oil reservoir, oil pump and all oil lines as described in Chapter Thirteen.

3. On Optimax models, remove the belt tensioner assembly from the power head.

4A. On carbureted models, refer to Chapter Six and remove the following:

a. Carburetors, fuel pump and fuel filter.

b. Fuel enrichment valve, intake manifold and reed blocks.

c. Fuel primer and fuel bleed (recirculation) lines.

4B. On EFI models, refer to Chapter Six and remove the following:

a. Induction manifold and vapor separator assembly.

b. Mechanical fuel pump and water separating fuel filter.

c. Intake manifold, reed blocks, and all fuel and fuel bleed (recirculation) lines.

4C. On Optimax models, refer to Chapter Six and remove the following:

a. Induction manifold and vapor separator assemblies.

b. Mechanical fuel pump, water separating fuel filter, and all fuel and fuel bleed (recirculation) lines.

c. Intake manifold and reed blocks.

d. Air compressor, the air/fuel rails, direct injectors, and all remaining air, fuel and bleed lines.

NOTE
Disconnect the shift switch leads from the engine harness bullet connectors and leave the switch installed on the bracket. All models are also equipped with an engine coolant temperature (ECT) sensor. The sensor may be removed or left in place, depending on the service to be performed. Disconnect the leads and/or remove the sensor before proceeding.

5A. On EFI and carbureted models, remove the remaining ignition and electrical components as an assembly. This includes the crankshaft position sensor, the ignition and fuel ECM (EFI models only), CDMs, and the electrical/ignition plate containing the starter solenoid and the trim/tilt relays. Do not disconnect electrical components from each other unless absolutely necessary; simply remove the mounting screws, cable clamps and tie-straps. See Chapter Seven.

5B. On Optimax models, remove the remaining ignition and electrical components as an assembly. This includes the stator assembly, crankshaft position sensor, the ECM, the electrical plate containing the starter solenoid, fuses and main power and trim/tilt relays, and the ignition plate containing the ignition coils. Do not disconnect electrical components from each other unless absolutely necessary, simply remove the mounting screws, cable clamps and tie-straps. Refer to Chapter Six and Chapter Seven as necessary.

6. Remove the bolt at the center of the throttle control arm located on the port side of the power head. Then remove the control arm and any remaining control linkage as an assembly. Position the bolt through the control arm, then install a suitable nut to keep the control arm components together.

7. Remove the shift and throttle cable anchor bracket and shift interrupt switch from the port lower side of the power head.

8. Remove the two cylinder head bolts (25, **Figure 42**) securing the thermostat housing to the top of each cylinder head. Remove both thermostat covers, gaskets and thermostats. Discard the gaskets.

9. Remove the two screws (1, **Figure 44**) securing the poppet valve assembly to the exhaust adapter plate at the top of the drive shaft housing. Remove the valve assembly from the adapter plate. Separate the inner and outer plates, then remove and discard both gaskets.

10. Reach into the adapter plate's poppet valve cavity and retrieve the grommet and grommet carrier from the cavity. See 11 and 12, **Figure 44**. Discard the grommet.

11. Remove the 18 remaining bolts (19, **Figure 42**) securing each cylinder head to the cylinder block. Carefully pull each head from the block, then remove and discard the three combustion chamber O-ring seals and the water jacket molded seal from each head. If necessary, tap each cylinder head with a soft-faced rubber or plastic hammer to break the seals. Do not damage the sealing surfaces during the removal process.

12. Remove the four bolts (12, **Figure 42**) securing the lower end cap to the power head. Do not remove the lower end cap at this time.

CAUTION
The crankcase cover and cylinder block are a matched, align-bored unit. Do not scratch, nick or damage the machined mating surfaces.

13. Remove the eight large main bearing and 14 small outer bolts securing the crankcase cover to the cylinder block. Carefully tap the cover with a soft-faced plastic or rubber hammer to break the crankcase seal. Then remove the crankcase cover. Locate and secure the locating dowel as necessary.

14. Mark the corresponding cylinder number on the pistons and connecting rods with a felt-tipped permanent marker. Mark the connecting rods and rod caps so the rod caps can be reinstalled in their original orientation.

NOTE
*Always store **all** components from each connecting rod and piston assembly together. They must be reinstalled in their original locations.*

15. Remove each connecting rod and piston assembly as follows:

a. Manually rotate the crankshaft to position the upper, cylinder No. 1 piston at the bottom of its cylinder bore. This will expose the connecting rod bolts (**Figure 30**, typical) for easy removal.

b. Use a 12-point socket to remove the connecting rod bolts from the upper, cylinder No. 1 connecting rod.

8

Alternately loosen each bolt a small amount until all tension is off both bolts.

c. Tap the rod cap with a soft metal (brass) mallet to separate the cap from the rod.

d. Remove the cap and rod from the crankshaft, then remove the roller bearings and cages from the crankshaft.

e. Carefully slide the piston and rod assembly from its cylinder bore. Be ready to catch the assembly as it leaves the cylinder bore (**Figure 31**, typical).

CAUTION
Each connecting rod and cap is a matched assembly and must not be mismatched. The cap must be installed in its original orientation.

f. Reinstall the rod cap to the connecting rod in its original orientation. Tighten the rod cap bolts finger-tight.

g. Store the roller bearings and cages in clean, numbered containers, corresponding to the cylinder number.

h. Repeat this procedure to remove the cylinders No. 2-6 connecting rod assemblies.

16. Lift the flywheel end of the crankshaft slightly and slide the upper caged needle bearing (3, **Figure 43**) from the crankshaft. Remove and discard the O-ring and seal from the bearing case.

17. Remove the lower end cap. Discard the O-ring, then drive the seals from the end cap with a suitable punch and hammer. Do not damage the end cap's seal bore during removal. Discard the seals.

18. Lift the crankshaft assembly straight up and out of the cylinder block (**Figure 33**, typical) and mount it vertically in a crankshaft stand (part No. 91-30591A-1 or an equivalent). Make sure the stand is securely clamped in a vise.

19. Locate and secure the crankshaft center main bearing locating dowels (3, **Figure 42**) as necessary. There are three dowels on these models.

20. Remove the retaining ring from around a center main bearing. See **Figure 34**, typical. Then remove the outer race halves and the double stack of loose roller bearings. Store the bearing components in marked containers so they can be reassembled in their original locations. Repeat the procedure for the remaining center main bearing.

CAUTION
Wear suitable eye protection for piston ring and piston pin retainer removal procedures.

21. Remove the piston rings from the pistons using a piston ring expander (part No. 91-24697 or an equivalent).

See **Figure 35**, typical. Keep the rings to clean the piston's ring grooves.

22. Use a lock ring remover (part No. 91-52952A-1) or a suitable awl to a remove all piston pin lock rings. See **Figure 36**, typical.

23. Place the piston pin tool (part No. 91-92973A-1 or an equivalent) into one end of the cylinder No. 1 piston pin bore. Support the bottom of the piston with one hand and drive the pin tool and pin from the piston. See **Figure 37**.

24. Remove the piston from the connecting rod. Remove the locating (thrust) washers and the 34 loose needle bearings (**Figure 38**). Store the components in clean, numbered containers corresponding to the cylinder number.

25. Repeat Steps 23 and 25 to separate the cylinders No. 2-6 pistons from their connecting rods.

26. If the crankshaft ball bearing and/or oil pump drive gear requires replacement, replace them as follows:

a. Remove the retainer ring with pliers (part No. 91-822778A-3) or Sears Craftsman part No. 4735.

b. Support the ball bearing in a knife-edged bearing separator, such as part No. 91-37241.

c. Press against the crankshaft using the power head stand as a mandrel until the bearing is free from the crankshaft. See **Figure 39**.

d. Discard the bearing.

e. Slide the oil pump drive gear off the crankshaft. Discard the gear.

27. Remove and discard the O-ring from inside the wear sleeve on the drive shaft end of the crankshaft.

NOTE
In the next step, it may be necessary to heat the wear sleeve with a heat lamp, such as part No. 91-63209 or an equivalent, to loosen the Loctite seal. Do not use an open flame.

28. If the wear sleeve on the crankshaft lower end is damaged or worn, pull it from the crankshaft with a pair of pliers. Do not damage the crankshaft surface during removal. Discard the wear sleeve.

CAUTION
*There are seven seal rings (18, **Figure 43**) that seal each crankcase chamber from the adjacent chamber(s). If the rings are damaged or broken, replace them. Do not remove any seal ring unless it is going to be replaced.*

29. If the crankshaft seal ring(s) must be replaced, remove the ring(s) using piston ring expander (part No. 91-24697 or an equivalent).

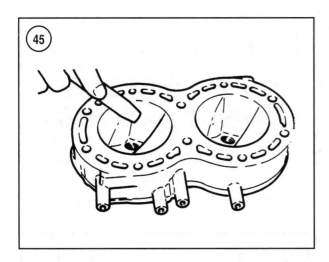

30. Refer to *Cleaning and Inspection* later in this chapter before beginning the reassembly procedure.

POWER HEAD CLEANING AND INSPECTION

Refer to Chapter Six, and clean and inspect the reed blocks and the fuel bleed (recirculation) system. Test all check valves in the fuel bleed system for correct function as described in Chapter Six.

Review *Sealing Surfaces, Fasteners and Torque* and *Sealants, Lubricants and Adhesives* located at the beginning of this chapter.

Replace all seals, O-rings, gaskets, connecting rod bolts, piston pin lock rings, piston rings and all bearings if the a power head is disassembled.

Perform the cleaning and inspection procedure in each of the following sections that applies to your engine *before* beginning assembly procedures.

Cylinder Block and Crankcase

Mercury and Mariner outboard cylinder blocks and crankcase covers are matched, align-bored assemblies. For this reason, do not attempt to assemble an engine with parts salvaged from other blocks. If the following inspection procedure indicates that the block or cover requires replacement, replace the cylinder block and crankcase cover as an assembly.

NOTE
Remove all fuel bleed components, such as hoses, T-fittings, threaded fittings, check valves and check valve carriers, if it is necessary to submerge the block and/or cover

in a strong cleaning solution. See Chapter Six.

1. Clean the cylinder block and crankcase cover thoroughly with clean solvent and a parts washing brush. Carefully remove all gasket and sealant material from mating surfaces.

2. Remove all carbon and varnish deposits from the combustion chambers, exhaust ports and exhaust cavities with a carbon removing solvent, such as Quicksilver Power Tune (part No. 92-15104). Use a hardwood dowel or plastic scraper to remove stubborn deposits. See **Figure 45**. Do not scratch, nick or gouge the combustion chambers or exhaust ports.

WARNING
Use suitable hand and eye protection when using muriatic acid products. Avoid breathing the vapors. Only use them in a well-ventilated area.

CAUTION
Do not allow muriatic acid to come into contact with the aluminum surfaces of the cylinder block.

3. If the cylinder bore(s) has aluminum transfer from the piston(s), clean loose deposits using a stiff bristle brush. Apply a *small* quantity of diluted muriatic acid to the aluminum deposits. Bubbling indicates that the aluminum is dissolving. Wait 1-2 minutes, then thoroughly wash the cylinder with hot water and detergent. Repeat this procedure until the aluminum deposits have been removed. Lightly oil the cylinder wall to prevent rusting.

4. Check the cylinder block and crankcase cover for cracks, fractures, stripped threads or other damage.

NOTE
On 105 jet, 115 Optimax and 135-200 hp (except 200 Optimax) models, the crankshaft sealing rings commonly wear grooves in the cylinder block and crankcase cover. The grooves present no problems unless the crankshaft must be replaced. If the seal rings on a new crankshaft do not perfectly align with the seal grooves in the original cylinder block/crankcase cover assembly, the crankshaft may bind. If this happens, replace the cylinder block.

5. Inspect gasket mating surfaces for nicks, grooves, cracks or distortion. Any defects may allow leakage. Check the surfaces for distortion as described in *Sealing Surfaces* in this chapter. Replace the component if the distortion is more than 0.004 in. (0.1 mm), unless otherwise

8

specified. Lap the component as described under *Sealing Surfaces* to remove smaller imperfections. **Figures 46-48** show typical directions in which to check for warp on the cylinder head and exhaust cover/manifold surfaces.

6. Check all water, oil and fuel bleed passages in the block and cover for obstructions. Make sure all pipe plugs are installed tightly. Seal pipe plugs with Loctite 567 PST pipe sealant (part No. 92-809822).

Cylinder bore inspection

Inspect the cylinder bores for scoring, scuffing, grooving, cracks or bulging and other mechanical damage. Inspect the cylinder block casting and cast-iron liner for separation or delamination. There should be no gaps or voids between the aluminum casting and the liner. Remove any aluminum deposits as described previously in this section. If the cylinders are in a visually acceptable condition, hone the cylinders as described in *Cylinder wall honing*. If the cylinders are in an unacceptable condition, rebore the defective cylinder bore(s) or replace the cylinder block and crankcase cover as an assembly.

> *NOTE*
> *It is not necessary to rebore all cylinders in a cylinder block. Only rebore the cylinders that are defective. It is acceptable to have a mix of standard and oversize cylinders on a given power head as long as the correct standard or oversize piston is used to match each bore. Always check the manufacturer's parts catalog for oversize piston availability and bore sizes before over-boring the cylinder(s).*

Cylinder bore honing

Only use a rigid type cylinder hone to deglaze the bore to aid in the seating of new piston rings. If the cylinder has been bored oversize, the rigid hone is used in two steps; a rough (deburring) hone removes the machining marks and a finish (final) hone establishes the correct cross-hatch pattern in the cylinder bore.

Do not use flex (ball type) hones and spring-loaded hones as they will not produce a true (straight and perfectly round) bore.

> *NOTE*
> *If you are not proficient with the correct use of a rigid cylinder hone, have a qualified machine shop or dealership perform the cylinder bore honing. The manufacturer recommends rigid hones from the Sunnen*

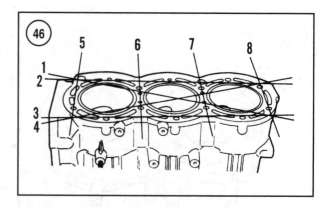

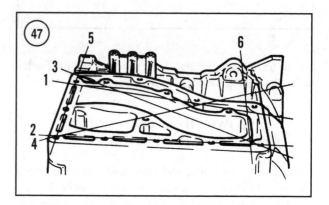

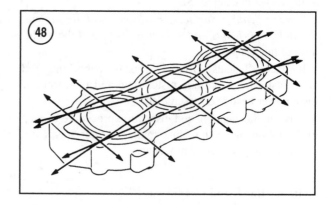

Products Company, 7910 Manchester Ace, St. Louis, Missouri 63143. Sunnen products are often available from tool and industrial suppliers.

If the cylinders are in a visually acceptable condition, prepare the cylinder bore for new piston rings and remove glazing, light scoring and/or scuffing by lightly honing the cylinders as follows:

1. Follow the rigid hone manufacturer's instructions when using the hone. Make sure the correct stones for the bore (cast-iron) are installed on the hone.

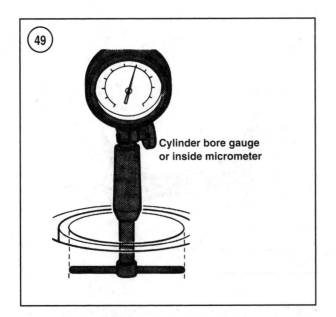

Cylinder bore gauge
or inside micrometer

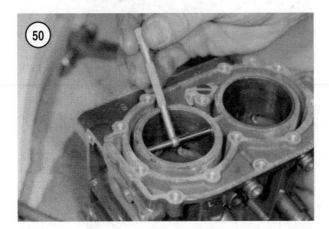

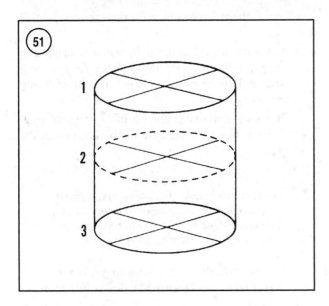

2. Pump a continuous flow of honing oil into the bore during the honing operation. If an oil pumping system is not available, have an assistant with an oil can keep the cylinder walls flushed with honing oil.

3. If the hone loads and slows down at one location in the bore, this is the narrowest portion of the bore. Localize the stroking in this location to remove stock until the hone maintains the same speed and load throughout the entire bore.

4. Frequently remove the hone from the cylinder bore and inspect the bore. Do not remove more material than necessary.

5. Attempt to achieve a stroke rate of approximately 30 cycles per minute. Adjust the speed of the hone to achieve a cross-hatch pattern with an intersecting angle of approximately 30°. Do not exceed a cross-hatch of more than 45°.

6. After honing, thoroughly clean the cylinder block using hot water, detergent and a stiff bristle brush. Remove all abrasive material from the honing process. After washing and flushing, coat the cylinder walls with a film of outboard motor oil to prevent rusting.

7. Check the cylinder bores' wear, taper and out-of-round in *Cylinder bore measurements*.

Cylinder bore measurements

Oversize bore specifications are simply the standard bore specification *plus* the oversize dimension. Check the parts catalog for available oversize dimensions. All standard bore specifications, maximum taper and out-of-round specifications are in **Table 3**. Record and compare the measurements to these specifications. The maximum wear limit on a given cylinder is equal to the standard bore plus the maximum taper specification.

Use a cylinder bore gauge (**Figure 49**), inside micrometer, or a telescoping gauge (**Figure 50**) and a regular micrometer to measure the entire area of ring travel in the cylinder bore. Take three sets of readings at the top, middle and bottom of the ring travel area (**Figure 51**).

1. Take the first reading at the top of the ring travel area (approximately 1/2 in. [12.7 mm] from the top of the cylinder bore) with the gauge aligned with the crankshaft centerline. Record the reading. Then turn the gauge 90° to the crankshaft centerline and record another reading.

2. The difference between the two readings is the cylinder out-of-round.

3. Take a second set of readings at the midpoint of the ring travel area (just above the ports) using the same alignment points described in Step 1. Record the readings. Calculate the cylinder out-of-round by determining the

8

difference between the two (or highest and lowest) readings.

4. Take a third set of readings at the bottom of the ring travel area near the bottom of the cylinder bore using the same alignment points described in Step 1. Record the readings. Calculate the cylinder out-of-round by determining the difference between the two readings.

5. To determine the cylinder taper, subtract the readings taken at the top of the cylinder bore in Step 1 from the readings taken at the bottom of the cylinder bore in Step 4. The difference in these readings is the cylinder taper.

NOTE
If the cylinder has already been bored oversize, add the oversize dimension to the standard bore dimension and the maximum out-of-round specification in the next step.

6. To determine if the cylinder is excessively worn, add the maximum taper specification (**Table 3**) to the standard cylinder bore. If any of the readings taken in Steps 1-4 exceed this calculation, the cylinder is excessively worn.

7. Repeat Steps 1-6 for each remaining cylinder.

8. If any cylinder is excessively out-of-round, tapered or worn, bore the cylinder(s) oversize or replace the cylinder block and crankcase cover as an assembly.

Piston

Service the piston and piston pin as an assembly. If either is damaged, replace them together. Reinstall piston pins in the pistons in which they were removed.

CAUTION
Do not use an automotive ring groove cleaning tool as it can damage the ring grooves and loosen the ring locating pins.

1. Clean the piston(s), piston pin(s), thrust (locating) washers and the piston pin needle bearing assemblies thoroughly with clean solvent and a parts washing brush. Do not use a wire brush on the piston as metal from the wire can be imbedded in the piston. This can lead to preignition and detonation.

2. Remove all carbon and varnish deposits from the top of the piston, piston ring groove(s) and under the piston crown with a carbon removing solvent, such as Quicksilver Power Tune (part No. 92-15104). Use a piece of hardwood or a plastic scraper to remove stubborn deposits. Do not scratch, nick or gouge any part of the piston. Do not remove stamped or cast identification marks.

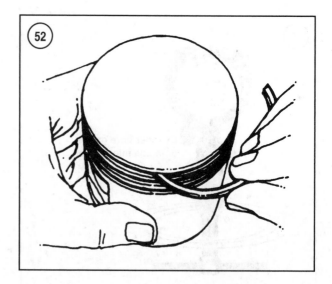

3. Clean stubborn deposits from the ring groove(s) as follows:

   a. Fashion a ring cleaning tool from the original piston ring(s). Rings are shaped differently for each ring groove. Use the correct original ring for each ring groove.

   b. Break off approximately 1/3 of the original ring. Grind a beveled edge onto the broken end of the ring.

NOTE
On keystone and semi-keystone rings, grind off enough of the ring taper to allow the inside edge of the broken ring to reach the inside diameter of the ring groove.

   c. Use the ground end of the ring to gently scrape the ring groove clean (**Figure 52**). Be careful to only re-

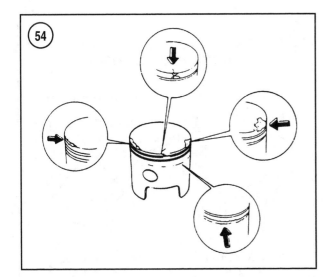

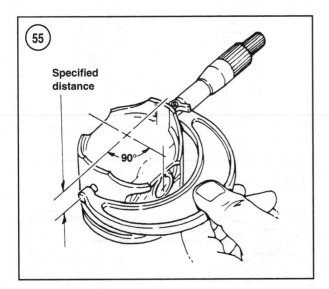

Specified distance

90°

move the carbon. Do not gouge the metal and damage or loosen the piston ring locating pin(s).

4. Polish nicks, burrs or sharp edges on and around the piston skirt with crocus cloth or 320 grit carborundum cloth. Do not remove cast or stamped identification markings. Wash the piston thoroughly to remove all abrasive grit.

5. Inspect the piston(s) overall condition for scoring (**Figure 53**), cracks, worn or cracked piston pin bosses, and other mechanical damage. Carefully inspect the crown and the top outer diameter for burning, erosion, evidence of ring migration and mechanical damage (**Figure 54**). Replace the piston and pin as necessary.

6. Check the piston ring grooves for wear, erosion, distortion and loose ring locating pins.

7. Inspect the piston pin for water etching, pitting, scoring, heat discoloration, excessive wear, distortion and mechanical damage. Roll the pin across a machinist's surface plate to check the pin for distortion.

8. Inspect the thrust (locating) washers and needle bearings for water damage, pitting, scoring, overheating, wear and mechanical damage.

Piston measurements

The pistons used in these engines are cam shaped; the piston is built out-of-round on purpose. The piston is engineered to fit the bore perfectly when at operating temperature and fully expanded, which makes the engine run more quietly and efficiently. Measure the piston at the specified point(s) or the readings will be inaccurate.

Measure each piston diameter with a micrometer as described in the following procedure and compare the readings to the specifications in **Table 4**.

To calculate the specified diameter dimension on oversize pistons, simply add the oversize dimension to the standard diameter in **Table 4**.

1. Using a micrometer, measure each piston diameter at a 90° angle to the piston pin bore and at the distance from the bottom of the skirt specified in **Table 4**. See **Figure 55**. Record the measurement. If the piston is not within the specification, replace the piston(s).

2. On 105 jet, 115 hp Optimax and 135-250 hp models, take a second diameter measurement at a point aligned with the piston pin bore, but at the same distance from the bottom of the skirt. Compare the second reading with the first reading. If the second reading is not within 0.008 (0.203 mm) of the first reading, replace the piston.

Connecting Rods

The connecting rods are the fractured cap design. The cap is broken from the rod during the manufacturing process, leaving a jagged (fractured) mating surface that mates perfectly if it is installed in its original orientation. If the cap is installed reversed and the rod bolts are tightened, the rod will distort and will have to be discarded.

While alignment marks are provided, always mark the rod and cap with a felt-tipped permanent marker for identification. Correct orientation is obvious if the time is taken to examine the mating surfaces of the rod and cap. Hold the connecting rod cap firmly in position while installing the bolts.

New connecting rod bolts must be installed during final assembly, but the old bolts can be used for cleaning and

8

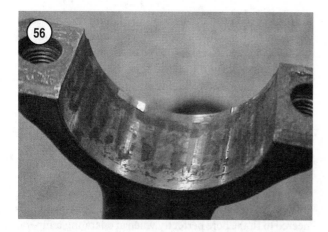

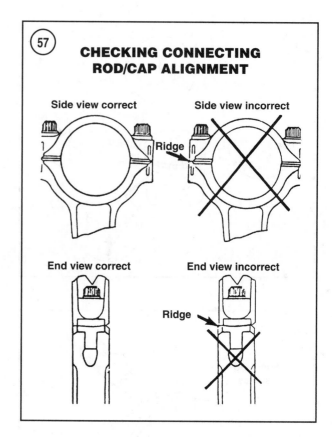

CHECKING CONNECTING ROD/CAP ALIGNMENT

Side view correct

Side view incorrect

Ridge

End view correct

End view incorrect

Ridge

inspection. All connecting rod bolt torque specifications are in **Table 1**.

Use *Torque and Turn* on all models to tighten the connecting rod bolts properly. Apply oil to the bolt threads and under the bolt head. Tighten the bolts to an initial torque (**Table 1**), and check the alignment of the rod cap. Then tighten the bolts to a second, higher torque (**Table 1**), and finally turn both bolts an additional 90°.

Clean and inspect the connecting rods as follows:

1. Clean the connecting rods thoroughly with clean solvent and a parts washing brush.

2. Check the connecting rod big and small end bearing surfaces for water damage (**Figure 56**), pitting, spalling, chatter marks, heat discoloration and excessive or uneven wear. If the defect can be felt when a pencil lead or a fingernail is dragged over it, discard the rod. Stains or marks that cannot be felt can be removed by polishing the bearing surface in later steps.

3. Assemble the rod cap to the connecting rod as follows:

   a. Clamp the cylinder No. 1 connecting rod securely in a vise with protective jaws.

   b. Install the matching connecting rod cap to the connecting rod in its original orientation. Carefully observe fracture and alignment marks to ensure correct installation (**Figure 57**).

   c. Lubricate the bolt threads and underside of the bolt head with outboard lubricant. Then, while holding the cap firmly in position, install the connecting rod bolts and thread them fully into the rod.

   d. Tighten each bolt to 15 in.-lb. (1.7 N•m). Run a fingernail or pencil lead over each edge of the rod to cap joint (**Figure 58**). No ridge should be seen or felt. Realign and retorque the cap as necessary.

   e. After checking the alignment, finish torquing the rod bolts as specified in **Table 1**. Make a final check of alignment after the final torque is applied.

   f. Repeat this procedure for each remaining rod.

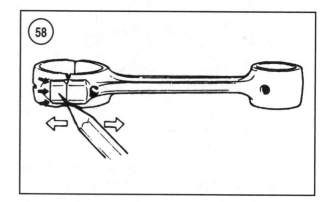

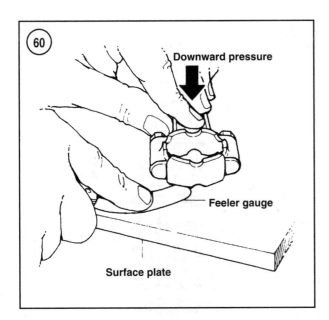

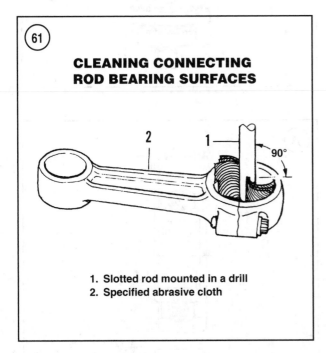

**CLEANING CONNECTING
ROD BEARING SURFACES**

1. Slotted rod mounted in a drill
2. Specified abrasive cloth

4. Rod bending may not be visually apparent (**Figure 59**). To check the rod straightness, place each rod/cap assembly on a machinist's surface plate and press downward on the rod beam. The rod should not wobble under pressure. While holding the rod against the plate, attempt to insert a 0.002 in. feeler gauge between the machined surfaces of the rod and the plate (**Figure 60**). If the feeler gauge can be inserted between any machined surface of the rod and the surface plate, the rod is bent and must be discarded.

*CAUTION
Use only crocus cloth or 320 carborundum cloth in the following steps. Do not substitute any other abrasive cloth to clean the connecting rod bearing surfaces. Clean both ends of the connecting rod in the following steps.*

5. If the connecting rod has passed all inspections to this point, slight defects noted in Step 2 in either bearing surface may be cleaned up as follows:

a. Fabricate a holder by cutting a 1 in. (25.4 mm) notch lengthwise into a 4 in. (102 mm) long, 5/16 in. (8 mm) shank, rod or bolt with a hacksaw.

b. On bearing assemblies with loose needle bearings, clean the bearing surface with a strip of 320 carborundum cloth mounted in the holder. Mount the holder in a drill. Spin the cloth using the drill as shown in **Figure 61** until the surface is polished. Maintain a 90° angle as shown and do not remove more material than necessary.

c. On bearing assemblies that use cages to position and space the needle bearings, clean the bearing surface with a strip of crocus cloth mounted in the holder. Mount the holder in a drill. Spin the cloth using the drill as shown in **Figure 61** until the surface is polished. Maintain a 90° angle as shown and do not remove more material than necessary.

d. Wash the connecting rod thoroughly in clean solvent to remove any abrasive grit, then inspect the bearing surfaces. Replace any connecting rod assembly that does not clean up properly.

e. Remove and discard the rod cap bolts. Wash the rod and cap again in clean solvent. Retag the rod and cap for identification. Lightly oil the bearing surfaces with outboard lubricant to prevent rust.

f. Repeat this process for each remaining connecting rod.

Crankshaft

1. Thoroughly wash the crankshaft and the main and connecting rod bearing assemblies with clean solvent and a parts washing brush.

2. Inspect the drive shaft splines, flywheel taper, flywheel key groove or splines and flywheel nut or bolt hole threads for corrosion, cracks, excessive wear and mechanical damage.

3. Inspect the upper and lower seal surfaces for excessive grooving, pitting, nicks or burrs. The seal surfaces may be polished with crocus cloth as necessary. If the crankshaft

is equipped with a wear sleeve on the drive shaft end, replace it if it is damaged.

4A. On 105 jet, 115 Optimax and 135-250 hp models, inspect each of the seven crankshaft seal rings (**Figure 62**, typical) for broken segments and excessive wear. Replace any seal ring that is damaged or worn.

4B. On all other models, inspect the seal ring groove at each center main journal location for wear and mechanical damage. Replace worn or damaged seal rings.

5. Check the crankshaft bearing surfaces for rust, water damage, pitting, spalling, chatter marks, heat discoloration and excessive or uneven wear. If the defect can be felt when a pencil lead or a fingernail is dragged over it, discard the crankshaft. Stains or marks that cannot be felt can be removed by polishing the bearing surface as follows:

    a. On bearing assemblies with loose needle bearings, clean the bearing surface with a strip of 320 carborundum cloth. Work the cloth back and forth evenly over the entire journal until the surface is polished. Do not remove more material than necessary.

    b. On bearing assemblies that use cages to position and space the needle bearings, clean the bearing surface with a strip of crocus cloth. Work the cloth back and forth evenly over the entire journal until the surface is polished. Do not remove more material than necessary.

6. Thoroughly clean the crankshaft again in clean solvent and recheck the crankshaft surfaces. Replace the crankshaft if it cannot be properly cleaned. If the crankshaft is in a visually acceptable condition, lightly oil the crankshaft to prevent rust.

7. Inspect the oil pump drive gear for worn or chipped teeth, heat damage or other damage. Replace the oil pump drive gear if it is damaged. On 105 jet and 135-200 hp models (except Optimax), the drive gear is located as shown in **Figure 62**. On all other models (except Optimax), the drive gear is on the drive shaft end of the crankshaft.

8. Inspect the bearings as follows:

    a. *Ball bearing*—Rotate the bearing. The bearing should rotate smoothly with no rough spots, catches or noise. There should be no discernible end or axial play (**Figure 63**) between the inner and outer races of the bearing. If the bearing shows visible signs of wear, corrosion or deterioration, replace it.

    b. *Roller/needle bearings*—Inspect the rollers and/or needles for water etching, pitting, chatter marks, heat discoloration and excessive or uneven wear. Inspect the cages for wear and mechanical damage. Replace bearings as an assembly. Do not attempt to replace individual rollers or needles.

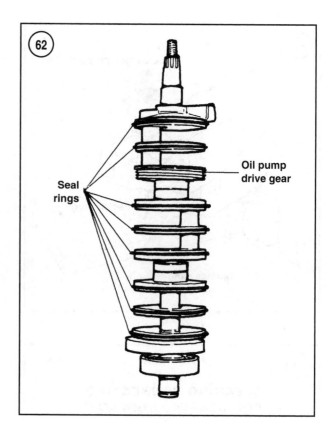

Seal rings

Oil pump drive gear

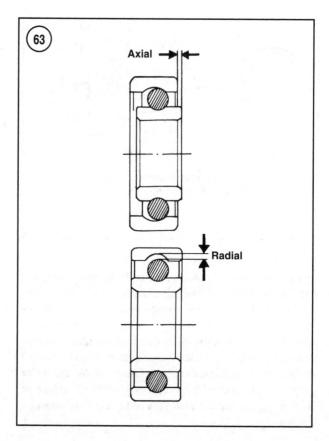

Axial

Radial

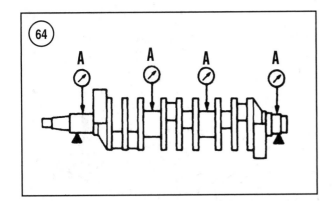

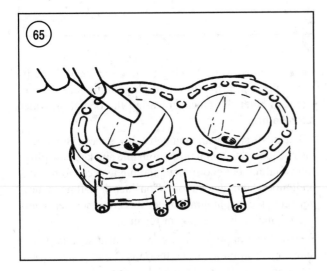

CAUTION
Some bearing cages retain the rollers, others do not. All or none of the rollers should be retained. If some rollers fall out of the cage, yet some are retained, replace the bearing assembly. If any bearing's condition is questionable, replace it.

9. Support the crankshaft assembly at the upper and lower main bearing journals as shown in **Figure 64**, typical. Rotate the crankshaft assembly and check the runout at each main journal with a dial indicator. Replace the crankshaft if runout exceeds 0.002 in. (0.051 mm).

End Cap(s), Cylinder Head(s), and Exhaust, Intake and Cylinder Block Cover(s)

If the engine is equipped with any or all of these components, clean and inspect each component as described in the following sections.

Cylinder head(s) or cylinder block cover

1. Clean the cylinder head(s) or block cover thoroughly with clean solvent and a parts washing brush. Carefully remove all gasket and sealant material from mating surfaces.

2. On cylinder heads, remove all carbon and varnish deposits from the combustion chambers with a carbon removing solvent, such as Quicksilver Power Tune (part No. 92-15104). A sharpened hardwood dowel or plastic scraper can be used to remove stubborn deposits (**Figure 65**, typical). Do not scratch, nick or gouge the combustion chambers.

NOTE
The cylinder head(s) on 1998 and 1999 105 jet, 1998 and 1999 150-200 hp models (except 200 hp Optimax) and all 135 hp models can be lapped or resurfaced to remove warp up to 0.010 in. (0.254 mm). Do not remove more than 0.010 in. (0.254 mm) of material. The cylinder heads on 115 Optimax, 2000-on 150-200 hp models and all 200 hp Optimax, 225 hp and 250 hp models use O-rings instead of a gasket and cannot be lapped or resurfaced.

3. Check the cylinder head(s) and block cover for cracks, fractures, distortion or other damage. Check the cylinder head(s) for stripped or damaged threads. Refer to *Sealing surfaces* at the beginning of this chapter and check the cylinder head(s) for warp. Maximum warp specifications are in **Table 3**. Minor imperfections can be removed by lapping the cylinder head as described in *Sealing Surfaces*.

4. Inspect all gasket surfaces, or O-ring and water seal grooves, for nicks, grooves, cracks, corrosion or distortion. Replace the cylinder head or block cover if the defect is severe enough to cause leaks.

5. Check all water, oil and fuel bleed passages in the head(s) for obstructions. Make sure all pipe plugs are installed tightly. Seal all pipe plugs with Loctite 567 PST pipe sealant (part No. 92-809822).

Exhaust cover/manifold/plate

1. Clean the exhaust cover, manifold and plate thoroughly with clean solvent and a parts washing brush. Carefully remove all gasket and sealant material from mating surfaces.

2. Remove all carbon and varnish deposits with a carbon removing solvent, such as Quicksilver Power Tune (part No. 92-15104). Use a hardwood dowel or plastic scraper

8

to remove stubborn deposits. Do not scratch, nick or gouge the mating surfaces.

3. Inspect the component and all gasket surfaces for nicks, grooves, cracks, corrosion or distortion. Replace the cover/manifold/plate if the defect is severe enough to cause leaks.

Intake cover(s)

1. Clean the intake cover(s) thoroughly with clean solvent and a parts washing brush. Carefully remove all gasket and sealant material from mating surfaces.

2. Inspect the cover and all gasket surfaces or O-ring grooves for nicks, grooves, cracks, corrosion or distortion. Replace the cover if the defect could cause leaks.

End caps

The upper end cap on 105 jet, 115 hp Optimax and 135-200 hp (except 200 hp Optimax) models contains a caged roller bearing assembly. If the bearing needs replacement, replace the upper end cap as an assembly, rather than attempting to remove the bearing from the end cap.

1. Clean the end cap(s) thoroughly with clean solvent and a parts washing brush. Carefully remove all sealant material from mating surfaces.

2. Inspect the seal bore(s) for nicks, gouges or corrosion that would cause the seal to leak around its outer diameter. Replace the end cap if the seal bore is damaged.

3. Inspect the end cap mating surface and O-ring groove for nicks, grooves, cracks, corrosion or distortion. Replace the end cap(s) if the defect could cause leaks.

4. If the end cap contains a bearing, inspect the bearing as described in *Crankshaft* under *Cleaning and Inspection* in this chapter.

Thermostat and Poppet Valve Assembly (Models So Equipped)

The thermostat regulates the water leaving the power head. V-6 models use one thermostat for each cylinder head. Consider replacing the thermostat during any major disassembly or repair. Correct thermostat operation is vital to engine break-in, spark plug life, smooth consistent idling, and maximum performance and durability.

The poppet valve assembly is controlled by water pressure in the block. At higher engine speeds, the water pump pressure will be sufficient to force the poppet valve open. When the poppet valve opens, it provides an additional exit for heated cooling water. This increased

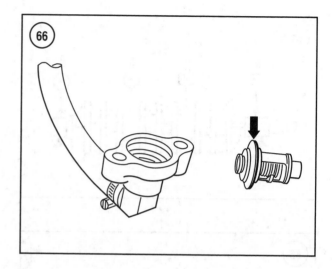

flow of heated water leaving the cylinder head, in addition to the thermostat flow, allowing additional cold inlet water to enter the block, lowering the operating water temperature.

The block stays warm enough at low speeds under thermostat control to maintain smooth idle and keep the plugs from fouling, but cools enough at high speeds to prevent preignition and detonation. Consider installing a new poppet valve diaphragm, poppet and grommet (seat) during any major disassembly or repair.

Refer to the appropriate power head disassembly procedure for illustrations of the thermostat and poppet valve assemblies specific to the model engine.

1. Carefully clean all gasket material from the thermostat housing, poppet valve inner and outer plates, and their mating surfaces. Most thermostats are sealed by a grommet around the thermostat and/or a gasket between the thermostat and the housing. **Figure 66** shows a typical grommet installation and thermostat cover for a V-6 power head.

2. Check thermostat covers and poppet valve inner and outer plates for cracks, corrosion or distortion, and replace them as necessary. **Figure 67** shows the poppet valve assembly for the 200 hp Optimax, 225 hp and 250 hp models. All poppet valves use a similar construction.

3. If the thermostat is to be reused, refer to *Engine Temperature and Overheating* in Chapter Three for inspection and testing procedures.

4. Inspect the poppet valve diaphragm for cracks, pin holes or deterioration. Replace the diaphragm if there is any doubt as to its condition.

5. Inspect the plastic poppet valve for melting and mechanical damage. Replace the poppet if there is any doubt as to its condition.

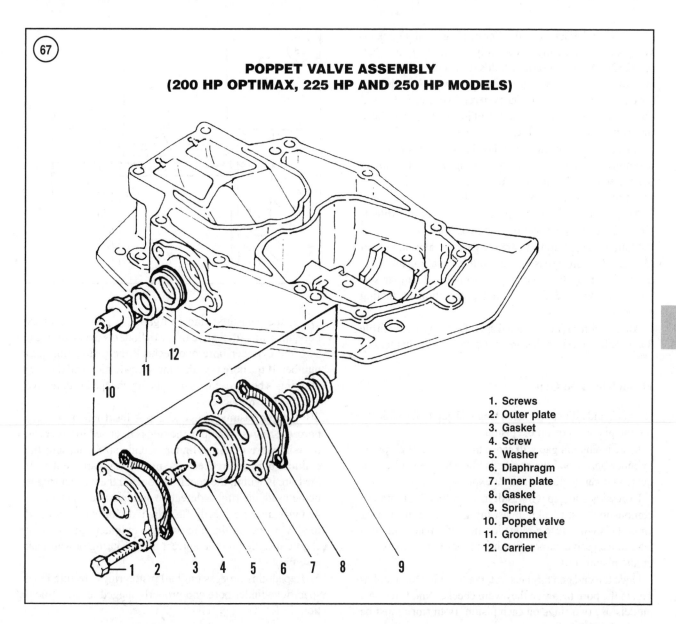

67

**POPPET VALVE ASSEMBLY
(200 HP OPTIMAX, 225 HP AND 250 HP MODELS)**

1. Screws
2. Outer plate
3. Gasket
4. Screw
5. Washer
6. Diaphragm
7. Inner plate
8. Gasket
9. Spring
10. Poppet valve
11. Grommet
12. Carrier

8

POWER HEAD ASSEMBLY

Before beginning assembly, complete all applicable sections of the *Cleaning and Inspection* in this chapter.

Review *Sealing Surfaces, Fasteners and Torque,* and *Sealants, Lubricants and Adhesives* in the beginning of this chapter.

Replace all seals, O-rings, gaskets, connecting rod bolts, piston pin lock rings, piston rings and all bearings any time a power head is disassembled. When reusing the original bearings, reinstall them in their original positions.

CAUTION
Never reuse the connecting rod bolts. Install new bolts for final assembly.

Identification marks on a piston ring must face up when installed. Some pistons use a combination of ring styles. Rings may be rectangular, semi-keystone, or full-keystone.

Rectangular and full keystone rings fit their grooves in either direction, but must be installed with the identification mark facing up.

Semi-keystone rings are beveled 7-10° on the upper surface only. These rings will not fit their grooves correctly if they are installed upside down. Carefully examine the construction of the rings and look for identification marks before installation. The beveled side is identified by a mark on the upper surface and must face up (matching the ring groove).

Lubricate the needle and roller bearings with Quicksilver Needle Bearing Assembly Grease (part No. 92-825265A-1). This grease holds the needles, rollers and cages in position during assembly. Lubricate all other internal components with Quicksilver two-Cycle TC-W3 outboard oil. Do not use a lubricant inside the power head that is not gasoline soluble.

A selection of torque wrenches is essential for correct assembly and to ensure maximum longevity of the power head assembly. Failing to torque items as specified will result in a premature power head failure.

All power head torque specifications are in **Table 1**. General torque specifications are in **Table 2**.

Mating surfaces must be free of gasket material, sealant residue, dirt, oil, grease or any other contaminant. Lacquer thinner, acetone, isopropyl alcohol and similar solvents can be used for the final preparation of mating surfaces.

All power head dimensional specifications are in **Table 3** and **Table 4**. All tables are at the end of the chapter.

Piston Ring End Gap

Check and adjust the piston ring end gap before installing the piston rings on the pistons.

Insufficient end gap will cause the piston to stick in the cylinder bore when the engine is hot. There must be adequate end gap to allow for heat expansion.

Excessive end gap will result in an excessive amount of combustion gases leaking past the gap between the ring ends. This will cause a reduction in performance and can lead to excessive carbon buildup in the ring grooves and on the piston skirt.

Once the end gap has been set, tag the rings for installation in the bore in which they were checked and fitted. All models use two rings on each piston. Both rings must be checked and fitted.

Excessive ring end gap can be caused by a worn or oversize bore. Recheck the cylinder bore as described previously in this chapter and/or make sure the correct piston rings are being used for the actual bore size.

Refer to **Figure 68** and **Figure 69**, and check the piston ring end gap as follows:

1. Select a piston ring and place it inside the cylinder No. 1 bore. Push the ring squarely into the bore using the piston (**Figure 68**). The ring must be square in the bore.

2. Measure the ring end gap with a feeler gauge as shown in **Figure 69**. If the ring gap is not within the specification in **Table 4**, repeat the measurement with the same ring in the cylinder No. 2 bore. Repeat the process as necessary until a bore is found that the ring fits correctly.

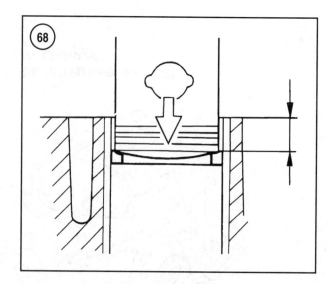

3A. If the measured ring end gap is excessive in every bore, the ring is defective or the cylinder is oversize. Measure the cylinder bore and recheck the piston ring part number. If the bore is within the specification and the correct ring is being used, the ring being checked is defective and must be replaced.

3B. If the measured ring end gap is insufficient in every bore, the ring is defective, the ring is intended for use in an oversize bore or the cylinder is undersize. Measure the cylinder bore and recheck the piston ring part number. If the bore is within the specification and the correct ring is being used, the ring is defective and must be replaced.

4. Once a ring correctly fits a cylinder or has been fitted to a cylinder, tag the ring with the cylinder number so it can be installed on the correct piston during power head assembly.

5. Repeat this process until all piston rings are fitted to a specific cylinder bore and properly tagged for identification.

Assembly (65 Jet and 75-125 hp [Except 105 Jet and 115 Optimax] Models)

These models are equipped with the capacitor discharge module (CDM) ignition system. The ignition system and most electrical components mount on a single plate on the starboard side of the power head.

Because this section covers three- and four-cylinder models, and since the three-cylinder models are essentially a shortened version of a four-cylinder model, the exploded illustrations are of the four-cylinder model. Any procedures specific to one model is identified in the text.

Refer to **Figure 70** and **Figure 71** for the following procedures.

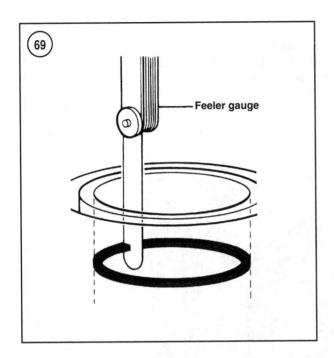

69

Feeler gauge

8

Crankshaft and pistons

1. Check the end gap of the new piston rings as described under *Piston Ring End Gap* in this chapter. The ring end gap must be within the specification in **Table 4**.

2. Assemble the lower end cap as follows:

   a. Coat the outer diameter of a new crankshaft lower seal (10, **Figure 70**) with Loctite 271 threadlocking adhesive (part No. 92-809819).

   b. Press the seal into the end cap until the seal is seated in the end cap bore. The lip of the seal must face up, toward the flywheel, when the end cap is installed.

   c. Grease a new O-ring (11, **Figure 70**) with Quicksilver 2-4-C Multi-Lube (part No. 92-825407). Install the O-ring into the end cap's groove.

> *CAUTION*
> *The wear sleeve is a very thin material and can easily be crushed or distorted during installation.*

3. If the wear sleeve was removed, install a new wear sleeve on the lower end of the crankshaft as follows:

   a. Coat the wear sleeve contact area of the crankshaft with Loctite 271 threadlocking adhesive.

   b. Pilot the wear sleeve over the lower end of the crankshaft.

   c. Using a suitable block of wood and a hammer, drive the wear sleeve onto the crankshaft until the sleeve seats on the crankshaft shoulder. Make sure the sleeve is driven straight and not crushed.

4. Grease a new O-ring with Quicksilver 2-4-C Multi-Lube. Carefully install the O-ring into the crankshaft's drive shaft bore. Position the O-ring between the wear sleeve and the end of the crankshaft.

5. If the oil pump drive gear and/or ball bearing were removed, install a new gear and/or bearing as follows:

   a. Lubricate the crankshaft and a new oil pump drive gear with outboard oil. Position the recessed side of the gear toward the crankshaft counterweight, align the keyway and seat the gear against the crankshaft shoulder.

   b. Lubricate a new ball bearing with outboard oil, then slide the bearing over the drive shaft end of the crankshaft with the numbered side facing away from the crankshaft.

   c. Support the crankshaft under the lower counterweight in a press. Press against the inner race of the bearing with a suitable mandrel (**Figure 72**) until the bearing is seated on the crankshaft.

6. Mount the crankshaft vertically on a power head (crankshaft) stand (part No. 91-812549 or an equivalent). Securely clamp the power head stand in a vise.

> *CAUTION*
> *If the original bearings are reused, install them in their original locations. Each crankshaft seal ring groove requires two seal rings to be installed. The open ends of seal rings must be 180° apart from each other.*

7. Assemble the two, on three-cylinder models, or three, on four-cylinder models, center main bearings as follows:

   a. Install two new seal rings (18, **Figure 71**) into the upper center main bearing journal's seal groove. Do not expand the rings any further than necessary to install them. Position the open ends of each seal ring 180° apart from each other.

   b. Apply a thick coat of needle bearing assembly grease (part No. 92-825265A-1) to the journal's twin bearing surfaces. Then install the 16 loose rollers to each bearing surface (32 rollers for each bearing assembly).

   c. Position the outer race halves over the bearing rollers and seal rings. The retaining ring groove must be positioned up, toward the flywheel.

   d. Carefully align the fracture lines, then install the retainer ring (**Figure 73**). Position the retaining ring to cover as much of both fracture lines as possible.

   e. Repeat this procedure as necessary to assemble the lower center main bearing on three-cylinder mod-

⑦⓪

CYLINDER BLOCK (65 JET AND 75-125 HP [EXCEPT 105 JET AND 115 HP OPTIMAX] MODELS) (FOUR-CYLINDER SHOWN)

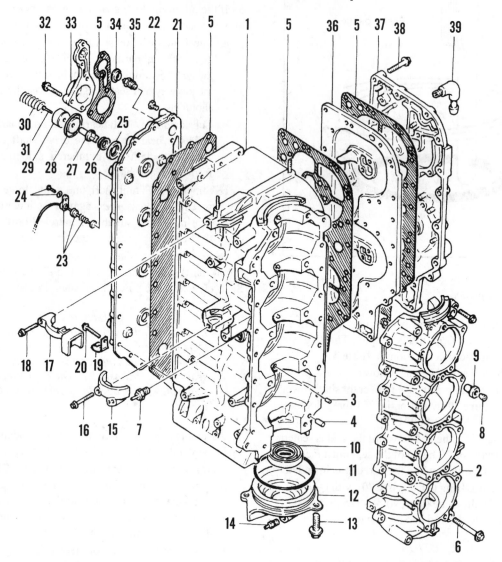

1. Cylinder block
2. Crankcase cover
3. Bearing locating dowel
4. Crankcase cover dowel
5. Gaskets
6. Crankcase cover bolts
7. Accelerator pump discharge nozzle
8. Check valve
9. Check valve carrier
10. Crankshaft lower seal
11. O-ring
12. Lower end cap
13. Bolt
14. Check valve
15. Lower starter bracket
16. Bolt
17. Upper starter bracket
18. Bolt
19. Clamp
20. Screw
21. Cylinder block cover
22. Brass pipe plug
23. Engine temperature switch
24. Screw and washer
25. Carrier
26. Grommet
27. Poppet valve
28. Diaphragm
29. Cup
30. Spring
31. Screw
32. Screw
33. Thermostat cover
34. Grommet
35. Thermostat
36. Exhaust manifold
37. Exhaust cover
38. Bolt
39. Water discharge (tell-tale) fitting

CRANKSHAFT ASSEMBLY (65 JET AND 75-125 HP [EXCEPT 105 JET AND 115 HP OPTIMAX] MODELS) (FOUR CYLINDER SHOWN)

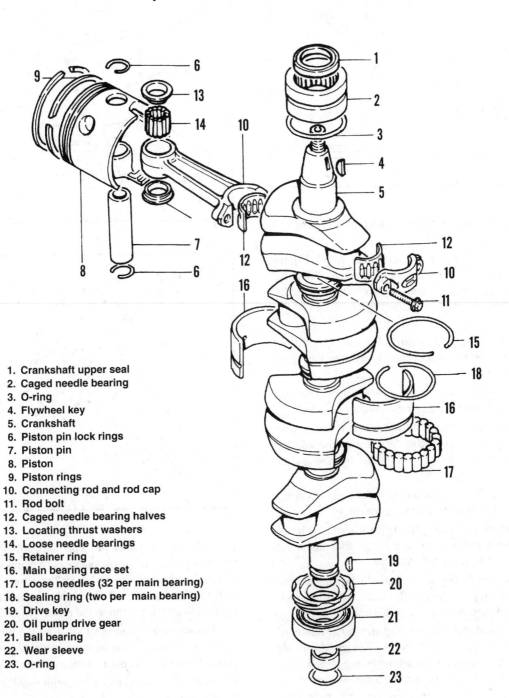

1. Crankshaft upper seal
2. Caged needle bearing
3. O-ring
4. Flywheel key
5. Crankshaft
6. Piston pin lock rings
7. Piston pin
8. Piston
9. Piston rings
10. Connecting rod and rod cap
11. Rod bolt
12. Caged needle bearing halves
13. Locating thrust washers
14. Loose needle bearings
15. Retainer ring
16. Main bearing race set
17. Loose needles (32 per main bearing)
18. Sealing ring (two per main bearing)
19. Drive key
20. Oil pump drive gear
21. Ball bearing
22. Wear sleeve
23. O-ring

8

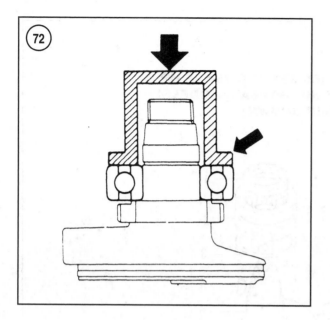

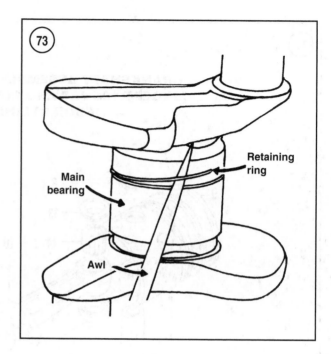

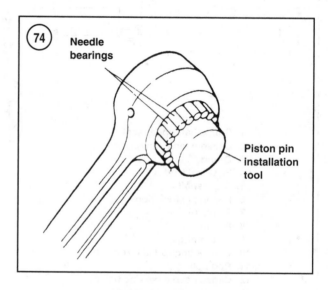

els, or the center and lower center main bearings on four-cylinder models.

8. Coat the outer diameter of a new upper seal (1, **Figure 71**) with Loctite 271 threadlocking adhesive. Press the seal into the upper main bearing with a suitable mandrel. The lip of the seal must face down, away from the flywheel.

9. Coat a new O-ring (3, **Figure 71**) with Quicksilver 2-4-C Multi-Lube and install the O-ring into the upper main bearing groove.

10. Lubricate the upper main bearing rollers with outboard oil, then install the bearing onto the crankshaft.

11. Begin assembling the connecting rods to the pistons by greasing the sleeve portion of the piston pin installation tool (part No. 91-76160A-2) with needle bearing assembly grease.

12. Position the No. 1 cylinder connecting rod in its original orientation, as marked during disassembly.

13. Hold the lower locating (thrust) washer (13, **Figure 71**) under the connecting rod small end, then insert the greased sleeve into the small end bore.

14. Lubricate the 29 needles with needle bearing assembly grease and insert them into the small end of the connecting rod and around the sleeve (**Figure 74**).

15. Position the upper locating (thrust) washer on top of the needles. Carefully slide the No. 1 cylinder piston over the rod with the stamped UP marking facing up and align the piston pin bores. Then insert the main body of piston pin tool (part No. 91-76160A-2) into the piston pin bore and through the connecting rod, pushing the sleeve out the other side of the piston pin bore. Remove the sleeve.

16. Lubricate the piston pin with outboard oil and pilot it into the open end of the piston pin bore. Support the piston and tool with one hand and drive the piston pin into the piston with a soft-faced rubber or plastic mallet. Allow the pin tool to be pushed out as the piston pin is driven in.

17. Remove the piston pin tool from the bottom of the piston, then insert it into the top of the piston pin bore and gently tap it until the pin is centered in the pin bore.

18. Make sure no needles or locating washers were displaced, then secure the piston pin with two new piston pin lock rings (6, **Figure 71**) using a lock ring installation tool (part No. 91-77109A-2) as follows:

**INSTALLING LOCKRING
INTO INSTALLATION TOOL**

75

76

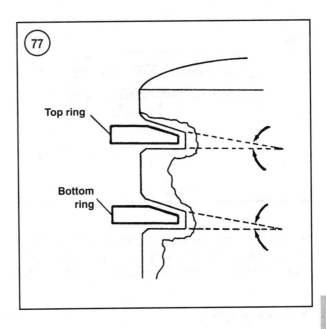

77

Top ring

Bottom
ring

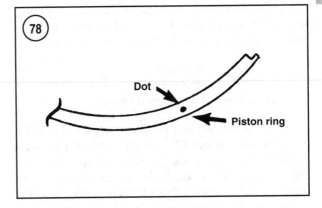

78

Dot

Piston ring

8

a. Position a new lock ring into the stepped, open end of the tool's sleeve (**Figure 75**).

b. Insert the drive handle into the opposite end of the sleeve.

c. Pilot the stepped end of the sleeve into either end of the cylinder No. 1 piston pin bore.

d. While holding the sleeve to the pin bore, press the drive handle quickly and firmly to install the ring.

e. Remove the handle and sleeve. Make sure the lock ring is completely seated in its groove in the piston pin bore.

f. Install the second lock ring in the opposite end of the piston pin bore in the same manner.

19. Repeat Steps 11-18 for the remaining pistons and connecting rods.

CAUTION
Install the piston rings on the pistons that match the cylinder bore for which the rings were fitted.

20. Install the two semi-keystone piston rings onto each piston using a ring expander (part No. 91-24697 or an equivalent). See **Figure 76**. The flat side of the rings face the piston skirt and the tapered side faces the piston dome (**Figure 77**). Install the bottom ring first, then install the top ring. Expand each ring just enough to slip over the piston. The identification mark (**Figure 78**, typical) on both rings must face upward.

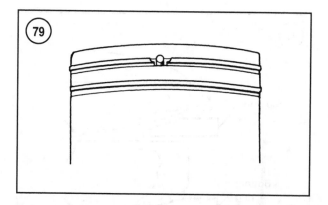

21. Make sure that each ring can be rotated freely in its groove, then position the end gap of each piston ring to straddle the ring locating pin in its groove. See **Figure 79**.

Power head assembly

1. Lubricate the piston rings, pistons and cylinder bores with outboard oil. Make sure the end gap of each piston ring is still straddling the locating pin in its groove.

NOTE
A ring compressor is not required as the cylinder bores have a tapered entrance.

2. Install each piston into its appropriate cylinder bore. Make sure the stamped UP marks are facing the flywheel end of the cylinder block and the connecting rods are aligned with the crankshaft throws. Rock each piston slightly to help it enter its cylinder bore, making sure the piston rings do not rotate or catch and break while entering the bore. Seat each piston at the bottom of its bore.

3. Insert a thin screwdriver through the exhaust port of each cylinder and depress each piston ring (**Figure 80**). If the ring does not spring back when the screwdriver is removed, the ring was probably broken during piston installation and must be replaced.

4. Make sure the upper and center main bearing locating dowels (3, **Figure 70**) are installed in the cylinder block. Then position the cylinder block so the block-to-crankcase cover mating surface is pointing upward. Position all connecting rods toward one side on the cylinder block.

5. Slowly lower the crankshaft assembly into the block. Rotate the crankshaft main bearing assemblies as necessary to align the hole in the bearing races with the bearing locating dowels (3, **Figure 70**).

CAUTION
Do not strike the end of the crankshaft directly or the wear sleeve will be destroyed.

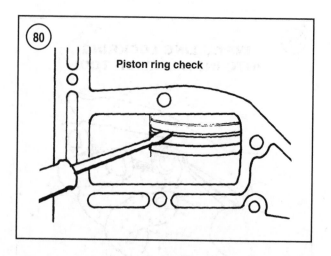

Piston ring check

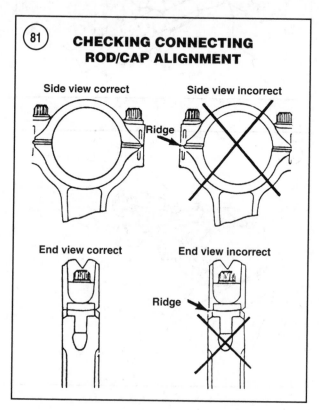

CHECKING CONNECTING ROD/CAP ALIGNMENT

Side view correct   Side view incorrect

Ridge

End view correct   End view incorrect

Ridge

6. Insert the power head (crankshaft) stand into the lower end of the crankshaft. Then carefully tap the stand with a soft hammer to seat the ball bearing in its bore.

7. Install the connecting rods to the crankshaft journals as follows:

   a. Apply a thick coat of needle bearing assembly grease (part No. 92-825265A-1) to the crankpin journals. Install the bearing cages and needle bearing to the journals. If the original bearings are reused, install them in their original position.

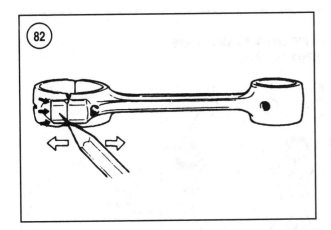

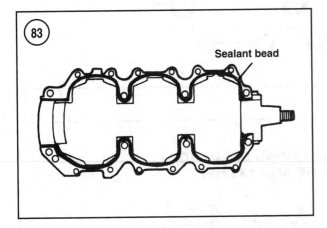

Sealant bead

check of the alignment after the final torque has been applied.

g. Repeat this procedure to install the remaining connecting rods to their respective crankshaft journals.

8. Use an oil- and wax-free solvent, such as acetone or lacquer thinner to clean the cylinder block and crankcase cover mating surfaces.

9. Install the crankcase dowel (4, **Figure 70**) into the cylinder block or crankcase cover if it is not already installed.

10. Install the lower end cap over the crankshaft. Coat the mating surfaces with Quicksilver Perfect Seal (part No. 92-34227-1). Align the bolt holes in the cylinder block and seat the end cap to the block. Install two bolts finger-tight to hold the end cap in position.

CAUTION
Loctite Master Gasket Sealant (part No. 92-12564-2) is the only sealant recommended to seal the crankcase cover-to-cylinder block mating surfaces. The sealant comes in a kit that includes a special primer. Follow the instructions included in the kit for preparing the surfaces and applying the sealant. Apply the sealant bead to the inner, crankshaft side of all crankcase cover bolt holes.

11. Following the instructions supplied with the sealant, apply a continuous bead of Loctite Master Gasket Sealant (part No. 92-12564-2) to the mating surface of the cylinder block. Run the sealant bead along the inside of all bolt holes as shown in **Figure 83**, typical. The bead of sealant must be continuous.

12. Install the crankcase cover into position on the cylinder block. Seat the cover to the block with hand pressure.

13. Insert the power head (crankshaft) stand into the lower end of the crankshaft. Tap against the stand with a soft hammer to make sure the ball bearing is seated in its bore.

14A. *Three-cylinder models*—Coat the threads of the eight large main bearing and 12 smaller outer crankcase cover bolts with Loctite 242 threadlocking adhesive (part No. 92-809821), then install the cover bolts. Tighten the large cover bolts to the specification in **Table 1** in a minimum of two progressive steps, following the pattern shown in **Figure 84**. Then tighten the smaller outer cover bolts to the specification in **Table 1** in a minimum of two progressive steps, following the pattern shown in **Figure 84**.

14B. *Four-cylinder models*—Coat the threads of the ten large main bearing and 16 smaller outer crankcase cover bolts with Loctite 242 threadlocking adhesive (part No. 92-809821), then install the cover bolts. Tighten the large

b. Pull the No. 1 cylinder rod and piston assembly up to the No. 1 crankpin journal and bearings. Rotate the crankshaft as necessary to allow mating of the rod and journal.

c. Install the matching connecting rod cap in its original orientation. Carefully observe fracture and alignment marks to ensure correct installation (**Figure 81**, typical).

d. Lubricate the bolt threads and underside of the bolt heads of the *new* connecting rod bolts with outboard lubricant. Then, while holding the cap firmly in position, install the connecting rod bolts and thread them fully into the rod.

e. Tighten each rod bolt to the initial torque specification in **Table 1**. Run a fingernail or pencil lead over each edge of the rod-to-cap joint (**Figure 82**). No ridge should be seen or felt. Realign and retorque the cap as necessary.

f. Once the alignment is correct, tighten each bolt in two progressive steps to the second torque specification in **Table 1**. Then apply the final torque by turning each rod bolt an additional 90°. Make a final

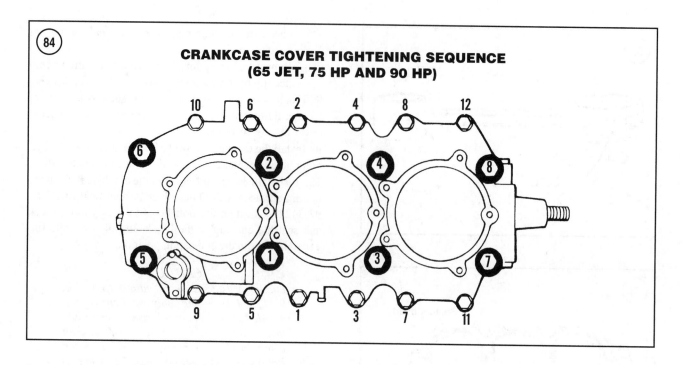

**CRANKCASE COVER TIGHTENING SEQUENCE
(65 JET, 75 HP AND 90 HP)**

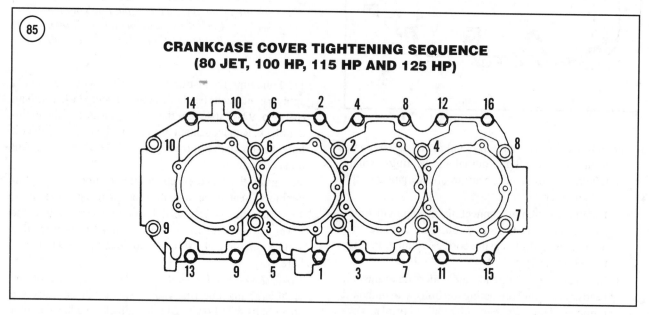

**CRANKCASE COVER TIGHTENING SEQUENCE
(80 JET, 100 HP, 115 HP AND 125 HP)**

main bearing cover bolts to the specification in **Table 1** in a minimum of two progressive steps, following the pattern shown in **Figure 85**. Then tighten the smaller outer cover bolts to the specification in **Table 1** in a minimum of two progressive steps, following the pattern shown in **Figure 85**.

15. Rotate the crankshaft several revolutions to check for binding or unusual noise. If there is binding or noise, disassemble the power head, and locate and correct the cause of the defect before proceeding.

16. Remove the lower end cap bolts installed previously. Coat the threads of the three lower end cap bolts with Loctite 242 threadlocking adhesive. Install and evenly tighten the bolts to the specification in **Table 1**.

17. Install the cylinder block cover (21, **Figure 70**) using a new gasket (5). Do not use any sealant on this gasket. Apply Loctite 242 threadlocking adhesive to the threads of the cover bolts. Install the 14 bolts on three-cylinder models or 18 bolts on four-cylinder models. Tighten the bolts finger-tight at this time.

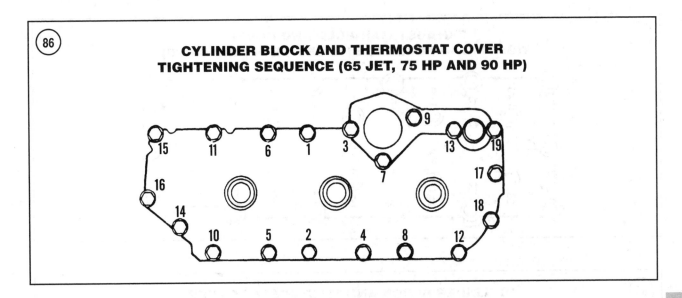

CYLINDER BLOCK AND THERMOSTAT COVER TIGHTENING SEQUENCE (65 JET, 75 HP AND 90 HP)

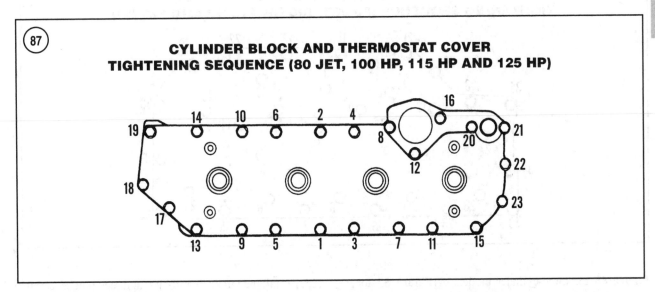

CYLINDER BLOCK AND THERMOSTAT COVER TIGHTENING SEQUENCE (80 JET, 100 HP, 115 HP AND 125 HP)

18. Assemble the thermostat housing as follows:

a. Install a new grommet around the thermostat and install the thermostat into the cylinder block cover with the sensing pellet facing the power head.

b. Install a new grommet (26, **Figure 70**) into the poppet valve cavity in the cylinder block cover.

c. Install the poppet valve assembly as shown in **Figure 70**.

d. Install the cover (33, **Figure 70**) using a new gasket (5) and secure the cover with four screws. Coat the screw threads with Quicksilver Perfect Seal. Tighten the screws finger-tight at this time.

19. Tighten the cylinder block cover and thermostat cover screws to the specification in **Table 1** in three progressive steps, following the pattern shown in **Figure 86**

for three-cylinder models or **Figure 87** for four-cylinder models.

20. Install the engine temperature switch (23, **Figure 70**) into the cylinder block cover. Secure the switch with a screw and washer (24, **Figure 70**). Tighten the screw securely.

21. Assemble the exhaust manifold and cover with two new gaskets. Do not use sealant on these gaskets. Sandwich the exhaust plate between the gaskets, then position the cover over the outer gasket and manifold. Position the assembly on the power head and secure it with 24 bolts on three-cylinder models or 35 bolts on four-cylinder models. Coat the bolt threads with Loctite 242 threadlocking adhesive and tighten them to the specification in **Table 1** in three progressive steps, following the pattern shown in

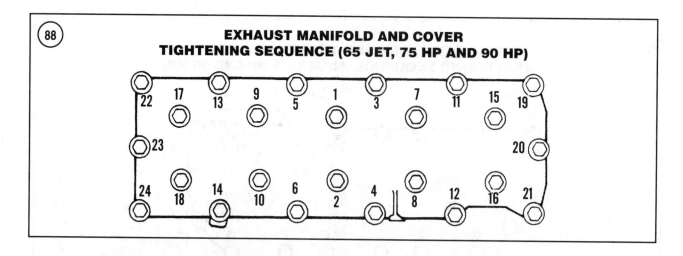

**EXHAUST MANIFOLD AND COVER
TIGHTENING SEQUENCE (65 JET, 75 HP AND 90 HP)**

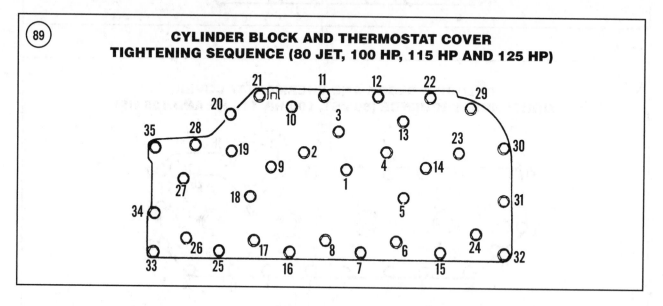

**CYLINDER BLOCK AND THERMOSTAT COVER
TIGHTENING SEQUENCE (80 JET, 100 HP, 115 HP AND 125 HP)**

Figure 88 for three-cylinder models or **Figure 89** for four-cylinder models.

22. Position the spark and throttle control arm assembly on its power head mounting boss. Install and tighten the arm's center bolt securely.

23. Install the ignition and electrical components as an assembly. This includes the stator assembly, trigger coil, trim/tilt relays, and the electrical/ignition plate containing the CDMs, voltage regulator and starter solenoid). If equipped with an rpm limit module, install it at this time. Secure all cables and harnesses with the original clamps and/or new tie-straps. See Chapter Seven.

24. Install the internal fuel bleed (recirculation) check valves and check valve carriers (8 and 9, **Figure 70**) into the crankcase cover openings for cylinders No. 2, 3 and 4. See Chapter Six for fuel bleed system information.

25. Install the intake manifold(s) and reed blocks, carburetors, fuel pump, fuel filter, fuel primer valve and all fuel, primer and fuel bleed (recirculation) lines as described in Chapter Six.

26. On four-cylinder models, install the accelerator pump system and adjust the pump clearance as described in Chapter Six.

27. Install the oil pump, oil reservoir, oil warning module and all oil lines as described in Chapter Thirteen.

28. Install the flywheel and electric starter as described in Chapter Seven.

Assembly (105 Jet, 115 hp Optimax and 135-200 hp [Except 200 hp Optimax] Models)

Refer to **Figure 90** and **Figure 91** for the following procedures.

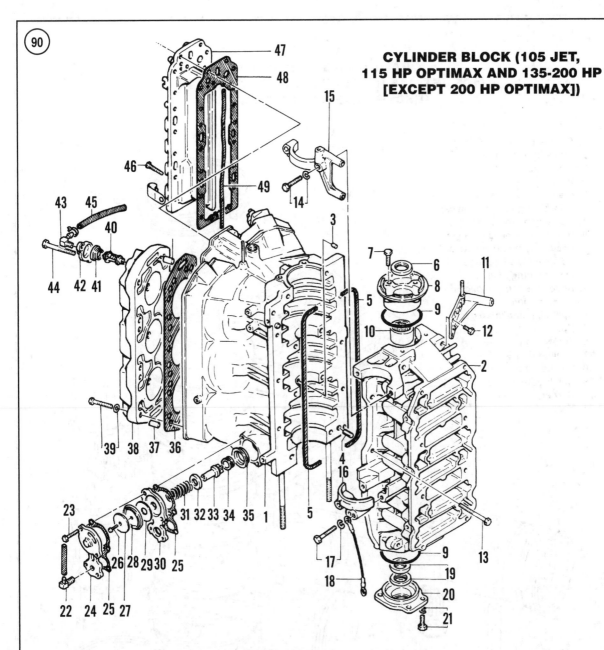

CYLINDER BLOCK (105 JET, 115 HP OPTIMAX AND 135-200 HP [EXCEPT 200 HP OPTIMAX])

90

8

1. Cylinder block
2. Crankcase cover
3. Bearing locating dowel
4. Crankcase cover dowel pin
5. Crankcase sealing ring
6. Crankshaft upper seal
7. Bolt
8. Upper end cap
9. O-ring
10. Caged needle bearing
11. Bracket
12. Bolt
13. Crankcase cover bolt

14. Bolt and washer
15. Upper starter bracket
16. Lower starter bracket
17. Bolt and washer
18. Ground wire
19. Crankshaft lower seals
20. Lower end cap
21. Bolt and washer
22. Fitting (water discharge)*
23. Screw
24. Outer plate
25. Gaskets

26. Screw
27. Washer
28. Diaphragm
29. Water deflector
30. Inner plate
31. Spring
32. Washer
33. Poppet valve
34. Grommet
35. Carrier
36. Head gasket*
37. Dowel pins

38. Cylinder head
39. Bolt and washer
40. Thermostat
41. Grommet
42. Thermostat housing
43. Fitting
44. Bolt
45. Hose (water discharge)
46. Bolt
47. Exhaust divider plate
48. Gasket
49. Sealing strip

*Not used on all models.

⟨91⟩

CRANKSHAFT ASSEMBLY
(105 JET, 115 HP OPTIMAX AND 135-200 HP
[EXCEPT 200 HP OPTIMAX])

1. Crankshaft
2. Piston pin lock rings
3. Piston pin
4. Piston
5. Piston rings
6. Connecting rod and rod cap
7. Connecting rod bolt
8. Roller bearings and cages
9. Locating (thrust) washers
10. Loose needle bearings
11. Main bearing race
12. Roller bearings an cages
13. Retainer ring
14. Split oil pump drive gear
15. Nut
16. Screw
17. Sealing ring
18. Ball bearing
19. Retainer ring
20. Carrier
21. Seal

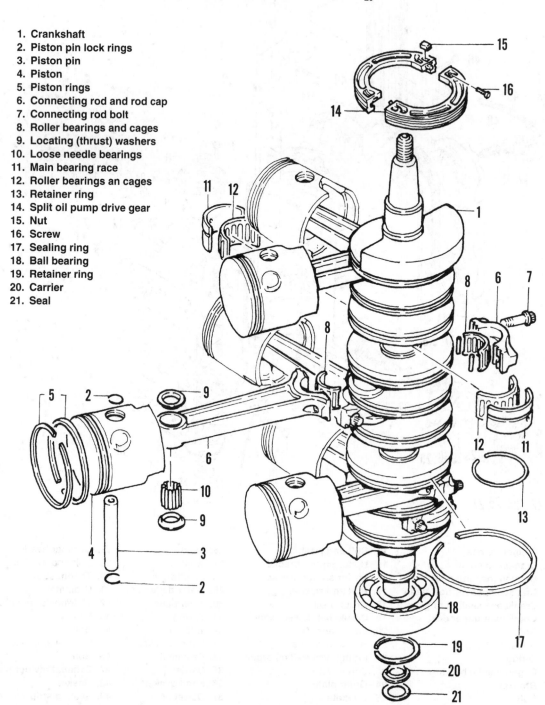

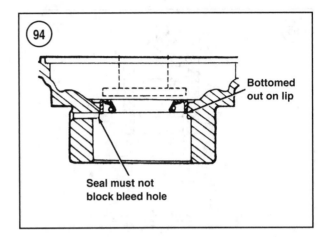

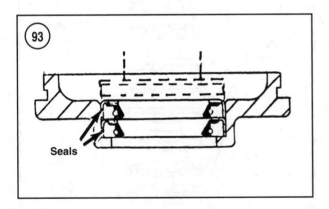

PISTON IDENTIFICATION AND ORIENTATION (105 JET, 115 HP OPTIMAX AND 135-200 HP MODELS [EXCEPT 200 HP OPIMAX])

Crankshaft replacement

If a new crankshaft is installed into a used cylinder block, inspect the crankshaft seal ring mating surfaces in the cylinder block and crankcase cover. If the original sealing rings wore grooves into the block and cover mating surfaces, the sealing rings of the new crankshaft must fit into the grooves or the crankshaft will bind.

Check for crankshaft binding as follows:

1. Check the seal rings grooves in the block and cover for burrs. Remove any burrs found.

2. Lubricate the crankshaft seal rings with outboard oil. Temporarily install the crankshaft and end caps into the cylinder block.

3. Rotate the crankshaft several turns while checking for binding or excessive drag. If there is binding or excessive drag, recheck the seal grooves for burrs and remove any found.

4. If there is still excessive drag or binding, replace the cylinder block and crankcase cover as an assembly.

Crankshaft and pistons

Each cylinder and piston is identified as shown in **Figure 92**. Install the pistons with their stamped markings positioned as shown in **Figure 92**.

1. Check the end gap of the new piston rings as described under *Piston Ring End Gap* in this chapter. The ring end gap must be within the specification in **Table 4**.

2. Refer to **Figure 93** and assemble the lower end cap as follows:

   a. Coat the outer diameter of the two new crankshaft lower seals (19, **Figure 90**) with Loctite 271 threadlocking adhesive (part No. 92-809819).

   b. Press the seals into the end cap one at a time and on top of each other using driver head part No. 91-55919, or an equivalent, until each seal is seated in the end cap bore. The lip of both seals must face down, toward the drive shaft when the end cap is installed. See **Figure 93**.

   c. Grease a new O-ring (9, **Figure 90**) with Quicksilver 2-4-C Multi-Lube (92-825407). Install the O-ring into the end cap's groove.

3. Refer to **Figure 94** and assemble the upper end cap as follows:

   a. Coat the outer diameter of a new upper seal with Loctite 271 threadlocking adhesive.

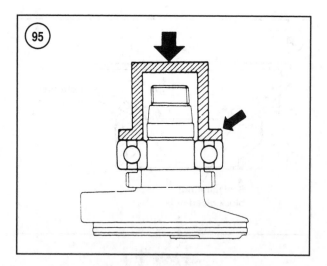

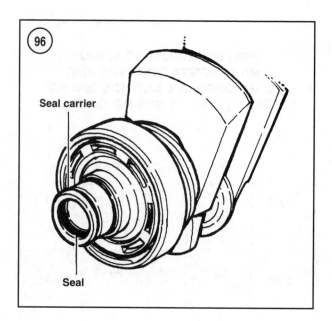

b. Press the seal into the end cap with a suitable mandrel. The lip of the seal must face down, toward the drive shaft and must not cover the bleed hole as shown in **Figure 94**.

4. If the ball bearing was removed, install a bearing as follows:

   a. Lubricate a new ball bearing with outboard oil, then slide the bearing over the drive shaft end of the crankshaft with the numbered side facing away from the crankshaft.

   b. Support the crankshaft under the lower counterweight in a press. Press against the inner race of the bearing with a suitable mandrel until the bearing is seated on the crankshaft. See **Figure 95**.

   c. Install the retainer ring (19, **Figure 91**) with snap ring pliers (part No. 91-922778A-3). Make sure the retainer ring fully seats in the crankshaft groove.

5. Install the seal carrier and seal (**Figure 96**, typical) to the lower end of the crankshaft as follows:

   a. Coat the carrier contact area of the crankshaft with Loctite 271 threadlocking adhesive.

   b. Pilot the carrier into the drive shaft bore at the lower end of the crankshaft.

   c. Using a suitable block of wood and a hammer, drive the carrier onto the crankshaft until the carrier is seated. Make sure the carrier is driven straight.

   d. Grease a new seal with Quicksilver 2-4-C Multi-Lube and install the seal into the carrier.

6. Mount the crankshaft vertically on a power head (crankshaft) stand (part No. 91-30591A-1 or an equivalent). Securely clamp the power head stand in a vise.

CAUTION
*The crankshaft seal rings (17, **Figure 91**)*
are brittle. Wear approved eye protection

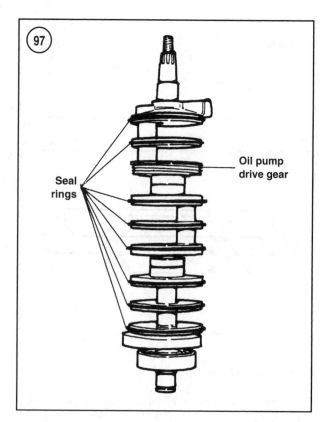

and do not expand the ring(s) any further
than necessary to install them.

7. If one or more of the seven crankshaft seal rings (**Figure 97**) are removed, expand the new ring(s) just enough to fit around the nearest crankpin journal. Then, install the

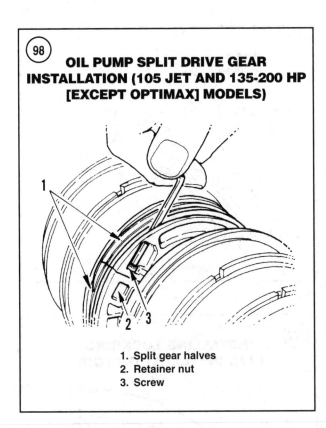

98

OIL PUMP SPLIT DRIVE GEAR INSTALLATION (105 JET AND 135-200 HP [EXCEPT OPTIMAX] MODELS)

1. Split gear halves
2. Retainer nut
3. Screw

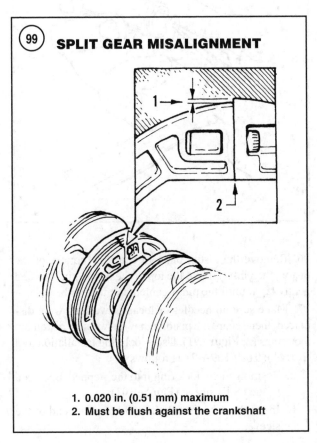

99

SPLIT GEAR MISALIGNMENT

1. 0.020 in. (0.51 mm) maximum
2. Must be flush against the crankshaft

ring(s) into the crankshaft groove(s) using piston ring expander part No. 91-24697 or an equivalent.

8. On 105 jet and 135-200 hp (except Optimax) models, if the oil pump drive gear was removed, install a new drive gear as follows:

   a. Position the split oil pump drive gear halves (14, **Figure 91**) around the crankshaft (**Figure 98**) with the screw and nut access holes facing the upper center main bearing. Make sure the alignment pins align, then seat the halves to each other.

   b. Coat the threads of the two screws (16, **Figure 91**) with Loctite RC680 retaining compound (part No. 92-809833). Position a retainer nut as shown in **Figure 98**, then install and tighten the screw finger-tight. Install the second screw and nut in the same manner.

   c. Evenly and carefully tighten both screws to the specification in **Table 1**. Make sure the gears halves pull down tightly and evenly.

   d. Check the gear tooth misalignment at both mating points. See **Figure 99**. The misalignment shouldn't exceed 0.020 in. (0.51 mm) at either mating point (**Figure 99**) or the gear will fail prematurely.

   e. If the misalignment is excessive, remove the gear and repeat the installation procedure. Make sure the gear seats against the crankshaft at the point shown in 2, **Figure 99**. Do not proceed until the misalignment is within specification.

CAUTION
If the original bearings are reused, install them in their original locations.

9. Assemble the two center main bearings as follows:

   a. Apply a thick coat of needle bearing assembly grease (part No. 92-825265A-1) to the upper center main bearing journal. Then install the roller bearing halves to the bearing surface.

   b. Position the outer race halves over the bearings. The retaining ring groove must be positioned up, toward the flywheel.

   c. Carefully align the fractured parting lines, then install the retainer ring (**Figure 100**). Position the retainer ring to cover as much of both fracture lines as possible.

   d. Repeat this procedure to assemble the lower center main bearing.

10. Begin assembling the connecting rods to the pistons by greasing the sleeve portion of piston pin installation tool (part No. 91-74607A-1) with needle bearing assembly grease.

8

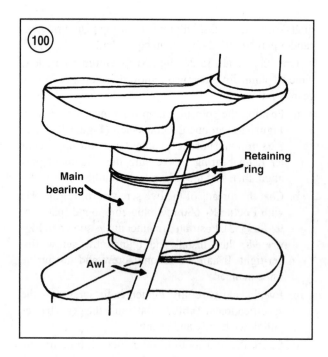

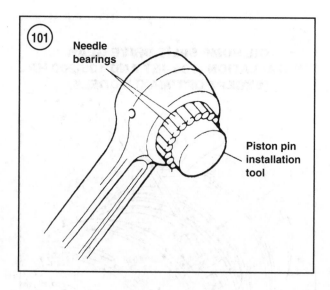

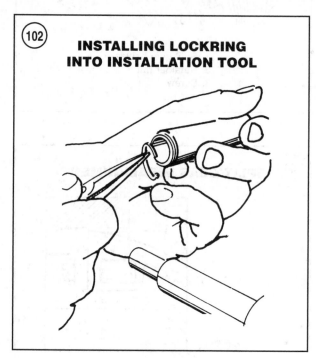

NOTE
All pistons are stamped UP to signify the top
of the piston. However, the cylinder No. 1, 3
*and 5 pistons are also marked with an **S**,*
signifying the starboard cylinder bank of the
engine. The cylinder No. 2, 4 and 6 pistons
*are marked with a **P**, signifying the port cyl-*
inder bank of the engine. Install each piston
*in its correct orientation. See **Figure 92**.*

11. Position the No. 1 cylinder connecting rod with its part number in the I-beam facing up.

12. Hold the lower locating (thrust) washer (9, **Figure 91**) under the connecting rod small end, then insert the greased sleeve into the small end bore.

13. Lubricate the 29 needles with needle bearing assembly grease and insert them into the small end of the connecting rod and around the sleeve (**Figure 101**).

14. Position the upper locating (thrust) washer (9, **Figure 91**) on top of the needles. Carefully slide the No. 1 piston over the rod with the UP marking facing up and align the piston pin bores. Then insert the main body of piston pin tool (part No. 91-74607A-1) into the piston pin bore and through the connecting rod, pushing the sleeve out the other side of the piston pin bore. Remove the sleeve.

15. Lubricate the piston pin with outboard oil and pilot it into the open end of the piston pin bore. Support the piston and tool with one hand and drive the piston pin into the piston with a soft-faced rubber or plastic mallet. Allow the pin tool to be pushed out as the piston pin is driven in.

16. Remove the piston pin tool from the bottom of the piston, then insert it into the top of the piston pin bore and gently tap it until the pin is centered in the pin bore.

17. Make sure no needles or locating washers were displaced, then secure the piston pin with two new piston pin lock rings (2, **Figure 91**). Use a lock ring installation tool (part No. 91-77109A-2) as follows:

   a. Position a new lock ring into the stepped, open end of the tool's sleeve (**Figure 102**).

   b. Insert the drive handle into the opposite end of the sleeve.

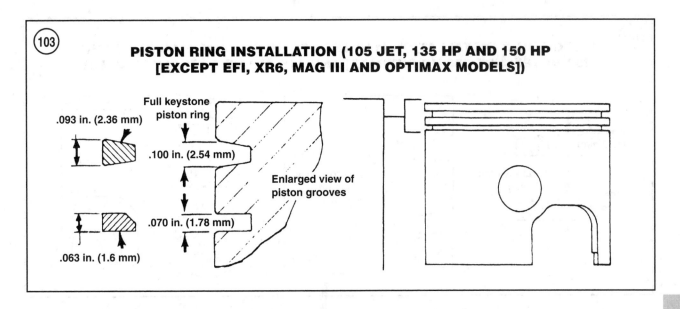

**PISTON RING INSTALLATION (105 JET, 135 HP AND 150 HP
[EXCEPT EFI, XR6, MAG III AND OPTIMAX MODELS])**

.093 in. (2.36 mm)

Full keystone piston ring

.100 in. (2.54 mm)

Enlarged view of piston grooves

.070 in. (1.78 mm)

.063 in. (1.6 mm)

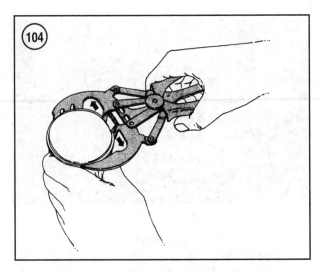

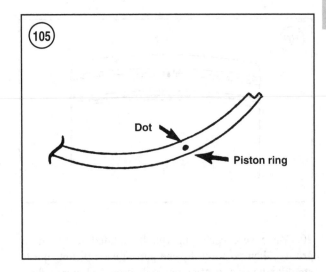

Dot

Piston ring

8

c. Pilot the stepped end of the sleeve into either end of the cylinder No. 1 piston pin bore.

d. While holding the sleeve to the pin bore, press the drive handle quickly and firmly to install the ring.

e. Remove the handle and sleeve. Make sure the lock ring completely seats in its groove in the piston pin bore.

f. Install the second lock ring in the opposite end of the piston pin bore in the same manner.

18. Repeat Steps 10-17 for the remaining pistons and connecting rods.

CAUTION
Install the piston rings onto the pistons that match the cylinder bore for which the rings were fitted.

19A. On 105 jet, 135 hp and 150 hp (except EFI, XR6, Mag III and Optimax) models, refer to **Figure 103** and install the piston rings onto each piston using ring expander part No. 91-24697 or an equivalent. See **Figure 104**. Install the bottom, rectangular ring first, then the top, full keystone ring, expanding each ring just enough to slip over the piston. The identification mark (**Figure 105**) on both rings must face up.

19B. On 140 jet, 150 EFI, XR6, Magnum III, 175-200 hp (except 200 Optimax) and 115-175 Optimax models, refer to **Figure 106** and install the two semi-keystone rings onto each piston using a ring expander part No. 91-24697 or an equivalent. See **Figure 104**. Install the bottom ring first, then the top ring, expanding each ring just enough to slip over the piston. The identification mark (**Figure 105**) on both rings must face up.

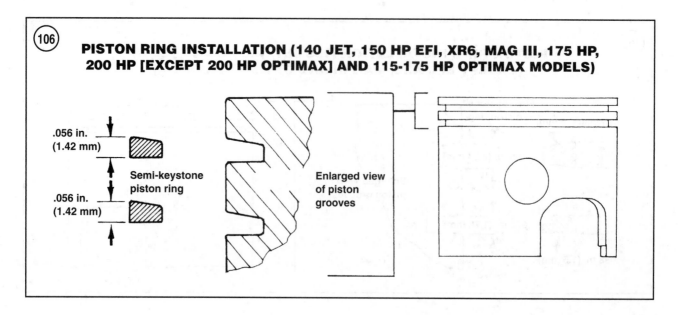

106

PISTON RING INSTALLATION (140 JET, 150 HP EFI, XR6, MAG III, 175 HP, 200 HP [EXCEPT 200 HP OPTIMAX] AND 115-175 HP OPTIMAX MODELS)

.056 in.
(1.42 mm)

Semi-keystone
piston ring

.056 in.
(1.42 mm)

Enlarged view
of piston
grooves

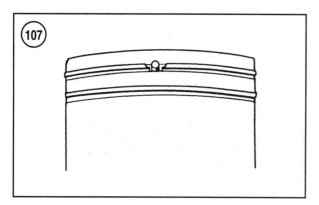

107

108

20. Make sure each ring can be rotated freely in its groove, then position the end gap of each piston ring to straddle the ring locating pin in its groove (**Figure 107**).

Power head assembly

1. Make sure the two center main bearing locating dowels (3, **Figure 90**) are installed in the cylinder block. Then position the cylinder block so the block-to-crankcase cover mating surface is pointing up.

2. Lubricate all seven seal rings and the oil pump drive gear with outboard oil.

3. Slowly lower the crankshaft assembly into the block (**Figure 108**). Rotate the crankshaft center main bearing assemblies as necessary to align the hole in the bearing races with the bearing locating dowels (3, **Figure 90**). Position each seal ring (17, **Figure 91**) so the ring end gap is pointing straight up.

CAUTION
Do not strike the end of the crankshaft directly or the seal carrier may be damaged.

4. Insert the power head (crankshaft) stand into the lower end of the crankshaft. Carefully tap the stand with a soft hammer to seat the ball bearing in its bore.

5. Install the upper (**Figure 109**) and lower end caps over their respective end of the crankshaft. Coat the mating surfaces with Quicksilver Perfect Seal (part No. 92-34227-1). Align the bolt holes of each end cap with the cylinder block and seat the caps against the block. Install two bolts finger-tight in each end cap to hold it in position.

6. Lubricate the No. 1 cylinder piston rings, piston and cylinder bore with outboard oil. Then, make sure the piston ring end gaps are still straddling the locating pin in each ring groove (**Figure 107**).

7. Install the cylinder No.1 piston and connecting rod assembly as follows:

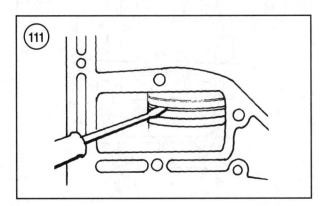

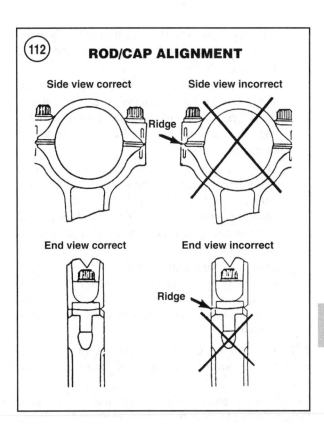

ROD/CAP ALIGNMENT

Side view correct

Side view incorrect

Ridge

End view correct

End view incorrect

Ridge

8

a. Lubricate the cylinder No. 1 piston, piston rings and cylinder bore.

b. Make sure the end gap of each piston ring is positioned over the ring locating pin in each ring groove.

c. Using the appropriate tapered sleeve ring compressor (part No. 91-65494 for a 3.125 in. bore or part No. 91-818773 for a 3.501 in. bore), install the No. 1 piston into the cylinder bore (**Figure 110**) with the

UP mark facing the flywheel and the connecting rod big end aligned with the crankshaft journal. Be careful to keep the rod's big end from damaging the cylinder bore and the crankshaft journal.

d. Insert a small screwdriver through the exhaust port and depress each piston ring. See **Figure 111**. If the ring does not spring back when the screwdriver is removed, the ring was probably broken during installation and must be replaced.

8. Install the No. 1 cylinder connecting rod to the crankshaft journal as follows:

a. Grease the crankpin journals with a thick coat of needle bearing assembly grease (part No. 92-825265A-1). Install the bearing cages and needle bearing to the journals. If the original bearings are reused, install them in their original positions.

b. Pull the No. 1 cylinder rod and piston assembly up to the No. 1 crankpin journal and bearings. Rotate the crankshaft as necessary to allow mating of the rod and journal.

c. Install the connecting rod cap in its original orientation. Carefully observe fracture and alignment marks to ensure correct installation (**Figure 112**, typical).

d. Lubricate the bolt threads and underside of the heads of the *new* connecting rod bolts with outboard lubricant. Then, while holding the cap firmly in position, install the connecting rod bolts and thread them fully into the rod.

e. Tighten each rod bolt to the initial torque specification in **Table 1**. Run a fingernail or pencil lead over each edge of the rod-to-cap joint (**Figure 113**). No ridge should be seen or felt. Realign and retorque the cap as necessary.

f. After checking the alignment, tighten each bolt in two progressive steps to the second torque specification in **Table 1**. Then apply the final torque by turning each rod bolt an additional 90°. Make a final check of the alignment after the final torque has been applied.

g. Rotate the crankshaft several revolutions to check for binding or unusual noise. If there is binding or unusual noise, remove the piston and connecting rod just installed and correct the defect before proceeding.

9. Repeat Steps 6-8 for the remaining piston and connecting rod assemblies. Refer to **Figure 92** for piston location and orientation.

10. Use an oil- and wax-free solvent, such as acetone or lacquer thinner to clean the cylinder block and crankcase cover mating surfaces.

11. Install the two dowel pins (4, **Figure 90**) into the cylinder block or crankcase cover if they are not already installed.

> *CAUTION*
> *Loctite Master Gasket Sealant (part No. 92-12564-2) is the only sealant recommended to seal the crankcase cover-to-cylinder block mating surfaces. The sealant comes in a kit that includes a special primer. Follow the instructions included in the kit for preparing the surfaces and applying the sealant. Apply the sealant bead to the inner, crankshaft side of all crankcase cover bolt holes.*

12. Following the instructions supplied with the sealant, apply a continuous bead of Loctite Master Gasket Sealant (part No. 92-12564-2) to the mating surface of the cylinder block. Run the sealant bead along the inside of all bolt holes and to within 1/16 in. (1.6 mm) of the seal rings and center main bearings. Make sure the bead is continuous.

13. On 1998-2000 models, install new crankcase sealing rings (5, **Figure 90**) into the grooves in the crankcase cover. Trim the ends of the rings flush with the end cap bores. Then install the crankcase cover into position on the cylinder block. Seat the cover to the block as far as

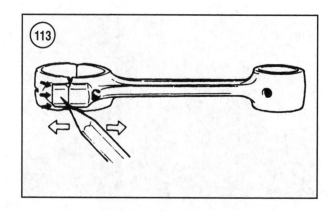

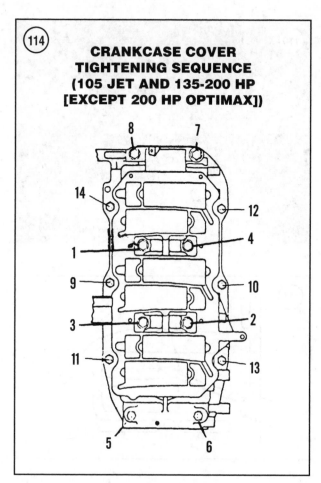

CRANKCASE COVER TIGHTENING SEQUENCE (105 JET AND 135-200 HP [EXCEPT 200 HP OPTIMAX])

possible with hand pressure. The seal rings prevent the cover from seating completely.

14. Insert the power head (crankshaft) stand into the lower end of the crankshaft. Tap against the stand with a soft hammer to make sure the ball bearing is seated in its bore.

15. Oil the threads and under the heads of the eight large main bearing crankcase cover bolts and coat the threads of

(115)

EXHAUST DIVIDER/COVER TIGHTENING SEQUENCE (105 JET AND 135-200 HP [EXCEPT 200 HP OPTIMAX])

18. Remove the end cap bolts installed previously. Coat the threads of the three lower and four upper end cap bolts with Loctite 242 threadlocking adhesive. Install and evenly tighten the upper end cap and lower end cap bolts to the specification in **Table 1**.

19. Install a new sealing strip (49, **Figure 90**) into the slot in the exhaust cavity.

20. Install the exhaust divider plate (47, **Figure 90**) using a new gasket (48). Coat the threads of the 20 bolts with Loctite 271 threadlocking adhesive (part No. 92-809819). Install and tighten the bolts to the specification in **Table 1** in three progressive steps, following the sequence shown in **Figure 115**.

NOTE
*All 2000-on 115 hp Optimax, 150 hp EFI, XR6, Mag III, 175 hp, 200 hp and all Optimax models use O-rings to seal the cylinder heads. 105 jet, 135 hp, 150 hp carbureted (except XR6 ad Mag III) and all 1998 and 1999 models use gaskets to seal the cylinder heads. See **Figure 116**.*

21A. On models with gaskets, install both cylinder heads to the power head using new gaskets.

21B. On models with O-rings, install new O-rings into the grooves on the cylinder head. The cross section of the O-ring is *not* round. The pointed side of the O-rings must face the cylinder head and the notched side must face the cylinder block. See **Figure 117**.

22. Position the thermostat pockets up, toward the flywheel. Coat the threads and under the head of each of the 12 head bolts with outboard oil. Install and tighten the bolts as follows:

    a. Tighten all 12 bolts hand tight.

    b. Torque the bolts to the initial torque specification in **Table 1** in three progressive steps, in the sequence shown in **Figure 118**.

    c. Turn each head bolt an additional 90°, following the pattern shown in **Figure 118**.

    d. Do not retorque the head bolts after this operation.

23A. On carbureted models, install the engine temperature switch into the port cylinder head, just below the No. 2 spark plug hole. Secure the switch with the plate and screw. Secure the switch's ground lead under the screw. Coat the screw threads with Loctite 242 threadlocking adhesive. Tighten the screw to the specification in **Table 1**.

23B. On EFI and Optimax models, install the engine coolant temperature sensor(s) into the cylinder head(s) as described in Chapter Six.

24. If equipped with an engine temperature gauge, install the temperature sensor unit into the starboard cylinder head, just below the No. 1 spark plug hole. Secure the

the six smaller outer cover bolts with Loctite 242 threadlocking adhesive (part No. 92-809821), then install the bolts. Evenly tighten the large main bearing cover bolts in small increments until the crankshaft seal rings are completely compressed and the crankcase cover seats against the cylinder block. Then tighten the six outer bolts finger-tight.

16. Torque the eight large main bearing bolts to the specification in **Table 1** in three progressive steps, following the sequence shown in 1-8, **Figure 114**. Then torque the six smaller outer bolts to the specification in **Table 1** in three progressive steps, following the sequence shown in 9-14, **Figure 114**.

17. Rotate the crankshaft several revolutions to check for binding or unusual noise. If there is binding or noise, disassemble the power head, and locate and correct the cause of the defect before proceeding.

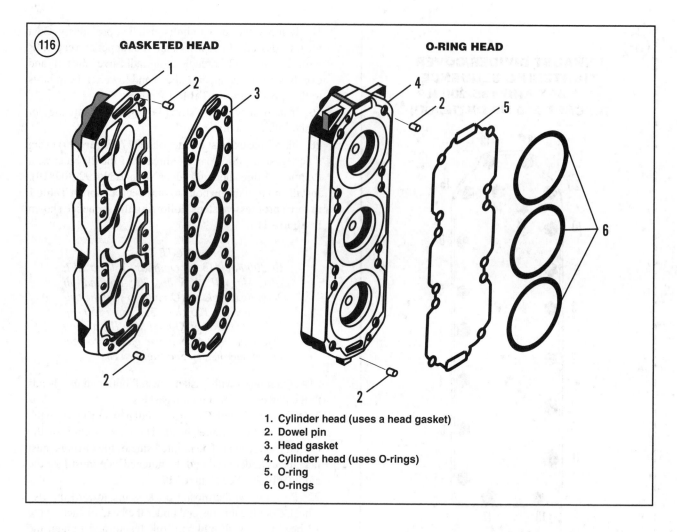

GASKETED HEAD   **O-RING HEAD**

1. Cylinder head (uses a head gasket)
2. Dowel pin
3. Head gasket
4. Cylinder head (uses O-rings)
5. O-ring
6. O-rings

sending unit with the plate and screw. Coat the screw threads with Loctite 242 threadlocking adhesive. Tighten the screw to the specification in **Table 1**.

25. Install a new grommet around each thermostat. Install a thermostat into each cylinder head with the sensing pellet facing the head. Install a thermostat cover over each thermostat and against each cylinder head. The water fittings on each thermostat cover must face towards each other. Coat the threads of the thermostat cover screws with Quicksilver Perfect Seal. Install and evenly tighten the screws to the specification in **Table 1**.

26. Connect the water discharge hose(s) to the thermostat cover fittings. Secure each connection with a new tie-strap.

27. Assemble and install the poppet valve as follows:

    a. Install a new grommet (34, **Figure 90**) into the poppet valve cavity in the cylinder block.

    b. Assemble the poppet valve components as shown in **Figure 90**. Tighten the poppet valve diaphram screw (26, **Figure 90**) to the specification in **Table 1**.

    c. Sandwich a new gasket between the outer and inner plates, then position the assembly to the cylinder head using another new gasket.

    d. Secure the assembly with four screws. Coat the screw threads with Quicksilver Perfect Seal. Evenly tighten the cover screws to the specification in **Table 1**.

    e. Connect the water discharge hose to the poppet valve fitting. Secure the connection with a new tie-strap.

28. Position the throttle and spark control arm to its mounting boss on the port side of the power head. Make sure the thrust washer is between the assembly and the power head, then install the center bolt and tighten it securely.

29. Install the shift and throttle cable anchor bracket to the port lower side of the power head. Coat the three mounting bolts with Loctite 271 threadlocking adhesive. Install the bolts and tighten them securely.

30. Install the ignition and electrical components as an assembly. This includes the stator assembly, trigger coil, both switch boxes, starter solenoid, idle stabilizer module,

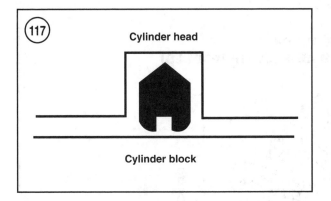

Cylinder head

Cylinder block

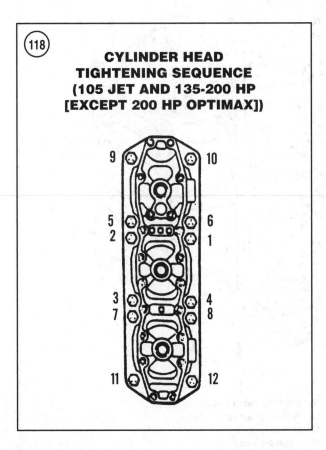

**CYLINDER HEAD
TIGHTENING SEQUENCE
(105 JET AND 135-200 HP
[EXCEPT 200 HP OPTIMAX])**

32A. On carbureted models, install the carburetors, fuel pump, fuel filter, fuel primer valve, intake manifold and reed blocks, and all fuel, primer and fuel bleed (recirculation) lines as described in Chapter Six.

32B. On EFI models, install the induction manifold assembly, ECM, mechanical fuel pump, vapor separator assembly, water separating fuel filter, water warning module, intake manifold and reed blocks, and all fuel and fuel bleed (recirculation) lines as described in Chapter Six.

32C. On Optimax models, install the induction manifold, ECM, mechanical fuel pump, fuel/air rails, air compressor, intake manifold, and all fuel and fuel bleed (recirculation) lines as described in Chapter Six.

33. On 200 hp EFI models, install the detonation sensor and module as described in Chapter Six.

34. Install the oil reservoir, oil pump, oil warning module and all oil lines as described in Chapter Thirteen.

35. Install the flywheel and electric starter as described in Chapter Seven.

**Assembly (200 hp Optimax,
225 hp and 250 hp Models)**

Refer to **Figure 119** and **Figure 120** for the following procedures. The poppet (water pressure relief) valve is mounted on the exhaust adapter plate, which is not removed with the power head. Be sure to reassemble the poppet valve when directed.

Crankshaft replacement concerns

If a new crankshaft was installed into a used cylinder block, inspect the crankshaft seal ring mating surfaces in the cylinder block and crankcase cover. If the original sealing rings wore grooves into the block and cover mating surfaces, the sealing rings of the new crankshaft must fit into the grooves or the crankshaft will bind.

Check for crankshaft binding as follows:

1. Check the seal ring's grooves in the block and cover for burrs. Remove any burrs found.

2. Lubricate the crankshaft seal rings with outboard oil. Temporarily install the crankshaft and lower end cap into the cylinder block.

3. Rotate the crankshaft several turns while checking for binding or excessive drag. If there is binding or excessive drag, recheck the seal grooves for burrs and remove any found.

4. If there is still excessive drag or binding, replace the cylinder block and crankcase cover as an assembly.

oil and overheat warning module, and the electrical/ignition plate containing the ignition coils, voltage regulators and trim relays. If equipped with an rpm limit module, install it at this time. Secure all cables and harnesses with the original clamps and/or new tie-straps. See Chapter Seven.

31. On models equipped with a shift switch, such as XR6, Mag III, Optimax models and any engines with this system added as an accessory, connect the shift switch leads to the engine harness bullet connector and connect the ring terminal to the engine ground.

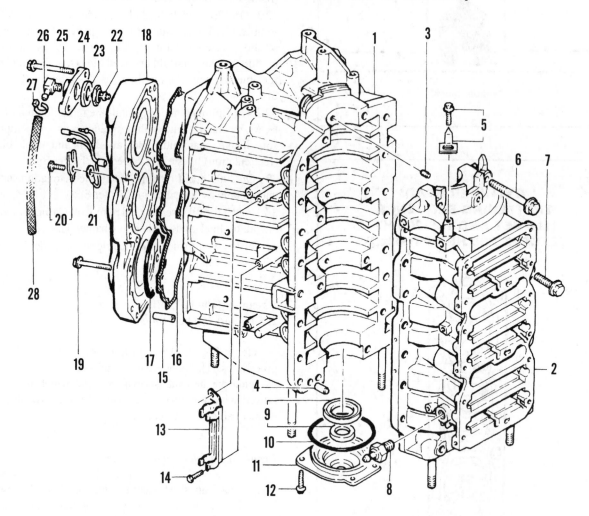

**CYLINDER BLOCK
(200 HP OPTIMAX, 225 HP AND 250 HP MODELS)**

1. Cylinder block
2. Crankcase cover
3. Bearing locating dowel
4. Crankcase dowel pin
5. Adjustable timing pointer*
6. Main bearing bolt (large)
7. Outer crankcase bolt (small)
8. Pulse fitting (remote oil tank)
9. Crankshaft lower seals
10. O-ring
11. Lower end cap
12. Bolt
13. Main harness connector bracket
14. Screw
15. Cylinder head dowel
16. Water jacket seal
17. O-ring
18. Cylinder head
19. Cylinder head bolt
20. Retainer plate and bolt
21. ECT sensor
22. Thermostat
23. Gasket
24. Thermostat housing
25. Thermostat housing/cylinder head bolt
26. Water discharge fitting*
27. Tie-strap
28. Water discharge hose

*Not used on all models

CRANKSHAFT ASSEMBLY
(200 HP OPTIMAX, 225 HP AND 250 HP MODELS)

1. O-ring
2. Crankshaft upper seal
3. Caged needle bearing
4. Flywheel key
5. Crankshaft
6. Piston pin lock rings
7. Piston pin
8. Piston
9. Piston rings
10. Locating (thrust) washers
11. Loose needle bearings
12. Connecting rod and cap
13. Connecting rod bolt
14. Needle bearings
15. Retainer ring
16. Double stacked loose roller bearings
17. Main bearing race
18. Sealing ring
19. Oil pump drive gear
20. Ball bearing
21. Retainer ring
22. O-ring

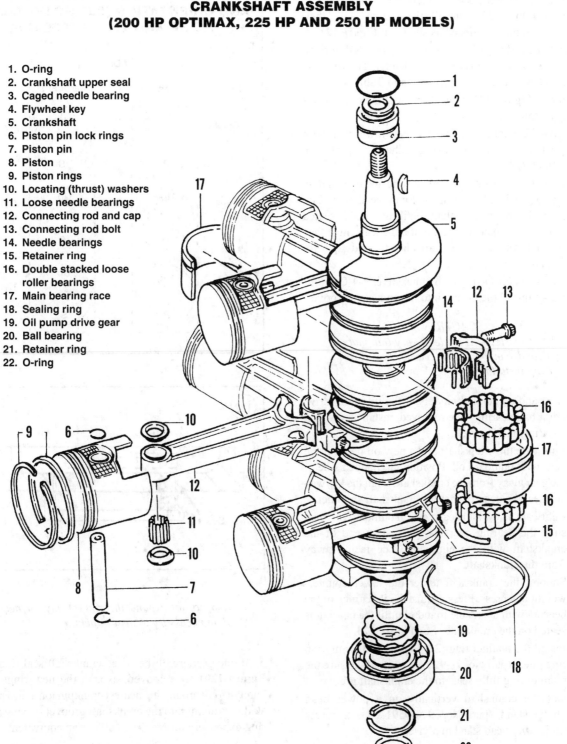

8

Crankshaft and pistons

Each cylinder and piston is identified (numbered) as shown in **Figure 121**. Install the pistons with their stamped markings positioned as shown in **Figure 121**.

1. Check the end gap of the new piston rings as described under *Piston Ring End Gap* in this chapter. The ring end gap should be within the specification in **Table 4**.

2. Refer to **Figure 122**, typical and assemble the lower end cap as follows:

   a. Coat the outer diameter of two new lower seals with Loctite 271 threadlocking adhesive (part No. 92-809819).

   b. Press the seals into the end cap one at a time and on top of each other using a driver head (part No. 91-55919 or an equivalent) until each seal is seated in the end cap bore. The lip of both seals must face down, toward the drive shaft when the end cap is installed.

   c. Grease a new O-ring with Quicksilver 2-4-C Multi-Lube. Install the O-ring into the end cap's groove.

> *CAUTION*
> *The wear sleeve is made of very thin material and can be easily crushed or distort during installation.*

3. On EFI and carbureted models, if the oil pump drive gear and/or ball bearing were removed, install a new gear and/or bearing as follows:

   a. Lubricate the crankshaft and a new oil pump drive gear with outboard oil. Position the flanged side of the gear away from the crankshaft, align the keyway and seat the gear against the crankshaft shoulder.

   b. Lubricate a new ball bearing with outboard oil, then slide the bearing over the drive shaft end of the crankshaft with the numbered side facing away from the crankshaft.

   c. Support the crankshaft under the lower counterweight in a press. Press against the inner race of the bearing with a suitable mandrel until the bearing is seated on the crankshaft. See **Figure 123**.

   d. Install the retainer ring (21, **Figure 120**) with snap ring pliers (part No. 91-922778A-3). Make sure the retainer ring fully seats in the crankshaft groove.

4. Mount the crankshaft vertically on a power head (crankshaft) stand (part No. 91-30591A-1). Securely clamp the power head stand in a vise.

> *CAUTION*
> *The crankshaft seal rings (18, Figure 120) are brittle. Wear approved eye protection*

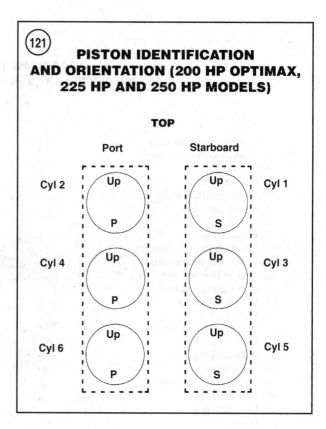

121 **PISTON IDENTIFICATION AND ORIENTATION (200 HP OPTIMAX, 225 HP AND 250 HP MODELS)**

TOP

Port   Starboard

Cyl 2 Up P   Up S Cyl 1

Cyl 4 Up P   Up S Cyl 3

Cyl 6 Up P   Up S Cyl 5

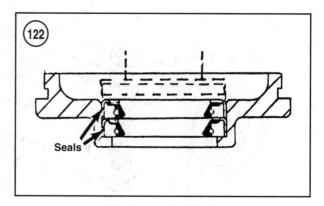

122

Seals

and do not expand the ring(s) any further than necessary to install them.

5. If one or more of the seven crankshaft seal rings (18, **Figure 120**) are removed, expand the new ring(s) just enough to fit around the nearest crankpin journal. Then install the ring(s) into the crankshaft groove(s) using piston ring expander part No. 91-24697 or an equivalent.

> *CAUTION*
> *If the original bearings are reused, install them in their original locations.*

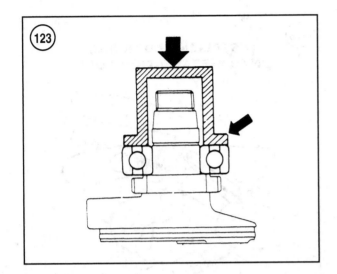

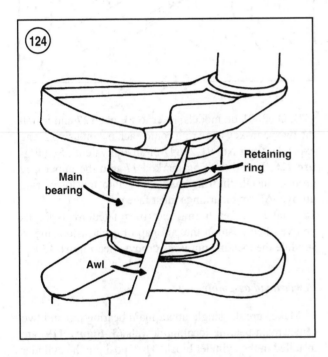

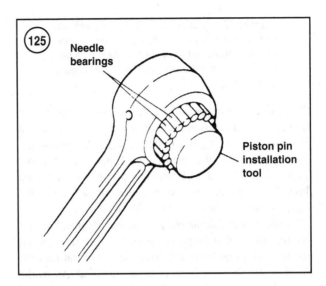

d. Repeat this procedure to assemble the lower center main bearing.

7. Assemble and install the upper main bearing as follows:

a. Coat the outer diameter of a new upper seal with Loctite 271 threadlocking adhesive (part No. 92-809819).

b. Position the seal in the open bore of the upper main bearing with the seal lip facing down.

c. Use a suitable mandrel to press the seal into the bearing until it is seated.

d. Coat a new O-ring (1, **Figure 120**) with Quicksilver 2-4-C Multi-Lube grease (part No. 92-825407) and install the O-ring into the bearing's groove.

e. Slide the bearing over the flywheel end of the crankshaft and seat it against the crankshaft shoulder.

8. Begin assembling of the connecting rods to the pistons by greasing the sleeve portion of the piston pin installation tool (part No. 91-92973A-1) with needle bearing assembly grease.

9. Position the No. 1 cylinder connecting rod in its original orientation, as marked during disassembly.

10. Hold the lower locating (thrust) washer (10, **Figure 120**) under the connecting rod small end, then insert the greased sleeve into the small end bore.

11. Lubricate the 34 needles with needle bearing assembly grease and insert them into the small end, around the sleeve as shown in **Figure 125**, typical.

NOTE
*All pistons are marked UP to signify the top of the piston. However, the cylinder No. 1, 3 and 5 pistons are also marked with an **S**, signifying the starboard cylinder bank of the*

6. Assemble the two center main bearings as follows:

a. Apply a thick coat of needle bearing assembly grease to the upper center main bearing journal. Then install the double stack of loose bearing rollers to the bearing surface.

b. Position the outer race halves over the bearing rollers and seal rings. The retaining ring groove must be positioned up, toward the flywheel.

c. Carefully align the fractured parting lines, then install the retainer ring (**Figure 124**). Position the retainer ring to cover as much of both fracture lines as possible.

*engine. The cylinder No. 2, 4 and 6 pistons
are also marked with a **P**, signifying the port
cylinder bank of the engine. Install each piston in its correct orientation. See **Figure
121**.*

12. Position the upper locating (thrust) washer on top of
the needles. Carefully slide the No. 1 piston over the rod
with the UP marking facing up and align the piston pin
bores. Then insert the main body of the piston pin tool
(part No. 91-92973A-1) into the piston pin bore and
through the connecting rod, pushing the sleeve out the
other side of the piston pin bore. Remove the sleeve.

13. Lubricate the piston pin with outboard oil and pilot it
into the open end of the piston pin bore. Support the piston
and tool with one hand and drive the piston pin into the
piston with a soft-faced rubber or plastic mallet. Allow the
pin tool to be pushed out as the piston pin is driven in.

14. Remove the piston pin tool from the bottom of the
piston, then insert it into the top of the piston pin bore and
gently tap it until the pin is centered in the pin bore.

15. Make sure no needles or locating washers were displaced, then secure the piston pin with two new piston pin
lock rings (6, **Figure 120**). Use a lock ring installation tool
(part No. 91-93004A-2) and proceed as follows:

    a. Position a new lock ring into the stepped, open end
        of the tool's sleeve (**Figure 126**).

    b. Insert the drive handle into the opposite end of the
        sleeve.

    c. Pilot the stepped end of the sleeve into either end of
        the No. 1 cylinder piston pin bore.

    d. While holding the sleeve to the pin bore, press the
        drive handle quickly and firmly to install the ring.

    e. Remove the handle and sleeve. Make sure the re-
        tainer completely seats in its groove in the piston
        pin bore.

    f. Install the second retainer in the opposite end of the
        piston pin bore in the same manner.

16. Repeat Steps 8-15 for the remaining pistons and connecting rods.

*CAUTION
Install the piston rings onto the pistons that
match the cylinder bore for which the rings
were fitted.*

17A. On 1998-2000 models, refer to **Figure 127** and install the two semi-keystone rings onto each piston using a
ring expander (part No. 91-24697 or an equivalent). See
Figure 128. Install the bottom ring first, then the top ring,
expanding each ring just enough to slip over the piston.
The identification mark (**Figure 129**) on both rings must
face up.

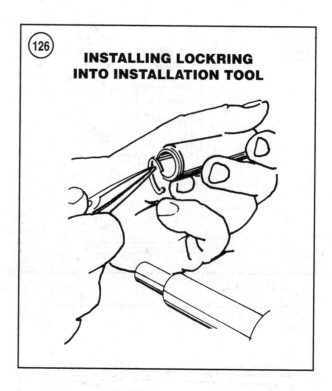

17B. On 2001-on models, refer to **Figure 127** and install
the two semi-keystone rings onto each piston using a ring
expander (part No. 91-24697 or an equivalent). See **Figure 128**. Install the ring marked *1T* into the upper ring
groove. Install the ring marked *2T* into the lower ring
groove. All ring markings must face up.

18. Make sure each ring can be rotated freely in its
groove, then position the end gap of each piston ring to
straddle the locating pin in its groove. See **Figure 130**.

Power head assembly

1. Make sure the single upper main bearing pin and two
center main bearing locating dowels (3, **Figure 119**) are
installed in the cylinder block. Then position the cylinder
block so the block-to-crankcase cover mating surface is
pointing upward.

2. Lubricate all seven seal rings (18, **Figure 120**) and the
oil pump drive gear (19) with outboard oil.

3. Slowly lower the crankshaft assembly into the block
(**Figure 131**, typical). Rotate the crankshaft center main
bearing assemblies as necessary to align the holes in the
bearing races with the bearing locating dowels (3, **Figure
119**). Position each seal ring (18, **Figure 120**) so the ring
end gap is pointing straight up.

*CAUTION
Do not strike the end of the crankshaft directly or the wear sleeve will be damaged.*

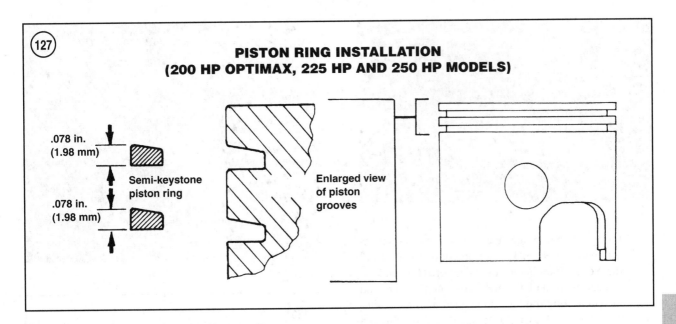

PISTON RING INSTALLATION
(200 HP OPTIMAX, 225 HP AND 250 HP MODELS)

.078 in.
(1.98 mm)

Semi-keystone
piston ring

.078 in.
(1.98 mm)

Enlarged view
of piston
grooves

8

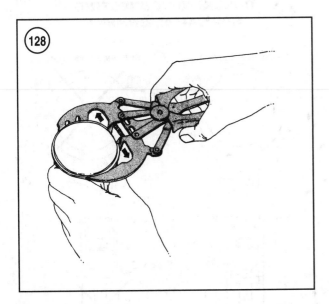

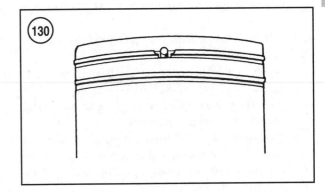

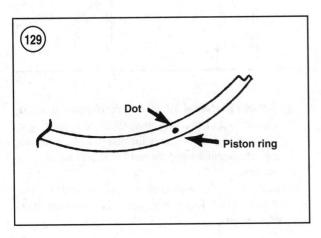

Dot

Piston ring

4. Insert the appropriate power head (crankshaft) stand into the lower end of the crankshaft. Carefully tap the stand with a soft hammer to seat the ball bearing in its bore.

5. Install the lower end cap over the crankshaft. Coat the mating surfaces with Quicksilver Perfect Seal (part No. 92-34227-1). Align the bolt holes with the cylinder block and seat the end cap to the cylinder block. Install two bolts finger-tight to hold the end cap in position.

6. Lubricate the No. 1 cylinder piston rings, piston and cylinder bore with outboard oil. Then make sure the piston ring end gaps are still straddling the locating pins in their ring grooves. See **Figure 130**.

7. Install the No. 1 cylinder piston and connecting rod assembly as follows:

   a. Lubricate the cylinder No. 1 cylinder bore, piston and piston rings.

   b. Make sure the end gap of each piston ring is positioned over the ring locating pin in its ring groove.

c. Using the appropriate tapered sleeve ring compressor (part No. 91-823237 or an equivalent), install the No. 1 piston into its cylinder bore (**Figure 132**, typical) with the UP mark facing the flywheel and the connecting rod big end aligned with the crankshaft journal. Be careful to keep the rod's big end from damaging the cylinder bore and the crankshaft journal.

8. Install the No. 1 cylinder connecting rod to the crankshaft journal as follows:

   a. Apply a thick coat of needle bearing assembly grease (part No. 92-825265A-1) to the crankpin journals. If the original bearings are reused, install them in their original position.

   b. Pull the No. 1 cylinder rod and piston assembly up to the No. 1 crankpin journal and bearings. Rotate the crankshaft as necessary to allow mating of the rod and journal.

   c. Install the connecting rod cap in its original orientation. Carefully observe fracture and alignment marks to ensure correct installation (**Figure 133**, typical).

   d. Lubricate the threads and underside of the heads of *new* connecting rod bolts with outboard lubricant. Then, while holding the cap firmly in position, install the connecting rod bolts and thread them fully into the rod.

   e. Tighten each bolt to the initial torque specification in **Table 1**. Run a fingernail or pencil lead over each edge of the rod-to-cap joint (**Figure 134**). No ridge should be seen or felt. Realign and retorque the cap as necessary.

   f. After checking the alignment, tighten both bolts in two progressive steps to the second torque specification in **Table 1**. Then apply the final torque by turning each rod bolt an additional 90°. Make a final check of the alignment after applying the final torque.

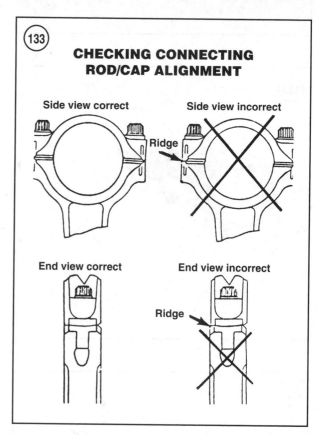

CHECKING CONNECTING ROD/CAP ALIGNMENT

Side view correct

Side view incorrect

Ridge

End view correct

End view incorrect

Ridge

   g. Rotate the crankshaft several revolutions to check for binding or unusual noise. If there is binding or an unusual noise, remove the piston and connecting rod just installed and correct the defect before proceeding.

9. Repeat Steps 6-8 for the remaining piston and connecting rod assemblies. Refer to **Figure 121** for piston location and orientation.

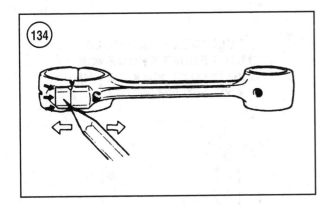

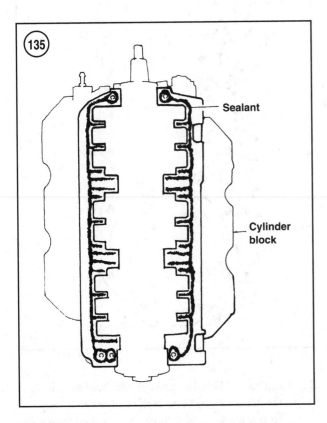

10. Use an oil- and wax-free solvent, such as acetone or lacquer thinner to clean the cylinder block and crankcase cover mating surfaces.

11. Install the dowel pin (4, **Figure 119**) into the cylinder block or crankcase cover if it is not already installed.

CAUTION
Loctite Master Gasket Sealant (part No. 92-12564-2) is the only sealant recommended to seal the crankcase cover-to-cylinder block mating surfaces. The sealant comes in a kit that includes a special primer. Follow the instructions included in the kit

for preparing the surfaces and applying the sealant. Apply the sealant bead to the inner, crankshaft side of all crankcase cover bolt holes.

12. Following the instructions supplied with the sealant, apply a continuous bead of Loctite Master Gasket Sealant (part No. 92-12564-2) to the mating surface of the cylinder block as shown in **Figure 135**. Run the sealant bead along the inside of all bolt holes and to within 1/16 in. (1.6 mm) of the seal rings and center main bearings. The bead must be continuous.

13. Install the crankcase cover into position on the cylinder block. Seat the cover to the block as far as possible with hand pressure. The seal rings prevent complete seating of the cover.

14. Insert the power head (crankshaft) stand into the lower end of the crankshaft. Tap the stand with a soft hammer to make sure the ball bearing seats in its bore.

15. Oil the threads and under the heads of the eight large main bearing crankcase cover bolts and coat the threads of the 14 smaller outer cover bolts with Loctite 242 threadlocking adhesive (part No. 92-809821), then install the bolts. Evenly tighten the large main bearing cover bolts in small increments until the crankshaft seal rings are completely compressed and the crankcase cover seats against the cylinder block. Then tighten the 14 outer bolts finger-tight.

16. Torque the eight large main bearing bolts as follows:
   a. Tighten all eight bolts snugly.
   b. Tighten all eight bolts in three progressive steps to the specification in **Table 1**, following the pattern in A, **Figure 136**.
   c. Turn each one of the eight bolts an additional 90°, following the pattern in A, **Figure 136**.

17. Torque the 14 smaller outer bolts in three progressive steps to the specification in **Table 1**, following the pattern in B, **Figure 136**.

18. Rotate the crankshaft several revolutions to check for binding or unusual noise. If there is binding or noise, disassemble the power head, and locate and correct the cause of the defect before proceeding.

19. Remove the end cap bolts installed previously. Coat the threads of the four lower end cap bolts with Loctite 242 threadlocking adhesive. Install and evenly tighten the bolts to the specification in **Table 1**.

20. Install both cylinder heads to the power head as follows:
   a. Grease the O-rings and water jacket seals (16 and 17, **Figure 119**) with Quicksilver 2-4-C Multi-Lube (part No. 92-8825407), and position them in each cylinder head's grooves.

8

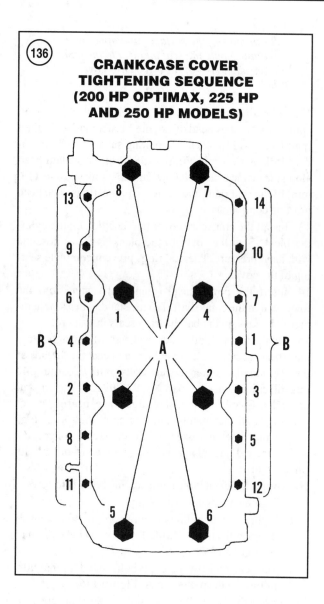

CRANKCASE COVER TIGHTENING SEQUENCE (200 HP OPTIMAX, 225 HP AND 250 HP MODELS)

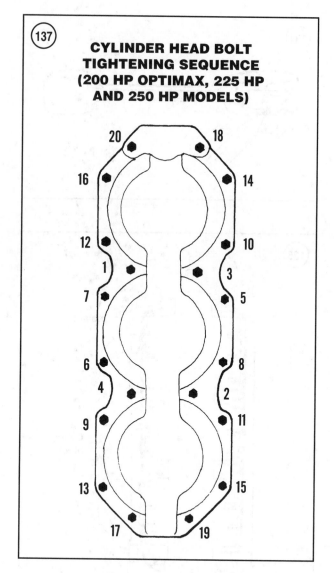

CYLINDER HEAD BOLT TIGHTENING SEQUENCE (200 HP OPTIMAX, 225 HP AND 250 HP MODELS)

b. Position the heads on the cylinder block with the thermostat pockets facing up, toward the flywheel.

c. Lubricate the 18 short bolts with clean engine oil. Apply oil to the threads and the bottom of the bolt heads.

d. Install the bolts in every hole except the two used by the thermostat covers. Tighten the 18 bolts on each head finger-tight at this time.

21. Install a new grommet around, or a new gasket over, each thermostat and install a thermostat into each cylinder head with the sensing pellet facing the head. Position a thermostat cover over each thermostat with the water fittings facing down and towards each other. Coat the threads and underside of the heads of the thermostat cover/cylinder head bolts with outboard oil. Install the bolts finger-tight at this time.

22. Torque all 20 bolts on each cylinder head as follows:

a. Tighten all 20 bolts on each head snugly.

b. Torque all 20 bolts in three progressive Steps to the specification in **Table 1**, following the pattern in **Figure 137**.

c. Torque the thermostat cover bolts to the specification in **Table 1**.

d. Turn each head and thermostat cover bolt an additional 90°, following the pattern in **Figure 137**.

e. Do not retorque the head bolts after this operation.

23. Assemble and install the poppet valve as follows:

a. Install a new grommet (11, **Figure 138**) into the poppet valve cavity in the exhaust adapter plate.

b. Assemble the poppet valve components as shown in **Figure 138**. Tighten the poppet valve diaphragm screw (4, **Figure 138**) to the specification in **Table 1**.

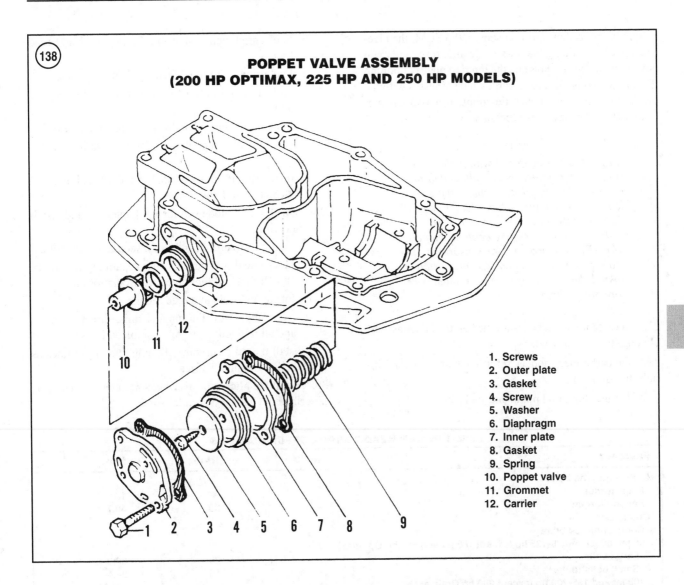

(138)

**POPPET VALVE ASSEMBLY
(200 HP OPTIMAX, 225 HP AND 250 HP MODELS)**

1. Screws
2. Outer plate
3. Gasket
4. Screw
5. Washer
6. Diaphragm
7. Inner plate
8. Gasket
9. Spring
10. Poppet valve
11. Grommet
12. Carrier

8

c. Sandwich a new gasket between the outer and inner plates, then position the assembly to the adapter plate using another new gasket.

d. Secure the assembly with two screws. Coat the screw threads with Quicksilver Perfect Seal. Evenly tighten the screws to the specification in **Table 1**.

24. Position the throttle and spark control arm to its mounting boss on the port side of the power head. Make sure the thrust washer is between the assembly and the power head, then install the center bolt and tighten it securely.

25. Install the shift and throttle cable anchor bracket and shift interrupt switch to the port lower side of the power head. Coat the three mounting bolts with Loctite 271 threadlocking adhesive (part No. 92-809819). Install the bolts and tighten them securely.

26A. On carbureted models, install the ignition and electrical components as an assembly. This includes the stator assembly, crankshaft position sensor, the ignition ECM (electronic control module), CDMs, and the electrical/ignition plate containing the starter solenoid and the trim/tilt relays. Secure all cables and harnesses with the original clamps and/or new tie-straps. See Chapter Seven.

26B. On EFI models, install the ignition and electrical components as an assembly. This includes the stator assembly, crankshaft position sensor, the ignition and fuel electronic control modules and mounting plate, CDMs, and the electrical plate containing the starter solenoid, fuse and the trim/tilt relays. Secure all cables and harnesses with the original clamps and/or new tie-straps. Refer to Chapter Six.

26C. On Optimax models, install the ignition and electrical components as an assembly. This includes the stator assembly, crankshaft position sensor, the ECM, the electrical plate containing the starter solenoid, fuses and main power and trim/tilt relays and the ignition plate containing the ignition coils. Secure all cables and harnesses with the original clamps and/or new tie-straps. Refer to Chapter Six and Chapter Seven as necessary.

NOTE
All models are equipped with a shift interrupt switch mounted on the shift and throttle cable anchor bracket. Connect the switch leads to the engine harness bullet connectors at this time. All models are also equipped with an engine coolant temperature (ECT) sensor. If the sensor was removed, refer to Chapter Six and install it. Install the sensor, or connect the leads before proceeding.

27. On Optimax models, install the belt tensioner assembly onto the power head.

28A. On carbureted models, refer to Chapter Six and install the following:

   a. Carburetors, fuel pump and fuel filter.

   b. Fuel enrichment valve, intake manifold and reed blocks.

   c. Fuel primer and fuel bleed (recirculation) lines.

28B. On EFI models, refer to Chapter Six and install the following:

   a. Induction manifold and vapor separator assembly.

   b. Mechanical fuel pump and water separating fuel filter.

   c. Intake manifold, reed blocks, and all fuel and fuel bleed (recirculation) lines.

28C. On Optimax models, refer to Chapter Six and install the following:

   a. Induction manifold and vapor separator assemblies.

   b. Mechanical fuel pump, water separating fuel filter, and all fuel and fuel bleed (recirculation) lines.

   c. Intake manifold and reed blocks.

   d. Air compressor, the air/fuel rails, direct injectors and all remaining air, fuel and bleed lines.

29. Install the oil reservoir, oil pump and all oil lines as described in Chapter Thirteen.

30. Install the alternator, flywheel and electric starter as described in Chapter Seven.

Table 1 POWER HEAD TORQUE SPECIFICATIONS

Fastener	in.-lb.	ft.-lb.	N•m
Connecting rod bolts			
Initial torque	15	–	1.7
Second torque	–	30	40.7*
Crankcase cover			
Connecting rod bolts			
65 jet, 80 jet and 75-125 hp (except 105 jet and 115 hp Optimax)			
Large bolts	–	25	33.9
Small bolts (outer)	–	18	24.4
105 jet and 135-200 hp (except 200 hp Optimax)			
Large bolts (inner)	–	38	51.5
Small bolts (outer)	–	15	20.3
200 hp Optimax, 225 hp and 250 hp			
Large bolts (inner)	–	30*	40.7*
Small bolts (outer)	–	28	37.9
Cylinder block cover bolts			
65 jet, 80 jet and 75-125 hp (except 105 jet and 115 hp Optimax)	–	18	24.4
Cylinder head bolts			
105 jet and 135-200 hp (except 200 hp Optimax)	–	30*	40.7*
200 hp Optimax, 225 hp and 250 hp	–	20*	27.1
End cap bolts			
65 jet, 80 jet and 75-125 hp (except 105 jet and 115 hp Optimax)	–	18	24.4
105 jet and 135-200 hp (except 200 hp Optimax)			
Upper cap	–	13	16.9
Lower cap	80	–	9.0
200 hp Optimax, 225 hp and 250 hp	85	–	9.6
Engine temperature switch/sensor screw	–	17	22.5
Exhaust manifold and cover			
65 jet, 80 jet and 75-125 hp (except 105 jet and 115 hp Optimax)	–	18	24.4

(continued)

Table 1 POWER HEAD TORQUE SPECIFICATIONS (continued)

Fastener	in.-lb.	ft.-lb.	N•m
Exhaust divider plate/cover			
105 jet and 135-200 hp (except 200 hp Optimax)	–	16.5	22.4
Lower cover (cowl) screws	65	–	7.3
Oil pump drive gear screws	8	–	0.9
Poppet valve cover			
115 hp Optimax and 135-200 hp (except 200 hp Optimax)	–	13	16.9
200 hp Optimax, 225 hp and 250 hp	–	20	27.1
Poppet valve diaphragm screw	25	–	2.8
Power head mounting nuts			
65 jet, 80 jet and 75-125 hp (except 105 jet and 115 hp Optimax)	–	45	61
105 jet and 135-200 hp (except 200 hp Optimax)	–	20	27.1
200 hp Optimax, 225 hp and 250 hp	–	50	67.8
Spark plug	–	20	27.1
Thermostat cover screw			
105 jet and 135-200 hp (except 200 hp Optimax)	–	16.5	22.4
200 hp Optimax, 225 hp and 250 hp	–	30	40.7

*Use the torque and turn method described in the text.

Table 2 GENERAL TORQUE SPECIFICATIONS

Screw or nut size	in.-lb.	ft.-lb.	N•m
U.S. Standard			
6-32	9	–	1.0
8-32	20	–	2.3
10-24	30	–	3.4
10-32	35	–	4.0
12-24	45	–	5.1
1/4-20	70	–	7.9
1/4-28	84	–	9.5
5/16-18	160	13	18
5/16-24	168	14	19
3/8-16	–	23	31
3/8-24	–	25	34
7/16-14	–	36	49
7/16-20	–	40	54
1/2-13	–	50	68
1/2-20	–	60	81
Metric			
M5	36	–	4
M6	70	–	8
M8	156	13	18
M10	–	26	35
M12	–	35	48
M14	–	60	81

Table 3 CYLINDER BORE SPECIFICATIONS

Measurement	Specification
Standard bore diameter	
65 jet and 75-125 hp (except 105 jet and 115 hp Optimax)	3.501 in. (88.925 mm)
135 hp	3.125 in. (79.375 mm)
105 jet and 150 hp (except 150 hp EFI, XR6 and Mag III)	3.125 in. (79.375 mm)
150 hp EFI, XR6, Mag III, 175 hp and 200 hp	3.501 in. (88.925 mm)
115-175 hp Optimax models	3.501 in. (88.925 mm)
200 hp Optimax, 225 hp and 250 hp	3.6265 in. (92.113 mm)

(continued)

8

Table 3 CYLINDER BORE SPECIFICATIONS (continued)

Measurement	Specification
Maximum cylinder diameter (wear limit)	
65 jet, 80 jet and 75-125 hp (except 105 jet and 115 hp Optimax)	3.504 in. (89.002 mm)
135 hp	3.128 in. (79.451 mm)
105 jet and 150 hp (except 150 hp EFI, XR6 and Mag III)	3.128 in. (79.451 mm)
150 hp EFI, XR6, Mag III, 175 hp and 200 hp	3.504 in. (89.002 mm)
115-175 hp Optimax models	3.504 in. (89.002 mm)
200 hp Optimax, 225 hp and 250 hp	3.6295 in. (92.189 mm)
Maximum out or round	0.003 in. (0.076 mm)
Maximum taper	0.003 in. (0.076 mm)
Maximum cylinder head warpage	
105 jet, 115 hp Optimax and 125-200 hp	
(except 200 hp Optimax)	0.004 in. (0.102 mm)
200 hp Optimax, 225 hp and 250 hp	0.005 in. (0.127 mm)

Table 4 PISTON SPECIFICATIONS

Piston diameter	
65 jet, 80 jet and 75-125 hp (except 105 jet and 115 hp Optimax)	3.495 in. (88.773 mm)
135 hp	3.113-3.117 in. (79.07-79.17 mm)
150 hp (except 150 hp EFI, XR6 and Mag III)	3.113-3.117 in. (79.07-79.17 mm)
150 hp EFI, XR6, Mag III, 175 hp and 200 hp	
(except hp Optimax models)	3.493-3.495 in. (88.722-88.773 mm)
115-175 hp Optimax models	3.492-3.493 in. (88.697-88.722 mm)
200 hp Optimax, 225 hp and 250 hp	3.6205-3.6215 in. (91.961-91.986 mm)
Piston measuring point	
65 jet, 80 jet and 75-125 hp (except 105 jet and 115 hp Optimax)	0.50 in. (12.7 mm)*
135 hp	
1998 and 1999	0.91 in. (23 mm)*
2000-on	0.50 in. (12.7 mm)*
150 hp (Except hp Optimax, 150 hp EFI, XR6 and Mag III)	
1998 and 1999	0.91 in. (23 mm)*
2000-on	0.50 in. (12.7 mm)*
150 hp EFI, XR6, Mag III, 175 hp and 200 hp	0.50 in. (12.7 mm)*
(except Optimax models)	
115-175 hp Optimax models	0.70 in. (17.8 mm)*
200 hp Optimax, 225 hp and 250 hp	1.0 in. (25.4 mm)*
Piston ring end gap	
65 jet, 80 jet and 75-125 hp	
(except 105 jet and 115 hp Optimax)	0.010-0.018 in. (0.25-0.46 mm)
105 jet and 135-200 hp (except Optimax models)	0.018-0.025 in. (0.46-0.64 mm)
115-175 hp Optimax models	0.010-0.018 in. (0.25-0.46 mm)
200 hp Optimax, 225 hp and 250 hp	0.010-0.018 in. (0.25-0.46 mm)

*Distance from the bottom of the piston skirt.

Table 5 ENGINE CHARACTERISTIC CODES

Code	Definition
C	Counter rotation gearcase
E	Electric start
EFI	Electronic fuel injection
H	Handle (tiller steering handle)
M	Manual start (rope recoil starter)
O	Oil injection
PT	Power trim and tilt
L	Long shaft (20 in.)
XL	Extra long shaft (25 in.)
XXL	Extra, extra long shaft (30 in.)

Chapter Nine

Gearcase

This section provides lower gearcase removal/installation, rebuilding and resealing procedures for all standard rotation models.

Table 1 lists specific application torque specifications. **Table 2** lists general torque specifications. Use the general torque specification for fasteners not listed in **Table 1**.

Table 3 lists gear tooth count and gearcase ratio specifications. **Table 4** and **Table 5** list gearcase service specifications.

All tables are located at the end of the chapter.

Illustrations of each lower gearcase are located in the appropriate *Disassembly* section and are helpful references for many service procedures. Since this chapter covers a large range of models, the gearcases shown in the accompanying illustrations are the most common models. While it is possible that the components shown may not be identical with those being serviced, the step-by-step procedures cover each model in this manual.

The lower gearcase can be removed from the outboard motor without removing the entire outboard from the boat.

The gearcases covered in this chapter differ in construction and require different service procedures. The chapter

is arranged in a disassembly/assembly sequence. When only a partial repair is required, follow the procedure(s) to the point where the faulty parts can be replaced, then procede to the appropriate assembly step to reassemble the unit.

GEARCASE OPERATION

A drive shaft transfers engine torque from the engine crankshaft to the lower gearcase. See **Figure 1**. A pinion (drive) gear on the drive shaft is in constant mesh with forward and reverse (driven) gears in the lower gearcase housing. These gears are spiral bevel cut to change the vertical power flow into the horizontal flow required by the propeller shaft. The spiral bevel design also provides quiet operation.

All models covered in this manual have full shifting capability. A sliding clutch, splined to the propeller shaft, engages the spinning forward or reverse gear. See **Figure 1**. This creates a direct coupling of the drive shaft to the propeller shaft. Since this is a straight mechanical engagement, shifting should only be done at idle speed. Shifting at higher speeds results in gearcase failure.

All lower gearcases incorporate a water pump to supply cooling water to the power head. All models require gearcase removal to service the water pump. Water pump removal and installation procedures are covered in this chapter.

All gearcases use precision shimmed gears. This means that the gears are precisely located in the gear housing by the use of very thin metal spacers, called shims (**Figure 2**). After assembly, verify correct shimming of the gears by measuring the *gear lash*, also called *backlash*. Gear lash is the clearance or air gap between a tooth on the pinion gear and two teeth on the forward or reverse gear.

If the gear lash is excessive the gear teeth are too far apart. This will cause excessive gear noise (whine) and a reduction in gear strength and durability since the gear teeth are not sufficiently overlapping.

If the gear lash is insufficient the gear teeth are too close together. Operation with insufficient gear lash leads to gear failure since there will not be enough clearance to maintain a film of lubricant. Heat expansion will compound the problem.

Gear Ratio

The gear ratio is the amount of gear reduction between the crankshaft and the propeller provided by the lower gearcase. Gear ratios range from as low as 2.30:1 to as high as 1.64:1. A gear ratio of 2.30:1 means that the crankshaft turns 2.3 times for every 1 turn of the propeller shaft. Higher number ratios are easier for the engine to turn. **Table 3** lists the recommended gear ratio and tooth count for all models.

If the gear ratio is suspected as being incorrect, the gear ratio can be determined by two different methods. The first method does not require removing the gearcase. Mark the flywheel and a propeller blade for counting purposes. Manually shift the gearcase into FORWARD gear. While counting, turn the flywheel in the normal direction of rotation (clockwise as viewed from the top of the flywheel) until the propeller shaft has made exactly 10 turns. Divide the number of flywheel rotations counted by ten and compare the result with the list of gear ratios in **Table 3**. Round the result to the nearest ratio listed.

The second method of determining gear ratio involves counting the actual number of teeth on the gears. This method requires at least partial disassembly of the gearcase. To determine the gear ratio, divide the driven gear forward or reverse gear tooth count by the drive gear (pinion or drive shaft gear) tooth count.

For example, on a gearcase with a 15:28 drive to driven tooth count, divide 28 (driven) by 15 (drive) = 1.87 ratio.

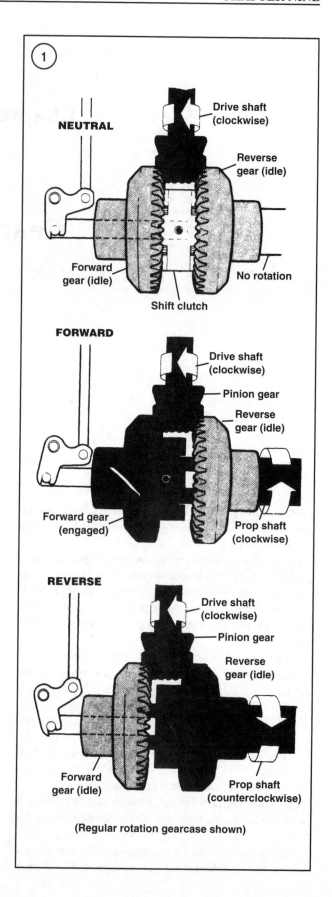
(Regular rotation gearcase shown)

The engine must be operated with the recommended gear ratio. Running the engine with an incorrect gear ratio can cause gearcase failure, poor performance, poor fuel economy and make it difficult or impossible to obtain the correct wide-open throttle engine speed, which will lead to expensive power head damage.

Some horsepower groups of engines that use the same gearcase housing will have several ratios, depending on the exact horsepower of the engine. Refer to **Table 3** for gear ratio specifications for each specific engine.

Regardless of which gear ratio is used, the engine must be operated within the recommended speed range at wide-open throttle. Change propeller pitch and diameter as necessary to adjust engine speed. Increasing pitch or diameter increases the load on the engine and reduces the wide-open throttle speed. Decreasing the pitch or diameter reduces the load on the engine and increases the wide-open throttle engine speed. Use an accurate shop tachometer for wide-open throttle engine speed verification.

High-Altitude Operation

On certain models, a high-altitude gear ratio set is available. The recommended gear ratio is adequate for altitudes up to 5000 ft. (1524 m). At higher altitudes, change the gear ratio to a higher number ratio to compensate for the loss of horsepower caused by the thinner air. Alternate gear ratios are in **Table 3**.

Also change the propeller to maintain the recommended wide-open throttle speed range.

If the boat is returned to lower altitudes, change the gear ratio back to the recommended ratio and adjust the wide-open throttle speed with propeller changes as necessary.

NOTE
If the boat is operated in a high-altitude environment temporarily, only change the pro-

peller to achieve the correct wide-open throttle speed during the stay. Change back to the original propeller when the boat is returned to its normal altitude.

Carbureted models

At high altitude, the lower density air also affects the engine's carburetor calibration, causing the engine's air/fuel mixture to become richer. Richer mixtures cause the engine to produce less horsepower and lead to fouled spark plugs, reduced fuel economy and accelerated carbon build-up in the combustion chamber.

All Mercury/Mariner carbureted engines are calibrated to operate efficiently between sea level and 2500 ft. (762 m). Mercury/Mariner recommends rejetting the carburetor for operation at altitudes of 5000 ft. (1524 m) or higher. Refer to Chapter Six for jetting information. If possible, have rejetting performed by a dealership located near the area and altitude where the engine is operated. Such dealerships are generally familiar with modifications required to achieve maximum performance at higher altitude.

SERVICE PRECAUTIONS

When working on a gearcase, keep the following precautions in mind to make the work easier, faster and more accurate.

1. Replace elastic locknuts each time they are removed.
2. Use special tools where noted. The use of makeshift tools can damage components and cause serious personal injury.
3. Use the appropriate fixtures to hold the gearcase housing whenever possible. Use a vise with protective jaws to hold smaller housings or individual components. If protective jaws are not available, insert blocks of wood or similar padding on each side of the housing or component before clamping.
4. Remove and install pressed-on parts with an appropriate mandrel, support and arbor or hydraulic press. Do not attempt to pry or hammer press-fit components on or off.
5. Refer to **Table 1** and **Table 2** for torque specifications. Proper torque is essential to ensure long life and satisfactory service from gearcase components.
6. To help reduce corrosion, especially in saltwater areas, apply Quicksilver Perfect Seal (part No. 92-34227-1) or an equivalent to all external surfaces of bearing carriers, housing mating surfaces and fasteners when no other sealant, adhesive or lubricant is recommended. Never apply sealing compound to surfaces where it can get into gears or bearings.

9

7. Discard all O-rings, seals and gaskets during disassembly. Apply Quicksilver 2-4-C Multi-Lube grease (part No. 92-825407) or an equivalent to new O-rings and seal lips to provide initial lubrication.

8. Tag all shims (**Figure 2**) with the location and thickness of each shim as it is removed from the gearcase. Shims are reusable as long as they are not damaged or corroded. Follow shimming instructions closely and carefully. Shims control gear location and/or bearing preload. Incorrectly shimming a gearcase can cause failure of the gears and/or bearings, or greatly reduce their service life.

9. Work in an area with good lighting and sufficient space for component storage. Keep an ample number of clean containers available for parts storage. Cover parts and assemblies with clean shop towels or plastic bags when they are not being worked on.

> *CAUTION*
> *Metric and American fasteners are used on Mercury/Mariner gearcases. Always match a replacement fastener to the original. Do not run a tap or thread chaser into a hole or over a bolt without first verifying the thread size and pitch. Check all threaded holes for Heli-Coil stainless steel locking thread inserts. Never run a tap or thread chaser into a Heli-Coil equipped hole. Heli-Coil inserts can be replaced, if they are damaged.*

10. Whenever a threadlocking adhesive is specified, first spray the threads of the threaded hole or nut and the screw with Locquic Primer (part No. 92-809824). Allow the primer to air dry before proceeding. Locquic primer will clean the surfaces and allow better adhesion. Locquic primer also accelerates the cure rate of threadlocking adhesives from an hour or longer, to 15-20 minutes.

CORROSION CONTROL

Sacrificial zinc or aluminum anodes are standard equipment on all models. The anodes must have good electrical continuity to ground or they will not function. Anodes are inspected visually and tested electrically. Anodes must not be painted or coated with any material.

The most common location for the anode is the anodic trim tab, but most newer models use a painted trim tab with an anode mounted on the side of the gearcase above the antiventilation plate. On all models, an anode is mounted across the bottom of the stern brackets (**Figure 3**). Refer to the exploded illustrations of each lower gearcase in the appropriate *Disassembly* section for exact anode location(s) for a specific gearcase.

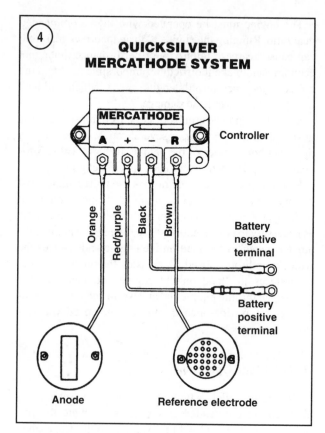

If the unit is operated exclusively in freshwater, magnesium anodes are available from Quicksilver Parts and Accessories. Magnesium anodes provide better protection in freshwater, but must *not* be used in saltwater. Magnesium anodes will overprotect the unit in saltwater and cause the paint to blister and peel from all surfaces contacting the water.

Electronic corrosion control, called the MerCathode system is also available from Quicksilver Parts and Accessories. The controller module is mounted inside the bilge, and the reference electrode and anode are mounted on the transom, below the waterline. See **Figure 4**.

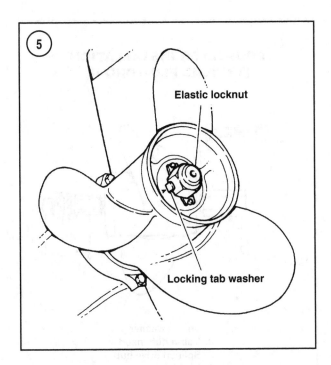

Elastic locknut

Locking tab washer

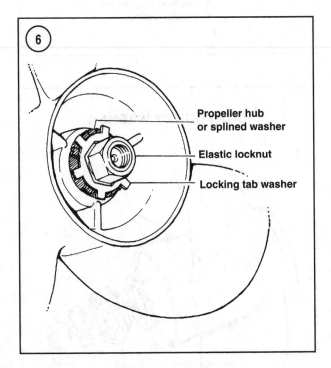

Propeller hub
or splined washer

Elastic locknut

Locking tab washer

Sacrificial Anode Visual Inspection

Check for loose mounting hardware, make sure the anodes are not painted and check the amount of deterioration present. Replace anodes if they are 1/2 their original size. Test the electrical continuity of each anode after installation as described in the next section.

Sacrificial Anode Electrical Testing

This test requires an ohmmeter.

1. Calibrate the ohmmeter on the lowest scale available.
2. Connect one ohmmeter lead to the anode being tested. Connect the other ohmmeter lead to a good ground point on the gearcase on which the anode is mounted. The meter should show a very low reading (zero or very near zero), which indicates electrical continuity.
3. If the reading is not very low, remove the anode and clean the mounting surfaces of the anode, gearcase and mounting hardware. Reinstall the anode and retest continuity.
4. Test the continuity of the gearcase to the engine and negative battery post by connecting one ohmmeter lead to the negative battery cable and the other ohmmeter lead to a good ground point on the lower gearcase. The meter should show a very low reading (zero or very near zero), which indicates electrical continuity.
5. If the reading is not very low, check the electrical continuity of the lower gearcase to the drive shaft housing, the upper drive shaft housing to the power head and the power head to the negative battery terminal. Check for loose mounting hardware, broken or missing ground straps, or excessive corrosion. Repair as necessary to establish a good electrical ground path.

GEARCASE LUBRICATION

To ensure maximum performance and durability, the gearcase requires periodic lubrication. Change the gearcase lubricant every 100 hours of operation or once each season.

The recommended lubricant for all models is Quicksilver Premium Blend Gear Lubricant. If the gearcase is subjected to severe duty, consider using Quicksilver High Performance Gear Lubricant.

Refer to Chapter Four to change the lower gearcase lubricant.

PROPELLER

The propeller pushes against a thrust washer that rides against a tapered step on the propeller shaft. The propeller is retained by an elastic locknut and a lock tab washer that engages two protrusions on the propeller hub *or* by a spline washer (built into the propeller on some models), a lock tab washer and an elastic locknut. After the elastic locknut is tightened, the locking tabs are either bent up against the nut (**Figure 5**) or driven down into the propeller hub or spline washer (**Figure 6**).

9

All propellers use a shock absorbing rubber or Delrin hub which is primarily designed to absorb the shock loads produced from shifting the unit into gear. When a hub fails, it will generally slip at higher throttle settings, but still allow the boat to return to port at reduced throttle. The defective rubber hub can be removed and a new hub pressed into the propeller using a hydraulic or arbor press (generally by a propeller repair station), or the propeller can be replaced.

Late model Quicksilver or Mercury/Mariner Propeller Company propellers use the Flo-Torq II square Delrin drive hub that can be replaced by the operator, without the use of a hydraulic or arbor press. See **Figure 7**. If the propeller was originally equipped with a square rubber hub, it may be possible to upgrade the propeller to the Flo-Torque II style hub. Consult a Mercury/Mariner dealership.

A continuity (toothed) washer, used on 135 hp and larger engines with the 4-3/4 in. (121 mm) diameter torpedo, is equipped with a rubber hub to ensure proper grounding of the propeller and mounting components to the gearcase. The continuity washer fits between the rear splined washer and the propeller hub as shown in **Figure 8**. Do not remove or discard the continuity washer on models so equipped. If the propeller shows signs of accelerated corrosion, check with a Mercury/Mariner dealership to see if the propeller should use a continuity washer. Flo-Torq II equipped propellers do not use a continuity washer.

Removal/Installation

> *WARNING*
> *To prevent accidental engine starting during propeller service, disconnect and ground all spark plug leads to the power head. Remove the ignition key and safety lanyard from models so equipped.*

Only the 135 hp and larger models, with the 4 3/4 in. (121 mm) diameter torpedo and with a rubber hub propeller, use the continuity washer and splined rear washer shown in **Figure 8**. All other models have the rear washer built into the propeller or drive hub (on Flo-Torq II models). All models use some type of locking tab washer and elastic locknut.

1. Pry the lock tab(s) up from the propeller or rear splined washer, or down from the elastic stop nut, with an appropriate tool.

2. Place a suitable block of wood between a propeller blade and the antiventilation plate to prevent propeller rotation. See **Figure 9**.

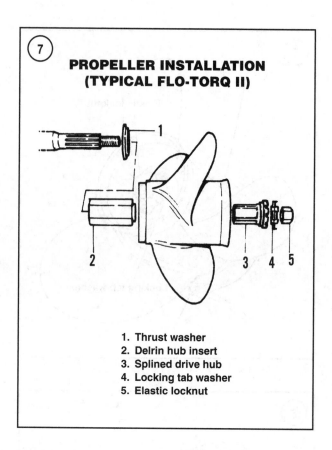

7

PROPELLER INSTALLATION (TYPICAL FLO-TORQ II)

1. Thrust washer
2. Delrin hub insert
3. Splined drive hub
4. Locking tab washer
5. Elastic locknut

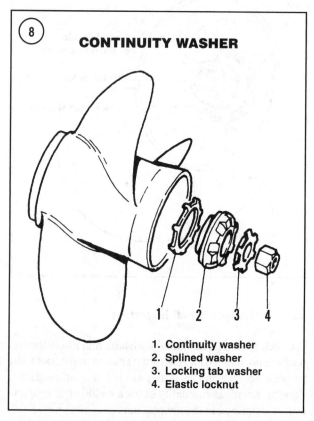

8

CONTINUITY WASHER

1. Continuity washer
2. Splined washer
3. Locking tab washer
4. Elastic locknut

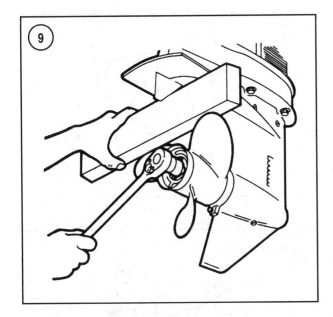

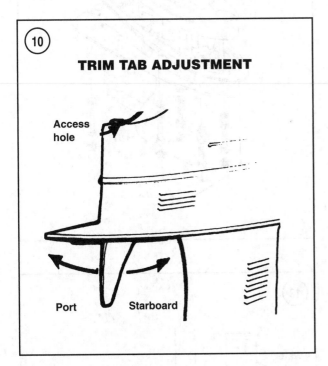

TRIM TAB ADJUSTMENT

3. Remove the propeller elastic stop nut with an appropriate socket. Replace the nut if it can be unthreaded by hand.

4. Slide the propeller and all related hardware from the propeller shaft.

5. Clean the propeller shaft thoroughly. Inspect the propeller shaft for cracks, wear or damage. Rotate the propeller shaft to check for a bent propeller shaft. Inspect the propeller thrust washer and rear washer(s) for wear or damage. Replace any damaged parts.

6. On Flo-Torq II models, inspect the Delrin hub for wear, deterioration, damage or failure.

7. Lubricate the propeller shaft liberally with 2-4-C Multi-Lube or Special Lubricant 101.

8. Slide the propeller thrust washer onto the propeller shaft.

9A. On rubber hub models, align the splines and seat the propeller against the thrust washer.

9B. On Flo-Torq II models, assemble the Delrin hub, propeller and drive hub as shown in **Figure 8**. Align the splines and seat the propeller and drive hub against the thrust washer.

10. Install the continuity washer (if equipped), splined washer (if equipped), locking tab washer and the elastic lock nut.

11. Place a suitable block of wood between a propeller blade and the antiventilation plate to prevent propeller rotation, and tighten the propeller nut to the specification in **Table 1**.

12. Secure the propeller nut in one of the following ways:

   a. Bend both lock tabs securely against the appropriate flats of the elastic stop nut. See **Figure 5**. If necessary, tighten the propeller nut slightly to align the tabs.

   b. Select three lock tabs that align with the notches in the propeller hub or rear splined washer. Drive the lock tabs into the notches with a hammer and punch. See **Figure 6**. If necessary, tighten the propeller nut slightly to align the tabs.

TRIM TAB ADJUSTMENT

Adjust the trim tab so the steering wheel will turn with equal ease in each direction at the normal cruising speed and trim angle. The trim tab can only provide neutral steering effort for the speed and trim angle for which it was set. Trimming the outboard out (up) or in (down), or changing engine speed will change the torque load on the propeller and the resultant steering effort.

To adjust the trim tab, run the boat at the speed and trim angle desired. If the boat turns more easily to starboard than port, loosen the trim tab retaining screw and move the tab trailing edge slightly to starboard. If the boat turns more easily to port, move the tab slightly to port. See **Figure 10**, typical. Tighten the trim tab retaining screw to the specification in **Table 1** after adjustment and before water testing.

On models equipped with an anodic trim tab, deterioration of the anode will reduce the effectiveness of the trim tab. Replace the anodic trim tab as necessary.

9

GEAR HOUSING

Removal/Installation (75-125 hp [Except 115 hp Optimax] Models)

Removal

1. Disconnect and ground the spark plug leads to the power head to prevent accidental starting.
2. Remove the propeller as described in this chapter.
3. Tilt the outboard to the fully *up* position and engage the tilt lock.
4. Shift the gearcase into the forward position. Rotate the propeller shaft while shifting to assist full gear engagement.
5. Mark the trim tab position with a white grease pencil or china marker. See **Figure 11**. Remove the retaining screw and trim tab.
6. Remove the four screws (two on each side) and washers, and one locknut and washer in the trim tab cavity securing the gearcase to the drive shaft housing. See **Figure 12**.
7. Pull the gearcase straight down and away from the drive shaft housing.
8. Place the gearcase in a suitable holding fixture or on a clean workbench.
9. If the water tube guide and seal remains on the water tube in the drive shaft housing, remove the water tube guide and seal from the water tube. Inspect the guide and seal, and replace it if it is damaged.

Installation

1. Make sure the water tube guide and seal are securely attached to the water pump housing. If the guide and seal are loose, glue the guide and seal to the water pump housing with Loctite 405 adhesive. See **Figure 13**.

> *CAUTION*
> *Do not apply lubricant to the top of the drive shaft in the next step. Excess lubricant between the top of the drive shaft and the engine crankshaft can create a hydraulic lock, preventing the drive shaft from fully engaging the crankshaft.*

2. Clean the drive shaft splines as necessary, then coat the splines with Quicksilver 2-4-C Multi-Lube grease (part No. 92-825407). Coat the shift shaft splines and inner diameter of the water tube seal in the water pump housing with the same grease. See **Figure 13**.
3. Shift the gearcase into forward gear. Rotate the propeller shaft to assist gear engagement. When forward gear is

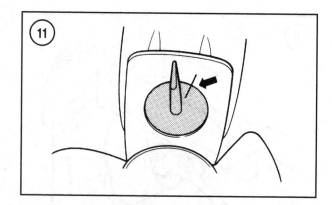

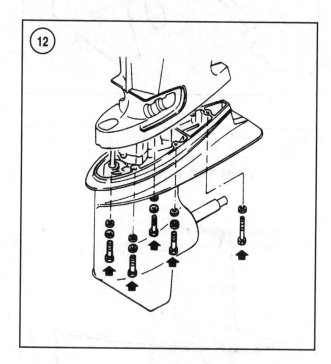

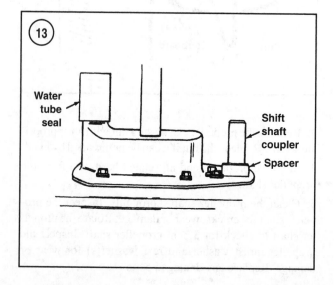

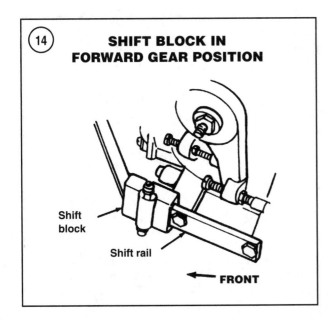

SHIFT BLOCK IN FORWARD GEAR POSITION

Shift block

Shift rail

← FRONT

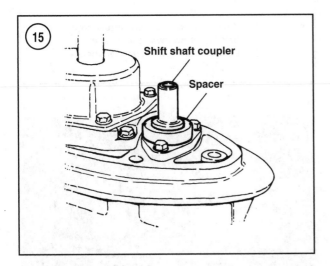

Shift shaft coupler

Spacer

with crankshaft splines and the shift shaft with the shift shaft coupler.

CAUTION
Do not rotate the flywheel counterclockwise in the next step or water pump impeller can be damaged. If necessary, rotate the shift mechanism slightly to engage the shift shaft splines with the gearcase shift rod splines.

8. Push the gearcase toward the drive shaft housing, rotating the flywheel clockwise as required to align the drive shaft and crankshaft splines. In addition, move the shift block *slightly* on the power head to align the shift shaft splines.

9. Make sure the water tube is seated in the water pump seal and the shift rod splines are engaged, then push the gearcase against the drive shaft housing.

10. Apply Loctite 271 threadlocking adhesive (part No. 92-809819) to the threads of the four mounting screws.

11. Secure the gearcase to the drive shaft housing with the four mounting screws and one locknut. Tighten the fasteners hand-tight at this time.

9

NOTE
If the gearcase does not shift as described in the next step, the shift shafts are incorrectly indexed. Remove the gearcase and repeat Steps 12-20.

12. Shift the outboard into FORWARD gear; the propeller shaft should lock when rotated counterclockwise. Shift into NEUTRAL; the propeller shaft should rotate freely in both directions. Shift into REVERSE gear; the propeller shaft should lock when rotated in the clockwise direction. If shift operation is not as specified, remove the gearcase from the drive shaft housing and re-index the upper shift shaft with the lower shift shaft coupler.

13. Once shift function is correct, evenly tighten the gearcase mounting screws to the specification in **Table 1**.

14. Install the trim tab and secure it with the screw and washer. Align the marks made during removal (**Figure 11**). Install the trim tab bolt and tighten it to the specification in **Table 1**.

15. Install the propeller as described in this chapter.

16. Release the tilt lock and return the outboard to the normal operating position.

17. Check the lubricant level or refill the gearcase with the recommended lubricant as described in Chapter Four.

18. If remote control shift cable adjustment is necessary, refer to Chapter Fourteen.

19. Reconnect the spark plug leads.

engaged and the propeller shaft is turned clockwise, the sliding clutch will ratchet.

4. Position the shift block on the power head in the full forward position. If the remote control cable is attached, make sure the block is traveling to the full forward position. See **Figure 14**.

5. Install the shift shaft spacer and coupler shaft to the gearcase shift shaft. Install the nylon spacer over the shift shaft. Then install the shift shaft coupler as shown in **Figure 15**.

6. Run a 1/4 in. (6.4 mm) bead of RTV sealant (part No. 92-809826) along the water dam at the rear of the water pump base.

7. Position the gearcase under the drive shaft housing. Align the water tube in the water pump, the drive shaft

Removal/Installation (115 hp Optimax and 135-200 hp [Except 200 hp Optimax] Models)

All 135-200 hp models use *not ratcheting* gearcases. This means that the propeller cannot overrun the sliding clutch during deceleration. The propeller will lock in either forward or reverse gear. In neutral, the propeller spins freely in either direction.

Removal

1. Disconnect and ground the spark plug leads. Remove the spark plugs from the engine.

2. Shift the outboard into NEUTRAL. The propeller should rotate freely in both directions.

3. Tilt the outboard to the fully UP position and engage the tilt lock.

4. Remove the propeller as described in this chapter.

5. Mark the trim tab position with a white grease pencil or china marker. See **Figure 11**.

6. Pry the plastic access plug from the rear of the drive shaft housing. Insert a suitable socket into the hole and remove the screw securing the trim tab or anodic plate. Remove the trim tab or anodic plate.

7. Remove the locknut and washer (or screw) (2, **Figure 16**) located inside the trim tab cavity.

8. Remove the two locknuts (or screws) (3, **Figure 16**) from the bottom of the antiventilation plate at the trailing edge of the gearcase strut.

9. Remove the upper lock nut and washer securing the gearcase to the leading edge of the drive shaft housing.

> *NOTE*
> *On badly corroded units, the gearcase might be frozen to the drive shaft housing. Apply penetrating oil to the mounting studs. Mild heat, such as a propane torch, and a soft mallet can be used to free the gearcase. In extreme cases, it may be necessary to pry the gearcase from the drive shaft housing. Avoid damaging the gearcase and drive shaft housing mating surfaces.*

10. Loosen the locknut on each side of the gearcase (**Figure 17**) one turn at a time, then move back to the other side. Remove one nut and washer, but leave the other nut threaded on 2-3 turns to prevent the gearcase from falling free.

11. If equipped with a gearcase speedometer pickup, disconnect the speedometer line from the connector fitting at the entrance to the swivel tube near the front of the lower motor mounts.

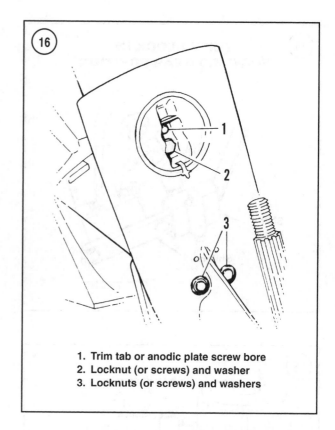

1. Trim tab or anodic plate screw bore
2. Locknut (or screws) and washer
3. Locknuts (or screws) and washers

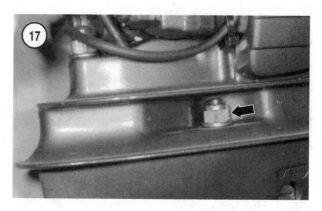

12. Holding the gearcase firmly, remove the last nut and washer, then pull the gearcase straight down and away from the drive shaft housing.

13. Mount the gearcase into a suitable holding fixture or place the gearcase on a clean workbench.

14. If the water tube guide and water tube seal are on the water tube in the drive shaft housing, remove the water tube guide and water tube seal from the water tube. If the water tube guide and water tube seal are in the water pump, remove the water tube guide and the water tube seal from the water pump housing. Discard the water tube seal.

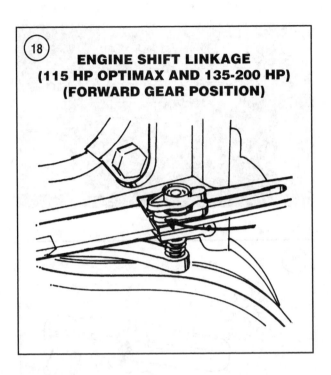

**ENGINE SHIFT LINKAGE
(115 HP OPTIMAX AND 135-200 HP)
(FORWARD GEAR POSITION)**

Installation

1. Install a new water tube seal into the water pump housing. Then install the water tube guide to the water pump housing.

> *CAUTION*
> *Do not apply lubricant to the top of the drive shaft and shift shaft in the next step. Excess lubricant between the top of the drive shaft and the engine crankshaft can create a hydraulic lock, preventing the drive shaft from fully engaging the crankshaft.*

2. Clean the drive shaft splines as necessary, then coat the splines with Quicksilver 2-4-C Multi-Lube grease (part No. 92-825407). Coat the shift shaft splines and inner diameter of the water tube seal in the water pump housing with the same grease.

3. Shift the gearcase into FORWARD gear by rotating the shift shaft fully clockwise while rotating the propeller shaft counterclockwise.

4. Run a thin bead of RTV Sealant (part No. 92-809826) across the top of the exhaust divider plate and set the trim tab retaining screw into the furthest aft hole on the gearcase deck.

5. Position the engine shift linkage in full FORWARD gear. The engine shift linkage guide block anchor pin should be positioned as shown in **Figure 18**.

6. Position the gearcase under the drive shaft housing. Align the water tube in the water pump, the drive shaft

with crankshaft splines and the shift shaft with the shift shaft coupler. Insert the speedometer hose through the shift shaft hole in the drive shaft housing and connect the hose to its connector.

> *CAUTION*
> *Do not rotate the flywheel counterclockwise in the next step or the water pump impeller may be damages. It may be necessary to rotate the shift mechanism slightly to engage the shift block splines with the shift rod splines.*

7. Push the gearcase toward the drive shaft housing, rotating the flywheel clockwise as required to align the drive shaft and crankshaft splines. In addition, move the shift linkage slightly on the power head to align the shift shaft splines.

8. Make sure the water tube is seated in the water pump seal and the shift rod splines are engaged, then push the gearcase against the drive shaft housing.

9. Install the locknut and washer (or screw) into the trim tab cavity (2, **Figure 16**). Tighten the fastener hand-tight to keep the gearcase from falling from the drive shaft housing.

10. Install the locknuts and flat washers on the sides (**Figure 17**), and the locknut and washer on the front of the gearcase. Tighten the locknuts hand-tight at this time.

11. Install the two locknuts and washers (3, **Figure 16**) under the antiventilation plate. Tighten the fasteners hand-tight at this time.

12. Verify correct shift rod engagement by first moving the engine shift linkage into full FORWARD gear. Manually rotate the flywheel clockwise as viewed from top while observing the propeller shaft; the shaft should turn clockwise. Then move the engine shift linkage to the NEUTRAL position. The propeller shaft should rotate freely in both directions. Finally, move the engine shift linkage to the full REVERSE position. Manually rotate the flywheel clockwise as viewed from the top while observing the propeller shaft; the shaft should turn counterclockwise. If shift operation is not as specified, remove the gearcase and re-index the shift shaft splines.

13. Once shift shaft indexing is correct, tighten all gearcase mounting hardware to the specification in **Table 1**.

14. Install the trim tab or anodic plate and secure it with the previously installed screw. Align the marks made during removal (**Figure 11**) and tighten the trim tab screw to the specification in **Table 1**.

15. Install the propeller as described in this chapter.

16. Release the tilt lock and return the outboard to the normal operating position.

9

17. Check the lubricant level or refill the gearcase with the recommended lubricant as described in Chapter Four.

18. If remote control shift cable adjustment is necessary, refer to Chapter Fourteen.

19. Install the spark plugs and connect the spark plug leads.

Removal/Installation (200 hp Optimax and 225-250 hp Models)

These models use *not ratcheting* gearcases. This means that the propeller cannot overrun the sliding clutch during deceleration. The propeller will lock in either forward or reverse gear. In neutral, the propeller spins freely in either direction.

Removal

1. Disconnect and ground the spark plug leads. Remove the spark plugs from the engine.

2. Shift the outboard into NEUTRAL. The propeller should rotate freely in both directions.

3. Tilt the outboard to the fully UP position and engage the tilt lock.

4. Remove the propeller as described in this chapter.

5. Mark the trim tab or anodic plate position with a white grease pencil or china marker. See **Figure 11**.

6. Pry the plastic access plug from the rear of the drive shaft housing. Insert a suitable socket into the hole and loosen the screw securing the trim tab. Remove the trim tab.

7. Remove the locknut and washer (or screw) (2, **Figure 16**) located inside the trim tab cavity.

8. Loosen the two locknuts (**Figure 19**) on each side of the gearcase. Loosen each nut one turn at a time, then move onto the next nut. Remove three of the nuts and washers, but leave one nut threaded on 2-3 turns, to prevent the gearcase from falling free.

9. If equipped with a gearcase speedometer pickup, disconnect the speedometer line from the connector fitting at the entrance to the drive shaft housing near the front of the lower motor mounts.

> *NOTE*
> *Some gearcases use a two-piece drive shaft. A splined coupler connects the upper and lower drive shafts just above the water pump housing.*

10. Holding the gearcase firmly, remove the last nut and washer, then pull the gearcase straight down and away from the drive shaft housing. If equipped with a two-piece drive shaft, be prepared to catch the upper drive shaft and coupler if they separate from the lower drive shaft.

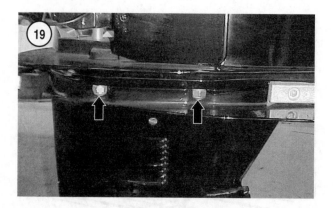

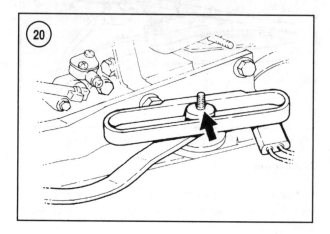

11. Mount the gearcase into a suitable holding fixture or place the gearcase on a clean workbench. Remove the trim tab or anodic plate screw.

12. Remove the water tube guide and seal assembly from the water pump housing. Remove and discard the two O-rings from the inner diameter of the guide.

Installation

1. Install two new water tube O-rings into the water tube guide. Lubricate the O-rings with Quicksilver 2-4-C Multi-Lube grease (part No. 92-825407). Then install the water tube guide to the water pump housing.

> *CAUTION*
> *Never apply lubricant to the top of the drive shaft. Excess lubricant between the drive shaft and the crankshaft can create a hydraulic lock, preventing the drive shaft from fully engaging the crankshaft.*

2. Clean the drive shaft splines as necessary, then coat the splines with Quicksilver 2-4-C Multi-Lube grease. Coat the shift shaft splines with the same grease.

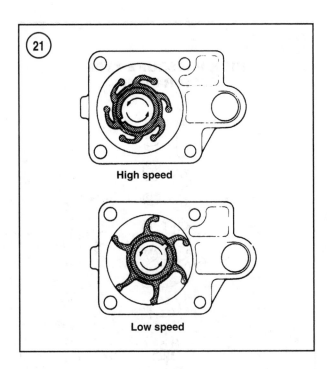

High speed

Low speed

3. On two-piece drive shaft models, install the drive shaft coupler and upper drive shaft to the lower drive shaft. Lubricate the splined areas of the shafts.

4. Shift the gearcase into NEUTRAL gear by rotating the shift shaft until the propeller spins freely in both directions.

5. If the water dam behind the water pump was removed, run a thin bead of RTV Sealant (part No. 92-809826) across both sides of the dam and install it into the gear housing.

6. Install the trim tab or anodic plate retaining screw into the furthest aft hole on the gearcase deck.

7. Position the engine shift linkage into the NEUTRAL gear position. The shift linkage guide block anchor pin should be positioned in the middle of its total travel as shown in **Figure 20**.

8. Position the gearcase under the drive shaft housing. Align the water tube in the water pump, the drive shaft with the crankshaft splines and the shift shaft with the shift shaft coupler. Insert the speedometer hose through its opening in the drive shaft housing and connect the hose to its connector.

CAUTION
Do not rotate the flywheel counterclockwise in the next step or the water pump impeller can be damaged. It might be necessary to rotate the shift mechanism slightly to engage the shift block splines with the shift rod splines.

9. Push the gearcase toward the drive shaft housing, rotating the flywheel clockwise as required to align the drive shaft and crankshaft splines. In addition, move the shift linkage slightly on the power head to align the shift shaft splines.

10. Make sure the water tube is seated in the water pump guide and the shift rod splines are engaged, then push the gearcase against the drive shaft housing.

11. Install the mounting locknut and washer (or screw) (2, **Figure 16**) located in the trim tab cavity. Tighten the fastener hand-tight to keep the gearcase from falling from the drive shaft housing.

12. Install the locknuts and flat washers (**Figure 19**). Tighten the locknuts hand-tight at this time.

13. Verify correct shift rod engagement by first moving the shift linkage into full FORWARD gear. Manually rotate the flywheel clockwise as viewed from the top while observing the propeller shaft; the shaft should turn clockwise. Then move the engine shift linkage to the NEUTRAL position. The propeller shaft should rotate freely in both directions. Finally move the engine shift linkage to the full REVERSE position. Manually rotate the flywheel clockwise as viewed from the top while observing the propeller shaft; the shaft should turn counterclockwise. If shift operation is not as specified, remove the gearcase and re-index the shift shaft.

14. Once shift shaft indexing is correct, tighten all gearcase mounting hardware to the specification in **Table 1**.

15. Install the trim tab or anodic plate and secure it with the previously installed screw. Align the marks made during removal (**Figure 11**). Tighten the trim tab screw to the specification in **Table 1**. Install the plastic access plug into the opening at the rear of the gearcase.

16. Install the propeller as described in this chapter.

17. Release the tilt lock and return the outboard to the normal operating position.

18. Check the lubricant level or refill the gearcase with the recommended lubricant as described in Chapter Four.

19. If remote control shift cable adjustment is necessary, refer to Chapter Fourteen.

20. Install the spark plugs and connect the spark plug leads.

WATER PUMP

All late model Mercury and Mariner outboard motors use an offset-center pump housing that causes the vanes of the impeller to flex during rotation. At low speed the pump operates as a positive displacement pump. At high speed, water resistance causes the impeller vanes to flex inward, causing the pump to operate as a centrifugal pump. See **Figure 21**.

9

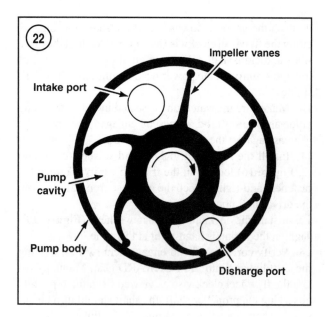

Impeller vanes

Intake port

Pump cavity

Pump body

Discharge port

The pump draws water into the intake port(s) as the vanes expand (flex outward) and pumps water out of the discharge port(s) as the vanes compress (flex inward) as shown in **Figure 22**.

Two basic water pump designs are used: the high-pressure pump (**Figure 23**, typical) and the high-volume pump (**Figure 24**, typical). The high-pressure pump develops more pressure than volume, while the high-volume pump delivers more volume than pressure.

A high-pressure pump is used on 105 jet, 115 hp Optimax and 135-200 hp (except 200 hp Optimax) models. All other models covered in this manual use a high-volume pump.

On all models, the pump is located on the gearcase upper deck and is driven by a key in the drive shaft. The impeller only operates in a clockwise rotation with the drive shaft or propeller shaft and is held in a flexed (compressed) position at all times. Over time, this causes the impeller to take a *set* in one direction. Turning an impeller over and attempting to turn it against its natural *set* will cause premature impeller failure and power head damage from overheating. Replace the impeller *every* time the water pump is disassembled. Only reuse the impeller if there is no other option. If the impeller must be reused, reinstall the impeller in its original position.

Replace the impeller and related seals and gaskets at the following intervals:

1. Replace the high-pressure pump once a year or every 100 hours of operation.

2. Replace the high-volume pump every three years or 300 hours of operation.

Individual operating conditions may dictate that the pump require service more often. Also service the water

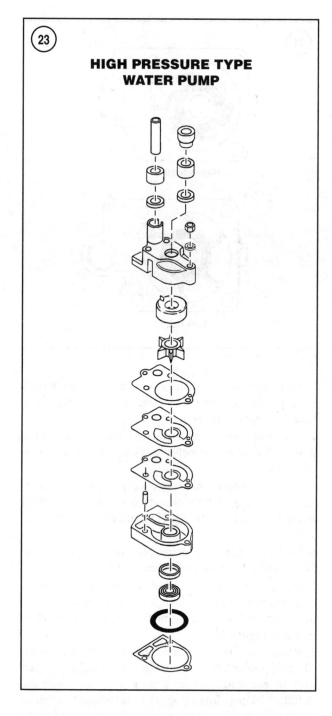

HIGH PRESSURE TYPE WATER PUMP

pump any time the lower gearcase or jet pump unit is removed for any type of service.

Removal and Disassembly

Replace all seals and gaskets whenever the water pump is disassembled. Since the drive shaft seals operate at crankshaft speed and are under motion when the engine is

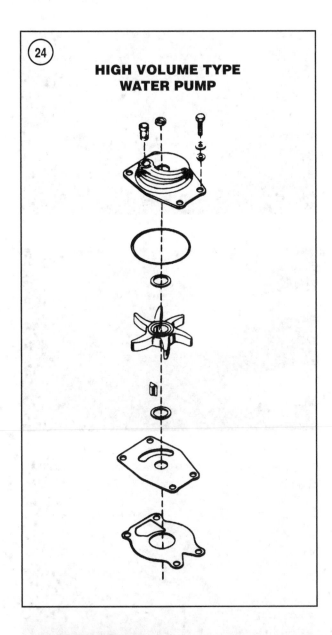

**HIGH VOLUME TYPE
WATER PUMP**

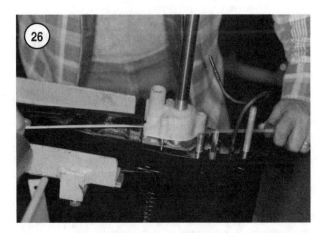

running, remove the water pump base (on models so equipped) and replace the drive shaft seals anytime the water pump is disassembled. Also replace the water pump impeller anytime the pump is disassembled.

105 jet and 135-200 hp (except 200 hp Optimax) models

1. Remove the gearcase as described previously in this chapter. Secure the gearcase in a suitable holding fixture or a vise with protective jaws. If protective jaws are not available, position the unit upright in a vise with the skeg between wooden blocks.

2. Remove the rubber centrifugal slinger (A, **Figure 25**) from the drive shaft.

3. Remove the water tube guide (B, **Figure 25**) and seal from the top of the pump housing. Discard the seal.

4. Remove the three elastic locknuts and washers and the single screw (C, **Figure 25**) at the rear of the housing holding the water pump housing to the gearcase.

5. Carefully insert screwdrivers at the fore and aft ends of the pump housing, and pry the housing upward. See **Figure 26**. Lift the housing up and off the drive shaft.

> *NOTE*
> *In extreme cases, it may be necessary to split
> the impeller hub with a hammer and chisel
> to remove it from the drive shaft in Step 6.*

6. Remove the impeller and drive key from the drive shaft (**Figure 27**). If necessary, drive the impeller upward on the shaft with a punch and hammer. Do not damage the drive shaft in the process.

7. Remove the impeller plate (**Figure 28**), and the top and bottom gaskets. Discard the gaskets.

8. Insert screwdrivers at the fore and aft ends of the pump base. Pad the pry areas under each screwdriver with clean

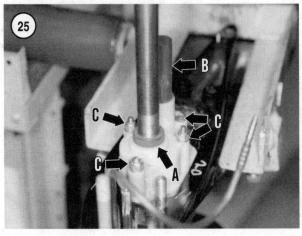

9

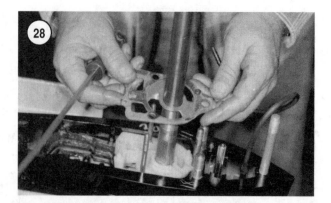

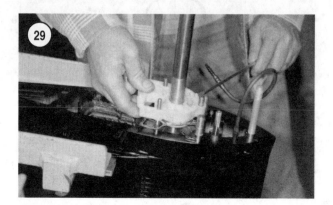

shop towels and pry the pump base loose. Remove the base from the shaft (**Figure 29**).

9. Remove and discard the pump base-to-gearcase O-ring (A, **Figure 30**).

10. Pry, or drive, the drive shaft seals (B, **Figure 30**) from the pump base from, or towards, the gearcase side of the base.

11. If the housing liner must be replaced and the housing is not melted or damaged, drive the liner from the pump cover using a punch and hammer inserted through the drive shaft bore. If the insert will not come out, carefully drill a 3/16 in. (4.8 mm) hole through the top, but not through the insert, on each side of the cover as shown in **Figure 31** and drive the insert out using a hammer and punch.

12. Inspect the water pump components as described under *Water Pump Cleaning and Inspection* in this chapter.

65 jet and 75-125 hp (except 105 jet and 115 hp Optimax) models

Refer to **Figure 32** for this procedure.

1. Remove the gearcase as described in this chapter. Secure the gearcase in a suitable holding fixture or a vise with protective jaws. If protective jaws are not available, position the unit upright in a vise with the skeg between wooden blocks.

2. Remove the water tube guide and seal (**Figure 33**) from the pump housing.

3. Remove the four pump housing screws (3, **Figure 32**). Lift the pump housing up and off the drive shaft (**Figure 34**). If necessary, carefully pry at each end with a suitable tool.

4. Remove the impeller from the drive shaft (**Figure 35**).

5. Remove the impeller drive key (5, **Figure 32**) from the drive shaft flat.

6. Remove the impeller plate (**Figure 36**) and the upper and lower gaskets (**Figure 37**). Discard the gaskets.

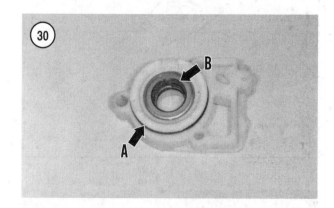

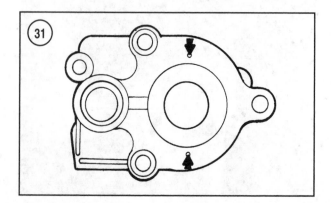

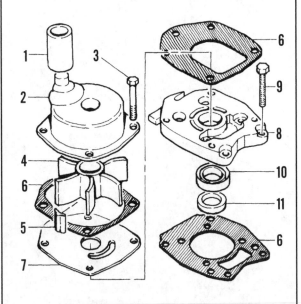

32

**WATER PUMP COMPONENTS
(65 JET AND 75-125 HP [EXCEPT
105 JET AND 115 HP OPTIMAX])**

1. Water tube guide and seal
2. Pump housing
3. Screw
4. Impeller
5. Impeller key
6. Gaskets
7. Impeller plate
8. Water pump base
9. Screw
10. Large drive shaft seal
11. Small drive shaft seal

9

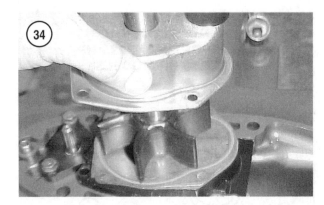

34

35

36

33

37

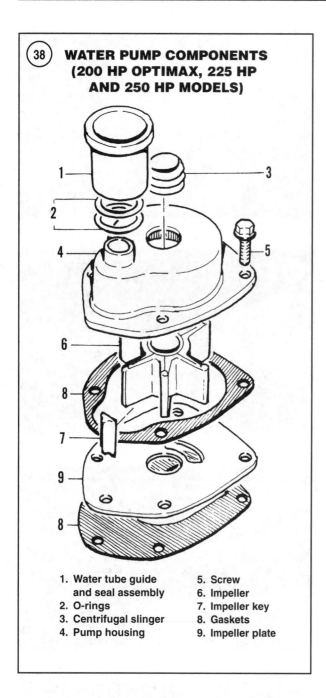

**38 WATER PUMP COMPONENTS
(200 HP OPTIMAX, 225 HP
AND 250 HP MODELS)**

1. Water tube guide
   and seal assembly
2. O-rings
3. Centrifugal slinger
4. Pump housing
5. Screw
6. Impeller
7. Impeller key
8. Gaskets
9. Impeller plate

7. Remove the six screws (9, **Figure 32**) securing the pump base to the gearcase. Dislodge the base from the gearcase by carefully prying at each end using two screwdrivers. Lift the base up and off the drive shaft. Remove and discard the base-to-gearcase gasket. Carefully pry the drive shaft seals (10 and 11, **Figure 32**) from the pump base.

8. Inspect the water pump components as described in *Water Pump Cleaning and Inspection* located later in this chapter.

200 hp Optimax, 225 hp and 250 hp models

Refer to **Figure 38** for this procedure.

1. Remove the gearcase as described in this chapter. Secure the gearcase in a suitable holding fixture or a vise with protective jaws. If protective jaws are not available, position the unit upright in a vise with the skeg between wooden blocks.

2. Remove the water tube guide (**Figure 39**) and seal assembly (**Figure 40**) from the pump housing. Remove and

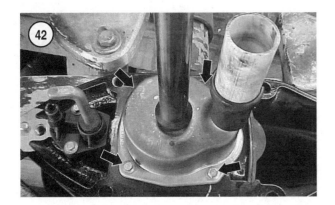

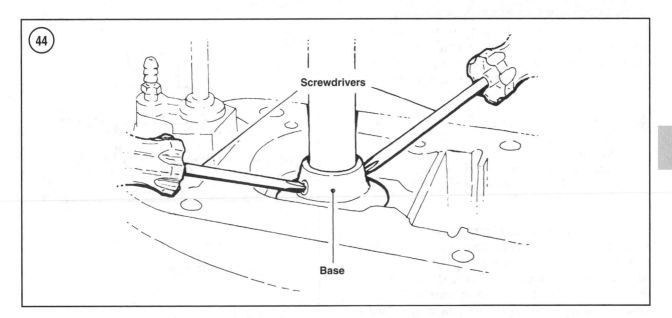

discard the two O-rings (2, **Figure 38**) in the seal assembly.

3. Remove the centrifugal slinger seal from the drive shaft. Slide the seal up and off the drive shaft (**Figure 41**). Discard the seal.

4. Remove the four pump housing screws (**Figure 42**). Lift the pump housing up and off the drive shaft. If necessary, carefully pry at each end with a suitable tool.

5. Remove the impeller (6, **Figure 38**) from the drive shaft.

6. Remove the impeller key (7, **Figure 38**) from the drive shaft flat.

7. Remove the impeller plate and the upper and lower gaskets (**Figure 43**). Discard the gaskets.

8. Insert two appropriately sized screwdrivers into the holes in the drive shaft seal carrier. Pry the seal carrier from the gearcase. See **Figure 44**. Remove the water dam seal from the gearcase (**Figure 45**).

9. Remove and discard the seal carrier O-ring. Then pry or drive out the drive shaft seal(s) from the carrier. Do not damage or distort the carrier during the removal process. Discard the seal(s).

10. Inspect the water pump components as described in *Water Pump Cleaning and Inspection* in this chapter.

Water Pump Cleaning and Inspection

1. Clean all metal parts in solvent and dry them with compressed air.

2. Clean all gasket material from all mating surfaces. Do not gouge or distort gasket sealing surfaces and do not allow gasket material to fall into the gearcase housing.

3. Check plastic pump housings, plastic pump bases and plastic drive shaft seal carriers for cracks or distortion from overheating or improper service procedures.

4. Check metal pump housings (A, **Figure 46**), pump bases and drive shaft seal carriers for excessive wear corrosion, distortion, and mechanical or other damage.

5. Check the lower plate and pump liner or housing for grooves, rough surfaces or excessive wear. Replace the pump liner insert or housing and lower plate as necessary. Grooves from the impeller sealing rings are not a concern.

> *NOTE*
> *The water pump impeller must be able to float on the drive shaft. Clean the impeller area of the drive shaft thoroughly using emery cloth. Make sure the impeller slides onto the drive shaft easily.*

6. Replace the impeller (B, **Figure 46**) anytime it is removed. If the impeller must be reused, check the bonding of the rubber to the impeller hub for separation. Check the side seal surfaces and blade ends for cracks, tears, excessive wear, or a glazed or melted appearance. If any of these defects are noted, do *not* reuse the impeller under any circumstances.

7. On metal pump housings, measure the thickness of the pump cover at the discharge slots. Replace the cover if the metal thickness is 0.060 in. (1.52 mm) or less.

8. Inspect the pump housing and impeller plate for grooves or excessive wear. Replace the housing and/or the impeller plate if grooves (except the impeller seal ring grooves) exceed 0.030 in. (0.76 mm) deep.

Assembly and Installation

105 jet, 115 hp Optimax and 135-200 hp (except 200 hp Optimax) models

1. If the pump housing liner was removed, lightly coat the liner area in the housing with Quicksilver Perfect Seal (part No. 92-34227-1). Align the insert tab with its respective recess in the housing and press the liner into the housing until it is seated.

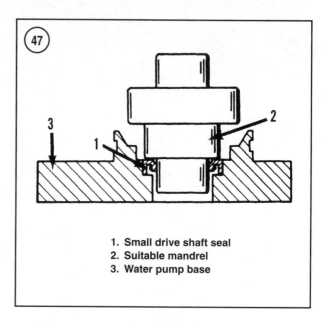

1. Small drive shaft seal
2. Suitable mandrel
3. Water pump base

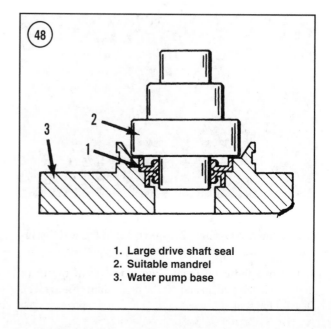

1. Large drive shaft seal
2. Suitable mandrel
3. Water pump base

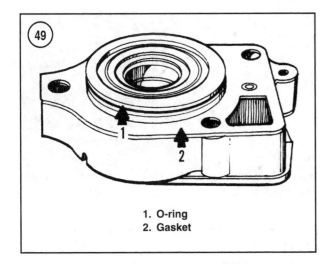

1. O-ring
2. Gasket

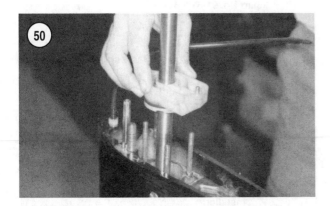

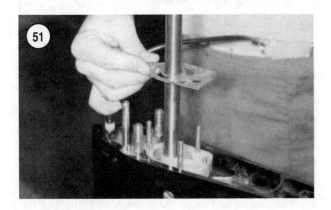

9

NOTE
If holes had to be drilled into the pump cover for insert removal, fill the holes with RTV sealant (part No. 92-809826). Allow the sealant to fully cure before operating the boat.

2. Position the pump base on a press. Apply Loctite 271 Threadlocking adhesive (part No. 92-809819) to the out-

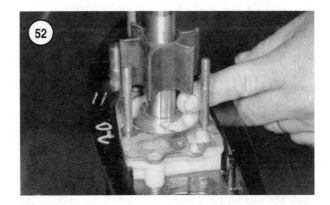

side diameter of two new drive shaft seals. Press the smaller diameter seal with the lip facing the impeller into the pump base until it is seated as shown in **Figure 47**. Then press the larger diameter seal with the lip facing the gearcase into the pump base until it is also seated as shown in **Figure 48**.

3. Lubricate a new pump base O-ring and the drive shaft seal lips with Quicksilver 2-4-C Multi-Lube grease (part No. 92-825407).

4. Install the lower gasket (2, **Figure 49**) onto the water pump base. Install the O-ring into its groove in the pump base (1, **Figure 49**).

NOTE
Be very careful not to damage the drive shaft seals when installing the pump base over the drive shaft and drive shaft spline. Remove any sharp burrs or nicks from the drive shaft and splines with emery cloth. If necessary, wrap tape over the splines.

5. Install the pump base over the drive shaft and into position in the housing. See **Figure 50**.

6. Install new lower and upper gaskets on the impeller plate. Install the plate and gaskets onto the pump base. See **Figure 51**. Make sure the dowel pins on the base properly engage the face plate and gaskets.

7. Lubricate the impeller key with Quicksilver 2-4-C Multi-Lube grease. Position the impeller key on the drive shaft flat.

8. Lubricate the impeller with Quicksilver 2-4-C Multi-Lube grease. Slide the impeller over the drive shaft and engage the impeller key (**Figure 52**).

9. Install a new water tube seal into the pump housing with the plastic side of the seal facing downward. Then install the water tube guide into the pump housing.

10. Slide the pump housing assembly over the drive shaft and into position over the impeller and onto the mounting studs. Turn the drive shaft clockwise and press the hous-

ing down to feed the impeller into the housing. Seat the pump housing against the plate.

> *CAUTION*
> *Do not over tighten the fasteners in the next step or the pump housing may crack during boat operation.*

11. Install the three elastic locknuts and washers and the one rear screw. Evenly tighten the nuts and screw to the specifications in **Table 1**.

12. Install the rubber centrifugal slinger over the drive shaft and against the pump cover. Install the gearcase to the outboard motor as described previously in this chapter.

75-125 hp (except 105 jet and 115 hp Optimax) models

Refer to **Figure 32** for this procedure.

1. Apply Loctite 271 Threadlocking adhesive (part No. 92-809819) to the outer diameter of two new drive shaft seals. Set the water pump base with the stepped side facing up into a press. Install the Teflon coated seal (flat brown/black color) with the spring facing the power head onto the longer stepped side of the seal installer (part No. 91-13949 or an equivalent). Press the seal into the water pump base until the tool bottoms. Install the non-Teflon coated seal (glossy black color) with the spring facing the gearcase onto the short stepped side of the same installer. Press the seal into the water pump base until the tool bottoms. Coat the seal lips with 2-4-C Multi-Lube grease (part No. 92-825407).

2. Place a new gasket (6, **Figure 32**) onto the gearcase. Slide the water pump base over the drive shaft and into position on the gasket (**Figure 53**). Be careful not to cut or damage the seals on the drive shaft splines. Make sure the water pump base is piloted into the gearcase bore and does not pinch the gasket in the gearcase bore.

3. Coat the six water pump base screws (9, **Figure 32**) with Loctite 271 threadlocking adhesive. Install the screws and washers. Evenly tighten the screws to the specification in **Table 1**.

4. Install a new gasket on top of the water pump base (**Figure 37**). Slide the impeller plate over the drive shaft and into position on the gasket (**Figure 36**). Then install a new housing gasket on the plate.

5. Grease the impeller key with 2-4-C Multi-Lube grease and position it on the drive shaft flat. Slide the impeller onto the drive shaft (**Figure 35**) and engage the key.

6. Slide the pump housing over the drive shaft and into position over the impeller (**Figure 34**). Turn the drive

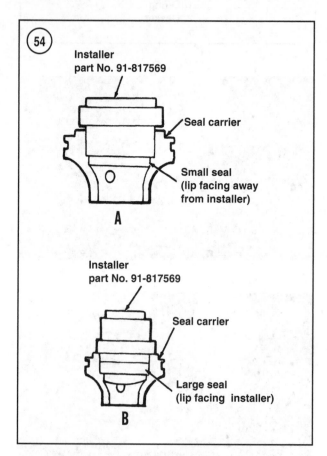

shaft clockwise and press the housing down to feed the impeller into the body. Seat the pump housing against the plate.

7. Coat the threads of the four housing screws with Loctite 271 threadlocking adhesive. Install and evenly tighten the screws to the specification in **Table 1**.

8. If the water tube guide and seal were removed, glue the guide and seal to the water pump housing (**Figure 33**) with Loctite 405 adhesive. Then lubricate the water tube seal with Quicksilver 2-4-C Multi-Lube grease.

9. Install the gearcase to the outboard motor as described previously in this chapter.

200 hp Optimax, 225 hp and 250 hp models

Refer to **Figure 38** for this procedure.

1. Apply Loctite 271 threadlocking adhesive (part No. 92-809819) to the outer diameter of two new drive shaft seals. Then set the drive shaft seal carrier into a press with the tapered end facing down.

   a. Install the upper seal with the lip facing the power head onto the longer stepped side of seal installer part No. 91-817569 or an equivalent. Press the seal into the carrier until the tool bottoms as shown in A, **Figure 54**.

   b. Install the lower seal with the lip facing the gearcase onto the short stepped side of the same installer. Press the seal into the carrier until the tool bottoms as shown in B, **Figure 54**.

2. Lubricate a new carrier O-ring with Quicksilver 2-4-C Multi-Lube grease (part No. 92-825407). Install the O-ring into the carrier groove.

3. Slide the drive shaft seal carrier over the drive shaft and into position in the gearcase bore. Be careful not to cut or damage the seal(s) on the drive shaft splines. Seat the carrier into the gearcase bore.

4. Insert the water dam seal into the slots in the gearcase (**Figure 45**).

5. Install a new gasket on top of the gearcase. Slide the impeller plate over the drive shaft and into position on the gasket. Then install a new housing gasket on the plate. See **Figure 43**. Make sure the gasket and plate holes are aligned with the gearcase holes.

6. Grease the impeller key with 2-4-C Multi-Lube grease and position it on the drive shaft flat. Slide the impeller onto the drive shaft and engage the key. See **Figure 35**.

7. Install two water pump alignment pins into the water pump housing screw holes in the gearcase. Use two opposing screw holes.

8. Slide the pump housing over the drive shaft and into position over the impeller (**Figure 34**). Turn the drive shaft clockwise and press the housing down to feed the impeller into the body. Seat the pump housing over the alignment pins and against the plate.

9. Coat the threads of the four housing screws with Loctite 271 threadlocking adhesive.

10. Install two screws finger-tight, then remove the alignment pins and install the last two screws finger-tight. Finally, tighten all four housing screws (**Figure 42**) evenly to the specification in **Table 1** .

11. Lubricate two new O-rings (2, **Figure 38**) with Quicksilver 2-4-C Multi-Lube grease. Install the O-rings into the seal assembly. Then install the seal (**Figure 40**) and guide (**Figure 39**) onto the pump housing.

12. Place the new centrifugal slinger seal over the drive shaft (**Figure 41**). Use the seal installation tool included with the seal to position the seal on the drive shaft (**Figure 55**). Remove the installation tool from the drive shaft.

GEARCASE DISASSEMBLY/ASSEMBLY

This section covers complete disassembly and reassembly procedures of the lower gearcase for each model covered in this manual. Once the gearcase is disassembled, refer to *Gearcase Cleaning and Inspection* before assembly.

On all models covered in this manual, shim the gears and verify the gear lash between forward gear and the pinion gear before continuing with assembly. On V-6 models (105 jet, 115 hp Optimax and 135-250 hp models), also verify the gear lash between reverse gear and the pinion gear. The assembly procedure refers to *Gearcase Shimming* at the proper time.

Disassembly (75-125 hp [Except 115 hp Optimax] Models)

The propeller shaft bearing carrier and propeller shaft can be removed without removing the gearcase from the drive shaft housing, if so desired. Refer to **Figure 56** for this procedure.

NOTE
If the forward gear or drive shaft roller bearings must be replaced, replace the bearing rollers and races as assemblies. Do not remove pressed-in bearings and/or races unless replacement is necessary.

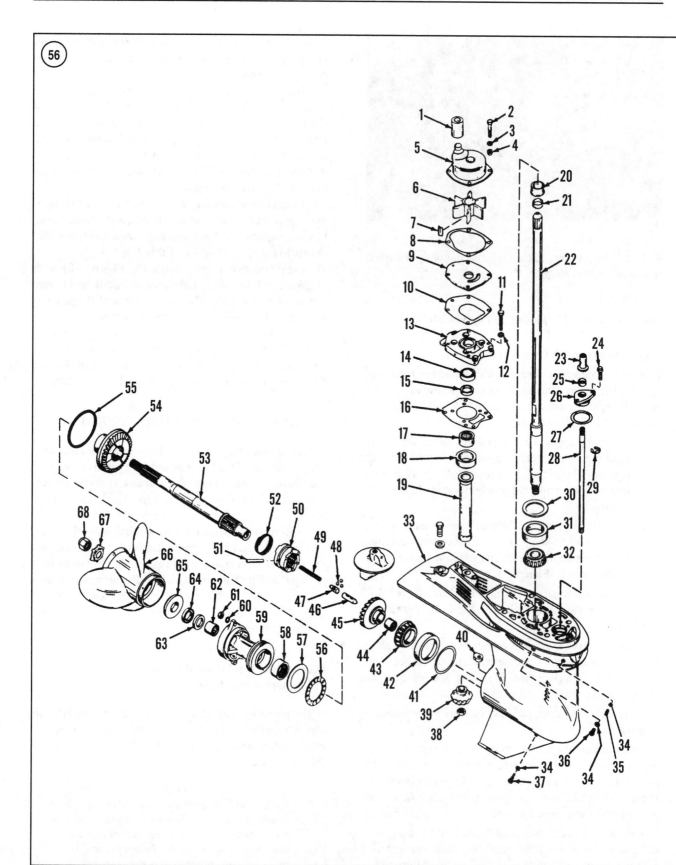

GEARCASE COMPONENTS
(65 JET AND 75-125 HP [EXCEPT 115 HP OPTIMAX] MODELS)

1. Water tube seal
2. Screw
3. Washer
4. Insulator*
5. Water pump cover
6. Impeller
7. Impeller drive key
8. Gasket
9. Plate
10. Gasket
11. Screw
12. Washer
13. Water pump base
14. Seal
15. Seal
16. Gasket
17. Roller bearing
18. Carrier
19. Sleeve
20. Wear sleeve
21. Seal ring
22. Drive shaft
23. Shift shaft coupler
24. Screw
25. Seal
26. Shift shaft retainer/bushing
27. O-ring
28. Shift shaft
29. E-clip
30. Shim pack
31. Bearing race
32. Tapered roller bearing
33. Gear housing
34. Gasket
35. Plug
36. Plug
37. Plug
38. Pinion gear nut
39. Pinion gear
40. Shift cam
41. Shim pack
42. Bearing race
43. Tapered roller bearing
44. Roller bearing
45. Forward gear
46. Shift cam follower
47. Spring guide
48. Three balls
49. Spring
50. Clutch
51. Cross pin
52. Clutch spring
53. Propeller shaft
54. Reverse gear
55. O-ring
56. Thrust bearing
57. Thrust bearing washer
58. Roller bearing
59. Bearing carrier
60. Flatwasher
61. Locknut
62. Needle bearing
63. Seal
64. Seal
65. Thrust hub
66. Propeller
67. Tab washer
68. Propeller nut

*Not used on all models

9

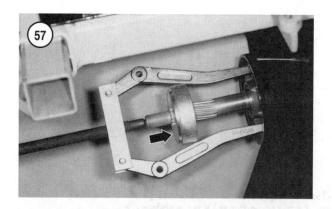

1. Remove the gearcase as described in this chapter.

2. Drain the gearcase lubricant as described in Chapter Four.

3. Remove the water pump and pump base as described in this chapter.

4. Remove the two elastic locknuts (61, **Figure 56**) and flat washers (60) securing the propeller shaft bearing carrier to the gearcase.

5. Install puller jaws part No. 91-46086A-1 and puller bolt part No. 91-85716 or an equivalent and pull the bearing carrier from the gearcase. If necessary, use a propeller thrust hub (**Figure 57**, typical) to prevent the puller jaws from sliding inward.

NOTE
If the needle bearing inside the bearing carrier must be replaced, also remove the propeller shaft seals during the bearing removal process. If needle bearing replacement is not necessary, remove and discard both propeller shaft seals at the same time using a suitable seal puller. Do not damage the seal bore in the process.

6. Remove the reverse gear (**Figure 58**), thrust bearing (**Figure 59**) and thrust washer (**Figure 60**) from the bear-

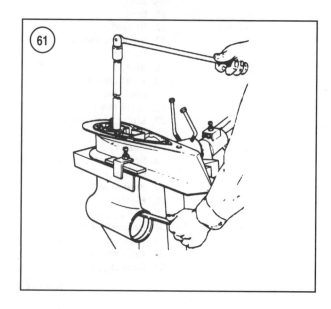

ing carrier. Then remove and discard the O-ring (55, **Figure 56**).

7. Pull the propeller shaft assembly from the gearcase. If the shift cam follower (46, **Figure 56**) falls out of the propeller shaft, retrieve it from the gearcase and reinstall it into the propeller shaft.

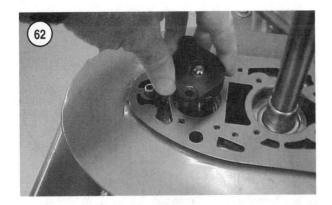

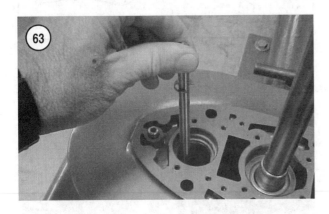

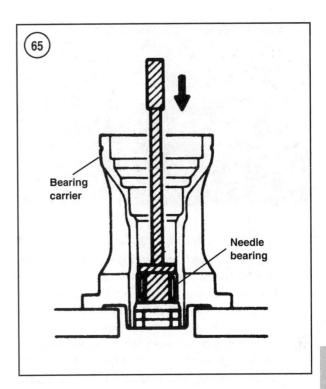

9

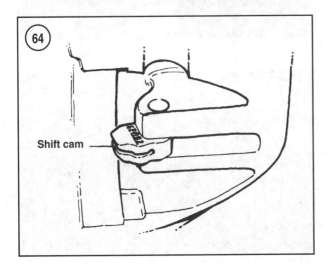

Shift cam

8. Remove the pinion nut by holding the nut with a suitable socket or wrench, then turning the drive shaft counterclockwise using spline socket part No. 91-817070 or equivalent until the nut is free from the drive shaft. See **Figure 61**.

9. Pull the drive shaft assembly from gearcase.

10. Remove the pinion gear, pinion gear roller bearing and forward gear assembly from the propeller shaft bore.

11. Remove the two screws securing the shift shaft retainer/bushing (26, **Figure 56**) to the gearcase. Carefully pry the shift shaft retainer loose from the gearcase. Remove the retainer (**Figure 62**). Then remove the shift shaft assembly from the gearcase (**Figure 63**).

12. Remove the shift cam from the front of the gearcase bore. See **Figure 64**.

13. Remove the O-ring (27, **Figure 56**) and seal (25) from the shift shaft bushing. Discard the seal and O-ring.

14. If the bearing carrier needle bearings must be replaced, replace them as follows:

    a. Clamp the carrier assembly into a vise with protective jaws or between wooden blocks.

    b. Pull the reverse gear needle bearing from the bearing carrier using a suitable slide hammer, such as part No. 91-34569A-1. Discard the bearing.

    c. Set the carrier in a press with the propeller end facing down.

    d. Assemble the mandrel part No. 91-26569 and driver rod part No. 91-37323, or an equivalent. Position the mandrel and driver rod in the carrier bore on top of the needle bearing.

    e. Press the propeller shaft needle bearing and seals from the carrier (**Figure 65**). Discard the bearing and seals.

15. Remove the forward gear/bearing and clutch from the propeller shaft as follows:

a. Hook the end of a small screwdriver over an end loop of the clutch spring (**Figure 66**). Carefully wind the spring from the clutch.

b. Place the shift cam follower against a solid surface and push on the propeller shaft to relieve spring pressure on the cross pin. See **Figure 67**.

c. Use a pin punch to push the cross pin from the clutch, propeller shaft and spring guide (**Figure 68**).

d. Pull the clutch from the propeller shaft (**Figure 69**).

e. Remove the shift cam follower (46, **Figure 56**), three steel balls (48), spring guide (47) and spring (49) from the propeller shaft.

16. Remove the forward gear roller bearing, the forward gear internal needle bearing and/or the forward gear bearing race as follows:

a. Pull the forward gear and bearing assembly from the gearcase (**Figure 70**).

b. Press the roller bearing from the forward gear. Support the bearing with a knife-edged bearing separator, such as part No. 91-37241. See **Figure 71**. Press on the gear hub using a suitable tool. Discard the roller bearing.

c. Clamp the gear in a vise with protective jaws with the gear engagement lugs facing up. Drive the internal needle bearing from the gear using a suitable punch and hammer. Discard the bearing.

d. To remove the forward gear bearing race from the gearcase, pull the race from the front of the propeller shaft bore using a suitable slide hammer, such as part No. 91-34569A-1. See **Figure 72**. Remove the shim(s) from the bearing bore. Measure and record the thickness of the shims for later reference. Discard the race if the roller bearing assembly must be replaced.

> *NOTE*
> *If the forward gear bearing race was only removed so the shim(s) and forward gear*

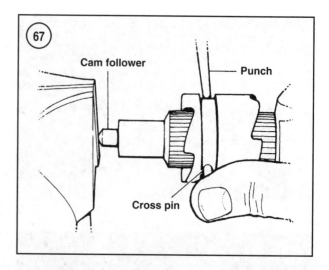

lash could be changed, do not discard the bearing race.

17. If the drive shaft wear sleeve and seal must be replaced, replace them as follows:

a. Support the drive shaft wear sleeve in a knife-edged bearing separator such as part No. 91-37241. The pinion gear end of the shaft must face down.

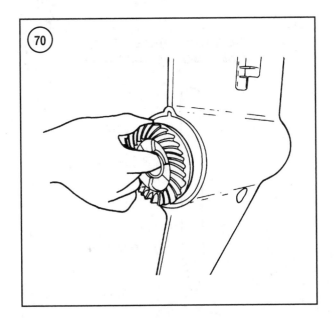

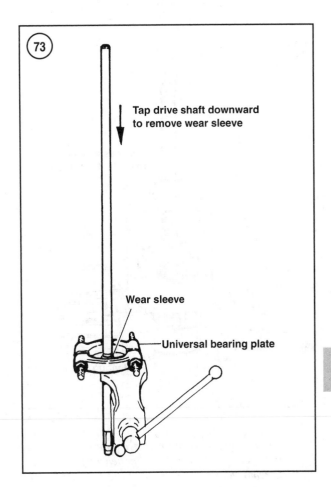

Tap drive shaft downward to remove wear sleeve

Wear sleeve

Universal bearing plate

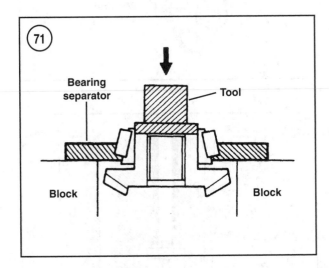

Bearing separator

Tool

Block

Block

b. Press on the crankshaft end of the drive shaft until the sleeve is free. See **Figure 73**. Discard the sleeve and rubber seal.

18. If the drive shaft upper bearing or the lubrication sleeve must be replaced, replace them as follows:

    a. Remove the bearing by pulling it out of the drive shaft bore using puller part No. 91-83165M or an equivalent two-jaw puller (**Figure 74**). Discard the bearing.

    b. Remove the bearing sleeve by also pulling it out of the drive shaft bore using puller part No. 91-83165M or an equivalent two-jaw puller (**Figure 74**). Discard the sleeve.

    c. Remove the lubrication sleeve by pulling it out of the drive shaft bore using puller part No. 91-83165M or an equivalent two-jaw puller. Discard the lubrication sleeve.

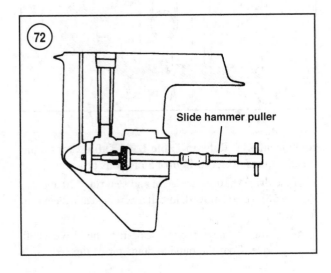

Slide hammer puller

NOTE
If the drive shaft roller bearing race was only removed so the shim(s) and the pinion gear depth could be changed, do not discard the bearing race. The drive shaft needle

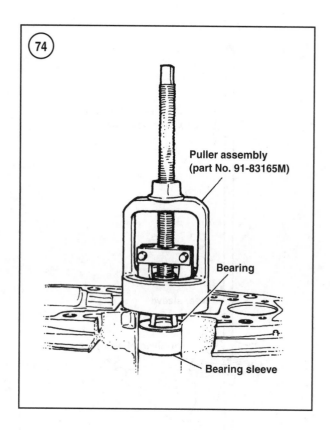

Puller assembly
(part No. 91-83165M)

Bearing

Bearing sleeve

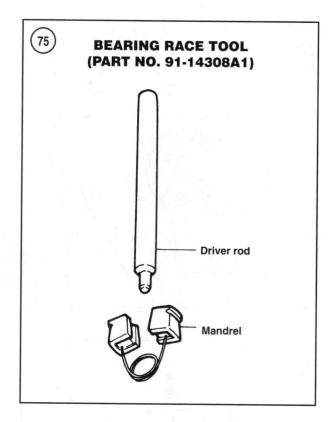

BEARING RACE TOOL
(PART NO. 91-14308A1)

Driver rod

Mandrel

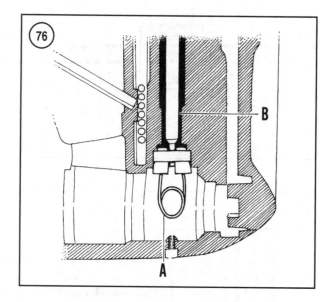

*bearing and lubrication sleeve do not have
to be removed before the roller bearing race
is removed.*

19. If the drive shaft roller bearing race must be removed
or replaced, proceed as follows:

    a. Remove the bearing race from the gearcase by driv-
ing it down into the propeller shaft bore with a bearing remover part No. 91-14308A-1 or an
equivalent. See **Figure 75**.

    b. Insert the puller jaws (A, **Figure 76**) from the pro-
peller shaft bore. Insert the driver (B, **Figure 76**)
through the drive shaft bore.

    c. Place a shop cloth under the bearing puller. Use a
suitable mallet to drive the bearing race out into the
propeller shaft bore. Discard the bearing race and
matching roller bearing.

20. Refer to *Gearcase Cleaning and Inspection*. Clean
and inspect all components as described before beginning
the reassembly procedure.

Assembly (75-125 hp Models)

Lubricate all internal components with Quicksilver Premium Blend gear oil or an equivalent. Do not assemble

components *dry*. Refer to **Table 1** and **Table 2** for torque
specifications. Refer to **Figure 56** for this procedure.

1. If the drive shaft wear sleeve and seal ring (20 and 21,
Figure 56) were removed, install a new seal and sleeve as
follows:

    a. Position a new rubber seal into the drive shaft
groove. Coat the outside diameter of the seal with

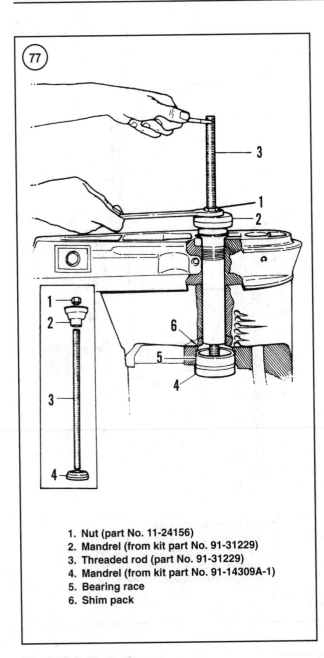

77

1. Nut (part No. 11-24156)
2. Mandrel (from kit part No. 91-31229)
3. Threaded rod (part No. 91-31229)
4. Mandrel (from kit part No. 91-14309A-1)
5. Bearing race
6. Shim pack

Loctite 271 threadlocking adhesive (part No. 92-809819).

b. Place a new wear sleeve into the holder from the sleeve installation kit part No. 91-14310A-1. Slide the drive shaft into the sleeve and holder.

c. Place the driver from the sleeve installation kit over the pinion end of the drive shaft. Place the drive shaft and tool assembly in a press. Press the driver against the holder until they contact each other.

d. Wipe excess Loctite from the drive shaft.

2. If the lower drive shaft bearing was removed, install the race into the gearcase as follows:

a. Lubricate the race and place the original shims on top of the race. If the original shims are lost or damaged beyond specification, install 0.025 in. (0.635 mm) shim(s).

b. Position the race into its bore with the tapered side facing down.

c. Assemble the bearing installer components as shown in **Figure 77**.

d. Tighten the nut to seat the race fully in the bearing bore.

3. If the drive shaft lubrication sleeve was removed, lubricate a new sleeve and press the sleeve into the gearcase as far as possible with hand pressure. Make sure the tab at the top of the sleeve points to the rear of the gearcase. The sleeve will be fully seated into the gearcase in the next step.

NOTE
The drive shaft oil sleeve must be installed before proceeding with the next step.

4. If the drive shaft needle bearing and sleeve were removed, install a new bearing assembly as follows:

a. If the new bearing is separate from the new bearing sleeve, lubricate both parts with Quicksilver 2-4-C Multi-Lube grease (part No. 825407). Set the sleeve with the tapered side down into a press. Position the bearing with the numbered side up into the sleeve and press it into the sleeve with a suitable mandrel until it is flush with the sleeve.

b. Lubricate the outside diameter of a new bearing assembly with Quicksilver 2-4-C Multi-Lube grease.

c. Position the bearing assembly into the drive shaft bore with the tapered (beveled) end facing down.

d. Assemble the installer components as shown in **Figure 78**.

e. Tighten the nut to seat the bearing assembly and lubrication sleeve into the drive shaft bore.

5. If the forward gear bearing race was removed, install the race into the gearcase as follows:

a. Position the original shims (A, **Figure 79**) into the bearing bore. If the original shims were lost, start with 0.010 in. (0.254 mm) shim(s).

b. Lubricate the bearing race (B, **Figure 79**) and set it into the gearcase bearing bore. Place mandrel part No. 91-31106 or an equivalent over the race.

c. Place the propeller shaft into the mandrel hole. Install the propeller shaft bearing carrier into the gearcase to keep the propeller shaft centered.

d. Thread a scrap propeller nut onto the propeller shaft. Use a mallet to drive the propeller shaft against the mandrel until the bearing race is fully seated in the gearcase bearing bore. See **Figure 79**.

9

e. Remove the propeller nut, propeller shaft, bearing carrier and mandrel.

6. If the forward gear roller bearing was removed, lubricate a new roller bearing and set it on the gear hub with the rollers facing up. Press the bearing fully onto the gear with mandrel part No. 91-37350 or an equivalent. See **Figure 80**. Do not press on the roller cage.

7. If the forward gear internal needle bearing was removed, install a new bearing as follows:

a. Position the forward gear in a press with the gear teeth facing down.

b. Lubricate the new needle bearing and position it in the gear bore with the numbered side facing up.

c. Press the bearing into the gear with a suitable mandrel until the bearing bottoms in the bore. Be careful not to damage the bearing by over-pressing.

8. If the bearing carrier needle bearings were removed, install new bearings as follows:

a. Set the carrier into a press with the propeller end facing down. Lubricate a new reverse gear needle bearing and position it into the carrier bore with its lettered end facing up.

b. Press the bearing into the carrier with bearing installer part No. 91-13945 or an equivalent. See **Figure 81**. Press until the tool bottoms.

c. Set the carrier in a press with the propeller end facing up, on bearing installer part No. 91-13945 or an equivalent to protect the carrier and reverse gear needle bearing.

d. Lubricate a new propeller shaft needle bearing and position it into the carrier bore with the lettered end facing up.

e. Press the bearing into the carrier with a suitable mandrel, such as part No. 91-15755, until the bearing bottoms in its bore and the bearing is below the seal bore. See **Figure 82**.

9. If the propeller shaft was disassembled, refer to **Figure 83** and reassemble it as follows:

a. Lubricate all components with Quicksilver 2-4-C Multi-Lube grease.

b. Align the cross pin holes of the sliding clutch with the slot in the propeller shaft. Position the grooved end of the sliding clutch toward the propeller and slide it onto the propeller shaft.

c. Install the shift spring into the propeller shaft. Then install the shift spring guide with the narrow end towards the shift spring. Install the three steel balls and finally install the cam follower with the beveled end facing out.

d. Press the cam follower against a solid object to compress the spring. Align the sliding clutch holes

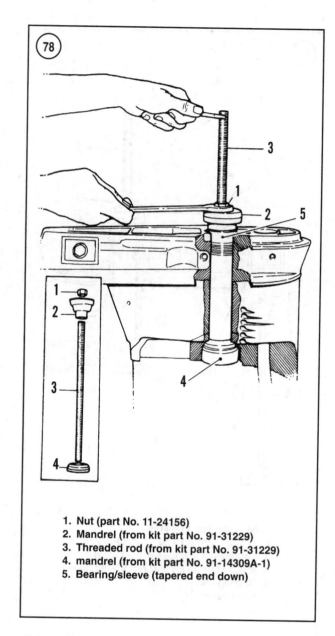

1. Nut (part No. 11-24156)
2. Mandrel (from kit part No. 91-31229)
3. Threaded rod (from kit part No. 91-31229)
4. mandrel (from kit part No. 91-14309A-1)
5. Bearing/sleeve (tapered end down)

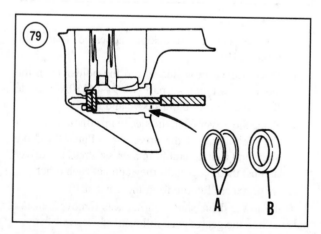

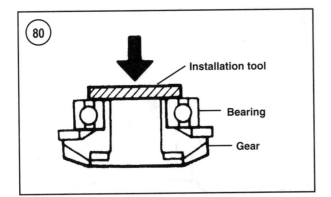

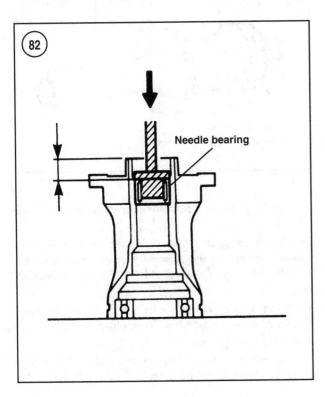

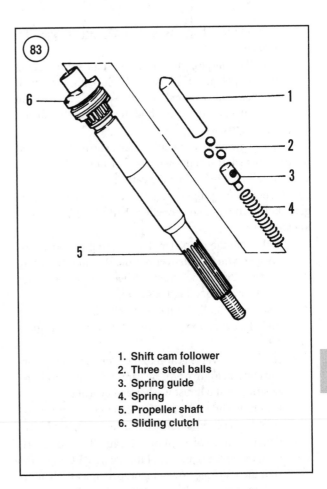

1. Shift cam follower
2. Three steel balls
3. Spring guide
4. Spring
5. Propeller shaft
6. Sliding clutch

9

with the spring guide's hole. A small punch may be used to ease alignment. See **Figure 67**, typical.

e. Insert the sliding clutch cross-pin into the clutch and through the spring guide's hole. The cross-pin must pass through the spring guide.

NOTE
The sliding clutch retaining spring must lay flat, with no overlapping coils.

f. Secure the pin to the sliding clutch with a new retainer spring. Do not open the spring any more than necessary to install it.

10. Install two new propeller shaft seals as follows:

a. Coat the outer diameter of two new propeller shaft seals with Loctite 271 threadlocking adhesive.

b. Set the carrier in a press with the propeller end facing up, on bearing installer part No. 91-13945 or an equivalent to protect the carrier and reverse gear needle bearing.

c. Install the small diameter seal with the spring facing the gearcase. Press the seal in with the large stepped end of mandrel part No. 91-31108 or an equivalent until the tool bottoms against the carrier. See **Figure 84**.

d. Install the large diameter seal with the spring facing the propeller. Press the seal in with the small stepped end of mandrel part No. 91-31108 or an equivalent until the tool bottoms against the carrier. See **Figure 84**.

11. Coat a new propeller shaft bearing carrier O-ring and the propeller shaft seal lips with 2-4-C Multi-Lube grease. Then install the O-ring into the carrier groove.

12. Assemble the propeller shaft bearing carrier, reverse gear and bearings, and propeller shaft assembly as follows:

a. Lubricate the propeller shaft bearing carrier thrust washer with Quicksilver Needle Bearing Assembly Grease. Install the thrust washer onto the propeller shaft carrier. See **Figure 60**.

b. Lubricate the thrust bearing with the same grease and place it on top of the thrust washer. See **Figure 59**.

c. Install the reverse gear into the propeller shaft bearing carrier (**Figure 58**). Be careful not to disturb the position of the thrust washer and bearing.

d. Carefully slide the propeller shaft into the carrier assembly. Be careful not to damage the carrier seals.

e. Obtain a piece of 1 1/4 or 1 1/2 in. (31.75 or 38.10 mm) diameter, 6 in. (152.4 mm) long PVC pipe. Install the PVC pipe over the propeller shaft, then install the propeller locking tab washer and propeller nut. Hand tighten the nut to hold the propeller shaft securely into the bearing carrier. See **Figure 85**.

13. Assemble and install the shift components as follows:

a. Coat the outer diameter of a new shift shaft seal with Loctite 271 threadlocking adhesive. Press the seal into the shift shaft retainer/bushing with a suitable mandrel until it is flush with the retainer bore.

b. Lubricate the seal lip and a new retainer O-ring with Quicksilver 2-4-C Multi-Lube grease. Install the O-ring into the shift bushing groove.

c. If the E-ring was removed, install it onto the shift shaft.

d. Lubricate the shift shaft with the same grease and carefully insert the shift shaft into the shift shaft retainer and seal.

e. Place the shift cam into the gear housing with the numbered side up as shown in **Figure 86**. Install the shift shaft assembly into the gearcase and engage the shift shaft splines to the shift cam internal splines.

f. Apply Loctite 271 threadlocking adhesive to the threads of the two shift shaft retainer screws. Install

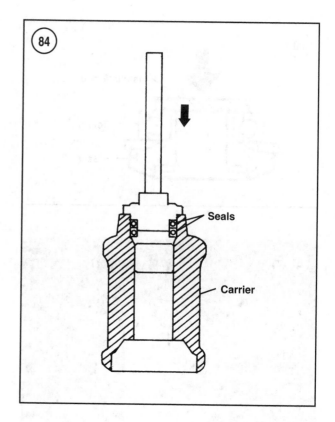

Seals

Carrier

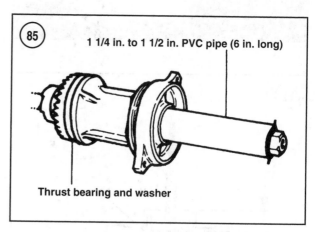

1 1/4 in. to 1 1/2 in. PVC pipe (6 in. long)

Thrust bearing and washer

and tighten the screws to the specification in **Table 1**.

14. Rotate the gearcase so the propeller shaft bore is pointing up. Install the forward gear assembly into the propeller shaft bore and into the forward gear bearing race.

15. Position the drive shaft roller bearing in the race at the bottom of the drive shaft bore, then place the pinion gear in position over the bearing.

16. Spray the threads of the drive shaft with Locquic primer (part No. 92-809824). Insert the drive shaft into the

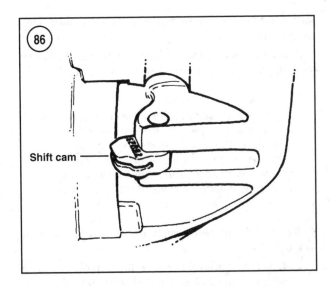

Shift cam

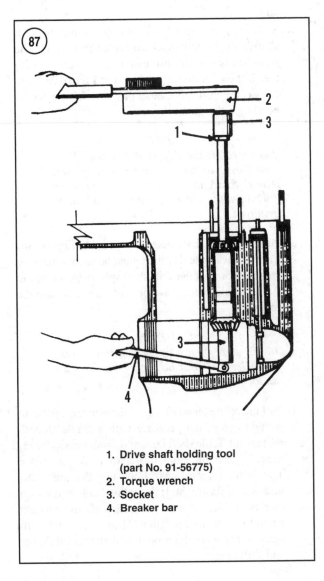

1. Drive shaft holding tool
   (part No. 91-56775)
2. Torque wrench
3. Socket
4. Breaker bar

drive shaft bore while holding the pinion gear and lower bearing in position. Rotate the shaft as necessary to engage the drive shaft splines to the pinion gear splines.

NOTE
*Apply Loctite 271 threadlocking adhesive to a **new** pinion nut **after** the pinion gear depth and forward gear lash have been verified. Install the original pinion nut without sealant to check the gear depth and forward gear lash.*

17. Install the original pinion nut with the recessed side facing *toward* the pinion gear. Tighten the nut finger-tight at this time.

18. Hold the pinion nut with a suitable wrench or socket. Attach spline socket part No. 91-56775 or an equivalent to a suitable torque wrench. Tighten the pinion nut to the specification in **Table 1**. See **Figure 87**, typical.

19. Refer to *Gearcase Shimming* to set the pinion gear depth. Do not continue until the pinion gear depth is correct.

20. Once the pinion gear depth is correct, install the propeller shaft assembly into the gearcase and into the forward gear internal needle bearing. Make sure the shift cam follower does not fall out during assembly.

21. Liberally lubricate the front and rear flanges of the propeller shaft bearing carrier with Quicksilver Special Lubricant 101 (part No. 92-13872A1). Install the carrier over the propeller shaft, being careful not to damage the carrier seals on the propeller shaft splines. Make sure the screw holes are aligned with the gearcase. Rotate the drive shaft to make sure the gear teeth are meshed, then seat the carrier into the gearcase bore.

22. Secure the bearing carrier with two locknuts and washers. Tighten the fasteners to the specification in **Table 1**. Then remove the propeller nut, washer and PVC pipe.

23. Refer to *Gearcase Shimming* in this chapter to set the forward gear lash. Do not continue until the gear lash is correct.

24. Once the gear lash is correct, remove the propeller shaft and bearing carrier, and install a *new* pinion nut with Loctite 271 threadlocking adhesive as described previously in this section. Then reinstall the propeller shaft and bearing carrier as described previously in this section. Coat the two bearing carrier studs with Loctite 271 threadlocking adhesive and install the screws or locknuts and washers. Tighten the two fasteners to the specification in **Table 1**.

25. Install the water pump assembly as described in this chapter.

26. Pressure test the gearcase as described in *Gearcase Pressure Testing*.

9

27. Fill the gearcase with the recommended lubricant as described in Chapter Four.

Disassembly (115 hp Optimax and 135-200 hp [Except 200 hp Optimax] Models)

All models covered in this section are equipped with an *E-Z Shift* gearcase. This gearcase uses a special shift cam and follower that provides positive sliding clutch engagement into and out of both gears.

On E-Z Shift models, the propeller shaft bearing carrier can be removed from the gearcase without removing the gearcase from the drive shaft housing, but the propeller shaft *cannot* be removed unless the gearcase is removed from the drive shaft housing.

NOTE
If the forward gear or drive shaft roller bearings must be replaced, replace the bearing rollers and races as assemblies. Do not remove a pressed in bearing and/or race unless replacement is necessary.

Refer to **Figure 88** and **Figure 89** for this procedure.

1. Remove the gearcase as described in this chapter.

2. Drain the gearcase lubricant as described in Chapter Four.

3. Remove the water pump and pump base as described in this chapter.

4. Bend the locking tab away from the propeller shaft bearing carrier retaining ring using a suitable punch and hammer. See **Figure 90**, typical.

NOTE
If the retaining ring is frozen in place and cannot be removed in the next step, apply penetrating oil and mild heat using an electric heat gun, heat lamp or propane torch. If removal is still difficult, drill through the ring in several places parallel to the propeller shaft and break the ring into several pieces with a suitable chisel and hammer. Do not drill into the gearcase threads or into the bearing carrier.

5. Remove the retaining ring using spanner wrench part No. 91-61069 or an equivalent (**Figure 91**). Turn the ring counterclockwise until it is free from the gearcase (**Figure 92**). If the ring is corroded or damaged, discard it. Then remove the locking tab washer (**Figure 93**).

6. Install puller jaws (part No. 91-46086A-1) and a puller bolt (part No. 91-85716) or an equivalent, and pull the bearing carrier from the gearcase. See **Figure 94**. If neces-

sary, use a propeller thrust hub to prevent the puller jaws from sliding inward.

7. Locate and secure the bearing carrier alignment key (if so equipped), then remove and discard the carrier O-ring.

NOTE
If the needle bearing inside the bearing carrier must be replaced, also remove the propeller shaft seals. If bearing replacement is not necessary, remove and discard both propeller shaft seals at this time using a suitable seal puller. Do not damage the seal bore during the process.

8. Remove the propeller shaft and shift mechanism as follows:

a. Unthread, but do not remove, the shift shaft bushing with bushing tool part No. 91-31107 or an equivalent.

b. Shift the gearcase into neutral by placing the shift shaft in the middle of its total rotational travel. The straight edge of the shift cam must be parallel with the shift cam follower as shown in **Figure 95**. Otherwise, the shift cam cannot pass through the needle bearing in the forward gear.

NOTE
Do not rotate the shift shaft in either direction during its removal in the next substep. The shift mechanism must be in neutral before the shift shaft and propeller shaft can be removed.

c. Pull the shift shaft assembly (38-44, **Figure 88**) from the gearcase. If pliers must be used to remove the shaft, protect the shift shaft splines by wrapping a strip of aluminum or other soft metal around the splines.

CAUTION
In this step, do not apply side force to the propeller shaft or it may break the clutch actuator rod neck.

d. Pull the propeller shaft, cam follower and shift cam straight out of the gearcase with a single smooth movement. If the shaft jams and cannot easily be removed, push the propeller shaft back into place against the forward gear. Look into the shift shaft hole with a flashlight. If the splined hole in the shift cam is visible, reinstall the shift shaft and rotate it again to the neutral position. Then remove the shift shaft and remove the propeller shaft, cam follower and shift cam.

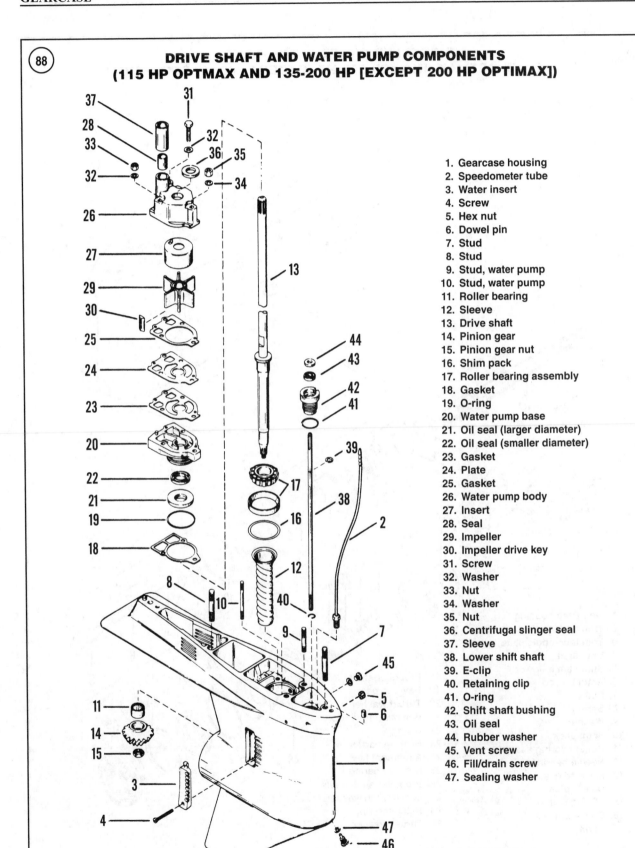

(88)

**DRIVE SHAFT AND WATER PUMP COMPONENTS
(115 HP OPTMAX AND 135-200 HP [EXCEPT 200 HP OPTIMAX])**

1. Gearcase housing
2. Speedometer tube
3. Water insert
4. Screw
5. Hex nut
6. Dowel pin
7. Stud
8. Stud
9. Stud, water pump
10. Stud, water pump
11. Roller bearing
12. Sleeve
13. Drive shaft
14. Pinion gear
15. Pinion gear nut
16. Shim pack
17. Roller bearing assembly
18. Gasket
19. O-ring
20. Water pump base
21. Oil seal (larger diameter)
22. Oil seal (smaller diameter)
23. Gasket
24. Plate
25. Gasket
26. Water pump body
27. Insert
28. Seal
29. Impeller
30. Impeller drive key
31. Screw
32. Washer
33. Nut
34. Washer
35. Nut
36. Centrifugal slinger seal
37. Sleeve
38. Lower shift shaft
39. E-clip
40. Retaining clip
41. O-ring
42. Shift shaft bushing
43. Oil seal
44. Rubber washer
45. Vent screw
46. Fill/drain screw
47. Sealing washer

9

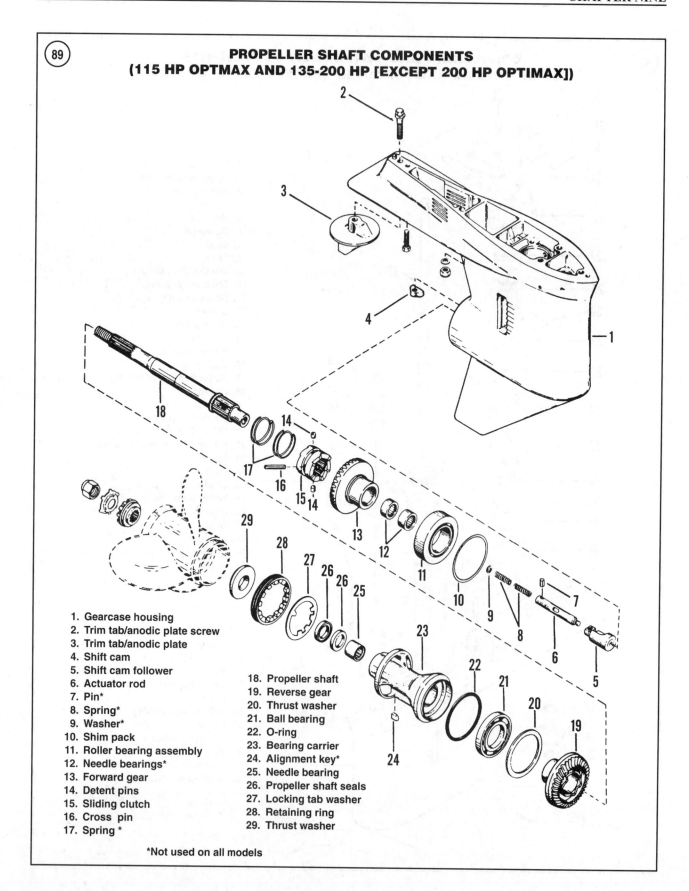

**PROPELLER SHAFT COMPONENTS
(115 HP OPTMAX AND 135-200 HP [EXCEPT 200 HP OPTIMAX])**

1. Gearcase housing
2. Trim tab/anodic plate screw
3. Trim tab/anodic plate
4. Shift cam
5. Shift cam follower
6. Actuator rod
7. Pin*
8. Spring*
9. Washer*
10. Shim pack
11. Roller bearing assembly
12. Needle bearings*
13. Forward gear
14. Detent pins
15. Sliding clutch
16. Cross pin
17. Spring *

18. Propeller shaft
19. Reverse gear
20. Thrust washer
21. Ball bearing
22. O-ring
23. Bearing carrier
24. Alignment key*
25. Needle bearing
26. Propeller shaft seals
27. Locking tab washer
28. Retaining ring
29. Thrust washer

*Not used on all models

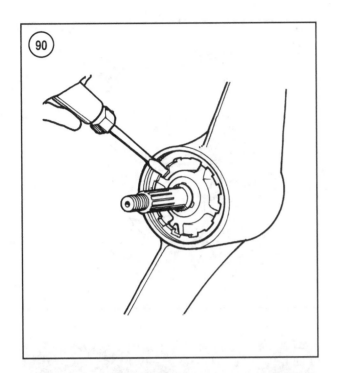

9

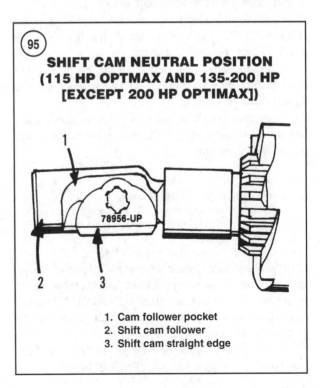

SHIFT CAM NEUTRAL POSITION (115 HP OPTMAX AND 135-200 HP [EXCEPT 200 HP OPTIMAX])

78956-UP

1. Cam follower pocket
2. Shift cam follower
3. Shift cam straight edge

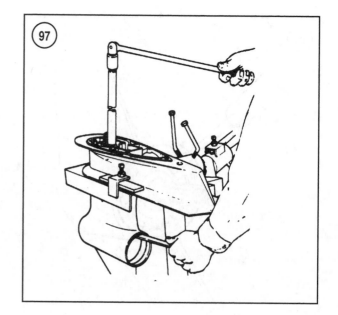

e. If the propeller shaft still cannot be removed, push the shaft back into place against the forward gear. Reinstall the propeller shaft bearing carrier to support the propeller shaft. Remove the gearcase from the holding fixture and lay it on its *port* side. Strike the upper leading edge of the housing with a rubber mallet to dislodge the shift cam from the cam follower. Remove the bearing carrier and pull the propeller shaft from the housing. Retrieve the shift cam after the forward gear is removed.

9. Remove the drive shaft upper bearing retainer (**Figure 96**) using retainer tool part No. 91-43506.

10. Install drive shaft spline socket part No. 91-90094 or an equivalent onto the drive shaft splines.

11. Hold the pinion nut using a suitable wrench or socket (**Figure 97**). Pad the area around the handle with shop towels to prevent housing damage.

12. Loosen and remove the pinion nut by turning the drive shaft counterclockwise. Remove the pinion nut and washer from the housing.

13. Clamp the drive shaft into a vise with protective jaws, or between wooden blocks. Clamp as close to the water pump studs as possible.

NOTE
The lower drive shaft bearing contains 18 loose rollers that may fall out during drive shaft removal. Be sure to retrieve all rollers from the housing.

14. Place a wooden block against the gearcase mating surface. With the aid of an assistant, hold the housing securely and tap the wooden block with a mallet until the drive shaft separates from the pinion gear. Then pull the gearcase housing off the drive shaft.

15. Remove the 18 loose bearing rollers from the drive shaft lower bearing race or propeller shaft bore.

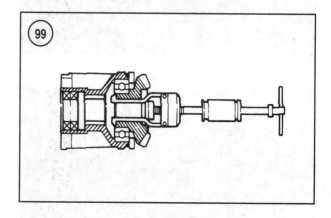

16. Remove the shim(s) from the drive shaft bearing bore (**Figure 98**). Measure and record the thickness of the shim(s) for later reference. Tag the shim(s) for identification during reassembly. Discard the race if the roller bearing assembly is being replaced.

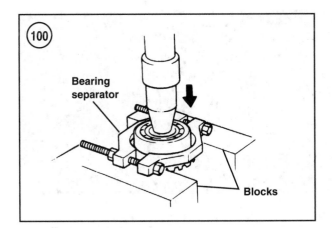

Bearing separator

Blocks

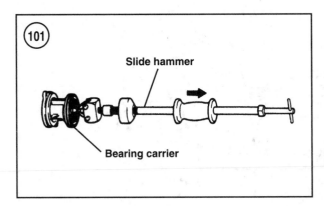

Slide hammer

Bearing carrier

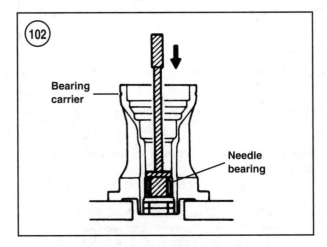

Bearing carrier

Needle bearing

Propeller shaft bearing carrier disassembly

The reverse gear rides on a ball bearing that is pressed into the carrier. The propeller shaft has a needle bearing located near the propeller shaft seals. Remove the reverse gear to service the propeller shaft needle bearing. Remove the reverse gear and bearing, and the propeller shaft needle bearing as follows:

1. Clamp the carrier in a vise with protective jaws or between two blocks of wood.

2. Pull the reverse gear assembly from the bearing carrier with a suitable slide hammer, such as part No. 91-34569A-1. See **Figure 99**.

3. If the reverse gear ball bearing must be replaced, replace it as follows:

    a. *Bearing remains on the reverse gear*—Support the ball bearing in a suitable knife-edged bearing separator, such as part No. 91-37241. Press against the gear hub with a suitable mandrel until the bearing is free from the gear. See **Figure 100**.

    b. *Bearing remains in the carrier*—Clamp the carrier in a vise with protective jaws or between two blocks of wood. Pull the bearing from the bearing carrier with a suitable slide hammer, such as part No. 91-34569A-1. See **Figure 101**.

    c. Remove the thrust washer (20, **Figure 89**) from the reverse gear or bearing carrier.

    d. Discard the bearing.

4. If the propeller shaft needle bearing must be replaced, replace it as follows:

    a. Set the carrier in a press with the propeller end facing down.

    b. Press the bearing and seals from the carrier with a suitable mandrel. See **Figure 102**.

    c. Discard the bearing and seals.

Propeller shaft disassembly

The propeller shaft has one cross pin retaining spring and one detent pin. The actuating rod is solid and does not have a spring, washer and pin.

1. Remove the shift cam from the cam follower.

2. Insert a thin-blade screwdriver or similar tool under the retaining spring(s). Lift the coil up and rotate the propeller shaft to unwind the spring from the sliding clutch. See **Figure 103**. Discard the spring.

9

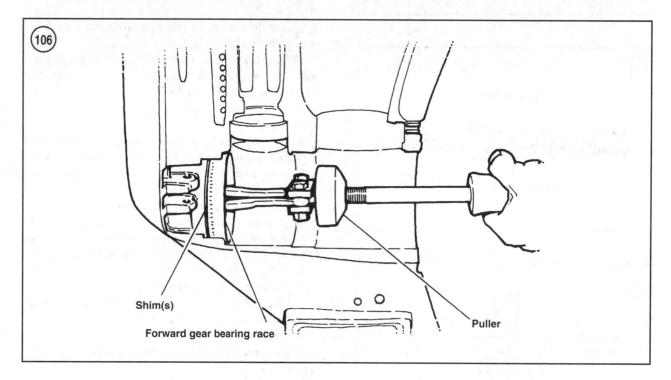

Shim(s)

Forward gear bearing race

Puller

3. Remove the detent pins (14, **Figure 89**) from the sliding clutch.

4. Push the cross pin through the clutch and propeller shaft using a suitable punch (**Figure 104**). Slide the clutch off the shaft (**Figure 105**).

5. Pull the shift cam follower (5, **Figure 89**) and clutch actuator rod (6) straight out of the propeller shaft. Do not move the cam follower up, down or side-to-side during removal.

6. Separate the clutch actuator rod from the cam follower.

Forward gear bearing removal

If the forward gear bearing race must be removed to adjust forward gear lash, or the roller bearing assembly or internal needle bearing(s) must be replaced, proceed as follows:

NOTE
If the forward gear bearing race was only removed so the shim pack and forward gear lash could be changed, do not discard the bearing race.

1. To remove the forward gear bearing race from the gearcase, pull the race from the front of the propeller shaft bore with a suitable slide hammer, such as part No. 91-34569A-1. See **Figure 106**, typical.

2. Remove the shim(s) from the bearing bore. Measure and record the thickness of the shims for later reference. Tag the shim(s) for identification during reassembly. Dis-

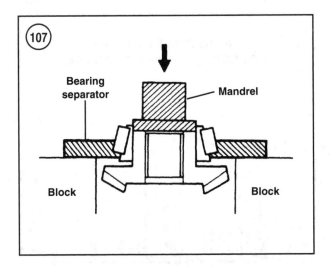

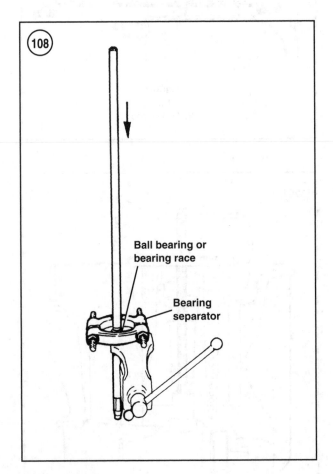

groove in the inner race to provide a lip for the knife-edged bearing separator.

3. To remove the roller bearing from the forward gear, support the bearing with a knife-edged bearing separator, such as part No. 91-37241. Press on the gear hub with a suitable mandrel until the bearing is free from the gear. See **Figure 107**. Discard the roller bearing.

4. To remove the internal needle bearing (12, **Figure 89**), clamp the gear in a vise with protective jaws with the gear engagement lugs facing up. Remove the snap ring (if so equipped) from the groove in the bearing bore. Drive the internal needle bearing from the gear with a suitable punch and hammer. Later models only use a single needle bearing. Discard the bearing.

Drive shaft bearing removal

A loose roller bearing supports the lower portion (pinion gear end) of the drive shaft and a single tapered roller bearing supports the upper portion of the drive shaft. The shims under the tapered roller bearing race control the pinion gear depth.

If the drive shaft upper roller bearing(s) and/or lower roller must be replaced, replace them as follows:

1. Remove the drive shaft roller bearing as follows:

   a. Place the drive shaft (pinion end down) into bearing separator supported by a vise (**Figure 108**). Open the separator enough to contact the roller bearing inner race, but not the drive shaft surface.

   b. Using a soft lead or plastic hammer, tap the drive shaft down, driving the bearing off toward the top of the shaft. Do not damage the drive shaft-to-crankshaft splines.

   c. Discard the bearing and its race.

   NOTE
   The drive shaft lower bearing contains 18 loose bearing rollers that may fall out of the race during drive shaft removal. Reinstall the bearing rollers into the outer race to provide a contact surface for the removal tool.

2. Remove the lower roller bearing at the bottom of the drive shaft bore as follows:

   a. Install the 18 loose bearing rollers into the lower bearing race. Use a suitable grease, such as Quicksilver Needle Bearing Assembly Grease (part No. 92-825265A 1), to hold the rollers in place.

   b. Use mandrel part No. 91-15755, pilot part No. 91-36571 and driver rod part No. 91-37323 or an

card the race if the roller bearing assembly is being replaced.

NOTE
In Step 3, it may be necessary to cut the roller cage from the bearing and grind a

9

equivalent, assembled as shown in **Figure 109**, to drive the bearing into the gear cavity.

c. Remove and discard the bearing. Locate all loose bearing rollers.

CAUTION
If the drive shaft lower bearing has failed, causing the outer race to spin in the housing, replace the gearcase housing. Otherwise, the new bearing will spin inside the damaged bore, and cause premature gear and/or bearing failure.

Assembly (115 hp Optimax and 135-200 hp [Except 200 hp Optimax] Models)

If the drive shaft bearings, forward gear bearing, reverse gear or propeller shaft bearings were removed, or if the propeller shaft was disassembled, install new bearings or reassemble the propeller shaft as described in the following sections. Then proceed to *Assembly*.

Lubricate all internal components with Quicksilver Premium Blend gear oil or an equivalent. Do not assemble components *dry*. Refer to **Table 1** for torque specifications. Refer to **Figure 88** and **Figure 89** for this procedure.

Drive shaft bearing installation

1. To install a new needle bearing or loose roller bearing at the bottom of the drive shaft bore, lubricate a new bearing with Quicksilver Needle Bearing Assembly Grease (part No. 92-825265A 1). Install the ten rollers into the bearing race.

2. Assemble the bearing installer components as shown in **Figure 110**. Use mandrel part No. 91-92788, pilot part No. 91-92790, plate part No. 91-29310 and threaded rod part No. 91-31229 (or an equivalent). The numbered side of the bearing must face up the drive shaft bore away from the pinion gear when installed.

3. Pull the bearing into the drive shaft bore by turning the nut (2, **Figure 110**) until the bearing seats in the drive shaft bore. Do not apply excessive force to the bearing.

4. To install the new roller bearing(s) onto the drive shaft, lubricate the bearing(s) and applicable area on the drive shaft with Quicksilver Needle Bearing Assembly Grease.

5. Slide the bearing over the drive shaft splines. The rollers must face the power head, away from the pinion gear. Support the bearing's inner race with a suitable round mandrel, such as a scrap drive shaft roller bearing inner race. Place the assembly in a press with the mandrel or scrap bearing race supported by a knife-edged bearing

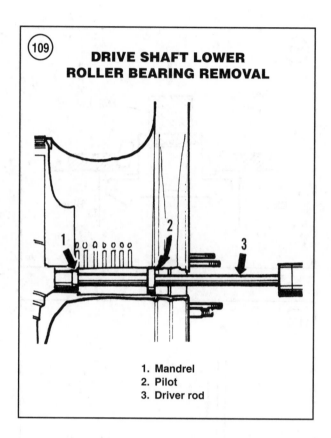

DRIVE SHAFT LOWER ROLLER BEARING REMOVAL

1. Mandrel
2. Pilot
3. Driver rod

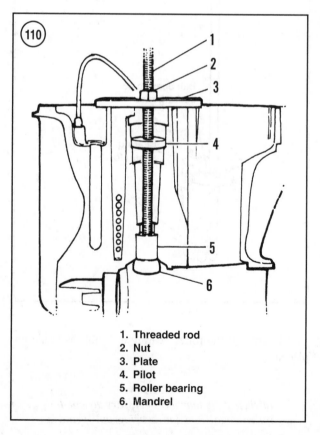

1. Threaded rod
2. Nut
3. Plate
4. Pilot
5. Roller bearing
6. Mandrel

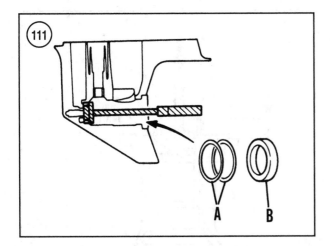

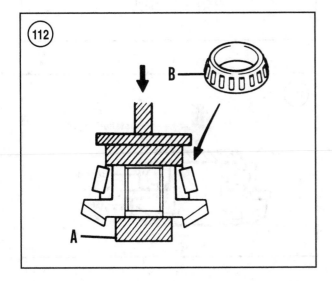

separator, such as part No. 91-37241. The pinion end of the shaft must face up.

6. Thread an old pinion nut onto the drive shaft threads to protect the threads. Press against the pinion nut until the bearing seats against the drive shaft shoulder.

Forward gear bearing installation

1. To install the forward gear roller bearing race into the gearcase housing, position the original shim pack (A, **Figure 111**) into the housing bearing bore (**Figure 98**). If the original shims were lost, start with a 0.010 in. (0.254 mm) shim pack.

2. Lubricate the bearing race (B, **Figure 111**) and set it into the gearcase bearing bore on top of the shim pack. Place the mandrel part No. 91-87120 or an equivalent over the race.

3. Place the propeller shaft into the mandrel hole. Install the propeller shaft bearing carrier into the gearcase to keep the propeller shaft centered.

4. Thread a scrap propeller nut onto the propeller shaft. Use a mallet to drive the propeller shaft against the mandrel until the bearing race is fully seated in the gearcase bearing bore.

5. Remove the propeller nut, propeller shaft, bearing carrier and mandrel.

6. If the forward gear roller bearing was removed, lubricate a new roller bearing (B, **Figure 112**) and set it on the gear hub with the rollers facing up. Place the gear on an additional mandrel (A, **Figure 112**) for support. Press the bearing fully onto the gear with a suitable mandrel. Do not press on the roller cage.

7. If the forward gear internal needle bearing (12, **Figure 89**) was removed, install the new bearing as follows:

   a. Position the forward gear in a press with the gear teeth facing down.

   b. Lubricate the new needle bearings. Position the bearing into the gear bore with the numbered side facing up.

   c. Press the bearing into the gear using the long-stepped side of the bearing installer (part No. 91-86943 or an equivalent) until the tool seats against the gear hub face. Install the snap ring into the groove in the needle bearing bore (if so equipped).

Propeller shaft bearing carrier assembly

1. Set the carrier in a press with the propeller end facing up.

2. Lubricate a new propeller shaft needle bearing and position it into the carrier bore with the lettered end facing up.

3. Press the bearing into the carrier bore with a mandrel (part No. 91-15755 or an equivalent). See **Figure 113**. Press the bearing into the carrier until the tool or bearing seats (whichever happens first). Do not over-press the bearing.

4. If the reverse gear was removed from the bearing carrier and/or if the ball bearing was removed from the reverse gear, proceed as follows:

   a. To install a new bearing to the reverse gear, lubricate the bearing and the reverse gear hub. Then set the gear into a press with the gear teeth facing down.

   b. Position the thrust washer over the gear hub with the larger diameter side of the washer facing toward the gear.

   c. Set the bearing on the gear hub with the numbered side facing up. Press the bearing onto the gear with a

9

suitable mandrel until the bearing is fully seated on the gear. See **Figure 114**. Press only on the bearing's inner race.

d. Lubricate the bearing carrier's reverse gear bearing bore and place the carrier over the reverse gear and ball bearing assembly. See **Figure 115**. Press against the propeller end of the carrier until the ball bearing is seated in the carrier bore.

Propeller shaft assembly

The gearcase uses one cross pin retaining spring and one detent pin. The actuating rod is solid and does not have a spring, washer and pin.

1. Lubricate all components with Quicksilver 2-4-C Multi-Lube grease (part No. 92-825407).

2. Align the cross pin holes of the sliding clutch with the slot in the propeller shaft and align the detent pin hole with the detent notch in the propeller shaft splines. Position the grooved end of the sliding clutch towards the propeller and slide it onto the propeller shaft. See **Figure 116**.

3. Connect the clutch actuator rod to the shift cam follower. Then insert the actuator rod into the propeller shaft bore.

> *NOTE*
> *The sliding clutch retaining spring must lay flat, with no overlapping coils.*

4. Align the actuator rod's cross pin bore with the cross pin holes in the sliding clutch and with the slot in the propeller shaft. See **Figure 117**. Use a small punch to help with alignment.

5. Insert the cross pin through the sliding clutch *and* actuator rod.

6. Install the detent pin (1, **Figure 117**) into the sliding clutch bore. Make sure the bore has been aligned with the notch in the shaft splines. Use Quicksilver Needle Bearing Assembly Grease (part No. 92-825265A 1) to hold the detent in position.

> *NOTE*
> *The sliding clutch retaining spring must lay flat, with no overlapping coils.*

7. Secure the cross pin and detent pin to the sliding clutch with a new retainer spring. Do not open the spring any more than necessary to install it.

Assembly

1. Assemble the shift shaft components as follows:

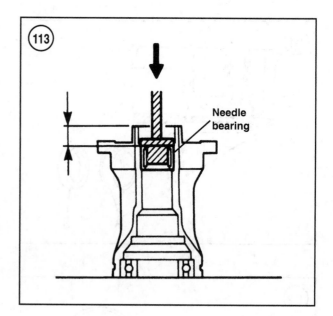

113

Needle bearing

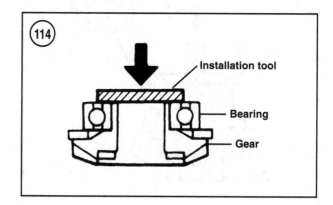

114

Installation tool

Bearing

Gear

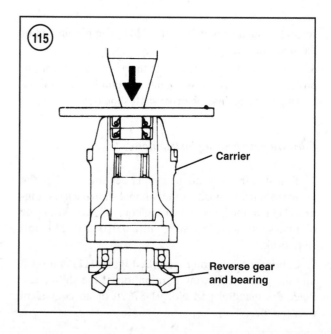

115

Carrier

Reverse gear and bearing

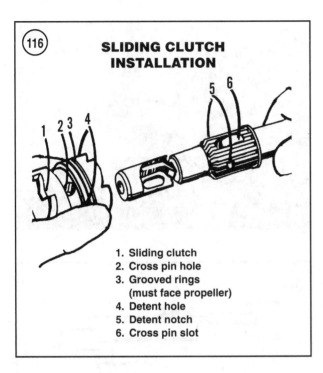

116

SLIDING CLUTCH INSTALLATION

1. Sliding clutch
2. Cross pin hole
3. Grooved rings
   (must face propeller)
4. Detent hole
5. Detent notch
6. Cross pin slot

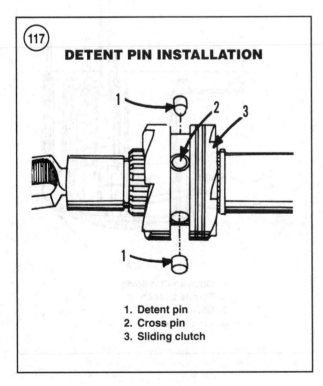

117

DETENT PIN INSTALLATION

1. Detent pin
2. Cross pin
3. Sliding clutch

a. Coat the outer diameter of a new shift shaft seal with Loctite 271 threadlocking adhesive (part No. 92-809819).

b. Press the seal into the shift shaft bushing with the lip side facing up using a suitable mandrel.

118

c. Coat the shift shaft and a new bushing O-ring with Quicksilver 2-4-C Multi-Lube grease (part No. 92-825407).

d. Carefully insert the shift shaft through the bushing. Be careful not to damage the seal with the shaft splines.

e. Install the E-clip into the shift shaft groove, on models so equipped. Then install the washer over the shift shaft and against the shift shaft seal.

2. If the 18 loose rollers are not installed into the lower drive shaft needle bearing, coat the rollers with Quicksilver Needle Bearing Assembly Grease (part No. 92-825265A 1) and install them into the bearing race.

3. Rotate the gearcase so the propeller shaft bore is pointing up. Install the forward gear assembly into the propeller shaft bore and into the forward gear bearing race.

4. Position the pinion gear over the lower drive shaft needle bearing.

5. Install the original shim(s) into the drive shaft bore (**Figure 98**). If the shims are lost or damaged, use an initial shim pack thickness of 0.010 in. (0.25 mm).

6. Spray the threads of the drive shaft with Locquic primer (part No. 92-809824). Insert the drive shaft into the drive shaft bore (**Figure 118**) while holding the pinion gear in position. Rotate the shaft as necessary to engage the drive shaft splines to the pinion gear splines.

NOTE
*Apply Loctite 271 threadlocking adhesive to a **new** pinion nut **after** the pinion gear depth and forward gear lash have been verified. Install the old pinion nut without sealant to check the gear depth and forward gear lash.*

7. Install the pinion nut washer, then install the original pinion nut with its flat side facing *away* from the pinion gear. Tighten the nut finger-tight at this time.

9

8. Install the drive shaft roller bearing race (**Figure 119**). Lubricate the threads of the drive shaft bearing retainer with Quicksilver Special Lubricant 101 (part No. 92-13872A 1), then thread the retainer into the bore. The *OFF* mark must face up.

9. Use the retainer tool (part No. 91-43506) to tighten the bearing retainer to the specification in **Table 1**.

10. Hold the pinion nut with a suitable wrench or socket. Attach the spline socket (part No. 91-90094 or an equivalent) to a suitable torque wrench. Tighten the pinion gear nut to the specification in **Table 1**. See **Figure 120**, typical.

11. Refer to *Gearcase Shimming* to set the pinion gear depth. Do not continue until the pinion gear depth is correct.

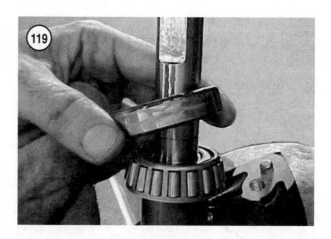

> *NOTE*
> *Do not install the shift shaft assembly and shift cam until the gear lash is correct.*

12. Once the pinion gear depth is correct, install the propeller shaft assembly into the gearcase and into the forward gear internal needle bearing(s). Do not install the shift cam at this time.

13. Liberally coat both flanges of the propeller shaft bearing carrier with Quicksilver Special Lubricant 101.

14. Align the alignment key slots (if so equipped) in the bearing carrier and gearcase, then install the carrier over the propeller shaft. Be careful not to damage the propeller shaft seals. Rotate the drive shaft as necessary to ensure the pinion and reverse gears mesh.

15. Push the bearing carrier into the gearcase as far as possible by hand.

   a. *Models with an alignment key*—Install the alignment key into the carrier and gearcase slots. Drive the key in with a suitable punch until it is flush with the carrier. See **Figure 121**.

   b. *Models without an alignment key*—Rotate the carrier to align the V-notch to the top side. The V-notch must align with the opening in the retainer threads.

16. Install a new tab washer into the gearcase bore and against the rear of the bearing carrier.

17. Liberally apply Quicksilver Special Lubricant 101 to the carrier retaining ring. Then install the retaining ring with the OFF mark facing out. Screw the ring into the gearcase as far as possible by hand.

18. Tighten the bearing carrier to the specification in **Table 1** using spanner wrench part No. 91-61069. See **Figure 91**.

19. Refer to *Gearcase Shimming* in this chapter to set the forward gear lash. Do not continue until the forward gear lash is correct.

20. Once the forward gear lash is correct, remove the propeller shaft bearing carrier and propeller shaft, and install

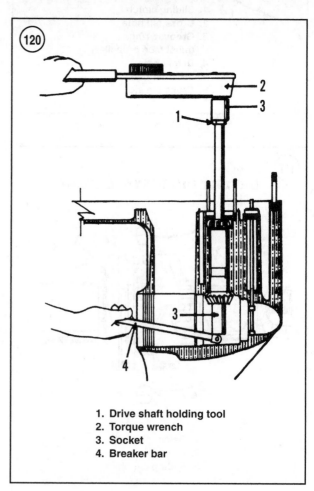

1. **Drive shaft holding tool**
2. **Torque wrench**
3. **Socket**
4. **Breaker bar**

a *new* pinion nut with Loctite 271 threadlocking adhesive as described previously in this section.

21. Install the shift shaft assembly, shift cam and propeller shaft as follows:

   a. Fill the shift cam follower pocket with Quicksilver 2-4-C Multi-Lube grease. See 1, **Figure 122**.

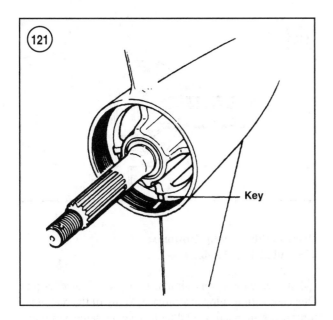

121

Key

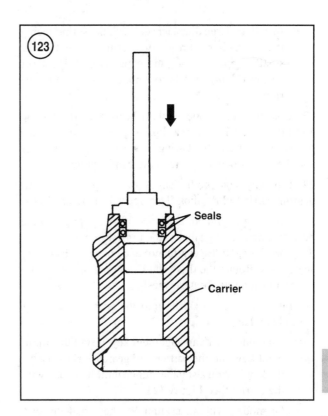

123

Seals

Carrier

9

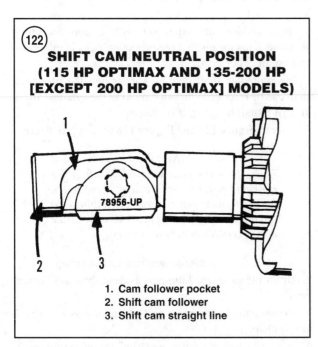

122

**SHIFT CAM NEUTRAL POSITION
(115 HP OPTIMAX AND 135-200 HP
[EXCEPT 200 HP OPTIMAX] MODELS)**

1

78956-UP

2   3

1. Cam follower pocket
2. Shift cam follower
3. Shift cam straight line

b. Place the shift cam into the cam follower cavity. Make sure the numbered side of the cam is facing up and the straight edge of the shift cam is parallel to the cam follower as shown in **Figure 122**.

CAUTION
Position the shift cam in neutral as shown in Figure 122 for propeller shaft installation.

c. Install the propeller shaft assembly into the gearcase, inserting the shift cam follower into the forward gear until the shaft is fully seated. Make sure the shift cam did not fall out of the follower.

CAUTION
Do not apply side (radial) load to the propeller shaft until the propeller shaft bearing carrier is installed. The neck of the clutch actuator rod can be easily broken by side-to-side or up-and-down propeller shaft movement.

d. Coat the shift bushing threads with Quicksilver Special Lubricant 101. Install the shift shaft assembly into the gearcase and engage the shift cam splines. If necessary, rotate the shift shaft back and forth slightly to engage the shift cam splines.

e. Tighten the shift shaft bushing finger-tight at this time.

22. Install two new propeller shaft seals as follows:

a. Coat the outer diameter of two new propeller shaft seals with Loctite 271 threadlocking adhesive.

b. Set the carrier in a press with the propeller end facing up. See **Figure 123**.

c. Install the small diameter seal with the spring facing the gearcase. Press the seal in with the large-stepped end of mandrel part No. 91-31108 (or an equivalent) until the tool bottoms against the carrier.

d. Install the large diameter seal with the spring facing the propeller. Press the seal in with the small-stepped end of mandrel part No. 91-31108 (or an equivalent) until the tool bottoms against the carrier.

23. Coat the new propeller shaft bearing carrier O-ring and the propeller shaft seal lips with 2-4-C Multi-Lube grease. Then install the O-ring between the thrust washer and the carrier beveled edge in the carrier groove.

24. Liberally coat both flanges of the propeller shaft bearing carrier with Quicksilver Special Lubricant 101.

25. Align the alignment key slots (if so equipped) in the bearing carrier and gearcase, then install the carrier over the propeller shaft. Be careful not to damage the propeller shaft seals. Rotate the drive shaft as necessary to ensure the pinion and reverse gears mesh.

26. Push the bearing carrier into the gearcase as far as possible by hand.

a. On models with an alignment key, install the alignment key into the carrier and gearcase slots. Drive the key in with a suitable punch until it is flush with the carrier. See **Figure 121**.

b. On models without an alignment key, rotate the carrier to align the V-notch to the top side. The V-notch must align with the opening in the retainer threads.

27. Install the tab washer into the gearcase bore and against the rear of the bearing carrier.

28. Liberally apply Quicksilver Special Lubricant 101 to the carrier retaining ring. Then install the retaining ring with the OFF mark facing out. Screw the ring into the gearcase as far as possible by hand.

29. Tighten the retaining ring to the specification in **Table 1** using spanner wrench part No. 91-61069.

30. Determine which locking tab (**Figure 124**, typical) aligns with a slot in the retaining ring. Bend the tab over firmly into the retaining ring slot. Then bend all remaining tabs forward.

31. Use bushing tool part No. 91-31107 or an equivalent to tighten the shift shaft bushing to the specification in **Table 1**.

32. Refer to *Gearcase Shimming* in this chapter to check the reverse gear lash.

33. Install the water pump base and water pump assembly as described previously in this chapter.

34. Pressure test the gearcase as described in *Gearcase Pressure Testing*.

35. Fill the gearcase with the recommended lubricant as described in Chapter Four.

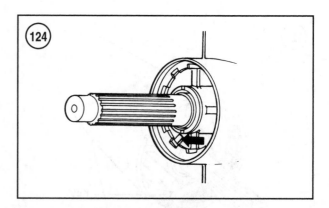

Disassembly (200 hp Optimax, 225 and 250 hp Models)

This gearcase is very similar to the MerCruiser Alpha One Generation II lower gearcase. Many of the manufacturer recommended special tools have the same part number.

These models are equipped with a non-ratcheting gearcase. This means that the propeller locks in either direction, in either gear.

The propeller shaft bearing carrier and the propeller shaft can be removed without removing the gearcase from the drive shaft housing, if so desired.

Refer to **Figure 125** and **Figure 126** for this procedure.

NOTE
If the forward gear or drive shaft roller bearings require replacement, replace the bearing rollers and races as assemblies. Do not remove a pressed in bearing and/or race unless replacement is necessary.

1. Remove the gearcase as described in this chapter.

2. Drain the gearcase lubricant as described in Chapter Four.

3. Remove the water pump and pump base as described in this chapter.

4. Bend the locking tab away from the propeller shaft bearing carrier retaining ring with a suitable punch and hammer. See **Figure 127**, typical.

NOTE
If the retaining ring is frozen in place and cannot be removed in the next step, apply penetrating oil and mild heat with an electric heat gun, heat lamp or propane torch. If removal is still difficult, drill through the ring in several places parallel to the propeller shaft and break the ring into several pieces with a suitable chisel and hammer.

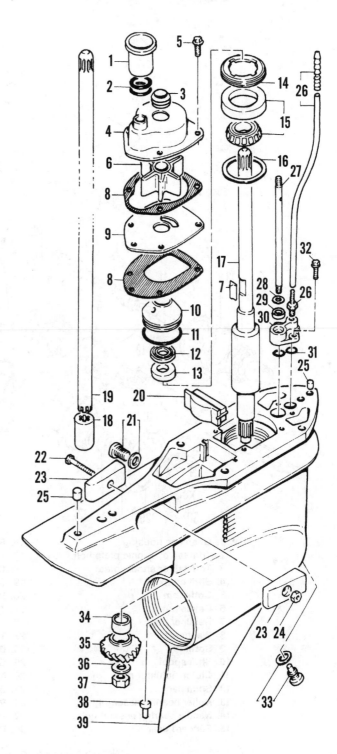

**DRIVE SHAFT AND WATER PUMP COMPONENTS
(200 HP OPTIMAX, 225 HP AND 250 HP MODELS)**

1. Water tube guide
2. O-rings
3. Centrifugal slinger seal
4. Pump housing
5. Screw
6. Impeller
7. Impeller key
8. Gaskets
9. Plate
10. Seal carrier
11. O-ring
12. Upper drive shaft seal
13. Lower drive shaft seal
14. Drive shaft bearing retainer
15. Roller bearing assembly
16. Shim pack
17. Drive shaft
18. Drive shaft coupler*
19. Upper drive shaft*
20. Water dam seal
21. Vent plug and seal
22. Screw
23. Anodes
24. Locknut
25. Dowel pins
26. Speedometer tube and fittings
27. Shift shaft
28. Washer
29. Shift shaft seal
30. Shift shaft retainer/bushing
31. O-rings
32. Retainer screw
33. Drain/fill plug and sealing washer
34. Lower drive shaft roller bearing
35. Pinion gear
36. Washer
37. Pinion nut
38. Pivot pin
39. Gearcase housing

*Not used on all models

9

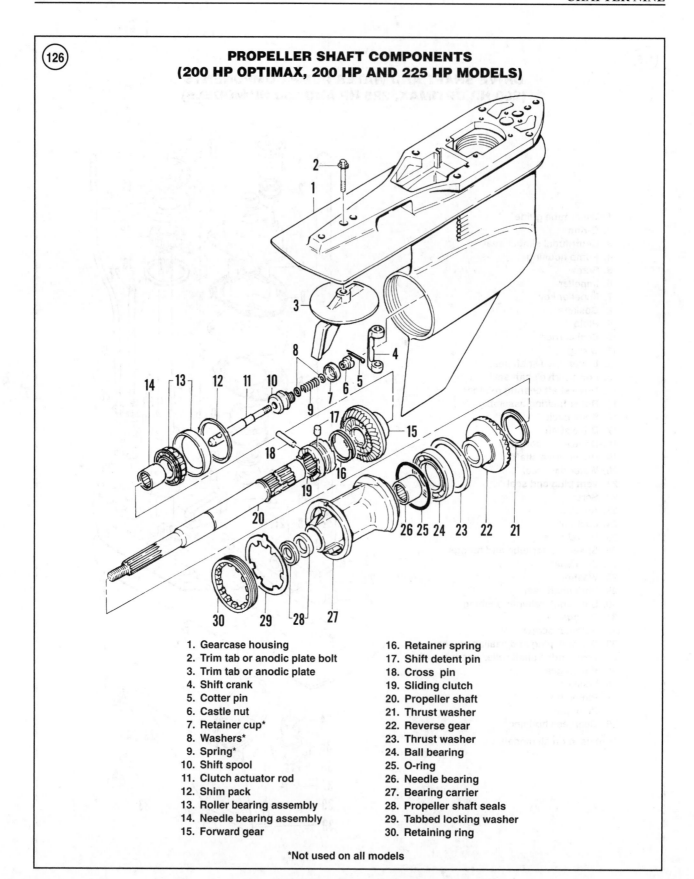

**PROPELLER SHAFT COMPONENTS
(200 HP OPTIMAX, 200 HP AND 225 HP MODELS)**

1. Gearcase housing
2. Trim tab or anodic plate bolt
3. Trim tab or anodic plate
4. Shift crank
5. Cotter pin
6. Castle nut
7. Retainer cup*
8. Washers*
9. Spring*
10. Shift spool
11. Clutch actuator rod
12. Shim pack
13. Roller bearing assembly
14. Needle bearing assembly
15. Forward gear
16. Retainer spring
17. Shift detent pin
18. Cross pin
19. Sliding clutch
20. Propeller shaft
21. Thrust washer
22. Reverse gear
23. Thrust washer
24. Ball bearing
25. O-ring
26. Needle bearing
27. Bearing carrier
28. Propeller shaft seals
29. Tabbed locking washer
30. Retaining ring

*Not used on all models

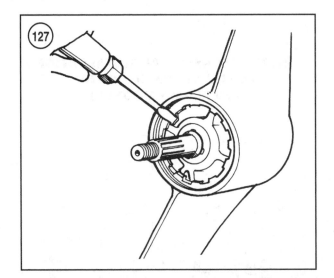

Do not drill into the gearcase threads or into the bearing carrier.

5. Remove the retaining ring using spanner wrench part No. 91-61069 or an equivalent. See **Figure 128**. Turn the ring counterclockwise until it is free from the gearcase

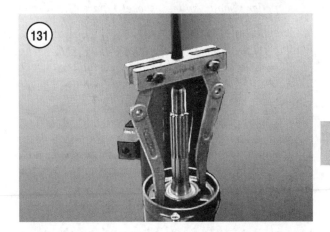

(**Figure 129**). If the ring is corroded or damaged, discard it. Then remove the locking tab washer (**Figure 130**).

6. Install puller jaws (part No. 91-46086A-1) and puller bolt (part No. 91-85716) or an equivalent and pull the bearing carrier and reverse gear assembly from the gearcase. See **Figure 131**. Position the puller jaws as close to the carrier bosses as possible. Remove and discard the carrier O-ring (25, **Figure 126**).

7. Reach into the propeller shaft bore and remove the reverse gear thrust washer (21, **Figure 126**) by sliding it off of the propeller shaft.

NOTE
If the needle bearing inside the bearing carrier requires replacement, remove the propeller shaft seals during the bearing removal process. If bearing replacement is not required, remove and discard both propeller shaft seals at this time with a suitable seal puller. Do not damage the seal bore in the process.

8. Install the drive shaft upper bearing retainer tool (part No. 91-43506) over the drive shaft and engage the retainer

lugs, but do not loosen or remove the retainer at this time. See **Figure 132**.

9. Install the drive shaft splined adapter (part No. 91-56775 or an equivalent) onto the drive shaft splines.

10. Insert the pinion nut tool (part No. 91-61067A-2 or an equivalent) over the propeller shaft and engage the *MR* slot to the pinion nut. If necessary, loosen the drive shaft retainer up to two full turns with part No. 91-43506 to allow the drive shaft to be raised high enough for the tool to engage the pinion nut. See **Figure 132**.

> *NOTE*
> *If the drive shaft is broken, install the propeller shaft spline socket (part No. 91-61077), which is included with pinion nut tool (part No. 91-61067A-2) (**Figure 133**), onto the propeller shaft splines. Shift the gearcase into FORWARD gear and rotate the propeller shaft 1/2 turn counterclockwise to loosen the pinion nut. Remove the drive shaft retaining nut before completely unthreading the pinion nut.*

11. Install the propeller shaft bearing carrier *backwards* over the propeller shaft into the gearcase bore and over the end of the pinion nut tool to stabilize the tool. Only the rear flange of the carrier will fit into the gearcase bore. See **Figure 132**.

12. Loosen the pinion nut by turning the drive shaft one full turn counterclockwise. Then completely unscrew the drive shaft bearing retainer with the previously installed retainer tool (part No. 91-43506 or an equivalent).

13. Remove the pinion nut by turning the drive shaft counterclockwise until the nut is free from the shaft. Then remove all tools.

> *NOTE*
> *The lower drive shaft bearing contains 18 loose rollers that may fall out during drive shaft removal. Retrieve all rollers from the housing.*

14. Lift the drive shaft straight up and out of the drive shaft bore (**Figure 118**). Remove the shim(s) from the drive shaft bearing bore (**Figure 134**). Measure and record the thickness of the shim(s) for later reference. Tag the shim(s) for identification during reassembly. Discard the race if the roller bearing assembly is being replaced.

15. Remove the pinion nut, washer and pinion gear by moving the rear of the propeller shaft to the lower port area of the propeller shaft bore and allow the components to fall into the propeller shaft bore from the drive shaft bore. Then remove the 18 loose bearing rollers from the drive shaft lower bearing race or propeller shaft bore.

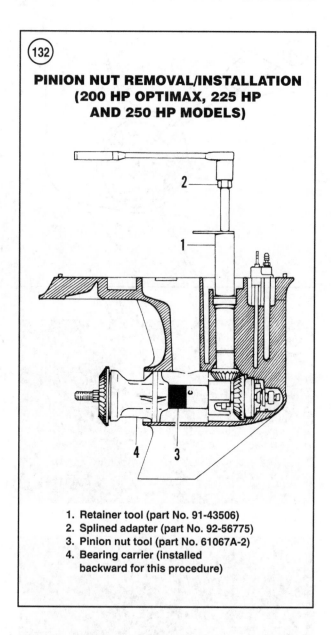

(132)

PINION NUT REMOVAL/INSTALLATION (200 HP OPTIMAX, 225 HP AND 250 HP MODELS)

1. Retainer tool (part No. 91-43506)
2. Splined adapter (part No. 92-56775)
3. Pinion nut tool (part No. 61067A-2)
4. Bearing carrier (installed backward for this procedure)

16. Remove the propeller shaft and forward gear assembly by moving the rear of the propeller shaft to the port side of the propeller shaft bore to disengage the shift crank from the shift spool. It may be necessary to rotate the shift shaft slightly while holding the shaft to port and pulling it rearward.

17. Remove the shift mechanism as follows:

  a. Remove the two screws securing the shift shaft retainer/bushing (30, **Figure 125**) to the gearcase. Carefully pry the shift shaft retainer from the gearcase, then remove the shift assembly from the gearcase.

  b. Pull the shift shaft from the shift shaft retainer. Locate and secure the washer (28, **Figure 125**).

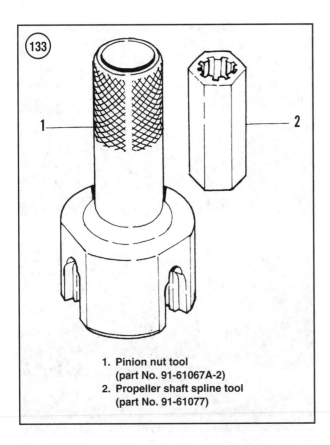

1. **Pinion nut tool**
   (part No. 91-61067A-2)
2. **Propeller shaft spline tool**
   (part No. 91-61077)

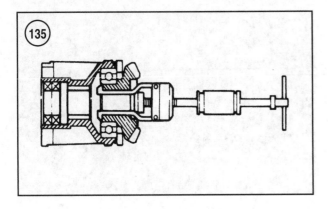

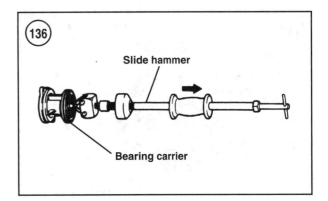

c. Remove and discard the two O-rings from the gearcase deck or shift shaft retainer.

d. Remove and discard the shift shaft seal from the shift shaft retainer.

e. Remove the shift crank (4, **Figure 126**) from the front of the gearcase bore. Lift the crank off of the lower pivot pin. Remove the crank from the gearcase.

Propeller shaft bearing carrier disassembly

The reverse gear rides on a ball bearing pressed into the carrier. The propeller shaft has a needle bearing located near the propeller shaft seals. Remove the reverse gear to service the propeller shaft needle bearing. Remove the reverse gear and bearing, and the propeller shaft needle bearing and seals as follows:

1. Clamp the carrier in a vise with protective jaws or between two blocks of wood.

2. Pull the reverse gear assembly from the bearing carrier with a suitable slide hammer, such as part No. 91-34569A-1. See **Figure 135**.

3A. If the ball bearing remains in the carrier, pull the bearing from the carrier with the slide hammer (**Figure 136**).

3B. If the ball bearing remains on the reverse gear, remove the bearing as follows:

a. Support the ball bearing in a suitable knife-edged bearing separator, such as part No. 91-37241.

b. Press against the gear hub with a suitable mandrel until the bearing is free from the gear. See **Figure 137**.

c. Remove the thrust washer from the reverse gear or bearing carrier.

d. Discard the bearing.

4. If the propeller shaft needle bearing must be replaced, replace it as follows:

a. Set the carrier in a press with the propeller end facing down.

9

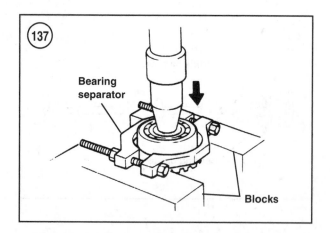

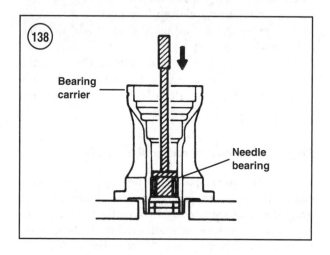

b. Press the bearing and seals from the carrier with a mandrel (part No. 91-36569) and driver rod (part No. 91-37323) or an equivalent. See **Figure 138**.

c. Discard the bearing and seals.

Propeller shaft disassembly

1. Insert a thin-blade screwdriver or similar tool under the retaining spring. Lift the coil up and rotate the propeller shaft to unwind the spring from the sliding clutch (**Figure 139**).

2. Remove the single detent pin from the sliding clutch. Then push the cross pin through the clutch and propeller shaft. See **Figure 140**.

3. Pull the shift spool and clutch actuator rod straight out of the propeller shaft. See **Figure 141**.

4. Slide the forward gear and bearing assembly off the propeller shaft. See **Figure 142**.

5. Slide the sliding clutch off the propeller shaft splines. See **Figure 143**.

6. Disassemble the shift spool and actuator rod as follows:

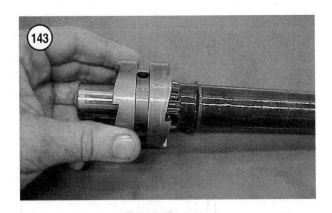

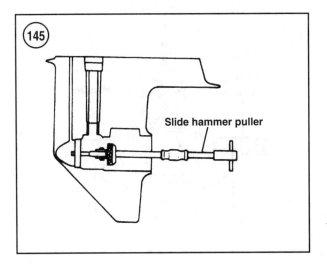

Slide hammer puller

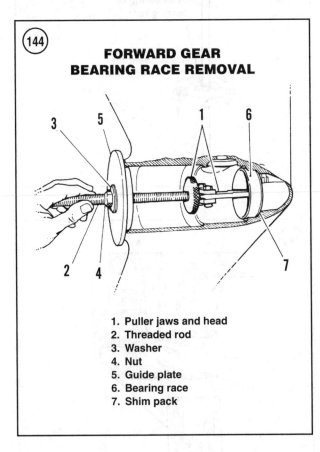

**FORWARD GEAR
BEARING RACE REMOVAL**

1. Puller jaws and head
2. Threaded rod
3. Washer
4. Nut
5. Guide plate
6. Bearing race
7. Shim pack

a. Remove the cotter pin (5, **Figure 126**) from the castle nut (6).

b. Unthread the castle nut from the actuator rod.

c. Slide the shift spool from the rod.

Forward gear bearing removal

If the forward gear bearing race must be removed to adjust forward gear lash, or if the roller bearing assembly or internal needle bearing(s) must be replaced, proceed as follows:

NOTE
If the forward gear bearing race was only removed so the shim pack and forward gear lash could be changed, do not discard the bearing race.

1. To remove the forward gear bearing race from the gearcase, pull the race from the front of the propeller shaft bore as shown in **Figure 144**, using the following tools:
   a. The puller head and jaws from slide hammer part No. 91-34569A-1 (or an equivalent).
   b. Puller shaft part No. 91-3229 or a suitable 5/8 in. fine-threaded rod.
   c. Washer part No. 11-24156 or a suitable 5/8 in. flat washer.
   d. Guide plate part No. 91816243 or an equivalent.

A suitable slide hammer, such as part No. 91-34569A-1, may be used, but the race must be pulled straight from its bore. See **Figure 145**.

2. Remove the shim(s) from the bearing bore. Measure and record the thickness of the shims for later reference. Tag the shim(s) for identification during reassembly. Discard the race if the roller bearing assembly is being replaced.

NOTE
In Step 3, it may be necessary to cut the roller cage from the bearing and grind a groove in the inner race to provide a lip for the knife-edged bearing separator.

3. To remove the roller bearing from the forward gear, support the bearing with a knife-edged bearing separator, such as part No. 91-37241. Press on the gear hub with a

9

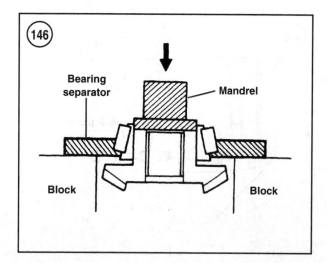

suitable mandrel until the bearing is free from the gear. See **Figure 146**. Discard the roller bearing.

4. To remove the internal needle bearing, clamp the gear in a vise with protective jaws. The gear engagement lugs must face up. Remove the snap ring (if so equipped) from the needle bearing bore. Drive the internal needle bearing from the gear with a suitable punch and hammer. Discard the bearing.

Drive shaft bearing removal

A loose roller bearing supports the lower portion (pinion gear end) of the drive shaft and a single, tapered roller bearing supports the upper portion of the drive shaft. The shims under the tapered roller bearing race control the pinion gear depth.

1. Remove the drive shaft tapered roller bearing as follows:

   a. Support the drive shaft in a knife-edged bearing separator, such as part No. 91-37241, clamped in a vise. See **Figure 147**. Position the drive shaft with the crankshaft end facing up. Open the separator enough to contact the inner bearing race without contacting the drive shaft surfaces.

   b. Press against the crankshaft end of the shaft until the bearing is free from the shaft.

   c. Discard the roller bearing and its race.

NOTE
The drive shaft lower bearing contains 18 loose bearing rollers that may fall out of the race during drive shaft removal. Reinstall the loose bearing rollers into the outer race to provide a surface for the removal tool to push against.

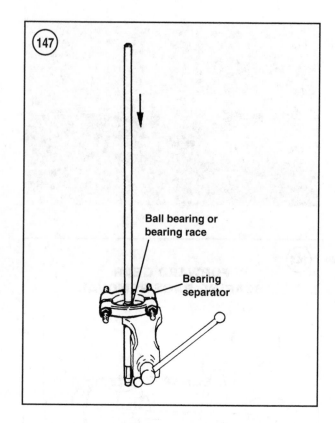

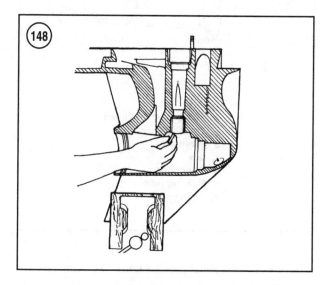

2. Remove the loose needle bearing at the bottom of the drive shaft bore as follows:

   a. Install the 18 loose bearing rollers into the lower bearing race (**Figure 148**). Use a suitable grease, such as Quicksilver Needle Bearing Assembly Grease to hold the rollers in place.

   b. Use mandrel (part No. 91-36569), pilot (part No. 91-36571) and driver rod (part No. 91-37323) or an

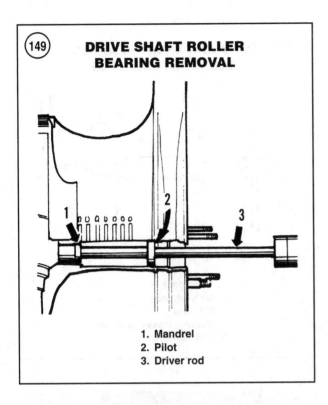

DRIVE SHAFT ROLLER BEARING REMOVAL

1. Mandrel
2. Pilot
3. Driver rod

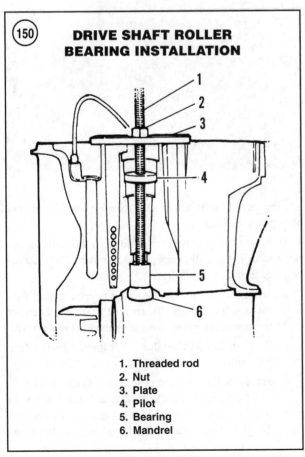

DRIVE SHAFT ROLLER BEARING INSTALLATION

1. Threaded rod
2. Nut
3. Plate
4. Pilot
5. Bearing
6. Mandrel

equivalent assembled as shown in **Figure 149**, typical to drive the bearing into the gear cavity.

c. Remove and discard the bearing. Locate all loose bearing rollers.

CAUTION
If the drive shaft lower bearing has failed, causing the bearing outer race to spin inside the housing, replace the gearcase housing. Using a new bearing in a damaged housing will result in bearing and/or gear failure.

Assembly (200 hp Optimax, 225 hp and 250 hp Models)

If the drive shaft bearings, forward gear bearing, reverse gear or propeller shaft bearings were removed, or if the propeller shaft was disassembled, install new bearings or reassemble the propeller shaft as described in the following sections. Then proceed to *Assembly*.

Lubricate all internal components with Quicksilver Premium Blend gear oil or an equivalent. Do not assemble components *dry*. Refer to **Table 1** for torque specifications. Refer to **Figure 125** and **Figure 126** as appropriate for this procedure.

Drive shaft bearing installation

1. To install a new roller bearing at the bottom of the drive shaft bore, lubricate a new bearing with Quicksilver Needle Bearing Assembly Grease (part No. 92-825265A-1). Install all 18 roller bearings (**Figure 148**).

2. Assemble the bearing installer components as shown in **Figure 150**. The numbered side of the bearing must face up, away from the pinion gear when installed. Use mandrel (part No. 91-38628), pilot (part No. 91-36571), plate (part No. 91-29310) and threaded rod (part No. 91-31229) or an equivalent.

3. Pull the bearing into the drive shaft bore by turning the nut (2, **Figure 150**) until the bearing seats in the drive shaft bore. Do not apply excessive force to the bearing.

4. To install the new roller bearing(s) onto the drive shaft, lubricate the bearing(s) and applicable area on the drive shaft with Quicksilver Needle Bearing Assembly Grease.

5. Slide the bearing over the drive shaft splines. The rollers must face the power head away from the pinion gear. Support the bearing's inner race with a suitable round mandrel, such as a scrap drive shaft roller bearing inner race. Place the assembly in a press with the mandrel or scrap bearing race supported by a knife-edged bearing

9

separator, such as part No. 91-37241. The pinion end of the shaft must face up.

6. Thread an old pinion nut onto the drive shaft threads to protect the threads. Press against the pinion nut until the bearing seats against the drive shaft shoulder.

Forward gear bearing installation

1. To install the forward gear roller bearing race into the gearcase housing, position the original shim(s) into the housing bearing bore. If the original shims were lost or damaged beyond measurement, start with a 0.020 in. (0.51 mm) shim(s).

2. Lubricate the bearing race and set it into the gearcase bearing bore on top of the shim(s). Place the mandrel (part No. 91-31106) or an equivalent over the race.

NOTE
Be careful to prevent cocking the bearing race in the gearcase bore.

3. Thread the bearing cup installation tool (part No. 91-18605A-1) or an equivalent into the propeller shaft bore until its threads are fully engaged in the retaining ring threads as shown in **Figure 151**. Tighten the hex head screw (5, **Figure 151**) to press the bearing into its bore. Make sure the bearing is fully seated.

4. Remove the installation tool and mandrel.

5. If the forward gear roller bearing was removed, lubricate a new roller bearing and set it on the gear hub with the rollers facing up. Press the bearing fully onto the gear using a suitable mandrel (**Figure 152**). Do not press on the roller cage.

6. If the forward gear internal needle bearing was removed, install a new bearing as follows:
   a. Position the forward gear in a press with the gear teeth facing down.
   b. Lubricate the new needle bearing and position it in the gear bore with the numbered side facing up.
   c. Press the bearing into the gear with a suitable mandrel until the bearing is seated in the gear bore. Do not over-press the bearing.
   d. Install the snap ring (if so equipped) into the groove in the needle bearing bore.

Propeller shaft bearing carrier assembly

1. Set the carrier in a press with the propeller end facing up.
2. Lubricate a new propeller shaft needle bearing and position it into the carrier bore with the lettered end facing up.
3. Press the bearing into the carrier bore with mandrel (part No. 91-15755) or an equivalent. Press the bearing

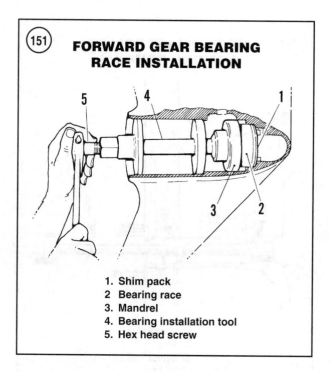

FORWARD GEAR BEARING RACE INSTALLATION

1. Shim pack
2. Bearing race
3. Mandrel
4. Bearing installation tool
5. Hex head screw

into the carrier until the tool seats. See **Figure 153**. Do not over-press the bearing.

4. If the reverse gear was removed from the bearing carrier and/or if the ball bearing was removed from the reverse gear, proceed as follows:
   a. To install a new bearing to the reverse gear, lubricate the bearing and the reverse gear hub. Then set the gear into a press with the gear teeth facing down.
   b. Position the thrust washer (23, **Figure 126**) over the gear hub.
   c. Set the bearing on the gear hub with the numbered side facing up. Press the bearing onto the gear with a suitable mandrel until the bearing is fully seated on the gear. See **Figure 154**. Press only on the bearing's inner race.

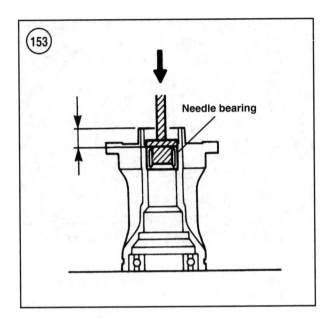

Needle bearing

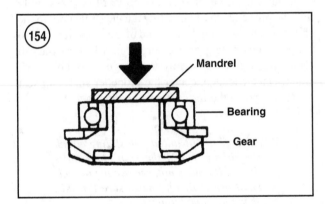

Mandrel

Bearing

Gear

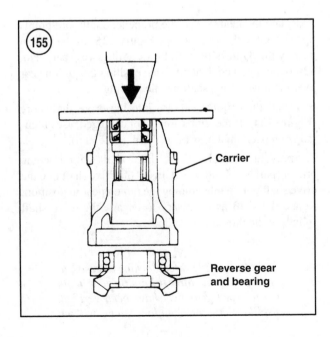

Carrier

Reverse gear
and bearing

d. Lubricate the bearing carrier's reverse gear bearing bore and place the carrier over the reverse gear and ball bearing assembly. Press against the propeller end of the carrier until the ball bearing is seated in the carrier bore. See **Figure 155**.

Propeller shaft assembly

The shift spool is secured by a castle nut and cotter pin. Adjust the castle nut to provide 0.002-0.010 in. (0.051-0.254 mm) end play between the shift spool and the actuator rod.

1. Lubricate all components with Quicksilver 2-4-C Multi-Lube grease (part No. 92-825407).

2. Align the cross pin holes of the sliding clutch with the slot in the propeller shaft and align the detent pin hole(s) with the detent notch in the propeller shaft splines. Position the grooved end of the sliding clutch towards the propeller and slide it onto the propeller shaft (**Figure 143**).

3. Assemble the shift spool and actuator rod as follows:

   a. Install the shift spool over the actuator rod.

   b. Install the castle nut and tighten the nut until it is lightly seated.

   c. Back off the castle nut just enough to align a set of slots in the nut with the cotter pin bore.

   d. Measure the spool end play on the actuator shaft. Adjust the nut as necessary. The shift spool must have 0.002-0.010 in. (0.051-0.254 mm) of end play between the shift spool and the actuator rod.

   e. Install a new cotter pin. Bend both ends of the cotter pin to provide a secure attachment.

4. Slide the forward gear and bearing assembly over the propeller shaft (**Figure 142**). Then insert the actuator rod and spool assembly into the propeller shaft bore (**Figure 141**).

5. Install the cross pin as follows:

   a. Align the actuator rod's cross pin bore with the cross pin holes in the sliding clutch and with the slot in the propeller shaft. Use a small punch to help with alignment.

   b. Insert the cross pin through the sliding clutch *and* actuator rod (**Figure 140**).

   c. Install the shift detent pin (17, **Figure 126**) into the sliding clutch bore. Make sure the bore is aligned with the notch in the shaft splines. Use Quicksilver Needle Bearing Assembly Grease (part No. 92-825265A-1) to hold the detent in position.

NOTE
The sliding clutch retaining spring must lay flat, with no overlapping coils.

d. Secure the cross pin and detent pin to the sliding clutch with the retainer spring. See **Figure 139**. Do not open the spring any more than necessary to install it.

Assembly

1. Assemble the shift shaft components as follows:
   a. Coat the outer diameter of a new shift shaft seal with Loctite 271 threadlocking adhesive (part No. 92-809819).
   b. Press the seal into the shift shaft retainer/bushing with the lip side facing up using a suitable mandrel.
   c. Coat the shift shaft and two new bushing O-rings with Quicksilver 2-4-C Multi-Lube grease (part No. 92-825407). Position the O-rings on the shift shaft retainer.
   d. Carefully insert the shift shaft through the bushing. Be careful not to damage the seal with the shaft splines.
   e. Install the washer over the shift shaft and against the shift shaft seal.
2. Install the shift crank and shift shaft assembly as follows:
   a. Position the shift crank in the gearcase bore with the splined end facing up and the cranked end facing port. See **Figure 156**. The crank must be piloted on the lower pivot pin.
   b. Install the shift shaft assembly into the gearcase and engage the shift crank splines.
   c. Make sure the shift retainer O-rings are still in position, then seat the retainer to the gearcase deck.
   d. Install and tighten the two retainer screws (32, **Figure 125**) to the specification in **Table 1**. Make sure the shift shaft and crank pivot freely, and the shift crank is positioned to the port side of the gearcase.
   e. Position the washer (28, **Figure 125**) over the shift shaft seal.
3. If the 18 loose rollers are not installed into the lower drive shaft needle bearing, coat the rollers with Quicksilver Needle Bearing Assembly grease (part No. 92-825265A 1) and install them into the bearing race (**Figure 148**).

NOTE
If the pinion gear depth will be set using the universal shim tool (part No. 91-12349A-2), the propeller shaft cannot be installed. Go directly to Step 5. After setting the pinion gear depth, return to this point and install the propeller shaft assembly. If the pinion gear depth will be set using the MerCruiser

shim tool (part No. 91-56048), install the propeller shaft at this time.

4. Install the propeller shaft and forward gear assembly into the propeller shaft bore. Engage the shift spool to the shift crank by holding the rear end of the propeller shaft to the port side of the gearcase bore. It may be necessary to rotate the shift shaft slightly to engage the spool to the crank. Once engaged, center the propeller shaft and seat the shaft against the forward gear bearing race.

NOTE
When correctly installed, the sliding clutch moves forward when the shift shaft turns clockwise. If it does not, remove the propeller shaft assembly and make sure the shift crank is positioned to port.

5. Rotate the gearcase so the propeller shaft bore points upward. Glue the washer (36, **Figure 125**) to the pinion gear with Quicksilver Bellows Adhesive (part No. 92-86166) or an equivalent. Then position the pinion gear over the lower drive shaft needle bearing.

6. Install the original shim(s) into the drive shaft bore (**Figure 134**). If the shims are lost or damaged, use an initial shim pack thickness of 0.038 in. (0.97 mm).

7. Spray the threads of the drive shaft with Locquic primer (part No. 92-809824). Insert the drive shaft into the drive shaft bore while holding the pinion gear in position. Rotate the shaft as necessary to engage the drive shaft splines to the pinion gear splines.

NOTE
*Apply Loctite 271 threadlocking adhesive to a **new** pinion nut **after** the pinion gear depth and forward gear lash have been verified. Install the old pinion nut without*

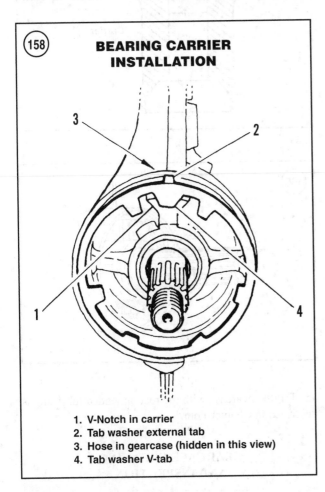

**BEARING CARRIER
INSTALLATION**

1. V-Notch in carrier
2. Tab washer external tab
3. Hose in gearcase (hidden in this view)
4. Tab washer V-tab

*threadlocking compound to check the gear
depth and forward gear lash.*

8. Position the pinion nut into the *MR* slot in the pinion
nut tool (part No. 91-61067A-02). Use a small amount of
grease to help hold the nut in position. Do not allow grease
to get on the threads.

9. Slide the pinion nut tool over the propeller shaft and
into position under the pinion gear. It may be necessary to
lift the drive shaft and pinion gear slightly to allow the
tool to pass under the gear and shaft.

10. Engage the pinion nut to the drive shaft by turning the
drive shaft clockwise until the nut is seated finger-tight.
Leave the pinion nut tool in position.

11. Install the drive shaft roller bearing race (**Figure
157**). Lubricate the threads of the drive shaft bearing retainer with Quicksilver Special Lubricant 101 (part No.
92-13872A 1), then install the retainer with the *OFF* mark
facing up. Thread the retainer in hand-tight at this time.

12. Use retainer tool (part No. 91-43506) to tighten the
bearing retainer to the specification in **Table 1**. See 1, **Figure 132**.

13. Install the propeller shaft bearing carrier *backward* as
shown in **Figure 132** to support the pinion nut tool.

14. Attach the spline socket part No. 91-56775 or an
equivalent to a suitable torque wrench. Tighten the pinion
gear nut to the specification in **Table 1**. See **Figure 132**.
Remove all tools when finished.

15. Refer to *Gearcase Shimming* to set the pinion gear
depth. Do not continue until the pinion gear depth is correct.

16. Once the pinion gear depth is correct, install the propeller shaft assembly, if it is not already installed, as described previously in this section.

17. Liberally coat both flanges of the propeller shaft
bearing carrier with Quicksilver Special Lubricant 101.

18. Install the carrier over the propeller shaft. Make sure
the *V*-shaped notch (casting) in the carrier is facing up, directly under the hole in the propeller shaft bore as shown
in **Figure 158**. Then push the carrier into the gearcase until it is seated. Rotate the drive shaft as necessary to align
and mesh the reverse gear teeth.

19. Install the locking tab washer. Position the external
tab into the hole at the top of the propeller shaft bore.
Make sure the *V* notch on the tab washer fits into the *V*
notch on the bearing carrier. See **Figure 158**.

20. Liberally apply Quicksilver Special Lubricant 101 to
the carrier retaining ring. Then install the retaining ring
and screw the ring into the gearcase as far as possible by
hand.

21. Tighten the retaining ring to the specification in **Table 1** using spanner wrench part No. 91-61069.

22. Refer to *Gearcase Shimming* in this chapter to set the
forward gear lash. Do not continue until the forward gear
lash is correct.

23. Once the forward gear lash is correct, remove the propeller shaft bearing carrier and install a *new* pinion nut
with Loctite 271 threadlocking adhesive as described in
this section.

9

24. Install two new propeller shaft seals as follows:
   a. Coat the outer diameter of two new propeller shaft seals with Loctite 271 threadlocking adhesive.
   b. Set the carrier in a press with the propeller end facing up.
   c. Install the inner seal with the spring facing the gearcase. Press the seal in with the large stepped end of mandrel (part No. 91-31108 or an equivalent) until the tool bottoms against the carrier. See **Figure 159**.
   d. Install the outer seal with the spring facing the propeller. Press the seal in with the small stepped end of mandrel (part No. 91-31108 or an equivalent) until the tool bottoms against the carrier. See **Figure 159**.

25. Coat a new propeller shaft bearing carrier O-ring and the propeller shaft seal lips with 2-4-C Multi-Lube grease. Then install the O-ring between the thrust washer and the carrier beveled edge.

26. Liberally coat both flanges of the propeller shaft bearing carrier with Quicksilver Special Lubricant 101.

27. Install the carrier over the propeller shaft. Make sure the *V* notch (casting) in the carrier is facing up, directly under the hole in the propeller shaft bore as shown in **Figure 158**. Then push the carrier into the gearcase until it is seated. Rotate the drive shaft as necessary to align and mesh the gear teeth.

28. Install the locking tab washer. Position the external tab into the hole at the top of the propeller shaft bore. Make sure the *V* notch on the tab washer fits into the *V* notch on the bearing carrier. See **Figure 158**.

29. Liberally apply Quicksilver Special Lubricant 101 to the carrier retaining ring. Then install the retaining ring and screw the ring into the gearcase as far as possible by hand.

30. Tighten the retaining ring to the specification in **Table 1** using spanner wrench part No. 91-61069.

> *CAUTION*
> *If necessary, tighten the retaining ring to align a locking tab. Do not loosen the ring to align a locking tab.*

31. Determine which locking tab (**Figure 160**, typical) aligns with a slot in retaining ring. Bend the tab over firmly into the retaining ring slot. Then bend all remaining tabs forward.

32. Refer to *Gearcase Shimming* later in this chapter to check the reverse gear lash, if so desired.

33. Install the water pump assembly as described in this chapter.

34. Pressure test the gearcase as described in *Gearcase Pressure Testing*.

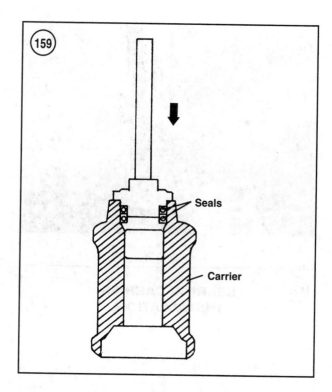

Seals

Carrier

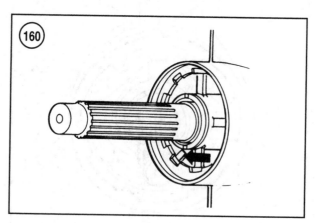

35. Fill the gearcase with the recommended lubricant as described in Chapter Four.

GEARCASE CLEANING AND INSPECTION

> *NOTE*
> *Do not remove pressed-on roller or ball bearings or pressed-in needle bearings, ball bearings or bushings unless replacement is necessary. A tapered roller bearing consists of the roller assembly and a bearing race. The roller and race are a matched assembly and must be replaced together.*

1. Discard all seals, gaskets and O-rings removed during disassembly.

2. Clean all parts in clean solvent and dry them with compressed air. Lightly lubricate all internal components to prevent rusting.

CAUTION
Metric and American fasteners are used on Mercury/Mariner gearcases. Always match a replacement fastener to the original. Do not run a tap or thread chaser into a hole or over a bolt without first verifying the thread size and pitch. Check all threaded holes for Heli-Coil stainless steel locking thread inserts. Never run a tap or thread chaser into a Heli-Coil equipped hole. Heli-Coil inserts are replaceable, if they are damaged.

3. Inspect all screws, bolts, nuts and other fasteners for damaged, galled or distorted threads. Replace any elastic locknuts that can be installed without the aid of a wrench. Clean all sealing compound, RTV sealant and thread-locking compound from the threaded areas. Correct minor thread imperfections with an appropriate thread chaser.

4. Clean all gasket and sealant material from the gearcase housing. Make sure all water and lubricant passages are clean and unobstructed. Make sure all threaded holes are free of corrosion, gasket sealant or threadlocking adhesive. Damaged or distorted threads can be repaired with stainless steel threaded inserts.

5. On models with propeller shaft bearing carrier retaining rings, remove corrosion from the gearcase threaded area with a suitable non-corrosive, brass or stainless steel wire brush. Use a thread file to repair minor thread defects. If the threads are severely damaged, replace the gearcase housing.

6. Inspect all castings on the gearcase, propeller shaft bearing carrier and all other seal or bearing carriers for cracks, porosity, wear, distortion and mechanical damage. Replace any housing that shows evidence of having a bearing spun in its bore.

7. If the gearcase is equipped with a speedometer pickup, make sure the pickup port is not clogged with debris. Use a very small drill bit mounted in a pin vise to remove any debris from the pickup port. Make sure air can flow freely from the pickup port to the speedometer hose connection.

8. Inspect all anodes as described at the beginning of this chapter. Replace any anode that has deteriorated to half of its original size.

9. Inspect the water inlet screen(s) for damage or obstructions. Clean or replace the screen(s) as necessary.

10. Inspect the drive shaft and propeller shaft for worn, damaged or twisted splines. Excessively worn drive shaft splines are usually the result of shaft misalignment caused by a distorted drive shaft housing or lower gearcase housing, due to impact with an underwater object. Replace distorted housings.

11. Inspect the drive shaft and propeller shaft threaded areas for damage. If equipped with an impeller drive pin, check the pin and propeller drive pin holes for wear, elongation and cracks.

12. Inspect each shaft's bearing and seal surfaces for excessive wear, grooving, metal transfer and discoloration from overheating. See **Figure 161**.

13. Check for a bent propeller shaft by supporting the propeller shaft with V-blocks at its bearing surfaces. Mount a dial indicator on the propeller splines. Rotate the propeller shaft while observing the dial indicator. A noticeable wobble or a reading of more than 0.006 in. (0.15 mm) indicates excessive shaft runout. Replace the propeller shaft if excessive runout is evident.

14. Check each gear for excessive wear, corrosion or rust and mechanical damage. Check the teeth for galling, chips, cracks, missing pieces, distortion or discoloration from overheating. Check the sliding clutch and each gear's engagement lugs (**Figure 162**) for chips, cracks and excessive wear.

9

15. Check the pinion gear and sliding clutch splines for wear, distortion or mechanical damage.

16. Inspect shift components and shift linkage for excessive wear and mechanical damage. Inspect the shift cam for wear or grooving. Replace the shift cam if it is damaged or worn. On rotary shift shaft models, inspect the shift shaft splines for corrosion, wear, distortion or twisting. Replace the shift shaft if it is corroded, damaged or worn.

17. Inspect all roller, ball and needle bearings for water damage, pitting, discoloration from overheating and metal transfer. Be sure to locate and inspect all internal needle bearings (**Figure 163**).

18. Check the propeller for nicks, cracks or damaged blades. Minor nicks can be removed with a file. Be careful to keep the original shape and contour of the blade. Replace the propeller or have it repaired if any blades are bent, cracked or badly chipped. If the propeller is excessively corroded, replace it.

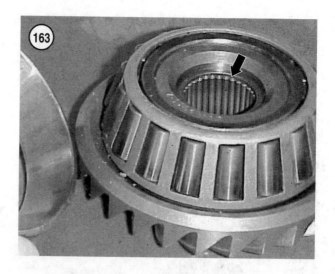

GEARCASE PRESSURE TESTING

If a gearcase has been disassembled, pressure test it after reassembly to ensure that no leaks are present. If the gearcase fails the pressure test, find and correct the source of the leak. Failure to correct leaks will result in major gearcase damage from water entering the gearcase or lubricant leaking out.

Do not fill the gearcase with lubricant until the pressure test has been satisfactorily completed.

NOTE
Drain the gearcase lubricant before pressure testing. Refer to Chapter Four if necessary.

Pressure test the gearcase as follows:

1. Make sure the gearcase lubricant is completely drained. Then make sure the fill/drain plug is installed and properly tightened. Always use a new sealing washer on the fill plug.

2. Remove the vent plug. Install the pressure tester (part No. FT-8950) into the vent hole. See **Figure 164**. Tighten the tester securely. Always use a new sealing washer on the pressure tester.

3. Pressurize the gearcase to 10 psi (69 kPa) for at least five minutes. During this time, periodically rotate the propeller and drive shafts, and move the shift linkage through its full range of travel.

4. The gearcase must hold pressure for a minimum of five minutes. If it does not, pressurize the gearcase again and

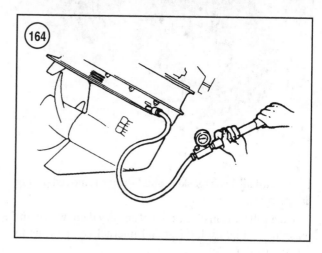

spray soapy water on all sealing surfaces or submerge the gearcase in water to locate the source of the leak.

5. Correct any leaks before proceeding

6. Refer to Chapter Four and fill the gearcase with the recommended lubricant.

GEARCASE SHIMMING

Proper pinion gear-to-forward/reverse gear engagement and the corresponding gear lash are crucial for smooth, quiet operation and long service life. Several shimming procedures must be performed to set up the lower gearcase properly. The pinion gear must be shimmed to the correct height (depth) and the forward gear must then be shimmed to the pinion gear for the proper backlash.

Reverse gear backlash is not adjustable, but should be checked to ensure the gearcase is properly assembled.

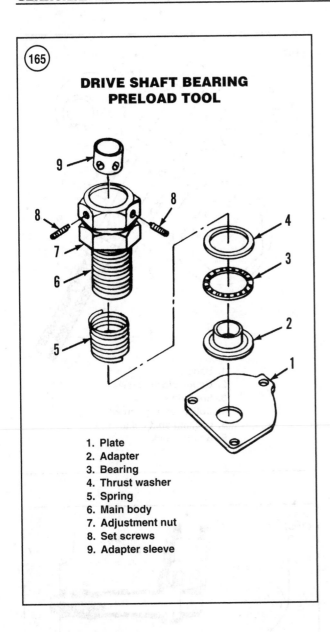

DRIVE SHAFT BEARING PRELOAD TOOL

1. Plate
2. Adapter
3. Bearing
4. Thrust washer
5. Spring
6. Main body
7. Adjustment nut
8. Set screws
9. Adapter sleeve

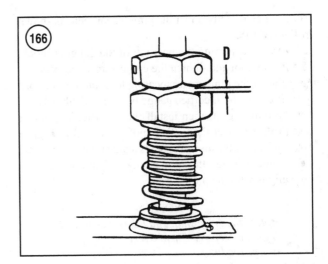

Pinion Gear Depth

1. Position the gearcase with the drive shaft facing up.

NOTE
A drive shaft bearing preload tool (part No. 91-14311A-1) is required to check/adjust pinion gear depth and gear backlash. The plate (1, Figure 165) is not required on 75-200 hp (except 200 hp Optimax) models. However, the engine's original impeller plate must be used on 200 hp Optimax and 225-250 hp models.

2. Install the bearing preload tool (part No. 91-14311A-1) onto the drive shaft in the order shown in **Figure 165**. Do

not install the plate (1, **Figure 165**). On 200 hp Optimax and 225-250 hp models, install the original impeller plate first to support the tool, then install the adapter (2, **Figure 165**).

   a. Make sure the thrust bearing and washer are clean and lightly oiled.

   b. Screw the adjustment nut (7, **Figure 165**) completely onto the main body (6), then securely tighten the set screws (8) making sure the holes in the adapter sleeve (9) are aligned with the set screws.

   c. Measure the distance (D, **Figure 166**) between the top of the nut and the bottom of the bolt head. Then screw the nut downward to increase the distance (D, **Figure 166**) by 1 in. (25.4 mm).

   d. Rotate the drive shaft 10-12 turns to seat the drive shaft bearing(s).

NOTE
The pinion gear locating tool (part No. 91-56048 [Mercruiser tool]) can be used on 200 hp Optimax, 225 hp and 250 hp models. This tool does not need setup or adjustments and can be used with the propeller shaft installed. Insert the tool into the propeller shaft bore and go to Step 7.

3. Assemble the pinion gear locating tool (part No. 91-12349A-2) as shown in **Figure 167**. Face the numbered side of the gauge block out so the numbers can be seen as the tool is being used. Tighten the split collar retaining screw to the point where the collar can still slide back and forth on the handle with moderate hand pressure.

4. Insert the tool into the gearcase, making sure the tool passes through the forward gear needle bearing. Slide the gauge block back and forth as necessary to position the

9

gauge block directly under the pinion gear teeth as shown in **Figure 168**.

5. Without disturbing the position of the gauging block, remove the tool and tighten the collar screw securely.

6. Reinsert the pinion gear locating tool into the forward gear. Position the specified gauge block flat (**Table 4**) under the pinion gear, then install the specified alignment disc (**Table 4**) over the tool's handle as shown in **Figure 169**. Make sure the disc fully seats against the bearing carrier shoulder inside the gear cavity and the disc access hole aligns with the pinion gear.

NOTE
Rotate the drive shaft and take several readings in Step 7. Then average the feeler gauge readings

7. Insert a 0.025 in. (0.64 mm) flat feeler gauge between the gauging block and pinion gear. See **Figure 170**. The average clearance between the gear and gauging block must be 0.025 in. (0.64 mm).

8A. On 75-125 hp (except 115 hp Optimax) models, if the average clearance in Step 6 is not exactly 0.025 in. (0.64 mm), proceed as follows:

   a. If the clearance is less than 0.025 in. (0.64 mm), remove the shims as necessary under the drive shaft roller bearing race.

   b. If the clearance exceeds 0.025 in. (0.64 mm), add shims as necessary under the drive shaft roller bearing race.

8B. On 115 hp Optimax and 135-250 hp models, if the average clearance in Step 6 is not exactly 0.025 in. (0.64 mm), proceed as follows:

   a. If the clearance is less than 0.025 in. (0.64 mm), add shims as necessary under the drive shaft roller bearing race.

   b. If clearance exceeds 0.025 in. (0.64 mm), remove the shims as necessary under the drive shaft roller bearing race.

9. Reassemble the drive shaft and pinion gear as described previously in this chapter, then recheck pinion gear depth as described in this section.

10. Leave the drive shaft bearing preload tool installed. Continue the assembly procedure.

Forward Gear Backlash Measurement

NOTE
*Check the pinion gear depth **before** attempting to adjust forward gear lash. The correct drive shaft bearing preload tool (part No. 91-14311A-1) must be installed for this procedure. Refer to **Pinion Gear Depth** in this*

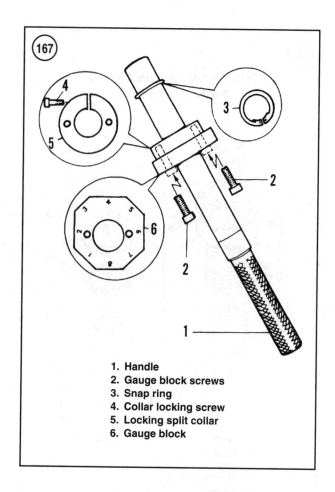

1. Handle
2. Gauge block screws
3. Snap ring
4. Collar locking screw
5. Locking split collar
6. Gauge block

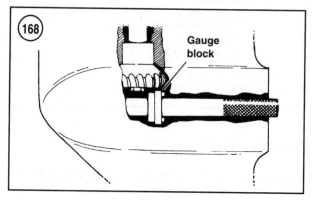

section to install the preload tool and check the pinion gear depth.

Forward gear lash (75-125 hp [except 115 hp Optimax], 200 hp Optimax, 225 hp and 250 hp models)

1. Assemble puller jaws (part No. 91-46086A1) and the threaded bolt (part No. 91-85716) or an equivalent. Install

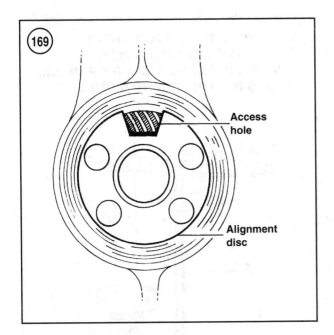

Access hole

Alignment disc

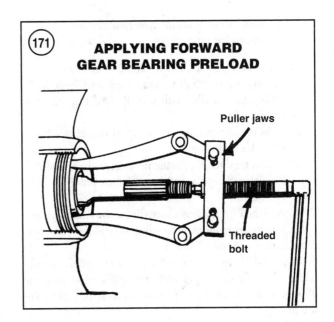

APPLYING FORWARD GEAR BEARING PRELOAD

Puller jaws

Threaded bolt

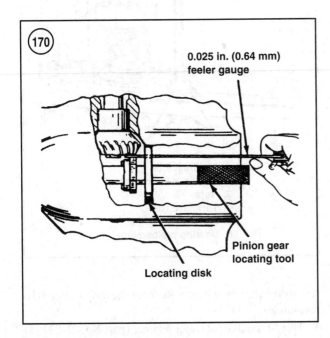

0.025 in. (0.64 mm) feeler gauge

Pinion gear locating tool

Locating disk

the assembly to the propeller shaft and bearing carrier as shown in **Figure 171**.

2. Tighten the puller bolt to 45 in.-lb. (5.1 N•m), then turn the drive shaft 5-10 revolutions to seat the forward gear bearing and race. This will preload the forward gear assembly in its bearing race. Recheck the torque after the 5-10 turns.

3. Fasten a suitable threaded rod to the gearcase using flat washers and nuts. Then install a dial indicator to the threaded rod. See **Figure 172**.

4A. On 75-125 hp (except 115 hp Optimax) models, install the specified backlash indicator tool onto the drive shaft. Align the tool with the indicator plunger and tighten the tool securely on the drive shaft. See **Figure 172**.

    a. *2.3:1 gear ratio*—Use indicator tool part No. 91-78473.

    b. *2.07:1 gear ratio*—Use indicator tool part No. 91-19660-1.

4B. On 200 hp Optimax, 225 and 250 hp models, install the specified backlash indicator tool onto the drive shaft. Align the tool with the indicator plunger and tighten the tool securely on the drive shaft. See **Figure 172**.

    a. *1.75:1 and 1.62:1 gear ratios*—Use indicator tool part No. 91-53459.

    b. *1.87:1 gear ratio*—Use indicator tool part No. 91-78473.

5A. On 75-125 hp (except 115 hp Optimax) models, adjust the dial indicator mounting so the plunger aligns with the specified line on the backlash indicator tool. Then zero the dial.

    a. *2.3:1 gear ratio*—Use line No. 4.

    b. *2.07:1 gear ratio*—Use line No. 1.

5B. On 200 hp Optimax, 225 hp and 250 hp models, adjust the dial indicator mounting so the plunger is aligned with the No. 1 line on the backlash indicator tool. Then zero the dial.

NOTE
The propeller shaft must not move during the gear lash measurement. Rotate the drive shaft just enough to contact a gear tooth in one direction, then rotate the drive shaft just

9

*enough in the opposite direction to contact
the opposing gear tooth.*

6A. On 200 hp Optimax, 225 hp and 250 hp models:

  a. Lightly rotate the drive shaft back and forth while observing the dial indicator. Record the indicator reading.

  b. Lift the indicator, then rotate the drive shaft 90° and reset the indicator.

  c. Take a new reading at the new drive shaft position. Repeat substeps a and b until four readings have been taken.

  d. Add the four readings, then divide the sum by four.

  e. The average indicator reading should be within the specification in **Table 5**.

6B. On 75-125 hp (except 115 Optimax) models, lightly rotate the drive shaft back and forth while observing the dial indicator. The gear lash should be as specified in **Table 5**.

7. If the gear lash is excessive, add shims behind the forward gear bearing race as necessary. If the gear lash is insufficient, remove the shims behind the forward gear bearing race as necessary.

> *CAUTION*
> *Once the backlash is correct, the gearcase can be completely assembled. However, use a new pinion nut secured with Loctite 271 threadlocking compound. On 75-125 hp models, also secure the propeller shaft bearing carrier screws with Loctite 271 (part No. 92-809819).*

8. Complete the remaining assembly procedure.

Forward gear lash (115 hp Optimax and 135-200 hp [except 200 hp Optimax] models)

> *NOTE*
> *Check the pinion gear depth **before** attempting to adjust the forward gear lash. Install the drive shaft bearing preload tool (part No. 91-14311A-2) for this procedure. Refer to **Pinion Gear Depth** in this section to install the preload tool and check the pinion gear depth.*

1. Assemble puller jaws part No. 91-46086A1 and threaded bolt part No. 91-85716 or an equivalent. Install the assembly to the propeller shaft and bearing carrier as shown in **Figure 171**.

2. Tighten the puller bolt to 45 in.-lb. (5.1 N•m), then turn the drive shaft 5-10 revolutions to seat the forward gear bearing and race. This will preload the forward gear as-

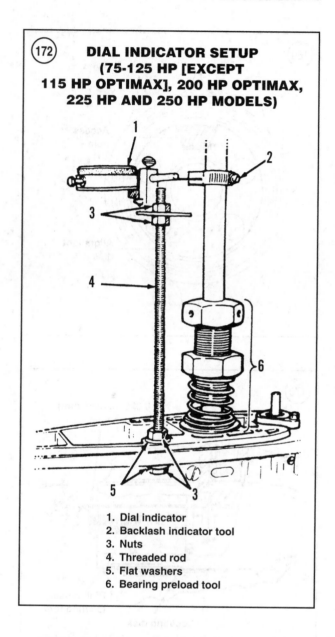

172

DIAL INDICATOR SETUP (75-125 HP [EXCEPT 115 HP OPTIMAX], 200 HP OPTIMAX, 225 HP AND 250 HP MODELS)

1. Dial indicator
2. Backlash indicator tool
3. Nuts
4. Threaded rod
5. Flat washers
6. Bearing preload tool

sembly into its bearing race. Recheck the torque after 5-10 revolutions.

3. Thread the dial indicator adapter (part No. 91-83155) onto one water pump stud, then install a dial indicator holder (part No. 91-89897) onto the adapter. Then install the dial indicator (part No. 91-58222A-1) onto the adapter. See **Figure 173**.

4. Place the backlash indicator tool (part No. 91-78473) onto the drive shaft, align the indicator tool with the dial indicator plunger, then tighten the tool securely to the drive shaft. See **Figure 173**.

5. Adjust the dial indicator mounting so the plunger is aligned with the specified line on the backlash indicator tool. Then zero the indicator gauge.

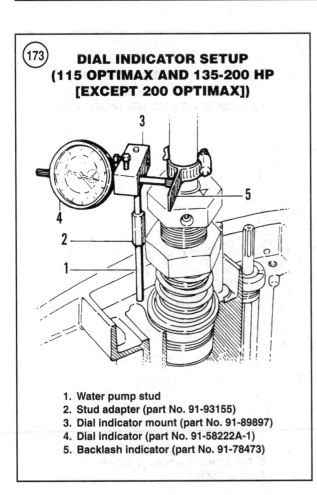

**DIAL INDICATOR SETUP
(115 OPTIMAX AND 135-200 HP
[EXCEPT 200 OPTIMAX])**

1. Water pump stud
2. Stud adapter (part No. 91-93155)
3. Dial indicator mount (part No. 91-89897)
4. Dial indicator (part No. 91-58222A-1)
5. Backlash indicator (part No. 91-78473)

a. *1.87:1 gear ratio*—Use line No. 1.
b. *2:1 gear ratio*—Use line No. 2.
c. *2.3:1 gear ratio*—Use line No. 4

NOTE
The propeller shaft must not move during gear lash measurement. Rotate the drive shaft just enough to contact a gear tooth in one direction, then rotate the drive shaft just enough in the opposite direction to contact the opposing gear tooth.

6. Lightly rotate the drive shaft back and forth while observing the dial indicator reading. The indicator reading should be within the specification in **Table 5**.

NOTE
A 0.001 in. (0.25 mm) change in forward gear bearing shim thickness changes forward gear backlash by approximately 0.00125 in. (0.032 mm).

7. If the gear lash is excessive, add shim(s) behind the forward gear bearing race as necessary. If the gear lash is insufficient, remove the shim(s) behind the forward gear bearing race as necessary.

CAUTION
Once the gear backlash is correct, the gearcase can be completely assembled. However, install a new pinion nut and washer, secured with Loctite 271 threadlocking adhesive (part No. 92-809819) before completing assembly. Also secure the bearing carrier retaining ring by bending the locking tab washers when assembly is complete.

8. Complete the assembly procedure.

Reverse Gear Lash

Reverse gear backlash is not adjustable; however, check it to ensure the gearcase is properly assembled.

115 hp Optimax and 135-200 hp (except 200 hp Optimax) models

Check the reverse gear lash after setting the forward gear lash and after installing the shift shaft and the shift cam. The propeller shaft and bearing carrier must be installed for this procedure.
1. Install the bearing preload tool as described under *Pinion Gear Depth*. Then install the dial indicator and backlash indicator tool as described under *Forward Gear Lash*.
2. Shift the gearcase into full reverse gear while rotating the propeller to ensure full clutch engagement.
3. Install a piece of 6 in. (152.4 mm) long, 1 1/2 in. (38.1 mm) diameter PVC pipe over the propeller shaft and against the bearing carrier. Tighten the pipe against the bearing carrier using the propeller nut and tab washer. Tighten only until the propeller shaft is pulled securely against the propeller shaft bearing carrier. Do not over-tighten.
4. Gently turn the drive shaft back and forth (the propeller shaft must not move) and note the dial indicator reading. The amount of drive shaft travel indicates reverse gear lash, which should be within the specification in **Table 5**.
5. If the lash is not within the specification, the bearing carrier/reverse gear is incorrectly assembled, or contains excessively worn components. Disassemble the gearcase, and determine and repair the problem before returning the gearcase to service.
6. If the lash is within the specification, complete the assembly procedure.

9

200 hp Optimax, 225 hp and 250 hp models

Check the reverse gear lash after setting the forward gear lash. The propeller shaft assembly and bearing carrier must be installed for this procedure.

1. Install the bearing preload tool as described under *Pinion Gear Depth*. Then install the dial indicator and backlash indicator tool as described under *Forward Gear Lash*.

2. Install pinion nut tool part No. 91-61067A-2 over the propeller shaft and against the propeller shaft bearing carrier. See **Figure 174**.

3. Install a flat washer, such as part No. 12-54048, over the propeller shaft and against the pinion nut tool. See **Figure 174**.

4. Install the propeller nut and tighten the nut to 45 in.-lb. (5.1 N•m). Rotate the drive shaft at least three full turns to seat the bearings, then retighten the propeller nut to 45 in.-lb. (5.1 N•m).

5. Gently turn the drive shaft back and forth (the propeller shaft must not move), and note the dial indicator reading. The amount of drive shaft travel indicates reverse gear lash, which should be within the specification in **Table 5**.

6. If the lash is not within specification, the bearing carrier/reverse gear is incorrectly assembled, or contains excessively worn components. Disassemble the gearcase, and determine and repair the problem before returning the gearcase to service. Make sure the reverse gear thrust washer (21, **Figure 126**) has been installed.

7. If the lash is within specification, complete the assembly procedure.

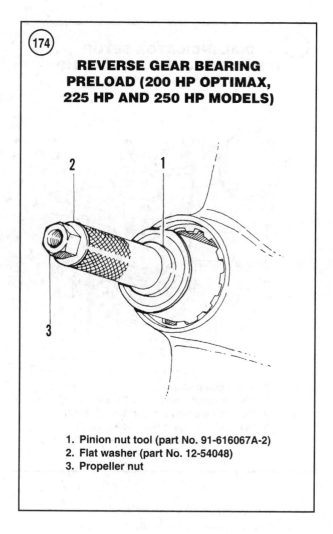

REVERSE GEAR BEARING PRELOAD (200 HP OPTIMAX, 225 HP AND 250 HP MODELS)

1. Pinion nut tool (part No. 91-616067A-2)
2. Flat washer (part No. 12-54048)
3. Propeller nut

Table 1 GEARCASE TORQUE SPECIFICATIONS

Fastener	in.-lb.	ft.-lb.	N•m
Anode (side of gearcase)	60	–	6.8
Bearing carrier			
75-125 hp (except 115 hp Optimax)	–	25	33.9
115 hp Optimax and 135-250 hp	–	210	284.7
Drain/fill and vent plugs	60	–	6.8
Drive shaft bearing retainer	–	100	135.6
Gearcase mounting			
75-125 hp (except 115 hp Optimax)	–	40	54.2
115 hp Optimax and 135-200 hp (except 200 hp Optimax)			
Bolts	–	30	41
Locknuts	–	50	68
200 hp Optimax, 200 hp and 225 hp			
Bolts	–	45	61
Locknuts	–	55	74.6
Pinion gear nut			
75-125 hp (except 115 hp Optimax)	–	70	95
115 hp Optimax and 135-250 hp	–	75	101.7

(continued)

Table 1 GEARCASE TORQUE SPECIFICATIONS (continued)

Fastener	in.-lb.	ft.-lb.	N•m
Propeller nut	–	55	74.5
Shift shaft bushing/retainer screws			
75-125 hp (except 115 hp Optimax)	35	–	3.9
115 hp Optimax and 135-200 hp (except 200 hp Optimax)	–	50	67.8
200 hp Optimax, 225 and 250 hp	60	–	6.8
Trim tab/anodic plate			
75-125 hp (except Optimax models)	–	22	29.8
150-250 hp	–	40	54.2
Water pump			
65 jet and 75-125 hp (except 105 jet and 115 hp Optimax)			
Water pump base	60	–	6.8
Water pump body	60	–	6.8
115 hp Optimax and 135-200 hp (except 200 hp Optimax)			
Nuts	50	–	5.6
Screw	35	–	3.9
200 hp Optimax and 225-150 hp	60	–	6.8

Table 2 GENERAL TORQUE SPECIFICATIONS

Screw or nut size	in.-lb.	ft.-lb.	N•m
U.S. Standard			
6-32	9	–	1.0
8-32	20	–	2.3
10-24	30	–	3.4
10-32	35	–	4.0
12-24	45	–	5.1
1/4-20	70	–	7.9
1/4-28	84	–	9.5
5/16-18	160	13	18
5/16-24	168	14	19
3/8-16	–	23	31
3/8-24	–	25	34
7/16-14	–	36	49
7/16-20	–	40	54
1/2-13	–	50	68
1/2-20	–	60	81
Metric			
M5	36	–	4
M6	70	–	8
M8	156	13	18
M10	–	26	35
M12	–	35	48
M14	–	60	81

Table 3 GEAR RATIO AND TOOTH COUNTS

Model	Pinion/driven gear tooth count	Gear ratio
75 hp and 90 hp	13/30	2.3:1
100-125 hp (except 115 hp Optimax)		
Standard ratio	14/29	2.07:1
High elevation ratio	13/30	2.3:1
115 hp and 135 hp Optimax models		
Standard ratio	14/28	2:1
High elevation ratio	13/30	2.3:1

(continued)

9

Table 3 GEAR RATIO AND TOOTH COUNTS (continued)

Model	Pinion/driven gear tooth count	Gear ratio
135 hp and 150 hp (except EFI, Optimax, XR6 and Mag III)		
Standard ratio	14/28	2:1
High elevation ratio	13/30	2.3:1
150 hp EFI, XR6, Mag III and 175 hp (except Optimax models)		
Standard ratio	15/28	1.87:1
High elevation ratio	14/28	2:10
150 hp and 175 hp Optimax models		
Standard ratio	15/28	1.87:1
High elevation ratio	14/28	2:1
200 hp (except Optimax)		
Standard ratio	15/28	1.87:1
High elevation ratio	14/28	2:1
200 hp Optimax, 225 hp and 225 hp		
Standard ratio	12/21	1.75:1
Alternate ratio	13/21	1.62:1
High elevation ratio	15/28	1.87:1

Table 4 PINION GEAR LOCATING TOOL SPECIFICATIONS

Model	Alignment disc	Measuring flat
75 hp and 90 hp	No. 3	No. 8
100-125 hp (except 115 hp Optimax)		
2.07:1 ratio	No. 3	No. 2
2.33:1 ratio	No. 3	No. 8
115 hp Optimax and 135-200 hp (except 200 hp Optimax)	No. 2	No. 7
200 hp Optimax, 225 hp and 225 hp	No. 2	No. 4

Table 5 GEARCASE BACKLASH SPECIFICATIONS

Model	Backlash specification
75 hp and 90 hp	0.012-0.019 in. (0.30-0.48 mm)
100-125 hp (except 115 hp Optimax)	
2.07:1 ratio	0.015-0.022 in. (0.38-0.56 mm)
2.33:1 ratio	0.012-0.019 in. (0.30-0.48 mm)
115 hp Optimax and 135-200 hp (except 200 hp Optimax)	
2.3:1 ratio	
Forward gear	0.018-0.023 in. (0.46-0.58 mm)
Reverse gear	0.030-0.050 in. (0.76-1.27 mm)
2.0:1 ratio	
Forward gear	0.015-0.022 in. (0.38-0.56 mm)
Reverse gear	0.030-0.050 in. (0.76-1.27 mm)
1.87:1 ratio	
Forward gear	0.017-0.028 in. (0.43-0.71 mm)
Reverse gear	0.030-0.050 in. (0.76-1.27 mm)
200 hp Optimax, 225 hp and 250 hp	
Forward gear	0.017-0.028 in. (0.43-0.71 mm)
Reverse gear	0.030-0.050 in. (0.76-1.27 mm)

Chapter Ten

Jet Drive

Jet drive models are based on the following basic outboard models. The standard lower gearcase has been removed and a jet pump unit has been installed. Rpm limiting circuits are incorporated into the ignition system on all jet drive models.

1. 65 jet—90 hp power head (three-cylinder).
2. 80 jet—115 hp power head (four-cylinder).
3. 105 jet—150 hp power head (V-6).
4. 140 jet—200 hp power head (V-6).

All jet drive models are carburetor equipped engines. Service to the power head, ignition, electrical, fuel, and power trim and tilt systems is the same as on propeller-driven outboard models. Refer to the appropriate chapter and service section for the engine models or component serviced. This chapter only covers service to the jet drive assembly. Refer to **Table 1** for specific torque values. Tighten fasteners not listed in **Table 1** to the general torque specification in **Table 2**.

A disadvantage of jet-drive propulsion is reduced efficiency compared to an equivalent propeller-driven unit. The performance of a jet drive is generally equivalent to 70% of the same outboard motor with a standard gearcase.

Jet Pump Operation

The major components of the jet drive include the impeller (1, **Figure 1**), volute tube (3) and discharge nozzle (4). One end of the impeller is connected to a shaft supported by bearings and the other end is connected to the crankshaft. Therefore, anytime the engine is running, the impeller is turning. The rotating impeller pulls water through the intake opening (2, **Figure 1**) and pushes it through the volute tube (3). The volute tube directs the water toward the discharge nozzle. Water flowing from the discharge nozzle provides thrust to move the boat. Thrust increases as the speed of the impeller increases.

Directional Control

The boat's operational direction is controlled by a thrust gate. The thrust gate is controlled by a remote control shaft cable. When the directional control lever is in the full forward position, the thrust gate uncovers the jet drive housing's outlet nozzle opening (see **Figure 2**) and seats securely against the rubber pad on the jet drive pump

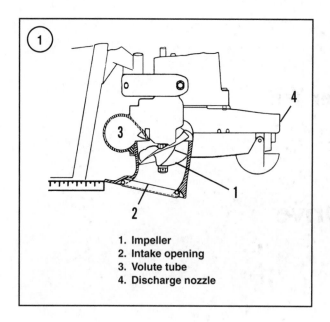

1. Impeller
2. Intake opening
3. Volute tube
4. Discharge nozzle

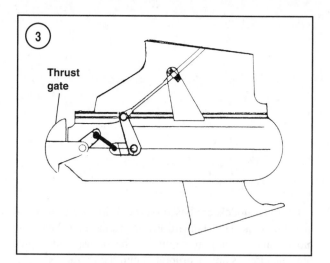

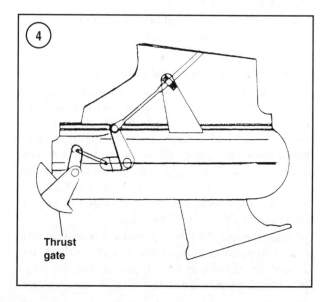

housing. When the directional control lever is in the full reverse position, the thrust gate closes off the pump housing's outlet nozzle opening (see **Figure 3**). Neutral is midway between complete forward and complete reverse position (see **Figure 4**).

Steering is accomplished as the engine is pivoted port or starboard as with the standard propeller-driven gearcases.

Outboard Mounting Height

A jet drive outboard must be mounted higher on the transom plate than an equivalent propeller-driven outboard motor. However, if the jet drive is mounted too high, air will enter the jet drive causing cavitation and power loss. If the jet drive is mounted too low, excessive drag, water spray and loss in speed will occur.

Water intake fin kits are available to reduce cavitation when running with the wind in rough water. The 65-140 jet water fin kits are available from Specialty Manufacturing Company, 2035 Edison Avenue, San Leandro, California 94577.

Set the initial height of the outboard motor as follows:
1. Place a straightedge against the boat bottom (not keel) so the end contacts the jet drive intake.
2. Align the front edge of the water intake housing with the top edge of the straightedge (**Figure 5**).
3. Secure the outboard motor at this setting, then test run the boat.
4. If cavitation occurs (over-revving and/or loss of thrust), lower the outboard motor in 1/4 in. (6.35 mm) increments until the operation is uniform.

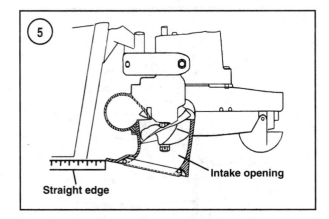

Straight edge — Intake opening

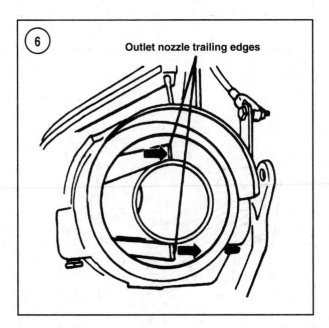

Outlet nozzle trailing edges

CAUTION
A slight amount of cavitation in rough water and during sharp turns is normal. However, excessive cavitation damages the impeller and can cause the power head to overheat.

5. If operation is uniform with the initial setting, raise the outboard motor in 1/4 in. (6.35 mm) increments until cavitation occurs. Then lower the motor to the last uniform setting.

NOTE
The outboard motor should be vertical when the boat is on plane. Adjust the motor trim setting as needed. If the outboard trim setting is altered, check and adjust the outboard motor height, if needed, as previously outlined.

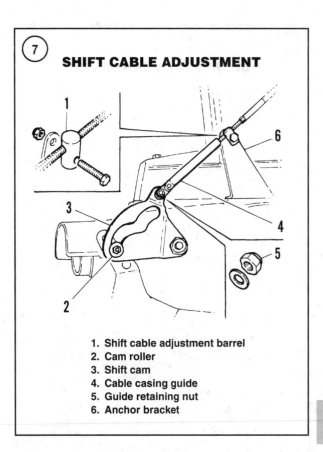

SHIFT CABLE ADJUSTMENT

1. Shift cable adjustment barrel
2. Cam roller
3. Shift cam
4. Cable casing guide
5. Guide retaining nut
6. Anchor bracket

10

Steering Torque

A minor adjustment to the trailing edge of the drive outlet nozzle can be made if the boat pulls in one direction when the boat and outboard are pointed straight-ahead. If the boat pulls to the starboard side, bend the top and bottom trailing edge of the jet drive outlet nozzle 1/16 in. (1.6 mm) toward the starboard side of the jet drive. See **Figure 6**.

Shift Cable Adjustment

The directional control cable is properly adjusted if the thrust gate cannot be moved into the neutral position by hand after placing the remote control lever in the full forward position.

WARNING
Shift cable adjustment must be correct or water pressure from the boat's forward movement can engage the thrust gate, causing reverse to engage unexpectedly.

Refer to **Figure 7** and adjust the remote control shift cable as follows:

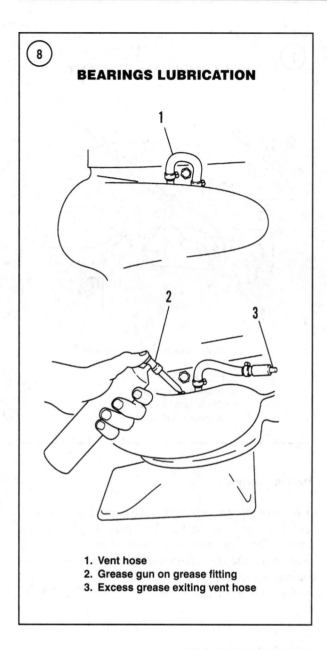

BEARINGS LUBRICATION

1. Vent hose
2. Grease gun on grease fitting
3. Excess grease exiting vent hose

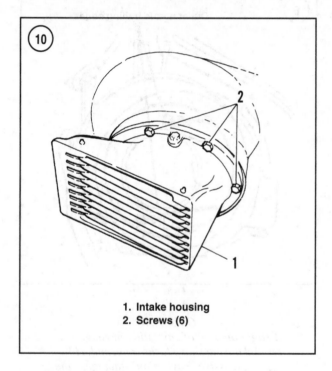

Feeler gauge

1. Intake housing
2. Screws (6)

1. Place the remote control shift lever into the full forward position. Remove the screw and locknut securing the shift cable adjustment barrel (1, **Figure 7**) to the shift cable anchor bracket.

2. Adjust the shift cable barrel to position the cam roller (2, **Figure 7**) just at the end of the shift cam slot. Secure the cable barrel to the anchor bracket with the screw and locknut. Tighten the locknut securely.

3. Shift the remote control to neutral, then back to the full forward position.

4. Attempt to move the thrust gate up, towards reverse. Readjust the cable barrel as necessary to prevent the gate from moving towards reverse.

5. After the adjustment is correct, tighten the screw and locknut securing the cable barrel to the anchor bracket.

6. Tighten the cable casing guide retaining nut (5, **Figure 7**) until it bottoms, then back the nut off 1/8 to 1/4 turn.

JET PUMP UNIT MAINTENANCE

Bearing Lubrication

Lubricate the jet pump bearing(s) after each operating period, after every 10 hours of operation and prior to storage. After every 30 hours of operation, pump ad-

IMPELLER REMOVAL/INSTALLATION

1. Impeller sleeve
2. Impeller
3. Drive key
4. Shims (upper and lower)
5. Locking tab washer
6. Impeller nut

Impeller Clearance Adjustment and Impeller Removal/Installation

If there is a loss of high boat speed performance and/or a higher than normal full throttle engine speed, check the clearance between the edge of the impeller and the water intake casing liner. Also, check the leading edge(s) of the impeller for wear or damage. If it is worn or damaged, refer to *Worn (dull) impeller* following this procedure.

NOTE
The impeller can wear quickly when the boat is operated in water with excessive silt, sand or gravel.

1. Disconnect the spark plug leads to prevent accidental starting.
2. Use a feeler gauge set to determine the clearance between the impeller blades and the intake liner. See **Figure 9**.
3. The impeller-to-liner clearance should be approximately 0.030 in. (0.8 mm).
4. If the clearance is not as specified, remove the six water intake housing mounting screws (2, **Figure 10**). Remove the intake housing (1, **Figure 10**).
5. Bend the tabs on the locking tab washer (5, **Figure 11**). Hold the impeller nut to allow a suitable tool to be installed on the impeller nut. Remove the nut, tab washer, lower shims impeller, drive key, plastic sleeve and upper shims. Note the number of lower and upper shims. See **Figure 11**.

NOTE
If the impeller is stuck to the drive shaft, use a suitable block of wood and a hammer to rotate the impeller in the opposite direction of normal rotation. Rotate the impeller just enough to free the drive key to allow impeller removal.

6. If the clearance is excessive, remove the lower shims as needed from below the impeller and position them above the impeller on the nut side.

NOTE
Lubricate the impeller shaft, impeller sleeve and drive key with Quicksilver 2-4-C Multi-Lube grease (part No. 92-825407) or Quicksilver Special Lubricant 101 (part No. 92-13872A 1) prior to reassembly.

7. Install the impeller with the selected number of shims. Hold the upper shims to the drive shaft with grease. Then position the plastic sleeve in the impeller and install the impeller, drive key and lower shims.

10

ditional grease into the bearing(s) to purge moisture. Lubricate the bearings by first removing the vent hose (1, **Figure 8**) on the side of the jet pump housing to expose the grease fitting. Use a grease gun to inject Quicksilver 2-4-C Multi-Lube grease (Part No. 92-825407) into the fitting until grease exits the end of the hose (3, **Figure 8**). Pump fresh grease into the fitting until all old grease is expelled and new grease exits from the end of the hose.

8. Install a new tab washer and impeller retaining nut on the drive shaft. Tighten the nut securely. Do not bend the tabs on the tab washer at this time.

9. Apply Quicksilver Perfect Seal (part No. 92-34227-1) to the threads of the intake housing retaining screws. Install the housing and screws. Tighten the screws finger-tight.

> *NOTE*
> *The intake housing can be moved slightly on its mounting to center the liner over the impeller.*

10. Rotate the impeller to check for rubbing or binding. Make sure the housing is centered over the impeller.

11. Repeat Steps 2 and 3 to recheck impeller clearance. Readjust the clearance as necessary.

12. After the clearance is correct, remove the intake housing screws and housing.

13. Tighten the impeller nut securely, then lock the nut in place with the tab washer. Make sure the tabs are bent up securely against the nut.

14. Reinstall the intake housing. Make sure the housing is centered on the impeller. Tighten the water intake housing screws in a crossing pattern to specification in **Table 1**.

Worn (dull) impeller

The leading edge(s) of the impeller wear due to ingestion of gravel, silt and other debris. If there is a noticeable performance loss, increased wide-open throttle speed, or difficulty getting the boat on plane, check the leading edge(s) of the impeller for wear or damage.

1. If the leading edge(s) is damaged, remove the impeller as described in the previous section.

2. Sharpen the impeller by removing material, with a flat file, from the lower surface of the leading edge(s) as shown in **Figure 12**. Do not remove material from the upper surface or alter the top side lifting angle of the impeller.

3. When finished, file or sand a 1/32 in. (0.8 mm) radius on the leading edge(s) as shown in **Figure 12**.

4. Reinstall the impeller and recheck the impeller clearance as described in the previous section.

Cooling System Flushing

The cooling system can become plugged by sand and salt deposits if it is not flushed occasionally. Clean the cooling system after each use in salt, brackish or silt-laden water. Refer to Chapter Four for cooling system flushing procedures.

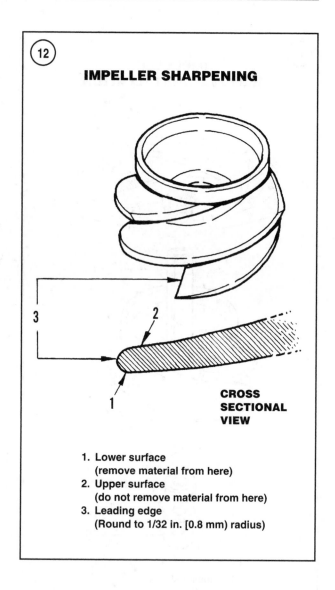

(12)

IMPELLER SHARPENING

CROSS SECTIONAL VIEW

1. **Lower surface**
   (remove material from here)
2. **Upper surface**
   (do not remove material from here)
3. **Leading edge**
   (Round to 1/32 in. [0.8 mm] radius)

Water Pump

All water pumps are the same as the pump used on the related power head model as described at the beginning of this section. The water pump is located at the top of the jet pump unit on all models.

On 65 jet and 80 jet models, the water pump adapter is retained by the same screws as the water pump housing. The screws are longer than those used on the standard gearcases. There is no gasket between the adapter and the pump unit housing.

On 105 jet and 140 jet models, a standard water pump base and gasket are mounted directly to the pump unit housing.

Since proper water pump operation is critical to outboard operation and durability, service the water pump anytime the jet pump unit is removed from the outboard. To service the water pump, remove the jet drive assembly

JET DRIVE REMOVAL/INSTALLATION (65 JET AND 80 JET)

1. Internal screws (4)
2. External screws

as described in this chapter and refer to the appropriate water pump service section in Chapter Nine for the related power head. Tighten the water pump mounting fasteners to the specification in **Table 1**.

JET PUMP UNIT REPAIR

If the jet drive mounting fasteners are corroded, discard them and install new ones. Apply Quicksilver Perfect Seal to the threads of the mounting screws during installation.

Jet Pump Unit Removal (65 Jet and 80 Jet Models)

1. Disconnect and ground the spark plug leads to the power head to prevent accidental starting.

2. Tilt the outboard to the fully UP position and engage the tilt lock lever, securely block the drive shaft housing or support the drive shaft housing with a suitable hoist.

3. Remove the shift cable adjustment barrel from the anchor bracket and remove the casing guide from the shift cam stud (**Figure 7**).

4. Remove the six water intake housing mounting screws. Remove the intake housing (**Figure 10**, typical).

5. Bend the tabs on the impeller nut tab washer (5, **Figure 11**) away from the impeller nut. Remove the impeller nut and tab washer. Discard the tab washer.

NOTE
Note the number and location of impeller adjustment shims for reference during reassembly.

6. Remove the shims (4, **Figure 11**) located below the impeller and note the number of shims. Remove the impeller (2, **Figure 11**) and the shims located above the impeller and note the number of shims.

7. Slide the impeller sleeve and drive key (1 and 3, **Figure 11**) from the drive shaft.

8. Remove the four bolts (1, **Figure 13**) located inside the impeller cavity. Then remove the bolt (2, **Figure 13**) at the rear of the drive shaft housing. Support the pump unit as the bolt is removed.

9. Remove the jet pump unit by pulling it straight down and away from the drive shaft housing until the drive shaft is free from the housing. Place the pump unit on a clean workbench.

10. Locate and secure the fore and aft dowel pins that align the jet pump unit to the drive shaft housing.

Pump Unit Installation (65 Jet and 80 Jet Models)

1. Make sure the water tube guide and seal are securely attached to the water pump housing. If the guide and seal are loose, glue the guide and seal to the water pump housing with Loctite 405 adhesive.

CAUTION
Do not apply lubricant to the top of the drive shaft in the next step. Excess lubricant between the top of the drive shaft and the engine crankshaft can create a hydraulic lock, preventing the drive shaft from fully engaging the crankshaft.

10

2. Clean the drive shaft splines as necessary, then coat the splines with Quicksilver 2-4-C Multi-Lube grease (part No. 92-825407). Coat the inner diameter of the water tube seal in the water pump housing with the same grease.

3. Make sure the fore and aft dowel pins are installed in either the drive shaft housing or the jet pump unit housing.

4. Position the pump unit under the drive shaft housing. Align the water tube in the water pump and the drive shaft with the crankshaft splines.

CAUTION
Do not rotate the flywheel counterclockwise in the next step or the water pump impeller can be damaged.

5. Push the pump unit toward the drive shaft housing, rotating the flywheel clockwise as required to align the drive shaft and crankshaft splines.

6. Make sure the water tube is seated in the water pump seal, then push the gearcase against the drive shaft housing.

7. Coat the threads of the mounting screws with Loctite 271 threadlocking adhesive (part No. 92-80819).

8. Secure the pump unit to the drive shaft housing with the five bolts. Tighten the bolts evenly to the specification in **Table 1**.

NOTE
Install the original amount of upper and lower impeller shims as noted on disassembly if the original impeller and intake liner are being used. If a new impeller or liner is being installed, start with no upper shims and carefully add shims until the clearance is correct.

9. Install the impeller and water intake housing, and check the impeller clearance as described in *Impeller Clearance Adjustment and Impeller Removal/Installation*.

10. Connect and adjust the shift cable as described previously in this chapter.

11. Reconnect the spark plug leads.

Jet Pump Unit Removal
(105 Jet and 140 Jet Models)

1. Disconnect and ground the spark plug leads to the power head to prevent accidental starting.

2. Tilt the outboard to the fully up position and engage the tilt lock lever, securely block the drive shaft housing or support the drive shaft housing with a suitable hoist.

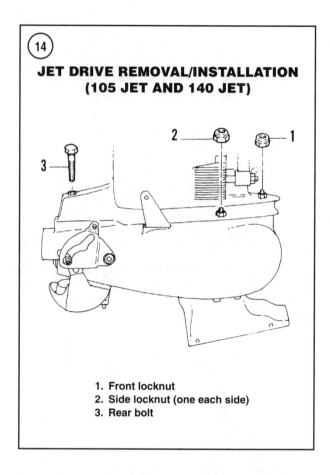

(14)

JET DRIVE REMOVAL/INSTALLATION
(105 JET AND 140 JET)

1. Front locknut
2. Side locknut (one each side)
3. Rear bolt

3. Remove the shift cable adjustment barrel from the anchor bracket and remove the casing guide from the shift cam stud. See **Figure 7**.

NOTE
It is not necessary to remove the impeller before removing the jet pump unit on these models.

4. Remove the front locknut (1, **Figure 14**) and two side locknuts (2). Then remove the bolt (3, **Figure 14**) at the rear of the drive shaft housing. Support the pump unit as the last screw is removed.

5. Remove the jet pump unit by pulling it straight down and away from the drive shaft housing until the drive shaft is free from the housing. Place the pump unit on a clean workbench.

6. Locate and secure the fore and aft dowel pins that position the jet pump unit to the drive shaft housing.

Pump Unit Installation (105 Jet and 140 Jet Models)

1. Make sure the water tube guide and seal are securely attached to the water pump housing.

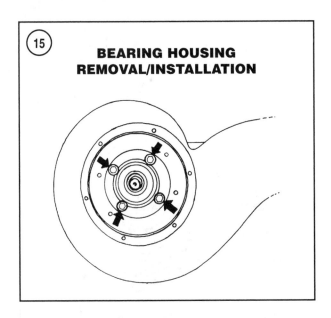

⑮ **BEARING HOUSING REMOVAL/INSTALLATION**

CAUTION
Do not apply lubricant to the top of the drive shaft in the next step. Excess lubricant between the top of the drive shaft and the engine crankshaft can create a hydraulic lock, preventing the drive shaft from fully engaging the crankshaft.

2. Clean the drive shaft splines as necessary, then coat the splines with Quicksilver 2-4-C Multi-Lube grease (part No. 92-825407). Coat the inner diameter of the water tube seal in the water pump housing with the same grease.

3. Make sure the fore and aft dowel pins are installed in either the drive shaft housing or the jet pump unit housing.

4. Position the pump unit under the drive shaft housing. Align the water tube in the water pump and the drive shaft with the crankshaft splines.

CAUTION
Do not rotate the flywheel counterclockwise in the next step or the water pump impeller can be damaged.

5. Push the pump unit toward the drive shaft housing, rotating the flywheel clockwise as required to align the drive shaft and crankshaft splines.

6. Make sure the water tube is seated in the water pump seal, then push the gearcase against the drive shaft housing.

7. Coat the threads of the rear mounting screw (not the locknuts) with Loctite 271 threadlocking adhesive (part No. 92-80819).

8. Secure the pump unit to the drive shaft housing with the three locknuts and one bolt (**Figure 14**). Tighten the fasteners to the specification in **Table 1**.

9. Connect and adjust the remote control shift cable as described previously in this chapter.

10. Reconnect the spark plug leads.

Drive Shaft Bearing Housing

Quicksilver part and accessories only sells the bearing housing and drive shaft as an assembly. Therefore, only removal and installation of the bearing housing and drive shaft assembly is covered.

Removal

1. Remove the pump unit as described previously in this chapter.

2. Remove the water pump assembly. Refer to the appropriate water pump servicing section in Chapter Nine.

3A. On 65 jet and 80 jet models, remove the water pump base adapter from the top of the pump unit housing.

3B. On 105 jet and 140 jet models, remove the water pump base and gasket from the pump unit housing if they have not already been removed.

4. Remove the four screws securing the bearing housing and drive shaft assembly to the pump unit housing. See **Figure 15**. Withdraw the bearing housing and drive shaft assembly from the pump unit housing and place it on a clean work bench.

5. Locate and secure the three O-rings from the bearing housing-to-drive shaft housing mating surface. See **Figure 16**.

Installation

1. Lubricate the three O-rings with Quicksilver 2-4-C Multi-Lube grease (part No. 92-825407). Position the O-rings into the recesses on the mating surface of the bearing housing as shown in **Figure 16**.

2. Install the housing and drive shaft assembly into the pump unit housing. Make sure the retainer screw holes are aligned and the O-rings are not displaced during installation.

3. Apply Loctite 271 threadlocking adhesive (part No. 92-80819) to the threads of the bearing housing screws.

4. Install the four housing retaining screws (**Figure 15**). Evenly tighten the screws to the specification in **Table 1**.

5A. On 65 jet and 80 jet models, install the water pump base adapter to the top of the pump unit housing. Coat the

10

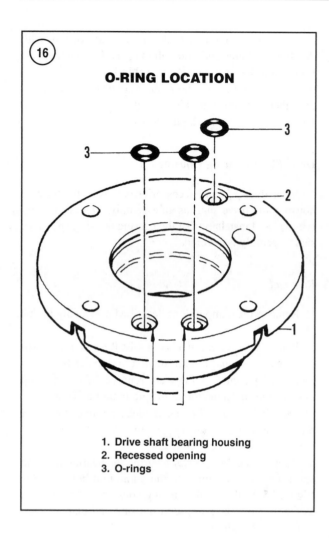

O-RING LOCATION

1. Drive shaft bearing housing
2. Recessed opening
3. O-rings

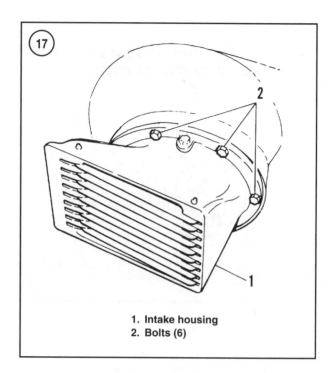

1. Intake housing
2. Bolts (6)

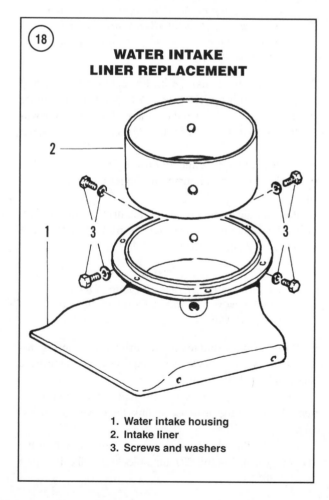

WATER INTAKE LINER REPLACEMENT

1. Water intake housing
2. Intake liner
3. Screws and washers

mating surfaces with Quicksilver Perfect Seal (part No. 92-34227-1).

5B. On 105 jet and 140 jet models, install the water pump base to the pump unit housing using a new gasket.

6. Install the water pump assembly as described in the appropriate water pump servicing section in this chapter.

7. Install the jet pump unit as described in this section. Lubricate the jet pump unit bearings before operation as described in this chapter.

Water Intake Housing Liner Replacement

1. Remove the six water intake housing mounting bolts (2, **Figure 17**). Pull the water intake housing (1, **Figure 17**) down and away from the pump unit housing.

2. Mark or tag the liner screws for reassembly in the same location, then remove the screws and washers (3, **Figure 18**).

3. Tap the liner loose by inserting a long drift punch through the intake housing grate. Place the punch on the edge of the liner and tap it with a hammer.

4. Withdraw the intake liner (2, **Figure 18**) from the liner housing (1).

5. Insert the new liner into the intake housing.

6. Align the liner screw holes with their respective intake housing holes. Gently tap the liner into place with a soft hammer if necessary.

7. Apply Quicksilver Perfect Seal (part No. 92-34227-1) to the threads of the liner retaining screws.

8. Install the liner retaining screws and washers. Evenly tighten the screws to the specification in **Table 1**.

9. Remove any burrs from the inner diameter of the liner and grind the end of the screws as necessary to ensure a flush inner surface.

10. Install the intake housing and set the impeller clearance as described under *Impeller Clearance Adjustment and Impeller Removal/Installation* in this chapter.

Table 1 JET DRIVE TORQUE SPECIFICATIONS

Fastener	in.-lb.	ft.-lb.	N•m
Cable anchor bracket	160	–	18.1
Cable barrel retainer bolt/nut	160	–	18.1
Drive shaft bearing housing	70	–	8
Intake housing liner			
65 jet and 80 jet	120	–	13.6
105 jet and 140 jet	100	–	11
Jet pump mounting			
65 jet and 80 jet			
Internal bolts	–	25	34
External bolt	–	23	31
105 jet and 140 jet			
Locknuts	–	50	68
Bolt	–	23	31
Water intake housing screws			
65 jet and 80 jet	120	–	13.6
105 jet and 140 jet	100	–	11
Water pump			
65 jet and 80 jet	60	–	6.8
105 jet and 140 jet			
Locknut	50	–	5.6
Bolt	35	–	4

Table 2 GENERAL TORQUE SPECIFICATIONS

Screw or nut size	in.-lb.	ft.-lb.	N•m
U.S. Standard			
6-32	9	–	1.0
8-32	20	–	2.3
10-24	30	–	3.4
10-32	35	–	4.0
12-24	45	–	5.1
1/4-20	70	–	7.9
1/4-28	84	–	9.5
5/16-18	160	13	18
5/16-24	168	14	19
3/8-16	–	23	31
3/8-24	–	25	34
7/16-14	–	36	49
7/16-20	–	40	54
1/2-13	–	50	68
1/2-20	–	60	81
(continued)			

10

Table 2 GENERAL TORQUE SPECIFICATIONS (continued)

Screw or nut size	in.-lb.	ft.-lb.	N•m
Metric			
M5	36	–	4
M6	70	–	8
M8	156	13	18
M10	–	26	35
M12	–	35	48
M14	–	60	81

Chapter Eleven

Trim and Tilt Systems

Different operating conditions and changes to the boat load will require frequent changes to the trim pin position to maximize boat performance and efficiency. Power trim and tilt was developed to provide an easy and convenient way to change the trim angle while under way and allow hands free tilting of the motor for trailer loading or beaching.

This section includes maintenance, component replacement and troubleshooting procedures for the trim and tilt systems. **Table 1** lists torque specifications for most trim and tilt system fasteners. **Table 2** lists standard tightening torque specifications. Use the standard torque specifications for fasteners not listed in **Table 1**. All tables are located at the end of the chapter.

Power Trim and Tilt System Description

A power trim/tilt system is standard equipment on all models covered in this manual. The typical system consists of:

1. A reversible electric motor controlled from the remote control or dash.
2. A hydraulic pump and fluid reservoir assembly.
3. A single hydraulic trim and tilt cylinder on 75-125 hp (except 115 hp Optimax and 105 jet), 65 jet and 80 jet models, or a separate tilt cylinder and two integral trim rams on 115 hp Optimax, 135-250 hp, 105 jet and 140 jet models.

4. Electrical wiring, a fuse and two relays.

Operation

Power trim/tilt systems incorporate several special hydraulic functions:

1. *Impact*—This circuit is designed to absorb and dissipate the energy of an impact with an underwater object, while in forward motion. It does *not* protect the unit from impact damage when backing up. The circuit allows the hydraulic system to act as a shock absorber. High-pressure springs and check balls in the tilt cylinder piston vent hydraulic fluid to the opposite side of the piston when the pressure caused by the impact reaches a predetermined value. When fluid is vented, the engine is allowed to tilt up as necessary, dissipating the energy of the impact.

2. *Memory piston*—The memory piston works with the impact circuit to return the engine to the trim angle it was at before the impact occurred. The memory piston stays in place during an impact as the tilt cylinder's piston pulls away. After the impact has passed, propeller thrust pushes against the tilt cylinder piston. A valve in the tilt piston allows the fluid between the tilt piston and memory piston to vent, allowing the tilt piston to move downward until it seats against the memory piston. Memory pistons contain no valves.

3. *Reverse lock*—Reverse lock is multiple circuits in the system that hold the gearcase in the water during reverse thrust. Reverse thrust occurs during deceleration and when in reverse gear. If the gearcase is not held in the water during deceleration and reverse gear operation, the operator will not have control of the boat.

4. *Manual release*—The manual release valve allows the operator to raise or lower the engine if the electric motor or hydraulic system does not function. The valve can be opened and the engine can be positioned as desired. After positioning the engine, the manual release valve must be closed in order for the engine to hold position and for the impact and reverse lock circuits to function. Manual release valves must never be completely unscrewed except during disassembly.

WARNING
Do not operate a boat with the manual re-
lease valve opened.

5. *Hydraulic trim limit*—All trim and tilt systems use hydraulic valving to limit the maximum amount of positive trim the engine can achieve while under way. The trim range is limited to approximately 20° positive trim. The engine can be tilted higher than this when the boat is operated below planing speeds (shallow water drive) or when trailering. If the unit is tilted above 20° positive trim and the operator attempts to plane out or accelerate the boat, propeller thrust will overcome the tilt relief valve(s) and the engine will move down to the maximum trim out position. If the operator tries to exceed the maximum trim out (up) limit while under way, the electric motor and pump will run, but the unit will not trim higher. The internal valving will bypass the pump's output and lower the hydraulic pressure to prevent additional trimming out.

Power Trim and Tilt System Identification

Power trim/tilt systems can be divided into two basic designs.

1. 75-125 hp (except 115 hp Optimax and 105 jet), 65 jet and 80 jet models use an integral single ram system (**Figure 1**) with a two wire electric motor controlled by relays. This trim system is commonly referred to as the *yellow plug trim* because the fluid fill plug is yellow. An optional trim indicator gauge sending unit is available from Quicksilver parts and accessories.

2. 135-225 hp, 115 hp Optimax, 105 jet and 140 jet models use an integral three ram system (**Figure 2**). There is one tilt cylinder and two trim rams. The trim ram cylinders are cast into the manifold assembly. The trim rams push against replaceable striker (wear) plates. The com-

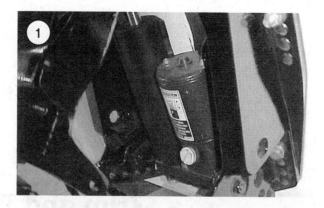

plete system is mounted between the stern brackets. This system uses a two wire (round) electric motor controlled by relays. A trim indicator gauge sending unit is standard equipment.

Electric Motor Operation

All models covered in this manual use a permanent magnet electric motor. Two strong permanent magnets are glued to the main housing. Never strike a permanent magnet motor with a hammer as this will crack the magnets and destroy the motor. The two motor leads are blue and green. When the blue wire is connected to positive and the green wire is grounded, the motor runs in the up direction. When the green wire is connected to positive and the blue wire is grounded, the motor runs in the down direction. Two relays switch the polarity of the green and blue leads to change the motor direction.

The electric motors used on 135-250 hp, 115 hp Optimax, 105 jet and 140 jet models incorporate a thermal switch. If the electric motor overheats for any reason, the thermal switch opens, interrupting electrical current flow to stop the motor. The switch resets after cooling for approximately one minute.

CAUTION
Activation of the thermal switch indicates an abnormal condition. Check for a faulty trim switch or defect within the electric motor if the thermal switch activates frequently.

Manual Release Valve Operation

All models incorporate a manual release valve. The valve is located at the lower outside corner of the starboard stern bracket. The valve may be accessed through a hole in the stern bracket or accessed directly, depending on model. See **Figure 3**, typical.

The manual release valve allows the engine to be raised and lowered to any position if the electric motor or hydraulic pump should fail.

WARNING
Do not operate the engine with the manual release valve in the open position. The reverse lock protection will be disabled. Nothing would prevent the engine from tilting out of the water when in reverse gear and when decelerating in forward gear. This will cause a loss of directional control. Retighten the manual release valve securely once the motor has been positioned as desired.

1. To raise or lower the motor manually, open the manual release valve (**Figure 3**) 3-4 full turns. Do not open the valve further than recommended.
2. Position the engine at the desired tilt or trim.
3. Securely tighten the manual release valve.

Maintenance

Periodically check the wiring system for corrosion and loose or damaged connections. Tighten loose connections, replace damaged components and clean corroded terminals as necessary. Coat the terminals and connections with anticorrosion grease or liquid neoprene. Check the reservoir fluid level as outlined in the following procedures.

Inspect the anode (**Figure 4**) for loose mounting hardware, loose or damaged ground straps (if equipped), and excessive deterioration. Replace the anode if it is reduced to one-half of its original size or less. Never paint or cover the anode with any substance. Replace the anode if paint or any other substance cannot be stripped from the surfaces.

Reservoir fluid check

On 75-125 hp (excluding 115 hp Optimax and 105 jet), 65 jet and 80 jet models, the fill plug (**Figure 5**) is located just below the electric motor.

On 135-250 hp, 115 hp Optimax, 105 jet and 140 jet models, the fill plug is located on the rear of the fluid reservoir (**Figure 6**).
1. Trim the outboard to the full up position. Clean the area around the fill plug. Carefully remove the fill plug while holding a shop cloth over the plug to block any oil spray.
2. The fluid level should be even with the bottom of the fill plug hole (**Figure 7**). If necessary, add Quicksilver

11

Power Trim Fluid (part No. 92-90100) or automatic transmission fluid (Dexron II) to bring the level up to the bottom of the oil level hole.

3. Install the fill plug and refer to *Bleeding air from the hydraulic system*.

4. Recheck the fluid level as described in Steps 1 and 2. Make sure the fill plug is tightened securely (see **Table 1**) when finished.

Bleeding air from the hydraulic system

All trim and tilt systems are considered self-bleeding. Simply cycle the unit fully up and down a total of 3-5 times to bleed all air from the system. Make sure the fluid level in the reservoir is maintained as described previously in this section. If the fluid appears foamy, allow the unit to sit for a minimum of 30 minutes to allow the air to separate from the fluid.

Maximum Trim In Limit Adjustment

An adjustable trim limit rod is used to limit the total amount of negative (down/in) trim an outboard can obtain. All models covered in this manual use a single long bolt (**Figure 8**) that passes through both stern brackets and is secured with a locknut.

Hydraulic Troubleshooting

If a problem develops in the trim/tilt system, first determine whether the problem is located in the electrical system or in the hydraulic system. If the electric motor runs normally, the problem is in the hydraulic system. If the electric motor does not run or runs slowly, go to *Electric system testing* in this chapter. It is possible for an internal hydraulic component problem to cause the pump to turn slowly or lock up completely, but it is unlikely.

If the electric motor seems to run abnormally fast in both directions (up and down), remove the electric motor and check for a sheared pump drive shaft or coupler.

If the unit will only tilt or trim partially, or the system's movement is jerky or erratic, check the reservoir fluid level as described previously in this chapter.

If the unit will not trim out (up) under load, but otherwise functions normally, the problem is probably in the pump assembly. On some units, the pump can be replaced without having to replace the valve body or manifold assembly. Consult a parts catalog or the appropriate illustrations in this chapter to determine the best course of action.

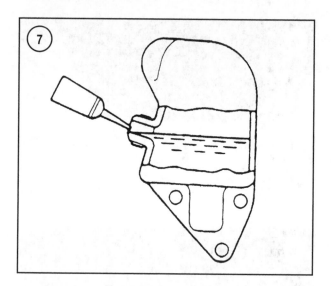

The recommended fluid for all trim systems covered in this manual is Quicksilver Power Trim and Steering Fluid (part No. 92-90100) or automatic transmission fluid (Dexron II). Lubricate all seals and O-rings with the recommended fluid during assembly. Apply Loctite 271 threadlocking adhesive (part No. 92-80819) to all threaded fasteners. If the manual release valve was removed, lubricate it with Quicksilver Special Lubricant 101 (part No. 92-13872A 1).

> *NOTE*
> *Always replace all O-rings, seals and gaskets that are removed. Clean the outside of the component before disassembly. Always use a lint-free cloth when handling trim/tilt components. Dirt or lint can block passages, causing valves to stick and preventing O-rings from sealing.*

The single-ram on 75-125 hp (except 115 hp Optimax and 105 jet), 65 and 80 jet models is removed and installed as an assembly. Specific troubleshooting procedures to

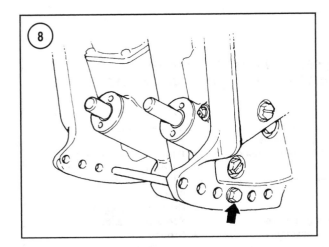

isolate the trim/tilt cylinder from the pump and manifold are not available. Parts to service most of the cylinder and pump/valve body components are available. Refer to **Figure 9** for component identification.

Three-ram systems on 135-250 hp, 115 hp Optimax, 105 jet and 140 jet models are removed and installed as an assembly. There is no specific troubleshooting procedure to isolate the tilt cylinder from the trim rams and manifold assembly. Parts to service most of the tilt cylinder, trim rams and manifold assembly are available. Refer to **Figure 10** or **Figure 11** as appropriate for component identification.

One-Piece, Single-Ram, Integral Trim/Tilt System Hydraulic Troubleshooting (75-125 hp [Except 115 hpOptimax and 105 Jet], 65 Jet and 80 Jet Models)

Unit leaks down

If the unit will not hold trim position in forward gear:

1. Remove, clean and inspect the manual release valve and O-ring (12, **Figure 9**). Replace the manual release valve if it or the O-ring(s) are damaged. Install the manual release valve and tighten the valve securely to prevent leaks. Retest the system for leak-down. Continue to the next step if leak-down persists.

2. Remove, clean and inspect the tilt relief valve and pilot valve assembly (13, **Figure 9**) components. Replace all of the tilt relief or pilot valve components if the assembly or any of the O-rings are damaged. Reassemble the unit and retest it for leak-down. Continue to the next step if leak-down persists.

3. Remove, clean and inspect the piston operating spool valve assembly (10, **Figure 9**). Replace the piston operating spool valve if any of the components are damaged.

Reassemble the unit and retest it for leak-down. Continue to the next step if leak-down persists.

4. Remove, clean and inspect the memory piston, the cylinder rod piston and the impact relief valves. If the O-rings are undamaged and the cylinder wall is not scored, replace the memory piston, and the cylinder rod and piston assembly.

   a. If the cylinder wall is scored or damaged, replace the cylinder assembly.

   b. Reassemble the unit with new seals and O-rings. Retest the system for leak-down. If leak-down is still evident, replace the pump and valve body assembly.

Unit has no reverse lock

If the unit kicks up in reverse or trails out on deceleration:

1. Remove, clean and inspect the manual release valve and O-ring(s) (12, **Figure 9**). Replace the manual release valve if it or the O-ring(s) are damaged. Install the manual release valve and tighten the valve securely to prevent leaks. Retest the system for reverse lock function. Continue to the next step if the reverse lock still does not function correctly.

2. Remove, clean and inspect the cylinder piston rod assembly for debris or damage to the impact relief (shock rod) valves. Replace the cylinder rod and piston assembly if there is any damage. Reassemble the unit with new O-rings and seals, and retest it for reverse lock function. Continue to the next Step if the reverse lock still does not function correctly.

3. Remove, clean and inspect the piston operating spool valve assemblies (10, **Figure 9**). Replace the piston operating spool valves if any of the valve components are damaged. Reassemble the unit with new O-rings and retest for reverse lock function. Replace the pump and manifold (valve body) assembly if the reverse lock still does not function correctly.

One-Piece, Triple Ram, Integral Trim/Tilt System Hydraulic Troubleshooting (135-250 hp, 115 hp Optimax, 105 Jet and 140 Jet Models)

Unit leaks down

If the unit will not hold trim position in forward gear:

1. Remove, clean and inspect the manual release valve and lock clip (27, **Figure 10** or 20, **Figure 11**). Replace the manual release valve if it or the O-ring(s) are damaged. Install the manual release valve and tighten the valve securely to prevent leaks. Retest the system for leak-down. Continue to the next step if leak-down persists.

11

⑨

SINGLE RAM TRIM SYSTEM (YELLOW CAP) (75-125 HP [EXCEPT 115 HP OPTIMAX AND 105 JET], 65 JET AND 80 JET MODELS)

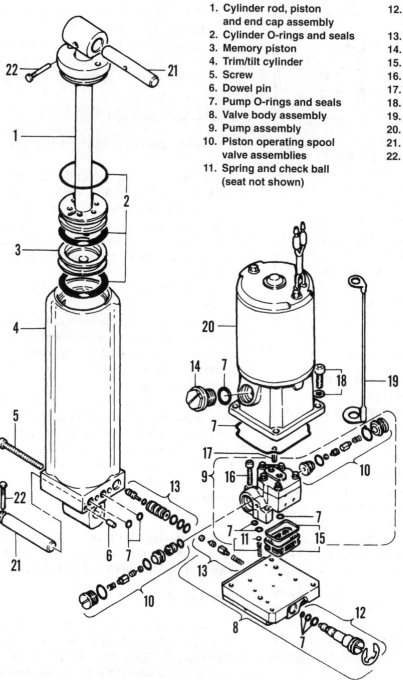

1. Cylinder rod, piston and end cap assembly
2. Cylinder O-rings and seals
3. Memory piston
4. Trim/tilt cylinder
5. Screw
6. Dowel pin
7. Pump O-rings and seals
8. Valve body assembly
9. Pump assembly
10. Piston operating spool valve assemblies
11. Spring and check ball (seat not shown)
12. Manual release valve and lock clip
13. Pilot valve assemblies
14. Fill plug
15. Filter and seal
16. Screw
17. Drive shaft (coupler)
18. Screw and washer
19. Ground wire
20. Electric motor
21. Pivot shaft
22. Trilobe or dowel pins

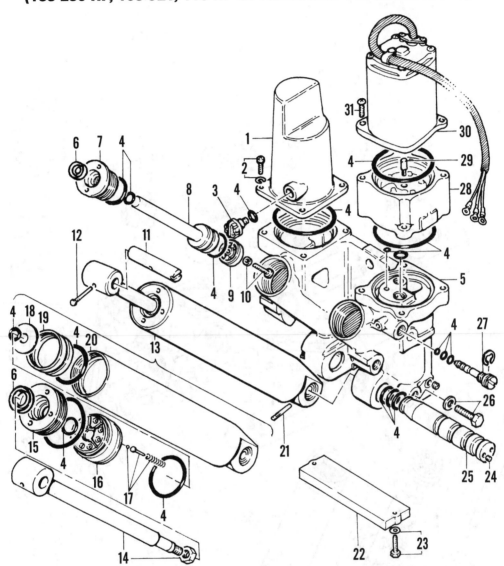

THREE RAM TRIM SYSTEM (1998 AND 1999)
(135-250 HP, 105 JET, 115 HP OPTIMAX AND 140 JET MODELS)

1. Fluid reservoir
2. Screw and washer
3. Fill plug
4. O-rings
5. Manifold
6. Wiper
7. Trim rod end cap
8. Trim rod (port)
9. Trim rod filter
   (port rod only)
10. Screw and washer
    (port rod only)
11. Upper pivot shaft
12. Trilobe or dowel pin
13. Tilt cylinder assembly
14. Tilt cylinder rod
    and locknut
15. Tilt cylinder end cap
16. Tilt cylinder piston
17. Spring, spring seat
    and check ball
18. Retaining washer
19. Memory piston
20. Tilt cylinder
21. Retaining pin
22. Anode
23. Screw and washer
24. Pipe plug(s)
25. Lower pivot shaft
26. Screw and washer
27. Manual release valve
    and lock clip
28. Pump and valve
    body assembly
29. Drive shaft (coupler)
30. Electric motor
31. Screw

11

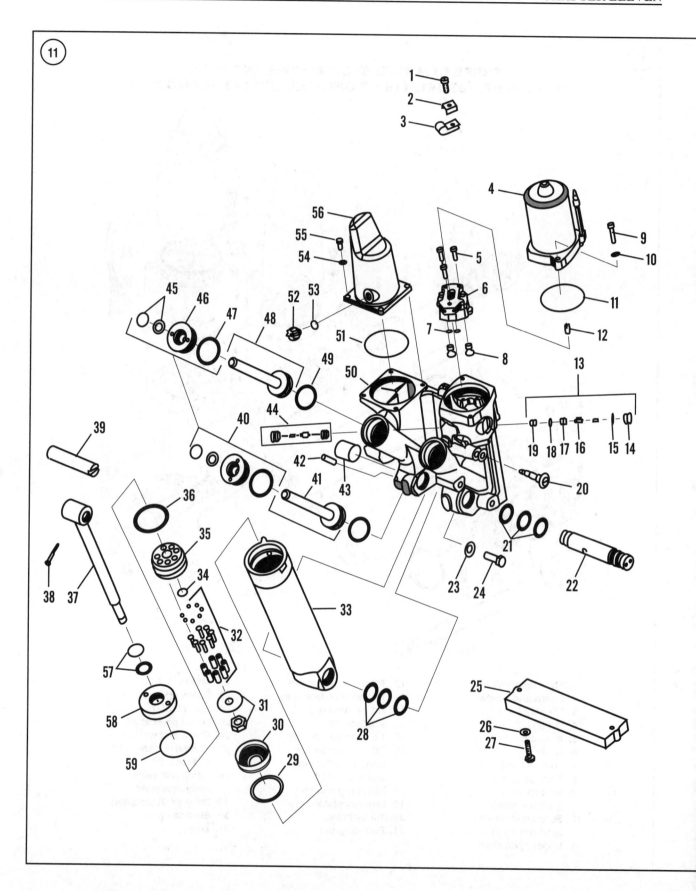

THREE RAM TRIM SYSTEM (2000-ON)
(135-250 HP, 105 JET, 115 HP OPTIMAX AND 140 JET MODELS)

1. Screw
2. Washer
3. Wire clamp
4. Electric motor
5. Screw
6. Pump
7. O-rings
8. Filter and O-ring
9. Screw
10. Washer
11. O-ring
12. Drive shaft (coupler)
13. Pilot valve assembly
14. Plug
15. O-ring
16. Pilot valve
17. Seat
18. O-ring
19. Spool
20. Manual release valve and lock clip
21. O-rings
22. Lower pivot shaft
23. Washer
24. Bolt
25. Anode
26. Washer
27. Bolt
28. O-rings
29. O-ring
30. Memory piston
31. Locknut and plate
32. Springs, balls and guides
33. Tilt cylinder
34. O-ring
35. Tilt cylinder piston
36. O-ring
37. Tilt cylinder rod
38. Trilobe pin
39. Upper pivot shaft
40. Trim rod end cap (starboard)
41. Trim rod (starboard)
42. Retaining pin
43. Bushing
44. Pilot valve assembly
45. Scraper and seal
46. Trim rod cap (port)
47. O-ring
48. Trim rod (port)
49. O-ring
50. Manifold
51. O-ring
52. Fill plug
53. O-ring
54. Washer
55. Screw
56. Fluid reservoir
57. Seal and scraper
58. Tilt cylinder end cap
59. O-ring

11

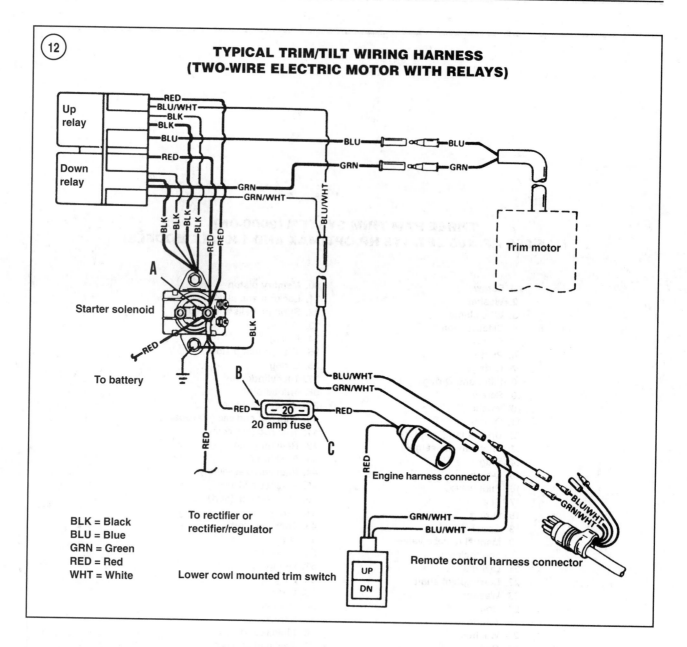

TYPICAL TRIM/TILT WIRING HARNESS
(TWO-WIRE ELECTRIC MOTOR WITH RELAYS)

2. Remove, clean and inspect the port trim ram rod (8, **Figure 10** or 48, **Figure 11**). Inspect the upper and lower check valves in the trim rod piston. If no dirt or debris is found in the check valves, replace the trim rod and reassemble the unit with new O-rings. Seal and retest for leak-down. Continue to the next step if leak-down persists.

3. Remove, clean and inspect the memory piston, cylinder rod piston and impact relief valves (14-20, **Figure 10** or 29-36, **Figure 11**).

   a. If the O-rings are undamaged and the cylinder wall is not scored, replace the memory piston and shock piston.

   b. If the cylinder wall is scored or damaged, replace the cylinder assembly.

   c. Reassemble the unit with new seals and O-rings. Retest the system for leak-down. Continue to the next step if leak-down is still noted.

4. Remove, clean and inspect the lower pivot shaft (25, **Figure 10** or 22, **Figure 11**). Reinstall the pivot shaft with new O-rings and retest leak-down. Continue to the next step if leak-down persists.

5A. On 1998 and 1999 models, if leak-down persists, replace the pump and valve body assembly (28, **Figure 10**).

5B. On 2000-on models, replace the pilot valve assemblies (13 and 44, **Figure 11**).

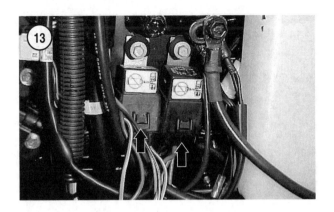

Unit has no reverse lock

If the unit kicks up in reverse or trails out on deceleration:

1. Remove, clean and inspect the manual release valve and O-rings (27, **Figure 10** or 20, **Figure 11**). Replace the manual release valve if it or the O-ring(s) are damaged. Install the manual release valve and tighten the valve securely to prevent leaks. Retest the system for reverse lock function. Continue to the next step if the reverse lock still does not function correctly.

2. Remove, clean and inspect the cylinder piston rod assembly (14-20, **Figure 10** or 29-36, **Figure 11**) for debris or damage to the impact relief (shock rod) valves. Replace the cylinder rod and piston assembly if there is any damage. Reassemble the unit with new O-rings and seals, and retest it for reverse lock function. Continue to the next step if the reverse lock still does not function correctly.

3. Remove, clean and inspect the lower pivot shaft (25, **Figure 10** or 22, **Figure 11**). Reinstall the pivot shaft with new O-rings and retest leak-down. Continue to the next step if leak-down persists.

4A. On 1998 and 1999 models, replace the pump and valve body assembly (28, **Figure 10**) if the reverse lock still does not function correctly.

4B. On 2000-on models, replace the pilot valve assemblies (13 and 44, **Figure 11**) and retest the unit for leak-down.

5. If the reverse lock still does not function, replace the tilt cylinder as an assembly. Reassemble the unit with new O-rings and retest the system for reverse lock function. If the reverse lock still does not function properly, replace the trim/tilt unit as a complete assembly.

Electrical System Troubleshooting

Blue-colored leads are primarily used for the up circuits. Green-colored leads are primarily used for the down circuits. The switching circuits for the trim/tilt system are normally protected by the main 20-amp fuse. Use a multimeter to perform electrical testing most accurately. Use a 12-volt test lamp and a self-powered continuity meter if a multimeter is unavailable. Before beginning troubleshooting with a test lamp, connect the test lamp directly to the battery and observe the brightness of the bulb. Reference the rest of the readings against this test. If the bulb does not glow as brightly as when it was hooked directly to the battery, low voltage is indicated. If a multimeter is used, take a battery voltage reading to reference all of the readings against. If the voltmeter reads 1 volt or more less than battery voltage, a definite problem is indicated. When continuity is checked with an ohmmeter, a zero reading is good. The higher the reading above zero, the worse the condition of the circuit.

Before attempting to troubleshoot any electrical circuit:

1. Make sure all connectors are properly engaged, and all terminals and leads are free of corrosion. Clean and tighten all connections as required.

2. Check and correct the battery charge level as described in Chapter Seven.

Trim relay operation

Refer to **Figure 12** for a typical relay-controlled system wiring diagram. Refer to the wiring diagrams at the end of the manual for specific models.

The two-wire motor is reversed by switching the polarity of the trim motor blue and green wires. There are two relays (**Figure 13**), one for each trim motor wire. Both relays connect their trim motor blue or green wire to ground when they are not activated. When the up relay is activated, the blue wire is switched to positive. The down relay is inactive and the green wire remains grounded. Current then flows from the positive terminal of the up relay to the trim motor and back to ground through the down relay causing the motor to operate in the up direction. When the down relay is activated, the green trim motor wire is switched to positive. The up relay is inactive and the blue wire remains grounded. Current then flows from the positive terminal of the down relay to the trim motor and back to ground through the up relay causing the motor to operate in the down direction. If the motor operates in one direction, but not the other, the problem *cannot* be in the trim motor.

Relay circuit test

> *NOTE*
> *Some models are equipped with an engine cover mounted trim switch (**Figure 14**) in addition to the remote control mounted*

11

switch. Either or both of the switches can fail and cause the system to malfunction. Test each trim switch separately.

1. Connect the test lamp lead to the positive terminal of the battery and touch the test lamp probe to metal anywhere on the engine block. If the lamp does not light or is dim, the battery ground cable connections are loose or corroded, or there is an open circuit in the battery ground cable. Check connections on both ends of the ground cable.

2. Connect the test lamp lead to a good engine ground.

3. Connect the test lamp probe to the starter solenoid input terminal. If the lamp does not light or is very dim, the battery cable connections are loose or corroded, or there is an open in the cable between the battery and the solenoid. Clean and tighten the connections or replace the battery cable as required.

4. Remove the 20 amp fuse and connect the test lamp probe to the input side of the 20 amp fuse. If the test lamp does not light, repair or replace the wire between the starter solenoid and the fuse holder.

5. Reinstall the fuse and connect the test lamp probe to the output side of the fuse. If the test lamp does not light, replace the fuse.

6. Disconnect the trim/tilt relays from their connector bodies.

7. Connect the test lamp probe to the input side of each relay (red terminal). If the test lamp does not light at each point, repair or replace the wire from the starter solenoid to each relay.

8. Connect the test lamp lead to the positive terminal of the battery and touch the test lamp probe to each of the two black wires at each relay connector. If the test lamp does not light at each point (a total of four wires), repair or replace each wire from the relay connector body to the ground that failed the test.

NOTE
*Refer to **Key (Ignition) Switch Test** in Chapter Three for more information on testing the ignition switch and the wire connections to the switch. Refer to the remote control harness wiring diagrams at the end of this manual.*

9. Connect the test lamp lead to a clean engine ground. Connect the test lamp probe to the red or red/purple wire (B, B+ or BAT terminal) at the ignition switch. If the lamp does not light, repair or replace the wire, or the main engine harness connector terminals between the starter solenoid positive terminal and the ignition switch terminal.

10. Connect the test lamp probe to the center terminal (red or red/purple wire) of each trim/tilt switch. If the test lamp

does not light, repair or replace the wire from the ignition switch red or red/purple wire (B, B+ or BAT terminal) connection to the defective trim/tilt switch center terminal.

11. Connect the test lamp probe to the blue/white terminal in the up relay connector body. Hold each trim switch in the up position and observe the test lamp. If the test lamp does not light as each switch is activated, connect the test lamp probe to the blue/white wire at each trim switch. Hold each trim switch in the up position and observe the test lamp. If the test lamp does not light when each trim switch is activated, replace the defective trim/tilt switch. If the test lamp lights at the trim switch, but not at the up relay blue/white terminal, repair or replace the blue/white wire from the suspect trim/tilt switch to the up relay connector.

12. Connect the test lamp probe to the green/white terminal in the down relay connector body. Hold each trim switch in the down position and observe the test lamp. If the test lamp does not light as each switch is activated, connect the test lamp probe to the green/white wire at each trim switch. Hold each trim switch in the down position and observe the test lamp. If the test lamp does not light when each trim switch is activated, replace the defective trim/tilt switch. If the test lamp lights at the trim switch, but not at the down relay green/white terminal, repair or replace the green/white wire from the suspect trim/tilt switch to the relay connector.

13. Reconnect the trim/tilt relays to the wiring harness connectors. Probing from the rear of the relay connector body, connect the test lamp probe to the large blue terminal in the up relay connector body. Hold the trim switch in the UP position and observe the test lamp. If the test lamp does not light, replace the up trim relay.

14. Probing from the rear of the relay connector body, connect the test lamp probe to the large green terminal in the down relay connector body. Hold the trim switch in the DOWN position and observe the test lamp. If the test lamp does not light, replace the down trim relay.

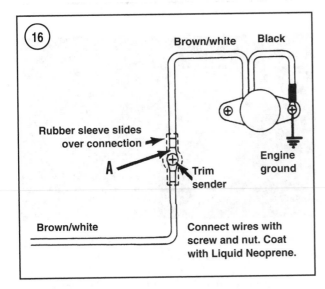

NOTE
The blue or green trim motor wire of each relay is grounded when the relay is not activated. Checks the relays ground path in Step 15.

15. Connect the test lamp lead to the positive terminal of the battery. Probing from the rear of each relay connector body, alternately touch the test lamp probe to the large blue terminal of the up relay and the large green terminal of the down relay. The test lamp does not light at each test point, replace the defective relay(s).

16. If all previous tests are satisfactory and the electric motor still does not operate correctly, repair or replace the electric motor.

Trim Sending Unit Test

The trim sender is standard equipment on 135-250 hp, 115 hp Optimax, 105 jet and 140 jet models. The sender is mounted on the swivel bracket (**Figure 15**). The rotor por-

tion of the sender fits into a slot in the upper pivot shaft and rotates as the engines tilts up and down, sending a varying voltage signal to the dash mounted trim gauge. The sender voltage corresponds to the trim angle of the engine.

1. Make sure the black trim sender wire has a good ground connection. Clean and tighten the connection as necessary.

2. Trim the outboard to its fully down position. Make sure the ignition switch is OFF.

3. Connect an ohmmeter calibrated to the R × 1 scale between a good engine ground and test point (A, **Figure 16**, typical).

4. Trim the outboard up while noting the meter reading.

5. The resistance should smoothly increase as the outboard trims up and smoothly decrease when the unit is trimmed down. If it does not, replace the trim sender.

6. Reconnect all wires when finished.

POWER TRIM AND TILT SYSTEM SERVICE

CAUTION
Metric and American fasteners may be found on trim/tilt units, stern brackets and swivel brackets. Always match a replacement fastener to the original. Do not run a tap or thread chaser into a hole or over a bolt without first verifying the thread size and pitch.

The recommended fluid for all integral systems is Quicksilver Power Trim and Steering Fluid (part No. 92-90100) or automatic transmission fluid. Lubricate all seals and O-rings with the recommended fluid during assembly. Apply Loctite 271 threadlocking adhesive (part No. 92-80819) to all threaded fasteners. If the manual release valve was removed, lubricate it with Quicksilver Special Lubricant 101 (part No. 92-13872A 1). Refer to **Table 1** and **Table 2** for torque specifications.

NOTE
Always replace all O-rings, seals and gaskets. Clean the outside of the component before disassembly. Always use a lint-free cloth when handling trim/tilt components. Dirt or lint can cause blocked passages, sticking valves and prevent O-rings from sealing.

Relieving System Pressure

WARNING
Before disassembling any trim/tilt system, relieve the internal pressure.

11

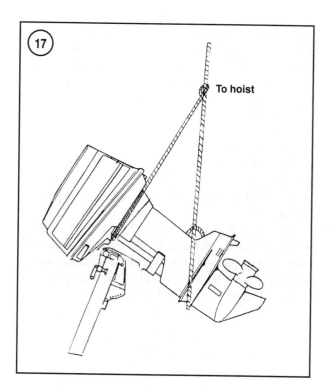

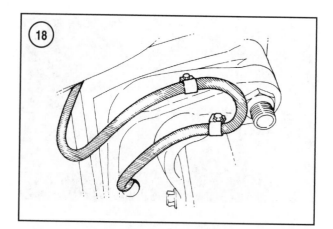

The trim/tilt cylinder ram or tilt cylinder and trim rams must be fully extended for all internal pressure to be safely relieved. If the trim/tilt unit has already been removed from the outboard motor, simply reconnect the electric motor leads to the relays and run the unit up until the ram(s) is fully extended.

1. Trim the outboard to the full up position.

2. Engage the tilt lock, securely block the outboard or support the outboard with a suitable hoist (**Figure 17**). Refer to the owner's manual for information on how the tilt lock works on a specific engine.

3. Open the manual release valve as described previously in this chapter and allow the outboard to settle onto the tilt lock, blocks or hoist.

4. Carefully remove the fill plug while covering the plug with a shop towel.

5. After the internal pressure has been relieved, reinstall the fill plug and close the manual release valve to minimize fluid leaks, if so desired.

75-125 hp (Except 115 hp Optimax and 105 Jet) 65 Jet and 80 Jet Models

The electric motor is not serviceable and must be replaced as an assembly with the reservoir. However, the hydraulic pump can be replaced without the complete valve body being replaced.

System removal/installation

1. Tilt the outboard to the full tilt position and engage the tilt lock, securely block the outboard or support the outboard with a suitable hoist. If it is necessary to use the manual release valve to tilt the outboard, do not open the manual release valve more than four full turns.

2. Disconnect the negative battery cable.

3. Remove the screws and clamps securing the trim motor harness to the starboard stern bracket. See **Figure 18**.

4. Carefully unplug the blue and green trim motor wires from the trim relay harness.

5. Route the trim motor harness out of the engine cover grommet and free from the starboard stern bracket.

NOTE
If the trilobe pin is difficult to remove in Step 6, the upper pivot shaft can be driven forcefully from its bore, shearing the trilobe pin. Remove all trilobe pin remnants. Clean the pivot shaft and trilobe pin bores, and inspect them for damage.

6. Use diagonal cutters to pull the trilobe pin from the cylinder rod and upper pivot shaft (**Figure 19**). Remove

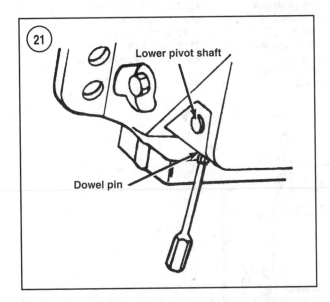

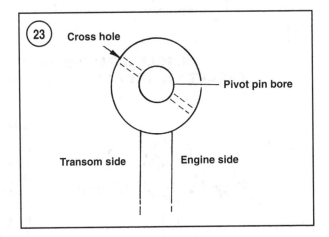

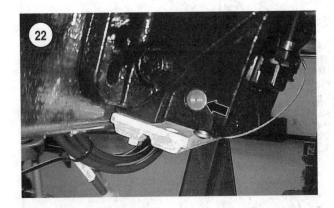

and inspect the trilobe pin. Replace the pin if it is damaged. Then drive the upper pivot shaft laterally from the bracket using a punch and hammer.

7. Remove the bolts (**Figure 20**) and the anode plate. Replace the plate if it is damaged or if it has lost 40% or more material.

8. Use a suitable punch to drive the dowel pin securing the lower pivot shaft upward. See **Figure 21**. Remove and inspect the dowel pin. Replace the dowel pin if it is damaged.

9. Remove the lower pivot shaft (**Figure 22**) from the trim/tilt unit and the stern brackets by driving it laterally with a suitable punch and hammer.

10. Note the position and routing of the trim motor ground wire.

11. Remove the trim/tilt system by pivoting the top of the trim/tilt cylinder out and away from the stern brackets.

12. To install the system, liberally apply Quicksilver 2-4-C Multi-Lube grease (part No. 92-825407) to the upper and lower pivot shafts, pivot shaft bores, dowel pin and trilobe pin bores, and the dowel and trilobe pin.

NOTE
Make sure the grooved end of the lower pivot shaft is positioned on the same side of the engine as the retaining pin bore.

13. Start the lower pivot shaft with the grooved end facing the dowel pin bore into its bore from the port side stern bracket, then start the lower dowel pin from the top of its bore. Do not drive either pin far enough to interfere with tilt unit installation.

14. Install the trim/tilt system, inserting the bottom into the stern brackets first, then rotating the trim/tilt cylinder towards the transom and into position. Route the motor harness out through the hole in the starboard stern bracket.

15. Drive the lower pivot shaft flush with the stern bracket or mounting bracket outer surfaces. Then use a suitable punch to drive the dowel pin in from the top until it is fully seated.

16. Align the upper pivot shaft bore with the trim/tilt cylinder rod eye. The cylinder rod eye must face as shown in **Figure 23**.

17. Install the upper pivot shaft into the swivel bracket bore and through the trim/tilt cylinder rod eye. The shaft

11

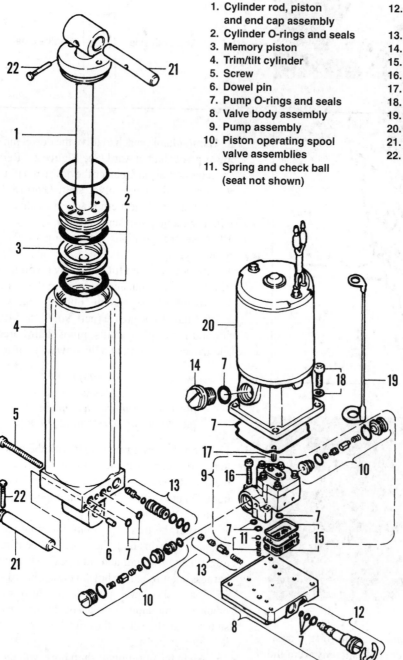

(24)

SINGLE RAM TRIM SYSTEM (YELLOW CAP) (75-125 HP
[EXCEPT 105 JET AND 115 HP OPTIMAX], 65 JET AND 80 JET MODELS)

1. Cylinder rod, piston and end cap assembly
2. Cylinder O-rings and seals
3. Memory piston
4. Trim/tilt cylinder
5. Screw
6. Dowel pin
7. Pump O-rings and seals
8. Valve body assembly
9. Pump assembly
10. Piston operating spool valve assemblies
11. Spring and check ball (seat not shown)
12. Manual release valve and lock clip
13. Pilot valve assemblies
14. Fill plug
15. Filter and seal
16. Screw
17. Drive shaft (coupler)
18. Screw and washer
19. Ground wire
20. Electric motor
21. Pivot shaft
22. Trilobe or dowel pins

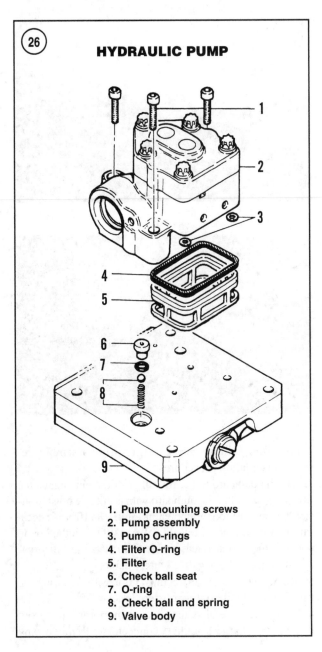

HYDRAULIC PUMP

1. Pump mounting screws
2. Pump assembly
3. Pump O-rings
4. Filter O-ring
5. Filter
6. Check ball seat
7. O-ring
8. Check ball and spring
9. Valve body

must be flush with the swivel bracket outer surfaces. Make sure the bores align, then drive the dowel pin or trilobe pin into its bore until it is fully seated.

18. Install the anode and connect the trim motor ground wire as noted on removal. Tighten the anode screws to the specification in **Table 1**.

19. Route the trim motor harness through the lower engine cover grommet and to the trim relay harness connections.

20. Install the screws and clamps to secure the trim motor harness to the starboard stern bracket as shown in **Figure 18**.

21. Connect the blue and green trim motor wires to their corresponding bullet connectors on the trim relay harness. Install any remaining clamps or tie-straps to the trim motor harness.

Electric motor removal/installation

Remove and install the electric motor and reservoir as an assembly. Refer to **Figure 24** for this procedure.

1. Remove the trim/tilt system as described in the previous section.

2. Relieve the internal pressure as described in this chapter. Then drain the reservoir into a suitable container.

3. Secure the system in a vise with protective jaws or between two suitable blocks of wood.

4. Note the position of the motor ground strap, then remove the four screws and washers securing the electric motor to the manifold assembly.

5. Carefully lift the electric motor and reservoir from the manifold (**Figure 25**). Locate and secure the pump coupler (drive shaft).

6. Remove and discard the motor O-ring or molded seal.

7. To install the motor, position the pump coupler (drive shaft) onto the hydraulic pump.

8. Install a new O-ring or molded seal on the electric motor/reservoir. Carefully align the motor armature shaft with the pump coupler (drive shaft) and install the motor/reservoir to the manifold. Be careful not to pinch the O-ring.

9. Install and evenly tighten the four screws and washers to the specification in **Table 1**. Make sure the ground strap is reinstalled under the starboard rear screw as noted on disassembly.

10. Reinstall the trim/tilt system as described in the previous section.

Hydraulic pump removal/installation

Refer to **Figure 24** for this procedure. The filter and filter O-ring are located beneath the hydraulic pump as shown in **Figure 26**.

11

1. Remove the electric motor as described in the previous section.

2. Remove the three pump mounting screws (1, **Figure 26**) securing the pump to the manifold. Do not remove the TORX head screws.

3. Lift the pump from the manifold (**Figure 27**). Remove and discard the pump O-rings (**Figure 28**).

4. Lift the filter O-ring and filter from the manifold (**Figure 29**). Clean and inspect the filter. Replace the filter if it cannot be cleaned or if it is damaged.

5. Remove and inspect the check ball seat (6, **Figure 26**) and discard the O-ring (7). Remove the check ball and spring (8, **Figure 26**) from the manifold. Replace any damaged or suspect components.

6. To reinstall the pump, place the spring into the manifold bore, followed by the check ball. Install a new O-ring on the check ball seat and press the seat and O-ring into the manifold bore.

7. Position two new O-rings on the base of the pump. Apply a light coat of Quicksilver Needle Bearing Assembly grease (part No. 92-825265) to hold the O-rings in place.

8. Position a new filter O-ring over the pump, then install the filter.

9. Install the pump assembly into the manifold. Be careful not to displace the pump O-rings or filter.

10. Secure the pump with three screws. Tighten the screws evenly to the specification in **Table 1**.

11. Install the electric motor/reservoir as described in this chapter.

135-250 hp, 115 hp Optimax, 105 Jet and 140 Jet Models

The trim system used on 2000-on models differs from the earlier systems in that it has replaceable pilot check valves. On 1998 and 1999 models, the hydraulic pump assembly must be replaced if the valves fail. Refer to **Figure 30** or **Figure 31** as appropriate during the repair procedures.

System removal/installation

> *WARNING*
> *Failure to support the outboard motor properly during power trim/tilt system removal/installation can result in severe personal injury and/or damage to the boat or motor.*

This procedure requires a suitable hoist, or a support tool fabricated from a used shift shaft or other 3/8 in. (9.53 mm) diameter rod as shown in **Figure 32**. Use the hoist (**Figure 33**) or the support tool to prevent the outboard

motor from falling during power trim assembly removal/installation procedures.

1. Tilt the outboard to the full tilt position and engage the tilt lock *and* secure the outboard with a suitable hoist or install the support tool as shown in **Figure 34**. If it is necessary to use the manual release valve to tilt the outboard, do not open the manual release valve more than four full turns.

2. Disconnect the negative battery cable.

3. Remove the screw and clamp (**Figure 35**) securing the trim harness to the starboard stern bracket.

4. Disconnect the blue and green trim motor wires from the engine harness bullet connectors. Remove any

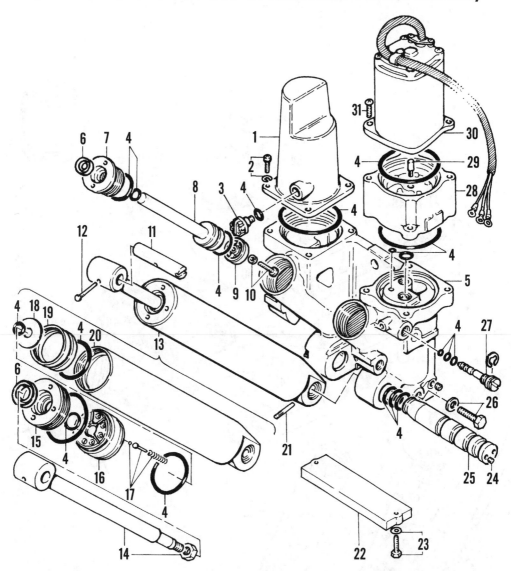

**THREE RAM TRIM SYSTEM (1998 AND 1999)
(135-250 HP, 105 JET, 115 HP OPTIMAX AND 140 JET MODELS)**

1. Fluid reservoir
2. Screw and washer
3. Fill plug
4. O-rings
5. Manifold
6. Wiper
7. Trim rod end cap
8. Trim rod
9. Trim rod filter
   (port rod only)
10. Screw and washer
    (port rod only)
11. Upper pivot shaft

12. Trilobe or dowel pin
13. Tilt cylinder assembly
14. Tilt cylinder rod
    and locknut
15. Tilt cylinder end cap
16. Tilt cylinder piston
17. Spring, spring seat
    and check ball
18. Retaining washer
19. Memory piston
20. Tilt cylinder
21. Retaining pin

22. Anode
23. Screw and washer
24. Pipe plug(s)
25. Lower pivot shaft
26. Screw and washer
27. Manual release valve
    and lock clip
28. Pump and valve
    body assembly
29. Drive shaft (coupler)
30. Electric motor
31. Screw

11

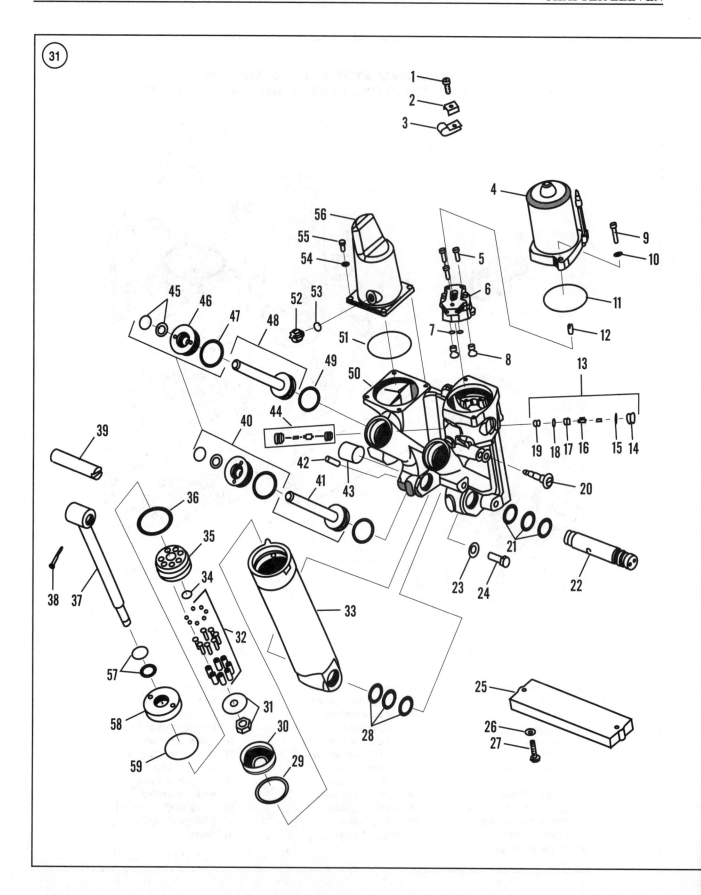

THREE RAM TRIM SYSTEM (2000-ON)
(135-250 HP, 105 JET, 115 HP OPTIMAX AND 140 JET MODELS)

1. Screw
2. Washer
3. Wire clamp
4. Electric motor
5. Screw
6. Pump
7. O-rings
8. Filter and O-ring
9. Screw
10. Washer
11. O-ring
12. Drive shaft (coupler)
13. Pilot valve assembly
14. Plug
15. O-ring
16. Pilot valve
17. Seat
18. O-ring
19. Spool
20. Manual release valve
    and lock clip
21. O-rings
22. Lower pivot shaft
23. Washer
24. Bolt
25. Anode
26. Washer
27. Bolt
28. O-rings
29. O-ring
30. Memory piston
31. Locknut and plate
32. Springs, balls and guides
33. Tilt cylinder
34. O-ring
35. Tilt cylinder piston
36. O-ring
37. Tilt cylinder rod
38. Trilobe pin
39. Upper pivot shaft
40. Trim rod end cap (starboard)
41. Trim rod (starboard)
42. Retaining pin
43. Bushing
44. Pilot valve assembly
45. Scraper and seal
46. Trim rod cap (port)
47. O-ring
48. Trim rod (port)
49. O-ring
50. Manifold
51. O-ring
52. Fill plug
53. O-ring
54. Washer
55. Screw
56. Fluid reservoir
57. Seal and scraper
58. Tilt cylinder end cap
59. O-ring

11

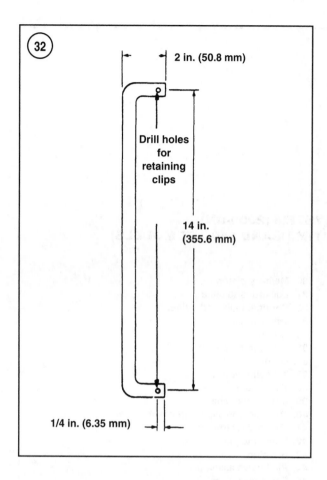

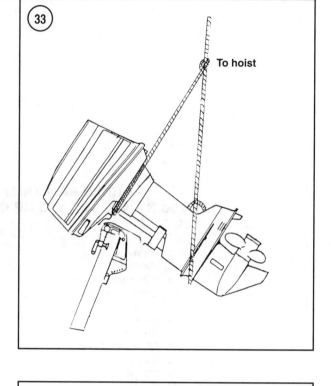

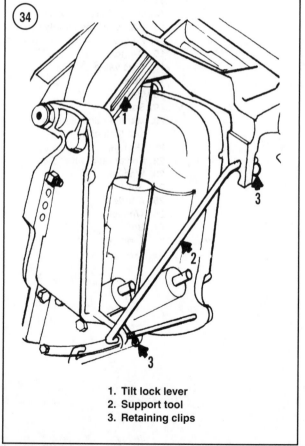

1. Tilt lock lever
2. Support tool
3. Retaining clips

tie-straps or clamps and pull the trim motor harness through the lower cowl.

5. Remove the anode at the bottom of the stern brackets.

6. Remove the trim-in limit adjustment bolt from the stern brackets (if present).

7. Attach a suitable wooden block under the engine swivel bracket with a large C-clamp to support the starboard side of the outboard. See **Figure 36**. The purpose of the block and C-clamp is to keep the engine from rotating away from the transom when the starboard stern bracket is removed.

8. Remove the cable retaining nut from the end of the tilt tube. It is not necessary to completely remove the steering cable from the motor.

9. On the starboard side of the outboard, remove the two transom bracket mounting bolts, nuts and washers (**Figure 37**). Remove the tilt tube nut (3, **Figure 36**) and the wave washer behind it.

10. Remove the three bolts and washers (**Figure 38**) holding the starboard stern bracket to the power trim/tilt system.

11. Move the starboard stern bracket away from the power trim assembly to allow the manual release valve to clear the bracket and allow the system to be removed.

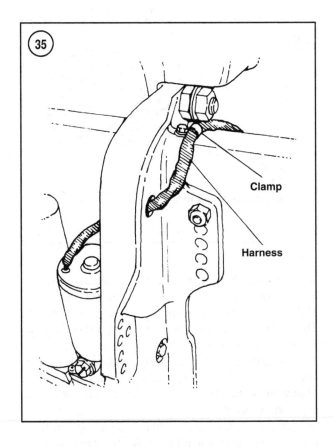

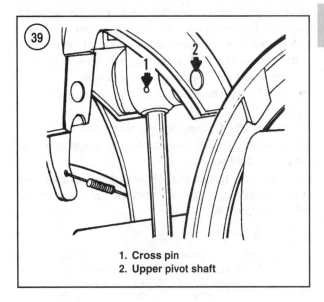

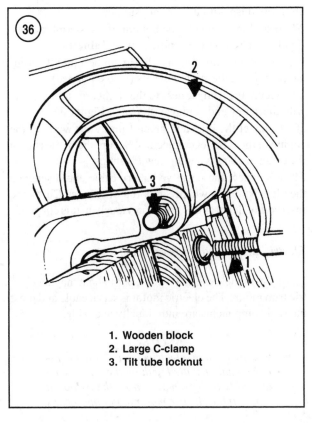

1. Wooden block
2. Large C-clamp
3. Tilt tube locknut

1. Cross pin
2. Upper pivot shaft

11

NOTE
*Do not reuse the cross pin that secures the tilt cylinder pivot shaft (**Figure 39**) once it has been removed.*

12. Drive out the cross pin (1, **Figure 39**) securing the tilt cylinder upper pivot shaft (2) with a suitable punch and

hammer. Discard the pin. Then drive the pivot shaft laterally from the swivel bracket bore with a suitable punch and hammer.

13. Remove the three bolts and washers holding the power trim/tilt system to the port transom bracket. Then remove the power trim assembly.

14. To reinstall the power trim assembly, apply Loctite 271 threadlocking adhesive (part No. 92-80819) to the threads of the three port side trim/tilt system mounting bolts. Install the system into the port transom bracket. Install the three bolts and washers, and tighten them finger-tight.

15. Lubricate the wave washer and the steering tube with Quicksilver 2-4-C Multi-Lube grease (part No. 82-825407). Then install the wave washer onto the tilt tube.

16. Route the power trim wiring harness through the hole in the top of the starboard stern bracket.

17. Apply Loctite 271 threadlocking adhesive to the threads of the three trim system mounting bolts that secure the system to the starboard stern bracket. Install the starboard stern bracket, then fasten the bracket to the trim/tilt system with the three bolts and washers. Be careful not to damage the power trim manual release valve. Tighten the three port and three starboard mounting bolts to the specification in **Table 1**.

18. Coat the shanks (not the threads) of the outboard mounting bolts with a suitable marine sealant, then reattach the starboard transom bracket to the boat transom with the bolts, flat washers and locknuts. The installation *must* be watertight. Tighten the bolts securely.

19. Install the tilt tube locknut (3, **Figure 36**) and tighten it securely.

20. Remove the C-clamp and wooden block.

21. Reinstall the cable retaining nut onto the tilt tube and tighten it securely.

22. Make sure the chamfered hole in the tilt cylinder rod eye faces the rear of engine. Rotate the rod eye as necessary. See **Figure 40**.

> *NOTE*
> *If the tilt ram overextends in Step 23, retract it by reversing the battery connections (green to positive and blue to negative).*

23. Connect the trim motor harness terminals to a 12-volt battery to extend the tilt ram enough to install the pivot shaft. Using a pair of suitable jumper leads, connect the trim motor blue wire to the positive battery terminal and the green wire to the negative battery terminal. When the end of the tilt ram aligns with the swivel bracket bore, disconnect the jumper leads.

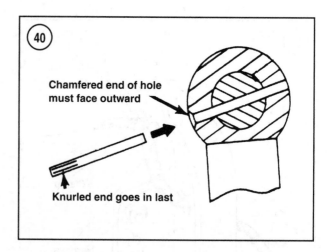

24. Align the tilt cylinder rod eye with the swivel bracket bore. Coat the pivot shaft with Quicksilver 2-4-C Multi-Lube grease and install the upper pivot shaft (1, **Figure 41**) into its bore with the slotted end of the shaft facing the port side of the engine.

25. Rotate the pivot shaft by engaging a large screwdriver in the slotted end. Align the cross pin holes as shown in **Figure 40**. A small tapered punch can be used to speed the alignment process.

26. Once the holes align, remove the punch and install a new cross pin as shown in **Figure 40**. Tap the cross pin in until it is flush with the tilt ram surface.

27. Install the anode to the bottom of the stern brackets. Tighten the screws to specification in **Table 1**.

28. Install the trim-in limit adjustment bolt into its original position in the stern brackets (if so equipped).

29. Secure the trim harness to the starboard stern bracket with the screw and clamp as shown in **Figure 35**.

30. Connect the blue and green trim motor wires to the engine harness bullet connectors. Secure the harness with the original clamps and/or new tie-straps.

31. Reconnect the negative battery cable and disengage the tilt lock or remove the support tool or hoist. Check the reservoir oil level as described previously in this chapter.

Electric motor removal/installation

All V-6 models use a two-wire, permanent magnet electric trim motor. The electric motor is serviceable and most internal components are individually available.

> *NOTE*
> *The pump and electric motor can be removed and installed without the power trim assembly being removed from the outboard motor. If the electric motor mounting screws*

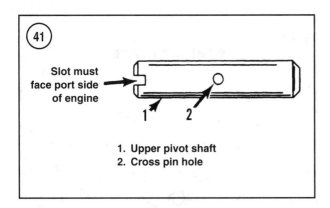

Slot must face port side of engine

1. Upper pivot shaft
2. Cross pin hole

cannot be accessed, remove the starboard stern bracket from the engine.

1. Relieve the internal pressure as described in this chapter. See *Relieving System Pressure*.

2. If the system is removed from the engine, drain the reservoir into a suitable container and secure the system in a vice with protective jaws or between two suitable blocks of wood.

3. If the system is installed on the engine, place a suitable drain pan under the stern brackets and trim/tilt system.

4. If the system is installed on the engine, disconnect the trim motor harness from the engine and remove the starboard stern bracket as described in Steps 2-11 under *System removal/installation* in this section.

5A. On 1998 and 1999 models, remove the two screws (31, **Figure 30**) securing the base of the electric motor to the pump and valve body assembly (28). Then remove the motor.

5B. On 2000-on models, remove the socket head screws (9, **Figure 31**) and washers (10) securing the electric motor to the manifold (50). Then remove the motor.

6. Locate and secure the pump/drive shaft coupler (29, **Figure 30** or 12, **Figure 31**). Then discard the motor O-ring (4, **Figure 30** or 11, **Figure 31**).

7. To install the motor, position the pump coupler (drive shaft) onto the hydraulic pump.

8. Install a new O-ring into the recess in the pump and valve body or manifold. Carefully align the motor armature shaft with the pump coupler (drive shaft) and install the motor to the manifold. Be careful not to pinch the O-ring.

9. Install and evenly tighten the screws to the specification in **Table 1**.

10. Reinstall the trim/tilt system or reinstall the starboard stern bracket and reconnect the trim motor harness as described in the previous section.

Hydraulic pump removal/installation

The hydraulic pump can only be serviced as an assembly.

1. Remove the electric motor as described in the previous section.

2A. On 1998 and 1999 models, remove the pump as follows:

   a. Remove the two socket head screws securing the pump and valve body assembly (28, **Figure 30**) to the manifold.

   b. Lift the pump from the manifold.

   c. Remove and discard the pump O-rings (4, **Figure 30**).

   d. Remove and clean the filter screens if equipped. Replace the screens if they cannot be thoroughly cleaned or if they are damaged.

2B. On 2000-on models, remove the pump as follows:

   a. Remove the three screws (5, **Figure 31**) securing the pump (6) to the manifold.

   b. Lift the pump from the manifold opening.

   c. Remove the O-rings (7, **Figure 31**) from the pump or manifold surface. Discard the O-rings.

   d. Remove the filters and O-rings (8, **Figure 31**) from the bottom of the pump. Discard the O-rings.

   e. Clean the filters. Replace them if they cannot be thoroughly cleaned or if they are damaged.

3A. On 1998 and 1999 models, install the pump and valve body assembly as follows:

   a. Fit the filter screens and three O-rings (4, **Figure 30**), if equipped, into their respective recesses in the manifold. A light coat of Quicksilver Needle Bearing Assembly grease (part No. 92-825265) can be used to hold the O-rings in place.

   b. Install the pump assembly into the manifold. Be careful not to displace the pump O-rings or filters. The casting in the flat of the side of the pump must face the starboard stern bracket.

   c. Secure the pump with two screws. Tighten the screws evenly to the specification in **Table 1**.

3B. On 2000-on models, install the pump as follows:

   a. Install new filter O-rings into the recesses on the bottom of the pump (6, **Figure 31**). Fit the filters into the recesses. The open end of the filters must face the pump.

   b. Fit new O-rings (7, **Figure 31**) into their respective recesses in the pump or manifold. A light coat of Quicksilver Needle Bearing Assembly grease (part No. 92-825265) can be used to hold the O-rings in place.

11

c. Align the screw holes, then install the pump into the manifold opening. Do not dislodge the O-rings or filters.

d. Secure the pump with the three screws. Tighten the screws evenly to the specification in **Table 1**.

4. Install the electric motor as described in the previous section.

Striker plate removal/installation

The striker plates (**Figure 42**) are the plates in the swivel bracket that the trim rods push against to trim the motor throughout the approximately 20° positive trim angle range. Replace the striker plates if they are damaged or worn. Worn or damaged plates create a popping noise during down trim system operation.

Simply remove the nut and lockwasher, then remove the striker plate. Replace the lockwasher if it is damaged or defective. To install the striker plate, position the plate in the swivel bracket bore and secure it with the lockwasher and nut. Tighten the nut to the specification in **Table 1**.

Trim sender removal, installation and adjustment

Refer to **Figure 43** for this procedure.

1. Tilt the outboard to its fully up position and engage the tilt lock lever, block the outboard securely or support the outboard with a hoist.

2. Disconnect the trim sender leads.

3. Remove the sender attaching screws. Then remove the sender.

4. To install the sender, position the sender in the swivel bracket and install the two screws finger-tight.

5. Connect the trim sender leads to the wiring harness.

> *NOTE*
> *Some 2000-on engines use Smartcraft gauges. The digital trim sender used with these gauges does not require adjustment.*

6. With the outboard in the fully down position, the trim indicator needle should point to the full down position on the gauge. If it does not, trim the engine to its fully up position and engage the tilt lock lever, block the outboard securely or support the outboard with a hoist.

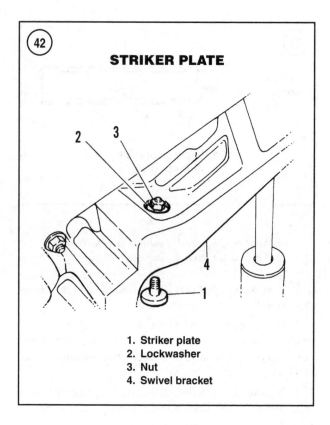

STRIKER PLATE

1. Striker plate
2. Lockwasher
3. Nut
4. Swivel bracket

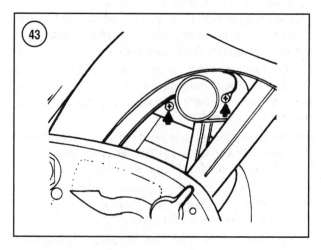

7. Loosen the trim sender attaching screws just enough to allow sender rotation. Rotate the sender unit slightly counterclockwise to raise, or rotate it slightly clockwise to lower, the trim indicator needle.

8. Repeat Steps 6 and 7 until the needle position is correct. Then securely tighten the attaching screws and make a final check of the needle position.

Table 1 TRIM AND TILT SYSTEM TORQUE SPECIFICATIONS

Fastener	in.-lb.	ft.-lb.	N•m
Anode screws			
75-125 hp (except 115 hp Optimax and 105 jet), 65 jet and 80 jet	60	–	6.8
135-250 hp, 105 jet, 115 hp Optimax and 140 jet	70	–	7.9
Check valve plug			
75-125 hp (except 115 hp Optimax and 105 jet), 65 jet and 80 jet	120	–	13.6
135-250 hp, 105 jet, 115 hp Optimax and 140 jet	120	–	13.6
Fill plug			
135-250 hp, 105 jet, 115 hp Optimax and 140 jet	22	–	2.5
Fluid reservoir			
135-250 hp, 105 jet, 115 hp Optimax and 140 jet	60	–	6.8
Manual relief valve			
135-250 hp, 105 jet, 115 hp Optimax and 140 jet	22	–	2.5
Mounting bolts			
135-250 hp, 105 jet, 115 hp Optimax and 140 jet	–	45	61
Pump to manifold			
75-125 hp (except 115 hp Optimax and 105 jet), 65 jet and 80 jet	70	–	8.1
135-250 hp, 105 jet, 115 hp Optimax and 140 jet	80	–	9
Relay mount	35	–	4
Shock piston to ram			
75-125 hp (except 115 hp Optimax and 105 jet), 65 jet and 80 jet	–	90	122
Shock piston plate (screws)			
75-125 hp (except 115 hp Optimax and 105 jet), 65 jet and 80 jet	35	–	4
Striker plate nuts			
135-250 hp, 105 jet, 115 hp Optimax and 140 jet	80	–	9
Tilt cylinder end cap			
135-250 hp, 105 jet, 115 hp Optimax and 140 jet	–	45	61
Tilt cylinder locknut			
135-250 hp, 105 jet, 115 hp Optimax and 140 jet	–	95	129
Trim cylinder end cap			
135-250 hp, 105 jet, 115 hp Optimax and 140 jet	–	70	95
Trim cylinder to manifold			
75-125 hp (except 115 hp Optimax and 105 jet) 65 jet and 80 jet	100	–	11.3
Trim motor to pump			
135-250 hp, 105 jet, 115 hp Optimax and 140 jet	80	–	9
Trim motor/reservoir			
75-125 hp (except 115 hp Optimax and 105 jet) 65 jet and 80 jet	80	–	9

11

Table 2 GENERAL TORQUE SPECIFICATIONS

Screw or nut size	in.-lb.	ft.-lb.	N•m
U.S. Standard			
6-32	9	–	1.0
8-32	20	–	2.3
10-24	30	–	3.4
10-32	35	–	4.0
12-24	45	–	5.1
1/4-20	70	–	7.9
1/4-28	84	–	9.5
5/16-18	160	13	18
5/16-24	168	14	19
3/8-16	–	23	31
3/8-24	–	25	34
7/16-14	–	36	49
7/16-20	–	40	54
1/2-13	–	50	68
1/2-20	–	60	81

(continued)

Table 2 GENERAL TORQUE SPECIFICATIONS (continued)

Screw or nut size	in.-lb.	ft.-lb.	N•m
Metric			
M5	36	–	4
M6	70	–	8
M8	156	13	18
M10	–	26	35
M12	–	35	48
M14	–	60	81

Chapter Twelve

Midsection and Tiller Control

This chapter provides replacement instructions for all midsection components.

Repairs to the midsection typically involve replacing worn motor mounts, corrosion-damaged components or components damaged because of impact with underwater objects.

Minor repair to the midsection involves the replacement of easily accessible components such as the lower motor mounts (**Figure 1**, typical) or tilt lock mechanism (**Figure 2**, typical).

Major repair may require removal of the power head and gearcase followed by complete disassembly of the midsection. Major service is required when repairing or replacing the stern brackets (**Figure 3**, typical), swivel housing or drive shaft housing (**Figure 4**, typical).

Refer to Chapter Eleven if it is necessary to remove the trim system components to access the midsection component(s).

Apply Quicksilver 2-4-C grease (part No. 92-825407) to all bushings, pins and pivot points during assembly. **Table 1** lists specific application torque specifications and

Table 2 lists general torque specifications. Tighten fasteners not listed in **Table 1** to the general torque specifications in **Table 2**. **Table 1** and **Table 2** are located at the end of this chapter.

> *WARNING*
> *Never work under any part of the engine without first providing suitable support. The engine-mounted tilt lock or hydraulic system may collapse and cause the engine to drop. Support the engine with blocks or an overhead cable before working under the engine.*

Tilt Lock Lever Replacement

Refer to **Figure 5** and **Figure 6** as appropriate during tilt lock lever replacement.

1. Place the engine in the full up position.

2. Use an overhead hoist to support the engine as indicated in **Figure 7**. Disconnect both cables from the battery.

3. Remove all springs, pins, washers and attaching nuts for the tilt lock lever (14, **Figure 5** or 37, **Figure 6**).

4. Inspect all pins, levers, bushings and springs for worn, corroded or damaged surfaces. Replace any components if defects are noted.

5. Lubricate all bushings and pivot points with Quicksilver 2-4-C grease (part No. 92-825407) prior to assembly. Install all bushings, pins and washers onto the stern brackets.

6. Make sure the tilt lock lever operates smoothly. Check for improper assembly if rough operation or binding is noted.

7. Carefully remove the overhead support from the engine. Connect the cables to the battery.

> *CAUTION*
> *Do not use sealant on the anode bolt threads. The anodes cannot protect the engine without electrical continuity to the engine ground. Check for electrical continuity after installation. Remove the anode and clean the bolts and bolt heads if there is no continuity or high resistance.*

Anode Replacement

Refer to **Figure 5** or **Figure 6** as appropriate for this procedure.

1. Place the engine in the full up position.

2. Use an overhead hoist to support the engine as indicated in **Figure 7**. Disconnect both cables from the battery.

3. Loosen and remove the anode mounting bolts, then pull the anodes from the stern brackets. Tap the anode loose with a rubber mallet if necessary.

4. Clean all corrosion from the stern brackets at the anode mating surface. Clean all corrosion from the threads of the anode bolt holes.

5. Clean all deposits from the anode surfaces. Sand the surfaces, if necessary, until they are clean.

6. Install the anode(s) and bolts. Securely tighten the anode bolts.

7. Use a multimeter to check for electrical continuity between the anode and a bare spot on the stern bracket. Remove the anode, and clean the bolts and bolts holes if there is high resistance or no continuity. Install the anode and check the continuity.

8. Carefully remove the overhead support from the engine. Clean the terminals and connect the cables to the battery.

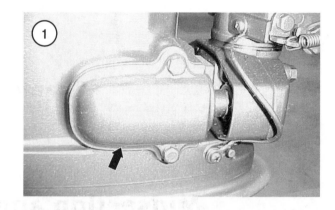

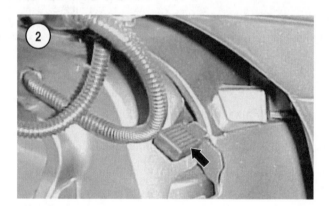

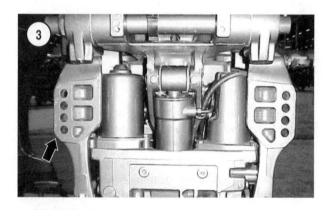

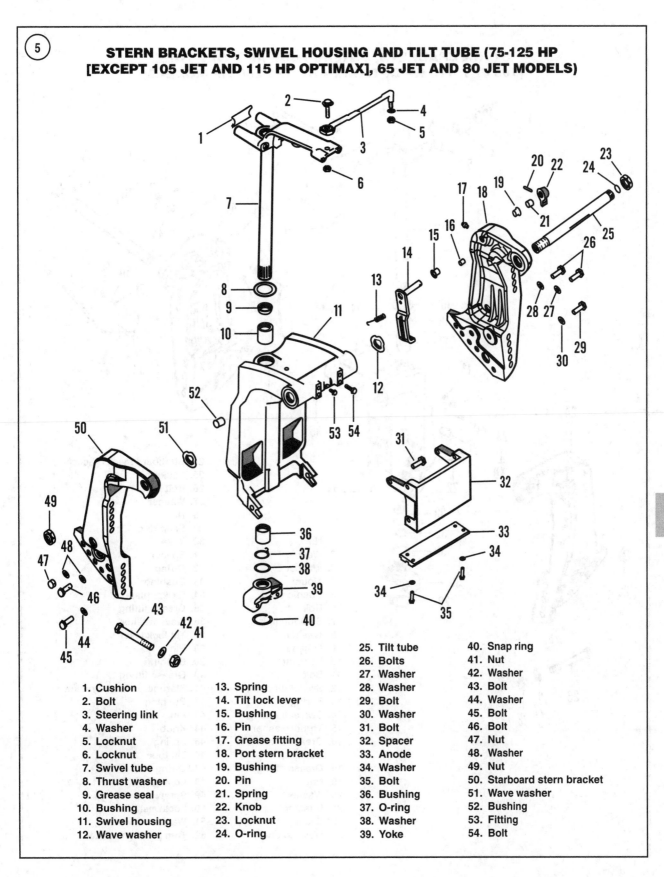

STERN BRACKETS, SWIVEL HOUSING AND TILT TUBE (75-125 HP [EXCEPT 105 JET AND 115 HP OPTIMAX], 65 JET AND 80 JET MODELS)

1. Cushion
2. Bolt
3. Steering link
4. Washer
5. Locknut
6. Locknut
7. Swivel tube
8. Thrust washer
9. Grease seal
10. Bushing
11. Swivel housing
12. Wave washer
13. Spring
14. Tilt lock lever
15. Bushing
16. Pin
17. Grease fitting
18. Port stern bracket
19. Bushing
20. Pin
21. Spring
22. Knob
23. Locknut
24. O-ring
25. Tilt tube
26. Bolts
27. Washer
28. Washer
29. Bolt
30. Washer
31. Bolt
32. Spacer
33. Anode
34. Washer
35. Bolt
36. Bushing
37. O-ring
38. Washer
39. Yoke
40. Snap ring
41. Nut
42. Washer
43. Bolt
44. Washer
45. Bolt
46. Bolt
47. Nut
48. Washer
49. Nut
50. Starboard stern bracket
51. Wave washer
52. Bushing
53. Fitting
54. Bolt

12

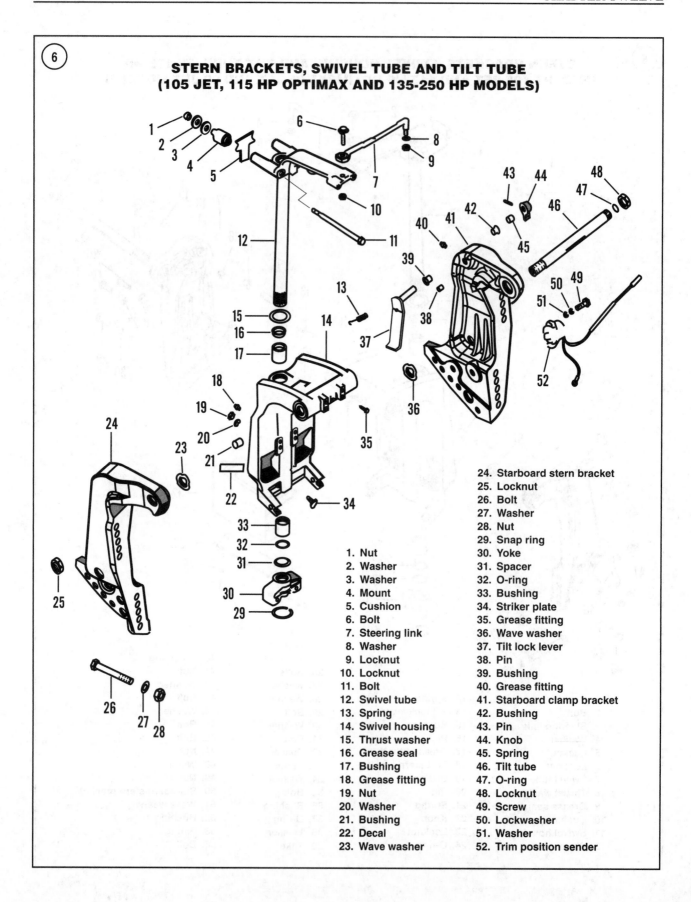

**STERN BRACKETS, SWIVEL TUBE AND TILT TUBE
(105 JET, 115 HP OPTIMAX AND 135-250 HP MODELS)**

1. Nut
2. Washer
3. Washer
4. Mount
5. Cushion
6. Bolt
7. Steering link
8. Washer
9. Locknut
10. Locknut
11. Bolt
12. Swivel tube
13. Spring
14. Swivel housing
15. Thrust washer
16. Grease seal
17. Bushing
18. Grease fitting
19. Nut
20. Washer
21. Bushing
22. Decal
23. Wave washer
24. Starboard stern bracket
25. Locknut
26. Bolt
27. Washer
28. Nut
29. Snap ring
30. Yoke
31. Spacer
32. O-ring
33. Bushing
34. Striker plate
35. Grease fitting
36. Wave washer
37. Tilt lock lever
38. Pin
39. Bushing
40. Grease fitting
41. Starboard clamp bracket
42. Bushing
43. Pin
44. Knob
45. Spring
46. Tilt tube
47. O-ring
48. Locknut
49. Screw
50. Lockwasher
51. Washer
52. Trim position sender

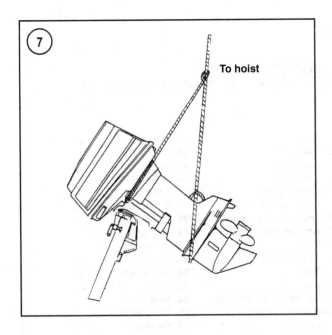

⑦

To hoist

Lower Engine Mount Replacement

Refer to **Figures 8-10** as appropriate for this procedure.

1. Place the engine in the full up position.

2. Use an overhead hoist to support the engine as indicated in **Figure 7**. Disconnect both battery cables.

3. Refer to **Figures 8-10** to locate the lower engine mounts.

4. Remove the small screws and the plastic lower engine mount cover. Remove the nut and washers that retain the mount bolts to the lower yoke.

5. Remove the bolts, washers and nuts that hold the lower mount bracket to the drive shaft housing. Carefully pull the mounts from both sides of the drive shaft housing.

6. Clean the mounting bolts, threaded bolt holes and mount contact surfaces.

7. Inspect all fasteners for wear, corrosion or damage. Replace any questionable or defective fasteners. Inspect the mounts for wear or damage. Replace the mount if there are any defects.

8. Inspect the mount contact surfaces in the drive shaft housing for cracked or damaged areas. Replace the drive shaft housing if they are cracked or excessively worn areas.

9. Insert the mount bolts with washers and grounding wires into the mounts. Fit the mounts into their recess in the drive shaft housing.

10. Install the lower mount bracket. Tighten the bracket bolts to the specification in **Table 1**.

11. Insert the mount bolt into the yoke. Fit the washer and nut over the mount bolt. Tighten the mount bolt and nut to the specification in **Table 1**.

12. Install the plastic mount cover. Tighten the plastic screw to the specification in **Table 1**.

13. Install all removed mount covers, ground wires, bumpers and brackets. Securely tighten all fasteners.

14. Carefully remove the overhead support from the engine. Clean the terminals and connect the cables to the battery.

Stern Brackets

NOTE
Replace all locking-type or tab washers with new ones when they are removed or disturbed.

NOTE
Note the connection points of the ground wires before disconnecting them to remove other components. Clean all corrosion or contaminants from wire contact surfaces. Make sure all ground wire terminals are securely tightened during assembly.

Refer to **Figure 5** or **Figure 6** as appropriate for this procedure.

1. Place the engine in the full up position.

2. Use an overhead hoist or wooden blocks to support the engine as indicated in **Figure 7**. Disconnect both cables from the battery.

3. Refer to **Figure 5** or **Figure 6** to locate the stern brackets and connected components or fasteners.

4. Refer to Chapter Eleven and remove the trim system from the engine. Remove the trim position sender (if so equipped) as described in Chapter Eleven.

5. Disconnect and remove the steering linkage and cables from the swivel tube and tilt tube. Remove the engine mounting bolts from the stern brackets and boat transom.

6. On 65 jet, 80 jet and 75-125 hp (except 115 hp Optimax) models, remove the bolts and washers (27-30, **Figure 5**) from the spacer (32).

7. Remove the large nut that retains the tilt tube to the stern brackets. Carefully pull the stern bracket from the engine. Clean the mounting bolt holes in the boat transom.

8. Clean the stern bracket, then inspect the stern bracket and related fasteners for cracks, wear or damage. Replace any defective components.

9. Place the stern bracket in position on the midsection. Align all bolts, nuts, spacers and brackets with their respective holes in the stern bracket.

10. Apply high quality marine-grade sealant to all surfaces of the mounting bolts and the bolt holes. Install the engine mounting bolts through the stern bracket and boat transom. Securely tighten the mount bolts.

12

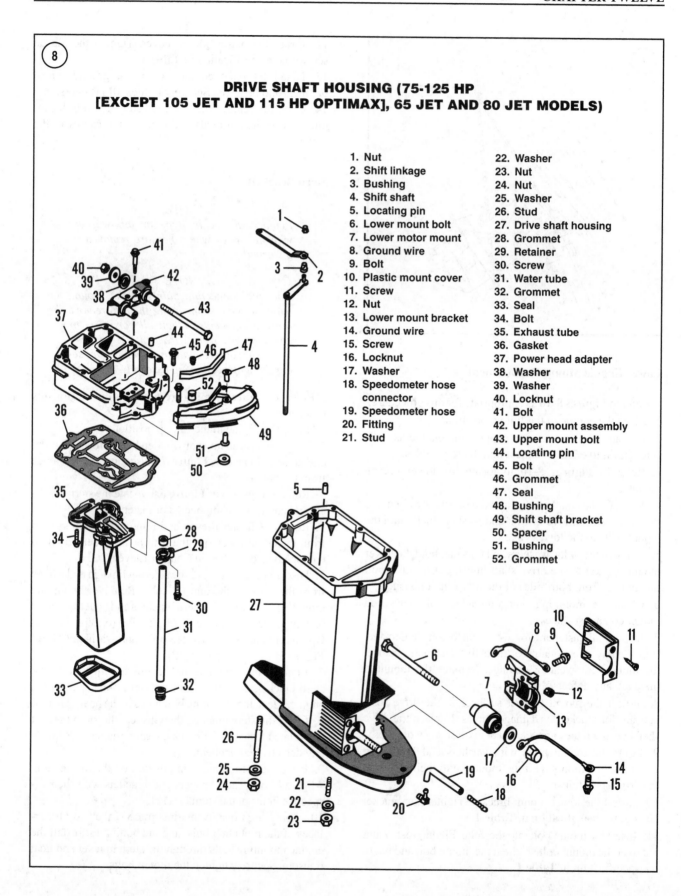

⑧

**DRIVE SHAFT HOUSING (75-125 HP
[EXCEPT 105 JET AND 115 HP OPTIMAX], 65 JET AND 80 JET MODELS)**

1. Nut
2. Shift linkage
3. Bushing
4. Shift shaft
5. Locating pin
6. Lower mount bolt
7. Lower motor mount
8. Ground wire
9. Bolt
10. Plastic mount cover
11. Screw
12. Nut
13. Lower mount bracket
14. Ground wire
15. Screw
16. Locknut
17. Washer
18. Speedometer hose connector
19. Speedometer hose
20. Fitting
21. Stud

22. Washer
23. Nut
24. Nut
25. Washer
26. Stud
27. Drive shaft housing
28. Grommet
29. Retainer
30. Screw
31. Water tube
32. Grommet
33. Seal
34. Bolt
35. Exhaust tube
36. Gasket
37. Power head adapter
38. Washer
39. Washer
40. Locknut
41. Bolt
42. Upper mount assembly
43. Upper mount bolt
44. Locating pin
45. Bolt
46. Grommet
47. Seal
48. Bushing
49. Shift shaft bracket
50. Spacer
51. Bushing
52. Grommet

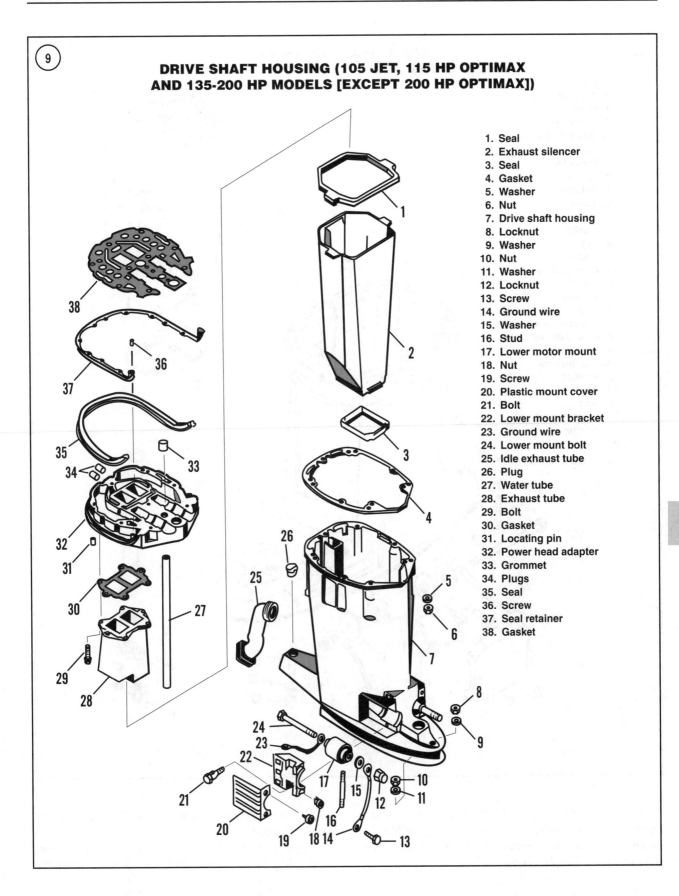

⑨

DRIVE SHAFT HOUSING (105 JET, 115 HP OPTIMAX AND 135-200 HP MODELS [EXCEPT 200 HP OPTIMAX])

1. Seal
2. Exhaust silencer
3. Seal
4. Gasket
5. Washer
6. Nut
7. Drive shaft housing
8. Locknut
9. Washer
10. Nut
11. Washer
12. Locknut
13. Screw
14. Ground wire
15. Washer
16. Stud
17. Lower motor mount
18. Nut
19. Screw
20. Plastic mount cover
21. Bolt
22. Lower mount bracket
23. Ground wire
24. Lower mount bolt
25. Idle exhaust tube
26. Plug
27. Water tube
28. Exhaust tube
29. Bolt
30. Gasket
31. Locating pin
32. Power head adapter
33. Grommet
34. Plugs
35. Seal
36. Screw
37. Seal retainer
38. Gasket

12

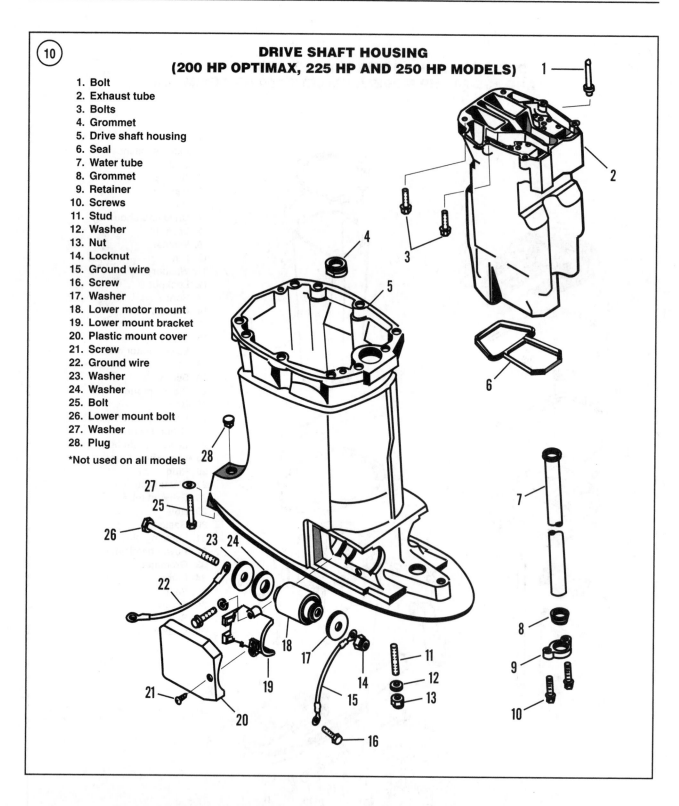

**DRIVE SHAFT HOUSING
(200 HP OPTIMAX, 225 HP AND 250 HP MODELS)**

1. Bolt
2. Exhaust tube
3. Bolts
4. Grommet
5. Drive shaft housing
6. Seal
7. Water tube
8. Grommet
9. Retainer
10. Screws
11. Stud
12. Washer
13. Nut
14. Locknut
15. Ground wire
16. Screw
17. Washer
18. Lower motor mount
19. Lower mount bracket
20. Plastic mount cover
21. Screw
22. Ground wire
23. Washer
24. Washer
25. Bolt
26. Lower mount bolt
27. Washer
28. Plug

*Not used on all models

11. On 65 jet, 80 jet and 75-125 hp (except 115 hp Optimax) models, position the spacer (32, **Figure 5**) between the stern brackets. Secure the spacer with the bolts and washers (27-30, **Figure 5**).

12. Refer to Chapter Eleven and install the trim system onto the engine.

13. Apply Quicksilver 2-4-C grease (part No. 92-825407) to the steering cable and tilt tube. Attach the

steering cable and linkage to the tilt tube and swivel tube. Securely tighten all fasteners, then engage any fastener locking devices.

14. Refer to Chapter Eleven and install the trim position sender (if so equipped).

15. Carefully remove the support from the engine. Clean the terminals and connect the cables to the battery.

16. Operate the trim and steering system through their entire operating range. Inspect the midsection for improperly installed components if there are unusual noises or binding. Repair as required.

Drive Shaft Housing
Removal and Installation

Refer to **Figures 8-10** as appropriate for this procedure.

1. Refer to Chapter Nine and remove the gearcase from the engine.

2. Refer to Chapter Eight and remove the power head from the engine.

3. Remove the lower engine mounts as described in this chapter.

4. Refer to **Figures 8-10** to identify the drive shaft housing components and their orientation.

5. Provide continual support for the drive shaft housing during this step. Remove the upper engine mount fasteners and pull the upper mounts from the drive shaft housing.

6. Remove all bolts, washers and nuts from the drive shaft housing, then carefully pry the adapter plate from the drive shaft housing. Remove and discard the adapter plate gaskets. On 105 jet, 115 hp Optimax and 135-200 hp (except 200 Optimax) models, remove the exhaust silencer (2, **Figure 9**) from the drive shaft housing.

7. Remove the exhaust tube only if it must be replaced. Remove its mounting bolts and carefully pry it from the adapter plate. Remove and discard the exhaust tube gaskets. Thoroughly clean all surfaces.

8. Clean the adapter plate, exhaust silencer, exhaust tube and drive shaft housing.

9. Inspect these components for wear, cracking or corrosion. Replace any defective components.

10. Inspect all alignment pins and their bores for worn or damaged pins or elongated holes. Replace any defective components.

11. Assembly is the reverse of disassembly. Note the following:

    a. Install new gaskets and seals at all locations during assembly.

    b. Apply Loctite 271 (part No. 92-809819) to the threads of all exhaust tube attaching bolts.

    c. Tighten all fasteners to the specification in **Table 1**.

12. Install the lower engine mounts as described in this chapter.

13. Refer to Chapter Eight and install the power head.

14. Refer to Chapter Nine and install the gearcase.

Swivel Housing Removal and Installation

Refer to **Figure 5** or **Figure 6** as appropriate for this procedure.

1. Refer to Chapter Eleven and remove the trim system.

2. Refer to Chapter Eight and remove the power head.

3. Refer to Chapter Nine and remove the gearcase.

4. Remove the lower engine mounts as described in this chapter.

5. Refer to **Figure 5** or **Figure 6** to identify the swivel housing components and their orientation.

6. Refer to *Stern Brackets* in this chapter and remove the stern brackets from the swivel housing. Remove the tilt lock lever as described in this chapter.

7. Clean the swivel housing. Inspect the housing for wear or damage. Replace the swivel housing if defects are noted.

8. Move the swivel tube through its full range of motion. Remove the swivel tube as described in this chapter if it binds or feels loose.

9. Refer to *Stern brackets* in this chapter and install the stern brackets on the swivel housing.

10. Install the lower engine mounts as described in this chapter.

11. Refer to Chapter Eight and install the power head.

12. Refer to Chapter Nine and install the gearcase.

13. Refer to Chapter Eleven and install the trim system. Install the tilt lock lever as described in this chapter.

14. Operate the trim and steering systems through their entire operating range. Inspect the midsection for improperly installed components if there are unusual noises or binding. Repair as required.

Swivel Tube Removal and Installation

Refer to **Figure 5** or **Figure 6** as appropriate for this procedure.

1. Remove the swivel housing as described in this chapter.

2. Refer to **Figure 5** or **Figure 6** to identify the swivel housing components and their orientation.

3. Remove the circlip from its groove on the lower end of the swivel tube. Inspect the circlip for corrosion, cracks or lost spring tension. Replace the circlip if defects are noted.

4. Support the yoke while pulling the swivel tube up and out of the swivel bracket.

5. Remove the yoke, spacers, O-ring and washers from the lower end of the swivel bracket in the swivel tube

12

bore. Remove the washers from the upper side of the swivel tube or swivel tube bore.

6. Inspect the bushings at the upper end of the swivel tube bore in the swivel housing. Remove and replace both bushings if they are worn or damaged.

7. Inspect the swivel tube for cracks, wear or corrosion. Replace the swivel tube if these or other defects are noted.

8. Assembly is the reverse of disassembly. Note the following:

   a. Apply Quicksilver 2-4-C grease (part No. 92-825407) to the swivel tube bushings and swivel tube.

   b. Push the grease seal (9, **Figure 5** or 16, **Figure 6**) into the bore with the seal lip facing the bushing.

   c. Install all washers and spacers as shown in **Figure 5** or **Figure 6**.

   d. Securely tighten all fasteners.

9. Install the swivel housing (11, **Figure 5** or 14, **Figure 6**) as described in this chapter.

Tilt Tube Removal and Installation

Refer to **Figure 5** or **Figure 6** for this procedure.

1. Place the engine in the full up position.

2. Use an overhead hoist or wooden blocks to support the engine as indicated in **Figure 7**. Disconnect both cables from the battery.

3. Refer to **Figure 5** or **Figure 6** to locate the stern brackets and connected components or fasteners.

4. Disconnect the steering linkage and cables from the swivel tube and tilt tube.

5. Remove the large nut that secures the tilt tube to the starboard stern bracket.

6. Use a 1 ft. section of pipe or tubing to drive the tilt tube through the stern brackets and swivel tube. The pipe must be slightly smaller in diameter than the tilt tube.

7. Provide just enough overhead support (**Figure 7**) to keep the tube from binding during removal. Do not use excessive force to remove the tube. Excessive force can cause the end of the tube to flare out, preventing removal. Use a wooden block as padding until the tube is flush with the stern bracket surface.

8. Carefully drive the tilt tube from the starboard side through the starboard stern bracket, swivel housing and port stern bracket. Support the engine, then slowly remove the driver tool. Retain the washers as they drop from the stern brackets and swivel housing. Remove the O-ring and nut from the port side of the tilt tube.

9. Thoroughly clean the tilt tube. Inspect the tilt tube for excessive wear, corrosion, cracking or damage. Replace the tilt tube if any defects are noted.

10. Thoroughly clean all surfaces of the swivel housing and stern brackets. Inspect the tilt tube bushings in the swivel housing for excessive wear, corrosion or damage. Remove the grease fittings and replace the bushings if defects are noted. Make sure the holes in the bushing bore align with the grease fitting openings. Install the grease fittings during installation of the bushings.

11. Apply Quicksilver 2-4-C grease (part No. 92-825407) to the tilt tube bore in the swivel bracket and stern brackets.

12. Place the wave washer between the stern brackets and swivel housing and align it with the tilt tube bore.

13. Apply a coat of Quicksilver 2-4-C grease to the external surfaces of the tilt tube. Place the tilt tube into its opening in the port stern bracket with the grooved end facing the port side. Align the tilt tube bores in the stern brackets, washers and swivel housing during installation of the swivel tube.

14. Using a block of wood for a cushion, carefully tap the tilt tube through the port stern bracket, swivel bracket and starboard stern bracket until the threaded end fully extends from the starboard stern bracket.

15. Install the large nuts, O-rings and washers on the stern brackets. Tighten the large nuts to the specification in **Table 1**.

16. Apply Quicksilver 2-4-C grease to the steering cable and tilt tube. Attach the steering cable and linkage to the tilt tube and swivel tube. Securely tighten all fasteners and engage any fastener locking devices.

17. Carefully remove the overhead support from the engine. Clean the terminals and connect the battery cables to the battery.

18. Operate the trim and steering systems through the entire operating range. Inspect the midsection for improperly installed components if there are unusual noises or binding. Repair as required.

Upper Engine Mount Replacement

1. Refer to Chapter Eight and remove the power head.

2. Remove all fasteners and lift the lower engine cover from the drive shaft housing.

3. Remove the attaching bolts (41, **Figure 8** typical) and lift each mount bracket from the power head adapter.

4. Support the drive shaft housing during the removal and installation of the upper engine mounts. Remove all bolts, nuts and washers that secure the upper mounts to the adapter plate and swivel tube.

5. Support the drive shaft housing and carefully pull both upper mounts from the adapter plate.

6. Clean the mount bolts, bolt holes and mount contact surfaces.

7. Inspect all mount fasteners for excessive wear, corrosion or damage. Replace any questionable fasteners. Inspect the mounts for worn surfaces or damage to the

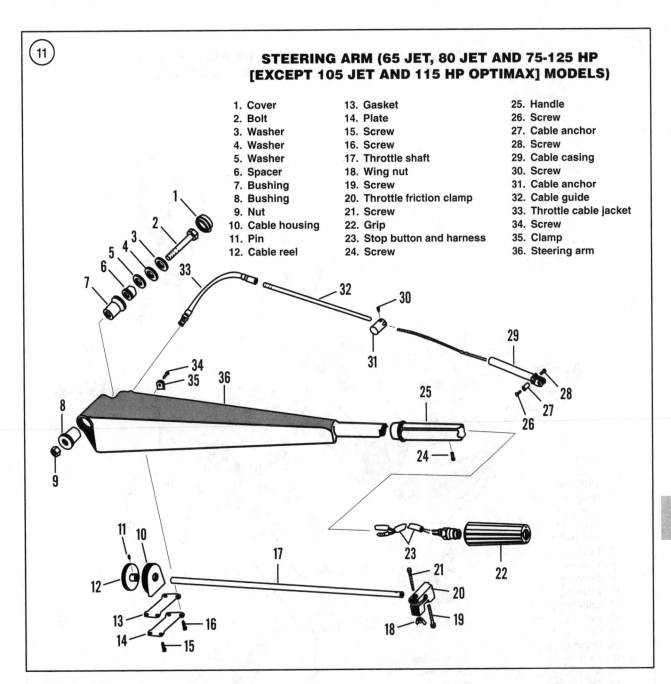

STEERING ARM (65 JET, 80 JET AND 75-125 HP [EXCEPT 105 JET AND 115 HP OPTIMAX] MODELS)

1. Cover
2. Bolt
3. Washer
4. Washer
5. Washer
6. Spacer
7. Bushing
8. Bushing
9. Nut
10. Cable housing
11. Pin
12. Cable reel
13. Gasket
14. Plate
15. Screw
16. Screw
17. Throttle shaft
18. Wing nut
19. Screw
20. Throttle friction clamp
21. Screw
22. Grip
23. Stop button and harness
24. Screw
25. Handle
26. Screw
27. Cable anchor
28. Screw
29. Cable casing
30. Screw
31. Cable anchor
32. Cable guide
33. Throttle cable jacket
34. Screw
35. Clamp
36. Steering arm

rubber portion of the mount. Replace the mount if any defects are noted.

8. Inspect the mount contact surfaces in the adapter plate for cracks or damage. Replace the adapter plate if it is cracked or excessively worn.

9. Assembly is the reverse of disassembly. Note the following:

   a. Apply 271 Loctite (part No. 92-809819) to the threads of all mount and mount bracket bolts.

   b. Tighten the mount fasteners to the specification in **Table 1**.

10. Install all ground wires, cushions and brackets. Securely tighten all fasteners.

11. Refer to Chapter Eight and install the power head.

Tiller Control

The tiller control is installed on some 75-125 hp (except 105 jet and 115 hp Optimax), 65 jet and 80 jet models. Refer to **Figure 11** and **Figure 12** to determine which components must be removed to access failed components.

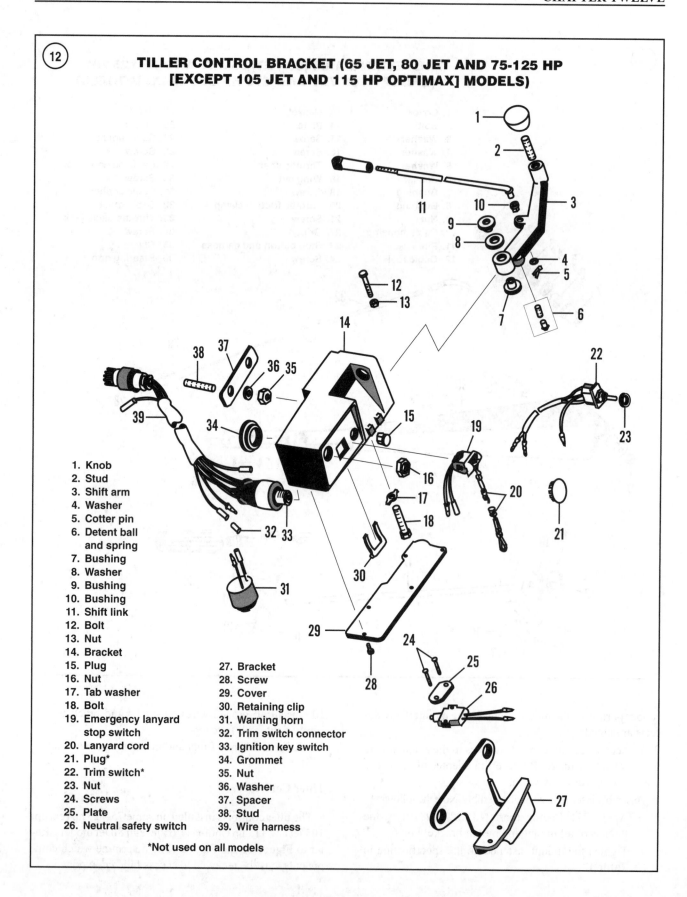

**TILLER CONTROL BRACKET (65 JET, 80 JET AND 75-125 HP
[EXCEPT 105 JET AND 115 HP OPTIMAX] MODELS)**

1. Knob
2. Stud
3. Shift arm
4. Washer
5. Cotter pin
6. Detent ball
   and spring
7. Bushing
8. Washer
9. Bushing
10. Bushing
11. Shift link
12. Bolt
13. Nut
14. Bracket
15. Plug
16. Nut
17. Tab washer
18. Bolt
19. Emergency lanyard
    stop switch
20. Lanyard cord
21. Plug*
22. Trim switch*
23. Nut
24. Screws
25. Plate
26. Neutral safety switch

27. Bracket
28. Screw
29. Cover
30. Retaining clip
31. Warning horn
32. Trim switch connector
33. Ignition key switch
34. Grommet
35. Nut
36. Washer
37. Spacer
38. Stud
39. Wire harness

*Not used on all models

Inspect all components and fasteners for wear or damage. Never reuse a questionable component. Apply Loctite 271 (part No. 92-809819) to the threads of all fasteners during assembly. Apply Quicksilver 2-4-C grease (part No. 92-825407) to all bushings, pins, rods and pivoting surfaces. Do not apply grease to the throttle friction mechanism.

The throttle cable jacket (33, **Figure 11**) is routed through the tiller handle and tiller bracket. Replace the cable if the cable jacket is worn or damaged. Push and pull the core wire while it is installed in the cable jacket. Replace the cable if the wire does not move smoothly. Refer to Chapter Five for cable adjustment instructions, and adjust the throttle and shift linkages anytime shift or throttle components are removed.

Inspect all bushings and pivot bolts or tubes. Replace these components if they are corroded, worn or damaged.

Check for proper steering, tilting, shifting and throttle movement when assembly is complete. Disassemble and check for worn, damaged or improperly installed components if binding or stiff operation occurs.

Table 1 MID-SECTION AND TILLER CONTROL TORQUE SPECIFICATIONS

Fastener	in.-lb.	ft.-lb.	N•m
Anode screw			
65 jet, 80 jet and 75-125 hp (except 105 jet and 115 hp Optimax)	60	–	6.8
Exhaust tube			
65 jet, 80 jet and 75-125 hp (except 105 jet and 115 hp Optimax)	–	25	33.9
105 jet and 135-200 hp (except 200 hp Optimax)	60	–	6.8
200 hp Optimax, 225 hp and 250 hp	–	21	28.5
Lower mount bolt/nut			
65 jet, 80 jet and 75-125 hp (except 105 jet and 115 hp Optimax)	–	50	68
105 jet and 135-200 hp (except 200 hp Optimax)	–	50	68
200 hp Optimax, 225 hp and 250 hp	–	90	122
Lower mount bracket bolts			
65 jet, 80 jet and 75-125 hp (except 105 jet and 115 hp Optimax)	–	14	18.9
105 jet and 135-200 hp (except 200 hp Optimax)	–	22	30
200 hp Optimax, 225 hp and 250 hp	–	20	27
Plastic mount cover screw			
105 jet and 135-200 hp (except 200 hp Optimax)	17	–	1.9
Power head adapter			
65 jet, 80 jet and 75-125 hp (except 105 jet and 115 hp Optimax)	–	25	34
105 jet and 135-200 hp (except 200 hp Optimax)	–	15	20.3
200 hp Optimax, 225 hp and 250 hp	–	25	34
Seal bracket screw			
105 jet and 135-200 hp (except 200 hp Optimax)	80	–	9
Shift shaft bracket			
65 jet, 80 jet and 75-125 hp (except 105 jet and 115 hp Optimax)	–	25	34
Stern bracket nuts			
65 jet, 80 jet and 75-125 hp (except 105 jet and 115 hp Optimax)	–	30	40.7
Tilt tube nut			
200 hp Optimax, 225 hp and 250 hp	–	45	61
Upper mount bolt			
65 jet, 80 jet and 75-125 hp (except 105 jet and 115 hp Optimax)	–	55	74.5
200 hp Optimax, 225 hp and 250 hp	–	20	27
Upper mount bracket			
65 jet, 80 jet and 75-125 hp (except 105 jet and 115 hp Optimax)	–	25	34
200 hp Optimax, 225 hp and 250 hp	–	20	27
Upper mount nut			
65 jet, 80 jet and 75-125 hp (except 105 jet and 115 hp Optimax)	–	80	108
200 hp Optimax, 225 hp and 250 hp	–	50	68
Water tube grommet retainer			
65 jet, 80 jet and 75-125 hp (except 105 jet and 115 hp Optimax)	–	15	20.3
200 hp Optimax, 225 hp and 250 hp	80	–	9

12

Table 2 GENERAL TORQUE SPECIFICATIONS

Screw or nut size	in.-lb.	ft.-lb.	N•m
U.S. Standard			
6-32	9	–	1.0
8-32	20	–	2.3
10-24	30	–	3.4
10-32	35	–	4.0
12-24	45	–	5.1
1/4-20	70	–	7.9
1/4-28	84	–	9.5
5/16-18	160	13	18
5/16-24	168	14	19
3/8-16	–	23	31
3/8-24	–	25	34
7/16-14	–	36	49
7/16-20	–	40	54
1/2-13	–	50	68
1/2-20	–	60	81
Metric			
M5	36	–	4
M6	70	–	8
M8	156	13	18
M10	–	26	35
M12	–	35	48
M14	–	60	81

Chapter Thirteen

Oil Injection System

All models, except the 115-225 hp Optimax models (direct fuel injection), are lubricated by mixing oil with the gasoline. On models that are not oil-injected, the boat operator premixes the oil and gasoline in the fuel tank(s). The recommended fuel/oil mixture for normal operation in all models without oil injection is 50 parts of fuel to 1 part of oil (50:1). This is the standard 6 gal. (22.7 L) of fuel to 1 pint (16 fl. oz. [473 mL]) of oil.

On oil-injected models (except Optimax models), the oil is automatically mixed with the gasoline. An engine-mounted oil pump injects oil into the fuel pump inlet line on carbureted models or into the vapor separator on EFI models. All models covered in this manual use variable rate oil injection. The fuel/oil ratio is changed based on throttle position. At wide-open throttle the fuel/oil ratio is approximately 50-60:1, while at idle speeds the ratio is approximately 80-100:1.

The various engine components are lubricated as the fuel and oil mixture passes through the crankcases and into the combustion chambers. The fuel/oil ratio required by the engine varies with engine load and speed. Oil demands are always highest at wide-open throttle.

The advantages of oil injection are that the operator only has to keep the oil reservoir(s) filled. No calculations must be made as to how much oil to add when refueling. Over-oiling and under-oiling from operator miscalculations are eliminated, along with the associated engine problems caused by under- or over-oiling.

Variable-ratio oil injection offers the additional benefits of reduced emissions and spark plug fouling at idle and low speeds, due to the reduced oil consumption.

All Optimax models (direct fuel injection) use an ECM controlled, electric oil pump that is mounted to a flange or bracket on the intake manifold. Oil is not mixed with the fuel. Straight oil flows from the oil pump through hoses to check valve fittings or passages in the intake manifold. The oil is discharged in front of each reed block. An external line delivers oil to the belt-driven air compressor.

Four different oil injection systems are used on models covered in this chapter:
1. Variable-ratio injection—75-125 hp and 65-80 jet models.
2. Variable-ratio injection—135-200 hp, 105 jet and 140 jet models.

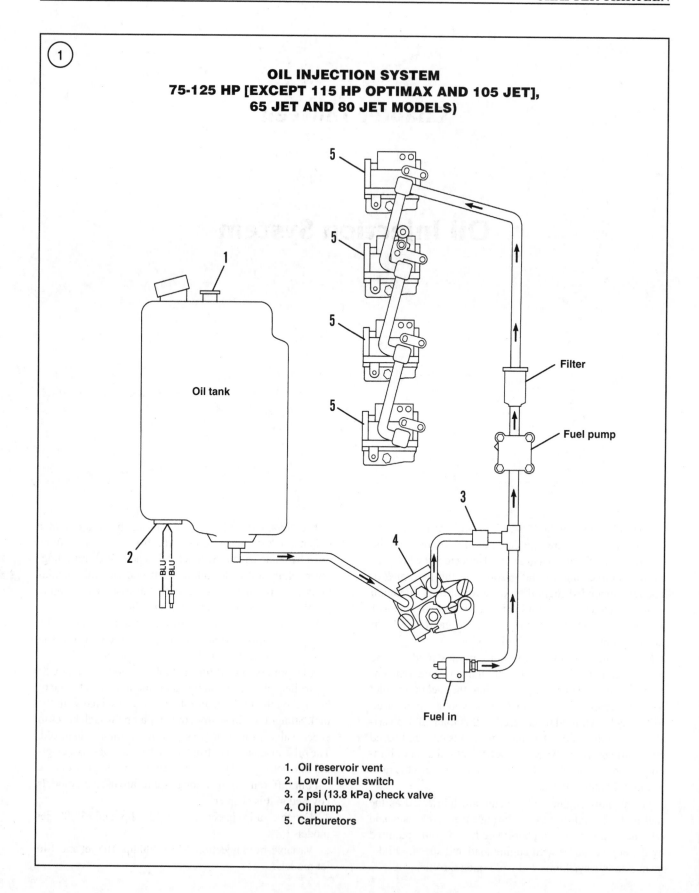

**OIL INJECTION SYSTEM
75-125 HP [EXCEPT 115 HP OPTIMAX AND 105 JET],
65 JET AND 80 JET MODELS)**

Oil tank

Filter

Fuel pump

Fuel in

1. Oil reservoir vent
2. Low oil level switch
3. 2 psi (13.8 kPa) check valve
4. Oil pump
5. Carburetors

3. Variable-ratio injection—225-250 hp models.

4. Variable-ratio electronically controlled injection—115-225 hp Optimax models.

Refer to Chapter Four for fuel and oil requirements, engine break-in procedures and reservoir filling procedures. Refer to Chapter Five for synchronizing the oil pump and throttle linkages on variable ratio models.

Table 1 lists specific application torque specifications. **Table 2** lists general torque specifications. Use the general torque specifications for fasteners not in **Table 1**. **Table 3** lists oil injection system specifications. All tables are at the end of the chapter.

VARIABLE RATIO OIL INJECTION (75-125 HP [EXCEPT 115 HP OPTIMAX AND 105 JET], 65 JET AND 80 JET MODELS)

A variable-ratio crankshaft driven oil injection pump is used on these models. The oil pump injects oil into the fuel line just before the fuel pump. The oil pump delivers oil relative to throttle lever position and engine speed. A linkage rod connects the oil pump control lever to the throttle linkage and varies the oil pump stroke according to throttle lever position. The fuel/oil ratio varies from approximately 80:1 at idle to approximately 50:1 at wide-open throttle.

WARNING
Although it is generally not necessary, a boat-mounted electric fuel supply may be installed along the fuel supply line. If so equipped, the fuel pressure must not exceed 4 psi (27.6 kPa) at the engine fuel line connector. If necessary, install a fuel pressure regulator between the electric fuel pump and engine fuel line connector. Adjust the regulator to a maximum of 4 psi (27.6 kPa) fuel pressure. The electric fuel

pump and all related fuel system components must conform to Coast Guard Safety standards for permanently installed fuel systems.

Operation

The 75-125 hp (except 115 hp Optimax and 105 jet), 65 jet and 80 jet models are equipped with the oil injection system shown in **Figure 1**.

The engine-mounted oil reservoir capacity is 3.2 qt. (3.0 L) on 75 hp, 90 hp and 65 jet models, and 5.13 qt. (4.9 L) on 100-125 hp and 80 jet models. This capacity provides sufficient oil for approximately 5 hours of operation at wide-open throttle. The reservoir cap has a dipstick to determine the oil level.

A check-valve vent at the top of the reservoir provides for atmospheric venting of the reservoir and prevents oil leaks when the outboard motor is tilted.

A low-oil level switch in the oil reservoir activates a warning horn when the oil level drops to 1 qt (0.95 L) or less. When the low-oil warning horn first sounds, enough oil remains for approximately 50-60 minutes of wide-open throttle operation. The warning horn also sounds if the engine temperature switch in the cylinder block closes to ground. If the warning horn sounds, either the power head is overheating or the oil level in the reservoir is low.

A 2 psi (13.8 kPa) check valve (**Figure 2**) is installed in the fuel line between the fuel line T-fitting and the oil pump discharge line. The check valve is used to prevent gasoline from entering the oil pump discharge line.

Warning System Troubleshooting

If a malfunction is suspected in the oil injection system (warning horn sounds), immediately stop the engine and check the oil level in the engine-mounted reservoir. If the oil is low, fill the reservoir with a recommended oil (Chapter Four). Refer to the wiring diagrams at the end of the manual and **Figure 1** for this procedure.

CAUTION
If an oil injection system malfunction is suspected, do not operate the outboard on straight gasoline. Operate the motor on a remote fuel tank containing a 50:1 fuel/oil mixture until the oil pump output test can be performed.

13

Warning horn does not sound
(with low oil level)

Perform this test if the oil level is low yet the warning horn fails to sound.

1. Clean and inspect the blue wires connecting the oil level switch to the main engine harness.

2. Disconnect the tan or tan/blue wire from the engine temperature switch located in the cylinder cover.

3. Turn the ignition switch to the ON position. Ground the wire to the engine using a suitable jumper wire. The warning horn should activate when the wire is grounded.

4. If the warning horn sounds when the lead is grounded, the oil level switch or wiring to the switch is faulty. Inspect the wiring for damaged or corroded terminals. Repair or replace the terminals or wiring. Test the oil level switch as described in this chapter.

5. If the warning horn does not sound when the lead is grounded, check the tan or tan/blue wire between the warning horn and the engine temperature switch bullet connector for an open circuit.

   a. *Tan/blue circuit is open*—Repair or replace faulty wiring or terminals.

   b. *Tan/blue circuit checks correctly*—Make sure the warning horn is receiving battery voltage at the purple wire. If the horn is receiving battery voltage, but does not sound when the tan or tan/blue wire is grounded, replace the warning horn.

Warning system sounds continuously
(all models)

Perform this test if the oil level is within the normal operating range yet the warning horn sounds.

1. Turn the ignition switch to the ON position.

2. Disconnect the engine temperature switch tan or tan/blue lead at its bullet connection to the engine temperature switch.

   a. If the warning horn stops sounding, the engine temperature switch is defective or the engine is overheating. Replace the defective switch or correct the cause of the engine overheat.

   b. If the warning horn continues to sound, disconnect the blue oil level switch wires from the main engine harness. If the warning horn stops, the switch is defective and must be replaced.

3. If the warning horn continues to sound after the temperature switch and oil level switch wires have been disconnected, the tan or tan/blue wire is shorted to ground somewhere between the warning horn and the engine tem-

perature switch/oil level switch bullet connectors. Repair or replace the wire as necessary.

Warning system sounds erratically

> **CAUTION**
> *Do not run the engine without an adequate water supply and do not exceed 3000 rpm without an adequate load. Refer to **Safety Precautions** at the beginning of Chapter Three or Chapter Five.*

1. Make sure the reservoir is full. Then disconnect the two oil level switch blue or light blue wires at the main engine harness.

2. Run the engine to check if the warning horn still sounds erratically. If the horn does not sound, replace the low oil level switch in the oil tank.

3. If the horn still sounds in Step 2, disconnect the engine temperature switch tan or tan/blue wire at its bullet connector.

4. Run the engine to check if the warning horn still sounds erratically. If the horn no longer sounds, the engine temperature switch is defective or the engine is overheating. Refer to Chapter Three for troubleshooting procedures.

5. If the horn still sounds in Step 4, the tan or tan/blue wire is shorted to ground somewhere between the warning horn and the engine temperature switch/oil level switch bullet connectors. Repair or replace the lead as necessary.

Oil level switch tests

> **NOTE**
> *On some models, the oil level switch is not available separately. On such models, replace the reservoir if the switch fails.*

1. Make sure the reservoir is full. Then disconnect the two oil level switch blue leads at the warning module bullet connectors.

2. Connect an ohmmeter calibrated on an appropriate scale to check continuity between the two oil level switch blue wires. If the meter does not indicate continuity when the reservoir is full, the oil level switch is defective and must be replaced.

Oil pump output test

> **CAUTION**
> *Do not run the engine without an adequate water supply and do not exceed 3000 rpm without an adequate load. Refer to **Safety***

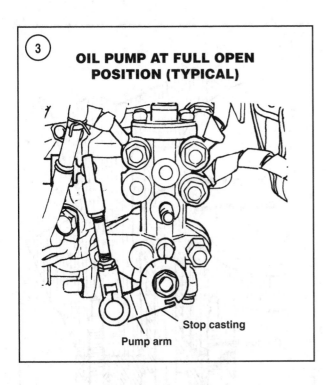

OIL PUMP AT FULL OPEN POSITION (TYPICAL)

Stop casting

Pump arm

Precautions in *Chapter Three or Chapter Five.*

Obtain a graduated container, capable of accurately measuring up to 50 cc, before continuing.

1. Connect a remote fuel tank containing a 50:1 fuel/oil mixture to the engine.

2. Disconnect the oil pump discharge line from the check valve fitting (**Figure 2**). Securely cap or plug the check valve fitting to prevent leaks.

3. Connect an accurate shop tachometer to the engine following the manufacturer's instructions.

4. Insert the disconnected end of the oil pump discharge line into the graduated container.

5. Disconnect the oil pump link rod from the oil pump control arm. Rotate the pump arm counterclockwise fully against the spring until the arm is against the stop casting. Hold the arm in this position.

6. Start the outboard motor and run it at 700 rpm for exactly 15 minutes.

NOTE
Oil pump output specifications are based on the test being performed at 70° F (21° C). If the ambient temperature is more or less, actual pump output can vary from the specification.

7. Stop the engine and check the quantity of oil in the graduated container. Oil pump output must meet or ex-

ceed the minimum specification in **Table 3**. If injection pump output is less than specified, replace the pump assembly as described in this chapter.

8. Reconnect the pump discharge line to the check valve fitting. Secure the connection with a new tie-strap. Then bleed the injection system as described in this chapter.

9. Reconnect the oil pump link rod to the control arm. Adjust the link rod as specified in Chapter Five.

Oil Injection System Service

Oil pump synchronization

Refer to Chapter Five for throttle linkage to oil pump linkage adjustment and synchronization procedures.

Bleeding the oil pump

If the pump has been removed, if any of the lines have been replaced, or if air is present in the oil pump lines, bleed air from the oil injection pump and lines as follows:

1. Place a shop towel beneath the oil pump.

2. Loosen the oil pump bleed screw 3-4 turns. A gasket is used on the bleed screw head.

3. Allow oil to flow from the bleed screw until no air bubbles are noted in the inlet hose.

4. Tighten the oil pump bleed screw to the specification in **Table 1**.

CAUTION
Do not run the engine without an adequate water supply and do not exceed 3000 rpm without an adequate load. Refer to Safety Precautions at the beginning of Chapter Three or Chapter Five.

5. If air is present in the pump discharge line, connect a remote tank containing a 50:1 fuel/oil mixture to the engine. Start the engine and run it at idle until no air bubbles are in the discharge hose. To speed the bleeding process, temporarily disconnect the pump link rod and rotate the pump arm to the full open position (see **Figure 3**).

Oil reservoir removal/installation

NOTE
On some models, the oil level switch is not available separately and cannot be removed from the oil reservoir.

1. Disconnect the negative battery cable.

2. Disconnect and ground the spark plug leads to the power head to prevent accidental starting.

13

3. Remove the two small screws securing the top oil reservoir bracket and the one larger screw securing the bottom rear corner of the reservoir to the power head.

4. Disconnect the oil level switch blue leads at the switch's bullet connectors.

5. Lift the reservoir enough to access the bottom of the tank. Cut the tie-strap securing the oil outlet hose to the reservoir, then disconnect the hose from the tank. Drain the oil from the reservoir.

6. Remove the reservoir from the power head.

7. Remove the screw securing the oil level switch to the bottom of the tank. Remove the switch.

8. To install the oil reservoir, install the oil level switch into the oil tank. Secure the switch with one screw. Tighten the screw securely.

9. Position the oil reservoir assembly to the power head. Then attach the oil outlet hose to the oil tank. Secure the hose with a new tie-strap.

10. Secure the reservoir with three screws. Tighten the oil reservoir screws to the specification in **Table 1**.

11. Connect the oil level switch leads to the wiring harness bullet connectors.

12. Fill the reservoir with the recommended oil (Chapter Four), then bleed the oil pump as described in this chapter. Reconnect the negative battery cable and the spark plug leads.

Oil pump removal/installation

Refer to Chapter Eight for oil pump drive gear removal/installation procedures. Refer to **Figure 4** for this procedure.

1. Disconnect the oil inlet and discharge lines from the pump.

2. Disconnect the link rod from the pump control arm, then remove the pump mounting screws.

3. Remove the pump assembly from the power head. If the pump adapter and/or driven gear remains in the engine block, retrieve them using needlenose pliers.

4. Remove and inspect the bushings from the adapter. Replace all worn or damaged components.

5. To install the pump, thoroughly lubricate the adapter and bushings with Quicksilver Needle Bearing Assembly Grease (part No. 92-825265). Install the bushings into the sleeve. Make sure the flanged bushing faces the oil pump driven gear.

6. Thoroughly lubricate the driven gear shaft with Quicksilver Needle Bearing Assembly Grease. Insert the driven gear into the bearing assembly, making sure the gear properly engages the pump shaft.

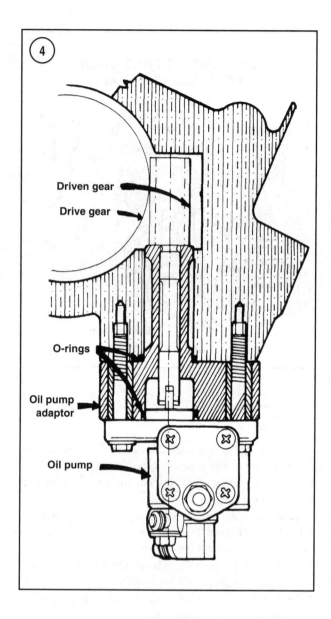

7. Install new O-rings onto the pump. Lubricate the O-rings with Quicksilver Needle Bearing Assembly Grease.

8. Install the pump assembly onto the power head. Apply Loctite 271 threadlocking adhesive to the threads of the oil pump mounting screws. Install the oil pump mounting screws and tighten them evenly to the specification in **Table 1**.

9. Reconnect the oil inlet and discharge hoses to the pump. Securely clamp the hoses to the pump using new tie-straps.

10. Reconnect the link rod to the pump control arm. Refer to Chapter Five for oil pump adjustment and synchronization procedures.

11. Perform the oil pump bleeding procedure as described in this chapter.

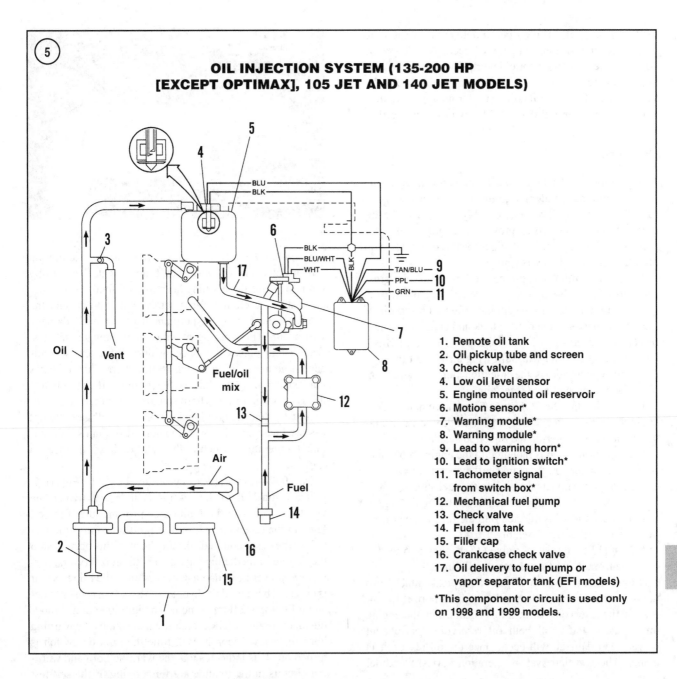

⑤

OIL INJECTION SYSTEM (135-200 HP [EXCEPT OPTIMAX], 105 JET AND 140 JET MODELS)

1. Remote oil tank
2. Oil pickup tube and screen
3. Check valve
4. Low oil level sensor
5. Engine mounted oil reservoir
6. Motion sensor*
7. Warning module*
8. Warning module*
9. Lead to warning horn*
10. Lead to ignition switch*
11. Tachometer signal
    from switch box*
12. Mechanical fuel pump
13. Check valve
14. Fuel from tank
15. Filler cap
16. Crankcase check valve
17. Oil delivery to fuel pump or
    vapor separator tank (EFI models)

*This component or circuit is used only
on 1998 and 1999 models.

13

VARIABLE-RATIO OIL INJECTION (135-200 HP [EXCEPT OPTIMAX MODELS], 105 JET AND 140 JET MODELS)

WARNING
Although it is generally not necessary, a boat-mounted electric fuel pump may be installed along the fuel supply line. If so equipped, the fuel pressure must not exceed 4 psi (27.6 kPa) at the engine fuel line connector. If necessary, install a fuel pressure regulator between the electric fuel pump and engine fuel line connector. Adjust the regulator to a maximum of 4 psi (27.6 kPa) fuel pressure. The electric fuel pump and all related fuel system components must conform to Coast Guard Safety standards for permanently installed fuel systems.

Refer to **Figure 5**, typical for a diagram of this oil injection system. A variable-ratio crankshaft driven oil injection pump is used on these models. The oil pump injects oil into the fuel line just before the fuel pump on carbureted models or into the bottom of the vapor separator on EFI models. The oil pump delivers oil relative to throttle lever position and engine speed. A linkage rod connects the oil pump control lever to the throttle linkage and varies the oil pump stroke according to the throttle lever position. The fuel/oil ratio varies from approximately 100:1 at idle to approximately 50:1 at wide-open throttle.

Operation

A 3 gallon (11.4 L) remote oil tank supplies oil to the reservoir mounted under the engine cowl (**Figure 6**, typical). The reservoir oil capacity is 0.94 qt. (0.89 L). The engine-mounted reservoir provides enough oil for approximately 30 minutes of wide-open throttle operation after the remote oil tank is empty.

The remote oil tank is pressurized by crankcase pressure through a one-way check valve, causing oil to flow from the remote tank to the engine-mounted reservoir. If the oil line between the remote tank and engine-mounted reservoir becomes restricted, the 2 psi (13.8 kPa) check valve (3, **Figure 5**) unseats, allowing air to vent through the hose, which allows the injection pump to draw oil from the engine-mounted reservoir.

The oil pickup tube (2, **Figure 5**) in the remote tank is equipped with a filter screen to prevent dirt or other contamination from entering the injection system.

The injection pump is mounted to the engine block and is driven by a gear on the crankshaft. On carbureted models, the oil pump injects the oil into the fuel stream before the mechanical fuel pump. On EFI (electronic fuel injection) models, the oil is injected into the fuel at the bottom of the vapor separator assembly.

A 2 psi (13.8 kPa) check valve (13, **Figure 5**) prevents gasoline from being forced into the oil lines.

A low-oil level switch (**Figure 7**, typical) attached to the reservoir fill cap activates the warning horn if the oil level in the reservoir is low. If this occurs, stop the engine immediately and refill both oil reservoirs; permanent power head damage will occur once the oil reservoir is empty. The warning system operation varies by model year.

On 1998 and 1999 models, a low-oil level switch (**Figure 7**, typical) attached to the reservoir fill cap activates the warning module (8, **Figure 5**) if the oil level in the reservoir is low. When activated, the warning module pulses the dash mounted warning horn. If this occurs, stop the engine immediately and fill both oil reservoirs; permanent power head damage will occur once the oil reservoir is empty. A motion sensor (6, **Figure 5**) detects movement of the oil pump shaft via a magnet inside the pump coupler. The warning module also receives a tachometer signal from the outer switch box, No. 2 cylinder primary

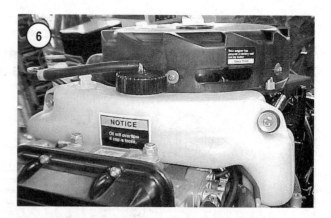

ignition coil lead. If the motor is running and the motion sensor detects no oil pump shaft movement, the warning module pulses the warning horn intermittently. If this occurs, stop the engine immediately. Find and correct the cause of the failure, or permanent power head damage will occur. The warning module incorporates a self test feature that pulses the warning horn for a few seconds each time the ignition switch is turned on. This indicates that the warning module is functioning. If the self test does not occur, or if the horn sounds intermittently or continuously after the ignition is switched on, do not attempt to start the engine. The warning horn also sounds if the engine temperature switch in the cylinder head(s) closes to ground.

On 2000-on models, a low-oil level switch (**Figure 7**, typical) attached to the reservoir fill cap activates the warning circuits in the ignition control module if the oil level in the reservoir is low. The ignition control module pulses the dash mounted warning horn. If this occurs, stop the engine immediately and refill both oil reservoirs; permanent power head damage occurs once the oil reservoir is empty. These models do not have a motion sensor to detect oil pump shaft movement. The ignition control module incorporates a self test feature that sounds the warning horn for a few seconds each time the ignition switch is turned on. This indicates that the warning horn and warning circuits in the module are functioning. If the self test does not occur, or if the horn sounds intermittently or continuously after the ignition is switched on, do not attempt to start the engine. The warning horn also sounds if the engine temperature switch in the cylinder head(s) closes to ground.

Warning System Troubleshooting

If a malfunction is suspected in the oil injection system (warning horn sounds), immediately stop the engine and check the oil levels in the remote oil tank and the en-

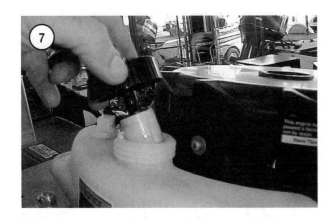

gine-mounted reservoir. If the oil is low, fill the oil tank and reservoir with a recommended oil (Chapter Four).

> **CAUTION**
> *If an oil injection system malfunction is suspected, do not operate the outboard on straight gasoline. Operate the motor on a remote fuel tank containing a 50:1 fuel/oil mixture until the oil pump output test can be performed.*

Each time the ignition switch is turned to the on from the off position, the warning module should briefly activate the warning horn, indicating the warning system is functioning. If an oil injection malfunction occurs, the warning module triggers a pulsing tone from the warning horn. If the power head overheats, the engine temperature switch triggers a continuous tone from the horn.

> **NOTE**
> *1998 and 1999 135-200 hp (except Optimax), 105 jet and 140 jet models use an oil pump motion sensor. If the warning horn is pulsing, yet both oil tanks (reservoirs) are full, the oil pump drive gear may have failed. Operate the motor on a remote fuel tank containing a 50:1 fuel/oil mixture until the oil injection system can be inspected.*

If the warning horn activates during operation, immediately shut down the engine and check the oil level in the engine-mounted reservoir. If necessary, fill the remote tank with a recommended oil. If the reservoir oil level is low, but the remote tank is full, proceed as follows:

1. Check the O-rings or gaskets in the reservoir fill cap for cracking, deterioration or other damage. Replace the O-rings or gaskets as necessary. Make sure the fill caps are screwed tightly on the reservoir and remote tank. Air leaks at the remote tank will prevent the movement of oil from the tank to the reservoir. Leaks at the reservoir result in oil spills.

2. Check the oil line between the remote tank and reservoir for kinks, restrictions or leaks. Repair or replace the line as required.

3. Check the crankcase pressure line between the crankcase check valve and remote tank for kinks, restrictions or leaks. Make sure the crankcase one-way check valve is functioning properly.

4. Check the oil pickup tube and filter for restrictions. Clean or replace the tube or filter as necessary.

5. Check all oil lines for kinks, cracks, deterioration, leaks or other damage. Make sure all connections are tightly clamped.

Warning system does not self test

Refer to the wiring diagrams at the end of the manual.

1. Check the warning module or ignition control module black lead for a clean, tight connection to ground. Clean and tighten the connection as necessary.

2. Turn the ignition switch to the ON position. Check the warning module or ignition control module purple wire for battery voltage. If voltage is not present, there is an open circuit or high resistance in the purple lead from the module bullet connector to the ignition switch. This includes the main harness connector and the ignition switch. Repair or replace the wire, connections or ignition switch as necessary.

3. Disconnect the engine temperature switch black wire from the terminal block connection to the tan or tan/blue main engine wire harness wire.

4. Turn the ignition switch to the ON position. Use a jumper lead to ground the tan/blue engine harness terminal. The warning horn should activate when the wire is grounded.

   a. If the warning horn sounds, replace the warning or ignition control module and recheck the self-test function.

   b. If the warning horn does not sound, check the tan or tan/blue wire between the warning horn and the engine temperature switch terminal for an open circuit. Repair or replace the wire as necessary. If the wire checks satisfactorily, make sure the warning horn is receiving battery voltage through its purple wire. If the horn is receiving battery voltage, but does not sound when the tan or tan/blue wire is grounded, replace the warning horn.

5. Reconnect all leads.

13

Warning system sounds continuously

Refer to the wiring diagrams and the end of the manual.
1. Turn the ignition switch to the ON position.
2. Disconnect the engine temperature switch black wire from the terminal block connection to the tan or tan/blue main engine harness wire. If the warning horn stops when the lead is disconnected, the engine temperature switch is defective or the engine is overheating. Replace the defective switch or correct the cause of the engine overheat.
3. If the warning horn continues to sound after the temperature switch wire is disconnected, disconnect the warning or ignition control module tan or tan/blue wire from the warning module bullet connector or terminal strip. If the warning horn stops when the wire is disconnected, the warning or ignition control module is defective and must be replaced.
4. If the warning horn continues to sound after the temperature switch and warning or ignition control module tan or tan/blue wires are disconnected, the tan or tan/blue wire is shorted to ground between the warning horn and the engine temperature switch/warning module bullet connectors. Repair or replace the wire as necessary.
5. Reconnect all wires.

Warning system sounds erratically

Refer to the wiring diagrams at the end of the manual.

> *CAUTION*
> *Do not run the engine without an adequate water supply and do not exceed 3000 rpm without an adequate load. Refer to **Safety Precautions** in Chapter Three or Chapter Five.*

1. Make sure both oil reservoirs are full. Then disconnect the two oil level switch blue or light blue wires at the warning module bullet connectors.
2. Run the engine to check if the warning horn still sounds erratically. If the horn does not sound, replace the low oil level switch in the oil reservoir.
3. If the horn still sounds in Step 2, disconnect the engine temperature switch black wire at the terminal strip junction with the tan or tan/blue main engine harness wire.
4. Run the engine to check if the warning horn still sounds erratically. If the horn does not sound, the engine temperature switch is defective or the engine is overheating. Refer to Chapter Three for troubleshooting procedures.
5. If the horn still sounds in Step 4, check for damaged wires or faulty terminals on the tan or tan/blue wire between the engine and the remote controls. If the wires test

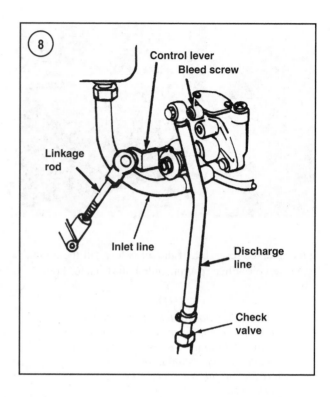

satisfactorily, replace the warning or ignition control module.

Oil level switch tests

1. Make sure the engine-mounted oil reservoir is full. Then disconnect the two oil level switch blue wires at the warning module bullet connectors.
2. Connect an ohmmeter, calibrated on an appropriate scale to check continuity, between the two oil level switch blue wires. The meter should indicate no continuity when the oil tank is full. If continuity is noted, the oil level switch is defective and must be replaced.

Motion sensor tests (135-200 hp [except Optimax], 105 jet and 140 jet models)

Perform this procedure only on 1998 and 1999 engines. 2000-on models are not equipped with a motion sensor. The following tests are intended to diagnose a problem in the warning system that produces a pulsing horn only when the engine is being cranked or is running. For this procedure, the low oil level switch should have already been tested as described in the previous section. Refer to the wiring diagrams at the end of the manual.
1. Disconnect and ground the spark plug leads to the power head to prevent accidental starting.

2. Inspect the green wire from the warning module to the outer switch box No. 2 cylinder primary lead terminal for loose connections, open circuits or high resistance. Correct any problems found.

3. Test the ignition system with an air gap tester as described in Chapter Three to make sure the No. 2 cylinder has adequate spark. If the primary voltage is incorrect, it can cause the warning module to malfunction, which can create false warning signals.

4. Disconnect the warning module white wire at its bullet connector between the module and the motion sensor. Connect a voltmeter between a good engine ground and the white wire from the module. Turn the ignition switch to the ON position and note the voltmeter. The voltage should be within 1 volt of battery voltage.

5. Reconnect the white wire to the module. Insert a suitable probe into the blue/white wire bullet connection between the motion sensor and warning module. A paper clip or piece of wire is sufficient.

6. Connect a voltmeter between the engine ground and the blue/white wire. Place the ignition switch in the ON position.

7. Using the emergency starting rope, rotate the flywheel while observing the voltmeter. The voltage should peak at 4-6 volts, then drop to less than 1.0 volt during every two revolutions of the flywheel.

8. If there is no voltage, the motion sensor is defective or the oil pump drive gear is not turning. Check the oil pump output as described in this chapter. If pump output is acceptable, replace the motion sensor as described later in this section, then recheck the voltage.

9. Reconnect the spark plug leads when finished.

Oil Pump Output Test (135-200 hp [except Optimax], 105 Jet and 140 Jet Models)

CAUTION
Do not run the engine without an adequate water supply and do not exceed 3000 rpm

*without an adequate load. Refer to **Safety Precautions** in Chapter Three or Chapter Five.*

Obtain a graduated container, capable of accurately measuring up to 50 cc, before continuing.

1. Connect a remote fuel tank containing a 50:1 fuel/oil mixture to the engine.

2. Disconnect the oil pump discharge line from the check valve fitting near the fuel pump on carbureted models (**Figure 8**) or from the bottom of the vapor separator on EFI models (**Figure 9**). Securely cap or plug the check valve fitting to prevent leaks.

3. Connect an accurate shop tachometer to the engine following the manufacturer's instructions.

4. Insert the disconnected end of the oil pump discharge line into the graduated container.

5. Start the outboard motor and run it at 1500 rpm for exactly 3 minutes.

NOTE
Injection pump output specifications are based on tests performed at 70° F (21° C). If the ambient temperature is more or less, actual pump output may vary from the specification.

6. Stop the engine and check the quantity of oil in the graduated container. Oil pump output should be within the specification in **Table 3**.

7. If the injection pump output is less than specified, replace the pump assembly as described in this chapter.

8. Empty the container. Disconnect the linkage rod from the injection pump control lever. See **Figure 8**. Rotate the control lever to the full open position, then repeat Steps 4 and 5.

9. Stop the engine and again check the quantity of oil in the graduated container. Oil pump output should be within the specification in **Table 3**.

10. If injection pump output is less than specified, replace the pump assembly as described in this chapter.

11. Reconnect the pump discharge line to the check valve fitting. Secure the connection with a new tie-strap. Then bleed the injection system as described in this chapter.

12. Reconnect the oil pump link rod to the control arm. Adjust the link rod as specified in Chapter Five.

Oil Injection System Service

Oil pump synchronization

Refer to Chapter Five for throttle linkage to oil pump linkage adjustment and synchronization procedures.

13

Bleeding the oil pump

If the pump has been removed, if any of the lines have been replaced, or if air is present in the oil pump lines, bleed air from the oil injection pump and lines as follows:
1. Place a shop towel beneath the oil pump.
2. Loosen the oil pump bleed screw 3-4 turns (**Figure 8**).
3. Allow oil to flow from the bleed screw until there are no air bubbles in the inlet hose.
4. Tighten the bleed screw to the specification in **Table 1**.

> *CAUTION*
> *Do not run the engine without an adequate water supply and do not exceed 3000 rpm without an adequate load. Refer to **Safety Precautions** in Chapter Three or Chapter Five.*

5. If air is present in the pump discharge line, connect a remote tank containing a 50:1 fuel/oil mixture to the engine. Start the engine and run it at idle until there are no air bubbles in the discharge hose. The pump link rod can be disconnected and the pump arm can be rotated to the full output position to speed the process.
6. On carbureted models, if necessary, gently pinch the fuel pump inlet hose between the injection pump T-fitting and remote fuel tank connector, causing the fuel pump to create a slight vacuum in the hose. This will quicken the bleeding process.
7. Continue running the outboard until all air is purged, then stop the engine and reconnect the linkage rod to the control lever if it was disconnected.

Warning module removal/installation (1998 and 1999 models)

1. Disconnect the negative battery cable.

> *NOTE*
> *The warning module is mounted on the port cylinder bank as shown in **Figure 10**. Note the warning module wiring routing for reference during installation.*

2. Disconnect the warning module purple and tan wires from the terminal block located on top of the engine. It may be necessary to remove the flywheel cover to access the terminal strip.
3. Disconnect the module blue, blue/white and white wires at the module's bullet connectors.

> *NOTE*
> *While normally connected to the outer switch box, the green wire from the warning module may be connected to either switch*

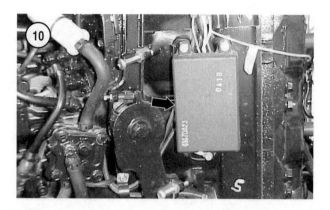

box. If it is connected to the inner switch box, separate the switch boxes as described in Chapter Seven.

4. Disconnect the green module wire from the appropriate switch box.
5. Remove the three module mounting screws and remove the module (**Figure 10**).
6. If the module black ground wire was not under a mounting screw, remove the ground wire from the power head.
7. To install the module, apply Loctite 242 threadlocking adhesive (part No. 92-809821) to the threads of the mounting screws. Install the module and tighten the three screws to the specification in **Table 1**. If the ground lead was under a mounting screw, reinstall the ground wire at this time. The module must be grounded to operate.
8. Connect the module wires at their respective locations. Route the module wires as noted during removal. The wires must not contact the flywheel or other moving components.
9. Reconnect the negative battery cable.

Ignition control module removal/installation (2000-on models)

Refer to Chapter Seven for ignition module removal/installation instructions.

Engine-mounted oil reservoir removal/installation

1. Disconnect the reservoir-to-oil pump line at the oil pump. If the reservoir contains oil, cap or plug the line to prevent leaks.
2. Disconnect the remote oil tank-to-engine reservoir input line from the top of the reservoir.
3. Disconnect the low-oil level switch leads at their bullet connectors or remove the fill cap from the reservoir.

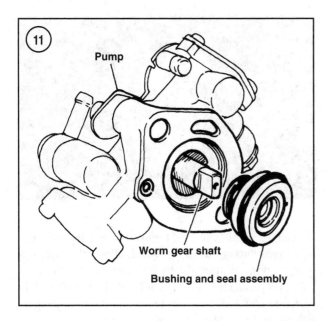

Pump

Worm gear shaft

Bushing and seal assembly

4. Remove the three reservoir mounting screws and remove the reservoir.

5. To install the reservoir, position the reservoir to the power head. Secure the reservoir with three screws. Apply Loctite 242 threadlocking adhesive (part No. 92-809819) to the threads of the mounting screws. Tighten the screws to the specification in **Table 1**.

6. Install the reservoir inlet and outlet lines. Securely clamp the oil lines using new tie-straps.

7. Reconnect the low-oil level switch leads.

8. Bleed the injection system as described in this chapter.

Oil pump removal/installation

Refer to Chapter Eight for oil pump drive gear removal/installation procedures.

1. Disconnect the inlet and outlet oil lines from the injection pump (**Figure 8**). Cap or plug the lines to prevent leaks or contamination.

2. Disconnect the link rod from the pump control lever. On EFI models, remove the vapor separator tank as described in Chapter Six.

3. Remove the two screws securing the pump to the cylinder block, then remove the pump assembly.

4. Grasp the worm gear shaft (**Figure 11**) with needlenose pliers. Then pull the gear, bushing and seal assembly from the pump. Be sure to retrieve the thrust washer located between the pump and worm gear.

5. Remove and discard the O-rings from the bushing. Replace the bushing if its inside seal is defective.

6. Grasp the oil pump coupler/bushing in the power head with needlenose pliers. Then carefully pull the coupler/bushing and driven gear from the opening.

7. Inspect all components for excessive wear or other damage. Replace all suspect components. If gray plastic material is found on the driven gear, the oil pump drive gear on the crankshaft has failed and must be replaced. See Chapter Eight.

8. Install new O-rings before installing the pump. Lubricate the O-rings and all components with Quicksilver Needle Bearing Assembly Grease (part No. 92-825265A 1).

9. Install the driven gear and coupler/bushing into the power head bore. The end of the gear must fit into the bushing in the block and the driven gear teeth must mesh with the drive gear teeth. Seat the assembly in the bore.

10. Install the worm gear into the pump assembly. Make sure the thrust washer is properly positioned at the bottom of the oil pump bore, between the pump body and worm gear.

11. Apply Loctite 271 threadlocking adhesive (part No. 92-80819) to the threads of the pump mounting screws. Align the worm gear shaft to the slot in the coupler/bushing. Then install the pump and tighten the bolts to the specification in **Table 1**.

12. Reconnect the oil inlet and outlet lines to the pump. Securely clamp the lines using new tie-straps.

13. Reconnect the link rod to the pump control arm. Refer to Chapter Five for oil pump adjustment and synchronization procedures. On EFI models, install the vapor separator tank as described in Chapter Six.

14. Perform the oil pump bleeding procedure as described in this chapter.

Motion sensor removal/installation

1. Remove the screw securing the motion sensor (**Figure 12**) to the oil pump.

13

2. Disconnect the sensor white and blue/white wires from the warning module bullet connectors. Remove the sensor black ground wire from the engine ground.

3. Remove the motion sensor.

4. Install the motion sensor by reversing the removal procedure. Tighten the sensor mounting screw to the specification in **Table 1**.

VARIABLE-RATIO OIL INJECTION (225 HP AND 250 HP [EXCEPT OPTIMAX] MODELS)

WARNING
Although it is generally not necessary, a boat-mounted electric fuel pump may be installed along the fuel supply line. If so equipped, the fuel pressure must not exceed 4 psi (27.6 kPa) at the engine fuel line connector. If necessary, install a fuel pressure regulator between the electric fuel pump and engine fuel line connector. Adjust the regulator to a maximum of 4 psi (27.6 kPa) fuel pressure. The electric fuel pump and all related fuel system components must conform to Coast Guard Safety standards for permanently installed fuel systems.

A variable-ratio crankshaft driven oil injection pump is used on these models. The oil pump injects oil into the fuel line just before the fuel pump on carbureted models or into the bottom of the vapor separator (**Figure 9**) on EFI (electronic fuel injection) models. The oil pump delivers oil relative to throttle lever position and engine speed.

A linkage rod connects the oil pump control lever to the throttle linkage and varies the oil pump stroke according to throttle lever position. The fuel/oil ratio varies from approximately 100:1 at idle to approximately 50:1 at wide-open throttle.

Operation

A 3 gallon (11.4 L) remote oil tank supplies oil to the reservoir mounted under the engine cowl (**Figure 13**). The reservoir oil capacity is approximately 51 fl. oz. (1.5 L) and is sufficient for approximately 30 minutes of wide-open throttle operation after the low oil level warning has sounded. Refer to **Figure 14** for the following description.

The remote oil tank is pressurized by crankcase pressure through a one-way crankcase check valve (12, **Figure 14**), causing oil to flow from the remote tank to the engine-mounted reservoir (5). If the oil line between remote tank and engine-mounted reservoir becomes re-

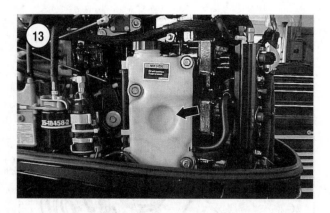

stricted, the check valve (3, **Figure 14**) unseats, allowing air to vent through the hose, which allows the injection pump to draw oil from the engine-mounted reservoir.

The oil pickup tube (2, **Figure 14**) in the remote tank is equipped with a filter screen to prevent dirt or other contamination from entering the injection system.

The oil injection pump (7, **Figure 14**) is mounted to the engine block and is driven by a gear on the crankshaft. On carbureted models, the oil pump injects the oil into the fuel stream before the mechanical fuel pump. On EFI (electronic fuel injection) models, the oil is injected into the fuel via a fitting at the bottom of the vapor separator assembly (**Figure 9**). A 2 psi (13.8 kPa) check valve is used at the injection point to prevent gasoline from being forced into the oil lines.

A low-oil level switch (4, **Figure 14**) attached to the engine-mounted reservoir activates the warning program in the ignition ECM (electronic control module), which triggers the warning horn and illuminates the warning panel if the oil level in the reservoir becomes low. If this occurs, stop the engine immediately and refill both oil reservoirs; permanent power head damage will occur once the oil reservoir is empty.

The ECM warning program incorporates a self test feature that should sound the warning horn briefly each time the ignition switch is turned on. This indicates that the warning system is functioning. If the self test does not occur, or if the horn sounds after the ignition is switched on, do not attempt to start the engine.

Warning System Troubleshooting

These models incorporate a warning panel (**Figure 15**) and a warning horn. When the ignition switch is first turned to the on position, the warning horn will beep momentarily as part of the warning system's self-test. The warning horn and warning panel are controlled by the ignition ECM on carbureted models and by the ignition and

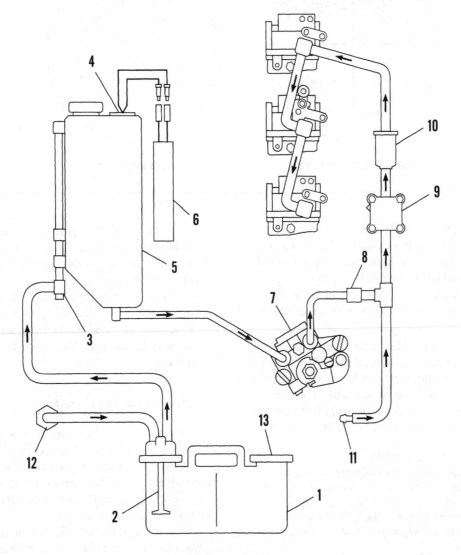

**OIL INJECTION SYSTEM (225 HP
[EXCEPT OPTIMAX] MODELS) (CARBURETOR MODEL)**

1. Remote oil tank
2. Oil pickup tube and screen
3. Check valve (vent)
4. Low oil level switch
5. Engine mounted oil reservoir
6. Ignition ECM (engine control module)
7. Oil injection pump
8. Check valve
9. Mechanical fuel pump
10. Fuel filter
11. Fuel inlet (from fuel tank)
12. Crankcase check valve
13. Filler cap

13

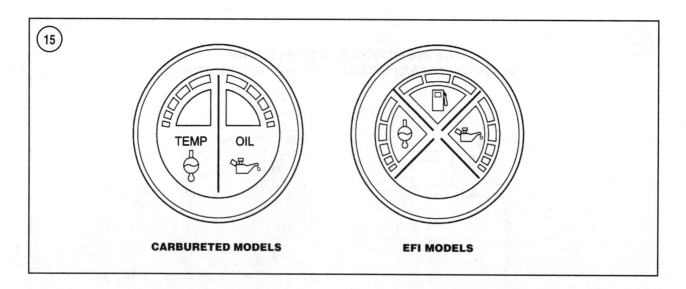

CARBURETED MODELS   **EFI MODELS**

fuel ECMs on EFI models. Refer to Chapter Three for a full explanation of the warning system. These systems are intended to be diagnosed with the Quicksilver digital diagnostic terminal (DDT). If the following procedure does not determine the cause of the problem, obtain a DDT or take the motor to a Mercury/Mariner dealership for diagnosis.

If a malfunction is suspected in the oil injection system (warning horn sounds and warning panel low oil level light illuminates), immediately stop the engine and check the oil levels in the remote oil tank and the engine-mounted reservoir. If the oil is low, fill the oil tank and reservoir with a recommended oil (Chapter Four).

CAUTION
If an oil injection system malfunction is suspected, do not operate the outboard on straight gasoline. Operate the motor on a remote fuel tank containing a 50:1 fuel/oil mixture until the oil pump output test can be performed.

If the reservoir oil level is low, but the remote tank is full, proceed as follows:

1. Check the O-rings or gaskets in the reservoir fill cap for cracking, deterioration or other damage. Replace the O-rings or gaskets as necessary. Make sure the fill caps are screwed tightly on the reservoir and remote tank. Air leaks at the remote tank will prevent the movement of oil from the tank to the reservoir. Leaks at the reservoir will result in oil spills.

2. Check the oil line between the remote tank and reservoir for kinks, restrictions or leaks. Repair or replace the line as required.

3. Check the crankcase pressure line between the crankcase check valve and remote tank for kinks, restrictions or leaks. Make sure the crankcase one-way check valve is functioning properly.

4. Check the oil pickup tube and filter for restrictions. Clean or replace the tube or filter as necessary.

5. Check all oil lines for kinks, cracks, deterioration, leaks or other damage. Make sure all connections are tightly clamped.

Warning system does not self test

Refer to the wiring diagrams at the end of the manual.
1. Turn the ignition switch to the ON position. Check the purple wire at the warning horn for battery voltage. The purple wire should show within 1 volt of battery voltage anytime the ignition switch is in the ON position. Repair or replace the lead as necessary.
2. With the ignition switch still in the ON position, ground the tan or tan/blue wire at the warning horn. If the horn does not sound, replace the warning horn.
3. Check the tan or tan/blue wire from the ignition ECM to the warning horn for continuity. Repair or replace the wire as necessary.
4. If all tests to this point are satisfactory, the ignition ECM may be defective. Check all ECM connections and ground wires for secure attachment.

Warning system sounds continuously

If the warning horn sounds continuously, check if any of the warning panel lights are illuminated. If the engine temperature light is illuminated, either the ECT sensor has

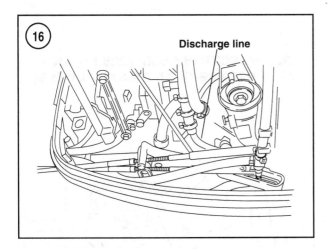

16

Discharge line

failed or the engine is overheating. Refer to Chapter Three for troubleshooting procedures. If no lights are illuminated, yet the horn is sounding continuously when the ignition switch is in the ON position, refer to the appropriate wiring diagram at the end of the manual, then proceed as follows:

1. Check the tan/blue wire from the ignition ECM to the warning horn for shorts to ground and damaged or missing insulation. Repair or replace the wire as necessary.
2. If the tan/blue wire is not shorted to ground or if it does not have damaged or missing insulation, the ignition ECM may be defective. Check all ECM connections and ground wires for secure attachment.

Oil level switch tests

1. Make sure the engine-mounted oil reservoir is full. Then disconnect the two oil level switch blue leads at the warning module bullet connectors.
2. Connect an ohmmeter, calibrated on an appropriate scale to check continuity, between the two oil level switch blue wires. The meter should indicate no continuity when the oil tank is full. If continuity is indicated, the oil level switch is defective and must be replaced.

Oil Pump Output Test

CAUTION
*Never run the engine without an adequate water supply and do not exceed 3000 rpm without an adequate load. Refer to **Safety Precautions** in Chapter Three or Chapter Five.*

Obtain a graduated container, capable of accurately measuring up to 50 cc, before continuing.

1. Connect a remote fuel tank containing a 50:1 fuel/oil mixture to the engine.
2. Disconnect the oil pump discharge line (**Figure 16**) from the check valve fitting below the Y-fitting which is just below the fuel pump on carbureted models or at the bottom of the vapor separator (**Figure 9**) on EFI models. Securely cap or plug the check valve fitting to prevent leaks.
3. Connect an accurate shop tachometer to the engine following its manufacturer's instructions.
4. Insert the disconnected end of the oil pump discharge line into the graduated container.
5. Start the outboard motor and run it at 1500 rpm for exactly 3 minutes.

NOTE
Injection pump output specifications are based on tests performed at 70° F (21° C). If the ambient temperature is more or less, actual pump output may vary from the specification.

6. Stop the engine and check the quantity of oil in the graduated container. Oil pump output must be within the specification (**Table 3**).
7. If injection pump output is less than specified, replace the pump assembly as described in this chapter.
8. Empty the container. Disconnect the control linkage (4, **Figure 17**) from the injection pump control lever. Rotate the control lever to the wide-open throttle position, then repeat Steps 4 and 5.
9. Stop the engine and again check the quantity of oil in the graduated container. Oil pump output should be within the specification in **Table 3**.
10. If injection pump output is less than specified, replace the pump assembly as described in this chapter.
11. Reconnect the pump discharge line to the check valve fitting. Secure the connection with a new tie-strap. Then bleed the injection system as described in this chapter.
12. Reconnect the oil pump link rod to the control arm. Adjust the link rod as specified in Chapter Five.

Oil Injection System Service

Oil pump synchronization

Refer to Chapter Five for throttle linkage to oil pump linkage adjustment and synchronization procedures.

Bleeding the oil pump

If the pump has been removed, if any of the lines have been replaced or if air is present in the oil pump lines, bleed air from the oil injection pump and lines as follows:

13

1. Place a shop towel beneath the oil pump.

2. Loosen the oil pump bleed screw (1, **Figure 17**) 3-4 turns.

3. Allow oil to flow from the bleed screw until there are no air bubbles in the inlet hose.

4. Tighten the bleed screw to the specification in **Table 1**.

CAUTION
*Do not run the engine without an adequate water supply and do not exceed 3000 rpm without an adequate load. Refer to **Safety Precautions** in Chapter Three or Chapter Five.*

5. If air is present in the pump discharge line, connect a remote tank containing a 50:1 fuel/oil mixture to the engine. Start the engine and run it at idle until there are no air bubbles in the discharge hose. Disconnect the pump link rod and rotate the pump arm to the full output position to speed the bleeding process.

6. On carbureted models, if necessary, gently pinch the fuel pump inlet hose (3, **Figure 17**) between the injection pump Y-fitting and the remote fuel tank connector, causing the fuel pump to create a slight vacuum in the hose. This will quicken the bleeding process.

7. Continue running the outboard until all air is purged, then stop the engine and reconnect the linkage rod to the control lever if it was disconnected.

Ignition ECM removal/installation

Refer to Chapter Seven for ignition ECM removal/installation procedures.

Engine-mounted oil reservoir removal/installation

1. Disconnect the inlet hose (3, **Figure 17**) from the oil pump. If the reservoir contains oil, cap or plug the line to prevent leaks.

2. Disconnect the remote oil tank-to-engine reservoir input line at the vent valve fitting at the front of the reservoir.

3. Disconnect the low-oil level switch wires at their bullet connectors.

4. Remove the three reservoir mounting screws and remove the reservoir.

5. Remove the screw securing the oil level switch to the top of the reservoir, then remove the oil level switch.

6. To install the reservoir, install the oil level switch into the top of the reservoir. Secure the switch with one screw. The sleeve must fit above the probe portion of the switch. Tighten the screw securely.

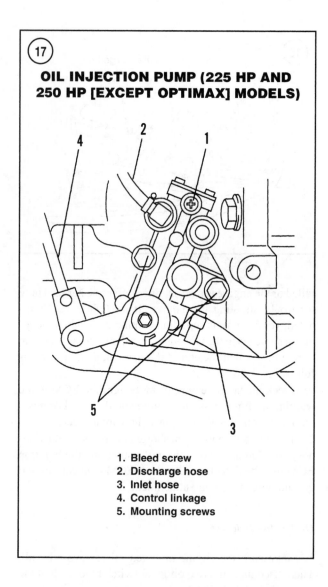

OIL INJECTION PUMP (225 HP AND 250 HP [EXCEPT OPTIMAX] MODELS)

1. Bleed screw
2. Discharge hose
3. Inlet hose
4. Control linkage
5. Mounting screws

7. Position the reservoir to the power head. Secure the reservoir with three screws. Apply Loctite 242 threadlocking adhesive (part No. 92-809821) to the threads of the mounting screws. Tighten the screws to the specification in **Table 1**.

8. Install the reservoir inlet and outlet lines. Securely clamp the oil lines using new tie-straps.

9. Reconnect the low-oil level switch leads or reinstall the fill cap to the reservoir.

10. Bleed the injection system as described in this chapter.

Oil pump removal/installation

Refer to Chapter Eight for oil pump drive gear removal/installation procedures.

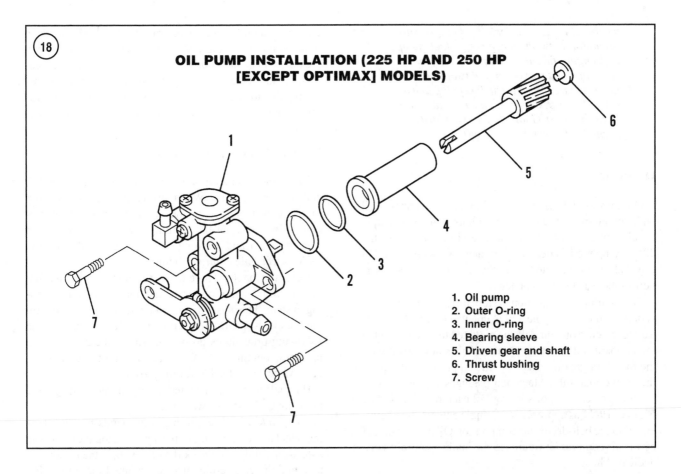

OIL PUMP INSTALLATION (225 HP AND 250 HP [EXCEPT OPTIMAX] MODELS)

1. Oil pump
2. Outer O-ring
3. Inner O-ring
4. Bearing sleeve
5. Driven gear and shaft
6. Thrust bushing
7. Screw

1. Disconnect the inlet (3, **Figure 17**) and discharge (2) oil lines from the injection pump. Cap or plug the lines to prevent leaks or contamination.

2. Disconnect the control linkage (4, **Figure 17**) from the pump control lever.

3. Remove the two screws (7, **Figure 18**) securing the pump (1) to the cylinder block, then remove the pump assembly. Grasp the driven gear shaft with needlenose pliers and pull the driven gear (5, **Figure 18**) and bearing sleeve (4) from the power head. Make sure the thrust bushing (6, **Figure 18**) is present in the end of the driven gear.

4. Inspect all components for excessive wear or other damage. Replace all suspect parts. If the teeth on the driven gear are damaged or contaminated with gray plastic material, the pump drive gear on the crankshaft has failed and must be replaced. See Chapter Eight.

5. Install new O-rings prior to installing the pump. Lubricate the O-rings and all components with Quicksilver Needle Bearing Assembly Grease (part No. 92-825625A 1).

6. Assemble the driven gear, bearing and thrust washer as shown in **Figure 18**. Use Quicksilver Needle Bearing Assembly Grease to keep the thrust bushing (6, **Figure 18**) in

place. Insert the gear and bearing assembly into the power head and seat it in its bore.

7. Apply Loctite 271 threadlocking adhesive (part No. 92-80819) to the threads of the pump mounting screws. Install the pump. Be careful to align the shaft and coupler. Tighten the screws to the specification in **Table 1**.

8. Reconnect the oil inlet and outlet lines to the pump. Securely clamp the lines using new tie-straps.

9. Reconnect the link rod to the pump control arm. Refer to Chapter Five for oil pump adjustment and synchronization procedures.

10. Perform the oil pump bleeding procedure as described in this chapter.

VARIABLE-RATIO ELECTRONICALLY CONTROLLED OIL INJECTION (OPTIMAX MODELS)

WARNING
Although it is generally not necessary, a boat-mounted electric fuel pump may be installed along the fuel supply line. If so equipped, the fuel pressure must not exceed 4 psi (27.6 kPa) at the engine fuel line con-

13

nector. If necessary, install a fuel pressure regulator between the electric fuel pump and engine fuel line connector. Adjust the regulator to a maximum of 4 psi (27.6 kPa) fuel pressure. The electric fuel pump and all related fuel system components must conform to Coast Guard Safety standards for permanently installed fuel systems.

Operation

Optimax models use the same 3 gal. (11.4 L) remote oil tank, engine-mounted reservoir with low oil level switch, check valve (vent) and crankcase check valve as the 225-250 hp models described in the previous section. Oil travels from the remote tank to the engine-mounted reservoir in the exact same manner.

The Optimax oil injection system differs in how the oil is delivered to the engine. Oil is injected by an ECM controlled, electric oil pump that is mounted to a flange on the intake manifold or intake plenum. Oil is not mixed with the fuel. Straight oil flows from the oil pump to fittings in the intake manifold. Machined passages or hoses direct the oil to discharge ports in front of each reed block. See **Figures 19-21** as appropriate. A single external line delivers oil to the belt-driven air compressor. Oil not consumed by the air compressor returns to the intake manifold via a dedicated hose.

The ECM constantly changes the output of the pump based on engine operating conditions. While fuel and oil are not mixed, the fuel/oil ratio varies from 300:1 at idle to 60:1 at wide-open throttle. The ECM also pulses the pump at each start up to purge air from the compressor line and intake passageways.

The ECM monitors the oil pump electrical circuits and the engine-mounted reservoir oil level at all times.

If the ECM detects that the engine-mounted oil tank level is low, the ECM illuminates the low oil level light (2, **Figure 22**) and sounds four short beeps from the warning horn every two minutes. When this occurs, stop the engine and refill both oil tanks as soon as possible. If the ECM detects an electrical fault in the oil pump circuits, the ECM illuminates the low oil level light (2, **Figure 22**) and the check engine light (3). The ECM also sounds the warning horn in a continuous tone and reduces engine speed to 3000 rpm or lower. Stop the engine immediately, and locate and repair the cause of the warning. Continued operation without oil flow will cause permanent power head damage.

During the first 120 minutes of new engine operation, the ECM double oils the engine to assist with break-in. After 120 minutes of run time (by the ECM internal

clock), oil pump operation returns to normal. The break-in must be initiated before starting a new engine and when the power head has been repaired or replaced. This procedure can also be used to purge air from the oil passages after repairs to the oil injection system. Instructions for initiating the break-in are included in this section.

Warning System Troubleshooting

These models incorporate a warning panel (**Figure 22**) and a warning horn. When the ignition switch is first turned to the ON position, the warning horn will beep momentarily as part of the warning system's self-test. The warning horn and warning panel are controlled by the ECM (electronic control module).

Refer to Chapter Three under ignition system and fuel system troubleshooting for a full explanation of the warning system. This system is intended to be diagnosed with the Quicksilver DDT (digital diagnostic terminal). If the following procedures do not determine the cause of the problem, obtain a DDT or take the motor to a Mercury/Mariner dealership for diagnosis.

If a malfunction is detected in the oil injection system, there are two possible warnings.

1. *Low oil level*—The warning horn sounds and the warning panel low oil level light illuminates. Stop the engine as soon as possible and check the oil levels in the remote oil tank and the engine-mounted reservoir. If the oil level is low, fill the oil tank and reservoir with the recommended oil (Chapter Four). If the warning continues, the engine can be operated, but the problem should be diagnosed as soon as possible.

2. *Electrical fault in the oil pump*—The warning horn sounds, the low oil level light illuminates, the check engine light illuminates and the maximum engine speed is reduced to 3000 rpm. This warning indicates the oil pump is probably not operating. Do *not* operate the outboard. Serious and expensive power head damage will occur with continued operation.

> *CAUTION*
> *If an oil injection system malfunction is suspected, do not operate the outboard. This engine cannot be run on a remote tank with a 50:1 fuel/oil mix. The DFI system does not pass fuel through the crankcase. The oil can only be injected into the crankcase through the electric oil pump system.*

If the reservoir oil level is low, but the remote tank is full, proceed as follows:

1. Check the O-rings or gaskets in the reservoir fill cap for cracking, deterioration or other damage. Replace the

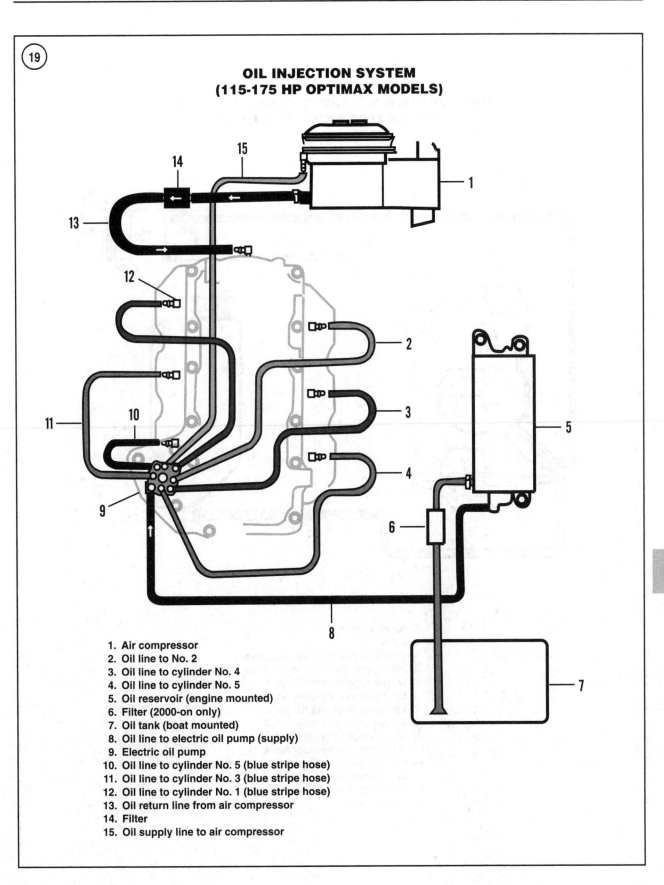

**OIL INJECTION SYSTEM
(115-175 HP OPTIMAX MODELS)**

1. Air compressor
2. Oil line to No. 2
3. Oil line to cylinder No. 4
4. Oil line to cylinder No. 5
5. Oil reservoir (engine mounted)
6. Filter (2000-on only)
7. Oil tank (boat mounted)
8. Oil line to electric oil pump (supply)
9. Electric oil pump
10. Oil line to cylinder No. 5 (blue stripe hose)
11. Oil line to cylinder No. 3 (blue stripe hose)
12. Oil line to cylinder No. 1 (blue stripe hose)
13. Oil return line from air compressor
14. Filter
15. Oil supply line to air compressor

13

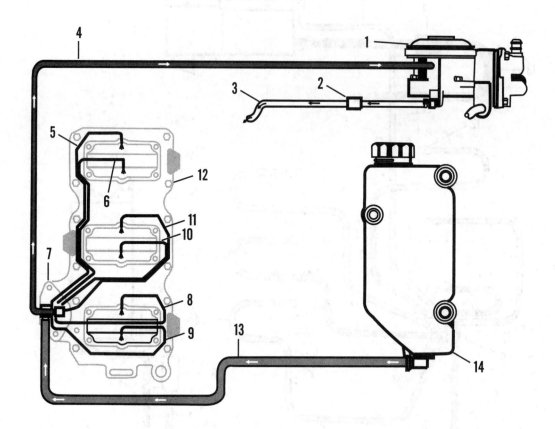

**OIL INJECTION SYSTEM (200 HP AND 225 HP
OPTIMAX 1998 AND 1999 MODELS)**

1. Air compressor
2. Filter
3. Oil return line from air compressor
4. Oil supply line to air compressor
5. Oil passage to cylinder No. 1
6. Oil passage to cylinder No. 2
7. Oil pump mounting flange
8. Oil passage to cylinder No. 5
9. Oil passage to cylinder No. 6
10. Oil passage to cylinder No. 4
11. Oil passage to cylinder No. 3
12. Intake manifold
13. Oil line to electric oil pump (supply)
14. Oil reservoir

OIL INJECTION SYSTEM (200 HP AND 225 HP OPTIMAX 2000-ON MODELS)

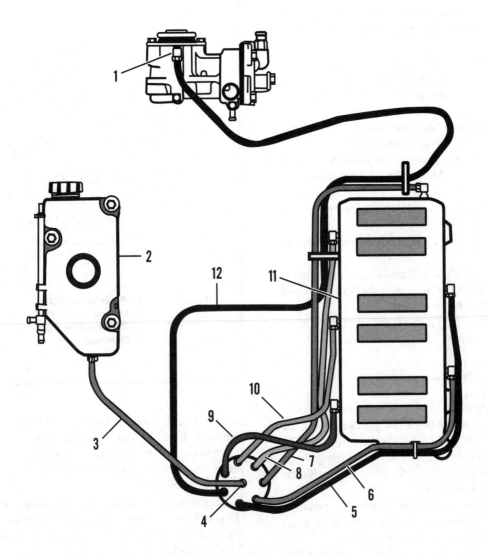

1. Air compressor
2. Oil reservoir
3. Oil line to electric oil pump (supply)
4. Inlet fitting to oil pump
5. Oil hose to No. 3 cylinder
6. Oil hose to No. 5 cylinder
7. Oil hose to No. 1 cylinder
8. Oil hose to No. 2 cylinder
9. Oil hose to No. 6 cylinder
10. Oil hose to No. 4 cylinder
11. Intake manifold
12. Oil supply line to air compressor

13

O-rings or gaskets as necessary. Make sure the fill caps are screwed tightly on the reservoir and remote tank. Air leaks at the remote tank will prevent the movement of oil from the tank to the reservoir. Leaks at the reservoir will result in oil spills.

2. Check the oil line between the remote tank and reservoir for kinks, restrictions or leaks. Repair or replace the line as required.

3. Check the crankcase pressure line between the crankcase check valve and remote tank for kinks, restrictions or leaks. Make sure the crankcase one-way check valve is functioning properly.

4. Check the oil pickup tube and filter for restrictions. Clean or replace the tube or filter as necessary.

5. Check all oil lines for kinks, cracks, deterioration, leaks or other damage. Make sure all connections are tightly clamped.

If an electrical fault in the electric oil pump is suspected, perform the following:

1. Check the wiring and connections to the electric oil pump.

2. Diagnose the fault using a digital diagnostic terminal (DDT). If a DDT is not available, have the fault diagnosed by a Mercury or Mariner dealership.

3. Replace the electric oil pump if the oil pump circuits are faulty and the wiring checks satisfactory.

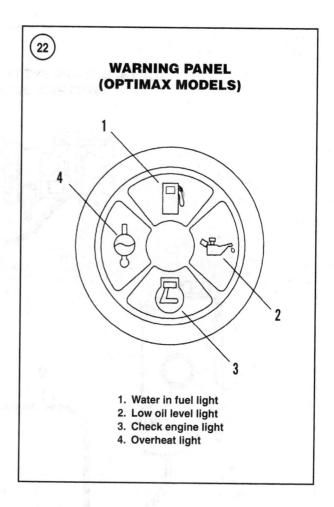

Warning system does not self test

Refer to the wiring diagrams at the end of the manual.

1. Turn the ignition switch to the ON position. Check the purple wire at the warning horn for battery voltage. The purple wire should show within 1 volt of battery voltage anytime the ignition switch is in the ON position. Repair or replace the lead as necessary.

2. With the ignition switch still in the ON position, ground the tan or tan/blue wire at the warning horn. If the horn does not sound, replace the warning horn.

3. Check the tan or tan/blue wire from the ECM to the warning horn for continuity. Repair or replace the lead as necessary.

4. If all tests to this point are satisfactory, the ECM may be defective. Check all ECM connections and ground leads for secure attachment.

Warning system sounds continuously

If the warning horn sounds continuously, check if any of the warning panel lights are illuminated. If the engine temperature light is illuminated, either the ECT sensor has failed or the engine is overheating. Refer to Chapter Three

for troubleshooting procedures. If no lights are illuminated, yet the horn is sounding continuously when the ignition switch is in the ON position, refer to the appropriate wiring diagram at the end of the manual, then proceed as follows:

1. Check the tan/blue wire from the ignition ECM to the warning horn for shorts to ground and damaged or missing insulation. Repair or replace the lead as necessary.

2. If the tan/blue wire is not shorted to ground and does not have damaged or missing insulation, the ECM may be defective. Check all ECM connections and ground leads for secure attachment.

Oil level switch tests

1. Make sure the engine-mounted oil reservoir is full. Then disconnect the two oil level switch blue wires at the warning module bullet connectors.

2. Connect an ohmmeter, calibrated on an appropriate scale to check continuity between the two oil level switch blue wires.

a. On 1998 and 1999 models, the meter should indicate no continuity when the oil tank is full. If continuity is indicated, the oil level switch is defective and must be replaced.

b. On 2000-on models, the meter should indicate continuity when the oil tank is full. If no continuity is indicated, the oil level switch is defective and must be replaced.

3. If the low oil level warning persists and the oil level switch tests correctly in Step 2, the wire between the switch and the ECM is open. Inspect the wire and repair it as needed. If the wire checks correctly and the alarm persists, the ECM or wire terminal is faulty.

Initiating Break-In and Air Purging

If the engine is new, the power head has been repaired or replaced, the oil pump has been removed, any of the lines have been replaced, or air is present in the oil pump lines, bleed air from the electric oil injection pump and lines as follows. This operation also resets the ECM to deliver the extra oil required for break-in.

1. Make sure the remote oil tank and engine-mounted reservoir are filled with the recommended oil (Chapter Four).

2. Put the remote control box in the neutral position.

3. Turn the ignition switch to the ON position. Do not start the engine.

4. Within 10 seconds, activate the shift interrupt switch five times by quickly shifting the engine from neutral to forward and back to neutral. The pump should start clicking and oil movement should be visible in the clear supply hose. Do not turn the ignition switch off until the clicking stops.

NOTE
The air purging process can take one minute or longer.

5. If air is still present, repeat Steps 2-4.

CAUTION
*Do not run the engine without an adequate water supply and do not exceed 3000 rpm without an adequate load. Refer to **Safety Precautions** in Chapter Three or Chapter Five.*

6. To purge the last of the air from the engine-mounted reservoir, loosen the reservoir cap slightly and run the engine at idle speed until oil begins to overflow the reservoir. Then tighten the cap securely.

Oil Injection System Service

If the oil distribution passages on 200 hp and 225 hp (1998 and 1999) models are suspected of having blocks, remove and clean the intake manifold as described in Chapter Six.

ECM removal/installation

ECM removal/installation is covered in Chapter Seven.

Engine-mounted reservoir removal/installation

1. Disconnect the reservoir-to-oil pump line from the electric oil pump. If the reservoir contains oil, cap or plug the line to prevent leaks.

2. Disconnect the remote oil tank-to-engine reservoir input line from the vent valve fitting at the front of the reservoir.

3. Disconnect the low-oil level switch leads at their bullet connectors.

4. Remove the three reservoir mounting screws. On 1998 and 1999 models, pull the fuel cooler slightly away from the engine and remove the reservoir.

5. Remove the screw securing the oil level switch to the top of the reservoir, then remove the oil level switch.

6. To install the reservoir, install the oil level switch into the top of the reservoir. Secure the switch with one screw. Tighten the screw securely.

7. Position the reservoir to the power head and behind the fuel cooler. Secure the reservoir with three screws. Apply Loctite 242 threadlocking adhesive (part No. 92-809821) to the threads of the mounting screws. Tighten the screws to the specification in **Table 1**.

8. Install the reservoir inlet and outlet lines. Securely clamp the oil lines using new tie-straps.

9. Reconnect the low-oil level switch leads or reinstall the fill cap to the reservoir.

10. Bleed air from the injection system as described in this chapter.

Electric oil pump removal/installation

If the machined oil distribution lines in the intake manifold are suspected of being blocked or restricted, refer to Chapter Six and remove the oil pump and intake manifold as an assembly. Oil pump mounting location varies by model and/or model year.

On 115-175 hp (1998-on) models, the oil pump mounts to a flange on the lower starboard side of the intake ple-

13

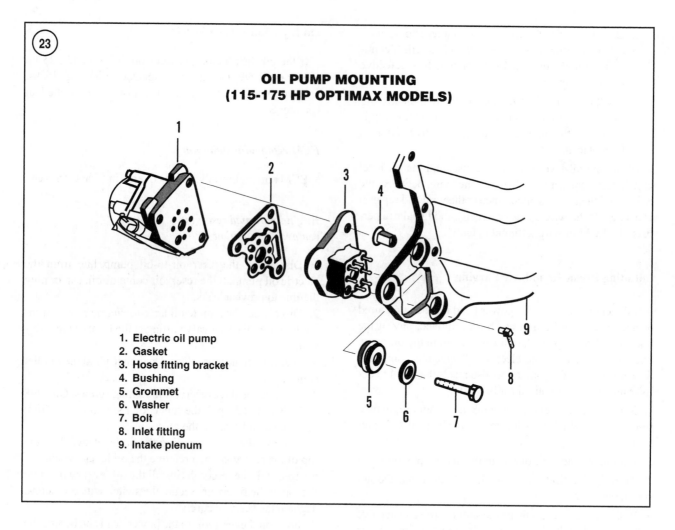

**OIL PUMP MOUNTING
(115-175 HP OPTIMAX MODELS)**

1. Electric oil pump
2. Gasket
3. Hose fitting bracket
4. Bushing
5. Grommet
6. Washer
7. Bolt
8. Inlet fitting
9. Intake plenum

num (**Figure 23**). The oil hose fittings are integrated in a bracket that mates to the oil pump.

On 200 and 225 hp (1998 and 1999) models, the oil pump mounts to a bracket on the lower starboard side of the intake manifold. Short hoses connect the oil pump outlet fittings on the oil distribution block (**Figure 24**).

On 200 and 225 hp (2000-on) models, the oil pump mounts to a flange on the lower starboard side of the intake plenum. The hoses to the individual cylinders attach directly to fittings on the oil pump.

Refer to **Figure 23-25** as appropriate.

1. Disconnect the negative battery cable.

2A. On 115-175 hp models, disconnect the oil supply hose from the inlet fitting (8, **Figure 23**). Plug the clear line.

2B. On 200 hp and 225 hp (1998 and 1999) models, disconnect the oil supply hose from the inlet fitting (5, **Figure 24**).

2C. On 200 hp and 225 hp (2000-on) models, disconnect the clear oil supply hose from its fitting on the electric oil pump (2, **Figure 25**). Plug or cap the clear oil supply line

from the engine-mounted reservoir to the electric oil pump intake manifold fitting.

3. Plug the clear line to prevent oil from leaking from the reservoir.

4. Disconnect the oil pump electrical connector.

5. Make notes or diagrams of the connection point and routing for each hose connected to the oil pump. Carefully disconnect each hose. Drain oil from the hoses.

6. Refer to **Figures 23-25** as appropriate to assist with component orientation. Then remove the oil pump mounting bolts.

7. Carefully pull the oil pump from the engine. Remove and discard any gaskets.

8. Clean all gasket material from the oil pump and intake manifold mating surfaces. Be careful not to scratch the mating surfaces. Do not allow debris to fall into the oil passages of the intake manifold and oil pump.

9. To install the oil pump, place the oil pump against the hose fitting bracket, mounting bracket or intake plenum flange using a new gasket (where applicable).

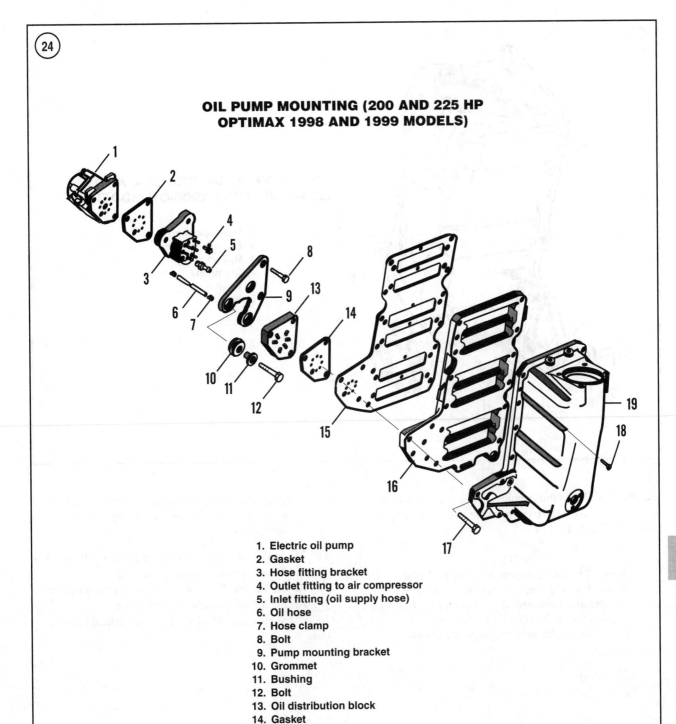

OIL PUMP MOUNTING (200 AND 225 HP OPTIMAX 1998 AND 1999 MODELS)

1. Electric oil pump
2. Gasket
3. Hose fitting bracket
4. Outlet fitting to air compressor
5. Inlet fitting (oil supply hose)
6. Oil hose
7. Hose clamp
8. Bolt
9. Pump mounting bracket
10. Grommet
11. Bushing
12. Bolt
13. Oil distribution block
14. Gasket
15. Plate
16. Intake manifold
17. Bolt
18. Allen screw
19. Intake plenum

13

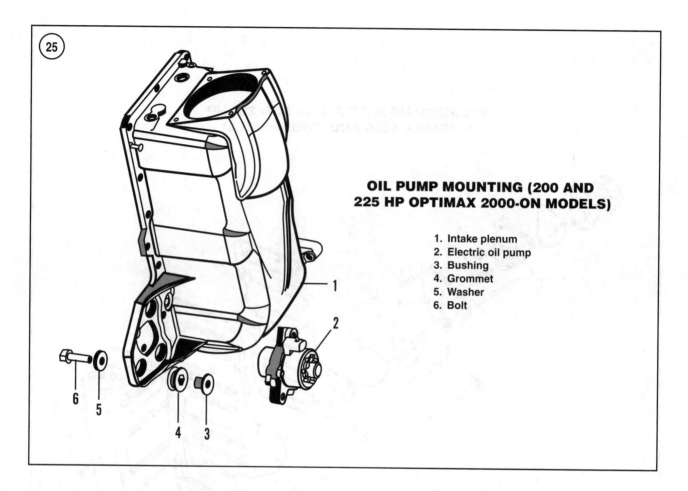

OIL PUMP MOUNTING (200 AND 225 HP OPTIMAX 2000-ON MODELS)

1. Intake plenum
2. Electric oil pump
3. Bushing
4. Grommet
5. Washer
6. Bolt

10. Install the mounting bolts, washer, grommets and bushings. Evenly tighten the mounting bolts to the specification in **Table 1**.

NOTE
Some 115-150 hp models are equipped with brass check valves in the oil hoses leading to the manifold fittings. If so equipped, the valves must be installed in the hose with the arrow on the side of the valve facing toward the intake manifold fittings. Never install the valves with the arrows facing the oil pump fittings.

11. Reconnect all hoses to their respective fittings. Secure each connection with a new tie-strap.
12. Reconnect the electrical connector to the oil pump.
13. Reconnect the negative battery cable.
14. Bleed air from the oil system as described in this section.

Table 1 OIL INJECTION SYSTEM TORQUE SPECIFICATIONS

Fastener	in.-lb.	ft.-lb.	N•m
Motion sensor screw	30	–	3.4
Oil pump bleed screw			
All models	25	–	2.8
Oil pump mounting bolts			
75-125 hp, 65 jet and 80 jet			
(except 115 hp Optimax and 105 jet)	60	–	6.8
135-200 hp (except Optimax) and 105 jet			
1998 and 1999	25	–	2.8
2000-on	55	–	6.2
115-225 hp (Optimax models)	–	16	21.7
225 hp and 250 hp (except Optimax)	55	–	6.2
Oil reservoir (engine mounted)			
75-125 hp, 65 jet and 80 jet			
(except 115 hp Optimax and 105 jet)	65	–	7.3
135-200 hp (except Optimax), 105 jet and 140 jet	25	–	2.8
225 hp and 250 hp (except Optimax)	–	14	19
115-225hp (Optimax models)	–	14	19
Warning module mounting	25	–	2.8

Table 2 GENERAL TORQUE SPECIFICATIONS

Screw or nut size	in.-lb.	ft.-lb.	N•m
U.S. Standard			
6-32	9	–	1.0
8-32	20	–	2.3
10-24	30	–	3.4
10-32	35	–	4.0
12-24	45	–	5.1
1/4-20	70	–	7.9
1/4-28	84	–	9.5
5/16-18	160	13	18
5/16-24	168	14	19
3/8-16	–	23	31
3/8-24	–	25	34
7/16-14	–	36	49
7/16-20	–	40	54
1/2-13	–	50	68
1/2-20	–	60	81
Metric			
M5	36	–	4
M6	70	–	8
M8	156	13	18
M10	–	26	35
M12	–	35	48
M14	–	60	81

13

Table 3 OIL INJECTION SYSTEM SPECIFICATIONS

Oil tank capacity	
75 hp, 65 jet and 90 hp	3.2 qt. (3.0 L)
100 hp, 115 hp, 125 hp and 80 jet (except 115 hp Optimax)	5.13 qt. (4.9 L)
135-200 hp (except Optimax) and 105 jet	
Remote oil tank	3.0 gal. (11.4 liter)
Engine mounted reservoir	.94 qt. (0.89 liter)
225 hp and 250 hp (except Optimax)	
Remote oil tank	3.0 gal. (11.4 liter)
Engine mounted reservoir	1.5 qt. (1.4 liter)

(continued)

Table 3 OIL INJECTION SYSTEM SPECIFICATIONS (continued)

Run time after warning horn sounds	
75 hp, 65 jet and 90 hp	Approximately 1 hour
100 hp, 115 hp, 125 hp and 80 jet (except 115 hp Optimax)	Approximately 50 minutes
135-200 hp (except Optimax) and 105 jet	Approximately 30 minutes
225 hp and 250 hp (except Optimax)	30-35 minutes
Oil pump output	
75 hp, 65 jet and 90 hp	22 cc minimum[1]
100 hp, 115 hp, 125 hp and 80 jet (except 115 hp Optimax)	29 cc minimum[1]
135 hp (except Optimax)	
@ 1500 rpm with link arm attached	6.1-7.5 cc[2]
@ 1500 rpm with link arm disconnected (full open)	15.3-18.7 cc[2]
150-200 hp (except Optimax), 105 jet and 140 jet	
@ 1500 rpm with link arm attached	7.4-9.0 cc[2]
@ 1500 rpm with link arm disconnected (full open)	17.3-21.1 cc[2]
225 and 250 hp (except Optimax)	
@ 1500 rpm with link arm attached	6.1-7.5 cc[2]
@ 1500 rpm with link arm disconnected (full open)	28.4.-.34.7 cc[2]

1. Oil pump output in 15 minutes at 700 rpm engine speed with oil pump lever at full open.
2. Oil pump output in 3 minutes at 1500 rpm engine speed.

Chapter Fourteen

Remote Control

The 1998-on Mercury/Mariner outboard motors primarily use the Commander 2000 or Commander 3000 series remote control box. The Commander 2000 control has a side-mount (**Figure 1**) configuration. The Commander 3000 control has flush-mount (**Figure 2**) or console mount (**Figure 3**) configurations.

These control boxes and engines use standard Quicksilver Mercury Mariner style control cables. Mercury Mariner control cables do not require adjustments in the control box, only at the engine.

Side mount control boxes are pre-wired and include the ignition switch, primer switch, emergency lanyard switch, warning horn and trim/tilt switch (on models so equipped). The main harness connector on these controls is the standard Mercury Mariner eight-pin connector. The harness includes additional connectors at each end for accessory gauges and warning system components. Remote control wiring diagrams are located at the end of the manual.

Panel and console mount controls include the neutral only start switch and tilt/trim switch (on models so equipped). The ignition switch, primer switch, emergency lanyard and warning horn connect to the instrument harness. The instrument harness connects to the engine harness using the standard Mercury Mariner eight-pin connector.

This chapter primarily covers throttle and shift cable removal, installation and adjustment.

Control Box Service

When servicing Mercury control boxes, lubricate all internal friction points with Quicksilver 2-4-C Multi-Lube grease or an equivalent. Apply Loctite 242 threadlocking (Mercury part No. 92-809821) adhesive to all internal threaded fasteners. A brass lock bolt secures the shift handle to the control on Commander 3000 type controls. Tighten the lock bolt to 150 in.-lb (17 N•m). Tighten all other control box fasteners to the standard torque specification in **Table 1**.

Refer to **Figure 4** for an exploded view of the Commander 2000 series control box internal components and **Figure 5** for an exploded view of the Commander 3000 series control box internal components.

Control Cable Removal/Installation/Adjustment (Engine)

Lubricate the control cable moveable casing guides, moveable barrel threads and attachment points with Quicksilver 2-4-C Multi-Lube grease (Mercury part No. 92-825407) before installation.

> *CAUTION*
> *Always install and adjust the shift cable first and the throttle cable last.*

> *NOTE*
> *Install the control cables into the control box before installating and adjusting the control box at the engine.*

Control cable removal (75-125 hp, 65 jet and 80 jet [except 115 hp Optimax] models)

1. Disconnect the negative battery cable. Disconnect and ground the spark plug leads to the power head to prevent accidental starting.
2. Carefully pull the rubber cable grommet (**Figure 6**) from the cables and lower engine cover.
3. Remove the elastic stop nut and nylon washer from each control arm attachment stud (**Figure 7**). Then pull the cables' casing guides from the control arm attachment studs.
4. Unlock both cables' barrels by rotating the cable retainer plate (**Figure 8**) to the full open position. Then pull both cables straight out of their anchor pockets. Remove both cables from the lower cowl grommet, then remove the cables from the engine.
5. To install the cables, route both cables through the grommet opening in the lower engine cover. Position each cable near the appropriate control arm stud and cable anchor barrel retainer bracket. Then refer to the appropriate cable installation/adjustment procedure, located later in this section.

Control cable removal (115 hp Optimax, 135-200 hp [except 200 hp Optimax] and 105-140 jet models)

1. Disconnect the negative battery cable.
2. Pull out on the spring-loaded throttle cable retainer (1, **Figure 9**) and rotate it in either direction. Lift up on the spring-loaded shift cable retainer (2, **Figure 9**) and rotate it in either direction. Then pull or lift each cable casing guide from its control arm attachment stud.
3. Unlock both cables' barrels by rotating the cable retainer plate (3, **Figure 9**) to the full open position. Then pull both cables straight out of their anchor pockets.

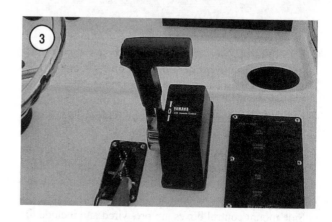

4A. On 1998 and 1999 models, remove the two screws and lift the upper half of the cable and hose clamp (**Figure 10**) from the lower engine cover. Lift the cables from the lower clamp.

4B. On 2000-on models, remove the plastic locking tie clamp (A, **Figure 11**) from the cable guide. Discard the clamp. Remove the two screws and lift the cable and hose guide (B, **Figure 11**) from the lower engine cover. Carefully remove the neoprene wrap from the cables and hoses. Lift the cables from the guide.

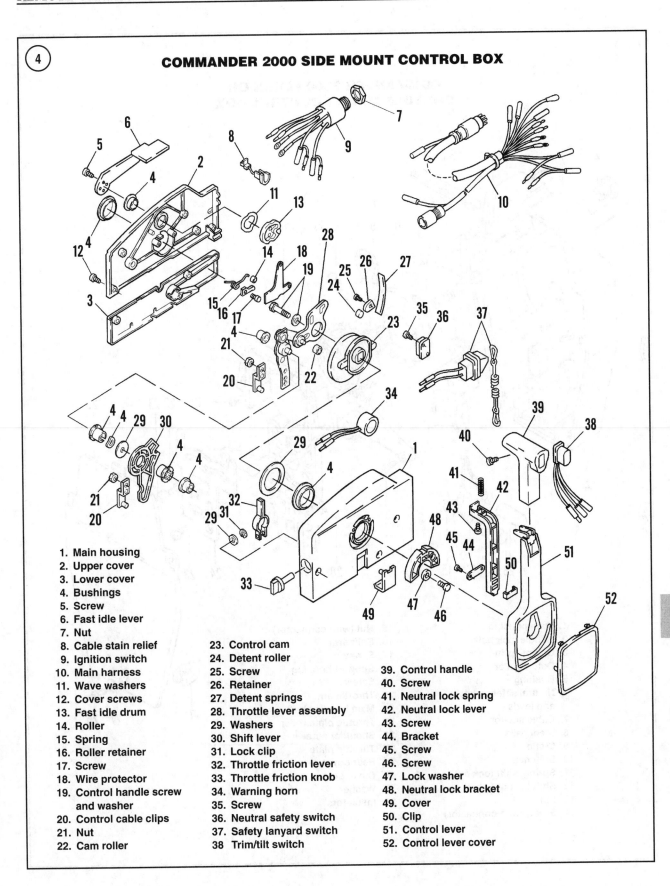

COMMANDER 2000 SIDE MOUNT CONTROL BOX

1. Main housing
2. Upper cover
3. Lower cover
4. Bushings
5. Screw
6. Fast idle lever
7. Nut
8. Cable stain relief
9. Ignition switch
10. Main harness
11. Wave washers
12. Cover screws
13. Fast idle drum
14. Roller
15. Spring
16. Roller retainer
17. Screw
18. Wire protector
19. Control handle screw
    and washer
20. Control cable clips
21. Nut
22. Cam roller

23. Control cam
24. Detent roller
25. Screw
26. Retainer
27. Detent springs
28. Throttle lever assembly
29. Washers
30. Shift lever
31. Lock clip
32. Throttle friction lever
33. Throttle friction knob
34. Warning horn
35. Screw
36. Neutral safety switch
37. Safety lanyard switch
38. Trim/tilt switch

39. Control handle
40. Screw
41. Neutral lock spring
42. Neutral lock lever
43. Screw
44. Bracket
45. Screw
46. Screw
47. Lock washer
48. Neutral lock bracket
49. Cover
50. Clip
51. Control lever
52. Control lever cover

14

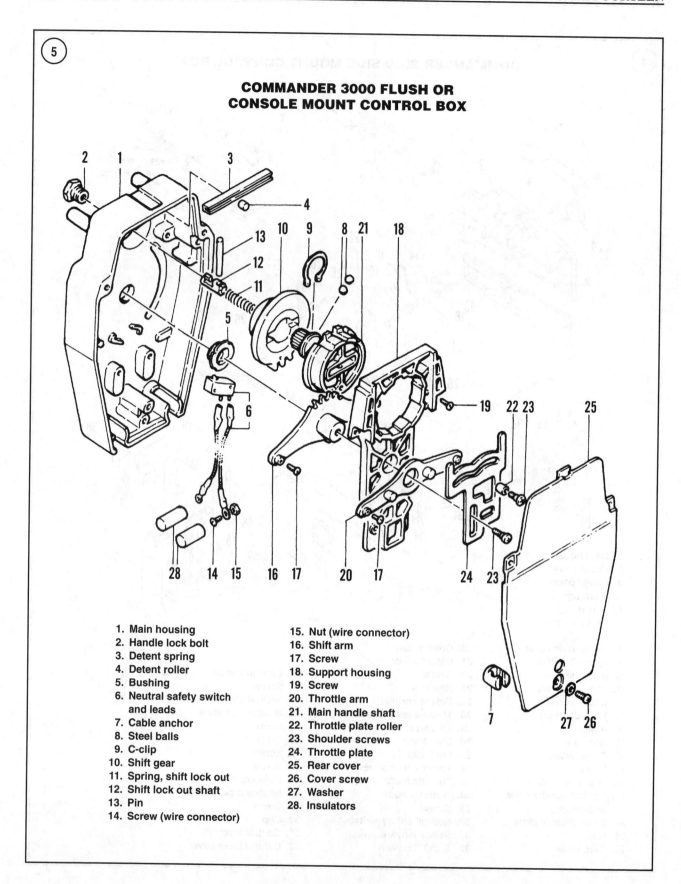

⑤

**COMMANDER 3000 FLUSH OR
CONSOLE MOUNT CONTROL BOX**

1. Main housing
2. Handle lock bolt
3. Detent spring
4. Detent roller
5. Bushing
6. Neutral safety switch
   and leads
7. Cable anchor
8. Steel balls
9. C-clip
10. Shift gear
11. Spring, shift lock out
12. Shift lock out shaft
13. Pin
14. Screw (wire connector)
15. Nut (wire connector)
16. Shift arm
17. Screw
18. Support housing
19. Screw
20. Throttle arm
21. Main handle shaft
22. Throttle plate roller
23. Shoulder screws
24. Throttle plate
25. Rear cover
26. Cover screw
27. Washer
28. Insulators

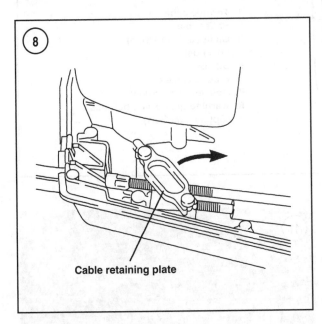

Cable retaining plate

5. To install the cables, route both cables through the lower cable and hose clamp or guide. Position each cable near the appropriate control arm pin and cable anchor barrel retainer bracket. Then refer to the appropriate cable installation/adjustment procedure in this section.

Control cable removal (200 hp Optimax and 225-250 hp models)

1. Disconnect the negative battery cable.

2. Remove the elastic stop nut and nylon washer (3, **Figure 12**) from each control arm attachment stud. Then pull the cables (1 and 2, **Figure 12**) casing guides from the control arm attachment studs.

3A. On 225-250 hp (except Optimax) models, remove the two screws and lift the upper half of the cable and hose clamp (**Figure 10**) from the lower engine cover. Lift the cables from the lower clamp.

3B. On 200 hp and 225 hp Optimax models (1998 and 1999), remove the two screws (1, **Figure 13**) and lift the cable and upper clamp assembly (2) from the lower engine cover (5). Remove the two screws (3, **Figure 13**) and the lower clamp (4) from the assembly.

3C. On 200 hp and 225 hp Optimax models (2000-on), remove the plastic locking tie clamp (A, **Figure 11**) from the cable and hose guide. Discard the clamp. Remove the two screws and lift the cable and hose guide (B, **Figure 11**) from the lower engine cover. Carefully remove the neoprene wrap from the cables and hoses. Lift the cables from the guide.

4. Unlock both cable's barrels by rotating the cable retainer plate (4, **Figure 12**) to the full open position. Then pull both cables straight out of their anchor pockets.

5. Remove the access plug (**Figure 14**). Then remove the three screws securing the lower engine covers to the drive shaft housing. The front screw is accessible from inside the cover. The middle screw is located on the lower port side of the cover. The rear screw is accessible from the access plug opening. Carefully remove the port side engine cover.

6. To install the cables, route both cables through the lower opening and position each cable near the appropriate control arm pin and cable anchor barrel retainer bracket. Then refer to the appropriate cable installation/adjustment procedure in this section.

Shift Cable Installation/Adjustment

NOTE
Some models may have a cast-in mark on the shift linkage indicating true neutral.

1. Shift the remote control into the NEUTRAL position. Center the free play in the shift cable by moving the casing guide back and forth, and positioning it in the middle of its free play.

   a. Push in on the casing guide as shown in A, **Figure 15** and make a mark on the cable sleeve as shown.

14

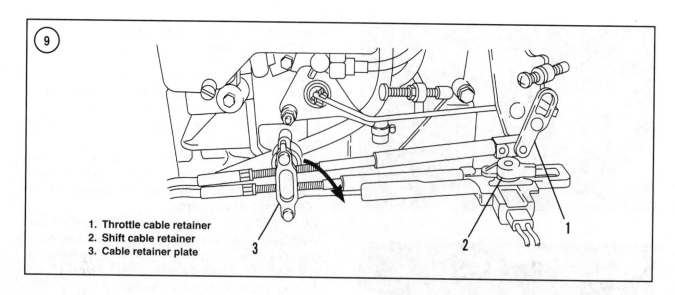

1. Throttle cable retainer
2. Shift cable retainer
3. Cable retainer plate

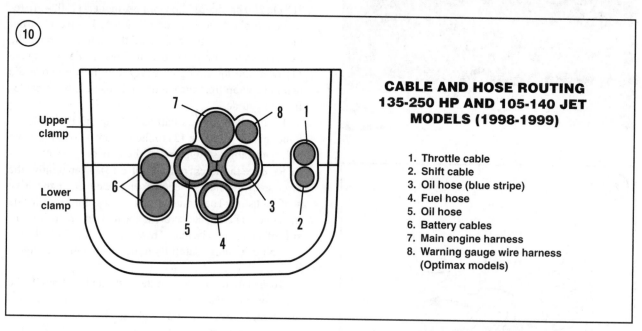

**CABLE AND HOSE ROUTING
135-250 HP AND 105-140 JET
MODELS (1998-1999)**

1. Throttle cable
2. Shift cable
3. Oil hose (blue stripe)
4. Fuel hose
5. Oil hose
6. Battery cables
7. Main engine harness
8. Warning gauge wire harness
   (Optimax models)

Upper clamp

Lower clamp

b. Pull out on the casing guide as shown in B, **Figure 15** and make a mark on the cable sleeve as shown.

c. Make a third mark on the cable sleeve in the exact middle of the *A* and *B* marks as shown in C, **Figure 15**. The third mark is true neutral of the remote control system.

NOTE
Rotate the propeller when shifting the gearcase in Step 2 to prevent shift linkage and gearcase damage.

2A. *75-125 hp (except 115 hp Optimax) and 65-80 jet models*—Adjust the shift cable as follows:

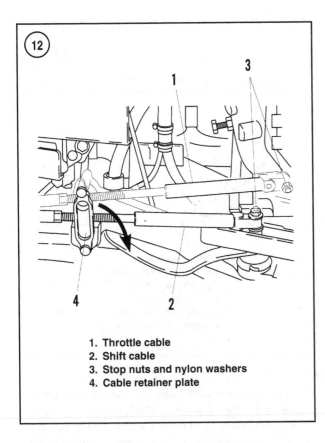

1. Throttle cable
2. Shift cable
3. Stop nuts and nylon washers
4. Cable retainer plate

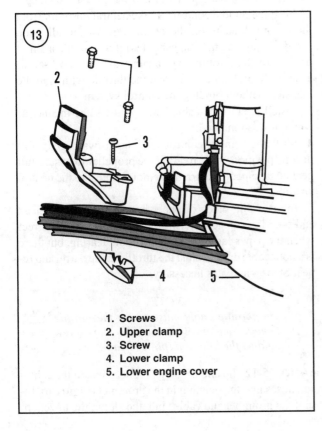

1. Screws
2. Upper clamp
3. Screw
4. Lower clamp
5. Lower engine cover

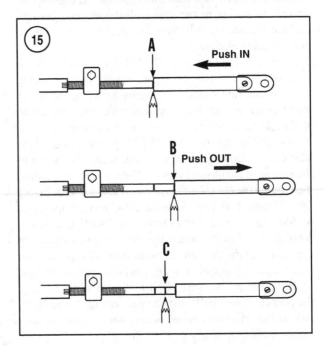

a. Manually move the engine shift linkage (1, **Figure 16**) to the neutral position. The propeller should spin freely in both directions.
b. Push the engine shift linkage rearward until there is slight resistance. Do not push the linkage into reverse gear.
c. Hold the linkage in this position and measure the distance (5, **Figure 16**) between the center of the shift linkage stud and the center of the opening in the barrel retainer (2).
d. Push the casing guide (3, **Figure 16**) lightly toward the barrel to remove slack from the cable. Measure the distance between the center of the barrel (4, **Figure 16**) and the center of the opening in the guide (3). Rotate the barrel until the measurement equals the distance shown in 5, **Figure 16** with all slack removed.

14

2B. *115 hp Optimax, 135-250 hp and 105-140 jet models*—Adjust the shift cable as follows:

    a. Manually move the engine shift linkage to the neutral position (the exact center of total shift linkage travel). The propeller should spin freely in both directions.

    b. Adjust the shift cable barrel to fit into its anchor when the center mark (C, **Figure 15**) is aligned with the casing guide or slightly pre-loaded toward the reverse gear.

3A. On 75-125 hp (except 115 hp Optimax) and 65-80 jet models, install the shift cable barrel into the retainer and the cable casing over the shift linkage stud (1, **Figure 16**). Secure the casing to the stud with the nut and washer. Tighten the nut securely, then loosen the nut 1/4 turn to prevent cable binding.

3B. On 115 hp Optimax, 135-200 hp (except 200 hp Optimax) and 105-140 jet models, install the cable casing over the shift cable retainer (2, **Figure 9**). Swing the spring load retainer over the casing to secure the cable. Install the shift cable barrel into the lower barrel retainer opening.

3C. On 200 hp Optimax and 225-250 hp models, install the shift cable casing over shift arm stud. Secure the casing to the stud with the nut and washer. Tighten the nut securely, then loosen the nut 1/4 turn to prevent cable binding. Install the shift cable barrel into the lower barrel retainer opening.

4. Shift the remote control into FORWARD gear while rotating the propeller, and make sure the gear engages in forward. Return the remote control to NEUTRAL and make sure the propeller spins freely in each direction. Shift the control box into REVERSE gear while rotating the propeller, and make sure the gear engages in reverse. Adjust the shift cable barrel as necessary if gear engagements are not satisfactory.

5. Install and adjust the throttle cable as described later in this section

NOTE

For best results, check the shift engagement with the boat in the water. Both forward and reverse gear engagements should each require the same amount of control box travel from the neutral detent. Both gears should fully engage before throttle cable movement occurs. Readjust the cables as necessary. Do not preload the shift linkages toward forward gear.

Throttle Cable Installation/Adjustment

Refer to Chapter Five for identification of the idle stop screw. Install and adjust the shift cable before attempting throttle cable installation and adjustment.

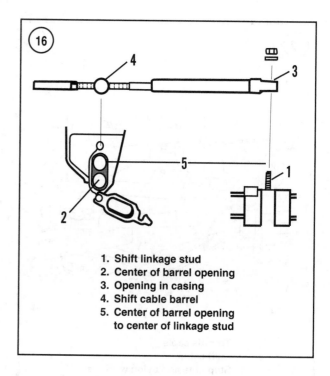

1. **Shift linkage stud**
2. **Center of barrel opening**
3. **Opening in casing**
4. **Shift cable barrel**
5. **Center of barrel opening to center of linkage stud**

1. Install the throttle cable casing guide onto the actuator pin or stud in the same manner as which it was removed. On models with locknuts and nylon washers, tighten the nut securely, then loosen the nut 1/4 turn to prevent cable binding.

2. Shift the remote control into the neutral position. Hold the throttle linkage on the engine against the idle stop screw. Adjust the throttle cable barrel to provide a slight preload of the throttle lever against the idle stop screw. This slight preload ensures that the throttle returns to the idle stop without binding the control system.

3. Install the throttle cable barrel in the same manner as which it was removed.

4. Shift the remote control into the forward gear, full throttle position while rotating the propeller to ensure full gear engagement. Return the remote control to the neutral position.

5. Insert a thin piece of paper between the power head and the idle stop screw. Throttle cable preload is correct when the paper can be removed without tearing, but there is a noticeable drag. Adjust the throttle cable barrel and repeat Steps 4 and 5 as necessary.

NOTE

The throttle cable must return the throttle linkage and position the idle stop screw against the idle stop (power head).

6A. On 75-125 hp and 65-80 jet models, install the cables and hoses into the opening in the grommet (**Figure 6**). Install the grommet and cables into the slot in the lower engine cover. Allow enough slack in the cables and hoses to prevent binding without interfering with other components.

6B. On 115 hp Optimax, 135-200 hp (except 200 hp Optimax) and 105-140 jet models (1998 and 1999), place the cables and hoses into the lower clamp (**Figure 10**). Install the upper clamp onto the lower clamp and secure it with the two screws. The hoses and cables must fit into the proper openings as shown in **Figure 10**. To prevent binding cables or pinched hoses, allow adequate slack in the cables and hoses before tightening the clamp screws.

6C. On 115 hp Optimax, 135-200 hp (except 200 hp Optimax) and 105-140 jet models (2000-on), route the cables and hoses though the guide opening in the lower engine cover. To prevent binding cables or pinched hoses, allow adequate slack in the cables and hoses before tightening the clamp screws. Wind the neoprene wrap over the cables and hoses. Install the cable and hose guide (B, **Figure 11**) to the lower engine cover and secure it with the two screws.

6D. On 225-250 hp (except Optimax) models, place the cables and hoses into the lower clamp (**Figure 10**). Install the upper clamp onto the lower clamp and secure it with the two screws. The hoses and cables must fit into the proper openings as shown in **Figure 10**. To prevent binding cables or pinched hoses, allow adequate slack in the cables and hoses before tightening the clamp screws.

6E. On 200 hp and 225 hp Optimax models (1998 and 1999), install the cable and hose clamp as follows:

   a. Route the cables and hoses though the upper clamp (2, **Figure 13**).

   b. Install the lower clamp (4, **Figure 13**) on the upper clamp as shown. Secure the clamp with the two screws (3, **Figure 13**). Do not tighten the screws at this time.

   c. Temporarily install the port side engine lower cover. Install the clamp assembly into the lower en-

gine cover. Pull on the cables and hoses to remove excess slack. The cables and hoses must not bind or interfere with other components.

   d. Securely tighten the two screws (3, **Figure 13**).

6F. On 200 hp and 225 hp Optimax models (2000-on), route the cables and hoses though the guide opening in the lower engine cover. To prevent binding cables or pinched hoses, allow adequate slack in the cables and hoses before tightening the clamp screws. Wind the neoprene wrap over the cables and hoses. Install the cable and hose guide (B, **Figure 11**) to the lower engine cover.

7. Rotate the cable retainer plate (**Figure 8**) to secure the barrels. Make sure the throttle cable and shift cable barrels are both secured before operating the engine.

8. Carefully install the port side engine lower cover onto the drive shaft housing. The exhaust relief grommet must fit into the opening at the rear of the cover. Make sure no hoses, cables or other components are pinched between the cover halves. Secure the cover halves to the engine with the three screws. Lubricate the access plug (**Figure 14**) with soapy water. Carefully fit the plug into the opening on the port side cover.

9A. On 115 hp Optimax, 135-200 hp (except 200 hp Optimax) and 105-140 jet models (2000-on), secure the front of the guide to the lower cover with a plastic locking tie clamp (A, **Figure 11**).

9B. On 200 hp and 225 hp Optimax models (1998 and 1999), install the upper clamp (2, **Figure 13**) into the lower engine cover (5). Secure the assembly to the cover with the two screws (1, **Figure 13**).

9C. On 200 hp and 225 hp Optimax models (2000-on), install the rear clamp plate to the rear of the guide. Secure the guide and clamp plate to the rear cable with the two screws. Secure the front of the guide to the lower cover with a plastic locking tie clamp (A, **Figure 11**).

10. Reconnect the negative battery cable and the spark plug leads.

14

Table 1 is on the following page.

Table 1 GENERAL TORQUE SPECIFICATIONS

Screw or nut size	in.-lb.	ft.-lb.	N•m
U.S. Standard			
6-32	9	–	1.0
8-32	20	–	2.3
10-24	30	–	3.4
10-32	35	–	4.0
12-24	45	–	5.1
1/4-20	70	–	7.9
1/4-28	84	–	9.5
5/16-18	160	13	18
5/16-24	168	14	19
3/8-16	–	23	31
3/8-24	–	25	34
7/16-14	–	36	49
7/16-20	–	40	54
1/2-13	–	50	68
1/2-20	–	60	81
Metric			
M5	36	–	4
M6	70	–	8
M8	156	13	18
M10	–	26	35
M12	–	35	48
M14	–	60	81

Index

15

15

WIRING
DIAGRAMS

65 JET, 75 HP AND 90 HP MODELS

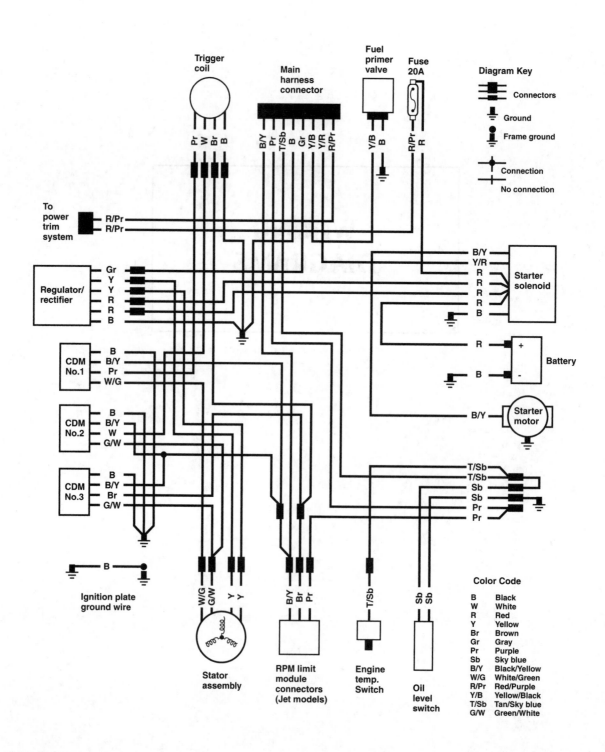

80 JET, 100 HP, 115 HP (EXCEPT OPTIMAX) AND 125 HP MODELS

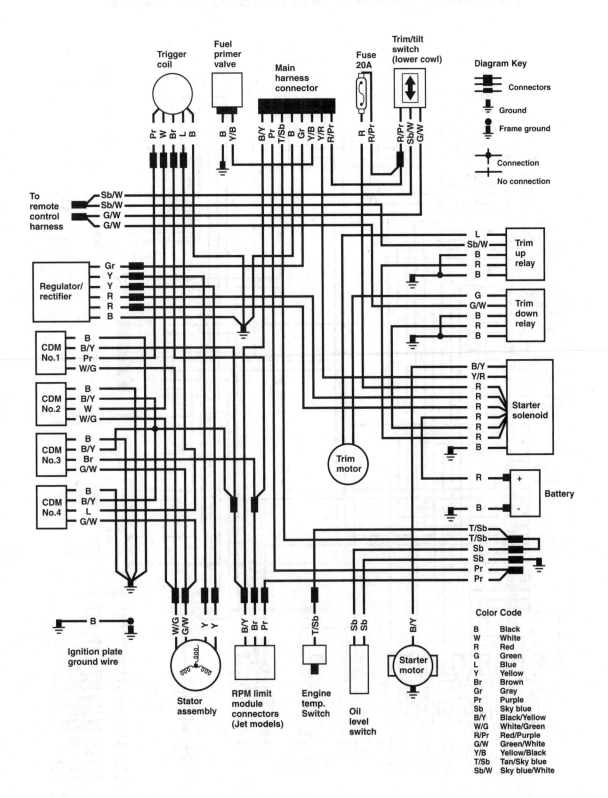

1998-1999 135-200 HP MODELS (CARBURETOR EQUIPPED)

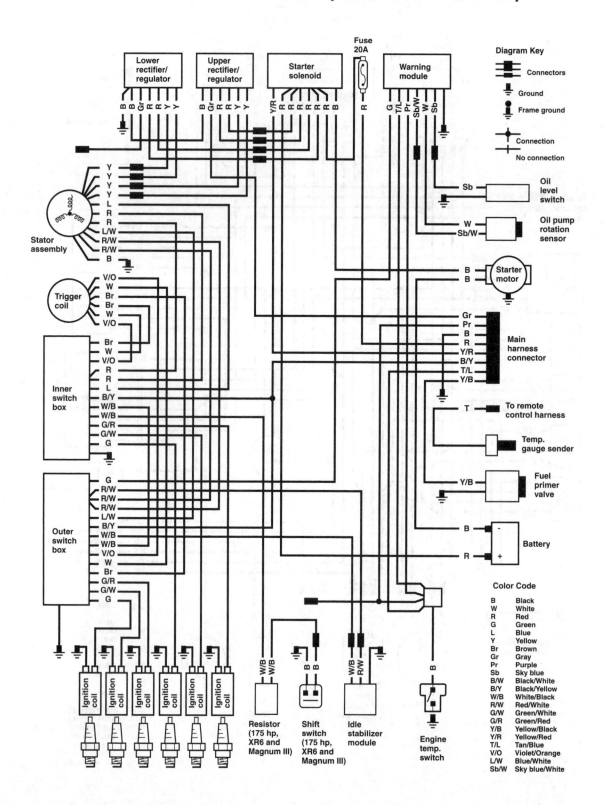

1998-1999 105 JET AND 140 JET MODELS

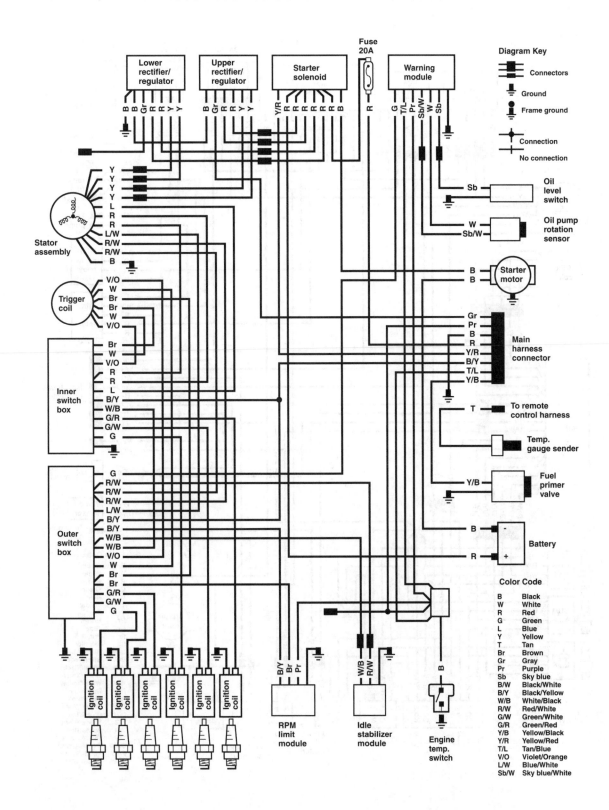

Diagram Key
- Connectors
- Ground
- Frame ground
- Connection
- No connection

Color Code

B	Black
W	White
R	Red
G	Green
L	Blue
Y	Yellow
T	Tan
Br	Brown
Gr	Gray
Pr	Purple
Sb	Sky blue
B/W	Black/White
B/Y	Black/Yellow
W/B	White/Black
R/W	Red/White
G/W	Green/White
G/R	Green/Red
Y/B	Yellow/Black
Y/R	Yellow/Red
T/L	Tan/Blue
V/O	Violet/Orange
L/W	Blue/White
Sb/W	Sky blue/White

16

105 JET, 140 JET AND 135-200 HP MODELS (CARBURETOR EQUIPPED [2000-ON])

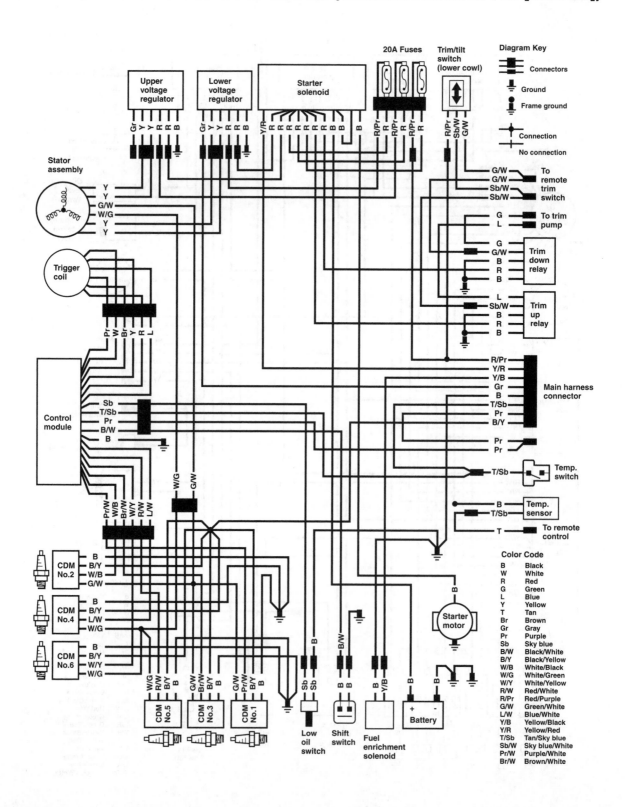

150-200 HP EFI MODELS
(FUEL MANAGEMENT SYSTEM [1998-1999])

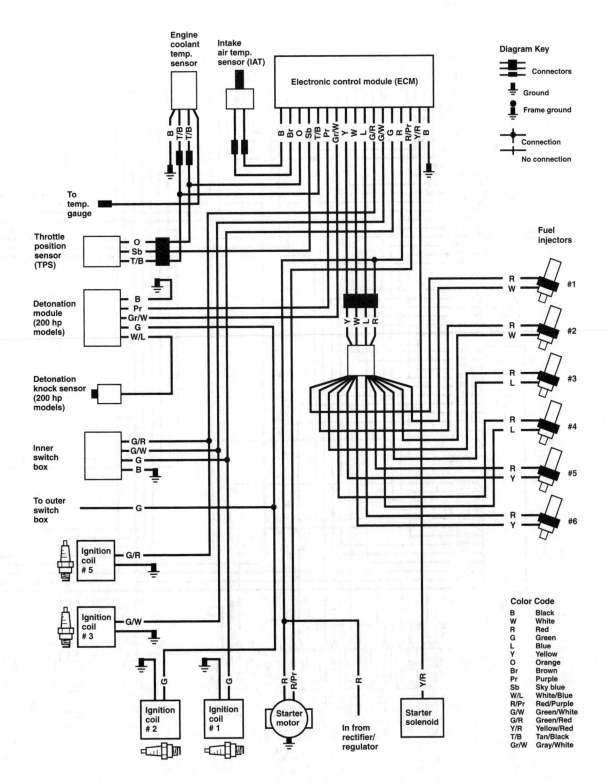

Diagram Key

Connectors

Ground

Frame ground

Connection

No connection

Engine coolant temp. sensor

Intake air temp. sensor (IAT)

Electronic control module (ECM)

To temp. gauge

Throttle position sensor (TPS)

Detonation module (200 hp models)

Detonation knock sensor (200 hp models)

Inner switch box

To outer switch box

Ignition coil # 5

Ignition coil # 3

Ignition coil # 2

Ignition coil # 1

Starter motor

In from rectifier/ regulator

Starter solenoid

Fuel injectors

#1 #2 #3 #4 #5 #6

Color Code

B	Black
W	White
R	Red
G	Green
L	Blue
Y	Yellow
O	Orange
Br	Brown
Pr	Purple
Sb	Sky blue
W/L	White/Blue
R/Pr	Red/Purple
G/W	Green/White
G/R	Green/Red
Y/R	Yellow/Red
T/B	Tan/Black
Gr/W	Gray/White

16

150 HP AND 175 HP EFI MODELS (1998-1999)

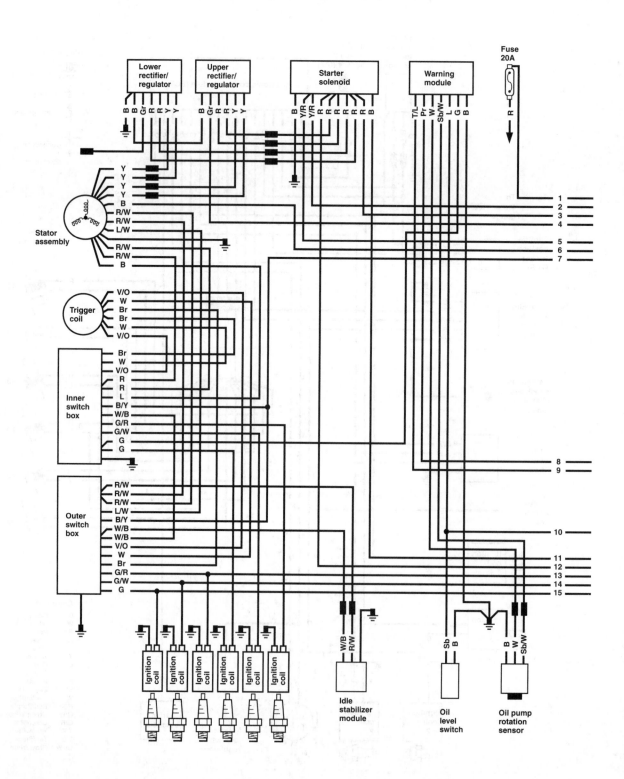

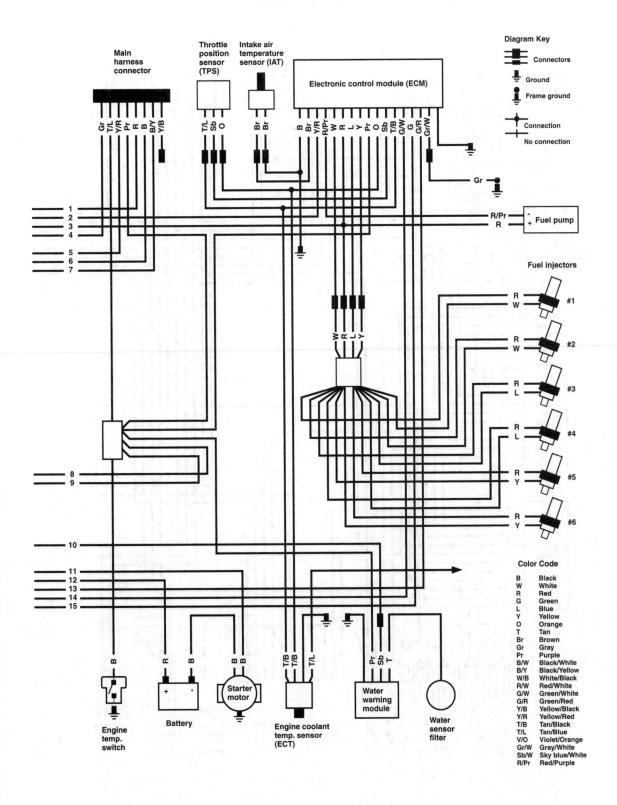

200 HP EFI MODELS (1998-1999)

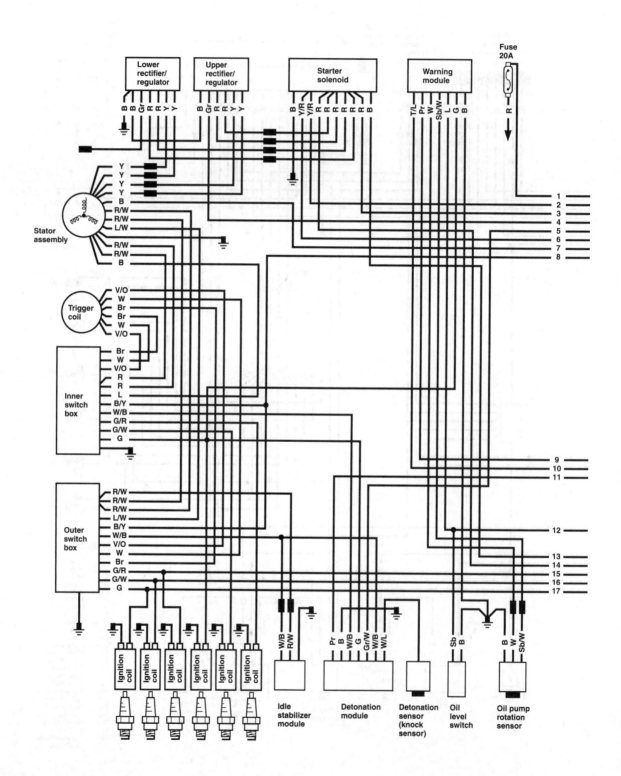

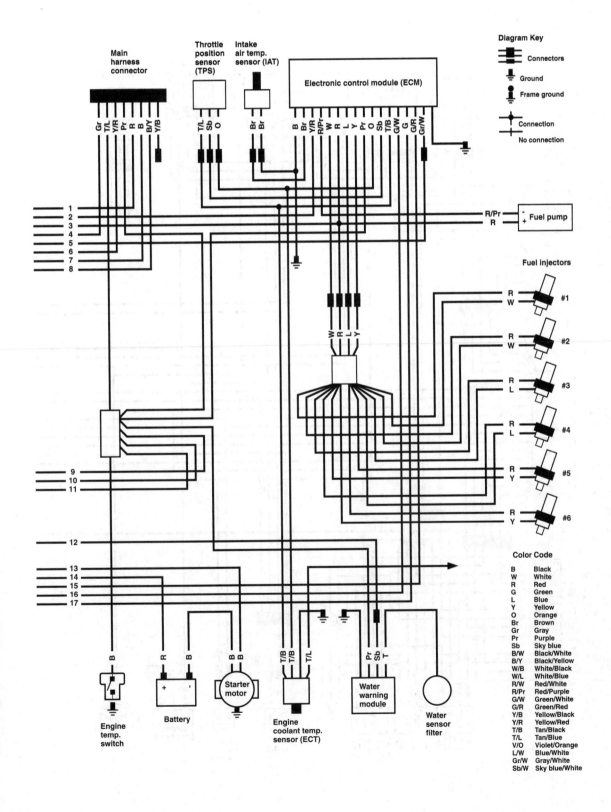

150 HP AND 175 HP EFI MODELS (2000-ON)

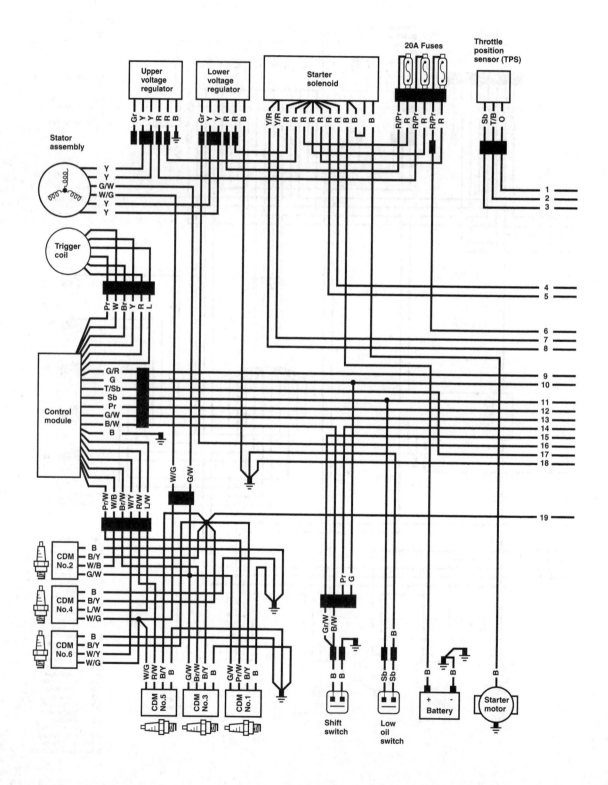

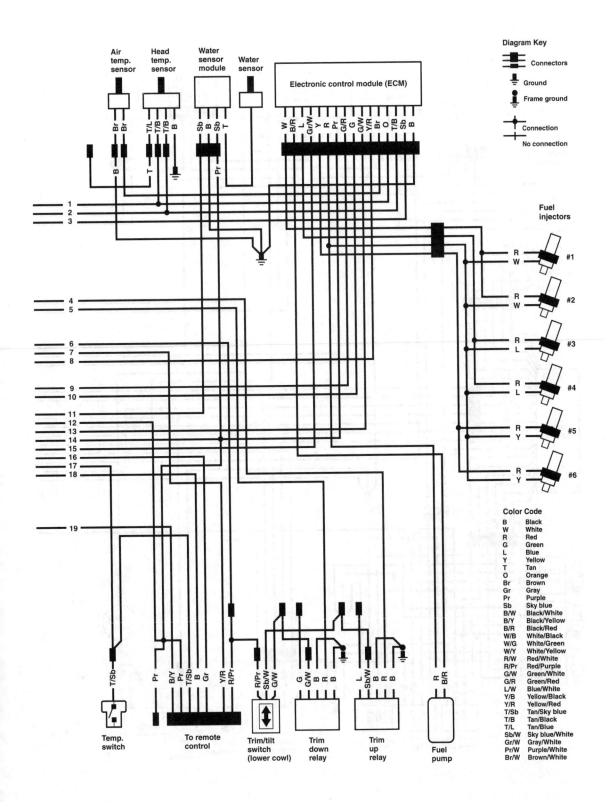

Diagram Key

Connectors

Ground

Frame ground

Connection

No connection

Air temp. sensor

Head temp. sensor

Water sensor module

Water sensor

Electronic control module (ECM)

Fuel injectors

#1
#2
#3
#4
#5
#6

Temp. switch

To remote control

Trim/tilt switch (lower cowl)

Trim down relay

Trim up relay

Fuel pump

Color Code

B	Black
W	White
R	Red
G	Green
L	Blue
Y	Yellow
T	Tan
O	Orange
Br	Brown
Gr	Gray
Pr	Purple
Sb	Sky blue
B/W	Black/White
B/Y	Black/Yellow
B/R	Black/Red
W/B	White/Black
W/G	White/Green
W/Y	White/Yellow
R/W	Red/White
R/Pr	Red/Purple
G/W	Green/White
G/R	Green/Red
L/W	Blue/White
Y/B	Yellow/Black
Y/R	Yellow/Red
T/Sb	Tan/Sky blue
T/B	Tan/Black
T/L	Tan/Blue
Sb/W	Sky blue/White
Gr/W	Gray/White
Pr/W	Purple/White
Br/W	Brown/White

16

200 HP EFI MODELS (2000-ON)

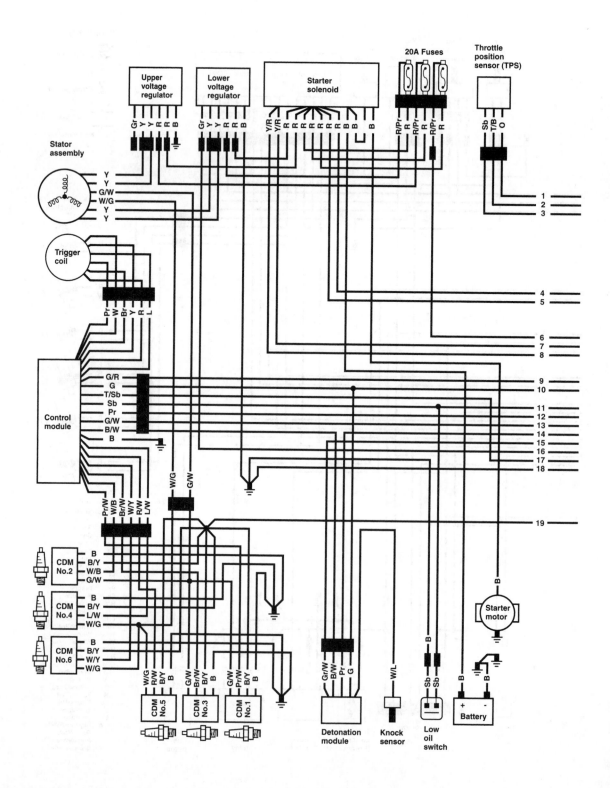

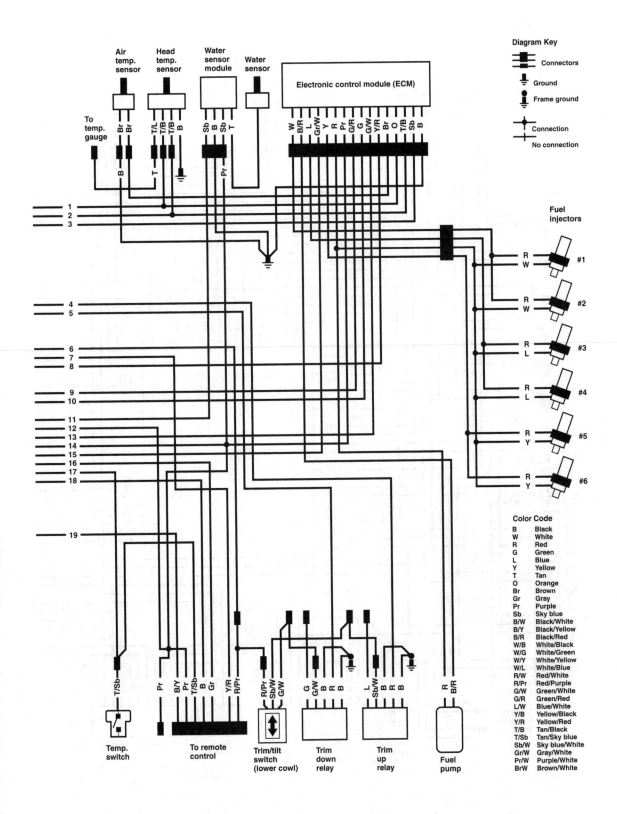

Diagram Key

- Connectors
- Ground
- Frame ground
- Connection
- No connection

Air temp. sensor

Head temp. sensor

Water sensor module

Water sensor

Electronic control module (ECM)

To temp. gauge

Fuel injectors

#1
#2
#3
#4
#5
#6

Color Code

B	Black
W	White
R	Red
G	Green
L	Blue
Y	Yellow
T	Tan
O	Orange
Br	Brown
Gr	Gray
Pr	Purple
Sb	Sky blue
B/W	Black/White
B/Y	Black/Yellow
B/R	Black/Red
W/B	White/Black
W/G	White/Green
W/Y	White/Yellow
W/L	White/Blue
R/W	Red/White
R/Pr	Red/Purple
G/W	Green/White
G/R	Green/Red
L/W	Blue/White
Y/B	Yellow/Black
Y/R	Yellow/Red
T/B	Tan/Black
T/Sb	Tan/Sky blue
Sb/W	Sky blue/White
Gr/W	Gray/White
Pr/W	Purple/White
Br/W	Brown/White

Temp. switch

To remote control

Trim/tilt switch (lower cowl)

Trim down relay

Trim up relay

Fuel pump

16

135-225 HP OPTIMAX MODELS (1998-1999)

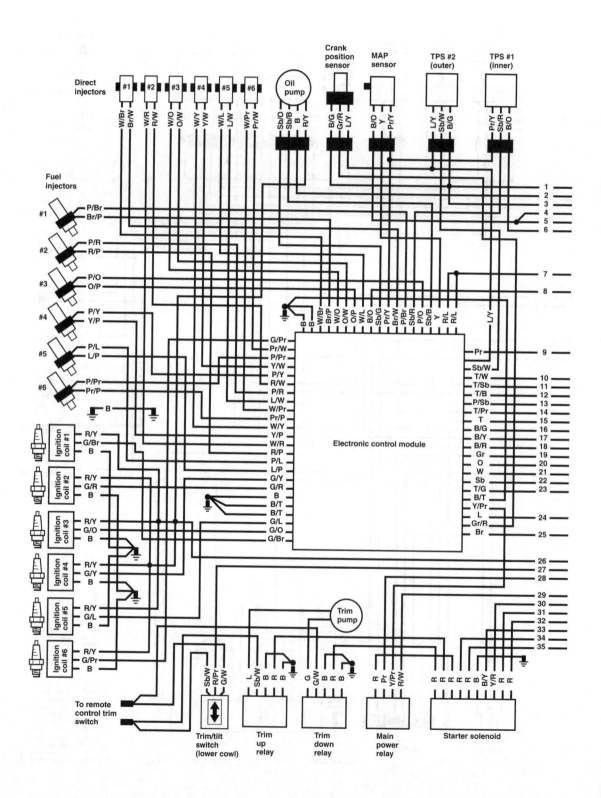

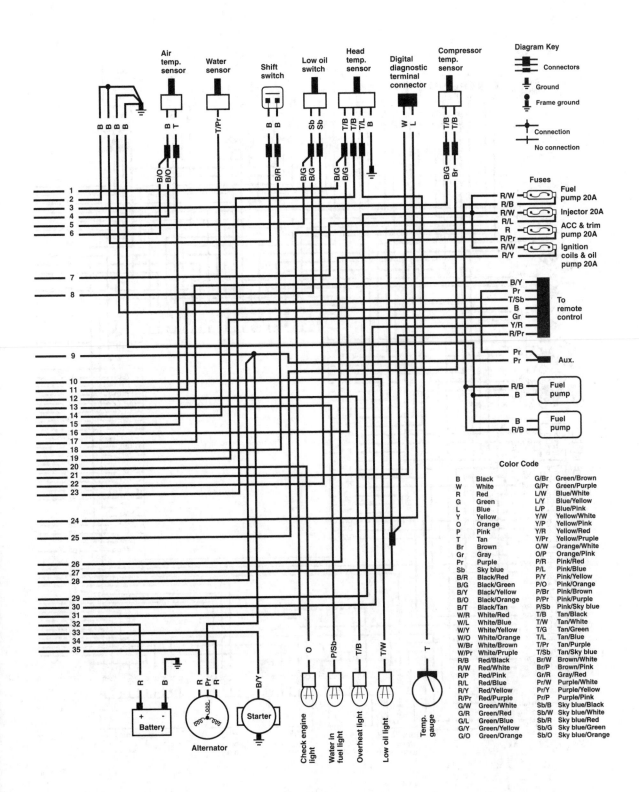

115-225 HP OPTIMAX MODELS (2000)

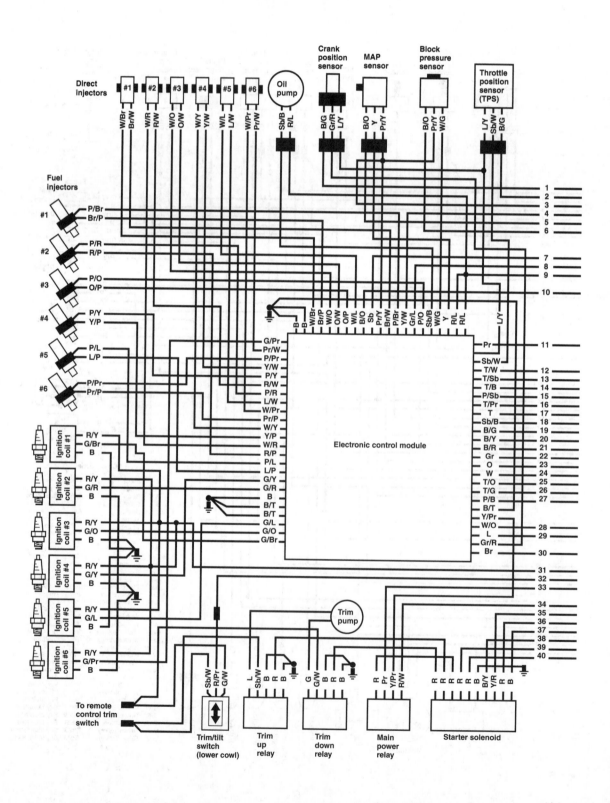

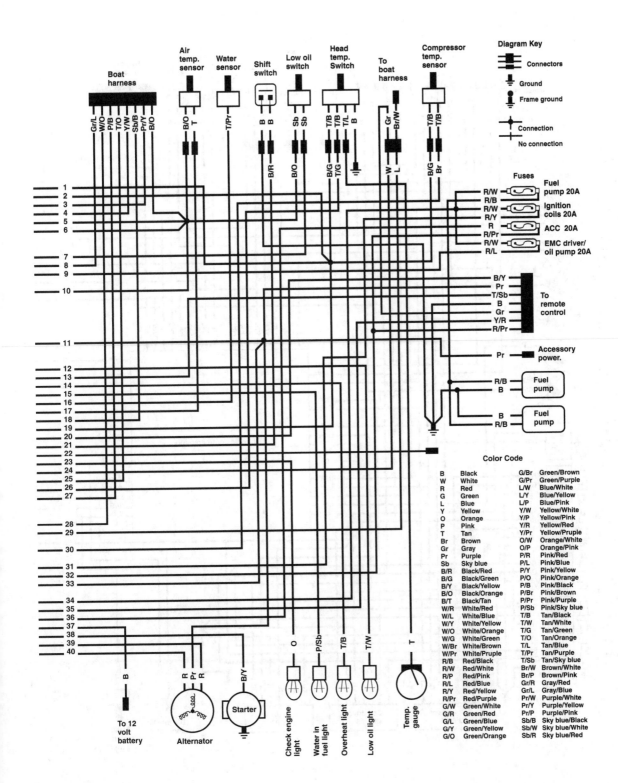

115-225 HP OPTIMAX MODELS (2001-ON)

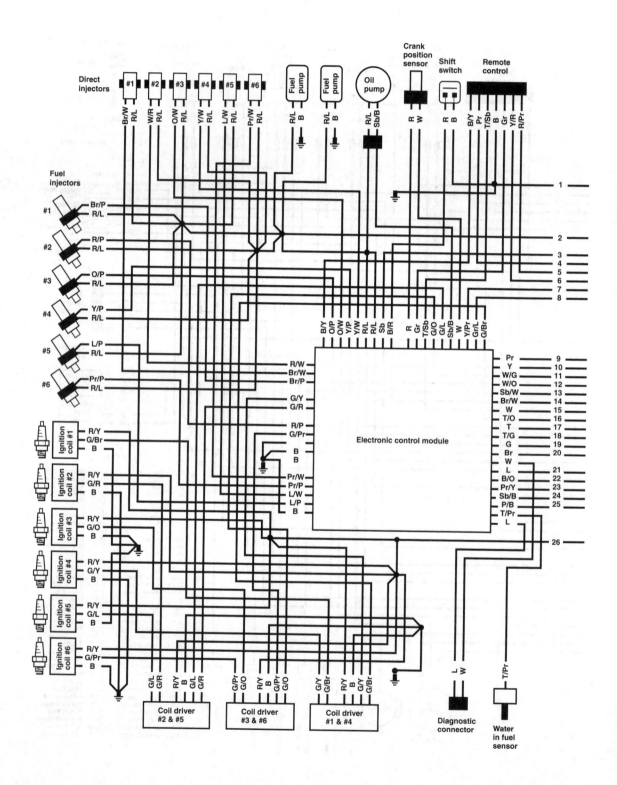

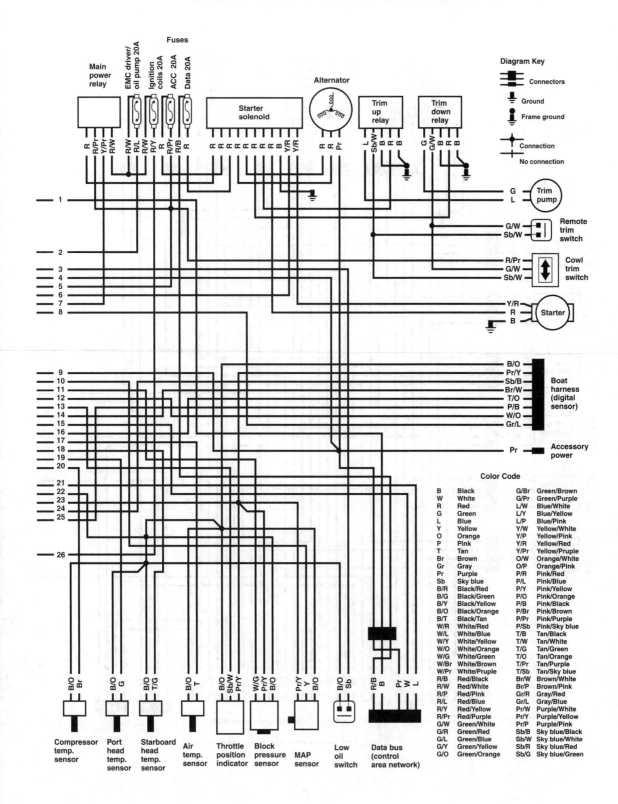

225 HP (CARBURETOR EQUIPPED [1998-ON])

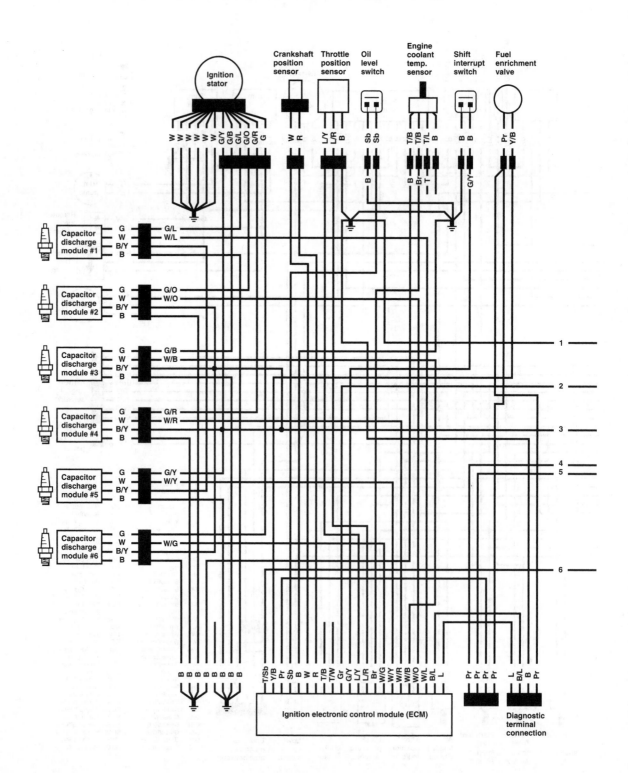

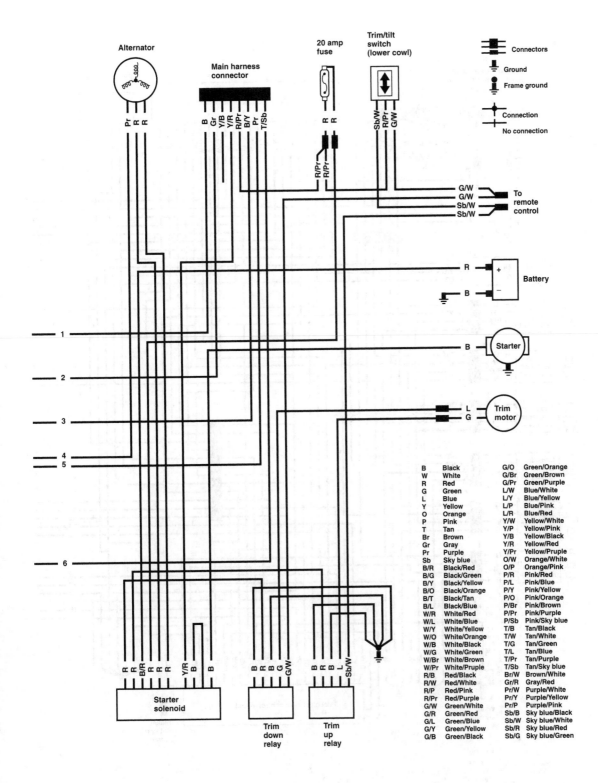

B	Black	G/O	Green/Orange
W	White	G/Br	Green/Brown
R	Red	G/Pr	Green/Purple
G	Green	L/W	Blue/White
L	Blue	L/Y	Blue/Yellow
Y	Yellow	L/P	Blue/Pink
O	Orange	L/R	Blue/Red
P	Pink	Y/W	Yellow/White
T	Tan	Y/P	Yellow/Pink
Br	Brown	Y/B	Yellow/Black
Gr	Gray	Y/R	Yellow/Red
Pr	Purple	Y/Pr	Yellow/Pruple
Sb	Sky blue	O/W	Orange/White
B/R	Black/Red	O/P	Orange/Pink
B/G	Black/Green	P/R	Pink/Red
B/Y	Black/Yellow	P/L	Pink/Blue
B/O	Black/Orange	P/Y	Pink/Yellow
B/T	Black/Tan	P/O	Pink/Orange
B/L	Black/Blue	P/Br	Pink/Brown
W/R	White/Red	P/Pr	Pink/Purple
W/L	White/Blue	P/Sb	Pink/Sky blue
W/Y	White/Yellow	T/B	Tan/Black
W/O	White/Orange	T/W	Tan/White
W/B	White/Black	T/G	Tan/Green
W/G	White/Green	T/L	Tan/Blue
W/Br	White/Brown	T/Pr	Tan/Purple
W/Pr	White/Pruple	T/Sb	Tan/Sky blue
R/B	Red/Black	Br/W	Brown/White
R/W	Red/White	Gr/R	Gray/Red
R/P	Red/Pink	Pr/W	Purple/White
R/Pr	Red/Purple	Pr/Y	Purple/Yellow
G/W	Green/White	Pr/P	Purple/Pink
G/R	Green/Red	Sb/B	Sky blue/Black
G/L	Green/Blue	Sb/W	Sky blue/White
G/Y	Green/Yellow	Sb/R	Sky blue/Red
G/B	Green/Black	Sb/G	Sky blue/Green

16

225 HP AND 250 HP EFI MODELS (1998-ON)

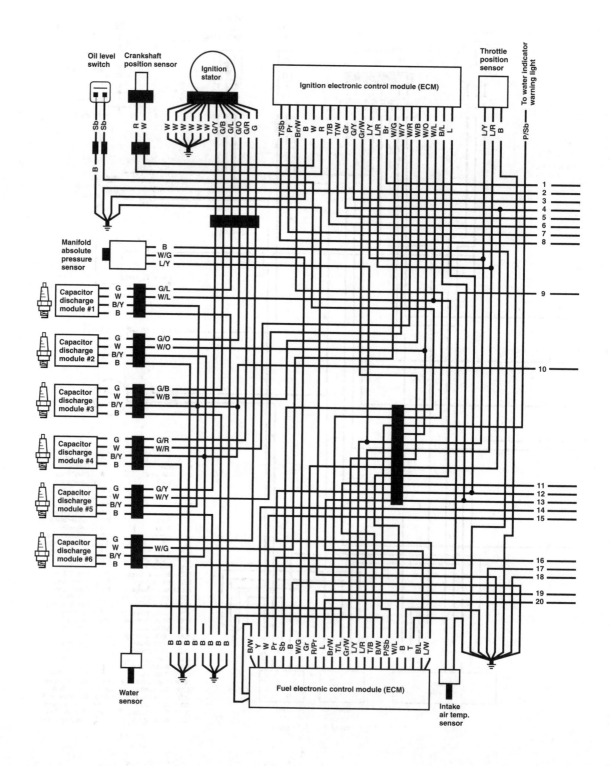

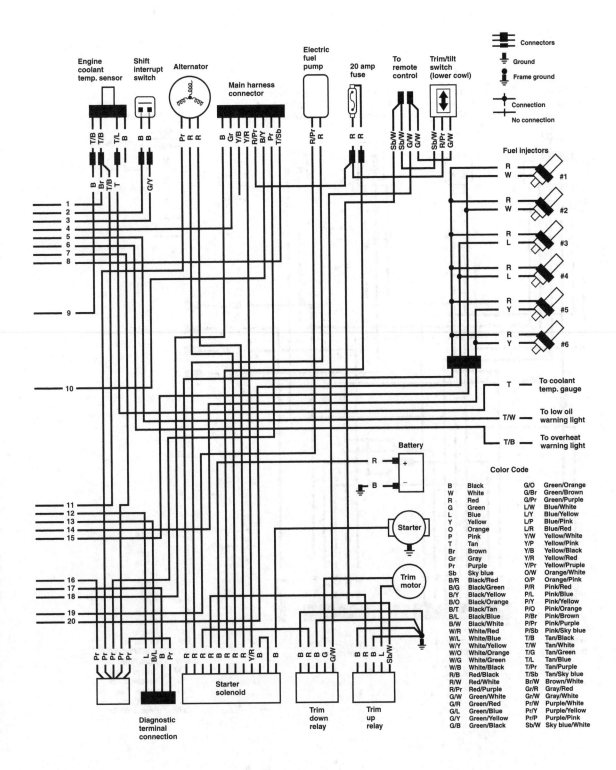

REMOTE CONTROL

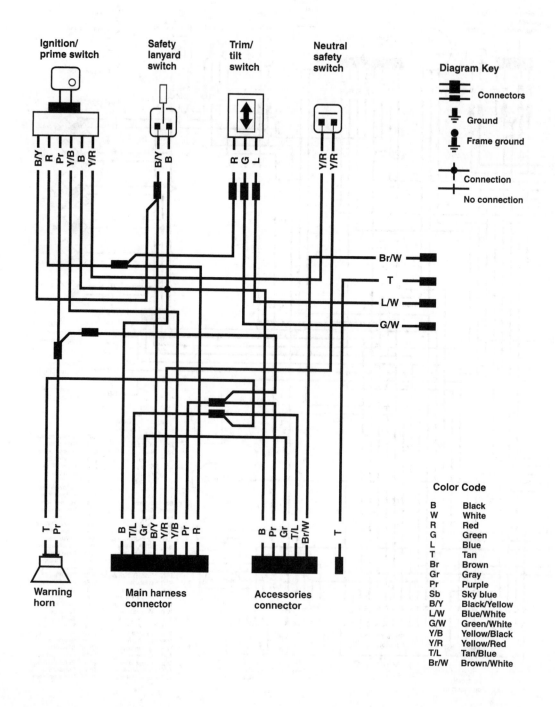

TILT AND TRIM SYSTEM (TYPICAL)

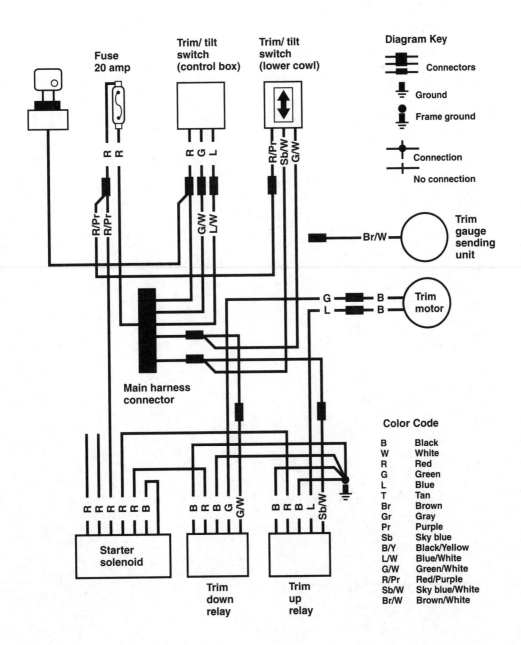

Fuse 20 amp

Trim/ tilt switch (control box)

Trim/ tilt switch (lower cowl)

Diagram Key

Connectors

Ground

Frame ground

Connection

No connection

Trim gauge sending unit

Trim motor

Main harness connector

Starter solenoid

Trim down relay

Trim up relay

Color Code

B	Black
W	White
R	Red
G	Green
L	Blue
T	Tan
Br	Brown
Gr	Gray
Pr	Purple
Sb	Sky blue
B/Y	Black/Yellow
L/W	Blue/White
G/W	Green/White
R/Pr	Red/Purple
Sb/W	Sky blue/White
Br/W	Brown/White

16

NOTES

NOTES

NOTES

NOTES

MAINTENANCE LOG

Date	Maintenance performed	Engine hours